Frommer's

W9-CCE-739

Europe by Rail

3rd Edition

Here's what the critics say about Frommer's:

"Amazingly easy to use. Very portable, very complete."

—*Booklist*

"Detailed, accurate, and easy-to-read information for all price ranges."
—*Glamour Magazine*

"Hotel information is close to encyclopedic."

—*Des Moines Sunday Register*

"If you're thinking about taking trains around Europe on your next visit, run—don't walk—to your nearest bookstore or website to get *Frommer's Europe by Rail.*"
—*Ed Perkins, SmarterTravel.com*

WILEY

Wiley Publishing, Inc.

Published by:

Wiley Publishing, Inc.

111 River St.
Hoboken, NJ 07030-5774

Copyright © 2008 Wiley Publishing, Inc., Hoboken, New Jersey. All rights reserved. No part of this publication may be reproduced, stored in a retrieval system or transmitted in any form or by any means, electronic, mechanical, photocopying, recording, scanning or otherwise, except as permitted under Sections 107 or 108 of the 1976 United States Copyright Act, without either the prior written permission of the Publisher, or authorization through payment of the appropriate per-copy fee to the Copyright Clearance Center, 222 Rosewood Drive, Danvers, MA 01923, 978/750-8400, fax 978/646-8600. Requests to the Publisher for permission should be addressed to the Legal Department, Wiley Publishing, Inc., 10475 Crosspoint Blvd., Indianapolis, IN 46256, 317/572-3447, fax 317/572-4355, or online at http://www.wiley.com/go/permissions.

Wiley and the Wiley Publishing logo are trademarks or registered trademarks of John Wiley & Sons, Inc. and/or its affiliates. Frommer's is a trademark or registered trademark of Arthur Frommer. Used under license. All other trademarks are the property of their respective owners. Wiley Publishing, Inc. is not associated with any product or vendor mentioned in this book.

ISBN 978-0-470-17498-2

Editor: Naomi P. Kraus
with Jamie Ehrlich, Anuja Madar, and Ian Skinnari
Production Editor: Michael Brumitt
Cartographer: Andrew Murphy
Photo Editor: Richard Fox
Production by Wiley Indianapolis Composition Services

Front cover photo: Bernina Express, Switzerland
Back cover photo: Glacier Express, Switzerland

For information on our other products and services or to obtain technical support, please contact our Customer Care Department within the U.S. at 800/762-2974, outside the U.S. at 317/572-3993 or fax 317/572-4002.

Wiley also publishes its books in a variety of electronic formats. Some content that appears in print may not be available in electronic formats.

Manufactured in the United States of America

5   4   3   2   1

Contents

List of Maps

About the Authors

Amy Eckert's love affair with travel began on a train in Europe and it hasn't stopped yet. As a college student Amy lived and worked in Southern Germany; as a travel writer she has returned many times since, traveling by train through a dozen countries including Germany, France, the Benelux nations, Italy, and Scandinavia.

After living several years in Germany as a freelance travel writer and in Tokyo as editor of *Far East Traveler*, **Beth Reiber** has written several Frommer's guides, including *Frommer's Japan, Frommer's Tokyo,* and *Frommer's Hong Kong.* She also contributes to *Frommer's USA* and is a blogger for japantravelinfo.com. She resides in Kansas with her two sons, a dog, and a cat.

George McDonald has lived and worked in both Amsterdam and Brussels as deputy editor of the KLM in-flight magazine and as editor-in-chief of the Sabena in-flight magazine. Now a freelance journalist and travel writer based in Germany, he is the author of *Frommer's Amsterdam* and *Frommer's Belgium, Holland & Luxembourg.*

Hana Mastrini is a native of the western Czech spa town of Karlovy Vary who became a veteran of the "Velvet Revolution" as a student in Prague in 1989. She began contributing to Frommer's guides while helping her husband, John, better understand his new home in the Czech Republic.

Olivia Edward is a British writer and photographer who specializes in travel and culture, and has contributed to guidebooks for MTV, *Time Out,* and DK. She loves sea air and raw fish, and was particularly happy researching the Scandinavian chapters for this guide. You can see more of her work at www.oliviaedward.com.

A freelance writer and editor, **Jocelyn Auerbach** grew up in both the U.S. and the U.K., and currently resides in France. Her childhood travels have created a strong desire to explore the world's vast number of cultures—and to capture them all in the written word. So far, she's managed to get to four continents . . . and counting.

Tania Kollias Eurailed her way through a gap-semester "On $10 a Day," which sparked a few more years of travel across four continents. Based in Athens, Greece, she is an accredited journalist and has worked as a copy editor, writer/reporter and editor for more than a decade.

Ryan James earned a doctorate in International and Multicultural Education from the University of San Francisco. He has been living in Budapest, Hungary since 2001, and has been a full time instructor in the American Studies Department at Eötvös Loránd University since 2002. He has traveled to forty-five countries, so far.

Darwin Porter, a native of North Carolina, was assigned to write the very first edition of a Frommer's guide devoted solely to one European country. Since then, he has written many best-selling Frommer's guides to all the major European destinations. In 1982, he was joined in his research efforts by **Danforth Prince,** formerly of the Paris bureau of the *New York Times,* who has traveled and written extensively about Europe.

Native New Yorker **Naomi Kraus** is a senior editor at Frommer's, a former travel agent, and a graduate of the Columbia Graduate School of Journalism. She's logged lots of miles on European trains over the years and rides the rails whenever she can.

An Invitation to the Reader

In researching this book, we discovered many wonderful places—hotels, restaurants, shops, and more. We're sure you'll find others. Please tell us about them, so we can share the information with your fellow travelers in upcoming editions. If you were disappointed with a recommendation, we'd love to know that, too. Please write to:

Frommer's Europe by Rail, 3rd Edition
Wiley Publishing, Inc. • 111 River St. • Hoboken, NJ 07030-5774

An Additional Note

Please be advised that travel information is subject to change at any time—and this is especially true of prices. We therefore suggest that you write or call ahead for confirmation when making your travel plans. The authors, editors, and publisher cannot be held responsible for the experiences of readers while traveling. Your safety is important to us, however, so we encourage you to stay alert and be aware of your surroundings. Keep a close eye on cameras, purses, and wallets, all favorite targets of thieves and pickpockets.

Acknowledgments

Many people worked behind the scenes and lent us a helping hand to keep this book on track. I'd like to give special thanks to **Cece Drummond** for her invaluable assistance. Rail Europe staffers who deserve lots of applause for their help: Beth DeMarte, Paul Kaufmann, Meredith Marks, Kathryn Seabrook, Patricia Timlin, and Michele Topper. You can't ask for a better cartographer than **Andrew Murphy**, the man behind all the maps in this book. Major kudos to **Jamie Ehrlich, Anuja Madar,** and **Ian Skinnari** at Frommer's for their generous assistance. And thanks to my family for making sure I stayed sane while juggling rail maps, timetables, and train itineraries for 6 months.

—Naomi P. Kraus

Other Great Guides for Your Trip:

Frommer's Star Ratings, Icons & Abbreviations

Every hotel, restaurant, and attraction listing in this guide has been ranked for quality, value, service, amenities, and special features using a **star-rating system.** In country, state, and regional guides, we also rate towns and regions to help you narrow down your choices and budget your time accordingly. Hotels and restaurants are rated on a scale of zero (recommended) to three stars (exceptional). Attractions, shopping, nightlife, towns, and regions are rated according to the following scale: zero stars (recommended), one star (highly recommended), two stars (very highly recommended), and three stars (must-see).

In addition to the star-rating system, we also use **five feature icons** that point you to the great deals, in-the-know advice, and unique experiences that separate travelers from tourists. Throughout the book, look for:

Finds	Special finds—those places only insiders know about
Moments	Special moments—those experiences that memories are made of
Tips	Insider tips—great ways to save time and money
Value	Great values—where to get the best deals
Warning	Warning—traveler's advisories are usually in effect

The following **abbreviations** are used for credit cards:

AE	American Express	DISC	Discover	V	Visa
DC	Diners Club	MC	MasterCard		

Frommers.com

Now that you have this guidebook to help you plan a great trip, visit our website at **www.frommers.com** for additional travel information on more than 3,600 destinations. We update features regularly to give you instant access to the most current trip-planning information available. At Frommers.com, you'll find scoops on the best airfares, lodging rates, and car rental bargains. You can even book your travel online through our reliable travel booking partners. Other popular features include:

- Online updates of our most popular guidebooks
- Vacation sweepstakes and contest giveaways
- Newsletters highlighting the hottest travel trends
- Online travel message boards with featured travel discussions

Touring Europe by Rail

Rich, ancient, and incredibly diverse, the nations of Europe offer a vast array of sights, climates, cultures, and cuisines. The 10 trips outlined below show the full reach of the European rail system; feel free to mix and match parts of them to create your ideal vacation.

Where possible, we've used overnight trains on these trips, as they save you the cost of a hotel night, maximize your sightseeing time, and are a rail experience in and of themselves. Remember that overnight trains, many high-speed lines, the Eurostar trains, French TGV trains, and Eurostar Italia require extra reservation fees over the price of your railpass. (See p. 38 for more on overnight trains.) Also note that advance reservations on high-speed rail lines and night trains are becoming more essential every day. If your itinerary depends on making specific connections or catching trains that run on specific schedules, reserve your seat or sleeping car as soon as possible (see "The Price of Rail Travel," in chapter 2, for more information on making train reservations).

We've recommended railpasses for those itineraries below that would make good use of them; where point-to-point tickets are cheaper, we've noted that as well. (For an overview of when to buy a pass and when to go point to point, see p. 44.)

Exact train times and prices are subject to change—the details in these pages were accurate as of August 2007, but you should double-check all train schedules when plotting out your journey. For more on navigating rail schedules, see p. 31.

1 1-Week Itineraries

The average North American vacation is a mere 7 days long (we know, too short!). To help you make the best of your time in Europe, we've put together six 1-week rail itineraries that will give you a taste of some of the best Europe has to offer. Whether you're a royalty fanatic who can't get enough of the Continent's magnificent palaces or a nature buff who'd rather tackle the magnificent scenery of Scandinavia, you'll find an itinerary below that will suit your needs. And if you happen to have more than a week to spend (lucky you!), you can mix and match these itineraries or check out the 2-week itineraries we offer in the next section.

ITINERARY 1   EUROPE'S BEST CASTLES & PALACES

Duration: 8 days, 7 nights
Best time of year: Spring or fall
Recommended passes: Second-class Eurail France–Germany 4-day railpass, plus Eurostar ticket
Arrive in: London
Depart from: Munich

Europe is practically overflowing with medieval castles and ornate palaces. And many of these world-famous residences (and former residences) are open to exploration by those of us whose blood isn't royal blue. Touring all these bastions of nobility could take years, but we've put together an itinerary that will introduce you to a few of the most noteworthy castles and palaces on the Continent and in London.

Day 1

Arrive in London (you'll need to take the red-eye, so catch some z's on the flight). After checking into your hotel, head for a tour of **Buckingham Palace** in the morning, if it's open (only in summer); otherwise, take in the adjacent **Royal Mews** and the magnificent **Queen's Gallery,** both of which are open year-round and feature lots of fabulous royal treasures. Spend the afternoon exploring the **Tower of London,** an imposing castle complex built by William the Conqueror and home to Britain's fabulous crown jewels. If you have time, indulge in a traditional afternoon tea, or try a night out at the theater. See "London" in chapter 10 for more sightseeing options in this historic city.

Day 2

Fortify yourself with a good English breakfast before taking the Eurostar train on a jaunt (trip time: 2 hr., 15 min.) to Paris. If you've got time once you've settled into your hotel, visit the **Louvre,** which would be the largest palace in the world, if it were still a palace and not one of the world's greatest art museums. Pay homage to the *Mona Lisa,* the *Venus de Milo,* and 300,000 or so of their fellow artworks. It's a royal treat, palace or not. See "Paris" in chapter 8 for other things to do in the city.

Day 3

Get an early morning start and take the RER C-line commuter train (show your railpass at the ticket booth and get your free ticket—the pass itself isn't enough) out to **Versailles** (p. 281) and spend a half-day touring Louis XIV's masterpiece,

a structure so magnificent that building it practically bankrupted the state treasury. Return to Paris in the afternoon for a stroll or some other sightseeing before taking an evening TGV high-speed train for the 1-hour ride to **Tours,** in the Loire valley. Check into your hotel (see "Tours" in chapter 8 for accommodations options) and rest up.

Day 4

If ever there were a spot for castle lovers, it's the **Loire valley.** Unfortunately, it's not the most train-friendly locale in France, so the best way to see the region's famous castles is to get up early and take a full-day bus tour of the Loire châteaux. Tours leave at 9am daily from the city's tourist office and, alas, Tours sightseeing tours aren't covered by railpasses. Should you wish to explore on your own, a few châteaux are reachable from Tours by rail. Try the Gothic and Renaissance **Château Royal d'Amboise** or the historic **Château Royal de Blois.** Stay in Tours a second night. See "Tours" in chapter 8 for more châteaux excursions out of Tours.

Day 5

More châteaux! Take a 25-minute train ride to **Chenonceaux** (p. 295), noted for its startling river-spanning castle. Return to Tours and take the 7:13pm train to St-Pier-Des-Cours, then hop immediately on the TGV to Gare Montparnasse in Paris, arriving at 8:25pm, to connect to the 10:45pm overnight train from Paris Est station to **Munich,** which arrives at 8:59am. (*Note:* You'll have to get from Montparnasse to Paris Est station by Metro or taxi, but you've got plenty of time to make the connection.)

Itinerary 1: Europe's Best Castles & Palaces

Day 6
Check into your hotel upon arriving in Munich, then head off to the **Nymphenburg Palace** (p. 364), Germany's largest baroque palace. If the weather's good, be sure to stroll the surrounding Nymphenburg Park. At night you can raise a stein or two inside of the city's famous beer halls. For other nightlife options, check out "Munich" in chapter 9.

Day 7
You've got a busy day. From the Munich Hauptbahnhof, take an early morning train to **Füssen** (trip time: 2 hr.). Take one of the hourly buses to **Neuschwanstein**

(p. 371), Mad King Ludwig's fairy-tale folly. (This was the model for Walt Disney's Cinderella Castle and the real thing is a heck of a lot better!) Next up is nearby **Hohenschwangau** (p. 371) and its famous murals. Tour that castle (waiting in line to get in should eat up the rest of your day) and then return to Munich for the evening.

Day 8
If you have an afternoon flight, you can tour the downtown **Residenz Palace** before heading off to the airport. Otherwise your castle hopping will come to an end as you fly home from Munich.

ITINERARY 2   SMALL CITIES OF THE BENELUX

Duration:	8 days, 7 nights
Best time of year:	Summer
Ideal passes:	Point-to-point tickets or Eurail Benelux Pass (more convenient, though more expensive)
Arrive in:	Amsterdam Schiphol
Depart from:	See below

Relaxing, romantic small cities can be an antidote to the typical European big-city bustle. Tack part of this itinerary onto a Paris or Amsterdam trip for a change of pace, or do the whole thing for a truly intimate week. All the Dutch and Belgian destinations in this itinerary are within a few hours of Amsterdam or Brussels, and you won't have to worry about catching a train at a specific time within Holland because all trains run on at least an hourly basis.

Day 1

Arrive at Amsterdam Schiphol airport, and take a train from the station beneath the airport terminal directly to The Hague, just 50 minutes away. Check into your hotel for a 3-night stay. Once you're settled in, head for **Madurodam,** a fascinating scale-model replica of dozens of Dutch landmarks and attractions. After you've had your fill of miniatures, and if you still have time, take tram 1 all the way up to the beach resort of **Scheveningen** to see how the Dutch spend sunny days. See p. 642 for more information on The Hague.

Day 2

Take local tram 1—not the train—from The Hague to **Delft** and spend the day in that charming city, strolling its atmospheric canals, touring its two churches, and visiting its renowned **Stedelijk Museum Het Prinsenhof** (p. 647). Head back in the evening to The Hague and relax.

Day 3

In the morning, grab a train to **Haarlem,** a compact town just 35 minutes away that's ideal for strolling. Start first at its impressive **Grote Markt (market square)** and catch a recital on the 98-foot-tall (29m) organ inside the **Church of St.**

Bavo. Finally, take in the city's finest attraction, the **Frans Hals Museum,** which sports both great art and a charming 17th-century setting. For more information on Haarlem, see p. 641. In the afternoon, head back to The Hague and tour the **Mauritshuis,** whose must-see art collection includes the quintessential Benelux city landscape—Vermeer's *View of Delft*—as well as Vermeer's famous *Girl with a Pearl Earring.*

Day 4

It's time to leave The Hague behind. Take a morning InterCity train to Antwerp's Centraal Station (trip time: 1 hr., 30 min.), store your luggage there, and then lose yourself on the streets of Antwerp, a hidden gem that's the capital of Europe's diamond trade. Don't miss the largest church in the Benelux, the **Cathedral of Our Lady,** situated right off the city's medieval and picturesque **Grote Markt.** For a touch of culture, visit the impressive **Rubens House,** where artist Peter Paul Rubens once lived and worked. For more on Antwerp, see p. 145. In the evening, head back to the rail station and catch a train (trip time 1 hr., 50 min.) to the city of Liège in the heart of Belgium's Wallonia province. Check into your hotel and give yourself a well-earned rest.

Itinerary 2: Small Cities of the Benelux

Day 5

Spend your day exploring the "Passionate City" of Liège. Don't miss the **Museum of Walloon Life** (p. 156), especially its fabulous puppet collection. The Romanesque **Church of St. Bartholomew** has a 12th-century baptismal font that's regarded as one of the greatest treasures in Belgium. For more options in Liège, see p. 154.

Day 6

Eat an early breakfast before catching a train to your final base in the Benelux—the World Heritage city of **Bruges.** The trip will take about 2 hours. Once you've settled into your hotel, wind your way through the medieval streets of Bruges, making sure to visit the city's famous **Belfry and Market Halls,** the **Begijn-hof,** and the **Church of Our Lady** with its sculpture by Michelangelo. See p. 147 for more on the city.

Day 7

If you can draw yourself away from Bruges for the day, get on a train for the 23-minute ride to **Ghent,** another breathtaking medieval city. Make sure to see its **St. Bavo's Cathedral,** the **Belfry,** and the grim **Castle of the Counts,** and then stroll along Graslei. Return to Bruges before dinner and spend the rest of the evening soaking up the city's medieval atmosphere. For more on Ghent, see p. 142.

Day 8

Bruges is close to several international airports: Brussels is about 1½ hours away, Amsterdam Schiphol is just under 3½ hours, and Charles de Gaulle in Paris is about 3 hours. Fly home from whichever airport works best for you.

<hr>

ITINERARY 3   RIDING THE SCENIC ROUTE

Duration:	8 days, 7 nights
Best time of year:	Spring; arrive on a Sunday or Monday, so you can ride the Semmering Pass weekend train
Ideal passes:	Second-class point-to-point tickets (cheapest) or first-class 6-day, three-country Eurail Select Pass (most comfortable and flexible, and only a little more expensive)
Arrive in:	Milan
Depart from:	Vienna

There's some intense rail riding on this weeklong trip, but you'll be rewarded with a number of the world's most thrilling and dramatic rail journeys as you travel across the Alps. Two noteworthy trains you'll be riding are the magnificent Centovalli Railway traversing Italy and Switzerland, and the only railway deemed worthy of UNESCO's World Heritage Site designation, the Semmering Pass Railway in Austria.

<hr>

Before leaving home: Call to make reservations to see Leonardo's *Last Supper* in Milan.

Day 1

Arrive in Milan in the morning. After checking into your hotel, see the **Duomo,** and then head for the *Last Supper* if you nabbed a reservation. Spend the afternoon in the **Brera Picture Gallery** and checking out the shops and antiques stores on the side streets off of **Via Brera,** which are open until 7:30pm on most evenings. See p. 606 for more information on the city.

Day 2

Today you head off on one of the best railroad journeys in Europe: a ride on the **Centovalli Railway.** Grab the 9:25am InterCity train to Bellinzona, arriving at 11:21am. Connect there to a noon train to Locarno, arriving at 12:19pm, and then get on the Centovalli Railway to Domodossola, one of the lesser-known scenic treasures of the Alps. The hourly frequency of the Centovalli line means you can get off at any of the charming villages it serves (we recommend Verdasio or Intragna for their cable cars) and get back on again. There are local and express Centovalli trains, so take a local (leaving at 12:42pm) if you want to stop and an express (leaving at 2:12pm) if you want to shoot straight through. If you take the local, make sure to get back on the train to arrive in Domodossola no later than 7pm, so you can catch the 7:42pm Cisalpino (reservations required) to Brig, and from there, connect to **Bern.** If you take the express train straight through, you'll arrive in Domodossola at 3:55pm; from there, hop the 4:10pm train to Bern, where you'll arrive around 6:30pm and can check into your hotel for a well-earned rest.

This all sounds very complicated, but the views offered by the Centovalli trains are exceptional, and these are common and frequent connections. The conductors on any of the trains we mention above will tell you where to go if you ask. And if you miss a train, there will usually be another one along in an hour or so.

Itinerary 3: Riding the Scenic Route

Day 3

Bern is lovely, but the best railway scenery is in nearby Interlaken. In the morning, make the 54-minute journey to the Interlaken Ost train station and you'll get a view of the mountains in the distance, the 13,000-foot (3,900m) peaks of the **Jungfrau** (p. 824). An intricate network of railways climbs these mountains, and you can ride one or two of them today out of the Interlaken station; a railpass doesn't cover these trains, but passholders do get a 25% discount. Rail Europe also sells Jungfrau tickets. Once you've had your fill of the magnificent scenery, head back to Bern and have dinner in one of the city's wine taverns. See p. 830 for more Bern nightlife options.

Day 4

Say goodbye to Bern, grab your luggage, and head back to Interlaken Ost. The famous **Golden Pass Line** (p. 850) heads through the mountains outside of Interlaken along an incredibly scenic route to Luzern (Lucerne). Take the 11:08am **Golden Pass Panoramic** train (reservations needed) from Interlaken Ost to Luzern (you'll arrive at 1:04pm), connecting there to Zurich.

From Zurich, make the 3¾-hour trip to Innsbruck, Austria (you will probably end up on the 5:40pm out of Zurich and won't arrive in Austria until after 9pm, so consider eating on the train, or wait to eat a late dinner after you check into your hotel). If you have some energy left (or you managed to snag an earlier train out of Zurich), take a tram to the **Hungerburg cable railway** (p. 119), which takes you up a mountain overlooking the city and offers especially beautiful nighttime views of Innsbruck. For more on the city, see p. 115.

Day 5

Spend the morning strolling the beautifully preserved **Altstadt** (Old Town) in **Innsbruck.** After an early lunch, catch the 1:30pm train to **Salzburg,** a 2-hour ride through spectacular Alpine scenery. Check into your hotel and then stroll through this picturesque city and see the **Residenz State Rooms,** where Mozart once played for royal guests. For more options in Salzburg, see p. 104.

Day 6

Take the 9:10am train from Salzburg to Vienna. After you arrive at 12:30pm, check into your hotel and eat lunch. Spend the afternoon visiting the **Schönbrunn palace,** summer seat of the Habsburg dynasty. For more on this city, see p. 93. Have a piece of the city's famous dessert, the *Sacher torte*—you've earned it.

Day 7

Trying to experience the 150-year-old **Semmering Pass Railway**—the only rail line on UNESCO's list of World Heritage Sites—on a speedy modern train is a lost cause. The best way to see it is to take a round-trip excursion on an old-fashioned Experience Train out of Vienna, though these depart only on Saturday and Sunday mornings. For more on this historic railway, see p. 80. Have dinner in a Viennese wine tavern and, if you can, attend a concert or theater performance. If you're an opera fan, the **Staatsoper (Vienna State Opera)** is one of the best in the world.

Start your day off at **St. Stephen's Cathedral** in the heart of Vienna. Climb its south tower for a panoramic view of the city, and then stroll down Kärntnerstrasse, the main shopping street. Stop off at one of the city's grand cafes at 11am for coffee. In the afternoon, visit the **Schönbrunn palace,** summer seat of the Habsburg dynasty. Have dinner in a Viennese wine tavern and, if you can, attend a concert or theater performance. If you're an opera fan, the **Staatsoper (Vienna State Opera)** is one of the best in the world.

Day 8

If there's time in the morning, try and see **St. Stephen's Cathedral** in the heart of Vienna. Climb its south tower for a panoramic view of the city, and then stroll down Kärntnerstrasse, the main shopping street, before flying home out of Vienna.

<hr />

ITINERARY 4   EASTERN EUROPE

Duration:	8 days, 7 nights
Best time of year:	Summer
Ideal passes:	Point-to-point tickets
Arrive in:	Prague
Depart from:	Budapest

Liberated and bustling, but also ancient, Eastern Europe is blooming as a rail destination. And, compared to Western Europe, it's cheap, too. This weeklong jaunt takes you to three very different but easily accessible capitals on both sides of the former Iron Curtain: hip Prague, historic Budapest, and cultured Vienna.

Itinerary 4: Eastern Europe

Day 1

Arrive in **Prague** in the morning. After checking into your hotel, walk the city's famous Royal Route, touring **Prague Castle** before walking across the Charles Bridge into **Old Town.** From there, head for **Wenceslas Square,** site of the demonstrations that led to the Velvet Revolution in 1989. See p. 169 for more on the city.

Day 2

Prague's greatest strengths are its architecture and atmosphere; both are best experienced by strolling and wandering the city's streets. So spend your day exploring Prague's **Old Town** and **Jewish Quarter** in more depth. In the Jewish Quarter

(Josefov), be sure to visit the **Old Jewish Cemetery.**

Day 3

Take an early morning train to beautiful, medieval **Český Krumlov,** changing trains in České Budějovice. Grab the 8:16am from Prague, which will get you into Krumlov around 1:21pm. Spend the day exploring this World Heritage Site (be sure to see the city's famous castle) and stay overnight. For more information on this picturesque town, see p. 190.

Day 4

It's another very early start. Hop the 8:06am train from Krumlov back to

České Budějovice. You'll have about 2½ hours to explore this former fortress town and original home of Budweiser beer. See p. 194 for sightseeing options in the town. Make sure you're back in the station in time to catch the 12:09pm train to Linz. You'll connect there to a train to Vienna and should arrive in the Austrian capital around 4:35pm. Check into your hotel, have dinner (don't skip dessert in this city renowned for its pastries!), and perhaps take in a concert. For more on Vienna, see p. 84.

Day 5

See Day 7 of the "Riding the Scenic Route" itinerary on p. 6.

Day 6

Take the 8:25am train out of Vienna to Budapest. After arriving at 11:18am, check into your hotel and eat lunch. Spend your afternoon exploring the **Inner City** and **Central Pest.** Walk down **Vaci útca,** the city's trendiest shopping street. Then stroll along the Danube to the neo-Gothic **Parliament** building. Have a hearty Hungarian dinner and, if you're an opera fan, join the rest of Budapest at the **Hungarian State Opera.** See p. 511 for more information on the city.

Day 7

Today, focus on Budapest's Castle District. Be sure to see the 13th-century **Matthias Church** and the **Budapest History Museum.** On your way back into Pest, stop for coffee and a slice of *dobos torta* (layer cake) at **Auguszt,** one of the city's classic coffeehouses. Then drop in at **St. Stephen's Church,** the country's largest, before heading over to the striking Moorish and Byzantine **Dohány Synagogue,** the largest in Europe. After dinner, take in one the city's many musical concerts.

Day 8

Fly home from Budapest.

ITINERARY 5   EXPLORING THE SCANDINAVIAN TRIANGLE

Duration:	8 days, 7 nights
Best time of year:	Summer
Ideal passes:	Point-to-point tickets or 5-day Eurail Scandinavia Pass
Arrive in:	Copenhagen
Depart from:	Stockholm

Summer in Scandinavia brings days that stretch forever. Take advantage of all those sunny hours to explore three of the region's key cities: Copenhagen, Stockholm, and Oslo.

Day 1

Arrive in Copenhagen in the morning and check into your hotel. Take a couple of hours to stroll the old city's cobblestone streets and its many canals. Spend the late afternoon at **Christiansborg Palace.** Early in the evening, sample the rides and entertainment at the city's famous **Tivoli.** See p. 202 for more sightseeing options.

Day 2

In the morning, visit **Amalienborg Palace,** see the changing of the guard there, and then walk to the statue of the **Little Mermaid.** In the afternoon, see the treasures of the **Nationalmuseet,** and in the evening, drop in on one of the city's many jazz clubs.

Itinerary 5: Exploring the Scandinavian Triangle

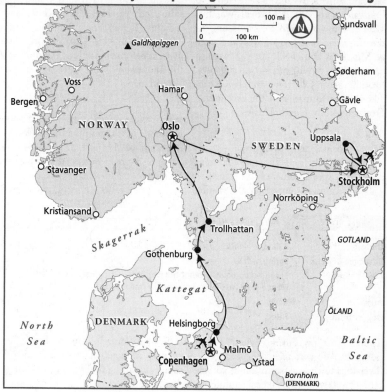

Day 3

Spend your morning perusing works by the Old Masters at **the Statens Museum for Kunst,** then have an early lunch and leave Copenhagen on the 1:23pm X2000 express train to Gothenburg, and switch there to the 5:50pm train to Oslo. Eat dinner on the train because you won't arrive in Oslo before 9:45pm. Check into your hotel and get some rest.

Day 4

After breakfast, stroll past the **Akershus Castle and Fortress** before catching the bus to the Bygdøy peninsula for the city's renowned ship museums. In the afternoon, if you have time, take in the

Edvard Munch Museum or head to the **Tryvannstårnet** tower for a panoramic view of Oslo. See p. 646 for more information.

Day 5

Get up early and spend your morning viewing the masterpieces hanging in the **Nasjonalgalleriet.** Then hop the 1:29pm train to Karlstad, where you can pick up the 4:23pm X2000 train to Stockholm, which will put you in the Swedish capital at 7:35pm. After checking into your hotel, head to Stockholm's **Gamla Stan (Old Town)** and have a late dinner at one of its restaurants. See p. 778 for information on Sweden's capital.

Day 6

Get an early start and take a ferry to Djurgården to visit the **Royal Warship Vasa** and the **Skansen** folk museum. In the afternoon, head to the **Royal Palace & Museums** and check out the Swedish crown jewels, among other royal treasures. Have dinner in Old Town and, if you can, take in a performance in the exceptional **Drottningholm Court Theater.**

Day 7

Take a morning train to **Uppsala**—trains leave every half hour and take 57 minutes—and spend some of the morning walking around the university and visiting its famous Gothic cathedral. After lunch, take the local bus to historic **Gamla Uppsala** and explore the archaeological remains there. For more sightseeing options, see p. 793. Return to Stockholm by train before dinnertime. For dinner, try the smorgasbord-style buffet at the **Grand Verandan.**

Day 8

If your flight doesn't leave until the afternoon, spend the morning in the **National Museum of Art.** Catch the 20-minute Arlanda Express train to the airport and fly home.

ITINERARY 6   WARM-WEATHER EUROPE

Duration:	8 days, 7 nights
Best time of year:	Spring or fall
Ideal passes:	Second-class point-to-point tickets (cheapest) *or* first-class 4-day France–Italy Pass (more comfortable and flexible)
Arrive in:	Rome
Depart from:	Nice

There's a mellow Europe, where 3-hour lunches and lounging on the beach is the norm. It's also an ancient and beautiful place, with numerous cultural and historical diversions to choose from should you need to do something other than work on your tan. This 1-week trip takes you along the Mediterranean coastline and lets you relax along the beaches of two sun-soaked countries. Bring plenty of sunblock!

Day 1

Arrive early in **Rome** and take the train (don't use your railpass for this inexpensive option) into town. Check into your hotel and spend the afternoon and evening touring the ruins of Ancient Rome, starting at the **Capitoline Hill** and walking along the **Via dei Fori Imperiali** to the ruins of the **Colosseum.** Have dinner near the **Piazza Navona,** then explore that famous square and see **Bernini's Fountain.** See p. 552 for more sightseeing options in the city.

Day 2

Spend today exploring the treasures of the Vatican. Take in **St. Peter's Basilica** in the morning and the **Vatican Museums** in the afternoon. Have dinner in Trastevere.

Day 3

Take a day-trip to the ancient city of **Pompeii,** just 2½ hours from Rome by train. Trains run via Naples and if you leave Rome at 9:25am and return from Pompeii at 5:06pm, you'll have time for dinner in Naples before returning to Rome.

Itinerary 6: Warm-Weather Europe

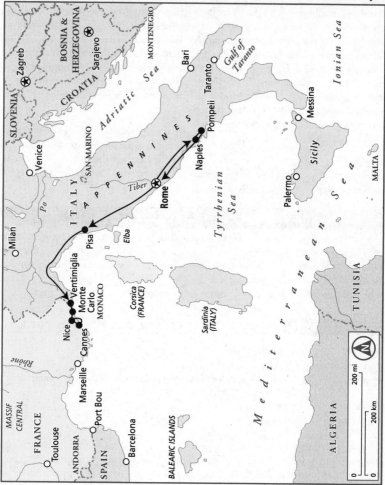

Day 4

During the morning, shop and stroll around the **Spanish Steps.** In the afternoon, take in another museum, such as the **Galleria Borghese,** or enjoy people-watching on the Piazza della Rotonda near the Pantheon. Take the 9:16pm overnight train to Nice.

Day 5

You'll arrive in Nice at 9:45am. Check into your hotel, and then head off to stroll the **promenade des Anglais.** Be sure to take in one of the city's many museums—perhaps the **Musée des Beaux-Arts?** For other sightseeing options in the capital of the Riviera, see p. 312.

Day 6
Head off to Cannes (a mere 34 min. by train) and spend the day ogling beachgoers (as Cannes's rocky beach isn't very comfortable), window-shopping on **La Croisette,** and pretending to be rich and famous. Or take a ferry from the port in Cannes to one of the Lérins Islands and sunbathe. See p. 305 for more on Cannes. Head back to Nice for dinner, and perhaps see a show or court lady luck in the **Cabaret du Casino Ruhl.**

Day 7
In the morning, catch a train (48 of them run each day; trip time: 20 min.) to glamorous Monte Carlo, capital of the tiny principality of Monaco. Spend the day soaking up the chic atmosphere of this wealthy playground, but don't miss the appropriately royal **Les Grands Appartements du Palais** and the amazing **Musée de l'Océanographie.** Eat dinner here before returning to Nice. For more on Monte Carlo, see p. 317.

Day 8
If you have time before your flight, visit another museum in Nice, or exploring **Le Château.** Then bid *adieu* to France and fly home out of Aéroport Nice–Côte d'Azur.

2 2-Week Itineraries

Though you can do a 1-week rail vacation in Europe if you limit your travels to a small region, if you want to cut a wider swath, you'll need at least 2 weeks to see things without feeling rushed. In this section we offer a couple of specialized itineraries for architecture buffs and food lovers, as well as a few "grand tour" suggestions for travelers who want to sample Europe's various regions and cities at a reasonable pace.

ITINERARY 7   EUROPE'S BEST ART & ARCHITECTURE

Duration:	15 days, 14 nights
Best time of year:	Spring
Ideal passes:	First-class 6- or 8-day, four-country Eurail Select Pass (most comfortable; and only a little more expensive than second-class)
Arrive in:	Brussels
Depart from:	Venice

This trip lets you bury yourself among the masterpieces of European art—it's a museum buff's dream. You'll hit four of the world's greatest museums—the Louvre, the Prado, the Vatican, and the Uffizi—as well as three open-air museums filled with great architecture in Bruges, Barcelona, and Venice.

Day 1
Arrive at Brussels National Airport, then take the train into Brussels Midi station and immediately connect to a train to **Bruges;** the entire train trip should take about 1½ hours. In Bruges, tour the medieval streets and enjoy the city's unique architecture. If you opt for the 6-day pass, then just buy a point-to-point ticket for this trip. See p. 147 for more on Bruges.

Day 2
Take one of the hourly trains that leave Bruges for Brussels, and then catch a Thalys trains to Paris. If you time it right, the entire trip should take about 2½ hours. Once you're settled in **Paris,** start off at the **Arc de Triomphe,** then stroll down the Champs-Elysées to the **Egyptian obelisk** at the Place de la Concorde.

Itinerary 7: Europe's Best Art & Architecture

Next up is the **Eiffel Tower**. Around sunset, head for **Notre-Dame Cathedral** to top off your Paris monuments tour. See p. 254 for more on the City of Light.

Day 3

If you're a fan of great art, then we don't have to tell you that the **Louvre** warrants an entire day. But if you need a change of pace in the afternoon, the **Centre Pompidou** will yank you into the 20th century.

Day 4

So many riches: The **Musée National Auguste Rodin**? The **Musée Picasso**? How about the **Musée d'Orsay**? Choose two, and enjoy one in the morning and one in the afternoon. After an early dinner,

head to Paris's Austerlitz station for the 7:43pm overnight train to Madrid's Charmartín station, arriving at 9:13am. This train, the *Francisco de Goya*, is an Elipsos Trenhotel (p. 258) and one of Europe's most luxurious rides.

Day 5

Check into your hotel, then start your day in Madrid at the **Royal Palace** and work your way east to the **Monasterio de las Descalzas Reales.** Spend the night as locals do by Tasca hopping. See p. 711 for more information.

Day 6

How does the **Museo del Prado** compare to the Louvre? Today's your day to find out. If there's time, head over to the **Museo Nacional Centro de Arte Reina Sofia,** home of Picasso's famous *Guernica.* If you aren't too exhausted, take in a flamenco show after dinner.

Day 7

Take the 10:25am high-speed train from Charmartín station to **Barcelona Sants,** arriving at 2:43pm. Spend the afternoon and evening strolling the **Barri Gòtic,** the city's Gothic quarter, or the famous promenade of **La Rambla.** For more sightseeing options in Barcelona, see p. 762.

Day 8

Start your morning with a tour of **La Sagrada Família;** then head either to **Parc Güell** for more Modernist masterpieces, or take in the **Fundació Joan Miró** or **Museu Picasso** museums. (This is a good time to take a break from museums, and lounge on a bench in Parc Güell staring at the sky.)

Take the 8:15pm Euro Night train out of Estacio de França to Milan, where you'll transfer to the 10am Eurostar Italia train bound for Rome, arriving at 2:30pm on Day 9.

Day 9

Check into your hotel in **Rome** and spend the afternoon and evening touring the ruins of Ancient Rome, starting at the **Capitoline Hill** and walking along the **Via dei Fori Imperiali** to the ruins of the **Colosseum.** See p. 543 for more sightseeing options in the city.

Day 10

Spend the entire day perusing the contents of the **Vatican Museums.** Seeing the **Sistine Chapel** is a given, but don't miss the **Pinacoteca** (picture gallery), which is loaded with masterpieces.

Day 11

Say goodbye to Rome and take a morning train—trains run twice an hour and reservations are necessary—for the 95-minute journey to **Florence.** Florence is fortunately compact, so once you've checked into your hotel, you can spend your day strolling the axis from the **Basilica di Santa Maria Novella** to **Il Duomo,** the **Palazzo Vecchio,** and **Giotto's Bell Tower.** See p. 563 for further details on the city.

Day 12

Check out of your hotel, stash your bags at the train station, and spend your entire day, if possible, submerged in the art of the **Galleria degli Uffizi.** Tear yourself away from the museum's masterpieces in order to grab your bags and board the 7:54pm train to Venice, arriving at 10:49pm. (Either have an early dinner in Florence or eat in the Eurostar Italia train's dining car.) See p. 580 for more details on Venice.

Day 13

Venice *is* art. Explore the **Piazza San Marco** in the morning—be sure to stop in at the **Ducale Palace & Bridge of Sighs** and **St. Mark's Basilica**—and then wander the city's many canals and bridges in the afternoon.

Day 14

Museum buffs should hit the **Galleria dell'Accademia** for older art, the **Collezione Peggy Guggenheim** for newer works, and **Ca' d'Oro,** where a multitude of masterpieces are hung in a grand setting in a former palace. If you prefer architecture to museums, take a *vaporetto* (water taxi) ride along the Grand Canal and visit several of Venice's beautiful churches and guild houses.

Day 15

Bid farewell to Europe and fly home out of Venice.

ITINERARY 8   EUROPE FOR FOOD LOVERS

Duration:	15 days, 14 nights
Best time of year:	Spring or fall
Ideal passes:	First-class three-country Eurail Select Pass (5 or 6 days depending on the side trips you take), plus Eurostar ticket
Arrive in:	London
Depart from:	Barcelona

This 2-week trip features a walk through some of the best and most recognized regional cuisine and dining experiences in Europe. We start you off in London, where you can take afternoon tea or dine on classic pub grub, then head off to indulge in the renowned food mecca of Paris plus the celebrated cuisines of Tuscany and Spain with a side trip to Provence as a bonus. Loosen your belt as you eat your way through Europe.

Before you leave: If you don't want to be left out in the cold, it is crucial to make dinner reservations by phone in advance before you leave home.

Day 1

Arrive in the morning in **London.** The city is actually a center of global cuisine where you can eat a different country's food every day for weeks—it's an often-underrated foodie capital that's about a lot more than fish and chips (though you should have those too!). Spend the day visiting the sites of Westminster: **Westminster Abbey, 10 Downing Street, Big Ben,** and the **Houses of Parliament.** For dinner, sample the festive Indian cuisine at **Mela.** Top off the evening with a pint at a pub near your hotel. See p. 415 and p. 408 for more on dining and sightseeing in the city.

Day 2

Today's a royal day in London. Spend a long morning at the **Tower of London,** have lunch, and then head off to **Kensington Palace.** Grab a pretheater dinner at Michelin-starred chef Nico Ladenis's **Incognico,** then head off to the West End and see a show.

Day 3

In the morning, visit the **British Museum.** Shop a bit in Covent Garden and stop in at one of Soho's many patisseries (**Maison Bertaux**'s our favorite) for a traditional afternoon tea. Then, head off to South Kensington and pop in at the **Victoria & Albert Museum.** For your final night in London, dine at the ultra-British but thoroughly modern cuisine at **Rules Restaurant.**

Day 4

After a good English breakfast, take a morning Eurostar train (trip time: 2 hr., 15 min.) ride to Paris. Your Eurail Select Pass gives you a discount on this speedy but expensive train. (See p. 395 for more on the Eurostar.) Spend the afternoon at the **Louvre** and have dinner in a traditional French brasserie. See p. 273 for dining options in Paris.

Day 5

Get acquainted with monumental Paris. Begin at the **Arc de Triomphe** and stroll down the Champs-Elysées to the **Egyptian obelisk;** then either stand in line for the Eiffel Tower or explore the **Ile St-Louis** and the **Quartier Latin.** Take a break at a Left Bank cafe for coffee and pastries, and around sunset, head for **Notre-Dame Cathedral** to top off your Paris monuments tour. Have dinner in a Left Bank bistro.

Itinerary 8: Europe for Food Lovers

Day 6

Explore a Parisian food market this morning to see where chefs get their inspiration. Then visit **Fauchon,** the ultimate gourmet food store, for the ingredients of a picnic lunch. Spend the rest of the day exploring the sights of the **Ile de la Cité** and **Le Marais** before seeing what all that three-star Michelin stuff is about at **L'Ambroisie** (just be prepared to empty your wallet). Get some rest—you'll have an early start and a very long day tomorrow.

Day 7

Depart Paris on the 10:20am TGV train to **Avignon,** in Provence (arriving at 12:57pm). This former capital of Christendom offers excellent dining and the magnificent **Palais des Papes (Palace of the Popes)** for touring. Have an early dinner because you'll need to hop the TGV back to Paris at 8:56pm to arrive at 11:40pm. Fall into bed and get a well-deserved night's sleep. See p. 300 for dining options in the city.

Day 8

Sleep in a little, have a leisurely breakfast, and then spend the day at the **Musée d'Orsay** and **Centre Pompidou.** Have lunch in one of the city's celebrated cafes (the avant-garde **Café Beaubourg** is just across from the Pompidou). You can bring along Parisian takeout or have dinner on the 7:06pm overnight train (out of Gare de Bercy) to Florence, your base for Tuscany. You'll arrive at 7:16am on Day 9.

Day 9

Work up your appetite today by strolling **Florence** from the **Basilica di Santa Maria Novella** to the Duomo, the **Palazzo Vecchio,** and finally Santa Croce. Have lunch at a simple Italian restaurant such as **Buca dell'Orafo** or **Da Ganino.** For dinner, eat at the legendary Tuscan restaurant **Paoli.** See p. 583 for more on dining in the city.

Day 10

It's excursion time: Catch the 9:33am train to the Tuscan city of Pisa. You'll arrive at 10:31am and should immediately set out for the famous **Leaning Tower.** For lunch, sample excellent Pisan cuisine at **Antica Trattoria Da Bruno,** near the tower. Then tour the **Duomo** and the **Baptistery** before returning to Florence on the 5:29pm train (arriving 6:33pm). Sample some more delectable Tuscan cuisine at dinner, then have dessert and coffee at one of the city's many sidewalk cafes and people-watch.

Day 11

Spend the morning at the **Boboli Gardens** and the **Palazzo Pitti.** Take a long lunch at **Cantinetta Antinori,** sampling the wines. After a siesta, do some shopping and have a final Tuscan dinner at **Trattoria Garga.**

Day 12

Get up early and spend the day in the **Galleria degli Uffizi,** one of the world's greatest art museums. Take the 4:14pm express train from Florence to Milan, where you'll have a 50-minute layover before connecting to the 7:50pm overnight train to Barcelona. Have dinner on the train or grab something in Milan's station before you depart. You'll arrive in Barcelona at 9:01am.

Day 13

Barcelona has an embarrassment of riches, both culinary and architectural. Check into your hotel and then start your day off at **La Sagrada Familia** cathedral, the city's famous cathedral, and wander the city's Gothic Quarter. Take lunch at **Garduña,** located in the back of Catalonia's best food market, before visiting the **Museu Picasso.** Retire to your hotel room for a siesta, then eat a late dinner and spend the night downing bubbly at Barcelona's numerous *cava* (champagne) bars. See p. 766 for more on dining in the city.

Day 14

Start your day off by visiting the **Parc Güell,** and the **Fundació Joan Miró.** Spend a relaxing afternoon sipping cava and munching tapas at **El Xampanyet,** and eat a late dinner at one of Barcelona's excellent Catalonian restaurants—**Jean Luc Figueras** is a good choice.

Day 15

Say *adios* to Europe and fly home from Barcelona.

ITINERARY 9   GREAT CITIES OF EUROPE

Duration:	15 days, 14 nights
Best time of year:	Spring or fall
Ideal passes:	First-class 5-day, four-country Eurail Select Pass, plus Eurostar tickets
Arrive in:	Rome
Depart from:	Berlin

Europe has been the center of many a globe-girdling empire. This 2-week trip gets you to the heart of the Continent's great cities—and gives you as much time as possible to explore their sights and sounds—and to meet their people.

Day 1

Land at Rome's Fiumicino airport, starting your European rail journey with the train shuttle to the Roma Termini Station (don't waste a day on your railpass for this ride, though—the ticket is very cheap). Check into your hotel before starting your exploration of ancient Rome, beginning at the **Capitoline Hill** and walking along the Via dei Fori Imperiali to the ruins of the **Colosseum.** Nearby you'll find the ruins of the **Roman Forum** and the **Palatine Hill.** Have dinner near the **Pantheon** and visit the **Trevi Fountain.** See p. 536 for more on the city.

Day 2

Spend today exploring the treasures of the Vatican. Take in **St. Peter's Basilica** in the morning and the **Vatican Museums** in the afternoon. Have dinner in Trastevere.

Day 3

During the morning, shop and stroll around the **Spanish Steps.** In the afternoon, take in another museum, such as the **Galleria Borghese,** or enjoy people-watching on the Piazza della Rotonda near the Pantheon. Around 5pm, head to Stazione Termini for your first major rail trip: the **Artesia France-Italy Night train** departing at 6:40pm from Rome, arriving at 9:10am the next morning in Paris.

Day 4

Get acquainted with Paris. Begin at the **Arc de Triomphe** and stroll down the Champs-Elysées to the **Egyptian obelisk;** then either stand in line for the **Eiffel Tower** or explore the **Ile St-Louis** and the **Latin Quarter.** Around sunset, head for **Notre-Dame Cathedral** to top off your day. Eat dinner in a Left Bank cafe. See p. 254 for more information on Paris.

Day 5

Start your day off exploring the **St-Germain-des-Prés** area. Move on to the Ile de la Cité, before heading to the **Place de la Bastille.** Finish your day off by touring fashionable Le Marais. Then eat dinner at a brasserie and spend the night people-watching at a sidewalk cafe.

Day 6

Spend the day at the **Louvre;** if you want a change of scenery, tack on a visit to the magnificent **Musée d'Orsay.** Be sure to indulge in some Parisian pastries before the day is through.

Day 7

Grab a croissant on the way to the Gare de Nord and take a morning Eurostar train to London. The just-over-2-hour journey rockets across France at up to 180 mph (290kmph). It may appear costly, but the passholder fare is no more expensive (and far more comfortable) than the combined fare for a high-speed ferry from Calais to Dover and a local train from Dover to London. (See p. 395 for more on Eurostar.)

You'll arrive in **London** around lunchtime. Leave your bags at your hotel and grab lunch at a nearby pub. Spend the afternoon touring the sights of Westminster: **Westminster Abbey, 10 Downing Street, Big Ben,** and the **Houses of Parliament.** Have dinner in Covent Garden. See p. 400 for more on the British capital.

Day 8

If you couldn't get into Westminster Abbey on Day 7, try again. Otherwise, spend the

Itinerary 9: Great Cities of Europe

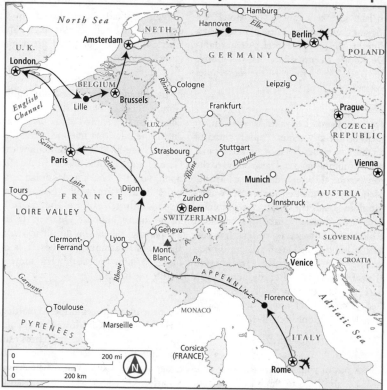

morning at the **British Museum,** and after lunch head over to the **Tower of London.** If you have time, take a ride on the **British Airways London Eye,** just across the river. After a quick dinner, head over to the West End and catch a show.

Day 9

If one of your days in London is a weekend, spend some time at one or two of the major markets, such as Portobello Road. If you're here midweek, wave hello to the lions in **Trafalgar Square** and tour the **National Gallery,** one of Europe's finest art museums (and it's free!). Grab some lunch, shop a bit at Covent Garden, and end your day at the **Victoria & Albert Museum**—home of the world's

greatest collection of decorative arts (don't miss the British Galleries).

Day 10

Fortify yourself with a good English breakfast this morning before heading to Waterloo station for the 10am Eurostar to **Brussels,** the capital of the European Union. The trip takes under 2 hours, but you'll arrive after 1pm thanks to a 1-hour time difference. See p. 129 for more on Brussels.

Once you arrive, stash your luggage at Gare du Midi, then hop a train to Gare Central and head to the medieval **Grand-Place,** a World Heritage Site, for some of the city's famous seafood and mussels. After dinner, head back to Gare du Midi and get on the 8:25pm InterCity train for the 2¾-hour trip to Amsterdam. You'll get in late, so take a cab to your hotel. We suggest staying near Centraal Station, at a hotel such as the **Hotel Amsterdam-De Roode Leeuw** or the **Amstel Botel.** See p. 629 in chapter 14 for more hotel options.

Day 11

You've only got 2 days in Amsterdam, so focus on the city center. Explore the core of the city either by foot or on a canal boat, stopping at the **Dam Square,** the picturesque **Flower Market** at **Muntplein,** the immense market at **Waterlooplein,** and the lively **Leidseplein.** After a late lunch, stop at the renowned **Rijksmuseum** to see its current "greatest hits" exhibition of Dutch art. For dinner, sample one of the city's **Indonesian rijsttafel buffets.** After dinner, if you dare, take an evening walk through the Red Light District on the way back to your hotel—it only gets livelier as it gets later.

Day 12

Check out of your hotel early, store your luggage, and head to the western part of the city this morning, past the Dutch Renaissance–style **Westerkerk,** to the haunting **Anne Frank House.** Have lunch at **De Prins,** right across the canal. Unwind with a coffee and "brown-cafe" style food while people-watching along the canal.

Make sure to be at Schiphol Station in time to catch the 2:51pm InterCity train to Berlin (alas, there are no decent overnight trains from Amsterdam to the German capital). Have dinner on the train and arrive in Berlin at 9:18pm. Check into your hotel and get a good night's sleep.

Day 13

In the morning, visit the **Brandenburg Gate,** symbol of Berlin, then walk down Unter den Linden and enjoy breakfast at one of the cafes that line the street. Head to the store-lined **Ku'damm** to witness German capitalism in action. In the afternoon, visit the Greek and Roman antiquities in the **Pergamon Museum,** then head south to explore the charming 16th-century **Nikolai Quarter.** If they are playing, when you are in town, the **Berlin Philharmonic Orchestra** is one of the best in the world. For more on Berlin, see p. 330.

Day 14

Visit the masterpieces at the **Gemäldegalerie,** then tour **Charlottenburg Palace** and its museums. Spend any leftover time strolling through Berlin, perhaps stopping at the Cold War's **Checkpoint Charlie.** Or take a day-trip to beautiful **Potsdam,** just 20 minutes away by train (trains depart throughout the day), and explore the **Sans Souci Palace** and its surrounding parkland. After dinner, do as Berliners do and have a drink at a Kneipe, the local version of a British pub.

Day 15

Fly back to your home from Berlin.

ITINERARY 10   THE GRAND TOUR

Duration:	15 days, 14 nights
Best time of year:	Any time
Ideal passes:	First-class 15-day Eurail Global Pass *or* point-to-point tickets (cheapest)
Arrive in:	Lisbon
Depart from:	Berlin

Itinerary 10: The Grand Tour

The European Union may have a single currency (well, minus a few pesky holdouts here and there), but it's got more than a dozen unique cultures. A dozen in 15 days is a bit too much of a challenge for us, but this long-distance journey lets you experience six distinctly different flavors of Europe without having to change your money once—the most diversity and least hassle you can get in 2 weeks. Note that the five rail legs used in this itinerary are night trains, so you'll save on hotel rooms, but will have to budget for sleeper supplements.

Day 1

Time your flight to arrive in Lisbon as early as possible. Start your day with a stroll through the **Alfama,** the most atmospheric quarter of Lisbon. Visit the city's 12th-century cathedral and take in a view of the city and the river Tagus from the **Miradouro de Santa Luzia.** Climb up to the **Castelo de São Jorge** and take in another breathtaking view from the castle's observation platform. Consider a nap before spending a late night at a **fado club** in the Alfama. See p. 688 for more information on the Portuguese capital.

Day 2

Head to the suburb of Belém to see the **Mosteiro dos Jerónimos,** the **Torre de Belém,** and the **Museu Nacional dos Coches.** After lunch, see the artworks at the **Museu de Fundação Calouste Gulbenkian,** or shop at the open-air **Feira da Ladra.** Take the overnight Lusitânia hotel train to Madrid (p. 674).

Day 3

Drop your luggage at your hotel, then start your day in Madrid at the **Royal Palace** and work your way east to the **Monasterio las Descalzas Reales.** After checking into your hotel, snack your way around the many tapas bars in the Plaza Mayor area. See p. 722 for more on Madrid.

Day 4

Check out the masterpieces at the **Museo Lázaro Galdiano** in the morning and shop the El Rastro flea market in the afternoon. Or take a day-trip to explore the Moorish architectural riches of **Córdoba**—hourly AVE express trains leave from Madrid's Atocha station for the 2-hour journey. See p. 748 for more on this Moorish city.

Day 5

Spend your last day in Madrid at the **Museo del Prado,** and take the overnight *Francisco de Goya* train to Paris. This train, one of the Elipsos series, is one of Europe's most luxurious regular trips; even the most basic accommodation is a four-berth sleeper, not a six-berth couchette room like those on many other trains (p. 258).

Day 6

See Day 4 of the "Great Cities of Europe" itinerary (p. 20).

Day 7

See Day 5 of the "Great Cities of Europe" itinerary (p. 20).

Day 8

Spend the day immersed in art at the **Louvre** and the **Musée d'Orsay.** Grab some gourmet French takeout at **Fauchon** for dinner and take the overnight train to Florence, departing Paris at 7:06pm and arriving at 7:16am.

Day 9

Florence is all about art. Spend your day strolling the city from the **Basilica di Santa Maria Novella** to the **Duomo,** the **Palazzo Vecchio,** and finally **Santa Croce.** Florence is all about food too, so load up on Tuscan cuisine at dinner. See p. 574 for dining options in Florence.

Day 10

Allot the entire day for the **Galleria degli Uffizi,** one of the world's greatest art museums. If you need a change of scenery, stroll the **Boboli Gardens** and take in the art at the **Palazzo Pitti.** Take the 10:14pm overnight train to Vienna, arriving at 8:52am.

Day 11

See Day 7 of the "Riding the Scenic Route" itinerary (p. 8).

Day 12

Explore other major Vienna attractions, such as the **Kaiserliche Hofburg (Imperial Court Palace)** and the **Kunsthistorisches Museum.** Get to the train station in time to take the 7:50pm overnight train to Berlin (arriving at 8:03am).

Day 13

You'll get to **Berlin** by breakfast time, so head for **Unter den Linden** and enjoy breakfast at one of the cafes that line the street. Head to the store-lined **Ku'damm** to shop until you feel like eating lunch. In the afternoon, visit the Greek and Roman antiquities in the **Pergamon Museum,** then head south to explore the charming 16th-century **Nikolai Quarter.** If they are playing, when you are in town, the **Berlin Philharmonic Orchestra** is one of the best in the world. For more on the city, see p. 330.

Day 14
Visit the masterpieces at the **Gemäldegalerie,** then tour **Charlottenburg Palace**

and its museums. Spend any leftover time strolling through Berlin, perhaps stopping at the Cold War's **Checkpoint Charlie.** Top off your trip with a drink at one of Berlin's vaunted wine cellars.

Day 15
Fly home from Berlin.

2

Planning Your European Rail Trip

Rails are the veins of Europe. When you travel on the Continent's speedy, affordable, and surprisingly complete rail system, you'll cross terrain where no cars go, make friends you would never otherwise have met, travel without the worries of traffic, parking, and airport security—and perhaps enjoy a good night's sleep, too.

Speedy trains zip across northern Europe at speeds up to 186 mph (300kmph); slower trains stop in the depths of Swiss mountain valleys and meander past quaint Dutch villages. And somehow, trains make people open up in ways they never would if they were traveling by air, bus, or car. In a car on a French night train, we once met a college student from Nashville, an artist from Florence, and five members of an Ethiopian soccer team. Riding a high-speed train along the backbone of Italy, we were charmed by a young man, heading to his exams for the *carabinieri,* who led us patiently through the chaos of Rome's Termini Station.

Thousands of students first see Europe from the inexpensive perch of a six-berth couchette, but more mature travelers who seek luxury are sure to find it in Europe's top-class trains, where cabins include private showers and waiters bring restaurant-quality meals straight to your room as the Pyrenees or the Mediterranean coast slide by your window.

Those who haven't traveled on European trains in a while will be startled by the range of ticket classes and the bewildering number of trains. But traveling by train doesn't have to be confusing: Take a deep breath, leave yourself some time at the station, and enjoy traveling the way Europeans do.

Modern trains are romantic, comfortable, and an easy way to get around, and they even get you to where you're going on time. What more can you ask?

1 Visitor Information

Your first step in planning your Europe trip should be to decide which countries or regions you'd like to visit. Browse chapters 3 through 19 and the appendix of this book to get an idea of the highlights of each major European country. The 33-nation **European Travel Commission** produces a customized electronic travel planner on its website that is also useful. (c/o Spring, O'Brien and Co., 50 W. 23rd St., 11th Floor, New York, NY 10010; ✆ **212/620-7100;** www.visiteurope.com). Should you want more detailed information to help you make your selections, contact the **European tourist offices** in your own country; for a complete list, see below:

AUSTRIAN NATIONAL TOURIST OFFICE

www.austria.info

IN THE U.S. & CANADA P.O. Box 1142, New York, NY 10110 (**© 212/944-6880;** fax 212/730-4568; travel@austria.info). No visitors.

BELGIAN TOURIST OFFICE

www.visitbelgium.com

IN THE U.S. & CANADA 220 E. 42nd St., Suite 3402, New York, NY 10017 (**© 212/758-8130;** fax 212/355-7675; info@visitbelgium.com). Open Monday to Friday 9:30am to 4:30pm.

VISIT BRITAIN

www.visitbritain.com

IN THE U.S. & CANADA 551 Fifth Ave., Suite 701, New York, NY 10176 (**©US: 800/462-2748; CANADA: 888/VISIT-UK;** travelinfo@visitbritain.org). Open Monday to Friday 9am to 5pm.

BULGARIAN STATE AGENCY FOR TOURISM

www.bulgariatravel.org

IN BULGARIA 1, Sveta Nedelia Sq., 1040 Sofia, Bulgaria (**© 359/2 933 5845;** fax 359/2 989 6939; info@bulgariatravel.org).

CROATIAN NATIONAL TOURIST BOARD

http://us.croatia.hr

IN THE U.S. & CANADA 350 Fifth Ave., Suite 4003, New York, NY 10118 (**© 800/829-4416,** 212/279-8672, or 212/279-8674; fax 212/279-8683; cntony@earthlink.net).

CZECH TOURIST AUTHORITY

www.czechtourism.com

IN THE U.S. 1109 Madison Ave., New York, NY 10028 (**© 212/288-0830;** fax 212/288-0971; info-usa@czechtourism.com). Open Tuesday, Wednesday and Friday, 9am to 5pm; Thursday 9am to 7pm.

IN CANADA 401 Bay St., Suite 1510, Toronto, ON M5H 2Y4 (**© 416/363-9928;** fax 416/363-0239; info-ca@czechtourism.com). Open Monday, Wednesday and Friday 9am to 1pm; Tuesday and Thursday noon to 4pm.

FRENCH GOVERNMENT TOURIST OFFICE

www.franceguide.com

IN THE U.S. 444 Madison Ave., 16th Floor, New York, NY 10022 (**© 514/288-1904;** fax 212/838-7855; info.us@franceguide.com).

IN CANADA 1800 av. McGill College, Suite 1010, Montreal, PQ H3A 3J6 (**© 514/288-2026;** fax 514/845-4868; canada@franceguide.com).

GERMAN NATIONAL TOURIST OFFICE

www.cometogermany.com

IN THE U.S. 122 E. 42nd St., Suite 2000, New York, NY 10168-0072 (**© 800/651-7010** or 212/661-7200; fax 212/661-7174; GermanyInfo@d-z-t.com).

IN CANADA 480 University Avenue, Suite 1500, Toronto, ON M5G 1V2 (**© 877/315-6237** or 416/968-1685; fax 416/968-0562; info@gnto.ca).

GREEK NATIONAL TOURISM ORGANIZATION

www.greektourism.com

IN THE U.S. Olympic Tower, 645 Fifth Ave., Suite 903, New York, NY 10022 (**© 212/421-5777;** fax 212/826-6940; info@greektourism.com).

IN CANADA 1500 Don Mills Rd., Toronto, ON M3B 3K4 (**© 416/968-2220;** fax 416/968-6533; grnto.tor@on.aibn.com).

HUNGARIAN NATIONAL TOURIST OFFICE

www.gotohungary.com

IN THE U.S. & CANADA 350 Fifth Ave., Suite 7107, New York, NY 10118

(© **212/695-1221;** fax 212/207-4103; info@gotohungary.com).

TOURISM IRELAND
www.discoverireland.com

IN THE U.S. & CANADA 345 Park Ave., New York, NY 10154 (© **800/223-6470** or 212/418-0800; fax 212/371-9052).

ITALIAN GOVERNMENT TOURIST BOARD
www.italiantourism.com

IN THE U.S. 630 Fifth Ave., Suite 1565, New York, NY 10111 (© **212/245-5618;** fax 212/586-9249). Open Monday to Friday 9:30am to 5pm.

IN CANADA 175 Bloor St. E., South Tower, Suite 907, Toronto, ON M4W 3R8 (© **416/925-4882;** fax 416/925-4799). Open 9am to 5pm.

LUXEMBOURG NATIONAL TOURIST OFFICE
www.visitluxembourg.com

IN THE U.S. & CANADA 17 Beekman Place, New York, NY 10022 (© **212/935-8888;** fax 212/935-5896; info@visitluxembourg.com).

NATIONAL TOURIST ORGANI-ZATION OF MONTENEGRO
www.visit-montenegro.com

IN MONTENEGRO C/o dBO Advertising Agency, Postanski fah, 28, 85310 Budva, Montenegro (© **381/86 40 20 30;** fax 381/86 40 20 31; info@visit-montenegro.com).

NETHERLANDS BOARD OF TOURISM
www.holland.com

IN THE U.S. & CANADA 355 Lexington Ave., 19th Floor, New York, NY 10017 (© **212/370-7360;** fax 212/370-9507; information@holland.com).

POLISH NATIONAL TOURIST OFFICE
www.polandtour.org

IN THE U.S. & CANADA 5 Marine View Plaza, Hoboken, NJ 07030 (© **201/420-9910;** fax 201/584-9153; pntonyc@polandtour.org).

PORTUGUESE TRADE & TOURISM OFFICE
www.visitportugal.com

IN THE U.S. 590 Fifth Ave., 4th Floor, New York, NY 10036 (© **646/723-0200;** fax 212/575-4737; tourism@portugal.org).

IN CANADA 60 Bloor St. W., Suite 1005, Toronto, ON M4W 3B8 (© **416/921-7376;** fax 416/921-1353; icep.toronto@icep.pt).

ROMANIAN NATIONAL TOURIST OFFICE
www.romaniatourism.com

IN THE U.S. & CANADA 355 Lexington Ave., 19th Floor, New York, NY 10017 (© **212/545-8484;** fax 212/251-0429; info@romaniatourism.com).

SCANDINAVIAN TOURIST BOARDS (DENMARK, FINLAND, NORWAY & SWEDEN)
www.goscandinavia.com, www.visitdenmark.com, www.gofinland.org, www.visitnorway.com, or www.visitsweden.com

IN THE U.S. & CANADA P.O. Box 4649, Grand Central Station, New York, NY 10163-4649 (© **212/885-9700;** fax 212/885-9710; info@goscandinavia.com).

NATIONAL TOURIST ORGANI-ZATION OF SERBIA
www.serbia-tourism.org

IN THE U.K. 7 Dering St., London W1S 1AE (© **44/207 629 2007;** fax 44/207 629 6500; sales@jatlondon.com).

SLOVAK REPUBLIC COMMERCIAL & TOURIST OFFICE

www.slovakiatourism.sk

IN THE SLOVAK REPUBLIC Namestie L. Stura 1, PO Box 35, 974 05 Banska Bystrica, Slovak Republic (© **48/413 61 46;** fax 48/413 61 49; sacr@sacr.sk).

SLOVENIAN TOURIST BOARD

www.slovenia-tourism.si

IN THE U.S. & CANADA 2929 E. Commercial Blvd., Suite 201, Ft. Lauderdale, FL 33308 (© **954/491-0112;** fax 954/771-9841; slotouristboard@kompas.net).

TOURIST OFFICE OF SPAIN

www.spain.info

IN THE U.S. 666 Fifth Ave., 35th Floor, New York, NY 10103 (© **212/265-8822;** fax 212/265-8864; nuevayork@tourspain.es).

IN CANADA 2 Bloor St. W., Suite 3402, Toronto, ON M4W 3E2 (© **416/961-3131;** fax 416/961-1992; toronto@tourspain.es).

SWITZERLAND TOURISM

www.myswitzerland.com

IN THE U.S. & CANADA 608 Fifth Ave., New York, NY 10020 (© **877/794-8037;** fax 212/262-6116; info.usa@myswitzerland.com).

TURKISH GOVERNMENT TOURIST OFFICES

www.tourismturkey.org

IN THE U.S. & CANADA 2525 Massachusetts Ave., Washington, DC 20008(© **202/612-6800;** fax 202/319-7446; dc@tourismturkey.org).

2 When to Go

Europe is a continent for all seasons, offering everything from a bikini beach party on the Riviera to the world's finest skiing in the Alps.

Europe has a continental climate with distinct seasons, but you can expect great temperature variations from one region to another. Northern Norway measures its snow in meters, while southern Italy remains far warmer in the winter. Still, the Gulf Stream keeps weather more temperate across the continent than you might imagine. Scandinavia is seldom colder than the northern U.S., and it's not unheard of for snow to fall even on the Greek Islands in winter. Generally speaking, in spite of its location north of most of the United States expect European temperatures to be somewhat warmer than those in North America.

The **high season** lasts from mid-May to mid-September, with the most tourists hitting the Continent from mid-June to August. In general, this is the most expensive time to travel, except in Austria and Switzerland, where prices are actually higher during the ski season. And because Scandinavian hotels depend on business clients instead of tourists, lower prices can often be found in the fleeting summer, when business travelers are scarce and a smaller number of tourists take over.

You'll find smaller crowds, fair weather, and moderate prices at hotels in the **shoulder seasons,** from Easter to mid-May and mid-September to mid-October. **Off season** (except at ski resorts) is from November to Easter, with the exception of December 25 to January 6. Much of Europe, especially Italy, traditionally takes August off from work, and August 15 to August 30 is vacation time for many locals. Some cities may well be devoid of natives, many of whom are flocking on the beaches instead. But this trend is slowly changing as Europeans step up efforts to attract a global tourism market.

Tips **What Time Is It, Anyway?**

Based on U.S. **Eastern Standard Time (EST),** Britain, Ireland, and Portugal are 5 hours ahead of New York City; Greece is 7 hours ahead of New York. The rest of the countries in this book are 6 hours ahead of New York. For instance, when it's noon in New York, it's 5pm in London and Lisbon; 6pm in Paris, Copenhagen, and Amsterdam; and 7pm in Athens. The European countries observe daylight saving time, but the time change doesn't occur on the same day as in the United States, so be advised that the time difference can vary by as much as 2 hours during those weeks when some countries have switched to or from daylight saving time ahead of North America.

If you plan to travel to Ireland or continental Europe from Britain, keep in mind that the time will be the same in Ireland and Portugal, 2 hours later in Greece, and 1 hour later in the other countries in this guide.

Note: Departure and arrival times on train schedules are always given in 24-hour military time. So a train leaving at 1:23pm would be listed as leaving at 13:23.

WEATHER

BRITAIN & IRELAND   Everyone knows it rains a lot in Britain and Ireland. Winters are rainier than summers; August and from September to mid-October are the sunniest months. Summer daytime temperatures average from the low 60s Fahrenheit (teens Celsius) to the mid-60s (20s Celsius), dropping to the 40s (single digits Celsius) on winter nights. Ireland, whose shores are bathed by the Gulf Stream, has a milder climate and the most changeable weather—a dark rainy morning can quickly turn into a sunny afternoon, and vice versa. The Scottish Lowlands have a climate similar to England's, but the Highlands are much colder, with storms and snow in winter.

CENTRAL EUROPE   In Vienna and along the Danube Valley the climate is moderate. Summer daytime temperatures average in the low 70s Fahrenheit (20s Celsius), falling at night to the low 50s (teens Celsius). Winter temperatures are in the 30s Fahrenheit (below 0 Celsius) and 40s (teens Celsius) during the day. In Budapest, temperatures can reach 80°F (25°C) in August and dip to 30°F (0°C) in January. Winter is damp and chilly, spring is mild, and May and June are usually wet. The best weather is in the late summer through October. In Prague and Bohemia, summer months have an average temperature of 65°F (18°C) but are the rainiest, while January and February are usually sunny and clear, with temperatures around freezing.

FRANCE & GERMANY   The weather in Paris is approximately the same as in the U.S. mid-Atlantic states, but like most of Europe, there's less extreme variation. In summer, the temperature rarely goes above the mid-70s Fahrenheit (mid-20s Celsius), though heat waves (such as the one that struck all of Europe in 2003) can occur. Summers are fair and can be hot along the Riviera. Winters tend to be mild, in the 40s Fahrenheit (teens Celsius), though it's warmer along the Riviera. Germany's climate ranges from the moderate summers and chilly, damp winters in the north to the mild summers and very cold, sunny winters of the Alpine south.

NORTHERN EUROPE   In the Netherlands, the weather is never extreme at any time of year. Summer temperatures average around 67°F (20°C) and the winter average is about 40°F (5°C). The climate is rainy and windy, the skies gray, with the driest months from February to May. From mid-April to mid-May, the tulip fields burst into color. The climate of northern Germany is very similar. Belgium's climate is moderate, varying from 73°F (23°C) in July and August to 40°F (5°C) in December and January. It does rain a lot, but the weather is at its finest in July and August.

SCANDINAVIA   Summer temperatures above the Arctic Circle average around the mid-50s Fahrenheit (midteens Celsius), dropping to around 14°F (–10°C) during the dark winters. In the south, summer temperatures average around 70°F (22°C), dropping to the 20s Fahrenheit (below 0 Celsius) in winter. Fjords and even the ocean are often warm enough for summer swimming, but rain is frequent. The sun shines 24 hours in midsummer above the Arctic Circle, where winter brings semi-permanent twilight. Denmark's climate is relatively mild by comparison. It has moderate summer temperatures and winters that can be damp and foggy, with temperatures just above the mid-30s Fahrenheit (0 Celsius).

SOUTHERN EUROPE   Summers are hot in Italy, Spain, and Greece, with temperatures around the high 80s Fahrenheit (30s Celsius) or higher in some parts of Spain. Along the Italian Riviera, summer and winter temperatures are mild, and except in the Alpine regions, Italian winter temperatures rarely drop below freezing (although Mediterranean winds can be cold). The area around Madrid is dry and arid, and summers in Spain are coolest along the Atlantic coast, with mild temperatures year-round on the Costa del Sol. Seaside Portugal is very rainy but has temperatures of 50°F to 75°F (10°C–25°C) year-round. In Greece, there's sunshine all year, and winters are usually mild, with temperatures around 50°F to 54°F (10°C–12°C). Hot summer temperatures are often helped by cool breezes. The best seasons to visit Greece are from mid-April to June and mid-September to late October, when the wildflowers bloom and the tourists go home.

SWITZERLAND & THE ALPS   The Alpine climate is shared by Bavaria in southern Germany, the Austrian Tyrol, and Italian Dolomites. Winters are cold and bright, and spring comes late, with snow flurries well into April. Summers are mild and sunny, though the Alpine regions can experience dramatic changes in weather any time of year.

3 Finding Your Rail Route

Thousands of trains run across Europe every day, and on many routes you can just show up at the station and be assured a train will leave pretty soon. But there are many reasons to plan your trip in advance. Some trains require advance reservations, some only run a few times a day, and most lines have both fast and slow trains. You will want to be especially mindful of reservations if you want a sleeping car or plan to travel via high-speed trains such as Thalys and Eurostar.

The **Rail Europe** website (**www.raileurope.com**) produces train schedules for routes between major European destinations. But many smaller towns and cities are missing from their site, and if you want to check intermediate stops on a given train, you'll have to look elsewhere. The site also offers prices for point-to-point tickets (a major plus when budgeting for a trip), seat reservations, passes when purchased in

National Railway Websites & Phone Numbers

Country	Website	Phone number (international)
All countries	www.raileurope.com	877/272-7245 (E)*
Austria	www.oebb.at	43/1 930 000
Belgium	www.b-rail.be	32/2 528 2828
Bulgaria	www.bdz.bg	359/2 932 41 90
Croatia	www.hznet.hr	385/60 333 444
Czech Republic	www.cd.cz	420/972 211 111
Denmark	www.dsb.dk	45/70 13 14 15 (E)
Finland	www.vr.fi	358/9 2319 2902 (E)
France	www.sncf.com	33/892 35 35 39 (E)
Germany	www.bahn.de	49/1805 996 633 (E)
Great Britain	www.nationalrail.co.uk	44/20 7278 5240 (E)
Greece	www.ose.gr	30/210 529 8838
Hungary	www.mav.hu	36/1 461 5500
Ireland	www.irishrail.ie	353/1 836 6222 (E)
Italy	www.ferroviedellostato.it	39/89 20 21
Luxembourg	www.cfl.lu	352/2489 2489
Netherlands	www.ns.nl	31/900 202 11 63
Norway	www.nsb.no	47/815 00 888 (E)
Poland	www.pkp.pl	48/22 511 6003 x 1 (E)
Portugal	www.cp.pt	351/808 208 208
Romania	www.cfr.ro	40/256 793 806
Serbia & Montenegro	www.zeleznicesrbije.com	381/360 28 99
Slovak Republic	www.slovakrail.sk	421/18188
Slovenia	www.slo-zeleznice.si	386/1 29 13 332
Spain	www.renfe.es	34/902 15 75 07
Sweden	www.sj.se	46/771 75 75 75 (E)
Switzerland	www.sbb.ch	41/512 20 11 11
Turkey	www.tcdd.gov.tr	90/212 527 7085

Note: *All phone numbers above are shown as you would dial them from North America (dial the international access code 011, then the number as listed above).*

*Phone numbers marked with an "E" respond immediately in English. For other countries, you'll have to wait through a taped message in the local language. Hang on—the operators usually speak, or can find someone who speaks, English.

North America (some passes can only be purchased on this side of the Atlantic), and a list of accommodations on night trains.

A better site for detailed timetables—and our personal favorite—is produced by German railway **Die Bahn (DB)** at **www.bahn.de** (click the "Internat.Guests" tab at the top of the Web page). The DB site covers all major rail lines in all Eurail countries. It also features many bus and ferry services, and will tell you which trains require reservations. Within Germany, it gives train prices and even tells you what tracks you can expect your trains to appear on.

But even the DB site is missing some small stations and lines, and it can be hard to find the correct station for smaller cities when the station name doesn't match the location name (we had a heck of a time getting the correct routing for some towns in Hungary). Note also that the DB website (like most European sites) uses local and not American spellings, so you won't be looking for Florence and Vienna, you'll be looking for Firenze and Wien.

If the DB site doesn't meet your needs, you'll need to go to the national rail site for the destination you're interested in. Choose your desired country from the "National Railway Websites & Phone Numbers" chart above, or from a more comprehensive list at **www.railfaneurope.net/links.html**. Many of the national rail sites will display prices for domestic itineraries only; if you are traveling through several countries, you'll need to call the national rail company or you can check Rail Europe's website. *Warning:* Keep in mind that some European national rail sites don't have English versions, so if you don't speak the local language, navigating these sites will be extremely difficult.

Off-line, the ultimate bible for European rail schedules is the **Thomas Cook European Timetable.** At over 500 pages, it's chunky, but it covers every major railway line on the Continent, as well as many bus and ferry services. It's updated monthly, so buy it as close to your travel date as you dare, allowing 2 weeks for delivery. The timetable is available online from Thomas Cook Publishing (www.thomascookpublishing.com) for £12.50 plus shipping to the U.S. (approximately $32 total). To order by phone (it'll cost you about 10% more), call ✆ **44/1733 416 477.**

4 Choosing the Train That's Right for You

If your time in Europe is limited, then speed will be an issue when selecting a train. There are many high-speed options that will zip you around the Continent, but it's admittedly hard to enjoy the scenery when you're flying by at 186 mph (300kmph), so consider a slower train now and then. (Those who suffer from motion sickness may find high-speed trains less pleasant than the slower, local variety.)

If your budget allows, you may enjoy the amenities and extra space in first class; those who prefer to spend their money on other things will find that second-class cars are a perfectly clean, comfortable option. And those who prefer to travel while they sleep will find a plethora of sleeping options on Europe's vast array of night trains. In this section, we outline all of the major train and accommodations options you'll encounter when traveling through Europe by rail. Read through the descriptions and then choose the train that best suits your needs.

HIGH-SPEED TRAINS

Note: See the tear-out map at the back of this book for a look at all of the major high-speed routes in Europe.

High-Speed vs. Regular Trains

Route	Fastest Regular Train	High-speed Train	Time Saved
Paris–Avignon	9 hr., 10 min.	2 hr., 38 min.	6 hr., 32 min.
Rome–Florence	2 hr., 27 min.	1 hr., 34 min.	53 min.
Munich–Berlin	7 hr., 27 min.	5 hr., 38 min.	1 hr., 49 min.
London–Paris	9 hr., 20 min.	2 hr., 15 min.	7 hr., 5 min.

High-Speed Trains in Europe

Country & Train Name	Route	Time	One-Way Fare (2nd Class)	Pass Fare/Res. Fee (2nd Class/1st Class)	Reservations
Belgium Thalys	Brussels–Paris	1 hr., 25 min.	$60	$26/$43	Yes
	Brussels–Cologne	2 hr., 16 min.	$32–$64	$26/$43	Yes
	Brussels–Amsterdam*	2 hr., 58 min.	$35–$71	$26/$43	Yes
Denmark X2000	Copenhagen–Stockholm	5 hr., 9 min.	$105	$13/$30	Yes
England Eurostar	London–Paris	2 hr., 50 min.	$149–$277	$83/$158	Yes
	London–Brussels	3 hr., 30 min.	$124–$177	$83/$158	Yes
Finland Pendolino	All major cities	Varies	Varies	$16/$21	Yes
France Artesia	Paris–Milan	6 hr., 46 min.	$85	$18/$18	Yes
TGV	Paris to many major cities	Varies	Varies	$11/$11	Yes
Germany ICE	All major cities	Varies	Varies	$11/$11 with reservation; otherwise, no charge	Optional
Italy Cisalpino	Florence–Zurich	7 hr.	$120	$13/$13	Yes
	Milan–Basel	4 hr., 7 min.	$91-$106	$13/$13	Yes
	Venice–Geneva	7 hr.	$126	$13/$13	Yes
Eurostar Italia (ES)	All major cities	Varies	Varies	$26/$26	Yes
Portugal Alfa	Lisbon–Porto	2 hr., 35 min.	$34	$11/$11 with reservation	Yes
Spain AVE	Madrid-Lerida	2 hr., 39 min.	$75	$18/$40 with reservation	Yes
	Madrid–Seville	3 hr., 13 min.	$78	$18/$40 with reservation	Yes
Talgo 200	Madrid–Malaga	3 hr., 50 min.	$71-$79	$18/$40 with reservation	Yes
Sweden X2000	All major cities	Varies	Varies	$13	Yes
Switzerland	Served by Cisalpino and Riviera trains from Italy, TGV trains from France, and ICE trains from Germany				

*Thalys trains from Belgium continue into the Netherlands at regular speed. We strongly recommend against spending extra to ride Thalys on this route as the trip takes just as long as it would on a normal express train.

Europe's high-speed trains are true marvels, traversing the countryside at speeds of 186 mph (300kmph) and faster. Some of them, such as the Pendolino and Cisalpino trains, tilt so they can glide through curves without having to slow down (trust us, you'll hardly feel a thing). In many cases, traveling on high-speed trains is faster than flying!

Italy, Germany, France, and Spain offer the most developed high-speed networks, but most European countries have some form of high-speed service. These trains are worth seeking out: TGV and Eurostar trains, especially, can turn a full day's journey into a 3-hour trip. In fact, in some cases it is difficult to travel between two major European cities any other way but via high-speed train.

You'll pay extra for the privilege of riding on one of these rail rockets, but shelling out the extra cash is worth it when you consider the time you'll save. An express ticket from Munich to Berlin, for instance, is 105€ ($137) if bought in Germany, with the ride taking about 5½ hours. You can pay as little as 70.30€ ($91.40) for a regular ticket, but you'll be forced to change trains at least twice en route and the trip could take as much as 10 hours!

High-speed trains are also generally more comfortable and posh than regional and local trains. First-class accommodations on these trains might include a newspaper, free drinks and meals, outlets for powering up cellphones and laptop computers, Internet access, or onboard music channels. If you want to sit in a nonsmoking section on a train, you're also more likely to find space in first class than you are in second. So if you're purchasing a railpass and you want legroom and luxury, go for first class.

For passholders, most high-speed trains require reservations and therefore a reservation fee (and some include extra fees on top of that). You'll still get a large discount over what nonpassholders pay, but the ride won't be free. (For the passholder fares listed below, we assume you've got a pass that covers all the countries the train travels through. For more on reservation fees, see p. 44.) In the "High-Speed Trains in Europe" chart above, we detail the high-speed trains in all of the Eurail-covered countries. We list second-class, one-way adult fares on the chart because those are what most leisure travelers with point-to-point tickets buy; first-class fares tend to be around 50% more. Most trains also have discounted children's, youth, and senior fares.

EXPRESS, REGIONAL & LOCAL TRAINS

Typically, there are four levels of trains below the posh, high-speed services, though some countries may have less or more (Germany has seven). As all of these trains typically cost the same—and all are included in a railpass—you should just take whichever is the fastest train that stops at your destination.

EuroCity (EC) trains are express trains, typically crossing borders. EC trains sometimes require reservations and additional supplements, so make sure to ask when booking your ticket.

InterCity (IC) trains are express trains, stopping at major cities. Some require reservations, so make sure to check.

Tips Getting the Quickest Trip

Before you assume that the very next train for Amsterdam is the one you want, take a close look at the train's arrival time. You may discover that the next fast train—perhaps one with a departure time 30 minutes later—actually delivers you to your desired destination *before* its slower counterpart.

First-class compartment, Euromed train. *(photo: Courtesy of Rail Europe)*

First Class

The photo features the standard first-class configuration on most modern European trains; older trains (such as the Corail trains in France) have compartment seating, but these are gradually being phased out.

Regional or **Local** trains have different names in every country. In Belgium they're "L" trains, in the Netherlands they're "stoptreins," and in Germany they're "Regional Bahn." Whatever they're called, these are the slow trains that stop at every tiny station, and you should avoid them whenever possible. (In Germany, there are two more classes of middling express trains called InterRegioExpress and Regional Express. These essentially split the difference between express and regional trains.)

Suburban trains connect major cities and nearby destinations, and may leave from a different train station than long-distance trains. Some of these may *not* be covered by a railpass, such as the Paris RER system (except for Paris RER Lines B and C to the airports and Versailles), the S-bahn in Berlin (except between city center DB stations), and Stockholm's S-togs. Also not covered are **local city transport systems** such as buses, trams, and subways.

FIRST VS. SECOND CLASS

Most European trains have two classes of seats: first and second class.

On **local, regional,** and most **express trains,** there's not as much difference between the classes as there is on the high-speed and premiere trains. First-class cars usually have either three seats per row (a seat on one side of the aisle, two seats on the other) or six seats per compartment; second-class cars have four seats per row (two on each side of the aisle) or eight per compartment. First class has more legroom, and the upholstery may be plusher or better kept.

Note that second class tends to fill up a lot faster than first class, so if you're traveling second class on a major route where reservations are not required, you'll likely need to show up a lot sooner at the train station in order to guarantee yourself a seat.

Second-class compartment, panoramic car on Switzerland's Glacier Express. *(photo: Courtesy of Rail Europe)*

Second Class

The photo features the second-class configuration on most modern panoramic European trains. Second-class seats on high-speed trains are usually far more comfortable than those on local and regional trains.

The major difference between first and second class on most trains is the clientele; the folks in the first-class compartment will be older and include more business travelers. Most families and young travelers will be in second class. Both classes, of course, get to their destinations at the same time.

On **high-speed trains,** first class often includes airline-style amenities (see "Fabulous in First," below, for some examples) and very spacious seating. In the individual country chapters in this book, we point out where the difference between second class and first class isn't enough to justify paying the higher fee. And we also point out

Fabulous in First

Country	Train	First-Class Bonus
Belgium/France/Netherlands	Thalys	Meals, wine, and newspapers served at seat
England/Belgium/France	Eurostar	Meals, wine, and newspapers served at seat, power ports, Wi-Fi lounges, dedicated business cars
Germany	ICE	Newspapers
Italy	Eurostar Italia	Drink and snack
Italy/Switzerland	Cisalpino	In-seat music system, power ports, drink, snack, newspapers
Norway	Signatur	Meals, phones, in-seat music, power ports
Spain	AVE/Talgo/Euromed	Meals and newspapers served at your seat, audio/video services
Sweden	X2000	Free meal, coffee/tea, in-seat music, newspapers, Internet access

Trenhotel restaurant car. *(photo: Courtesy of Rail Europe)*

Restaurant Cars

Though most long-distance trains feature some type of dining option, premiere trains, such as Spain's luxurious Elipsos Trenhotel, feature top-quality restaurant cars.

instances where going first-class (on older trains in Greece, for example) is almost a must if you want to have anything approaching a comfortable ride.

If you feel like switching classes, first-class pass and ticket holders can sit in second class any time they like. Second-class ticket holders can upgrade on board the train by paying the price difference if a seat is available.

NIGHT TRAINS

Most major European cities that are at least 7 hours apart by rail are connected by night trains. Not only do night trains save you the price of a hotel, they give you more time to sightsee. And some night trains even have hotel-style amenities, such as private bathrooms with showers. We recommend taking night trains whenever possible.

Tips Tasty Train Rides

Unless you're traveling in some Eastern European countries, if you don't have time to eat before you get on the train, don't worry: Long-distance trains in Europe have dining cars or will send an attendant past your seat with a rolling cart serving up drinks and snacks which, while not always healthy, are at least edible. Expect prices to be very high for what you get.

Premium-class tickets on many high-speed and night trains (for instance, on AVE, Eurostar, and Thalys) include meals, and if you're in a first-class sleeper on one of the premier night trains, they'll even serve you breakfast in your cabin. Ask about food arrangements when making your reservation.

Snack bar on Eurostar train. *(photo: Courtesy of Rail Europe)*

Snack Bars

Most new or upgraded high-speed and international trains have a fast-food snack bar where passengers can get a quick bite.

The average European night train will have sleeper cars, which sleep between one and four people; couchettes, which are affordable compartments for four to six people with less-comfortable, but serviceable bunk beds; and airline-style reclining coach seats. True cheapskates can sleep in coach seats on trains that offer this option, but because a berth in a six-bunk couchette costs passholders only $32 on most trains, there's no need to give yourself a neck cramp. Keep in mind that some trains require that you have a first-class pass to sleep in certain types of cabins. Except in France and Italy, however, there are no first-class couchettes—you can go second class only. Note that we've had enough reports about substandard conditions in second-class couchettes in several countries (and theft issues in certain countries) that we recommend you stick to either first-class couchettes or to sleeper cars. **Note:** Couchettes, except in a few countries (see below), are not gender specific.

Sleepers offer a somewhat more posh travel experience than other train sleeping arrangements: You have a steward to deliver snacks, drinks, and (possibly) a complimentary breakfast to your room. All sleeper cabins also have sinks (and some have bathrooms with showers), while couchette cabins don't.

Whether you're traveling in a couchette or sleeper, the compartment you sleep in will start out with benches or sofas during the evening (unless your departure is after 10pm). At some point after dark, an attendant will come by to snap down the bunks and make them up as beds (or give you the necessary equipment to make your own), with sheets included. The attendant will also take your passport if you're traveling across a border with passport control so there's no need to wake you for it later (this doesn't apply at Eastern European borders).

After the bunks are down, everyone's expected to be quiet. In couchettes, nobody undresses; just stash away your shoes, curl up under the covers, and let the rocking of the train lull you to sleep. (Be sure to cuddle up with your valuables or you may wake up without them!)

The attendant will wake you up in time for your stop, but if you want to have control over your morning, you can bring your own alarm clock. Forget sleeping in: When morning comes around, the attendant will return to the car to turn the bunks back into seats.

If you're a woman creeped out by the idea of sleeping near strangers of the opposite sex, French and Austrian couchettes offer the option of women-only cars. (Sorry, guys, you don't get any couchette cars to yourselves.) Otherwise, your only option is to get a bed in a sleeper: Sleepers are segregated by sex unless you're booking the whole sleeper at once.

All sleeping compartments are supposed to have locks, but with the number of strangers coming in and out of a couchette, you shouldn't count on the lock to protect your valuables. Lock your bags and chain them to seats or bunks if possible.

Parents concerned about their children's safety in bunk beds can request "safety nets" on French sleepers at no charge; this webbing prevents the kids from rolling out of bed. Still, if you want complete control over your environment, get a sleeper rather than couchettes or reserve the entire compartment (*note:* you will need a ticket for each berth in that case).

LUXURY SLEEPERS

A few luxury sleeper services don't have couchettes, which means you either have to settle for a reclining seat or shell out for a bunk in a four-berth room. Here's a selection of some of the best luxury options in Europe:

- **Elipsos Trenhotel.** The bane of the budget traveler, but absolutely perfect for someone looking for a high-end rail travel experience, this super-classy overnight service is available between Madrid and Paris/Loire Valley; Barcelona and Zurich/Milan/Paris. The train has a full restaurant on board and individually air-conditioned sleepers. Opt for the top "Gran Class" and you'll get all meals and a private bathroom with shower. The minimum passholder fare on those routes during the tourist high season is $26 for a second-class (Tourist Class) reclining seat; to stay in a second-class (Tourist Class) four-bed sleeper, the price runs $117 and climbs to $337 for a single Gran Class cabin. Find out more at **www.elipsos.com** or **www.raileurope.com**.

- **Artesia Night Train.** This train runs between major French and Italian cities, including Paris, Chambery, Dijon, Rome, Milan, Florence, and Venice. Six-person couchettes begin at $36 for passholders. Single sleepers in first class begin at $160 for passholders.

- **CityNightLine.** These trains run various routes through Germany, Switzerland, the Netherlands, and Austria. The trains offer deluxe single and double sleeper cabins with private bathrooms and showers, as well as economy six-bed cabins with shared bathrooms and reclining seats. All cabins have electronic locks, and are air-conditioned and nonsmoking. Passholders can get a reclining seat reservation starting at $38. A bed in a four-berth sleeper starts at $64 for passholders; double sleepers start at $103 a person. To find out more, check out **www.rail europe.com**.

Train Sleeping Accommodations

Regular sleeper, Spanish night train

REGULAR SLEEPERS

- One to four beds per cabin
- Secure compartments with reserved bathrooms
- Available in either first- or second-class (on some trains)
- Air conditioning in most cabins
- Sink, mirror, and luggage storage space
- Mineral water
- Breakfast often included in the rate

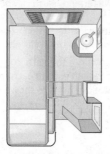

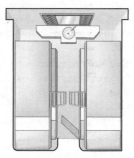

Deluxe sleeper, Trenhotel Elipsos

DELUXE SLEEPERS

- One to three beds per cabin
- Secure compartments with private attendant
- Private bathroom with shower and toiletries
- Sitting area (only on some trains)
- Electronic door locks, luggage storage areas, panoramic windows, individual climate controls
- Mineral water
- Breakfast always included in rate

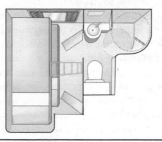

Tips Cleaning Up

If you can't stand the idea of an overnight ride without a shower, these trains provide showers:

Private Showers
- Spanish hotel trains between Madrid and Barcelona
- Paris–Germany night trains between Paris and Munich, Frankfurt, Bremen, Hamburg, Hannover, or Berlin
- Elipsos trains from Madrid to Paris, Barcelona to Paris, Barcelona to Zurich, or Barcelona to Milan in "Gran" class
- Lusitania Trenhotel from Madrid to Lisbon in "Gran" class
- CityNightLine trains throughout Germany, Switzerland, Austria, and the Netherlands in "Deluxe" two-bed cabins
- Sweden's Northern Arrow from Gothenburg to Stockholm and Östersund in "Exclusive" class

Some other night train accommodations offer corridor showers. In certain cars, you'll find washbasins as well as one shower at both ends of each coach. And if all else fails, many large European train stations provide showers for a nominal fee.

Other luxury night trains include Swedish night trains (Oslo-Stockholm/Malmo), Spanish night trains (Madrid-Barcelona/Santiago de Campostela and Barcelona-Malaga/Granada/Seville), the Lusitania Trenhotel (Lisbon-Madrid), and Paris-Germany night trains (Paris to Munich, Hamburg, Berlin, or Hannover). For more information, check out **www.raileurope.com**.

TYPES OF ACCOMMODATIONS

If the last time you rode on a European night train was as a college student, crammed into a six-berth couchette compartment, you'll be pleasantly surprised by the range of accommodations on modern night trains. At their best, they bring back the classic age of train travel, with a uniformed attendant serving you an aperitif as you board, air-conditioning, private showers, and attendant-call phones in every room. Of course, a top-class bed will cost you; a full-fare ticket for a single, private, top-class compartment from Paris to Madrid runs $700 and more.

Not every train has every one of these accommodations, but the range of accommodations on night trains usually includes the ones listed below.

Seats are the cheapest way to travel overnight. These are airline-style seats, with toilets and sinks at one end of the car. Reservations will usually cost you around $15. We recommend you add another $20 to upgrade to a couchette.

Couchettes (aka **T6**) are the sleeping cars of the masses, and they're where you'll find most budget travelers. Second-class couchette accommodations cost $35 for passholders on most European trains. The compartment has two long, benchlike seats during the day, with three people sitting on each side and two top bunks up near the ceiling; at night, the back of each bench snaps up to become a middle bunk. Couchette cars have toilets and sinks at one end, but no showers.

First-class couchettes are offered on some French trains. They seat and sleep four (two on each side) and usually cater to an older, more business-oriented clientele than second-class couchettes.

Four-berth sleepers (aka **T4**) have two beds on each side. These are most often seen on high-class night trains such as the Elipsos hotel trains, which don't offer couchettes. On those trains, these are the cheapest beds.

Triple sleepers (aka **T3**) have three beds that fold down from one side of the compartment, with a table and a sink on the other side. These are sometimes gender specific unless occupied entirely by one group.

Double sleepers (aka **T2** or **Dbl**) offer two bunk beds, a table, and a sink. These are always gender specific unless occupied entirely by one group.

Single sleepers (aka **Special** or **Sgl**) give you the most personal space you'll have on a train: a compartment all to yourself, complete with sink and locking door.

Top-class or **deluxe sleepers** are available on hotel trains such as the Elipsos and CityNightLine series. Many of these have private showers, and you're sure to get very attentive service.

5 The Price of Rail Travel

RESERVATIONS & SUPPLEMENTS

A railpass means you've paid up front and can just hop on a train, right?

Alas, no. Most high-speed trains (including some EuroCity and InterCity), scenic trains, and all sleepers require reservations—and reservation fees will cost you over and above the price of your railpass. Some fast trains have "Passholder Fares," which are essentially reservation fees.

Some exceptions: Reservations aren't necessary on German high-speed trains (although they're helpful, as they guarantee you a seat). They're also unnecessary on certain Spanish and Portuguese trains, British trains (except on some routes to Scotland), or Swiss trains (except certain scenic trains).

We say, don't nickel and dime yourself to avoid reservation fees. The difference in speed between regular and high-speed trains is so striking that for your extra $20 you'll usually get several hours more at your destination.

You can often reserve within just a few hours of departure at European train stations, and you probably won't have to worry about most trains selling out. You'll also likely save money by making reservations in Europe: While the reservation fee on most trains begins at $11 if booked from the U.S., it can be as little as 4€ ($5.20) if you're booking in Europe.

There are cases when you will want to reserve before you leave home. If you're traveling on popular routes (especially night trains) in the summer or during a holiday period, we advise you always to reserve in advance through **Rail Europe** (② **877/272-RAIL** [7245] in North America; www.raileurope.com). We let you know in the individual country chapters when a reservation should be made before you leave home. You can make reservations up to 120 days in advance for Eurostar; up to 90 days in advance for Thalys, Elipsos, and German, Swiss, and French TGV trains; and up to 60 days in advance for most other trains. Reservations in Bulgaria, Greece, Portugal, and Ireland can't be made from North America.

Note: If you did reserve a seat, there is one quirk you might want to watch out for. Some countries (Greece, for example) don't mark seats as reserved and confusion occasionally reigns when people occupy seats they didn't know were reserved. If you show

Reservation Fees*		
Country	**Train**	**Res. Fee/Pass Fare in US**
England–France/Belgium	Eurostar	from $83
France	TGV	from $11
France–Belgium/Netherlands	Thalys	from $26
France–Italy	Artesia (day)	from $18
Italy	Eurostar Italia	from $26
Italy–Switzerland	Cisalpino	from $13
Most countries	Night trains	from $35 (couchette)
Most countries	High-speed trains	from $11
Spain	AVE	from $18
Spain	Talgo 200	from $18
Spain–France/Italy	Elipsos night trains	from $76
Spain–Portugal	Lusitania	from $13 (seat), $50 (T4)
Switzerland	Glacier Express	from $33
Switzerland	William Tell Express	from $42
Switzerland	Bernina Express	from $18 ($28 for bus train)
Switzerland	Golden Pass Line	from $18

Unless otherwise noted, all reservation fees above were calculated for second-class seats and accommodations.

up at your reserved seat and someone's sitting in it, politely but firmly inform him or her that you have a reservation and ask him or her to vacate. Don't let them talk you out of your own seat (and some people will try to do just that). Ask a porter if you need assistance.

PASSES VS. POINT-TO-POINT TICKETS

Ah, the great debate: to buy a pass or to buy point-to-point tickets?

That depends on what kind of traveler you are. If you're on a tight budget, are staying in only a few cities, or if you plan out your trip in advance and travel second class, you may find that point-to-point tickets are cheaper. But if you plan to cover a lot of territory, love the freedom of traveling on a whim, crave convenience, or want to know with some certainty how much your European adventure is going to cost you, you'll find railpasses will likely save you money and time. Rail Europe's website (**www.rail europe.com**) has an interactive railpass finder that will help you compare point-to-point tickets up against a pass.

PASS PLUSES

- **Passes allow for spontaneity.** Many itineraries are cheaper if you buy point-to-point tickets rather than a pass. But what a pass gives you is the flexibility to dodge ticket lines and vending machines, and often to ignore schedules—you simply show up at the station to hop onto the next train to anywhere.

(Tips) Protecting Your Pass

Railpasses are expensive and may be lost or stolen. Get peace of mind through Rail Europe's Rail Protection Plan, which reimburses you for your pass's remaining value if the pass disappears. We strongly recommend buying the Rail Protection Plan for Eurail Global Passes and Eurail Select Passes ($14), and for single-country and regional passes ($10). Rail Europe also sells a Rail Protection Plan for individual tickets, for $10 per ticket. While that's a great idea for a $180 round-trip TGV ticket, you can probably do without it for a $17 hop from Amsterdam to Delft. *Note:* The Rail Protection Plan doesn't cover sleepers or reservations, so keep a very close eye on that $617 Gran Class sleeper ticket from Madrid to Paris.

If you're a peripatetic traveler who wants to see every new day in a different city, or a spontaneous traveler who wants to follow your whims, railpasses are for you. You'll still have to make reservations for high-speed or overnight trains, but if you choose to avoid the reservation counter entirely, you may find your trip made more spontaneous on a slower train that stops in fascinating small towns along the way.

Consider also that a single full-fare TGV round-trip between Paris and Avignon can cost up to $220. That's only $50 less than a full-fare 3-day France Railpass, and only $7 less than a second-class France Railpass, either of which will allow you 3 days of unlimited travel throughout the country within a 30-day period. Clearly, the pass is the way to go if you're going first class over long distances.

- **Speedy trains mean big savings for passholders.** Generally, if you're traveling several long-distance legs on high-speed trains, especially within large countries such as France or Germany, a single-country pass will pay off. The triangular route of Berlin-Munich-Frankfurt-Berlin will cost you $369 for point-to-point tickets in second class. But a 4-day second-class German Rail Pass for the same trip will only run $234—a big cost savings, and you'll have an extra rail day left on the pass.
- **If you're staying in one or two countries and taking long trips, passes are winners.** The France–Italy Pass is a good deal, because it reduces the huge fare on overnight trains between those two countries to a cool $36 (if you're sleeping in a couchette). Even if you're just going from Paris to Rome and Venice and back, you end up saving $6 by getting a France–Italy Pass over buying point-to-point tickets. Not a huge cost savings, but enough to buy lunch—and you enjoy the added flexibility that a railpass offers.
- **Railpasses are usually discounted if you buy in volume.** BritRail offers a Party Pass for adult passengers traveling together. The third through ninth passholders traveling together receive a 50% pass discount. Many Eurail passes offer "saver" varieties for two or more people traveling together; these discount the per-person rate.
- **Railpasses lock in your transportation costs.** If you're waffling between buying point-to-point tickets or railpasses, consider this: You can purchase a railpass up to 6 months in advance of your trip, while most European trains won't sell tickets sooner than 30 to 60 days prior to travel. Buying in advance means you can firm up your budget early and head off currency fluctuations down the road.

No Passes Please, We're Basque

Some trains in Europe won't take *any* railpass. You'll have to buy point-to-point tickets on these trains whether or not you have a pass:

- Regional trains in Spain not run by RENFE (along the northern coast, in the Basque country, around Valencia, and FGC-run trains around Barcelona) don't take passes. You'll have to pay cash for these tickets, and you can't buy the tickets from Rail Europe.
- The private InterConnex train in Germany isn't covered by railpasses and Rail Europe will not book tickets on this train. The good news: Regular EC and IC trains also ply the InterConnex routes, and they *are* covered.
- Scenic private railways in Switzerland and Austria don't take passes. A number of scenic railways (the famous Jungfrau trains in Switzerland, for example) aren't covered by your railpass, though it will get you a discount. Rail Europe will help you book the tickets on these railways.

POINT-TO-POINT ADVANTAGES

- **If you're not traveling far, don't bother with a pass.** It's almost impossible to make the Benelux Pass pay off because trips in Belgium and the Netherlands are so short and cheap. Even if you cram Amsterdam, Haarlem, Leiden, Delft, The Hague, Antwerp, Bruges, Ghent, and Brussels into your trip, you'll only have spent around $87 on point-to-point tickets if you buy them in Europe—well short of the $207 you'd pay for a Benelux Pass.

  In Italy, a 3-day Italy Pass starts at $196 (plus reservation fees if you're taking Eurostar Italia trains). But if you plan to travel between only two or three cities (say Rome to Florence to Venice—an itinerary that costs only $90 in point-to-point tickets), you're not covering enough ground to warrant the purchase of a pass.
- **A quick trip across a border is best done point-to-point.** If you're just slipping from the Benelux into Germany, a Eurail Benelux–Germany Pass is overkill. Get a single-country pass for the country you're spending more time in, and supplement it with a point-to-point ticket or two. Look into getting two one-country passes (or two-country combo passes such as the France–Italy or France–Spain passes) only if you're spending considerable time in two countries. Some international high-speed trains offer pass 2 rates that are valid when only one of the countries you're traveling through is covered by a railpass.
- **Eastern Europe is really cheap.** Point-to-point tickets in Eastern Europe are so inexpensive that railpasses become difficult to justify unless you're continually hopping on and off trains or traveling very long distances.

HOME OR AWAY?

If you're buying point-to-point tickets, you've got to decide whether to get them while you're in North America or when you arrive in Europe. We'd advise buying all tickets on high-speed or overnight trains from Rail Europe. For other tickets, it's up to how adventurous you feel.

It's always a good idea to buy long-distance tickets as far in advance as you can, whether through Rail Europe's website or a local European rail company's website. For a full list of European rail websites, see p. 32.

Rail Europe's prices are generally competitive with European prices for high-speed trains such as the French TGV and German ICE. For other trains, you may want to compare Rail Europe's website prices to the prices on a local European rail site. Most European rail companies, including the railways in France, Spain, Italy, and Germany, let you buy tickets through their websites with a credit card and pick them up at a train station, or print them out on your home printer. If you buy tickets in advance and are willing to put up with restrictions, you can get some amazing discounts.

For instance, a ticket from Paris to Milan for the next day bought at a train station can run you up to $135 if the train isn't entirely sold out (which happens during the summer). On Rail Europe's website, a Paris-Milan ticket bought a month in advance costs $129. Buy that advance-purchase ticket through **www.voyages-sncf.com** (the French rail website) and it can be as little as $78.

Dealing with local European railway sites isn't for the timid. If you buy your tickets through Rail Europe, you deal with friendly, English-speaking agents who know the needs of North American travelers and will make sure you get all your tickets and necessary reservations before you leave home. Accommodation arrangements on night trains, especially, can be complicated. And inexperienced visitors to Europe may relish a patient walk-through from an experienced agent.

If you're taking short trips—practically any train in Belgium or the Netherlands, from Denmark to Sweden, or on local trains in Spain and Italy will qualify—it makes sense to buy the tickets on the spur of the moment from a vending machine at a local train station. So much sense, in fact, that Rail Europe doesn't sell certain short-distance tickets online, such as rides between Barcelona and Girona in Spain or between Delft and Haarlem in the Netherlands. In Europe, you can generally buy unreserved tickets at vending machines, avoiding long lines at ticket counters. (Make sure to have enough change, though, as some vending machines don't take bills.) Even the short-haul tickets that Rail Europe does sell are usually much cheaper in Europe than they are in North America.

FARE DISCOUNTS

There's one other advantage to buying tickets in Europe: You can get discounts that aren't offered when you're buying your tickets in North America. Often these discounts require buying tickets in advance, but you can usually buy them over the phone, with a credit card, by calling the relevant national rail system's phone number, or through the rail system's website (see the "National Railway Websites & Phone Numbers" chart on p. 32).

A few other notable discounts can apply whether you buy your tickets in person, over the phone, or over the Internet. In **France,** the "Decouverte à Deux" fare gives parties of two to nine people a 25% discount on tickets for TGV trains (except overnight trains) and couchettes on non-TGV trains. **German** trains offer two big discounts. The

---

Don't Wait until the Last Minute!

If you wait until the last minute to order your railpass from Rail Europe, you'll incur a $36 overnight shipping fee. It pays to plan ahead.

Pricing the Difference: Fast vs. Slow Trains

Route	Rail Europe Price	Sample European Price (Next Day Travel)
Fast or Long-Distance Trains		
Munich-Berlin	$155	$137
Paris-Avignon	$117	$89.20
Madrid-Seville	$87	$73.05
Rome-Venice	$72	$52.65
Paris-Milan	$156	$137
London-Paris	$177	$301
Slow or Short-Distance Trains		
Amsterdam-Haarlem	$6	$4.70
Bruges-Ghent	$12	$7.15
London-Cambridge	$35	$34.60
Nice-Monaco	$11	$3.50
Cologne-Aachen	$23	$17.30

"Sparpreis 25" fare gives you 25% off a round-trip ticket bought at least 3 days in advance. The "Sparpreis 50" fare bumps the discount up to 50% if you stay over a Saturday night. Both special fares require that you make reservations, and both are of limited availability and nonrefundable. Tickets connecting Germany to certain international destinations also enjoy these price reductions.

British trains have a complex system of advance purchase fares; rest assured that the further you buy in advance, the lower the fare will probably be.

European nations differ in the ages eligible for **children's fares,** but most offer considerable discounts, charging approximately 50% the adult fare for kids between ages 4 to 11. Kids under 4 usually ride free. In Belgium, the "Large Families" discount is available to parents with three children under age 25: Adults and children age 12 and over get 50% discounts on first- and second-class tickets, while children under 12 get a 75% discount in first class and travel free in second class, even if they are traveling alone. In the Netherlands, the Railrunner ticket is just for kids ages 4 to 11 and costs only 2€ ($2.60) when accompanied by an adult. In Sweden, all children under 16 ride for 20 SEK ($2.80) when accompanied by an adult. If you will be traveling with kids on your rail trip, ask ahead of time about available discounts.

For more country-specific fare discounts, see the individual country chapters.

6 The Train Passes

So you've decided you're going with a pass. Rail Europe offers dozens of passes, and the choices can be overwhelming. Decided on the appropriate railpass by answering four questions:

1. How much ground do you want to cover?

If you want to stay in one country, look for a single-country pass (or point-to-point tickets; see p. 46). For up to five countries, look for a multiple-country pass. For six or more countries, look at the Eurail Global Pass or Eurail Select Pass.

2. **Will you be continually on the move, or do you want to linger in some places for a few days?**

If you're continually on the move, **a consecutive-day** pass allows unlimited travel during a specified period. If you'll be staying in cities for several days at a time, a **nonconsecutive** pass gives you a certain number of travel days, and lets you stay put for the rest.

Once you've determined your best kind of railpass, answering two more questions will help you get the best price:

3. **How old are you?**

If you are under 26, **youth passes** are available. Children travel at reduced rates, usually half price or free. If you are at least 60, discounted **senior passes** are the way to go.

4. **How many people are you traveling with?**

If at least two people are traveling together, look for **two-person and group discounts.**

In this section, we divide all the passes into six categories so you can find the one that's best for you, and then describe youth, senior, and group savings options.

ONE-COUNTRY, CONSECUTIVE-DAY PASSES

Consecutive passes are available for whirlwind journeys within the U.K. or Switzerland. As with all one-country passes, they're not always cheaper than point-to-point tickets, especially for brief trips, but they offer ultimate flexibility.

BritRail Consecutive Pass: Covers 4, 8, 15, 22 days, or 1 month of unlimited travel in England, Scotland, and Wales. **First-class prices:** Start at $349 for 4 days. **Second-class prices:** Start at $232 for 4 days. You may use the tickets for rail service between Heathrow and Gatwick to London. Special passholder fare available on Eurostar to Paris and Brussels.

BritRail England Consecutive Pass: Covers 4, 8, 15, 22 days, or 1 month of unlimited travel in England. **First-class prices:** Start at $279 for 4 days. **Second-class prices:** Start at $185 for 4 days. Special passholder fare available on Eurostar to Paris or Brussels.

Swiss Pass: Covers 4, 8, 15, 22 days, or 1 month of unlimited travel in Switzerland. **First-class prices:** Start at $291 for 4 days. **Second-class prices:** Start at $194 for 4 days.

Discounts & Bonuses: Includes lake steamers, city transportation lines, and scenic trains (reservations required). Free travel from Le Chatelard to Chamonix

---

Is the U.K. Okay?

The one glaring omission from the Eurail system is that its passes don't touch England, Scotland, or Wales. But there are still several railpass options for travelers going to Britain. **BritRail** passes cover the mainland U.K.; the **BritRail England Pass, BritRail London Plus Pass,** and **Scottish Freedom Pass** focus on specific parts of the kingdom. The **BritRail Pass + Ireland** lets you roam freely in all of the U.K. and Ireland, and includes a round-trip by ferry.

If you're traveling with children in the U.K., be sure to request the **BritRail Family Pass,** which allows one child age 5 to 15 to travel for free with each fully paying adult or senior. Additional children age 5 to 15 pay approximately half price, and all children under 5 ride for free.

(SNCF). 50% discount on most mountain railways. Free entrance to 400 museums. Discounts on tours and events available at major train stations through Rail-Away, a travel and events company run by the Swiss Federal Railways. Discounts on city tours and hotels. Special price on bike rentals at major railway stations.

ONE-COUNTRY, NONCONSECUTIVE PASSES

If you're planning to explore one country for a week or two, this is the kind of pass to get. Watch out when buying these passes: In many cases, especially with short pass durations or in very small countries (such as the Netherlands), point-to-point tickets will be cheaper.

One-country passes can also be used as add-ons to regional passes, or stacked on top of each other for a two-country trip. If you're going to France and Germany, for instance, the combined price of two one-country passes can often be cheaper than point-to-point tickets.

All passes covering Britain or France give you access to the special passholder fare on Eurostar.

Austrian Railpass: Covers 3 to 8 days of travel within a 15-day period. **Price for 3 days:** $199 first class, $136 second class. **Additional days:** $27 first class, $25 second class.

  Discounts: Discounts on sightseeing ferries (p. 62) and Danube River trips. First-class passengers have access to ÖBB-lounges in Wien Süd station, Wien West station, Klagenfurt, Innsbruck, and Salzburg Hbf.

BritRail Flexipass: Covers 4, 8, or 15 days of travel within a 2-month period in England, Scotland, and Wales. **First-class prices:** Start at $436 for 4 days. **Second-class prices:** Start at $293.

BritRail England Flexipass: Covers 4, 8, or 15 days travel within a 2-month period in England. **First-class prices:** Start at $349. **Second-class prices:** Start at $235.

BritRail London Plus Pass: Covers 2 or 4 days of travel within an 8-day period or 7 days of travel within a 15-day period in Southeast England. **First-class prices:** Start at $113. **Second-class prices:** Start at $74.

Britrail Scottish Freedom Pass: Covers 4 days of travel within an 8-day period or 8 days of travel within a 15-day period throughout Scotland. Includes certain ferry routes to the islands and travel on the Glasgow Underground. **Second-class prices only:** Start at $217.

Croatia Pass: Covers 3, 4, 6, or 8 days of travel within a 1-month period. **First-class prices:** Start at $148. **Second-class prices:** Start at $115.

Czech Flexipass: Covers 3 to 8 days of travel within a 15-day period. **First-class prices:** Start at $125. **Second-class prices:** Start at $86. **Additional rail days:** $17 in first class, $13 in second class.

Finland Pass: Covers 3, 5, or 10 days of travel within a 1-month period in Finland. **First-class prices:** Start at $256. **Second-class prices:** Start at $171.

  Discounts: Receive up to 30% off ferry service between Hanko and Rostock, Germany.

France Railpass: Covers 3 to 9 days of travel within a 1-month period. **First-class prices:** Start at $267. **Second-class prices:** Start at $227. **Additional days:** $39 in first class, $34 in second class.

Discounts: A wide variety of discounts apply, ranging from SeaFrance ferries (p. 64) and Seine River cruises to museums, shopping, ferries, scenic trains, skiing, theme parks, and hotels, and free passage on Paris' RER underground trains.

German Rail Pass: Covers 4 to 10 days of travel within a 1-month period. **First-class prices:** Start at $303. **Second-class prices:** Start at $234. **Additional days:** $42 in first class, $28 in second class.

Discounts & Bonuses: Free travel on select KD Rhine River cruises, and discounts on Lake Constance cruises. Discounts on sightseeing ferries (p. 62) and on Romantic Road and Castle Road Europabus routes (reserve 2 working days in advance through **Deutsche Touring GmbH** at ✆ **49-69-790-30;** www.deutsche-touring.de).

Greece Pass: Covers 3 to 10 days of travel within a 1-month period. **First-class prices only:** Start at $132.

Discounts & Bonuses: Price reductions on various high-speed ferries to Italy, cruises and sightseeing excursions.

Holland Pass: Covers 3 or 5 days travel within a 1-month period. **First-class prices:** Start at $137. **Second-class prices:** Start at $92.

Discounts: Fare reduction on certain ferry crossings to the U.K.

Hungary Pass: Covers 5 within 15 days or 10 days travel within a 1-month period. **First-class prices only:** Start at $97.

Discounts & Bonuses: 50% reduction on supplements for select nostalgic train rides and on admission to the Hungarian Heritage Railway Park.

Ireland Pass: Covers 5 days of travel within a 1-month period. Includes discounts on certain ferry crossings. **First-class prices only:** Start at $197.

Discounts & Bonuses: 30% reduction on standard passenger fares on select ferry crossings on Irish Ferries and Stena Line.

Italy Pass: Covers 3 to 10 days of travel within a 2-month period. **First-class prices:** Start at $245. **Second-class prices:** Start at $196. **Additional days:** $30 in first class, $25 in second class.

Discounts & Bonuses: Free passage on the Leonardo Express train between Fiumicino Airport and Roma Termini rail station for first-class pass holders. Free ferry passage to all card holders traveling to Messina, Sicily, and discounts on ferry travel to Greece, Spain, France, and Tunisia (p. 64).

Norway Pass: Covers 3 to 8 days within a 1-month period. **Second-class prices only:** Start at $243.

Discounts: Reduced fares on select ferry lines and bus travel (p. 64).

Portugal Pass: Covers 3, 4, or 6 days of travel within a 1-month period. **First-class prices only:** Start at $130.

Romania Pass: Covers 5 or 10 days of travel within a 2-month period. **First-class prices only:** Start at $176.

Spain Pass: Covers 3 to 10 days of travel within a 2-month period. **First-class prices:** Start at $253. **Second-class prices:** Start at $197. **Additional days:** $40 in first class, $33 in second class. Pass is not accepted on Catalonian rail lines.

Discounts: 50% reduction on Catalonian rail lines, as well as a reduction in HUSA-Hotels and Grimaldi Ferries to Civitavecchia, Italy (p. 64).

Swiss Flexipass: Covers 3, 4, 5, 6, or 8 days of travel within a 1-month period. **First-class prices:** Start at $276. **Second-class prices:** Start at $184.

Discounts & Bonuses: Valid as a half-fare card offering 50% discount on rail, postal bus, and boat travel on days you do not wish to activate a travel day. Discount only valid during validity period of the pass. For more bonuses, see "Swiss Pass," above.

REGIONAL, CONSECUTIVE-DAY PASSES

There is only one regional, consecutive-day pass. The **Scanrail Pass** has an option that gives you 21 consecutive days of travel in Denmark, Finland, Norway, and Sweden for $539. Otherwise, the classic Eurail Global Pass (p. 55) or the regional nonconsecutive Scanrail Pass, below, may make sense for you.

REGIONAL, NONCONSECUTIVE PASSES

Most travelers on 1-week or 2-week trips are going to go for this kind of pass, which lets you take a few defined trips covering a specific chunk of Europe.

The king of the regional passes is the do-it-yourself **Eurail Select Pass.** The Select Pass allows you to cover 3 to 5 adjoining countries for 5, 6, 8, 10, or 15 days of travel within a 2-month period. The following count as one country: the Benelux (Belgium/the Netherlands/Luxembourg), Croatia-Slovenia, and Bulgaria/Serbia/Montenegro. The ultimate do-it-yourself pass, the Select Pass will satisfy most desires for trips up to a month long.

There are many other predefined regional passes that are cheaper than the Select Pass. These include:

Austria–Croatia–Slovenia Pass: Covers 4 to 10 days of travel within a 2-month period in Austria, Croatia, and Slovenia. **First-class prices only:** Start at $261. **Additional days:** Start at $40.

Discounts & Bonuses: For bonuses see "Austrian Railpass" above; discounts on sightseeing ferries (p. 62).

Austria–Czech Republic Pass: Covers 4 to 10 days of travel within a 2-month period in Austria and the Czech Republic. **First-class prices only:** Start at $238. **Additional days:** $35.

Discounts & Bonuses: For bonuses see "Austrian Railpass" and "Czech Flexipass" above.

Austria–Germany Pass: Covers 5, 6, 8, or 10 days of travel within a 2-month period. **First-class prices:** Start at $378. **Second-class prices:** Start at $320.

Discounts & Bonuses: For bonuses see "Austrian Railpass" and "German Rail Pass" above.

And Norway Connects to Denmark . . .

The Eurail Select Pass applies to "adjoining" countries. Most of these are obvious—countries that share a border, such as France and Germany, are adjoining. But there are a few tricks. Ireland and France are considered adjoining, as are Greece and Italy; Norway and Denmark; and Germany, Sweden, and Finland—all of those countries are connected by ferry lines. Norway and Finland share a border, but they're *not* considered adjoining as no rail or ferry line crosses that border.

Select a Price

Pricing on the Eurail Select Pass depends both on how many days of travel you want and on how many countries you will be traveling in. Further complicating things, there are discounts for couples, groups, and people under 26. At press time, the prices for one person over 26 traveling first class were as follows: three countries from $429; four countries from $478; and five countries from $527. Passes are also available for 6, 8, 10, and 15 days of travel within a 2-month period. For more information, check out **www.raileurope.com**.

Austria–Hungary Pass: Covers 4 to 10 travel days within a 2-month period. **First-class prices only:** Start at $238. **Additional days:** $35.

  Discounts & Bonuses: For bonuses see "Austrian Railpass" above.

Austria–Switzerland Pass: Covers 4 to 10 travel days within a 2-month period. **First-class prices only:** Start at $368. **Additional days:** $43.

  Discounts & Bonuses: For bonuses in Austria, see "Austrian Railpass" above. In Switzerland, receive free lake and river sailings; discounts available on cable cars and mountain-top funiculars, certain scenic private railroads, and the Transport Museum in Lucerne. Discounts on sightseeing ferries (p. 62).

Balkan Flexipass: Covers 5, 10, or 15 days of travel within a 1-month period in Bulgaria, Greece, Macedonia, Romania, and Turkey, including Serbia and Montenegro. **First-class prices only:** Start at $225.

  Discounts & Bonuses: A wide variety of discounts are available on numerous ferry crossings and cruises, flights between various Greek destinations, hotels, excursions, and sightseeing tours. Discounts on sightseeing ferries; see p. 62. All benefits can be obtained locally at Ionian Travel in Athens (see p. 460).

Benelux–France Pass: Covers 4, 5, 6, 8, or 10 days travel within a 2-month period in Belgium, the Netherlands, Luxembourg, and France. **First-class prices:** Start at $334. **Second-class prices:** Start at $292.

  Discounts & Bonuses: Special passholder fare on Eurostar and Brussels–France TGV, as well as a wide variety of discounted ferry tickets, hotels, museums, and scenic trains and free passage on Paris' RER underground trains.

Benelux–Germany Pass: Covers 5, 6, 8, or 10 days of travel within a 2-month period in Belgiuim, the Netherlands, Luxembourg, and Germany. **First-class prices:** Start at $394. **Second-class prices:** Start at $296.

  Discounts & Bonuses: Special passholder fare on Eurostar, as well as a wide variety of discounted ferry tickets, hotels, museums, and scenic trains. Free cruises on select KD Rhine Line boats, and free travel on Germany's S-Bahn system in most major cities. Discounts on sightseeing ferries (p. 62).

BritRail Pass + Ireland: Covers 5 or 10 days of travel within a 1-month period in the U.K. and Ireland. **First-class prices:** Start at $636. **Second-class prices:** Start at $462.

  Discounts & Bonuses: Includes passage on trains servicing Gatwick and Heathrow, as well as round-trip Stena Line or Irish Ferries service between Britain and Ireland (p. 64). Special passholder fare on Eurostar.

⌒Tips **Train Pass Tip**

If you are not a European resident and have already arrived in Europe and want to buy a pass, in the U.K. contact Rail Europe at ℂ **08708/306-050;** in Germany contact Euraid at ℂ **089/593-889.**

Denmark–Germany Pass: Covers 5, 6, 8, or 10 days of travel within a 2-month period. **First-class prices:** Start at $360. **Second-class prices:** Start at $296.

Discounts & Bonuses: Includes discounts under "German Rail Pass" above, as well as select scenic railways and ferry lines in Denmark (p. 64).

European East Pass: Covers 5 to 10 days of travel within a 1-month period in Austria, the Czech Republic, Hungary, Poland, and Slovakia. **First-class prices:** Start at $272. **Second-class prices:** Start at $191. **Additional days:** $32 in first class, $25 in second class.

Discounts: For bonuses in Austria, see "Austrian Railpass," above. Discounts in Hungary include the Children's Railway in Budapest, the Double Chair Lift in Jànoshegy (Libegoe), select scenic railways, and the Hungarian Railway Heritage Park.

France–Germany Pass: Covers 4, 5, 6, 8, or 10 days of travel within a 2-month period. **First-class prices:** Start at $373. **Second-class prices:** Start at $335.

Discounts & Bonuses: For bonuses, see "France Railpass" and "German Rail Pass" above. Discounts on sightseeing ferries (p. 62).

France–Italy Pass: Covers 4 to 10 days of travel within a 2-month period. **First-class prices:** Start at $352. **Second-class prices:** Start at $306. **Additional days:** $40 in first class, $35 in second class.

Discounts & Bonuses: For bonuses, see "France Railpass" and "Italy Pass" above. Discounts on sightseeing ferries (p. 62).

France–Spain Pass: Covers 4 to 10 days of travel within a 2-month period. **First-class prices:** Start at $352. **Second-class prices:** Start at $306. **Additional days:** Start at $40 in first class, $35 in second class.

Discounts & Bonuses: For bonuses, see "France Railpass" and "Spain Pass" above. Discounts on sightseeing ferries (p. 62).

France–Switzerland Pass: Covers 4 to 10 days of travel within a 2-month period. **First-class prices only:** Start at $368. **Additional days:** $43.

Discounts & Bonuses: For bonuses, see "France Railpass" and "Swiss Flexipass" above. Discounts on sightseeing ferries (p. 62).

Germany–Switzerland Pass: Covers 5, 6, 8, or 10 days of travel within a 2-month period. **First-class prices only:** Start at $401.

Discounts & Bonuses: For bonuses see "German Rail Pass" and "Swiss Flexipass" above.

Greece–Italy Pass: Covers 4 to 10 days of travel within a 2-month period. **First-class prices:** Start at $343. **Second-class prices:** Start at $274. **Additional days:** Start at $35 in first class, $28 in second class.

Discounts & Bonuses: For bonuses, see "Greece Pass" and "Italy Pass" above. Discounts on sightseeing ferries (p. 62).

Hungary–Croatia–Slovenia Pass: Covers 5, 6, 8, or 10 days of travel within 2 months. **First-class prices only:** Start at $242.

Discounts & Bonuses: Discounts in Hungary on select scenic railways and the Hungarian Railway Heritage Park

Hungary–Romania–Pass: Covers 5, 6, 8, or 10 days travel within 2 months. **First-class prices only:** Start at $248.

Discounts & Bonuses: Discounts in Hungary on select scenic railways and the Hungarian Railway Heritage Park. Additional discounts on select Romanian hotels.

Italy–Spain Pass: Covers 4 to 10 days of travel within a 2-month period. **First-class prices only:** Start at $352. **Additional days:** $40.

Discounts & Bonuses: For discounts see "Italy Pass" and "Spain Pass" above.

Portugal–Spain Pass: Covers 3 to 10 days of travel throughout Spain and Portugal within a 2-month period. **First-class prices only:** Start at $289. **Additional days:** $40.

Discounts & Bonuses: For discounts see "Spain Pass" above. Discounts on sightseeing ferries (p. 62).

Scandinavia Pass: Covers 5, 8, or 10 days of travel within a 2-month period in Denmark, Sweden, Norway, and Finland. **Second-class prices only:** Start at $318.

Discounts & Bonuses: Free or discounted travel on selected ferries (p. 62), boats, scenic trains, and buses throughout Scandinavia.

ALL-EUROPE, CONSECUTIVE-DAY PASSES

The classic Eurail Global Pass is best if you want the ultimate in flexibility or you're covering very long distances. With the 15-day pass, you've got to take some very long trips or be on the train constantly for the price to make sense, but as the pass durations get longer, the Eurail Global Pass compares better and better to point-to-point tickets.

Eurail Global Pass: Covers 15 or 21 days, or 1, 2, or 3 months travel. **First-class prices only:** Start at $675. For complete list of bonuses and discounts, refer to Rail Europe's website at **www.raileurope.com**.

ALL-EUROPE, NONCONSECUTIVE PASSES

Plot your trip out before comparing the prices for the Eurail Global Pass and the Eurail Global Pass Flexi. For many trips, you'll find the original Global Pass is a better deal. The Flexi is good, for instance, if you're visiting eight cities over the course of 2 months without taking many side trips.

Eurail Global Pass Flexi: Covers 10 or 15 days of travel within a 2-month period. **First-class prices only:** Start at $798. For complete list of bonuses and discounts, refer to Rail Europe's website at **www.raileurope.com**.

Point-to-Point-to-Point

Unreserved point-to-point tickets in Europe let you get off and back on again at any number of stops, as long as you start and end your trip on the same day. So you don't need to book two tickets or use a pass if you want to visit Orléans on the way from Paris to Tours. If you're using high-speed trains, though, you'll need separate reservations for each segment of the journey.

AN ADD-ON PASS: THE SWISS CARD

The **Swiss Card** adds a trip from the Swiss border to one Swiss destination and back within 1 month's time. The card also nets you 50% discounts on all Swiss railways, lake steamers, postal buses, and on excursions to most mountaintops for the length of the pass. The price is $187 for first class, $139 for second class. Compare the price of this pass with that of a single round-trip ticket into the country, then factor in the savings you'll receive from additional discounted travel to see whether it makes sense for you.

RAIL-DRIVE & RAIL-FLY PASSES

Not all of Europe is accessible by train—many charming small towns and rural areas are best visited by car, and you've got to take a boat or a plane to get to the Greek Islands. So Rail Europe offers a range of passes combining car rentals or plane tickets with railpasses. Remember to factor in gas, though, which can exceed US$6 per gallon. *Note:* Unlike a regular car rental, car days on a rail 'n drive pass need not be used consecutively.

The price of rail 'n drive passes is based on the class of car you drive, and the available cars vary from country to country, so check out **www.raileurope.com** for the full details. Generally, you'll pay a big premium for an automatic transmission.

Car rentals in Europe are generally much more expensive than in North America, and although these passes are discounted, U.S. and Canadian travelers may get hit by sticker shock. For instance, an add-on car day for a tiny economy car with the Eurail Global Pass 'n Drive is $56; for a car with automatic transmission, you'll pay $105 a day. Single-country passes vary widely in affordability and the availability of automatic transmission. In France, a compact car is $57 per day and a full-size is $120; in Spain, an economy car will cost you only $42, but a compact car costs $114 per day. Germany is the most economical country, charging between $46 and $88 per day depending upon the size and transmission you select, but the prices are still rather high. Before you decide you absolutely need a car, make sure you can't get where you need to go by train or bus.

These passes are all for nonconsecutive days. **Rail 'n drive** passes include:

Eurail Global Pass 'n Drive: Covers 4 days of train travel and at least 2 days' car rental within a 2-month period in Austria, Belgium, Denmark, Finland, France, Germany, Greece, Holland, Hungary, Italy, Luxembourg, Norway, Portugal, Republic of Ireland, Romania, Spain, Sweden, and Switzerland. Manual and automatic-transmission cars are available through Hertz, although automatics are not available in every city. Beware that the largest cars available are "intermediate," seating five. **Price:** From $569 and up.

Discounts: Includes all the bonuses listed under the single-country passes detailed above.

Eurail Select Pass 'n Drive: Covers 3 to 15 days of train travel, and at least 2 days' car rental within a 2-month period in 3, 4, or 5 adjoining European countries. Rent manual and automatic-transmission cars (where available) from Hertz, but beware that the largest cars available are "intermediate," seating five. **Price:** From $432.

Discounts: Bonuses available, depending on the countries selected.

BritRail Pass 'n Drive: Covers 4 days of train travel, and 2 to 7 days Hertz car rental within a 2-month period in England, Scotland, and Wales. Manual and automatic-transmission cars are available; the largest car seats five. **Price:** From $418 and up.

Discounts: Special passholder fare on Eurostar.

France Rail 'n Drive: Covers 2 to 5 days of train travel and at least 2 days' Avis car rental within a 1-month period. Manual and automatic-transmission cars are available; largest car is a minivan. **Price:** From $325.

    Discounts: For bonuses, see "France Railpass" earlier.

German Rail 'n Drive: Covers 2 to 4 days of train travel, and at least 2 days' Hertz car rental within a 1-month period. Manual and automatic-transmission cars are available; largest car seats five. **Price:** From $252.

Italy Rail 'n Drive: Covers 3 days of train travel, and at least 2 days Hertz car rental within a 2-month period. Manual and automatic-transmission cars are available; largest car seats five. **Price:** From $330.

    Discounts & Bonuses: Discounted fares on Artesia day and night trains, and Elipsos (Barcelona–Milan) trains; ferry service to Sicily (Villa S. Giovanni–Messina); theft protection; and collision damage waiver.

Scandinavia 'n Drive: Covers 3 to 10 days of train travel and at least 2 days Hertz car rental within a 2-month period in Denmark, Norway, Finland, and Sweden. Automatic and manual transmission cars are available; largest car seats five. **Price:** From $307.

    Discounts: For bonuses, see "Scandinavia Pass" above.

Spain Rail 'n Drive: Covers 3 to 10 days of train travel, and at least 2 days' Hertz car rental within a 2-month period. Manual and automatic-transmission cars are available; largest car seats five. **Price:** From $307.

Eurail no longer offers the **Greek Rail 'n Fly Pass** as travelers once knew it. Travelers who want the benefit of hopping through several Greek islands can get discounted airline tickets by purchasing the **Balkan Flexipass.** You won't get free flights, but you will get discounted prices on short hops between Athens and various destinations, including Mykonos, Kalamata, and Chania, Crete. Reservations must be made through **Ionian Travel** (© **210/523-9609** or 210/523-4774). But compare these prices to the other big European discounters before you whip out your credit card. See the "When to Fly" section in this chapter (p. 61) for more advice.

DISCOUNTS
YOUTH & SENIOR DISCOUNTS
Many railpasses offer discounted versions for travelers under 26 and over 60.

All **youth passes** except the Balkan, BritRail, French, Greek, Romanian, and Swiss versions are for second-class travel only, but they offer big savings. There are youth versions of all of the multiple-country passes we've discussed, with the exception of the BritRail Pass + Ireland, the European East Pass, and the Portugal–Spain Pass. In the U.K., you can take advantage of the BritRail Consecutive Youth Pass, BritRail Flexipass Youth, BritRail England Consecutive Youth Pass, BritRail England Youth Flexipass, and BritRail London Plus Youth Pass. There are also youth versions of most single-country passes, including those from Croatia, France, Germany, Hungary, Ireland, Italy, the Netherlands, Norway, Romania, Switzerland, and Italy. Eurail Global and Eurail Select Youth Passes are also available.

    Senior passes, for travelers over 60, are just like the standard versions—but cheaper. Senior passes include the Balkan Flexipass, France Pass, Norway Pass, and Scandinavia Pass, as well as the BritRail Consecutive Senior Pass, BritRail Senior Flexipass, BritRail England Consecutive Senior Pass, and BritRail England Senior Flexipass.

Validating Your Pass

You must validate your railpass before you step on your first train. There are two ways to do this. Head to a ticket office at any European train station and ask the ticket agent to validate your pass. The agent will write in the first and last days you can use your pass, and you're on your way.

Single-country and multi-country passes have to be validated in the country they're being used for (except when using the passholder rate on the Eurostar). For instance, if you've got a France Railpass and you're heading to the Riviera from Barcelona, buy a ticket from Barcelona to the border; then the French conductor will validate the pass and you can use it for the rest of your journey.

If you're using a Saverpass or another kind of pass that affects more than one person, all the relevant people must be present when the pass is validated—but not necessarily every time it's used (except in France).

If you're using a nonconsecutive day pass such as a Eurail Select Pass, there's one more thing you have to do after validation. Each day you plan to use the pass, write the day and month in ink in one of the boxes below "Last Day." If you're taking an overnight train that leaves after 7pm, write in the next day's date. (You get the evening part of the train free!) This is called the **7pm Rule,** but it may not apply to all passes; inquire at time of booking. All trips must be completed in the days marked on your pass. Be sure to write in the date before you get on the train or you might get fined when the conductor comes around.

Note: Dates should be entered European style—date first, then month. So May 10 would be written 10-5 and not 5/10.

Children get discounted rates on most passes, usually 40% to 50% off the adult rate. Qualifying ages vary by country. Adults with a Swiss Pass, Swiss Flexipass, or Swiss Card can also get the free Swiss Family Card, which will let them tote along any number of their own children under 16 at no additional charge. Adults holding any type of BritRail Pass can request the free BritRail Family Pass, which allows one child, age 5 to 15, to travel free with each full-paying adult.

COUPLE, GROUP & FAMILY DISCOUNTS

If more than one person is traveling, more discounts are available. Saver and Party passes offer discounts to small groups (including couples). Generally, if you're under 26, the youth discount is better than the saver discount, so go with a youth pass instead. If there's no youth pass available in the country you want to visit, check out the group passes instead.

Saver passes or group discounts include the following multicountry and regional passes: All rail 'n drive passes, Eurail Global Pass, Eurail Select Pass, Austria–Czech Saverpass, Austria–Croatia–Slovenia Saverpass, Austria–Germany Saverpass, Austria–Hungary Saverpass, Austria–Switzerland Saverpass, Benelux–France Saverpass, Benelux–Germany Pass Saver, Denmark–Germany Saverpass, France–Germany

Saverpass, France–Italy Saverpass, France–Spain Saverpass, France–Switzerland Saverpass, Germany–Switzerland Saverpass, Greece–Italy Saverpass, Hungary–Croatia–Slovenia Saverpass, Hungary–Romania Pass Saver, Portugal–Spain Saverpass and the Italy–Spain Saverpass. **Note:** If you are traveling with a group of 10 or more people, Rail Europe's EuroGroups department can assist you through **www.eurogroups.com**.

Single-country passes that allow for group discounts include Croatia, France, Greece, Hungary, Italy, Romania, and Britain (which offers fun-sounding Party Passes).

Note: British passes require three or more people to constitute a group; other passes require only two.

7 The Rail Experience

AT THE TRAIN STATION

If you're traveling Europe by rail, you'll spend a lot of time in train stations. That's not a bad thing. Many European train stations are masterpieces of architecture—glorious palaces of glass and light that will inspire your wanderlust. In practical terms, European stations are generally clean, safe, and well kept, though you should keep an eye on your bags in any public place.

Many European cities have more than one train station: Paris has six, London has nine, and Brussels has four. Make sure you know which station your train leaves from, as they can be miles apart and stations aren't necessarily connected to each other by efficient means. If you have to transfer between stations in a major city, check the appropriate country chapter in this book to see how long it takes to switch stations.

In some cases, the station most trains come into isn't the most convenient one for downtown tourist attractions. See if you can hop a short-distance train to get to the more central station. In Madrid, for instance, you can take the local *cercanias* trains (valid with a pass) between the Chamartin and Atocha stations.

If you're just in town for a few hours, most train stations offer lockers for around $5 per day—but the lockers only take coins, so make sure you've got plenty of change on you. Train station lockers can fit even sizeable suitcases. Some stations that lack lockers have luggage checkrooms where you can leave your bags. If a station has porters, they'll be uniformed. Never hand your bag over to a guy on the platform who isn't wearing a clearly identifiable uniform.

Feeling hungry? Most train stations have fast-food restaurants (or at least a vending machine or two). Larger stations have sit-down restaurants and pubs. Some stations have minigroceries—ideal for buying picnic essentials. If you need cash, stations generally have ATMs and (in major cities) currency-exchange windows. ATMs offer the best exchange rate and they work just like at home; if you need to use an exchange window, local banks generally have a better rate than train stations.

When you need to use the restroom, check your pockets. While European train stations have bathrooms, they almost all cost money to use. (Usually, the price is around 50¢.) Paid toilets mean clean, safe, and well-attended toilets; the pay turnstile will often be handled by a live attendant, who makes sure things are kept neat and tidy. Larger stations offer showers, also for pay.

As you go to buy your ticket, remember that many stations have separate domestic and international reservations counters. Even though some European countries are tiny, "International" still means just that—a ticket from the Netherlands to Belgium must be booked at the international counter.

To help you find the right train, stations offer printed schedules and departure boards. Printed schedules are usually posted up on gigantic boards, both by the tracks and in the main hall of the station. Departure schedules are usually on a yellow background; arrival schedules are on a white background. On the schedules, train times are shown according to a 24-hour clock, with fast trains in red and slower trains in black. Larger stations have computerized departure boards.

You'll find local transport, like trams, buses and taxis, outside the stations. Taxi touts working inside stations may be scam artists. Walk past them to the official taxi stand instead.

GETTING ON BOARD

Be on the platform a few minutes before your train is due to arrive. European trains are seldom early—don't worry if you see no sign of your train 5 minutes before its departure. On the other hand, trains wait for no one, and stops can be as short as a minute.

When your train shows up, don't just jump into the first door you see (unless you're in a real hurry). While you're safe with most short-distance trains, some long-distance trains tend to split and rejoin, with different cars going to different destinations. Ask a conductor on the platform which cars are going your way. If you're in a hurry, get on board and ask the conductor once the train leaves which car you need to be in—you'll be able to move between cars using the connecting doors (except on some high-speed trains).

You'll also need to pay attention to whether you're in a first-class or second-class car: Classes are marked by a big "1" or "2" on the side of the carriage. There may also be a yellow stripe on the car for first class, and a green stripe for second class. And if you are sensitive to smoke, be sure you get yourself into a nonsmoking car or section (just be advised that nonsmoking signs tend to be ignored a lot more in Europe than they are in North America).

If you have a reservation, you can locate your car by checking the train diagram (composition de train) on the platform so you'll know just where to stand when the train pulls into the station. Once on board, you'll need to match up your car number and seat number. Car numbers are listed right by the outside car doors. Seat numbers are usually over the seats, inside the train. If you're in a hurry, jump onto the train and sort things out after the train gets moving.

Most train cars have a space for luggage near the entrance and baggage racks above the seats. If you have more baggage than you can handle, check it; we don't recommend letting your bags out of your sight. Theft is common enough that you'll need to be vigilant. If you're traveling by rail in Europe, also remember that you'll be walking up and down a lot of stairs and along a lot of long platforms. Pack as lightly as possible.

(Tips Special Needs

Many, but not all, trains and stations in Europe have accessible toilets, ramps, and elevators for mobility-impaired passengers. If you think you'll need help or want to scope out the situation in advance, ask Rail Europe or your travel agent when you make your train reservation. Station staff are willing to help travelers with mobility issues to the best of their abilities, but help must be reserved in advance.

8 When a Train Just Won't Do

Trains are the best way to see Europe, but there are times when you find alternative forms of transportation will get you someplace faster; in some of the more remote locations, a train may simply not be an option. Sometimes, a quick trip by air, a short bus leg, a ferry ride, or a rental car can save you a long, roundabout trip by train—and it may save you a little money, too.

WHEN TO FLY

Trains are usually the cheapest and most efficient way to get from Point A to Point B in Europe. But scheduling a flight can help you cover a great distance very quickly (for instance, from London to Italy, or from Dublin to pretty much anywhere else) if you're short on time. So if you want to travel to a number of countries that aren't all that close together and have a limited amount of time in Europe, a quick flight used in conjunction with your railpass may make sense.

Holders of the **Balkan Flexipass** are entitled to discounted airfares from Athens to various Greek destinations, including Mykonos, Kalamata, and Chania, Crete. Reservations must be made through **Ionian Travel** (② **30/210 523 9609**). But compare the pass prices to the other big European air discounters before you choose this option.

The lowest one-way fares in Europe are available from **low-fare airlines** that offer no meal service, no intercontinental connections, and often fly from satellite airports well outside their target cities. It's not uncommon to get a flight halfway across Europe for as little as $40 to $70, including taxes and fees.

The two biggest low-fare players in Europe are **Ryanair** (② **353/1 249 7799,** with toll-free numbers in many European countries; www.ryanair.com) and **easyJet** (② **44/ 870 600 0000;** www.easyjet.com). Both are profitable, solid carriers. Ryanair has major bases in Dublin, London, Frankfurt, Milan, Rome, Stockholm, and northern Spain. easyJet offers the most flights out of London and Berlin, but both airlines cover dozens of European destinations.

A wild array of smaller budget carriers blankets Europe as well, with nearly every country having its own budget-flight solution. To find out where these carriers fly and get links to their websites, go to **www.flybudget.com**, an independent and regularly updated guide to low-fare airlines. **SkyScanner (www.skyscanner.com)** is another good site, offering a map of low-fare airlines' routes and tools to help you figure out the best days to fly for the best fares.

Warning: When pricing and timing planes against trains, factor in the price of getting to the airport and the time you'll need to spend in the airport before getting anywhere. For example, even though it isn't covered by the Eurail Global Pass, the Eurostar is actually a far more economical choice than flying from London to Paris once you've factored in the time and cost of getting to the airport.

WHEN TO TAKE A BUS

Local buses pick up where the rail network leaves off, and they can be lifesavers. Taking a train from Portugal's Algarve to Spain's Costa Del Sol is a 19-hour agony; by bus, the ride is a mere 1½ hours. Many small towns in Ireland, archaeological sites in Greece, and small villages in Eastern Europe are also only reachable by bus.

The most useful bus services for rail travelers are small, local outfits that will be discussed in each of the following country chapters. Likewise, the best way to get information about their routes, schedules, and prices is to contact them locally. The major international bus company **Eurolines** (© **44/870 514 3219;** www.eurolines.com) will hook you up with routes in Ireland and some Eastern European countries, but not anything in Greece. If you're truly adventurous, the website **www.busstation.net** offers hundreds of links to local bus companies. (Many of the bus companies' websites are in the local languages, and you usually can't buy tickets online in advance.)

WHEN TO TAKE A FERRY

Many ferries are covered by the Eurail Global Pass, including international routes from Italy to Greece, from Germany to Sweden, from Denmark to Norway, and from Germany and Sweden to Finland. The Global Pass also offers discounted fares on several other routes, including ferries from Ireland to France. On many routes—especially the Scandinavian, Mediterranean, and Adriatic ones—the modern, comfortable ferryboats are great ways to cross borders while you sleep. Note that in order to take advantage of discounted tickets, your pass must be valid in either the country of departure or the country of arrival. For free tickets, your pass must be valid in *both* the country of departure and the country of arrival. For either free or reduced travel within a single country, your pass must be valid in that country. Free tickets require the use of 1 travel day on your pass (either the day of departure or arrival).

European ferries are generally even more plush than European trains. They may have onboard swimming pools, movie theaters, sit-down restaurants, or even casinos. On the Adriatic ferries, accommodations range from chaises on the deck to luxurious, hotel-room-like private cabins equipped with showers, refrigerators, and TVs, with views of the water. In colder waters, nobody's forced to sleep on the deck—accommodations start with reclining, airline-style seats or four-berth cabins and work their way up to two-berth cabins with a view.

Note, however, that your railpass usually covers only the lowest possible fare. Depending on the route, that may give you an unreserved seat, a bed in a four-berth cabin, or a little space on the deck overnight. If you want better accommodations, you'll have to pay more. You'll also likely have to pay port fees (6€/$7.80–20€/$26) and/or high-season supplements, even if you have a railpass. These fees are usually payable at the port when you're about to board the ferry, so have some cash on you.

Keep an eye on schedules, too. Ferry schedules vary from season to season, and some ferries don't run every day. You can get schedules from the individual ferry firms' websites (see "Major European Ferry Lines," below, for the major ferry company websites).

If possible, reserve your ferry in advance. Ferries do sell out, just like overnight trains. Many ferry companies allow you to book seats and cabins online; though you usually can't book online if you're holding a railpass, you can make a reservation by calling the ferry company direct.

Complicating the issue, a growing number of ferry companies now offer airline-style pricing. Irish Ferries, for instance, has seven price levels, varying by individual sailing. If you're intending to take a ferry, you can save lots of money by planning ahead and getting on one of the cheap sailings—dropping the fare from Ireland to France from 110€ ($143) to 60€ ($78).

Two of these ferry routes are so well trodden by low-fare airlines and other options, they're not worth taking unless you're unwilling to plan ahead. The ferries between Ireland and France are 19-hour trips, and they don't even leave daily. But if you plan ahead and book a flight on low-fare Ryanair well in advance, you can shrink that trip to 2½ hours for as little as 25€ ($32.50).

The Calais-Dover ferry, meanwhile, is a lousy way to get from Paris to London—the trip takes more than 6 hours, and you've got to buy a Dover-London train ticket on the U.K. end. You might as well take Eurostar or fly Ryanair.

Aside from the major international ferry routes, your railpass also gives you discounts on a wide range of sightseeing boats. None of these smaller boats are the most efficient way to get from point A to point B, but many are scenic. Discounts on these scenic options include:

Austria: 20% off DDSG Blue Danube Schiffahrt GmbH (© **43/1 588 80;** www.ddsg-blue-danube.at) boats between Melk and Krems, between Vienna and Dürnstein (on Sun), and sightseeing trips by boat in Vienna. Special price on Wurm and Köck steamers (© **43/732 783 607;** www.wurm-koeck.de) between Linz and Passau (Germany). 50% off BSB, SBS, ÖBB boats on Lake Constance from May to October.

Germany: Free passage on KD German Rhine Line (© **49/2 21 20 88 318;** www.k-d.com) between Köln and Mainz on the Rhine and between Koblenz and Cochem on the Mosel (with some limitations). 50% off BSB, SBS, ÖBB boats on Lake Constance from May to October. 50% off on URh (© **41/52 634 0888;** www.urh.ch) boats from Constance to Schaffhausen (Switzerland). Special price on Wurm and Köck steamers (© **49/851 929 292;** www.wurm-koeck.de) between Linz (Austria) and Passau.

Greece: 20% off 1-day cruises from Athens to Aegina, Poros, and Hydra with Ionian Travel (© **30/210 523 9609;** www.greeka.com).

Switzerland: Free sailings on URh (© **41/52 634 0888;** www.urh.ch) boats from Constance to Schaffhausen (Switzerland). Free sailings on various steamers on the lakes of Biel, Brienz, Genève, Luzern, Murten, Neuchâtel, Thun, and Zürich (© **41/33 334 52 11,** www.bls.ch; © **41/848 811 848,** www.cgn.ch; © **41/32 329 88 11,** www.bielersee.ch; © **41/44 487 13 33,** www.zsg.ch) and on the river Aare between Biel and Solothurn (©**41/32 329 88 11;** www.bielersee.ch).

WHEN TO DRIVE

Train and bus services honeycomb much of Europe, but there are still rural areas where you might want to drive—especially in such countries as Ireland, Portugal, and Greece, where the rail networks aren't as comprehensive as in the rest of Europe. We recommend using a car only to explore small towns and wilderness areas—traffic and parking in major European cities can be nightmarish and expensive!

Though we mostly stick to the rails in this book, there are a few spots in Europe that we point out are better explored by car (the Ring of Kerry in Ireland, for example). This is when the Rail 'n Drive passes we detail on p. 56 may come in handy.

Warning: Those rail 'n drive passes don't include any of the following: gas, the collision damage waiver (CDW—included on the Italy 'n Drive pass only), personal accident insurance (PAI), other insurance options, fees for an additional and/or young driver, airport surcharges, registration tax, or car group upgrades made locally. Note that the minimum age for rentals on a rail 'n drive pass ranges from 23 to 25 depending on the country you're visiting. Also note that in some countries, or for a few car groups, a service charge is due on one-way rentals. And keep in mind that, unlike North America, most rental cars in Europe have manual transmission; automatic will cost you more.

Major European Ferry Lines

Countries	Routes	Ferry Line	Contact
Denmark–Norway	Hirtshals–Bergen Hirtshals–Stavanger Hirtshals–Larvik Hirtshals–Kristiansand Frederikshavn–Oslo Strömstad–Sandefjord	Color line	www.colorline.com; ☎ 47/810 00 811
France–England	Calais–Dover	SeaFrance	www.seafrance.com; ☎ 33/825 0825 05
Germany–Denmark	Puttgarden–Rødby	Scandlines	www.english.scandlines.dk; ☎ 45/331 51 51
Germany–Finland	Rostock–Helsinki	Superfast Ferries	www.superfast.com; ☎ 358/9 180 41
Germany–Sweden	Sassnitz–Trelleborg Rostock-Trelleborg	Scandlines	www.english.scandlines.dk; ☎ 45/331 51 51
Greece–Italy	Patras–Ancona Igoumenitsa–Ancona	Minoan Lines	www.minoan.gr; ☎ 30/281 039 9800 (Greece); ☎ 877/465-2697 (USA)
Greece–Italy	Patras–Bari Patras–Ancona Igoumenitsa–Bari Igoumenitsa–Ancona	Blue Star/Superfast Ferries	www.superfast.com; ☎ 30/210 891 9000 (Greece); ☎ 800/424-2471 (USA)
Ireland–France	Rosslare–Cherbourg Rosslare–Roscoff	Irish Ferries	www.irishferries.com; 353/818 300 400 (Ireland); 772/563-2856 (USA)
Italy–Sicily	Villa S. Giovanni–Messina	Trenitalia	www.trenitalia.com; ☎ 39/89 20 21
Italy–Spain/Tunisia	Civitavecchía–Barcelona Salerno–Tunis Palermo–Tunis	Grimaldi Ferries	www.grimaldi-ferries.com; ☎ 39/081 496 444
Netherlands–England	Hoek van Holland–Harwich	Stena Line	www.stenaline.com; ☎ 44/8705 70 70 70
Norway	Stavanger–Bergen	HSD-Flaggruten ANS	www.hsd.no; ☎ 47/55 23 87 00

Excluding some holidays. Check schedules before departing.

Length of trip	Frequency	Passholder Discount/ Regular One-Way Fare
21½ hr. (overnight); 18½ hr. (overnight) 11–12 hr. (day); 11–12 hr. (overnight) 5½ hr. (day); 5–10 hr. (day and overnight) 2½–5 hr. 45 min. 8½ hr. (day); 11–12 hr. (overnight) 2½ hr.	3 per week* 3-4 per week* 1-2 daily* 1–5 per day* 6 per week* 1-6 per day*	50% off day sailings only/24€–80€
1¼ hr.	15 per day	50%/£6-12
45 min.	Every 30 min.	Free/4€–7€
24-25 hr. (overnight)	Daily*	Free/from 91€
3 hr. 45 min. 5 hr. 45 min.	5 per day 3 per day	Free (only on night ferry carrying the night train from Malmo–Berlin)/95€–117€ 105€–152€
20–21 hr. (overnight) 15–16 hr. (overnight)	6 per week* 1 per day*	Free, plus 15€ June and Sept and 30€ July and Aug/from 54€
15½ hr.; 17 hr. (overnight) 20–21 hr. (overnight) 9½ hr. (most overnight) 15–16 hr. (overnight)	1 per day* 6 per week* 6 per week* 1 per day*	Free, plus 10€ June and Sept and 20€ July and Aug/from 52€
19½ hr.; 17½ hr. (overnight) 18 hr.; 13½ hr. (overnight)	Up to 4 per week 1 per week mid-March–Oct	30%/56€-69€
40 min.	25 per day	Free/N/A
20 hr. (overnight) 21–35 hr. (overnight) 11–15 hr. (overnight)	4-7 per week 2 per week 1-2 per week	20% off/29€–79 € 39€–99€
5½-8½ (some overnight)	2 per day	30% off/30€
4½ hr.	1-4 per day	50%/NOK310–NOK640

Continues

Major European Ferry Lines

Countries	Routes	Ferry Line	Contact
Sweden–Denmark	Helsingborg–Helsingør	Scandlines	www.english.scandlines.dk; ℂ 45/331 51 51
	Göteborg–Frederikshavn	Stena Line	www.stenaline.com (Swedish only); ℂ 44/8705 70 70 70
Sweden–Finland	Stockholm–Helsinki	Silja Line	www.silja.fi;
	Stockholm–Turku		ℂ 358/9 18041

When reserving your car, be sure to ask what these extras cost, because they can make a big difference in your bottom line. Gasoline is very expensive in Europe. The CDW and other insurance might be covered by your credit card if you use the card to pay for the rental; check with your card issuer to be sure.

If your credit card doesn't cover the CDW (and it probably won't in Ireland), **AIG Travel Guard,** 1145 Clark St., Stevens Point, WI 54481 (ℂ **800/826-4919** or 715/345-0505; www.travelguard.com), offers it at reasonable rates. Avis and Hertz, among other companies, require that you purchase a theft-protection policy in Italy.

The Rules of the Road: Driving in Europe

- First off, know that European drivers tend to be more aggressive than their American counterparts.
- Drive on the right except in England, Scotland, Wales and Ireland, where you drive on the left. And *do not drive* in the left lane on a four-lane highway; it is truly only for passing.
- If someone comes up from behind and flashes his lights at you, it's a signal for you to slow down and drive more on the shoulder so he can pass you more easily (two-lane roads here routinely become three cars wide).
- Except for the German autobahn, most highways do indeed have speed limits of around 60 to 80 mph (100–135kmph).
- Remember that everything's measured in **kilometers** here (mileage and speed limits). For a rough conversion, 1 kilometer = 0.6 miles.
- Be aware that although gas may look reasonably priced, the price is per liter, and 3.8 liters = 1 gallon—so multiply by four to estimate the equivalent per-gallon price. (Gas prices in North America don't look so bad now, do they?)
- Never leave anything of value in the car overnight, and don't leave anything visible any time you leave the car (this goes double in Italy, triple in Naples).

Length of trip	Frequency	Passholder Discount/ Regular One-Way Fare
20 min.	1-3 per hour	Free/3€–67€
2–3½ hr.	5-6 per day	30% off/SEK165–SEK250
16½ hr. (overnight)	1 per day	Free w/ Eurail, 50% w/ Scandinavia/ 116€–157€ (inc. cabin)
9 hr., 45 min.–14 hr. (overnight to Turku)	1 per day	Free w/ Eurail, 50% w/ Scandinavia/ 11€–33€

Should you wish to rent a car on your own for a day-trip, the main car-rental companies are **Avis** (© 800/331-1212; www.avis.com), **Budget** (© 800/527-0700; www.budget.com), **SIXT** (© 888/749-8227; www.e-sixt.com), **Hertz** (© 800/654-3001; www.hertz.com), **Dollar** (© 800/800-3665; www.dollar.com), and **National** (© 800/227-7368; www.nationalcar.com).

U.S.-based companies specializing in European rentals are **Auto Europe** (© 800/223-5555; www.autoeurope.com), **Europe by Car** (© 800/223-1516 or 212/581-3040; www.europebycar.com), and **Kemwel** (© 877/820-0668; www.kemwel.com). Europe by Car, Kemwel, and **Renault Eurodrive** (© 800/221-1052; www.renault usa.com) also offer a low-cost alternative to renting for longer than 17 days: **short-term leases** in which you technically buy a fresh-from-the-factory car and then sell it back when you return it. All insurance and taxes are included, from liability and theft to personal injury and CDW, with no deductible. And unlike many rental agencies, who won't rent to anyone under 25, the minimum age for a lease is 18.

The **AAA (www.aaa.com)** supplies good maps to its members. **Michelin** maps (© 800/423-0485; www.viamichelin.com) are made for European visitors. The maps rate cities as "uninteresting" (as a tourist destination); "interesting"; "worth a detour"; or "worth an entire journey." They also highlight particularly scenic stretches of road in green, and have symbols pointing out scenic overlooks, ruins, and other sights along the way.

9 Getting to Europe

FLYING FROM NORTH AMERICA

There's no train from North America to Europe (that pesky ocean gets in the way), so you'll have to fly. Most major airlines fly to Europe, but fares can vary wildly depending on the time of year and who's having a sale at any given moment.

Railpass travelers have unusual flexibility in choosing their destination; if you're going to be covering five or six countries, you can choose the cheapest one to fly into. Generally, flying into a capital city (such as Paris) is cheaper than flying to a provincial city (such as Marseille), but there are exceptions: For Germany, you'll often find better fares into **Frankfurt** than into Berlin, and fares to Milan and Rome are often equal.

London is the cheapest European destination to fly to from North America, followed by **Paris** and **Amsterdam. Frankfurt** and **Brussels** are also competitive hubs. If you're heading for Eastern Europe, **Prague** may be cheaper than Vienna or Budapest.

The time of week and time of year you fly is critical. Midweek flights are almost always cheaper than weekend flights. **Low season** stretches from November to March, except December 14 to January 1, and fares of around $600 from the East Coast of the U.S. to various European destinations are the norm. **Shoulder season** is from April to May, mid-September to October, and December 14 to January 1. In **high season,** from June to early September, expect to pay $800 to $1,200 for a round-trip ticket to Europe.

As with all air travel, however, prices vary widely, sometimes from one day to the next. Follow airfares into a couple of acceptable European cities over the course of several weeks so you know what airfare norms are. Then you'll recognize a deal when you see one.

Note: The cheapest way to fly to Europe is usually to fly into and out of the same city—flying into one city and out of another can sometimes add several hundred dollars to your airfare. The best way to travel by rail, however, is usually to start off in one city and end your journey in another, and unless you're covering a small region, backtracking to your starting point could cost you valuable travel time. We suggest you add up the costs and time of doing your rail trip as both a one-way or round-trip journey and then decide which option works best for your schedule and budget.

Check the "Essentials" section in chapters 3 through 19 for a list of the major airlines that service each European country's major cities out of North America.

FINDING THE LOWEST FARES ONLINE

Shopping online provides an easy way of finding low fares. The "big three" online travel agencies, **Expedia.com, Travelocity.com,** and **Orbitz.com,** sell most of the air tickets bought on the Internet. (Canadian travelers should try expedia.ca and travelocity.ca.) Each has different business deals with the airlines and may offer different fares on the same flights, so it's wise to shop around. Expedia and Travelocity will also send you **e-mail notification** when a cheap fare becomes available to your favorite destination. Of the smaller travel agency websites, **SideStep** (www.sidestep.com) has gotten the best reviews from Frommer's authors. It's a browser add-on that purports to "search 140 sites at once," but in reality only beats competitors' fares as often as other sites do. **Kayak** (www.kayak.com) and **Mobissimo** (www.mobissimo.com) are also "aggregators" who pull together other websites' fare results.

Also remember to check **airline websites.** Don't neglect checking prices on low-fare carriers such as easyJet or Ryanair, whose fares are often misreported or simply missing from travel agency websites. Even with major airlines, you can often shave a few bucks from a fare by booking directly through the airline and avoiding a travel agency's transaction fee. Some airlines reserve their best deals for their own websites, so it's wise to use the consolidators to compare prices between major carriers and then check the airlines' own websites before you click "Buy Now." The best prices available through the airlines themselves are only available by **booking online:** Most airlines now offer online-only fares that even their phone agents know nothing about.

If you're willing to give up some control over your flight details, use an **opaque fare service** such as **Priceline** (www.priceline.com; www.priceline.co.uk for Europeans) or **Hotwire** (www.hotwire.com). Both offer rock-bottom prices in exchange for travel on

> ⌒Tips **Alternative Airlines**
>
> A few airlines fly between the U.S. and Europe from destinations you'd never think of, and often at lower fares than U.S. or European carriers. The most reliable include:
>
> **Singapore Air** (800/742-3333; www.singaporeair.com), which flies from Newark to Frankfurt.
>
> **Air India** (800/223-7776; www.airindia.com, but buy tickets via www.expedia.com), which flies from New York to London and Paris and from Chicago to London.
>
> **Air New Zealand** (800/262-1234; www.airnz.com), which flies from Los Angeles to London.
>
> **Air Tahiti Nui** (877/824-4846; www.airtahitinui-usa.com), which flies from Los Angeles to Paris.

a "mystery airline" at a mysterious time of day, often with a mysterious change of planes en route. The mystery airlines are all major, well-known carriers—and the possibility of being sent from Philadelphia to Paris via Chicago is remote; the airlines' routing computers have gotten a lot better than they used to be. But your chances of getting a 6am or 11pm flight are pretty high. Hotwire tells you flight prices before you buy; Priceline usually has better deals than Hotwire, but you have to play their "name our price" game. If you're new at this, pick up a copy of *Priceline.com For Dummies* (Wiley Publishing, Inc., 2004; $19.99), the only easy, comprehensive guide to using Priceline.

PACKAGE TOURS & TRAVEL AGENTS

Packages aren't guided tours—rather, they're a way to save by buying your airfare, rail-pass, and accommodations from the same agent. Especially during high season, you can often get a better deal this way than if you booked all the pieces independently. You lose some freedom, though, and the hotels chosen by packagers are usually personality-free international-style boxes. Getting a travel agent to construct a custom package may cost a bit more, but it can take a lot of stress out of the planning process and you'll get exactly the trip you want.

The **Society of International Railway Travelers** (© 800/478-4881; www.irtsociety.com) knows so much about rail that they publish a newsletter entirely about great train journeys. They offer organized rail tours and are also willing to function as a travel agent to design your ideal air/hotel/rail combination.

Ray Hanley, a former board member of the American Society of Travel Agents, runs **Travel Pro Network** (© 800/947-8728; www.travelpro.net), a travel agency specializing in designing European trips involving rail travel.

10 Money Matters

Here's the bad news: The U.S. dollar has been on a slow slide against every European currency for several years now. During the 2005–06 period, the dollar dropped by about 5% against the euro, and fell 15% against some Eastern European currencies, and those rates haven't improved. If you haven't been to Europe in a while, expect severe sticker shock, even in "cheap" countries.

The *euro,* Western Europe's joint currency, will batter your wallet, but it is convenient. As long as you stay in Austria, Belgium, Finland, France, Germany, Greece, Ireland, Italy, Luxembourg, the Netherlands, Portugal, and Spain, you won't need to change your money once. Montenegro also uses the euro because that country refuses to use the Serbian dinar.

One euro is broken into 100 cents. There are coins of 1, 2, 5, 10, 20, and 50 cents, and one and two euros; bills are 5, 10, 20, 50, 100, 200, and 500 euros. (Five-hundred-euro bills, a common counterfeiters' target, aren't accepted at many shops.) Bills look the same in every euro country, but each country is allowed to design one side of its euro coins. They're like the "50 states" U.S. quarters—interchangeable, but collectable—and it's a great game for kids to try to find all 96 varieties.

At press time, 1€ equaled $1.30. The exchange rate directly affects the planning of your rail journey—when the euro is low, it becomes much cheaper to buy some point-to-point tickets in Europe than to buy them at home. Check the latest currency rates in your local newspaper's business pages or by going to **www.oanda.com** before traveling.

OTHER FOREIGN CURRENCY

Fifteen other countries in this book don't use the euro. Great Britain, Denmark, and Sweden are members of the European Union (EU) that have "opted out" of the euro. The Czech Republic, Hungary, Poland, Slovakia, and Slovenia are brand-new members of the EU who are still aligning their economies to ready themselves for the euro. Bulgaria, Croatia, Norway, Romania, Serbia and Montenegro, Switzerland, and Turkey are not members of the EU. (Businesses in Hungary, Turkey, and the Balkans often post prices in euros or dollars as hedges against inflation; those businesses will accept both the posted currency and their own local cash.) Here's how the "outsider" currencies break down and their rates against the U.S. dollar at press time:

GETTING CASH

It's a good idea to exchange at least some money—just enough to cover airport incidentals and transportation to your hotel—before you leave home, so you can avoid lines at airport ATMs (but you will assuredly find ATMs in whatever airport you land in). You can exchange money at your local American Express or Thomas Cook office or your bank. If you're far away from a bank with currency-exchange services, **American Express** (© 800/528-4800; www.americanexpress.com) offers traveler's checks and foreign currency, though you'll pay a $15 order fee and additional shipping costs. (Note, however, that fewer and fewer European businesses are willing to accept traveler's checks.)

The easiest and best way to get cash away from home is from an ATM. They are ubiquitous, even in Europe. The **Cirrus** (© 800/424-7787; www.mastercard.com) and **PLUS** (© 800/843-7587; www.visa.com) networks span the globe; look at the back of your bank card to see which network you're on, then call or check online for ATM locations at your destination. Be sure you know your personal identification number (PIN) before you leave home and be sure to find out your daily withdrawal limit before you depart. Also keep in mind that many banks impose a fee every time a card is used at a different bank's ATM, and that fee can be higher for international transactions (up to $5 or more) than for domestic ones. On top of this, the bank from which you withdraw cash may charge its own fee.

You can also get cash advances on your credit card at an ATM. Keep in mind that credit card companies try to protect themselves from theft by limiting the funds

Non-Euro Countries

Bulgaria	Leva (BGN)	100 stotinki	$1 = 1.45 BGN
Croatia	Kuna (HRK)	100 lipa	$1 = 5.44 HRK
Czech Republic	Koruna (Kč)	100 haléru	$1 = 21Kč
Denmark	Krone (DKK)	100 øre	$1 = 5.90 DKK
Hungary	Forint (Ft)	no smaller unit	$1 = 183.35 Ft
Norway	Kroner (NOK)	100 øre	$1 = 6.50 NOK
Poland	Zloty (Zl)	100 groszy	$1 = 2.80 Zl
Romania	New Lei (RON)	100 bani	$1 = 2.38 RON
Serbia	Dinar	100 para	$1 = 61 Dinar
Slovakia	Koruna (Sk)	100 halieru	$1 = 25 Sk
Slovenia	Tolar (SIT)	100 stotini	$1 = 177.9 SIT
Sweden	Krona (SEK)	100 oüre	$1 = 7.20 SEK
Switzerland	Franc (CHF)	100 centimes	$1 = CHF 1.23
Turkey	New Lira (YTL)	100 kurus	$1 = 1.31 YTL
United Kingdom	Pound (£)	100 pence	$1.90 = 1£

someone can withdraw outside their home country, so call your credit card company before you leave home.

CREDIT CARDS

Credit cards are a safe way to carry money, they provide a convenient record of all your expenses, and they generally offer good exchange rates. You can also withdraw cash advances from your credit cards at banks or ATMs, provided you know your PIN. If you've forgotten yours, or didn't even know you had one, call the number on the back of your credit card and ask the bank to send it to you. It usually takes 5 to 7 business days, though some banks will provide the number over the phone if you tell them your mother's maiden name or some other personal information. However, you should beware that you'll be charged interest from the day you withdraw your cash, not from the day your credit card bill is due, as is the case with credit card purchases. If you charge foreign purchases to your card, your bankcard company will likely charge a commission (1% or 2%) on every foreign purchase you make, but don't sweat this small stuff; for most purchases, you'll still get the best deal with credit cards when you factor in traveler's check exchange rates.

Within Europe, Visa and MasterCard are almost universally accepted (though some smaller establishments or places in rural areas will still only take cash). And American Express is useful, if somewhat less omnipresent than the Big Two. Leave your Discover Card at home.

VALUE-ADDED TAX (VAT)

All European countries charge a **value-added tax (VAT)** of 15% to 34% on goods and services—it's like a sales tax that's already included in the price. Rates vary from country to country (as does the name—it's called the IVA in Italy and Spain, the TVA in France, MOMS in Sweden, and so on), though the goal in EU countries is to arrive at a uniform rate of about 15%. Citizens of non-EU countries can, as they leave the country, usually get back most of the tax on purchases (not services) if they spend

> **Tips Dear Visa: I'm off to Paris!**
>
> Some credit card companies recommend that you notify them of any impending trip abroad so that they don't become suspicious when the card is used numerous times in a foreign destination and your charges are blocked. Even if you don't call your credit card company in advance, you can always call the card's toll-free emergency number if a charge is refused—a good reason to carry the phone number with you. But perhaps the most important lesson here is to carry more than one card with you on your trip; a card might not work for any number of reasons, so having a backup is the smart way to go.

above a designated amount (usually $80–$200) in a single store (and, in some cases, if they don't use the items while in the country in which they were purchased).

Regulations vary from country to country, so inquire at the tourist office when you arrive to find out the procedure; ask what percentage of the tax is refunded, and if the refund is given to you at the airport or mailed to you later. Look for a TAX FREE SHOPPING FOR TOURISTS sign posted in participating stores. Ask the storekeeper for the necessary forms, and, if possible, keep the purchases in their original packages. Save all your receipts and VAT forms from each EU country to process all of them at the **"Tax Refund"** desk in the airport of the last country you visit before flying home (allow at least an extra 30 min. at the airport to process forms).

To avoid VAT refund hassles, ask for a Global Refund form at a store where you make a purchase. When leaving a European country, have it stamped by customs, after which you take it to the Global Refund counter at more than 700 airports and border crossings in Europe. Your money is refunded on the spot. For information, contact **Global Refund** (© **800/566-9828;** www.globalrefund.com).

11 Tips on Accommodations

Traditional European hotels tend to be simpler than American ones and emphasize cleanliness and friendliness over amenities. For example, even in the cheapest American chain motel, free cable is as standard as indoor plumbing. In Europe, however, few hotels below the moderate level have in-room TVs.

Unless otherwise noted, all hotel rooms in this book have **private bathrooms.** However, the standard European hotel bathroom might not look like what you're used to. For example, the European concept of a shower is to stick a nozzle in the bathroom wall and a drain in the floor. Shower curtains are optional. In some cramped private bathrooms, you'll have to relocate the toilet paper outside the bathroom before turning on the shower and drenching the whole room. Another interesting fixture is the "half tub," in which there's only room to sit, rather than lie down. The half tub usually sports a shower nozzle that has nowhere to hang—so your knees get very clean and the floor gets very wet. Hot water may be available only once a day and not on demand—this is especially true with shared bathrooms. Heating water is costly, and many smaller hotels do it only once daily, in the morning.

A few other differences to note:

- **Think small.** European hotel rooms are generally smaller than hotel rooms in North America. Many have been squeezed into historic and older buildings. As a result, these hotels offer an atmosphere that more modern hotels lack, but they also occasionally end up with some odd room configurations.

- **Double up.** Or not. When we use the term "double" in referring to hotel rates inside this book, we mean a room for two people. But you need to be careful when booking a hotel room in Europe because in many instances, if you ask for a double, what you'll get is a room with one double bed (and beds are smaller in Europe, too!). A twin room, on the other hand, has two beds. King beds are exceptionally rare.

- **Cooling off.** Air-conditioning is far from a common amenity in most European hotels, and the hotels that do have it tend to fall into the top price categories. So if you must have air-conditioning, be prepared to pay for it.

GETTING THE BEST ROOM AT THE BEST RATE

The **rack rate** is the maximum rate that a hotel charges for a room. Hardly anybody pays this price, however. To lower the cost of your room:

- **Ask about special rates or other discounts.** Always ask whether a less-expensive room than the first one quoted is available, or whether any special rates apply to you. You may qualify for corporate, student, senior, or other discounts. Find out the hotel policy on children—do kids stay free in the room (this is uncommon in Europe) or is there a special rate? Do you get a discount if you book a minimum number of days?

- **Dial direct.** When booking a room in a chain hotel, you'll often get a better deal by calling the individual hotel's reservation desk than the chain's main number.

- **Book online.** Many hotels offer Internet-only discounts, or supply rooms to Priceline, Hotels.com, Lodging.com, or Expedia at rates much lower than the ones you can get through the hotel itself.

- **Shop around!** A little-known gem, **Travelaxe (www.travelaxe.com)** offers a free, downloadable price comparison program that will make your hotel search infinitely easier. The program searches a host of discount travel websites for the best prices for your city (and it covers most major European cities) and your travel dates. Click on the price you like and the program will send you straight to the website offering it. And, unlike most websites, Travelaxe prices almost always include hotel tax, so you actually see the total price of the room.

- **Remember the law of supply and demand.** Many hotels have high-season and low-season prices, and booking the day after "high season" ends can mean big discounts. For example, Paris hotel rates usually drop in August as natives leave town en masse for their summer vacations, and if you hit the Netherlands right after the major tulip bloom season, you'll still see plenty of colorful flora but will pay a whole lot less for your hotel room.

- **Avoid excess charges and hidden costs.** When you book a room, ask whether the hotel charges for air-conditioning (some do in the Mediterranean countries). Use your own cellphone (keeping in mind that North American phones don't generally work in Europe), pay phones, or prepaid phone cards instead of dialing direct from hotel phones, which usually have exorbitant rates. And don't be tempted by the room's minibar offerings: Most hotels charge through the nose for water, soda, and snacks. Finally, ask about local taxes and service charges, which can increase the cost of a room by 15% or more.

Tips **A Traveler's Tip**

If you call a hotel from home to reserve a room, *always follow up with a confirmation fax or e-mail.* Not only is it what most hotels prefer, but it is also printed proof you've booked a room. Keep the language simple—state your name, number of people, what kind of room (such as "double with bathroom and one bed" or "twin with bathroom and two beds"), how many nights you'd like to stay, and the starting date for the first night. Remember that Europeans abbreviate dates day/month/year, not month/day/year.

HOTEL BOOKING SERVICES

When you arrive in town, don't be snookered by hotel hawkers who peg you as a traveler as soon as you hop off the train—they're probably scam artists. A desk in the train station or at the tourist office (look for the sign with the *i* for information) acts as a central hotel reservation service for the city. Tell them your price range, where you'd like to be in the city, and even the style of hotel, and they'll use a computer database to find you a room that meets your demands.

The advantages of booking services are that they do all the room-finding work for you—for a nominal fee—and always speak English, while individual hoteliers may not. When every hotel in town seems to be booked up (during a convention or festival or just in high season), they can often find space for you at inns not listed in guidebooks or other main sources. On the downside, hotels in many countries often charge higher rates to people booking through such a service. Our recommendation: Unless you're the happy-go-lucky type, plan an itinerary and make your hotel reservations in advance, even if it's only a few days in advance. And remember that even inexpensive hostels frequently allow online reservations.

RAILPASS HOTEL BONUSES

If you've got a European railpass, you can get discounted rates at many European hotels. Be aware, though, that the discount almost always applies to the hotel's sky-high rack rates and the final price may still be higher than what you'd get through an online reservation service such as hotels.com or Priceline.

Eurail Global Pass, Eurail Global Pass Flexi, and Eurail Select Pass: Discounts of 30% off of maximum double room rates in many major European cities. You must book via Hilton's worldwide toll-free number at ✆ **00800/444 58667** (✆ **800/774-1500** in the U.S. and Canada), quote the discount code "P96ERW," and show your pass at check-in. See also the country-specific discounts listed below, including passes in Benelux, France, Greece, Romania, Spain, and Switzerland.

Balkan Flexipass: Discounted prices at the Hotel Beograd (11070 10 Vladimira Popovica) in Belgrade, Serbia; and the Hotel Zeleznicar in Vrnjacka Banja, and the Klimetica in Ohrid, Macedonia. Discount of 15% off hotels in Athens booked via Ionian Travel (✆ **30/210 523 9609**).

Benelux–France, Benelux–Germany, France–Germany, France–Italy, France–Spain, France–Switzerland, Italy–Spain Pass, Portugal–Spain, and **Spain Passes:** Up to 40% discount for passholders on HUSA-Hotels.

France Railpass: Discounts on the Accor Group Hotels (© 33/146 62 44 40; www.accorhotels.com), including 10% reductions at Mercure, Novotel, and Suitehotel brands; and a 5% discount on Sofitel, Lucien, and Barrière brands, weekends only. Also, receive a 10% discount on Citadines Apart'hotels (© 33/1 41 05 79 05; www.citadines.com), which offer fully furnished studio apartments with hotel services.

Greece Pass and **Greece–Italy Pass:** 15% off hotels in Athens booked via **Ionian Travel** (© 30/210 523 9609).

Romania Pass and Hungary–Romania Pass: Receive 50% off rooms at the Crowne Plaza Bucharest (© 40/212 240 034; www.bucharest-crowneplaza.com). Get 30% off rooms at the Hotel Alexandros in Busteni (©40/244 320 138; www.hotel-alexandros.ro); and at the Hotel Europa and Asian Health Spa in Eforie Nord (© 40/241-741 710; www.anahotels.ro).

Swiss Pass: 10% discount on Swiss Budget Hotels when booked online (© 41/848 805 508; www.rooms.ch); and on Unikat Hotels (© 41 [0]56 664 56 84; www.unikathotels.ch).

3

Austria

Rivaled only by Switzerland for its soaring Alpine peaks and scenic grandeur, Austria is one of the world's greatest destinations for rail travelers. Much of the country's spectacular scenery can be seen outside your train window as you ride the rails in this once-great empire that was a major world power during the 18th and 19th centuries. You'll pass unspoiled mountain villages, ocher-colored baroque buildings, onion-domed churches, and miles and miles of rugged scenery in a country that is 75% mountainous.

Though Austria is just smaller than the state of Maine, its geography is among the most varied in Europe. Castles and dense forests disappear as ancient glacial lakes come into view, lapping up against old spas that are bordered by acres of vineyards. But nothing can compete with the Alps, with some of the most panoramic and dramatic mountain peaks in the world—most of which you'll be able to see and reach easily through the country's extensive rail system, which stretches for nearly 3,600 miles (5,800km) of tracks.

Since ancient times, Austria has stood at the crossroads of Europe, and that is even truer today for the rail traveler. Austria is bordered by Germany and the Czech Republic to the north, Slovakia and Hungary to the east, Slovenia and Italy to the south, and Switzerland and Liechtenstein to the west. As such, Austria is smack in the middle of most of Europe's rail networks and is easily connected to almost anywhere you're going except Britain and Scandinavia.

And you won't have much trouble getting around once you board your train. Austria's rail system is among the most intricate, efficient, and sophisticated in the world, and a passenger will find that getting around, even in the mountains, is easy and fast because of amazing engineering advances in rail technology, including aerial cableways.

Another plus: Austrians are taught English beginning in grade school, so language is hardly a barrier. A final allure: Austria is a biseasonal country, attracting sightseers and hikers in summer and skiers in winter. The skiing here is equaled in the world only by neighboring Switzerland.

HIGHLIGHTS OF AUSTRIA

The three most popular destinations in Austria are Vienna, Salzburg, and Innsbruck. All three are easily reached by rail, and, most importantly for the rail traveler, none of the major routes between these cities usually suffers any snow delays or closures during the popular winter ski season.

Vienna, the capital of Austria, is not centrally located but rather lies in one of the easternmost provinces of the nation. So, unlike the country's two other major cities, it is not on the main north-south rail lines of Europe. If, however, you're flying into Austria or arriving by rail from Eastern Europe, this will assuredly be your first stop in the country and is, therefore, where we start you off in this chapter. And if your rail trip

will include an overview of Europe (western, central, and eastern) as a whole, then designate Vienna your crossroads: A dividing point between the Continent's western and eastern frontiers, it makes a grand stopover of at least 3 days, especially if you're traveling by rail farther east to such cities as Budapest or Prague.

Vienna is actually a worthy destination itself, as it's filled with scenic grandeur that rivals or even surpasses most of the other capitals of Europe. The Habsburg dynasty left a legacy of grandiose monuments constructed during their centuries of imperial rule, and the city offers some of Europe's greatest museums and palaces.

The second city of Austria, **Salzburg,** is easily reached by rail from such cities as Vienna, Innsbruck, Munich, Zurich, or Milan. As a rail destination, it's particularly convenient for passengers who also want to see Munich and parts of Italy on the same journey. Allow at least 2 days for a hurried visit to this city of Mozart and the von Trapps, made famous in the fabled 1965 musical *The Sound of Music.* Rich with the splendors of the baroque age, Salzburg is one of Europe's premier architectural gems and is famous throughout the world for one of the Continent's most prestigious music festivals. Little wonder that many rail travelers rate Salzburg among their favorite destinations in Europe.

Moments Festivals & Special Events

Given Austria's major contributions to the field, it's no wonder that many of the country's special events revolve around music. Since the 1920s, the **Salzburg Festival,** held the end of July to the end of August, has been one of the premier cultural events of Europe, sparkling with opera, chamber music, plays, concerts, appearances by world-class artists, and many other cultural presentations. Always count on stagings of Mozart operas. Performances are staged at various venues throughout the city. For tickets, contact the **Salzburg Festival,** Postfach 140, A-5020 Salzburg (© **0662/8045-500;** www.salzburgfestival.at), several months in advance.

Other big annual events include the **Wiener Festwochen (Vienna Festival)** in May and June, featuring primarily new and avant-garde theater productions, as well as jazz and classical concerts and art exhibits; and the **Donauinselfest (Danube Island Festival),** a gigantic open-air party held in Vienna the last weekend in June on the banks of the Danube, complete with rock, pop, and folk music and an evening fireworks display. For more information on Vienna's many events, contact **Vienna Tourist Information** (© **01/24 555;** www.vienna.info).

Most rail passengers entering Austria from the west make a stopover in **Innsbruck,** the capital of the Tyrolean state. It's a two-season city, being both a summer resort and a winter ski center, and is full of Alpine flavor. Its Old Town has a distinct medieval flair, with mountain peaks soaring virtually everywhere you look. Innsbruck is actually the third most important city to visit in Austria after Vienna and Salzburg, but if you're traveling by rail, it's the most central of the major Austrian cities. It's a stopover on the major rail link between Zurich and Vienna, making it an ideal introduction to Austria, especially if you want to concentrate on the Alpine grandeur of this small nation. Most rail visitors usually settle for a 2-night visit to Innsbruck before heading off to other countries, with the promise of a return on another occasion.

1 Essentials

GETTING THERE

From the United States and Canada, you can fly directly to Vienna on **Austrian Airlines** (© **800/843-0002** in the U.S. and Canada; www.aua.com), the national carrier of Austria. There's nonstop service from New York, Washington, D.C., Chicago, and Toronto to Vienna. **British Airways** (© **800/AIRWAYS** in the U.S. and Canada; www.ba.com) provides excellent service to Vienna through London. Flights on **Lufthansa** (© **800/645-3880** in the U.S. and Canada; www.lufthansa.com), the German national carrier, depart from North America frequently for Frankfurt and Munich, with connections to Vienna.

AUSTRIA BY RAIL

Rail travel is superb in Austria, with fast, clean trains taking you through scenic regions. Trains will carry you nearly every place in the country, except for remote hamlets tucked away in almost-inaccessible mountain districts. Many other services tie in with railroad travel, among them car or bicycle rental at many stations, bus transportation links, and package tours, including boat trips and cable-car rides.

High-tech **InterCity Express (ICE)** trains, complete with audio connections at every seat and video displays in first class, connect Vienna with all major cities in the country, including Salzburg and Innsbruck, with express IC trains on other lines. **EuroCity (EC)** trains also connect cities within Austria as well as with several international trains. A few **EuroNight (EN)** and **CityNightLine (CNL)** trains travel through the night to connect Vienna with Paris, Venice, Florence, Rome, Zurich, Berlin, and other international destinations. Avoid the slower RegionalExpress and RegionalBahn trains unless you have no other alternative, as the other rail options in the country are faster and have more amenities.

One of the great train rides of Europe is the 7-hour journey from Venice northeast to Vienna. This is a stunning route set against an Alpine backdrop, taking in vistas at every turn, including mountain lakes, vast woodlands, and towering peaks. On this trip, arrangements can be made for you to get off in Ljubljana to explore its attractions.

And one final noteworthy route, combining two Alpine nations, is the 9-hour Zurich–Vienna run, which passes through panoramic valleys and takes in magnificent Alpine vistas, especially around the Arlberg Pass. This trip passes some of the most beautiful and unspoiled villages in Europe before stopping at Innsbruck and Salzburg as the train heads east toward Vienna. If Innsbruck and Salzburg are the only two cities in Austria on your itinerary, you can change directions at Innsbruck, because that Tyrolean city lies on the main rail route between Munich in the north and Venice in the southeast.

For more information, to order tickets, and to obtain schedule information, go to the **Austrian Federal Railroad (ÖBB)** website at www.oebb.at. In Austria, information on trains and schedules can be obtained by calling © **05/1717** from anywhere in the country.

TICKETS & PASSES

For information on the **Eurail Global Pass, Eurail Select Pass, Eurail Global Pass Flexi,** and other multicountry options, see chapter 2. In addition to these popular passes, the **Austria Railpass** grants 3 to 8 days of nonconsecutive unlimited train travel in a 15-day period with a choice of first- or second-class seats. Bonuses built in to this pass include various discounts, including Danube river trips between Melk and Krems and between Vienna and Dürnstein. The 3-day pass starts at $199 in first class or $136 in second class. There is also an **Austria–Switzerland Pass,** valid for 4 to 10 days of nonconsecutive unlimited train travel within 2 months, with the 4-day pass costing $347 for first class.

If you're traveling in first class on any of the passes mentioned above, you're also entitled to use the first-class lounges at Vienna's Südbahnhof and Westbahnhof stations, Salzburg Hauptbahnhof, and Innsbruck Hauptbahnhof.

All of the passes mentioned should be purchased in North America prior to your departure. To buy a pass, contact **Rail Europe** (© **877/272-RAIL** [7245] in North America; www.raileurope.com) or your travel agent. *Note:* Children under 6 travel free in Austria; kids ages 6 to 12 are offered a discount. Other discount fares and tickets available in Austria at most rail stations include:

ÖBB VORTEILScard The VORTEILScard provides a 50% reduction on domestic train fares and 25% reduction in international travel through most European countries.

Moments Riding Historic Rails

One of the most breathtaking and dramatic train rides in Alpine Europe is the **Semmering Pass Railway** ✮✮✮, one of the world's greatest feats of railway engineering. This UNESCO-protected site (the only rail line on UNESCO's Heritage list) dates from 1842 and still pays tribute to the engineers of imperial Austria.

Through limestone cliffs with craggy rocks and across wide valleys, the rail lines take you across 16 viaducts, through 15 tunnels, and across 129 bridges, a distance of 25 miles (41km). The railway, for the most part, is wholly preserved in its original state. The Semmering Pass itself is 56 miles (90km) southeast of Vienna and marks the boundary between the provinces of Styria and Lower Austria. At the peak of the pass, constructed on terraces between 3,231 and 3,973 feet (969 and 1,192m), is a winter sports center and mountain spa.

The Semmering rail links Vienna's Südbahnhof with the city of Leoben, 106 miles (176km) southwest of Vienna. Although modern trains make this run, the best way to experience this breathtaking ride is aboard the slower **Erlebniszug** (Experience Train), a regular train with old-fashioned coaches. It departs Vienna's Südbahnhof every Saturday and Sunday morning and travels through Semmering to Mürzzuschlag before heading back to Vienna, with more than a dozen stops along the way. Passengers can get off the train wherever they like and reboard it later in the day on its return trip to Vienna (passholders can ride for free). For departure times and more information, call ✆ **05/1717** or go to **www.erlebnis-bahn-schiff.at**.

Price of the card is 99€ ($129) and is valid for 1 year; a photo is required. Seniors (women 60 years of age and over and men age 65 and over) can have the same benefits with the VORTEILScard Senior, which costs 26.90€ ($35) and requires proof of age along with a passport photo. All VORTEILScard are available at all railroad stations.

FOREIGN TRAIN TERMS

English speakers should have no trouble getting around and riding the rails of Austria. The people of Austria, including those who run the rails, are among the most well educated on earth, and most are nearly as fluent in English as they are in their native German.

It's helpful to know that the Austria Federal Railroad is called **Österreichische Bundesbahn (ÖBB)** and that yellow poster-size signs announce departure times, called *Ausfahrt,* and that white signs announce arrivals, known as *Ankunft.* For more train terms in German, see chapter 9.

PRACTICAL TRAIN INFORMATION

Vienna has rail links to all the major cities of Europe. Rail travel within Austria itself is superb, with fast, clean trains taking you just about anywhere in the country and going through some incredibly scenic regions.

Any train depot in Austria will sell you an individual ticket. At major stations these are also sold at automated machines. You can often hop aboard a train and purchase a ticket from a conductor, although you're assessed a small surcharge (usually 3€/$3.90) for this service. Nearly all major stations accept credit cards such as American Express, Visa, and MasterCard.

For more on Austria's railways, Check out the ÖBB's website at **www.oebb.at**.

RESERVATIONS   Although not always required, it is still advisable to make a reservation for travel on an Austrian rail line. A seat reservation is not guaranteed even with a railpass, and it's worth the 3.50€ ($4.55) extra investment for the greater security in travel. During holiday seasons or busy times—such as the peak winter ski season in Innsbruck—reservations are imperative. Your railpass will cover most high-speed trains such as EuroCity or InterCity, and though no supplement is charged within Austria, you may be charged a supplement for the portion of your travels outside the Austrian border.

Austria is a relatively small country, and you can usually get where you're going without any long overnight hauls, so sleeping arrangements are rarely a factor. If, however, you're heading for an international destination, you might consider getting a *couchette* (a fold-down bunk bed; see chapter 2 for more details). These are usually clean and comfortable on Austrian trains. Reservations can be made through travel agents or in person at any rail station in Austria. Most seat reservations only require a few hours' notice. However, for a couchette reservation, a few days' notice is advised, especially during high season. *Note:* Because the price of couchette and seat reservations is the same in the U.S. as it is in Austria, if you have a firm travel itinerary, we recommend getting your train reservations from Rail Europe (see above) before you leave North America. Another option, if you wish to travel in style, is to splurge on your own private sleeper compartment, complete with bathroom, on the EuroNight or City Nightline trains that cross the country or pass through it.

SERVICE & AMENITIES   All InterCity and EuroCity trains have dining cars. And all, except for local commuter trains going to the suburbs of Vienna, feature mini-bars—which on European trains is a trolley-style snack bar (also serving liquor) that's rolled on wheels through the train carriages.

The bad news is that drinking and dining on Austrian railways is prohibitively expensive for travelers on strict budgets, who are better advised to bring along some food and drink and have an on-train picnic while taking in all that panoramic Austrian scenery. Most stations have well-stocked kiosks that are only slightly more expensive than regular supermarkets. In Vienna, food or drink is no problem, as the two big stations have delicatessens that keep long hours, even on Sundays.

Trains & Travel Times in Austria

From	To	Type of Train	# of Trains	Frequency	Travel Time
Vienna	Salzburg	ICE, IC, EC, EN	29	Daily	2 hr., 37 min.– 3 hr., 18 min.
Vienna	Innsbruck	ICE, IC, EC, EN	11	Daily	4¹/₂ hr.
Salzburg	Innsbruck	ICE, EC, EN	11	Daily	2 hr.

FAST FACTS: Austria

Area Codes   The country code for Austria is **43**. The area code for Vienna is **01**; for Salzburg, **0662**; and for Innsbruck, **0512**.

Business Hours   Banking hours vary according to the region. In Vienna, they're open Monday to Friday 8am to 3pm (to 5:30pm Thurs). The exchange counters at airports and railroad stations are open longer (from the first to the last plane at airports), including weekends. Shop hours are generally Monday to Friday 9 or 9:30am to 6:30 or 7pm and Saturday from 9am to 5 or 6pm. Shops in small towns or outside city centers may close for lunch from noon to 1pm or 2pm. Most businesses and shops are closed on Sunday, but convenience stores at train stations are open and sell basic necessities.

Climate   In Austria the temperature varies greatly depending on your location. The national average ranges from a low of 9°F (–13°C) in January to a high of 68°F (20°C) in July. However, in Vienna the January average is 32°F (0°C), for July 68°F (20°C). Snow falls in the mountainous sectors by mid-November, but it rarely affects the major rail routes. The winter air is usually crisp and clear, with many sunny days. The winter snow cover can last from late December through March in the valleys, from November through May at about 6,000 feet (1,800m), and all year at above 8,500 feet (2,550m). The ideal times for visiting Vienna are spring and fall, when you'll find mild, sunny days. "Summer" generally means from Easter until about mid-October. By the end of July, Alpine wildflowers are in full bloom.

Documents Required   Americans, Canadians, and Australians need only a valid passport for travel to Austria. European Union (EU) citizens traveling to Austria face lesser requirements. In general, a national identity card with photo ID will be sufficient. But check with a travel agent or the Austrian embassy in your home country to be absolutely certain.

Electricity   Austria operates on 220 volts AC (50 cycles). That means that U.S.-made appliances that don't come with a 110/220 switch will need a transformer (sometimes called a converter) and an adaptor plug. Many Austrian hotels stock adapter plugs but not power transformers.

Embassies & Consulates   The main building of the Embassy of the **United States** is at Boltzmanngasse 16, A-1090 Vienna (② **01/31339-0**). However, the consulate is at Parking 12a, A-1010 Vienna (② **01/31339-7573**; U-Bahn: Stadtpark); it handles lost passports, tourist emergencies, and other matters and is open for emergency services Monday to Friday 8:30am to 5pm.

The Embassy of **Canada,** Laurenzerberg 2 (② **01/531 38-3000**; U-Bahn: Schwedenplatz), is open Monday to Friday 8:30am to 12:30pm and 1:30 to 3:30pm.

Health & Safety   You'll encounter few health issues while traveling in Austria. The tap water is generally safe to drink, the milk is pasteurized, and health services are good. Occasionally, the change in diet and water may cause some minor gastric disturbances, so you may want to talk to your doctor. As for safety, no particular caution is needed, other than what a discreet person would maintain anywhere. Compared to the rest of the world, Austria is a very safe country in which to travel.

Holidays Bank holidays in Austria are as follows: January 1, January 6 (Epiphany), Easter Monday, May 1, Ascension Day, Whitmonday, Corpus Christi Day, August 15, October 26 (Austria National Day), November 1, December 8, and December 25 and 26.

Legal Aid If arrested or charged with a crime, you can obtain a list of private lawyers from the U.S. Embassy to represent you.

Mail **Post offices** *(Das Postamt)* in Austria are usually located in the heart of the town, village, or urban district they service. If you're unsure of your address in any particular town, correspondence can be addressed c/o the local post office by labeling it either POST RESTANTE or POSTLAGERND. If you do this, it's important to clearly designate the addressee, the name of the town, and its postal code. To claim any correspondence, the addressee must present his or her passport.

The postal system in Austria is, for the most part, efficient and speedy. You can buy stamps at a post office or from the hundreds of news and tobacco kiosks, designated locally as Tabak-Trafik. Mailboxes are painted yellow. Both postcards and airmail letters weighing less than 20 grams cost 1.25€ ($1.65) for delivery to North America.

Police & Emergencies Dial ✆ **133** anywhere in Austria to summon the police. Emergency phone numbers throughout the country (no area code needed) are as follows: ✆ **133** for the police, **144** for an ambulance, and **122** to report a fire.

Telephone If you're on a tight budget, do not dial abroad directly from your hotel room unless it's an emergency. Austrian hotels routinely add 40% surcharges, and some will add as much as 200% to your call. If you do place a call from your room, for help dialing, contact your hotel's operator; or dial ✆ **09** for placement of long-distance calls within Austria or for information about using a telephone company credit card; dial ✆ **1611** for directory assistance; and dial ✆ **08** for help in dialing international long distance.

Coin-operated phones can be found all over Austria. Despite the increasing automation of many aspects of local life, many public phones are still operated by coins instead of by credit card. It costs .10€ (15¢) to make a 1-minute local phone call, but you must insert a minimum of .20€ (25¢) to place the call. Insert several coins to prevent being cut off. The phone will return whatever unused coins remain at the end of your call (in theory, at least).

Avoid carrying lots of coins by buying a **telephone card,** available at post offices for 15€ ($19.50). It saves about 15% on the price of a call and there are cards for both domestic and international calls. There are also cheaper telephone cards for 3.60€ ($4.70) and 6.90€ ($9), but these do not provide discounts.

Tipping A service charge of 10% to 15% is included on hotel and restaurant bills, but it's a good policy to leave something extra—about 10% of the bill—for waiters and 2€ ($2.60) per day for your hotel maid.

Your hairdresser should be tipped 10% of the bill, and the shampoo person will be thankful for a 2€ ($2.60) gratuity. Toilet attendants are usually given .50€ (65¢) and coat-check attendants expect .50€ to 1.50€ (65¢–$1.95), depending on the establishment.

2 Vienna ★★★

From the time the Romans selected the site of a Celtic settlement for location of one of its most important Central European forts, *Vindobona,* the city that grew up in the Vienna Basin of the Danube has played a vital role in European history. Austria developed around the city into a mighty empire, but the Viennese character that formed during the long history of the country is a rich amalgam of the blending of cultures that have made Vienna what it still is today: a cosmopolitan city whose people devote themselves to enjoyment of the good life. It is also one of Europe's most visually striking capitals.

The Habsburgs, Austria's rulers for 6 centuries, left a rich architectural legacy of magnificent baroque and rococo buildings and palaces, beautifully landscaped gardens, and fabulous art collections from the far corners of their empire. Music, art, literature, theater, architecture, education, food, and drink (perhaps wine from the same slopes where the Romans had vineyards in the 1st c. A.D.)—all contribute to the warm congenial atmosphere, the *Gemütlichkeit,* of Vienna.

For the rail traveler exploring Austria, Vienna should, and likely will, be your introduction to the country. Most flights into Austria from North America land here, and the city is the center hub for the Austrian rail system. In addition, it's a springboard for travel to or from Budapest, Prague, and other Eastern European destinations.

STATION INFORMATION
GETTING FROM THE AIRPORT TO THE TRAIN STATION
Vienna International Airport (© **01/7007-22233;** www.viennaairport.com) is 12 miles (19km) southeast of the city center. For a list of air carriers flying into Vienna, see "Getting There," earlier in this chapter.

A branch office of the **Vienna Tourist Information Office,** located in the arrivals hall, is open daily 8am to 9pm. A shuttle bus, the **Vienna Airport Line** (© **01/7007 32300**), departs every 30 minutes for Schwedenplatz in the heart of the city. The trip takes about 20 minutes, and Schwedenplatz is easily connected to the rest of the city via tram, bus, and U-Bahn (subway). Shuttle buses also depart the airport every 30 minutes for the Südbahnhof (a 25-min. trip) and the Westbahnhof (a 35-min. trip), Vienna's two train stations. In any case, the cost of the shuttle to Schwedenplatz or the train stations is 6€ ($7.80) one-way or 5€ ($6.50) if you have the Vienna Card (see "City Transportation on the Cheap," below).

A cheaper alternative is to take **Schnellbahn (Rapid Transit) 7** from the airport to Wien Mitte, a train/subway station located just east of the Old City. The trip costs 3€ ($3.90) one-way and takes about 25 minutes, with departures every half hour. But if you're in a hurry, you can take the same trip aboard the **City Airport Train** (CAT; www.cityairporttrain.com), which delivers you to Wien Mitte in 16 minutes for 9€ ($12), with departures every 30 minutes.

Taxis charge about 26€ to 30€ ($34–$39) for the same trip the shuttle buses make.

INSIDE THE STATIONS
Vienna has two main rail stations, which offer frequent connections to all Austrian cities and towns and from all major European cities. For train and station information, call © **05/1717** from anywhere in Austria.

The **Westbahnhof (West Station),** Mariahilferstrasse 132, serves trains arriving from western Austria, France, Germany, Switzerland, and some Eastern European countries (Hungary, for one). It has frequent links to major Austrian cities such as Salzburg, Innsbruck, and Linz, with longer connections to such cities as Hamburg, Amsterdam, Munich, Zurich, and Budapest. Trains arrive on the second level of the two-level station. For reservations, rail information, and pass validation, head for an office marked **Reisebüro am Bahnhof** (© 01/93000-33598) on the main level. Here, in the same office, is a **Verkehrsbüro** travel agency that can book sightseeing tickets and arrange hotel reservations for 4.50€ ($5.85). It's open Monday to Friday 8am to 7pm and Saturday 8am to 1pm. The Westbahnhof also has a money exchange office, *Exchange–Wechselstube,* located to the left of the escalators on the main level, that is open daily from 7am to 10pm. There are lockers for luggage. Westbahnhof connects with local trains, the U3 and U6 underground lines, and several tram and bus routes.

Südbahnhof (South Station), Wiedner Gürtel, has train service to southern and eastern Austria and is also linked to local rail service and tram and bus routes. At this trilevel terminal, the train platforms are located on the middle and top levels. Trains depart for such destinations as Graz or Villach in southern Austria, as well as Rome, Venice, Krakow, Prague, and other cities. Its currency exchange office *(Exchange–Wechselstube)* is on the lowest level of the station, immediately to the left of the main stairwell, and is open daily from 6:30am to 10pm. Its **Reisebüro am Bahnhof** (© 01/93000-35685) is open Monday to Friday 8am to 7pm and Saturday 8am to 1pm.

INFORMATION ELSEWHERE IN THE CITY

For a free map, brochures, and details on Vienna (including the current showings and times for the opera, theater, Spanish Riding School, and Vienna Boys' Choir), drop by the main office of **Vienna Tourist Information,** on the corner of Albertinaplatz and Maysedergasse (© 01/24 555; www.vienna.info; U-Bahn: Stephansplatz), off Kärntner Strasse north of the Staatsoper. It will book hotel rooms for 2.90€ ($3.75). Be sure to pick up the free monthly *Wien-Programm*—it tells what's going on in Vienna's concert halls, theaters, and opera houses. If you're looking for detailed historic information on Vienna's many beautiful buildings, be sure to buy the 3.60€ ($4.70) English-language booklet *Vienna from A to Z.* Its listings are keyed to the unique numbered plaques affixed to the front of every building of historic interest. You'll spot these plaques everywhere: They're heralded by little red-and-white flags in summer. The tourist office is open daily 9am to 7pm

CITY LAYOUT

Vienna's **Altstadt (Old City)** is delightfully compact, filled with tiny cobblestone streets leading to majestic squares. In the center is **Stephansplatz,** with Vienna's most familiar landmark, Stephansdom (St. Stephen's Cathedral). From here it's a short walk

---

⌒Tips Can't Get There from Here

Most of Vienna's train stations do not have interconnecting rail service, so you must take public transportation or a taxi to get between them if you are only switching trains in Vienna. If you opt for public transportation, it can take up to an hour to get from Westbahnhof to Südbahnhof aboard tram 18. As a result, be sure to leave plenty of time to catch a train if your journey will require switching stations.

Vienna

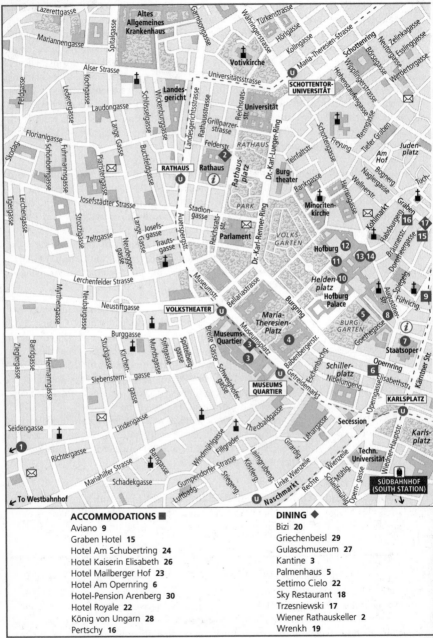

ACCOMMODATIONS ■
Aviano **9**
Graben Hotel **15**
Hotel Am Schubertring **24**
Hotel Kaiserin Elisabeth **26**
Hotel Mailberger Hof **23**
Hotel Am Opernring **6**
Hotel-Pension Arenberg **30**
Hotel Royale **22**
König von Ungarn **28**
Pertschy **16**

DINING ◆
Bizi **20**
Griechenbeisl **29**
Gulaschmuseum **27**
Kantine **3**
Palmenhaus **5**
Settimo Cielo **22**
Sky Restaurant **18**
Trzesniewski **17**
Wiener Rathauskeller **2**
Wrenkh **19**

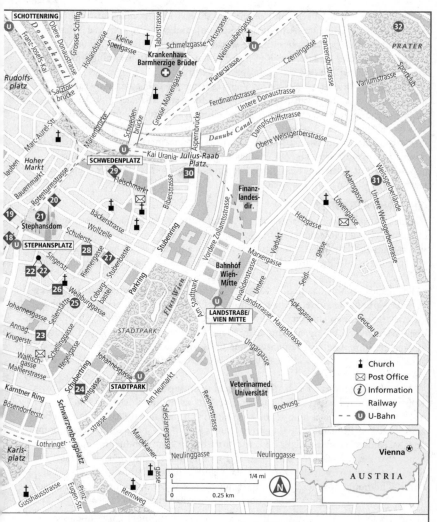

ATTRACTIONS ●

Albertina **8**
Burgkapelle **13**
Haus der Musik **25**
Hofburg **10**
Kaiserappartements **12**
Kunsthaus Wien **31**
Kunsthistorisches Museum **4**
Leopold Museum **3**

MUMOK **3**
Prater **32**
Schatzkammer **11**
Schönbrunn **1**
Silberkammer **12**
Sisi Museum **12**
Spanische Reitschule **14**
Stephansdom **21**
Staatsoper **7**

to the Hofburg (official residence of the Habsburgs) and its many attractions, the Kunsthistorisches Museum (Art History Museum), and MuseumsQuartier Wien, one of the largest museum complexes in the world and home to the prestigious Leopold Museum. **Kärntner Strasse,** much of it pedestrian, is the main shopping street, leading from Stephansplatz past the Staatsoper to Karlsplatz.

Circling the Altstadt is the Ring, as Vienna's **Ringstrasse** is commonly called. This impressive circular boulevard, 2½ miles (4km) long and 187 feet (56m) wide, was built in the mid-1800s along what used to be the city's fortifications (hence its shape as a circle around the Altstadt). Trams run along the tree-shaded Ring. Everything inside the Ring is known as the *First Bezirk* (First Precinct), denoted by the 1010 postal code in addresses. The rest of Vienna is also divided into various precincts.

Schönbrunn, Vienna's top sight, is a few miles southwest of the city center, easily reached by U-Bahn from Karlsplatz.

GETTING AROUND

Vienna's transit network consists of five U-Bahn (subway) lines, trams, buses, and several rapid transit and commuter trains. The free map given out by the tourist office shows tram and bus lines, as well as subway stops, although you'll need a magnifying glass to read it. Luckily, most of Vienna's attractions are within walking distance of one another.

For details on Vienna's public transport system, visit the **Informationsdienst der Wiener Verkehrsbetriebe,** in the underground Opernpassage at Karlsplatz, in the U-Bahn station at Stephansplatz, or at the Westbahnhof U-Bahn station. All three are open Monday to Friday 6:30am to 6:30pm and Saturday, Sunday, and holidays 8:30am to 4pm. The staff can answer questions, such as which bus to take to reach your destination. You can also call *©* **01/79 09-100** or check the website at **www.wienerlinien.at**.

A **single ticket** (good for the tram, day and night buses, S-Bahn, or U-Bahn) costs 1.50€ ($1.95) if bought in advance and permits as many transfers as you need to reach your destination as long as you keep moving in the same direction. You can buy advance tickets from automated ticket machines in U-Bahn stations and ticket booths or tobacconists. Tickets bought on board from bus or tram conductors, on the other hand, cost 2€ ($2.60). For all tickets, you must validate them yourself by inserting them into little boxes at the entry of S-Bahn and U-Bahn platforms or on buses and trams. Children up to 6 can travel free, while those 7 to 14 travel for half fare, except on Sunday, holidays, and Vienna school holidays, when they travel free.

U-BAHN (SUBWAY)   Most of the top attractions in the Inner City can be seen by foot, tram, or bus, but the U-Bahn is your best bet to get across town quickly or to reach the suburbs. It consists of five lines labeled as U-1, U-2, U-3, U-4, and U-6 (there is no U-5). The most important U-Bahn line for visitors is U-4, which stops at Schwedenplatz and Karlsplatz before continuing to Kettenbrückengasse (site of Vienna's outdoor market and weekend flea market) and Schönbrunn. U-2 travels around part of the Ring (with plans to extend it east past the Danube over the next few years), while U-1 and U-3 have stations at Stephansplatz (U-3 connects the Westbahnhof with Stephansplatz). U-4, U-2, and U-1 all converge at Karlsplatz. The underground runs daily 6am to midnight.

TRAM (STREETCAR)   Although the U-Bahn and buses have taken over most of the tram *(Strassenbahn)* routes, the city's red-and-white trams are not only a practical

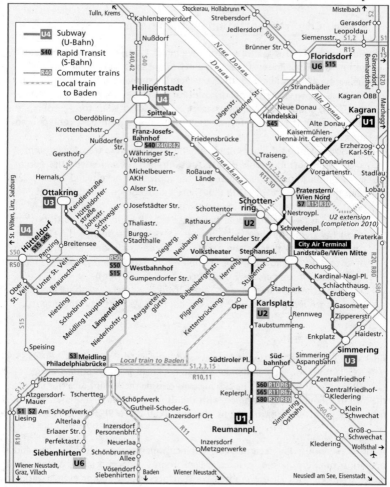

way to get around, but they're also a great way to see the city. They're heavily used for traveling around the Ring (trams 1 and 2) and for transportation between the Süd-bahnhof and the Ring (tram D). Tram 18 travels between the Westbahnhof and the Südbahnhof (see "Can't Get There from Here," above, for more on traveling between train stations).

BY BUS   Buses *(Autobus)* traverse Vienna in all directions and operate daily from 5 or 6am to around midnight, depending on the route. However, only 1A, 2A, and 3A (mostly minibus size) travel inside the Ring, Monday to Saturday. Twenty-two buses operate throughout the night from Schwedenplatz, Oper, or Schottentor to the suburbs (including Grinzing), with departures every half hour.

BY TAXI   Taxis are easy to find within the city center, but be warned that fares can add up quickly. The base fare is 2.50€ ($3.25), plus 1.20€ ($1.55) per kilometer. For night

---

Value   City Transportation on the Cheap

The **Vienna Card** is useful when traveling a lot by public transportation within the city limits. It's extremely flexible and functional for visitors because it allows unlimited travel on Vienna's subways, buses, and trams for 72 hours, along with nominal discounts at city museums, attractions, restaurants, and shops. You can purchase a Vienna Card valid for 72 hours for 18.50€ ($24) at tourist information offices, public transport centers, and some hotels.

Another option if you plan to ride a lot on the city's transport system is to buy transportation-only tickets. A ticket valid for unlimited rides during any 24-hour period costs 5€ ($6.50); an equivalent ticket valid for any 72-hour period goes for 12€ ($15.60). There's also a green ticket, priced at 24€ ($31), that contains eight individual partitions, each good for 1 day of unlimited travel (an individual can opt to use all eight of the partitions for his or her own use, thereby gaining 8 days of cost-effective travel on the city's transport system; or, the partitions can be subdivided among a group of several riders, allowing—for example—two persons 4 days each of unlimited rides or three persons 2 days each of unlimited rides).

These tickets are available at Tabak-Trafiks, as well as vending machines in underground stations, at the two main train stations, and the airport.

---

rides after 11pm, and for trips on Sundays and holidays, the base fare is 2.60€ ($3.40), plus 1€ ($1.30) for each additional kilometer. There is an additional charge of 2€ ($2.60) if ordered by phone. The fare for trips outside the Vienna area (for instance, to the airport) should be agreed upon with the driver in advance, and a 10% tip is the norm. Taxi stands are marked by signs, or you can call ✆ **01/31 300**, 60 160, or 40 100.

WHERE TO STAY

Aviano ⭐ *Value*   This centrally located pension, between Stephansplatz and the opera just off Kärntnerstrasse, offers elegant rooms decorated in old Vienna Biedermeier style but with all the modern conveniences. Some rooms even have kitchen nooks and some feature double-pane windows facing Kärntner Strasse.

Marco-d'Aviano-Gasse 1 (off Kärntner Strasse), A-1010 Wien. ✆ 01/512 83 30. Fax 01/512 83 30-6. www.secret homes.at. 17 units. 105€–157€ ($137–$204) double. Rates include buffet breakfast. AE, DC, MC, V. U-Bahn: Stephansplatz or Oper. *In room:* Hair dryer.

Graben Hotel   Established in 1918 at the collapse of the Austrian empire, this hotel is great for shoppers, as it lies near some of the most famous shopping streets of Vienna, including Kärntnerstrasse. Franz Kafka used to frequent this hotel in the days when he was called a bohemian. The mostly Art Nouveau, minimalist bedrooms are a bit small and spartan but individually designed with high ceilings. It's a longtime favorite of devotees who like the atmosphere of the old city and like having their coffee at the fabled Café Hawelka across the street, where the Kafka of today might be seen hanging out.

Dorotheergasse 3, A-1010 Vienna. ℂ **01/512 15 31-0.** Fax 01/512 15 31-20. www.kremslehnerhotels.at. 41 units. 150€–180€ ($195–$234) double. Rates include buffet breakfast. AE, DC, MC, V. U-Bahn: Karlsplatz. **Amenities:** Restaurant; nonsmoking rooms. *In room:* Hair dryer.

Hotel Am Opernring   Just across from the State Opera on the Ring, this hotel doesn't seem to promise much from its characterless lobby, but rooms, which range from midsize to quite spacious, are comfortable and provide free wireless Internet service. All have tall ceilings and modern furnishings; some have balconies. Double-glazed windows keep the street noise at bay.

Opernring 11, A-1010 Vienna. ℂ **01/587 55 18.** Fax 01/587 55 18 29. www.opernring.at. 46 units. 155€–240€ ($202–$312) double; 280€ ($364) suite. Rates include buffet breakfast. AE, DC, MC, V. U-Bahn: Karlsplatz. **Amenities:** Laundry; nonsmoking rooms. *In room:* A/C (not all rooms), hair dryer.

Hotel Am Schubertring ⚜   This imposing hotel stands in the heart of the city on the famous Ring, near the opera and the Stadtpark (one of the city's loveliest parks). It has more Austrian style and old-world tradition than many of its nearby competitors, with mostly midsize rooms decorated in Art Nouveau or Belle Epoque furnishings (some also have kitchenettes). All rooms are located on the top floor, and though some have views over the rooftops, others have only skylights or windows too high to look out of.

Schubertring 11, A-1010 Vienna. ℂ **01/717 02-0.** Fax 01/713 99 66. www.schubertring.at. 39 units. 128€–218€ ($165–$283) double. Rates include buffet breakfast. AE, DC, MC, V. U-Bahn: Karlsplatz or Stadtpark. **Amenities:** Bar; laundry. *In room:* A/C, hair dryer.

Hotel Kaiserin Elisabeth ⚜⚜   For those nostalgic for old Vienna, this hotel is a good choice, having hosted such musical greats as Liszt, Wagner, and Mozart over the years. Named for the wife of Emperor Franz Joseph and featuring her portrait in an elegant lobby, the hotel lies in the vicinity of the cathedral inside the Ring. Though it has many trappings of the 19th century, rooms have been disappointingly updated to a bland uniformity, though Oriental carpeting and natural wood help give them some character.

Weihburggasse 3, A-1010 Vienna. ℂ **01/515 26.** Fax 01/515 267. www.kaiserinelisabeth.at. 63 units. 208€–230€ ($270–$299) double. Rates include buffet breakfast. AE, DC, MC, V. U-Bahn: Stephansplatz. **Amenities:** Bar; laundry; nonsmoking rooms. *In room:* A/C (not all rooms), hair dryer.

Hotel Mailberger Hof ⚜⚜ *(Finds)*   This property dates from the 14th century and once served as a mansion for the knights of Malta. It was converted into a small baroque palace in the 17th century before being completely recast in 1976 as a stately hotel. Classified today as a historical monument, it's located off Vienna's main thoroughfare, Kärntnerstrasse, in the heart of the city. Many old-fashioned touches remain, such as wooden doors, vaulted ceilings, and even a cobblestone courtyard. The atmosphere is intimate and cozy, with midsize bedrooms that have been comfortably modernized with a bit of style, though most of the latter is reserved for the public lounges.

Annagasse 7, A-1010 Vienna. ℂ **01/512 06 41.** Fax 01/512 06 41 10. www.mailbergerhof.at. 40 units. 180€–240€ ($234–$312) double. Rates include buffet breakfast. AC, DC, MC, V. U-Bahn: Karlsplatz. **Amenities:** Restaurant; bar; laundry; nonsmoking rooms. *In room:* A/C (not all rooms), hair dryer.

Hotel–Pension Arenberg   This small, quaint hotel, under the Best Western banner, occupies the second and third stories of a six-floor apartment house dating from the late 1890s. A few minutes from the Danube canal, the well-run hotel offers tall-ceilinged, average-size bedrooms with soundproof windows and mostly spacious bathrooms. There's a certain old-fashioned charm here, though the attempt to integrate both modern and antique furnishings doesn't always work.

Stubenring 2, A-1010 Vienna. © **800/633-6548** in the U.S., or 01/512-52 91. Fax 01/513 93 56. www.arenberg.at. 22 units. 138€–208€ ($179–$270) double. Rates include breakfast. AE, DC, MC, V. U-Bahn: Schwedenplatz or Stubentor. **Amenities:** Restaurant; laundry; nonsmoking rooms. *In room:* A/C (not all rooms), hair dryer.

Hotel Royal ★★   Less than a block from St. Stephan's but on a quiet side street, this property is unusual in that it shelters two of the city's best Italian restaurants: Firenze Enoteca and Settimo Cielo (see "Where to Dine," later in this chapter). In the lobby is the original piano on which Wagner composed *Die Meistersinger von Nürnberg*. Most of the midsize to spacious bedrooms are furnished in an Art Nouveau style that combines antiques with reproductions. Corner rooms, with their large foyers, are the most desirable.

Singerstrasse 3, A-1010 Vienna. © **01/515 68-0.** Fax 01/513 96 98. 85 units. 145€–175€ ($189–$228) double; 195€–250€ ($254–$325) suite. Rates include buffet breakfast. AE, DC, MC, V. U-Bahn: Stephansplatz. **Amenities:** Restaurants; bar; laundry; nonsmoking rooms. *In room:* A/C, hair dryer.

König von Ungarn ★★★   A top choice in boutique hotels within the Ring, this property dates from 1746 and hosted Hungarian royalty during the days of the Austro-Hungarian empire. The overall atmosphere is of a dignified, country inn. Its lounge occupies a handsome courtyard atrium topped by a glass cupola, while guest rooms—no two alike—are nicely decorated with chandeliers, rich fabrics, walk-in closets, and large bathrooms with two basins. Its location, near Stephansplatz, is superb.

Schulerstrasse 10, A-1010 Vienna. © **01/515 84-0.** Fax 01/515 848. www.kvu.at. 33 units. 203€ ($264) double. Rates include breakfast. AE, DC, MC, V. U-Bahn: Stephansplatz. **Amenities:** Restaurant; bar; laundry. *In room:* A/C, hair dryer.

Pertschy ★★ *(Value)*   Inside the Ring between the Hofburg and St. Stephan's, the Pertschy occupies several floors of a 1723 palace built for a count and now a historic landmark. Rooms are outfitted in updated Biedermeier style, with high, vaulted stucco ceilings, chandeliers, and modern bathrooms. Some rooms have kitchenettes. To get from room to room, you walk along an enclosed catwalk on a balcony tracing around a courtyard, giving it a certain old-world charm.

Habsburgergasse 5 (a few steps off Graben, near Stephansplatz), A-1010 Wien. © **01/534 49-0.** Fax 01/534 49 49. www.pertschy.com. 55 units. 100€–177€ ($130–$230) double. Rates include buffet breakfast. AE, DC, MC, V. U-Bahn: Stephansplatz. **Amenities:** Nonsmoking rooms. *In room:* Hair dryer.

TOP ATTRACTIONS & SPECIAL MOMENTS

After deliverance from the dreaded plague and the equally dreaded Turks, the empire entered into a period of great power and prosperity that reached its zenith under the long reign of Maria Theresa from 1740 to 1780. Many of the sights we describe below can be traced directly to that great empress of the Age of Enlightenment, who welcomed Mozart to her court at Schönbrunn when he was only 6 years old—a child prodigy indeed.

SCHÖNBRUNN PALACE

Schönbrunn ★★★ *(Finds)*   A baroque summer palace with an astounding 1,441 rooms, the lovely Schönbrunn was built between 1696 and 1730 and is an absolute must-see for the Vienna visitor. Empress Maria Theresa left the greatest imprint on the palace. In the course of having 16 children (one of whom was the ill-fated Marie Antoinette) in 20 years, running the country, and fighting a war for her right to sit on the Austrian throne, she found time to decorate and redesign the palace (1744–49), and it remains virtually as she left it. Franz Josef I, who was born in the palace and reigned for 68 years, was the last emperor to live here. His wife, Elisabeth, popularly known as Sisi, was famed for her beauty (her hair reached to the ground), intelligence, and independent spirit.

You can tour the inside of the predominantly white-and-gilt palace on your own, choosing either the 50-minute **Grand Tour** through 40 state rooms or the 35-minute **Imperial Tour** through 22. Both include use of an English-language audio guide and allow you to see the **private apartments** of Franz Josef and Elisabeth; **Maria Theresa's nursery** with portraits of her children; the **Hall of Mirrors** where the 6-year-old Mozart played for Maria Theresa; the exotic **Chinese Cabinets** with inlaid lacquerware; the **Hall of Ceremonies** with a portrait of Maria Theresa; the impressive **Large Gallery,** fashioned after a room in Versailles and used in a 1961 meeting between Kennedy and Khrushchev; and more. The Grand Tour then continues on through, among others, the **Chinese Lacquered Room** and the **Millions Room,** decorated with 260 precious parchment miniatures brought from Constantinople and set under glass in the paneling.

If you have children in tow, they can have their own tour of Schönbrunn, called the **Schönbrunn Palace Experience,** which is both educational and fun. After dressing in period clothing, children are led by English-speaking guides (make reservations online or by phone) through original rooms outfitted with hands-on displays that give an insider's view of court life, from why people wore wigs to how folding fans were used to communicate intentions. Tours are given three times a day daily during school vacations and only on weekends and holidays the rest of the year.

Be sure to explore the 500 acres (200 hectares) of **palace grounds,** one of the most important baroque gardens in the French style. At the top of the hill opposite the palace is the **Gloriette,** a monument to soldiers and the site of a cafe with glorious views of Schönbrunn and the spread of Vienna beyond. Among the many other things to see, standouts include the **Wagenburg,** a museum with 36 imperial carriages, and the beautifully designed **Tiergarten Schönbrunn,** founded in 1752 and considered the world's oldest zoo.

Schönbrunner Schlossstrasse. (𝄞 **01/811 13-239.** www.schoenbrunn.at. Imperial Tour 9.50€ ($12) adults, 8.50€ ($11) students, 4.90€ ($6.35) children 6–15 (free for children under 6). Grand Tour 12.90€ ($17) adults, 11.40€ ($15) students, 6.90€ ($9) children. Schönbrunn Palace Experience 6.50€ ($8.45) adults, 4.50€ ($5.85) children. July–Aug daily 8:30am–6pm; Apr–June and Sept–Oct daily 8:30am–5pm; Nov–Mar daily 8:30am–4:30pm. U-Bahn: Schönbrunn.

THE HOFBURG PALACE COMPLEX

The Hofburg was the Imperial Palace of the Habsburgs for more than 6 centuries, during which time changes and additions were made in several architectural styles—Gothic, Renaissance, baroque, rococo, and classical. The entire Hofburg occupies 47 acres in the heart of Vienna; it's a virtual city within a city, with more than 2,600 rooms.

Hofburg Kaiserappartements (Imperial Apartments), Hofburg Silberkammer (Imperial Silver Collection), and Sisi Museum ✹✹✹   The Imperial Apartments, Silver Collection, and Sisi Museum share the same entrance and are included in the same ticket price. The **Imperial Apartments,** which served as the winter residence of the Habsburgs, might seem a bit plain if you've already seen the splendor of

Schönbrunn, but the Hofburg is so conveniently located it's a shame to pass it up. You can wander at leisure through 19 official and private rooms once belonging to Franz Josef and his wife, Elisabeth. Known as Sisi, she was talented, artistic, and slightly vain—she'd no longer sit for portraits after she turned 30. She was an excellent rider, and in the Hofburg is her own small gymnasium, where she kept in shape (much to the disgust of the court, which thought it improper for a lady). The **Sisi Museum** describes her somewhat tragic life and includes many personal mementos. She came from the Wittelsbach family of Munich in 1854 to marry Franz Josef at 16. Her son, Crown Prince Rudolf and the only male heir to the throne, committed suicide in a hunting lodge at Mayerling with his young mistress. Elisabeth was assassinated in 1898 by an anarchist in Geneva.

Dating from the 15th century onward, the **Imperial Silver Collection** of silverware, dinnerware, and tableware provides insight into the imperial household, royal banquets, and court etiquette. It displays items of daily use as well as valuable pieces, everything from cooking molds and pots and pans to table linens, elaborate centerpieces, crystal, silver serving sets, gilded candelabras, silverware, and porcelain table settings.

Michaeler Platz 1. ✆ 01/533 75 70. www.hofburg-wien.at. Admission 8.90€ ($12) adults, 7€ ($9.10) students, 4.50€ ($5.85) children. Daily 9am–5pm (to 5:30pm July–Aug; you must enter 30 min. before closing). U-Bahn: Stephansplatz or Herrengasse. Tram: 1, 2, D, or J to Burgring.

Schatzkammer (Treasury) ☆☆

The Schatzkammer displays a stunning collection of the secular and ecclesiastical treasures of the Habsburgs. Its priceless imperial regalia and relics of the Holy Roman Empire include royal crowns inlaid with diamonds, rubies, pearls, sapphires, and other gems (the two most impressive are the Crown of the Holy Roman Empire from ca. 962 and the Austrian Emperor's Crown from 1602), as well as swords, imperial crosses, jewelry, altars, christening robes, coronation robes, and other richly embroidered garments. However, because descriptions are only in German, it's worth forking over the extra 3€ ($3.90) for an audio guide.

Two prized heirlooms are believed to have mystical and religious significance: the **Agate Bowl (Achat Schale),** carved in Constantinople in the 4th century from a single piece of agate and once thought to be the Holy Grail; and the **Ainkhörn,** a huge narwhal tusk, considered a symbol of the unicorn and associated with the Virgin Mary and Christ. Other objects on display include the Holy Lance, which was once thought to be the lance used to pierce Christ's side during the crucifixion; and a reliquary containing what's regarded as a piece of the cross.

Among other great Schatzkammer prizes is the **Burgundian Treasure,** seized in the 15th century and rich in vestments, oil paintings, gems, and robes. The artifacts connected with the Order of the Golden Fleece, that romantic medieval order of chivalry, are the highlight of this collection.

Schweizerhof 1, Hofburg. ✆ 01/533 79 31. www.khm.at. Admission 10€ ($13) adults, 7.50€ ($9.75) seniors/ students; 3.50€ ($4.55) children. Wed–Mon 10am–6pm. U-Bahn: Stephansplatz or Herrengasse. Tram: 1, 2, D, or J to Burgring.

Spanische Reitschule (Spanish Riding School) ☆☆☆

This prestigious school has roots dating back more than 400 years, when Spanish horses were brought to Austria for breeding. The famous graceful Lipizzaner horses are a cross of Berber and Arabian stock with Spanish and Italian horses. They're born with dark coats that turn white only between the ages of 4 and 10. In addition to being beautiful, they are also the world's most classically styled equine performers. Many North Americans have seen them in the States, but to watch the Lipizzaners perform their "airs above the ground" dressage to the music of Johann Strauss or a Chopin polonaise in their baroque, chandeliered 18th-century hall is a pleasure you should not miss.

There are several ways to see the Lipizzaners at work. Most impressive are the 80-minute regular performances. However, tickets for these often sell out so it's best to order them in advance online. The least expensive and easiest way to see the horses are at their regular Morning Exercise Sessions with music. When the horses are gone on tour, the Horses' Workout features the youngsters, who come to the school when they're 4 years old and spend the next 6 years training. Tickets for the Morning Exercise and Horses' Workout are sold on a first-come, first-served basis at the visitor center, Michaelerplatz 1, Tuesday to Saturday from 9am to 4pm, and in the inner courtyard of the Imperial Palace at Josefsplatz, gate 2, on days of morning exercise. Finally, you can also join a 1-hour guided tour for a look behind the scenes of the Spanish Riding School (reservations suggested).

Josephsplatz, Hofburg. (©) 01/533 90 31. www.srs.at. Regular performances, seats 35€–135€ ($46–$176), standing room 20€–25€ ($26–$33); Morning Exercise Sessions 12€ ($16) adults, 9€ ($12) seniors, 6€ ($7.80) students/children; Horses' Workout 6€ ($7.80); guided tours 15€ ($20) adults, 12€ ($16) seniors, 8€ ($10) students/children. Regular performances Feb–June and Sept–Oct, most Sun at 11am and occasionally Fri or Sat at 11am or Fri at 7pm; Morning Exercise Sessions Feb–June and Sept–Oct and Dec, Tues–Sat 10am–noon; Horses' Workout Nov to mid-Dec Tues–Sat 10am–noon; guided tours year-round Tues–Sun (no tours given on days of performances) usually at 2, 3, and 4pm. U-Bahn: Stephansplatz or Herrengasse.

Wiener Sängerknaben (Vienna Boys' Choir) 🎈🎈🎈 The Vienna Boys' Choir was founded in 1498 to sing at church services for the Royal Chapel of the Imperial Palace. Joseph Haydn and Franz Schubert sang in the choir, which now consists of four choirs, two of which are usually on world tours. January to June and mid-September to Christmas, you can hear the choir, accompanied by Vienna State Opera orchestra members, every Sunday and some religious holidays at 9:15am Mass in the Burgkapelle of the Hofburg. Order seats at least 10 weeks in advance by contacting the Hofmusikkapelle, Hofburg, A-1010 Wien (fax 01/533 99 27-75; whmk@chello. at). Don't enclose money or a check, but rather pay and pick up your ticket at the Burgkapelle on the Friday preceding the performance 11am to 1pm or 3 to 5pm, as well as Sunday 8:15 to 8:45am. Unsold tickets go on sale at the Burgkapelle on Friday 11am to 1pm and 3 to 5pm for the following Sunday. (It's wise to get there at least 30 min. before tickets go on sale.) Otherwise, standing room is free, but there's room for only 20 people on a first-come, first-served basis.

Burgkapelle, Hofburg (entrance on Schweizerhof). (©) 01/533 99 27. Fax 01/533 99 27-75. www.wsk.at. Mass: Seats 5€–29€ ($6.50–$38), standing room free. Mass performed Sun and some religious holidays at 9:15am mid-Sept to June. U-Bahn: Stephansplatz or Herrengasse.

THE TOP MUSEUMS

Albertina Museum 🎈 Occupying the southern tip of the Hofburg, this museum is renowned for its graphic arts collection of hand-drawn sketches, drawings, posters, and lithographs dating from the late 15th to 20th centuries. Included in the collection are works by all the great masters—Raphael, Rubens, Rembrandt, Michelangelo, da Vinci, and Dürer, as well as works by Klimt, Schiele, Kokoschka, and other Austrian artists. Exhibitions change every 3 months, drawing on the museum's own collection and international contributions. Several elegant State Rooms are also open for viewing.

Albertinaplatz 1. (©) 01/534 83-540. www.albertina.at. Admission 9.50€ ($12) adults, 8€ ($10) seniors, 7€ ($9.10) students/children, 21.50€ ($28) families. Daily 10am–6pm (to 9pm Wed). U-Bahn: Karlsplatz, Stephansplatz. Tram: 1, 2, D, or J to Oper.

Haus der Musik   For a one-stop lesson in the origins of sound, the history of the Viennese Philharmonic Orchestra, and the lives of Austria's most famous composers, take in this unique hands-on museum. Exploring the world of sound through audio-visual displays, visitors can play futuristic instruments, conduct an orchestra, listen to the gnashing of teeth (and other bodily functions), create a CD (for an extra fee), and listen to an audio guide as they wander through rooms devoted to Haydn, Mozart, Beethoven, Schubert, and other famous composers.

Seilerstätte 30 ⓒ 01/516 48-51. www.hdm.at. Admission 10€ ($13) adults, 8.50€ ($11) students/seniors, 5.50€ ($7.15) children. Daily 10am–10pm. U-Bahn: Stephansdom or Oper.

KunstHausWien 🎨🎨 *(Finds)*   This one-of-a-kind museum showcases the lifelong works of painter/designer Friedensreich Hundertwasser, famous for his whimsical, fantastical, and dramatically colorful paintings, prints, and architecture. Created from a former Thonet chair factory, the museum houses about 300 of his works, including paintings, prints, tapestries, and architectural models. Temporary shows feature the works of international artists. Typical of Hundertwasser (who died in 2000), the building itself is one of the exhibits, a colorful protest against the mundane gray of modern cities. Be sure to see the **Hundertwasser Haus,** an apartment complex Hundertwasser designed on the corner of Kegelgasse and Löwengasse in the mid-1980s (about a 5-min. walk away). On Kegelgasse is also **Kalke Village,** another Hundertwasser architectural conversion, this time a former stable and gas station turned into a small shopping complex.

Untere Weissgerberstrasse 13. ⓒ 01/712 04 91. www.kunsthauswien.com. Admission 9€ ($12) adults, 7€ ($9.10) seniors/students/children, free for children under 10, temporary exhibits extra, 50% discount Mon (except holidays). Daily 10am–7pm. Tram: N or O to Radetzkyplatz.

Kunsthistorisches Museum (Museum of Fine Arts) 🎨🎨🎨   This great museum owes its existence largely to the Habsburgs, who for centuries were patrons and collectors of art. There are several collections, of which the **Egyptian-Oriental Collection**—with sarcophagi, reliefs, statues, and portraits of kings—and the **Picture Gallery** are the most outstanding. Other displays feature coins and medals, as well as sculpture and applied arts from the medieval, Renaissance, and baroque periods. The Picture Gallery, on the first floor, contains paintings by **Rubens, Rembrandt, Dürer, Titian, Giorgione, Tintoretto, Caravaggio,** and **Velázquez.** The high point of the museum is the world's largest collection of **Bruegels,** including the *Turmbau zu Babel (Tower of Babel), Die Jäger im Schnee (The Hunters in the Snow*—you can hardly believe it's not real), the *Kinderspiel* (in which children have taken over an entire town), and *Die Bauernhochzeit (The Peasant Wedding*—notice how the bride is isolated in front of the green cloth, barred by custom from eating or talking).

Maria-Theresien-Platz. ⓒ 01/525 24-403. www.khm.at. Admission 10€ ($13) adults, 7.50€ ($9.75) seniors/students/children, 20€ ($26) families; free for children under 7. Tues–Wed and Fri–Sun 10am–6pm; Thurs 10am–9pm. U-Bahn: Volkstheater or MuseumsQuartier. Tram: 1, 2, D, or J to Burgring.

Leopold Museum 🎨🎨🎨   The centerpiece of the MuseumsQuartier, Vienna's impressive museum district, is this outstanding collection of Austrian modernist masterpieces covering movements from the late Romantic period to the mid-1900s, including art produced during the Jugendstil, Secessionist, and Expressionist periods. Major works by Gustav Klimt, Oskar Kokoschka, Richard Gerstl, Herbert Boeckl, Alfred Kubin, Ferdinand Georg Waldmüller, and Anton Romako are on display, but the absolute highlight of the museum is the world's largest collection of paintings by

Moments **Boating on the "Blue" Danube**

Its waters aren't as idyllic as the Strauss waltz would lead you to believe, and its color is usually muddy brown rather than blue. But despite these drawbacks, many visitors to Austria view a day cruise along the Danube as a highlight of their trip. Until the advent of railroads and highways, the Danube played a vital role in Austria's history, helping to build the complex mercantile society that eventually became the Habsburg Empire.

The best cruises are operated by the **DDSG Blue Danube Steamship Co.** (© **01/588 80-0;** www.ddsg-blue-danube.at). Boats cruise the Danube during the warmer months, departing from a pier next to the Schwedenbrücke (U-Bahn: Schwedenplatz) or from the Reichsbrücke (U-Bahn: Vorgartenstrasse). Various tours are available, from standard sightseeing trips costing 16.80€ ($22) to themed cruises like the Sound of W.A. Mozart tour featuring musical entertainment and a three-course meal for 38€ ($49). DDSG also offers cruises to Budapest.

Egon Schiele, who produced 330 oil canvases and more than 2,500 drawings and watercolors before dying at 28; the museum owns some 200 of his works. Also on display are major objects of Austrian arts and crafts such as furniture and glassware from the late 19th and 20th centuries, with works by Otto Wagner, Adolf Loos, Josef Hoffmann, Kolo Moser, and Franz Hagenauer. A must-see.

Museumsplatz 1. © 01/525 70-0. www.leopoldmuseum.org. Admission 9€ ($12) adults, 7€ ($9.10) seniors, 5.50€ ($7.15) students/children. Wed–Mon 10am–7pm (to 9pm Thurs). U-Bahn: Volkstheater or MuseumsQuartier.

MUMOK (Museum of Modern Art Stiftung Ludwig Wien) ★★   This museum in the MuseumsQuartier showcases international 20th-century art, with an emphasis on "classical modern" art from expressionism and cubism to abstraction, pop art, photo realism, and contemporary media art. The museum's biggest contribution to the art world is its preservation of Viennese Actionism, which emerged in the 1960s at the same time as performance art was gaining attention in the United States and shocked audiences with its aggressive attacks on social taboos. Works by Picasso, Kokoschka, Kandinsky, Warhol, Rauschenberg, Roy Lichtenstein, Nam June Paik, Joseph Beuys, Günther Brus, and many others are presented in both permanent and temporary exhibits.

Museumsplatz 1. © 01/525 00. www.mumok.at. Admission 9€ ($12) adults, 7.20€ ($9.35) seniors, 6.50€ ($8.45) students, 2€ ($2.60) children. Tues–Sun 10am–6pm (to 9pm Thurs). U-Bahn: Volkstheater or MuseumsQuartier.

OTHER LEADING ATTRACTIONS

Prater   Prater is Vienna's amusement park, opened to the general public in 1766 on the former grounds of Emperor Maximilian II's game preserve. Most notable is its **Riesenrad,** a giant Ferris wheel constructed in the 1890s (then rebuilt after its destruction in World War II). If you saw the film classic *The Third Man,* you may recall the park's Ferris wheel in the scene where it appeared that Orson Welles was going to murder Joseph Cotton. Measuring 200 feet (60m) in diameter, it offers 20-minute rides and great views of Vienna, especially at night. There are also some 200 booths and both old and new attractions, including the usual shooting ranges, amusement rides ranging from bumper cars and miniature train rides to roller coasters and a bungee ejection-seat, game arcades, restaurants, beer halls, and beer gardens (only a limited number of attractions, including the Riesenrad, operate in winter). Compared to today's slick amusement parks, Prater seems endearingly old-fashioned; kids, of course, love it.

Prater Hauptallee. ⒸⒻ 01/728 05 16. www.prater.wien.info. Park free; amusement rides, charges vary (the Ferris wheel and its museum cost 8€/$10 adults, 3.20€/$4.15 children). May–Sept daily 9am–midnight; Mar–Apr and Oct daily 10am–10pm; Nov–Feb daily 10am–8pm. U-Bahn: Praterstern.

Stephansdom (St. Stephen's Cathedral) ★★
In the heart of old Vienna, Stephansdom is the city's best-known landmark. Built in the 12th century and then enlarged and rebuilt over the next 800 years, it's Vienna's most important Gothic structure and boasts staggering dimensions—352 feet long (106m) with a nave 128 feet high (38m). The highest part is its 450-ft.-high (135m) **south tower,** completed in 1433, with 343 spiral steps. From its high vantage point, watchkeepers of earlier days kept vigil over the city. This tower is open to the public (entrance outside the church on its south side) and affords one of the best city views. If you don't like to climb stairs, you can take an elevator (entrance inside the church) to the top of the **north tower,** which was never completed and is only about half as high as the south tower.

Stephansdom is inextricably linked with Viennese and Austrian history. It was here that mourners attended Mozart's "pauper's funeral" in 1791, and it was on the cathedral door that Napoleon posted his farewell edict in 1805. The chief treasure of the cathedral is the carved wooden **Wiener Neustadt altarpiece** dating from 1447, richly painted and gilded, found in the Virgin's Choir. The **catacombs** contain copper urns bearing the intestines of the Habsburg family. May to November, organ concerts are given every Wednesday at 8pm; there are also choirs and other concerts throughout the year (pick up a brochure at the cathedral).

Stephansplatz. ⒸⒻ 01/515 52-3689. Cathedral free; south tower 3€ ($3.90) adults, 1€ ($1.30) children; north tower elevator 4€ ($5.20) adults, 1.50€ ($1.95) children; catacombs 4€ ($5.20) adults, 1.50€ ($1.95) children. Cathedral Mon–Sat 6am–10pm, Sun 7am–10pm; south tower daily 9am–5:30pm; north tower daily in summer 9am–6pm, daily in winter 8:30am–4:30pm; catacombs Mon–Sat 10–11:30am and 1:30–4:30pm, Sun and holidays 1:30–4:30pm. U-Bahn: Stephansplatz.

WHERE TO DINE

Bizi (Value ITALIAN This popular self-service restaurant is a top choice for many Viennese in search of a quick tasty meal inside the Ring. It offers a variety of pizzas and pastas, such as ravioli, gnocchi, tagliatelle, and tortellini, all with a choice of sauces. There's also a salad bar, daily specials, and a selection of wines and beer. The decor is upbeat and pleasant, with modern art on the walls, and there's even a nonsmoking section.

Rotenturmstrasse 4 (at the corner of Wollzeile, north of Stephansplatz). ⒸⒻ 01/513 37 05. Main courses 5.50€–7€ ($7.15–$9.10). No credit cards. Daily 10:30am–10:30pm. U-Bahn: Stephansplatz or Schwedenplatz.

GriechenBeisl ★ AUSTRIAN All Viennese know the GriechenBeisl, and many of their ancestors have probably dined here—it dates from the 15th century, built on Roman foundations inside the Ring. Prominent diners have included Beethoven, Schubert, Wagner, Strauss, Brahms, and Twain. Housed in an ancient-looking vine-covered building, Vienna's oldest restaurant offers typical Viennese food from its English menu, including *Tafelspitz* (boiled beef with vegetables), Wiener schnitzel, Gulasch, and ragout of venison with burgundy sauce. There's live music from 7:30pm and, in summer, outdoor seating.

Fleischmarkt 11. (✆ 01/533 19 77. Meals 15€–20€ ($19.50–$26). AE, DC, MC, V. Daily 11:30am–11:30pm (last order). U-Bahn: Stephansplatz or Schwedenplatz.

Gulaschmuseum AUSTRIAN   Despite its name, this is not a museum dedicated to that favorite Austrian dish imported from Hungary, but it does offer walls covered with fine art for customers to gaze upon as they dine on more than a dozen variations of Gulasch (goulash). Probably the world's only restaurant dedicated to Gulasch, it serves traditional Hungarian *Gulasch* (a spicy beef and paprika ragout), as well as innovative renditions like fish or mushroom Gulasch. A large selection of desserts rounds out the English menu.

Schulerstrasse 20. (✆ 01/512 10 17. Reservations recommended for dinner. Main dishes 8.30€–13.60€ ($11–$18). MC, V. Daily 10am–midnight. U-Bahn: Stephansplatz.

Kantine AUSTRIAN/CONTINENTAL   Of the handful of restaurants in the MuseumsQuartier, this casual establishment is one of the most inviting, with seating at tables or on sofas and a long bar under a high vaulted ceiling. Its atmosphere is of a coffee shop, diner, and bar rolled into one (maybe that's why it says "essen, trinken und mehr"—eat, drink and more—on its menu). You can order breakfast until noon (to 6pm on weekends) or opt for one of the pita sandwiches, soups, salads, or meat or vegetarian selections. You'll find it next to the Prachner bookshop, on the east end of MuseumsQuartier.

Museumsplatz 1. (✆ 01/523 82 39. Main courses 5€–10€ ($6.50–$13). AE, DC, MC, V. Mon–Sat 9am–2am; Sun 9am–midnight. U-Bahn: MuseumsQuartier.

Palmenhaus ✦ MODERN AUSTRIAN   This stylish, airy restaurant is a good place for a meal on a dreary or rainy day. It occupies the middle section of the Schmetterlinghaus (Butterfly House), an early 1900s Art Nouveau greenhouse, set in the midst of the formal Burggarten park. On fine summer days, you can dine on the outdoor terrace overlooking greenery. It offers a variety of fresh grilled fish and daily specials, as well as what could be described as nouveau Austrian cuisine. On Fridays there's a DJ from 9pm.

In the Schmetterlinghaus, Burggarten, Opernring. (✆ 01/533 10 33. Main dishes 10€–19€ ($13–$25). DC, MC, V. Daily 10am–11:30pm (last order). Closed Mon–Tues Jan–Feb. U-Bahn: Karlsplatz, Stephansplatz, or Museums-Quartier. Tram: 1, 2, D, or J to Opernring or Burgring.

Settimo Cielo ✦ *Finds* ITALIAN   Walk through the lobby of the Hotel Royal to elevators that will whisk you to seventh heaven—a glass-enclosed restaurant with great views over Vienna's rooftops. The menu focuses on fresh fish, lobster, and seafood, but such traditional dishes as chicken with sage are not neglected.

Hotel Royal, Singerstrasse 3. (✆ 01/512 38 75. Reservations recommended. Main dishes 17.50€–26€ ($23–$34). AE, DC, MC, V. Mon–Sat noon–2:30pm and 6–11:30pm. U-Bahn: Stephansplatz.

Sky Restaurant ✦ AUSTRIAN/INTERNATIONAL   Located on the top floor of Steffl department store, this restaurant offers fine views over roofs of the Stephansdom. The menu offers a variety of dishes, from *Tafelspitz* and Wiener schnitzel to poached filet of char. During the day, you can still enjoy the view at either the Sky Café, which offers a limited menu Monday to Saturday 9:30am to 6pm, or the Sky Bar, open Monday to Saturday 1pm to 3am and Sunday 6pm to 2am.

Moments   Coffeehouses inside the Ring

As Paris has its sidewalk cafes, Vienna has its coffeehouses. All offer news-papers for leisurely perusal, and many also offer live classical music a few times a week. Introduced 300 years ago by the Turks during their unsuc-cessful attempt to conquer Vienna, coffee as served in Viennese coffee-houses has become an art form. Among the many kinds are the *kleiner Schwarzer*, a small cup without milk; *kleiner Brauner*, a small cup with cream; *Melange*, a large cup with frothy milk; *Melange mit Schlag*, coffee topped with whipped cream; *Mokka*, strong black Viennese coffee; and *Türkischer*, Turkish coffee boiled in a small copper pot and served in a tiny cup. Coffee is always served with a glass of water.

Founded in 1785 by a pastry chef who later served as the pastry supplier to the royal family, **Demel**, Kohlmarkt 14 (© **01/535 17 17-23**; U-Bahn: Stephansplatz), is Vienna's most expensive and most famous coffeehouse. Its elegant interior looks like the private parlor of a count, and in summer there's sidewalk seating. It's open daily 10am to 7pm.

Equally famous is the 19th-century **Café Sacher**, in the Hotel Sacher Vienna behind the Staatsoper, Philharmonikerstrasse 4 (© **01/514 56-0**; www.sacher.com; U-Bahn: Karlsplatz), where you can taste the famous *Sacher torte*, created in 1832 by 16-year-old Franz Sacher, whose son later founded this hotel. The cafe is open daily 8am to 11:30pm.

Kärntner Strasse 19. © **01/513 17 12-26**. Meals 18€–25€ ($23–$33). AE, DC, MC, V. Mon–Sat 6:30am–11:30pm. U-Bahn: Stephansplatz.

Trzesniewski ⋆ SANDWICHES   This cafeteria is a Viennese institution—and rightly so. It's so small that the mealtime line often snakes through the entire store; try coming at off-peak times, as seating is limited. Trzesniewski is a buffet of small open-face finger sandwiches covered with spreads like salami, egg salad, tuna fish, hot peppers, tomatoes, and two dozen other selections. This is a most satisfying choice unless you are ravenously hungry or want a leisurely meal.

Dorotheergasse 1 (just off Graben). © **01/512 32 91**. Sandwiches .90€ ($1.15). No credit cards. Mon–Fri 8:30am–7:30pm; Sat 9am–5pm. U-Bahn: Stephansplatz.

Wiener Rathauskeller ⋆⋆ AUSTRIAN   The Rittersaal (Knights' Hall), in the cellar of Vienna's City Hall, offers elegant a la carte dining in a historical setting. The attractive decor features medieval-style murals on the vaulted ceilings, stained-glass windows, beautiful lamps, and flowers and candles on the tables. The English menu lists traditional Viennese dishes, as well as such in-house specialties as grilled loin of veal. In the evenings, there's live classical music. Farther down the hall, in the Grinzinger Keller, the Austrian Dinner Show (© **01/274 90 46**) features a fixed-price meal with traditional Viennese entertainment, offered mid-April to mid-October Tuesday to Saturday from 8 to 10:30pm.

Rathausplatz. © **01/405 12 10**. www.wiener-rathauskeller.at. Reservations recommended for fixed-price meal with traditional entertainment. Meals 8.30€–18.20€ ($11–$24); Austrian Dinner Show 39€ ($51). AE, DC, MC, V. Mon–Sat 11:30am–3pm and 6–10pm (last order). U-Bahn: Rathaus. Tram: 1, 2, or D to Burgtheater/Rathausplatz.

Wrenkh ✦ VEGETARIAN/INTERNATIONAL   If you're a vegetarian or simply tired of Austria's meat obsession, head to this hip restaurant and treat yourself to innovative dishes influenced by Mediterranean and Asian cuisine. You might start with one of the tofu dishes (like the appetizer plate of smoked tofu with five spices), followed by glass noodles in a tomato-coconut sauce. There are also seafood dishes, like the tuna on spinach and red beet in caramel, with a honey-mustard sauce. The chef of this restaurant has become so well known, he even has his own cooking school next door.

Bauernmarkt 10 (west of Stephansplatz). ⓒ **01/533 15 26.** Meals 12.50€–15.50€ ($16–$20). AE, DC, MC, V. Mon–Fri noon–4pm and 6–11pm; Sat 6–11pm. U-Bahn: Stephansplatz.

SHOPPING

Vienna's most famous **shopping streets** are inside the Ring in the city center, including the pedestrian-only Kärntner Strasse, Graben, Kohlmarkt, and Rotenturmstrasse. **Ö.W. (Österreichische Werkstatten),** Kärntnerstrasse 6 (ⓒ **01/512 24 18;** U-Bahn: Stephansplatz), a three-floor, well-run store, sells hundreds of handmade art objects from Austria. Leading artists and craftspeople throughout the country organized this cooperative to showcase their wares, and it's only half a minute's walk from St. Stephan's. There's an especially good selection of pewter, along with modern jewelry, reproduction Art Nouveau jewelry, glassware, brass, baskets, ceramics, candles, and more.

If during your exploration of Vienna you should happen to admire a crystal chandelier, there's a good chance that it was made by **J. & L. Lobmeyr,** Kärntnerstrasse 26 (ⓒ **01/512 05 08;** U-Bahn: Stephansplatz). Established in 1823, Lobmeyr was named as a purveyor to the imperial court of Austria in the early 19th century and it has maintained an elevated position ever since. In addition to chandeliers of all shapes and sizes, the store also sells hand-painted Hungarian porcelain, along with complete breakfast and dinner services.

If you prefer to wear your crystal, stop by the elegant **Swarovski Store Wien,** Kärntnerstrasse 8–9 (ⓒ **01/512 90 32),** Vienna's outlet for the famous Tyrolean crystal manufacturer. The well-stocked **Steffl Kaufhaus,** Kärntnerstrasse 19 (ⓒ **01/514 31-0;** U-Bahn: Stephansplatz), rising five floors above the pedestrian traffic of inner Vienna's most appealing shopping street, is the city's most prominent department store.

The state-owned **Dorotheum,** Dorotheergasse 17 (ⓒ **01/515 60-0;** www. dorotheum.com; U-Bahn: Stephansplatz), is Europe's oldest auction house, founded by Emperor Joseph I in 1707 as an auction house where impoverished aristocrats could fairly (and anonymously) get good value for their heirlooms. The objects for sale cover a wide spectrum, including exquisite furniture and carpets, delicate objets d'art, valuable paintings, and decorative jewelry.

If flea markets are more your style, then visit the city's best known, held just past the Naschmarkt outdoor market on **Linke Wienzeile** near the Kettenbrücken U-Bahn station. This is the most colorful (and crowded) place to look for curios, antiques, jewelry, ethnic clothing, and junk. Be sure to haggle. It's open Saturday about 8am to dusk (about 6pm in summer). It's also worth a trip to the adjoining **Naschmarkt,** Vienna's outdoor food-and-produce market, open Monday to Friday 6am to 6:30pm and Saturday 6am to 5pm.

NIGHTLIFE

Everything in Vienna is somewhat theatrical, perhaps because of its majestic baroque backdrop. Small wonder that opera reigns supreme. It would be a shame if you came all this way without experiencing something that's very dear to the Viennese heart.

One of the world's leading opera houses, and under the musical direction of Seiji Ozawa since 2002, the **Staatsoper,** Opernring 2 (© **01/514 44-2250;** www.wiener-staatsoper.at; U-Bahn: Karlsplatz), stages grand productions throughout the year, except July and August. It's traditional to start each year with Johann Strauss's operetta *Die Fledermaus,* followed by a repertoire of 40 operatic works each season. Opera or ballet, accompanied by the Viennese Philharmonic Orchestra, is presented nightly September to June. (In Aug, an operetta is sometimes performed as well.) A staff of about 1,200—including the stage crew, singers, and production workers—make sure everything runs smoothly. At 5,300 square feet (488 sq. m), the stage area is one of Europe's largest and is even much larger than the spectator floor of the opera house.

For advance ticket sales, head to the **Bundestheaterkassen,** cater-cornered from the opera at Operngasse 2 (© **01/5144-7880;** U-Bahn: Karlsplatz). It's open Monday to Friday 8am to 6pm and Saturday, Sunday, and holidays 9am to noon. Tickets for most productions are 10€ to 178€ ($13–$231). There are also 500 standing-room tickets available only on the night of the performance that cost 2€ to 3.50€ ($2.60–$4.55).

Almost equally dear to the Viennese heart are the city's many historic wine cellars. With a history stretching back to the 19th century, the **Augustiner Keller,** located below the Albertina Museum at Augustinerstrasse 1 (© **01/533 10 26;** U-Bahn: Karlsplatz or Stephansplatz), boasts wooden floors, a vaulted brick ceiling, and a long narrow room that once served as a monastery cellar. A *Heuriger* (wine tavern) serving wine from its own vineyards, it offers free traditional *Heurigenmusik* daily starting at 6:30pm and a menu of traditional Austrian specialties. It's open daily 11am to midnight. **Zwölf Apostelkeller,** Sonnenfelsgasse 3 (© **01/512 67 77;** U-Bahn: Stephansplatz), is a huge wine cellar two levels deep. The vaulting of the upper cellar is mainly 15th-century Gothic, while the lower cellar is early baroque. Its Apostel wine is the specialty of the house. It's open daily 4:30pm to midnight.

Loos American Bar, Kärntnerdurchgang 10 (© **01/512-3283;** U-Bahn: Stephansplatz), is one of the most unusual and interesting bars in the center of Vienna. Once a private men's club designed by the noteworthy architect Adolf Loos in 1908, this closet-size establishment now welcomes a crowd that tends to be bilingual and very hip, including clients from Vienna's arts and media scene. It's open daily noon to 4am. On the opposite end of the spectrum is **Esterházykeller,** Haarhof 1 (© **01/533 34 82;** U-Bahn: Stephansplatz), a brick-vaulted cellar with scarred wooden tables and permeated with the aroma of endless pints of spilled beer and smoke (there is, however, a no-smoking section). Famous since 1683, it attracts a mostly older crowd and offers a self-service food counter selling meat dishes and snacks. If you decide this place is for you, choose the left-hand entrance (*not* the right-hand entrance), grip the railing firmly, and begin your descent down very steep stairs. It's open Monday to Friday 11am to 11pm and Saturday and Sunday 4 to 11pm.

Somewhere in between is the plebian **Bermuda Bräu,** Rabensteig 6 (© **01/532 28 65;** U-Bahn: Schwedenplatz), which caters to a mixed professional crowd with a varied international menu and beer on tap, while the next-door **Krah Krah,** Rabensteig 8 (© **01/533 81 93**), is famous for its large selection of beer. Both are located in **Rabensteig,** about a 3-minute walk north of Stephansplatz, in the center of the Ring's most popular nightspot, popularly referred to as the Bermuda Triangle. Both bars are open daily 11am to 2am.

Jazzland, Franz-Josefs-Kai 29 (© **01/533-2575;** www.jazzland.at; U-Bahn: Schwedenplatz), is the most famous jazz pub in Austria, noted for the quality of its U.S. and

Moments The Heurige of Grinzing

Heurige are Viennese wine taverns featuring local Viennese wines (called Heurige as well). Today there are about 400 families still cultivating vine-yards in and around Vienna, spread over several wine-growing districts on the outskirts of Vienna. Of these, **Grinzing,** at the edge of the Vienna Woods, is probably the best known, with about 20 Heurige clustered together along a charming main street lined with fairy-tale-like houses, their thick walls built around inner courtyards where grape arbors shelter Viennese wine drinkers on summer nights. Almost all Heurige also offer evening *Heurigenmusik* and a buffet with cold cuts, cheeses, salads, and meats such as grilled chicken, smoked pork, and Schweinebraten. Or you can buy a quarter-liter mug of wine and linger as long as you want. Most Heurige are open 4pm to midnight, and although some are closed November to March, you'll always find Heurige that are open. Look for the sprig of pine, usually hung above the entrance, and a small plaque with EIGENBAU written on it, which means the grower serves his or her own wine.

Although it's probably easiest to wander about and choose a Heuriger that suits your fancy, for a specific recommendation you might try the **Altes Presshaus,** Cobenzlgasse 15 (© **01/320 02 03**), uphill from the tram stop. Built in 1527, it's the oldest Heuriger in Grinzing, with an interior filled with wood paneling and antique furniture and a pleasant garden terrace that blossoms throughout summer. **Mayer am Pfarrplatz,** Pfarrplatz 2 (© **01/370 33 61**), has been owned by the Mayer family since 1683. The house remains unchanged since Beethoven lived here in the summer of 1817, when he is said to have worked on his Ninth Symphony here.

Grinzing is only 5 miles (8km) from the city center. From Schottentor, take tram 38 to the last stop, a 20-minute ride.

Central European–based performers. Open for more than 35 years, it's in a deep, 200-year-old cellar and is open Monday to Saturday 7pm to 1am, with music beginning at 9pm. Cover charge is 11€ to 18€ ($14–$23).

3 Salzburg ★★★

Salzburg, surrounded by magnificent Alpine scenery, boasts one of the world's most striking cityscapes—a medieval fortress perched above a perfectly preserved baroque inner city filled with architectural wonders. With only 150,000 inhabitants, Salzburg is also one of Europe's leading cultural centers, especially for classical music. Mozart was born here, and Salzburg boasts one of the grandest music festivals in the world.

For passengers doing a rail tour of the Continent, Salzburg stands at the crossroads of Europe. It makes a grand stopover on the lines running between Munich and Italy and also lies on the main rail route linking Switzerland in the west with Vienna (and ultimately, Budapest) in the east. Because Vienna is somewhat remotely located in the east end of Austria rather than its center, Salzburg is actually a more convenient gateway into the country if you're arriving by rail.

On the most rushed of itineraries, Salzburg (at least its highlights) can be viewed in a day, though it's better to devote at least 2 days to explore its architectural treasures and soak in its refined atmosphere. The best months to visit—unless you're planning a winter ski trip to Land Salzburg, one of Europe's greatest winter playgrounds—is from May to September, though the sight of Salzburg covered in a delicate layer of snow is equally breathtaking. On the downside, all this *Sound of Music* atmosphere and great beauty carries a high price tag, as Salzburg is one of the most expensive cities in Central Europe.

GETTING THERE

For some visitors, Salzburg—not Vienna—is their aerial gateway to Austria. Once in Salzburg, it's possible to begin a rail journey not only to the cities of Vienna and Innsbruck, but to all the remote corners of this little Alpine nation.

Salzburg Airport–W.A. Mozart, Innsbrucker Bundesstrasse 95 (© **0662/8580;** www.salzburg-airport.com), is 2 miles (3km) southwest of the city center. It has regularly scheduled air service to all Austrian airports, as well as to Amsterdam, London, Frankfurt, Berlin, Paris, and other major European destinations. Major airlines serving the Salzburg airport are **Austrian Airlines** (© **0662/85 45 33**), **Lufthansa** (© **0810/1025 8080**), and **Tyrolean** (© **0662/85 45 33**).

STATION INFORMATION

GETTING FROM THE AIRPORT TO THE TRAIN STATION

There is no direct rail service from the airport into the city center. Bus no. 2 runs between the airport and Salzburg's main rail station. Departures are frequent, and the 20-minute trip costs 1.80€ ($2.35) one-way. By taxi it's only about 15 minutes, but you'll pay at least 13€ to 15€ ($17–$19.50).

INSIDE THE STATION

Salzburg's main rail station, **Salzburg Hauptbahnhof,** Südtirolerplatz, is connected to all the major rail lines of Europe, with frequent arrivals not only from all the main cities of Austria but also from a host of European cities, especially Munich (see "Munich," in chapter 9). Trains from Vienna arrive approximately every hour or so (trip time: about 3 hr. or less) and from Innsbruck every 2 hours (trip time: 2 hr.). From Munich, trains arrive every hour or less (trip time: 2 hr. or less).

The rail station has a currency exchange office, open Monday to Friday 8:30am to 7pm and Saturday 8:30am to 2:30pm, as well as luggage-storage lockers. There's a small tourist information kiosk on Platform 2A of the Hauptbahnhof, where you can obtain a free map, buy a more detailed city map for .70€ (90¢), or make hotel reservations by paying a 2.20€ ($2.85) fee and a 12% deposit. The office is open daily 8:45am to 8pm in summer and 8:45am to 7pm in winter. For train information, the **Reisebüro am Bahnhof,** in the main hall (© **0662/93000-3161**), is open Monday to Friday 9am to 6pm.

From the train station, buses depart to various parts of the city, including the *Altstadt* (**Old Town**). Or you can walk from the rail station to the Altstadt in about 20 minutes.

INFORMATION ELSEWHERE IN THE CITY

A larger **Salzburg Tourist Office (Tourismus Salzburg)** is in the heart of the Altstadt at Mozartplatz 5. May to September it's open daily 9am to 7pm; October to April, hours are Monday to Saturday 9am to 6pm. The office also books hotel rooms, sells

Salzburg

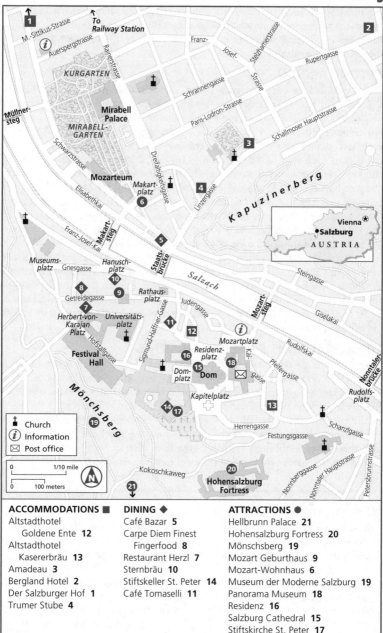

ACCOMMODATIONS ■

Altstadthotel
  Goldene Ente **12**
Altstadthotel
  Kasererbräu **13**
Amadeau **3**
Bergland Hotel **2**
Der Salzburger Hof **1**
Trumer Stube **4**

DINING ◆

Café Bazar **5**
Carpe Diem Finest
  Fingerfood **8**
Restaurant Herzl **7**
Sternbräu **10**
Stiftskeller St. Peter **14**
Café Tomaselli **11**

ATTRACTIONS ●

Hellbrunn Palace **21**
Hohensalzburg Fortress **20**
Mönchsberg **19**
Mozart Geburthaus **9**
Mozart-Wohnhaus **6**
Museum der Moderne Salzburg **19**
Panorama Museum **18**
Residenz **16**
Salzburg Cathedral **15**
Stiftskirche St. Peter **17**

city maps, stocks brochures, and sells sightseeing, concert, and theater tickets. Be sure to pick up a free copy of *Veranstaltungen,* a monthly brochure listing the concerts in Salzburg's many music halls. For more information, call ✆ **0662/889 87-0** or check the website www.salzburginfo.at.

GETTING AROUND
Walking around Salzburg, especially in the Altstadt with its many pedestrian zones, is a pleasure. In fact, because Salzburg is rather compact, you can walk to most of its major attractions. The Altstadt is only a 20-minute walk from the train station. Otherwise, buses provide quick, comfortable service between the Hauptbahnhof and Altstadt and to Salzburg's outskirts. The cost per ticket for a single journey, including transfers to reach your final destination, is 1.80€ ($2.35) for adults and half price for children (children under 6 travel free). If you think you'll be traveling a lot by bus, consider buying a 4.20€ ($5.45) *24 Stundenkarte,* valid for 24 hours of unlimited travel. If you purchase tickets in advance (not from the bus driver but from tobacco shops or vending machines at the train station), prices are slightly cheaper: 1.60€ ($2.10) for a single journey and 3.40€ ($4.40) for the 24-hour ticket. For more info about the **public transportation system,** call ✆ **0662/44 801 500.**

You'll find taxi stands scattered at key points all over the city center and in the suburbs. In and around the Altstadt, convenient taxi stands are at Hanuschplatz, Residenzplatz, Max-Reinhart-Platz, and the Mönchsberg Lift; on the opposite side of the river taxi stands are at the train station, Makartplatz, and Auerspergstrasse. Fares start at 3€ ($3.90); 10pm to 6am and all day Sundays and holidays, fares start at 3.70€ ($4.80). To phone for **a taxi,** call ✆ **8111.**

TOP ATTRACTIONS & SPECIAL MOMENTS
Most of Salzburg's attractions are on the left bank of the **Salzach River,** in the **Altstadt (Old City).** Much of the Altstadt is a pedestrian zone, including picturesque Getreidegasse with its many shops, Domplatz, and Mozartplatz. This is where you'll find such attractions as Mozart's Geburtshaus (Mozart's Birthplace), the Festival House complex, the cathedral, the Catacombs of St. Peter, and Salzburg's landmark, the **Hohensalzburg.** In fact, it's this fortress, towering above the Altstadt on a sheer cliff, that makes Salzburg so beautiful, even from afar. It's lit up at night, making a walk along the Salzach river one of the most romantic in Austria.

Value **A Discount Pass**

If you plan on traveling to Salzburg's outskirts and visiting most of the city's attractions, you might consider investing in the **Salzburg Card,** which allows unlimited use of the city's public transportation system and includes free admission to most of the city's attractions, including Mozart's birthplace, the Hohensalzburg fortress, the Residenz gallery, and the world-famous water fountain gardens at Hellbrunn. The card comes with a brochure with maps and sightseeing hints. Sold at any tourist office and most hotels, cards are valid for 24, 48, and 72 hours and cost 21€ ($27), 29€ ($38), and 34€ ($44), respectively, except from June through October, when 2€ ($2.60) is added to the prices above. Children pay half fare.

Just a short walk across the Salzach from the Altstadt is the **Neustadt (New City),** though even it boasts medieval buildings and Mozart's Wohnhaus (Mozart's Residence), as well as the pretty Mirabellgarten.

Festung Hohensalzburg (Hohensalzburg Fortress) ✦✦✦, Mönchsberg 34 (© **0662/84 24 30-11;** www.salzburg-burgen.at), is Salzburg's overwhelming landmark. Dominating the city from a sheer cliff, this impressive medieval fortress was built between the 11th and the 17th century as a residence for the prince-archbishops who ruled Salzburg for more than 500 years. It has the honor of being both Central Europe's largest completely preserved fortress and Europe's largest fortress from the 11th century. It contains the **State Rooms** of the former archbishops and two related museums, which you can visit on a guided tour in which each participant receives an audio guide that describes the most important rooms. There's even an audio guide geared toward kids, with less history and more anecdotes. The tour takes you through dark corridors and unfurnished chambers, including a dismal torture chamber filled with hideous instruments of pain. You'll also see the archbishops' living quarters, with carvings of gold leaf and a late Gothic porcelain stove from 1501—the most valuable item in the fortress—as well as a huge open-air barrel organ (dating from 1502) once used to signal the daily opening and closing of the city's gates.

Included in the tour is a visit of the **Rainermuseum,** a military museum displaying armor, swords, uniforms, and other related items. You'll also tour the **Burgmuseum (Fortress Museum),** which provides a historic overview of the fortress with displays of weapons used in peasant revolts, furniture from the 14th and 15th centuries, and a macabre collection of medieval torture devices. And, finally, you'll see the **Sound and Vision Show,** a multimedia presentation of the fortress's history, and **Welt der Marionetten,** a museum displaying marionettes from Salzburg and around the world.

The easiest way to reach the fortress is by **funicular,** but if you want a workout, you can hike to the fortress. A path leading from the Altstadt and winding up the hill, offering changing vistas on the way, makes for a pleasant and slightly strenuous walk. As an alternative, you might want to go up by funicular and descend on foot.

A combination ticket for the funicular, fortress tour, and museums costs 10€ ($13) adults, 5.70€ ($7.40) children, and 23.10€ ($30) families. It's open daily: October to April 9:30am to 5pm, May to June and September 9am to 6pm, and July and August 9am to 7pm (you must enter at least an hour before closing).

Below the fortress, in the heart of the Altstadt, is the 180-room **Residenz,** Residenzplatz 1. It dates from the mid–12th century but was rebuilt extensively in the 16th, 17th, and 18th centuries, offering a tour through 200 years of classical architecture. It served as the official residence of the archbishops when it was deemed safe for them to move down from the fortress into the city. (After you've toured both places, you won't blame them for preferring the more elegant Residenz.) You can tour 15 **Residenz Prunkräume (State Rooms;** © **0662/80 42-26 90;** www.salzburg-burgen.at) with the aid of an audio guide; you'll see the throne room (the most beautiful, and one of several in which Mozart performed), the bedroom of the archbishop, the library, the audience chamber (the most lavishly decorated, with original furnishings), and other chambers, most with inlaid wooden floors, marble portals, ceiling frescoes relating the heroics of Alexander the Great, tapestries, and precious furniture.

Also in the Residenz is the **Residenzgalerie** (© **0662/84 04 51-0;** www.residenzgalerie. at), a 15-room gallery of European art from the 16th to the 19th century, with works by Dutch, French, Italian, and Austrian baroque artists, including **Rembrandt, Rubens, Bruegel, Friedrich Loos, Ferdinand Georg Waldmüller,** and **Hans Makart.** Of special interest are paintings depicting Salzburg through the centuries.

A combination ticket for both the State Rooms and Residenzgalerie is 8.20€ ($11) adults, 6.20€ ($8.05) seniors/students, and 2.60€ ($3.40) children. The State Rooms are open daily 10am to 5pm (closed 2 weeks before Easter and for special events). The Residenzgalerie is open Tuesday to Sunday 10am to 5pm.

At the south side of Residenzplatz, where it flows into **Domplatz** (here you'll see a 1771 statue of the Virgin Mary), stands the **Dom (Salzburg Cathedral)** ✵ (𝄞 **0662/ 80 47-1860**), world renowned for its 4,000-pipe organ. When a previous edifice was destroyed by fire in 1598, Prince-Archbishop Wolf Dietrich followed up the start of work on the Residenz by commissioning construction of a new cathedral, but his over-throw prevented the finishing of the project. His successor, Archbishop Markus Sit-tikus Count Hohenems, commissioned the Italian architect Santino Solari to build the present cathedral, which was consecrated in 1628 by Archbishop Paris Count Lodron. Hailed as the "most perfect" Renaissance building in the Germanic countries, the cathedral has a marble facade and twin symmetrical towers. This is where Mozart was baptized and engaged as a court organist. The interior is in rich baroque style with elaborate frescoes, the most important of which, along with the altarpieces, were designed by Mascagni of Florence. The Dom, free to the public, is open daily 8am to 7pm (to 5pm in winter).

Although the Dom is Salzburg's most commanding cathedral, the **Stiftskirche St. Peter (St. Peter's Church)** ✵✵, St.-Peter-Bezirk (𝄞 **0662/84 45 78-0**), boasts the most picturesque setting, nestled at the foot of Mönchsberg and surrounded by one of the prettiest cemeteries you're likely to see anywhere. Many of the aristocratic fam-ilies of Salzburg are buried here, as well as many other noted persons, including Nan-nerl Mozart, sister of the composer. Four years older than her better-known brother, Nannerl was also an exceptionally gifted musician. It's also possible to take a tour through the early Christian catacombs in the cliff above the church cemetery, where you'll see rooms and chapels carved into the cliff, the first dating from A.D. 250 and built by Roman Christians for secret religious ceremonies (be forewarned: There are lots of stairs to climb). Admission to the cemetery is free; the catacombs cost 1€ ($1.30) adults, .60€ (80¢) children. The cemetery is open daily 6:30am to 6pm. The catacombs are open May to September Tuesday to Sunday 10:30am to 5pm; October to April, Wednesday and Thursday 10:30am to 3:30pm and Friday to Sunday 10:30am to 4pm.

Of course, the reason many music fans are drawn to Salzburg is because of the city's most famous citizen: Wolfgang Amadeus Mozart. The most heavily visited attraction in Salzburg is the **Mozart Geburtshaus (Mozart's Birthplace)** ✵, Getreidegasse 9 (𝄞 **0662/84 43 13;** www.mozarteum.at), located in the heart of the Altstadt on its most picturesque street. Mozart was born in this simple third-floor apartment in 1756 and lived in these four rooms with his family until 1773. The museum contains his clavichord, a copy of his pianoforte (he started composing when he was 4), and the violin he played as a boy. Of the several paintings of Amadeus, his sister Nannerl, and his family, only one is known to be a true likeness of the genius—the unfinished one by the pianoforte, done by his brother-in-law. Another is thought to be of the musi-cian when he was 9. In addition to the rooms where the family lived, there are a few

Moments **The Hills Are Alive . . .**

Bob's Special Tours (📞 **0662/84 95 11**; www.bobstours.com), which has specialized in personable English-language tours for more than 30 years, offers personalized tours in buses seating 8 to 20. The 4-hour *"Sound of Music* Tour" includes a short city tour and takes in most of the major film locations, such as Leopoldskron Palace (which served as the von Trapp film home), the Lake district where the opening scene was filmed, and the gazebo at Hellbrunn Palace. It costs 38€ ($49) adults and 33€ ($43) children.

adjoining rooms decorated in the style of a typical burgher's house in Mozart's time. You'll also find changing exhibits related to Mozart's works.

More worthwhile, however, if you have time for only one Mozart attraction, is the **Mozart-Wohnhaus (Mozart's Residence)** ✸✸✸, Makartplatz 8 (📞 **0662/87 42 27-40**; www.mozarteum.at), on the other side of the Salzach River in the Neustadt. It strives to chronicle the musician's life and the influence his family—particularly his father—had on his career, making it more informative than his birthplace for those who know little about the genius's life. A teenage Mozart and his family moved from their small Getreidegasse home to this more spacious elegant residence in 1773; it dates from 1617 and was once used for dancing classes for the aristocracy. Amadeus lived here until 1780, composing symphonies, serenades, piano and violin concertos, and sacred music. His father died here in 1787. Today the home, heavily damaged during World War II and completely rebuilt, contains a museum dedicated to Mozart and his family, period furniture, Mozart's pianoforte, and original music scores. Best, however, are the audio guides that are automatically activated by the various displays, complete with music, and the movie depicting the child prodigy's life in Salzburg and his tours of Europe. You can spend the better part of an hour here, more if you're a Mozart fan.

Both the Geburtshaus and Wohnhaus are open September to June daily 9am to 6pm and July and August daily 9am to 7pm (you must enter 30 min. before closing). A combination ticket to both costs 9.50€ ($12) adults, 7.50€ ($9.75) seniors and students, 3€ ($3.90) children 15 to 18, 2.50€ ($3.25) children 5 to 14 (free for children under 6), and 21€ ($27) families. Otherwise, a ticket to either costs 6€ ($7.80), 5€ ($6.50), 2€ ($2.60), 1.50€ ($1.95), and 14€ ($18) respectively.

Kids will probably find **Miracle's Wax Museum,** located next to Mozart's Birthplace at Getreidegasse 7 (📞 **0662/84 22 580;** www.miracleswaxmuseum.com), more to their liking. Designed to resemble Salzburg in 1791, it's an audiovisual tour through mock winding narrow streets, people's homes, and shops ranging from a shoemaker and goldsmith to a pharmacist and tooth puller, with life-size figures and media installations explaining everything from the fashion of the times to Mozart's music. It's open daily from 9am to 7pm and charges 12€ ($16) adults, 6€ ($7.80) students and children, and 24€ ($31) families.

If you're in Salzburg between the end of March and October, it's worth a trip 3 miles (5km) south of the city to see the unique **Hellbrunn Palace and its trick gardens** ✸✸, Fürstenweg 37 (📞 **0662/82 03 72-0;** www.hellbrunn.at). Built as a hunting lodge/ summer residence for Salzburg's prince-bishops in the early 17th century, this Italian

Moments   **A Panoramic Stroll**

For the best view of Hohensalzburg Fortress towering above Salzburg and the Salzach River, hike along the heavily forested ridge that stretches from the fortress to **Mönchsberg.** The hike takes about 30 minutes, and features changing vistas along the way. On Mönchsberg is the **Museum der Moderne Salzburg Mönchsberg** (© **0662/84 22 20-401;** www.museumdermoderne.at), which features changing exhibitions of art and photography from the 20th and 21st centuries. It's open Tuesday to Sunday 10am to 6pm (to 9pm Wed) and charges 8€ ($10) adults and 6€ ($7.80) seniors, students, and children.

From here, you can take the **Mönchsberg Lift** (© **0662/44 80-9772;** www.moenchsbergaufzug.at) back down to the Altstadt. It operates daily 8am to 7pm (to 10pm Wed), except in July and August when it's open daily 8am to 1am. It costs 1.80€ ($2.35) one-way for adults and .90€ ($1.15) for children.

Or, for more scenic hiking, continue walking west another 20 minutes to the **Augustiner Bräustübl,** Salzburg's famous brewery and beer garden (see "Nightlife," below).

Renaissance–style country villa is an impressive example of the luxury enjoyed by absolute rulers during the Renaissance. The most intriguing features are its water gardens—dozens of trick fountains and water sprays hidden in the large Renaissance gardens, with mysterious grottoes and mythical statues. (You almost invariably get doused, to the delight of children.) Guided tours of the garden last 30 to 40 minutes and depart every half hour daily: April and October 9am to 4:30pm (last tour); May, June, and September 9am to 5:30pm; and July and August 9am to 6pm. During July and August, evening guided tours that take in only the illuminated trick fountains are also given at 7, 8, 9, and 10pm.

The cost of the tour is 8.50€ ($11) adults, 6€ ($7.80) students, 3.80€ ($4.95) children, and 22€ ($29) families. Included in the price (except during the evening tours), is a visit to the palace, which you tour on your own with an audio guide. To reach the palace, take bus no. 55 to Hellbrunn.

Finally, history buffs may want to see the **Panorama Museum,** located next to the post office at Residenzplatz 9 (© **0662/620 808-730**). It displays Salzburg's first advertising campaign, a huge 360-degree panorama of Salzburg painted in 1829 by J. M. Sattler, who then traveled to Munich, Vienna, Prague, Dresden, Berlin, Amsterdam, and beyond to promote his masterpiece. An interactive display allows visitors to compare the Salzburg of 1829 with today, but most fun are the 24 *cosmoramas* (panoramas) of cities from around the world as they looked in the 19th century, identified only by number so you can guess which cities they represent (hint: Boston, New York, and London are included). It's open daily 9am to 6pm (to 8pm Thurs) and charges 2€ ($2.60) adults, 1.70€ ($2.20) seniors and students, and 1€ ($1.30) children.

WHERE TO STAY & DINE

Located in the heart of the Altstadt in a 650-year-old house, **Altstadthotel Goldene Ente,** Goldgasse 10 (© **0662/84 56 22;** www.ente.at; bus: 3, 5, 6, 7, 8, or 25), looks as ancient as it is, with thick walls, worn stone stairways attesting to centuries of use, tiny bathrooms, and wood furnishings. The entire house is nonsmoking, and there's a ground-floor restaurant serving traditional Austrian cuisine. Doubles are 110€ to 140€ ($143–$182), including buffet breakfast (there's a computer in the breakfast room with free Internet use).

Lying a few blocks from the Dom (cathedral), **Altstadthotel Kasererbräu,** Kaigasse 33 (© **0662/84 24 45;** www.kasererbraeu.at; bus: 5 or 25), is a 650-year-old house constructed on Roman walls in the center of the city. Each of its 43 rooms is different; those decorated with baroque and Biedermeier furnishings have more character than those with modern furniture. Guests have free access to a steam room and sauna, and there's a pizzeria on the ground floor. Some units are large enough to be classified as apartments, and are suitable for two to four persons. Double rates are 118€ to 198€ ($148–$257) and include buffet breakfast. Apartments cost 176€ to 218€ ($229–$283).

Occupying a 15th-century building and owned by the same family for three generations, **Amadeus** ★★, Linzer Gasse 43–45 (© **0662/87 14 01;** www.hotelamadeus. at; bus: 1, 3, 5, 6, or 25), has a great location in the city center, across the river from the Altstadt. You have your choice of rooms facing either a pedestrian shopping street or a peaceful cemetery (where Mozart's wife is buried). Rooms are pleasant, with both traditional furniture and modern touches. There's a computer in the lobby with free Internet use, and the hotel's second-floor terrace overlooking the cemetery is a good place to relax in the sun or spend an evening with drinks. Double rates are 120€ to 155€ ($156–$203), with off-season discounts available. Rates include substantial buffet breakfasts.

Der Salzburger Hof, Kaiserschützenstrasse 1 (© **0662/46 97-0;** www.dersalzburger hof.at), is a worthy and convenient choice for rail travelers, as it lies only 2 blocks from the Hauptbahnhof. It's a small, older hotel, with a friendly staff and 34 theme-decorated rooms, ranging from Mozart to the Sound of Music. Its restaurant offers Austrian, Indian, and Italian cuisine. Room rates are 114€ to 141€ ($148–$183) double and include buffet breakfast.

Trumer Stube ★★, Bergstrasse 6 (© **0662/87 47 76** or 0662/87 51 68; www.trumer-stube.at; bus: 1, 3, 5, 6, or 25), is a 20-room, personable hotel in the city center, across the river from the Altstadt and within a 5-minute walk of both Mozart's Birthplace and Residence. Ideal for couples and families, it's managed by friendly Silvia Rettenbacher, who speaks English and is happy to give sightseeing tips, make restaurant and guided tour reservations, and do whatever else guests desire. The pension offers cheerful, cozy, and spotless rooms (all nonsmoking), decorated with a feminine touch, as well as a lobby computer guests can use for a small fee. Doubles are 96€ to 135€ ($125–$176), including buffet breakfast.

Although not as conveniently located as those above, another good choice is the **Bergland Hotel,** Rupertgasse 15 (© **0662/87 23 18-0;** www.berglandhotel.at), an all-nonsmoking pension owned by the Kuhn family for more than 95 years. A 15-minute walk from the train station and a 10-minute walk from the Altstadt (rental bikes are available), it is managed by the friendly English-speaking Peter Kuhn, who has decorated the pension with his own artwork, oversees breakfast, and is on hand most evenings to converse with guests in the cozy bar/lounge. Doubles here are 93€ ($121), including buffet breakfast.

A dining favorite, **Restaurant Herzl** ✦✦, Getreidegasse 35 or Karajanplatz 7 (© **0662/8084 889;** bus: 1, 4, 8, 18, or 24), stands next door to the city's most glamorous hotel, Goldener Hirsch, and is entered from either Karajanplatz or Getreidegasse in the center of the city. It's especially popular during the Salzburg Festival, drawing some of the leading performers with its relaxed country-inn atmosphere and its finely tuned take on Austrian and Viennese specialties. Come here for old-fashioned favorites such as Wiener schnitzel and Nürnberger sausages. Main courses run 10.50€ to 21€ ($14–$27). It's open daily 11:30am to 9:30pm.

The Austro-Hungarian army used to eat at **Sternbräu,** Griessegasse 23 (© **0662/84 21 40;** bus: 1, 4, 8, 18, or 24), opened more than 500 years ago as a brewery. Located in the Altstadt, it's a huge place, with various dining halls and two courtyard gardens, including a beer garden shaded by chestnut trees. The Austrian food is more hearty and filling than refined, but that—and the brew served here—is why the place is so popular. Main courses with side dishes cost 8€ to 15€ ($10–$19.50). It's open daily 10am to 11pm.

Stiftskeller St. Peter ✦✦, near St. Peter's Monastery at the foot of the Mönchsberg, St. Peter-Bezirk (© **0662/84 12 68-0;** bus: 3, 5, 6, 7, 8, 25, or 26), is probably Salzburg's most popular first-class restaurant. It's under the management of St. Peter's Monastery and was first mentioned in documents dating from 803, making it Europe's oldest restaurant. There are various dining rooms, each unique but all with a medieval ambience. The changing English menu lists international dishes as well as local specialties, such as fresh trout, boiled beef with chives, veal schnitzel, and numerous daily specials. For wine you might select the Prälatenwein (prelate's wine), the grapes of which are grown in the convent's own vineyards in Wachau. The traditional desserts are great—try the *Salzburger Nockerl,* a dessert soufflé made of eggs, flour, butter, and sugar. For a real splurge, there's the Mozart Dinner Concert, held in the restaurant's elegant Baroque Hall and featuring Mozart music played by period-costumed musicians and a three-course meal based on traditional 17- and 18th-century recipes, costing 45€ ($58.50). Otherwise, main courses here are 12€ to 24€ ($16–$31). It's open daily 11:30am to 2:30pm and 6 to 10:30pm.

Although it looks out of place in the Altstadt, the hottest restaurant for casual dining is **Carpe Diem Finest Fingerfood,** Getreidegasse 50 (© **0662/84 88 00;** bus: 1, 4, 8, 18, or 24), where famous chef Jörg Wörther offers innovative finger food, served mostly in crispy cones and ranging from yellow fin tuna and avocado salad with ginger in a pumpkin cone to beef tartar with potato puree and rocket salad in a potato cone. Most cones cost 3.80€ to 7.60€ ($4.95–$9.90) and the restaurant is open daily 8:30am to midnight.

SHOPPING

Austrian artisanship is of high quality, with correspondingly high prices for Austrian traditional **sweaters, dirndls, leather goods, jewelry, petit point,** and other local goods, including **chocolates.** Most shops are concentrated in the Altstadt along **Getreidegasse** and **Alter Markt,** as well as across the river along **Linzergasse.** Most stores in Salzburg are open Monday to Saturday 9am to 6pm. Some shops may close an hour or two at noon or Saturday afternoon.

Established in 1408 and owned by the same family for four generations, **Jahn-Markl,** Residenzplatz 3 (© **0662/84 26 10**), is a small and elegant store with a forest-green facade trimmed with brass and wrought-iron detailing. Located in the center

Moments   Cafe Society

Salzburg is famous for its coffeehouses and pastry shops, where you can linger over pastry and coffee or a glass of wine, read the newspapers (including the *International Herald Tribune*), and watch the passersby. In summer, most cafes have outdoor seating. **Café Bazar**, Schwarzstrasse 3, on the Neustadt side of the Salzach near the Staatsbrücke (© **0662/87 42 78**), features large windows and a great terrace affording stunning views of the river and fortress and is popular with locals. It serves breakfast all day, as well as snacks and daily specials and is open Monday to Saturday 7:30am to 11pm and Sundays and holidays 9am to 6pm.

Opened in 1705 and one of Austria's oldest coffeehouses, **Café Tomaselli**, in the heart of the Altstadt at Alter Markt 9 (© **0662/84 44 88**), is still going strong. It's so popular you might have to wait to get a seat. In summer, extra chairs are placed out on the cobblestone square and an upstairs balcony. Have a *Melange* (a large coffee with frothy milk) and dessert, or choose from the pastry tray or display case. It's open Monday to Saturday 7am to 9pm.

of the Altstadt, it carries Lederhosen for all sizes and sexes, leather skirts, and a full line of traditional Austrian coats and blazers.

Salzburger Heimatwerk, Residenzplatz 9 (© **0662/84 41 10**), is one of the best places in town to buy Austrian handcrafts. It's a dignified stone building next to the post office, with a discreet (and hard to see) sign announcing its location. Items for sale include Austrian silver and garnet jewelry, painted boxes, candles, glassware, woodcarvings, copper and brass ceramics, tablecloths, and patterns for cross-stitched samplers in Alpine designs.

Wiener Porzellanmanufaktur Augarten Gesellschaft, Alter Markt 11 (© **0662/ 84 07 14**), is the premier shop in Salzburg for Austrian porcelain, specializing in Augarten ware. Its most famous item, which it still turns out, is a black-and-white coffee set created by architect/designer Josef Hoffmann.

NIGHTLIFE

As the birthplace of Mozart and site of the Salzburg Festival, the city boasts a musical event almost every night of the year. To find out what's going on where, stop by the **City Tourist Office**, Mozartplatz 5 (© **889/889 87-0**), to pick up a free copy of the monthly *Veranstaltungen.*

The cheapest way to secure theater tickets is by buying them directly at the theater box office. Otherwise, the **Salzburg Ticket Service,** which charges a 20% commission, is at the City Tourist Office on Mozartplatz (© **0662/84 03 10**). Selling tickets for all concerts, it's open Monday to Friday 9am to 6pm and Saturday 9am to noon (mid-July to Aug Mon–Sat 9am–7pm and Sun 10am–6pm).

All the premier opera, ballet, and concerts are staged at the **Festspielhaus**, Hofstallgasse 1 (© **0662/80 45-0;** bus: 1, 3, 5, 6, 7, 15, 25, or 26), as are major events of the Salzburg Festival. Performances are in the 1,324-seat Haus für Mozart or the 2,170-seat Grosses Haus (Large House), and it's best to buy tickets in advance; for the

Salzburg Festival, months in advance for major performances. The box office for the Salzburg Festival is at Herbert-von-Karajan-Platz (© **0662/80 45-500**). It's open Monday to Friday 9:30am to 3pm, except from July 1 to the start of the festival, when it's open Monday to Saturday 9:30am to 5pm, and during the festival, when it's open daily 9:30am to 6:30pm. For orchestra concerts, given September to June, you'll find the box office at Kulturvereinigung, Waagplatz 1A (© **0662/84 53 46**), near the tourist office. It's open Monday to Friday 8am to 6pm; performances are usually at 7:30pm. Tickets for orchestra concerts start at 8€ ($10), while opera tickets begin at 22€ ($29).

Orchestra concerts and chamber music are presented in the **Mozarteum,** Schwarzstrasse 26 (© **0662/87 31 54;** bus: 1, 3, 5, 6, or 25). The Mozarteum is on the river's right bank, near Mirabellgarten. Its box office is open Monday to Thursday 9am to 2pm and Friday 9am to 4pm. Performances are at 11am and/or 7:30pm, with most tickets at 9€ to 38€ ($12–$49).

The **Salzburger Schlosskonzerte (Salzburg Palace Concerts)** take place year-round in the Marble Hall of Mirabell Palace, Mirabellplatz (© **0662/84 85 86;** www.salzburger-schlosskonzerte.at; bus: 1, 3, 5, 6, 51, or 25). The chamber-music series presents mostly Mozart's music, as well as music by other renowned composers such as Haydn, Beethoven, Schubert, and Vivaldi. Concerts, generally at 8 or 8:30pm 3 to 7 nights a week, are held in intimate baroque surroundings, much as they were in Mozart's time. The box office, at Theatergasse 2, is open Monday to Friday 9am to 5:30pm. Tickets are 29€ to 35€ ($38–$46).

Salzburg's landmark, the **Hohensalzburg Fortress,** Mönchsberg 34 (© **0662/82 58 58;** www.mozartfestival.at; take the funicular from Festungsgasse), features concerts called the **Salzburger Festungskonzerte** in the medieval Prince's Chamber, performed by the Salzburger Mozart-Ensemble, as well as guest musicians. The box office, at A.-Adlgasser-Weg 22, is open daily 9am to 9pm; performances are given almost daily at 7:30, 8 or 8:30pm. Tickets are 31€ or 38€ ($40 or $49). Both the Salzburg Palace and Fortress concerts can be combined with preconcert dinners.

The **Salzburger Marionettentheater,** Schwarzstrasse 24 (© **0662/87 24 06;** www.marionetten.at; bus: 1, 3, 5, 6, or 25), was founded in 1913 and tours the world as one of Europe's largest and most famous marionette theaters. Using recordings made by top orchestras and singers, it presents operas and operettas Easter through September, during Christmas, and some dates in January, including *The Magic Flute, Die Fledermaus, The Barber of Seville, The Marriage of Figaro,* and *Don Giovanni.* The box office is open Monday to Saturday 9am to 1pm and 2 hours before the start of each performance; performances are usually Monday to Saturday at 7:30pm, with occasional matinees. Tickets run 18€ to 35€ ($23–$45.50).

Outside the cultural venues, the most entertaining evenings in Salzburg are at the **Augustiner Bräustübl,** Augustinergasse 4 (© **0662/43 12 46;** bus: 27). Founded in 1621 by Augustine monks, this brewery, about a 10-minute walk from the Altstadt, is a Salzburg institution and a great place for a meal in the huge outdoor beer garden or upstairs in one of the huge beer halls. Counters sell sausages and cold cuts, cheese, pretzels, hamburgers, grilled chicken, soup, salads, boiled pork with horseradish, beef with creamed spinach and potatoes, and more. It's a crowded, noisy place, as a brewery should be. It's open Monday to Friday 3 to 10:30pm and Saturday and Sunday 2:30 to 10:30pm.

4 Innsbruck ✶✶

Rivaling Vienna and Salzburg for the title of Austria's most beautiful city, Innsbruck is the capital of Tyrol, one of the world's greatest Alpine playgrounds. Its name—translated as "bridge over the Inn," the Inn being the river that flows through the city—is testimony to its importance as a major crossroad through the centuries, and today it serves as a major rail transportation hub for western Austria. But it is also a destination in itself, boasting a picture-perfect medieval Old Town (Altstadt) of narrow cobbled streets and Gothic, Renaissance, and baroque buildings in kaleidoscopic colors, with majestic mountain peaks rising above the rooftops virtually everywhere you look. Little wonder the Winter Olympics were held here in 1964 and 1976—it's a skier's paradise almost year-round, due to the nearby Stubai Glacier, and is the rail gateway to such winter ski resorts as Seefeld, Zell am Ziller, and Kitzbühel. In summer, the surrounding countryside offers hiking and other fair-weather pursuits.

In short, Innsbruck is a perfect place to unwind and escape the big city (pop. 120,000) and is also a convenient stopover for those doing a grand rail tour of Europe. By train, the German border is only 45 minutes to the north, while the Italian frontier is just 30 minutes to the south. While its major attractions can be seen in a day, 2 days are needed to do the city justice. And though it's not cheap, it's less expensive than Salzburg.

STATION INFORMATION
GETTING FROM THE AIRPORT TO THE TRAIN STATION
Although its airport is much smaller than Munich's and Salzburg's, Innsbruck's airport, **Flughafen Innsbruck-Kranebitten,** Fürstenweg 180 (✆ **0512/22525;** www. innsbruck-airport.com), serves as a gateway for air passengers who prefer to begin their rail journey of Austria in the Tyrolean Alps. Though there is no direct service from North America, there is regularly scheduled air service from Amsterdam, Frankfurt, London, Vienna, and a few other cities on flights operated by **Austrian Airlines** and **Air Alps.** From the airport, 2 miles (3km) west of the city, there is no direct rail service into town, but bus F travels to the main train station in the exact center of town in 18 minutes. Tickets cost 1.70€ ($2.20). A taxi ride takes about 10 minutes and costs 8€ ($10) and up, depending on traffic.

MORE STATION INFORMATION
Innsbruck is connected to all the major cities of Europe by international railway links. At least eight direct trains arrive daily from Munich (trip time: 1 hr., 50 min.) and 12 direct daily trains from Salzburg (2 hr.). Train travel from Vienna ranges from 4½ hours to about 5 hours, depending on the train you take. Trains arrive at the newly remodeled main railway station, the **Hauptbahnhof,** Südtiroler Platz, about a 10-minute walk from the Altstadt and connected to the rest of the city by tram and bus. Call ✆ **05/1717** for rail information or visit the **Reisebüro am Bahnhof** (✆ **0512/93000-5000**), open Monday to Friday 9am to 5:30pm.

There's an **Innsbruck Information Office** in the main hall of the train station, where you pick up city maps for 1€ ($1.30) and reserve accommodations for free. It's open daily 9am to 7pm. A bank (open weekdays only), post office, and lockers are also in the train station.

INFORMATION ELSEWHERE IN THE CITY

Innsbruck-Information, Burggraben 3 (© **0512/59850**), in the Altstadt just off Maria-Theresien-Strasse, is open daily 9am to 6pm. Here you can stock up on printed information about Innsbruck (and other parts of Tyrol) and ask questions about virtually any feature of the town. You can also buy bus tickets, exchange money (even on weekends), purchase tickets to concerts and cultural events, and book hotel rooms for free. You can visit Innsbruck's home page at **www.innsbruck.info**.

GETTING AROUND

Most of Innsbruck's major sights are clustered in or around the Altstadt, within easy walking distance from one another. Otherwise, trams and buses provide public transportation around Innsbruck and its environs. A **single ticket,** which permits transfers, costs 1.70€ ($2.20) and can be bought from the driver. Other options, available from the tourist information office, tobacco shops, and automated vending machines, include a **24-hour transportation pass** for 3.80€ ($4.95) or a **group of four tickets** for 5.70€ ($7.40). Best for tourists, however, is the **Sightseer,** a red trolley that travels to the Alpenzoo, the Altstadt, and other tourist attractions, with runs every 30 minutes in summer and every hour in winter. A single ticket costs 2.80€ ($3.65), but best is the **Day Ticket** for 8.80€ ($11). For information about various routes, call the **Innsbrucker Verkehrsbetriebe** (© **0512/5307-500**).

Otherwise, the best deal that combines transportation and sightseeing is the **Innsbruck Card,** available for 24, 48, or 72 hours for 23€ ($30), 28€ ($36), or 33€ ($43) respectively (children pay half fare). It provides unlimited transportation (including the Sightseer and shuttle bus to Swarovski Kristallwelten) along with free entry to all Innsbruck's attractions.

Taxi stands are scattered at strategic points throughout the city, or you can call a radio car (© **0512/5311**).

TOP ATTRACTIONS & SPECIAL MOMENTS

First mentioned in 12th-century documents, Innsbruck gained international stature under Maximilian I, who became German emperor in 1507, made the town the seat of the Holy Roman Empire, and constructed the most important buildings. Today, these buildings stand at the center of the compact medieval **Altstadt,** which contains most of the city's main attractions.

Most striking is Innsbruck's famous landmark, the **Goldenes Dachl (Golden Roof),** Herzog-Friedrich-Strasse 15, easily recognized by its gleaming balcony made of 2,657 gilded copper tiles. Built in the late 15th century by Emperor Maximilian to celebrate his marriage to his second wife, Bianca Maria Sforza, it was used as a royal box for watching civic events in the square below, including tournaments between armored knights, dances, and theatrics. If you look closely at the building's reliefs, you can see images of Maximilian and his two wives. (His first wife, Mary of Burgundy, died in a riding accident and was much grieved; his second wife brought him great wealth and went largely ignored.) Today the building's facade is the most photographed sight in Innsbruck. In summer, Tyrolean Folk Art Evenings are staged in the square on Thursday at 8:30pm.

Just a stone's throw away is the **Stadtturm (City Tower),** Herzog-Friedrich-Strasse 21 (© **0512/56 15 00-3**), built in 1450 and at 185 feet tall (56m) still one of the Altstadt's highest structures. Its viewing platform, reached via 148 stairs, offers magnificent

© 2007 Travelocity.com LP. LSI # 20BbS7Z-20.

I don't speak sign language.

A hotel can close for all kinds of reasons.
Our Guarantee ensures that if your hotel's undergoing construction, we'll let you know in advance. In fact, we cover your entire travel experience. See www.travelocity.com/guarantee for details.

travelocity®
You'll never roam alone.

Frommers.com

Frommers.com makes the going fast and easy.

Find a destination. ✓ Buy a guidebook. ✓ Book a trip. ✓ Get hot travel deals.
Enter to win vacations. ✓ Check out the latest travel news.
Share trip photos and memories. ✓ Download podcasts. ✓ And much more.

Frommers.com

Rated #1 Travel Web Site by *PC Magazine*®

Innsbruck

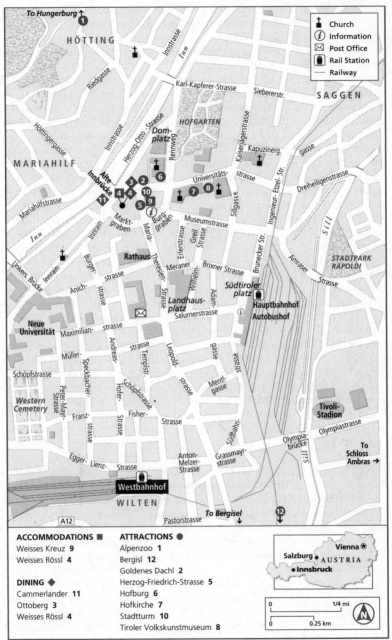

Legend:
- ✝ Church
- ⓘ Information
- ✉ Post Office
- 🚉 Rail Station
- — Railway

To Hungerburg ↑ **1**

HÖTTING

Riedgasse

Innstrasse

Inn

Karl-Kapferer-Strasse

Siebererstr.

SAGGEN

Höttingergasse

HOFGARTEN

Herzog-Otto-Strasse

Rennweg

Dom-platz

Kaiserjägerstrasse

Kapuzinerg.

gasse

MARIAHILF

Innrain

Alte Innbrücke

Mariahilfstrasse

Universitäts- strasse

Sillgasse

Dreiheiligenstrasse

Ingenieur-Etzel Str.

3 **2**
4 **4** **10** **6**
11 **5** **9**
ⓘ

7 **8**

Markt-graben

Burg-graben

Maria-Theresien-Strasse

Museumstrasse

Erlerstrasse

Greil Strasse

Brunecker Str.

Amraser Strasse

Sill

STADTPARK RAPOLDI

Univers. Brücke

Innrain

Rathaus

Burger-strasse

Anich-strasse

Meraner Strasse

Wilhelm-Greil

Brixner Strasse

Adam-gasse

Südtiroler platz

Hauptbahnhof
Autobushof

Neue Universität

Landhaus-platz

Salurnerstrasse

Maximilian-strasse

Andreas-strasse

Templstr.

Leopold-strasse

gasse

strasse

Müller-strasse

Speckbacher-strasse

Hofer-strasse

Schöpfstrasse

Mentl-gasse

Schöpfstrasse

Peter-Mayr-Strasse

Franz-strasse

Fisher-Strasse

Strasse

Südbahn-strasse

Tivoli-Stadion

Olympiastrasse

Western Cemetery

Egger- Lienz- Strasse

Anton-Melzer-Strasse

Grassmayr-strasse

Olympia-brücke

Sill

To Schloss Ambras →

Westbahnhof

WILTEN

A12

Pastorstrasse

To Bergisel ↓

12

Vienna ✦
Salzburg ●   AUSTRIA
● Innsbruck

0   1/4 mi
0   0.25 km

N

panoramic views of the city and Alps. It's open daily 10am to 5pm (to 8pm in summer) and admission is 3€ ($3.90) adults, 2.50€ ($3.25) seniors/students, 1.50€ ($1.55) children, and 6€ ($7.80) families.

Innsbruck's most imposing building remains the **Kaiserliche Hofburg (Imperial Court Palace)** *𝕮𝕮*, Rennweg 1 (© **0512/58 71 86;** www.tirol.com/hofburg-ibk). It's to Innsbruck what Versailles is to Paris—but on a much smaller scale. Built in 1460 and enlarged by Emperor Maximilian in the 1500s as a residence for his second wife, it was reconstructed in the baroque style by Empress Maria Theresa in the mid–18th century. On view are the **Kaiserappartements** used by Maria Theresa and her family whenever they visited, including the royal chapel, dining rooms, and bedrooms, all with original furnishings, tapestries, paintings, and portraits. The most fascinating of the 20-some open rooms is the **Giant's Hall,** lavishly decorated in rococo style with elaborate stucco designs and a painted ceiling. What's most striking about the room, however, are the portraits of Maria Theresa and her 16 children, including her youngest daughter, Antonia, who went on to become that ill-fated queen of France, Marie Antoinette. Admission is 5.50€ ($7.15) adults, 4€ ($5.20) seniors and students, 2.50€ ($3.25) children aged 15 to 18, and 1.10€ ($1.45) children 6 to 14 (free for children under 6). It's open daily 9am to 5pm (you must enter by 4:30pm).

A minute's walk east of the Kaiserliche Hofburg is the **Hofkirche (Court Church),** Universitätsstrasse 2 (© **0512/58 43 02;** www.hofkirche.at), conceived by Maximilian as his memorial and place of burial. Inside is his elaborate tomb, decorated with reliefs depicting scenes from the emperor's life and surrounded by 28 larger-than-life bronze statues representing his ancestors, relatives, and peers, including his father, two wives, son, and daughter; two of the statues are from designs by German artist Albrecht Dürer. The tomb, however, is empty—Maximilian died before the church was built and was buried in Wiener Neustadt. Several other important figures are interred here, however, including Tyrolean freedom fighter Andreas Hofer and Archduke Ferdinand II. You'll find Ferdinand's final resting place up the stairs in the **Silberne Kapelle (Silver Chapel);** just outside the chapel's iron gate is the tomb of Ferdinand's wife, Philippine Welser, who, as a mere commoner, wasn't allowed to be buried beside her husband. It's open Monday to Saturday 9am to 5pm and Sunday and holidays 12:30 to 5pm, with admission at 3€ ($3.90) adults and 1.50€ ($1.95) children.

For adults, the best deal is to buy a combination ticket for 6.50€ ($8.45) that also includes a visit to the **Tiroler Volkskunstmuseum (Tyrolean Folk Art Museum)** *𝕮𝕮𝕮* (© **0512/58 43 02;** www.tiroler-volkskunstmuseum.at), housed in a former monastery adjoining the Court Church (and sharing the same entry). Our favorite museum in Innsbruck, it's one of Austria's best folk art museums, with a collection of items used by common folk in the Tyrol from the Middle Ages to the 20th century. Included are sleighs; a beautiful collection of painted furniture *(Bauernmöbel);* ornamental bells for sheep, goats, and cows (you should see the size of some); farming tools and cooking utensils; religious artifacts; traditional clothing; glassware; displays on cottage industries ranging from weaving to woodcarving; and a fascinating collection of nativity scenes *(Krippe).* It also contains more than a dozen reconstructed Tyrolean rooms taken from inns, farmhouses, and patrician homes and furnished in Gothic, Renaissance, and baroque styles. It's open Monday to Saturday 9am to 5pm and Sunday and holidays 10am to 5pm. If you want to see only the museum and not the Hofkirche, it costs 5€ ($6.50) adults and 1.50€ ($1.95) children.

Moments **The Most Beautiful Spot in Tyrol**

The **Hungerburg** ✧✧ mountain plateau at 2,860 feet (858m) is the most beautiful spot in Tyrol, affording the best view of Innsbruck, especially on summer nights when much of the city, including fountains and historic buildings, is brightly lit. Beyond it is the Hafelekar, a paradise for snow-boarders and skiers alike.

To reach the Hungerburg plateau, take the new funicular from Congress Innsbruck, located in downtown Innsbruck just north of the Altstadt, 25 minutes to the mountain. Once you reach the plateau, you progress even farther into the Alpine wilds via the **Nordkette cable railway (Nordketten-bahn).** It will take you up to the Seegrube and the Hafelekar 7,655 feet (2,297m) for a sweeping view of Alpine peaks and glaciers. This is the starting point of high mountain walks, climbing expeditions, and skiing. A round-trip ticket from Hungerburg to Hafelekar costs 19.10€ ($25) for adults and 9.60€ ($12) children. A day ski pass for the Nordpark skiing area costs 25€ ($33) and 12.50€ ($16) respectively. For schedules and information, call ✆ **0512/29 33 44** or go to **www.nordpark.at.**

Note: None of the railways above are covered by railpasses.

Although it's not in the Altstadt, very much worth a visit—especially if you have children in tow—is Europe's highest-elevation zoo, the **Alpenzoo (Alpine Zoo)** ✧, Weiherburggasse 37 (✆ **0512/29 23 23;** www.alpenzoo.at), boasting great views from its location above the city on the slopes of the Hungerburg. This is the place to see all those animals native to the Alps and Alpine region, such as European bison, wolves, lynx, marmots, otters, beavers, vultures, owls, eagles, buzzards, elk, Alpine ibex, rabbits, brown bears, and local fish. There's also a section devoted to domesticated Alpine animals, including cows, goats, and sheep. Admission to the zoo, open daily 9am to 6pm (to 5pm in winter), is 7€ ($9.10) adults, 5€ ($6.50) seniors/students, and 3.50€ ($4.55) children. To reach the zoo, take bus W or the Sightseer to the Alpenzoo bus stop.

If you're staying overnight in Innsbruck, we highly recommend an excursion to nearby **Wattens** to visit the fantastic **Swarovski Kristallwelten (Crystal Worlds)** ✧✧✧, Kristallweltenstrasse 1 (✆ **05224/51080;** http://kristallwelten.swarovski.com), which you can reach in about 15 minutes by bus from the Innsbruck Busbahnhof (next to the Hauptbahnhof). Buses depart for Wattens every 30 minutes (every 60 min. on Sun and holidays); get off at the Kristallwelten stop. There is also a Swarovski shuttle bus four times a day from Innsbruck's Hauptbahnhof, at a round-trip fare of 8.50€ ($11).

Even if you know what Swarovski is—the world's leading producer of full-cut crystal—you won't be prepared for this experiment in fantasy, with theatrical three-dimensional displays that give this attraction a Disneyesque quality and have catapulted it into the region's top tourist draw. Kristallwelten itself is subterranean, hidden from view by a man-made hill but attracting attention with a giant head spouting water. Designed by Viennese multimedia artist Andre Heller, the interior consists of more than a dozen magical cavernlike chambers, with displays relating to crystal. You'll see the world's largest cut crystal (137 lb.); a glass-enclosed wall containing 12 tons of crystal; works by artists ranging from Salvador Dalí to Keith Haring; and costumes, art, and other displays about crystal, including a crystal dome that gives one a pretty good idea of what it would be like to be encapsulated inside a crystal. New Age music adds a dreamlike quality. Admission is 9.50€ ($12), free for children under 12. Open daily 9am to 6:30pm (you must enter by 5:30pm).

WHERE TO STAY & DINE

If you can afford it, stay in the Altstadt, just a 10-minute walk from the train station (or tram 3 to the second stop, Maria-Theresien-Strasse). A top pick is the **Weisses Rössl** ⚜⚜, Kiebachgasse 8, 6020 Innsbruck (© **0512/58 30 57;** www.roessl.at). This delightful inn, built in 1410 and recently renovated to enhance its rustic splendor, offers 12 rooms that have been updated in a contemporary style yet retain their medieval simplicity. A restaurant features local favorites. Rates are 110€ to 130€ ($143–$169) double, including breakfast buffet.

Also in the Altstadt is the **Weisses Kreuz** ⚜⚜, Herzog-Friedrich-Strasse 31, 6020 Innsbruck (© **0512/59 4 79;** www.weisseskreuz.at), with an enviable location down the street from the Goldenes Dachl and boasting a 500-year history. Mozart stayed here when he was 13, during a 1769 journey with his father to Italy. Although the inn has been updated with modern conveniences, including an elevator, it remains true to its historic atmosphere, offering 40 white-walled rooms furnished with modern or traditional pine furniture. Doubles here are 91€ to 115€ ($118–$150), including buffet breakfast.

For hearty, reasonably priced Austrian cuisine, head to the **Weisses Rössl,** Kiebachgasse 8 (© **0512/58 30 57**), described above. Up on the first floor, this old-fashioned restaurant with a covered outdoor terrace offers an English menu with photographs of Schnitzel, beef filet, Gulasch, *Gröstl* (a local stew made of potatoes, beef, and onions), and other meals costing 9€ to 17.50€ ($12–$23). Be sure to top off your meal with Apfelstrudel. It's open Monday to Saturday 11:30am to 2:30pm and 6 to 10pm; it's closed for 2 weeks in April and November.

For a splurge, there's no better place for a taste of Tyrolean history and cuisine than the atmospheric medieval-era **Ottoburg** ⚜, Herzog-Friedrich-Strasse 1 (© **0512/58 43 38**), in the Altstadt between the Goldenes Dachl and the Inn River. First mentioned in 12th-century documents, when it was listed as an apartment house (Maximilian lived here for a year), it was converted to a restaurant 150 years ago. The building is topped by a 1494 Gothic tower and contains four intimate dining rooms with carved wooden ceilings and neo-Gothic decor. In summer, there's outdoor seating on the Altstadt's most famous pedestrian lane. Local and house specialties on the English menu include Gulasch, Wiener schnitzel, and Ottoburg pork filet and steak with an herb sauce and Austrian-style gnocchi, with meals costing 13.80€ to 22€ ($18–$29). It's open Tuesday to Sunday from 11:30am to 2pm and 6 to 10pm, closed 2 weeks in January.

If you're tired of the hearty and somewhat heavy Austrian cuisine, try the **Cammerlander,** Innrain 2 (© **0512/58 63 98**), conveniently located beside the Inn River and offering an outdoor terrace in summer with a view of the mountains. It serves a variety of international dishes, including pizza, pasta, salads (including a salad bar), Schnitzel, fish, Japanese-style noodles, steaks, and more, with most dishes priced 7.90€ to 22.50€ ($10–$29). It's open daily 8:30am to 1am.

Moments A Leap of Faith

Less than a mile from the center of Innsbruck, easily reached by the Sightseer bus and then funicular (8.30€/$11 adults, 4€/$5.20 children), looms the sleek, futuristic-looking **Bergisl** (© 0512/58 92 59-0; www.bergisel.info). Its raison d'être is its famous ski jump, first built in 1925, but the new tower also beckons with an observatory and the Café im Turm offering continental food, snacks, and desserts. Enclosed by glass on three sides, the cafe boasts panoramic views of Innsbruck, lofty mountain peaks, the ski jump, and, at the bottom of the hill, Innsbruck's largest cemetery. Bergisl is open daily 9am to 6pm (9:30am–5pm in winter).

SHOPPING

On their home turf, you can purchase such Tyrolean specialties as lederhosen, dirndls, leather clothing, woodcarvings, loden cloth, and all sorts of skiing and mountain-climbing equipment. Stroll around such shopping streets as the **Maria-Theresien-Strasse,** the **Herzog-Friedrich-Strasse,** and the **Museumstrasse,** ducking in and making discoveries of your own.

Here are a few recommendations if you're seeking something special:

Tiroler Heimatwerk, Meraner Strasse 2 (© 0512/58 23 20), is one of the best stores in Innsbruck for such handcrafted Tyrolean items as sculpture, pewter, textiles, woolen goods, hand-knitted sweaters, lace, and bolts of silk for do-it-yourselfers. You can purchase regionally inspired fabrics and dress patterns, which you can whip into a dirndl (or whatever) as soon as you get home. Also for sale are carved chests, mirror frames, and furniture.

Lodenbaur, Brixner Strasse 4 (© 0512/58 09 11), is the closest thing you'll find to a department store in Innsbruck devoted to regional Tyrolean dress. Most of the goods are made in Austria, including a full array of lederhosen, coats, dresses, dirndls, and accessories for men, women, and children. Be sure to check out the basement as well.

NIGHTLIFE

The **Tiroler Landestheater,** Rennweg 2 (© 0512/52 07 44; www.landestheater.at), is Innsbruck's most important venue for performances of opera, operetta, and theater. Tickets for opera run 9€ to 39.50€ ($12–$51). The box office is open Monday to Saturday 8:30am to 8:30pm and, on night of performances, Sunday and holidays 5:30 to 8:30pm.

For an evening of Tyrolean entertainment, including traditional music, yodeling, and folk dancing, see the **Tiroler Alpenbühne** (© 0512/26 32 63; www.tiroler alpenbuehne.com), held in the Gasthaus Sandwirt am Inn, Reichenauerstrasse 151, or in the Messe-Saal at Ing.-Etzel Strasse 33. Held daily at 8:30pm May through October, it costs 20€ ($26), including a free drink.

South of the Altstadt is a very popular microbrewery, **Theresien-Bräu,** Maria-Theresien-Strasse 51 (© 0512/58 75 80). It offers an Austrian menu and is open Monday to Wednesday 11:30am to 1am, Thursday to Saturday 11:30am to 2am, and Sunday 11:30am to midnight. Nearby, at Maria-Theresien-Strasse 9, is **Limerick**

Bill's Irish Pub (© 0512/58 20 11), a popular trilevel gathering place for English speakers; it's open daily 4pm to 6am.

In summer there's no finer place to be—judging by the crowds—than the **Hofgarten Cafe** (© 0512/58 88 71), located in the Hofgarten just north of the Altstadt and offering indoor and outdoor seating and live music. Many natives make it a tradition to stop off for a beer after work—and then perhaps another, and another. In summer, it's open daily 10am to 2am; in winter, hours are Tuesday to Saturday 6pm to 2am.

4

Belgium

The home of continental Europe's first railway, built way back in 1835, Belgium has one of Europe's most extensive rail networks—nearly 2,200 miles (3,500km) of track. About the size of Maryland and with 10 million inhabitants, Belgium is a small country, but not so small that if you blink you'll have missed it—it does take almost 4 hours to cross by train, after all. But it's compact enough that a couple of hours of riding the rails will get you from the capital, Brussels, to just about any corner of the realm you care to mention. Yet the variety of culture, language, history, and cuisine crammed into this small space would do credit to a country many times its size, making this the ideal destination for the rail traveler on a tight time budget.

Belgium's diversity is a product of its location at Europe's cultural crossroads. The boundary between the Continent's Germanic north and Latin south cuts clear across the country's middle, leaving Belgium divided into two major ethnic regions, Dutch-speaking Flanders in the north and French-speaking Wallonia in the south. (No matter where you end up on your journey, however, you'll likely find someone who speaks English.)

The country is also at the crossroads of some of Europe's major rail networks and serves as a major hub for international train travel. If you're planning a grand jaunt across the Continent, Belgium makes an easy and convenient transfer point—don't miss it.

HIGHLIGHTS OF BELGIUM

Because **Brussels** has Belgium's only real international airport and is the country's rail net hub, it's likely you'll visit this centrally located city first. That's not a bad proposition. Brussels may not be the Continent's most exciting city, but the "capital of Europe" has its fair share of history and world-class attractions, and much to savor when it comes to dining and drinking. If you can set aside a few days for Belgium on your rail trip, devoting one to Brussels will be time well spent, though ideally you need 2 or 3 days to do the place any kind of justice.

If, instead, you want to head straight to a historic Flemish city of art and culture, you can do no better than **Bruges.** Art, history, and Gothic architecture are what this marvel of a city is all about. It's less than an hour from Brussels by train and is small enough to be doable in a day, if all you want is to soak up the atmosphere and visit a few of its highlights.

Ghent and **Antwerp** are even closer to Brussels than Bruges. Though these two handsome Flemish cities can't boast as much sheer old-fashioned charm as Bruges, each one is brimful with art and history yet has far less of a tourist-swamped, museum-exhibit setting.

Moments **Festivals & Special Events**

A major event in Brussels is the **Ommegang,** a historic pageant that takes place on the Grand-Place on the first Tuesday and Thursday in July. It represents the "joyous entry" into Brussels of Emperor Charles V and his entourage in 1549. For more information, contact **Brussels International Tourism & Congress** (© 02/513-89-40).

A striking spectacle that should not be missed if you're in town is the **Carpet of Flowers,** on the Grand-Place, Brussels. During this event—held in mid-August in even-numbered years—the historic square is carpeted with two-thirds of a million begonias arranged in a kind of tapestry. Contact **Brussels International Tourism & Congress** (© 02/513-89-40).

Finally, if you're in Bruges on Ascension Day (fifth Thurs after Easter), don't miss the **Procession of the Holy Blood.** A relic of the blood of Christ is carried through the streets, while costumed characters act out biblical scenes. Contact **In&Uit Brugge** (© 050/44-46-46).

To compete with the Flemish art cities and the Flanders region's North Sea coast, the Wallonia region offers fresh air and scenic landscapes in the Ardennes and the Meuse River valley. Sadly, the sparsely populated Ardennes has few rail lines, and travel by bus is slow. You really need your own transportation and the time to take advantage of it. For a taste of francophone Belgium, however, a day trip to a Meuse River city like **Liège** is an acceptable substitute easily done by train from Brussels.

And as a final option, a fairly easy side trip is **Luxembourg.** The Grand Duchy may be a pocket-size nation, but size isn't everything. Its capital, Luxembourg City, is one of Europe's small, hidden gems—off the beaten track but worth a visit in its own right.

1 Essentials

GETTING THERE
Carriers with flights to Brussels from North America include **Air Canada** (© 888/247-2262; www.aircanada.ca), **American Airlines** (© 800/433-7300; www.aa.com), **Continental Airlines** (© 800/231-0856; www.continental.com), **Delta Airlines** (© 800/241-4141; www.delta.com), and **United Airlines** (© 800/538-2929; www.united.com).

Brussels National Airport (© 0900/70-000 in Belgium, or 02/753-77-53 from abroad; www.brusselsairport.be), at Zaventem, 7 miles (11km) northeast of the center city, is Belgium's principal airport and handles virtually all the country's international flights. From here there is direct train service to Brussels, from where you can travel onward to Bruges, Ghent, Antwerp, and all other points in Belgium, as well as to Paris, Amsterdam, and Cologne.

BELGIUM BY RAIL
Four different kinds of high-speed trains zip into Belgium from neighboring countries: The **Eurostar** linking Great Britain to the Continent runs from London to Brussels in only 2 hours and 20 minutes; **Thalys** links Brussels, Antwerp, Liège, and other Belgian cities with Paris, Amsterdam, and Cologne (trip times to Brussels from these

Belgium

three cities are, respectively, 1 hr., 20 min., 2 hr., 40 min., and 2 hr., 20 min.); **ICE** trains speed into Brussels from Frankfurt (3 hr., 30 min); and **TGV** trains arrive in Brussels from around France. In addition, Belgium is linked to most European capitals by slower **EuroCity (EC), EuroNight (EN),** and other international trains.

Although one or more high-speed services stop at several Belgian cities, distances inside the country are so short and local trains fast enough that using the fast-movers is rarely worth the additional expense and ticket regulations. Besides, all important tourist destinations in Belgium can be reached easily in a day-trip by train from Brussels on the excellent rail network of the **Société Nationale des Chemins de Fer Belges/SNCB,** also known as NMBS in Dutch (Belgian Railways; ✆ **02/528-28-28;** www.b-rail.be). There are the fast and comfortable **InterCity (IC)** trains; the somewhat slower and less comfortable **Inter-Regional (IR)** trains; and the **Local (L)** trains that stop at every station on the way and can get uncomfortable over long distances (or what passes for long distances in Belgium). By InterCity train from Brussels's Gare Centrale, Antwerp is just 45 minutes away; Ghent, 32 minutes; Bruges, 58 minutes; and Liège, 54 minutes.

Note that many train stations around the country have bicycles for rent.

PASSES

For details on purchasing multicountry options, such as the **Eurail Global Pass,** see chapter 2. The **Benelux Pass** allows 5 days of unlimited travel in 1 month in Belgium, the Netherlands, and Luxembourg, for $207 in second class and $314 in first class. Two to five adults traveling together should purchase the **Benelux Saverpass,** to benefit from a discount of around 18%. For passengers ages 12 to 25, the **Benelux Youth Pass** (available in second class only) costs $158. Children ages 4 to 11 pay about half the adult fare, and children under 4 travel free. These passes must be purchased in North America and can be obtained from **Rail Europe** (© **877/272-RAIL** [7245] in North America; www.raileurope.com) or through your travel agent.

Valid only in Belgium, and available from train stations in Belgium, the **Rail Pass** is valid for 10 single journeys anywhere on the Belgian Railways network (except for stations at international borders), for 69€ ($90) in second class, and 106€ ($138) in first class. The same pass for passengers ages 4 to 25 (traveling in second class only), is called a **Go Pass,** and costs 45€ ($58).

In addition to Belgian Railways's regular single *(billet simple/enkele reis)* and return *(aller et retour/retour)* tickets, look for discounted **B-Excursion** and **Weekend Ticket** options.

Note: The words "single" and "return," when used in reference to trains in Belgium, mean one-way and round-trip respectively.

Tickets should be purchased onboard Belgian trains only if the station where you board has no sales point; if you were merely in too much of a hurry, you need to inform the train conductor before boarding or immediately after, in which case your ticket will cost an additional 2.70€ ($3.50). The fine for riding a train without a valid ticket is 12.50€ ($16), when paid on the spot; and 60€ ($78) for adults and 30€ ($39) for minors, when paid within 14 days; plus the fare.

FOREIGN TRAIN TERMS

A train is *un train* in French and a *trein* in Dutch and there are three kinds of trains in Belgium. Class is *classe* in French and *klas* in Dutch. Second class is *deuxième classe/tweede klas,* and first class is *premier classe/eerste klas.* A station is a *gare/station.* In big cities like Brussels and Antwerp, which have more than one station, the main station is called *Gare Centrale/Centraal Station* (Central Station). Platform is *quai/spoor* (in Dutch it rhymes with "boar").

In French, departure and arrival are pretty easy: *départ* and *arrivée;* in Dutch you'll need to get by with *vertrek* and *aankomst* (announcements are also made in English in the most important stations). Information is *Renseignements* in French and *Informatie* in Dutch.

PRACTICAL TRAIN INFORMATION

Belgian trains are often crowded, and because reservations for individual passengers are not available, it makes sense not to travel during peak hours, when you may need to stand (reservations are available on international trains). On the other hand, distances between stations are short, and a bunch of people are sure to get out at whatever the next one is; so, you could just wait and grab a seat when it becomes vacant.

All trains, even the smallest, have a first-class section or cars. Smoking is forbidden both on trains and in stations.

Train Frequency & Travel Times in Belgium*

	Ghent	Antwerp	Bruges	Ostend	Liège
Time	32 min.	45 min.	58 min.	73 min.	54 min.
Train frequency**	4	4	2	2	3

*Travel times are calculated using Brussels Gare Centrale as the departure point and assume you'll be traveling by the fastest Inter-City train.
**Frequency is average number of trains out of Brussels Gare Centrale per hour during daytime (for Ghent, Antwerp, and Liège, these may include slower InterRegional [IR] and Local [L] trains).

Due to the country's small size, no Belgian trains have restaurant cars (international trains generally do), but on long-distance InterCity trains an attendant pushes around a small cart, from which coffee, tea, mineral water, sandwiches, potato chips, and other snacky items are dispensed. These cost more than the same things bought from a supermarket, so if you are on a tight budget, buy them before traveling. Similarly, a lack of long-distance lines means there are no sleeper cars on trains within Belgium.

Some trains, employed most often during rush hours in urban areas, are double-deckers; these often get very crowded, but an upstairs window seat affords a great view of whatever there is to be seen.

Note that Belgium has two main national languages, French and Dutch (there's also a small community of German speakers who provide a third national language). Depending on where you are in the country, a station might be listed or announced using a name you are not familiar with. Station name boards are written in the local language, except in Brussels, where they are in both French and Dutch. The following are some common examples:

English	French	Dutch
Brussels	Bruxelles	Brussel
Bruges	Bruges	Brugge
Ghent	Gand	Gent
Antwerp	Anvers	Antwerpen
Liège	Liège	Luik
Ostend	Ostende	Oostende
Namur	Namur	Namen
Ypres	Ypres	Ieper

FAST FACTS: Belgium

Area Codes When making phone calls within Belgium (and this includes if you're calling another number within the same area code), you always need to dial the area codes shown in this book. The area code for Brussels is **02**. Other area codes are: Bruges **050**; Ghent **09**; Antwerp **03**; Liège **04**. Luxembourg has no area codes; when calling a local number from anywhere within the Grand Duchy, you need only dial the local number.

Business Hours Banks are generally open Monday to Friday from 9am to 1pm and 2 to 4:30 or 5pm, and some branches are also open on Saturday morning. Stores generally are open Monday to Saturday from 10am to 6pm, though some also are open on Sunday. Most department stores stay open on Friday to 8 or 9pm.

Climate Belgium's climate is moderate, with few extremes in temperature either in summer or winter. It rains a lot. You're well advised to pack a fold-up umbrella at any time of year. Likewise, carry a raincoat (with a wool liner for winter). Temperatures are lowest in December and January, when they average 42°F (6°C), and highest in July and August, when they average 73°F (23°C). Pack a sweater or two (even in July) and be prepared to layer your clothing at any time of year. Don't worry: May through October you're allowed to leave some space for T-shirts, skimpy tops, and sneakers.

Documents Required For stays of up to 3 months, U.S. and Canadian citizens need only to have a valid passport. For stays longer than 3 months, a visa is required.

Electricity Belgium runs on 230 (220–240) volts electricity (North America uses 110 volts). So, for any small appliance, you need to take a small voltage transformer (available in drug and appliance stores and by mail order) that plugs into the round-holed European electrical outlet and converts the Belgian voltage from 230 volts down to 110 volts.

Embassies These are both in Brussels. **U.S.:** bd. du Régent 27 (© **02/508-21-11;** www.usembassy.be; Métro: Arts-Loi). **Canada:** av. de Tervuren 2 (© **02/741-06-11;** www.international.gc.ca/brussels; Métro: Merode).

Health & Safety For day or night emergency medical service in Brussels, call **Médi Garde** © **02/479-18-18** or **SOS Médecins** © **02/513-02-02;** for emergency dental service, call © **02/426-10-26.** For both prescription and nonprescription medicines, go to a pharmacy (*pharmacie* in French; *apotheek* in Dutch). Regular pharmacy hours are Monday to Saturday from 9am to 6pm (some close earlier on Sat). Each pharmacy has a list of late-night and weekend pharmacies posted on its door; schedules are also available by calling © **0900/10-500** or heading online to www.pharmacie.be.

Holidays January 1 (New Year's Day); Easter Sunday and Monday; May 1 (Labor Day); Ascension Day; Pentecost Sunday and Monday; July 21 (Independence Day); August 15 (Assumption Day); November 1 (All Saints' Day); November 11 (World War I Armistice Day); and December 25 (Christmas). In Flanders only, July 11 is Flemish Community Day. In Wallonia only, September 27 is French Community Day.

Mail Postage for a priority-mail *(Prior)* postcard or standard letter to the U.S. and Canada is .90€ ($1.15), and for nonpriority mail .75€ ($1).

Police & Emergencies For emergency police assistance, call © **101;** for an ambulance or the fire department, © **100.**

Taxes On top of a 16% service charge, there's a value-added tax (TVA) of 6% on hotel bills and 21.5% on restaurant bills. The higher rate is charged on purchased goods, too. If you spend over 125€ ($163) in some stores, and you are not a resident in a European Union country, you can recover it from some stores by having the official receipt stamped by Belgian Customs on departure and returning the stamped receipt to the store. Your refund should arrive by check or be credited to your credit card within a few weeks. Not all stores participate in this scheme so it pays to ask first, particularly for major purchases.

Telephone **To call Belgium:** If you're calling from the United States, dial the international access code (011), followed by the country code for Belgium (32), then the area code (2 for Brussels) and the number. So the whole number you'd dial would be **011-32-2-000-0000.**

To make international calls: To make international calls from Belgium, first dial 00 and then the country code (U.S. and Canada 1). Next you dial the area code and number.

For information in English, both in Belgium and international, dial ✆ **1405.**

You can use pay phones with a Belgacom *télécarte* (phone card), which costs 5€ ($6.50), 10€ ($13), and 25€ ($33) from post offices, train ticket counters, tourist information offices, some tobacconists, and newsstands. Some pay phones take credit cards. A few pay phones take coins, of .10€ (15¢), .20€ (25¢), .50€ (65¢), 1€ ($1.30), and 2€ ($2.60).

To charge a call to your calling card, dial **AT&T** (✆ **0800/100-10**); **MCI** (✆ **0800/100-12**); **Sprint** (✆ **0800/100-14**); or **Canada Direct** (✆ **0800/100-19**).

Tipping The prices on most restaurant menus already include a service charge of 16%, so it's unnecessary to tip. If service is good, however, it's usual to show appreciation with a tip. It's enough to round up the bill to the nearest convenient amount, if you wish, rather than leave a full-fledged tip. Otherwise, 10% is adequate (and more than most Belgians would leave). Service is included in your hotel bill as well. Taxis include the tip in the meter reading. You can round up the fare if you like, but need not add a tip unless you have received an extra service like help with luggage. For other services: Leave 20% for hairdressers (with the cashier when you pay up) and 1€ to 2€ ($1.30–$2.60) per piece of luggage for porters.

2 Brussels

A city with a notable history, Brussels is carving out a bright future for itself and is unquestionably the place to start your train journey through Belgium. The "capital of Europe" has begun to act like Europe's Washington, D.C., a focus of economic and political power, where decisions are made that affect the lives of people around the world. Headquarters of the European Union (EU), Brussels both symbolizes the Continent's vision of unity and is a bastion of officialdom, a breeding ground for the regulations that govern and often exasperate the rest of Europe.

Bruxellois have ambivalent feelings about their city's transformation into a power center. At first, the waves of Eurocrats brought a new cosmopolitan air to a somewhat provincial city, but old neighborhoods have been leveled to make way for office towers, leaving people wondering whether Brussels is losing its soul. After all, this city doesn't only mean politics and business—it helped inspire surrealism and Art Nouveau, worships comic strips, prides itself on handmade lace and chocolate, and serves each one of its craft beers in its own unique glass.

Brussels

Church ✝
Information ⓘ
Post Office ✉
Railway ┄┄┄

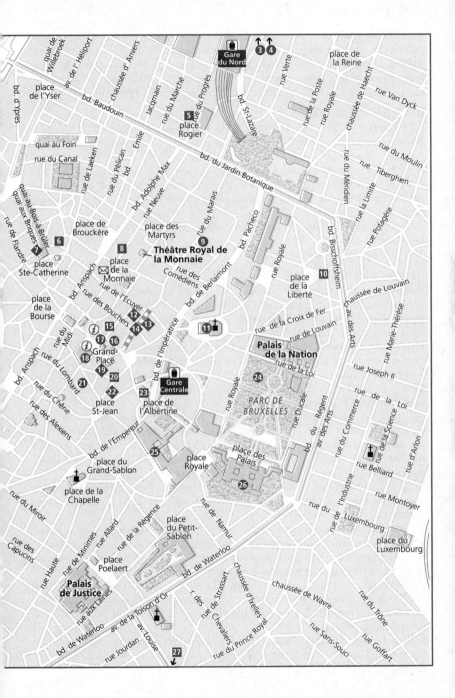

Fortunately, not all of Brussels's individuality has been lost in this transition, and though the urban landscape has suffered from wanton "development," the city's spirit survives in traditional cafes, bars, bistros, and restaurants. Whether elegantly Art Nouveau or eccentrically festooned with posters, curios, and knickknacks, such centuries-old establishments provide a warm, convivial ambience that is peculiarly Belgian.

STATION INFORMATION
GETTING FROM THE AIRPORT TO THE TRAIN STATION

There's **train** service to Brussels's Nord, Centrale, and Midi stations from Brussels National Airport (see "Getting There," earlier in this chapter) every 20 minutes or so between 5:30am and 11:30pm, for a one-way fare starting at 2.80€ ($3.65). The trip is free if you hold a validated train pass. Most airport trains have wide corridors and extra space for baggage and are the best and easiest way into town. The ride to Gare Centrale takes 35 minutes.

You'll find **taxi** stands in front of the airplane terminal building if you prefer to head into town that way. All taxis from the airport are metered. Expect to pay around 32€ ($42) to get to the center city.

INSIDE THE STATIONS

Brussels has three major train stations. High-speed Eurostar trains from London; Thalys from Paris, Amsterdam, and Cologne; TGV from France; and ICE from Germany arrive at **Gare du Midi/Zuidstation,** rue de France, south of the center city; other international trains also arrive at Gare du Midi. A few blocks from the Grand-Place, **Gare Centrale/Centraal Station,** Carrefour de l'Europe, is the station closest to many attractions in the center city. **Gare du Nord/Noordstation,** rue du Progrès, is north of the center city. Trains arriving from around Belgium generally stop at all three stations. Only Gare Centrale has environs that are worth exploring on foot, and even then not if you are hefting a backpack or other luggage.

Boards and screens provide constantly updated train departure and arrival information. Note that Gare Centrale does not have a train information desk, and you cannot make train reservations or validate a railpass here. Gare Centrale and Gare du Midi have room reservations desks that do not accept phone bookings. Tourist information is not available in any of Brussels's train stations.

All three stations offer currency exchange, luggage storage, waiting rooms, fast-food restaurants, bars, cafes, snack kiosks, and stores, with Gare du Midi being the best-outfitted in all these services.

Note: Watch out for pickpockets and for your bags, in particular at Gare du Midi, but at the other two stations as well. The environs of Gare du Midi have been popular with muggers preying on international travelers, and though this seems to be less of a problem than it once was, it might be better to access and depart the station by public transportation or taxi than on foot. The north exit from Gare du Nord leads into Brussels's scuzzy red-light district and is best avoided; the south exit has some slightly classier red-light haunts mixed in with upmarket hotels and modern office towers, and is generally okay.

Both Gare du Midi and Gare du Nord have stops for tram (streetcar) lines and a bus station; Gare Centrale has an adjacent Métro (subway) station and multiple bus stops outside. All three stations have taxi stands outside.

INFORMATION ELSEWHERE IN THE CITY

The centrally located **Brussels International Tourism & Congress** office is in the Hôtel de Ville (Town Hall), Grand-Place (© **02/513-89-40;** www.brusselsinternational.be; Métro: Gare Centrale). The office, which can make hotel reservations, is open April to October, daily from 9am to 6pm; November to December, Monday to Saturday from 9am to 6pm, and Sunday from 10am to 2pm; and January to March, Monday to Saturday from 9am to 6pm.

GETTING AROUND

Once in town, your feet are almost always the best way to get around, and the center of town is small enough to allow you to use your own leg power. Be sure to wear good walking shoes, as those charming cobblestones on the sidewalks and streets will get under your soles and onto your nerves after a while. When crossing the street, watch out for trams and bikes.

Maps of the integrated public transit network—Métro, tram, and bus—are available free from the tourist office, from offices of the public transportation company, **STIB,** Galérie de la Toison d'Or 15 (© **0900/10-310;** www.stib.irisnet.be), and from the Porte de Namur, Rogier, and Gare du Midi Métro stations. In addition, all stations and most tram and bus stops have transit maps. The full system operates from 6am to midnight, after which a limited night-bus service takes over.

The **Métro** (subway) net covers the center city and reaches out to the suburbs and to the Bruparck recreation zone in the north of town. Stations are identified by signs with a white letter M on a blue background. An extensive network of **tram** (streetcar) lines provides the ideal way to get around the city. Trams are generally faster and more comfortable than **buses.**

Tickets are 1.50€ ($1.95) for a single journey (known as a *direct*) and 6.70€ ($8.70) for a five-ride card, both of which you can buy from the driver; 10.50€ ($14) for a 10-ride card available from Métro stations and train stations; and 4€ ($5.20) for a 1-day ticket valid on all urban services. You validate your ticket by inserting it into the orange electronic machines that stand inside buses and trams and at the access to Métro platforms. Though the ticket must be revalidated each time you enter a new vehicle, you are allowed multiple transfers within a 1-hour period of the initial validation, so you can hop on and off Métro trains, trams, and buses during that time and only one journey will be deducted from your card by the electronic scanner. If more than one person is traveling on one ticket, the ticket must be validated each time for each traveler. Children under 12 ride free on the STIB transit network.

The minimum rate for **taxis** is 2.40€ ($3.10) during the day and 4.40€ ($5.70) at night. Charges per kilometer vary from 1.25€ to 2.45€ ($1.60–$3.20), depending on location and time. Tip and taxes are included in the meter price. You can round up the fare but need not add an extra tip unless there has been extra service, such as helping with heavy luggage. All taxis are metered. You cannot hail them in the street, but there are taxi stands on many principal streets, particularly in the center, and at train stations. To request a cab by phone, call **Taxis Bleus** (© **02/268-00-00**); **Taxis Oranges** (© **02/349-43-43**); or **Taxis Verts** (© **02/349-49-49**).

WHERE TO STAY

Arlequin Grand-Place   You can't get closer to the heart of the city than this, with a restaurant-lined rue des Bouchers right outside the hotel's back entrance, and fine views from some rooms of the Town Hall spire on the neighboring Grand-Place, and of the Old City's rooftops and narrow medieval streets from the top-floor breakfast room. The guest rooms themselves are not quite so spectacular, but all are tastefully contemporary and most get plenty of natural light.

Rue de la Fourche 17–19 (off rue des Bouchers), 1000 Bruxelles. ✆ **02/514-16-15.** Fax 02/514-22-02. www.arlequin.be. 92 units. 95€–230€ ($124–299) double. Rates include buffet breakfast. AE, DC, MC, V. Métro: Bourse. **Amenities:** Laundry. *In room:* Hair dryer.

Comfort Art Hotel Siru ✿

What sets the Siru, opposite Gare du Nord, apart is that the owner of this art-gallery-cum-hotel in a redeveloped business district persuaded 130 Belgian artists to "decorate" each coolly modern, well-equipped room and the corridors with a work on travel. Given the unpredictable nature of reactions to modern art, it should come as no surprise that some clients reserve the same room time after time, while others ask for a room change in the middle of the night.

Place Rogier 1, 1210 Bruxelles. ✆ **800/228-3323** in the U.S. and Canada, or 02/203-35-80. Fax 02/203-33-03. www. comforthotelsiru.com. 101 units. 85€–250€ ($85–$325) double. Rates include buffet breakfast. AE, DC, MC, V. Métro: Rogier. **Amenities:** Restaurant; laundry; nonsmoking rooms. *In room:* Hair dryer.

De Boeck's

In a quiet, well-maintained 19th-century town house off chaussée de Charleroi and a short walk from Place Stephanie, this graceful hotel has some unusually spacious rooms and some so small you'll need to shoehorn yourself and your luggage into them. None measures up to the Victorian elegance of the public spaces, but they are adequately furnished, with comfortable beds, soft carpeting, and floral-pattern curtains. Some rooms, good for families and small groups, can be used as quads or even quints.

Rue Veydt 40, 1050 Bruxelles. ✆ **02/537-40-33.** Fax 02/534-40-37. www.hotel-deboecks.be. 46 units. 62€–100€ ($81–$130) double. Rates include buffet breakfast. AE, DC, MC, V. Métro: Louise. *In room:* Hair dryer.

Le Dixseptième ✿✿

This graceful, 17th-century house was once the Spanish ambassador's official residence and stands close to the Grand-Place (2 blocks from Gare Centrale) in a neighborhood of restored dwellings. Rooms have wood paneling and marble chimneys and are as big as suites in many hotels; some have balconies. All are in 18th-century style and are named after Belgian painters from Bruegel to Magritte. Two elegant lounges are decorated with carved wooden medallions and 18th-century paintings.

Rue de la Madeleine 25, 1000 Bruxelles. ✆ **02/517-17-17.** Fax 02/502-64-24. www.ledixseptieme.be. 24 units. 200€ ($260) double. Rates include buffet breakfast. AE, DC, MC, V. Métro: Gare Centrale. **Amenities:** Lounge; laundry. *In room:* Hair dryer.

Métropole ✿✿✿

An ornate, marble-and-gilt interior distinguishes this late-19th-century landmark from 1895 (Brussels's sole surviving 19th-c. hotel), just a few blocks away from the Grand-Place. Soaring ceilings, potted palms, and lavishly decorated public spaces on the ground floor add to the Belle Epoque allure. The spacious rooms, some in Art Deco style, have a mix of classic and elegant modern furnishings. Both the French restaurant L'Alban Chambon and the Café Métropole are worth a visit in their own right.

Place de Brouckère 31 (close to Centre Monnaie), 1000 Bruxelles. ✆ **02/217-23-00.** Fax 02/218-02-20. www. metropolehotel.be. 305 units. 329€–429€ double ($428–$558). Rates include buffet or continental breakfast. AE, DC, MC, V. Métro: De Brouckère. **Amenities:** Restaurant; lounge; cafe; sidewalk cafe; laundry. *In room:* Hair dryer.

Mozart ✿

Can you guess which famous composer's music wafts through the lobby here? The Mozart is located a flight of stairs up from the busy, cheap-eats at street

Value **Passport to Brussels**

One of the city's best discounts is the **Brussels Card,** available from the Brussels International tourist office on the Grand-Place, and from hotels, museums, and STIB city transit authority offices, for 30€ ($39). Valid for 3 days, it allows free use of public transportation; free and discounted admission to 30 city museums and attractions; and discounts at restaurants and other venues, and on some guided tours.

level, a block away from the Grand-Place. Salmon-colored walls, plants, and old paintings create a warm, intimate ambience that's carried into the rooms. Furnishings are in Louis XV style and exposed beams lend each unit a rustic originality. Several are duplexes with a sitting room underneath the loft bedroom. Top rooms afford great views.

Rue du Marché aux Fromages 23, 1000 Bruxelles. ✆ **02/502 66-61.** Fax 02/502-77-58. www.hotel-mozart.be. 47 units. 95€–115€ ($124–$150) double. AE, DC, MC, V. Métro: Gare Centrale. **Amenities:** Lounge.

Sabina This small hostelry off place des Barricades is like a private residence, presided over by hospitable owners. A grandfather clock in the reception area and polished wood along the restaurant walls give it a warm, homey atmosphere. Rooms vary in size, but all are comfortable and simply yet tastefully done in modern style with twin beds. Three rooms have kitchenettes.

Rue du Nord 78, 1000 Bruxelles. ✆ **02/218-26-37.** Fax 02/219-32-39. www.hotelsabina.be. 24 units. 75€–82€ ($98–$107) double. Rates include buffet breakfast. AE, DC, MC, V. Métro: Madou. *In room:* Hair dryer.

Welcome 🏵🏵 The smallest hotel in the center city, this little gem of a place lives up to its name in full. You can think of it as a country *auberge* (inn) in the heart of town, on the old Fish Market square. Rooms are styled on individual themes—Savannah, Provence, Japan, Thailand, India, Tibet, Bali, and Laura Ashley—and furnished and decorated from both local designer and antiques stores with what can best be described as tender loving care.

Quai au Bois à Brûler 23, 1000 Bruxelles. ✆ **02/219-95-46.** Fax 02/217-18-87. www.hotelwelcome.com. 15 units. 85€–130€ ($111–$169) double. Rates include buffet breakfast. AE, DC, MC, V. Métro: Ste-Catherine. **Amenities:** Lounge. *In room:* Hair dryer.

TOP ATTRACTIONS & SPECIAL MOMENTS
THE GRAND-PLACE 🏵🏵🏵

Ornamental gables, medieval banners, gilded facades, sunlight flashing off gold-filigreed rooftop sculptures, a general impression of harmony and timelessness—there's a lot to take in all at once when you first enter the **Grand-Place** (Métro: Gare Centrale or Bourse), a World Heritage Site. Its present composition dates mostly from the late 1690s, but the Town Hall dates from the early 1400s. Don't miss the cafes lodged within the opulent wooden interiors of old guild houses; their upper-floor windows overlooking the Grand-Place afford some of the best views in Europe.

And be sure to take in the *son-et-lumière* on summer evenings on the Grand-Place. Appropriately grand music plays at this sound-and-light show as the historic square's buildings are dramatically highlighted. Or you can stop by at noon, when the Maison du Roi's tower bells play golden carillon chimes reminiscent of an earlier European era.

THE PRINCIPAL MUSEUMS

Musée de la Ville de Bruxelles (Museum of the City of Brussels) ⭐⭐ In the neo-Gothic King's House (which, despite its name, has never housed a king), this museum documents the history of Brussels. Among the most fascinating displays are old paintings and modern scale reconstructions of the historic center, including some that depict activity along the now-vanished Senne River. There also are exhibits on traditional arts and crafts, such as tapestry and lace. The museum's pride, however, is its collection of more than 750 costumes—including an Elvis outfit—donated to clothe Brussels's famous *Manneken-Pis* statue (see "Key Monuments & Public Buildings," below), each equipped with a strategically positioned orifice so that the little sculpture's normal function is not impaired.

Grand-Place 1. ⓒ 02/279-43-50. www.brucity.be. Admission 3€ ($3.90) adults; 2.50€ ($3.25) seniors, students; 1.50€ ($1.95) children 6–15; children under 6 free. Tues–Sun 10am–5pm. Métro: Bourse.

Musées Royaux des Beaux-Arts de Belgique (Royal Museums of Fine Arts of Belgium) ⭐⭐⭐ In a vast museum of several buildings at place Royale, this complex combines the **Musée d'Art Ancien** and the **Musée d'Art Moderne** under one roof (connected by a passage). The collection shows off works, most of them Belgian, from the 14th to the 20th century, including Hans Memling's portraits from the late 15th century, which are marked by sharp lifelike details; works by Hieronymus Bosch; and Lucas Cranach's *Adam and Eve.* Be sure to seek out the rooms featuring Pieter Bruegel, including his *Adoration of the Magi* and *Fall of Icarus.* Don't miss his unusual *Fall of the Rebel Angels,* with grotesque faces and beasts. But don't fear—many of Bruegel's paintings, such as those depicting Flemish village life, are of a less fiery nature. Later artists represented include Rubens, Van Dyck, Frans Hals, and Rembrandt.

Next door, in a circular building connected to the main entrance, the modern art section has an emphasis on underground works—if only because the museum's eight floors are all below ground level. The overwhelming collection includes works by van Gogh, Matisse, Dalí, Tanguy, Ernst, Chagall, Miró, and local boys Magritte, Delvaux, De Braekeleer, and Permeke.

Moments **Special Brussels Experiences**

- **Watching the *Son-et-Lumière* on Summer Evenings in the Grand-Place.** This sound-and-light show in which a series of colored lamps on the Hôtel de Ville (Town Hall) are switched on and off in sequence to a piece of appropriately grand music is admittedly kind of kitsch. But who cares? It's also magical.

- **Snapping Up a Bargain at the Flea Market.** Each day, from 7am to 2pm, the Marché aux Puces on place du Jeu de Balle in the Marolles district offers everything from the weird to the wonderful at rock-bottom prices.

- **Pigging Out on Belgian Chocolates.** Those devilish little creations—hand-made Belgian pralines—are so addictive they should be sold with a government health warning attached. Try the Wittamer chocolatier on place du Grand Sablon, and eat your fill.

Moments   A Neat Little Park

Once a hunting preserve belonging to the dukes of Brabant, the **Parc de Brux-elles (Brussels Park)**, rue Royale (Métro: Parc), between Parliament and the Royal Palace, was laid out in the 18th century as a landscaped garden. In 1830, Belgian patriots fought Dutch troops here during the War of Independence. Later it was a fashionable place to stroll and to meet friends. Although not very big, the park manages to contain everything from carefully trimmed borders to rough patches of trees and bushes, and has fine views along its main paths, which together with the fountain form the outline of Masonic symbols.

Rue de la Régence 3. ⓒ 02/508-32-11. www.fine-arts-museum.be. Admission 5€ ($6.50) adults, 3.50€ ($4.55) seniors, 2€ ($2.60) students, children under 13 free; free for all visitors 1st Wed afternoon of the month (except special exhibits). Tues–Sun 10am–5pm. Métro: Parc.

KEY MONUMENTS & PUBLIC BUILDINGS

Two blocks from the Grand-Place, the famous *Manneken-Pis* **statue** 𝕶, on the corner of rue du Chêne and rue de l'Etuve, is Brussels's favorite little boy, gleefully doing what a little boy's gotta do. It's known that the boy's effigy has graced the city since at least the time of Philip the Good, who became count of Flanders in 1419. Among the speculations about his origins are that he was the son of a Brussels nobleman who got lost and was found while answering nature's call, and also that he was a patriotic Belgian kid who sprinkled a hated Spanish sentry passing beneath his window. Perhaps the best theory is that he saved the Town Hall from a sputtering bomb by extinguishing it—like Gulliver—with the first thing handy.

Atomium 𝕶 *Kids*   There's nothing quite like this cluster of giant spheres representing the atomic structure of an iron crystal enlarged 165 billion times. The model was constructed for the 1958 World's Fair. It rises 335 feet (102m) like a giant plaything of the gods that's fallen to earth. The view from the viewing deck is marvelous, and you can even wander around inside the spheres.

Bd. du Centenaire, Heysel. ⓒ 02/475-47-77. www.atomium.be. Admission 9€ ($12) adults; 6€ ($7.80) students, seniors, children 12–18; free for children under 12. Daily 10am–6pm. Métro: Heysel.

Cathédrale des Sts-Michel-et-Gudule 𝕶   Begun in 1226, this magnificent Gothic church, off boulevard de l'Impératrice 2 blocks west of Gare Centrale, was officially consecrated as a cathedral only in 1961. The 16th-century Emperor Charles V donated its superb stained-glass windows. Aside from these, the spare interior decoration focuses attention on its soaring columns and arches, and the bright exterior stonework makes a fine sight.

Parvis Ste-Gudule. ⓒ 02/217-83-45. www.cathedralestmichel.be. Admission: Cathedral free; crypt 1€ ($1.30), treasury 1€ ($1.30), archaeological zone 2.50€ ($3.25). Mon–Fri 7am–7pm (Oct–Mar 6pm), Sat–Sun 8:30am–7pm (Oct–Mar 6pm); tourist visits not permitted during services Sat from 3:30pm, Sun until 2pm. Métro: Gare Centrale.

Hôtel de Ville (Town Hall) 𝕶𝕶   The facade of the dazzling Town Hall, dating back to 1402, shows off Gothic intricacy at its best, complete with dozens of arched windows and sculptures—some of them, such as the drunken monks, a sleeping Moor and his harem, and St. Michael slaying a female devil, display a perfectly medieval sense of humor. A 215-foot (65m) tower sprouts from the middle, yet it's not placed

exactly in the center. A colorful but untrue legend has it that when the architect realized his "error," he jumped off the summit of the tower. The building is still the seat
of civic government of the Brussels *commune*, and its wedding room is a popular place
to tie the knot. Its spectacular Gothic Hall, open for visits when the aldermen are not
in session, is replete with baroque decoration. In other chambers are 16th- to 18th-
century tapestries; one depicts the Spanish duke of Alba, whose cruel features reflect
the brutal oppression he imposed on the Low Countries; others show scenes from the
life of Clovis, the king of the Franks.

Grand-Place. ✆ 02/279-43-65. Admission (for guided tours in English) 3€ ($3.90) adults; 2.50€ ($3.15) seniors,
students; 2€ ($2.60) children 6–15; children under 6 free. Apr–Sept Tues–Wed 3:15pm, Sun 10:45am, 12:15pm;
Oct–Mar Tues–Wed 3:15pm. Métro: Gare Centrale.

Palais Royal (Royal Palace)   The palace, which overlooks the Parc de Bruxelles,
was begun in 1820 and had a grandiose Louis XVI–style face-lift in 1904. The older
wings date from the 18th century and are flanked by two pavilions. Today, the palace
is used for state receptions. It also contains the offices of King Albert II, though he
and Queen Paola do not reside here.

Place des Palais. ✆ 02/551-20-20. www.monarchie.be. Free admission. 3rd week July to late Sept (exact dates
announced yearly) Tues–Sun 10:30am–4:30pm. Métro: Parc.

POPULAR CITY ATTRACTIONS
Centre Belge de la Bande Dessinée (Belgian Center for Comic-Strip Art) ⃰
Dubbed the CéBéBéDé, the center, off boulevard de Berlaimont, is dedicated to
comic strips and takes a lofty view of its "Ninth Art." As icing on the cake, it's housed
in a restored Art Nouveau department store from 1903, the Magasins Waucquez,
designed by Victor Horta. A model of the red-and-white checkered rocket in which
Tintin and Snowy flew to the Moon, long before Armstrong and Aldrin did it in mere
fact, takes pride of place at the top of the elegant staircase. Beyond is a comic strip
wonderland. All the big names appear in a library of 30,000 books and in permanent
and special exhibits, including Tintin, Asterix, Thorgal, Lucky Luke, the Smurfs,
Peanuts, Andy Capp, Suske and Wiske—yes, even Superman, Batman, and the Green
Lantern—along with many lesser heroes.

Rue des Sables 20. ✆ 02/219-19-80. www.cbbd.be. Admission 7.50€ ($9.75) adults; 6€ ($7.80) students, seniors;
3€ ($3.90) children under 12. Tues–Sun 10am–6pm. Métro: Gare Centrale.

Mini-Europe ⃰   Stroll among highlights from European Union member states, all
meticulously detailed at a scale is 1:25. There's London's Big Ben, Berlin's Brandenburg Gate, the Leaning Tower of Pisa, the Bull Ring in Seville (complete with simulated sounds of fans yelling *¡Olé!*), and Montmartre in Paris, as well as more modern
emblems of continental achievement such as the Channel Tunnel and the Ariane
rocket. Mt. Vesuvius erupts, gondolas float around the canals of Venice, and a Finnish
girl dives into the icy waters of a northern lake.

Bruparck, Heysel. ✆ 02/478-05-50. www.minieurope.com. Admission 12.20€ ($16) adults; 9.20€ ($12) children
under 13; children under 4 ft. (1.2m) accompanied by parents free. Late Mar to June and Sept daily 9:30am–6pm;
July–Aug daily 9:30am–8pm (except Aug Sat–Sun 9:30am–midnight); Oct–Dec and 1st week Jan 10am–6pm. Closed
rest of Jan to late Mar. Métro: Heysel.

WHERE TO DINE
Chez Léon BELGIAN/MUSSELS   Think of it as "the mussels from Brussels," since
this big, basic restaurant right off the Grand-Place is the city's most famous purveyor

Moments Les Marolles

The working-class Marolles district is a special place where the old Brussels dialect, *Brusseleir,* can still be heard. It's a generally poor community, threatened by encroachment and gentrification from neighboring, wealthier areas. Most visitors to Brussels get their Marolles initiation by visiting the daily flea market on place du Jeu de Balle, which opens at 7am and closes at 2pm (take the Métro to Porte de Hal and then walk several blocks up rue Blaes). Here the weird and wonderful is commonplace. It makes a refreshing change to wander around for an hour or two in this other Brussels, a simple neighborhood of homes, welcoming cafes, and great, inexpensive restaurants.

of that marine delicacy. Léon has been flexing its mussels since 1893 and now has clones all over Belgium. The mollusks in question are served in a variety of styles. If you don't like mussels, there are plenty of other fishy delights—like eels in green sauce, cod, and bouillabaisse.

Rue des Bouchers 18. ✆ 02/511-14-15. www.chezleon.be. Main courses 9€–22€ ($12–$29); *menu Formule Léon* 14€ ($18). AE, DC, MC, V. Daily Sun–Thurs 11:30am–11pm; Fri–Sat 11:30am–11:30pm. Métro: Gare Centrale.

De l'Ogenblik ✻ FRENCH/BELGIAN Set in the elegant Galeries Royales St-Hubert, this restaurant supplies good taste in a Parisian bistro-style setting. It often gets busy, but the ambience in the split-level, wood-and-brass-outfitted dining room, with a sand-strewn floor, is convivial, though a little too tightly packed when it's full. Look for garlicky meat and seafood menu dishes, and expect to pay a smidgeon more for atmosphere than might be strictly justified by results on the plate.

Galerie des Princes 1. ✆ 02/511-61-51. www.ogenblik.be. Main courses 22€–28€ ($29–$36); *plat du jour* (lunch only) 11€ ($14). AE, DC, MC, V. Mon–Thurs noon–2:30pm and 7pm–midnight; Fri–Sat noon–2:30pm and 7pm–12:30am. Métro: Gare Centrale.

François ✻✻ SEAFOOD A bright and cheerful ambience complements fine cuisine at this restaurant on the ground floor of a 19th-century *maison de maître* (town house). The building has housed fishmongers since 1922, and that tradition is taken seriously. The presentation is professional yet relaxed. In fine weather, you can dine on a great sidewalk terrace across the street out on the old Fish Market square. If you're dining indoors, try to get a window table overlooking the square.

Quai aux Briques 2. ✆ 02/511-60-89. www.restaurantfrancois.be. Main courses 18€–58€ ($24–$75); fixed-price menu 24.50€–36€ ($32–$47). AE, DC, MC, V. Tues–Sat noon–2:30pm and 7–11:30pm. Métro: Ste-Catherine.

In 't Spinnekopke ✻✻ *Finds* TRADITIONAL BELGIAN Occupying a 1762 stagecoach inn off rue Van Artevelde, "In the Spider's Web" is just far enough off the beaten track downtown to be frequented mainly by those in the know. You dine in a tilting, tiled-floor building, at plain tables. This is one of Brussels's most traditional cafe/restaurants—so much so, in fact, that the menu lists its hardy standbys of regional Belgian cuisine in the old Bruxellois dialect.

Place du Jardin aux Fleurs 1. ✆ 02/511-86-95. www.spinnekopke.be. Main courses 11€–22€ ($14–$29); *plat du jour* 11€ ($14). AE, DC, MC, V. Mon–Fri noon–3pm and 6–11pm; Sat 6pm–midnight (bar Mon–Fri 11am–midnight; Sat 6pm–midnight). Métro: Bourse.

La Manufacture ✦ FRENCH/INTERNATIONAL   Even in its former incarnation, this place was a purveyor of style—it used to be the factory of chic Belgian leather goods maker Delvaux. Fully refurbished, with hardwood floors, leather banquettes, polished wood, and stone tables set amid iron pillars and exposed air ducts, it produces trendy world cuisine on a French foundation. On sunny days in summer, you can dine outdoors on a terrace shaded by giant bamboo plants. It's something of a hike from the Bourse Métro station, past place du Jardin aux Fleurs, but well worth the walk.

Rue Notre-Dame du Sommeil 12–20. ℂ 02/502-25-25. www.manufacture.be. Main courses 12€–21€ ($16–$27); *menu du jour* (lunch only) 14€ ($18); fixed-price menus 30€–65€ ($39–$85). AE, DC, MC, V. Mon–Fri noon–2pm and 7–11pm; Sat 7pm–midnight. Métro: Bourse.

L'Auberge des Chapeliers ✦ *(Value)* TRADITIONAL BELGIAN   In a 17th-century building off the Grand-Place that was once the hatmakers' guild house, the Auberge preserves its historic charm. Behind a venerable brick facade, the first two floors are graced with timber beams and paneling and connected by a narrow wooden staircase. The food is typical hearty Belgian fare, with an accent on mussels in season and dishes cooked in beer.

Rue des Chapeliers 1–3. ℂ 02/513-73-38. Reservations recommended on weekends. Main courses 10€–18€ ($13–$23); set-price menus 15€–21€ ($20–$27). AE, DC, MC, V. Mon–Thurs noon–2pm and 6–11pm; Fri noon–2pm and 6pm–midnight; Sat noon–3pm and 6pm–midnight; Sun noon–3pm and 6–11pm. Métro: Gare Centrale.

Le Scheltema ✦ BELGIAN   This is one of those solid restaurants in the Ilot Sacré district off rue des Bouchers that keep going day in, day out, year after year, serving up much the same fare but never forgetting that quality counts. Good service and fine atmosphere complement the seafood specialties at this brasserie-style restaurant, which in some ways is similar to others in the district but always goes the extra mile in terms of class and taste.

Rue des Dominicains 7. ℂ 02/512-20-84. www.scheltema.be. Main courses 20€–52€ ($26–$68); seafood platter 68€ ($85). AE, DC, MC, V. Mon–Thurs noon–3pm and 6–11:30pm; Fri–Sat noon–3pm and 6pm–12:30am. Métro: Gare Centrale.

't Kelderke ✦✦ TRADITIONAL BELGIAN   Despite being on the Grand-Place—the square that is the focus of tourism in Brussels—this is far from being a tourist trap. As many Bruxellois as tourists throng the long wooden tables in a 17th-century, brick-arched cellar, and all are welcomed with time-honored respect. Memorable traditional Belgian fare, with little in the way of frills, is served up from an open kitchen. This is a great place to try local specialties.

Grand-Place 15. ℂ 02/513-73-44. Main courses 10€–19€ ($13–$25); *plat du jour* 8.50€ ($11). AE, DC, MC, V. Daily noon–2am. Métro: Gare Centrale.

SHOPPING

One of Europe's oldest malls, the **Galeries Royales St-Hubert** (Métro: Gare Centrale) is a light and airy triple-galleried arcade hosting boutiques, cafe terraces, and street musicians playing classical music. Built in Italian neo-Renaissance style and opened in 1847, architect Pierre Cluysenaer's gallery offers shopping with a touch of class and is well worth strolling through even if you have no intention of even looking in a store window. The Galeries Royales St-Hubert is near the Grand-Place, between rue du Marché aux Herbes and rue de l'Ecuyer, and split by rue des Bouchers.

Among the finest—and most addictive—of Belgian specialties are the country's handmade pralines. Two good places to buy these are **Neuhaus,** Galerie de la Reine

25–27 (© **02/512-63-59;** Métro: Gare Centrale), and **Wittamer,** place du Grand Sablon 12 (© **02/512-37-42;** tram: 92 or 93). And while you're in sweet-tooth mode, for spicy *speculoos* cookies (made with cinnamon, ginger, and almond) and *pain à la grecque* (a thin, spicy biscuit), check out **Dandoy,** rue au Beurre 31 (© **02/511-03-26;** Métro: Bourse).

Lace isn't far behind as a Brussels shopping highlight. Two fine, centrally located stores that retail top-quality handmade Belgian lace are **Maison Antoine,** Grand-Place 26 (© **02/512-48-59;** Métro: Gare Centrale), and **Manufacture Belge de Dentelle,** Galerie de la Reine 6–8 (© **02/511-44-77;** Métro: Gare Centrale).

At the **Flea Market** on place du Jeu de Balle (Métro: Louise), a large square in the Marolles district, you can find some exceptional decorative items, many recycled from the homes of the "recently deceased," as well as unusual postcards, clothing, and household goods. The market is held daily from 7am to 2pm.

Every weekend, place du Grand Sablon hosts a fine **Antiques Market** (tram: 92, 93, or 94). The salesmanship is low-key, the interest pure, the prices not unreasonable (but don't expect bargains), and the quality of the merchandise—which includes silverware, pottery, paintings, and jewelry—high. The market is open Saturday from 9am to 6pm and Sunday from 9am to 2pm.

Near the Grand-Place, at the top end of rue du Marché aux Herbes, in a square loosely called the Agora, there's a weekend **Crafts Market** (Métro: Gare Centrale), with lots of handmade jewelry and other items, mostly inexpensive.

NIGHTLIFE

The superb and historic **Théâtre Royal de la Monnaie** ✿✿, place de la Monnaie (© **070/23-39-39;** www.lamonnaie.be; Métro: De Brouckère), founded in the 17th century, is home to the Opéra National and l'Orchestre Symphonique de la Monnaie. Ballet performances are also presented here. The present resident dance company is local choreographer Anne Theresa de Keersmaeker's Group Rosas. **BOZAR** (or, to purists, the Palais des Beaux-Arts), rue Royale 10 (© **02/507-82-00;** www.bozar.be; Métro: Gare Centrale), is home to Belgium's National Orchestra.

Théâtre Royal de Toone VII, in a room in the Toone cafe, is the latest in the Toone line of puppet theaters, which dates from the early 1800s—the title being passed from one puppet master to the next. At Toone, Puppet Master José Géal presents his adaptation of such classic tales as *The Three Musketeers, Faust,* and *Hamlet* in the Brussels dialect, but also in English, French, Dutch, and German. Impasse Schuddeveld 6, Petite rue des Bouchers 21 (© **02/511-71-37;** www.toone.be. Métro: Gare Centrale). Ticket prices and performance times vary.

Jazz is a popular but ever-changing scene. **L'Archiduc,** rue Antoine Dansaert 6 (© **02/512-06-52**), puts on jazz concerts on Saturday and Sunday. **Le Sounds,** rue de la Tulipe 28 (© **02/512-92-50**), has daily jazz concerts, and a workshop on Mondays at 7:30pm. For those who like their licks a tad restrained, there's a jazz brunch at the **Airport Sheraton Hotel,** facing the terminal building (© **02/725-10-00**), every Sunday from noon to 3pm.

BARS & CAFES   A Brussels favorite, **A la Mort Subite,** rue Montagne aux Herbes Potagères 7 (© **02/513-13-18**), is a bistro of rather special character whose name translates to "Sudden Death," which is also the name of a beer you can buy here. The decor consists of stained-glass motifs, old photographs, paintings, and prints on the walls, and plain wooden chairs and tables on the floor.

Moments   Puppet Shows

A special word is in order about a special sort of theater—that of the wooden marionettes that have entertained Belgians for centuries. In times past, puppet theaters numbered in the hundreds nationwide (Brussels alone had 15), and the plays were much like our modern-day soap operas. The story lines went on and on, sometimes for generations, and working-class audiences returned night after night to keep up with the *Dallas* of the times. Performances were based on folklore, legends, or political satire.

Specific marionette characters came to personify their home cities: a cheeky ragamuffin named Woltje (Little Walloon) was from Brussels; Antwerp had the cross-eyed, earthy ne'er-do-well Schele; Pierke, from Ghent, was modeled on the traditional Italian clown; and Liège's Tchantchès stood only 16 inches high and always appeared with patched trousers, a tasseled floppy hat, and his constant companion, the sharp-tongued Nanesse (Agnes).

Hidden away at the end of a narrow alleyway, **Au Bon Vieux Temps,** impasse St-Michel, rue du Marché aux Herbes 12 (© **02/217-26-26**), is a gloomily atmospheric old tavern that seems to hearken back to a bygone era. You should try the appropriately named *Duvel* (Devil) beer here. **A l'Imaige de Nostre-Dame,** impasse des Cadeaux, rue du Marché aux Herbes 8 (© **02/219-42-49**), is a decent, quiet place to drink and read or reflect if you're alone, or to converse with a companion without having to compete with a blaring jukebox.

A legendary 1904 Art Nouveau tavern, enlivened with a dash of Art Deco and rococo, **Le Falstaff,** rue Henri Maus 17–25 (© **02/511-87-89**), has stunning decor, stained-glass scenes in the style of Pieter Bruegel the Elder depicting Shakespeare's Falstaff tales, and reasonably priced brasserie food. **Rick's,** av. Louise 344 (© **02/647-75-30**), brings a touch of Humphrey Bogart and Ernest Hemingway, accompanied by American and Mexican food, to the stylish avenue Louise.

AN EXCURSION TO GHENT 🏵🏵

When it comes to tourism, Ghent (Gent) is often considered a poor relation of Bruges (p. 147). Its historical monuments and townscapes are not quite as pretty as those in its sister city, and are to be viewed only if there is time after visiting Bruges. There is some truth in this—but not too much. An important port and industrial center, Ghent compensates for its less precious appearance with a vigorous social and cultural scene.

ESSENTIALS

GETTING THERE   Ghent is just a half-hour train ride from Brussels (trains depart from all three of Brussels's main stations), and there are around four trains an hour from the capital. The city's main train station, **Gent-Sint-Pieters Station,** or Gand-Saint-Pierre as you also may see it written in French on timetables on Koningin Maria-Hendrikaplein, 1½ miles (2km) south of the center city, dates from 1912 and has a more-than-decent station restaurant. For schedule and fare information, call © **02/528-28-28.**

To get quickly and easily to the heart of town, take tram 1 from the nearest tram platform under the bridge to your left as you exit the station, and get out at Korenmarkt—it may be just a bit too far to walk there, and the way is none too interesting.

VISITOR INFORMATION   Ghent Tourist Office's **Infokantoor (Info Office)** is in the cellar of the Belfry and Cloth Hall, Botermarkt 17A (© **09/266-56-60;** www. visitgent.be). It's open April to October daily from 9:30am to 6:30pm, and November to March daily from 9:30am to 4:30pm.

Moments   **Heading Out to Waterloo** ⚔

The Battle of Waterloo was Europe's Gettysburg, and the battlefield remains much as it was on June 18, 1815. To visit it, you don't go to the town of Waterloo, 6 miles (10km) south of Brussels. The battle was not actually fought there. A stretch of rolling farmland dotted with stoutly built manor-farmhouses several miles to the south got that "honor." By bus from Brussels, take TEC line W from Gare du Midi to the **Centre Visiteur (Visitor Center),** route du Lion 252–254 (© **02/385-19-12;** www.waterloo1815.be), where an audiovisual presentation on the tactical background plus an extract from a fictional film version of the conflict will give you an idea of the battle's immense scale.

The view from atop the **Butte du Lion (Lion Mound),** next to the Visitor Center, is worth the 226-step climb, though it takes an active imagination to fill the peaceful farmland below you with slashing cavalry charges, thundering artillery, and 200,000 colorfully uniformed, struggling soldiers. Across the road from the Visitor Center is the **Musée des Cires (Waxworks Museum),** where Napoleon, Wellington, Blücher, and other leading participants appear as rather tatty wax figures. Also next to the Center is the **Panorama de la Bataille (Battlefield Panorama),** featuring a painted diorama of the massive French cavalry charge led by Marshal Ney. It was a sensation in the pre-cinema era.

These four sites are open daily April to October from 9:30am to 6:30pm; and November to March from 10am to 5pm. Admission to the Visitor Center is free. Admission to its audiovisual presentation and the four on-site attractions is 8.70€ ($11) for adults, 6.70€ ($8.70) for seniors and students, 5.50€ ($7.15) for children ages 7 to 17, and free for children under 7.

In Waterloo itself is the well-ordered **Musée Wellington (Wellington Museum),** chaussée de Bruxelles 147 (© **02/354-78-06;** www.museewellington. be), in an old Brabant coaching inn that was the Duke's headquarters. It was from here that Wellington sent his historic victory dispatch. The museum is open daily April to September from 9:30am to 6:30pm; and November to March from 10am to 5pm. Admission is 5€ ($6.50) for adults, 4€ ($5.20) for students and seniors, 2€ ($2.60) for children ages 6 to 12, and free for children under 6.

TOP ATTRACTIONS & SPECIAL MOMENTS

Even if you see nothing else in Ghent, you shouldn't miss **Sint-Baafskathedraal (St. Bavo's Cathedral)** ✿✿✿, Sint-Baafsplein (© 09/269-20-45; www.sintbaafskathedraal-gent.be). Don't be put off by the exterior's uncertain mix of Romanesque, Gothic, and baroque. The interior has priceless paintings, sculptures, screens, memorials, and carved tombs. About midway along the vaulted nave is a remarkable pulpit in white marble entwined with oak, reminiscent of Bernini. St. Bavo's showpiece is Jan van Eyck's 24-panel altarpiece *The Adoration of the Mystic Lamb,* completed in 1432. The cathedral is open April to October, Monday to Saturday from 8:30am to 6pm, and Sunday from 1 to 6pm; November to March, Monday to Saturday from 8:30am to 5pm, and Sunday from 1 to 5pm. Admission to the cathedral is free; to the *Mystic Lamb* chapel 3€ ($3.90) for adults, 1.50€ ($1.95) for children ages 6 to 18, and free for children under 6.

Across the square from the cathedral, the richly ornate Gothic **Belfort en Laken-halle (Belfry and Cloth Hall)** ✿, Emile Braunplein (© 09/269-37-30), together form a glorious medieval ensemble. The Cloth Hall from 1425 to 1445 is where cloth was stored and traded and was the gathering place of wool and cloth merchants. A UNESCO World Heritage Site, the Belfry, dating from 1313 to 1380, is 298 feet high (89m) and has a gilded copper dragon at its summit. It holds the great bells that have rung out Ghent's civic pride down through the centuries. Take the elevator up to the Belfry's upper gallery, at a height of 215 feet (65m), to see the bells and fantastic panoramic city views. The attraction is open mid-March to mid-November, daily from 10am to 12:30pm and 2 to 6pm (and mid-Nov to mid-Mar for prebooked guided tours for groups) only. Admission is 3€ ($3.90) for adults, 2.50€ ($3.25) for seniors and students, and free for children under 13. Free guided tours are available May to October, at 2:10, 3:10, and 4:10pm.

"Grim" is the word that springs to mind when you first see the **Gravensteen (Castle of the Counts)** ✿, Sint-Veerleplein (© 09/225-93-06). The fortress, built by Philip of Alsace in 1180, crouches like a gray stone lion over the city. If the castle's 6-foot-thick (1.8m) walls, battlements, and turrets failed to intimidate attackers, the count could always turn to a well-equipped torture chamber inside. Climb to the ramparts of the high building in the center, the donjon, where your reward is a great view of Ghent's rooftops and towers. The castle is open April to September, daily from 9am to 6pm; and October to March, daily from 9am to 5pm. Admission is 6€ ($7.80) for adults, 1.20€ ($1.55) for seniors, students and visitors ages 12 to 26, and free for children under 12.

WHERE TO DINE

In a town where the Middle Ages are *big,* **Brasserie Pakhuis** ✿✿, Schuurkenstraat 4 (© 09/223-55-55; www.pakhuis.be), located down a narrow lane off Veldstraat, is

---

(Moments **A Stroll through History**

Graslei and **Korenlei** ✿✿, two elegant canal-side rows that face each other across a waterway that once formed the city's harbor, are home to towering, gabled guild houses built between the 1200s and 1700s. To appreciate their majesty, walk across the connecting bridge over the Leie to view each one from the opposite bank, then return to stroll past each.

almost modern. In a vast, beautifully restored 19th-century warehouse, it's replete with painted cast-iron pillars, soaring wrought-iron balconies, and oak and marble tables with specially designed table settings, and has a granite mosaic floor. Although maybe too conscious of its own sense of style, Pakhuis is all stocked up in matters of taste and serves excellent Flemish cuisine. Main courses range from 11€ to 20€ ($14–$26).

Convivial and trendy, **Keizershof** ⨍, Vrijdagmarkt 47 (© **09/223-44-46;** www. keizershof.net), on the historical market square, has an attractively informal ambience and a good menu of continental fare. Behind its narrow facade are plain wood tables on multiple floors around a central stairwell. The decor beneath the timber ceiling beams is spare, tastefully tattered, and speckled with paintings by local artists. Service for office workers doing lunch is fast; in the evenings you're expected to linger. In summertime, you can dine al fresco in a courtyard at the back. An entree will set you back 9€ to 17€ ($12–$22).

AN EXCURSION TO ANTWERP ⨍

Antwerp, the acknowledged "Diamond Center of the World," is one of Western Europe's most hidden gems. Many people think of it only as a port and center of the diamond trade, yet it is also easygoing, stylish, and filled with the monuments of a wealthy medieval and Renaissance period. Only 40 minutes by train from Brussels, and compact enough for walking, it's an ideal day-trip out of the capital city.

ESSENTIALS

GETTING THERE   You can count on around four trains an hour from Brussels. Antwerp's main station is **Antwerpen Centraal Station,** or Anvers-Centrale as you may see it written in French on timetables, 1 mile (1.5km) east of the Grote Markt, on the edge of the center city. Centraal Station is a domed, cathedral-like edifice constructed between 1895 and 1905 (and with a superb station cafe, the Art Deco **De Gulden Kroon**). Antwerp is on the **Thalys** high-speed train network that connects Paris, Brussels, and Amsterdam. Reservations are required for Thalys. For schedule and fare information, call © **02/528-28-28.**

To get quickly from Centraal Station to the heart of the Old Town, take tram 2, 3, 5, or 15 and get out at Groenplaats. It's a short walk from there to the Grote Markt.

VISITOR INFORMATION   There is an **Info Desk** of the Antwerp Tourist Office on Koningin Astridplein, inside Antwerpen Centraal Station that is open the same hours as the main office. Pick up a very useful map of the city at the office; it'll cost you 1€ ($1.30). The main **Antwerp Tourist Office (Toerisme Antwerpen),** Grote Markt 13, 2000 Antwerpen (© **03/232-01-03;** www.antwerpen.be), is open Monday to Saturday from 9am to 5:45pm, and Sunday from 9am to 4:45pm.

TOP ATTRACTIONS & SPECIAL MOMENTS

Housed in an impressive neoclassical building, the **Koninklijk Museum voor Schone Kunsten Antwerpen (Antwerp Royal Museum of Fine Arts)** ⨍⨍⨍, Leopold de Waelplaats 2 (© **03/238-78-09;** www.kmska.be), has a collection of paintings by Flemish masters that is second to none in the world. Among them are more Rubens masterpieces in one place than anywhere else. To view them, pass through the ground-floor exhibits of canvases by modern artists (including works by Ensor, Magritte,

Permeke, and Delvaux). Ascend to the second floor, where you'll find works by Rubens, Jan van Eyck, Rogier van der Weyden, Dirck Bouts, Hans Memling, the Bruegel family, and by the Dutch artists Rembrandt and Frans Hals. The museum is open Tuesday to Saturday from 10am to 5pm, and Sunday from 10am to 6pm. Admission is 6€ ($7.80) for adults, 4€ ($5.20) for seniors and students, and free for children under 19; admission on the last Wednesday in the month is free.

A masterpiece of Brabant Gothic architecture, the towering **Onze-Lieve-Vrouwe-kathedraal (Cathedral of Our Lady)** ✿✿✿, Handschoenmarkt (© **03/213-99-51;** www.dekathedraal.be), off the Grote Markt, is the largest church in the Low Countries. Begun in 1352 and completed by around 1520, it has 7 aisles and 125 pillars, but of the original design's five towers, only one was ever completed. This one is the tallest church spire in the Low Countries, 403 feet (123m) high. A mix of baroque and neo-classical, the cathedral houses four Rubens altarpieces. Our Lady is open Monday to Friday from 10am to 5pm, Saturday from 10am to 3pm, and Sunday and religious holidays from 1 to 4pm. Admission is 2€ ($2.60), and free for children under 12.

To touch Antwerp's cultural heart, a visit to the **Rubenshuis (Rubens House)** ✿✿, Wapper 9–11 (© **03/201-15-55;** http://museum.antwerpen.be/rubenshuis), a short walk east of the center, is essential. Antwerp's most illustrious son, the artist Peter Paul Rubens (1577–1640), lived and worked here. Rubens amassed a tidy fortune from his paintings that allowed him to build this impressive mansion in 1610, along what was then a canal, when he was 33. Today, you can stroll past the baroque portico into its reconstructed period rooms and through a Renaissance garden, and come away with a good idea of the lifestyle of a patrician Flemish gentleman of that era. Examples of Rubens's works, and others by master painters who were his contemporaries, are scattered throughout. The house is open Tuesday to Sunday from 10am to 5pm. Admission is 6€ ($7.80) for adults, 4€ ($5.20) for seniors and persons ages 19 to 26, and free for seniors and children under 19; admission on the last Wednesday in the month is free.

A medieval fortress on the banks of the Scheldt, **De Steen** ✿, Steenplein 1 (© **03/ 201-93-40;** http://museum.antwerpen.be/scheepvaartmuseum), is Antwerp's oldest building. The glowering fortress has served a number of purposes over the centuries. Today, it houses the **Nationaal Scheepvaartmuseum (National Maritime Museum),** containing exhibits about the development of the port, and Belgian maritime history in general. The most eye-catching are models of old-time sailing ships, like the Belgian East India Company clippers. The museum is open Tuesday to Sunday from 10am to 5pm. Admission is 4€ ($5.20) for adults, 3€ ($3.90) for seniors and persons ages 19 to 26, and free for children under 19.

The Diamond Quarter

Some 80% of the world's rough diamonds, 50% of cut diamonds, and 40% of industrial diamonds are traded here annually. The diamond cutters of Antwerp are world-renowned for their skill, which you can admire in the Diamond Quarter, a surprisingly down-at-the-heels-looking area, only steps away from Centraal Station. More than 12,000 cutters and polishers work here in hundreds of workshops, serving thousands of firms, brokers, and merchants. Browsing the various store windows in the quarter is a highly enjoyable activity and won't cost you a thing.

WHERE TO DINE

The attractive **In de Schaduw van de Kathedraal** ✿, Handschoenmarkt 17–21 (© **03/232-40-14**), in the center city, features traditional Belgian cuisine gussied up

---

(Moments Cruising the Harbor

Do take a cruise around Antwerp's awesome harbor, which handles 16,000 ships and 100 million tons of cargo a year. Most departures are from the Steen waterfront on the Scheldt. **Flandria Line** (© **03/231-31-00;** www.flandriaboat. com) runs a varied program of harbor cruises. Their signature 2½-hour cruise is 12€ ($16) for adults, 10€ ($13) for seniors and children ages 3 to 12, and free for children under 3.

---

just a bit. Mussels and eel assume several guises on the menu, and beef is also well represented. If the prices here seem a little inflated, it's due to the excellent location; after all, this restaurant lies, as its name says, "in the shadow of the cathedral." Main courses cost 18€ to 45€ ($23–$59).

Rooden Hoed ⚔, Oude Koornmarkt 25 (near the Cathedral; © **03/233-28-44;** www.roodenhoed.be), a pleasant, old-fashioned restaurant is the oldest in Antwerp, having been in business for more than 250 years. It serves good, hearty food—a mix of old-style regional cuisine and trendy new forms—at moderate prices. Mussels, a delicious *choucroute d'Alsace* (sausages with sauerkraut and mashed potatoes), chicken *waterzooï,* and fish specialties are all featured on the menu. Try an aperitif, or a snack, in the medieval cellar under the restaurant. Main courses run 12€ to 20€ ($15–$25); fixed-price menus cost 25€ to 40€ ($31–$50).

A location amid the delightful 16th-century Vlaeykensgang courtyard's jumble of cafes, restaurants, and antique apartments all but guarantees a pleasant atmosphere at **Sir Anthony Van Dijck** ⚔⚔, Oude Koornmarkt 16 (© **03/231-61-70**). This used to be a Michelin Star–rated restaurant, until owner and chef Marc Paesbrugghe got tired of staying on the Michelin treadmill. Reopened as a relaxed French brasserie-restaurant, in a sparely elegant setting that's flooded with light that streams in from the old-world Vlaeykensgang courtyard through big, arched windows, it retains a commitment to good food. Main courses run 27€ to 30€ ($35–$39).

3 Bruges ⭐⭐⭐

The graceful, small city of Bruges (Brugge) has drifted down the stream of time with all the self-possession of the swans that cruise its canals. To step into the old town is to be transported back to the Middle Ages, when Bruges was among the wealthiest cities of Europe. UNESCO has recognized the cultural importance of the historic center by awarding it World Heritage status. The city is the pride and joy of all Flanders.

Medieval Gothic architecture is the big deal here. Sure, there's a layer of Romanesque; a touch of Renaissance, baroque, and rococo; a dab of neoclassical and neo-Gothic; and a smidgen of Art Nouveau and Art Deco. But Gothic is what Bruges provides, in quantities that come near to numbing the senses—and likely would if it weren't for the city's contemporary animation.

GETTING THERE

Trains arrive every half hour or so from Brussels, Antwerp, and Ghent, and from the North Sea resort and ferry port of Ostend (Oostende) and the ferry port of Zeebrugge. Journey time is about 1 hour by train from Brussels and Antwerp, 30 minutes from Ghent, and 15 minutes from Ostend and Zeebrugge.

From Paris, you can take the Thalys high-speed trains through Brussels to Bruges, or the slower and cheaper International trains, changing in Brussels. A train from Lille in northern France connects there with the Eurostar trains through the Channel Tunnel from London to Paris and Brussels. From Amsterdam, you can go via Antwerp or Brussels, either on the Thalys, or the normal International and InterCity trains.

STATION INFORMATION

Although the city is called Bruges in English and French, in Dutch it's "Brugge," and that's what the train station destination boards say. The station is on Stationsplein, about 1 mile (1.6km) south of the center of town. You can even get started on sightseeing here—inside the station is a large wall mural depicting scenes from Bruges's history and everyday life. And when leaving, the elegant **Perron Brasserie** is a good place for a pre-train snack or drink. For schedule and fare information, call ✆ **02/528-28-28.** There's a small booth for tourist information and hotel bookings inside the train station.

It's a 20-minute walk to the town center or a short bus or taxi ride—choose any bus labeled CENTRUM from the bus stops outside the station and get out at the Markt.

INFORMATION ELSEWHERE IN THE CITY

Bruges's main tourist information office, **In & Uit Brugge,** Concertgebouw, 't Zand 34, 8000 Brugge (✆ **050/44-46-46;** www.brugge.be), is inside the city's ultramodern Concert Hall, about midway between the train station and the heart of town. The office is open daily from 10am to 6pm (Thurs until 8pm).

GETTING AROUND

Narrow streets fan out from two central squares, the **Markt** and the **Burg.** A network of canals threads its way to every section of the small city, and the center is almost encircled by a canal that opens at its southern end to become a swan-filled lake, the **Minnewater**—this translates as Lake of Love, though the name actually comes from the Dutch *Binnen Water,* meaning Inner Harbor—bordered by the Begijnhof and a fine park.

Walking is by far the best way to see Bruges, since the center of town is traffic-free (but wear good walking shoes, as those charming cobblestones can be hard going). A bicycle is a terrific way to get around. You can rent a bike from the train station for 9€ ($12) a day, plus a deposit. Some hotels and stores rent bikes, for 6€ to 10€ ($7.80–$13) a day.

De Lijn city buses (✆ **070/22-02-00;** www.delijn.be) depart from the bus station outside the train station, and from the big square called 't Zand, west of the Markt. Several bus routes pass through the Markt. There's a taxi rank outside the train station (✆ **050/38-46-60**), and another at the Markt (✆ **050/33-44-44**).

TOP ATTRACTIONS & SPECIAL MOMENTS

In the **Markt (Market Square),** heraldic banners float from venerable facades. This square, along with the Burg (see below), is the heart of Bruges and the focal point of your sightseeing. Most major points of interest in the city are no more than a 5- or 10-minute walk away.

A part of the **Belfort en Hallen (Belfry and Market Halls)** ✿✿, Markt (✆ **050/44-87-11**), the bell tower was, and is, the symbol of Bruges's civic pride. The tower itself stands 272 feet high. Its lower section dates from around 1240, with the corner turrets added in the 14th century and the upper, octagonal section in the 15th century. If you have the stamina, climb the 366 steps to the Belfry's summit for a

Bruges

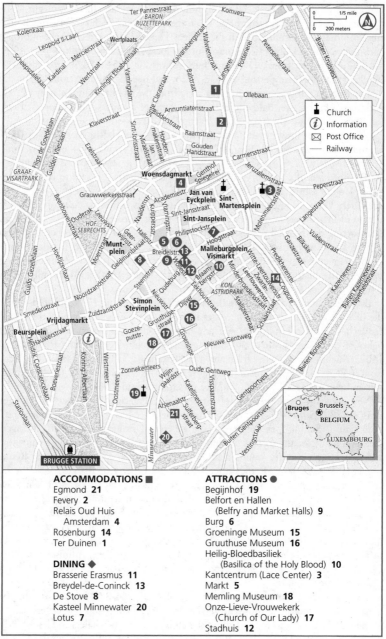

Church
(i) **Information**
✉ **Post Office**
— **Railway**

Bruges
Brussels
✪
BELGIUM
LUXEMBOURG

BRUGGE STATION

ACCOMMODATIONS ■
Egmond **21**
Fevery **2**
Relais Oud Huis
    Amsterdam **4**
Rosenburg **14**
Ter Duinen **1**

DINING ◆
Brasserie Erasmus **11**
Breydel-de-Coninck **13**
De Stove **8**
Kasteel Minnewater **20**
Lotus **7**

ATTRACTIONS ●
Begijnhof **19**
Belfort en Hallen
    (Belfry and Market Halls) **9**
Burg **6**
Groeninge Museum **15**
Gruuthuse Museum **16**
Heilig-Bloedbasiliek
    (Basilica of the Holy Blood) **10**
Kantcentrum (Lace Center) **3**
Markt **5**
Memling Museum **18**
Onze-Lieve-Vrouwekerk
    (Church of Our Lady) **17**
Stadhuis **12**

panoramic view over Bruges and the surrounding countryside. Its magnificent 47-bell carillon peals out every quarter hour. From the 13th to the 16th century, much of the city's commerce was conducted in the Hallen. These halls have recently been brought back into use for exhibits by a consortium of local art dealers. The complex is open Tuesday to Sunday from 9:30am to 5pm. Admission is 5€ ($6.50) for adults, 3€ ($3.90) for seniors and persons ages 13 to 26, and free for children under 13.

The **Burg,** a public square just steps away from the Markt, holds an array of stellar buildings. On this site, Baldwin Iron Arm, Count of Flanders, built a fortified castle (or "burg"), around which a village grew up that developed into Bruges.

A Romanesque basilica with a Gothic upper floor, the **Heilig-Bloedasiliek (Basilica of the Holy Blood)** ✿, Burg 10 (© **050/33-67-92;** www.holyblood.com), houses a venerated relic of Christ. Since 1149, it has been the repository of a fragment of cloth embedded in a rock-crystal vial and stained with what is said to be the coagulated blood of Christ, wiped from his body by Joseph of Arimathea after the crucifixion. Every year, in the colorful Procession of the Holy Blood on Ascension Day, the bishop of Bruges carries the relic through the streets, accompanied by costumed residents acting out biblical scenes. The basilica is open April to September, daily from 9:30 to 11:50am and 2 to 5:50pm; October to March, Thursday to Tuesday from 10 to 11:50am and 2 to 3:50pm, and Wednesday from 10 to 11:50am. Admission to the basilica is free; to the museum, 1.50€ ($1.95) for adults, 1€ ($1.30) for children ages 5 to 18, and free for children under 5.

Bruges's unmatched Gothic **Stadhuis (Town Hall)** ✿, Burg 12 (© **050/44-87-11**), the oldest town hall in Belgium, dates from the late 1300s. Don't miss the upstairs **Gotische Zaal (Gothic Room)** ✿✿ and its ornate decor, wall murals depicting highlights of the town's history, and the illuminated vaulted oak ceiling from 1385 to 1402, which features scenes from the New Testament. The Town Hall is open daily from 9:30am to 5pm. Admission is 2.50€ ($3.25) for adults, 1.50€ ($1.95) for seniors and persons ages 13 to 26, and free for children under 13.

Next door, the **Landhuis van het Brugse Vrije (Palace of the Liberty of Bruges),** Burg 11 (© **050/44-87-11**), dates mostly from 1722 to 1727, when it replaced a 16th-century building as the seat of the Liberty of Bruges—the Liberty being the medieval name for the district around Bruges. The palace later became a courthouse and now houses the city council's administration. Inside, at no. 11A, is the **Renaissancezaal Brugse Vrije (Renaissance Hall of the Liberty of Bruges)** ✿✿, the Liberty's council chamber, which has been restored to its original 16th-century condition. The hall has a superb black-marble fireplace decorated with an alabaster frieze and topped by an oak chimney piece carved with statues of Emperor Charles V, who visited Bruges in 1515, and his grandparents: Emperor Maximilian of Austria, Duchess Mary of Burgundy, King Ferdinand II of Aragon, and Queen Isabella I of Castile. The palace is open daily from 9:30am–12:30pm and 1:30 to 5pm. Admission is 2.50€ ($3.25) for adults, 1.50€ ($1.95) for seniors and persons ages 13 to 26, and free for children under 13.

The **Groeninge Museum** ✿✿✿, Dijver 12 (© **050/44-87-11**), ranks among Belgium's leading traditional museums of fine arts, with a collection that covers painting in the Low Countries from the 15th to the 20th century. The Gallery of Flemish Primitives holds some 30 works by painters such as Jan van Eyck, Rogier van der Weyden, Hieronymus Bosch, and Hans Memling. Works by Magritte and Delvaux also are exhibited. The museum is open Tuesday to Sunday from 9:30am to 5pm. Admission is 8€ ($10) for adults, 6€ ($7.80) for seniors and visitors ages 13 to 26, and free for children under 13.

Lodewijk van Gruuthuse, a Flemish nobleman and herb merchant who was a coun-selor to the Dukes of Burgundy in the 1400s, lived in this ornate Gothic mansion, now the **Gruuthuse Museum** ⚘, Dijver 17 (© **050/44-87-11**). Among the 2,500 antiques in the house are paintings, sculptures, tapestries, lace, weapons, glassware, and richly carved furniture. The museum is open Tuesday to Sunday from 9:30am to 5pm. Admission is 8€ ($10) for adults, 6€ ($7.80) for seniors and visitors ages 13 to 26, and free for children under 13.

In the former Sint-Janshospitaal (Hospital of St. John), where the earliest wards date from the 13th century, is housed the **Memling Museum** ⚘⚘, Mariastraat (© **050/44-87-11**). Visitors come primarily for the magnificent paintings by the German-born artist Hans Memling (ca. 1440–94), who moved to Bruges in 1465 and became a prominent city artist. Among his masterpieces here is the three-paneled altarpiece of St. John the Baptist and St. John the Evangelist. The museum is open Tuesday to Sun-day from 9:30am to 5pm. Admission is 8€ ($10) for adults, 5€ ($6.50) for seniors and visitors ages 13 to 26, and free for children under 13.

It took 2 centuries (from the 13th–15th) to build the **Onze-Lieve-Vrouwekerk (Church of Our Lady)** ⚘, in Mariastraat (© **050/34-53-14**), whose soaring 396-foot (119m) spire can be seen from miles around. Among the many art treasures within is an outstanding Carrara marble *Madonna and Child* ⚘⚘⚘, by Michelan-gelo. This sculpture, created in 1504, was the only one of Michelangelo's works to leave Italy during his lifetime. It was bought by a Bruges merchant, Jan van Mouskroen, and donated to the church in 1506. The church also holds a painting, the *Crucifixion,* by Anthony Van Dyck, and the impressive side-by-side bronze **tomb sculptures** of the duke of Burgundy, Charles the Bold, who died in 1477, and his daughter, Mary of Burgundy, who died at age 25 in 1482. The church is open Tues-day to Saturday from 9am to 5pm (Sat 4:45pm), and Sunday from 1:30 to 5pm. Admission to the church and *Madonna and Child* altar is free; to the chapel of Charles and Mary and the museum, is 2.50€ ($3.25) for adults, 1.50€ ($1.95) for children ages 13 to 18, and free for children under 13.

A combination workshop, museum, and sale room, the **Kantcentrum (Lace Cen-ter)** ⚘, Peperstraat 3A (© **050/33-00-72;** www.kantcentrum.com), is where the ancient art of making lace by hand gets passed on to the next generation. The center is open Monday to Saturday from 10am to noon and 2 to 6pm (Sat 5pm). Admission is 2.50€ ($3.25) for adults, 2€ ($2.60) for seniors and students, and free for children under 7.

Through the centuries, since it was founded in 1245 by the Countess Margaret of Constantinople, the **Prinselijk Begijnhof ten Wijngaarde (Princely Beguinage of**

(Moments Strolling the Back Streets

You don't need to visit the top 10 highlights to enjoy Bruges. Shut your guide-book, put away the street map, and just wander, taking time out to make your own discoveries. Bruges's inhabitants live their everyday lives in absurdly beau-tiful surroundings and aren't always engaged in putting on a show for the tourists.

Moments **Bruges by Boat**

Be sure to take a **boat trip** ✻✻✻ on the canals, onboard one of the open-top tour boats that cruise year-round from five departure points around the center, all marked with an anchor icon on maps available from the tourist office. The boats operate March to November, daily from 10am to 6pm. A half-hour cruise is 5.70€ ($7.40) for adults, 2.80€ ($3.65) for children ages 4 to 11 accompanied by an adult, and free for children under 4.

---

the Vineyard) ✻✻, Wijngaardstraat (© **050/33-00-11**), at the Lake of Love, has long been one of Bruges's most tranquil spots. *Begijns* were religious women, similar to nuns, who accepted vows of chastity and obedience, but drew the line at poverty, preferring to earn a living by looking after the sick and making lace. The begijns are no more, but the Begijnhof is occupied by the Benedictine nuns of the Monasterium De Wijngaard, who try to keep their traditions alive. This handsome little cluster of 17th-century whitewashed houses surrounding a lawn with poplar trees and flowers makes a marvelous escape from the hustle and bustle outside. The Begijnhof courtyard is always open and admission is free.

A fine example of the *godshuizen* (houses of God, or almshouses), built by the rich in Bruges from the 13th century onward as refuges for widows and the poor, is the **Godshuis de Vos (De Vos Almshouse),** from 1713, at the corner of Noordstraat and Wijngaardstraat, near the Begijnhof. The moneybags weren't being entirely altruistic, since the residents had to pray for their benefactors' souls twice a day in the chapel that was an integral part of an almshouse's facilities. The pretty courtyard garden here is surrounded by a chapel and eight original houses, since converted to six, which are owned by the city and occupied by seniors. Admission is not permitted, but you can view the complex from over a low wall out front.

WHERE TO STAY

Egmond ✻ There are just eight rooms in this rambling mansion next to the Minnewater Park, but the lucky few who stay here will find ample space, plenty of family ambience, abundant local color, and lots of peace and tranquillity. All rooms are furnished in an individual style, and all have views on the garden and the Minnewater Park. Every afternoon, free coffee and tea are served on the garden terrace or in the lounge.

Minnewater 15, 8000 Brugge. © **050/34-14-45.** Fax 050/34-29-40. www.egmond.be. 8 units. 103€–125€ ($134–$163) double. Rates include buffet breakfast. No credit cards. **Amenities:** Nonsmoking rooms (all rooms). *In room:* Hair dryer.

Fevery A family-owned hotel, the Fevery is on a quiet side street off Langerei in a quiet part of town. The modern and comfortably furnished guest rooms, enlarged through a rebuilding program that ended in 2002, are cheery and immaculate, with new bathrooms and monogrammed pressed sheets. The proprietor Mr. Asselman is a wealth of local information and clearly takes great pride in his establishment.

Collaert Mansionstraat 3, 8000 Brugge. © **050/33-12-69.** Fax 050/33-17-91. www.hotelfevery.be. 10 units. 60€– 85€ ($78–$111) double. Rates include buffet breakfast. AE, MC, V. **Amenities:** Lounge; nonsmoking rooms (all rooms). *In room:* Hair dryer.

Relais Oud Huis Amsterdam 👍👍 Rooms in this large canal-side building, parts of which date from the 1300s, are large and sumptuously furnished. Some bathrooms feature whirlpool tubs. The elegant guest rooms in the front overlook the canal; those in back overlook the garden and picturesque rooftops. In the rear, there's a charming little courtyard with umbrella tables and a garden off to one side—the setting for Sunday concerts in June.

Spiegelrei 3, 8000 Brugge. ✆ **050/34-18-10.** Fax 050/33-88-91. www.oha.be. 44 units. 218€–278€ ($283–$361) double. AE, DC, MC, V. **Amenities:** Bar; laundry; nonsmoking rooms. *In room:* Hair dryer.

Rosenburg 👍 This ultramodern brick hotel is set alongside a lovely canal, a short walk west from the center of Bruges. The hotel is an artful combination of old Bruges style and contemporary amenities and fittings. Its spacious guest rooms are restfully decorated in warm colors like peach and furnished with bamboo and rattan beds. Most have views of the canal at Coupure.

Coupure 30, 8000 Brugge. ✆ **050/34-01-94.** Fax 050/34-35-39. www.rosenburg.be. 27 units. 140€–195€ ($182–$254) double. Rates include buffet breakfast. AE, DC, MC, V. **Amenities:** Laundry; nonsmoking rooms. *In room:* Hair dryer.

Ter Duinen 👍 This charming hotel is an ideal marriage of classical style and modern conveniences. Guest rooms are ample in size, brightly decorated, and have modern furnishings. Some rooms have wooden ceiling beams, and some have a great view overlooking the tranquil Langerei canal, just north of the town center and an easy walk away. Proprietors Marc and Lieve Bossu-Van Den Heuvel take justified pride in their hotel and extend a friendly welcome to guests.

Langerei 52, 8000 Brugge. ✆ **050/33-04-37.** Fax 050/34-42-16. www.terduinenhotel.be. 20 units. 105€–149€ ($137–$194) double. Rates include full breakfast. AE, DC, MC, V. **Amenities:** Lounge; laundry. *In room:* A/C, hair dryer.

WHERE TO DINE

Brasserie Erasmus FLEMISH Small but popular, this is a great stop after viewing the cathedral and nearby museums. It serves a large variety of Flemish dishes, all prepared with beer. Try the typically Flemish souplike stew dish *waterzooï,* which is very good here and is served with fish, as it's supposed to be, although they also make it with chicken, a style that has become the norm elsewhere.

Wollestraat 35. ✆ **050/33-57-81.** www.hotelerasmus.com. Main courses 12.50€–17.50€ ($16–$23); fixed-price menu from 20€ ($26). MC, V. Daily noon–3:30pm and 6–10pm.

Breydel-de-Coninck SEAFOOD The wood beam ceilings and plaid upholstery here are cheerful, but the real attraction is the seafood. The specialties are mussels, eels, and lobsters prepared with white wine, cream, or garlic sauces that enhance the seafood without overwhelming it. Try a pail full of plain mussels, or go for something with a little more zest, such as the *moules Provençal* (mussels in a light red sauce with mushrooms, peppers, and onions).

Breidelstraat 24. ✆ **050/33-97-46.** Main courses 9.90€–21€ ($12.85–$27.30); fixed-price menus 16€–36€ ($21–$47). AE, MC, V. Thurs–Tues noon–3pm and 6–9:30pm.

De Stove 👍👍 FLEMISH/SEAFOOD This small (there's space for just 20 diners), family-owned restaurant combines a rustic atmosphere with a more contemporary style than is usual in Bruges. The seafood specialties are well worth a try, particularly the Flemish fish stew, and the menu of the month is always well considered.

Kleine Sint-Amandsstraat 4 (close to the Markt). ✆ **050/33-78-35.** www.restaurantdestove.be. Reservations recommended on weekends. Main courses 16€–30€ ($21–$36); fixed-price menu 44€ ($57). AE, MC, V. Fri–Tues noon–1:45pm and 6:30–9:30pm.

Kasteel Minnewater ★★ BELGIAN/FRENCH Old paintings on the walls, a marble fireplace, chandeliers, and fine table linen, all complement this château-restaurant's superb location on the *Minnewater* (Lake of Love). It exudes an unstuffy charm that makes château dining not just something for lords and ladies, and though prices have been edging up, it still provides a good deal considering the setting.

Minnewater 4. ✆ **050/33-42-54.** Main courses 25€–45€ ($33–$59); Markt-menu 30€ ($39). V. Summer daily 11am–11pm; winter Mon–Fri noon–2:30pm and 6:30–11pm, Sat–Sun 11am–11pm.

Lotus ★ VEGETARIAN Even nonvegetarians will likely enjoy the inventive food here. There are just two menu options—but at least you can choose from a small, medium, or large serving—each with a hearty assortment of imaginatively prepared ingredients, served in a tranquil but cheery Scandinavian-style dining room.

Wapenmakersstraat 5. ✆ **050/33-10-78.** Fixed-price lunch menus 9€–11€ ($12–$14). No credit cards. Mon–Sat 11:45am–2pm.

4 Liège

Fervent, lively Liège—its nickname is *la Cité Ardente* (the Passionate City)—exudes the aura of an aging industrial gloom, but that seems to fade next to its gracefully down-at-the-heels 19th-century monuments and remnants from the time of its powerful prince-bishops.

GETTING THERE

There are between two and four trains an hour to Liège from Brussels and Antwerp, one an hour from Maastricht and Cologne, and one every 2 hours from Luxembourg. The Thalys high-speed train, arrives via Brussels, from Paris, and direct from Cologne; ICE high-speed trains arrive from Frankfurt, Germany.

STATION INFORMATION

The main train station is **Liège Guillemins,** rue des Guillemins, just south of the center city. The smaller, more centrally located station **Liège Palais,** on rue de Bruxelles, is used by some local and connecting trains. Both stations are served by multiple bus lines. For schedule and fare information, call ✆ **02/528-28-28.** There is no tourist information office at either station.

INFORMATION ELSEWHERE IN THE CITY

The city tourist office, the **Office du Tourisme,** Féronstrée 92, 4000 Liège (✆ **04/221-92-21;** www.liege.be), is open Monday to Friday from 9am to 5pm.

GETTING AROUND

The **Old City,** which has most of Liège's sightseeing attractions, and nighttime entertainment in the student-filled **Carré** district, is on the west bank of the Meuse, bounded by rue de l'Université, boulevard de la Sauvenière, and rue Pont-d'Avroy. On the east bank, the **Outremeuse** (Across the Meuse) district has a big choice of lively bars, discothèques, and cabarets. Along the river are tree-lined walkways.

Sightseeing highlights in the Old City are close together, so downtown Liège makes for easy walking, though traffic can be frenetic. **Buses,** useful for getting to sights outside the Old City, cost 1.30€ ($1.70) for a ride. You can buy discounted eight-ride tickets from booths at major route stops and at train stations. The excellent bus system is not hard to figure out, since many stops have network maps posted. Place St-Lambert, an important interchange point downtown, is reached from Guillemins train station

Liège

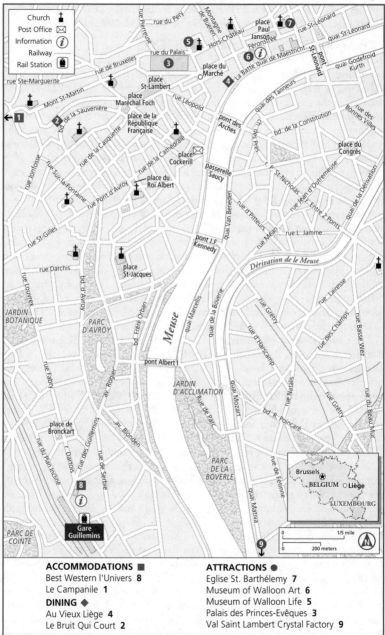

Legend	
Church	✝
Post Office	✉
Information	ⓘ
Railway	-----
Rail Station	🚉

ACCOMMODATIONS ■
Best Western l'Univers **8**
Le Campanile **1**

DINING ◆
Au Vieux Liège **4**
Le Bruit Qui Court **2**

ATTRACTIONS ●
Eglise St. Barthélemy **7**
Museum of Walloon Art **6**
Museum of Walloon Life **5**
Palais des Princes-Evêques **3**
Val Saint Lambert Crystal Factory **9**

by lines 1, 2, 3, and 4. City bus information is available from **TEC** (© **04/361-94-44;** www.infotec.be). For a taxi, call **Liège-Tax** (© **0800-32-200** or 04/367-50-40).

TOP ATTRACTIONS & SPECIAL MOMENTS

A small but impressive collection of works by Walloon (French-speaking Belgian) artists from the 16th century to the present graces the **Musée de l'Art Wallon (Museum of Walloon Art)** ⚔, Ilot St-Georges, Féronstrée 86 (© **04/221-92-31**), by the river in the center of town. Among these artists are Paul Delvaux, Constant Meunier, Antoine Wiertz, Félicien Rops, René Magritte, Roger Somville, and Pierre Alechinsky. The museum is open Tuesday to Saturday from 1 to 6pm, and Sunday from 11am to 4:30pm. Admission is 3.80€ ($4.95) for adults; 2.50€ ($3.25) for seniors, students, and children ages 12 to 18; and free for children under 12.

An incredible array of exhibits bring to life the days of 19th-century Walloons and their traditions and customs, at the newly refurbished **Musée de la Vie Wallonne (Museum of Walloon Life)** ⚔⚔, Cour des Mineurs (© **04/237-90-40**), in the center city, north of place St-Lambert. Housed in a 17th-century former Franciscan convent, the collection features examples of popular art, crafts, recreation, and even the workings of a coal mine. Here, too, is a marvelous puppet collection, which includes the city's beloved Tchantchès. *Note:* The museum was closed for renovation at this writing, but was due to reopen some time in the spring of 2008. The latest practical information available was that the museum would be open Tuesday to Saturday from 10am to 5pm, and Sunday from 10am to 4pm. Admission (which will no doubt increase somewhat on the museum's reopening) was 2.50€ ($3.25) for adults, 1.50€ ($1.95) for children ages 6 to 18, and free for children under 6.

The twin-towered Romanesque **Eglise St-Barthélemy (Church of St. Bartholomew),** place St-Barthélemy (© **04/221-89-44**), dates from 1108. Its **Fonts-Baptismaux (Baptismal Font)** ⚔ is counted among "Belgium's Magnificent Seven" most important historical treasures. The copper-and-brass font, cast in the early 1100s by master metalsmith Renier de Huy, a masterpiece of medieval Mosan Art, rests on the backs of ten sculpted oxen and is surrounded by five biblical scenes. The church is open to visitors Tuesday to Saturday from 10am to noon and 2 to 5pm, and Sunday from 2 to 5pm. Admission is 2.50€ ($3.25) for adults, and 1.50€ ($1.95) for children.

The prince-bishops, who ruled the city and the surrounding territory from 980 to 1794, constructed for themselves the largest secular Gothic structure in the world. Of primary interest at the **Palais des Prince-Evêques (Palace of the Prince-Bishops)** on place St-Lambert are the two inner courtyards, one lined with 60 carved columns depicting the follies of human nature, and the other housing an ornamental garden. Today, this historic building is Liège's Palace of Justice, housing courtrooms and administrative offices. The palace is open Monday to Friday from 10am to 5pm. Admission to the courtyards is free; contact the tourist office for guided tours.

A visit to the factory of **Val Saint Lambert,** rue du Val 245, Seraing (© **04/330-38-00;** www.val-saint-lambert.com), next to the Meuse River, just southwest of Liège, on N90, allows you to watch the company's craftsmen at work making the renowned, handblown Val Saint Lambert crystal. You can also buy the finished product—including slightly flawed pieces at a considerable discount—from the factory store. Workshop visits are Monday to Thursday at 10:30am and 2:30pm, and Friday at 10:30am. The workshop is sited within a complex that contains the remains of a 13th-century Cistercian abbey, a 16th-century Mosan Renaissance château, and examples of industrial archaeology from the 18th and 19th centuries. Housed in the château, the **Musée** du Cristal (Crystal Museum) displays particularly fine antique pieces, and is open daily from 9am to 5pm. Admission is 6€ ($7.80) for adults, 5€ ($6.50) for seniors, 3.75€ ($4.90) for children ages 5 to 16, and free for children under 5.

WHERE TO STAY

The 51-room **Best Western l'Univers** ⚔, rue des Guillemins 116 (𝒞 **04/254-55-55;** www.bestwestern.com), close to Gare des Guillemins, is a reasonably good value. The guest rooms are modest in decor but quite comfortable. Though there's no restaurant on the premises, several are within walking distance. Rates here are 80€ to 100€ ($104–$130) double.

Guest rooms at **Le Campanile,** rue Jules de Laminne 18 (𝒞 **04/224-02-72;** www. campanile.fr), are spacious and comfortable, if not much inflected with character, at this modern hotel, which has a reputation for its value. The suburban setting won't appeal to anyone who wants to be in the heart of town, but it's just 5 to 10 minutes by bus to the center city. Rates run 60€ to 75€ ($78–$98) double and don't include breakfast.

WHERE TO DINE

Set in a four-story 16th-century town house furnished with antiques of that era, **Au Vieux Liège,** Quai de la Goffe 41 (𝒞 **04/223-77-48;** www.vieux-liege.be), serves food that outshines even the excellent setting. Dinner is by candlelight, and the waiters wear formal attire. Almost any fish dish is a good choice, but there's more experimental fare including rare-cooked *escargots niçoises* (snails) and lobster ravioli. Main courses run from 25€ to 49€ ($33–$64).

An imposing 19th-century building, formerly a bank, houses **Le Bruit Qui Court,** bd. de la Sauvenière 142 (𝒞 **04/232-18-18;** www.bruitquicourt.be), and confers upon it a certain amount of class, which is matched by a refined cuisine. Light menu dishes, such as salads and quiches, predominate and mix flavors in a manner that often is unexpected. You can even dine in the ground-floor strong room, behind the original heavily armored door. A main course runs 8€ to 15€ ($10–$20).

SHOPPING

On Sunday mornings, a **street market** is strung out for about a mile along the quai de la Batte on the bank of the Meuse. You'll find brass, clothes, flowers, foodstuffs, jewelry, birds, animals, books, radios, and more; the list is simply endless. Shoppers from as far away as Holland and Germany join what seems to be at least half the population of Liège.

5 An Excursion to Luxembourg City ★★

Luxembourg City, the Grand Duchy's diminutive capital, is a marvelously contrasting mix of the old and the new. The old part of town runs along a deep valley beneath brooding casemates, while the more modern part of town crowns steep cliffs overlooking the old. The city is the headquarters of the European Court of Justice and of the European Investment Bank, and is one of the three seats of the European Parliament (along with Brussels and Strasbourg). Despite the many banks and the Euro-office towers, Luxembourg City has retained plenty of small-scale, provincial ambience.

GETTING THERE   Luxembourg City has good rail connections from Belgium, Germany, and France (in 2007, a high-speed TGV service from Paris was introduced).

Luxembourg City

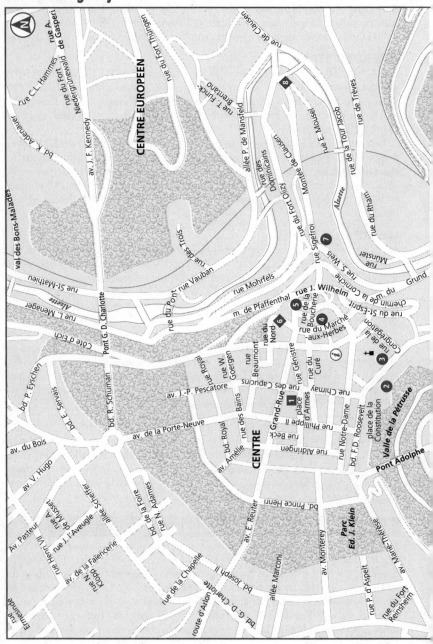

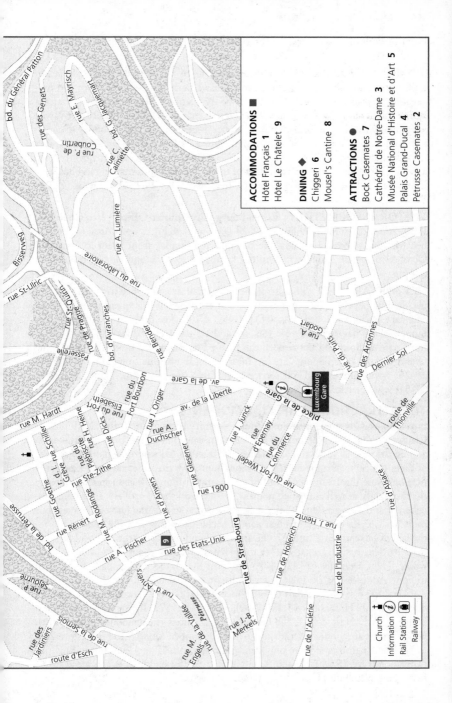

ACCOMMODATIONS ■
Hôtel Français **1**
Hôtel Le Châtelet **9**

DINING ◆
Chiggeri **6**
Mousel's Cantine **8**

ATTRACTIONS ●
Bock Casemates **7**
Cathédral de Notre-Dame **3**
Musée National d'Histoire et d'Art **5**
Palais Grand-Ducal **4**
Pétrusse Casemates **2**

Church
Information
Rail Station
Railway

159

From Brussels, the fastest time by **InterCity** train (departing from Gare du Midi) is 3 hours.

STATION INFORMATION **Luxembourg Gare** (✆ **49-90-49-90**), the main train station, in the southern part of town, has a currency-exchange office and luggage-storage facilities inside. The Luxembourg National Tourist Office operates a **Bureau d'Acceuil (Welcome Desk)** at Gare Centrale (✆ **42-82-82-20**; www.visit luxembourg.lu). This information desk is open June to September, Monday to Saturday from 9am to 7pm, and Sunday from 9am to 12:30pm and 1:45 to 6pm; October to May, daily from 9:15am to 12:30pm and 1:45 to 6pm. Buses run frequently from a depot outside the station to the center of town. For train information (and bus service outside Luxembourg City), contact **Chemins de Fer Luxembourgeois** (✆ **24-89-24-89**; www.cfl.lu).

VISITOR INFORMATION **Luxembourg City Tourist Office,** place Guillaume II 30, 1648 Luxembourg-Ville (✆ **22-28-09**; www.lcto.lu), is open April to September, Monday to Saturday from 9am to 7pm, and Sunday from 10am to 6pm; and October to March, Monday to Saturday from 9am to 6pm, and Sunday from 10am to 6pm.

GETTING AROUND Because of the city's small size, you may have little need to use the **bus** network. Service is extensive and efficient but infrequent on some lines. The fare (valid for 1 hr.) is 1.50€ ($1.95); a 10-ticket pack costs 10€ ($13). A money-saving **day ticket** for 5€ ($6.50), and a 5-day pack for 20€ ($26), available from train stations and the airport, can be used on buses and trains throughout the Grand Duchy. Luxembourg City bus information is available from **ADL** (✆ **47-96-29-75**; www.autobus.lu). **Taxi** service is available from **Benelux Taxis** (✆ **800/2-51-51**; www.beneluxtaxi.lu).

TOP ATTRACTIONS & SPECIAL MOMENTS

Luxembourg City grew up around Count Sigefroi's 10th-century castle at Montée de Clausen on the Bock promontory. In time, there came to be three rings of battlements around the city, 15 forts, and an exterior wall interspersed with nine more forts, three of them cut right into the rock. Even more impressive than these aboveground fortifications were the 16 miles (25km) of underground tunnels that sheltered troops by the thousands, as well as their equipment, horses, workshops, artillery, arms, kitchens, bakeries, and even slaughterhouses. Legend says that within the fortress's tremendous rocky walls sits a beautiful maiden named Mélusine, whose knitting needles control the fate of Luxembourg. In 1867, the Treaty of London ordered the dismantling of all these battlements, and what you see today represents only about 10% of the original works. The **Casemates** (✆ **22-28-09**) are open March to October, daily from 10am to 5pm. Admission is 2€ ($2.60) for adults, and 1.50€ ($1.95) for children.

The oldest part of the **Palais Grand-Ducal (Palace of the Grand Dukes)** ✿✿, rue du Marché aux Herbes (✆ **47-96-27-09**), dates from 1572. Its "new" right wing was built in 1741. Next door is the Chamber of Deputies (Luxembourg's Parliament). Guided tours are conducted mid-July to mid-September, Monday to Friday from 2:30 to 5pm (in English at 4:30pm only), and Saturday from 10 to 11am (not in English). Admission is 6€ ($7.80) for adults, and 3€ ($3.90) for children; tickets are available from the Luxembourg City Tourist Office on place d'Armes.

The **Musée National d'Histoire et d'Art (National Museum of Art and History)** ✿, Marché aux Poissons (© 47-93-30-1; www.mnha.lu), in the oldest part of town, holds fascinating archaeological, geological, and historical exhibits. In addition, there's the exquisite Bentinek-Thyssen Collection of works of art by Low Countries artists from the 15th to the 18th century, among them Rubens, van Dyck, Bruegel, and Rembrandt. The museum is open Tuesday to Sunday from 10am to 5pm. Admission is 5€ ($6.50) for adults, 3€ ($3.90) for seniors and students, and free for children under 19.

A magnificent Gothic structure built between 1613 and 1621, the **Cathédrale de Notre-Dame (Notre-Dame Cathedral)** ✿, boulevard F.D. Roosevelt (entrance also on rue Notre-Dame), contains the royal family's vault and a remarkable Treasury (it can only be viewed on request). This is the offsetting for the **Octave of Our Lady of Luxembourg,** an annual ceremony on the fifth Sunday following Easter, when thousands of pilgrims arrive to pray to the miraculous statue of the Holy Virgin for protection. They then form a procession to carry the statue from the cathedral through the streets to an alter covered with flowers in avenue de la Porte Neuve, north of place d'Armes. The cathedral is open daily from 10am to noon and 2 to 5:30pm. Admission is free.

WHERE TO STAY

Small and central, the **Hôtel Français** ✿, place d'Armes 14 (© 47-45-34; www.hotel francais.lu), is a nice, moderately priced hotel. The 21 guest rooms have been recently refurbished and redecorated in a bright, modern style, though some are on the small side. The hotel is in a pedestrian-only zone, but cars and taxis are allowed to drop off and pick up people and baggage. Rates run 125€ ($163) double and include continental breakfast.

The small **Hôtel Le Châtelet** ✿, bd. de la Pétrusse 2 (© 40-21-01; www.chatelet.lu), close to the Pétrusse Valley, is a longtime favorite of visiting academics and businesspeople. Its rooms are divided between two lovely old Luxembourg homes; all have modern, comfortable, and attractive furnishings. Rates are 108€ to 130€ ($141–$169) double and include a buffet breakfast.

WHERE TO DINE

The remarkable **Chiggeri** ✿, rue du Nord 15 (© 22-99-36; www.chiggeri.lu), off Grand-Rue is in a rambling mansion on a quiet side street. The main dining room employs African-influenced decorative motifs and has a friendly but professional style. The menu changes seasonally, and the Mediterranean dishes with Asian influences are always inventive. When the weather's good, you may want to dine on the cafe section's outdoor terrace. Main courses in the cafe cost 11€ to 14€ ($14–$18), and in the restaurant 23€ to 32€ ($30–$42); fixed-price menus run 13€ to 21€ ($17–$27).

Next door to the Mousel Brewery, down beside the Alzette River, the excellent **Mousel's Cantine,** Montée de Clausen 46 (© 47-01-98), is a great place to sample regional treats. The decor is rustic, with plain wooden tables and oil paintings in the back room, and the front room overlooks the quaint street outside. The menu majors on hearty portions of Luxembourg favorites such as sauerkraut with sausage, potatoes, and ham. To wash this down, try a stein of the unfiltered local Mousel brew. A main course will set you back 11€ to 23€ ($14–$30) and there's a *plat du jour* for 11€ ($14).

5

The Czech Republic

The Czech Republic, comprising the ancient kingdoms of Bohemia, Moravia, and Silesia, is the westernmost of the former Soviet satellite countries and probably the easiest way to explore what used to be the other side of the Iron Curtain. The republic is actually a lot more modernized than most of its former East Bloc neighbors. The European Union put the Czech Republic at the head of its new intake of states in May 2004.

Three years into EU membership the Czech Republic has been included in the Schengen border free zone. As of January 2008, there will be completely open borders with all neighboring countries and passport checks will not be required. Although it still will be several years until the euro is adopted here, this country already has the attitude of a mature Western European state, and the tourists and investments keep flowing in.

For rail travelers, however, the republic still has some work to do in the modernizing department. New SuperCity Pendolino trains now serve riders on several top routes within the country and to neighboring Vienna. But with the exception of a handful of international trains crisscrossing the country, most local routes in the country are served by ubiquitous, prompt, and cheap-but-oh-so-grungy trains. And the Republic isn't covered by the Eurail Global Pass—a negative if you plan on covering a number of countries on your trip. Nevertheless, once at your destination, few countries in Europe can match the mix of history of this one. And the Republic is renowned as a value destination, so rail travelers' dollars will go a lot further here than in many other countries.

HIGHLIGHTS OF THE CZECH REPUBLIC

The capital, **Prague,** is widely regarded as one of the most beautiful cities in Europe. This quirky and compact heart of Bohemia is a jumble of architecture. Gothic bestrides baroque, Renaissance adjoins Cubist, with a splash of Socialist Realism and postmodern kitsch thrown in for good measure. It's also unquestionably the first stop on any rail traveler's itinerary. Most international trains arrive here and it's the only Czech city that welcomes direct flights from North America.

But Prague isn't the Czech Republic's only draw. For castle-hoppers, the majestic **Karlštejn Castle** (p. 185) is an easy day trip by train from Prague and one of the country's most popular destinations. And visitors are venturing more and more into West Bohemia, where one of the world's best-known spas **(Karlovy Vary)** has been restored to its Victorian-era splendor, and where castles abound in the surrounding countryside. These are old-world spas—not New Age health farms—villages where you get your system replenished by drinking the waters, strolling the promenades, and soaking up the ambience. And though some of the Czech Republic isn't efficiently accessed by rail—hence the absence of Moravia from this chapter—the cities in this region generally make for easy rail trips out of Prague. In addition to the spa towns,

The Czech Republic

if you have the time in your schedule, don't pass up the opportunity to visit Southern Bohemia's jewel of cities, **Český Krumlov,** named a World Heritage Site by UNESCO for its magnificent old-world architecture and atmosphere. You can reach this town on your way through **České Budějovice,** the hometown of the original Budweiser brand and a convenient rail base for exploring southern Bohemia.

1 Essentials

GETTING THERE

BY PLANE **CSA Czech Airlines** (**www.csa.cz/en**), the national airline offers flights to Prague from a number of U.S. cities, including New York, Atlanta, Chicago, Los Angeles, or Washington, D.C. From Canada, you can fly to Prague out of Toronto and Montreal.

To make a reservation call toll-free ✆ **800/223-2365** (NYC), ✆ **1-800/641-0641** (Toronto), or ✆ **00-440-870-4443-747** (London). For more information, call the nonstop call center in Prague ✆ **00-420-239-007-007.**

The only major U.S. airline that flies to Prague (though always with a stopover somewhere in Europe) is **Delta Airlines** (✆ **800/241-4141;** www.delta.com). Other airlines that service Prague out of Europe and that offer connecting services to several

⌒**Moments** **Festivals & Special Events**

The world famous **Prague Spring International Music Festival** is a 3-week series of classical music performances and concerts that usually takes place the last 3 weeks of May. Details on the festival can be found online at **www. festival.cz.** There is also an autumn version of the festival in September (**www.pragueautumn.cz**) with a similarly impressive mix of internationally recognized orchestras, conductors, and soloists.

After being banned during communism, **The Festival of the Five-Petaled Rose** in Český Krumlov has made a triumphant comeback and is now in its 22nd year. It's held each year on the summer solstice. Residents of Český Krumlov dress up in Renaissance costume and parade through the streets. Afterward, the streets become a stage with plays, chess games with people dressed as pieces, music, and even duels "to the death." Information is available online at **www.ckrumlov.cz.**

---

major U.S. airlines include **Lufthansa** (© **800/645-3880;** www.lufthansa.com) and **British Airways** (© **800/AIRWAYS;** www.ba.com).

All flights arrive in modern **Ruzyně Airport** (© **00-420/220-111-111;** www.csl.cz), which is 12 miles (19km) west of the city center. At the airport, you'll find currency exchange offices Travelex, Acron, or AVE (open daily 7am–9pm), telephones, and several car-rental offices.

THE CZECH REPUBLIC BY RAIL
PASSES
Note: The Czech Republic is not covered by the Eurail Global Pass, though the **European East Pass** and the **Austria–Czech Republic Railpass** (see chapter 2) are accepted. The Republic does have a country-specific pass option.

The **Czech Flexipass** pass entitles you to 3 to 8 nonconsecutive days of unlimited train travel in a 15-day period. It starts at $130 (£ 68.90) for first class and $90 (£ 47.70) for second class. The **Prague Excursion Pass** entitles you to one round-trip journey from any Czech border to Prague (your trip may not originate in Prague), and costs $104 (£ 55.10). Both passes should be purchased in North America before you leave on your trip. You can buy one on the phone or online from **Rail Europe** (© **877/272-RAIL** [7245] in North America; www.raileurope.com) or your travel agent.

FOREIGN TRAIN TERMS
In Prague, many of the international ticket window agents at the main train station will speak English. It may not be the most pleasant experience—Czech sales assistants in any trade tend to be surly—but you should get along fairly well.

As you get farther afield from Prague, you may not find such convenience, but with a little patience and a bit of preparation before you join the line, you should be able to be understood enough in English to get to where you want to go, and at the appropriate fare. Many destinations are often hard to pronounce, so be sure to write them down clearly on a piece of paper to show to the agent, or to circle your end station in this guide book or on a train timetable.

Note that you will see signs bearing the following terms in train terminals and major attractions: **Vchod** (entrance); **Východ** (exit); *Informace* (information); *Odjezd/Odlet* (Departures); and the all-important *Toalety* (restrooms).

PRACTICAL TRAIN INFORMATION

The train network in the Czech Republic is run by **Czech Railways (České Dráhy)**, which uses a number of trains of different quality. For a list of the trains, their abbreviations on timetables, and an explanation of their features, see "Train Designations in the Czech Republic," below. Ordinary passenger trains (marked Os for *osobní* on timetables) don't require reservations or supplements and offer first- and second-class seating. They are also slow as molasses and usually very uncomfortable—avoid them if you can. If you get stuck, splurge on first-class to make the trip as painless as possible.

The train network itself is pretty extensive and connects to a number of major cities in both Eastern and Western Europe. Major cities with InterCity or EuroCity connections to Prague include Vienna, Munich, Berlin, Budapest, and Warsaw. Locally, the routings are a little odd and getting to some of the country's smaller towns and out of the way spots is, as a result, often faster by bus. Stick to the major cities and towns we discuss in this chapter and you'll be fine. To find out about timetables of all connections within the Czech Republic and from/to abroad go to **www.jizdnirady.cz**.

RESERVATIONS   Reservations on Czech trains are mandatory only if an R surrounded by a box is listed on the timetable next to your departure, or if you are traveling on an SC train. That said, trains can get very crowded, and if you plan on traveling in high season or on weekends, make a reservation way in advance so you can assure yourself of a seat and avoid standing in lines in the station. Reservations on

Useful Czech Train & Travel Terms

Where is the . . . ?	**Kde je . . . ?**	*gde* yeh . . .
train station	**nádraží**	*nah*-drah-zhee
How much is the fare?	**Kolik je jízdné?**	*koh*-leek yeh yeesd-neh
I am going to . . .	**Pojedu do . . .**	*poh*-yeh-doo doh . . .
I would like a . . .	**Chci . . .**	khtsee . . .
one-way ticket	**Jízdenka**	*yeez*-den-kah
round-trip ticket	**Zpáteční jízdenka**	*zpah*-tech-nee *jeez-den*-kah
I'm looking for . . .	**Hledám . . .**	*hleh*-dahm . . .
the city center	**centrum**	*tsent*-room
the tourist office	**cestovní kancelář**	*tses*-tohv-nee *kahn*-tseh-larsh
Where is the nearest telephone?	**Kde je nejbližší telefon?**	gde yeh *nay*-bleesh-ee *tel*-oh-fohn
I would like to buy . . .	**Chci koupit . . .**	khtsee *koh*-peet . . .
a map	**mapu**	*mahp*-oo

Train Designations in the Czech Republic

Name	Abbreviation	Explanation
SuperCity	SC	Czech trains with a high standard of quality and consist of modernized first-class coaches only and a restaurant car. A reservation is necessary and special prices apply (see "Reservations" in this section for more on pricing).
EuroCity	EC	European trains that are guaranteed to meet an international standard. These have first- and second-class coaches and a restaurant car. A supplement is required and reservations are possible but not mandatory.
InterCity	IC	These trains offer a certain level of guaranteed quality, and have first- and second-class coaches, and a restaurant car. A supplement is required and reservations are possible but not mandatory.
Express	Ex *(EN)*	Express trains offer fast connections between selected Czech cities, and have first- and second-class coaches. Night trains are indicated by the letters *EN* in a timetable. Reservations are possible. There is no supplement.

express trains must be made at least 2 hours before departure and can be made inside almost all of the Republic's train stations. A reservation costs 30Kč ($1.40/70p). Note that reservations on local trains in the Czech Republic cannot be made in North America, though you can buy open tickets through Rail Europe.

Reservations for sleeper accommodations on night trains in the Czech Republic and on international night trains to and from Prague are a must. Reserve these as soon as you can (most international trains allow you to reserve up to 3 months in advance). You can reserve most international sleepers and couchettes through Rail Europe before you depart North America. Sleeper supplement prices are variable; a single couchette costs 462Kč ($22/£11).

Note: Even if you have a railpass of any type, you'll still have to pay a travel supplement of about 60Kč ($2.85/£1.45) one-way, when traveling on IC and EC trains.

You pay a fixed price for any route taken on an SC train, regardless of distance or time. The fee is 200Kč ($9.50/£4.75).

SERVICES & AMENITIES Generally, Czech trains do not have a very good reputation in terms of comfort and cleanness. They are old, lack most creature comforts, and run on old-style single tracks. That said, they still run pretty reliably and for reasonable prices. First-class travel (the only way to go) in the republic is far less expensive than in Western European countries.

Trains & Travel Times in Czech Republic

From	To	# of Trains	Frequency	Travel Time
Prague	Karlovy Vary	9	Daily	3 hr., 26 min.
Český Krumlov	České Budějovice	9	Daily	55 min.
Prague	České Budějovice	12	Daily	2 hr., 50 min.

Sleeping accommodations—ranging from simple couchettes to private single rooms—are available on long-haul trains within the Czech Republic and on international trains running through or terminating in Prague. Sleepers tend to be expensive (though often less than a hotel room) and the quality of the accommodations varies widely. *Warning:* Theft is common from couchette compartments, so if you opt for a couchette, keep a close eye on your belongings.

Restaurant cars are available on SC, EC, and IC trains. They are not available, however, on Express trains, so bring lots of food—and lots of bottled water. (Do not drink tap water on trains, or anywhere else for that matter.)

In Prague's main station, České Budějovice's station, and in other selected cities' train stations the Czech railways have a **"ČD center,"** providing complete services—reservations and ticket sales, timetable info, international train connections info, hotel booking, currency exchange, and so on. You also can check their website on **www.cd.cz**, where you will find timetable information and an on-line reservation service.

FAST FACTS: Czech Republic

Area Codes The **country code** for the Czech Republic is **420.** The **city codes** are connected to the local number in front so the entire 9-digit number must be dialed locally. For directory assistance in English and for information on services and rates calling abroad, dial ⓒ **1181.**

Business Hours Most **banks** are open Monday to Friday 8am to 6pm. Pubs are usually open daily 11am to midnight. Most restaurants are open for lunch 11am to 3pm and for dinner 6 to 11pm; only a few stay open later.

Climate Prague's average summer temperature is about 63°F (18°C), but some days can be quite chilly and others uncomfortably sultry. In winter, the temperature remains close to freezing. During an average January, it's sunny and clear for only 50 hours the entire month. Pollution, heaviest in the winter, tends to limit the snowfall in Prague, though the city's been blanketed for quite a long period of winter the last couple of years.

Currency The basic unit of currency is the koruna (plural, koruny) or crown, abbreviated Kč. Each koruna is divided into 100 haléřů or hellers. At this writing, $1 = approximately 21Kč or 1Kč = 4.7¢, and £1 = 42Kč.

Documents Required North American citizens need only passports and no visa for stays less than 90 days; passports must be valid for a period of at least 90 days beyond the expected length of stay in the Czech Republic. For more information, go to **www.czech.cz**.

Electricity Czech appliances operate on 220 volts and plug into two-pronged outlets that differ from those in America and the United Kingdom. Appliances designed for the U.S. or U.K. markets must use an adapter and a transformer.

Embassies The **U.S. Embassy** is at Tržiště 15, Praha 1 (© **257-022-000**). The **Canadian Embassy** is at Muchova 6, Praha 6 (© **272-101-800**).

Health & Safety You will likely feel safer in Prague than in most Western cities, but always take common-sense precautions. Don't walk alone at night around Wenceslas Square—one of the main areas for prostitution. All visitors should be watchful of pickpockets in heavily touristed areas, especially on Charles Bridge, in Old Town Square, and in front of the main station. Be wary in crowded buses, trams, and trains.

If you need any common medicine, you can purchase it from a pharmacist. Czech pharmacies are called *lékárna* and are recognized by a green cross on a white background. The most centrally located one is at Václavské nám. 8, Praha 1 (© **224-227-532**), open Monday to Friday from 8am to 6pm. If you need a doctor or dentist and your condition isn't life-threatening, you can visit the **Polyclinic at Národní,** Národní 9, Praha 1 (© **222-075-120;** for an emergency call mobile phone number © **720-427-634;** Metro: Můstek), during walk-in hours, from 8am to 5pm. For emergency medical aid, call the **Foreigners' Medical Clinic,** Na Homolce Hospital, Roentgenova 2, Praha 5 (© **257-272-174;** Metro: Anděl, then bus 167).

Holidays Official holidays are observed on January 1 (New Year's Day); Easter Monday; May 1 (Labor Day); May 8 (Liberation Day from Fascism); July 5 (Introduction of Christianity); July 6 (Death of Jan Hus); September 28 (St. Wenceslas Day); October 28 (Foundation of the Republic); November 17 (Day of student movement in 1939 and 1989); December 24 and 25 (Christmas); and December 26 (St. Stephen's Day). On these holidays, most business and shops (including food shops) are closed, and buses and trams run on Sunday schedules.

Mail Post offices are plentiful and are normally open Monday to Friday from 8am to 6pm. Mailboxes are orange and are usually attached to the side of buildings. If you're sending mail overseas, make sure it's marked "Par Avion" so it doesn't go by surface. If you mail your letters at a post office, the clerk will add this stamp for you. Mail can take up to 10 days to reach its destination. For a regular letter to a European country you need a 11Kč (52¢/26p) stamp, and you need a 12Kč (57¢/29p) stamp to send a regular letter to North America.

Police & Emergencies Dial the European emergency number © **112** from any phone in case of emergency. You can reach Prague's police and fire services by calling © **158** or **150.** For an ambulance call © **155.**

Telephone The **country code** for the Czech Republic is **420.** The **city codes** are connected to the local number in front so the entire number is dialed locally and has nine digits. For directory assistance in English and for information on services and rates for calling abroad, dial © **1181.**

There are two kinds of pay phones. One accepts coins and the other operates only with a phone card, available from post offices and newsdealers in denominations ranging from 50Kč to 500Kč ($2.40–$23.80/£1.20–£11.90). The minimum cost of a local call is 4Kč (15¢/7p) in coin-op phones. The more efficient phone card telephones deduct the price of your call from the card. If you're calling home, get a phone card with plenty of cash on it, as calls run about 20Kč (95¢) per minute to the United States. Charging to your phone credit card from a public telephone is often the most economical way to call home.

A fast, convenient way to call home from Europe is via services that bypass the foreign operator and automatically link you to an operator with your long-distance carrier in your home country. The access number in the Czech Republic for **AT&T USA Direct** is ✆ **00-800-222-55288,** for **MCI Call USA** ✆ **00-800-001-112.** Canadians can connect with **Canada Direct** at ✆ **00-800-001-115,** and Brits with **BT Direct** at ✆ **00-800-001-144.** From a pay phone in the Czech Republic, your local phone card will be debited only for a local call.

Tipping At most restaurants and pubs, locals just round the bill up to the nearest few crowns. When you're given good service at tablecloth places, a 10% tip is proper. Washroom and cloakroom attendants usually demand a couple of koruny, and porters in airports and rail stations usually receive 20Kč (95¢/45p) per bag. Taxi drivers should get about 10%, unless they've already ripped you off.

2 Prague

More than 80 years after native-son Franz Kafka's death, Prague's mix of the melancholy and the magnificent, set against some of Europe's most spectacular architecture, still confounds all who live or visit here. Its tightly wound brick paths have felt the hooves of kings' horses, the jackboots of Hitler's armies, the heaving tracks of Soviet tanks, and the shuffle of students in passive revolt. Fate tested the city once again in August 2002 when record floodwaters from the River Vltava engulfed much of Lesser Town and part of Old Town putting many restaurants and attractions near the riverfront out of business. But the city has recovered very quickly. The 6-centuries-old Charles Bridge is today jammed with visitors and venture capitalists looking for memories or profits from a once-captive city now enjoying yet another renaissance.

For the rail traveler, Prague is *the* city to visit in the Czech Republic—if you can visit only one place in the country, this is the one you want to see. It's also the one you most likely *will* see. The central hub for most of the country's trains, the city is also a convenient stop on rail routes heading from the west into Eastern Europe. It's about 5 hours by train from Berlin and Vienna, and 7 hours from Frankfurt and Budapest.

If the Czech Republic is the first stop on your rail trip, Prague is home to the only airport that serves direct flights from the U.S. And on the convenience front, though it's cheaper than many other European capitals, it's the most modern of the Eastern European cities, so you'll have access to most of the creature comforts of home, even while surrounded by centuries of medieval architecture. If your schedule allows it, plan on spending at least 2 days here, though you could spend more than a week and not discover all of the city's treasures.

STATION INFORMATION
GETTING FROM THE AIRPORT TO THE TRAIN STATION
Plenty of taxis line up in front of Ruzyně Airport (p. 164), but know that most drivers will try to take advantage of you and getting an honestly metered ride out of the

Prague

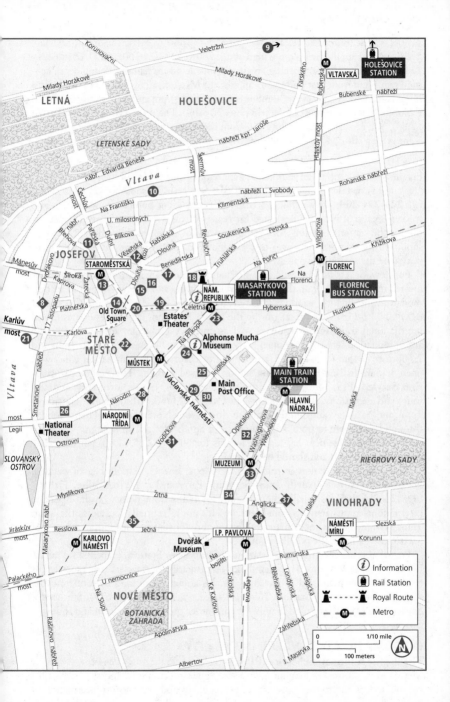

airport is next to impossible. The fare from the airport to Hlavní nádraží (the Main Train Station) should be no more than about 700Kč ($33/£16.60). **CEDAZ** (© 220-114-296; www.cedaz.cz) operates an airport shuttle bus to náměstí Republiky in central Prague and from that point you can take the Metro to all of Prague's train stations. It leaves the airport daily every 30 minutes from 6am to 9pm and stops near the náměstí Republiky Metro station (Line B; trip time: 30 min.). The shuttle costs 120Kč ($5.70/£2.85). You can also take **city bus 119** from the airport to the Dejvická Metro station (Line A) for 20Kč (95¢/45p; trip time: 60 min.).

INSIDE THE STATIONS

Prague has two central rail stations: Hlavní nádraží and Nádraží Holešovice.

Of the two, **Hlavní nádraží (Main Train Station),** Wilsonova třída 80, Praha 2 (© 224-224-200; www.cdrail.cz), is grander and more popular; however, it's also seedier because it has been neglected for years. At this writing, a massive reconstruction of the station's building complex is under way. It will be a lengthy process that should bring significant changes to the station's main hall interior as well as revitalization of the surrounding areas.

For now, tickets for domestic and international trains are available at the windows located in the main hall on the ground level. There are also several visitor and accommodation information windows situated in the main hall. Useful is the **ČD center** (© 840-112-113; www.cd.cz) run by the Czech Railways. It provides domestic and international **train information** as well as currency exchange, airline tickets, and accommodation services. It is open daily from 7am to 11am, 11:30am to 2pm, and 2:30pm to 5:45pm. Visa and MasterCard are accepted. An information window is open 3:15am to 12:40am (the train station is closed 1–3am). The **Prague Information Service (PIS)** office helps with accommodations, tickets for events, and city tours and excursions. It is open April to October Monday through Friday 9am to 7pm, and Saturday and Sunday 9am to 4pm; from November to March Monday through Friday 9am to 6pm and Saturday and Sunday from 9am to 5pm.

The station's basement has luggage lockers for 60Kč ($2.85/£1.40) per day. They aren't secure though and should be avoided.

The main train station is reachable by Metro line C, station Hlavní nádraží. **Nádraží Holešovice (North Train Station),** Partyzánská at Vrbenského, Praha 7 (© 224-615-865), is usually the terminus for trains from points north, especially international trains arriving from Germany. It's not as centrally located as the Main Train Station, but its more manageable size and convenient location at the end of Metro line C, make it a popular choice.

Prague also has two smaller rail stations. **Masarykovo Station,** Hybernská, Praha 1 (© 221-111-122; Metro: nám. Republiky), is primarily for travelers arriving on trains from other Bohemian and Moravian cities. It's about 10 minutes by foot from the main station. **Smíchov Station,** Nádražní ulice, Praha 5 (© 224-617-686; Metro: Smíchovské Nádraží), is used mainly for commuter trains from western and southern Bohemia.

INFORMATION ELSEWHERE IN THE CITY

The **Prague Information Service (PIS),** Rytířská 31, Praha 1 (© 12444; www.pis.cz; Metro: Můstek), makes lodging reservations, gives touring tips, and sells tickets for cultural events and tours. Its website offers regularly updated tourism information in

English. It's open April to October daily 9am to 7pm; November to March daily 9am to 6pm.

The city's **Cultural and Information Center,** on the ground floor of the Municipal House (Obecní dům), nám. Republiky 5, Praha 1 (© **222-002-101;** www.obecni dum.cz; Metro: nám. Republiky) offers advice, tickets, souvenirs, refreshments, and restrooms. It's open daily 9am to 7pm.

On the Web, the well-designed **www.czechsite.com** offers tips on getting around, attractions, museums, galleries, and restaurants. You can book your lodging on the site.

GETTING AROUND

In order to easily get around town, you'll first need a quick explanation of the city's layout. The River Vltava bisects Prague. **Staré Město (Old Town)** and **Nové Město (New Town)** are on the east (right) side of the river, while the **Hradčany (Castle District)** and **Malá Strana (Lesser Town)** are on the west (left) bank.

Bridges and squares are the most prominent landmarks. **Charles Bridge,** the oldest and most famous of those spanning the Vltava, is at the epicenter and connects Old Town with Lesser Town and the Castle District. Several important streets radiate from Old Town Square, including fashionable **Pařížská** to the northwest, historic **Celetná** to the east, and **Melantrichova,** connecting to Wenceslas Square (Václavské nám.) to the southeast. On the west side of Charles Bridge is **Mostecká,** a 3-block-long connection to **Malostranské náměstí,** Malá Strana's main square. **Hradčany,** the Castle District, is just northwest of the square, while a second hill, **Petřín,** is just southwest.

BY PUBLIC TRANSPORTATION   Prague's public transport network is a vast system of subways, trams, and buses. Adults can ride through a maximum of five stations on the Metro (not including the station of validation) or 20 minutes on a tram or bus, without transfers (on the Metro you can change from lines A, B, and C within 30 min.), for 14Kč (65¢/35p); children 6 to 15 years old ride for 7Kč (35¢/15p), those under 6 ride free. You usually won't need more than the maximum 5 stations for trips in the historic districts. Rides of more than five stops on the Metro, or longer tram or bus rides, with unlimited transfers for up to 75 minutes (90 min. Sat–Sun, public holidays, and after 10pm on weekdays) after your ticket is validated, cost 20Kč (95¢/45p). You can buy tickets from coin-operated orange machines in Metro stations or at most newsstands. Hold on to your ticket (which you must validate at the orange or yellow stamp clocks in each tram or bus when you get on board or at the entrance to the Metro) during your ride—you'll need it to prove you've paid if a ticket collector asks. If you're caught without a valid ticket, you have to pay a 500Kč ($23.80/ £11.90) fine to a ticket controller on the spot.

Tips Reading Maps

When reading maps or searching for addresses, keep in mind that *ulice* (abbreviated ul.) means "street," *třída* means "avenue," *náměstí* (abbreviated nám.) is a "square" or "plaza," a *most* is a "bridge," and *nábřeží* is a "quay." In Czech, none of these terms are capitalized. In addresses, street numbers usually follow the street name (like Václavské nám. 25). Each address is followed by a district number, such as Praha 1 (Praha is "Prague" in Czech).

Warning: Oversize luggage (larger than carry-on size) requires a transfer ticket for 10Kč (45¢/25) for each piece. You may be fined 50Kč ($2.40/£1.20) for not having tickets for your luggage. Also, beware the pickpockets common on the trams and metro.

Metro trains operate daily from 5am to midnight and run every 3 to 8 minutes. The most convenient stations are Můstek, at the foot of Václavské náměstí (Wenceslas Sq.); Staroměstská, for Old Town Square and Charles Bridge; and Malostranská, serving Malá Strana and the Castle District.

The electric **tramlines** run practically everywhere. You never have to hail trams; they make every stop. The most popular, **no. 22** and **no. 23,** run past top sights such as the National Theater and Prague Castle. Regular bus and tram service stops at midnight, after which selected routes run reduced schedules, usually only once per hour. If you miss a night connection, expect a long wait for the next bus.

Passes   You can purchase discounted transport passes for the public transport system. A 1-day pass good for unlimited rides is 80Kč ($3.80/£1.90); a 3-day pass 220Kč ($10.45/£5.20); a 7-day pass 280Kč ($13.35/£6.65); and a 15-day pass 320Kč ($15.25/£7.60). You can buy the day passes at the "DP" windows at any Metro station.

BY FUNICULAR   A cog railway makes the scenic run up and down Petřín Hill every 10 minutes or so from 9am to 11:30pm, with an intermediate stop at the Nebozízek Restaurant in the middle of the hill overlooking the city. It requires the same 20Kč (95¢/50p) ticket as other public transportation, and discounted transport passes are accepted. The funicular departs from a small house in the park just above the middle of Újezd in Malá Strana.

BY TAXI   *Avoid taxis!* If you must, hail one in the streets or in front of train stations, large hotels, and popular attractions, but be forewarned that many drivers simply gouge tourists. The best fare you can hope for is 25Kč ($1.20/60p) per kilometer, but twice or three times that isn't rare. The rates are usually posted on the dashboard, making it too late to haggle once you're in and on your way. Negotiate a price and have it written down before getting in. Better yet, go on foot or by public transport. Somewhat reputable companies with English-speaking dispatchers are **AAA Taxi** (© **140 14** or 222-333-222) and **SEDOP** (© **271-722-222**).

WHERE TO STAY

Prague's full-service hotels have had to tighten efficiency in the face of heavier international competition, but due to low supply, room rates still top those of many similar or better-quality hotels in Western Europe. Pensions with limited services are cheaper than hotels, but compared with similar western B&Bs, they're pricey. The best budget accommodations are rooms in private homes or apartments.

All kinds of private housing are offered by several local agencies. The leader now is Prague-based **E-TRAVEL.CZ,** which offers all types of accommodation at their main website, or you can tap their large pictured database of apartments at **www.apartments.cz**. The office is near the National Theater at Divadelní 24, Praha 1 (© **224-990-990;** www.travel.cz; Metro: Národní třída). Another agency, especially for those arriving late by train or air, is **AVE Travel Ltd.** (© **251-551-011;** www.avetravel.cz). It has an outlet at the airport (open 7am–10pm).

Andante *Value*   One of the best value choices near Wenceslas Square, the understated Andante is tucked away on a darker side street, about 2 blocks off the top of the square. Despite its less than appealing neighborhood (it's in the local red-light district), this is the most comfortable property in the moderate price range. The clean and comfortable guest rooms have been modernized.

Ve Smečkách 4, Praha 1. ℭ **222-210-021.** Fax 222-210-591. www.andante.cz. 32 units. 4,018Kč ($191/£95) double; 5,453Kč ($259/£129) suite. Rates include breakfast. AE, MC, V. Metro: Muzeum. **Amenities:** Restaurant; bar; laundry. *In room:* No A/C.

Hotel Cloister Inn ★ *Value*   Between Old Town Square and the National Theater (a 3-min. walk from the Charles Bridge), the Cloister Inn occupies a building that the secret police once used to hold prisoners. It sounds ominous, but it offers sparse, clean accommodations at an unbeatable price for the location. The hotel's owner has refurbished the property and installed comfortable Czech wooden furniture in the guest rooms.

Konviktská 4, Praha 1. ℭ **224-211-020.** Fax 224-210-800. www.cloister-inn.cz. 73 units with en suite showers. 3,100Kč-4,200Kč ($147–$200/£73–£100) double. Rates include breakfast. AE, MC, V. Metro: Národní třída. **Amenities:** Breakfast room, laundry. *In room:* Hair dryer.

Hotel Esplanade   Located on a side street at the top of Wenceslas Square and across from the Main Train Station, the Esplanade began life as a bank and the offices of an Italian insurance company. Rooms are bright and airy, some with standard beds, others with French provincial headboards, and others with extravagant canopies.

Washingtonova 19, Praha 1. ℭ **224-501-111.** Fax 224-229-306. www.esplanade.cz. 74 units. From 3,128Kč ($148/£74) double; from 5,711Kč ($271/£135) suite. Rates include breakfast. AE, MC, V. Metro: Muzeum. **Amenities:** Restaurant; cafe; bar; laundry. *In room:* Hair dryer.

Hotel Meran *Value*   This used to be part of Hotel Evropa, the bigger Art Deco landmark that draws so much attention to its gilded facade. The family-run and cozier Meran has had a face-lift to make it a fair midrange choice on Wenceslas Square, within walking distance of the Main Train Station. The lobby interior has retained some original Art Nouveau accents, although the furnishings in the spotless rooms have few.

Václavské nám. 27, Praha 1. ℭ **222-244-373.** Fax 224-23-411. www.hotelmeran.cz. 20 units. 3,950Kč ($188/£94) double. Rates include breakfast. AE, DC, MC, V. Metro: Muzeum or Můstek. **Amenities:** Concierge; exchange. *In room:* Hair dryer.

Hotel Paříž ★★   At the edge of náměstí Republiky (very close to the Metro) and across from the Municipal House, the Paříž provides a rare glimpse back into the gilded First Republic. Each light fixture, etching, and curve at this Art Nouveau landmark recalls the days when Prague was one of the world's richest cities. For a glimpse of the hotel's atmosphere, rent the film *Mission Impossible;* you can see Tom Cruise plotting his revenge from within one of the fine suites. The high-ceilinged guest rooms are comfortable, with modern Art Deco accents.

U Obecního domu 1, Praha 1. ℭ **222-195-195.** Fax 222-195-907. www.hotel-pariz.cz. 94 units. 4,800Kč ($228/£114) double; from 8,400Kč ($400/£200) suite. Rates include breakfast. AE, DC, MC, V. Metro: nám. Republiky. **Amenities:** Restaurant; cafe; relaxation club, laundry. *In room:* Hair dryer.

Hotel Ungelt   It's not very opulent, but the Ungelt offers airy, spacious suites. Each contains a living room, a full kitchen, and a bathroom. Rooms have standard-issue beds; some have hand-painted ceilings. The Old Town Square is just around the corner and the train station is less than half a mile away.

Štupartská 1, Praha 1. ℭ **224-828-686.** Fax 224-828-181. www.ungelt.cz. 10 units. From 4,075Kč ($194/£97) 1-bedroom suite for 2; 5,740Kč ($273/£136) 2-bedroom suite for 1 or 2. Rates include breakfast. AE, MC, V. Metro: Staroměstská or nám. Republiky. **Amenities:** Bar; laundry. *In room:* Hair dryer.

Palace Hotel ⌖   The Palace is a top, upscale property, a block from Wenceslas Square and within walking distance of the Main Train Station, although I think the nearby Paříž (see above) has far more character. The 1903 Art Deco property is nevertheless a favorite with visiting celebrities (from Caruso to Steven Spielberg) and offers excellent service. Guest rooms are some of the largest and most modern luxury accommodations in Prague, each with an Italian marble bathroom.

Panská 12, Praha 1. ⓒ **224-093-111.** Fax 224-221-240. www.palacehotel.cz. 124 units. from 6,084Kč ($289/£144) double; from 7,462Kč ($355/£177) suite. Rates include breakfast. AE, DC, MC, V. Metro: Můstek. **Amenities:** 2 restaurants; 2 lounges; laundry; 2 rooms for those w/limited mobility. *In room:* A/C, hair dryer.

U Krále Karla ⌖   This Castle Hill property does so much to drive home its Renaissance roots, King Charles's heirs should be getting royalties. Replete with period-print, open-beamed ceilings and stained-glass windows, the atmosphere is almost Disneyesque in its pretense, but somehow appropriate for this location at the foot of Prague Castle. This is a fun, comfortable choice, with heavy period furniture and colorful angelic accents everywhere, though it is pretty far from a train station.

Nerudova-Úvoz 4, Praha 1. ⓒ **257-533-594.** Fax 257-533-591. www.romantichotels.cz. 19 units. 5,500Kč ($261/£130) double; 7,900Kč ($376/£188) suite. Rates include breakfast. AE, MC, V. Tram: 22 or 23 to Malostranské nám. **Amenities:** Restaurant; cafe; bar; laundry. *In room:* Hair dryer.

TOP ATTRACTIONS & SPECIAL MOMENTS

Most of Prague's special features are best viewed while slowly wandering through the city's heart. Except for the busy main streets, where you may have to dodge traffic, Prague is ideal for walking. Actually, walking is really the only way to explore Prague. Most of the town's oldest areas are pedestrian zones, with motor traffic restricted. If you have the time and energy, absorb the grand architecture of Prague Castle and the Old Town skyline (best from Charles Bridge) at sunrise and then at sunset. You'll see two completely different cities.

Prague Castle (Pražský Hrad) ⌖⌖⌖ *Moments*   The huge hilltop complex known collectively as Pražský Hrad encompasses dozens of towers, churches, courtyards, and monuments. A visit could easily take an entire day or more. Still, you can see the top sights in the space of a morning or an afternoon. Make sure not to miss **St. Vitus Cathedral (Chrám sv. Víta)** ⌖ constructed in A.D. 926 as the court church of the Premyslid princes. It was named for a wealthy 4th-century Sicilian martyr and has long been the center of Prague's religious and political life. The cathedral's architecture is a mix of Gothic, baroque, and neo-Gothic elements.

The **Royal Palace (Královský palác)** ⌖, in the third courtyard of the castle grounds, served as the residence of kings between the 10th and the 17th centuries. Vaulted Vladislav Hall, the interior's centerpiece, was used for coronations and is still used for the inauguration of the Czech presidents and special occasions. You'll find a

---

⌒*Tips*   **Prague in a Day**

If you are doing a quick stopover in Prague and have only 1 day to see the city, do what visiting kings and potentates do on a short visit: Walk the **Royal Route** from the top of the Hradčany hill (tram 22 or 23 or a taxi is suggested for the ride up unless you're very fit). Tour **Prague Castle,** and then stroll across Charles Bridge on the way to the winding alleys of **Old Town (Staré Město).**

good selection of guidebooks, maps, and other related information at the entrance. Other must-sees include **St. George's Basilica (Kostel sv. Jiří)**, which houses a museum of historic Czech art; **Golden Lane (Zlatá ulička)**, a picturesque, fairy-tale street of tiny 16th-century servants' houses; and the **Powder Tower (Prašná věž,** aka Mihulka), a laboratory for the 17th-century alchemists serving the court of Emperor Rudolf II.

Tickets are sold at the **Prague Castle Information Center** (© 224-373-368), in the third courtyard after passing through the main gate from Hradčanské náměstí. The center also arranges tours in various languages and sells tickets for individual concerts and exhibits.

Hradčanské nám., Hradčany, Praha 1. © 224-373-368. Fax 224-310-896. www.hrad.cz. Grounds free. Combination ticket for tour to 5 main attractions (St. Vitus Cathedral, Royal Palace, St. George's Basilica, Powder Tower, Golden Lane) 350Kč ($16.65/£8.35) adults, 175Kč ($8.35/£4.15) students without guide; English-speaking guide 100Kč ($4.75/£2.40) per person and hour (4 hr. minimum). Guided tours Tues–Sun 9am–4pm. V. Ticket valid 2 days, can be reserved by e-mailing tourist.info@hrad.cz. Castle open daily 9am–6pm (to 4pm Nov–Mar), gardens daily 10am–6pm (Apr–Oct only). Metro: Malostranská, then tram 22 or 23, up the hill 2 stops.

THE JEWISH MUSEUM

The Jewish Museum manages all the Jewish landmarks in Josefov, the Jewish Quarter, which is the northwest quarter of Old Town. The museum offers guided package tours with an English-speaking guide as part of a comprehensive admission price. The package includes the Ceremonial Hall, Old Jewish Cemetery, Pinkas Synagogue, Klaus Synagogue, Maisel Synagogue, and Spanish Synagogue.

Maisel Synagogue   Maisel Synagogue is used as the exhibition space for the Jewish Museum. Most of Prague's ancient Judaica was destroyed by the Nazis during World War II. Ironically, those same Germans constructed an "exotic museum of an extinct race," thus salvaging thousands of objects, such as the valued Torah covers, books, and silver now displayed here.

Maiselova 10 (between Široká and Jáchymova 3), Praha 1. © 222-317-191. Fax 222-317-181. www.jewishmuseum.cz. Admission to museum sites listed above is 290Kč ($13.80/£6.90) adults, 190Kč ($9.05/£4.50) students. Apr–Oct tours for groups of 10 or more on the hour starting 9am (last tour 5pm). Nov–Apr tours leave whenever enough people gather in the same language, open 9am–4:30pm Sun–Fri. Metro: Staroměstská.

Old Jewish Cemetery (Starý židovský hřbitov) ⋇   Dating from the mid–15th century and a block away from the Old-New Synagogue, this is one of Europe's oldest Jewish burial grounds. It's also one of the most crowded because the city restricted Jewish burials—a 1-block zone is filled with more than 20,000 graves. The most renowned occupant: Rabbi Yehuda Loew (d. 1609), also known as the Maharal, who created the legendary Golem (clay creature) to protect the Jews of Prague.

U Starého hřbitova 3A. © 222-317-191. Fax 222-317-181. www.jewishmuseum.cz. Admission to all Jewish Museum sites 290Kč ($13.80/£6.90) adults, 190Kč ($9.05/£4.50) students. Apr–Oct Sun–Fri 9am–6pm; Nov–Mar Sun–Fri 9am–4:30pm. Metro: Staroměstská.

Old-New Synagogue (Staronová synagoga) ⋇   First called the New Synagogue to distinguish it from an even older one that no longer exists, the Gothic-style Old-New Synagogue, built around 1270, is Europe's oldest Jewish house of worship. Note that this is the one site in Josefov not included in the Jewish Museum tour package.

Červená 3. © 222-317-191. Admission 200Kč ($9.50/£4.75) adults, 140Kč ($6.65/£3.35) students. Sun–Thurs 9am–6pm; Fri 9am–5pm. Metro: Staroměstská.

Moments Charles Bridge

Dating from the 14th century, the **Charles Bridge (Karlův most)** ✶✶✶, Prague's most celebrated structure, links Prague Castle to Staré Město. For most of its 600 years, the 1,700-foot (510m) span has been a pedestrian promenade, although for centuries walkers had to share the concourse with horse-drawn vehicles and trolleys. Today, the bridge is filled with hordes walking among folksy artists and street musicians. Strolling the bridge is a quintessential Prague experience and should not be missed.

THE NATIONAL GALLERY

The national collection of fine art is grouped for display in the series of venues known collectively as the **National Gallery (Národní Galerie; www.ngprague.cz)**. *Tip:* Admission to all of the National Gallery's exhibits is free from 3pm to 8pm on the first Wednesday of every month.

St. Agnes Convent (Klášter sv. Anežky české)   This complex of early Gothic buildings and churches dates from the 13th century. The convent, tucked in a corner of Staré Město, is appropriately home to a collection of medieval and Renaissance art.

U milosrdných 17, Praha 1. ✆ **224-810-628.** Admission 100Kč ($4.75/£2.40) adults, 50Kč ($2.40/£1.20) children; 50Kč ($2.40/£1.20) adults, 30Kč ($1.40/70p) children after 4pm. Tues–Sun 10am–6pm. Metro: Staroměstská.

Šternberk Palace (Šternberský palác) ✶   The jewel in the National Gallery crown, the gallery at Šternberk Palace, adjacent to the main gate of Prague Castle, was overhauled in 2002–03. It now has an exhibition of ancient Greek and Roman art, though the primary collection still features European artworks from the 14th through the 18th centuries. You'll find small sculptures mixed along with Renaissance oils from Dutch masters. Pieces by Rembrandt, El Greco, Goya, Dürer, and Van Dyck are mixed among numerous pieces from Austrian imperial-court painters.

Hradčanské nám. 15, Praha 1. ✆ **233-090-570.** Admission 130Kč ($6.20/£3) adults, 60Kč ($2.85/£1.40) students and children; 80Kč ($3.80/£1.90) adults, 40Kč ($1.90/95p) students and children after 4pm. Tues–Sun 10am–6pm. Metro: Malostranská or Hradčanská; tram: 22 or 23.

St. George's Convent at Prague Castle (Klášter sv. Jiří na Pražském hradě)   Dedicated to displaying traditional Czech art, the castle convent is especially packed with Gothic and baroque Bohemian iconography as well as portraits of patron saints. The most famous among the unique collection of Czech Gothic panel paintings are those by the master of the Hohenfurth Altarpiece and the master Theodoricus. There's also a noteworthy collection of Czech Mannerist and baroque paintings from the 17th and 18th centuries.

Jiřské nám. 33. ✆ **257-531-644.** Admission 130Kč ($6.20/£3) adults, 60Kč ($2.85/£1.40) students; 80Kč ($3.80/£1.90) adults, 40Kč ($1.90/95p) students and children after 4pm. Daily 10am–6pm. Metro: Malostranská or Hradčanská; tram: 22 or 23.

Kinský Palace (Palác Kinských) ✶   This rococo palace houses graphic works from the National Gallery collection, including pieces by Georges Braque, André Derain, and other modern masters. Good quality international exhibits have included Max Ernst and Rembrandt retrospectives.

Staroměstské nám. 12, Praha 1. © **224-810-758**. Admission 100Kč ($4.75/£2.40) adults, 50Kč ($2.40/£1.20) children; 50Kč ($2.40/£1.20) adults, 30Kč ($1.40/70p) children after 4pm. Tues–Sun 10am–6pm. Metro: Line A to Staroměstská.

Veletržní Palace   This 1925 constructivist palace, built for trade fairs, holds the bulk of the National Gallery's collection of 20th- and 21st-century works by Czech and other European artists. Three atrium-lit concourses provide a comfortable setting for some catchy and kitschy Czech sculpture and multimedia works. Alas, the best cubist works from Braque and Picasso, Rodin bronzes, and many other primarily French pieces have been relegated to the second floor; the museum's 19th-century collection is here as well.

Veletržní at Dukelských hrdinů 47, Praha 7. © **224-301-111**. Admission 160Kč ($7.60/£3.80) adults, 80Kč ($3.80/£1.90) students; 100Kč ($4.75/£2.40) adults, 50Kč ($2.40/£1.20) children after 4pm. Tues–Sun 10am–6pm. Metro: Vltavská or tram 5, 12, or 17 to Veletržní stop.

FAMOUS SQUARES
The most celebrated square, **Old Town Square (Staroměstské nám.),** is surrounded by baroque buildings and packed with colorful craftspeople, cafes, and entertainers. In ancient days, the site was a major crossroad on central European merchant routes. In its center stands a memorial to Jan Hus, the 15th-century martyr who crusaded against Prague's German-dominated religious and political establishment. Unveiled in 1915, on the 500th anniversary of Hus's execution, the monument's most compelling features are the asymmetry of the composition and the fluidity of the figures.

The **Astronomical Clock (orloj)** at **Old Town Hall (Staroměstská radnice)** performs a glockenspiel spectacle daily on the hour from 8am to 8pm. Originally constructed in 1410, the clock has long been an important symbol of Prague. **Wenceslas Square (Václavské nám.),** a former horse market, has been the focal point of riots, revolutions, and national celebrations.

MORE ATTRACTIONS
Cathedral of St. Nicholas (Chrám sv. Mikuláše) ★ (Moments)   This church is critically regarded as one of the best examples of the high baroque north of the Alps. K. I. Dienzenhofer's 1711 design was augmented by his son Kryštof's 260-foot (78m) dome, which has dominated the Malá Strana skyline since its completion in 1752. Prague's smog has played havoc with the building's exterior, but its gilded interior is stunning. Gold-capped marble-veneered columns frame altars packed with statuary and frescoes.

Malostranské nám., Praha 1. © **257-534-215**. Free admission. Daily 9am–5pm, concerts are usually held at 6pm. Metro: Malostranská, then tram 12, 22, or 23 one stop to Malostranské nám.

PARKS & GARDENS
From **Vyšehrad,** Soběslavova 1 (© **224-920-735;** tram 3 from Karlovo nám. to Výtoň south of New Town), legend has it that Princess Libuše looked out over the Vltava valley toward the present-day Prague Castle and predicted the founding of a great state and capital city. Vyšehrad was the seat of the first Czech kings of the Premyslid dynasty before the dawn of this millennium. Today, within the confines of the citadel, lush lawns and gardens are crisscrossed by dozens of paths, leading to historic buildings and cemeteries. From here you'll see one of the city's most panoramic views.

The **Royal Garden (Královská zahrada)** at Prague Castle, once the site of the sovereigns' vineyards, was founded in 1534. Dotted with lemon trees and surrounded by

16th-, 17th-, and 18th-century buildings, the park is laid out with abundant shrub-bery and fountains. Enter from U Prašného mostu street north of the castle complex.

In Hradčany, the **Garden on the Ramparts (Zahrada na Valech),** a park below the castle with a gorgeous city panorama, was reopened in spring 1995 after being thor-oughly refurbished. Open daily 10am to 6pm (Apr–Oct only).

WHERE TO DINE

The true Czech dining experience can be summed up in three native words: *vepřo-knedlo-zelo*—pork, dumplings, and cabbage. If that's what you want, try most any *hostinec* (Czech pub). Most offer a hearty *guláš* or pork dish with dumplings and cab-bage for about 80Kč to 150Kč ($3.80–$7.15/£1.90–£3.55). After you wash it down with Czech beer, you won't care about the taste—or your arteries.

Menu prices include VAT. Tipping has become more commonplace in restaurants where the staff is obviously trying harder; rounding up the bill to about 10% or more is usually adequate.

Warning: Some restaurants gouge customers by charging exorbitant amounts for nuts or other seemingly free premeal snacks left on your table. Ask before you eat.

Bohemia Bagel *(Value* BAGELS/SANDWICHES The roster of golden-brown, hand-rolled, stone-baked bagels at these restaurants (the original one at the base of Petřín Hill, one near the Jewish Quarter at Masná 1, and one near Charles Bridge at Lázeňská 19), is stellar. Plain, cinnamon raisin, garlic, or onion provides a sturdy but tender frame for Scandinavian lox and cream cheese or jalapeño-cheddar cheese (on which you can lop Tex-Mex chili for the Sloppy Bagel).

Újezd 16, Praha 1. ✆ 257-310-831. www.bohemiabagel.cz. Bagels, sandwiches, and wraps 30Kč–169Kč ($1.40–$8/70p–£4). No credit cards. Daily 9am–midnight. Tram: 6, 9, 12, 22, or 23 to Újezd.

Bonante Restaurant INTERNATIONAL Our favorite choice above Wenceslas Square in Vinohrady, it is one of the best values in Prague and especially great for shunning the cold of an autumn or winter evening near the roaring fire in the brick cellar dining room. Bonante is a bridge between Italian cuisine and other continental foods. There are also vegetarian and low-calorie, chicken-based selections. Jazz com-bos play on some nights from a small stage in the corner.

Anglická 15, Praha 2. ✆ 224-221-665. www.bonante.cz. Reservations recommended. Main courses 105Kč–295Kč ($5–$14/£2.50–£7). AE, MC, V. Daily 11am–11pm. Metro: I. P. Pavlova or nám. Míru.

Café-Restaurant Louvre CZECH/INTERNATIONAL This big, breezy upstairs dining hall in New Town is great for a coffee, an inexpensive pre-theater meal, or an upscale game of pool. A fabulous Art Nouveau interior with huge original chandeliers buzzes with shoppers, businessmen, and students. Main dishes range from Czech beef goulash to grilled salmon steak. Avoid the always-overcooked pastas and stick to the basic meats and fish. In the snazzy billiards parlor in back, you can have drinks or a light meal.

Národní třída 20, Praha 1. ✆ 224-930-949. www.cafelouvre.cz (for reservations). Main courses 99Kč–499Kč ($4.70–$23.75/£2.35–£11.90); breakfast menu 39Kč–249Kč ($1.85–$11.85/90p–£5.90). AE, DC, MC, V. Mon–Sat 8am–11:30pm; Sun 9am–11:30pm. Metro: Národní třída.

Creperie Café Gallery Restaurant *(Value* FRENCH This convenient and afford-able French eatery rests at the foot of Charles Bridge on the Old Town side. Occupy-ing a wing of the St. Francis church complex, the Creperie creates the feel of a cozy farmhouse with old wooden chairs and hand-stitched pillows thrown on sturdy benches. The savory galettes are filled with spinach, tangy niva cheese, or chicken and make a good light lunch after a heavy morning of trudging. The sweet crepes with chocolate, fruit compote, or whipped cream are good for an afternoon break or for dessert following an evening stroll across the bridge.

Křížovnické nám. 3, Praha 1. ✆ 221-108-240. Reservations accepted. Crepes and galettes 75Kč–129Kč ($3.55–$6.15/£1.80–£3). AE, MC, V. Daily 10am–midnight. Metro: Staroměstská.

Hergetova Cihelna ✰✰ INTERNATIONAL/PIZZA   Set inside a much-renovated 18th-century former brick factory *(cihelna)*, this dining complex consists of a restaurant, cocktail bar, cafe, and music lounge. One of Prague's top dining experiences, it's worth a splurge. The food is good; we enjoyed their homemade pizza quattro stagioni and Czech goulash served with herbed gnocchi. From the large summer terrace you'll get an exciting and unforgettable view of the river and Charles Bridge.

Cihelná 2b, Praha 1. ✆ 296-826-103. www.cihelna.com. Reservations accepted on website. Main courses 295Kč–695Kč ($14–$33/£7–£16.55). AE, MC, V. Daily 11:30am–1am. Metro: Malostranská.

Kogo ✰✰ *(Value)* ITALIAN   This ristorante-pizzeria in the middle of Old Town is very trendy and popular. Fresh and well-prepared salads, pizza, pasta, and Italian specialties are served by an above-average waitstaff in a pleasant atmosphere. Beyond the standard and tasty pasta roster, the roasted veal is a good choice or try the rare (for Prague) tasty mussels in white wine and garlic.

A second Kogo restaurant is located at Na Příkopě 22, Praha 1 (✆ **221-451-259;** Metro: Můstek).

Havelská 27, Praha 1. ✆ 224-214-543. www.kogo.cz. Reservations recommended. Main courses 190Kč–448Kč ($9–$21.35/£4.50–£10.65). AE, MC, V. Mon–Fri 8am–11pm, Sat–Sun 9am–11pm(Havelská). Daily 11am–11pm(Na Příkopě). Metro: Můstek.

Osmička ✰ *(Value)* *(Kids)* CZECH/INTERNATIONAL   At first sight, the "Number 8" reveals a tourist-geared cellar restaurant with tawny eclectic colors, local art for sale on the walls, and a menu dominated by Italian standbys, fresh salads, and a variety of sandwiches. But once a Czech sits down, he or she quickly recognizes the neighborhood secret: This is still a good ol' Bohemian *hospoda* (pub) with *vepřo-knedlo-zelo* and other indigenous fare at local prices—all of it served on new solid wood furniture by a nicer-than-normal staff. If you're staying in Vinohrady, Osmička should be on your itinerary. Look closely for the dark metal triangle marking the location, next to one of the only golf pro shops in town.

Balbínova 8, Praha 2. ✆ 222-826-888. Main courses 54Kč–328Kč ($2.60–$15.60/£1.30–£7.80). MC, V. Mon–Sat 11am–midnight; Sun noon–midnight. Metro: I. P. Pavlova or Náměstí Míru.

Pizzeria Rugantino ✰ PIZZA   This restaurant's wood-fired stoves and handmade dough result in a crisp, delicate crust, a perfect platform for a multitude of cheeses, vegetables, and meats. The Diabolo with fresh garlic bits and very hot chiles goes nicely with a cool iceberg salad and a pull of Czech Bernard beer. The constant buzz, nonsmoking area, and heavy childproof wooden tables make this place near the Jewish quarter a family favorite. More spacious Rugantino II was opened at Klimentská 40, Praha 1 (✆ **224-815-192;** Metro: Florenc or Nám. Republiky) with a children's corner and plasma TV.

Dušní 4, Praha 1. ✆ 222-318-172. www.rugantino.cz. Individual pizzas 80Kč–225Kč ($3.80–$10.70/£1.90–£5.35). No credit cards. Mon–Sat 11am–11pm; Sun 5–11pm. Metro: Staroměstská.

Moments   Kavárna Society

Cafe life is back in a big way in Prague. From dissident blues to high society, these are the places where nonpub Praguers spend their afternoons and evenings, sipping coffee and smoking cigarettes while reading, writing, or talking with friends.

The **Kavárna (Cafe) Slavia** ✿, Národní at Smetanovo nábřeží 2, Praha 1 (© **224-218-493**; Metro: Národní třída), reopened in 1997, after a half-decade sleep. The restored crisp Art Deco room recalls the Slavia's 100 years as the meeting place for the city's cultural and intellectual crowd. You'll still find a relatively affordable menu of light fare served with the riverfront views of Prague Castle and the National Theater. Reservations are possible on **www.cafeslavia.cz**. It's open daily 8am to 11pm.

The biggest draw of the **Grand Café**, Staroměstské nám. 22, Praha 1 (© **221-632-520**; Metro: Staroměstská), is a great view of the Orloj, the astronomical clock with the hourly parade of saints on the side of Old Town Square's city hall. It's open daily 10am to midnight.

Of all the beautifully restored spaces in the Municipal House, the **Kavárna Obecní dům** ✿, nám. Republiky 5, Praha 1 (© **222-002-763**; Metro: nám. Republiky), might be its most spectacular room. Lofty ceilings, marble accents and tables, an altarlike mantel, huge windows, and period chandeliers provide the awesome setting for coffees, teas, and other drinks, along with pastries and light sandwiches. It's open daily 7:30am to 11pm.

A New Age alternative to the clatter of the kavárnas is **Dahab** ✿✿, Dlouhá 33, Praha 1 (© **224-827-375**; Metro: nám. Republiky). This tearoom was founded by Prague's king of tea, Luboš Rychvalský, who introduced Prague to Eastern and Arabic tea cultures soon after the 1989 revolution. Here you can choose from about 20 varieties of tea and more than 10 kinds of coffee. Arabic soups, hummus, tahini, couscous, pita, and tempting sweets are also on the menu. It's open daily from noon to 1am.

Radost FX ✿✿ Value VEGETARIAN   In vogue and vegetarian, Radost is a clubhouse for hip New Bohemians that's a short walk from the Main Train Station. The veggie burger is well seasoned and substantial on a grain bun, and the soups, such as lentil and onion, are light and full of flavor. The dining area is a dark rec room of upholstered armchairs, chaise lounges, couches from the 1960s, and coffee tables on which you eat. It serves as an art gallery and cafe as well.

Bělehradská 120, Praha 2. © 224-254-776. www.radostfx.cz. Main courses 60Kč–285Kč ($2.85–$13.55/£1.40–£6.80). MC, V. Daily 11am–5am. Metro: I. P. Pavlova.

Restaurant U Čížků ✿ Value CZECH   One of the city's first private restaurants, this cozy cellar-cum-hunting lodge on Charles Square is still an excellent value. The fare is purely Czech, and the massive portions of game, smoked pork, and other meats will stay with you for a while. The traditional *Staročeský talíř* (local pork meat, dumplings, and cabbage) is about as authentic Czech as it gets.

Karlovo nám. 34, Praha 2. ☎ **222-232-257**. www.restaurantucizku.cz. Reservations recommended. Main courses 120Kč–290Kč ($5.71–$13.80/£2.85–£6.90). AE, MC, V. Daily 11am–10:30pm.

U medvídků ★★ CZECH   Bright and noisy, the House at the Little Bears serves a better-than-average *vepřo-knedlo-zelo*. The pub, on the right after entering, is much cheaper and livelier than the bar to the left. It's a hangout for locals, German tour groups, and foreign journalists in search of the original Czech Budweiser beer, Budvar. In high season, an oompah band plays in the beer wagon.

Na Perštýně 7, Praha 1. ☎ **224-211-916**. www.umedvidku.cz. Main courses 99Kč–290Kč ($4.70–$13.80/£2.35–£6.90). AE, MC, V. Daily 11am–11pm. Metro: Národní třída.

SHOPPING

Czech porcelain, glass, and cheap but well-constructed clothing draw hordes of day-trippers from Germany. Private retailers have been allowed to operate here only since late 1989, but many top international retailers have already arrived. Shops lining the main route from Old Town Square to Charles Bridge are also great for browsing. For clothing, porcelain, jewelry, garnets, and glass, stroll around Wenceslas Square and Na Příkopě, connecting Wenceslas Square with náměstí Republiky.

For glass and crystal, try **Moser,** at Na Příkopě 12, Praha 1 (☎ **224-211-293**; Metro: Můstek), or at Malé nám. 11, Praha 1 (☎ **224-222-012**; Metro: Můstek). The Moser family began selling Bohemia's finest crystal in central Prague in 1857, drawing customers from around the world. It's open from Monday to Friday 10am to 8pm, Saturday and Sunday 10am to 7pm.

Celetná Crystal, Celetná 15, Praha 1 (☎ **222-324-022**; Metro: nám. Republiky), has a wide selection of world-renowned Czech crystal, china, arts and crafts, and jewelry displayed in a spacious three-floor showroom right in the heart of Prague. At **Cristallino,** Celetná 12, Praha 1 (☎ **224-225-173**; Metro: nám. Republiky), you'll find a good selection of stemware and vases in traditional designs. The shop's central location belies its excellent prices.

Havelský trh (Havel's Market), Havelská ulice, Praha 1 (Metro: Můstek), is on a short street running perpendicular to Melantrichova, the main route connecting Staroměstské náměstí with Václavské náměstí. This open-air market (named well before Havel became president in 1989) features dozens of private vendors selling seasonal homegrown fruits and vegetables. Other goods, including flowers and cheese, are also for sale. Since this place is designed primarily for locals, the prices are exceedingly low by Western European standards. The market is open Monday to Friday 7am to 6pm.

NIGHTLIFE

Prague's nightlife has changed completely since the Velvet Revolution—for the better if you plan to go clubbing, for the worse if you hope to sample the city's classical offerings. Still, seeing *Don Giovanni* in the Estates' Theater, where Mozart first premiered it, is worth the admission cost. Ticket prices, while low by Western standards, have become prohibitively high for the average Czech. You'll find, however, the exact reverse in the rock and jazz scene. Dozens of clubs have opened, and world-class bands are finally adding Prague to their European tours.

Turn to the *Prague Post* (www.praguepost.cz) for listings of cultural events and nightlife around the city; it's available at most newsstands in Old Town and Malá Strana. Once in Prague, you can buy tickets at theater box offices or from any one of dozens of agencies throughout the city center. Large, centrally located agencies (take the Metro to Můstek for all) are the **Prague Tourist Center,** Rytířská 12, Praha 1 (© **224-212-209**), open daily 9am to 8pm; **Bohemia Ticket International,** Na Příkopě 16, Praha 1 (© **224-215-031**); and **Čedok,** Na Příkopě 18, Praha 1 (© **224-197-640**).

THE PERFORMING ARTS Although there's plenty of music year-round, the symphonies and orchestras all come to life during the **Prague Spring Music Festival** (see "Festivals & Special Events," on p. 164). Tickets for festival concerts run from 250Kč to 2,000Kč ($11.90–$95/£5.95–£47.50).

The **Czech Philharmonic** and **Prague Symphony** orchestras usually perform at the **Rudolfinum,** náměstí Jana Palacha, Praha 1 (© **227-059-227;** Metro: Staroměstská). The Czech Philharmonic is the traditional voice of the country's national pride, often playing works by native sons Dvořák and Smetana; the Prague Symphony ventures into more eclectic territory. Tickets are 40Kč to 600Kč ($1.90–$28.50/95p–£14.30). Ticket orders and purchases can be made in advance (and you are advised to book well in advance) through the agencies listed above. Any remaining tickets are sold at the venues of the performances, which have various opening hours, but few seats usually remain within a month of the festival.

In a city full of spectacularly beautiful theaters, the massive pale-green **Estates' Theater** (Stavovské divadlo), Ovocný trh 1, Praha 1 (© **224-901-448;** Metro: Můstek), is one of the most awesome. Built in 1783 and the site of the premiere of Mozart's *Don Giovanni* (conducted by the composer), the theater now hosts many of the classic productions of European opera and drama. Simultaneous English translation, transmitted via headphone, is available for most performances. Tickets cost 30Kč to 1,000Kč ($1.40–$47.60/70p–£23.80). Lavishly constructed in the late-Renaissance style of northern Italy, the gold-crowned **Národní divadlo (National Theater),** Národní třída 2, Praha 1 (© **224-901-448;** Metro: Národní třída), overlooking the Vltava River, is one of Prague's most recognizable landmarks. Completed in 1881, the theater was built to nurture the Czech National Revival—a grassroots movement to replace the dominant German culture with that of native Czechs. Today, classic productions are staged here in a larger setting than at the Estates' Theater, but for about the same ticket prices.

The **National Theater Ballet** performs at the National Theater. The troupe has seen most of its top talent go west since 1989, but it still puts on a good show. After critics complained that Prague's top company had grown complacent, choreographer Libor Vaculík responded with humorous and quirky stagings of off-the-wall ballets such as *Some Like It Hot* and *Psycho.* Tickets cost 30Kč to 800Kč ($1.40–$38/70p–£19). **Laterna Magika,** Národní třída 4, Praha 1 (© **224-931-482;** Metro: Národní třída), is a performance-art show in the new wing of the National Theater. The multimedia show, which combines live theater with film and dance, was once considered radical and is not for those easily offended by nudity. Tickets are 680Kč ($32/£16).

JAZZ CLUBS Upscale by Czech standards, **AghaRTA Jazz Centrum,** Železná 16, Praha 1 (© **222-211-275;** Metro: Můstek), regularly features some of the best music in town, from standard acoustic trios to Dixieland, funk, and fusion. Bands usually begin at 9pm. The club is open daily 6pm to 1am. **Reduta Jazz Club,** Národní třída 20, Praha 1 (© **224-933-487;** Metro: Národní třída), is a smoky subterranean room that looks exactly like a jazz cellar should. An adventurous booking policy, which even included a

Moments An Excursion to Karlštejn Castle

By far the most popular day-trip from Prague is to **Karlštejn Castle**, 18 miles (30km) southwest of Prague, which was built by Charles IV in the 14th century to safeguard the crown jewels of the Holy Roman Empire and has been restored to its original state.

As you approach the castle by train from the Prague, little will prepare you for your first view: a spectacular castle perched high on a hill, surrounded by lush forests and vineyards. The Holy Rood Chapel is famous for the more than 2,000 precious and semiprecious inlaid gems that adorn its walls, and the Chapel of St. Catherine was King Karel IV's private oratory. Both the Audience Hall and the Imperial Bedroom are impressive, despite being stripped of their original furnishings. To see the Holy Rood Chapel you need to make a reservation (© **274-008-154**; www.spusc.cz or www. hradkarlstejn.cz).

Admission for a shorter tour is 220Kč ($10.50/£5.25) adults and 120Kč ($5.70/£2.85) students, and the longer one with the Holy Rood Chapel is 300Kč ($14.30/£7.15) adults, 150Kč ($7.15/£3.55) students. It's open Tuesday through Sunday: May, June, and September 9am to noon and 12:30 to 5pm; July and August 9am to noon and 12:30 to 6pm; April and October 9am to noon and 1pm to 4pm; November, December, January and March 9am to noon and 1pm to 3pm; closed February.

Most trains leave from Prague's Hlavní nádraží to the castle on an hourly basis throughout the day (trip time: 43 min.) and less frequently from Smíchov Station (Metro: Smíchovské nádraží), from which the trip time is only 34 minutes. One-way second-class fare is 46Kč ($2.20/£1.10) from the main train station or 40Kč ($1.90/95p) from Smíchov station. For train schedules, go to **www.jizdnirady.cz**. The castle is a 1¼-mile (1.9km) walk from the train station, though the stroll uphill to the castle—and the views that come with it—is one of the main highlights of the experience.

There is no official tourist center in Karlštejn, but the ticket and castle information booth can help you. On the main street heading up to the castle itself you will find a number of stores and restaurants. Take a break in **Restaurace Blanky z Valois**, where pizzas range from 80Kč to 190Kč ($3.80–$9.05/£1.90–£4.50). It is open daily from 11am to 10pm.

saxophone gig with a U.S. president in 1994, means that different bands play almost every night. It's open from 9pm (when the music usually starts) to midnight.

PUBS & BARS You'll experience true Czech entertainment in only one kind of place—a smoky local pub serving some of the world's best beer. Remember to put a cardboard coaster in front of you to show you want a mug, and never wave for service, as the typically surly waiter will just ignore you.

Originally a brewery dating from 1459, **U Fleků**, Křemencova 11, Praha 2 (© **224-934-805;** Metro: Národní třída), is Prague's most famous beer hall, and one of the only pubs that still brews its own beer. This huge place has a myriad of timber-lined rooms and a large, loud courtyard where an oompah band performs. Tourists come here by the busload, so U Fleků is avoided by disparaging locals who don't like its German atmosphere anyway. The pub's special dark beer is excellent, however, and not available anywhere else. It's open daily 9am to 11pm.

One of the most famous Czech pubs, **U Zlatého tygra (At the Golden Tiger),** Husova 17, Praha 1 (② **222-221-111;** Metro: Staroměstská or Můstek), was a favorite watering hole of ex-president Havel and the late writer Bohumil Hrabal. Particularly smoky, and not especially tourist-friendly, it is nevertheless a one-stop education in Czech culture. Then-presidents Havel and Clinton joined Hrabal for a traditional Czech pub evening here during Clinton's 1994 visit to Prague. It's open daily from 3pm to 11pm.

3 Western & Southern Bohemia

The Czech Republic is composed of two geographic regions: Bohemia and Moravia. The larger of the two, Bohemia, occupying the central and western areas of the country, has for centuries been caught between a rock (Germany) and a hard place (Austria). Bohemia was almost always in the center of regional conflicts, both secular and religious. But the area also flourished, as witnessed by the wealth of castles that dot the countryside and the spa towns that were once the playgrounds of the rich and famous. The good news for the rail traveler is that the region is small enough that you can visit these towns as separate day-trips from Prague, or once in the region, you can hop from one place to the other.

KARLOVY VARY (CARLSBAD)

The discovery of Karlovy Vary (Carlsbad), 75 miles (120km) west of Prague, by Charles IV reads something like a 14th-century episode of *The Beverly Hillbillies.* According to local lore, the king was out huntin' for some food when up from the ground came a-bubblin' water (though discovered by his dogs, not an errant gunshot). Knowing a good thing when he saw it, Charles immediately set to work building a small castle, naming the town that evolved around it Karlovy Vary (Charles's Boiling Place). The first spa buildings were built in 1522, and before long, notables such as Russian czar Peter the Great, and later Bach, Beethoven, Freud, Goethe, and Marx all came to take the waters.

After World War II, East Bloc travelers (following in the footsteps of Marx, no doubt) discovered the town, and Karlovy Vary became a destination for the proletariat. On doctors' orders, most workers enjoyed regular stays of 2 or 3 weeks, letting the mineral waters ranging from 110.3°F to 161.6°F (43.5°C–72°C) from the town's 12 spas heal their tired and broken bodies. Even now, most spa guests are there by doctor's prescription.

GETTING THERE There is no fast rail connection from Prague to Karlovy Vary and train travel takes much longer than a trip by bus, so although it's the most popular of the towns to visit (and thus the one we mention first), it's actually easier to get here by bus or by train from one of the other Bohemian towns.

The train from Prague goes through the northern region of Bohemia and reaches the spa town in about 4 hours. There are two trains leaving from Prague's main station and nádraží Holešovice in the morning and two from Masaryk station in the late afternoon. The fare is 274Kč ($13.05/£6.50).

Moments Spa Cures & Treatments

Most visitors to Karlovy Vary come specifically to get a spa treatment, a therapy that usually lasts 1 to 3 weeks. After consulting with a spa physician, guests are given a regimen of activities that may include mineral baths, massages, waxings, mudpacks, electrotherapy, and pure oxygen inhalation. After spending the morning at a spa, guests are then usually directed to walk the paths of the town's surrounding forest.

The common denominator of all the cures is an ample daily dose of hot mineral water, which bubbles up from 12 springs. This water definitely has a distinct odor and taste. You'll see people chugging it down, but it doesn't necessarily taste very good. Some thermal springs actually taste and smell like rotten eggs. You might want to take a small sip at first.

You'll also notice that almost everyone in town seems to be carrying "the cup," basically a mug with a built-in straw that runs through the handle. Young and old alike parade through town with their mugs, filling and refilling them at each new thermal water tap. You can buy these mugs everywhere for as little as 80Kč ($3.80/£1.90) or as much as 500Kč ($23/£11.90); they make a quirky souvenir. *Warning:* None of the mugs can make the hot springs taste any better!

Most rail travelers won't have the 1-week minimum most major spas demand, but many of the local hotels also offer spa and health treatments, so ask when you book your room. Most will happily arrange a treatment if they don't provide it directly. Visitors to Karlovy Vary for just a day or two can experience the waters on an "outpatient" basis. The **Sanatorium Baths III,** Mlýnské nábřeží 7 (*©* **353-223-473**), welcomes day-trippers with mineral baths, massages, saunas, and a cold pool. It's open Monday to Friday 7am to 2pm for spa treatments, and the swimming pool and sauna are open Monday to Friday 3pm to 6pm, Saturday 1 to 5pm.

For more information and reservations for spa packages contact **Čedok,** Na Příkopě 18, Praha 1 (*©* **224-197-777;** www.cedok.cz), in Prague.

Karlovy Vary's **Horní (upper) train station** is connected to the town center by city bus no. 11. If you are coming via Mariánské Lázně there are about seven trains daily. The 1½ hour-trip costs 76Kč ($3.60/£1.80) and you will end up at Karlovy Vary's **Dolní (lower) nádraží.** Just a 5-minute walk from this station is the main stop for all city buses **(Městská tržnice)** and the city center.

By Bus Taking a bus to Karlovy Vary is much more convenient if you're leaving from Prague. Frequent express buses leave from Prague's Florenc bus station and arrive in Karlovy Vary in 2¼ hours. The trip costs 140Kč ($6.65/£3.35). Take a 10-minute walk or local bus no. 4 into Karlovy Vary's spa center. Note that you must have a ticket to board local transport. You can buy tickets for 10Kč (45¢/25p) at the bus station stop, or, if you have no change, the kiosk across the street sells tickets during regular business hours. Alternatively, you can purchase the ticket for 15Kč (70¢/35p) from the bus driver. For timetable information, go to **www.jizdnirady.cz.**

VISITOR INFORMATION   Infocentrum města Karlovy Vary is located near the main Mlýnská kolonáda, on Lázeňská 1 (© **353-321-176**), and is open April to October Monday to Friday from 7am to 5pm, Saturday and Sunday from 9am to 3pm; and November to March on Monday to Friday from 7am to 4pm. The office also has a window at the terminal of the **Dolní (lower) nádraží** bus and train station, Západní ulice (© **353-232-838**). These are the official town's information centers, which will answer your questions, and help you make hotel reservations, sell you tickets for entertainment in the city, and so on.

Be sure to pick up the *Promenáda* magazine, a comprehensive collection of events with a small map of the town center.

For Web information on festivals and events in the city, go to **www.karlovyvary.cz**.

TOP ATTRACTIONS & SPECIAL MOMENTS

The town's slow pace and pedestrian promenades, lined with Art Nouveau buildings, turn strolling into an art form. Nighttime walks take on an even more mystical feel as the sewers, river, and many major cracks in the roads emit steam from the hot springs underneath. A good place to start is the **Hotel Thermal** at the north end of the old town's center, an easy walk from the bus station. The 1970s glass, steel, and concrete structure, between the town's eastern hills and the Ohře River, sticks out like a sore communist thumb amid the 19th-century architecture. Nonetheless, you'll find three important places here: its outdoor pool, the only centrally located outdoor public pool; its upper terrace, boasting a spectacular view of the city; and its cinema, Karlovy Vary's largest, which holds many of the local film festival's premier events.

As you enter the heart of the town on the river's west side, you'll see the renovated, ornate, white wrought-iron **Sadová kolonáda** adorning the beautifully manicured park **Dvořákovy sady.** Continue following the river, and about 330 feet (99m) later you'll encounter the **Mlýnská kolonáda,** a long, covered walkway housing several Karlovy Vary springs, which you can sample 24 hours a day. Each spring has a plaque beside it telling which mineral elements are present and the temperature of the water. Bring your own cup or buy one just about anywhere to sip the waters; most are too hot to drink from your hands.

When you hit the river bend, the majestic **Church of St. Mary Magdalene** sits perched atop a hill, overlooking the **Vřídlo,** the hottest spring in town. Built in 1736, the church is the work of Kilian Ignac Dientzenhofer, who also created two of Prague's more notable churches—both named St. Nicholas. Housing Vřídlo, which blasts water some 50 feet (15m) into the air, is the glass building called the **Vřídelní kolonáda.** It was built in 1974 and houses several hot springs you can sample for free. The building also holds several kiosks selling postcards, stone roses, and drinking cups. Heading away from the Vřídelní kolonáda are Stará and Nová Louka streets, which line either side of the river. Along **Stará (Old) Louka** you'll find several fine cafes and glass and crystal shops. Crystal and porcelain are Karlovy Vary's other claims to fame. Dozens of places throughout town sell everything from plates to chandeliers. **Nová (New) Louka** is lined with hotels and the historic **Town's Theater.**

Both streets lead to the **Grandhotel Pupp.** After a massive reconstruction that erased nearly 50 years of communism (it was temporarily called the Grand Hotel Moskva), the Pupp is once again the crown jewel of the town. Regardless of capitalism or communism, the Pupp remains what it always was: the grande dame of hotels in the area. Once catering to nobility from all over Central Europe, the Pupp still houses one of the town's finest restaurants, the Grand, and its grounds are a favorite with the hiking crowd.

If you still have the energy, atop the hill behind the Pupp stands the **Diana Lookout Tower.** Footpaths leading through the forests eventually spit you out at the base of the tower, as if to say, "Ha, the trip is only half over." If you are not up to the five-story climb, you can use the lift and enjoy the view of the town from above. Alternatively, a cable car runs to the tower from the base located right next to the Grandhotel Pupp. A one-way ticket on the cable car is 36Kč ($1.70/85p); round-trip, it's 60Kč ($2.85/£1.40). The cable car runs every 15 minutes daily from 9am to 7pm (to 6pm Apr, May, Oct; to 5pm Feb, Mar, Nov–Dec).

WHERE TO STAY & DINE

Some of the town's major spa hotels accommodate only those who are paying for complete treatment, unless their occupancy rates are particularly low. The hotels listed below accept guests for stays of any length.

One of Karlovy Vary's best hotels, the 116-room **Grandhotel Pupp** ★★★, Mírové nám. 2 (© **353-109-630;** www.pupp.cz), was built in 1701 and is also one of Europe's oldest. While the hotel's public areas ooze with splendor and charm, guest rooms aren't as consistently enchanting. The best tend to be on the upper floors facing the town center; only some rooms have air-conditioning. The Grand Restaurant serves up as grand a dining room as you'll find, with the food to match. The hotel's rates are quoted in euros to combat the volatility of the crown and run 149€ ($203/£101) double; from 350€ ($478/£239) for a suite. Breakfast is included.

Parkhotel Pupp ★, Mírové nám. 2 (© **353-109-111;** www.pupp.cz), is housed within the same complex as its five-star cousin, and was recently refurbished. The rooms are large and all the same facilities are available. Rates are 143€ ($195/£97.50) double; 350€ ($478/£239) suite. Rates include breakfast.

Less stylish but still in a great location is **Hotel Dvořák,** Nová Louka 11 (© **353-102-111;** www.hotel-dvorak.cz). Part of the Vienna International hotel/resort chain, the Dvořák has improved immensely, especially in terms of service. If the Pupp has the history and elegance, the Dvořák has the facilities. However, the rooms, for all their creature comforts, lack the old-world charm found at the Pupp. Rates run 98€ ($133/£67) double, including buffet breakfast. A daily exchange rate is used for those who want to pay in hard Czech currency.

Family-run hotel **Embassy** ★★, Nová Louka 21 (© **353-221-161;** www.embassy.cz), manages to evoke the turn of the 20th century with elegantly decorated rooms. Although smaller than those at the Pupp, they're impeccably furnished and overlook the river. The restaurant downstairs is where a lot of movers and shakers at the Karlovy Vary film festival get away from the glitz and get down to business. You can stay here for 2,660Kč to 3,440Kč ($126–$163/£63–£81.90) double; 3,600Kč ($171/£85.70) suite. Rates include breakfast. On the ground floor of the hotel is the **Embassy** restaurant (© **353-221-161**), which has a pub on one side and an intimate dining room on the other. On a cold day, the pub works wonders with a hearty goulash soup. But the dining room is the Embassy's hidden treasure. What the meals lack in flair, they make up for with sophistication. Main courses cost 145Kč to 895Kč ($6.90–$42/£3.45–£21).

Look for the restaurant **Promenáda** ★, Tržiště 31 (© **353-225-648**), if you'd like to dine in an intimate atmosphere. Across from the Vřídelní kolonáda, the Promenáda serves the best food around, offering a wide selection of generous portions. The daily menu usually includes well-prepared wild game, but the mixed grill for two and the chateaubriand, both flambéed at the table, are the chef's best dishes. Main courses run 210Kč to 599Kč ($10–$28.50/£5–£14.25).

ČESKÝ KRUMLOV

If you have time for only one day-trip, consider making it Český Krumlov, 96 miles (155km) south of Prague. One of Bohemia's prettiest towns, Krumlov is a living gallery of elegant Renaissance-era buildings housing charming cafes, pubs, restaurants, shops, and galleries. In 1992, UNESCO named Český Krumlov a World Heritage Site for its historic importance and physical beauty.

Bustling since medieval times, the town, after centuries of embellishment, is exquisitely beautiful. In 1302, the Rožmberk family inherited the castle and used it as their main residence for nearly 300 years. Looking out from the Lazebnický bridge, with the waters of the Vltava below snaking past the castle's gray stone, you'll feel that time has stopped. At night, with the castle lit up, the view becomes even more dramatic.

GETTING THERE   The only way to reach Český Krumlov by train from Prague is via České Budějovice (see below), a slow ride that deposits you at a station relatively far from the town center (trip time ranges from 3 hr., 46 min. to 4 hr., 41 min). Nine trains leave daily from Prague's Hlavní nádraží, and the fare is 224Kč ($10.65/£5.35).

If you are already in České Budějovice and you want to make a trip to Krumlov, numerous trains connecting these two cities run throughout the day. It takes about 60 minutes and costs 46Kč ($2.20/£1.10). For timetables go to **www.jizdnirady.cz**.

The Český Krumlov train station is situated in a northern suburb of the city. You can take a city taxi (parked in front of the station building) to get to the town center. The 10- to 15-minute ride costs about 100Kč ($4.75/£2.40).

VISITOR INFORMATION   On the main square, in a renovated Renaissance building, the **Infocentrum**, nám. Svornosti 2, 381 01 Český Krumlov (©/fax **380-704-621**), offers a complete array of services from booking accommodations to ticket reservations for events, as well as a phone and fax service. It's open daily 9am to 6pm (Apr–May and Oct), 9am to 7pm (June, Sept), 9am to 8pm (July–Aug), and 9am to 5pm (Nov–Mar). For more information about Český Krumlov visit its well-organized website, **www.ckrumlov.cz**, which features a very cool interactive map of the city.

TOP ATTRACTIONS & SPECIAL MOMENTS

Bring a good pair of walking shoes and be prepared to wear them out. Český Krumlov not only lends itself to hours of strolling, but its hills and alleyways demand it. No

---

⌒Tips Avoiding the Crowds

Consider yourself warned: Word has spread about Český Krumlov. The summer high season can be unbearable, as thousands of visitors blanket its medieval streets. If possible, try to visit in the off season—we suggest autumn to take advantage of the colorful surrounding hills—when the crowds recede, the prices decrease, and the town's charm can really shine. Who knows? You might even hear some Czech! For more details about the town go to **www.ckrumlov.cz**.

Moments Seeing the Český Krumlov Château

Reputedly the second-largest castle in Bohemia (after Prague Castle), the **Český Krumlov Château** was constructed in the 13th century as part of a private estate. Throughout the ages, it has passed to a variety of private owners, including the Rožmberk family, Bohemia's largest landholders, and the Schwarzenbergs, the Bohemian equivalent of the Hilton family. Perched high atop a rocky hill, the château is open from April to October only, exclusively by guided tours.

Follow the path at the entrance for the long climb up to the castle and first to greet you is a round 12th-century tower—painstakingly renovated—with a Renaissance balcony. You'll pass over the moat, now occupied by two brown bears. Beyond it is the **Dolní Hrad (Lower Castle)** and then the **Horní Hrad (Upper Castle)**. There are two guided tours. The first tour begins in the rococo **Chapel of St. George,** and continues through the portrait-packed **Renaissance Rooms,** and the **Schwarzenberg Baroque Suite,** outfitted with ornate furnishings that include Flemish wall tapestries, European paintings. You'll also see the extravagant 17th-century **Golden Carriage.** Tour two includes the **Schwarzenberg portrait gallery** as well as its 19th-century suite. Tours last 1 hour and depart frequently. Most are in Czech or German, however. If you want an English-language tour, arrange it ahead of time (© 380-704-721; www.castle.ckrumlov.cz). The guided tours cost 160Kč ($7.60/£3.80) adults, 80Kč ($3.80/£1.90) students (Tour 1); 140Kč ($6.60/£3.35) adults and 70Kč ($3.35/£1.65) students (Tour 2). The tickets are sold separately. The castle hours are from Tuesday to Sunday: June to August 9am to 6pm; April, May, September, and October 9am to 5pm (no Tour 2 in Apr). The last entrance is 1 hour before closing.

Tip: Once past the main castle building, you can see one of the more stunning views of Český Krumlov from **Most Na Plášti,** a walkway that doubles as a belvedere over the Inner Town. Even farther up the hill lies the castle's riding school and gardens.

---

cars, thank goodness, are allowed in the historic town, and the cobblestones keep most other vehicles at bay. The town is split into two parts—the Inner Town and Latrán, which houses the city's famous castle. They're best tackled separately, so you won't have to criss cross the bridges several times.

Begin at the **Regionální Muzeum (Regional Museum;** © **380-711-674)** at the top of Horní ulice and to the right of the Main Square. Once a Jesuit seminary, the three-story museum now contains artifacts and displays relating to Český Krumlov's 1,000-year history. The highlight of this mass of folk art, clothing, furniture, and statues is a giant model of the town that offers a bird's-eye view of the buildings. Admission is 50Kč ($2.40/£1.20), and it's open daily 10am to 5pm (May–June and Sept), daily 10am to 6pm (July–Aug); Tuesday to Friday from 9am to 4pm and Saturday and Sunday 1 to 4pm (Apr and Oct–Dec).

Across the street is the **Hotel Růže (Rose),** which was once a Jesuit student house. Built in the late 16th century, the hotel and the prelature next to it show the development of architecture in the city—Gothic, Renaissance, and rococo influences are all present. Continue down the street to see the impressive late Gothic **St. Vitus Cathedral;** admission is free.

As you continue down the street, you'll come to **náměstí Svornosti.** For such an impressive town, the main square is a little disappointing, with few buildings of any character. The **Radnice (Town Hall),** at nám. Svornosti 1, is one of the few exceptions. Its Gothic arcades and Renaissance vault inside are exceptionally beautiful in this otherwise run-down area. From the square, streets fan out in all directions. Take some time just to wander through them.

One of Český Krumlov's most famous residents was Austrian-born 20th-century artist Egon Schiele. He was a bit of an eccentric who, on more than one occasion, raised the ire of the town's residents (many were distraught with his use of their young women as his nude models); his stay was cut short when residents' patience ran out. But the town readopted the artist in 1993, setting up the **Egon Schiele Foundation** and the **Egon Schiele Centrum** in Inner Town, Široká 70–72, 381 01, Český Krumlov (© **380-704-011;** www.schieleartcentrum.cz). The center documents his life and work, housing a permanent selection of his paintings as well as exhibitions of other 20th-century artists. Admission 120Kč ($5.70/£2.85). It's open daily from 10am to 6pm.

For a different perspective on what the town looks like, take the stairs from the **Městské divadlo (Town Theater)** on Horní ulice down to the riverfront and rent a boat from **Maleček boat rentals** at Rooseveltova 28 (© **380-712-853;** www.malecek. cz) at 350Kč ($16.60/£8.35) per half hour. Always willing to lend his advice, the affable Pepa Maleček will tell you what to watch out for and where the best fishing is (no matter how many times you say that you don't want to fish!).

WHERE TO STAY & DINE

Hotels are sprouting up, or are getting a "new" old look; PENSION and ZIMMER FREI signs line Horní and Rooseveltova streets and offer some of the best values in town. For a comprehensive list of area hotels and help with bookings, call or write the Infocentrum listed above.

We recommend **Hotel Konvice,** Horní ul. 144 (© 380-711-611), as a good value choice. If you can get a room with a view out the back, take it immediately. Rooms themselves are small but clean and comfortable, with nice parquet floors and well-appointed bathrooms. As you overlook the river and the castle on the opposite bank, you'll wonder why people would stay anywhere else. Rates are 1,200Kč to 1,980Kč ($57–$94/£28.50–£47) double; 2,300Kč to 2,970Kč ($109–$141/£54.50–£70.70) suite. Rates include breakfast.

Along "pension alley," **Pension Anna** ✿, Rooseveltova 41 (©/fax **380-711-692;** www.pensionanna.euweb.cz), is a comfortable and rustic choice. The friendly management and the homey feeling you get as you walk up to your room make it a favorite. Forget hotels—this is the kind of place where you can relax. The owners even let you buy drinks and snacks at the bar downstairs and take them to your room. Rates include breakfast and run 1,250Kč ($59.50/£29.75) double; 1,550Kč ($73.80/£36.90) suite.

Moments Dining at the Castle

Most visitors don't realize that beyond the tourist sections of **Český Krumlov Château** they can have one of the Czech Republic's finest dining experiences at **Krčma Markéta** *&*, Zámek 62 (*©* **380-714-067**; www.auviex.cz), a Renaissance pub. To get there, walk all the way up the hill through the castle, past the Upper Castle and past the Castle Theater. Walk through the raised walkway and into the Zámecká zahrada (Castle Garden), where you'll eventually find the pub. Going inside is like leaving this century and the atmosphere hasn't changed much over the centuries. There's a wide variety of roasted meat on the menu. The waiter/cook will bring bread and a slab of spiced pork fat (considered a good base for drinking), but don't worry—refusing to eat it won't raise anyone's ire. Instead, wait until the entree comes. Krčma Markéta is open Tuesday to Sunday (Apr–Oct only) from 3 to 10pm and main courses cost 75Kč to 155Kč ($3.55–$7.40/£1.80–£3.70).

For a typical Czech dining experience visit **Hospoda Na louži,** Kájovská 66 (*©* **380-711-446;** www.nalouzi.cz), which offers diners good value for their money. The large wooden tables encourage you to get to know your neighbors in this Inner Town pub, located in a 15th-century house near the main square. The atmosphere is fun and the food above average. If no table is available, stand and have a drink; the seating turnover is pretty fast, and the staff is accommodating. Main courses cost 58Kč to 158Kč ($2.75–$7.50/£1.40–£3.75).

Located in the former cooling room of the local Eggenberg Brewery near the castle, **Restaurant Eggenberg,** Latrán 27 (*©* **380-711-426;** www.eggenberg.cz), is one of the few big beer halls in town, with some of the freshest drafts anywhere. Traditional meat-and-dumplings-style Czech food is augmented by vegetarian dishes. Main courses cost 98Kč to 280Kč ($4.65–$13.35/£2.35–£6.65).

ČESKÉ BUDĚJOVICE

This fortress town was born in 1265, when Otakar II decided that the intersection point of the Vltava and Malše rivers would be the perfect site to protect the approaches to southern Bohemia. Although Otakar was killed at the battle of the Moravian Field in 1278, and the town was subsequently ravaged by the rival Vítkovic family, the construction of the city continued, eventually taking the shape originally envisaged.

Today, České Budějovice, hometown of the original Budweiser brand beer, is more a bastion for the beer drinker than a protector of Bohemia. But its slow pace, relaxed atmosphere, and interesting architecture make it a worthy stop for the rail traveler, especially as a base for exploring southern Bohemia or as a quick stopover for those heading on to Austria.

GETTING THERE   By Train   Twelve express trains from Prague's Hlavní nádraží make the trip to České Budějovice in about 3 hours. The fare is 204Kč ($9.70/£4.85). From the train station, take city bus no. 1, 3, or 4 to the city center; the ride costs 8Kč (40¢/20p). For timetable information go to **www.jizdnirady.cz.**

Moments For Beer Lovers: Touring a Beer Shrine

On the town's northern edge sits a shrine for those who pray to the gods of the amber nectar. This is where it all began, where **Budějovický Budvar,** the original brewer of Budweiser brand beer, has its one and only factory. Established in 1895, Budvar draws on more than 700 years of Bohemian brewing tradition to produce one of the world's best beers. For information, contact Budvar n.p., Karolíny Světlé 4, České Budějovice (② **387-705-341;** exkurse@budvar.cz).

Tours can be arranged by phoning ahead, but only for groups. If you're traveling alone or with only one or two other people, ask a hotel concierge at one of the bigger hotels (we suggest the Zvon; see below) if he or she can put you in with an already scheduled group. Failing that, you might want to take a chance and head up to the brewery, where, if a group has arrived, another person or two won't be noticed.

Trolley buses no. 2, 4, 6, and 8 stop by the brewery; this is how it ensures that its workers and visitors reach the plant safely each day. The trolley costs 10Kč (45¢/25p) to the brewery. You can also hop a cab from the town square for about 100Kč to 150Kč ($4.75–$7.15/£2.40–£3.60).

VISITOR INFORMATION The **ČD center** (② **972-544-361**) at the train station is open nonstop (except the lunch break 12:30–1pm and midnight–3:30am) and provides train information, makes hotel bookings, and sells event tickets.

The Tourist Information Centre, nám. Přemysla Otakara II 2 (②/fax **386-801-412;** www.c-budejovice.cz), in the main square, sells maps and guidebooks, and finds lodging.

TOP ATTRACTIONS & SPECIAL MOMENTS
You can comfortably see České Budějovice in a day. At its center is one of central Europe's largest squares, the cobblestone **náměstí Přemysla Otakara II.** The square contains the ornate **Fountain of Sampson,** an 18th-century water well that was once the town's principal water supply, plus a mishmash of baroque and Renaissance buildings. On the southwest corner is the **town hall,** an elegant baroque structure built by Martinelli between 1727 and 1730. On top of the town hall, the larger-than-life statues by Dietrich represent the civic virtues: justice, bravery, wisdom, and diligence.

One block northwest of the square is the **Černá věž (Black Tower),** visible from almost every point in the city. Its 360 steps are worth the climb to get a bird's-eye view in all directions. The most famous symbol of České Budějovice, the 232-foot (70m), 16th-century tower was built as a belfry for the adjacent **St. Nicholas Church.** This 13th-century church, one of the town's most important sights, was a bastion of Roman Catholicism during the 15th-century Hussite rebellion. You shouldn't miss the flamboyant white-and-cream 17th-century baroque interior.

WHERE TO STAY & DINE
Several agencies can locate reasonably priced private rooms. Expect to pay about 500Kč ($23.80/£11.90) per person, in cash. The Tourist Information Centre (see

"Visitor Information," above) can point you toward a wide selection of conveniently located rooms and pensions.

Location is everything for the city's most elegant hotel, **Grandhotel Zvon,** nám. Přemysla Otakara II 28 (© **381-601-601;** www.hotel-zvon.cz), which occupies several historic buildings on the main square. Upper-floor rooms have been renovated and tend to be more expensive, especially those with a view of the square, which are not only brighter, but larger and nicer, too. Others are relatively plain and functional. There's no elevator, but if you don't mind the climb, stay on the fourth floor. One of the biggest improvements here in recent years has been the staff, which seems to be learning that guests like respect and quality treatment. Rooms cost 2,287Kč to 5,366Kč ($108–$255/£54.45–£128) double.

Around the corner from the Zvon you can find **Hotel Malý Pivovar (Small Brewery)** ★★, Ulice Karla IV. 8–10 (© **386-360-471;** www.malypivovar.cz). A renovated 16th-century microbrewery combines the charms of a B&B with the amenities of a modern hotel. Rooms are bright and cheery, with antique-style wooden furniture. It's definitely worth consideration if being only 100 feet (30m) from the sometimes-noisy main square isn't a problem. Rates are 3,300Kč ($157/£78.55) double; 3,800Kč ($180/£90) suite. Rates include breakfast.

The town is also home to a typical Czech-style restaurant serving up hearty food at reasonable prices. **U královské pečeti (At the Royal Seal),** Karla IV. 8-10 (© **386-360-471**), has a wide main menu selection, ranging from goulash with dumplings for 98Kč ($4.65/£2.35) to rib-eye steak for 198Kč ($9.40/£4.70).

6

Denmark

With one of Europe's best rail networks, the maritime nation of Denmark is easily viewed from the window of a train. It may not offer the dramatic and often hair-raising train trips of nearby Norway, but you'll pass by sweet fishing villages, rustic hamlets with half-timbered houses, Renaissance castles, Viking ruins, and gorgeous dune-backed beaches along the North Sea.

Touring Denmark by rail has been made easier in the last decade, thanks to the tunnel and bridge crossing The Great Belt. The "Belt" is a body of water separating the island of Zealand (on which Copenhagen sits) from the island of Funen. Funen is the island between Zealand and the peninsula of Jutland, which is connected geographically to Germany and the rest of continental Europe. These rail links mean the three landmasses can be reached without having to take the formerly unavoidable ferry. Nowadays, high-speed diesel trains link the major cities of Denmark, such as Copenhagen and Århus, at faster speeds than ever before.

The county's international rail links were also dramatically improved in the summer of 2002 when a 10-mile (16km) rail and motorway tunnel and bridge complex linked the northeast of Denmark (including Copenhagen) with southern Sweden (through Malmö).

Though Denmark is a very expensive destination for the rail traveler, its small size and extensive and efficient rail system mean you'll only need 3 to 4 days to take in its scenic highlights.

HIGHLIGHTS OF DENMARK

All visitors to Denmark seem to arrive in **Copenhagen,** the capital. It's not only the gateway to the country—by both rail and air—but also the country's major attraction. Historically known as the "fun" capital of Europe, contemporary Copenhagen focuses on all things hip, with designer hotels, bars, and restaurants springing up alongside the more functional old-fashioned equivalents. Yes, it's expensive: According to the U.K.'s Economic Intelligence Unit, Copenhagen was the third most expensive city in the world in 2007, outranked by only Paris and Oslo. But it is also clean and safe (although crime is increasing) and packed with things to see and do: museums, theaters, castles, old churches, and interesting shops. Plus, there's a noticeable lack of car fumes, as half of the city's 1.7 million residents apparently prefer to pedal around their hill-free city on bikes.

If time allows, day-trip to **Helsingør,** 25 miles (40km) to the north of Copenhagen, easily reached by train. Here you'll find Hamlet's Castle, known as **Kronborg Slot.** Yes, it's true, Shakespeare never actually visited the city, but it's still one of Denmark's proudest heritage sites.

Another free day? Take the train to Odense (97 miles/156km west of Copenhagen) on the neighboring island of Funen. This ancient town was the birthplace of Hans

Scandinavia

Moments   **Festivals & Special Events**

The **Roskilde Festival** in Roskilde (a half hour from Copenhagen) is one of Europe's biggest outdoor festivals, going strong since 1971. Taking place in late June/early July, it's 4 days of big names from pop, rock, and hip-hop playing on four stages. Bring a tent. For more information or to buy tickets ($255/£138), go to the official website, **www.roskilde-festival.dk**. If jazz appeals more to your musical tastes, international jazz musicians play in the streets, squares, and theaters during the **Copenhagen Jazz Festival** in early July. Pick up a copy of *Copenhagen This Week* (**www.ctw.dk**) to find the venues. For information, call ⓒ **33-93-20-13** or check out **www.jazzfestival. dk**. Early July.

At **Århus Festival Week** in late August/early September, a wide range of cultural activities—including opera, jazz, classical, and folk music, ballet, and theater—are presented. It's the largest multi-cultural festival in Scandinavia. Sporting activities and street parties abound as well. For more information, call ⓒ **89-40-91-91** or go to the festival website at **www.aarhus festuge.dk**.

Christian Andersen, and fans can explore his humble boyhood home and a museum devoted to the master storyteller.

For most visitors, Odense will mark the end of a rail tour of Denmark. Those with more time can continue by rail into Jutland, a peninsula of heather-covered moors, fjords, farmland, lakes, and sand dunes.

Here, the most interesting city is **Århus,** 109 miles (175km) west of Copenhagen and easily reached by train. Århus is the capital of Jutland and Denmark's second largest city, university town, and cultural center with a lively port life.

For most visitors, it's then back to Copenhagen, or on to the port of **Frederikshavn,** 238 miles (381km) northwest of Copenhagen, for overnight ferry connections to Oslo in Norway.

1 Essentials

GETTING THERE

From North America, nonstop flights to Copenhagen from the greater New York area take about 7½ hours; from Chicago, 8½ hours; and from Seattle, 9½ hours.

SAS (ⓒ **800/221-2350;** www.scandinavian.net) has more nonstop flights to Scandinavia from North American than any other airline, and more flights to and from Denmark and within Scandinavia than any other airline. North American carriers flying to Copenhagen include **Air Canada** (ⓒ **888/247-2262;** www.aircanada.ca), **American Airlines** (ⓒ **800/433-7300;** www.aa.com), **Delta Airlines** (ⓒ **800/221-1212;** www.delta.com), and **United Airlines** (ⓒ **800/864-8331;** www.united.com).

In the United Kingdom, **British Airways** (ⓒ **800/AIRWAYS** in the U.S., or 0870/850-9850 in the U.K.; www.ba.com) offers convenient connections through Heathrow to Copenhagen. Other European airlines with connections through their home countries to Copenhagen include **Icelandair** (© **800/223-5500;** www.icelandair. com), **Northwest/KLM** (© **800/225-2525;** www.klm.com), and **Lufthansa** (© **800/ 645-3880;** www.lufthansa-usa.com). Note that it's best to make your flight arrangements in North America before you go or you might find some of these flights prohibitively expensive. If you can get a cheap flight into London, **EasyJet** (© **0905/821-0905** in the U.K. at a rate of $1.25/65p per minute, or 01144870/600-0000 in the U.S.; www.easyjet.com) offers no-frills, daily flights from London Stansted to Copenhagen.

DENMARK BY RAIL
PASSES
For information on the **Eurail Global Pass, Eurail Global Pass Flexi, Eurail Denmark–Germany Pass, Eurail Denmark Pass,** and **Eurail Scandinavia Pass,** see chapter 2. Note that if you will be confining your travel to Denmark and the other Scandinavian countries, the Eurail Scandinavia Pass is your best option.

All Denmark train passes are best purchased in North America and are available from **Rail Europe** (© **877/272-RAIL** [7245] in North America; www.raileurope. com) or **ScanAm World Tours,** 108 N. Main St., Cranbury, NJ 08512 (© **800/545-2204;** www.scandinaviantravel.com), which sells Eurail Scandinavia Passes if booked together with other land arrangements such as hotels.

FOREIGN TRAIN TERMS
Almost everyone in Denmark, where schoolchildren start learning English in grade school, speaks English, so there's no need to worry about a language barrier.

PRACTICAL TRAIN INFORMATION
Flat, low-lying Denmark, with its hundreds of bridges and absence of mountains, has a large network of railway lines connecting virtually every hamlet with the largest city, Copenhagen. For **information, schedules,** and **fares** anywhere in Denmark, call © **70-13-14-15.** Waiting times for a person on this number can be lengthy. An alternative way to gather schedules and prices, and even reserve a seat on specific trains, involves surfing over to the website maintained by the **Danish State Railways (www. dsb.dk).**

A word you're likely to see and hear frequently is *Lyntog* (Express Trains), which are the fastest trains presently operational in Denmark. Be warned in advance that the

Trains & Travel Times in Denmark

From	To	Type of Train	# of Trains	Frequency	Approx. Travel Time
Copenhagen	Odense	InterCity	Every 30 min.	Daily	1 hr., 30 min.
Copenhagen	Odense	Lyntog	Every hour	Daily	1 hr., 19 min.
Copenhagen	Århus	InterCity	Every hour	Daily	3 hr., 15 min.
Copenhagen	Århus	Lyntog	Every hour	Daily	3 hr., 01 min.
Copenhagen	Helsingør	Regional	Every 30 min.	Daily	1 hr., 04 min.
Århus	Aalborg	InterCity	Every hour	Daily	1 hr., 35 min.
Århus	Aalborg	Lyntog	Every hour	Daily	1 hr., 23 min.
Århus	Aalborg	Regional	3	Mon–Sat	1 hr., 42 min.
Aalborg	Frederikshavn	Regional	12 (9 on Sun)	Daily	1 hr., 20 min.
Aalborg	Frederikshavn	Lyntog	10 (6 on Sun)	Daily	1 hr., 11 min.

most crowded times on Danish trains are Fridays, Sundays, and national holidays, so plan your reservations accordingly. *Note:* Aside from Lyntog, Danish "train lingo" is hardly a consideration in a nation where English is so widely spoken.

The Danish government offers dozens of discounts on the country's rail networks—depending on the age of a traveler, days or hours traveled, and destination. On any train within Denmark, children between the ages of 12 and 15 are charged half price if they're accompanied by an adult, and up to two children under 12 can travel for free with any adult on any train in Denmark. Seniors (age 65 or older) receive a discount of between 25% for travel on Fridays, Sundays, and holidays, and discounts of 50% every other day of the week. No identification is needed when you buy your ticket, but the conductor who checks your ticket may ask for proof of age.

RESERVATIONS   The **Danish State Railways (DSB)** runs all train services except for a few private lines and the outfit is one of the best and most reliable in Europe. Reservations are strongly recommended on the new, sleek **InterCity (IC)** trains unless you board after 8pm or are traveling on the line from Aalborg to Frederikshavn, where overnight ferries leave for Norway. Expect to pay a small booking fee when making the reservation.

You can reserve both first-class or second-class cars on all IC trains. In Denmark, second-class travel is generally quite comfortable, so you may not want to pay the extra money for a first-class seat.

The other major type of train, the **Regional (R),** is upgrading its cars, and aims to replace all the older ones by the time you are reading this. The trains are a bit slower and there is no first-class section. Seat reservations are optional on these trains, which don't tend to be crowded except at major holidays or during peak travel periods, especially July—the single biggest travel month in Denmark. In most cases, you'll be able to find a seat without a reservation, but you may not want to take that chance. Note that reservation fees aren't covered by railpasses, so you'll have to pay extra for them.

SERVICES & AMENITIES   Because Denmark is so small, long overnight hauls aren't a factor. There are also no dining cars on trains though most trains do have carts selling snacks and drinks. "Snacks" usually consist of expensive smørrebrød (open-faced sandwiches), though drinks are more reasonably priced.

FAST FACTS: Denmark

Area Code   The country code for Denmark is **45**. It precedes any call made to Denmark from another country. There are no city area codes. Every telephone number has eight digits.

Business Hours   Most **banks** are open Monday to Friday from 9:30am to 4pm (Thurs until 6pm), but outside Copenhagen, banking hours vary. **Stores** are generally open Monday to Thursday from 9:30/10am to 5:30pm, Friday 9:30/10am to 7 or 8pm, and Saturday noon to 2pm (although they are allowed to stay open until 5pm on the first Sat of every month); most are closed Sunday (although they can open on the first Sun of the month and Sun in Dec).

Climate   Denmark's climate is mild for Scandinavia—New England farmers experience harsher winters. Summer temperatures average 61° to 77°F (16°C–25°C).

Winter temperatures seldom go below 30°F (–1°C), thanks to the warming waters of the Gulf Stream, though cold snaps and snow are common, and wintry winds can cut sharply. From a weather perspective, mid-April to November is a good time to visit.

Currency The basic unit of currency is the krone (crown), or DKK, made up of 100 øre. At this writing, $1 = approximately 5. 9DKK and £1 = 11DKK. Some major stores may also show prices in euros and accept euros as payment but they are not obliged to and may give back change in kroner.

Documents Required Americans and Canadians can stay up to 3 months in Denmark with just a passport, but it must be valid for 3 months beyond their planned departure day.

Electricity Voltage is generally 220 volts AC, 50 to 60 cycles, and appliances use round two-pin plugs. In many camping sites, 110-volt power plugs are also available. Adapters and transformers may be purchased in Denmark. It's always best to check at your hotel desk before using an electrical outlet.

Embassies All embassies are in Copenhagen. The embassy of the **United States** is at Dag Hammärskjölds Allé 24, DK-2100 København (✆ **33-41-71-00;** www.us embassy.dk). **Canada**'s embassy is at Kristen Bernikowsgade 1, DK-1105 København K (✆ **33-48-32-00;** www.canada.dk).

Health & Safety You will have few health issues to worry about in Denmark. You don't need to get shots, most foodstuffs are safe, and the water in cities and towns is potable. If you're concerned, order bottled water. Prescriptions can be filled in towns and cities at any *"apotek"* (make sure your doctor fills out prescriptions using generic and not brand names), and nearly all areas have English-speaking doctors in hospitals with well-trained medical staffs. Doctors will also make house calls to your hotel.

Denmark is one of the safest European countries for travelers. Copenhagen, the major population center, naturally experiences the most crime, much of it alcohol-related hooliganism, although muggings are known to occur. There are also tensions between the police and the citizens of the free state of Christiania that can erupt into rioting, as happened in 2007. If you are concerned, stay away from the area, or check the current situation with hotel staff. Crimes of violence are exceedingly rare. Exercise the usual precautions you would when traveling anywhere.

Holidays Some of the dates below may vary slightly each year, so check with a local tourist office or online at **www.visitdenmark.com**. Danish public holidays are New Year's Day (Jan 1), Maundy Thursday, Good Friday, Easter Sunday, Easter Monday, Labor Day (May 1), Common Prayers Day (4th Fri after Easter), Ascension Day (mid-May), Whitsunday (late May), Whitmonday, Constitution Day (June 5), Christmas Day (Dec 25), and Boxing Day (Dec 26).

Legal Aid While traveling in Denmark, you are, of course, subject to that country's laws. If arrested or charged, you can obtain a list of private lawyers from the U.S. Embassy to represent you.

Mail Post office opening hours vary widely. Most post offices are open Monday to Friday from 9 or 10am to 5 or 6pm. Some close on Saturdays. Others open from 9am to noon. All post offices close on Sundays and Bank Holidays. A standard letter weighing up to 50 grams (1.7 oz.) to North America costs 8DKK ($1.35/70p). Mailboxes are painted red and display the embossed crown and trumpet of the Danish Postal Society. To find post offices in Denmark check out **www.postdanmark.dk**.

Police & Emergencies Dial ⓒ **112** for the fire department, the police, an ambulance, or to report a disaster of any kind. Emergency calls from public telephone kiosks are free (no coins needed).

Telephone The country code of **45** should precede any call made to Denmark from another country. Danish phones are fully automatic. Dial the eight-digit number; there are no city area codes. At public telephone booths, use two 50-øre coins or a 1-krone or 5-krone coin only; insert the coins only when your party answers. You can make more than one call on the same payment if your time hasn't run out. Emergency calls to ⓒ 112 are free.

Tipping Tips are seldom expected. Porters charge fixed prices, and tipping hairdressers or barbers is not customary. Service is built into the system, and hotels, restaurants, and even taxis include a 15% service charge in their rates. Rounding up when paying a restaurant bill or for your taxi is the norm, but you generally need tip only for special services.

2 Copenhagen ⭐⭐⭐

The capital of Denmark, home to almost a quarter of the country's population, is booming, bustling, and cosmopolitan. In summer—the time to visit—the entire city seems to flock outdoors to enjoy some precious sunshine after the gloomy, cold months of winter. Cafe culture flourishes, and locals flood the Strøget (the pedestrian-only mall in the heart of town) or go boating on the city's lakes. But mainly they bike: Danes cycle an average of 375 miles (604km) per year. At night, the Tivoli Gardens explode into a burst of light with entertainment for the masses. All this makes Copenhagen a veritable summer festival before it settles down once more in September for a long winter's nap.

For the rail passenger, Copenhagen is the gateway to all of Scandinavia, including Norway and Sweden. Trains will carry you from Copenhagen to Stockholm in just 5½ hours and to Oslo in 8½ to 9½ hours. And Copenhagen's train connections to Germany are great, especially to Hamburg and Berlin, two of Europe's best rail hubs.

Copenhagen is also the rail hub of Denmark even though it's in the far eastern section of the country. The city offers easy rail links to all major attractions on the island of Zealand (on which Copenhagen lies) and to the eastern island of Funen, which is most often visited by those wishing to explore Odense, the birthplace of Hans Christian Andersen. You'll also find convenient connections to the major cities and towns on the peninsula of Jutland, including Århus.

STATION INFORMATION
GETTING FROM THE AIRPORT TO THE TRAIN STATION

Flights into Copenhagen land at **Kastrup Airport** (ⓒ **32-31-32-31;** www.cph.dk), 7¼ miles (12km) from the center of Copenhagen. Trains link the airport with Copenhagen's Central Railway Station, in the center of the hotel zone. The trip takes a mere

13 minutes and costs 27DKK ($4.60/£2.45). Located right under the airport's arrivals and departures halls, the Air Rail Terminal is a short escalator ride from the gates. It has ticketing offices (where you can validate a railpass), information desks, restaurants, and fast-food chains. You can also take an SAS bus to the city terminal; the fare is 26DKK ($4.40/£2.35) A taxi to the city center costs between 150DKK and 200DKK ($25.50–$34/£13.50–£18).

INSIDE THE STATION
Trains arrive at the **København Hovedbanegård (Central Rail Station),** Copenhagen's main train hub, in the center of Copenhagen near the Tivoli Gardens and Rådhuspladsen (Town Hall Square). The station is frequently abbreviated København H on train schedules. Call ℭ **70-13-14-15** for local rail information.

Visitor information and hotel reservations are not available inside the rail station but you'll find both at the Tourist Information Center, which is nearby and well marked (follow the signs from the station). Several ATMs can be found on the streets outside the station. Inside the station is a currency exchange kiosk open daily 7am to 9pm. It doesn't charge commission and will exchange any remaining kroner you have at the end of your trip if you keep your receipt. There is also an on-site luggage storage kiosk, charging 25DKK to 35DKK ($4.50–$6.30) per bag for 24 hours; service is Monday to Saturday 5:30am to 1am, Sunday 6am to 1am. Several restaurants and a few shops are also located in the station. For more details, see **www.hovedbanen.dk**. From the Central Station, you can easily connect with the local subway system, the **S-tog.** Trains depart from platforms within the terminal.

INFORMATION ELSEWHERE IN THE CITY
The **Copenhagen Tourist Information Center,** Vesterbrogade, 4A (ℭ **70-22-24-42;** www.visitcopenhagen.dk), is across from the main entrance to the Tivoli and around the corner from the rail station. The center is open 9am to 4pm Monday through Friday, and 9am to 2pm Saturday for September through April; open 9am to 6pm Monday through Saturday in May and June and Monday to Saturday 9am to 8pm, and Sunday 10am to 6pm in July and August. It's closed Easter Monday; December 25, 26, and 31; and New Year's Day.

The staff here will make hotel reservations for 100DKK ($17/£9) or you can book a room yourself using one of their computers for 30DKK ($5.10/£2.70). While here, pick up a copy of *Copenhagen This Week* (www.ctw.dk); its events calendar has good listings for sightseeing and entertainment.

GETTING AROUND
Touring Copenhagen is best done on foot, but you'll need public transport to reach some of the sights. A joint fare system covers the Metro, buses, and trains, meaning you can travel on Copenhagen Transport buses, the State Railway and S-tog trains in Copenhagen and North Zealand, plus some private railway routes within a 25-mile (40km) radius of the capital on one ticket.

BASIC FARES The Greater Copenhagen area consists of seven different transportation zones and fares vary depending on the zones you travel through. All bus stops and transit stations display a color-coded zone map to help you calculate your fare. A *grundbillet* (basic ticket) for both buses and trains costs 18DKK ($3.10/£1.60), allowing you to travel on as many different forms of public transport as you like, in two zones, for up to an hour. Up to two children ages 11 and under ride for

Copenhagen

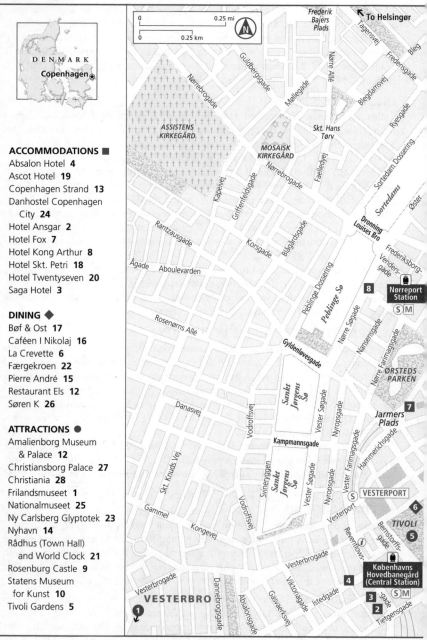

DENMARK
Copenhagen

ACCOMMODATIONS ■
Absalon Hotel **4**
Ascot Hotel **19**
Copenhagen Strand **13**
Danhostel Copenhagen
    City **24**
Hotel Ansgar **2**
Hotel Fox **7**
Hotel Kong Arthur **8**
Hotel Skt. Petri **18**
Hotel Twentyseven **20**
Saga Hotel **3**

DINING ◆
Bøf & Ost **17**
Caféen I Nikolaj **16**
La Crevette **6**
Færgekroen **22**
Pierre André **15**
Restaurant Els **12**
Søren K **26**

ATTRACTIONS ●
Amalienborg Museum
    & Palace **12**
Christiansborg Palace **27**
Christiania **28**
Frilandsmuseet **1**
Nationalmuseet **25**
Ny Carlsberg Glyptotek **23**
Nyhavn **14**
Rådhus (Town Hall)
    and World Clock **21**
Rosenburg Castle **9**
Statens Museum
    for Kunst **10**
Tivoli Gardens **5**

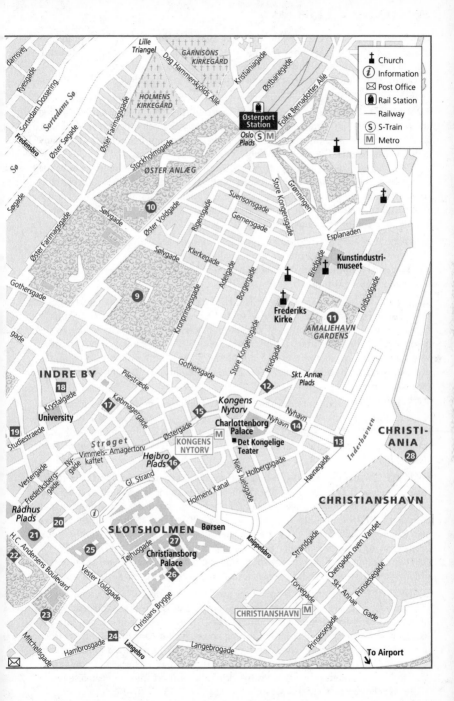

half fare when accompanied by an adult. For 105DKK ($17.85/£9.45) you can purchase a ticket allowing 24-hour bus and train travel through nearly half of Zealand; it's half price for children 7 to 11, and free for children 6 and under.

Eurail passes and **Nordturist Pass** tickets (which can be purchased at any train station in Scandinavia) can be used on local trains in Copenhagen.

DISCOUNT PASS The **Copenhagen Card** entitles you to free and unlimited travel by bus and rail throughout the metropolitan area (including North Zealand), 25% to 50% discounts on crossings to and from Sweden, and free admission to many sights and museums. The card is available for 1 or 3 days and costs 199DKK ($33.85/ £17.90) and 429DKK ($72.95/£38.60), respectively. Up to two children under the age of 10 are allowed to go free with each adult card. If you have three or more children, a 50% discount is granted. Buy the card at tourist offices, the airport, train stations, and most hotels. For more information contact the Copenhagen Tourist Information Center (see above).

BY BUS Copenhagen's well-maintained buses mostly leave from Rådhuspladsen in the heart of the city. Buses run along the major routes every 10 to 15 minutes. Fares are integrated into the existing zonal systems (see "Basic Fares," above). For information, call ☎ **36-13-14-15.**

BY METRO In 2002, Copenhagen launched its first Metro line, taking passengers from east to west across the city or vice versa. Operating 24 hours, the Metro runs as far west as Vanlose or as far south as Vestmager. Nørreport is the transfer station to the **S-tog** system, the commuter rail link to the suburbs. Metro trains run every 2 minutes during rush hours and every 15 minutes at night. Check online at **www.m.dk/ en/route** for a map and schedule. Fares are integrated into the existing zonal systems (see "Basic Fares," above).

BY S-TOG The S-tog connects the heart of Copenhagen, most notably the Central Station, with the city's suburbs. Use of the tickets is the same as on the buses and metro (see "Basic Fares," above). You can transfer from a bus line to an S-tog train on the same ticket. Rail passholders generally ride free. For more information, call ☎ **70-13-14-15.**

BY TAXI Watch for the FRI (free) sign or green light to hail a taxi, and be sure the taxis are metered. **Taxa 4x35** (☎ **35-35-35-35**) operates the largest fleet of cabs. Tips are included in the meter price (although rounding up and leaving a little change is common): 19DKK to 32DKK ($3.25–$5.45/£1.70–£2.90) at the drop of the flag and 12DKK ($2.05/£1.10) per kilometer thereafter, Monday to Friday 7am to 4pm. From 6pm to 6am, and all day Saturday and Sunday, the cost is 15DKK ($2.55/ £1.10) per kilometer. Many drivers speak English. *Note:* You will be charged more for ordering a taxi by phone—it's cheaper to hail one or find a taxi stand.

BY BICYCLE Copenhagen is one of the most bike-friendly cities in Europe, resulting in a noticeable lack of pollution. Beware of cyclists as you walk around—they have right of way on bike paths and if you hear a bell, move over. If you want to join the locals, there is a great rental scheme allowing you to pick up one of 2,000 bikes from one of 110 racks for a refundable deposit of 20DKK ($3.40/£1.80). You then return it to any bike rack across the city and get your deposit back. The scheme runs from May to November annually. See **www.bycyklen.dk** for more info. You can also rent a bike at **Copenhagens Cyklebors,** Gothersgade 157 (☎ **33-14-07-17**). Depending on the bike, daily rates range from 60DKK to 150DKK ($10.20–$25.50/£5.40–£13.50) with deposits from 200DKK to 300DKK ($34–$51/£18–£27). Hours are Monday to Friday 8:30am to 5:30pm and Saturday 10am to 1:30pm.

WHERE TO STAY

Note: Air-conditioning is not a standard amenity in Scandinavia, where it rarely gets very hot in summer. So, unless noted below, your hotel won't have any. And for those on tight budgets, look for hotels offering weekend packages to counteract the city's high rack rates.

Absalon Hotel *(Value)* Long the most popular and most affordable budget hotel near the Central Station, this well-managed, family-run lodging has been putting up rail travelers since 1938. It is actually two hotels in one: the government-rated three-star Absalon Hotel and the one-star Absalon Annex. The rooms in the main building are more comfortable and spacious (best of all being the 19 luxury rooms and suites on the top floor); the Annex is more of a hostel, without private bathrooms.

Helgølandsgade 15, DK-1653 København. ✆ **32-24-22-11.** Fax 33-24-34-11. www.absalon-hotel.dk. 262 units. 900DKK–1,150DKK ($153–$196/£81–£104) double; 1,100DKK–1,300DKK ($187–$221/£99–£117) triple; 1,260DKK–1,810DKK ($214–$308/£113–£163) suite. Rates include buffet breakfast. AE, DC, MC, V. Closed Dec 14–Jan 2. Bus: 6, 10, 16, 27, or 28. **Amenities:** Breakfast room; lounge; laundry; nonsmoking rooms. *In room:* Hair dryer (in some).

Ascot Hotel *(Value)* One of Copenhagen's better midsize hotels, in the very heart of town, near the Central Station and a 2-minute walk from Rådhuspladsen. Dating from 1902 (with a 19th-c. ex-bathhouse annexed in 1994), it's seen many changes and alterations over the years but could now do with a little sprucing up. Bedrooms are simply furnished. The finest open onto the street, but the units in the rear get better air circulation and more light. There's also a fitness center.

Studiestraede 61, DK-1554 København. ✆ **33-12-60-00.** Fax 33-14-60-40. www.ascothotel.dk. 120 units. 1,090DKK–1,480DKK ($185–$252/£98.10–£133) double; 1,695DKK–2,560DKK ($288–$435/£153–£230) suite. Rates include buffet breakfast. AE, DC, MC, V. Bus: 14 or 16. **Amenities:** Restaurant; bar; laundry; nonsmoking rooms. *In room:* Hair dryer.

Copenhagen Strand *(★)* This old brick and timber warehouse has been skillfully converted into a charming modern hotel. The waterfront Strand sports a vaguely maritime decor heavy on the *hygge,* a Danish word loosely translating as cozy or warm, but meaning so much more. The higher-priced rooms open onto views of the harbor. Standard rooms are well furnished and on the small end of midsize; each has a well-kept bathroom with a tub (some have showers). In 2007 the Strand started offering guests free Internet access.

Havnegade 37, DK-1058 København. ✆ **33-48-99-00.** Fax 33-48-99-01. www.copenhagenstrand.com. 174 units. Mon–Thurs 1,670DKK–2,360DKK ($284–$401/£150–£212) double, 2,875DKK–3,290DKK ($489–$559/£259–£296) suite; Fri–Sun 1,330DKK–1,875DKK ($226–$319/£120–£169) double, 2,085DKK–3,115DKK ($354–$529.55/£188–£280) suite. Tram: 1 or 6. **Amenities:** Breakfast room; bar; laundry; nonsmoking rooms; rooms for those w/limited mobility. *In room:* Hair dryer.

Danhostel Copenhagen City *(★)* Staying in a hostel can be risky, but we recommend this one because it's more stylish than most. The furniture has been supplied by GUBI, the same design company chosen to furnish New York's Museum of Modern Art, *and* the whole place is clean, central (less than 1km from the rail station) and cheap compared to most Copenhagen accommodations. Private rooms sleep between four and six, but if you pay for the whole room you can keep it all to yourself.

H.C. Andersens Blvd. 50, DK-1553 København. ✆ **33-18-83-32.** Fax 33-11-85-88. www.danhostel.dk. 192 en-suite units. 520DKK–660DKK ($88.40–$112/£46.80–£59.40) 4-bed private room. AE, DC, MC, V. Bus: 5A. **Amenities:** Breakfast room; laundry; entire hostel is nonsmoking; rooms for those w/limited mobility. *In room:* No phone.

Hotel Ansgar   Only a 3-minute walk from the Central Station, this hotel lies in the heart of Copenhagen but on a fairly tranquil one-way street. The five-story building dates from 1885, and has recently been upgraded and extensively modernized (meaning the prices went up but it's still good value). It's a family favorite because of its two dozen spacious rooms with extra beds. Rooms are comfortable, cozy, and modern with Danish designs and a marble, shower-only bathroom.

Colbjørnsensgade 29, DK-1652 København. ✆ **33-21-21-96.** Fax 33-21-61-91. www.ansgar-hotel.dk. 81 units. 850DKK–1,250DKK ($145–$213/£77–£113) double. Rates include buffet breakfast. AE, DC, MC, V. Bus: 6, 10, 28, or 41. **Amenities:** Breakfast room; lounge; laundry; nonsmoking rooms. *In room:* Hair dryer

Hotel Fox ✦✦   In 2005 Volkswagen launched its new Fox car and wanted somewhere supercool to put up the visiting journalists and execs. They couldn't find anywhere so decided to equip an old hotel to suit their needs. The result was this highly recommended hotel, where all the rooms have been decorated by 21 hip local designers. Choices now range from kitsch Heidi-inspired boudoirs to boxing dens. To top it off, there's an eco-loving Nordic eatery and free Internet access throughout.

Jarmers Plads 3, DK-1551 Copenhagen. ✆ **33-13-30-00.** Fax 33-14-30-33. www.hotelfox.dk. 61 units. Doubles 945DKK–1,620DKK ($161–$275/£85.05–£146). Rates include breakfast. AE, DC, MC, V. Bus: 14 or 16. **Amenities:** Restaurant; bar; laundry; all rooms are nonsmoking. *In room:* Hair dryer.

Hotel Kong Arthur ✦ *Value*   This 1882 hotel and former orphanage enjoys a tranquil residential setting opening out onto a string of city lakes. Completely renovated and modernized over the years, it's a very welcoming and intimate choice with a small atrium garden where breakfast is served in summer. The comfortable guest rooms have spacious tiled bathrooms. The helpful staff will do anything from cleaning shoes to getting theater tickets. It was once owned by Frommer's founder Arthur Frommer, hence the name.

Nørre Søgade 11, DK-1370 København. ✆ **33-11-12-12.** Fax 33-32-61-30. www.kongarthur.dk. 117 units. 1,520DKK–1,720DKK ($258–$292/£137–£155) double; from 3,020DKK ($513/£272) suite. Rates include buffet breakfast. AE, DC, MC, V. Bus: 5, 7, or 16. **Amenities:** 4 restaurants; bar; laundry; nonsmoking rooms. *In room:* Hair dryer.

Hotel Skt. Petri   This luxe hotel is a celebrity magnet offering trendy elegance in a charming neighborhood nicknamed the "Latin Quarter." Originally a graceless modern department store, the windows of this well-renovated property offer fine views of St. Peter's Church, the old library, and the Rundetårn (Round Tower), just 2 blocks away. The rooms have all of the amenities you could wish for, and marvelously comfy beds with feather pillows and cotton sheets. Prices are very high and the standard rooms are small, so definitely ask about their deals.

Krystalgade 22, DK-1172 København. ✆ **33-45-91-00.** Fax 33-45-91-10. www.hotelsktpetri.com. 268 units. 1,395DKK–2,195DKK ($237–$373/£126–£198) small double; from 3,395DKK ($577/£306) suite. Breakfast buffet is an additional 165DKK ($28.05/£14.85). AE, DC, MC, V. S-tog: Nørreport. Bus: 6a. **Amenities:** Restaurant; cafe; bar; laundry; nonsmoking floors; rooms for those w/limited mobility. *In room:* Hair dryer.

Hotel Twentyseven ✦✦   Within easy walking distance of Copenhagen's central station, Hotel Twentyseven is the city's latest design hotel and a place where we like to stay. Rooms are light and bright, featuring current Scandinavian styling and unique touches such as black slate bathrooms. There's no restaurant as such but The Wine Room does allow for some global grazing while the attached ice bar is an interesting experience that requires the donning of a thermal hooded cape. Free Wi-Fi is available throughout the hotel.

Løngangstræde 27, DK-1468 København. ⓒ 70-27-56-27. Fax 70-27-96-27. www.hotel27.dk. 200 units. 1,725DKK ($293/£155) double. Rates include breakfast. AE, DC, MC, V. Bus: 6a. **Amenities:** 3 bars; laundry; hotel is completely nonsmoking. *In room:* Hair dryer.

Saga Hotel   Close to the rail station, this longtime budget favorite of foreign visitors and students was created in 1947 by combining two late-19th-century apartment buildings. Only 31 of the comfortably but simply furnished bedrooms have private bathrooms. The shared hallway bathrooms are adequate. Many of the bedrooms are spacious, with three to four beds—great for friends traveling together. *Warning:* The five-story building has no elevator, and the cheaper rooms are often at the top.

Colbjørnsensgade 18-20, DK-1652 København. ⓒ 33-24-49-44. Fax 33-24-60-33. www.sagahotel.dk. 79 units. 480DKK–750DKK ($81.60–$128/£43–£68) double without bathroom; 600DKK–950DKK ($102–$162/£54–£86) double with bathroom. Rates include breakfast. AE, DC, MC, V. Bus: 6, 10, 16, 28, or 41. **Amenities:** Breakfast room; lounge; nonsmoking rooms.

TOP ATTRACTIONS & SPECIAL MOMENTS

Like many rail travelers, you may have only 1 day to spend in Copenhagen. That's far too little time, but start the day off by strolling the old city's cobblestone streets and along its canals. Spend the afternoon at **Christiansborg Palace,** on Slotsholmen ("Palace Island"), where the queen receives guests. Early in the evening, head to the **Tivoli.** If it's winter, explore **Kongens Nytorv (King's New Square)** and the charming old sailor's quarter called Nyhavn, bristling with boats, bars, and cozy restaurants. At some point in the day, climb the Rundetårn (Round Tower) for a glorious panorama of Copenhagen.

If you have a second day, visit **Amalienborg Palace,** the queen's residence. Try to time your visit to see the changing of the guard. It doesn't have the precision or pomp of the changing of the guard at Buckingham Palace (p. 410), but nonetheless remains a Kodak moment. Continue beyond the palace to the city's most famous statue, *The Little Mermaid,* perched upon a rock in the harbor. In the afternoon, see the art treasures of **Ny Carlsberg Glyptotek.**

Amalienborg Museum and Palace ✿✿   Amalienborg museum is inside Amalienborg Palace, the 18th-century French-style rococo home of the Danish royal family since 1794. Amalienborg opens onto Copenhagen's most beautiful square and is the setting for the changing of the guard ceremony at noon. The ceremony only takes place when the queen is in residence, which is signaled by the raising of a swallowtail flag. In 1994, the overflow of royal treasures at Rosenborg Castle was accommodated in a museum on the ground floor, and since then other rooms of Amalienborg have been opened to the public, revealing lavish private and state rooms. Two of the most interesting rooms are the **study of Christian IX** (1863–1906) and the **drawing rooms of Queen Louise** (1817–98). These rooms are furnished with gifts from their far-flung children in honor of their unofficial status as "parents-in-law to Europe."

Amalienborg Museum. ⓒ 33-12-21-86. www.ses.dk. Admission 50DKK ($8.50/£4.50) adults, 30DKK ($5.10/£2.70) students, 15DKK ($2.55/£1.35) children 5–12, free for children 4 and under. May–Oct daily 10am–4pm; Nov–Apr daily 11am–4pm. Closed Mon. Bus: 1, 6, 9, or 10.

Finds A "Free City" within Copenhagen

Not for everybody, but worth a look, is a trip to the **Free City of Christiania,** on the island of Christianshavn (take bus no. 8 from Rådhuspladsen). Since 1971, some 1,000 squatters have taken over 130 former army barracks (spread across 85 acres/34 hectares) and declared themselves a free city, whose hippie-style liberation included communal living, ecological stewardship, hashish cafes, and general tolerance of alternative lifestyles. You can shop, dine, and talk to the natives about the experimental community, which has its own doctors, clubs, and stores. It even flies its own flag. On January 1, 2006, the settlement was sold to private developers by the Danish government, who would like to see it become "like any other neighborhood," and who hope to quash the fabled anarchic spirit of the place. This led to a riot in May 2007 and increased tension between police and residents. Caution also needs to be exercised in the area as it's a favorite of pickpockets and "Pusher Street" attracts just the kind of crowd its name suggests.

Christiansborg Palace ★★★   Since 1167, five royal palaces have stood on this site on Slotsholmen, a small island separated from the heart of the city by a moatlike canal, pierced by several bridges. The present granite-and-copper palace dates from 1928. For 8 centuries, this has been the center of political power in Denmark, and the Christiansborg complex today is home to the houses of parliament, the prime minister's offices, and the Danish Supreme Court. Of more interest to visitors is a tour of the lushly decorated Royal Reception Salons, taking in such attractions as the Throne Room, the Banqueting Hall, and the Queen's Library.

In the courtyard, an equestrian statue of Christian IX (1863–1906) guards the grounds, and on the north end you'll find the **Kongeliege Stalde & Kareter (Royal Stables & Coaches).** Especially interesting here are the regal coaches and the grand carriages used in days of yore. There's a separate admission charge to the stables of 10 DKK ($1.70/90p) adults, free for children under 12. The site can be visited May to October Saturday to Sunday 2 to 4pm.

Christiansborg Slotsplads. (© **33-92-64-92.** www.ses.dk Guided tour of Royal Reception Rooms 60DKK ($10.20/£5.40) adults, 25DKK ($4.25/£2.25) children 4–17. Admission to castle ruins 40DKK ($6.80/£3.60) adults, 15DKK ($2.55/£1.35) children 4–17. Free admission to parliament. Guided tours of Reception Rooms May–Sept daily at 11am, 1pm, and 3pm; Oct–Apr Tues–Sun at 3pm. Ruins May–Sept daily 10am–4pm; Oct–Apr Tues–Sun 10am–4pm. English-language tours of parliament daily 11am, 1pm, and 3pm year-round. Bus: 1, 2, 5, 8, or 9.

Frilandsmuseet (Open-Air Museum) ★★   Covering 86 acres (35 hectares) in Lyngby, on the fringe of the city, this museum re-creates rural Denmark in the 19th century and does so exceedingly well. It's a 2-mile (3.2km) walk around the entire compound, where you'll come across cottages once inhabited by fishermen, a farmstead from the 1700s on a remote Danish island, a primitive longhouse from the remote Faeroe Islands, and even tower windmills and a potter's workshop from the 1800s. Buildings were shipped from all over Denmark and reassembled here. Organized activities often take place here on summer afternoons. Sometimes dancers perform Danish folkloric shows, or you might see demonstrations of lace-making and loom-weaving. The park is a 9-mile (14km) ride from the Central Station, and there is a restaurant serving lunch on the grounds.

Kongevejen 100. (© 33-13-44-11. www.natmus.dk. Free admission. Easter–Oct Tues–Sun 10am–5pm. Closed most Mon. Phone ahead to check. S-tog: Copenhagen Central Station to Sorgenfri (trains leave every 20 min.). Bus: 184 or 194.

Nationalmuseet (National Museum) ✻✻✻   One of the great museums of Scandinavia, this is the treasure-trove of Denmark, a gigantic repository of artifacts that allows visitors to stroll through 10,000 years of history in beautiful rooms that have been recently modernized without losing their charm. The vast complex takes in the Prinsens Palae or prince's palace constructed in 1744. There are six different departments in all, beginning with Danish prehistory, spanning the period from 13,000 B.C. to A.D. 1000. Among the stunning exhibits is the "Sun Chariot" found in a bog and dating from 1200 B.C. Finds from the Viking epoch include runic stones from Jutland in the 10th century. Religious objects and other exhibits, such as a 12th-century golden altar from Århus, fill a lot of the rooms devoted to the Middle Ages and the Renaissance. Lesser rooms feature the Danish collections of 1660 to 1830 (mainly antiques), Near-Eastern and Classical Antiquities, the Ethnographical Collections (among the finest in the world), and the Royal Collection of Coins and Medals. If it all seems like too much, free English audio guides can whisk you around the museum's highlights in an hour.

Ny Vestergade 10. (© 33-13-44-11. www.natmus.dk. Free admission. Tues–Sun 10am–5pm. Closed Dec 24, 25, and 31. Bus: 1, 2, 5, 6, 8, 10, or 41.

Ny Carlsberg Glyptotek ✻✻✻   Carl Jacobsen, Mr. Carlsberg Beer himself, originally opened this major art museum behind the Tivoli more than a century ago. It's now one of the greatest art collections in Europe. Jacobsen was a feverish collector of classical art, and the museum still reflects his 19th-century taste, though the beer baron's original collection has been beefed up considerably over the years and now includes a treasure-trove of works by French Impressionists. It was started with a gift of some three dozen Paul Gaugin pieces, but today you'll also see paintings by Monet, Manet, Degas, and Renoir, as well French sculpture, such as Rodin's *Burgers of Calais.* Cézanne's much-reproduced *Portrait of the Artist* also hangs here.

The antiquities collection is filled with sculpture and art from ancient Greece and Egypt, as well as Italy in the Etruscan and Roman eras. The most notable prize in the Egyptian collection is a prehistoric rendering of a hippopotamus. Impressive Greek originals, such as a headless Apollo and Niobe's tragic children, are on view with Roman copies of original Greek bronzes, including a 4th-century Hercules. The Etruscan art display is especially notable, with its sarcophagi, winged lions, bronzes, and pottery. The entire museum reopened in June 2006 after a 3-year renovation that cost 100 million DKK ($17 million/£9 million), part of which was spent on the construction of a wing called "The Ancient Mediterranean World."

Dantes Plads 7. (© 33-41-81-41. www.glyptoteket.dk. Admission 50DKK ($8.50/£4.50) adults, free for under 18s; free for everyone on Sun. Tues–Sun 10am–4pm. Closed Jan 1, June 15, and Dec 24–25. Bus: 1, 5, 10, 550S, or 650S.

Rådhus (Town Hall) and World Clock   We have never been able to work up much enthusiasm for this towering monument, the City Hall of Copenhagen. It was said to have been inspired by the main tower at the Piazza del Campo in Siena. The original is magnificent, the one in Copenhagen a bit dull. The architect, Martin Nyrop, wanted to create a building to "give gaiety to everyday life and spontaneous pleasure to all." We're not so sure he succeeded, but check it out anyway. Statues of Hans Christian Andersen and Niels Bohr (the Nobel Prize–winning physicist) are worth a look. Jens Olsen's **World Clock** is open for viewing Monday to Friday 10am to 4pm

Moments   **The Old Sailor's Port at Nyhavn**

Nothing quite captures the spirit of maritime Copenhagen the way **Nyhavn** ★★★ does. This colorful canal was dug in the late 1600s to permit seafaring vessels to go right up to Kongens Nytorv, the city's largest square, with an equestrian statue of Christian IV in the center. Here mariners would unload their cargo from the remote corners of the globe at the old warehouses once located here. Because so many sailors were in the area at night, a series of rowdy bars, cafes, and bordellos were opened to serve them.

In time, the area became gentrified and many of the most famous Copenhageners preferred to live here, including Hans Christian Andersen who resided at various addresses: 20, 67, and 18 Nyhavn in that chronological order. Today, charming little restaurants, cafes, and a scattering of bars line the canal, and this is one of the most favored places for absorbing Copenhagen's unique flavor. The northern side of Nyhavn is a pedestrian area crowded with locals and visitors alike. High-speed craft come and go from here all day, linking Copenhagen with Malmö, Sweden.

and Saturday at 1pm. Frederik IX set the clock on December 15, 1955. The clockwork is so exact that it's accurate to within half a second every 300 years. Climb the tower for an impressive view, though it's not for the faint of heart—300 steps with no elevator.

To the east of the Rådhus is one of Copenhagen's most famous landmarks, the **Lurblæserne** (Lur Blower Column), topped by two Vikings blowing an ancient trumpet called a *lur*. There's a bit of artistic license taken here. The *lur* actually dates from the Bronze Age (ca. 1500 B.C.), while the Vikings lived some 1,000 years ago. But it's a fascinating sight anyway.

Rådhuspladsen. © **33-66-25-82.** Admission to Rådhus 30DKK ($5.10/£2.70); 5DKK (85¢/45p) children. Guided tour of Rådhus 30DKK ($5.10/£2.70) Mon–Fri 3pm; Sat 3pm. Guided tour of tower Oct–May Mon–Sat noon; June–Sept Mon–Fri 10am, noon, and 2pm, Sat noon. Bus: 1, 6, or 8.

Rosenborg Castle ★★   Inspired by Dutch Renaissance architecture, this *slot* (castle) was constructed of red brick and decorated with sandstone, and it's rather the same as it was in 1633 except for the absence of the original moat. First laid out in 1606, *Kongens Have* ("king's garden") remains a delightful oasis of tranquility within the bustling city. Danish royals used Rosenborg as their summerhouse until 1710, when King Frederik IV pronounced it "too small for a king." The castle is filled with royal treasures ranging from Narwhal tusk and ivory coronation chairs to Frederik VII's baby shoes. The **crown jewels and regalia**—the single most impressive treasure—is on exhibit in the Treasury. In the Knights Hall you can see the coronation seat and other royal relics from the 18th century. The most lavish royal bedroom, Room 3, is decorated with Asian lacquer art with a stucco ceiling. Christian IV died in this room surrounded by mourners. *Warning:* The castle is currently undergoing major renovations and won't be fully reopen until April 2008. Until then, many areas are closed.

Øster Voldgade 4A. © **33-15-32-86.** www.rosenborgslot.dk. Admission 65DKK ($11.05/£5.85) adults, 40DKK ($6.80/£3.60) students and seniors, free for children under 17. Palace and treasury (royal jewels), Jan–Apr Tues–Sun 11am–4pm; May and Sept–Oct daily 10am–4pm; June–Aug daily 10am–5pm; Nov to mid-Dec Tues–Sun 11am–4pm. Closed Dec 17–26, Dec 31, and Jan 1. S-tog: Nørreport. Bus: 5, 10, 14, 16, 31, 42, 43, 184, or 185.

Statens Museum for Kunst (Royal Museum of Fine Arts) ★★★   We could spend an entire day here and always find some new artistic discovery. If you can't afford so much time, give it at least 2 hours, even more if you can spare it. The largest museum in Denmark houses painting and sculpture from the 13th century to the present. Its collection of Flemish and Dutch paintings from the 15th to the 18th centuries is especially impressive: an era of golden age landscapes and marine paintings by Rubens and his school, and remarkable portraits by every artist from Rembrandt (in 2006, after much international research, the museum discovered two of its paintings were genuine Rembrandts) to Frans Hals. The European art section is rich in works from the Italian school from the 14th to the 18th centuries, and the French school from the 17th and 18th centuries. The Statens is also one of the grandest showcases for showing the development of Danish painting in the 19th century. Notable paintings, each a world masterpiece, displayed here include *Workers Coming Home* by Edvard Munch; *Interior with a Violin* by Matisse; *Alice* by Modigliani; *The Guitar Player* by Juan Gris; and *The Judgement of Paris* by Harald Giersing. The museum also

---

⟨ Moments   The Town's Hottest Date: Half Woman, Half Fish

The Little Mermaid ★ is the most famous statue in Scandinavia, and every visitor wants to see her. Described by some cynics as "Copenhagen's greatest disappointment," this life-size bronze of *Den Lille Havfrue* was inspired by Hans Christian Andersen's *The Little Mermaid,* one of the world's most famous fairy tales. Edvard Eriksen's sculpture, unveiled in 1913, rests on rocks right off the shore. In spite of its small size, the statue is as important a symbol to Copenhageners as the Statue of Liberty is to New Yorkers. The mermaid has fallen prey to vandals over the years. In the early 1900s, her arm was cut off and later recovered. She was decapitated on April 25, 1964, and the head was never returned. (The original mold exists, so missing body parts can be recast.) In January 1998, she lost her head again, and most of the city responded with sadness. "She is part of our heritage, like the Tivoli, the queen, and stuff like that," said local sculptor Christian Moerk.

Although not taking blame for the attack, the Radical Feminist Faction sent flyers to newspapers to protest "the woman-hating, sexually fixated male dreams" allegedly conjured by the statue's nudity. The head mysteriously turned up at a TV station, delivered by a masked figure. Welders restored it, making the seam invisible.

But the japes and protests continue; since 2006 *The Little Mermaid* has sported a bra, a burka, a dildo, and various shades of paint. Copenhagen officials have responded by suggesting moving their city's symbol farther out to sea.

houses an impressive collection of Viking artifacts and has a sculpture garden filled with both classical and contemporary works. In 1998, a concert hall, Children's Art Museum, and a glass wing were added, the latter devoted to temporary exhibitions.

Sølvgade 48-50. ℭ 33-74-84-94. www.smk.dk. Free admission. Tues and Thurs–Sun 10am–5pm; Wed 10am–8pm. Bus: 6A, 14, 26, 40, 42, 43, 184, 185, 150S, or 173 E.

Tivoli Gardens ✿✿✿ *Moments*   Created in 1843, the Tivoli gardens gave Walt Disney an idea, and look what he did with it. The original is still here, standing in a 20-acre (8-hectare) garden in the center of Copenhagen. Its greatest admirers call it a pleasure park or flower garden; its critics say it's one giant beer garden.

Let's face it: The Tivoli is filled with schmaltz, but somehow with its glitz, glamour, and gaiety it manages to win over hardened cynics. Children prefer it during the day, but adults tend to like it better at night, when more than 100,000 specially made soft-glow light bulbs and at least a million regular bulbs are turned on—what an electric bill!

It features thousands of flowers, a merry-go-round, pinball arcades, slot machines, a Ferris wheel of hot-air balloons, an Arabian-style fantasy palace, and two-dozen expensive restaurants. The latest attraction at Tivoli, "The Star Flyer," is the world's tallest carousel at 264 ft. (80m) high, giving the brave amazing views of the city below. There's also a playground for children.

A parade of the red-uniformed Tivoli Boys Guard takes place on weekends at 5:20 and 7:20pm (also on Wed at 5pm), and their regimental band gives concerts on Saturday at 3pm on the open-air stage. The oldest building at Tivoli, the Chinese-style Pantomime Theater with its peacock curtain, offers pantomimes in the evening.

For more on the nighttime happenings in Tivoli—fireworks, bands, orchestras, discos, variety acts—see "Nightlife," below.

Vesterbrogade 3. ℭ 33-15-10-01. www.tivoligardens.com. Admission 75DKK ($12.75/£6.75) adults, 40DKK ($6.80/£3.60) children 3–11, free kids under 2. For all rides 200DKK ($34/£18) adults, 150DKK ($25.50/£13.50) children 3–11. Family ticket (2 adults, 2 kids) 575DKK ($97.75/£51.75). Closed mid-Sept to mid-Apr. Bus: 1, 16, or 29.

WHERE TO DINE

Bøf & Ost FRENCH/DANISH   Popular with university students, this relatively affordable restaurant—Beef & Cheese in English—is housed in an 18th-century building with an outdoor terrace overlooking Greyfriars Square, one of the landmark plazas in Copenhagen's Old Town. Its cellars were created out of the ruins of a medieval monastery. You don't get a lot of surprises here but you do get good, solid, home-style cooking (try the char-grilled streak), and one of the best cheese boards in Copenhagen.

Gråbrødretorv 13. ℭ 33-11-99-11. www.boef-ost.dk. Reservations required. Main courses 149DKK–199DKK ($25.35–$33.85/£13.40–£17.90); fixed-price lunch menu 118DKK ($20.60/£10.60). DC, MC, V. Mon–Sat 11:30am–10:30pm. Closed Jan 1. Bus: 5.

Caféen I Nikolaj DANISH   Set in an old church, this reasonably priced lunch and teatime venue is one of the most attractive eateries in the medieval Latin Quarter. Tables and chairs are set up outside in the summer months, while the building's large leaded-glass windows add atmosphere inside. Produce is bought in straight from the market so the menu changes seasonally but should always include innovative dishes such as mature cheddar cheese on rye with aspic jelly, drippings, and Jamaican rum.

Nikolaj Plads, 12. ⓒ **70-26-64-64**. www.nikolajkirken.dk. Reservations not accepted. Main courses 70DKK–178DKK ($11.90–$30.25/£6.30–£16). AE, DC, MC, V. Mon–Sat 11:30am–5pm; July–Aug and 2 weeks before Christmas Mon–Sat 11:30am–11pm.

Færgekroen DANISH

Tivoli is not a place for cheap dining, which makes this affordable lakeside restaurant, housed in a pink half-timbered Danish cottage, all the more delightful. Sit on its outdoor terraces on a sunny day, and enjoy honest, straight-forward fare such as fried meatballs, curried chicken, or pork chops with red cabbage. To complement the farm-style food the owners have recently added a microbrewery, producing two types of wonderfully tasty beer.

Vesterbrogade 3, Tivoli Gardens. ⓒ **33-12-94-12**. www.faergekroen.dk. Reservations recommended for outdoor ter-race tables. Main courses 110DKK–205DKK ($18.70–$34.85/£9.90–£18). AE, DC, MC, V. Daily 11am–midnight (hot food until 9:45pm).

La Crevette ✿✿ SEAFOOD/CONTINENTAL

For a really big splurge, reserve a table at this classic Tivoli restaurant, housed in a 1909 pavilion with an outdoor ter-race. Some of the city's best seafood is served here by chefs who dare to be innovative while still adhering to classic culinary principles. Most dishes here are "sure bets," including the terrine of Norwegian salmon baked with smoked eel and wild mush-rooms, or the skin-fried summer cod with warm lobster salad and green beans.

Vesterbrogade 5, Tivoli Gardens. ⓒ **33-14-60-03**. www.nimb.dk. Reservations required. Main courses 255DKK–315DKK ($43.35–$53.55/£22.95–£28.35); 4-course fixed-price dinner 455DKK ($77.35/£40.95). AE, DC, MC, V. Open during the Tivoli summer season only from mid-Apr to mid-Sep and mid-Nov to late Dec, daily noon–midnight.

Pierre André ✿✿✿ FRENCH

A great opportunity to enjoy world-class cuisine in a relaxed atmosphere. Entering his second decade with Michelin star firmly in hand, chef/owner Phillip Houdet serves fine French cuisine, while wife Sussie (who runs the dining room) offers a warm Danish welcome. Menu highs include carpaccio of foie gras served with shaved Parmesan and truffles, and wild venison with a bitter choco-late sauce. Children are welcome and dishes are adapted for their younger palates.

Ny Ostergarde 21 ⓒ **33-16-17-19**. www.pierreandre.dk. Reservations required. Main courses 275DKK–395DKK ($46.75–$67.15/£24.75–£35.55); fixed-price menus 400DKK–755DKK ($68–$128/£36–£67.95). AE, DC, MC, V. Tues–Sat noon–2pm and 6–10pm. Closed 3 weeks July–Aug. Bus: 6, 10, or 14.

Restaurant Els DANISH/FRENCH

With its original 1854 decor intact, this for-mer coffeehouse is now one of Copenhagen's most respected and traditional restau-rants. It's certainly the best decorated—just look at the 19th-century murals. Hans Christian Andersen dined here in his day; John Irving stopped by more recently. Pop in at lunch for one of the delectable open-faced Danish sandwiches, or book in the evening for market-fresh food such as grilled scallops with chestnuts or saddle of rein-deer with baked apple and cranberries.

Store Strandstraede 3, off Kongens Nytorv. ⓒ **33-14-13-41**. Reservations recommended. www.restaurant-els.dk. Main courses 158DKK–265DKK ($26.85–$45.05/£14.20–£23.85); sandwiches (lunch only) 50DKK–85DKK ($8.50–$14/£4.50–£7.65); 5-course prix-fixe dinner from 495DKK ($84/£45). AE, DC, MC, V. Mon–Sat noon–3pm; daily 5:30–10pm. Bus: 1, 6, or 10.

Søren K ✿ INTERNATIONAL

Named after Denmark's most celebrated philoso-pher, this minimalist dining room on the ground floor of the Royal Library is deco-rated in monochromatic tones, with big windows overlooking the canal. The chefs here cook without butter, cream, or high-cholesterol cheese—a heresy in a land known for its "butter-and-egg men"—and consequently some Danes boycott it, though foreign visitors, especially dieters, love it. Try the oyster soup or the roasted venison served with nuts and seasonal berries.

On the ground floor of the Royal Library's Black Diamond Wing, 1 Søren Kierkegaards Plads 1. (© **33-47-49-49.** www.soerenk.dk. Reservations recommended. Main courses 92DKK–145DKK ($15.65–$24.65/£8.30–£13.05) at lunch, 195DKK–225DKK ($33.15–$38.25/£17.55–£20.25) at dinner; fixed-price 3-course dinner 395DKK ($67.15/ £35.55). AE, DC, MC, V. Mon–Sat 11am–10:30pm. Bus: 1, 2, 5, 8, or 9.

SHOPPING

Much of the action takes place on **Strøget,** the pedestrian street in the heart of the capital. Note that "Strøget" is a description, not a place name; it's pronounced "stroll," which is what you do on it. Strøget begins as Frederiksberggade, north of Rådhus-pladsen, and winds to Østergade, which opens onto Kongens Nytorv. The jam-packed street is lined with stores selling everything from porcelain statues of *Youthful Boldness* to pizza slices. The hurried visitor searching for Danish design might head first for **Illum,** Ostergade 52 (© **33-14-40-02;** www.illum.dk), one of Copenhagen's leading department stores, filled with top-notch Danish designs as well as those from other Scandinavian countries. Another elegant department store is **Magasin,** Kongens Nytorv (© **33-11-44-33;** www.magasin.dk), which offers the tops in Scandinavia fashion, plus lots of fine glass and porcelain along with handicrafts.

Those seeking the best of top-grade Scandinavian sweaters or Icelandic cardigans will find a vast selection at the **Sweater Market,** Nytorv 19 (© **33-15-27-73;** www. sweatermarket.com). All sweaters are made of natural fibers—mostly wool, some cotton—and there are also mittens, caps, and socks on offer. Those who flock to flea markets will find **Det Blå Pakhus,** Holmbladsgade 113 (© **32-95-17-07;** www.blaa pakhus.dk), to their liking. Charging an entrance fee of 15DKK ($2.55/£1.35), "The Blue Warehouse" (its English name) is the country's largest indoor market, with 325 vendors hawking everything from antiques and carpets to assorted bric-a-brac.

For Copenhagen's world-renowned porcelain head to **Royal Copenhagen Porcelain,** in the Royal Scandinavia retail center, Amagertorv 4 (© **33-13-71-81**). Founded in 1775, the company's trademark of three wavy blue lines is now a world-famous symbol, and the showroom attracts some serious collectors.

NIGHTLIFE

To find out what's on in Copenhagen when you're there, pick up a free copy of *Copenhagen This Week* at the tourist information center or look online at **www.ctw.dk**.

For the summer visitor nothing competes with the **Tivoli Gardens** (p. 214) after dark. On an open-air stage in the center of the garden, vaudevillelike acts such as aerialists perform at 10pm on Friday evenings and on an arbitrary, oft-changing schedule varying from week to week and summer to summer. These performances are free, and are often a venue for jazz or folkloric entertainment. More than a dozen commedia dell'arte productions are performed at the **Pantomime Theater,** with a Chinese stage and peacock curtain. The free shows are staged Tuesday to Thursday at 6:15pm and 8:15pm; Friday at 7:30pm and 9pm; Saturday at 8:15pm and 8:30pm; and Sunday at 4:30pm and 6:30pm.

Grand concerts, everything from symphony to opera, are presented in the 2,000-seat **Tivolis Koncertsal** or concert hall, with tickets costing from 200DKK to 700DKK ($34–$119/£18–£63) when major artists are performing, but most performances are free. Concerts ranging from symphony to opera take place Monday to

Saturday at 7:30pm (sometimes at 8pm, depending on the event). For more information and to book tickets, call ✆ **33-15-10-12.**

Copenhagen is also filled with music clubs featuring jazz, rock, and blues, and has many dance clubs. Some of the best jazz artists in the world perform at **Copenhagen JazzHouse,** Niels Hemmingsensgade 10 (✆ **33-15-26-00;** www.jazzhouse.dk), with shows beginning at 8:30pm nightly, and a cover ranging from 65DKK to 280DKK ($11.05–$47.60/£5.85–£25.20), depending on the artists booked. Small and cozy (60 people max), **La Fontaine,** Kompagnistraede 11 (✆ **33-11-60-98**), presents jazz artists Friday and Saturday beginning around 11:30pm. Otherwise, it's a lively bar open daily from 8pm to 6am. When music is presented, there's a cover charge of 50DKK ($8.50/£4.50).

Considered the best place for clubbing and concerts in the city, **Rust,** Guldbergsgade 8 (✆ **35-24-52-00;** www.rust.dk), has made an interesting transition from its first incarnation as a political coffeehouse to two floors of cutting-edge cool and great music, both live and DJ'd. It's in the neighborhood of Norrebro, which can be reached by Bus 5A, 69, and 250S, and it's worth the ride, especially as it stays open till 5am from Wednesday to Saturday. Entrance is 50DKK ($8.50/£4.50), though concerts cost extra. A trendy joint, **Vega,** Enghavevej 40, Vesterbrø (✆ **33-25-70-11;** www.vega.dk), is the biggest venue in Copenhagen, with three floors of entertainment and three separate venues for concerts, clubbing, and cocktail lounging. International names such as Bjork, Prince, and David Bowie have played here, so keep an eye on the website for info on upcoming events. Opening hours vary, as does the cover, which ranges from free to 60DKK ($10.20/£5.40); concert ticket prices depend on who's playing but are usually between 100DKK and 180DKK ($17–$30.60/£9–£16.20). For a taste of the homegrown Danish rock scene, stop by **The Rock,** Skindergade 45-47 (✆ **33-91-39-13;** www.the-rock.dk), located in an old courthouse. Bands usually start up around 9pm, powering through until midnight when the venue morphs into a "rock club." Cover ranges from 55DKK to 225DKK ($9.35–$38.25/£4.95–£20.25).

Copenhagen also has a number of atmospheric old bars, of which our favorite is **Det Lille Apotek,** Stor Kannikestraede 15 (✆ **33-12-56-06;** www.det-lille-apotek. dk), The Little Pharmacy. Copenhagen's oldest restaurant (dating from 1720) offers an antique atmosphere and is a student favorite. It is open daily from 11am to midnight (except on Sun when it opens at midday). Although spruced up today, **Nyhavn 17,** Nyhavn 17 (✆ **33-12-54-19;** www.nyhavn17.dk), is one of the remaining honkytonks left over from the days when this gentrified quarter was a sailors' haunt. Maintaining a maritime flavor, it mixes up a wide selection of grog with live music most nights of the week. Open Sunday to Thursday 10am to 2am, Friday and Saturday until 3am.

EXCURSION TO HELSINGØR (HAMLET'S CASTLE) ✿

Does it really matter to the pilgrims flocking to this town that Hamlet never existed? Or that William Shakespeare never visited Helsingør? To the pilgrims wanting to see "Hamlet's Castle," the power of legend is what really matters.

After making the 25-mile (40-km) journey north from Copenhagen, make your way through the noisy, congested crowds and the fast-food stalls, and move deeper into Helsingør, where you'll find that it has a certain charm, with a market square, medieval lanes, and old half-timbered and brick buildings, many constructed by ships' captains in the heyday of the 19th-century shipping industry.

The Danish Riviera with its sandy but windy and cold beaches separates Helsingør from Copenhagen. To the east, a fleet of ferries link Helsingør across a 2½-mile (4km) strait with the town of Helsingborg, Sweden. Helsingør became important to merchants and mariners because of its strategic position at the entrance to the Øresund, a narrow strip of water connecting the Baltic Sea to the North Sea.

GETTING THERE   Helsingør lies at the end of the northern line of trains heading from Copenhagen into the final reaches of North Zealand. A one-way trip takes 50 minutes, and trains leave frequently throughout the day from Copenhagen's Central Station.

Ferries, covered by the Eurail Global Pass and Eurail Scandinavia Pass, ply the waters of the narrow channel separating Helsingør (Denmark) from Helsingborg (Sweden) in less than 25 minutes. They're operated around the clock by **Scandlines** (© **33-15-15-15**; www.scandlines.dk), which charges 21DKK ($3.55/£1.90) each way for a pedestrian. Between 6am and 11pm, departures are every 20 minutes; 11pm to 6am, departures are timed at intervals of 40 to 80 minutes. Border formalities during the crossing between Denmark and Sweden are perfunctory, and although you should carry a passport, you might not even be asked for it.

VISITOR INFORMATION   The **Helsingør Tourist Office,** Havnepladsen 3 (© **49-21-13-33;** www.visithelsingor.dk), is open Monday to Friday 10am to 4pm and Saturday 10am to 1pm; June 20 to August 31 Monday to Friday 10am to 5pm, and Saturday 10am to 3pm.

TOP ATTRACTIONS & SPECIAL MOMENTS

For most visitors there is only one site here worthy of making the trip: **Kronborg Slot** ★★★, Kronborg (© **49-21-30-78**; www.kronborgcastle.com), a sandstone-and-copper Dutch Renaissance castle known in English as "Elsinore Castle." The most famous castle in Scandinavia lies on a peninsula jutting out into the Øresund, and it's said to be the home of Holger Danske (Holger the Dane), a mythological hero who sleeps beneath the castle. Though he never saw it, literary historians believe that the Bard had heard enough about the castle from some well-traveled friends to use this dank and gloomy place as the setting for his *Hamlet,* repeatedly staged at the castle since 1816. There have been numerous British productions here: Lawrence Olivier, John Gielgud, and Kenneth Branagh are just a few of the Hamlets who've fretted and strutted their hour upon the courtyard of Elsinore. Dating from 1426, the castle was completely rebuilt in 1585 and restored again after a fire gutted it in 1629. Several rooms, including the state apartments, are open to the public, although the place is rather starkly furnished. The **Great Hall** is the largest in northern Europe, but only seven of its original 40 tapestries—each commissioned by Frederik II in 1585—remain. The whole castle is undergoing major renovations until 2010 so visitors can expect new exhibitions and some areas to be temporarily closed.

Also on the premises is the **Danish Maritime Museum** (© **49-21-06-85;** www.maritime-museum.dk), which explores the history of Danish shipping. Unless you're really nautical, you might skip this but that would mean missing the world's oldest surviving ship's biscuit, dating from 1852.

The castle is ½ mile (.8km) north of the Helsingør train depot. Admission to the castle and maritime museum is 85DKK ($14.45/£7.65) for adults, 60DKK ($10.20/£5.40) for young people aged between 15 and 18, and 15DKK ($2.55/£1.35) for children under 15. The castle is open from May to September daily from 10:30am to

5pm; in April and October from Tuesday to Sunday from 11am to 4pm, and from November to March from Tuesday to Sunday from 11am to 3pm. It's closed December 24 and 25.

WHERE TO DINE

Typical Danish hot meals, such as *hakkebof* (hamburger steak), *frikadeller* (Danish rissoles or meatballs), rib roast with red cabbage, cooked or fried flounder or herring, and *æggekage* (egg cake) with bacon, are served in the local restaurants. You'll also find many fast-food places, and won't want to miss the celebrated ice-cream wafers.

Restaurant-wise, try the appealing **Ophelia Restaurant,** in the Hotel Hamlet, Bramstraede 5 (© **49-21-05-91**), named after the Shakespeare heroine. The chef combines his Danish recipes with classics from French and Italian kitchens. Specialties include "Hamlet veal steak" and calorie-rich desserts. Main courses cost 90DKK to190DKK ($15.30–$32.30/£8.10–£17.10).

Alternatively, for good value and self-service, try **San Remo,** Stengade 53 (© **49-21-00-55**), which dishes out good, hearty Danish food—and plenty of it—in a most uncafeteria-style dining room with crystal chandeliers. The location is in a shopping mall near the harbor. Main courses cost 32DKK to 95DKK ($5.45–$16.15/£2.90–£8.55).

AN EXCURSION TO ODENSE ✦✦

After Helsingør, the second most popular rail trip from Copenhagen is to the ancient town of Odense, the third largest in Denmark, situated 97 miles (156km) west of Copenhagen. This was the birthplace of Hans Christian Andersen (1805–75), Scandinavia's most famous storyteller, still as popular today as he was more than a century ago.

Odense lies on the island of Funen, which separates Zealand (site of Copenhagen) from Jutland, attached to the European mainland. Even without the Andersen connection, Odense is a lively little town of quaint charm.

GETTING THERE   From Copenhagen's Central Station, a dozen trains per day make the 90-minute trip west to the city of Odense.

Note: Every hotel in Odense is located within a 1-mile (1.6km) radius of the railway station, and even the main shopping streets (Kongensgade and Vestergade) are on the opposite side of a verdant downtown park (Kongens Have) from the railway station.

VISITOR INFORMATION   The **Odense Tourist Bureau,** at Rådhuset, Vestergade 2A (© **66-12-75-20;** www.visitodense.com), is open mid-June to late August, Monday to Friday 9am to 6pm, Saturday and Sunday 10am to 3pm; early September to mid-June, Monday to Friday 9:30am to 4:30pm, Saturday 10am to 1pm. Should you wish to stay overnight, the staff here will reserve you a hotel room for 35DKK ($5.95/£3.15).

Besides helping arrange excursions, the tourist bureau sells the value-laden **Odense Adventure Pass.** It gives you access to 16 of the city's museums, the Odense Zoo, six indoor swimming pools, and unlimited free travel on the city buses and DSB trains within the municipality. It also entitles you to discounts on river cruises. Passes are valid for 1 or 2 days. A 1-day pass is 125DKK ($21.25/£11.25) for adults, 65DKK ($11.05/£5.85) for children under 14; 2-day passes cost 160DKK ($27.20/£14.40) for adults and 85DKK ($14.45/£7.65) for kids.

GETTING AROUND   Most Odense buses originate or terminate at the railway station. You can hop aboard a bus at various stops and buy your ticket once you're aboard; you must have exact change. Buses cost 16DKK ($2.70/£1.45) per ride within

Odense city center (on the buses with two-digit numbers), and are each valid for transfers within a 60-minute period of their issue.

You can rent a bike from **City Cykler,** Vesterbvro 27 (© **66-13-97-83;** www.city cykler.dk), for prices ranging from 99DKK to 175DKK ($16.85–$29.75/£8.90–£15.75) per day, depending on the type of cycle. A deposit, starting at 750DKK ($128/£67.50), is required.

TOP ATTRACTIONS & SPECIAL MOMENTS

Odense Tourist Bureau (see above) offers 2-hour **walking tours** in July and August, every Tuesday, Wednesday, and Thursday at 11am, from a meeting place behind its office. Covering the town's major sites, it costs 50DKK ($8.50/£4.50) for adults and 25DKK ($4.25/£2.25) for children. Reservations are recommended.

Other than the Hans Christian Andersen monuments (see below), you can visit the chief attraction, **Funen Village/Den Fynske Landsby** ★★, Sejerkovvej 20 (© **65-51-46-01;** www.museum.odense.dk), a large open-air museum of regional artifacts and buildings 1½ miles (2.4km) south of the historic center and reached by bus no. 21 or 22 from Flakhaven, a street in the center of Odense. This is really a living museum to Funen in the 18th and 19th centuries. Old structures from all over Funen were brought here and reassembled, including a village school, vicarage, jail, windmill, farmstead, and weaver's shop. Everything is authentically furnished, and you can visit workshops to see craftspeople at work, and later enjoy plays and folkloric dances at the Greek-style theater. Opened in 2006, an exhibition in the visitor center helps aid the transition from modern life to Hans Christian Andersen times. Admission to the village is 60DKK ($10.20/£5.40) for adults and free for children under 18, except from late-October to the end of March when admission drops to 40DKK ($6.80/£3.60) for adults as visitors are not allowed inside the individual houses. It's open Mid-June to mid-August daily 9:30am to 7pm, then April to mid-June and mid-August to mid-October Tuesday to Sunday 10am to 5pm, and mid-October to March Sunday 11am to 3pm.

H.C. Andersen's Hus ★★, Bangs Boder 29 (© **65-51-46-01;** www.odmus.dk), is the goal of most pilgrims to Odense. Popular with children of all ages, this museum is devoted to keeping alive the memory of Andersen, whose centenary in 2005 was honored with a spiffing up of the museum and yearlong celebrations. Precious memorabilia include his top hat, battered suitcase, and even his celebrated walking stick. Rare artifacts include letters to fellow writer Charles Dickens in London, and to "the Swedish nightingale," Jenny Lind, on whom Andersen had developed a crush. Reprints of his books in countless languages are on view. Admission is 60DKK ($10.20/£5.40) for adults and free for children under 17. Open mid-June to mid-August daily 9am to 6pm; mid-August to mid-June Tuesday to Sunday 10am to 4pm.

The other site associated with the writer is the **H.C. Andersen's Barndomshjem (Andersen's Childhood Home),** Munkemøllestræde 3-5 (© **65-51-47-01**). The house is a grim little place, which no doubt fueled the fairy-tale writer's imagination, as he grew from age 2 to 14 within its tiny confines. He was a gawky boy, a true ugly duckling, made fun of by his schoolmates. Life didn't get better after school, when he went home to a drunken, superstitious mother who worked as a washerwoman. But all is serene at the cottage today, and the "garden still blooms," as it did in *The Snow Queen.* Admission is 25DKK ($4.25/£2.25) for adults and free for children under 17; hours from mid-June to mid-August are daily 10am to 4pm; mid-August to mid-June Tuesday to Sunday 11am to 3pm.

Before bidding adieu to Odense, head for **St. Canute's Cathedral** ✿, Kloster-bakken 2 (© **66-12-03-92;** www.odense-domkirke.dk), the most impressive Gothic style building in Denmark. Work on this cathedral began in the 13th century, but it wasn't completed until the 15th century. Note the gold altar screen with an elegant **triptych** ✿✿✿ carved by Claus Berg in 1526 at the request of Queen Christina. The admission-free church stands opposite City Hall. Open April to October Monday to Saturday 10am to 5pm, Sunday and holidays noon to 2pm; and November to March Monday to Saturday 10am to 4pm.

WHERE TO DINE

While you're exploring the historic core of Odense, you'll find a number of atmospheric restaurants serving good food, including **Den Gamle Kro,** Overgade 23 (© **66-12-14-33;** www.den-gamle-kro.dk). A refined French and Danish cuisine based on fresh ingredients from the surrounding countryside is served at this old town center inn dating from 1683. Dine in one of two intimate and antique-filled rooms, or have a drink in the cellar bar. Main courses cost 179DKK to 278DKK ($30.45–$47.25/ £16.10–£25), with fixed-price meals going for between 298DKK and 358DKK ($50.65–$60.85/£26.80–£32.20).

The landmark **Under Lindetraeet,** Ramsherred 2 (© **66-12-92-86;** www.under lindetraet.dk), a centuries-old inn across from the much-visited H. C. Andersen's Hus, is noted for its fresh, top-quality ingredients and skillfully prepared Danish dishes. It serves some of the best meat and shellfish dishes in the area—including tender Danish lamb and filet of plaice with butter sauce—while also dishing out *lobscouse,* the fabled sailors' hash. Main courses cost 225DKK to 495DKK ($38.25–$84.15/ £20.25–£44.55).

3 Highlights of Jutland

From the islands of Zealand, on which Copenhagen sits, and Funen, whose heart is Odense, we move to the largest land mass of Denmark: Jutland. It's a peninsula of heather-covered moors, fjords, lakes, sandy dunes, and farmland. For your final look at Denmark, head via fast train to Jutland's major city, Århus.

ÅRHUS ✿✿

The capital of Jutland and Denmark's second-largest city, Århus lies 109 miles (175km) west of Copenhagen. A university town with a lively port, it's the cultural center of Jutland and a major industrial center as well. Pronounced *Ore*-hoos, Århus is self-styled "the world's smallest big city," and has some good museums and historic buildings. But we prefer to amble through the cobblestone streets before people-watching in the city's bars and sidewalk cafes, or picnicking in one of the city parks or sandy beaches.

GETTING THERE   Nearly 40 trains leave Copenhagen's Central Station each day, reaching Århus in 3 to 3½ hours. The city's railway station, Århus Hovedbanegard, lies on the south side of the town center.

VISITOR INFORMATION   **Tourist Århus** Banegårdspladsen 20 (© **87-31-50-10;** www.visitaarhus.com), just a few minutes' walk from the train station, is open July to mid-September Monday to Friday 9:30am to 6pm, Saturday 9:30am to 3pm, and Sunday 9:30am to 1pm; mid-September to June Monday to Thursday 9:30am to 5pm, Friday 9:30am to 4pm, Saturday 9:30am to 1pm, closed on Sunday.

GETTING AROUND   A regular bus ticket, to cover a journey in the city center through up to two zones, can be purchased on the rear platform of all city buses for 18DKK ($3.05/£1.60).

Or go eco and borrow one of Århus' 250 free city bikes. You'll find them at 30 stands dotted around the city. All you need to liberate a bike is a returnable 20-kroner coin. For more information about where to find a stand ask at the tourist office (see above).

The value-filled **Århus Pass** allows unlimited travel by public transportation and free admission to many museums and attractions. A 2-day pass costs 149DKK ($25.35/£13.40) for adults, 67DKK ($11.40/£6) for children 3 to 12; 1-week passes are 206DKK ($35/£18.50) for adults and 91DKK ($15.45/£8.20) for children under 16. The Århus Pass is sold at the tourist office, many hotels, camping grounds, and kiosks throughout the city.

TOP ATTRACTIONS & SPECIAL MOMENTS

For an introduction to Århus, head to the town hall's tourist office, from which all sorts of different walking tours depart every weekday. Themes range from "Architecture and art in Århus" to "The Latin Quarter." Each one lasts 2 hours and costs 125DKK ($21.25/£10) for adults or 75DKK ($12.75/£6) for children. Call the tourist office (above) for more information.

The late Gothic **Cathedral of St. Clemens (Århus Domkirke),** Bispetorvet (© **86-20-54-00**), is the longest in Denmark, with a 315-foot (96m) nave. Begun in the 13th century in the Romanesque style, it was completely overhauled in the 15th century into a rather flamboyant Gothic overlay. Admission is free and the cathedral is open May to September 9:30am to 4pm; October to April Monday to Saturday 10am to 3pm. Get there on bus no. 3, 11, 54, or 56.

The town's other crowning achievement is its **Rådhuset (Town Hall),** Rådhuspladsen (© **89-40-20-00**), built from 1936 to 1941 to commemorate the 500th anniversary of the town charter. Arne Jacobsen, Denmark's most famous architect, was one of the designers of this marble-plated building. You can take either an elevator or brave 346 steps to get to the top of the 194-foot (59m) tower, which opens onto a panoramic view of Århus and the countryside around it. A guided tour costs 10DKK ($1.70/90p); otherwise, admission to the tower is 5DKK (85¢/45p). Guided tours are offered Monday through Friday at 11am; additional tours of the tower take place at noon and 2pm. Closed September to June 23.

The biggest attraction of all, **Den Gamle By** ✸✸✸, an open-air museum, is located 1½ miles (2.4km) west of the train station, just outside of town, at Viborgvej 2 (© **86-12-31-88**; www.dengamleby.dk). The little community of more than 75 buildings lies in a park west of the town center. Re-created in a botanical garden, urban life from the 16th- to the 19th-centuries comes alive here. You can wander at leisure through workshops watching craftspeople at work, including carpenters, hatters, bookbinders, and so on. You can also explore old-fashioned buildings such as a schoolhouse, pharmacy, or post office, as well as the Burgomaster's House, the half-timbered 16th-century home of a rich merchant. Summer music programs are staged, and on the grounds you'll find a tea garden, bakery, beer cellar, and full-service restaurant. Admission is 90DKK ($15.30/£8.10) for adults from April to December, 50DKK ($8.50/£4.50) from January to March, and free for children 16 and under year-round. Opening hours are mid-September to mid-November and April to June daily 10am to 5pm; mid-November to Christmas weekdays 9am to 7pm, weekends 10am to 7pm; mid-February to March daily 10am to 4pm; January to mid-February daily 11am to 3pm; July to mid-September daily 9am to 6pm. To get here, take bus no. 3, 14, 25, or 55 (trip time: 3–5 min.) or walk (about 15–20 min.) from the train station.

WHERE TO STAY & DINE

With a history dating from 1907, **Teater Bodega,** Skolegade 7 (© **86-12-19-17;** www.teaterbodega.dk), is still going strong, serving excellent Danish meals, including delectable open-faced sandwiches at lunch, across from the Århus Cathedral. Theater buffs and art lovers, among others, are drawn to the atmosphere of thespian memorabilia and the Danish country-style cooking, including hash, Danish roast beef, and freshly caught fish. Lunch smørrebrød costs 48DKK to 89DKK ($8.15–$15.15/£4.30–£8), and main courses run 89DKK to 198DKK ($15.15–$33.65/£8–£17.80).

For the finest food in town, head to the periphery of the historic center and eat at **Prins Ferdinand** ✿✿✿, Viborgvej 2 (© **86-12-52-05;** www.prinsferdinand.dk), established in 1988 by Peter Brun and Lotte Norrig, who offer an applause-worthy repertoire of dishes. Flickering candles and fresh flowers set a romantic atmosphere as you dine on turbot with Russian caviar or boneless pigeon stuffed with fresh gooseliver served with a raspberry sauce. Main courses cost 140DKK to 175DKK ($23.80–$29.75/£12.60–£15.75); fixed-price menus at lunch run 175DKK to 235DKK ($29.75–$39.95/£15.75–£21.15).

Should you wish to stay overnight, the chain-run **Scandic Plaza** ✿, Banegårdsplads 14, DK-8100 (© **87-32-01-00;** www.scandic-hotels.com), is in the center of town, close to the Town Hall and major attractions. A remake of an original 1930s hotel, the 162-room property was vastly renovated and overhauled in 1997 to provide tastefully decorated and comfortably furnished bedrooms. Rates, which include breakfast, are 1,025DKK to 1,695DKK ($174–$288/£92.95–£153) double; from 1,865DKK ($317/£168) for a suite.

FREDERIKSHAVN

The embarkation ferry departure point for Norway, the coastal town of Frederikshavn, 238 miles (381km) northwest of Copenhagen, is the final stop for rail passengers in North Jutland.

In lieu of major attractions, you get stores loaded with Danish goods. Swedes and Norwegians arrive by sea in droves to shop for Danish food products that are much cheaper than back in their hometowns.

GETTING THERE   Frederikshavn is the northern terminus of the DSB rail line. About 11 direct trains leave daily from Århus to Frederikshavn; travel time is roughly 2¾ hours. Trains leaving out of Copenhagen take 5¾ hours.

VISITOR INFORMATION   The **Frederikshavn Turistbureau,** Brotorvet 1 (© **98-42-32-66;** www.frederikshavn-tourist.dk), near the ferry dock and a short walk down Havnepladsen from the train station, is open in midsummer Monday to Saturday from 9am to 6pm, Sunday from 11am to 2pm. In the off season, hours are Monday to Friday 9am to 4pm, Saturday 11am to 2pm. Staff can recommend and reserve local hotel rooms for you at no charge.

Ferries to Sweden & Norway

Stena Line (© **96-20-02-00**; www.stenaline.dk), one of Europe's largest and most reliable ferryboat operators, runs the two most popular routes in and out of town. Passengers heading to Norway can take a daily, daytime 9-hour ferryboat between Frederikshavn and Oslo. Foot passengers pay 180DKK ($30.60/£16.20). Be warned in advance that southbound boats originating in Oslo depart after dark, and consequently, all passengers are required to rent an overnight cabin for the 9-hour evening transit. Cabins, each suitable for two passengers, rent for between 380DKK and 1,560DKK ($64.60–$265/ £34.20–£140). Stena also has seven departures daily between the Swedish port of Gothenburg and Frederikshavn. Transit time is between 2 and 3¾ hours, depending on the boat. Passengers pay between 130DKK and 220DKK ($22.10–$37.40/£11.70–£19.80) each way, though Eurail passholders get a 30% reduction on this ferry. Stena also operates three catamaran crossings every day that are much faster than the ferries. Stena Line charges 40DKK ($6.80/£3.60) for phone reservations but Internet reservations are free.

Color Line (© **81-00-08-11**) also sails from Frederikshavn to Oslo, operating one or two daily ferry services that take 8½ hours. Eurail passholders get discounts of 50% on this ferry route (on day crossings only). For more info go to **www.colorline.no**.

THE TOP ATTRACTIONS & SPECIAL MOMENTS

Worth exploring, the oldest part of Frederikshavn, **Fiskerkylyngen,** lies north of the fishing harbor and is filled with well-preserved homes, many dating from the 1600s. Otherwise, attractions are minor except for the **Bangsbo Museum** ⊕, Dronning Margrethesvej (© **98-42-31-11**; www.bangsbo.com), an open-air museum in the north of Jutland, 1¾ miles (3km) south of the town center in a deer park. Several 18th-century buildings lie near the ruins of a 14th-century manor house. Many mementos of Denmark of yesterday are found here, including a barn from 1580 (one of the oldest in Denmark), farm equipment, and a large display of World War II relics. An ancient ship, similar to vessels used by the Vikings, is also displayed. Admission is 45DKK ($7.65/£4.05) for adults, free for children under 18. Open June to October daily 10:30am to 5pm; November to May Tuesday to Sunday 10:30am to 5pm.

WHERE TO STAY & DINE

Near the harbor in an 1850s building, **Restaurant Baachus,** Lodsgade 8A (© **98-43-29-00**), is an unpretentious bistro serving a mix of Italian and Mexican food at affordable prices. Its 40-seat old-fashioned dining room turns out quick fillers such as pizza, succulent pastas, burritos, and a spicy chili con carne. Main courses cost 95DKK to 160DKK ($16.15–$27.20/£8.55–£14.40) with set menus going for 75DKK to 210DKK ($12.75–$35.70/£6.75–£18.90).

For something a little grander head to the **Restaurant GråAnden (Gray Duck Restaurant)** in the Radisson SAS Jutlandia Hotel (see below), Havnepladsen (© **98-42-42-00**; www.hotel-jutlandia.dk), where you'll be one of a handful of diners eating in a dining room overlooking the blue-gray expanse of the sea. The food is a mix of French and Danish. It might include seafood cocktail followed by lemon sole in a ragout of mussels and curried cream, or quail with foie gras and a red-wine flambé. During July and August there is a buffet in the evening. Year-round, mains go from 132DKK to 189DKK ($22.40–$32.15/£11.90 £17), with set meals starting at 178DKK ($30.26/£16) for two courses.

The 95-room **Radisson SAS Jutlandia Hotel,** Havnepladsen, DK-9900 (© **98-42-42-00;** www.hotel-jutlandia.dk), is the best-rated place to stay in town, situated close to the embarkation point for the boats to Gothenburg. Scandinavian design and first-class comfort are found here, especially in the midsize and comfortably furnished bedrooms. Rates, including breakfast, range from 1,170DKK to 2,450DKK ($199–$417/£105–£221) for a double

A more affordable choice is the 28-room **Hotel 1987,** Damsgaards Plads 8E, DK-9900 (© **98-43-19-87;** www.hotel1987.dk), carved out of a 130-year-old marine warehouse in 1987. Completely modernized, the intimate and cozily furnished bedrooms are comfortable and equipped with shower-only bathrooms. Doubles cost 600DKK to 750DKK ($102–$128/£54–£67.50), including breakfast.

7

Finland

Finland often gets lumped in with the Scandinavian countries: Norway, Denmark and Sweden. But it's not actually a Scandinavian country at all. It's a Nordic country. And although it shares many similar traits—stunning wild landscapes and modern urban environments—there's something different about Finland. Maybe it's the Russian influence (Finland was part of the Russian Empire for over a century and you can still taste the remnants of this in the Helsinki restaurants dishing out bear steaks and caviar), or the fact it's one of the least populated countries in the world (with only 5.3 million people and a density of 14.8 inhabitants per sq. km—Japan has 327), or that its location on the top edge of Europe (it is one of the northernmost countries in the world, with nearly one-third of its land, Lapland, north of the Arctic Circle) has given its residents more mental freedom, more imagination. They are dreamy, outdoor-loving souls, given to escaping off to their ramshackle summerhouses in the warmer months, to spend the season cooking over a campfire, foraging for wild food, and doing what everyone imagines Finnish people should be doing—swimming in cold lakes and taking saunas.

Of the countries sitting on the "roof" of Europe, Finland is the most difficult to reach by rail. But once arriving in Helsinki, the Finnish capital, you'll have access to two unique travel opportunities. From Helsinki, you can take one of two daily trains to St. Petersburg in Russia, where you can visit the Hermitage, one of the great depositories of world art. Helsinki is also the gateway to the newly emerging Baltic countries, especially Estonia, which is only a short boat ride from the Finnish capital.

And even though Finland has the most difficult connections to European rail networks, it nonetheless is an easy ferry trip from Stockholm, which enjoys excellent rail links to other Scandinavian capitals and, consequently, the rest of continental Europe. With a Eurail pass, you can, for example, get on a train in Rome and ride the rails all the way to Stockholm where you can make the final run by ferry into Helsinki. Once in Helsinki, you can hook up with efficient rail lines in what is increasingly emerging as the "crossroads" between the east and west of Europe.

Finland also possesses a number of other pluses as a rail destination. The Finnish rail system is one of the most modern in the world, linking all the country's major towns and cities, except those in the remote north. Even though Finland is a large country, it's easy to get around by rail. And, in what may be the most literate country in the world, there is no language barrier as almost all Finns speak English, and rather fluently at that.

Summer is the best season to visit (although it's also when the Finns take their long summer vacations, so prepare for some restaurants and shop closures in Helsinki), when the country's endless scenic vistas of vast green forests and blue lakes can be seen from your train window. Many rail passengers visit in summer just to enjoy the Midnight Sun, best seen from Rovaniemi, the capital of Finnish Lapland.

Moments **Festivals & Special Events**

After a long, cold winter, most Helsinki residents turn out to celebrate the arrival of spring at the **Walpurgis Eve Celebration,** held on April 30. Celebrations are held at Market Square, followed by May Day parades and other activities the next morning.

A major Scandinavian musical event, the **Helsinki Festival** presents orchestral concerts by outstanding soloists and ensembles, chamber music and recitals, exhibitions, ballet, theater, and opera performances, along with jazz, pop, and rock concerts. For complete information about the program, contact the **Helsinki Festival,** Lasipalatsi Mannerheimintie 22–24 Finland–00100 Helsinki (✆ **09/6126-5100;** www.helsinkifestival.fi). The festival takes place from mid-August to early September.

Since the 1700s, the annual **Baltic Herring Market** has taken place along the quays of Market Square in early October. Fishermen continue the centuries-old tradition of bringing their catch into the city to sell from their boats. Prizes and blue ribbons go to the tastiest herring.

HIGHLIGHTS OF FINLAND

Of course, an entire book could be written on the lakes and untamed wilderness of Finland, which contrast nicely with the country's small, ultramodern cities. But the remoteness of the country's location means a rail visitor who makes it to this part of the world (mostly by boat or air from Stockholm), usually descends on Helsinki for a visit of only 2 or 3 days before moving on to other points on the Continent.

Now that the Iron Curtain is long gone, many adventurous travelers also stop off in Finland before ferrying over to Tallin, the capital of Estonia, or taking the train to Russia's St. Petersburg (the former Leningrad).

As the capital of Finland, **Helsinki** lies at the crossroads between eastern and western Europe. It's also the country's rail hub. You can begin your adventure in this city by heading for **Market Square** to test the pulse of the capital, followed by visits to two of the most important attractions, one of the three museums making up the **Finnish National Gallery** and the **Mannerheim Museum,** the latter the former home of World War II hero and Finnish president Baron Carl Gustaf Mannherheim. The following morning you can spend in the **National Museum of Finland,** followed by an afternoon at the **Seurasaari Open-Air Museum** and **Suomenlinna Fortress,** the "Gibraltar of the North." At some point in your journey, enjoy an authentic Finnish sauna in the land where the institution was invented.

1 Essentials

GETTING THERE

With more flights to Helsinki from more parts of the world (including Europe, Asia, and North America) than any other airline, **Finnair** (✆ **800/950-5000** in the U.S.; www.finnair.com) is the only airline that flies nonstop from North America to Finland (an 8-hr. trip). Departures take place from New York; most flights from major U.S. cities will transfer to a nonstop flight at Kennedy International Airport.

Several other airlines fly from North America to gateway European cities and then connect to Helsinki. Foremost among these is **British Airways (BA;** © **800/247-9297** in the U.S., or 0845/773-3377 in London; www.ba.com). **Finnair** (© **0870/241-4411** in London; www.finnair.com) also offers more frequent service to Helsinki from several airports in Britain.

If you're stopping in Finland after traveling by train through the Continent, it's likely you'll head here via modern ferry service from Stockholm on **Silja Line (www.silja.com)** or **Viking Line (www.vikingline.fi).** Eurail or Scandinavia passholders get a 50% discount on these routes, and a 50% discount on a bed in a four-berth cabin on the Silja route (passes must be valid in both Sweden and Finland to obtain these discounts). More comfort costs extra and prices depend on the class of cabin, the number of passengers per room, and the line you take.

If you take the ferry from Stockholm to Turku (an 11-hr. journey—also discounted with a Eurail pass), the county's former capital on the west coast of Finland, you can catch one of the seven daily trains (including a high-speed Pendolino) taking passengers across southern Finland to Helsinki. The trip takes 2¼ hours. Most passengers, however, take a ferry directly from Stockholm to Helsinki without any extra rail travel. Ferry service, with Silja Line, is also available from Rostock, Germany to Hanko but we do not recommend this option as it takes over 24 hours to make the crossing. If you do want to go this way, a bus service operated by Silja Line connects Hanko with Helsinki, approximately 90 minutes away. Passengers with a railpass, even if it is just for Finland, get a 30% reduction on this journey.

FINLAND BY RAIL
PASSES

For information on the **Eurail Global Pass,** the **Eurail Global Pass Flexi,** the **Eurail Select Pass,** the **Eurail Scandinavia Pass,** and other multicountry options, see chapter 2.

The Eurail Finland Pass entitles holders to unlimited travel for any 3, 5; or 10 days within a 1-month period on all passenger trains of the VR Ltd. Finnish Railways. Travel days may be used either consecutively or nonconsecutively. Prices start at $171 in second class. Children 6 to 16 are charged half the full fare (proof of age required); children 5 and under ride free when accompanied by a full-fare adult (they do not, however, get a seat).

The Eurail Finland Pass should be purchased before you leave home and can be obtained from **Rail Europe** (© **877/272-RAIL** [7245] in North America; www.raileurope.com) or through your travel agent.

Note: Second-class trains in Finland are comparable to first-class trains in many other countries, so splurging on a first-class ticket or pass is unnecessary.

Trains & Travel Times for Finland

From	To	Type of Train	# of Trains	Frequency	Travel Time
Stockholm	Helsinki	Ferry	3	Daily	14 hr., 30 min.
Helsinki	St. Petersburg	*Sibelius*	1	Daily	5 hr., 28 min.
Helsinki	St. Petersburg	*Repin*	1	Daily	5 hr., 31 min.
Helsinki	St. Petersburg	*Tolstoi*	1	Daily	6 hr., 13 min.
Helsinki	Tallinn	Jet Boat	6	Daily	1 hr., 40 min.

Finland

Moments **Speeding to Estonia**

One of the added advantages of traveling as far east as Helsinki is the chance to take a day-trip to the city of Tallinn, capital of Estonia. You can't get to Tallinn by train, but Nordic Jet Line's high-speed catamarans, launched in the spring of 2003, run quickly and efficiently between Helsinki and the Estonian city.

Tallinn, with its German spires, Russian domes, and Scandinavian towers, is quickly becoming a top choice for offbeat travel in Europe, and you can easily spend a day here exploring **Vanalinn (Old Town),** which is home to Europe's oldest town hall. The suds flow in its outdoor cafes, and local troupes will entertain you all summer.

Both the HSC *Baltic Jet* and HSC *Nordic Jet* zip you to Tallin in just over 90 minutes. Boat tickets can be purchased at both rail stations and travel agents in Finland or by calling © **09/681-700,** or 06/137-000 for reservations. For more information, check out the company's website at **www-eng.njl.fi**.

Depending on the time of departure, one-way tickets range from 27€ to 70€ ($20.25–$52.50); the cheapest deals being available online only.

FOREIGN TRAIN TERMS

Forget trying to learn Finnish; to speak it, you pretty much need to be born there, as it's one of the world's most difficult languages. The good news for English-speakers is that Finnish "train lingo" is hardly a consideration because school children in Finland start learning English in grade school and you won't have problems finding someone at any of the major stations who speaks English.

PRACTICAL TRAIN INFORMATION

Finland's extensive and reliable rail network is run by VR Ltd. Finnish Railways, and all major Finnish cities are linked by rail to Helsinki. Most trains are new (or close to it) and operate on a timely basis. And Finland's rail engineers now offer some of the most modern and high-speed trains in Europe. For example, the new high-tech Pendolino (they "tilt" as they take corners) trains have cut traveling time between Helsinki, the present capital, to Turku, the ancient capital, to under 2 hours. There are a total of four types of trains that operate in the country: **InterCity (IC)** trains, high-speed **Pendolino (EP)** express trains, regular express trains, and slower local and commuter trains.

The good news for budget travelers: Finnish trains are cheaper than those in the rest of Scandinavia. And if you choose to purchase open round-trip (return) tickets, they are valid for 15 days.

For a Finnish Railways journey planner, check **www.vr.fi**.

RESERVATIONS   Seat reservations are included in the price of an advance ticket on Pendolino, InterCity, and express trains but not on the regional trains, where seats are unreservable. If you buy your ticket on board a train you can't reserve a seat either. We recommend booking in advance, if you can, and getting a reserved seat, as Finnish trains tend to be crowded. If you have a Eurail pass, you can also make a reservation before you leave North America through Rail Europe for $11 or in Finland itself for prices from 6€ ($7.80) on the InterCity trains and from 11€ ($14.30) on the Pendolino trains, with prices getting steeper as the length of the journey increases. *Warning:* Reserved seats are not marked so you'll never know if you're taking someone's seat or not unless the passenger shows up to evict you.

SERVICES & AMENITIES   It's not possible to reserve couchettes on Finnish rails as there are none. You can reserve two- and three-berth compartments, however. Twenty new sleeper cars debuted in late 2006, each with two beds per compartment; some compartments have their own shower and toilet. All sleepers should be reserved as far in advance as possible, especially during the peak times of July, August, Christmas, and the skiing season between February and April. To reserve in advance, contact Rail Europe or your travel agent. Prices for accommodations vary, so ask when you make the reservation.

Most express trains are air-conditioned and offer nonsmoking sections, music channels, and facilities for those with mobility issues. Some Finnish trains, such as the double-decker InterCity2 trains, have outlets peddling snacks and drinks. Prices, however, are lethal. If you're watching your euros, it's far better to pick up a supply of food and drink for your journey at the rail station before boarding the train.

FAST FACTS: Finland

Area Code the international country code for Finland is **358**. The city area code for Helsinki is **09**.

Business Hours Most **banks** are open Monday to Friday from 9am to 4:15pm. You can also exchange money at the railway station in Helsinki daily from 8am to 9pm, and at the airport daily from 6:30am to 11pm. **Store** hours vary. Most are open Monday to Friday from 9am to 6pm and Saturday from 9 or 10am to 5 or 6pm. Some department stores and malls stay open until 9pm on weekdays. Shops are allowed to open on Sundays during the summer months and in the run-up to Christmas. Many do, including **R-kiosks,** which sell candy, tobacco, toiletries, cosmetics, and souvenirs all over Helsinki and elsewhere; they're open Monday to Saturday 8am to 9pm and Sunday from 9 or 10am to 9pm.

Climate Spring arrives in May and the summers are short—a standing joke in Helsinki claims summer lasts from Tuesday to Thursday. July is the warmest month, with temperatures averaging around 59°F (15°C). The coldest months are January and February, when the Finnish climate is comparable to that of New England. Snow usually arrives in December and lasts until April.

Currency As part of the European Union, Finland uses the euro as its currency. At press time 1€ = $1.30, or $1 = 75p.

Documents Required American and Canadian citizens need only a valid **passport** to enter Finland. You need to apply for a visa only if you want to stay more than 3 months.

Electricity Finland operates on 220 volts AC. Plugs are usually of the continental type with rounded pins. Always ask at your hotel desk before plugging in any electrical appliance. Without an appropriate transformer or adapter, you'll destroy the appliance.

Embassies & Consulates The Embassy of the **United States** is at Itäinen Puistotie 14B, FIN-00140 Helsinki (© **09/616-250;** www.usembassy.fi); and the Embassy of **Canada** is at Pohjoisesplanadi 25B, FIN-00100 Helsinki (© **09/228-530;** www.canada.fi). If you're planning to visit Russia after Finland and need information about visas, the **Russian Embassy** is at Tehtaankatu 1B, FIN-00140 Helsinki (© **09/661-877**). It's better, however, to make all your travel arrangements to Russia before you leave home. The visa service has a website (**www.russianconsulate.org**) and a toll-free number in the U.S. (© **800/553-9034**).

Health & Safety Finland's national health plan does not cover U.S. or Canadian visitors. Any medical expenses that arise must be paid in cash. (Medical costs in Finland, however, are generally more reasonable than elsewhere in Western Europe.) British and other European Union (EU) citizens can get reduced cost/free medical care in Finland with a European Health Insurance Card, which replaces the E111 form and covers emergencies in Finland and all other EU countries.

Finland is one of the safest countries in Europe, although the recent arrival of desperately poor immigrants from former Communist lands to the south means the situation is not as tranquil or as safe as before.

Holidays The following holidays are observed in Finland: January 1 (New Year's Day); Epiphany (Jan 6); Good Friday, Easter Monday; May 1 (May Day); Ascension Day (mid-May); Whitsun (late May/early June); Midsummer Eve and Midsummer Day (Fri and Sat of the weekend closest to June 24); All Saints' Day (Nov 6); December 6 (Independence Day); and December 25 and 26 (Christmas and Boxing days).

Mail Airmail letters take about a week to 10 days to reach North America; surface mail—sent by boat—takes 1 to 2 months. Parcels are weighed and registered at the post office, which may ask you to declare the value and contents of the package on a preprinted form. Stamps are sold at post offices in all towns and cities, at most hotels, sometimes at news kiosks, and often by shopkeepers who offer the service for customers' convenience. In Finland, mailboxes are bright yellow with a trumpet embossed on them. Airmail letters cost .65€ (85¢) for up to 20 grams. For postal information, call © **0200/71-000.**

Police & Emergencies In Helsinki, for emergencies dial © **112.**

Telephone To make **international calls** from Finland, first dial the international prefix of 00, 990, 994, or 999, then the country code, then the area code (without the general prefix 0), and finally the local number. For information on long-distance calls and tariffs, call © **02-02-08.** To place calls to Finland, dial whatever code is needed in your country to reach the international lines (for example, in the United States, dial **011** for international long distance), then the country code for Finland **(358)**, then the area code (without the Finnish long-distance prefix 0), and finally the local number. To make long-distance calls within Finland, dial 0 to get a long-distance line (the carrier is chosen at random), the area code, and the local number. (Note that all area codes in this guide are given with the prefix 0.) For phone number information, dial ℂ **02-02-02.** Besides phone booths and hotels, calls can be made from local post and telephone offices.

Tipping Tipping is not really part of the culture in Finland, but if you think someone has done something really well you can show your appreciation with a tip. It's standard for **hotels** and **restaurants** to add a service charge of 15%, and usually no further tipping is necessary, although it's usual to leave the small change in restaurants. **Taxi drivers** don't expect a tip. It is appropriate to tip **doormen** at least 1€ ($1.30) and **bellhops** usually get 1€ ($1.30) per bag (in most Finnish provincial hotels, guests normally carry their own luggage to their room). At railway stations, **porters** are usually tipped 1€ ($1.30) per bag. Hairdressers and barbers don't expect tips. **Coat check charges** are usually posted; there's no need for additional tipping.

2 Helsinki ⚑⚑⚑

A rail hub situated at the crossroads of Eastern and Western Europe, Helsinki is the capital of the Independent Republic of Finland and is home to some 560,000 people. Although Helsinki is most often reached by a boat cruise from Stockholm, the city contains a vast network of rail lines coming in from all over Finland, and even extending south to Russia for those who want to go to either Moscow or St. Petersburg. You can visit every major town or city in Finland via Helsinki.

The city was founded in 1550 at the mouth of the Vantaa River by Swedish King Gustav Vasa, when Finland was a part of Sweden, and was later relocated on the Vironniemi peninsula in the place now known as Kruununhaka. It was not the capital of Finland until after the Napoleonic Wars of the early 19th century. Russia, concluding a peace with the French, annexed Finland to its empire and moved the capital from Turku to Helsinki, which was closer to St. Petersburg.

Perhaps the city's greatest allure for the rail traveler is its individuality—it is distinct from all other European capitals and has a flavor all its own. Unlike Athens, you'll find no ancient temples here, for Finland is a decidedly modern nation with granite neoclassical structures. And, unlike Vienna, Helsinki is not full of unicorns, gargoyles, palaces, and tombs that testify to architectural splendor and the glory of empire. All the kings who've ruled the city have been foreigners; instead of glorifying monarchy, the Finns are more likely to honor an athlete or a worker in their sculpture. As proof, just take a look at the figures standing proudly, even defiantly, in front of Stockmann's Department Store: three nude blacksmiths.

STATION INFORMATION
GETTING FROM THE AIRPORT TO THE TRAIN STATION
Helsinki–Vantaa Airport (ℂ **0200/14-636;** www.helsinki-vantaa.fi) is 12 miles (19km) north of the center of town, about a 30-minute bus ride from the center of the city. Bus no. 615 goes back and forth from the airport and Railway Square, site of the main train terminal. A bus departs two to three times an hour from 5:30am to 10:20pm, for 3.40€ ($4.40) one-way. A taxi from the airport to the rail station in the center of Helsinki costs around 25€ to 30€ ($32.50–$39) one-way.

Helsinki

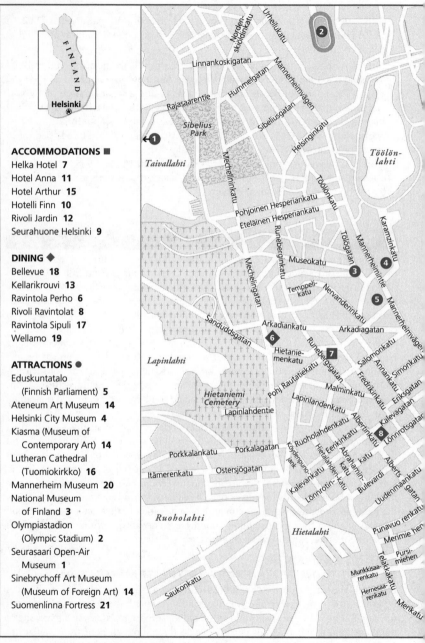

INSIDE THE STATION

Trains arrive in the center of the city at the **Central Helsinki Railway Station,** Kaivokatu (© **03/072-0900**). Designed by Eliel Saarinen (1873–1950) in the early 20th century, the station itself is a national monument and a classic example of the Art Nouveau style. And it's an especially good station for English speakers: All information in the station is posted in both Finnish and English.

Trains heading to St. Petersburg and ultimately to Moscow, the latter a 13-hour journey from Helsinki, depart from here. Trains also leave from this station for all major cities in Finland, including Tampere and Turku (both just 2 hr. away). You can catch a northbound train from here to Rovaniemi, the capital of Finnish Lapland (about three direct trains leave daily). The Lapland trip takes 10 to 13 hours, depending on the train.

If you don't want to go to the tourist office (see below), you'll find a hotel booking service, **Hotellikeskus** (© **09/2288-1400;** www.helsinkiexpert.fi), in the main central hall of the station, straight in front of you as you exit from the trains. There's a fee of 5€ ($6.50) per person if you show up and speak to a staff member; the service is free by phone, online, or if you e-mail **hotel@helsinkiexpert.fi**. Here you'll also find a small tourist information point, linked to the larger one (see "Information Elsewhere in the City," below) in the center of town.

You can store your luggage at the office on the far right of the main hall as you emerge from the trains. Lockers cost 3€ ($3.90) per day. A money exchange kiosk is also located in the main hall and is open daily from 7am to 9pm. For rail information, you can visit the **Train Information Center** (© **0307/29-900**) on the right-hand side of the main hall. It's possible to make seat reservations on Finnish trains at counters 1 through 10 Monday to Friday 8am to 9:30pm and Saturday and Sunday 9:30am to 9:30pm. To validate a railpass, go to counters 14 through 17.

INFORMATION ELSEWHERE IN THE CITY

From the train station, walk 2 blocks down Keskuskatu, make a left onto Pohjoisesplanadi, and you'll arrive at the **Helsinki City Tourist Office,** Pohjoisesplanadi 19 (© **09/3101-3300;** www.visithelsinki.fi). For a more general overview of the country, created specifically for U.S. and Canadian visitors, see **www.gofinland.org**. The tourist office is open May 2 to September 30 Monday to Friday 9am to 8pm and Saturday and Sunday 9am to 6pm; off season Monday to Friday 9am to 6pm, Saturday and Sunday 10am to 4pm. Staff here hand out free brochures and maps, alongside information on the city and its sights and events

Helsinki Expert/Tourshop (© **09/2288-1500**), a service offered from the same premises as the Helsinki City Tourist Office, is your best bet for booking tours once you reach Helsinki. The Tour Shop will also make hotel reservations for 5€ ($6.50), and sells bus and cruise tickets, and the money-saving **Helsinki Card** (see below).

GETTING AROUND

Helsinki is small enough to be explored on foot, but some of its best attractions lie outside the city center, and you'll need to take a taxi or public transportation to get to them.

Visitors to Helsinki can buy the **Helsinki Card,** which offers unlimited travel on the city's public buses, trams, subway, and ferries, and a free guided sightseeing bus tour (in summer daily, off season on Sun), as well as free entry to about 50 museums and other sights in Helsinki. The Helsinki Card is available for 1-, 2-, or 3-day periods. The price of the card for adults is 29€ ($37.70) for 1 day, 42€ ($54.60) for 2 days, and 53€ ($68.90) for 3 days. A card for children costs 11€ ($14.30), 14€

($18.20), and 17€ ($22.10) for 1-, 2-, and 3-day cards. Cards are sold at over 50 sales points in the Helsinki area, including the Helsinki City Tourist Office, Tour Shop, and hotel reception desks. Or you can buy them online at **www.helsinkiexpert.fi**.

You can also buy a **Tourist Ticket** for travel over a 1-, 3-, or 5-day period. This ticket lets you travel as much as you like within the city limits on all forms of public transportation except regional buses. A 1-day ticket costs 6€ ($7.80) for adults, 3€ ($3.90) for children ages 7 to 16; a 3-day ticket is 12€ ($15.60) for adults, 6€ ($7.80) child's fare; a 5-day ticket goes for 18€ ($23.40) for adults, 9€ ($11.70) child's fare. Children under 7 travel free. Tickets can be purchased at many places throughout Helsinki, including the Helsinki City Tourist Office and transportation service depots, such as the Railway Square Metro Station.

A single ticket bought from an automatic machine costs 2€ ($2.60) for adults, 1€ ($1.30) for children. A single ticket is valid for 60 minutes from the moment of purchase and allows passengers to transfer between different lines or types of transport.

You can order **taxis** by telephone (© 0100/0700), find them at taxi ranks, or hail them on the street. All taxis have an illuminated yellow sign that reads: TAKSI/TAXI. The basic fare costs 4.50€ ($5.85) and rises on a per-kilometer basis, as indicated on the meter. In the evening (8pm–6am Mon–Fri and 4–6pm Sat) and on Sunday the basic fare is 7€ ($9.10).

WHERE TO STAY

Helka Hotel ★★Value   This 1928 hotel is a budget oasis in a sea of expensively priced hotels and close to the train station. Completely refurbished in 2006, the centrally located property is also pretty stylish for the price. Guest rooms are minimalist, spacious, and filled with light-wood Scandinavian furniture. Each has a private bathroom with shower attached. Double windows cut down on the noise. The on-site Finnish restaurant is surprisingly hip and there's free Internet access throughout the building.

Pohjoinen Rautatiekatu 23, Helsinki 00100. © 09/613-580. Fax 09/441-087. www.helka.fi. 150 units. 109€–166€ ($142–$216) double; 185€–260€ ($241–$338) suite. Rates include breakfast. AE, DC, MC, V. Tram: 3B or 3T. Metro: Kamppi. **Amenities:** Restaurant; bar; laundry; rooms for those w/limited mobility; nonsmoking rooms. *In room:* Hair dryer.

Hotel Anna Value   In a residential neighborhood, this well-run and affordable hotel was converted from a 1926 apartment building that survived World War II Russian bombardment. Convenient to shopping and museums, the hotel retains a lot of its original charm, even though it was practically rebuilt in 1985, with additional upgrades completed in 2002, including the installation of an upgraded ventilation system. The small to midsize bedrooms are comfortably decorated.

Annankatu 1, FIN-00120 Helsinki. © 09/616-621. Fax 09/602-664. www.hotelanna.fi. 64 units. 160€–175€ ($208–$228) double; 205€ ($267) suite. Rates include breakfast buffet. AE, DC, MC, V. Tram: 3B, 3T, or 10. **Amenities:** Breakfast room; laundry; nonsmoking rooms. *In room:* Hair dryer.

Hotel Arthur Value   In high-priced Helsinki, the privately owned Arthur is an affordable stopover for the frugal rail traveler. A 4-minute walk from the rail station, the hotel is in a turn-of-the-20th-century building with an annex dating from 1950. Rooms are small and furnished in a standard motel fashion and the cramped bathrooms have full plumbing. In 2007, 25 new rooms were added to the seventh floor. Breakfasts are tasty, and lunch buffets are generous and reasonably priced.

Vuorikatu 19, FIN-00100 Helsinki. © 09/173-441. Fax 09/626-880. www.hotelarthur.fi. 168 units. 92€–135€ ($120–$176) double; 250€ ($325) suite. Rates include breakfast. Additional bed 20€ ($26). AE, DC, MC, V. Tram: 1, 3, 6, or 7. Metro: Kaisaniemi. **Amenities:** Restaurant; bar; laundry; nonsmoking rooms. *In room:* Hair dryer.

Hotelli Finn *(Value)*   This small hotel is less than 1,000 feet (300m) from the rail station, set on the fifth and sixth floors of a dignified but rather austere city office building. It's a welcoming place, however, and has been in the hands of the same family owners since 1960. Rooms can comfortably house two to four guests; furnishings are basic but better than the average college dorm lodgings. The Finn's owners pride themselves on being one of the least expensive hotels in central Helsinki.

Kalevankatu 3B, FIN-00100 Helsinki. ✆ 09/684-4360. Fax 09/6844-3610. www.hotellifinn.fi. 27 units. 70€ ($91) double without bathroom; 85€ ($111) double with bathroom. AE, DC, MC, V. Tram: 3, 4, 7, or 10. **Amenities:** Breakfast room; lounge.

Rivoli Jardin 🕊🕊   This recently renovated and well-managed hotel is one of the best boutique hotels in Helsinki, and is just over ¼ mile (.4km) from the rail stations. Custom designed as a hotel in 1984, it has stayed abreast of the times with frequent refurbishing, and a warm welcome awaits you in its stone- and marble-clad lobby. All the midsize bedrooms are individually decorated, for the most part, with lovely furniture and exquisite woodcarvings. Rooms have wall-to-wall carpeting or Asian rugs placed on hardwood floors, and each has an attractively tiled bathroom.

Kasarmikatu 40, FIN-00130 Helsinki. ✆ 09/681-500. Fax 09/656-988. www.rivoli.fi. 55 units. 239€ ($311) double; 339€ ($441) suite. Rates include breakfast. AE, DC, MC, V. Tram: 10. **Amenities:** Breakfast room; bar; laundry; nonsmoking rooms; 1 room for those w/limited mobility. *In room:* Hair dryer.

Seurahuone Helsinki 🕊   Originally opening in 1833, this hotel moved to its current location in a five-story Art Nouveau town house across from Helsinki's railway station in 1913. Since then, it has been expanded, most recently in 2006, as part of a series of comprehensive upgrades, one of which included a new wing. Rooms are moderate in size, mostly with twin beds, along with combination bathrooms (both showers and tubs). The public rooms are often crowded, as the hotel hosts many public organizations.

Kaivokatu 12. FIN-00100. Helsinki. ✆ 09/691-41. Fax 09/691-4010. www.hotelliseurahuone.fi. 118 units. 127€–227€ ($165–$295) double; 350€–400€ ($455–$520) suite. Rates include breakfast. AE, DC, MC, V. Tram: 3B, 3T, or 4. **Amenities:** Restaurant; bar; laundry. *In room:* Hair dryer.

TOP ATTRACTIONS & SPECIAL MOMENTS

Ateneum Art Museum 🕊🕊   Part of The Finnish National Gallery, Finland's largest selection of sculpture, painting, and graphic art is displayed at this museum. The Finnish National Gallery is an umbrella term for three independent museums: the **Ateneum Art Museum**, the **Kiasma (Museum of Contemporary Art)**, and the **Sinebrychoff Art Museum (Museum of Foreign Art)**. The first museum is housed in the Ateneum building across from the railway station. More than a century old, it was designed by Theodore Höijer. The Museum of Finnish Art has the largest collection of Finnish artists, from the mid-1700s to 1960, as well as the works of some 19th- and 20th-century international artists. The remaining two museums are listed separately below.

Kaivokatu 2. ✆ 09/173-361. www.fng.fi. Admission 6€ ($7.80) adults, 4€ ($5.20) students and seniors, free for children under 18. Special exhibits 8€ ($10.40) adults, 6.50€ ($8.45) student/seniors, free for children under 18. Free admission every Wed from 5–8pm. Tues and Fri 9am–6pm; Wed–Thurs 9am–8pm; Sat–Sun 11am–5pm. Tram: 3 or 6.

Eduskunta (Finnish Parliament)   Near the post office and only a few blocks from the rail station, this building of reddish Kavola granite (built in 1931) houses the 200 members of the one-chamber parliament (40% of whose members are women). The building looks austere on the outside, but it's much warmer inside. The goal was to use all Finnish material and artists in its construction, and there are nearly 1,000 art

Moments Paying Homage to Finlandia & Sibelius

Jean Sibelius (1865–1957), composer of *Finlandia*, lived for more than half a century at **Ainola Ainolantie** (© 09/287-322; www.ainola.fi) in Järvenpää, 24 miles (39km) from Helsinki. Few countries seem as proud of one of their native composers as the Finns are of Jean Sibelius. In 1903, while he was skiing with his brother-in-law, Sibelius discovered a forested hill, which inspired him to commission construction of what would eventually become his family home. He named it after his wife, Aino, and from 1904 maintained a residence there with his children for many years. Today, he and his wife are buried on the property, which has become a shrine for music lovers. Some claim that they can hear the first notes of his violin concerto as they approach the house on a still day.

Visitors can tour the interior of the Art Nouveau house, which remains as the maestro left it. There are no great antiques or art—in fact, Ainola is simplicity itself—just as Sibelius preferred. In many places, the log walls remain in their natural state, and traditional tiled heating stoves are visible. The highlight of the exhibits is the grand piano. Some of the walls are decorated with paintings from the composer's private collection.

To get to the house, hop on a train from Central Helsinki Railway Station to Järvenpää. Admission is 5.5€ ($7.15) adults, 1€ ($1.30) children. Open May to September, Tuesday to Sunday 10am to 5pm.

---

pieces in the collection, including five impressive bronze statues by Wäinö Aaltonen. The architect, J. S. Sirén, who wanted to celebrate the new republic, chose a modernized neoclassic style.

Mannerheimintie 30. © 09/432-2027. www.eduskunta.fi. Free admission. Tours given Sat at 11am and 12:30pm, Sun at noon and 1:30pm. Tram: 3B, 3T, 4, 7A, 7B, and 10.

Helsinki City Museum   At Villa Hakasalmi, about ¼ mile (.4km) from the railway station, the museum presents the history of Helsinki from its founding up to modern times. A small-scale model of the town in the 1870s is on display. There is also an exhibit of home decorations from the 18th and 19th centuries, glass, porcelain, and toys.

Sofiankatu 4 (by Senate Sq.). © 09/3103-6630. www.hel2.fi/kaumuseo. Admission 4€ ($5.20), free for children under 18, free for everyone on Thurs. Mon–Fri 9am–5pm; Sat–Sun 11am–5pm. Tram: 1, 3B, or 3T.

Kiasma (Museum of Contemporary Art)   Part of the Finnish National Gallery (see the Ateneum Art Museum, above), this museum opened in 1998 and houses Finland's finest collection of contemporary art. An American architect, Steven Hall, designed the stunning 14,400-square-foot (1,338 sq. m) structure, which is ideally lit for displaying modern art. The permanent collection exhibits post-1960 Finnish and international art, but also features changing exhibitions. Based on the word *chiasma*, which refers to crossovers in genetics and rhetoric, the name for the new museum suggests Finland's special ability to achieve crossovers between the worlds of fine art and high technology. A "mediatheque" concentrates on displaying the museum's media collections.

Mannerheiminaukio 2. ℂ **09/1733-6501.** www.kiasma.fi. Admission 6€ ($7.80) adults, 4€ ($5.20) students and seniors, free for those under 18. Free admission every Fri from 5–8:30pm. Tues 10am–5pm; Wed–Sun 10am–8:30pm. Tram: 3B or 3T.

Lutheran Cathedral (Tuomiokirkko) ⋒   Dominating the city's skyline is one of the city's most visible symbols, a green-domed cathedral erected between 1830 and 1852. Built during the Russian administration of Finland in a severe, almost stark interpretation of the glory of ancient Greece and Rome, the Lutheran Cathedral was designed by German architect Carl Ludwig Engel. It was inaugurated as part of the 19th-century reconstruction of Helsinki—mostly in the neoclassical style—after a fire had destroyed most of the city. Called St. Nicholas until Finland became independent from Russia in 1917, the church has always been Lutheran and today's services conform to the Evangelical Lutheran denomination. Extensive renovations in 1998, both to the cathedral and to its crypt, brought it back to its original beauty.

Senaatintori. ℂ **09/2340-6120.** www.muuka.com. Free admission. June–Aug daily 9am–midnight,; Sept–May daily 9am–6pm. No sightseeing access is allowed during services. Tram: 1, 3B, 3T, 4, 7A, or 7B.

Mannerheim Museum ⋒⋒   Visit the home of the late Baron Carl Gustaf Mannerheim, Finland's former president and WWII field marshal—he's a sort of George Washington in this country. Now a museum, his former residence houses his collection of European furniture, Asian art and rugs, and personal items (uniforms, swords, decorations, gifts from admirers) that he acquired during his long career as a military man and statesman. The house remains the same as it was when he died in 1951. It's quite a hike from the train station, so take the tram.

Kallionlinnantie 14. ℂ **09/635-443.** www.mannerheim-museo.fi. Admission (including guided tour) 8€ ($10.40) adults; 6€ ($7.80) children 12–16, students and seniors, free for children under 12. Fri–Sun 11am–4pm. Tram: 3B or 3T.

National Museum of Finland ⋒⋒   This museum was designed in the style called National Romantic. Opened in 1916, it contains three major sections—prehistoric, historic, and ethnographic. The country's prehistory in the light of archaeological

---

Moments **Olympic Memories & a Flying Finn**

Way back in 1952 Helsinki hosted the Olympic Games at its impressive **Olympiastadion,** Paavo Nurmi tie 1 (ℂ **09/440-363;** www.stadion.fi). You can ascend to the top of a tower by elevator for a panoramic view of the city and the archipelago. The stadium, 1¼ miles (2km) from the city center, was originally built in 1938, but the Olympic Games scheduled for Finland that year were cancelled when World War II broke out. The seating capacity of the stadium is 40,000, larger than any other arena in the country. The stadium was closed and rebuilt between 1992 and 1994, and today is a first-rate sports venue. Outside the stadium is a statue by Wäinö Aaltonen of the great athlete Paavo Nurmi, "The Flying Finn." The runner is depicted in full stride and is completely nude, a fact that caused considerable controversy when the statue was unveiled in 1952. Admission is 2€ ($2.60) adults, 1€ ($1.30) children under 16. Open Monday to Friday 9am to 8pm, Saturday and Sunday 9am to 6pm. Tram: 3B, 3T, 4, or 10.

⟨Moments⟩ Exploring the Fortress of Finland

The 18th-century **Suomenlinna Fortress** ✶✶ (✆ **09/684-1880**; www.suomenlinna.fi) is known as the "Gibraltar of the North," and lies on the archipelago guarding the approach to Helsinki. With its walks and gardens, cafes, restaurants, museums, shops, and old frame buildings, the island makes for one of the most interesting outings from Helsinki. Originally built in the mid–18th century when Finland was a part of Sweden, the fortress was taken over by the Russians in 1808. After Finland gained independence in 1917, the fortress was given its present name, Suomenlinna, which means "the fortress of Finland." It served as part of the nation's defenses until 1973. The fortification work involved six islands, but today the main attraction is the part of the fortress on **Susisaari** and **Kustaanmiekka** islands, now joined as one land body. Kustaanmiekka is a small, well-preserved fort with defense walls and tunnels. The main fortress is on Susisaari, which is also home to a number of parks and squares.

You can take a **ferry** from Market Square to Suomenlinna year-round beginning at 6am daily. The boats run about once an hour, and the last one returns from the island at 1:45am. The round-trip ferry ride costs 3.80€ ($4.95) for adults and 1.90€ ($2.50) for children.

The island has no "streets," but individual attractions are signposted. Suomenlinna has a visitor center, situated by the bridge on Tykistölahti Bay (✆ **09/684-1880**) open year-round from January to April and October to December daily from 10am to 4pm, and May to September daily from 10am to 6pm. The center serves as the starting point for **guided tours**—offered in English—of the fortress with a focus on its military history. Tours are scheduled between June and August daily at 11am and 2pm, and between September and May on weekends only at 1:30pm. They cost 6.50€ ($8.45) for adults and 3€ ($3.90) for children.

finds may be seen, revealing that after the Ice Age and at the dawn of the Stone Age humans made their homes in Finland. Of particular interest are the Finno-Ugric collections representing the folk culture of the various peoples of northeastern and Eastern Europe as well as northwestern Siberia who speak a language related to Finnish. Church art of the medieval and Lutheran periods, folk culture artifacts, folk costumes and textiles, furniture, and an important coin collection are exhibited.

Mannerheimintie 34. ✆ 09/4050-9544. www.nba.fi. Admission 6€ ($7.80) adults, 4 € ($5.20) students, free for children under 18. Free admission on Tues from 5:30–8pm. Tues–Wed 11am–8pm; Thurs–Sun 11am–6pm. Tram: 4, 7A, 7B, or 10.

Seurasaari Open-Air Museum ✶✶   In a national park on the island of Seurasaari (a short boat trip from the mainland) is a wondrous re-creation of Old Finland—about 100 buildings (authentically furnished), a 17th-century church, and a gentleman's manor dating from the 18th century and containing period furnishings. In addition, visitors can see one of the "aboriginal" saunas, which resemble a smokehouse. The best time to visit this collection of historic, freestanding buildings is during the summer months, when you can visit the interiors, and when an unpretentious restaurant serves coffee, drinks, and platters of food. Although the buildings are locked during the winter months, you can still view the exteriors and explore the parkland that surrounds them. A wintertime walk through this place is not as far-fetched an idea as you might think—it's a favorite of strollers and joggers, even during snowfalls.

Seurasaari Island. ℂ 09/4050-9660. www.seurasaari.fi. Admission 5€ ($6.50) adults, 4€ ($5.20) students, free for children under 18. May 15–31 and Sept 1–15 Mon–Fri 9am–3pm, Sat–Sun 11am–5pm; June 1–Aug 31 daily 11am–5pm. Closed Sept 16–May 14. Bus: 24 from the Erottaja bus stop, near Stockmann Department Store, to the island. The 3-mile (4.8km) ride takes about 15 min., and costs 2€ ($2.60) each way.

Sinebrychoff Art Museum (Museum of Foreign Art) ★ *Finds* Part of the Finnish National Gallery (see Antaneum Art Museum, above), this museum was built in 1840 and still displays its original furnishings. It houses an extensive collection of foreign paintings from the 14th to the 19th centuries and has a stunning collection of foreign miniatures. The collection originated from the wealthy Sinebrychoff dynasty, a family of Russians who owned a local brewery and occupied this yellow and white neo-Renaissance mansion. They were great collectors of antiques, their taste leaning toward the opulent in furnishings. Their art collection was wide ranging, especially noted for its Dutch and Swedish portraits from the 17th and 18th centuries. There is also a stunning collection of porcelain. Outdoor concerts in summer are often staged in the formerly private park surrounding the estate.

Bulevardi 40. ℂ 09/1733-6460. www.sinebrychoffintaidemuseo.fi. Admission 7.50€ ($9.75) adults, 6€ ($7.80) students/seniors, children under 18 free. Tues and Fri 10am–6pm; Wed–Thurs 10am–8pm; Sat–Sun 11am–5pm. Tram: 6.

WHERE TO DINE

Bellevue RUSSIAN Immensely popular, this restaurant dates from 1917 and is still serving the time-tested specialties that put it on the Helsinki culinary map in the first place. With Russian wines as a side offering, the menu offers all those favorites that delighted Finland's former czarist rulers, including blinis, caviar, Russian-style herring, stuffed cabbage, and even bear steak. The Bellevue is located in the center of the city, near the Uspenski Orthodox Cathedral.

Rahapajankatu 3. ℂ 09/179-560. www.restaurantbellevue.com. Reservations required. Main courses 18€–65€ ($23.40–$84.50). AE, DC, MC, V. Mon–Fri 11am–midnight; Sat 5pm–midnight. Tram: 4.

Kellarikrouvi ★ FINNISH/INTERNATIONAL Built at the turn of the 20th century, this restaurant is installed in a former storage cellar for firewood and "winter potatoes." When it opened in 1965, it became the first restaurant in Helsinki to serve beer from a keg, which it still does today in great abundance. The cuisine is inspired, combining local Finnish recipes with innovative continental influences.

Pohjoinen Makasiinikatu 6. ℂ 09/686-0730. www.ravintolaopas.net/kellarikrouvi. Reservations recommended for dinner. Main courses 15€–28€ ($19.50–$36.40). AE, DC, MC, V. Mon–Sat 5pm–midnight. Tram: 3B.

Ravintola Perho ★ FINNISH/CONTINENTAL Owned and managed by the Helsinki Culinary School, this restaurant is staffed by students and trainees. What's on offer depends on the day's cooking lesson but could include smoked whitebait with mustard sauce, a terrine of smoked reindeer, and glow-fried Arctic char with creamed asparagus and herbed potatoes. The youthful enthusiasm of the staff is infectious. Ask them to recommend a beer, as there's a small brewery onsite.

Mechelininkatu 7. ℂ 09/5807-8649. www.perho.fi. Reservations not accepted. Main courses 10€–20€ ($13–$26). AE, DC, MC, V. Mon–Fri 11am–11pm. Closed late June to early Aug. Tram: 8.

⌒ Moments The Art of Crayfish Eating

Every Finn looks forward to the crayfish season, which runs between mid-July and mid-September. Some 225,000 pounds of this delicacy are caught yearly in inland waters and you'll find it in virtually every restaurant in Helsinki. Called *rapu,* the crayfish is usually boiled in salt water and seasoned with dill. For Finns, the eating of crayfish is an art form, and they suck out every morsel of flavor. Of course, with all this slurping and shelling, you'll need a bib. After devouring half a dozen, Finns will down a glass of schnapps, but unless you're accustomed to schnapps, we suggest you order a beer or glass of white wine instead.

Ravintola Sipuli 🐟🐟   In the 1800s this was a warehouse, taking its name of *Sipuli* (onion) from the onion-shaped domes of the Orthodox Upenski Cathedral in the vicinity. Architects successfully turned the structure into a restaurant of atmosphere and charm, with thick beams, paneling, and brick walls. Today, the chef is known for his robust flavors and clever use of Finnish products, especially reindeer meat shipped down from Lapland.

Kanavaranta 7. ⓒ **09/622-9280.** www.royalravintolat.com/sipuli. Reservations recommended. Main courses 26€–32€ ($33.80–$41.60). AE, DC, MC, V. Mon–Fri 6pm–midnight. Closed late June to early Aug. Tram: 2 or 4.

Rivoli Ravintolat SEAFOOD/FRENCH/FINNISH   Visit this Art Nouveau restaurant for some of the best and freshest tasting Finnish seafood, such as the grilled rainbow trout or freshly caught salmon from very chilly local rivers. Or try something more warming, such as the roasted duck breast with fig sauce and goats cheese polenta. The tasty dishes are prepared with market-fresh ingredients, and some are inspired by French cooking techniques.

Albertinkatu 38. ⓒ **09/643-455.** www.ravintolaopas.net/rivoli. Reservations recommended. Main courses 14€–29€ ($18.20–$37.70). AE, DC, MC, V. Mon–Fri 11am. Tram: 6. Bus: 14.

Wellamo 🐟 *Finds* FINNISH/FRENCH/RUSSIAN   On the residential island of Katajanokka, but easily reached by tram from the heart of the city, this elegant restaurant draws a steady stream of habitués. The menu features many dishes evocative of a Paris bistro, but also heads east to chilly Siberia for such delights as a regional ravioli stuffed with minced lamb, fresh herbs, mushrooms, and sour cream. The chef is also known for his many game dishes.

Vyökatu 9. ⓒ **09/663-139.** Reservations recommended. Main courses 12€–21€ ($15.60–$27.30). AE, MC, V. Tues–Fri 11am–2pm and 5–11pm; Sat 5–11pm; Sun 1–8pm. Tram: 4.

SHOPPING

Most stores are open Monday to Friday 9am to 6 or 7pm (with small shops shutting earlier and department stores and shopping centers staying open until 9pm) and on Saturday 9 or 10am to 5 or 6pm (with small shops opening for fewer hours). A government regulation now allows shopping on Sunday in May, June, July, August, and in the run-up to Christmas. As a result, many shops will open for sometime between noon and 6pm on Sunday during these months, with some staying open as late as 9pm.

The most important shopping neighborhoods are in the center of the city. They include **Esplanadi,** for those seeking the finest of Finnish design—but at high prices.

(Moments Traveling on to St. Petersburg

Known as Leningrad in its Communist heyday, St. Petersburg is hailed as one of the most beautiful cities on the globe. Home of the famous Hermitage museum, the city is only a 5- or 6-hour train ride from Helsinki and is a popular destination with rail travelers. For around 56€ ($73) one-way, you can head out daily from Helsinki on either a Finnish morning train, *Sibelius,* or the Russian afternoon and evening trains, *Repin* or *Tolstoi,* to St. Petersburg (the *Tolstoi* continues on to Moscow). You can also purchase tickets before leaving North America through Rail Europe.

All the trains offer first- and second-class service. The *Repin* and *Tolstoi* use old-style compartment seating (with sleeping berths in the first-class section on the *Tolstoi*), while the *Sibelius* employs the modern style seen on most trains in Europe. Both the Russian and Finnish trains have first-class restaurant cars, and the *Sibelius* also has a coffee bar.

Border formalities when traveling between the two countries are now at a minimum, and currency exchange and tax-free refunds are all smoothly handled on the trains. You don't even have to clear Customs unless you have something to declare.

Tip: Bring along your own supply of drinking water.

You no longer have to purchase tickets through a designated Intourist agency to get to St. Petersburg. Any travel agent in Helsinki can sell you a ticket. Note that reservations are mandatory and must be made at least 48 hours in advance of departure.

Arrivals in St. Petersburg are at the rail station, **Finlandski Vokzal,** 71 Zanevski Prospekt, where you can catch a taxi to your hotel. You can arrange your hotel through a Helsinki travel agent before leaving Finland. For more information on train service to St. Petersburg, head online to **www.vr.fi.**

Note: You will need a visa to enter Russia. Visas are issued by the nearest Russian embassy or consulate. Some agencies advertising travel to Russia can also help you obtain a visa. For information about visa assistance, check **www.visatorussia.com**. In the United States, contact the Russian Embassy, 2650 Wisconsin Ave. NW, Washington, DC 20007 (© **202/298-5700;** www. russianembassy.org).

Even if you don't buy anything, it's a delightful promenade in summer, and loaded with shops filled with the best of Finnish crafts, as well as a number of art galleries.

Esplanadi leads from the commercial heart of town all the way to the waterfront. Bordering the water is **Market Square (Kauppatori),** a fresh open-air market that's open Monday to Friday 6:30am to 6pm and Saturday 6:30am to 4pm, and on Sundays in the summer from 10am to 5pm. In winter, turn up early, as the cold sends many of the vendors scurrying back to their homes by 2pm.

In summer, peddlers set up trolleys and tables to display their wares. Most of the goods for sale are produce (some of them ideal for picnic food), but there are souvenir and gift items as well.

The other main shopping section is called simply **Central,** beginning at Esplanadi and extending to the famous Central Helsinki Railway Station. Many of the big names in Finnish shopping are located here. One of the main shopping streets is **Aleksanterinkatu,** which runs parallel to Esplanadi, stretching from the harborfront to Mannerheimintie.

Other shopping streets, all in the center, include **Iso Roobertinkatu** and **Bulevardi,** lying off Esplanadi. Bulevardi starts at the Klaus Kurki Hotel and winds its way to the water.

Helsinki's largest department store, **Stockmann,** Aleksanterinkatu 52B (© **09/1211;** www.stockmann.fi; tram: 3B), is also Finland's finest and oldest. Stockmann has a little bit of everything, with the most diversified sampling of Finnish and imported merchandise of any store: glassware, stoneware, ceramics, lamps, furniture, furs, contemporary jewelry, clothes and textiles, handmade candles, reindeer hides—everything.

The **Forum Shopping Center,** Mannerheimintie 20 (**09/565-7450;** www.city forum.fi; tram: 3B, 3T, 7A, or 7B), covering an entire block, houses over 100 shops, a seven-story atrium, restaurants, and service enterprises—making it the number-one shopping center in Finland. You'll find a wide array of merchandise here, including art, gold, jewelry, food, clothing, leather, glasses, rugs, and watches.

NIGHTLIFE

The ballet and opera performances of the **Finnish National Opera,** Helsinginkatu 58 (© **09/4030-2211;** www.operafin.fi; tram: 3B), are internationally acclaimed and the stage was thoroughly renovated in the summer of 2007. The ticket office is open April to May and August to September Monday to Friday 10am to 5pm. On performance nights, the ticket office stays open until the performance begins. The opera and ballet season runs from late August to early June and tickets are 12€ to 95€ ($15.60–$124).

Although it has been reconfigured, redecorated, and reincarnated many times since it was established in 1915, **Baker's,** Mannerheimintie 12 (© **09/612-6330;** www. ravintolabakers.com; tram: 3B), is the most deeply entrenched, long-lived drinking and dining complex in Helsinki. It sprawls across three floors (it's got a nightclub, a bar, a pub, and a restaurant) and on a busy night is often crammed with clubbers—many of them single. Most people come for the cafe, open Monday to Friday 7am to 4am, Saturday 10am to 4am and Sunday 1pm to 4am, or for one of the bars open Tuesday to Thursday from 4:30pm to 10pm, Friday and Saturday 4:30pm to 4am.

Studio 51, Fredrikinkatu 51–53, (©**09/612-9900;** www.studio51.fi; tram: 3 or 4), is a glittering gold disco evocative of New York's Studio 54 in its 1970s heyday. Drawing a clientele aged 20 to 40, it also has a VIP lounge. There is no cover unless a special band has been imported for the evening's festivities. Otherwise, you get music spun by a DJ. It's open Wednesday to Saturday 10pm to 4am. Cover varies between free and 8€ ($10.40).

Storyville, Museokatu 8 (© **09/408-007;** www.storyville.fi; tram: 4, 7, or 10), is the busiest and most active live music venue in Helsinki and was named after the fabled red-light district of New Orleans. The music offered includes blues, jazz, Dixieland, soul, and funk Monday to Saturday from 8pm to 4am. The cover is 6.50€ to 8€ ($8.45–$10.40).

8

France

Throughout time, France, its civilization, its history, and its way of life—the savoir-faire of its people—has lured rail travelers from around the world. The fact that it is among the easiest countries to travel by train makes it all the more appealing. Smaller than the state of Texas, France is the global leader of rail technology. Its TGV trains hold the world's friction rail speed record at 320 mph (515kmph). Rail lines, stretching some 19,188 miles (30,880km), go almost anywhere—and rapidly.

Often referred to as "the garden of Europe," France is a land to be savored, not sped through. Each region is so intriguing and varied that it's easy to immerse yourself in one province for too long. Overall, it's better to get to know a few regions intimately rather than trying to explore them all.

Of course, the primary language of the country is French, which might intimidate nonspeakers, though it shouldn't—most tourism officials and rail personnel speak at least some English. So you should have little trouble riding the rails and getting your questions answered. And, as a final plus, though train travel is not cheap in France when compared to other countries, it's unquestionably the most economical way to see the country.

HIGHLIGHTS OF FRANCE

On the tightest of schedules, particularly if you're traveling by rail to other European capitals such as London or Rome, you'll need 3 days for Paris—the logical starting point for any journey in France, as it's the country's rail hub. While in Paris, see world-class museums (including the **Musée du Louvre** and **Musée d'Orsay**); tour famous monuments, such as the **Eiffel Tower** and **Arc de Triomphe;** and bask in the glorious architecture of the city's magnificent churches, including **Ste-Chapelle** and, of course, the cathedral of **Notre-Dame.** But the city is also full of marvelous and evocative neighborhoods just waiting to be explored: Like Sartre, have a coffee and croissant on the **Left Bank,** then explore **St-Germain-des-Prés,** the ancient **Ile de la Cité,** the glamorous **Ile St. Louis,** the historic **Le Marais,** and, an absolute must-do—stroll down the famous **Champs-Elysées.**

Set aside a fourth day to journey south by rail to the magnificent palace of **Versailles,** an easy day-trip from the French capital.

But don't make the mistake of limiting your visit to Paris, unless you'd call a trip to New York a look at America. France has a number of scenic and sight-filled provinces (enough to fill a whole book—*Frommer's France,* for example) just waiting to be explored. Note, however, that we've limited ourselves in this chapter to the most popular regions that are also easily reached by rail out of Paris. So you will find plenty about the Loire Valley, Provence, and the Riviera, but you won't see Brittany or Normandy (including the famous abbey of Mont-St-Michel) because it's very difficult to get to some of those places by train.

About 120 rail miles (193km) southwest of Paris stretches the "green heart of France," the breathtakingly beautiful region of the **Loire Valley.** The towns of this area have magical names, but they also read like Joan of Arc's battle register—Orléans, Blois, Tours. Every hilltop has a castle or palace; there are vineyards as far as your eye can see; the Loire river winds like a silver ribbon and walled cities cluster around medieval churches. It is estimated that the average visitor spends only 3 nights in the Loire Valley. A week would be better. Even then, you will have only skimmed the surface. If you're severely hampered by lack of time, then try at least to see the following châteaux: **Chenonceau, Amboise, Azay-le-Rideau, Chambord,** and **Blois.**

Regardless, the most central location with the best rail connections is the ancient city of **Tours.** Many visitors also like to pay a rail visit first to the city of **Orléans**—another good base—with its evocative memories of Joan of Arc.

Moments **Tidbits on French Food Culture**

The French know how to enjoy their food, drink, and daily breaks. Embracing this tradition will make your rail-travel experience far more complete. Wherever you stay, take a daily trip to the local *boulangerie* (bakery) for a baguette, sandwich, or pastry; or create a picnic feast of fresh baguette, *du fromage* (cheese), *des tomates* (tomatoes), and *du poulet rotisserie* (roasted chicken) from the local marché. Marketplaces are common on different days in every region, but try to find one in Provence (see "Arles," on p. 300) if you travel there. You should also stop for an afternoon *goûter* (snack) on a city square—perhaps a crêpe avec nutella, sorbet, or café au lait—where you can relax, people-watch, and soak up the local atmosphere.

To continue your rail journey through France, head for **Provence,** where you'll need at least 3 days. High-speed TGV trains have put the south of France within an easy commute of Paris, speeding you to where you want to go in record times. The chief centers of the region are **Avignon,** seat of the popes during the 14th century; **Arles,** which once cast a spell over van Gogh and inspired some of his greatest paintings; and **Aix-en-Provence,** home to Provence's most celebrated son, the artist Paul Cézanne.

To conclude your French rail trip, head to France's vacation hot spot par excellence for 2 to 3 days. Known to the world as the **Cote d'Azur** (the French name for its Riviera), this is a short stretch of curving coastline near the Italian border with a veritable bounty of hotels and resorts. It's also a land drenched in sunshine, sprinkled with vineyards and olive groves, and dotted with some of the world's most fascinating tourist meccas.

For the rail traveler, the resort of **Cannes** in the west and the city of **Nice** in the east make the best centers. Both have high-speed train connections to Paris. For a more sophisticated beach-style ambience, head to Cannes for at least 2 days, enjoying its glamour and style. But for a more typically Provençal city, make it Nice, which is also the best for sightseeing as it has far more museums and monuments, and is the better center for day excursions to hill towns such as **Vence, St-Paul-de-Vence,** and especially to **Monaco.**

1 Essentials

GETTING THERE

The French national carrier, **Air France** (© 800/237-2747; www.airfrance.com), offers daily or several-times-a-week flights out of several North American cities to Paris.

Other major carriers offering direct flights to Paris out of North America include **American Airlines** (© 800/433-7300; www.aa.com); **Continental Airlines** (© 800/525-0280; www.continental.com); **Delta Air Lines** (© 800/241-4141; www.delta.com); **US Airways** (© 800/428-4322; www.usairways.com), and **Air Canada** (© 888/247-2262; www.aircanada.ca).

British Airways (© 800/AIRWAYS; www.britishairways.com) offers connecting flights to Paris from 18 U.S. cities, with a stop in either Heathrow or Gatwick airport in England. Other carriers offering connecting flights to Paris include **Aer Lingus**

(© **800/IRISH-AIR;** www.aerlingus.com) and **Northwest/KLM** (© **800/225-2525;** www.nwa.com).

Flight time to Paris varies according to the departure city, but it generally takes 7 to 11 hours to get to France's capital from most major North American cities.

FRANCE BY RAIL

The *Société Nationale des Chemins de Fer* (SNCF) is the French National Railway and it runs more than 3,000 train stations, supervises more than 19,188 miles (30,880km) of track, and is fabled for its on-time performance. About 181 of the country's cities are linked by some 665 TGVs (some of the world's fastest trains), and you can get from Paris to just about anywhere in a matter of hours. For information, check out **www.sncf.com** or **www.raileurope.com**.

France is also well connected to the major international rail lines running through Europe. High-speed **Artesia** trains connect Paris and Lyon to Milan in Italy; the **Eurostar** connects Paris with both London and Brussels; **Thalys** trains link Paris with several cities in Belgium, the Netherlands, and Cologne in Germany; **TGV** trains connect many French cities with Brussels and Switzerland; and **Elipsos** overnight hotel trains connect Paris with both Madrid and Barcelona. The newly opened (2007) TGV

Moments **Festivals & Special Events**

Parades, boat races, music, balls, and fireworks are all part of the ancient **Carnival of Nice,** which draws visitors from all over Europe and North America. This "Mardi Gras of the Riviera" begins sometime in February, usually 12 days before Shrove Tuesday, celebrating the return of spring with 3 weeks of parades, *corsi* (floats), and *veglioni* (masked balls). The climax is the century-year-old tradition of burning King Carnival in effigy, after *Les Batailles des Fleurs* (Battles of the Flowers), when teams pelt each other with flowers. Make reservations well in advance. For information, contact the **Nice Convention and Visitors Bureau** (© **08-92-70-74-07**).

The world-class **Festival d'Avignon** (first 3 weeks in July) has a reputation for exposing new talent to critical acclaim. The focus is usually on avant-garde works in theater, dance, and music by groups from around the world. Much of the music is presented within the 14th-century courtyard of the Palais de l'Ancien Archeveché (the Old Archbishop's Palace). Other events occur in the medieval cloister of the Cathédral St-Sauveur. Part of the fun is the bacchanalia that takes place nightly in the streets. The prices for rooms and meals skyrocket, so make reservations far in advance. For more information contact the **Bureaux du Festival,** Espace Saint-Louis, 20 rue du portail Boquier, 84000 Avignon (© **04-90-27-66-50;** www.festival-avignon.com). Tickets cost 13€ to 36€ ($16.90–$46.80).

One of France's most famous festivals, the **Festival d'Automne** (mid-Sept to late Dec) in Paris, is one of its most eclectic, focusing mainly on modern music, ballet, theater, and modern art. For more information contact the Festival d'Automne (© **01-53-45-17-00;** www.festival-automne.com).

Est connects Paris to eastern France, Luxembourg, Zurich, and a number of German cities. These connections make Paris one of Europe's busiest rail junctions.

PASSES

For information on the **Eurail Global Pass, Eurail Global Pass Flexi,** and other multicountry options, see chapter 2.

The **France Rail Pass** provides unlimited rail transport in France for any 3 days within 1 month, from $278 in first class and from $237 in second. You can purchase up to 6 more days for an extra $41 per person per day. Children 4 to 11 get a discounted rate.

The **France Rail 'n Drive Pass** is best used by arriving at a major rail station, then striking out to explore the countryside by car. It includes 2 days' use of France Rail in first class (see above), and 2 days' use of a rental car (cheapest is economy size with unlimited mileage) within a given month. The pass starts at $286 per person (based on two people traveling together). Note that second class is not an option for this pass. For more on rail 'n drive passes, see chapter 2.

The railpasses mentioned above, as well as point-to-point rail tickets within France, are available through most travel agencies or through **Rail Europe** (© 877/272-RAIL [7245] in North America; www.raileurope.com).

FOREIGN TRAIN TERMS

Welcome officers (called *Agents d'accueil*) wear electric-blue jackets and caps, and are found at major rail stations to help answer your questions. Most officers speak English (to ask, say: *Parlez vous anglais?*).

Ticket windows are marked *guichets* and generally have signs for *billets* (tickets)— you can ask about your *résa* (reservation); a lost-luggage office is called *consigne.* SNCF's time schedules are *horaires.* Sleepers are known as *voitures-lits,* and in second-class sections you can often request *sieges inclinables* (reclining seats) for an extra fee.

A *supplement* is a supplement—they are color coded. SNCF calendars designate days for rail travelers as *période bleue* or *période rouge.* Trips in the blue period get many discounts; trips in the red period are peak periods where you get no discounts. There is also a *période blanche* or white, when moderate discounts are available. To be eligible for a discount, each leg of your rail trip must begin during a period of the appropriate color. For a complete list of these red, white, and blue periods, request a *Calendrier Voyageurs* at any rail station information office.

PRACTICAL TRAIN INFORMATION

SNCF-operated, the heavily state-subsidized French rail system is one of the world's greatest. Trains radiate out from Paris like the spokes of a wheel, taking you to all parts of France, though service may not be as extensive in some regions as in others.

The country also has **Transilien** trains, servicing the Paris suburban area (Ile-de-France), **T.E.R.** (Train Regional express) trains, and **Corail (TRN)** trains. T.E.R. trains are regional trains that link smaller cities to such transportation hubs as Paris, Nimes, and Toulouse. The Corail Teoz trains offer modern comfort, are air-conditioned, and travel at speeds of about 81 to 93 mph (130–150kmph). These trains are used on many major city routes.

Tickets are most often valid for up to 2 months following purchase. In some very large train stations, such as those in Paris, separate ticket windows are set aside for different types of trains: long haul is *grandes-lignes; banlieue* is for suburban lines. You can, of course, purchase tickets on board a train but you'll be hit with a hefty surcharge; and travel agents will sell you a rail ticket, but will charge you a stiff handling fee. Here, rail travel can get very expensive, so if you plan to travel quite a bit, a railpass makes sense. Railpasses should be hand-stamped at a designated rail station ticket window before you get on the first leg of your journey.

We'll admit that there is great freedom in seeing France by car, but the high price of gasoline/petrol, the never-ending high *autoroute* tolls, and the stiff car-rental fees make driving superexpensive. Trains are a whole lot cheaper. If you want to drive, even a little, consider the **France Rail 'n Drive Pass** (see above).

For one-way travel, request *un billet aller-simple;* for round-trip journeys, ask for *un billet aller-retour.* In all cases, round-trips are less expensive.

For SNCF routes, timetables, and information check **www.sncf.com** or **www.rail europe.com**.

RESERVATIONS   Although you can travel on most French trains without reserva-
tions, they are compulsory on Eurostar, Thalys, Artesia, Elipsos, TGVs, and Corail Teoz, and are available on regional trains. If you're heading into or out of Paris on an interna-
tional train, make reservations at least 2 to 3 days in advance. Reservations can be made as early as 90 days in advance of departure online at SNCF's website or through Rail Europe. During holiday periods, at Easter, and in July and August (especially Aug), reservations should be made as far in advance as possible.

If you're taking an overnight train, be sure to reserve your sleeping accommodations (see "Services & Amenities," below) far in advance. Having a railpass does not exempt you from reservation fees.

SERVICES & AMENITIES   Nearly all the country's trains, including the TGV, offer both first- or second-class seating, the first-class carriages designated by the number 1. Second-class travel on French trains is usually the equivalent of first-class travel in many parts of the world.

On overnight trains, you can reserve a couchette, although you must reserve one in advance (up to 1¼ hr. before departure). The second-class couchette compartments are crowded with six berths, while there are only four in first class. Note that we've had reports of unpleasant experiences (dirty cars, crowding) aboard couchettes in France, so we recommend traveling during the day.

The elegant and expensive (and more comfortable) way to go is with a sleeper (called *voitures-lits*), filled with real beds. Sleepers hold up to four people and prices

Train Schedules & Travel Times in France

From	To	Type of Train	# of Trains	Frequency	Travel Time
Paris	Tours	TRN	13	Daily	2 hr., 30 min.–3 hr., 14 min.
Paris	Tours	TGV	6	Daily	1 hr., 10 min.
Paris	Orleans	TRN	17	Daily	1 hr., 30 min.–1hr., 42min.
Paris	Avignon	TGV	14	Daily	2 hr., 30 min.–3 hr., 30 min.
Paris	Arles	TGV	2	Daily	3 hr., 52 min.–4hr., 3min.
Paris	Aix-en-Provence	TGV	11	Daily	2 hr., 55 min.–3 hr., 14min
Paris	Cannes	TRN	5	Daily	4 hr., 58 min.–5hr., 41min.
Paris	Nice	TRN	5	Daily	5 hr., 25 min.–6hr., 16min.
Nice	Monaco	TER	43	Daily	16 min.–22min.

run $45 to $420 per person. Hotel trains that run in France include the Trenhotel Ellipsos running between Spain and France, the Paris–Germany night train, and the Artesia Nuit trains that run between France and Italy.

Although food and drink are served aboard most French trains, especially long-haul ones, if you want to save money, board a train with enough bottled water and food for the length of your journey as the prices are very high indeed (equivalent to buying a drink in a New York theater at intermission). Most major rail stations have restaurants and bars, but prices there are also ridiculously high. If you have time, you can often leave the station and find a local *boulangerie* (bakery that usually serves delicious sandwiches) or grocery store where the prices are far more reasonable.

SNCF operates a special telephone line (© **0800/15-47-53**) for rail travelers with disabilities who might face accessibility issues. For information online, head to **www.sncf.com/voyageurs-handicapes**.

Note: The frequency of trains listed below is for weekdays; there are often fewer trains on weekends.

FAST FACTS: France

Area Code All French telephone numbers consist of 10 digits, the first two of which are like an area code. If you're calling anywhere in France from within France, just dial all 10 digits—no additional codes are needed. If you're calling from the United States, dial 0-11-33 and then drop the initial zero of the local area code.

Business Hours Business hours are erratic. Most banks are open Monday to Friday 9:30am to 4:30pm. Many, particularly in small towns, take a 2-hour lunch break, most often from 12:30pm to 2:30pm, but this varies. Hours are usually posted on the door. Most museums close 1 day a week (often Mon or Tues), and they're generally closed on national holidays. Refer to the individual listings for hours.

Offices tend to be open Monday to Friday 9am to 5pm, but always call first. In Paris and other big French cities, stores are open from 9 or 10am to 6 or 7pm without a break for lunch. Some shops, particularly those operated by foreigners, open at 8am and close at 8 or 9pm. In some small stores, the lunch break can last 3 hours, but this is more common in the south than in the north.

Climate France's weather varies by region and even sometimes by town separated by only 12 miles (19km). Despite its northern latitude, Paris never gets very cold—snow is a rarity. Rain usually falls in a kind of steady drizzle and rarely lasts more than a day. May is the driest month. The Mediterranean coast has the driest climate. When it does rain, it's heaviest in spring and autumn. (Cannes sometimes receives more rainfall than Paris.) Summers are comfortably dry. Provence dreads *le mistral* (an unrelenting, hot, dusty wind), which most often blows in winter for a few days but can last for up to 2 weeks.

Documents Required All foreign (non-French) nationals need a valid passport to enter France. The French government no longer requires visas for U.S. citizens, providing they're staying in France for less than 90 days. Citizens of Canada do not need visas.

Electricity In general, expect 200 volts or 50 cycles, though you'll encounter 110 and 115 volts in some older places. Adapters are needed to fit sockets. It's best to ask your concierge before plugging in any appliance.

Embassies & Consulates If you have a passport, immigration, legal, or other problem, contact your consulate. Call before you go, as they often keep odd hours and observe both French and home-country holidays. The Embassy of the **United States,** at 2 rue St-Florentin (© **01-43-12-22-22;** Métro: Concorde), is open Monday to Friday 9am to 6pm. Passports are issued at the Consulate at 2 rue St-Florentin (© **01-43-12-22-22;** Métro: Concorde). The Embassy of **Canada** is at 35 av. Montaigne, 8e (© **01-44-43-29-00;** Métro: F.D.-Roosevelt or Alma-Marceau), open Monday to Friday 9am to 5pm.

Health & Safety In general, France is viewed as a "safe" destination. You don't need to get shots; most food is safe and the water is potable. For tap water, order *une carafe d'eau* but if you're concerned, order bottled water *(une bouteille d'eau).* It is easy to get a prescription filled in French towns and cities, and nearly all places have English-speaking doctors at hospitals with well-trained staff. For minor health problems, local pharmacies (marked by a green cross) are extremely helpful.

The most common menace, especially in large cities, is pickpockets and gangs of Gypsy children who surround you, distract you, and steal your purse or wallet (especially in Métro stations). Also protect your valuables on French trains, where most robberies occur while passengers are asleep. Much of the country, particularly central France, remains relatively safe, though no place in the world is crime-free. Try to carry a backpack or purse that is difficult to get into (with the wallet hidden)—or hold it in front of you when walking in crowded areas.

Holidays In France, holidays are *jours feriés.* The main holidays include New Year's Day (Jan 1), Easter Sunday and Monday, Labor Day (May 1), V-E Day in Europe (May 8), Whit Monday (May 19), Ascension Thursday (40 days after Easter), Bastille Day (July 14), Assumption of the Blessed Virgin (Aug 15), All Saints' Day (Nov 1), Armistice Day (Nov 11), and Christmas (Dec 25). Monaco's National Day is Nov 19.

Mail Most post offices are open Monday to Friday 8am to 7pm (smaller ones close for lunch) and Saturday 8am to noon. Allow 5 to 8 days to send or receive mail from your home. Airmail letters within Europe cost .60€ (78¢); to the United States, Canada, Australia, and New Zealand, .85€ ($1.10). You can exchange money at post offices. Many hotels, post offices, and cafes displaying a red TABAC sign outside sell stamps.

Police & Emergencies If your wallet gets stolen, go to the police station in person (ask at your hotel's front desk for the nearest one). Otherwise, you can get help anywhere in France by calling © **17** for the police or © **18** for the fire department *(pompiers).*

Telephone The French use a Télécarte, a phone debit card, which you can purchase at railway stations, tabacs, and post offices. Sold in two versions, it allows you to use either 50 or 120 charge units (depending on the card) by inserting the card into the slot of most public phones. Depending on the type of card you buy, the cost is 6€ to 15€ ($7.80–$19.50). At some public phones (for a hefty fee) you can insert your credit card and call directly.

If possible, avoid making calls from your hotel, as some French establishments will double or triple the charges.

Tipping The law requires all bills to say *service compris,* which means the tip has been included. But French diners often leave some small change as an additional tip.

In general, locals *only* tip for exceptional services; the money is assumed to be included in the employee's pay check. That being said, restroom and cloakroom attendants are usually left a few coins. Taxi drivers, tour guides, and hotel staff are left 1 to 2 euros if the employee has gone out of his/her way for you (with luggage, children, elderly, and so on).

2 Paris ✳✳✳

Paris has been celebrated in such a torrent of media that for millions of people, the capital of France is an abstraction rather than a city. To most North American visitors, the city is still "Gay Paree," the fairy-tale town inviting you for a fling, the hub of everything "European," and the epitome of that nebulous attribute known as "chic." Paris remains the metropolis of pleasure, the picture postcard of blooming chestnut trees and young couples kissing by the Seine.

Paris is the glamour capital of the globe; by day a stone mosaic of delicate gray and green, by night a stunning, unforgettable sea of lights—white, red, orange. Broad, tree-lined boulevards open up before you, the mansions flanking them looming tall, ornate, and graceful. Everywhere you look are trees, squares, and monuments—and train stations. For Paris is also the center of France's extensive web of rail networks and a major international rail hub—a natural spot to begin a multicountry rail tour of Europe.

STATION INFORMATION
GETTING FROM AIRPORTS TO TRAIN STATIONS

Paris has two international airports: **Aéroport d'Orly,** 8½ miles (14km) south of the city, and **Aéroport Roissy–Charles de Gaulle,** 14¼ miles (23km) northeast of the city. A shuttle (**www.paris-airport-shuttle.com**), costing 19.90€ ($25.85) per person, makes the 50- to 74-minute journey between the two airports about every 30 minutes from 5am to 8pm. There is an additional fee of 3€ ($3.90) for rides outside of these hours.

At **Charles de Gaulle** (✆ 01-48-62-22-80; www.paris-cdg.com), foreign carriers use Aérogare (Terminal) 1, while Air France and other airlines flying to European destinations wing into Aérogare 2. From Aérogare 1, you take a moving walkway to the checkpoint and Customs. The two terminals are linked by the CDG VAL (automated light-rail shuttle). The CDG VAL also transports you to the **Roissy rail station (Terminal 3),** from which fast **RER** (Réseau Express Régional) trains leave every 15 minutes heading to such Métro stations as Gare du Nord (see below), Châtelet, Luxembourg, Port-Royal, and Denfert-Rochereau. A typical fare from Roissy to any point in central Paris is 8.20€ ($10.65). From terminals 2 and 3 you can access the RER line B to Paris Gare du Nord (departs every 10 to 15 min.; trip time: 30 min.) from approximately 5am to midnight.

Note: Underneath Aérogare 2 is a TGV rail station. If you're headed for Avignon, Tours, or Brussels, you can catch a train here.

You can also take an **Air France Coach** (© 08-92-35-08-20; transfer.airport-paris. com) to central Paris for 9€ to 14€ ($11.70-$18.20). It stops at the Palais des Congrès (Port Maillot), and then continues on to place Charles-de-Gaulle-étoile, where subway lines can carry you to any point in Paris. Depending on traffic it takes between 45 and 55 minutes. The shuttle departs about every 15 minutes between 5:45am and 11pm daily.

Another option is the **Roissybus** (© 08-92-68-77-14), departing from the airport daily from 5:45am to 11pm and costing 8.60€ ($10.40) for the 45- to 60-minute ride. Departures are about every 15 to 20 minutes, and the bus will take you near the corner of rue Scribe and place de l'Opéra in the heart of Paris.

A **taxi** from Roissy to the central Paris rail stations will cost about 42€ to 48€ ($54.60-$62.40), but from 8pm to 7am the fares are 40% higher. Long lines for taxis form outside each of the airport's terminals and are surprisingly orderly. Be sure to ask for an estimate of the fee *before* you get in the taxi.

Orly Airport (© 01-49-75-15-15) has two terminals—Orly *Sud* (south) for international flights and Orly *Ouest* (West) for domestic flights. They're linked by a free shuttle bus (trip time: 15 min).

Air France Coaches leave from gate K of Orly Sud, Orly Ouest, and Gate E arrival level every 15 minutes between 6am and 11pm for a major rail terminus, Gare des Invalides; the fare is 7.50€ ($9.75). Returning to the Airport, buses leave the Invalides terminal for Orly Sud or Orly Ouest every 15 minutes, taking about 30 minutes.

Another way to central Paris is via the free **shuttle bus** that leaves Orly's terminals about every 15 minutes for the nearby Métro and RER train station (Pont-de-Rungis/Aéroport-d'Orly). RER trains take 35 minutes. A trip to Les Invalides, for example, is 8.20€ ($10.65).

A **taxi** from Orly to central Paris costs about 36€ to 42€ ($46.80-$54.60), more at night. Don't take a meterless taxi from Orly—it's much safer (and usually cheaper) to hire one of the metered cabs, which are under the scrutiny of a police officer.

INSIDE THE STATIONS

There are six major train stations in Paris and seven **Welcome Centers,** two of which are located in the city's rail stations (**Gare de Lyon** and **Gare de Nord**). They can give you free maps, brochures, and a selection of magazines listing current events and

---

Tips The Airport Shuttle

Cheaper than a taxi for one or two people but more expensive than airport buses and trains, the **Paris Shuttle** (© 01-43-90-91-91; www.parisshuttle.com) will pick you up in a minivan at Charles de Gaulle or Orly and take you to your hotel or rail station for 25€ ($32.50) for one person or 19€ ($24.70) per person for parties of two or more. It'll take you to the airports from your hotel for the same price. **Blue Vans** (© 01-30-11-13-00; www.paris-blue-airport-shuttle.fr) offers a similar service, charging 25€ to 28€ ($32.50-$36.40) for one passenger or 34€ to 36€ ($44.20-$46.80) for two. Both accept major credit cards, but only if you book online.

Paris

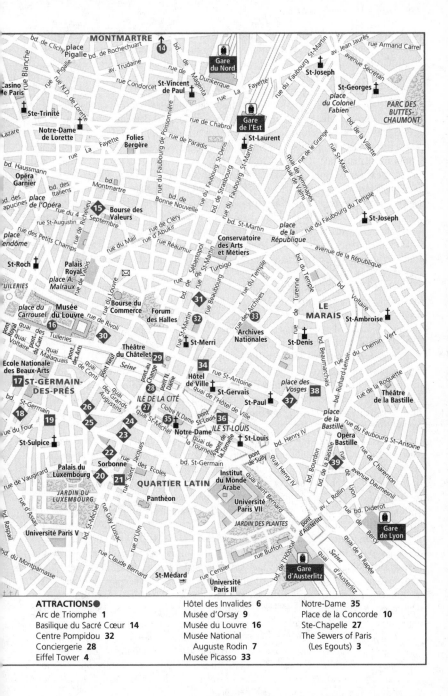

MONTMARTRE

place Pigalle
bd. de Clichy
bd. de Rochechouart
av. Trudaine
rue Condorcet
St-Vincent de Paul

Gare du Nord

rue du Faubourg St-Martin
av. Jean Jaurès
rue Armand Carrel
avenue Secrétan

St-Joseph

St-Georges
place du Colonel Fabien

PARC DES BUTTES-CHAUMONT

Casino de Paris
rue Blanche
rue Pigalle
rue N.D. de Lorette
Ste-Trinité

Notre-Dame de Lorette
Folies Bergère

Gare de l'Est
St-Laurent

rue de la Grange
rue St-Maur
bd. de la Villette

St-Lazare
bd. Haussmann
Opéra Garnier
bd. des Italiens
place de l'Opéra
rue du 4 Septembre

15 Bourse des Valeurs

rue St-Augustin
place des Petits Champs
place Vendôme

St-Roch
Palais Royal
place A. Malraux

TUILERIES

place du Carrousel
16 Musée du Louvre

quai Voltaire
Ecole Nationale des Beaux-Arts

17 ST-GERMAIN-DES-PRÉS

bd. St-Germain
18 **19**
rue du Four
26 **25**
St-Sulpice

22 Sorbonne
20 **21**
Palais du Luxembourg

JARDIN DU LUXEMBOURG

Université Paris V

bd. du Montparnasse
bd. Raspail
rue d'Assas
rue de Vaugirard

14

Bourse des Valeurs
Conservatoire des Arts et Métiers

place de la République

avenue de la République

bd. de la Villette

St-Joseph

Bourse du Commerce
Forum des Halles
30
Théâtre du Châtelet
29
28
ILE DE LA CITÉ
27 **35** **36**
Notre-Dame
24 **23**
ILE ST-LOUIS
St-Louis

31
32
St-Merri
34
Hôtel de Ville
St-Gervais
St-Paul

33
Archives Nationales
St-Denis

LE MARAIS
St-Ambroise

place des Vosges **38**
37

place de la Bastille
Opéra Bastille
39

Théâtre de la Bastille

rue de la Roquette

QUARTIER LATIN
Institut du Monde Arabe
Panthéon
Université Paris VII
JARDIN DES PLANTES

Université Paris III
St-Médard

Gare de Lyon

Gare d'Austerlitz

Seine

ATTRACTIONS●

Arc de Triomphe **1**	Hôtel des Invalides **6**	Notre-Dame **35**
Basilique du Sacré Cœur **14**	Musée d'Orsay **9**	Place de la Concorde **10**
Centre Pompidou **32**	Musée du Louvre **16**	Ste-Chapelle **27**
Conciergerie **28**	Musée National	The Sewers of Paris
Eiffel Tower **4**	Auguste Rodin **7**	(Les Egouts) **3**
	Musée Picasso **33**	

performances, as well as museum passes and hotel reservations. If you need a hotel room and you arrive at another station, visit the city's main tourist office or other Welcome Centers located around the city (see "Information Elsewhere in the City," below).

Paris' North Station or **Gare du Nord,** 18 rue de Dunkerque (Métro: Gare du Nord), is a major gateway to France. Passengers from the English Channel ports of Boulogne and Calais arrive here, as do trains from the Netherlands, Belgium, and Germany. It is also the termination point for Eurostar trains arriving from London and for Thalys trains from Brussels and Amsterdam. For rail information and tickets, go to the office across from platform #1 daily 6am to 11pm. Seat reservations on TGV trains and sleeping car reservations can be made here. Across from platform #3 is a kiosk that exchanges money and there are also ATMs scattered throughout the station. **Eurostar** (www.eurostar.com) has its own terminal and reservations offices in the building, and there's a special waiting room upstairs from the main terminal. For more on Eurostar, see chapter 10 and check out **www.raileurope.com**.

Daily from 8am to 6pm, a **Welcome Center,** located beneath the glass roof in the Ile-de-France zone, sells museum passes and will make hotel reservations and bookings for excursions.

Gare de Lyon, 20 bd. Diderot (Métro: Gare de Lyon), is the best equipped in Paris, and is the gateway station for passengers heading for Burgundy, Provence, and the French Riviera, as well as Italy and western Switzerland. Train information and reservations are handled at an office in the center of the station; open Monday to Saturday 8am to 10pm, Sunday 8am to 7pm.

The **Welcome Center** here is found in the station's main ticket hall. It's open Monday to Saturday 8am to 6pm. For hotel reservations fees, see "Information Elsewhere in the City," below. This station is also the site of **Restaurant Le Train Bleu (② 01-43-43-09-06;** www.le-train-bleu.com), the most elegant train station restaurant in Europe. Open since 1901, the restaurant serves good food in a fanciful Belle Epoque–style dining room.

The East Station or **Gare de l'Est,** place de 11 Novembre 1918 (Métro: Gare de l'Est), is the main terminal for departures into eastern France, with continuing service to such countries as Switzerland, Austria, Germany, and Luxembourg. The Rail Information Center here lies between platforms #6 and #7 and is open daily 8:45am to 8pm. You can make seat reservations here but only from Monday to Saturday. A currency-exchange kiosk is located in the main terminal opposite platforms #25 and #26, and ATMs are also available.

Gare d'Austerlitz, 55 quai d'Austerlitz (Métro: Gare d'Austerlitz), is the arrival and departure point for night trains heading into the central and southwestern sections of France and going on to Iberia (Spain and Portugal). The grand Train Hotel Elipsos trains to Madrid *(Francisco de Goya)* and Barcelona *(Joan Miró)* depart from and arrive in this station. In the foyer of the station (not the main hall) is a Train Information Center open Monday to Saturday 7:30am to 7:45pm. Seat reservations can also be made here. There is a currency-exchange office in the main hall.

Two other major stations are **Gare St-Lazare** (Métro: Gare St-Lazare), with trains departing for Normandy, and **Gare de Montparnasse** (Métro: Montparnasse-Bienvenue), with trains going to Brittany and TGV departures to southwestern France and day trains to Spain. The Artesia de Nuit night trains from Italy pull into **Gare de Bercy** (Métro: Bercy) near Gare de Lyon and Gare d'Austerlitz.

The stations above are not connected to each other by rail, but all are linked by bus, which is preferable to the Métro if you have luggage. All stations have cafes, bars, washing facilities, and waiting rooms. For information and reservations call ⓒ **08-92-35-36-35**. *Warning:* The stations and surrounding areas are usually seedy and frequented by pickpockets, hustlers, hookers, and addicts. Be alert, especially at night.

INFORMATION ELSEWHERE IN THE CITY

The main **Tourist Information Office** is at 127 av. Des Champs-Elysées, 8e (ⓒ **08-92-68-31-12;** Métro: Georges-V), where you can get details about Paris and the provinces. It's open April to October, daily 9am to 8pm (closed May 1), and November to March, daily 11am to 6pm (closed Dec 25). The staff reserves same-day hotel rooms only, charging 3€ ($3.90) for a one-star hotel, 4€ ($5.20) for a two-star; 6€ ($7.80) for a three-star; and 7.50€ ($9.75) for a four-star.

There are five **Welcome Centers** located outside of the train stations at strategic points around Paris. For general information about them, call ⓒ **08-92-68-30-00** or head online to **http://en.parisinfo.com**. The **Pyramides** center, 25 rue des Pyramides, 1er (Métro: Pyramides), is open from 10am to 7pm from Monday to Saturday and from 11am to 7pm on Sundays. The **Opéra-Grands Magasins** center, 11 rue Scribe, 9e (Métro: Opéra), is open from Monday to Saturday from 9am to 6:30pm. The **Tour Eiffel** center (Métro: Bir-Hakeim), located between the east and north pillar, is open from March 25 to October 31 daily 11am to 6:40pm.

The **Montmartre** center, 21 place du Tertre, 18e (Métro: Abbesses), is open daily from 10am to 7pm. The **Carrousel du Louvre** center, 99 rue de Rivoli, 1e (Métro: Palais Royal-Musée du Louvre), is open daily from 10am to 6pm. Neither of these two centers handles hotel reservations.

THE CITY LAYOUT

Paris is surprisingly compact and an excellent city for strollers. Occupying 432 square miles (696 sq. km), it's home to more than 10 million people. The River Seine divides Paris into the *Rive Droite* (**Right Bank**) to the north and the *Rive Gauche* (**Left Bank**) to the south. These designations make sense when you stand on a bridge and face downstream (west)—to your right is the north bank, to your left the south. A total of 32 bridges link the Right Bank and the Left Bank, some providing access to the two islands at the heart of the city—**Ile de la Cité,** the city's birthplace and site of Notre-Dame; and **Ile St-Louis,** a moat-guarded oasis of 17th-century mansions.

The "main street" on the Right Bank is, of course, **avenue des Champs-Elysées,** beginning at the Arc de Triomphe and running to place de la Concorde. Avenue des Champs-Elysées and 11 other avenues radiate like the arms of an asterisk from the Arc de Triomphe, giving it its original name, place de l'étoile (*étoile* means "star"). It was renamed place Charles-de-Gaulle following the general's death; today, it's often referred to as place Charles-de-Gaulle-étoile.

ARRONDISSEMENTS IN BRIEF The heart of medieval Paris was the **Ile de la Cité** and the areas immediately surrounding it. As Paris grew, it absorbed many of the once-distant villages, and today each of these *arrondissements* (districts) retains a distinct character. They're numbered 1 to 20 starting at the center and progressing in a clockwise spiral. The key to finding any address in Paris is to look for the arrondissement number rendered either as a number followed by "e" or "er" (1er, 2e, and so on). If the address is written out more formally, you can tell what arrondissement it's in by looking at the postal code. For example, the address may be written with the street name, then "75014 Paris." The last two digits, 14, indicate that the address is in the 14th arrondissement, Montparnasse.

On the Right Bank, the **1er** is home to the Louvre, place Vendôme, rues de Rivoli and St-Honoré, Palais Royal, and Comédie-Française—an area filled with grand institutions and grand stores. At the center of the **2e** is the Bourse (Stock Exchange), making it the city's financial center. Most of the **3e** and the **4e** is referred to as the Marais, the old Jewish quarter that in the 17th century was home to the aristocracy—today, it's a trendy area of boutiques and restored mansions as well as the center of Paris's gay and lesbian community. On the Left Bank, the **5e** is known as the Latin Quarter, home to the Sorbonne and associated with the intellectual life that thrived in the 1920s and 1930s. The **6e,** known as St-Germain-des-Prés, stretches from the Seine to boulevard du Montparnasse. It is associated with the 1920s and 1930s and known as a center for art and antiques; it boasts the Palais and Jardin du Luxembourg. The **7e,** containing both the Tour Eiffel and Hôtel des Invalides, is a residential district for the well heeled.

Back on the Right Bank, the **8e** epitomizes monumental Paris, with the triumphal avenue des Champs-Elysées, the Elysées Palace, and the fashion houses along avenue Montaigne and the Faubourg St-Honoré. The **18e** is home to Sacré-Coeur and Montmartre and all that the name conjures of the bohemian life painted most notably by Toulouse-Lautrec. The **14e** incorporates most of Montparnasse, including its cemetery, whereas the **20e** is where the city's famous lie buried in Père-Lachaise and where today the recent immigrants from North Africa live. Beyond the arrondissements stretch the vast *banlieue,* or suburbs, of Greater Paris, where the majority of Parisians live.

GETTING AROUND

BY METRO (SUBWAY)   The Métro (© **01-58-76-16-16**) is the fastest and most efficient means of transportation in Paris. All lines are numbered, and the final destination of each line is clearly marked on subway maps, in the underground passageways, and on the train cars. The Métro runs daily from 6:30am to around 1:15am. It's reasonably safe at any hour, but beware of pickpockets.

Note: To familiarize yourself with Paris's Métro, check out the **color map** on the inside front cover of this book.

To make sure you catch the correct train, find your destination on the map, then follow the rail line it's on to the end of the route and note the name of the final destination—this final stop is the direction. In the station, follow the signs labeled with your direction in the passageways until you see it labeled on a train.

Transfer stations are *correspondances*—some require long walks; Châtelet is the largest, but most trips require only one transfer. When transferring, follow the orange CORRESPONDANCE signs to the proper platform. Don't follow a SORTIE (EXIT) sign or you'll have to pay another fare to get back on the train.

Many of the larger stations have maps with push-button indicators that light up your route when you press the button for your destination.

The urban lines cost 1.40€ ($1.80). At the turnstile entrances, insert your ticket and pass through. At some exits, platforms, and on trains, tickets are occasionally checked, so hold on to yours.

BY BUS   Buses are much slower than the Métro, and the majority run from 7am to 8:30pm (a few operate until 12:30am, and 10 operate during early morning hours). Service is limited on Sunday and holidays. Bus and Métro fares are the same; you can use the same tickets on both. Most bus rides require one ticket, but some require two.

Value Saving on Travel

When purchasing Métro tickets, a *carnet* (book of coupons) is the best buy—10 tickets for 10.90€ ($14.20). You can also purchase a **Paris-Visite,** a tourist pass valid for 1, 2, 3, or 5 days on the public transportation system, including the Métro, buses, and RER (Réseau Express Régional) trains (most not included on a railpass). (The RER has both first- and second-class compartments, and the pass lets you travel in first class.) As a bonus, the funicular ride to the top of Montmartre is included. The cost ranges from 8.25€ ($10.75) for a 1-day pass to 26.65€ ($34.65) for 5 days. The card is available at RATP (Régie Autonome des Transports Parisiens), tourist offices, or the main Métro stations (© 08-36-68-77-14). The Paris-Visite is also available in advance from Rail Europe, with prices starting at $26 for a 1-day pass.

Another discount pass is **Carte Mobilis,** which allows unlimited travel on all bus, subway, and RER lines during a 1-day period for 5.50€ ($7.15) within Paris (zones 1-2). The price increases as the zone gets farther from Paris. Ask for it at any Métro station.

Most economical, for anyone who arrives in Paris early in the week, is a **Carte Orange.** Sold at large Métro stations, it allows 1 week of unlimited Métro or bus transit within central Paris for 16€ ($20.80) for zones 1 and 2 and 21.20€ ($27.30) for zones 1 to 3. They're valid from any Monday to the following Sunday, and are sold only on Mondays, Tuesdays, and Wednesdays. You'll have to submit a passport-size photo in order to buy the pass.

At certain stops, signs list the destinations and numbers of the buses serving that point. Most stops are also posted on the sides of the buses. During rush hours, you may have to take a ticket from a dispensing machine, indicating your position in the line at the stop.

If you intend to use the buses a lot, pick up an RATP bus map at the office on place de la Madeleine, 8e, or at the tourist office at RATP headquarters, 54 quai de la Rapée, 12e. For recorded information call © 08-92-68-77-14.

BY TAXI   It's impossible to get one at rush hour, so don't even try. Taxi drivers are organized into a lobby that keeps their number limited to 15,000.

Watch out for common rip-offs. Always check the meter to make sure you're not paying the previous passenger's fare. Beware of cabs without meters, which often wait outside nightclubs for tipsy patrons, or settle the tab in advance. You can hail regular cabs on the street when their signs read LIBRE. Taxis are easier to find at the many stands near Métro stations.

The flag drops at 1.50€ ($1.95), and from 7am to 7pm you pay 1€ ($1.30) per kilometer (⅔ mile). From 7pm to 7am, you pay 1.10€ ($1.45) per kilometer. On airport trips, you're not required to pay for the driver's empty return ride.

You're allowed several pieces of luggage free if they're transported inside and are l ess than 11 pounds. Heavier suitcases carried in the trunk cost 1.50€ to 2€ ($1.95–$2.60) apiece. Tip 12% to 15%—the latter usually elicits a *"Merci."* For radio cabs, call ✆ **01-44-52-23-58**—note that you'll be charged from the point where the taxi begins the drive to pick you up.

WHERE TO STAY

Although Paris hotels are quite expensive, there is some good news. Scores of lackluster Paris lodgings have been renovated and offer much better value in the moderate-to-inexpensive price range.

Hot weather doesn't last long in Paris (though it can get brutal every now and then), so many hotels don't have air-conditioning (we note those that don't in the listings below). To avoid a noise problem when you have to open windows, request a room in the back when making a reservation.

Galileo Hotel ⭐ *Finds*   This charming and elegant town house hotel is only a short walk from the Champs-Elysées, the Arc de Triomphe, and close to Gare St-Lazare. Owners Roland and Elisabeth Buffat have built up a good reputation with their attractively furnished and affordable bedrooms, which are filled with modern comforts. The most coveted and spacious are rooms 100, 200, 501, and 502, each opening onto a glass-covered veranda.

54 rue Galilée, 75008 Paris. ✆ **01-47-20-66-06**. Fax 01-47-20-67-17. www.galileohotel.com. 27 units. 148€–157€ ($192–$204) double. AE, DC, MC, V. Métro: Georges-V or Etoile. RER: Etoile. **Amenities:** Laundry; nonsmoking rooms; rooms for those w/limited mobility. *In room:* Hair dryer.

Grand Hôtel St-Michel   Located near the Luxembourg Gardens and a 10-minute walk from Notre-Dame, this 19th-century building is in the heart of the Latin Quarter. The hotel has been tastefully restored and decorated with antique reproductions and elegant fabrics. Its sixth-floor bedrooms open onto views over the rooftops of Paris; the most desirable rooms have balconies with views of the Sorbonne and the Pantheon. Most rooms have showers and tubs (the rest have showers only).

19 rue Cujas, 75005 Paris. ✆ **01-46-33-33-02**. Fax 01-40-46-96-33. www.parisby.com/stmichel. 46 units. 130€–170€ ($169–$221) double; 190€–220€ ($247–$286) suite. AE, DC, MC, V. Métro: Cluny–La Sorbonne or Odéon. RER: Luxembourg or St-Michel. **Amenities:** Breakfast room; bar; laundry; nonsmoking rooms; rooms for those w/limited mobility. *In room:* Hair dryer.

Hôtel Aviatic   Deep in the heart of Montparnasse, this hotel has been completely remodeled. Many of its old architectural touches remain, including an inner courtyard with a vine-covered wall lattice, and a lobby with marble columns, antiques, and crystal chandeliers. Its conservatory is an oasis of plants and natural light, and its Empire Lounge is a relaxing retreat. Run by the same family for over a century, Aviatic offers midsize bedrooms with thoughtful extras such as air-conditioning and good reading lamps.

105 rue de Vaugirard, 75006 Paris. ✆ **01-53-63-25-50**. Fax 01-53-63-25-55. www.aviatic.fr. 43 units. 144€–260€ ($187–$299) double. AE, DC, MC, V. Métro: Montparnasse-Bienvenue or St-Placide. **Amenities:** Breakfast room; lounge; laundry; nonsmoking rooms. *In room:* Hair dryer.

Hôtel Britannique   This attractive and well-furnished boutique hotel enjoys a privileged position close to the Louvre and Saint-Chapelle. The French call it a *hotel de charme,* and so it is, with a slightly English aura as suggested by its name. The public rooms could be the setting for an Agatha Christie novel, and the immaculate and soundproof bedrooms in this renovated 19th-century town house are studies in taste and comfort.

20 av. Victoria, 75001 Paris. ℭ **01-42-33-74-59.** Fax 01-42-33-82-65. www.hotel-britannique.fr. 39 units. 156€–199€ ($203–$258) double; 222€–297€ ($288–$386) suite. AE, DC, MC, V. Métro: Châtelet. **Amenities:** Laundry. *In room:* Hair dryer.

Hôtel Burgundy ⭐ (Value)

Two British-born entrepreneurs took a former bordello and an adjacent 1830s boarding house (where Baudelaire wrote poetry in the 1860s) and turned them into this seamless and stylish hotel. Just off the place de Madeleine, this tastefully furnished mansion is an exceptional value for its location and offers handsomely decorated bedrooms with modern conveniences. It's a favorite of visiting North Americans.

8 rue Duphot, 75001 Paris. ℭ **01-42-60-34-12.** Fax 01-47-03-95-20. www.burgundyhotel.com. 89 units. 150€–243€ ($204–$315) double. AE, DC, MC, V. Métro: Madeleine or Concorde. **Amenities:** lounge; bar; laundry. *In room:* Hair dryer, no A/C.

Hôtel de la Place des Vosges ⭐ (Value)

Built 350 years ago in the Marais district, this hotel is a 2-minute walk from the beautiful city square from which it takes its name. Author Victor Hugo lived around the corner of this well-managed and small-scale property, which was once a stable for the horses of Henri IV. Last renovated in 2002, the hotel offers cozy bedrooms with beamed ceilings and adjoining tile-clad bathrooms (with tub or shower).

12 rue de Birague, 75004 Paris. ℭ **01-42-72-60-46.** Fax 01-42-72-02-64. www.hotelplacedesvosges.com. 16 units. 107€–140€ ($139-$182) double. AE, MC, V. Métro: Bastille or St. Paul. **Amenities:** breakfast room; laundry. *In room:* Hair dryer, no A/C.

Hôtel de l'Université ⭐

This *hotel de charme,* a restored 300-year-old town house, is popular with North American visitors. Its Left Bank location (close to the Musée d'Orsay) is much favored by the literati, and it is filled with atmospheric touches such as antiques-filled rooms, splendid staircases and fireplaces (evocative of its status as a former convent), rattan beds, vaulted ceilings, and oak pillars. Try for room no. 35, which has a fireplace and opens onto a courtyard with a fountain. All bedrooms have a private terrace.

22 rue de l'Université, 75007 Paris. ℭ **01-42-61-09-39.** Fax 01-42-60-40-84. www.hoteluniversite.com. 27 units. 170€–180€ ($228–$243) double. AE, MC, V. Métro: St-Germain-des-Prés or Rue du Bac. **Amenities:** Lounge; breakfast room; laundry. *In room:* Hair dryer.

Hôtel du Pas-de-Calais

This hotel is a good choice for those nostalgic for some of that old St-Germain-des-Prés bohemian atmosphere—in fact Jean-Paul Sartre worked on his play, *Dirty Hands,* in room no. 41. A much-needed renovation at the dawn of the millennium transformed the hotel's once-dowdy atmosphere into something a bit lighter and brighter. The inner bedrooms open onto a secluded courtyard with garden tables set out.

59 rue des Sts-Pères, 75006 Paris. ℭ **01-45-48-78-74.** Fax 01-45-44-94-57. www.hotelpasdecalais.com. 40 units. 205€–240€ ($266–$312) double; 300€ ($390) suite. AE, DC, MC, V. Métro: St-Germain-des-Prés or Sèvres-Babylone. RER: St. Michel. **Amenities:** Breakfast room; laundry. *In room:* Hair dryer.

Hotel Le Tourville ⭐

Between the Eiffel Tower and Les Invalides, this small luxe hotel is located in a town house that dates from the Belle Epoque era of the 1890s. Today it's been renovated and tastefully furnished with old paintings, antiques, and contemporary chairs and sofas. The four best accommodations open onto a terrace. The bedrooms are light in color and have such homey touches as quilted bedspreads; the large bathrooms are clad in black marble and white tiles.

16 av. de Tourville, 75007 Paris. ℂ **800-3767-831** in the U.S., or 01-47-05-62-62. Fax 01-47-05-43-90. www.hotel letourville.com. 30 units. 150€–270€ ($ 204–$356) double; 420€ ($546) suite. AE, DC, MC, V. Métro: Ecole Militaire. **Amenities:** Bar; breakfast room; lounge; laundry; nonsmoking rooms. *In room:* Hair dryer.

Hôtel Queen Mary ✦   A model of charm and homey comfort, this hotel is housed in a restored turn-of-the-20th-century building with an iron-and-glass canopy. All the midsize bedrooms and spacious suites have deep mahogany furnishings, comfortable beds, and luxurious fabrics. All but five bathrooms have both tubs and showers (others are shower only). Other grace notes include a flowery patio and a liberal sprinkling of antiques.

9 rue Greffulhe, 75008 Paris. ℂ **01-42-66-40-50.** Fax 01-42-66-94-92. www.hotelqueenmary.com. 36 units. 189€– 219€ ($245–$285) double; 299€ ($388) suite. AE, DC, MC, V. Métro: Madeleine, Saint-Lazare or Havre-Caumartin. **Amenities:** Bar; breakfast room; nonsmoking rooms; rooms for those w/limited mobility. *In room:* Hair dryer.

Hôtel St-Louis ✦ *Value*   This most affordable hotel occupies some of the most expensive real estate in Paris. Filled with antiques and loaded with atmosphere, this restored 17th-century town house lies on the romantic Ile St-Louis, right between the Left and Right Banks. The bedrooms are small but charming. If you opt for one of the top-floor rooms, you might get a small balcony opening onto some of the Paris's best cityscapes.

75 rue St-Louis-en-l'Ile, 75004 Paris. ℂ **01-46-34-04-80.** Fax 01-46-34-02-13. www.hotelsaintlouis.com. 19 units. 140€–155€ ($182–$202) double; 220€ ($286) suite. MC, V. Métro: Pont Marie, St-Michel, or St-Paul. **Amenities:** Breakfast room; laundry. *In room:* Hair dryer.

Hôtel Saint-Merry ✦ *Finds*   This former bordello, with its 18th-century ceiling beams still intact, is today a little boutique hotel that's a choice address for an arts-oriented crowd. Rooms are a bit small but are handsomely furnished and comfortable, with a lot of atmosphere, including neo-Gothic architectural details. Once in total decay, the surrounding Marais quarter has now been completely gentrified and is the center of gay Paris (about half the hotel's clientele consists of gay travelers)—it's a great place for strolling about.

78 rue de la Verrerie, 75004 Paris. ℂ **01-42-78-14-15.** Fax 01-40-29-06-82. www.hotelmarais.com. 12 units. 160€– 230€ ($208–$299) double; 335€ ($436) suite. Métro: Hôtel de Ville or Châtelet. **Amenities:** Laundry. *In room:* Hair dryer, no A/C.

TOP ATTRACTIONS & SPECIAL MOMENTS

The French capital is home to some of the world's greatest museums and monuments, but the main attraction of Paris is the city itself. From the moment you start sightseeing you are liable to become so ensnared by the vistas you find en route to a particular sight that you run the risk of never getting there. The city streets lure you into hours of aimless rambling when you should be steering resolutely toward some three-star edifice.

There are people—and you well might agree with them—who find visiting museums in Paris redundant. Why sacrifice the sunshine to pursue art and culture through dim museum corridors when every Seine-side stroll reflects paintings of the masters and every city square is a model of architectural excellence?

If that is your view, stick with it. Of the almost 100 highly worthy Paris museums, only two or three are "required viewing" for the world traveler: the Louvre, Centre Pompidou, and the Musée d'Orsay. So, before we hit the must-see museums, here are the greatest districts for wandering, with monuments galore.

PLACE DE LA CONCORDE ✰✰✰   Regarded by many as the most beautiful urban square in the world, this immense 765,000-square-foot (71,071 sq. m) expanse is so vast that your eye can't take it in at one glance. The center of the oval is swarming with cars, a motorist's nightmare, but the hugeness of the place seems to swallow them up.

In the middle, looking pencil-small, rises a 3,300-year-old obelisk from Egypt, flanked by cascading fountains. Grouped around the outer edges are eight statues, each representing a different French city. Near the statue of Brest was the spot where the guillotine stood during the French Revolution. On Sunday morning January 21, 1793, King Louis XVI lost his royal head there, and was followed by 1,343 other victims, including Marie Antoinette and subsequently Danton and Robespierre, the very men who had launched the Reign of Terror.

The square borders the Tuileries Gardens on the east, and on the west, is the second great showpiece of Paris, the Champs-Elysées.

CHAMPS-ÉLYSÉES ✰✰✰   This is the world's most famous promenade. Pointing from the place de la Concorde like a broad, straight arrow to the Arc de Triomphe at the far end, this avenue is at its best when lit at night.

Automobile showrooms and gift stores have marred the once-impeccable elegance of this stretch, but this is still the greatest vantage point from which to watch Paris pass you by, preferably while sipping a cold drink at one of the many cafes that line the sidewalk.

TROCADERO   This is actually a series of adjoining sights, which a master touch of city planning has telescoped into one (a characteristic Parisian knack). From the place du Trocadéro, you can step between the two curved wings of the **Palais de Chaillot** and gaze out on a view that is nothing short of breathtaking. At your feet lies the **Jardins de Trocadéro,** centered by fountains. Directly in front, pont d'Iéna spans the Seine. Then, on the opposite bank, rises the iron immensity of the **Tour Eiffel.** And beyond, is the **Champ de Mars,** once a military parade ground but now a garden landscape with arches, grottoes, lakes, and cascades.

THE SEINE ISLANDS ✰✰✰   **Ile de la Cité,** the "egg from which Paris was hatched," lies quietly in the shadow of Notre-Dame. The home of French kings until the 14th century, the island still has a curiously medieval air, with massive gray walls rising up all around you, relieved by tiny patches of parkland.

Just behind Notre-Dame, sunken almost to the level of the river, is the **Memorial de la Déportation,** the monument to the thousands of French men, women, and children who perished in Nazi concentration camps from 1940 to 1945. You step down into a series of granite chambers with narrow, iron-barred windows. Hewn into the stone walls are the nightmarish names of the camps.

Back on the ground level, you'll see an iron bridge leading over to **Ile St-Louis**—the smaller and quieter of the river islands. It has remained almost exactly as it was in the 17th century, after it had been divided up into private building lots. Sober patrician houses stand along the four quays, and the fever-beat of the city seems a hundred miles away.

PLACE VENDÔME ✰✰✰   This is *the* textbook example of classical French architecture, a pure gem set in the fashionable heart of the Right Bank. The pillared palaces encircling the square include the Ritz Hotel as well as the Ministry of Justice. The center is crowned by a 144-foot-high (44m) column, erected to commemorate Napoleon's greatest victory—Austerlitz. The actual column is stone, but the enclosing spiral band of bronze was cast from the 1, 200 cannons captured by the emperor in the battle. The statue on top of the pillar is, of course, Napoleon, restored here after being pulled down twice: once by Royalist reactionaries, the second time by Communard revolutionaries.

A TOUR OF LE MARAIS ✿✿✿   Very few cities on earth boast an entire district that can be labeled a sight. Paris has several. The Marais or marshland is the vaguely defined maze of streets north of the **place de la Bastille.**

During the 17th century this was a region of the aristocratic. Today, Le Marais is increasingly chic, and many artists and craftspeople have moved in and restored once-decaying mansions.

In addition to the galleries, boutiques, and history, this is the old Jewish quarter of Paris. Wander around **rue des Rosiers** and perpendicular streets to find kosher patisseries, grocery stores, bookstores, schools, restaurants (including amazing and inexpensive falafels at **L'As du Fallafel,** 34 rue des Rosiers), commemorative plaques above doorways for lives lost in the Holocaust, and signs to the nearby **Musée Temple d'Art et d'Histoire du Judaisme.** The quarter shuts down on the Sabbath.

Take the Métro to the place de la Bastille to begin your tour of the neighborhood. The actual Bastille no longer exists but it once housed such illustrious tenants as "The Man in the Iron Mask" and the Marquis de Sade. The mob attack on the fortress on July 14, 1789, touched off the French Revolution and Bastille Day, a major French holiday that commemorates the storming of the prison.

The **Colonne de Juillet,** in the middle of the square, honors the victims of the July Revolution of 1830 that marked the supremacy of Louis-Philippe. The winged god of liberty crowns the column.

From place de la Bastille, head up rue Saint-Antoine, cutting right on rue des Tournelles, with its statue honoring Beaumarchais *(The Barber of Seville).* Take a left again onto the Pas-de-la-Mule, "the footsteps of the mule," which takes you to place des Vosges.

PLACE DES VOSGES ✿✿✿   Charming backstreets from place de la Bastille lead you to the oldest and most entrancing square in Paris.

Laid out in 1605 by order of King Henry IV, it was once called "Palais Royale" and was the scene of innumerable cavaliers' duels. The Revolutionary government changed its name but—luckily—left its structure intact. In the middle is a tiny park, and on three sides an arcaded walk supported by arches and paved with ancient flagstones. At No. 6 on the square is the **Maison De Victor Hugo.** Victor Hugo, known as a literary great, lived and worked here from 1832 to 1848; today it is a miniature museum full of Hugo's lesser-known drawings, carvings, paintings, and pieces of furniture. The windows of his study overlook the square—it's easy to see where he drew his inspiration.

QUARTIER LATIN ✿✿✿   The Latin Quarter lies in the 5th Arrondissement on the Left Bank and consists of the streets winding around the Paris University, of which the **Sorbonne** is only a part.

The logical starting point for touring this area is the **Place Saint-Michel,** right on the river, decorated by an impressive fountain. This was the scene of some of the most savage fighting of the French Resistance in August 1944. Here—as in many, many other spots—you'll see the little name tablets, marking the place where a Resistance fighter fell: *"Ici est Tombé . . . le 19 Août 1944. Pour la Libération de Paris."*

Running straight south is the main thoroughfare of the quarter, the wide, pulsating **boulevard St-Michel.** But turn left instead and dive into the warren of dogleg alleys

---

Finds A Surreal Moment

Hidden around the corner from Montmartre's place de Tertre is, **Espace Dalí,** 11 rue Poulbot, 18e (© **01-42-64-40-10;** www.daliparis.com; Métro: Anvers, Abbesses), a tribute to surrealist Salvador Dalí, who made his home in this artistic haven during the 1930s. A rare French collection of over 300 of Dalí's sketches, sculptures, lithographs, and paintings is on display in this modest museum. Admission is 10€ ($13) adults, 7€ ($9.10) seniors, 6€ ($7.80) students and children ages 9 to 26, free ages 8 and under. Open daily 10am to 6pm.

---

adjoining the river—**rue de la Huchette, rue de la Harpe, rue St-Séverin.** Thronged with students, shoppers, and tourists, exotic smells of Middle Eastern, African, and Asian cooking permeate the surroundings. Narrow, twisting, and noisy, the alleys resemble an Oriental bazaar more than a European city. Emerge at the **Church of St-Séverin** and you're back in Paris again. This flamboyant 13th century Gothic edifice acts like a sanctuary of serenity away from the crowded streets.

Head down the **rue St-Jacques** and Paris reasserts herself completely. The next crossing is the **boulevard St-Germain,** lined with sophisticated cafes and some of the most avant-garde fashion shops in town.

MONTMARTRE ⚜⚜⚜ This name has caused confusion in many an unwary visitor. So just to make things clear—there are three of them in Paris.

The first is the **boulevard Montmartre,** a busy commercial street nowhere near the mountain. The second is the tawdry amusement belt along the **boulevard de Clichy,** culminating at **place Pigalle** (the "Pig Alley" of World War II GIs). The third—*the Montmartre we're talking about*—lies on top, on the slopes of the actual *Mont.*

The best way to get here is to take the Métro to **Anvers,** then walk to the nearby rue de Steinkerque, and ride the curious little funicular to the top.

Montmartre used to be the city's artists' village, glorified by masters such as Utrillo and has been painted, sketched, sculpted, and photographed by 10,000 lesser lights. The tourists, building speculators, and nightclub entrepreneurs came and most of the artists went, but a few still linger. And so does some of the village charm that once drew them.

The center point, **place de Tertre,** is a bustling square filled with terraced restaurants, cafes, and crêperies. Artists and caricaturists are entertaining to watch as they bargain with tourists tirelessly. Just a few minutes away, the lively atmosphere is quickly contrasted by the peaceful and powerful presence of the **Basilica of Sacré-Coeur.** Behind the church and clinging to the hillside below are steep and crooked little streets that seem—almost—to have survived the relentless march of progress. **Rue des Saules** still has Montmartre's last vineyard. **Rue Lepic** still looks—almost—the way Renoir and the melancholy van Gogh and the dwarfish genius Toulouse-Lautrec saw it. This—almost—makes up for the blitz of portraitists and souvenir stores and postcard vendors up on top.

Arc de Triomphe ⚜⚜⚜ At the western end of the Champs-Elysées, the Arc de Triomphe is the largest triumphal arch in the world, about 163 feet high (50m) and 147 feet wide (45m). Its central location is unequalled in the city, but don't try crossing the busy square to reach it! Take the underground passage.

Commissioned by Napoleon in 1806 to commemorate his Grande Armée's victories, the arch wasn't completed until 1836, under Louis-Philippe. The arch is engraved with the names of the 128 victories of Napoleon and the 600 generals who participated in them. You can take an elevator or stairs to the top, where there are lithographs and photos depicting the arch throughout its history. From the observation deck, you have a panoramic view of the Champs-Elysées, the Louvre, the Eiffel Tower, and Sacré-Coeur.

Underneath the arch burns the Flame of Remembrance that marks the Tomb of France's Unknown Soldier—the effect at night is magical.

Place Charles de Gaulle-Etoile, 16e. ℂ **01-55-37-73-77**. www.monum.fr. Admission 8€ ($10.40) adults, 5€ ($6.50) ages 18–25, free for 17 and under. Apr–Sept daily 10am–11pm; Oct–Mar daily 10am–10:30pm. Métro: Charles de Gaulle-Etoile. Bus: 22, 30, 31, 52, 73, or 92.

Basilique du Sacré-Coeur ✶✶✶ Montmartre's crowning achievement is the white church that, along with the Eiffel Tower, dominates the skyline of Paris. Its gleaming white domes and campanile (bell tower) tower over Paris like a Byzantine church of the 12th century. But it's not that old: After France's defeat by the Prussians in 1870, the basilica was planned as an offering to cure the country's misfortunes; rich and poor alike contributed. Construction began in 1873, but the church wasn't consecrated until 1919. The interior is decorated with mosaics, the most striking of which are the ceiling depiction of Christ and the mural of the Passion at the back of the altar. The crypt contains what some believe is a piece of the sacred heart of Christ—hence the church's name.

On a clear day, the vista from the dome can extend for 35 miles (56km). You can also walk around the inner dome of the church, peering down like a pigeon (one is likely to be keeping you company).

Place St-Pierre, 18e. ℂ **01-53-41-89-00**. www.sacre-coeur-montmartre.com/us. Free admission to basilica; joint ticket to dome and crypt 5€ ($6.50) adults. Basilica daily 6am–11pm; dome and crypt daily 9am–7pm (6pm in winter). Métro: Abbesses; take the elevator to the surface and follow the signs to the *funiculaire*, which goes up to the church for the price of a Métro ticket (if you don't want to walk).

Centre Pompidou ✶✶✶ Dreamed up in 1969 by then-French president Georges Pompidou, this temple for 20th-century art was designed by Richard Rogers and Renzo Piano, opened in 1977, and became the focus of immediate controversy. Its bold exoskeletal architecture and the brightly painted pipes and ducts crisscrossing its transparent facade (green for water, red for heat, blue for air, and yellow for electricity) created a toy factory–like impression that was jarring in the old Beaubourg neighborhood. Relaunched in 2000, in what has been called "the most avant-garde building

---

Moments **Watching Twilight Fall over Paris**

Even if you have only 24 hours in Paris and can't explore most of the sights recommended in this chapter, try to make it to Sacré-Coeur at dusk. Here, as you sit on the top steps, the church at your back, the Square Willette in front of you, nighttime Paris comes alive. First, a twinkle like a firefly; then all of the lights go on. One young American got carried away describing it all: "Here, away from the whirling taxis, concierges, crazy elevators, and tipping problems, the sound of Paris permeates by osmosis." Try to see it.

in the world," the newly restored Pompidou Center is packing in the art-loving crowds again.

The **Musée National d'Art Moderne** ✿✿✿ housed in the center offers a large collection of 20th-century art. With some 40,000 works, only 850 can be displayed at one time. Minor Cubists are represented alongside such giants as Braque and Picasso (many of his harlequins). The permanent collection includes works ranging from the Fauves to Icelandic conceptual art. Among the sculpture, which leans heavily on the use of 20th-century metals, is a walk-through Calder and his ironic wire portrayal of the late Josephine Baker. Other sculpture includes works by Henry Moore and Jacob Epstein. Seasonally, special exhibitions are organized.

Place Georges-Pompidou, 4e. ✆ **01-44-78-12-33**. www.centrepompidou.fr. Admission 10€ ($13) adults, 8€ ($10.40) students ages 18–25, free for under age 18. Special exhibits 9€ ($11.70) adults, 7€ ($9.10) students, free for under age 18. Wed–Mon 11am–10pm. Métro: Rambuteau, Hôtel de Ville, or Châtelet–Les Halles.

Conciergerie ✿✿   The most sinister building in France squats on the north bank of the Ile de la Cité (near the pont au Change) and forms part of the huge Palais de Justice. Its name is derived from the title *concierge* (constable), once held by a high official of the Royal Court, but its reputation stems from the Revolution.

Here, as nowhere else in Paris, you can see the tall, square shadow of the guillotine. For, after the fall of the Bastille, this became the country's chief prison. When the Reign of Terror got under way, the Conciergerie turned into a kind of stopover depot en route to the "National Razor."

The conciergerie has the splendid remnants of a medieval royal palace, complete with refectory and giant kitchen. But most memorable are the rows of cells in which prisoners sat waiting for their ride to the blade. Famous prisoners who had a brief stay here before an even briefer trip to the guillotine include Marie Antoinette (you can visit her cell), Madame du Barry, Danton, and Robespierre. Among the few who stayed here and lived to write about it, was America's Thomas Paine, who remembered chatting in English with Danton.

1 quai de l'Horloge, 1er. ✆ **01-53-40-60-93**. www.monum.fr. Admission 6.50€ ($8.45) adults, 4.50€ ($5.85) ages 18–25, free for children under 18. Combination ticket with Ste-Chapelle 8€ ($10.40) adults, 7.50€ ($9.75) ages 18–25. Mar–Oct daily 9:30am–6pm; Nov–Feb daily 9am–5pm. Métro: Cité, Châtelet or St-Michel. RER: St-Michel.

Eiffel Tower ✿✿✿   Strangely enough, this symbol of Paris wasn't meant to be a permanent structure at all. Gustave-Alexandre Eiffel erected it specifically for the Universal Exhibition of 1889, and it was destined to be pulled down a few years later. But Parisians loved it, and, when wireless telegraphy and radio appeared on the scene, the 985-foot (296m) tower—the tallest on the earth—presented a handy signaling station. During the German advance on Paris in 1914, the powerful beam from the top of the tower effectively jammed the enemy's field radios. Today, the tower has a TV antenna tacked on the top and is 1,056 feet (317m) tall.

But forget all of the statistics and just stand underneath the tower and look straight up. If nothing else, it is a fantastic engineering achievement.

The view is the reason most people go to the third landing at the top of the tower, and this extends for 42 miles (68km), theoretically. In practice, weather conditions tend to limit it. Nevertheless, it's fabulous, and the best time for visibility is about an hour before sunset.

Champ de Mars, 7e. ✆ **01-44-11-23-23**. www.tour-eiffel.fr. Admission (elevator) to 1st landing 4.50€ ($5.85), 2nd landing 7.80€ ($10.15), 3rd landing 11.50€ ($14.95). Stairs to 2nd landing 4€ ($5.20). Jan 1–June 14 daily

9:30am–11:45pm; June 15–Sept 1 9am–12:45am; Sept 2–Dec 31 9:30am–11:45pm. Fall and winter, stairs open only to 6:30pm. Métro: Trocadéro, Ecole Militaire, or Bir-Hakeim. RER: Champs de Mars–Tour Eiffel.

Hôtel des Invalides ✦✦✦   This is not a "hotel," but rather a combined palace and church, which today houses a great museum, dozens of military administration offices, and the tomb of Napoleon. The monumental ensemble was originally built by Louis XIV as a stately home for invalid soldiers (hence the name). Most of the enormous space is taken up by the military-themed **Musée de l'Armée,** housing a collection that includes Viking swords, Burgundian basinets, 14th-century blunderbusses, Balkan khandjars, American Browning machine guns, and suits of armor worn by kings and dignitaries. You can gain access to the **Musée des Plans-Reliefs** through the west wing. This collection shows scale models of French towns and monuments (the model of Strasbourg fills an entire room), as well as models of military fortifications since the days of the great Vauban.

Napoleon's Tomb beneath the golden dome is one of Paris's greatest showpieces. Napoleon rests in a sarcophagus of red granite on a pedestal of green granite. Surrounding the tomb are 12 figures of victories and 6 stands of captured enemy flags. The pavement of the crypt consists of a mosaic of laurel leaves. First buried at St. Helena, Napoleon's remains were returned to Paris in 1840. Also interred here are Napoleon's brothers, Joseph and Jerome, his son (who was never crowned), and Marshal Foch, who led the Allied armies to victory in 1918.

Place des Invalides, 7e. ✆ **01-44-42-37-72.** www.invalides.org. Admission to Musée de l'Armée, Napoleon's Tomb, and Musée des Plans-Reliefs 8€ ($10.40) adults, 6€ ($7.80) students under 26, free for children under 18. Oct–Mar daily 10am–5pm; Apr–Sept daily 10am–6pm. Closed 1st Mon of every month and Jan 1, May 1, Nov 1, and Dec 25. Métro: Latour-Maubourg, Varenne, or Invalides.

Musée d'Orsay ✦✦✦   Rail travelers will feel right at home in the neoclassical Gare d'Orsay train station, which has been transformed into one of the world's greatest art museums. It contains an important collection devoted to the pivotal years from 1848 to 1914. Across the Seine from the Louvre and the Tuileries, it is a repository of works by the Impressionists as well as the Symbolists, Pointillists, Realists, and late Romantics. Artists represented include van Gogh, Manet, Monet, Degas, and Renoir. It houses thousands of sculptures and paintings across 80 galleries, plus Belle Epoque furniture, photographs, objets d'art, architectural models, and a cinema.

One of Renoir's most joyous paintings is here: *Moulin de la Galette* (1876). Another celebrated work is by James McNeill Whistler—*Arrangement in Gray and Black: Portrait of the Painter's Mother.* The most famous piece in the museum is Manet's 1863 *Déjeuner sur l'herbe* (Picnic on the Grass).

1 rue de Bellechasse or 62 rue de Lille, 7e. ✆ **01-40-49-48-14.** www.musee-orsay.fr. Admission 7.50€ ($9.75) adults, 5.50€ ($7.15) ages·18–25 and seniors, free for children 17 and under. Tues-Sun 9:30am–6pm (Thurs until 9:45pm). Métro: Solférino. RER: Musée d'Orsay.

Musée du Louvre ✦✦✦   The largest palace in the world (converted into a museum after the revolution), the Louvre is also one of the world's greatest museums, housing a collection of up to 208,500 works of art. The collection is both impressive and exhausting.

To enter the Louvre, you pass through the 71-foot (21m) **I. M. Pei glass pyramid** in the courtyard (or to try to avoid lines and enter through the underground shopping mall—a less impressive entrance—off of rue de Rivoli). Commissioned by Francois Mitterrand and completed in 1989, the pyramid received mixed reviews. There's so

Tips **The Handy Museum Pass**

The Paris Museum Pass (www.parismuseumpass.com) is available at any branch of the Paris Tourist Office, and at some of the included museums. It offers entrance to 70 monuments and museums in Paris and the Ile de France. The longer you stay in Paris and the more places you plan to visit, the more likely the pass will be a good buy for you. A 2-day pass is 30€ ($39), a 4-day pass 45€ ($59), and a 6-day pass 60€ ($78).

much to see, so many endless nightmare hallways to get lost in, that—regardless of how much you may enjoy exploring a museum on your own—here we suggest you start with a **guided tour** (in English), which lasts about 90 minutes. These start under the pyramid at the station marked ACCEIL DES GROUPES. Once you've gotten the lay of the land, you can always go back and see what you missed.

The collections are divided into seven departments: Asian antiquities; Egyptian antiquities; Greek, Etruscan, and Roman antiquities; sculpture; paintings; prints and drawings; and objets d'art. Three items are standouts and usually top everybody's must-see list. To the left of the main entrance, at the crest of a graceful flight of stairs, stands *The Winged Victory.* In the Department of Greek Antiquities, on the ground floor, stands the supple statue of *Venus de Milo,* the warm marble subtly tinted by sunlight. Upstairs, in a room of her own, and covered with bulletproof glass and surrounded by art students, photographers, and awe-struck visitors, hangs the gently chiding portrait of the *Mona Lisa.*

Note: Though the $1.2-billion Grand Louvre Project, a 15-year-long project, is officially complete, refurbishment of individual galleries and paintings continues. For up-to-date information, check out **www.louvre.fr.**

34–36 quai du Louvre, 1er. Main entrance in the glass pyramid, Cour Napoléon. ✆ 01-40-20-53-17, or 01-40-20-51-51 for recorded message. www.louvre.fr. Admission 9€ ($11.70) before 6pm, 6€ ($7.80) after 6pm, free for children 17 and under, free for art students with ID, free 1st Sun of every month. Wed and Fri 9am–10pm; Thurs, Sat–Mon 9am–6pm. (Parts of the museum begin to close at 5:30pm.) Métro: Palais Royal–Musée du Louvre.

Musée National Auguste Rodin ✿✿   Auguste Rodin, the man credited with freeing French sculpture of Classicism, once lived and had his studio in the charming 18th-century mansion **Hôtel Biron,** across the boulevard from Napoléon's Tomb in the Hôtel des Invalides. Today the house and garden are filled with his works, a soul-satisfying feast for the Rodin enthusiast. In the cobbled Court of Honor, within the walls as you enter, you'll see *The Thinker* crouched on his pedestal to the right of you; *the Burghers of Calais* grouped off to the left of you; and to the far left, the writhing *Gates of Hell,* atop which *The Thinker* once more meditates. There's a third *Thinker* inside the museum before the second-floor window. In the almost too-packed rooms, men, women, and angels emerge from blocks of marble, hands twisted in supplication, and the nude torso of Balzac rises up from a tree.

In the Hôtel Biron, 77 rue de Varenne, 7e. ✆ 01-44-18-61-10. www.musee-rodin.fr. Admission 6€ ($7.80) adults, 4€ ($5.20) ages 18–25, free for children 17 and under, 1€ ($1.30) for garden entry (without museum ticket). Apr–Sept Tues–Sun 9:30am–5:45pm (gardens open until 6:45); Oct–Mar Tues–Sun 9:30am–4:45pm. Métro: Varenne or Invalides.

Musée Picasso ✿✿✿   When it opened in the beautifully restored Hôtel Salé in the Marais, the press hailed it as a "museum for Picasso's Picassos," meaning those he chose not to sell. The world's greatest Picasso collection, acquired by the state in lieu of $50 million in inheritance taxes, consists of 203 paintings, 158 sculptures, 16 collages, 19 bas-reliefs, 88 ceramics, and more than 1,500 sketches and 1,600 engravings, plus 30 notebooks. These works span some 75 years of Picasso's life and changing styles.

The range of paintings includes a 1901 self-portrait and embraces such master-pieces as *Le Baiser* (The Kiss). Other masterpieces are *Reclining Nude* and *the Man with a Guitar* and the delightfully wicked *Jeune garçon à la langouste (Young Man with a Lobster)*. The museum also owns several studies for *Les Demoiselles d'Avignon*, the painting that launched Cubism in 1907.

In the Hôtel Salé, 5 rue de Thorigny, 3e. ☎ 01-42-71-25-21. www.musee-picasso.fr. Admission 6.50€ ($8.45) adults, 4.50€ ($5.85) ages 18–25, free for children 17 and under. Apr–Sept Wed–Mon 9:30am–6pm; Oct–Mar Wed–Mon 9:30am–5:30pm. Métro: St-Paul, St-Sébastien Froissart, or Chemin Vert.

Notre-Dame ✿✿✿

The Cathedral of Paris and one of civilization's greatest edifices replaced two Romanesque churches (Ste. Mary and St. Stephen), which stood on the spot until 1160. Then Bishop Maurice de Sully, following the example of Suger, the abbot of St. Denis, undertook the new structure, and building continued for more than 150 years. The final result was a piece of Gothic perfection. The rose window above the main portal, for instance, forms a halo 31 feet (9.3m) in diameter around the head of the statue of the Virgin. You'll have to walk around the entire structure to appreciate this "vast symphony of stone" with its classic flying buttresses. Better yet, cross the bridge to the Left Bank and view it from the quay.

More than any other building, Notre-Dame is the history of a nation. Here, the boy-monarch Henry VI of England was crowned king of France in 1422, during the Hundred Years War when—but for Joan of Arc—France would have become an English dominion. Here, Napoleon took the crown out of the hands of Pope Pius VII, and crowned himself and Josephine emperor and empress. Here, General de Gaulle knelt before the altar on August 26, 1944, to give thanks for the liberation of Paris—imperturbably praying while sniper bullets screeched around the choir galleries. Because of the beauty of its ornaments and of its symbolic meaning of redemption of all evil, Notre-Dame is a joyous church—though those devils and gargoyles grinning from its ledges add a genuinely macabre touch. You can almost see Victor Hugo's hunchback peering from behind them. You can climb the 402 steps up the 225-foot (69m) flat-topped twin towers to complete this image—and for a panoramic view of the city.

6 place de Parvis Notre-Dame, 4e. ☎ 01-53-10-07-02. www.monum.fr. Admission free to cathedral; towers 7.50€ ($9.75) adults, 4.80€ ($6.24) ages 18–25 and seniors, free for children under 18; treasury 3€ ($3.90) adults, 2.50€ ($3.25) ages 12–25 and seniors, free for children under 5. Cathedral open year-round daily 7:45am–6:45pm. Towers and crypt Apr–June and Sept daily 9:30am–6:30pm; July–Aug Mon–Fri 9:30-6:30, Sat–Sun open until 11pm, Oct–Mar daily 10am–5:30pm. Museum Wed and Sat–Sun 2:30–5pm.

The Sewers of Paris (Les Egouts) ✿

Some say Baron Haussmann will be remembered mainly for erecting this vast, complicated network of Paris sewers. They were made famous by Victor Hugo's *Les Misérables*. "All dripping with slime, his soul filled with a strange light," Jean Valjean in his desperate flight through the sewers of Paris is one of the heroes of narrative drama.

The *égouts* of the city are constructed around a quartet of principal tunnels, one of them 18 feet wide (5.5m) and 15 feet high (4.5m). These underground passages are truly mammoth, containing pipes bringing in drinking water and compressed air, as well as telephone and telegraph lines. Furthermore, each branch pipe bears the number of the building to which it is connected—like an underground city. Tours begin at Pont de l'Alma on the Left Bank. However, you often have to wait in line as much as 2½ hours.

Pont de l'Alma, 7e. 📞 **01-53-68-27-82.** Admission 4.10€ ($5.30) adults, 3.30€ ($4.30) students, seniors, and children 5–12, free for children under 5. May–Sept Sat–Wed 11am–6pm; Oct–Apr Sat–Wed 11am–5pm. Last ticket sold 1 hr. before closing. Closed 2 weeks in Jan. Métro: Alma-Marceau. RER: Pont de l'Alma.

Ste-Chapelle ✿✿✿   One of the oldest, most beautiful medieval churches in the world, Sainte Chapelle was built in 1246 to house the relics of the Crucifixion obtained from Constantinople. But the relics were later transferred to Notre-Dame, leaving Sainte Chapelle as an empty showcase, although a magnificent one.

The church actually has two levels: one humble, the other superb. You enter through the lower chapel (originally for servants), supported by flying buttresses and ornamented with fleurs-de-lis. The upper chapel, reached by a spiral staircase, was used by the royal household. You can still see the small grated window from which Louis XI could participate in services without being noticed.

Fifteen unforgettable stained-glass windows flood the church's interior with sunshine and colored light—deep blue, ruby, and dark green—and depict more than a thousand scenes from the Bible.

Ste-Chapelle stages concerts in summer, with tickets running 20€ to 30€ ($26–$39). Call 📞 **01-42-77-65-65** from 11am to 6pm daily for details.

Palais de Justice, 4 bd. du Palais, 1er. 📞 **01-53-40-60-80.** www.monum.fr. Admission 6.50€ ($8.45) adults, 4.50€ ($5.85) students 18–25, free for children 17 and under; combination ticket with conciergerie 10€ ($13) adults, 7.50€ ($9.75) students 18-25. Mar–Oct daily 9:30am–6pm; Nov–Feb daily 9am–5pm. Métro: Cité, St-Michel, or Châtelet–Les Halles. RER: St-Michel.

BOAT TOURS

A boat tour on the Seine provides vistas of the riverbanks and Notre-Dame. Many boats have sun decks, bars, and restaurants. **Bateaux-Mouche** (📞 **01-40-76-99-99;** Métro: Alma-Marceau) cruises depart from the Right Bank of the Seine, adjacent to pont de l'Alma, and last about 70 minutes. Between May and October, tours leave daily at 30-minute intervals from 10am to 8pm and at 20-minute intervals from 8pm to 11pm. Between November and April, departures are daily at 11am, 2:30pm, 4pm, 6pm, and 9pm, with changes according to demand and the weather. Fares start at 9€ ($11.70) for adults and 4€ ($5.20) for children under 12. Paris dinner-cruise tickets can be obtained from Rail Europe. Dinner cruises depart nightly at 8:30pm, last 2 hours and 15 minutes, and cost from 136€ ($177), depending on which of the fixed-price menus you order. On dinner cruises, jackets and ties are required for men.

WHERE TO DINE

Alcazar Bar & Restaurant ✿ MODERN FRENCH   This is what the French Parisians call a *brasserie de luxe.* The creation of famous British restaurateur Sir Terence Conran, it features an avant-garde decor in its street-level dining room and chic bar upstairs. The menu is personal, creative, perfumed with herbs, and constantly changing with the addition of new taste sensations such as magret of duckling with white radishes and sesame oil.

62 rue Mazarine, 6e. 📞 **01-53-10-19-99.** Reservations recommended. Main courses 16€–27€ ($20–$35); fixed-price menu 20€–30€ ($26-$39) lunch, 40€ ($52) dinner. AE, DC, MC, V. Daily noon–3pm and 7pm–2am. Métro: Odéon.

Allard ✿ TRADITIONAL FRENCH   This is one of the most fashionable Left Bank bistros, with a tradition dating from 1931. Following a long decline, it has bounced back to reclaim its former prestige when it catered to Left Bank artists and even an occasional French prime minister. Here you can try famous dishes considered typically French: foie gras, escargots, cassoulet Toulousian, and, of course, the inevitable frogs' legs. Many platters, such as roast duck with olives, are served for two.

41 rue St-André-des-Arts, 6e (Entrance on the corner of rue de l'Eperon). ✆ 01-43-26-48-23. Reservations recommended. Main courses 19€–39€ ($24.70–$50.70); fixed-price menu 25€ ($32.50) lunch, 34€ ($44.20) dinner. AE, DC, MC, V. Mon–Sat noon–2pm and 7–11:30pm. Closed 3 weeks in Aug. Métro: St-Michel or Odéon.

Angélina ✷✷ TEA/TRADITIONAL FRENCH   This *salon de thé,* or tea salon, is well known in Paris for its intensely rich, dark drinking chocolate served with freshly whipped cream—a treat for the true chocolate lover. In an elegant setting of carpets and high ceilings, Angélina also offers a constantly changing plat du jour, and serves old French favorites, such as steak tartare or sole meunière, as main courses. A dessert specialty—designed to go well with tea—is the Mont Blanc, a combination of chestnut cream and meringue.

226 rue de Rivoli, 1er. ✆ 01-42-60-82-00. Reservations accepted for lunch, not for teatime. Pot of tea for 1 6€ ($7.80); pot of drinking chocolate for 1 6.80€ ($8.85); breakfast 15€ ($19.50) or 25€ ($32.50); sandwiches and salads 10€–15€ ($10.30–$19.50); main courses 17€–24€ ($22.10–$31.20). AE, MC, V. Daily 9am–5pm (lunch 11:45am–3pm). Métro: Tuileries or Concorde.

Aux Charpentiers *(Value)* TRADITIONAL FRENCH   In days of yore, it seemed that practically every frugal traveler to Paris made this notation: Visit the Louvre and dine at Aux Charpentiers. This St-Germain-des-Prés bistro (with a patio downstairs), in business for a century and a half, is still going strong serving the *cuisine bourgeoise* that made it such a legend in the '50s and '60s. Feast on one of the plats du jour, invariably an example of French home-style cookery, featuring the likes of stuffed cabbage, or *boudin noire* (black pudding).

10 rue Mabillon, 6e. ✆ 01-43-26-30-05. Reservations required. Main courses 15€–30€ ($19.50–$39); fixed-price menu 19.50€ ($25.35) lunch, 27€ ($35.10) dinner. AE, DC, MC, V. Daily noon–3pm and 7–11pm. Métro: St-Germain-des-Prés or Mabillon.

Aux Lyonnais ✷ LYONNAIS/FRENCH   This 1890 bistro offers the finest Lyonnaise cuisine in Paris—especially the pork dishes. (The menu proclaims that in Lyon *"le cochon est roi"*—pig is king.) The *fin de siècle* atmosphere is set by frosted globe chandeliers, floral tiled walls, and stuffed deer and boar heads. Start with *la salade verte au lard avec de saucisson chaud* (a green salad with bacon and hot sausage). The chicken in a velvety-smooth cream sauce with tarragon and mushrooms is a classic.

32 rue St-Marc, 2e. ✆ 01-42-96-65-04. Reservations recommended. Main courses 21€–25€ ($27.30–$32.50); fixed-price menu 30€ ($39). AE, MC, V. Tues–Fri noon–2pm; Tues–Sat 7:30–11pm. Métro: Bourse or Richelieu-Drouot.

Bofinger ✷ ALSATIAN/FRENCH   The oldest Alsatian brasserie in Paris traces its origins from 1864. It successfully retains the palatial style of that era: lots of leaded glass, creamy macramé curtains, lampshades shaped like tulips, antique mirrors, mahogany pieces, dark-gray benches, a revolving main door, and a central dome of stained glass. In other words, Émile Zola would feel right at home here. At night, many members of the Parisian slumming chic venture into the Bastille district for beer and sauerkraut complete with sausages, smoked bacon, and pork chops. An excellent alternative for those wining and dining is to share one of the impressive three-tiered seafood displays.

5–7 rue de la Bastille, 4e. ✆ 01-42-72-87-82. Reservations recommended. Main courses 16€–30€ ($20.80–$39); fixed-price menu lunch 23.50€ ($30.55); dinner 3.50€ ($44.85); after 11pm 23.50€ ($30.55). AE, MC, V. Mon–Fri noon–3pm and 6:30pm–1am; Sat–Sun noon–1am. Métro: Bastille.

Brasserie Balzar *✿* TRADITIONAL FRENCH   If they visited Paris, chances are your grandfather (maybe even your great-grandfather), your father, or your ancestors, dined at this 1886 cheerful Left Bank bistro near the Sorbonne that Sartre, Camus, James Thurber, and a host of international journalists called their favorite. Count on the most traditional of French cookery—we're talking onion soup, pepper steak, sole meunière, fried calves' liver, and even pigs' feet.

49 rue des Ecoles, 5e. ✆ 01-43-54-13-67. www.brasseriebalzar.com. Reservations strongly recommended. Main courses 15€–25€ ($19.50–$32.50); after 10pm fixed-price menu 22.50€ ($29.25). AE, DC, MC, V. Daily 8am–midnight. Métro: Cluny–La Sorbonne.

Crémerie–Restaurant Polidor *✿* TRADITIONAL FRENCH   Along with the previously recommended Aux Charpentiers, this is one of the most famous and traditional of French bistros, serving a *cuisine familiale* (family cuisine) since the early 1900s. Over the years it has attracted the literati, including Hemingway and Kerouac, but today is likely to be filled with students and area artists. Nothing is as French as their *boeuf bourguignon* or *blanquette de veau*. For dessert, get a chocolate, raspberry, or lemon tart—the best in all of Paris.

41 rue Monsieur-le-Prince, 6e. ✆ 01-43-26-95-34. Main courses 10€–15€ ($13–$19.50); fixed-price menu 12€ ($15.60) lunch (Mon–Fri), 39€ ($50.70) dinner. No credit cards. Daily noon–2:30pm and 7pm–12:30am (Sun until 11pm). Métro: Odéon.

L'Ambassade d'Auvergne *✿* AUVERGNAT/FRENCH   In an obscure district of Paris, this rustic tavern not only oozes charm but also dispenses *cuisine bourgeoise* of Auvergne, the heartland of France. You enter through a busy bar, with heavy oak beams, hanging hams, and ceramic plates. At the entrance is a display of the chef's specialties: jellied meats and fowls, pâté cakes, plus an assortment of regional cheese and fresh fruit of the season. Rough wheat bread is stacked in baskets, and rush-seated, ladder-back chairs are placed at tables, along with a jug of mustard to go with all those pork products.

22 rue de Grenier St-Lazare, 3e. ✆ 01-42-72-31-22. www.ambassade-auvergne.com. Reservations recommended. Main courses 14€–22€ ($18.20–$28.60); fixed-price menu 28€ ($36.40). AE, MC, V. Daily noon–2pm and 7:30–10:30pm. Métro: Rambuteau.

L'Ambroisie *✿✿✿* MODERN & TRADITIONAL FRENCH   One of Paris's most talented chefs, Bernard Pacaud, draws world attention (and three coveted Michelin stars) with his vivid flavors and expert skill. Expect culinary perfection but a cool reception at this early-17th-century town house in Le Marais, with three high-ceilinged salons whose decor recalls an Italian palazzo. Dishes change seasonally; one of our favorite dishes in all Paris is the *poulard de Bresse demi-deuil homage à la Mère Brazier* (chicken roasted with black truffles and truffled vegetables in a style invented by a Lyonnais matron after World War II).

9 place des Vosges, 4e. ✆ 01-42-78-51-45. Reservations required far in advance. Main courses 82€–142€ ($107–$185); lunch fixed price menu (Mon–Fri) 70€ ($91). AE, MC, V. Tues–Sat 9am–3pm and 7pm–midnight. Métro: St-Paul or Bastille.

La Petite Hostellerie *✿* *Value* TRADITIONAL FRENCH   Since 1902, the fixed-price dinners here have kept many a struggling Left Bank artist from starvation. That is true even today, and the good news is that the old-fashioned cuisine—favorites such as duck à l'orange and coq au vin—is still a good bargain. Select a table on the bustling ground floor, or else head upstairs where the ambience, with its 18th-century woodwork, is more formal.

Moments The Famous Cafes of Paris

Whatever your pleasure—reading, meeting a lover, writing your memoirs, or drinking yourself into oblivion—you can do it at a French cafe.

Brasserie Lipp, 151 bd. St-Germain, 6e (© **01-45-48-53-91;** Métro: St-Germain-des-Prés), has an upstairs dining room, but it's more fashionable to sit in the back room. For breakfast, order traditional black coffee, baguette, and croissants. At lunch or dinner, the specialty is pork and *choucroute* (sauerkraut)—the best in Paris. Open daily from 11am to 2am, although restaurant service is available only from 11:45am to 12:45am—it's fashionable to arrive late.

On one of the main corners across from the Centre Pompidou, the avant-garde **Café Beaubourg,** 100 rue St-Martin, 4e (© **01-48-87-63-96;** Métro: Rambuteau or Hôtel-de-Ville), boasts soaring concrete columns and a minimalist decor by the architect Christian de Portzamparc. In summer, tables are set on the sprawling terrace, providing a panoramic view of the neighborhood's goings-on. Open daily from 8am to midnight (2am on weekends).

Jean-Paul Sartre came to **Café de Flore,** 172 bd. St-Germain, 6e (© **01-45-48-55-26;** Métro: St-Germain-des-Prés). It's said he wrote his trilogy, *Les Chemins de la Liberté (The Roads to Freedom)* here. The cafe is still going strong, though the celebrities have moved on. Open daily 7:30am to 1:30am.

Next door, the legendary **Deux Magots,** 6 place St-Germain-des-Prés, 6e (© **01-45-48-55-25;** Métro: St-Germain-des-Prés), is still the hangout for sophisticated residents and a tourist favorite in summer. Inside are two Asian statues that give the cafe its name. Open daily from 7:30am to 1am.

Fouquet's, 99 av. des Champs-Elysées, 8e (© **01-47-23-50-00;** www.fouquets-barriere.com; Métro: George-V), is the premier cafe on the Champs-Elysées. The outside tables are separated from the sidewalk by a barricade of potted flowers. Inside is an elegant grill room, private rooms, and a restaurant. The cafe and grill room are open daily 8am to 2am; the restaurant is open daily noon to 3pm and 7pm to midnight.

At **La Coupole,** 102 bd. Montparnasse, 14e (© **01-43-20-14-20;** www.lacoupoleparis.com; Métro: Vavin), the crowd ranges from artists' models to young men dressed like Rasputin. Perhaps order a coffee or cognac VSOP at one of the sidewalk tables. People don't come here for the cuisine; it's more on the see-and-be-seen circuit. Try the sole meunière or cassoulet. A buffet breakfast is served Monday to Friday 8:30 to 11am. Open Monday to Friday 8am to 1am, Saturday and Sunday 8:30am to 1:30am.

35 rue de la Harpe (a side street north of bd. St-Germain, just east of bd. St-Michel), 5e. © 01-43-54-47-12. All main courses 9€–10€ ($11.70–$13); fixed-price menu 7.80€–19.50€ ($10.15–$25.35). MC, V. Daily 11am–11pm. Métro St-Michel or Cluny–La Sorbonne.

Le Fumoir ✦ INTERNATIONAL   This is the place to dine after you've seen the masterpieces of the Louvre, as this bustling brasserie is only a few steps away. If you want to dine light, try the freshly made salads, the lavish pastries, and various snacks.

If you want more substantial and well-prepared fare based on market-fresh ingredients, you have come to the right place. Currently, it's one of the most fashionable places in Paris to be seen eating or drinking—or even reading one of the 6,000 books that provide a sophisticated backdrop to the schmoozing. Happy hour (with special menu) runs from 6 to 8pm, when you'll get cocktails at the discount price of 6€ ($7.80).

6 rue de l'Amiral-Coligny, 1er. (℧ 01-42-92-00-24. www.lefumoir.com. Reservations recommended. Main courses 16€–26€ ($20.80–$33.80); fixed-price menu 13€–22€ ($16.90–$28.60) lunch; 30€ ($39) dinner. Salads, pastries, snacks, and bar daily 11am–2am; full menu daily noon–3pm and 7–11:30pm; Sun brunch noon–3pm. AE, V. Métro: Louvre-Rivoli.

Ze Kitchen Galerie ★ *(Finds* FRENCH/INTERNATIONAL   Since William Ledeuil established this place in 2001, he's attracted the likes of First Lady Laura Bush. The setting—a block from the Seine and winding backstreets full of art galleries—is a colorful loft space in an antique building, with an open-to-view showcase kitchen. Menu items change about every 5 weeks; main courses are divided into meats and fish that are usually grilled *"a la plancha"* (on an iron skillet). The best examples include platters of oysters, mussels, and sea urchins served with herb sauce and *crostini;* and grilled shoulder of wild boar with tamarind sauce.

4 rue des Grands-Augustins, 6e. (℧ 01-44-32-00-32. Reservations required. Main courses 22€–33€ ($28.60–$42.90); fixed-price with wine 26€–70€ ($33.80–$91). Daily 12:15–2pm and 7:30–10:45pm. AE, DC, MC, V. Métro: Saint-Michel.

SHOPPING

Perfumes and **cosmetics,** including such famous brands as Guerlain, Chanel, Schiaparelli, and Jean Patou, are almost always cheaper in Paris than in the United States. Paris is also a good place to buy Lalique and Baccarat **crystal.** They're expensive but still priced below international market value. **Lingerie** is another great French export. Top lingerie designers are represented in boutiques and in the major department stores, Galeries Lafayette and Le Printemps.

Directly across from the Louvre, **Le Louvre des Antiquaires,** 2 place du Palais-Royal, 1er (℧ 01-42-97-29-86; www.louvre-antiquaires.com; Métro: Palais-Royal), is the largest repository of antiques in central Paris. More than 250 dealers display their wares on three floors, specializing in objets d'art and small-scale furniture of the type that might have been favored by Mme de Pompadour.

Viaduc des Arts, 1–129 av. Daumesnil (between rue de Lyon and av. Diderot), 12e (℧ 01-44-75-80-66; www.viaduc-des-arts.com; Métro: Bastille, Ledru-Rollin, Reuilly-Diderot, or Gare-de-Lyon), occupies the vaulted spaces beneath a 19th-century railway access route into the Gare de Lyon. Around 1990, crafts artists, including furniture makers, potters, glassblowers, and weavers, began occupying the then-empty niches beneath the viaduct, selling their wares to homeowners and members of Paris's decorating trades.

Purveyor to kings and presidents since 1765, **Baccarat** has a central location at place de la Madeleine, 8e (℧ 01-40-22-11-22; www.baccarat.fr; Métro: Madeleine), and an even larger showroom at 11 place des Etats-Unis, 16e (℧ 01-40-22-11-22; Métro: Boissière or Ièna)—site of the **Musée du Cristal Baccarat,** a repository of some of the most extravagant crystal items the organization has ever made.

Boutique Lalique, 11 rue Royale, 8e (℧ 01-53-05-12-12; www.cristallalique.fr; Métro: Concorde), famous for its clear- and frosted-glass sculpture, Art Deco crystal, and perfume bottles, has recently branched out into sales of other types of merchandise, such as silk scarves meant to compete with Hermès and leather belts with Lalique buckles.

One of the few regional handcrafts stores in Paris worth going out of your way to find, **La Tuile à Loup,** 35 rue Daubenton, 5e (© **01-47-07-28-90;** www.latuilealoup. com; Métro: Censier-Daubenton), carries beautiful pottery and faience from many regions of France. Look for figures of Breton folk on the faïence of Quimper as well as garlands of fruits and flowers from the *terre vernissée* (varnished earth, a charming way to define stoneware) from Normandy, Savoy, Alsace, and Provence.

After you've admired the architecture of one of Europe's most famous department stores, step inside **Au Printemps,** 64 bd. Haussmann, 9e (© **01-42-82-50-00;** departmentstoreparis.printemps.com; Métro: Havre-Caumartin), for a view of all it offers. Inside the main building is **Printemps de la Mode,** which occupies the bulk of the structure, and a housewares shop, **Printemps de la Maison.** Upstairs are wares of every sort, especially clothing. An affiliated store across the street is **Le Printemps de l'Homme,** the menswear division. Behind the main store is a branch of **Prisunic,** Printemps's workaday but serviceable dime store, which contains groceries. At **Galeries Lafayette,** 40 bd. Haussmann, 9e (© **01-42-82-34-56;** www.galerieslafayette. com; Métro: Havre-Caumartin), stand under "the Dome"—a stained-glass cupola that towers above the arcaded store. Built in 1912, Galeries Lafayette is divided into several stores: **Galfa** men's store, **Lafayette Sports,** and two other general-merchandise stores, both known simply as **"GL."**

Anna Lowe, 104 rue du Faubourg St-Honoré, 8e (© **01-42-66-11-32;** www.anna lowe.com; Métro: Miromesnil), is one of the premier boutiques for the woman who wishes to purchase a little Chanel or perhaps a Versace at a discount. Many clothes are runway samples; some have been gently worn. The inventory at **Réciproque,** 88–123 rue de la Pompe (between av. Victor-Hugo and av. Georges-Mandel), 16e (© **01-47-04-30-28;** Métro: Pompe), is scattered over five buildings. Everything is secondhand, clustered into sections devoted to Chanel, Versace, Lacroix, Hermès, and Mugler. Women will find gowns, suits, sportswear, and shoes.

At the place de la Madeleine stands one of the most popular sights in the city—not La Madeleine church but **Fauchon,** 26 place de la Madeleine, 8e (© **01-47-42-60-11;** www.fauchon.fr; Métro: Madeleine), which offers a wider choice of upscale gourmet products than any other store in the world.

Almost every working woman around place de la Madeleine shops at **Catherine,** 7 rue Castiglione, 1er (© **01-42-61-02-89;** Métro: Concorde). It resembles a high-volume pharmacy more than a boutique; flacons of perfume move in and out of the premises very fast. You get a 30% discount on most brands of makeup and perfume and a 20% discount on high-end brands such as Chanel and Dior.

NIGHTLIFE

Opéra Garnier, place de l'Opéra, 9e (© **08-92-89-90-90;** www.operadeparis.fr; Métro: Opéra), is the premier stage for dance and opera. Painstaking restorations have returned the Garnier to its former glory: Its boxes and walls are again lined with flowing red and blue damask, the gilt gleams, the ceiling (painted by Marc Chagall) has been cleaned, and air-conditioning has been added. The box office is open Monday through Saturday from 9am to 6pm and on Sunday from 9am to 1pm. The controversial building known as the **Opéra Bastille,** place de la Bastille, 120 rue de Lyon (© **08-92-89-90-90** or 01-72-29-35-35; www.operadeparis.fr; Métro: Bastille), was designed by the Canadian architect Carlos Ott, with curtains created by fashion designer Issey Miyake. The main hall is the largest of any French opera house, with 2,700 seats, but music critics have lambasted the acoustics. Both traditional opera performances and symphony concerts are presented here. Tours (75 min.) of the opera house are offered, though the schedule varies, and sometimes there are free concerts on French holidays; call before your visit.

Conceived by the Mitterrand administration, **Cité de la Musique,** 221 av. Jean-Jaurès, 19e (© **01-44-84-44-84** for tickets and information; www.cite-musique.fr; Métro: Porte-de-Pantin), has been widely applauded. At the city's northeastern edge in what used to be a run-down neighborhood, the $120-million stone-and-glass structure, designed by Christian de Portzamparc, incorporates a network of concert halls, a library, research center, and a museum. The complex hosts a variety of concerts, ranging from Renaissance to 20th-century programs. As an added convenience, they offer a bus service to various locations within Paris after evening concerts.

Picasso and Utrillo once patronized **Au Lapin Agile,** 22 rue des Saules, 18e (© **01-46-06-85-87;** www.au-lapin-agile.com; Métro: Lamarck-Caulaincourt), formerly known as the Cabaret des Assassins and housed in a cottage near the top of Montmartre. For decades, it has been the heart of French folk music. You'll sit at wooden tables in a dimly lit room with walls covered by bohemian memorabilia, listening to French folk tunes, love ballads, army songs, and sea chanteys. It's open Tuesday through Sunday nights from 9pm to 2am with a cover charge of 24€ ($31.20; 17€/ $22.10 for students), which includes the first drink.

The **Crazy Horse Saloon,** 12 av. George-V, 8e (© **01-47-23-97-90;** www.lecrazy horseparis.com; Métro: George-V or Alma-Marceau), a sophisticated strip joint, has thrived for decades thanks to good choreography and a sly, flirty theme that celebrates and exalts the female form. Shows last 1¾ hours and the cover (including two drinks) is 50€ to 110€ ($65–$143), with the dinner spectacle costing 135€ to 170€ ($176–$221). The **Folies-Bergère,** 34 rue Richer, 9e (© **01-44-79-98-90;** www.folies bergere.com; Métro: Grands-Boulevards or Cadet), is a Paris institution; foreign visitors have been flocking here since 1886. Don't expect the naughty permissive skin-and-glitter revue that used to be the trademark of this place—today, it's a conventional 1,600-seat theater devoted to a frequently changing roster of big-stage performances, in French, many of which are adaptations of Broadway blockbusters. Hours and days of spectacles vary according to the performance, but shows are usually Tuesday through Saturday at 9pm, Sunday at 3pm and the cover is 40€ to 60€ ($52–$78).

As it moves deeper into the millennium, **Lido de Paris,** 116 bis av. des Champs-Elysées, 8e (© **01-40-76-56-10;** www.lido.fr; Métro: George-V), has changed its feathers and modernized its shows. Its $15-million production, *C'est Magique,* reflects a dramatic reworking of the classic Parisian cabaret show, with eye-popping special effects, water technology using more than 60,000 gallons per minute, even aerial and aquatic ballet. On select dates there is a lunch show at 1pm or 3pm for 115€ ($150) to 125€ ($163); daily dinner dance is at 7pm and the show is at 9:30pm and costs 140€ to 250€ ($182–$325); seeing the show only (9:30pm and 11:30pm) costs 90€ to 100€ ($117–$130).

Moulin Rouge, 82 bd. de Clichy, 18e (© **01-53-09-82-82;** www.moulinrouge.fr; Métro: Blanche), is a camp classic with a long history of famous performers, events, and visitors—including King Edward VI and Queen Elizabeth II. Try to get a table, as the view is much better on the main floor than from the bar. Handsome men and girls, girls, girls—virtually all topless—keep the place going. Dance finales usually include two dozen belles ripping loose with a topless cancan. Revues are nightly at 9 and 11pm. The cover charge, including champagne, is 89€ to 99€ ($116–$129); 7pm dinner and show 145€ to 175€ ($189–$228). *Note:* Elegant attire is required.

Some Paris-watchers consider **Nouveau Casino,** 109 rue Oberkamp, 11e (© **01-43-57-57-40;** www.nouveaucasino.net; Métro: Saint-Maur, Parmentier, or Ménilmontant), the epitome of the counterculture and hyperhip context that blossoms along the rue Oberkampf nightly. Every weeknight live concerts take place between 7:30pm and midnight; and Thursday, Friday, and Saturday, the party continues from midnight till dawn with a DJ who spins out some of the most avant-garde dance music in Paris. Entrance to the concerts costs from 12€ to 20€ ($15.60–$26); entrance to the disco costs an additional 8€ to 10€ ($10.40–$13), depending on the DJ of the night.

Jazz lovers go to **Baiser Salé,** 58 rue des Lombards, 1er (© **01-42-33-37-71;** www.lebaisersale.com; Métro: Châtelet), a cellar transformed with its jazz-related paintings, large bar, and an ongoing roster of videos that show great jazz players (Charlie Parker, Miles Davis) of the past. Everything is mellow and laid-back, with an emphasis on the music. Open daily 5pm to 6am. Shows generally start at 7pm, 9pm, or 10pm, and the cover charge ranges from 15€ to 20€ ($19.50-$26) though there is a discount if you buy your tickets 2 days in advance. **Le Bilboquet/Club St-Germain,** 13 rue St-Benoît, 6e (© **01-45-48-81-84;** jazzclub.bilboquet.free.fr; Métro: St-Germain-des-Prés), the restaurant/jazz club/piano bar where the film *Paris Blues* was shot, offers some of the best music in the city. Jazz is featured on the upper level in the restaurant, where greats such as Miles Davis, Duke Ellington, and Charlie Parker once performed. Under separate management, the downstairs disco, Club St-Germain, charges no cover—but drinks cost a staggering 18€ ($23.40). You can walk from one club to the other, but have to buy a new drink each time you change venues.

If you are in the mood for dancing, go to **Batofar,** facing 11 quai François Mauriac, 13e (© **01-53-60-17-30;** www.batofar.org; Métro: Quai de la Gare). Self-consciously proud of its status as a club that virtually everybody views as hip, Batofar is housed in a converted barge that floats on the Seine, sometimes filled with hundreds of gyrating dancers, most of whom are in their 20s and 30s. In the music department, you'll find house, garage, techno, reggae, hip-hop, and live jazz from musicians from around the world. It's generally open daily from 10pm to 5 or 6am; closed November to March. The cost (always reasonable) and hours vary depending on bands, DJs, dance classes (free summer ones), and special events. Call or check out their website in advance. Established in 1936, **La Balajo,** 9 rue de Lappe, 11e (© **01-47-00-07-87;** www.balajo.fr; Métro: Bastille), is the place where Edith Piaf won the hearts of Parisian music lovers. Sessions held on Thursday (2:30–6:30pm; senior citizen discount) and Sunday (3–7:30pm) afternoons focus on tangos, pasodobles, and waltzes, and are more staid than their late-night counterparts. Then, Rock 'n Roll night is Wednesday from 9pm to 3am, Hot Hot Salsa Night/'80s Night is Thursday from 10 to 5am, and disco, funk, Latino, and R&B play on Friday and Saturday from 11pm to 5:30am. The cover is 8€ ($10.40) for afternoon sessions; 10€ to 20€ ($13–$26) for nighttime sessions (ladies often get discounts). The entrance fee generally includes the first drink. **Les Bains Douches,** 7 rue du Bourg-l'Abbé, 3e (© **01-48-87-01-80;** www.lesbainsdouches.net; Métro: Étienne Marcel), got its name thanks to this hot spot's former life as a Turkish bath. Dancing begins at midnight, and a supper club–like restaurant is located upstairs, open Wednesday to Sunday. Meals cost 30€ to 50€ ($39–$65). On certain nights this is the hottest party atmosphere in Paris, and there is a special "morning" gay dance Sunday 6am to noon. It's open daily 11pm to 6 or 8am and the cover for nondiners (including one drink) is 20€ ($26), but it's 15€ ($19.50) if you arrive before 1am.

Many Parisians now prefer the wine bar to the traditional cafe or bistro—the food is often better and the ambience more inviting. **Au Sauvignon,** 80 rue des Sts-Pères, 7e (© **01-45-48-49-02;** Métro: Sèvres-Babylone), is a tiny corner spot with tables overflowing onto a covered terrace and a decor featuring old ceramic tiles and frescoes done by Left Bank artists. Wines range from the cheapest Beaujolais to the most expensive Puligny-Montrachet. A glass of wine costs 5€ to 6€ ($6.50–$7.80), with an additional charge of 1€ ($1.30) to consume it at a table. For a midafternoon snack choose a traditional tartine, made with the local *pain poilâne* (sold around the corner at **Poilâne,** 49 bd. de Grenelle). Hours are daily 8am to 10pm (closed in Aug). Close to the Opéra Garnier, **Les Bacchantes,** 21 rue Caumartin, 9e (© **01-42-65-25-35;** Métro: Havre-Caumartin), prides itself on offering more wines by the glass—at least 25 varieties—than any other wine bar in Paris; prices range from 3€ to 5.40€ ($3.90–$7). It also does a hefty restaurant trade in well-prepared cuisine bourgeoise, with platters running from 11€ to 23.50€ ($18.20–$30.55). Wines are mainly from France, but you'll also find examples from neighboring countries of Europe. Hours are from noon to 3pm and 7pm to midnight. **Willi's Wine Bar,** 13 rue des Petits-Champs, 1e (© **01-42-61-05-09;** www.williswinebar.com; Métro: Bourse, Louvre, or Palais-Royal), offers about 250 kinds of wine, including a dozen "wine specials" you can taste by the glass for 5€ to 16€ ($6.50–$20.80). Daily specials are likely to include lamb brochette with cumin or Lyonnais sausage in truffled vinaigrette, plus a spectacular dessert such as chocolate terrine. The fixed-price menu runs 19€ to 34€ ($24.70–$44.20). The restaurant is open from Monday to Saturday noon to 2:30pm and 7 to 11pm, while the bar goes from Monday to Saturday noon to midnight.

Barrio Latino, 46 rue du Faubourg St-Antoine, 12e (© **01-55-78-84-75;** www.buddhabar.com; Métro: Bastille), is a multistory emporium of good times, Gallic flair, and Latino charm. Tapas bars, dance floors, and a Latino restaurant each take up a different floor. The food isn't too great and the drinks are pricey, but the club is a fun experience. Clientele is mixed, mostly straight, partly gay, and 100% blasé about matters such as an individual's sexuality. Open daily noon to 2am. There is a cover charge of 20€ ($26) for nondiners Thursday, Friday, and Saturday after 9pm (includes one drink). Sunday brunch and salsa classes, held noon to 4pm, cost 28€ ($36.40). **Harry's New York Bar,** 5 rue Daunou, 2e (© **01-42-61-71-14;** www.harrys-bar.fr; Métro: Opéra or Pyramides), was opened on Thanksgiving Day, 1911, by an expat named MacElhone. It's the spot where members of the World War I ambulance corps drank themselves silly. In addition to being Hemingway's favorite, Harry's is where the White Lady and Sidecar cocktails were invented; it's also the alleged birthplace of the Bloody Mary and the headquarters of a loosely organized fraternity of drinkers known as the International Bar Flies (IBF). The cocktail bar (with food) is open Monday to Saturday, 10am to 4pm; the piano bar (downstairs) is open Monday to Thursday from 10pm to 2am and on Friday and Saturday until 3am.

AN EXCURSION TO VERSAILLES

The town of Versailles, 13 miles (21km) southwest of Paris, is a stodgily formal place, but the palace here is the sight of a lifetime.

GETTING THERE   To get to Versailles, catch the **RER** line C at the Gare d'Auster-litz, St-Michel, Musée d'Orsay, Invalides, Ponte de l'Alma, Champ de Mars, or Javel stop, and take it to the Versailles Rive Gauche station, from which the château is a 5-minute walk. The RER departs every 15 minutes and the trip takes about 20 minutes. Railpass holders travel free on the RER, but need to show their pass at the ticket kiosk near any RER entrance to get an RER ticket. Or you can take one of the regular **SNCF trains** that make frequent runs from Gare St-Lazare and Gare Montparnasse in Paris to Versailles: Trains departing from Gare St-Lazare arrive at the Versailles Rive Droite railway station; trains departing from Gare Montparnasse arrive at Versailles Chantiers station. Both stations are a 10-minute walk from the château (follow the signs).

VISITOR INFORMATION   The **Office de Tourisme** is at 2 bis av. de Paris (© **01-39-24-88-88**), a short walk from the rail station and close to the main entrance to Versailles. Open April to September Tuesday to Sunday 9am to 7pm, Monday 10am to 6pm; October to March Tuesday to Saturday 9am to 6pm, Sunday and Monday 11am to 5pm.

TOP ATTRACTIONS & SPECIAL MOMENTS

The unbelievably vast **Château de Versailles** ✿✿✿ (© **01-30-83-78-00;** www.chateauversailles.fr) is as ornately artificial as a jewel box. Here, the kings of France built a whole glittering private world for themselves, as remote from the grime and noise and bustle of Paris as a gilded planet. Begun in 1661, the construction of the château involved 32,000 to 45,000 workmen, some of whom had to drain marshes—often at the cost of their lives—and move forests. Louis XIV set out to create a palace that would awe all Europe, and the result was a symbol of pomp and opulence that was to be copied, yet never quite duplicated.

For viewing purposes, the palace is divided up into sections. The first section features the six magnificent **Grands Appartements** ✿✿✿, done in the Louis XIV style; each takes its name from the allegorical painting on its ceiling. The most famous room in this section is the recently restored 236-foot (71m) **Hall of Mirrors** ✿✿✿ (where the Treaty of Versailles was signed). Begun by Mansart in 1678, it was decorated by Le Brun with 17 large arched windows matched by beveled mirrors in simulated arcades.

Highlights in other sections include the **Opera House** designed by Gabriel for Louis XV in 1748, though it wasn't completed until 1770. Also of interest are the **apartments of Mme de Pompadour,** the queen's private suites, the salons, the **Royal Chapel,** and the **Museum of the History of France.**

The Grands Appartements, the Royal Chapel, and the Hall of Mirrors can be visited without a guide. There are various opening times for other parts of the château. Seeing all of it can take up an entire morning and leave you pretty exhausted.

For a little relaxation, head for the **Gardens of Versailles** ✿. This park is the ultimate in French landscaping perfection—every tree, shrub, flower, and hedge disciplined into a frozen ballet pattern and blended with soaring fountains, sparkling little lakes, grandiose steps, and hundreds of marble statues. Try to save time to visit the **Grand Trianon,** which is a good walk across the park. The pink-and-white marble structure was designed by Hardouin-Mansart for Louis XIV in 1687. You can also visit the **Petit Trianon,** which was built by Gabriel in 1768 as a retreat for Louis XV and his mistress, Mme du Barry. Later on, it was the favorite residence of Marie Antoinette, who could escape the rigors of court here.

The latest attraction is the **Grande Ecourie,** the stables of Louis XIV. For 2 centuries, these historic stables have been closed to the public. They once housed more than 600 horses of the king. Today, they are home to 20 cream-colored Lusitanian horses from Portugal. Visitors are taken on a brief guided tour and then witness morning dressage demonstrations.

The château is open from April 3 to October 31, Tuesday through Sunday from 9am to 6:30pm (5:30pm the rest of the year). It's closed December 25 and January 1. The grounds are open daily from dawn to dusk; the Trianons are open from noon to 6pm. Individual attractions may have earlier opening and closing times.

Call or visit the website for a complete fee schedule (which varies, depending on which attractions you visit and the time of year). An unguided day pass covering many of the attractions costs 20€ ($26) April 3 to October 31 and 16€ ($20.80) the rest of the year; free for ages 18 and under. A visit to the Grands Appartements costs 13.50€ ($17.55) adults. Access to the gardens is free.

3 The Loire Valley ⋆⋆⋆

Val de Loire, the Loire Valley, is known popularly around the world as "châteaux country." Bordered by vineyards, the winding Loire Valley cuts through the soft contours of the land of castles deep in the heart of France. When royalty and nobility built châteaux throughout this valley during the Renaissance, sumptuousness was uppermost in their minds. An era of excessive pomp reigned here until Henri IV moved his court to Paris.

The Valley of the Loire has also played a major part in the national consciousness. Joan of Arc, the maid of Orléans, came this way looking for her dauphin, finding him at Chinon. A now legendary list of mistresses, ranging from Agnés Sorel (the mistress of Charles VII) to Diane du Poitiers (the mistress of Henri II), were carried from castle to castle. In his heyday, the Chevalier King brought Leonardo da Vinci from Florence, installing him at Amboise. Catherine de Médici and her "flying squadron" of beauties, Henry III and his handsome minions—these historical figures and events make for a rich tapestry.

The Loire has a fascinating tale to tell. Its sights and curiosities are multifarious, ranging from Renaissance, medieval, and classical châteaux to residences where Balzac wrote or Rabelais lived, to Romanesque and Gothic churches, to Roman ramparts, to art treasures. Attempts to explore the valley in 2 to 3 days are doomed, but that is all the time most rail passengers have to spare. If your schedule can accommodate it, allow at least a week. Autumn or spring is ideal for a visit, though most of the intriguing *son-et-lumiére* (sound-and-light) programs take place in summer when the châteaux are floodlit and their stories are told.

The cities of **Orléans, Tours,** and **Blois,** all within easy rail reach of Paris, are the major transportation hubs for the Loire Valley. Tours makes the best base because it is better connected by rail and public transport to the major châteaux: **Chenonceau, Amboise, Azay-le-Rideau, Chambord,** and **Blois.**

ORLÉANS ⋆

Orléans suffered heavy damage in World War II, so those hoping to see how it looked when the Maid of Orléans was here are likely to be disappointed. However, the reconstruction of Orléans has been judiciously planned, with many rewarding targets.

Orléans is the chief town of Loiret, on the Loire River, 74 miles (119km) southwest of Paris. Joan of Arc freed the city in 1429 from the attacks of the Burgundians and the English. That deliverance is celebrated every year on May 8, the anniversary of her victory. An equestrian statue of Joan of Arc stands in the **Place du Martroi,** which was created by Foyatier in 1855.

From that square, you can head down the **rue Royale**—rebuilt in the 18th-century style—across the **Pont George V,** erected in 1760. After crossing the bridge you'll have a good view of the town. A simple cross marks the site of the Fort des Tourelles, which Joan of Arc and her men captured.

GETTING THERE   Seventeen trains per day arrive from Paris's Gare d'Austerlitz (trip time: 1 hr., 3min.); there are also thirteen connections from Tours (trip time: 1 hr., 3min.). The one-way fare from Paris is 16.90€ ($21.95); from Tours it's 16.80€ ($21.85). The Orléans station is about a 10- to 15-minute walk from the town center.

VISITOR INFORMATION   The **Office de Tourisme** is at 2 place de l'Etape (© **02-38-24-05-05;** www.ville-orleans.fr), connected to the town hall, which is across from the cathedral. Hours are Tuesday to Saturday 9:30am to 1pm and 2 to 6:30pm. They will make hotel reservations for you for 1€ ($1.30), but you have to be in the office in person and the reservation must be for that same day.

TOP ATTRACTIONS & SPECIAL MOMENTS

In the heart of town stands **Cathédrale Ste-Croix** ⚔, place Ste-Croix (© **02-38-77-87-50**), begun in 1287 in the High Gothic style, although burned by the Huguenots in 1567. The first stone on the present building was laid by Henry IV in 1601, and work continued on the cathedral until 1829. Inside, the church of the Holy Cross contains a gigantic 17th-century organ, and some magnificent 18th-century woodwork in the chancel. You'll need a guide to tour the chancel, the crypt, and the treasury with its Byzantine enamels and textiles, its 15th- and 16th-century goldwork, and its Limoges enamels. Admission is free, but you should tip the tour guide. Visitors are welcome at daily services. Hours are daily 9:30am to 6:30pm (July–Aug until 7pm). In the winter they often close for lunch from noon and 2pm. Guided visits can be arranged by the tourist office for 4€ ($5.20) adults, 2€ ($2.60) children 6 to 13. Tours are given in July and August Monday to Saturday at 10:30am and 2:30pm and on Sunday at 2:30pm only.

Hôtel Groslot, place de l'Etape (northwest of the cathedral, across from the town hall; © **02-38-79-22-30**), is a Renaissance mansion begun in 1550 and embellished in the 19th century. François II (first husband of Mary Queen of Scots) lived in it during the fall of 1560 and died on December 5 of the same year. Between the revolution and the mid-1970s, it functioned as the town hall. Marriage ceremonies, performed by the town's magistrates, still occur here. Romance is nothing new to this building: It was here that Charles IX met his lovely Marie Touchet. The statue of Joan of Arc praying (at the foot of the flight of steps) was the work of Louis Phillipe's daughter, Princess Marie d'Orléans. In the charming garden in the back, you can see remains of the 15th-century Chapelle St-Jacques. Admission is free and guided tours in French and English are offered every hour on the hour. Open daily from 10am to 12pm and 2pm to 6pm (9am–6pm July–Aug). Often closed Saturdays for weddings.

After visiting the Groslot, you can backtrack to the cathedral square and walk down rue Jeanne-d'Arc, across rue Royale, to see a small museum dedicated to Orléans's favorite mademoiselle, the **Maison Jeanne-d'Arc,** 3 place de Gaulle

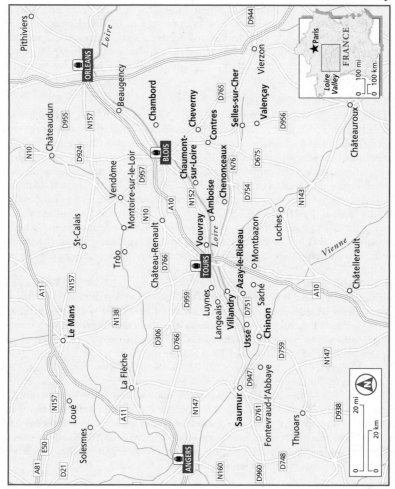

(© **02-38-52-99-89**). The house is a 20th-century reproduction of the 15th-century house where Joan of Arc, the liberator and patron of Orléans, stayed during her local heroics. The original house was destroyed by bombing in 1940. The first floor has temporary exhibitions, and the second and third floors contain Joan-related models and memorabilia. Admission is 2€ ($2.60) adults, 1€ ($1.30) seniors and students, free for children under 17. Hours are May to October Tuesday to Sunday 10am to 12:30pm and 1:30 to 6:30pm; November to April Tuesday to Sunday 1:30 to 6pm.

The **Musée des Beaux-Arts** ✿✿, 1 rue Fernand-Rabier (© **02-38-79-21-55**), occupies the 16th-century town hall, known as Hôtel des Créneaux. It mainly houses French works from the 15th to 19th centuries. Some of the art here once hung in Richelieu's château. Other pieces include busts by Pigalle and a fine array of portraits, including one of Mme de Pompadour, of whom, when she crossed the Pont George V, the people of the town remarked: "Our bridge has just borne France's heaviest weight." The collection also includes works by Georges de La Tour, Correge, Le Nain, Phillippe de Champaigne, La Hire, Boucher, Watteau, and Gauguin, as well as a salon of pastels by Perronneau, and a lovely Velásquez. Admission is 3€ ($3.90) adults, 2.50€ ($3.25) students and under 15. Hours are Tuesday to Sunday 9:30am to 12:15pm, 1:30 to 5:30pm.

WHERE TO STAY & DINE

Hôtel d'Arc, 37 rue de la République, 45000 Orléans (© **02-38-53-10-94;** www. hoteldarc.fr), a 35-room hotel with an Art Deco facade, sits in the middle of the town center and is close to nearly everything, including the train station and the city's pedestrian-only shopping streets. The 1920s structure has been considerably modernized; its average-size bedrooms are tastefully furnished. Avoid rooms facing rue de la République—they tend to be noisy. Rates are 93€ to 145€ ($121–$189) double.

If you seek more modern comfort, **Mercure Orléans Centre** ✦, 44 quai Barentin, 45000 Orléans (© **02-38-62-17-39;** www.mercure.com), is the town's finest address. Along the river, adjacent to pont Joffre, this 109-room bandbox structure is within walking distance of place du Martroi and its Joan of Arc statue. The air-conditioned bedrooms are done in an impersonal chain style but are nevertheless comfortable and inviting. Rates are 90€ to 155€ ($117–$207) double.

La Vieille Auberge, 2 rue de Faubourg St-Vincent (© **02-38-53-55-81;** www.la vieilleauberge.fr), is one of the most dignified-looking and best restaurants in Orléans. Menu items include sophisticated treatments of Loire Valley whitefish, game, and local produce, all accompanied by regional Loire wines that blend well with the cuisine. Main courses cost 16€ to 30€ ($20.80–$39) and a fixed-price menu is offered at 25€ to 49€ ($32.50–$63.70). Closed Sunday nights.

La Mangeoire, 28 rue de Poirier (© **02-38-68-15-38;** www.lamangeoire.fr), is a bistro usually filled with lively locals who are not in a hurry. Owner/chef Florent Dubois uses his American-influenced culinary skills to create plate-sized "tartines," a grilled open-faced sandwich loaded with combinations of melted cheeses, meats, and potatoes. Fish, pasta dishes, and large salads are also popular. Main courses cost 10€ to 16€ ($13–$20.80). Closed Sundays. (Dubois also owns the new **BaraFlor,** quai du Chatelet, on the promenade; it's connected to a 19th-century replica paddleboat, adding a little dash of New Orleans to the original Orléans.)

TOURS ✦

With a population of 130,000, Tours is known for its fine food and wine. Although without a major château itself, this industrial and residential city is the traditional center for exploring the Loire Valley.

At the heart of the châteaux country, Tours is 144 miles (232km) southwest of Paris and 70 miles (113km) southwest of Orléans. At the junction of the Loire and Cher rivers, it was one of the great pilgrimage sites of Europe in the Middle Ages. The townspeople are fond of pointing out that Tours, not Paris, is actually the logical site for the capital of France. And it virtually *was* the capital in June of 1940, when Churchill flew here to meet with Paul Reynaud during World War II.

Because many of the city's buildings were bombed in World War II, 20th-century apartment towers have taken the place of stately châteaux. It is, however, still at the doorstep of some of the most magnificent châteaux in France. And while most Loire

Orléans

Valley towns are rather sleepy, Tours is where the action is, as you'll see by its noisy streets and cafes. A quarter of the residents are students, who add a vibrant touch to the city.

GETTING THERE **Trains** to Tours/St. Pierre des Corps depart from Paris from two stations, Gare Montparnasse and Gare d'Austerlitz. The quickest transits are usually from Gare Montparnasse, departure point for up to 6 TGV trains per day, charging 38.40€ ($49.90) one-way for the 70-minute trip. Most of the conventional—slower—trains to Tours depart from the Gare d'Austerlitz. Transit time on these trains is about 2½ hours, and they cost 28.70€ ($37.30) one-way.

Trains arrive in Tours at place du Maréchal-Leclerc, 3 rue Edouard-Vaillant (© **08-92-35-35-35** for information), just a stone's throw from most of the city's major attractions. The city itself is easily navigable on foot and most hotels are close to the train station.

VISITOR INFORMATION The **Office de Tourisme** is at 78 rue Bernard-Palissy (© **02-47-70-37-37**), just across the place du Géneral-Leclerc from the train station (with the large blue fluorescent lights). Hotels can be reserved here for no charge. Hours are mid-April to mid-October, Monday to Saturday 8:30am to 7pm and Sunday

10am to 12:30pm and 2:30 to 5pm. Off-season hours are Monday to Friday 9am to 12:30pm and 1:30 to 6pm; Sunday 10am to 1pm.

TOP ATTRACTIONS & SPECIAL MOMENTS

Cathédrale St-Gatien, 5 place de la Cathédrale (© **02-47-70-21-00**), the chief attraction of Tours, honors an evangelist of the 3rd century. Its facade is in the flamboyant Gothic style, flanked by two towers, the bases of which date from the 12th century, although the lanterns are Renaissance. The choir was built in the 13th century, with new additions taking place up until the 16th century. Sheltered inside is the handsome 16th-century tomb of the children of Charles VIII. Some of the stained-glass windows, the building's glory, date from the 13th century. Admission is free and hours are daily 8:30am to 8pm. You can also visit the cloisters for 3€ ($3.90); free for children under 18; cloister hours are Monday to Sunday 9:30am to 12:30pm and 2pm to 6pm (closed Sun mornings due to services).

The **Musée des Beaux-Arts,** 18 place François-Sicard (© **02-47-05-68-73**), is housed in an archbishop's palace of the 17th and 18th centuries, complete with Louis XVI woodwork and Tours silk-damask hangings. Among the foreign acquisitions, the most outstanding paintings are Mantegna's *Christ in the Garden of Olives* and *The Resurrection.* Other foreign works include an early Rembrandt *(Flight into Egypt),* plus canvases by Rubens, Luca Giordano, and Mattäus Günther. The French school is represented by Le Sueur, Fouquet, Boucher, Vernet, Vuillard, David, Ingres, Degas *(Calvary),* Delacroix *(Comedians and Buffoons),* and Monet. The most important sculpture is by Houdon and Lemoyne. Free entrance to gardens daily from 7am to 8pm. Admission to the museum is 4€ ($5.20) adults, 2€ ($2.60) students and seniors, free for children under 13. Hours are Wednesday to Monday 9am to 12:45pm and 2 to 6pm.

WHERE TO STAY & DINE

The **Best Western Le Central,** 21 rue Berthelot, 37000 Tours (© **800/528-1234** in the U.S. and Canada, or 02-47-05-46-44; www.bestwestern.com), is within walking distance of the river and cathedral, surrounded by gardens, lawns, and trees. Built in 1850, this 41-room hotel is a modest but economical choice, with homey bedrooms that come in a variety of shapes and sizes, all of them renovated in 2003. About half the bathrooms have showers only. Rates are 97€ to 137€ ($126–$178) double.

The 19th-century **Hôtel du Manoir,** 2 rue Traversière, 37000 Tours (© **02-47-05-37-37;** site.voila.fr/hotel.manoir.tours), is situated on a quiet street near the train station, shops, and restaurants. This 20-room family-run residence provides guests with a comfortable, cheerful place to stay. The midsize bedrooms offer simple furnishings and lots of windows; half the bathrooms have showers only. Rates run 54€ to 60€ ($70.20–$78) double.

One of the hottest chefs in town, Alain Couturier, blends new and old techniques at **La Roche le Roy** ✿✿, 55 rte. St-Avertin (© **02-47-27-22-00;** www.rocheleroy. com), in a steep-gabled 18th-century manor south of the town center. Couturier's repertoire includes such delights as scalloped foie gras with lentils, cod with saffron cream, and pan-fried scallops with truffle vinaigrette. Main courses run 18€ to 32€ ($23.40–$41.60); a fixed-price menu is 35€ ($45.50) at lunch, 55€ to 70€ ($71.50–$91) at dinner. To get here, follow avenue Grammot south from town center until you pass over a bridge and the street becomes route St-Avertin.

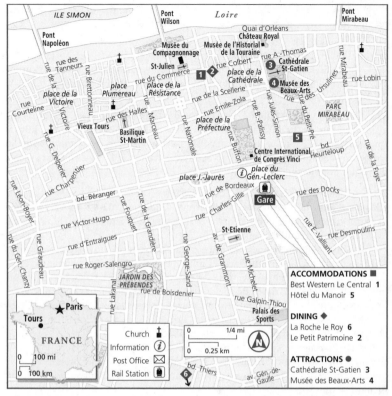

ACCOMMODATIONS ■
Best Western Le Central 1
Hôtel du Manoir 5

DINING ◆
La Roche le Roy 6
Le Petit Patrimoine 2

ATTRACTIONS ●
Cathédrale St-Gatien 3
Musée des Beaux-Arts 4

Le Petit Patrimoine, 58 rue Colbert (☏ **02-47-05-71-21**), is small, cozy, and extremely popular with locals as well as tourists. Generous-sized regional dishes include *rillons* (similar to bacon) and *chèvre* (goat's cheese)—both of which are in their specialty pie, the *tourte tourangelle aux rillons.* For dessert, try the local *poire tapée de Rivarennes* (reyhdrated pears with red wine). Main courses cost 11€ to 15€ ($14.30–$19.50); the fixed-price menu is 15.80€ to 25€ ($20.50–$32.50). Reservations are strongly recommended (at least a day in advance).

EXCURSIONS FROM TOURS

If you wish to see at least five or six of the greatest châteaux in Europe (previewed below), Tours is your best choice as a transportation hub, although some connections can be a bit difficult and are not always via a rail line. Once you land on your feet in these Loire towns, you can go immediately to the châteaux without feeling you're missing out on a lot of other attractions.

AZAY-LE-RIDEAU

This sleepy little town is 13 miles (21km) southwest of Tours. Now named after its château, the village was once known as Azay-le-Brûlé or "Azay the Burnt." Passing through with his court in 1418, the dauphin, later Charles VII, was insulted by the

Burgundians. The result: A whole garrison was killed and the village and its fortress razed. Today's château was built upon the ruins of the destroyed structure.

GETTING THERE   To reach Azay-le-Rideau, take one of three daily shuttles run by the SNCF (Tours-Chinon line) from Tours. Trip time is about 45 minutes; the one-way fare is 4.80€ ($6.25). The station is in an isolated spot 1¼ miles (2km) outside of town. There's no public transport, but visitors can call a **taxi** (© 02-47-45-26-26).

VISITOR INFORMATION   The **Office de Tourisme** (in town center) is on 5 place de l'Europe (© 02-47-45-44-40; www.ot-paysazaylerideau.com). July and August hours are Monday to Saturday 9am to 7pm and Sunday 10am to 6pm. September to June hours are Monday to Saturday 9am to 1pm and 2 to 6pm and Sunday 10am to 1pm and 2 to 5pm.

TOP ATTRACTIONS & SPECIAL MOMENTS

Château d'Azay-le-Rideau ★★, 37190 Azay-le-Rideau (© 02-47-45-42-04), despite its medieval appearance and defensive architecture, was actually created as a private residence during the Renaissance.

Gilles Berthelot, the financial minister of François I, built the château beginning in 1518. Actually, his big-spending wife, Phillipa, supervised its construction. So elegant and harmonious, so imposing was their creation that the Chevalier King grew immensely jealous. In time, Berthelot fled and the château reverted to the king. François I didn't live there, however, but started the custom of granting it to "friends of the crown." After a brief residency by Prince Frederick of Prussia in 1870, the château became the property of the state in 1905.

Before entering you can circle the mansion, enjoying its near-perfect proportions, the crowning achievement of the French Renaissance in Touraine. Architecturally, its most fancifully ornate feature is a great bay enclosing a grand stairway with a straight flight of steps.

The largest room, the **Banqueting Hall,** is adorned with four 17th-century Flemish tapestries representing scenes from the life of Constantine (it took a crafts person

---

Finds **A Romantic Getaway in the Loire**

In the hills of Vouvray, 8 miles (13km) from Tours and 7 miles (11km) from Amboise, the 15th-century **Château de Jallanges,** 37210 Vouvray (© 02-47-52-06-06; www.jallanges.com) is a journey into the past. With seven spacious rooms/suites (including bathrooms) and access to beautiful gardens, an outdoor heated pool (June–Sept), and close to some of the Loire Valley's most well-known châteaux (they're all within 25 miles/40km), you're certain to feel like royalty if you stay here. Carriage rides through Vouvray vineyards, hot-air-balloon and helicopter excursions, and wine tastings of local wines can all be arranged by request.

Rates run 145€ to 210€ ($189–$273) double; and 170€ to 290€ ($221–$377) for a suite (a buffet breakfast is included). The closest train station is St-Pierre-de-Corps (the hotel can arrange taxi pickup for 15€–20€/$19.50–$26) outside of Tours; your best option, however, would be to rent a car using the **France Rail 'n Drive Pass** (p. 250).

1 year just to weave 4 sq. ft/.35 sq. m). In the kitchen is a collection of utensils, including a wooden mold capable of making 45 designs on cakes.

In the dining room is a trio of 16th-century Flemish tapestries. The fireplace is only a plaster molding of a chimney piece made by Rodin for the Château of Montal. The fireplace masterpiece, however, is in a ground-floor bedroom containing a 16th-century four-poster bed. Over the stone fireplace hovers a salamander, the symbol of François I.

The château is open daily during July and August from 9:30am to 7pm; April to June and September from 9:30am to 6pm; and October to March from 10am to 12:30pm and 2 to 5:30pm. Admission is 7.50€ ($9.75) for adults and 4.80€ ($6.25) for ages 18 to 25 and seniors, free for children under 18. Allow 2 hours for a visit. From May to July, *son-et-lumière* (sound and light) performances (1 hr.) with recorded music and lights beaming on the celebrated exterior of the château, begin at 10pm nightly during July and August and on weekends in September. Tickets are 12€ ($15.60) for adults and 7€ ($9.10) for ages 18 to 25; 5€ ($6.50) for ages 12 to 18, and free for those under 12.

AMBOISE

On the banks of the Loire, Amboise is a real Renaissance town in the center of vineyards known as Touraine-Amboise. Leonardo da Vinci spent his last years in this ancient city at **Clos Lucé.** Dominating the town is the **Château of Amboise,** the first in France to reflect the impact of the Italian Renaissance. Amboise is the most important day-trip from Tours. The town is 22 miles (35km) east of Tours and 136 miles (219km) southwest of Paris.

GETTING THERE   Amboise lies on the main Paris-Blois-Tours rail line, with 19 trains per day arriving from both Tours and Blois (see below). The trip from Tours takes about 20 minutes and costs 4.60€ ($6) one-way; the trip from Blois also takes 20 minutes and costs 5.40€ ($7). About eight conventional trains per day depart from Paris's Gare d'Austerlitz from Paris (trip time: 2½ hr.), and several high-speed TGV trains leave from the Gare Montparnasse for St-Pierre-des-Corps (trip time: 1 hr.), less than a ½ mile (1km) from Tours. From St-Pierre-des-Corps, you can transfer to a conventional train bound for Amboise. One-way fares from Paris to Amboise cost 26.50€ ($33.80).

VISITOR INFORMATION   **Office de Tourisme,** quai du Général-de-Gaulle (© 02-47-57-09-28; www.amboise-valdeloire.com), is open October to May, Monday to Saturday 10am to 1pm and 2 to 6pm, Sunday 10am to 3pm; June and September, Monday to Saturday 9:30am to 1pm and 2 to 6:30pm, Sunday 10am to 1pm, 2 to 5pm; July and August, Monday to Saturday 9am to 8pm, Sunday 10am to 6pm. To get here from the train station, walk across the bridge over the river and turn right. Be sure to visit the *marché* (marketplace) nearby if you have time. The château is a short walk away. *Note:* The office sells a discount pass (skip lines!) that includes Château Royal d'Amboise, Clos Lucé, and Château de Chenonceau. Admission runs 28.50€ ($37.05) for adults, 25.50€ ($33.15) for students, and 19.20€ ($24.95) for children ages 6 to 14.

TOP ATTRACTIONS & SPECIAL MOMENTS

Château Royal d'Amboise 🐟🐟 (© 02-47-57-00-98; www.chateau-amboise.com) is a combination of Gothic and Renaissance architecture. This 15th-century château suffered during the French Revolution (only about a quarter of the original structure remains), and is mainly associated with Charles VIII, who built it on a rock spur separating the valleys of the Loire and the Amasse. Born at Amboise on June 30, 1470, Charles returned to France at the age of 25 following an Italian campaign, and with him, he brought artists, designers, and architects from "that land of enchantment." In a sense, he brought the Italian Renaissance to France.

You visit first the flamboyant **Gothic Chapel of St. Hubert,** distinguished by its lacelike tracery. It allegedly contains the remains of da Vinci. Actually, the great artist was buried in the castle's Collegiate Church, which was destroyed between 1806 and 1810. During the Second Empire, excavations were undertaken on the site of the church, and bones discovered were "identified" as those of Leonardo.

The **Logis du roi (the king's apartment),** its facade, pierced by large double mullioned windows and crowned by towering dormers and sculptured canopies, survived the Revolution intact. Alas, Charles VIII's own apartment caused his death: He died at Amboise on April 8, 1498, after accidentally banging his head against a wall. At the end of the terrace, near the room of his queen, Anne of Brittany is a low doorway where it is said the mishap took place.

Adjoining the apartment are two squat towers, the Hurtalt and the Minimes, which contain ramps of huge dimensions so that cavaliers on horseback or nobles in horse-drawn chariots could ascend them.

Today, the walls of the château are hung with tapestries, the rooms furnished in the style of *"La Belle Époque."* From the terraces are panoramic views of the town and the Loire Valley. Admission is 8.50€ ($11.05) adults, 7€ ($9.10) students, 5€ ($6.50) children ages 7 to 14, free for children 6 and under. Hours are July to August daily 9am to 7pm; April to June 9am to 6:30pm; September to October daily 9am to 6pm; November 2 to 15 daily 9am to 5:30pm; November 16 to January daily 9am to 12:30pm and 2 to 4:45pm; February to March daily 9am to noon and 1:30 to 5pm; March 1 to 31 9am to 5:30pm.

Clos-Lucé ⚐, 2 rue de Clos-Lucé (© **02-47-57-00-73;** www.vinci-closluce.com), is a 15th-century manor house of brick and stone about a 2-mile (3.2km) walk from the Château d'Amboise. In what had been an oratory for Anne of Brittany, François I installed "the great master in all forms of art and science," Leonardo da Vinci. Loved and venerated by the Chevalier King, da Vinci lived there for 3 years, dying at the manor in 1519. (Incidentally, those deathbed paintings depicting Leonardo in the arms of François I are probably symbolic; the king was supposedly out of town when the artist died.)

From the window of his bedroom Leonardo liked to look out at the château where François lived. Whenever he was restless, the king would visit Leonardo via an underground tunnel.

Inside, the rooms are well furnished, some containing reproductions from the period of the artist. The downstairs is reserved for da Vinci's designs, models, and inventions, including his plans for a turbine engine, an airplane, and a parachute. Admission is 12€ ($15.60) adults, 9.50€ ($12.35) students and seniors, 7€ ($9.10) children 6 to 15, free for children 5 and under. In January, hours are daily 10am to 5pm. It opens at 9am the rest of the year, but closes at various times: February, March, November, and December at 6pm; April, June, September, and October at 7pm; July and August at 8pm.

BLOIS

Just 37 miles (60km) northeast of Tours, the small town of **Blois** ("Blwah") is often called the center of the châteaux country. Although Blois does not have the same liveliness as Tours, it is a convenient base for rail travelers as it is between Tours and Orléans. It lies on the right bank of the Loire and is often visited by rail passengers in the morning, who then spend the afternoon at the château nearby, Chambord (see below). In 1429, Joan of Arc launched her expeditionary forces from Blois to oust the English from Orléans.

GETTING THERE   The Paris-Austerlitz line via Orléans delivers 17 **trains** per day from Paris (trip time: 1 hr., 5 min.), at a cost of 16.90€ ($21.95) one-way. From Tours, 15 trains arrive per day (trip time: 30 min.–1 hr.), at a cost of 9.10€ ($11.85) one-way.

The train station is at place de la Gare. Once here, you can take the **bus** (© 02-54-90-41-41), to tour various châteaux in the area, including Chambord. One bus a day departs from the train station from May to August only. The Château de Blois and tourist office are an easy 5-minute walk southeast of the rail station.

VISITOR INFORMATION   The **Office de Tourisme** is located at 23 place du Chateau (© 02-54-90-41-41; www.bloispaysdechambord.com). Summer hours are Monday to Saturday 9am to 7pm and Sunday 10am to 7pm. The off-season hours are 9am to 12:30pm and 2 to 6pm; often closed Sundays—if open, hours are 10am to 4pm.

TOP ATTRACTIONS & SPECIAL MOMENTS

Château Royal de Blois ★★★ (© 02-54-90-33-33) is forever linked to one of the most famous murders in French history, that of the Duke of Guise, *Balafre* (Scarface), on December 23, 1588. His archrival, Henri III, ordered the murder. The château and scene of this famous assassination was begun in the 13th century by the counts of Blois. Charles d'Orléans, the "poet prince," lived at Blois after his release from 25 years of English captivity. He had married Mary of Cleves and brought a "court of letters" to Blois. In his 70s, Charles became father of the future Louis XII, who was to marry Anne of Brittany, and Blois was launched in its new role as a royal château. In time it would be called the second capital of France, and Blois itself, the city of kings.

Blois, however, eventually became a palace of banishment. Louis XIII sent his interfering mother, Marie de Médici, here, but the plump matron escaped by sliding on a coat down a mound of dirt left by the builders and into the moat. In 1626, the king sent his conspiring brother, Gaston d'Orléans, here. He actually stayed put.

If you stand in the courtyard of the great château, you'll find it's like an illustrated storybook of French architecture. The **Hall of the Estates-General** is a beautiful work from the 13th century; the so-called **gallery of Charles d'Orléans** was actually built by Louis XII between 1498 and 1501, as was the **Louis XII wing.** The **François I** wing is a masterpiece of the French Renaissance; the **Gaston d'Orléans** wing was constructed by François Mansart between 1635 and 1637. Of them all, the most remarkable is the François I wing, which contains a spiral staircase with elaborately ornamented balustrades and the king's symbol, the salamander. In the Louis XII wing, seek out paintings by Antoine Caron, court painter to Henri III, depicting the persecution of Thomas More.

The château presents a *son-et-lumière* show in French from May to September, beginning at 10:15pm and lasting 45 minutes (in English on Wed night). As a taped lecture is played, colored lights and dramatic readings evoke the age in which the château was built. The show costs 7€ ($9.10) for adults, 5€ ($6.50) for students, 3€ ($3.90) for children, ages 6 to 17. Admission to the château is 9€ ($11.70) adults, 7€ ($9.10) students, 3€ $3.90) for children ages 6 to 17, free for children 5 and under. There are also several options for combination tickets (for the château, sound-and-light show, and *maison de la magie*—the magic museum), so be sure to consider these depending on your interests. Hours are daily January to March and October to December 9am to 12:30pm and 1:30 to 5:30pm; April to September 9am to 6:30pm.

WHERE TO STAY

Situated 5 minutes from the train station, the town center, and the Château Royal de Blois, the cozy hotel **Anne de Bretagne,** 31 av. Jean Laigret (© **02-54-78-05-38;** annedebretagne.free.fr), makes rail travel easy (the closest castles are Chambord and Chaumont-sur-Loire). The 27 warmly painted rooms have a Provençal feel with either a bathtub or shower, and the multilingual staff does everything to make guests comfortable. Rates run 51€ to 53€ ($66.30–$68.90) double.

CHAMBORD

In the village of Chambord, 11 miles (18km) east of Blois (see above), and 118 miles (190km) southwest of Paris, stands a château where the French Renaissance in architecture reached its peak.

GETTING THERE   This is one place you can't get to by rail alone; you'll need to take a train to Blois (see above), then travel here by other means. From May 16 to September 4, **Transports du Loir et Cher** (© **02-54-58-55-61**) operates bus service Monday through Saturday to Chambord, leaving Blois at 12:15pm and returning at 6:45pm. You can also rent a bicycle in Blois and ride the 11 miles (18km) to Chambord, or take one of the tours to Chambord leaving from Blois in summer.

VISITOR INFORMATION   The **Office de Tourisme,** on place St-Michel (© **02-54-33-39-16**), is open daily April to September Monday to Saturday 10am to 6pm; Sunday 9:30am to 1pm and 3 to 6pm.

TOP ATTRACTIONS & SPECIAL MOMENTS

Work on **Château de Chambord** ✶✶✶, 41250, intersection of route de Bracieux and route de la Commission (© **02-54-50-50-00**), was begun in 1519 by 2,000 laborers. After 20 years, the largest château in the Loire Valley emerged. It was ready for the visit of Charles V of Germany, who was welcomed by nymphets in transparent veils tossing wildflowers in the emperor's path.

French monarchs—Henri II, Catherine de Medici, and Louis XIII—came and went from Chambord, but it was the favorite of François I, the Chevalier King (who is said to have carved the following on one of the window panes with his diamond ring: "A woman is a creature of change; to trust her is to play the fool.").

The château was restored in part by the brother of Louis XIII, Gaston d'Orléans. His daughter, "La Grand Mademoiselle" (Mademoiselle de Montpensier), wrote that she used to force her father to run up and down Chambord's famous double spiral staircase after her. Because of its corkscrew structure, he never caught her (one person may descend at one end and another ascend at the other without ever meeting).

The château is set in a park of more than 13,000 acres (5,200 hectares), enclosed within a wall stretching 20 miles (32km). At its lowest point the château was used as a munitions factory. The state acquired Chambord in 1932. Its facade is characterized by four monumental towers. The keep contains a spectacular terrace, on which the ladies of the court used to stand to watch the return of their men from the hunt. From that platform, you can inspect the dormer windows and the richly decorated chimneys, some characterized by winged horses. The apartments of **Louis XIV** (the Sun King paid nine visits here), including his redecorated bedchamber, are also in the keep.

Finds **Chinon: For History Buffs**

Located between the "chalk cliff" and the river (La Vienne), the 2,000-year-old charming city of **Chinon** (1hr. 10 min. from Tours) should not be missed by historical enthusiasts. Visit the château remains (an uphill trek) that overlook the old city's streets, reflecting a long history marked by battles and such historic residents as Henry II (Middle Ages), Charles VII (Hundred Years War), and Joan of Arc (1429). If you get hungry, have lunch or dinner at **Brasserie le Gandoyau** (connected to **Hostellerie Gargantua,** a cozy place to stay), 73 rue Voltaire (*©* **02-47-93-04-71;** www.hostelleriegargantua.com), where traditional French food is complemented by a peaceful terrace in the midst of the city walls and rooftops. Main courses run 12€ to 16€ ($15.60–$20.80); it's closed Wednesday.

The château is open April to September daily 9am to 5:45pm and October to March 9am to 4:45pm. For horse enthusiasts, there are shows presented on the grounds from May to September at 11:45am and/or 4:30pm. Admission is 8.50€ to 9.50€ ($11.05–$12.35) for adults, 6.50€ to 7.50€ ($8.45–$9.75) for ages 18 to 25, and free for children 17 and under. Allow 1½ hours to go through the château.

CHENONCEAUX

Only 16 miles (26km) east of Tours is the tiny village of Chenonceaux, home to the fairy-tale-like château, Chenonceau (notice the missing "x").

GETTING THERE   There are 8 daily **trains** from Tours to Chenonceaux (trip time: 30 min.), costing 5.70€ ($7.40) one-way. The train deposits you at the base of the château.

VISITOR INFORMATION   The **Syndicat d'Initiative** (tourist office), 1 rue Bretonneau (*©* **02-47-23-94-45**), is open from Easter to September daily 10am to 1pm and 2 to 6:30pm (off season, open until 5pm and closed Sun).

TOP ATTRACTIONS & SPECIAL MOMENTS

The Renaissance masterpiece **Château de Chenonceau** ✸✸✸ (*©* **02-47-23-90-07;** www.chenonceau.com) is known for the series of famous *dames de Chenonceau* who occupied it. François I seized the château in 1524 from a wealthy Tours family and in 1547, Henri II gave Chenonceau to his mistress, Diane de Poitiers, who was 20 years his senior. For a time, this remarkable woman was virtually the queen of France. But when Henri died in a jousting tournament in 1559, his jealous wife, Catherine de Médici, became regent of France and immediately forced Diane de Poitiers to abandon her beloved Chenonceau in exchange for Chaumont (see below). Catherine added her own touches to the château, building a two-story gallery across the bridge—obviously inspired by her native Florence. The long gallery running along the Cher River contains a black-and-white diamond floor.

It was at Chenonceau that Catherine received a pair of teenage honeymooners: her son, François II, and his bride, Mary Stuart (aka Mary, Queen of Scots). And it was here, in the 18th century, that Rousseau declared his undying love for the mistress of the château, Madame Dupin, the grandmother of George Sand, and was promptly rebuffed.

Many of the château's walls today are covered with Gobelin tapestries, including one depicting a woman pouring water over the back of an angry dragon, another of a

Moments   **Nature & Art in Chaumont-sur-Loire**

Travelers interested in nature merged with art should be sure to visit Chaumont-sur-Loire. The rail station for the town is Onzain (© **02-54-20-72-15**); it's an 8-minute train ride from Blois, and 30 minutes from Tours. On the grounds of the Château de Chaumont is an annual **Festival International des Jardins** (© **02-54-20-99-22**; www.chaumont-jardins.com; late Apr to mid-Oct), where an average of 30 fabulous outdoor garden exhibits are created by artists, students, architects, engineers, and designers from around the world. Admission is 9€ ($11.70) adults, 6.50€ ($8.45) students, 3.50€ ($4.55) for ages 6 to 10, and free for ages 6 and under.

The **Château de Chaumont** ☆☆ (© **02-54-51-26-26**) was built next to the Loire River during the reign of Louis XII by Charles d'Amboise. The original fortress was dismantled by Louis XI, and in 1560 Chaumont was acquired by Catherine de Médici and then became the home (by force) of Diane Poitiers, mistress of Henry II. The château was later privately owned until it was taken over by the state in 1938. It is one of the Loire Valley's most well-known castles but is currently being renovated. Some rooms and the stables are still open to the public (admission is free during renovation), so they are also worth a visit if you're in Chaumont-Sur-Loire for the garden festival. Call or check the website of the **Office de Tourisme,** 24 rue du Maréchal-Leclerc (© **02-54-20-91-73**; www.chaumontsurloire.info) for updates. *Note:* It's a long uphill trek to the château from the rail station.

three-headed dog and a seven-headed monster. The chapel contains a delicate marble Virgin and Child, plus portraits of Catherine de Médici in her traditional black and white. There's even a portrait of the stern Catherine in the former bedroom of her rival, Diane de Poitiers. But in the Renaissance-style bedchamber of François I, the most interesting portrait is that of Diane de Poitiers as the huntress Diana, complete with a sling of arrows on her back. *The Three Graces* are by Van Loo. The château opens daily at 9am from April to November and at 9:30am the rest of the year. There are various closing times: November 5 to February 9 at 5pm; February 10 to March 15 and October 28 to November 4 at 6pm; October 1 to 27 at 6:30pm; March 16 to May 31 at 7pm; January 1 to 30 and September 1 to 30 at 7:30pm; and July 1 to August 31 at 8pm. Admission is 9.50€ ($12.35) for adults and 7.50€ ($9.75) for students and children 7 to 18. Allow 2 hours to see this château.

4 Provence & the Riviera

The French Riviera, known to the world as the fashionable Côte d'Azur, is actually part of the greater region of sunny Provence that sweeps across the southern tier of France—it's an easy train ride from Paris.

Provence has its own language and customs. The region is bounded on the north by the Dauphine, the west by the Rhône, the east by the Alps, and the south by the Mediterranean. In this section we cover the northern area of this region, what's traditionally thought of as Provence (and whose most evocative cities include **Avignon,**

Avignon

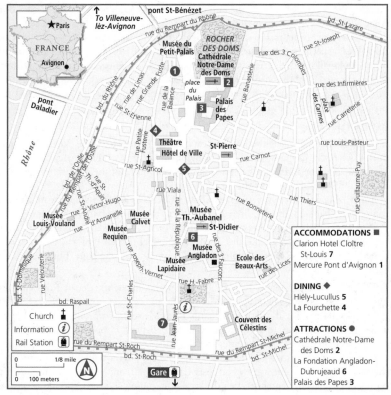

ACCOMMODATIONS ■
Clarion Hotel Cloître
St-Louis 7
Mercure Pont d'Avignon 1

DINING ◆
Hiély-Lucullus 5
La Fourchette 4

ATTRACTIONS ●
Cathédrale Notre-Dame
des Doms 2
La Fondation Angladon-
Dubrujeaud 6
Palais des Papes 3

Aix-en-Provence, and **Arles**), and then head down to the French Riviera and its two grandest resorts, **Cannes** and **Nice**—from which you can easily visit the principality of **Monaco.** The good news for rail travelers is that no matter what section you choose, you'll have very few problems getting around by train.

Of course, easy rail access isn't necessarily the big draw in this region. The weather isn't bad either. The winter temperature is higher in the Riviera than the rest of France, mainly because of the Alpine chain that protects the Côte d'Azur from cold, continental winds. The Riviera's high season used to be winter and spring only. However, with changing tastes, July and August have become the most crowded months, and reservations are imperative. The average summer temperature is 75°F (24°C); the average winter temperature, 49°F (10°C). If you can, we recommend coming here in May or October when crowds thin, prices drop, but the weather remains lovely, giving you exactly what the travel posters promise.

Another compelling trait of the Riviera is the incredible number of artists who are/were drawn to its shores and hillside villas, leaving behind a rich legacy. At Cagnes, Renoir praised the "light effects" of the region. Matisse chose Nice in which to spend the last years of his life (you can visit his remarkable museum there and his Chapelle du Rosaire in Vence). Cocteau decorated a chapel for the fishermen of Villefranche.

Picasso left an art legacy from one end of the Riviera to the other, as did Cezanne in Aix-en-Provence, and van Gogh in Arles.

Many visitors come to Provence specifically to dine, so do try some of the region's specialties, especially the *salade niçoise,* which essentially includes fresh vine-ripened tomatoes, small radishes, green peppers, potatoes, and green beans. The thick, saffron-flavored fish soup of the Mediterranean, the *bouillabaisse,* is eagerly ordered by diners, as is *ratatouille* (a mixture of small eggplants, tomatoes, miniature squash, and red peppers simmered in olive oil).

AVIGNON ✦✦✦

In the 14th century, Avignon was the capital of Christendom; the popes lived here during what the Romans called "the Babylonian Captivity." The legacy left by that "court of splendor and magnificence" makes Avignon one of the most interesting and beautiful of Europe's cities of the Middle Ages.

Today, this walled city of some 100,000 residents is a major stopover on the rail route from Paris to the Mediterranean and is the transportation hub for inland Provence. It is increasingly known as a cultural center. Artists and painters have been moving here, especially to rue des Teinturiers. Experimental theaters, galleries, and cinemas have brought diversity to the city. The popes are long gone, but life goes on exceedingly well.

GETTING THERE   From Paris, TGV Med trains frequently depart from Gare de Lyon, the trip taking 2 hours and 35 minutes. A one-way fare costs 76.80€ to 80.15€ ($99.85–$104). Trains also arrive frequently from Marseilles (trip time: 35 min.), with a ticket costing 21.30€ to 25.60€ ($27.70–$33.30); and from Arles the SNCF runs nine buses (trip time: 45 min.), with a fare of 7.50€ ($9.75). For train information and reservations, check out **www.raileurope.com**. The TGV train station has a shuttle bus, the *navette,* which runs frequently and costs 1.10€ ($1.70) one-way. The 10-minute trip terminates in the city center between the local train station and the Office de Tourisme.

VISITOR INFORMATION   The **Office de Tourisme** is at 41 cours Jean-Jaurès (© **04-32-74-32-74;** www.avignon-tourisme.fr), about 600 feet (180m) north of the train station. Off-season (Nov–Mar) hours are Monday to Friday 9am to 6pm, Saturday 9am to 5pm, and Sunday 10am to noon. Summer (Apr 2–Oct 31) hours are Monday to Saturday 9am to 6pm and Sunday 10am to 5pm. During the month of July, hours are extended to 7pm Monday to Saturday. This office does not reserve hotel rooms. Here you can also pick up "Avignon Passion," a pass that gives you a discounted rate for most of the attractions.

TOP ATTRACTIONS & SPECIAL MOMENTS

Even more famous than the papal residency is the ditty *"Sur le pont d'Avignon, l'on y danse, l'on y danse,"* echoing through every French nursery and around the world. Ironically, **pont St-Bénézet** ✦✦ was far too narrow for the *danse* of the rhyme. Spanning the Rhône and connecting Avignon with Villeneuve-lèz-Avignon, the bridge is now a ruin, with only 4 of its original 22 arches. According to legend, it was inspired by a vision that a shepherd named Bénézet had while tending his flock. The bridge was built between 1177 and 1185 and suffered various disasters from then on. (In 1669, half the bridge fell into the river.) On one of the piers is the **Chapelle St-Nicolas**—one story in Romanesque style, the other in Gothic. The remains of the bridge are open daily (times and dates are same as Palais des Papes, listed below). Admission (includes a free audio guide) is 4€ ($5.20) for adults and 3€ ($3.90) for students and seniors, free for ages 7 and under.

The **Palais des Papes** ᛘᛘᛘ, 6 rue Pente Rapide (© **04-90-27-50-00**), dominates Avignon. In 1309, a sick man, nearing the end of his life, arrived in Avignon. His name was Clement V, and he was the leader of the Christian world. Lodged as a guest of the Dominicans, he died in the spring of 1314 and was succeeded by John XXII. The new pope lived modestly in the Episcopal Palace. When Benedict XII took over, he greatly enlarged and rebuilt the palace. Clement VI, who followed, built an even more elaborate extension, the New Palace. After Innocent VI and Urban V, Pope Gregory XI did no building. Inspired by Catherine of Siena, he was intent upon returning the papacy to Rome, and he succeeded. In all, seven popes reigned at Avignon. Under them art and culture flourished, as did vice. Prostitutes blatantly went about peddling their wares in front of fat cardinals, rich merchants were robbed, and innocent pilgrims from the hinterlands were brutally swindled.

From 1378, during the Great Schism, one pope ruled in Avignon, another in Rome. The reign of the pope and the "anti-pope" continued, one following the other, until both rulers were dismissed by the election of Martin V in 1417. Rome continued to rule Avignon until it was joined to France during the French Revolution.

You're shown through the palace today on a guided 50-minute tour, taking in the Chapelle St-Jean, known for its 14th-century frescoes, and the Grand Tinel or banquet hall, about 135 feet long (41km). The pope's bedroom is on the second floor of the Tour des Anges, and other attractions include the Great Audience Hall containing frescoes attributed to Giovanetti and painted in 1352.

Admission (including a tour with a guide or cassette recording) is 9.50€ ($12.35) adults, 7.50€ ($9.75) students and seniors, free for ages 7 and under. It is 11.50€ ($14.95) for a combination ticket to the palace and the bridge. Hours are daily November 2 to March 14 from 9:30am to 5:45pm; March 15 to March 31 from 9:30am to 6:30pm; April 1 to June 30 and September 16 to November 1 from 9am to 7pm; July and September 1 to 15 from 9am to 8pm; and in August 9am to 9pm. The on-site **Musée du Petit Palais** contains an important collection of paintings from the Italian schools from the 13th through the 16th centuries, including works from Florence, Venice, Sienna, and Lombardy. In addition, salons display Roman and Gothic sculptures and 15th-century paintings created in Avignon.

The ramparts (still standing) around Avignon were built in the 14th century, and are characterized by their machicolated battlements, turrets, and old gates. The fortifications were rebuilt in the 19th century by Viollet-le-Duc, the busiest man in France, who also restored Notre-Dame in Paris and the fortified walls at Carcassonne.

Admission is 6€ ($7.80) adults and 3€ ($3.90) for students. Hours are Wednesday to Monday October to May 9:30am to 1pm and 2 to 5:30pm; June to September 10am to 1pm and 2 to 6pm. Nearby is **Cathédrale Notre-Dame des Doms,** place du Palais (© **04-90-86-81-01**), dating from the 12th century and containing the flamboyant Gothic tomb of John XXII, who died at the age of 90. Benedict XII is also buried there. Crowning the top is a gilded statue of the Virgin from the 19th century. From the cathedral, you can enter the **Promenade du Rocher des Doms,** strolling through its garden and enjoying the view across the Rhône to Villeneuve-lés-Avignon. Admission is free. Hours vary according to religious ceremonies, but are generally daily 9am to noon and 2 to 6pm.

It's been decades since the death of Jacques Doucet (1853–1929), the Belle Epoque dandy, dilettante, and designer of Parisian haute couture, but his magnificent art collection is on view to the general public at **La Fondation Angladon-Dubrujeaud** ★★, 5 rue Laboureur (© **04-90-82-29-03;** www.angladon.com). When not designing, Doucet collected the early works of a number of artists, among them Picasso, Max Jacob, and van Gogh. Today, you can wander through Doucet's former abode, viewing rare antiques; 16th-century Buddhas; Louis XVI chairs designed by Jacob; and canvases by Cézanne, Sisley, Degas, and Modigliani. Doucet died in 1929 at 76, his fortune so diminished that his nephew paid for his funeral, but his rich legacy lives on here. Admission is 6€ ($7.80) adults, 4€ ($5.20) students and teens 15 to 18, 1.50€ ($1.95) children 7 to 14, free for children under 7. Hours are Tuesday to Sunday April to November 1 to 6pm; Wednesday to Sunday (same hours) the rest of the year; open 3 to 6pm on holidays.

WHERE TO STAY & DINE

Not far from the rail station, the 80-room **Clarion Hotel Cloître St-Louis** ★, 20 rue Portail Boquier, 84000 Avignon (© **800/CLARION** in the U.S., or 04-90-27-55-55; www.cloitre-saint-louis.com), is housed in a former Jesuit school built in the 1580s. While public areas retain many original features, the bedrooms are more functional. Their decor is rather dull and severe; some overlook a patio. A newer wing, designed by world-class architect Jean Nouvel, has been added, and its rooms feature sleek modern lines. Rates are 145€ to 200€ ($189–$260) double; 300€ ($390) suite.

Mercure Pont d'Avignon, quartier de la Balance, rue Ferruce, 84000 Avignon (© **04-90-80-93-93;** www.mercure.com), is one of the best in Avignon, and is a good value for what it offers. The 87 midsize bedrooms are well maintained and simply though comfortably furnished, with small bathrooms. It lies within the city walls, at the foot of the Palace of the Popes. Rates are 90€ to 135€ ($117–$176) double; 200€ ($260) suite.

Hiély-Lucullus ★★, 5 rue de la République (© **04-90-86-17-07;** www.hiely lucullus.com), is a supremely good Relais Gourmand in Avignon. The owner/chef and his wife, Hervé, and Judith Mina, offer reasonable fixed-price menus—the best in town. The pièce de résistance is *cote de veau* (veal chop). Fixed-price menu prices are 38€ to 83€ ($49.40–$108). Reservations are required. It's open daily, noon to 2pm and 7:30 to 9:30pm.

La Fourchette, 17 rue Racine (© **04-90-85-20-93;** bus: 11), offers creative French cooking at a moderate price, although it shuts down on the weekends. The dining rooms are light and airy thanks to large windows. For a main course, we recommend the filet of daurade with shellfish sauce or daube of beef with a gratin of macaroni. Fixed-price lunches are 25€ to 27€ ($32.50–$35.10) and dinners cost 31€ ($40.30). Hours are Monday to Friday 12:15 to 1:45pm and 7:15 to 9:45pm.

ARLES ★★★

It's been called "the soul of Provence," though it was known as "the little Rome of the Gauls" when Constantine the Great named it the second capital in his empire in A.D. 306. Art lovers, archaeologists, and historians have all been attracted to this town on the Rhône. Many of its scenes, painted so luminously by van Gogh in his declining years, remain to delight. The great Dutch painter left Paris for Arles in 1888—same year that he cut off part of his left ear. But here he painted some of his most celebrated works, including *Starry Night, The Bridge at Arles, Sunflowers,* and *L'Arlésienne.*

Befitting its glorious past, Arles is still well connected—by rail that is. It's linked to both Paris and Avignon (where you usually need to change trains to get here) by high-speed lines and also offers connections to other cities in Provence.

GETTING THERE **Trains** leave from Paris's Gare de Lyon and arrive at Arles's **Gare SNCF** (av. Paulin-Talabot), a short walk from the town center. Two high-speed direct TGV trains travel from Paris to Arles each day (trip time: 4 hr.; 69.20€–99.60€/$89.95–$129). For other trains, you must change in Avignon. There are nine bus connections run by the SNCF between Arles and Avignon (trip time: 45 min.) with a fare of 7.50€ ($9.75); from Marseille (trip time: 49 min; 12.70€–15€/ $16.50–$19.50); and Aix-en-Provence (trip time: 1½ hr. with a stop in Marseille; 19€–21€/$24.70–$27.30). For rail schedules and information, check out **www.rail europe.com**.

VISITOR INFORMATION The **Office de Tourisme,** where you can buy a *billet global* (see below), is on the boulevard des Lices (© **04-90-18-41-20;** www.arles tourisme.com). Hours are April 1 to September 30 daily 9am to 6:45pm; October 1 to December 31 and January 2 to March 31 Monday to Saturday 9am to 4:45pm and Sunday 10am to 1pm.

TOP ATTRACTIONS & SPECIAL MOMENTS

At the tourist office (see "Essentials," earlier in this chapter), buy a *billet global* ✦, a combination pass that admits you to the town's museums, Roman monuments, and major attractions, at a cost of 13.50€ ($17.55) for adults and 12€ ($15.60) students 12 to 18, free for children 11 and under.

The town is full of Roman monuments. The general vicinity of the old Roman forum is occupied by **place du Forum,** shaded by plane trees. Once, the Café de Nuit, immortalized by van Gogh, stood on this square. Two Corinthian columns and pediment fragments from a temple can be seen at the corner of the Hôtel Nord-Pinus. South of here is **place de la République** (also known as the place de l'Hôtel de Ville), the principal plaza, dominated by a 50-foot (15m) blue porphyry obelisk. On the north is the impressive Hôtel-de-Ville (town hall) from 1673, built to Mansart's plans and surmounted by a Renaissance belfry.

One of the city's great classical monuments is the Roman **Théâtre Antique** ✦✦, rue de la Calade (© **04-90-49-36-25**). Begun by Augustus in the 1st century, only two Corinthian columns remain. The theater was where the *Venus of Arles* was discovered in 1651. Take rue de la Calade from city hall. The theater is open daily, as follows: November to February from 10 to 11:30am and 2 to 4:30pm; March, April, and October from 9 to 11:30am and 2 to 5:30pm; and May to September from 9am to 6pm. Admission costs 3€ ($3.90) for adults, 2.20€ ($2.85) for students and ages 12 to 18. It's free for children under 12.

Nearby is the **Amphithéâtre (Les Arènes Romaines)** ✦✦, rond-point des Arènes (© **04-90-49-36-86**), also built in the 1st century. It seats almost 25,000 and still hosts bullfights in summer. Be careful as the stone steps are uneven, and much of the masonry is worn. For a good view, you can climb the three towers that remain from medieval times, when the amphitheater was turned into a fortress. Hours are daily as follows: November to February 10am to 4:30pm; March, April, and October 9am to 11:30am and 2pm to 5:30pm; and May to September 9am to noon and 2 to 6pm. Admission costs 5.50€ ($71.50) for adults, 4.50€ ($5.85) for students and persons age 12 to 18, free for ages 11 and under. The ticket also includes entrance into the

Thermes de Constantin, the roman public baths that are a 10-minute-walk from the amphitheater.

Perhaps the most memorable sight in Arles, **Les Alyscamps** ✿, rue Pierre-Renaudel (© **04-90-49-36-87**), was once a necropolis established by the Romans. After being converted into a Christian burial ground in the 4th century, it became a setting for legends and was even mentioned in Dante's *Inferno.* Today, it's lined with poplars and the remaining sarcophagi. Admission is 3.50€ ($4.55) adults, 2.60€ ($3.40) ages 12 to 18, free for ages 12 and under. Hours are November to February 10am to 11:30am and 2pm to 4:30pm; March, April, and October 9 to 11:30am and 2 to 5:30pm; and May to September 9am to 6pm.

Half a mile (.8km) south of the town center, you'll find the **Musée de l'Arles et de la Provence antiques** ✿✿, Presqu'île du Cirque Romain (© **04-90-18-88-88**), with an incredible collection of Roman Christian sarcophagi, plus a rich ensemble of sculptures, mosaics, and inscriptions from the Augustinian period to the 6th century A.D. Eleven detailed models show ancient monuments of the region as they existed in the past. Admission is 5.50€ ($7.15) adults, 4€ ($5.20) students, and free for children 18 and under. Hours are April 1 to October 31 daily 9am to 7pm; November 1 to March 31 daily 10am to 5pm.

Museon Arlaten ✿, 29 rue de la République (© **04-90-93-58-11**), was founded by poet Frédéric Mistral, leader of a movement to establish modern Provençal as a literary language using the money from his Nobel Prize for literature in 1904. This is a folklore museum, with regional costumes, portraits, furniture, dolls, a music salon, and one room devoted to mementos of Mistral. Among its curiosities is a letter (in French) from Theodore Roosevelt to Mistral, bearing the letterhead of the Maison Blanche in Washington, D.C. Admission is 1€ ($5.20) adults; and free for children 18 and under. Hours are Tuesday to Sunday September, April, and May 9:30am to 12:30pm and 2 to 6pm; October to March 9:30am to noon and 2 to 4:30pm; and daily June to August daily 9:30am to 1pm and 2 to 6pm.

WHERE TO STAY & DINE

Because of its reasonable rates, **Hôtel Calendal** ✿, 5 rue Porte de Laure, 13200 Arles (© **04-90-96-11-89;** www.lecalendal.com), is a bargain hunter's favorite. On a quiet square near the arena, this 38-unit hotel offers rooms with bright colors, high ceilings, and a sense of spaciousness. Most have views of the hotel's peaceful garden, where guests can read a book or enjoy breakfast under the palm trees. Rates run 49€ to 119€ ($63.70–$155) double.

Hôtel d'Arlatan ✿✿, 26 rue du Sauvage, 13631 Arles (© **04-90-93-56-66;** www.hotel-arlatan.fr), the former residence of the comtes d'Arlatan de Beaumont, has been managed by the same family since 1920. It was built in the 15th century on the ruins of an old palace begun by Emperor Constantine. Rooms are furnished with authentic Provençal antiques and walls covered by tapestries. Rates are 85€ to 175€ ($111–$228) double; 195€ to 245€ ($254–$319) suite.

A few steps from the arena, **Le Bout du Monde,** 49 rue des Arènes (© **04-90-96-68-59**), offers unique cuisine and a relaxed setting at reasonable prices. It's outfitted with a decor inspired by India but with a European twist. The seasonally changing menu items include dishes from France, Thailand, Vietnam, and India, with an emphasis on curries and such French staples as a pâté of foie gras (made in-house). Main courses run 12€ to 19€ ($15.60–$24.70).

Moments **A Trip to the Market**

While in Provence, be sure to experience the magic of wandering through a bustling **marché** (market). On certain days (check with the tourism office—it depends on the season) in Arles, the boulevard des Lices is filled with seemingly endless market stalls brimming with fruits, vegetables, cheeses, olives, honey, breads, clothing, antiques, pottery, lavender, flowers, and more. The market can take up an entire morning—and you will end up with enough goodies for a great picnic lunch!

Lou Marquès ✿✿, at the Hôtel Jules-César, 9 bd. Des Lices (© **04-90-52-52-52**), part of a luxury hotel, has the highest reputation in town for its creative twists on Provençal specialties. As a main course, try *papeton d'aubergine* (a Mediterranean eggplant dish) or *steak du toro* (beef steak with a rich *Chateau Neuf du Pape* red wine sauce). Main courses (change seasonally) run 26€ to 33€ ($33.80–$42.90); fixed-price menus run 21€ to 28€ ($27.30–$36.40) at lunch, from 40€ to 60€ ($52–$78) at dinner.

AIX-EN-PROVENCE ✿✿✿

The celebrated son of this old capital city of Provence, Paul Cézanne, immortalized the countryside nearby. Just as he saw it, Montagne Sainte-Victoire still looms over the town, although a string of high-rises have now cropped up on the landscape. The most charming center in all of Provence, this faded university town was once a seat of the aristocracy, its streets walked by counts and kings. Aix still has much of the atmosphere it acquired in the 17th and 18th centuries before losing its prestige to Marseille, 20 miles (32km) to the south.

GETTING THERE   The city is easily accessible, with frequent buses (trip time: 50–70 min) from Marseilles replacing trains during the reconstruction until December 2008. A newer train station designed for the high-speed TGV Med trains is at Vitroll, 9 miles (5.5km) to the west of Aix. There are 15-minute-long bus *(navette)* links, costing 3.70€ ($4.80) one-way, from Vitroll into the center of Aix. For more information, call © **08-92-35-35-35.**

VISITOR INFORMATION   The **Office de Tourisme** is at 2 place du Général-de-Gaulle (© **04-42-16-11-61;** www.aixenprovencetourism.com). To get here from the train station, stroll up avenue Victor-Hugo (bearing left) and you'll eventually see it on your left. The office will reserve hotel rooms for you at no charge. Hours are Monday to Saturday 8:30am to 7pm (open until 8pm in June and until 9pm July–Aug) and Sunday 10am to 1pm and 2 to 6pm (until 8pm July–Aug).

TOP ATTRACTIONS & SPECIAL MOMENTS

Aix's main street, **cours Mirabeau** ✿✿, is one of Europe's most beautiful. Plane trees stretch their branches across the top like an umbrella, shading it from the hot Provençal sun and filtering the light into shadows that play on the rococo fountains below. Shops and sidewalk cafes line one side of the street; sandstone *hôtels particuliers* (mansions) from the 17th and 18th centuries fill the other. The street begins at the 1860 fountain on place de la Libération, which honors Mirabeau, the revolutionary and statesman.

Moments **Aix through the Eyes of Cézanne**

The best experience in Aix is a walk along the *route de Cézanne* (D17), which winds eastward through the countryside toward Ste-Victoire. From the east end of cours Mirabeau, take rue du Maréchal-Joffre across boulevard Carnot to boulevard des Poilus, which becomes avenue des Ecoles-Militaires and finally D17. The stretch between Aix and the hamlet of Le Tholonet is full of twists and turns where Cézanne often set up his easel to paint. The entire route is a lovely 3½-mile (5.5km) stroll. Le Tholonet has a cafe or two where you can refresh yourself while waiting for one of the frequent buses back to Aix.

Cézanne was the major forerunner of Cubism. **Atelier de Cézanne,** 9 av. Paul-Cézanne (outside town; ✆ **04-42-21-06-53**), surrounded by a wall and restored by American admirers, is where he worked. Admission is 5.50€ ($7.15) adults, 2€ ($2.60) students, and free for children ages 13 and under. Hours are daily January to March 10am to noon and 2pm to 5pm; April to June daily 10am to noon and 2 to 6pm; July to September 9, 10am to 6pm; September 10 to 30, 10am to noon and 2 to 6pm; October to December 10am to noon, 2 to 5pm. Reservations required (must be made at Office de Tourisme).

Cathédrale St-Sauveur ✿, place des Martyrs de la Résistance (✆ **04-42-23-45-65**), is dedicated to Christ under the title St-Sauveur (Holy Savior or Redeemer). Its baptistery dates from the 4th and 5th centuries, but the complex as a whole has seen many additions. It contains a 15th-century Nicolas Froment triptych, *The Burning Bush.* Masses are conducted every Sunday at 10am, and 7pm. Admission is free and hours are daily 8am to noon and 2 to 6pm. There are daily tours of the cloisters (except Sun) every half hour from 10am to 11:30am and 2:30 to 5pm.

Three series of tapestries from the 17th and 18th centuries line the gilded walls of **Musée des Tapisseries** ✿, 28 place des Martyrs de la Résistance (✆ **04-42-23-09-91**), a former archbishop's palace. *The History of Don Quixote,* by Natoire; *The Russian Games,* by Leprince; and *The Grotesques,* by Monnoyer were paintings collected by archbishops to decorate the palace. Admission is 2.50€ ($3.25) adults, free for ages 25 and under. Hours are Wednesday to Monday 10am to 6pm.

WHERE TO STAY & DINE

Grand Hôtel Nègre Coste, 33 cours Mirabeau, 13100 Aix-en-Provence (✆ **04-42-27-74-22;** www.hotelnegrecoste.com), a former 18th-century town house, is popular with the dozens of musicians who flock to Aix for the summer festivals. The higher floors of this 37-room hotel overlook cours Mirabeau and the old city. The soundproof rooms contain interesting antiques and good bathrooms. Room rates are 75€ to 145€ ($97.50–$189) double and 180€ ($234) for an apartment for five.

Not everything is state of the art, but to many, **Hôtel Cardinal,** 24 rue Cardinale (✆ **04-42-38-32-30**), is still the best value in Aix. Guests stay in the 30 simply furnished rooms either in the main building or in the high-ceilinged 18th-century annex up the street, site of most of the hotel's suites. Bathrooms tend to be small but good. Rates are 69€ ($89.70) double; 105€ ($137) suite.

Antoine Côté Cour, 19 cours Mirabeau (✆ **04-42-93-12-51**), is in an 18th-century town house a few steps from place Rotonde. A simple wine, such as Côtes-du-

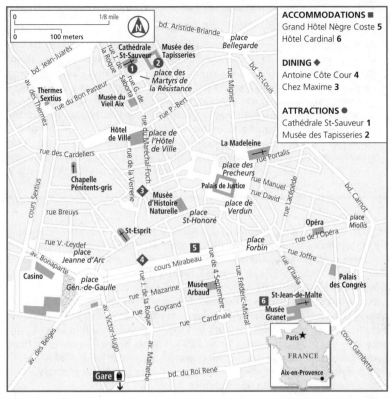

Aix-en-Provence

ACCOMMODATIONS ■
Grand Hôtel Nègre Coste **5**
Hôtel Cardinal **6**

DINING ◆
Antoine Côte Cour **4**
Chez Maxime **3**

ATTRACTIONS ●
Cathédrale St-Sauveur **1**
Musée des Tapisseries **2**

Rhône, goes nicely with the hearty Mediterranean fare, which might include a memorable pasta Romano flavored with calves' liver, cèpes (flap mushrooms), and tomato sauce; ravioli with goat cheese; *osso buco;* or at least half a dozen kinds of fresh fish. The bulk of the menu is composed of grilled fish, grilled meats, and pastas. Main courses run 12€ to 26€ ($15.60–$33.80).

Chez Maxime, 12 place Ramus (© **04-42-26-28-51;** www.restaurantchezmaxime. com), located in the pedestrian zone, reflects the skills and personality of its new owner, Madame Monnier, who replaced longtime manager Felix Maxime. Specialties include as many as 19 kinds of grilled meat or fish, cooked over an oak-burning fire. The wine list features more than 500 vintages, including many esoteric bottles from the region. Main courses run 12€ to 23€ ($15.60–$29.90); fixed-price menus 12€ to 30€ ($15.60–$39) lunch, 18.50€ to 33.80€ ($24.05–$43.95) dinner.

CANNES ✸✸✸

Popular with celebrities, Cannes is at its most frenzied during the **International Film Festival** at the **Palais des Festivals** on the promenade de la Croisette. Held in May, it attracts not only film stars but those with similar aspirations. On the seafront boulevards flashbulbs pop as the starlets emerge, pose, and set new trends. International

Moments Celebrity-Watching in Cannes

At the end of May, the **International Film Festival** is held at the Palais des Festivals on promenade de la Croisette. It attracts not only film stars, but seemingly every photographer in the world. You've got a better chance of being named prime minister of France than you do of attending one of the major screenings. (Hotel rooms and tables at restaurants are equally scarce during the festival.) But the people-watching is fabulous. If you find yourself here at the right time, you can join the thousands of others who line up in front of the Palais des Festivals, aka "the bunker," where the premieres are held. With paparazzi shouting and gendarmes holding back the fans, the guests parade along the red carpet, stopping for a moment to strike a pose and chat with a journalist. *C'est Cannes!*

regattas, galas, *concours d'élégance,* even a Mimosa Festival in February—something is always happening at Cannes, except in November, which is traditionally a dead month.

Sixteen miles (26km) southwest of Nice, Cannes is sheltered by hills. It is said that the Prince of Wales (before he became Edward VII) contributed to its original cost. But he was a Johnny-come-lately to Cannes. Setting out for Nice in 1834, Lord Brougham, a lord chancellor of England, was turned away because of an outbreak of cholera. He landed at Cannes and liked it so much he decided to build a villa there. Returning every winter until his death in 1868, he proselytized it in London, drawing a long line of British visitors. In the 1890s, Cannes became popular with Russian grand dukes (it is said more caviar was consumed there than in all of Moscow). One French writer claimed that when the Russians returned as refugees in the 1920s, they were given the garbage-collection franchise.

A port of call for cruise liners, the seafront of Cannes is lined with hotels, apartment houses, and chic boutiques. Many of the bigger hotels, some dating from the 19th century, claim part of the beaches for the private use of their guests, though there are public areas.

GETTING THERE   Cannes is connected to Nice, Paris, and the rest of France by rail. **Trains** arrive frequently throughout the day. Cannes is only 11 minutes by train from Antibes and only 30 minutes from Nice. The TGV from Paris via Marseille makes stops at Cannes, taking 5 hours and costing 108€ ($141). For rail information, check out **www.raileurope.com**.

In case you want to fly into Nice and begin your rail journey on the Riviera, the **Nice International Airport** (© 08-20-42-33-33) is a 20-minute drive northeast of Cannes. **Buses** pick up passengers at the airport about every 30 minutes during the day, delivering them in Cannes to the rail station, **Gare Routière,** place de l'Hôtel de Ville (© 04-93-39-11-39).

VISITOR INFORMATION   The **Office de Tourisme** is in the Palais des Festivals, esplanade Georges-Pompidou (© 04-92-99-84-22; www.cannes.fr), a short walk along the quays, which parallel the edge of the harbor, from the railway station (there is a smaller office next to the train station). Hours are daily 9am to 7pm (until 8pm July–Aug). The office can reserve a hotel room for you.

Cannes

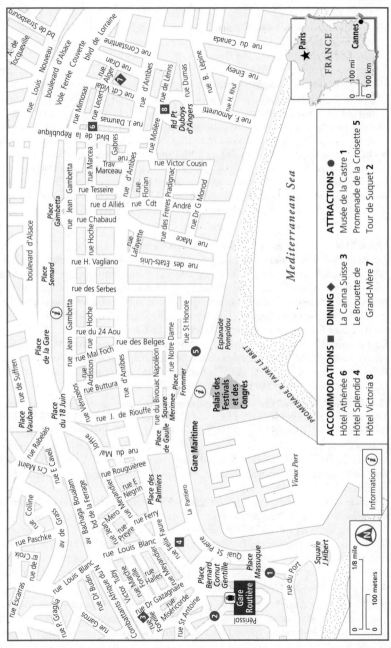

ATTRACTIONS ●
Musée de la Castre **1**
Promenade de la Croisette **5**
Tour de Suquet **2**

DINING ◆
La Canna Suisse **3**
Le Brouette de
Grand-Mère **7**

ACCOMMODATIONS ■
Hôtel Athénée **6**
Hôtel Splendid **4**
Hôtel Victoria **8**

Information ⓘ

Mediterranean Sea

FRANCE
Paris ★
Cannes
0   100 mi
0   100 km

TOP ATTRACTIONS & SPECIAL MOMENTS

Cannes is sheltered by hills. For many visitors, it might as well consist of only one street, **promenade de la Croisette** ★★ (or just La Croisette), curving along the coast and split by islands of palms and flowers.

Above the harbor, the old town of Cannes sits on Suquet Hill, where you'll see the 14th-century **Tour de Suquet,** which the English dubbed the Lord's Tower.

Nearby is the **Musée de la Castre** ★, in the Château de la Castre, Le Suquet (© 04-93-38-55-26), devoted to ethnography that includes objects from all over the world: from the Pacific islands to Southeast Asia to Peruvian and Mayan pottery to relics of Mediterranean civilizations, from the Greeks to the Romans, and the Cypriots to the Egyptians. Five rooms display 19th-century paintings. The museum is open Tuesday to Sunday: April to June, and September 10am to 1pm and 2 to 6pm, October to March 10am to 1pm and 2 to 5pm, and daily June to August 10am to 7pm (until 9pm Wed night June–Sept). Admission is 3.20€ ($4.15), 2€ ($2.60) for ages 25 and under, free for students 26 and under, children 18 and under, and on the first Sunday of each month.

FERRYING TO THE ILES DE LERINS ★★

Across the bay from Cannes, the Lérins Islands are the most interesting excursion from the port. Ferryboats depart at 30-minute intervals throughout the day, beginning at 9am (though some early-bird boats depart at 7:30am) and lasting until 5pm. Return boats begin at noon and end service at 6pm—make sure you're on time or you'll be stranded until the next morning. The largest of the ferryboat companies in Cannes is **Compagnies Estérel-Chanteclair** (© 04-93-39-11-82), but other contenders include **Compagnie Maritime Cannoise** (© 04-93-38-66-33); and **Trans-Côte d'Azur** (© 04-92-98-71-30). Departures are from the Gare Maritime des Iles, 06400 Cannes. Round-trip passage costs 11€ ($13) per adult, 9€ ($11.70) for students, and 5.50€ ($7.15) for children 5 to 10, free for children under 5.

ILE STE-MARGUERITE   This island was named after St-Honorat's sister, Ste-Marguerite, who lived here with a group of nuns in the 5th century. Today it is a youth center whose members (when they aren't sailing and diving) are dedicated to the restoration of the fort. From the dock, you can stroll along the island (signs point the way) to the Fort de l'Ile, built by Spanish troops from 1635 to 1637. Below is the 1st-century B.C. Roman town where the *Man in the Iron Mask* was imprisoned. You can visit his cell.

Musée de la Mer, Fort Royal (© 04-93-38-55-26), traces the history of the island, displaying artifacts of Ligurian, Roman, and Arab civilizations, plus the remains discovered by excavations, including paintings, mosaics, and ceramics. It's open daily October to March 10:30am to 1:15pm and 2:15pm to 4:45pm; April to May 10:30am to 1:15pm and 2:15 to 5:45pm; June to September 10am to 5:45pm. Admission is 3.20€ ($4.15) for adults, 2€ ($2.60) for reduced tickets and free for students, children ages 18 and under, and on the first Sunday of each month.

ILE ST-HONORAT ★★   Only a mile (1.6km) long, but richer in history than its sibling islands, Ile St-Honorat is the site of a monastery whose origins go back to the 5th century. Today, **Abbaye de Notre Dame de Lérins** ★, Ile St-Honorat, 06406 Cannes (© 04-92-99-54-00; www.abbayedelerins.com), boasts a combination of medieval ruins and early-20th-century ecclesiastical buildings, and a community of about 30 Cistercian monks. Under controlled circumstances, if space is available, well-intentioned outsiders can visit and spend the night, but only for prayer and meditation. Most visitors opt to avoid the monastery, wandering through the pine forests on the island's western side, and sunbathing on its beaches.

WHERE TO STAY & DINE

Note: During major festivals in Cannes, hotels often increase their rates significantly and reservations can be difficult to obtain.

On a quiet street about 4 blocks from the seafront, **Hôtel Athénée,** 6 rue Lecerf (*©* **04-93-38-69-54;** www.athenee.fr), occupies the second floor of a four-story building constructed in the 1970s. The 15 bedrooms are well maintained, furnished unpretentiously but comfortably, and are relatively affordable in high-priced Cannes. Rates are 70€ to 90€ ($91–$117) double; 250€ to 400€ ($325–$520) per week for studio apartment (2–3 persons). The 64-room **Hotel Splendid** ⋇, 4 and 6 rue Félix-Faure (*©* **04-97-06-22-22;** www.spledid-hotel-cannes.fr), is an ornate white building with wrought-iron accents looking out onto the sea, the old port, and a park. The rooms boast antique furniture and paintings; about half have kitchenettes. It's a favorite of actors, musicians, and politicians. Rates are 124€ to 244€ ($161–$317) double; 214€ to 264€ ($278–$343) apartment in the attic (no balcony).

Hôtel Victoria ⋇, rond-point Duboys-d'Angers (*©* **04-92-59-40-00;** www.hotel-victoria-cannes.com), a stylish modern hotel (recently renovated) in the heart of Cannes, offers accommodations with period reproductions and refrigerators. Nearly half of the 25 rooms have balconies overlooking the small park and the hotel pool (worth the extra cost). Rates are 105€ to 290€ ($137–$338) double. Closed November 18 to December 29. No rooms are available to the public during festivals (check website for exact dates).

Two sisters own **La Canna Suisse** ⋇, 23 rue Forville (le Suquet; *©* **04-93-99-01-27;** www.cannasuisse.com), a 33-year-old restaurant in Vieux Cannes that's decked out like a Swiss chalet and which specializes in the cheese-based cuisine of Switzerland's Alps. The menu features only two kinds of fondue—a traditional version concocted from six kinds of cheese and served in a bubbling pot with chunks of bread on skewers, plus another that adds either morels or cèpes to the blend, depending on your wishes. Main courses run 16€ to 24€ ($20.80–$31.20).

Few other restaurants in Cannes work so successfully at establishing a cozy testimonial to the culinary skills of old-fashioned French cooking as **La Brouette de Grand-Mère,** 9 bis rue d'Oran (*©* **04-93-39-12-10**). Owner Didier has taken over from father, Christian Bruno, who revitalized the recipes that many of the chic and trendy residents of Cannes remember from their childhood (or from an idealized version of their childhood). Memories are evoked in a way that Proust might have appreciated through seasonally changing dishes that might include *les cailles rôties à la niçoise* (roasted quail served with a niçoise sauce), and *magret de canard aux griottes* (duck filet with morello cherries). A fixed-price menu, including half a bottle of wine is 35€ ($45.50).

CANNES AFTER DARK

Palm Beach Casino, place F.D.-Roosevelt (58 bd. de la Croisette; *©* **04-97-06-36-90;** www.lepalmbeach.com), lies on the southeast edge of La Croisette. The casino maintains slot machines that operate daily from 11am to 5am (4am in the winter); plus suites of rooms devoted to *les grands jeux* (blackjack, roulette, and baccarat) that are open nightly 8pm to 5am (4am in the winter). The cover charge is 11€ ($14.30) for access to les grands jeux, where presentation of a passport or an identity card is required.

An English-speaker's oasis is **Morrison's Irish Pub,** 10 rue Teisseire (© **04-92-98-16-17;** www.morrisonspub.com), which offers live music, an international crowd, and big-screen TVs for soccer, golf, and rugby fans. Prices here are a welcome relief from the usual wallet-emptying costs of Cannes; there's even a happy hour from 5 to 8pm. Sunday is Ladies' Night. Expect lots of French girls and some American students. Live music plays Wednesday, Thursday, and Sunday nights. Hours are daily from 5pm to 2:30am.

NICE ✮✮✮

The Victorian upper class and czarist aristocrats loved Nice in the 19th century, but it is solidly middle class today. In fact, of all the major resorts of France, from Deauville to Biarritz to Cannes, Nice is the least expensive. It is also the best excursion center on the Riviera and has the best rail connections.

Nice is the capital of the Riviera, the largest city between Genoa and Marseille (also one of the most ancient, having been founded by the Greeks, who called it "Nike," or victory). Because of its brilliant sunshine and relaxed living, artists and writers have been attracted to Nice for years. Among them were Matisse, Dumas, Nietzsche, Appollinaire, Flaubert, Victor Hugo, Guy de Maupassant, George Sand, Stendhal, Chateaubriand, and Mistral.

GETTING THERE Trains arrive at **Gare Nice-Ville,** avenue Thiers. From here you can ride to Cannes, Monaco, and Antibes, with easy connections to anywhere else along the Mediterranean coast. There's a small-scale tourist center (© **08-92-70-74-07**) at the train station, open mid-September to mid-June, Monday to Saturday 8am to 7pm, and Sunday 10am to 5pm. In the summer, hours are Monday to Saturday 8am to 8pm and Sunday 9am to 7pm. The staff makes hotel reservations at no charge. If you face a long delay, you can eat at the cafeteria and even take showers at the station (or head to the beach—10 min. away).

Transatlantic and intercontinental flights land at **Aéroport Nice–Côte d'Azur** (© **08-20-42-33-33**). From here, municipal bus no. 98 departs at 20-minute intervals from the airport for Nice's bus station, Gare Routière, charging 4€ ($5.20) per person (day pass). To return to the airport, the no. 98 leaves at 20 and 40 minutes past the hour from Gare Routière. Bus no. 99 goes from the airport to the train station; bus no. 23 leaves from Gare Routière every 15 minutes and costs 1.30€ ($1.70), but only goes to/from terminal 1 (there is a free shuttle waiting at terminal 1 to take passengers to terminal 2). A somewhat more luxurious mode of transport involves a specially conceived yellow-sided shuttle bus *(la navette de l'aéroport)* that also charges 4€ ($5.20) for a ride between the airport and Nice's train station. A **taxi** ride from the airport to the station will cost at least 26€ to 32€ ($33.80–$41.60) each way (ask the price before getting in the taxi). Trip time is about 30 minutes.

VISITOR INFORMATION Of the city's three tourist offices, the largest and most central is at 5 promenade des Anglais (© **08-92-70-74-07;** www.nicetourism.com), near place Masséna (about a ¾-mile/1.2km walk from the train station). The staff can make a same-day hotel reservation at no charge. Hours are June to September, Monday to Saturday 8am to 8pm, Sunday 9am to 7pm; October to March Monday to Saturday 9am to 6pm.

GETTING AROUND Most of the local bus routes in Nice connect with one another at their central hub, the **Station Central,** 10 av. Félix-Faure (© **04-93-13-53-13**), a very

Nice

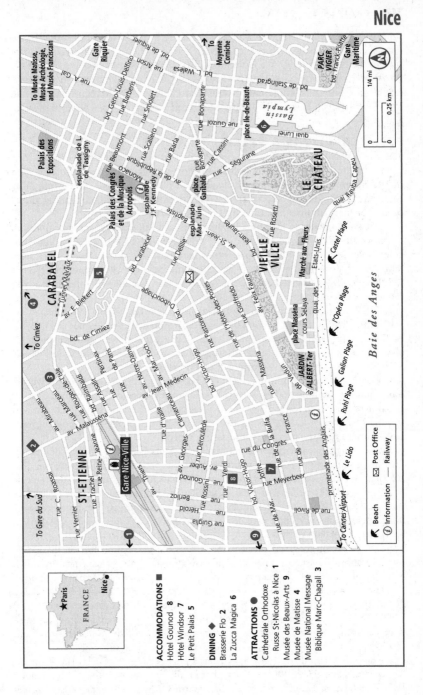

ACCOMMODATIONS ■
Hôtel Gounod **8**
Hôtel Windsor **7**
Le Petit Palais **5**

DINING ◆
Brasserie Flo **2**
La Zucca Magica **6**

ATTRACTIONS ●
Cathédrale Orthodoxe
Russe St-Nicolas à Nice **1**
Musée des Beaux-Arts **9**
Musée de Matisse **4**
Musée National Message
Biblique Marc-Chagall **3**

FRANCE
★Paris
Nice ●

Baie des Anges

LE CHÂTEAU

VIEILLE VILLE

CARABACEL

ST-ETIENNE

Gare Nice-Ville

Gare Riquier

Gare Maritime

PARC VIGIER

Bassin Lympia

Palais des Expositions

Palais des Congrès et de la Musique Acropolis

place Garibaldi

place Masséna

JARDIN ALBERT-1er

place Île-de-Beauté

esplanade J.F. Kennedy

esplanade Mar. Juin

esplanade de L. de Tassigny

To Musée Matisse, Musée Archéologie, and Musée Franciscain

To Moyenne Corniche

To Cimiez

To Gare du Sud

To Cannes Airport

Marché aux Fleurs

Castel Plage
l'Opéra Plage
Galion Plage
Ruhl Plage
Le Lido

promenade des Anglais

quai des États-Unis
cours Saleya
quai des

quai Lunel
quai Rauba Capeu

bd. de Stalingrad
bd. France-Pilatte

bd. L. Walesa
rue Arson
rue de Riquier
rue A. Gal
bd. Geno-Louis-Delfino
rue Barberis
rue Smolett
rue Bonaparte
rue Cassini
rue C. Ségurane
rue Rosetti
av. St-Jean-Jean-Jaurès
av. Félix Faure
rue Giofredo
rue de l'Hôtel-des-postes
rue Pastorelli
bd. Dubouchage
bd. Carabacel
rue Delille
bd. Malraux
av. E. Bieckert
bd. de Cimiez
av. Notre-Dame
av. Jean Médecin
rue de France
rue de
rue du Congrès
rue de la Buffa
av. de Verdun
av. Georges-Clemenceau
rue d'Italie
rue de Paris
rue Pertinax
rue Assalit
rue Raimbaldi
bd. Jean-Jaurès
rue Rossetti
rue Guiglia
rue de Mar.
rue de Rivoli
rue Meyerbeer
rue Joffre
Joffre
rue Masséna
bd. Victor-Hugo
av. Georges-Déroulède
av. Auber
av. Verdi
av. Gounod
av. Berlioz
av. Rossini
av. Hérold
rue Trachel
rue Reine-Jeanne
rue Vernier
rue C. Roassal
av. Mirabeau
av. de la République
av. Malaussena
av. Thiers
av. Mar-Foch
rue de Beaumont
rue Scaliero
rue Barla
rue Bonaparte
rue Guizot
rue Smolett
rue de Monaco
Tunnel Malraux

Baie des Anges

⚓ Beach ⊠ Post Office
ⓘ Information — Railway

1/4 mi
0.25 km

311

short walk from place Masséna. Municipal buses each charge 1.30€ ($1.70). To save money, consider buying a 10-ticket *carnet* for 10€ ($13). Bus no. 98 makes frequent trips to the beach. In 2007 the city introduced a brand new **tram system** (② 08-11-00-20-06); line 1 is from Las planas to Pont Michel. You can use the tram to reach popular areas of Nice such as the train station (Gare Thiers), Place Masséna, and the Old town (Vieille Ville). Each ride is 1.30€ ($1.70) and includes transfers between the tram and bus.

TOP ATTRACTIONS & SPECIAL MOMENTS

There's a higher density of museums in Nice than in many comparable French cities. If you decide to skip the beach and devote your time to visiting seven of the most impressive museums in the south of France, you can buy a **Carte Passe-Musée** that costs 6€ ($7.80) for 7 days. You can buy it at any of the museums or from the tourist office. For more information, call ② 04-97-03-82-20.

If you would prefer to tour on a hop-on, hop-off bus (with an open-air top deck), try **Gray Line's "Nice Le Grand Tour"** (② 04-92-29-17-00; www.grayline.com) around the city sights. Buses depart from the promenade des Anglais (across from Jardin Albert 1er—Albert Gardens) every 30 minutes from 9:30am and cost 17.70€ ($23) for a 1-day pass and 20€ ($26) for a 2-day pass. The tour is 1½ hours, but you can get on and off at any of the stops all day.

In 1822, the orange crop at Nice was bad and the workers faced a lean time. So the English residents put them to work building the **promenade des Anglais** ⚸⚸, a wide boulevard fronting the bay, split by "islands" of palms and flowers and stretching for about 4 miles (6.5km). Fronting the beach are rows of grand cafes, the Musée Masséna, villas, and hotels—some good, others decaying.

Crossing this boulevard in the briefest of bikinis or thongs are some of the world's most attractive bronzed bodies. They're heading for the **beach**—"on the rocks," as it's called here. Tough on tender feet, the beach is made not of sand but of pebbles (and not-too-small ones). It's one of the least attractive aspects of the cosmopolitan resort city. Many bathhouses provide mattresses for a fee.

In the east, the promenade becomes **quai des Etats-Unis,** the original boulevard, lined with some of the best restaurants in Nice, all specializing in bouillabaisse. Rising sharply on a rock is the site known as **Le Château,** the spot where the ducs de Savoie built their castle, torn down in 1706. The hill has been turned into a garden of pines and exotic flowers. To reach the site for the view, you can take an elevator for .80€ ($1.05) one-way (and walk down) or 1.10€ ($1.45) round-trip. The park is open daily from 8am to dusk.

At the north end of Le Château is the famous old **graveyard** of Nice, the largest one in France. It's visited primarily for its lavish monuments, which form their own enduring art statement. To reach it, you can take a small, canopied **Train Touristique de Nice** (② 06-16-39-53-51), which departs from the Jardin Albert-1er. It makes a 40-minute sightseeing transit past many of Nice's most heralded sites leaving every 30 to 60 minutes daily from 10am to 5pm (until 6pm Apr–May and Sept–Dec, until 7pm June–Aug). There's no service between mid-November and mid-December and during most of January. The price is 6.50€ ($7.80) per person.

Cathédrale Orthodoxe Russe St-Nicolas à Nice ⚸, avenue Nicolas-II (off bd. du Tzaréwitch; ② 04-93-96-88-02), was ordered built by none other than Czar Nicholas II. This is the most beautiful religious edifice of the Orthodoxy outside Russia. It dates from the Belle Epoque, when some of the Romanovs and their entourage turned the

Finds **Secrets of Nice**

British expatriate Patricia Fortune has lived in Nice since 2001. Enthusiastic, welcoming, and extremely helpful, she offers small "themed" tours under the categories of "mystery," "anticipation," and "pleasure." Her tours give you a chance to experience Nice at a local level; discovering hidden gems of the city—off the tourist path. Tours last 4 hours and accommodate two to six people. They cost 45€ ($23.40) per person, which includes a refreshing coffee/tea break and lunch. For more information contact Patricia directly at **envelopetours@orange.fr**.

Riviera into their own stomping ground. Admission is 3€ ($3.90) adults, 2€ ($2.60) students, free for children under 12. Hours are May to September daily 9am to noon and 2:30 to 6pm; October 9:15am to noon and 2:30 to 5:30pm; November 1 to February 15 9:30am to noon and 2:30 to 5pm; February 16 to April 30 9:15am to noon and 2:30pm to 5:30pm. Celebration of the Russian Orthodox liturgy occurs every Sunday at 10am (open to public for worship only). From the central rail station, head west along avenue Thiers to boulevard Gambetta; then go north to avenue Nicolas-II.

The villa housing the **Musée des Beaux-Arts** *&&*, 33 av. des Baumettes (© 04-92-15-28-28), was built in 1878 for the Ukrainian Princess Kotschoubey. The city of Nice has converted the villa into a museum of local history and decorative art. The first-floor gallery exhibits Niçoise primitives and masterpieces—paintings, sculptures, plates, and jewelry decorated with enamel (Limoges)—from the 15th to the 18th centuries. On the second floor are 19th-century collections devoted to sculptures, portraits, impressionists, and post-impressionists, including works by Monet, Rodin, and Viullard, as well as rooms featuring the history of Nice (and local artist Raoul Dufy). Admission is 4€ ($5.20) adults, 2.50€ ($3.25) students; free for children ages 18 and under. Hours are Tuesday to Sunday 10am to 6pm.

In the hills of Cimiez above Nice, the single-story **Musée National Message Biblique Marc-Chagall** *&&*, avenue du Dr.-Ménard (© 04-93-53-87-20; www.musee-chagall.fr), cannot be missed! It is devoted to Marc Chagall's treatment of biblical themes. Born in Russia in 1887, Chagall became a French citizen in 1937. The artist and his wife donated the works—the most important collection of Chagall ever assembled—to France in 1966 and 1972. Displayed are 450 of his vibrant oil paintings, gouaches, drawings, pastels, lithographs, sculptures, ceramics, a mosaic, three stained-glass windows, and a tapestry. Admission is 6.50€ ($8.45) adults, 4.50€ ($5.85) students, free for children under 18. Hours are Wednesday to Monday 10am to 5pm (open until 6pm July–Sept). To get to Cimiez: catch bus no. 15 on rue Gioffredo next to place Masséna (it costs 1.30€/$1.70). There is a free shuttle between the museum and the Matisse museum (ask at front desk).

While in Cimiez, visit the charming **Musée de Matisse** *&&*, 164, av. des Arènes de Cimiez (© 04-93-81-08-08; www.musee-matisse-nice.org). The 17th-century Genoese villa is filled with an impressive collection of Henri Matisse's drawings, sculptures, and paintings done from 1890 to 1953 (including sketches/models for his Chapelle du Rosaire in Vence). Admission is 4€ ($5.20) adults, 2.50€ ($3.25) students, and free for children ages 18 and under. Hours are Wednesday to Monday, 10am to 6pm. *Tip:* Across from the museum are the gardens of the Cimiez monastery, which offer a great view of Nice.

WHERE TO STAY & DINE

The 46-room **Hôtel Gounod** ⚔, 3 rue Gounod (© **04-93-16-42-00;** www.gounod-nice.com), is situated in the city center, a 5-minute walk from the sea. The high-ceilinged guest rooms are comfortable and quiet, usually overlooking the gardens of private homes. There aren't many amenities, but guests have free unlimited use of the pool and Jacuzzi at the Hôtel Splendid next door. Rates are 105€ to 145€ ($137–$189) double; 140€ to 250€ ($182–$325) suite.

The 57-room **Hôtel Windsor** ⚔, 11 rue Dalpozzo (© **04-93-88-59-35;** www.hotel windsornice.com), one of the most arts-conscious hotels in Provence, is set within a *maison bourgeoise* (near the Negresco and the promenade des Anglais), built by disciples of Gustav Eiffel in 1895. Inside, you'll find an artsy ambience and comfortable, individually furnished bedrooms. A one-of-a-kind series of frescoes adorns each of the midsize guest rooms. In the back is a quaint patio with parrots, a small pool, and an abundance of tropical flora. Rates are 105€ to 140€ ($137–$182) double.

The 25-room **Le Petit Palais** ⚔, 17 av. Emile-Bieckert, 06000 Nice (© **04-93-62-19-11;** www.hotel-petit-palais.com), occupies a mansion built around 1890; in the 1970s it was the home of the actor and writer Sacha Guitry, a name that's instantly recognized in millions of French households. The preferred rooms—the most expensive—have balconies offering sea views during the day and sunset-watching at dusk. Rooms are Art Deco and Italianate in style; the shower-only bathrooms are small. Rates are 85€ to 170€ ($111–$221) double.

Housed in a restored turn-of-the-20th-century building near place Masséna, **Brasserie Flo,** 2–4 rue Sacha-Guitry (© **04-93-13-38-38**), is brisk, stylish, reasonably priced, and fun. The seasonal menu items might include an array of grilled fish, *choucroute* (sauerkraut) Alsatian style, steak with brandied pepper sauce, and fresh oysters and shellfish. Main courses run 15€ to 29€ ($19.50–$52.40); fixed-price menus at lunch (not available on Sun) run 14.50€ ($18.85); at dinner they cost 22.50€ ($29.25) and 34.50€ ($44.85), including half a bottle of wine.

The chef at **La Zucca Magica (The Magic Pumpkin)** ⚔, 4 bis quai Papacino (© **04-93-56-25-27**), is the best Italian chef in Nice. Chef Marco serves refined vegetarian cuisine at reasonable prices, using recipes from Italy's Piedmont region and updating them with no meat or fish. Be warned that this is not your typical restaurant: There is no written menu, and everything is served here as part of a set-price "menu surprise." Four courses, plus a dessert, will be brought to your table unannounced and unheralded, but because everything is fresh and tasty, nobody leaves disappointed. Set menus cost 19€ ($24.70) at lunch, 29€ ($37.70) at dinner. Closed Sunday and Monday.

NICE AFTER DARK

OPERA The major cultural center on the Riviera is the **Opéra de Nice,** 4 and 6 rue St-François-de-Paule (© **04-92-17-40-00;** www.opera-nice.org), built in 1885 by Charles Garnier, fabled architect of the Paris Opéra. A full repertoire is presented, with emphasis on serious, often large-scale operas as well as concerts and recitals. In one season you might see *Tosca, Les Contes de Hoffmann,* Verdi's *Macbeth,* Beethoven's *Fidelio,* and *Carmen,* as well as a *saison symphonique,* dominated by the Orchestre Philharmonique de Nice. Tickets are available up to about a day or two prior to any performance. You can show up at the box office (Mon–Thurs, Sat 9am–5:45pm; Fri 9am–8pm; closed Sun) or buy tickets in advance by phoning © **04-92-17-40-79.**

Tickets run from 8€ ($10.40) for nosebleed (and we mean it) seats to 85€ ($111) for front-and-center seats on opening night.

Cabaret du Casino Ruhl, in the Casino Ruhl, 1 promenade des Anglais (© **04-97-03-12-77**), is Nice's answer to the cabaret glitter that appears in more ostentatious forms in Monte Carlo and Las Vegas. It includes a medley of cross-cultural jokes and nostalgia for the old days of French *chanson.* The cover of 16€ ($20.80) includes the first drink; dinner and the show (plus a bottle of wine) costs 65€ ($84.50). Shows are presented every Friday and Saturday at 10:30pm; dinners begin at 8pm. No jeans or sneakers.

AN EXCURSION TO ST-PAUL-DE-VENCE ✿✿

Of all the perched hill towns of the Riviera, St-Paul-de-Vence, 19 miles (31km) north of Nice, is the best known. It was popularized in the 1920s when many noted artists and writers (including Henri Matisse, Marc Chagall—buried in the local cemetery, and expat James Baldwin) lived here, occupying the little 16th-century houses that flank the narrow cobblestone streets. The hill town was originally built to protect its inhabitants from Saracens raiding the coast. The feudal hamlet grew up on a bastion of rock, almost blending into it. Its ramparts (allow 30 min. to encircle them) overlook a peaceful setting of flowers and olive and orange trees. As you make your way through the warren of streets you'll pass endless souvenir shops, art galleries, a charming old fountain carved in the form of an urn, and a Gothic church from the 13th century.

GETTING THERE   The nearest rail station is in Cagnes-sur-Mer, from which buses depart every 45 minutes for St-Paul-de-Vence. Rail passengers who arrive in Nice usually rent a car or opt for 1 of about 20 buses a day (bus no. 400), departing from Gare Routière, near the Nice railway station (trip time: 1 hr.). For bus information, call **Cie SAP** (© **04-93-58-37-60**). Buses stop in St-Paul near the post office, on the route de Vence, about ¼ mile (.4km) from the town center. Bus fare is 1.30€ ($1.70) one-way.

VISITOR INFORMATION   The **Office de Tourisme,** 2 rue Grande (© **04-93-32-86-95;** www.saint-pauldevence.com), is open June to September daily 10am to 7pm; October to May daily 10am to 6pm. It's closed year-round between 1 and 2pm.

TOP ATTRACTIONS & SPECIAL MOMENTS

Foundation Maeght ✿✿✿, outside the town walls (© **04-93-32-81-63**), is the most important attraction in St-Paul. On the slope of a hill in pine-studded woods, the Maeght Foundation is like a Shangri-la. Not only is the architecture daringly avant-garde (designed by José Luis Sert), but the building itself houses one of the finest collections of contemporary art on the Riviera.

Calder and Miró's stark sculptures welcome visitors from the grassy lawns. In a courtyard, the elongated bronze works of Giacometti form a surrealistic garden, creating a hallucinatory mood. The museum is built on several levels, its many glass walls providing an indoor-outdoor vista. Everywhere you look, you'll see 20th-century art: mosaics by Chagall and Braque, Miró ceramics in the "labyrinth," and Ubac and Braque stained glass in the chapel. Bonnard, Kandinsky, Léger, Matisse, Hepworth, and many other artists are well represented. Scattered throughout are cheerful photographs, newspaper clippings, and videos—all reflecting happy times; it feels as if Aimé and Marguerite Maeght and the many artists who touched their lives are still very much present in this peaceful space.

The foundation, a gift "to the people" from the Maeghts, also provides a showcase for new talent. Exhibitions are always changing.

Admission is 11€ ($14.30) adults, 9€ ($11.70) students and ages 10 to 25, free for children ages 10 and under. Hours are July to September daily 10am to 7pm; October to June daily 10am to 12:30pm and 2:30 to 6pm.

AN EXCURSION TO VENCE ★★

Travel up into the hills northwest of Nice—across country studded with cypresses, olive trees, and pines, where bright flowers, especially carnations, roses, and oleanders, grow in profusion—and Vence comes into view. Outside the town, along boulevard Paul-André, two old olive presses carry on with their age-old duties. But the charm lies in the **Vieille Ville (Old Town).**

GETTING THERE   It's easier to reach Vence by bus than by train. Frequent **buses** (no. 94 direct or 400, which stops in St-Paul-de-Vence, 5 min. away) originating in Nice take about an hour to reach Vence, and cost 1.30€ ($1.70) each way. For bus information, contact the **Compagnie SAP** at ✆ 04-93-58-37-60 for schedules. The nearest **rail station** is in Cagnes-sur-Mer, about 4½ miles (7km) from Vence. For rail info, call ✆ 08-92-35-35-35.

VISITOR INFORMATION   The **Office de Tourisme** is on 8 place Grand-Jardin (✆ 04-93-58-06-38; www.vence.fr/-Tourism-Office-.html). It's open June to August Monday to Sunday 9am to 7pm; September to May 9am to 6pm.

TOP ATTRACTIONS & SPECIAL MOMENTS

Visitors invariably have themselves photographed on **place du Peyra** in front of the urn-shaped **Vieille Fontaine (Old Fountain),** a background shot in several motion pictures. The 15th-century **square tower** is also a curiosity.

If you're wearing the right kind of shoes, the narrow, steep streets of the old town are worth exploring. Dating from the 10th century, the **cathedral** on place Godeau is unremarkable except for some 15th-century Gothic choir stalls. But if it's the right day of the week, most visitors quickly journey 15 minutes north of Vence's city center to the Chapelle du Rosaire.

The **Chapelle du Rosaire** ★★, avenue Henri-Matisse (✆ 04-93-58-03-26), was built by the great Henri Matisse at age 77. After a turbulent personal search, the artist set out to create "the culmination of a whole life dedicated to the search for truth." Just outside Vence, Matisse created a Chapel of the Rosary for the Dominican nuns of Monteils, who continue to administer it today.

Matisse wrote: "What I have done in the chapel is to create a religious space . . . in an enclosed area of very reduced proportions and to give it, solely by the play of colors and lines, the dimensions of infinity." The light picks up the subtle coloring in the simply rendered leaf forms and abstract patterns: sapphire-blue, aquamarine, and lemon-yellow. In black-and-white ceramics, St. Dominic is depicted in only a few lines. The most remarkable design is the black-and-white-tiled Stations of the Cross with Matisse's self-styled "tormented and passionate" figures. The bishop of Nice came to bless the chapel in the late spring of 1951 and, his masterpiece completed, Matisse died 3 years later.

Admission is 2.80€ ($3.65) adults, 1.50€ ($1.95) kids 16 and under; contributions to maintain the chapel are welcomed. Hours are Tuesday and Thursday 10 to 11:30am and 2 to 5:30pm; Monday, Wednesday, and Saturday 2 to 5:30pm. Sunday Mass is at 10am, followed by visit at 10:45am. Closed Friday, and November 15 to December 15.

> ### *Finds* For Art Lovers
>
> To witness an artist's life and work in process, visit the **N.A.L.L Art Association** (Nature Art and Life League), 232 bd. de Lattre, Vence (© **04-93-58-13-26** or 06-19-22-46-01; www.nall.org), a hidden gem. In 1997 American artist Nall, and his wife, Tuscia, purchased 9 acres (3.6 hectares) of land in Vence's serene valley. Today they run a small museum and offer apprenticeships to young artists. Inspired by Dalí, Dures, Bellmer, and Seraphim, Nall's own mosaics combine collected materials from around the world with watercolors, creating vibrant, thought-provoking, and spiritual images. The association is a 10-minute walk from the no. 400 bus stop (follow the signs). Tours last 1 hour and cost 5€ ($6.50) per person on weekends and 10€ ($13) per person on weekdays. Reservations are required in advance.

WHERE TO DINE

If you, like most rail passengers, visit both St-Paul-De-Vence and Vence in a single day, one of the best and most affordable places for lunch (noon–2pm) in the area is in Vence.

La Farigoule, 15 rue Henri-Isnard (© **04-93-58-01-27**), is set within a century-old house in Vence that opens onto a rose garden, where tables are set out during summer. This restaurant specializes in Provençal cuisine, including an array of dishes that feature a *bourride Provençal* (a bouillabaisse with a dollop of cream and lots of garlic), or a shoulder of roasted lamb with a ragout of fresh vegetables, served with fresh thyme. The fixed-price menu runs 25€ ($32.50) at lunch, and 29.50€ to 39.50€ ($38.35–$51.35) at dinner. Closed for lunch on Wednesday and Saturday, and all day Tuesday.

AN EXCURSION TO MONACO ✦✦✦

The outspoken Katharine Hepburn called it "a pimple on the chin of the south of France." She wasn't referring to the principality's lack of beauty, but rather to the preposterous idea of having a little country, a feudal anomaly, taking up some of the choicest coastline along the Riviera. Hemmed in by France on three sides and facing the Mediterranean, Monaco staunchly maintains its independence. Even Charles de Gaulle couldn't force the late Prince Rainier to do away with his tax-free policy (Monegasques do not pay taxes).

Monaco, or rather its capital of Monte Carlo, has for a century been a symbol of glamour. Its legend was further enhanced by the marriage in 1956 of the world's most eligible bachelor, Prince Rainier, to an American film star, Grace Kelly. She met the prince when she attended the Cannes Film Festival to promote the Hitchcock movie she made with Cary Grant, *To Catch a Thief.* Following the death of his father in 2005, Prince Albert II became the ruler of the principality.

Monaco became property of the Grimaldi clan, a Genoese family, as early as 1297. With shifting loyalties, it has maintained something resembling independence ever since. In a fit of impatience, the French annexed it in 1793, but the ruling family recovered it in 1814, although the prince at the time couldn't bear to tear himself away from the pleasures of Paris for "dreary old Monaco."

The second-smallest state in Europe (Vatican City is first), Monaco consists of the old town, **Monaco-Ville,** sitting on a promontory, the Rock, 200 feet high (60m)—the seat of the royal palace and the government building, as well as the famous Oceanographic Museum (see below). On the west of the bay, **La Condamine,** the home of the Monegasques, is at the foot of the old town, forming its harbor and port sector.

Up from the port (walking is steep in Monaco) is **Monte Carlo,** once the playground of European royalty and still the center for the wintering wealthy, the setting for the casino and its gardens and the deluxe hotels, such as the Hôtel de Paris. The fourth part of Monaco, **Fontvieille,** is an industrial suburb, surprisingly neat; but this entire principality is kept tidy.

Ironically, **Monte Carlo Beach,** at the far frontier, is on French soil. It attracts a chic, well-heeled crowd, including movie stars. The resort consists of a freshwater swimming pool, an artificial beach, and sea-bathing establishment.

GETTING THERE Monaco has rail connections to other coastal cities. There are 48 from Nice, only 20 minutes away for 3€ ($3.90). **Trains** arrive from Cannes, Menton, and Antibes. For more rail information and schedules, call ✆ **08-92-35-35-35.** Monaco's railway station (Gare SNCF) is on avenue Prince Pierre. It's a long steep walk uphill from the train station to Monte Carlo. If you'd rather take a **taxi** but can't find one at the station, call ✆ **93-15-01-01;** the ride into town will cost about 10€ ($13).There are no border formalities for anyone entering Monaco from mainland France. If there is a train strike at the time of your visit, you can take the no. 100 bus from Nice for 1.30€ ($1.70).

VISITOR INFORMATION The **Direction du Tourisme** office is in Monte Carlo at 2A bd. des Moulins (✆ **92-16-61-16;** www.monaco-tourisme.com). They do not reserve rooms for visitors. Hours are Monday to Saturday 9am to 7pm and Sunday 10am to noon. *Note:* November 19 is Monaco's National Day and most museums and attractions are closed.

TOP ATTRACTIONS & SPECIAL MOMENTS

During summer, most day-trippers from Nice head to **Les Grands Appartements du Palais** ✿, place du Palais (✆ **93-25-18-31**), wanting to see the home of Monaco's royal family, the Palais du Prince, which dominates the principality from "the Rock." A tour of the Grands Appartements allows you a glimpse of the Throne Room and some of the art (including works by Bruegel and Holbein), as well as the late Princess Grace's state portrait. The palace was built in the 13th century, and part of it dates from the Renaissance. The ideal time to arrive is 11:55am to watch the 10-minute **Relève de la Garde (Changing of the Guard).**

In a wing of the palace, the **Musée du Palais du Prince (Souvenirs Napoléoniens et Collection d'Archives),** place du Palais (✆ **93-25-18-31**), has a collection of mementos of Napoléon and Monaco itself. When the royal residence is closed, this museum is the only part of the palace the public can visit.

A single ticket to the Grands Apartments costs 7€ ($9.10) for adults, 3.50€ ($4.55) for children aged 8 to 14 and students. A single to the Musée du Palais is 4€ ($5.20) for adults, 2€ ($2.60) for children aged 8 to 14 and students. A combination ticket is 9€ ($11.70) for adults, 4.50€ ($5.85) children 8 to 14, free for children ages 8 and under. Grands Apartments hours are April daily 10:30am to 6pm; May to September 9:30am to 6:30pm; October 10am to 5:30pm. Museum hours are June to

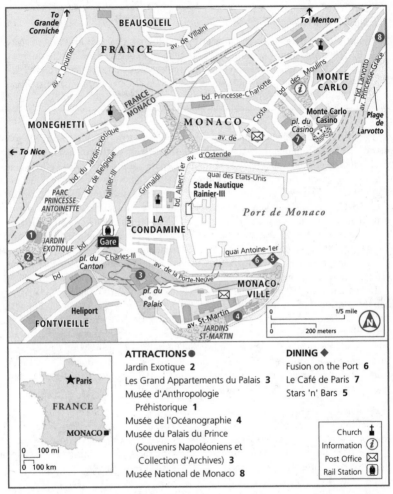

Monaco

ATTRACTIONS ●
Jardin Exotique **2**
Les Grand Appartements du Palais **3**
Musée d'Anthropologie
    Préhistorique **1**
Musée de l'Océanographie **4**
Musée du Palais du Prince
    (Souvenirs Napoléoniens et
    Collection d'Archives) **3**
Musée National de Monaco **8**

DINING ◆
Fusion on the Port **6**
Le Café de Paris **7**
Stars 'n' Bars **5**

Church ✝
Information ⓘ
Post Office ✉
Rail Station 🚉

September daily 9:30am to 6:30pm; October daily 10am to 5:30pm; December 1 to March 31 10:30am to 5pm. Closed December 25, January 1, and all of November.

Built on the side of a rock, the **Jardin Exotique** ✹✹, 62 bd. du Jardin-Exotique (© **93-15-29-80**), is known for its cactus collection, which was begun by Prince Albert I, who was a naturalist and scientist, and great-great-grandfather to the present prince. He spotted some succulents growing in the palace gardens and created this garden from them. You can also explore the grottoes here, as well as the **Musée d'Anthropologie Préhistorique** (© **93-15-80-06**). The view of the principality is splendid. Admission to garden and museum costs 6.90€ ($9) adults, 5.30€ seniors ($6.90), 3.60€ ($4.70) students and children 6 to 18, free for children under 6. It's open mid-May to mid-September daily 9am to 7pm; mid-September to mid-May daily 9am to 6pm or until sunset, whichever comes first.

Finds   **Fabulous & Fake**

Bijoux Marlene, Les Galeries du Metropole, 207 av. des Spélugues (© **93-50-17-57**), sells only imitation gemstones. They're shamelessly copied from the real McCoys sold by Cartier and Van Cleef & Arpels. Made in Italy of gold-plated silver, the fake jewelry (the staff refers to it as *Les Bijoux Fantaisies*) costs from 20€ ($26) to 700€ ($910) per piece.

The **Musée de l'Océanographie** ✿✿, avenue St-Martin (© **93-15-36-00**; www.oceano.mc), was founded in 1910 by Albert I. In the main rotunda is a statue of Albert in his favorite costume: that of a sea captain. Displayed are specimens he collected during 30 years of expeditions. The aquarium, one of the finest in Europe, contains more than 90 tanks. Some of the exotic creatures you'll see were unknown before he captured them. Skeletons of specimens are located on the main floor, including a whale that drifted ashore at Pietra Ligure in 1896. The skeleton is remarkable for its healed fractures, sustained when a vessel struck the animal as it was drifting on the surface. Admission is 12.50€ ($16.25) adults, 6€ ($7.80) students and children 6 to 18, free for children under 6. Hours are daily January to March and October to December 10am to 6pm; April to June, and September 9:30am to 7pm; July to August 9:30am to 7:30pm.

In a villa designed by Charles Garnier (architect of Paris's Opéra Garnier), the **Musée National de Monaco** ✿ 17 av. Princesse-Grace (© **98-98-91-26**; www.nmnm.mc), stems from an 18th- and 19th-century trend to create magnificent displays of antique mechanical toys and dolls. See the 18th-century Neapolitan crib, which contains some 200 figures. This collection, assembled by Mme de Galea, was presented to the principality in 1972. Admission is 6€ ($7.80) adults, 3.50€ ($4.55) students and children 6 to 14, free for children under 6. Open daily 10am to 6pm. Closed January 1, May 1, May 24 to May 27, November 19, and December 25.

WHERE TO DINE

Le Café de Paris ✿, place du Casino (© **92-16-20-20**), provides you with a front-row view of the comings and goings of the nerve center of Monte Carlo. Menu items change frequently. The platters are appreciated by local office workers, especially at lunchtime, because they can be served and consumed relatively quickly. Main courses run 17€ to 43€ ($22.10–$55.90).

Stars 'n' Bars, 6 quai Antoine-1er (© **97-97-95-95**; www.starsnbars.com/en), is modeled on the sports bars popular in the U.S. with Tex-Mex, steaks, pizza, sandwiches, and salads—and a happy hour! (Tues–Fri 5:30–7:30pm). On weekends (11am–3pm) they offer the "Brunch of Champions," a great addition to the all-round American experience at one of Monte Carlo's hotspots. You might even see a celebrity while you're there! Steaks run 18€ to 45€ ($23.40–$58.50) and other items cost 9€ to 26€ ($11.70–$33.80).

Fusion on the Port, 6 quai Antoine-1er (© **97-97-95-90**; www.starsnbars.com), is the chic upstairs addition to Stars 'n' Bars, with an excellent view of Monaco's port. The Pan-Asian menu "fuses" fresh, local products with traditional Japanese, Chinese, Thai, and Indian cooking techniques. On the terrace, diners can opt for the Fusion or Stars menu—plenty of choice for everyone! Main courses run 15€ to 28€ ($19.50–$36.40).

9

Germany

Although it's only about half the size of Texas, Germany is a large country by European standards. It also has an enviable location smack-dab in the center of the Continent, offering comprehensive rail links to most other major European nations. Within Germany, traveling by train is a snap, due to one of the world's most efficient and speedy—though by no means least expensive—rail networks. These networks crisscross a multitude of inspiring landscapes, from Alpine peaks to low-lying coastal plains, from dense forests to river valleys, passing hillside vineyards, craggy bluffs topped by medieval castles, and other scenes straight from the fairy tales.

Germany's cities beckon, too, even though many of them, on the surface at least, share a similar trait of bland modernity—they were blown to bits during World War II bombings and rebuilt in haste in the postwar period. But throughout Germany an impressive array of the finest of the lost architectural and cultural treasures has been re-created, and this work continues apace. And in many smaller towns that were spared the hard hand of war, historic cores of astonishing harmony and beauty seduce travelers just as they have for centuries. In short, Germany is both an easy and a fascinating stop on any rail traveler's journey though Europe.

HIGHLIGHTS OF GERMANY

Covering all of the fascinating towns and sights of Germany could easily take an entire book and several months of travel. Because most rail travelers won't have more than a week or so to visit the country, in this chapter we stick to the regions and cities we feel give the visitor a good yet varied look at the best Germany has to offer, from bustling metropolises to quaint villages, from the Bavarian charm of the south to the imposing grandeur of cities that were once part of former East Germany. We've also stuck to places that can easily be reached by rail. So while many people fly into the commercial hub of Frankfurt, we don't cover it beyond telling you how to board a train out of the city because there are far better places for travelers on a limited timetable to explore.

To say that Germany's capital, **Berlin,** had its ups and downs during the century just past would be an understatement of monumental proportions. Berlin has seen it all: proud imperial capital through defeat in World War I; 1920s instability and decadence; Hitler and the Holocaust; total destruction and defeat in World War II; occupation; partition by the Cold War "iron curtain" of the Berlin Wall; peaceful reunification; and national capital once again. And guess what? Berlin is back! It boasts the nation's greatest museums, a wealth of other attractions linked to its checkered past, and Germany's hottest nightlife. As the capital city and a major rail junction in the North, it's a natural starting point for many a visitor, and we rank it first on our tour of the country as well. While you can get a quick glimpse of Berlin in a

Moments   Festivals & Special Events

Oktoberfest, Germany's most famous festival, takes place in Munich from mid-September to the first Sunday in October. Millions show up, and hotels are packed. Most activities are at Theresienwiese, where local breweries sponsor gigantic tents that can hold up to 6,000 beer drinkers and there are many amusement rides and booths. Contact **Munich Tourist Information** (© 089/233 96 500; www.muenchen.de) for particulars, or just show up. However, always reserve hotel rooms well in advance. Munich's other big bash is **Fasching** (Carnival), which culminates Shrove Tuesday in a parade through town and a festive atmosphere at Viktualienmarkt.

At the other end of the spectrum is Dresden's annual **Striezelmarkt,** Germany's oldest Christmas Market, held in the Altmark from the end of November to Christmas Eve and featuring *Striezel* (braided baked bread). Contact **Dresden Tourist Information** at © 351/49 192 100 or www.dresden.de. In Heidelberg, there are monthly fireworks displays and a spectacular illumination of its castle during summer months. For more information, contact **Heidelberg Tourist Information** (© 06221/1 94 33; www.cvb-heidelberg.de).

couple of hours from the top deck of an open-top tour bus, as with all the world's great cities you need to take time to explore, to settle in, and to allow a little of the city's unique atmosphere to seep into your psyche. For those with limited time, we recommend spending 3 days in Berlin before you set out to see more of Germany. On the outskirts of Berlin is **Potsdam,** a charming small town with a quaint historic core and a lovely palace set amid an expansive garden.

Down south is another great city, **Munich,** the exuberant capital of the highly independent state of Bavaria. It, too, serves as one of Germany's most important cultural centers and is graced with an impressive architecture that includes royal residences, steepled churches, grand squares, and ornate monuments. A worthy side trip is **Neuschwanstein,** a picture-perfect castle perched on a cliff and famous as the model for Walt Disney's Sleeping Beauty castle at Disneyland.

A good contrast to the bustling cities of Berlin and Munich is **Heidelberg,** a medieval jewel and a thriving university town, famous for its massive castle that looms above the town's narrow, picturesque streets. Just a short train ride from Frankfurt, it's a perfect first-night stopover after a long transatlantic flight. Another great town worthy of a stopover, this time in former East Germany, is **Dresden,** once one of Germany's most important cultural centers and almost completely reconstructed in time for its 800th birthday celebration in 2006. It lies about halfway between Berlin and Prague by rail.

Finally, while Germany may not have a reputation as a land of romance, it does have its own **Romantic Road,** a route that stretches from **Würzburg** south to Füssen, connecting some of Europe's best-preserved medieval towns and monuments along the way.

Germany

1 Essentials

GETTING THERE

Germany's own **Lufthansa** (© **800/645-3880**; www.lufthansa.com) operates the most frequent service from around 16 gateway cities in the U.S. and Canada and flies to the greatest number of Germany's airports.

Other major North American carriers that fly to Germany include **American Airlines** (© 800/443-7300; www.aa.com), **Continental Airlines** (© 800/231-0856; www.continental.com), **Delta Airlines** (© 800/241-4141; www.delta.com), **United Airlines** (© 800/241-6522; www.united.com), **US Airways** (© 800/428-4322; www.usairways.com), and **Air Canada** (© 888/247-2262; www.aircanada.com).

Germany's major international gateway—and continental Europe's busiest airport—is **Flughafen Frankfurt/Main** (© 069/690 0; www.airportcity-frankfurt.com), which lies 7 miles (11km) from the city center at the Frankfurter Kreuz, the intersection of two major expressways. The airport consists of two terminals, Terminal 1 and Terminal 2, connected by a people-mover system, Sky Line, which provides quick transfers (the airport's standard connection time is 45 min. maximum). There are connecting flights to all major German airports. Flying time from Frankfurt to either Berlin or Munich is approximately 1 hour.

At the **Airport Train Station** beneath Terminal 1, you can connect to German InterCity and commuter trains that go directly to other German cities, such as Munich, and a few other European cities, including Vienna and Basel. Otherwise, local trains link the airport to Frankfurt's main rail station, the **Hauptbahnhof,** in about 15 minutes, with connections to all major German cities.

GERMANY BY RAIL

The national rail corporation in Germany, **Deutsche Bahn (German Railways)**— **DB** for short—spreads its silvery tentacles into the remotest corners of the land and manages more than 22,320 miles (36,000km) of rail track. The rail system is renowned for its timeliness and reach; German trains even crank their way up more than a few Alpine mountainsides. The busiest stations, in places such as Berlin, Munich, and Frankfurt, see hundreds of arrivals and departures—regional, national, and international—every day. For more information, to order tickets, and for the best European train timetables on the Web, check out DB's website at **www.bahn.de** (click on "Internat. Guests"). From outside Germany, you can obtain train schedules, purchase tickets, and make seat reservations by calling © 49/1805/99 66 33. Within Germany, dial © 11861. An automated toll-free service for train schedules is available by calling © 0800/150 70 90. Once you begin traveling, you'll find **Travel Centres** in major stations helpful for purchasing tickets and planning routes, while the **ServicePoint,** available in about 90 stations, provides quick answers to questions about connections, rail travel, timetables and local information (if the local tourist office is closed, you may be able to pick up a city map here).

TICKETS & PASSES

For details on purchasing multicountry options, such as the **Eurail Global Pass,** and for information on the **German Rail Pass,** see chapter 2. In addition to the German Rail Pass, DB also offers a **Twinpass** for two adults traveling together that's a real bargain. This pass costs $470 for 4 days in 1 month for first class or $346 for second class (price is for two, not per person). The passes above must be purchased in North America through your travel agent or **Rail Europe** (© 877/272-RAIL [7245] in North America; www.raileurope.com).

Other discount fares and tickets available in Germany at most rail stations include:

BahnCard A range of cards—BahnCard 25, 50, and 100—offer reduced-rate travel for people who intend to do a lot of traveling by train in Germany over an extended period of time. The BahnCard 25, for example, is worth purchasing for rail travel costing more than 200€ ($260), the equivalent of traveling round-trip between Hamburg and Munich; it costs 103€ ($134) for first class and 51.50€ ($69) for second class and provides a 25% discount off regular and special train fares.

Gruppe & Spar Tickets for groups of six or more people traveling together, offering savings from 50% to 70%, depending on how far in advance you buy them (up to 14 days).

Länder-Tickets In some of the German *Länder* (states) a range of reduced-rate tickets is offered on particular routes for individuals and groups of up to five people. The Bayern-Ticket, for example, allows nearly unlimited travel on local trains in Bavaria for 19€ ($25) for an individual and 27€ ($35) for up to five people if bought at a ticket machine; tickets bought at a ticket counter cost 2€ ($2.60) more.

Schönes-Wochenende-Ticket The Beautiful-Weekend-Ticket is valid for up to five people traveling on local trains throughout Germany on a Saturday or Sunday for 33€ ($43) if bought from a ticket machine, or 35€ ($46) if bought at a ticket window.

FOREIGN TRAIN TERMS

The rail network as a whole is known as *Die Bahn.* A *Zug* is a train. A fast regional train is known as a *Schnellzug* or *Eilzuge.* Night trains are known as *Nachtzüge.* A *Zuschlag* is a supplement, which you'll need to pay only on ICE high-speed German trains, if not using a railpass.

Class is *Klasse. Zweite (2.) Klasse* is second class and *Erste (1.) Klasse* is first class. A station is a *Bahnhof.* In towns and cities that have more than one station, the main station is often called the *Hauptbahnhof (Hbf).* The German term for platform is *Bahnsteig; Gleis* means track. The bigger stations have separate counters for selling domestic tickets *(Inlandsreisen)* and international tickets (*Auslandsreisen,* or just plain International). A *Fahrkarte* or *Fahrschein* is a ticket. A timetable is a *Fahrplan.* Platforms are generally subdivided into sections—A, B, C, D, and so on—and you are often informed of what section *(Abschnitt)* you will board or vacate the train at. If you have baggage you want to store for a time, look for the *Gepäckaufbewahrung.* Arrival and departure are *Ankunft* and *Abfahrt,* respectively. And if you need to change trains, the word for transfer is *Umsteigen.*

PRACTICAL TRAIN INFORMATION

As Berlin strengthens its role as capital, increasing numbers of trains are speeding their way into town. All points of the country, especially Frankfurt, Munich, and Bonn, maintain excellent rail connections, with high-tech, high-speed improvements being made to the country's railway system virtually all the time. Unlike many other European countries whose rail service is highly centralized, Germany uses a multihub system, which means you rarely have to wait long for a train.

Germany's high-speed **InterCity Express (ICE)** trains are sleek, comfortable, and among the fastest in Europe, reaching speeds of 186 mph (300kmph). These trains run on most major rail corridors in the country (and a limited number of international routes as well), with each train making a few stops along the way. There are actually several different types of ICE trains, ranging from the older but incredibly spacious domestic ICE 1 trains to the newer ICE T trains that use tilting technology and travel internationally.

All ICE trains offer state-of-the-art amenities, which may include electronic seat reservation displays, personal audio systems (and even personal video screens in first class), luggage storage lockers, fold-down tabletops, and computer ports. Some ICE trains have panoramic lounges that offer excellent views of the surrounding landscape.

The ICE network significantly reduces travel time, making transits north to south or east to west across the country easily in the course of a single day.

Slightly slower are the hundreds of **InterCity (IC)** passenger trains, traveling up to 124 mph (200kmph) with service every hour or two to the centers of some 60 German cities. IC trains have adjustable cushioned seats and individual reading lights. Bars, lounges, and dining rooms are available, too. A network of **EuroCity (EC)** trains connecting Germany with 13 other countries offers the same high standards of service as those of IC.

Interregio-Express (IRE) trains, some with double-decker compartments, handle inter-regional service and stop at more stations than the InterCity trains. *Regionalverkehr* (RV, RB, and RE) trains are local trains that stop at every station on their route.

CityNightLine (CNL) trains are exceptionally comfortable, including some double-decker night trains that run domestically as well as between Germany and surrounding countries, such as the route from Berlin to Zurich, or Frankfurt to Vienna or Copenhagen. They offer four categories of comfort, from private cabins with bathrooms to reclining seats. Similarly, the **EuroNights** provide night service on major international routes, including Munich to Budapest.

RESERVATIONS   German trains are invariably crowded, and even though they aren't required on most IC or ICE routes, many people reserve seats. We strongly recommend that you do, too, if you don't want to end up standing. Reservations cost 1.50€ to 3.50€ ($1.95–$4.55) extra; reservations for the ICE Sprinters cost 11€ ($14) extra. Reservations on all night trains and ICE Sprinters are mandatory and should be made as far in advance as possible, especially if you're traveling on an international route; sleeper reservations are normally included in the price of the ticket or pass supplement that you pay. Seat reservations can be made at all train stations or can be reserved in North America through Rail Europe.

SERVICES & AMENITIES   All German trains, even the smallest, have a first-class section or cars (offering more leg space and comfier seats). Trains are generally clean and comfortable. All trains are nonsmoking.

ICE trains have a buffet or restaurant car (called BordBistro or BordRestaurant) that sells drinks, meals, and snacks. The quality is usually good. IC trains generally have an attendant who pushes around a small cart from which coffee, tea, mineral water, sandwiches, potato chips, and other snack items are dispensed. These are more expensive than the same things bought from a supermarket, so if you're on a tight budget buy them before boarding the train.

Trains & Travel Times in Germany

From	To	Type of Train	# of Trains	Frequency	Travel Time
Frankfurt	Berlin	ICE	18	Daily	4 hr.
Frankfurt	Heidelberg	ICE, IC, RB	34	Daily	1 hr.
Frankfurt	Munich	ICE, IC	18	Daily	3 hr., 45 min.
Berlin	Munich	ICE, IC	13	Daily	6 hr.
Berlin	Potsdam	RE	29	Daily	25 min.
Berlin	Dresden	EC, IC	7	Daily	2 hr.
Munich	Heidelberg	IC	7	Daily	3 hr., 15 min.

Night trains offer first and tourist class. Sleeping accommodations in first class include single or double compartments with shower and toilet and are equipped with key cards, phones for wake-up service, luggage storage, and other amenities. Tourist class offers four-bed cabins with shared bathrooms as well as open seating with *sleeperettes* (reclining seats). Trains are equipped with a restaurant and bistro car, and breakfast is included in the first-class fare.

DB will arrange assistance for travelers with disabilities (getting to and boarding trains, among other things), provided you call their **Mobility Assistance Centre** (© **01805/512-512**) at least a day in advance.

FAST FACTS: Germany

Area Codes The country code for Germany is **49.** To call Germany from North America, dial 011 (the international access code), followed by the country code, the local area code minus the first zero (see below), and telephone number.

When making local calls in Germany, you don't need to use the area code for the city you're in. You do, however, need to use an area code when making a long-distance call to another town or city. The area code for Berlin is **030.** Other area codes used in this book include: Munich **089;** Heidelberg **06221;** and Dresden **0351.**

Business Hours Most **banks** are open Monday to Friday 8:30am to 12:30pm and 1:30 to 3:30pm (Thurs to 5:30pm), though hours vary from city to city. Money exchanges at airports and major train stations are generally open daily from about 6 or 7am to 10pm. Most **stores** are open Monday to Saturday from 9 or 10am to 6pm, though department stores generally stay open until 8pm. In small towns, some shops close for lunch about 12:30 to 2 or 2:30pm. Stores are closed on Sunday, though convenience stores are open at major train stations.

Climate The most popular tourist months are May to October, although winter travel to Germany is becoming increasingly popular, especially to the ski areas in the Bavarian Alps. Germany's climate varies widely. In the north, winters tend to be cold and rainy; summers are most agreeable. In the south and in the Alps, it can be very cold in winter, especially in January, and very warm in summer, but with cool, rainy days even in July and August. Spring and fall are often stretched out.

Documents Required For stays of up to 3 months, citizens of the U.S. and Canada need only to have a valid passport. A visa is required for stays of longer than 3 months.

Electricity Germany operates on 220 volts electricity (North America uses 110 volts). So you'll need a small voltage transformer that plugs into the round-holed European electrical outlet for any small appliance up to 1,500 watts. When in doubt, ask your hotel's front desk for advice before plugging anything in.

Embassies & Consulates The following are in Berlin: **United States:** Clayallee 170, Dahlem (© **030/238 51 74;** U-Bahn: Dahlem-Dorf), open Monday to Friday 8:30 to noon; **Canada:** Leipziger Platz 17 (© **030/203 12-0;** U-Bahn: Potsdamer Platz), open Monday to Friday 8:30am to 12:30pm and 1:30 to 5pm. In Munich, the consulate of the **United States** is at Königstrasse 5 (© **089/288 80;** bus: 53), open Monday to Friday 1 to 4pm, and the consulate of **Canada** is at Tal Strasse 29 (© **089/219 95 70;** S-Bahn: Isartor), open Monday to Friday 9am to noon.

Health & Safety Should you get ill while in Germany, hotels and tourist offices usually keep a list of English-speaking doctors and dentists, and the country's medical system is excellent. At least one pharmacy in every major city is open all night. Water is safe to drink in all major cities, but you should not drink any mountain stream water, no matter how pure it looks.

Germany is a reasonably safe country in which to travel, although neo-Nazi skinheads, especially in the eastern part of the country, have sometimes attacked black or Asian travelers. One of the most dangerous places, especially at night, is around the large railway stations in such cities as Frankfurt, Munich, Berlin, and Hamburg. Some beer halls get especially rowdy late at night.

Holidays January 1 (New Year's Day), Easter (Good Friday and Easter Monday), May 1 (Labor Day), Ascension Day (10 days before Pentecost/Whitsunday, the seventh Sun after Easter), Whitmonday (day after Pentecost/Whitsunday), October 3 (Day of German Unity), and December 25 to 26 (Christmas). In addition, the following holidays are observed in some German states with high Catholic populations, including Bavaria: January 6 (Epiphany), Corpus Christi (10 days after Pentecost), August 15 (Assumption), and November 1 (All Saints' Day).

Mail General delivery—mark it POSTE RESTANTE—can be used in any major town or city in Germany. You can pick up your mail upon presentation of a valid identity card or passport. Street mailboxes are painted yellow. It costs 1.70€ ($2.20) for the first 20 grams (about .7 oz.) to send an airmail letter to the United States or Canada, and 1€ ($1.30) for postcards. To mail a package, go to one of the larger post offices, preferably the main branch in the area.

Police & Emergencies Throughout Germany the emergency number for **police** is © **110;** for fire or to call an ambulance, dial © **112.**

Telephone Local and long-distance calls may be placed from public telephone booths, most of which nowadays require an advance-payment telephone card. **Telekom,** the German telephone company, offers phone cards at post offices in denominations of 5€ ($6.50), 10€ ($13) and 15€ ($20). Otherwise, insert a minimum of .20€ (25¢) for a 90-second local call. In any case, don't make phone calls from a hotel, where rates are often quadruple the standard.

German phone numbers are not standard and come in various formats. Hyphens in a telephone number indicate an extension. But because all the area codes are the same, these various configurations should have little effect on your phone usage once you get used to the fact that numbers are inconsistent and vary from place to place.

Tipping If a restaurant bill says *Bedienung*, that means a service charge has already been added, so just round up to the nearest euro.

If not, add 10% to 15%. Round up to the nearest euro for taxis. Bellhops get 1€ ($1.30) per bag, as does the doorperson at your hotel, restaurant, or nightclub. Room-cleaning staffs get small tips in Germany (about 1€/$1.30 a night), as do concierges who perform some special favors such as obtaining hard-to-get theater or opera tickets. Tip hairdressers or barbers 5% to 10%.

2 Berlin ✶✶✶

With its field of new skyscrapers, hip clubs, and fashion boutiques, Berlin is positioning itself as the Continent's new capital of cool. As one hip young Berliner, Joachim Stressmann, put it: "We don't know where we're going, but we know where we've been, and no one wants to go back there."

Before World War II, the section of the city that became East Berlin was the cultural and political heart of Germany, where the best museums, the finest churches, and the most important boulevards lay. The walled-in East Berliners turned to restoring their important museums, theaters, and landmarks (especially in the Berlin-Mitte section), while the West Berliners built entirely new museums and cultural centers. Today, museum collections have either merged or are in the process of being merged, and it's difficult to see much difference between the former East and West. Former East Berlin, in particular, has changed wildly in the past decade and a half, with renovated historic buildings, spanking new ones, and the city's hottest nightlife. If you've never been to Berlin—or even if you have—it will be hard to imagine that the city was ever divided.

Given its history and its wide range of attractions, hotels, and restaurants, the city is a natural starting point for a rail tour of the country, even if you end up flying into a more popular airport such as Frankfurt. Situated in the northeast of Germany, Berlin offers excellent rail connections to all of the major cities of Germany and has direct rail connections to many major cities, including Paris, Brussels, Vienna, Zurich, Budapest, and Prague.

STATION INFORMATION
GETTING FROM THE AIRPORT TO THE TRAIN STATION

Note: If you fly into Frankfurt, a popular airport for flights out of North America, follow the directions listed under "Getting There," earlier, for getting to the Frankfurt main train station, and then hop a train to Berlin. It takes approximately 4 hours by train to get to Berlin from Frankfurt's main train station, with trains departing every hour or less.

In 2011, the new **Airport Berlin Brandenburg International (BBI)** will open in Schönefeld to replace the east and west sectors' former airports. Until then, **Berlin-Tegel Airport,** 5 miles (8km) northwest of the city center, is the city's busiest. If you're arriving via Lufthansa, Air Berlin, or any other of the other airlines serving Berlin from Frankfurt, Munich, or Western Europe, you'll likely arrive here. The best and easiest way to get into town, particularly if your destination is one of the hotels on or around Kurfürstendamm, is by **city bus 109,** which costs 2.10€ ($2.75) one-way and departs every 10 to 15 minutes from outside the arrivals hall. It travels along Kurfürstendamm, where many hotels are located, to Bahnhof Zoologischer Garten (usually shortened to Bahnhof Zoo) in about 30 minutes. **Bus X9** travels a more direct route, with fewer stops (it does *not* travel along Kurfürstendamm), between Tegel Airport and Bahnhof Zoo in less than 20 minutes for the same fare. If you're staying near Berlin-Mitte, take one of the buses above to Bahnhof Zoo and transfer to the S-Bahn, or take the **JetExpressBus TXL** directly to Berlin-Mitte's Unter den Linden for 2.10€ ($2.75). If you think you'll be using public transportation more than one more time during the rest of the day, consider purchasing a *Tageskarte* (day ticket); see "Getting Around," below. The trip by **taxi** to Bahnhof Zoo is about 16€ ($21).

Western Berlin

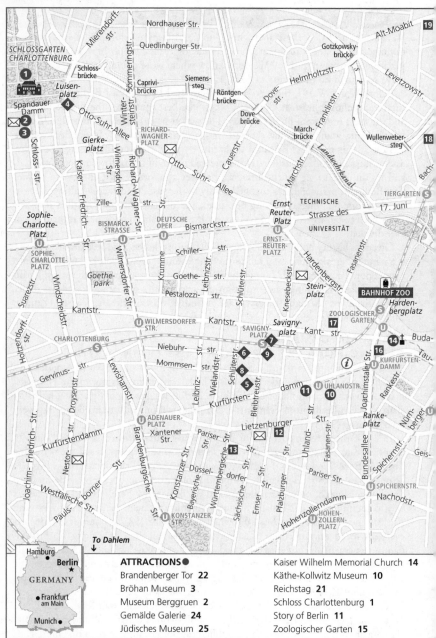

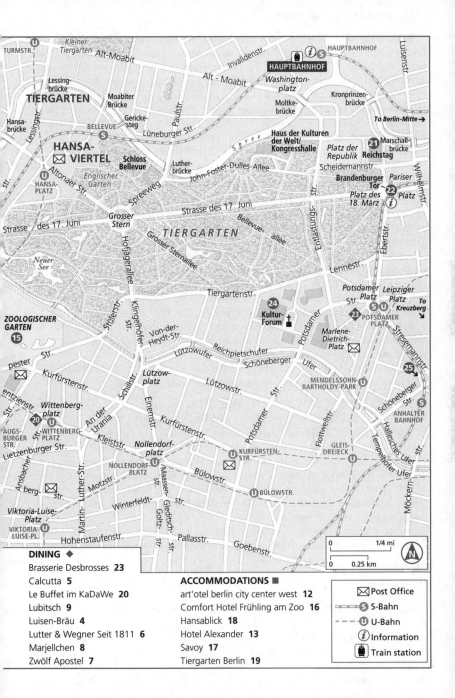

DINING ◆
Brasserie Desbrosses **23**
Calcutta **5**
Le Buffet im KaDaWe **20**
Lubitsch **9**
Luisen-Bräu **4**
Lutter & Wegner Seit 1811 **6**
Marjellchen **8**
Zwölf Apostel **7**

ACCOMMODATIONS ■
art'otel berlin city center west **12**
Comfort Hotel Frühling am Zoo **16**
Hansablick **18**
Hotel Alexander **13**
Savoy **17**
Tiergarten Berlin **19**

⊠ Post Office
Ⓢ S-Bahn
Ⓤ U-Bahn
ⓘ Information
🚉 Train station

0   1/4 mi
0   0.25 km

Schönefeld Airport, which once served as East Berlin's major airport, also receives both domestic and international flights, including many from Eastern Europe. The fastest way to get from Schönefeld to the city center is by the AirportExpress train, which delivers you from Schönefeld Station (a 5-min. walk from the airport) to the Hauptbahnhof (main train station) in about 30 minutes or to or Bahnhof Zoo (where many hotels are located) in about 40 minutes. The **S-Bahn S-9** makes the run to Bahnhof Zoo in about 50 minutes. Both trains cost 2.10€ ($2.75). **Berlin-Templehof Airport,** which is seldom used, is closing down in 2008.

For information on Berlin's airports, call ✆ **01805-00 01 86** or head online to **www.berlin-airport.de.**

INSIDE THE STATIONS

Berlin is easily reached from Frankfurt (trip time: 4 hr.), Munich (7 hr.), and Dresden (2 hr.). Most arrivals are at Berlin's contemporary **Hauptbahnhof,** which opened in 2006 and serves some 1,100 long-distance, regional, and rapid-transit trains daily. The S-Bahn train system connects the train station to the rest of the city. A money exchange office, ATMs, lockers for luggage, and restaurants are in the station. For information on Berlin, stop by the BERLIN infostore, located on the ground floor's north exit and open daily 8am to 10pm. In addition, **EurAide,** in the Reise Zentrum, is an English-language information counter for train travel and local sightseeing. It's open daily 10am to 8pm in summer and Monday to Friday 11am to 6:30pm in winter.

Bahnhof Zoologischer Garten, nicknamed "Bahnhof Zoo," is just three stops by S-Bahn from the Hauptbahnhof. It's just a few minutes' walk from the Kurfürstendamm and its many hotels and restaurants.

For information on train services, prices, and reservations, call ✆ **11 8 61** (available from within Germany only) or go to **www.bahn.de.**

INFORMATION ELSEWHERE IN THE CITY

In addition to the Hauptbahnhof, there's a **BERLIN infostore** conveniently located at Kurfürstendamm 21, at the Neues Kranzler Eck, where you can obtain a map and get sightseeing advice. It's open Monday to Saturday 10am to 8pm and Sunday 10am to 6pm. Other convenient tourist offices are at **Brandenburg Gate,** Unter den Linden, open daily April through October 9:30am to 6pm and November through March 10am to 6pm; and in the **Berlin Pavilion** at the Reichstag, Scheidemannstrasse, open daily April through October daily 8:30am to 8pm and November through March 10am to 6pm.

For more information or to book a hotel reservation, call **Berlin Tourismus** at ✆ **030/ 25 00 25.** For information online, check out **www.berlin-tourist-information.de.**

CITY LAYOUT

Berlin consists of 12 precincts. Berlin's greatest concentration of hotels, restaurants, and shops is clustered around the **Kurfürstendamm,** located in former West Berlin and affectionately called the **Ku'damm.** About 2½ miles (4km) long, it starts at the Kaiser-Wilhelm Gedächtniskirche (Memorial Church), a ruin left standing as a reminder of the horrors of war. Near the church are the Bahnhof Zoologischer Garten and a large park called the Tiergarten. To the northwest, easily reached by bus, are Charlottenburg Palace and a cluster of fine museums, including the Berggruen Sammlung with its Picasso collection and Bröhan Museum with its decorative arts.

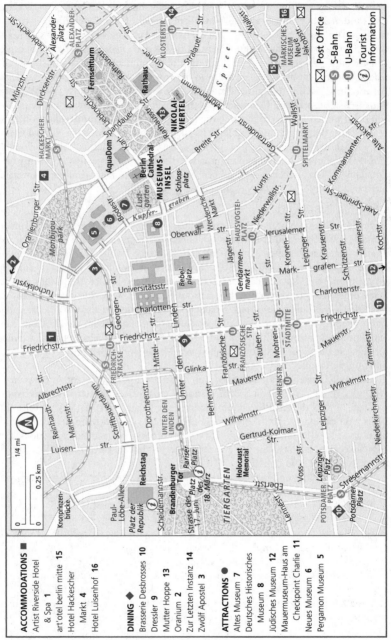

Berlin Mitte

Post Office ⊠
S-Bahn Ⓢ
U-Bahn Ⓤ
Tourist Information ⓘ

ACCOMMODATIONS ■
Artist Riverside Hotel
& Spa **1**
art'otel berlin mitte **15**
Hotel Hackescher
Markt **4**
Hotel Luisenhof **16**

DINING ◆
Brasserie Desbrosses **10**
Dressler **9**
Mutter Hoppe **13**
Oranium **2**
Zur Letzten Instanz **14**
Zwölf Apostel **3**

ATTRACTIONS ●
Altes Museum **7**
Deutsches Historisches
Museum **8**
Jüdisches Museum **12**
Mauermuseum-Haus am
Checkpoint Charlie **11**
Neues Museum **6**
Pergamon Museum **5**

Berlin's other well-known street—and historically much more significant—is **Unter den Linden,** in a precinct called **Berlin-Mitte** (literally, Central Berlin). This was the heart of Old Berlin before World War II, its most fashionable and lively street, and thereafter was part of East Berlin. Today, Mitte has once again become the city center and contains the city's highest concentration of monuments, tourist attractions, and federal government buildings. At the head of the wide, tree-lined Unter den Linden is Berlin's most readily recognized landmark, the Brandenburg Gate. The boulevard leads to **Museum Island (Museum Island),** which boasts the outstanding Pergamon and other museums, and to the drab modern square called **Alexanderplatz,** once the heart of East Berlin and easily found by its tall TV tower. Nearby is the **Nikolai Quarter,** a reconstructed neighborhood of shops, bars, and restaurants built to resemble Old Berlin. Berlin's other important museum district, the **Tiergarten,** is in Mitte near **Potsdamer Platz,** which has blossomed into a major business, retail and entertainment hub.

GETTING AROUND

Berlin has an excellent public transport network, including the U-Bahn (Underground), the S-Bahn (inner-city railway), buses, and trams (in eastern Berlin only). All use the same ticket and fare system and are run by the **Public Transport Company Berlin–Brandenburg** (**BVG;** ✆ 030/194 49; www.bvg.de), which maintains an information booth outside Bahnhof Zoo on Hardenbergplatz, at Alexanderplatz, and many other stations, most open daily 6am to 10pm. They provide details on how to reach destinations and the various ticket options available and also sell tickets. Public transportation throughout the city operates from about 4:30am to 12:30am daily, with special night buses (marked with an "N" in front of their numbers) running throughout the night and supplemented by U-Bahn and S-Bahn lines operating all night on weekends.

Although Greater Berlin is divided into three fare zones, A, B, and C (zone maps are posted at all U-Bahn and S-Bahn stations), most places of interest to you require purchase only of the **AB Einzelfahrausweis** single ticket at 2.10€ ($2.75). With this ticket, you can travel all of the U-Bahn system, most of the S-Bahn network, and all buses and trams, including travel to Berlin's two airports and its major attractions. The only exception is Potsdam, for which you must buy a three-zone ABC Einzelfahrausweis for 2.60€ ($3.40).

If you're traveling only a short distance (six stops by bus or three by subway), you need only buy a **Kurzstreckenkarte** for 1.20€ ($1.55).

If you don't want to hassle with individual tickets and plan to travel more than twice on a given day, consider buying a **Tageskarte** (day ticket) for 5.80€ ($7.55). If you're going to Potsdam, buy the 6€ ($7.80) Tageskarte valid for all three zones; it's good for local travel within Potsdam as well.

Tickets should be purchased before boarding (though standard single tickets are available on buses) from vending machines and then time-punched by one of the small red boxes found at the entrances to city buses and Underground stations.

Note that railpasses are valid only on Berlin's S-Bahn lines that connect DB train stations, such as the S-7 that connects the Hauptbahnhof with the Lichtenberg and Zoo stations.

Taxis are available throughout Berlin. The meter starts at 2.55€ ($3.30), plus 1.55€ ($1.80) per kilometer after that. Visitors can flag down taxis that have a T-sign illuminated. For a **taxi,** call ✆ **21 01 01,** 68 99 00, or 69 0 22.

Value **The WelcomeCard**

If you're going to be in Berlin for a few days and think you'll be traveling a lot by public conveyance, consider purchasing a **WelcomeCard** for 16€ ($21) valid for 2 days or 21€ ($27) valid for 3 days for most areas of Berlin. If you're traveling to Potsdam, get the WelcomeCard valid for all three zones for 17.50€ ($23) and 24€ ($31) respectively. The card entitles you to 48 or 72 hours of free travel on public transportation, as well as a 25% to 50% reduction on sightseeing tours and a small selection of museums, attractions, and theaters. Be sure to ask for a list of participating establishments, however, to see whether they're attractions you're interested in; the SchauLUST Museen Berlin ticket (described below) may be a better fit for you. The WelcomeCard is valid for one adult and up to three children 13 or younger. It's available at BERLIN infor-stores, many hotels, and BVG ticket offices.

WHERE TO STAY

Artist Riverside Hotel & Spa ★★ *Value*   This boutique hotel is my top choice in fast-changing Berlin-Mitte. Although it's in a nondescript Communist-era building, it has a great location beside the Spree River, near Museum Island and the Oranienburger Strasse nightlife. But what sets it apart is its design concept, from the hand-painted Jugendstil detailing in each room to the comfortable cafe with outdoor seating beside the Spree. A spa offers everything from massages and body treatments to saunas and baths. For individuals who revel in the offbeat, this place is a true find.

Friedrichstrasse 106, 10117 Berlin. © 030/28 49 00. Fax 03/28 49 04 9. www.great-hotel.com. 40 units. 99€–190€ ($129–$247) double; 279€–379€ ($363–$493) suite. Discounts available for artists. Buffet breakfast 9€ ($12). MC, V. S-/U-Bahn: Friedrichstrasse. **Amenities:** Bar; nonsmoking rooms. *In room:* Hair dryer, no A/C.

art'otel berlin city center west ★   Dedicated to Andy Warhol, this sleek hotel near the Ku'damm is decorated with the artist's works, photographs of Warhol, and furniture in pop-art colors of lime green, purple, and deep red. Unfussy rooms of various sizes combine modernity with functionality, including wireless access. A must-see: the sixth-floor exhibition of Warhol's works.

Lietzenburger Strasse 85, 10719 Berlin. © 800/814-7000 in the U.S. and Canada, or 030/88 77 77-0. Fax 030/88 77 77-777. www.artotel.de. 91 units. 130€–197€ ($169–$256) double; 170€–217€ ($221–$282) suite. Buffet breakfast 13€ ($17). AE, DC, MC, V. U-Bahn: Uhlandstrasse. **Amenities:** Restaurant; bar; laundry; nonsmoking rooms; rooms for those w/limited mobility. *In room:* Hair dryer.

art'otel berlin mitte ★   Sister hotel to the one above, this one doesn't have quite as convenient a location but is within walking distance of Berlin-Mitte's many attractions and boasts artwork by one of Germany's most contemporary artists, Georg Baselitz. Although most of the hotel is modern, including sixth-floor suites with balconies and kitchenettes, its glass-topped restaurant incorporates the ornate facade of the adjoining historic Emerlerhaus in its design (famous for its rococo rooms but open now only for private functions).

Wallstrasse 70–73, 10179 Berlin. © 800/814-7000 in the U.S. and Canada, or 030/240 62-0. Fax 030/240 62-222. www.artotel.de. 109 units. 160€–210€ ($208–$273) double; 180€–260€ ($234–$338) suite. Buffet breakfast 14€ ($18). AE, DC, MC, V. U-Bahn: Märkisches Museum. **Amenities:** Restaurant; bar; laundry; nonsmoking rooms; rooms for those w/limited mobility. *In room:* Hair dryer.

Berlin U-Bahn & S-Bahn

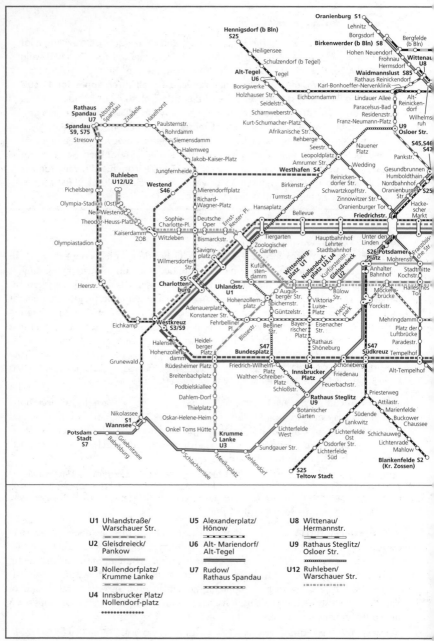

U1 Uhlandstraße/
Warschauer Str.

U2 Gleisdreieck/
Pankow

U3 Nollendorfplatz/
Krumme Lanke

U4 Innsbrucker Platz/
Nollendorf-platz

U5 Alexanderplatz/
Hönow

U6 Alt- Mariendorf/
Alt-Tegel

U7 Rudow/
Rathaus Spandau

U8 Wittenau/
Hermannstr.

U9 Rathaus Steglitz/
Osloer Str.

U12 Ruhleben/
Warschauer Str.

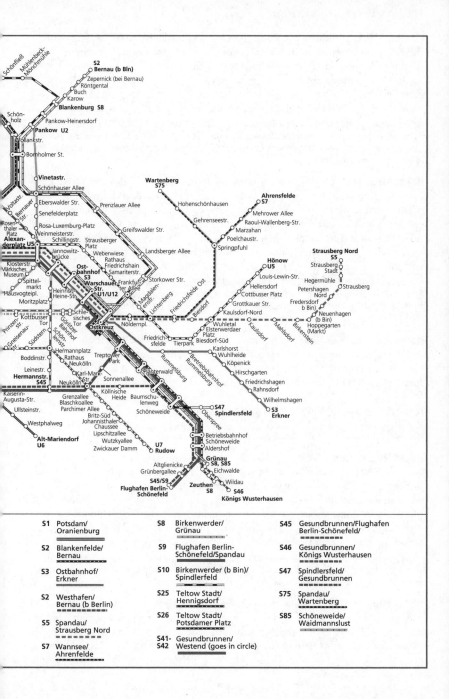

S1 Potsdam/
Oranienburg

S2 Blankenfelde/
Bernau

S3 Ostbahnhof/
Erkner

S2 Westhafen/
Bernau (b Berlin)

S5 Spandau/
Strausberg Nord

S7 Wannsee/
Ahrenfelde

S8 Birkenwerder/
Grünau

S9 Flughafen Berlin-
Schönefeld/Spandau

S10 Birkenwerder (b Bln)/
Spindlerfeld

S25 Teltow Stadt/
Hennigsdorf

S26 Teltow Stadt/
Potsdamer Platz

S41- Gesundbrunnen/
S42 Westend (goes in circle)

S45 Gesundbrunnen/Flughafen
Berlin-Schönefeld/

S46 Gesundbrunnen/
Königs Wusterhausen

S47 Spindlersfeld/
Gesundbrunnen

S75 Spandau/
Wartenberg

S85 Schöneweide/
Waidmannslust

Comfort Hotel Frühling am Zoo   If being close to the Bahnhof Zoo and right on the Ku'damm is important, this hotel is your best bet. Just a couple of minutes' walk from the train station, it's an older hotel with high, stucco ceilings but fairly standard, small rooms, with tiny bathrooms big enough for only one person. Although double-paned windows block out noise from the busy boulevard, those who insist on a good night's sleep will want to reserve a room facing the quiet inner courtyard.

Kurfürstendamm 17, 10719 Berlin. ☎ **800/654-6200** in the U.S. and Canada, or 030/889 11-0. Fax 030/889 11-150. www.frueling.com. 75 units. 113€–160€ ($147–$208) double; 143€–201€ ($186–$261) suite. Buffet breakfast 13€ ($17). AE, DC, MC, V. S/U-Bahn: Bahnhof Zoologischer Garten, Kurfürstendamm. **Amenities:** Bar; nonsmoking rooms. *In room:* Hair dryer, no A/C.

Hansablick 🌟🌟 *(Finds)*   One S-Bahn station or a 15-minute walk north of Bahnhof Zoo, this hotel is located on a quiet residential street beside the Spree River, lined with willows, and is only a few minutes' walk from the Tiergarten park (and a great week-end flea market). The rooms, in an early 1900s building without an elevator, come in different sizes and are a sophisticated blend of antique and modern, with wood floors, stucco ceilings, high-tech lighting, and modern furniture. The best rooms are those with views of the Spree, the largest (and most expensive) of which even has a balcony.

Flotowstrasse 6, 10555 Berlin. ☎ **030/39 04 80-0.** Fax 030/392 69 37. www.hotel-hansablick.de. 29 units. 101€– 121€ ($131–$157) double. Rates include buffet breakfast. A 10% reduction for guests who show this Frommer's guide. AE, DC, MC, V. S-Bahn: Tiergarten. U-Bahn: Hansaplatz. **Amenities:** Bar; nonsmoking rooms. *In room:* Hair dryer, no A/C.

Hotel Alexander 🌟 *(Value)*   Just a few-minutes' walk from the Ku'damm, this hotel combines the patina of age with contemporary furnishings, most which were custom-built by an artist in 1990. Rooms are simple but tastefully decorated, with all the crea-ture comforts you'd expect in medium-range accommodations, including wireless Internet access.

Pariser Strasse 37, 10707 Berlin. ☎ **030/88 71 65-0.** Fax 03/88 71 65-65. www.hotelalexander.de. 18 units. 125€– 155€ ($161–$202) double; 155€–175€ ($202–$228) suite. Off-season discounts available. Buffet breakfast 10€ ($13). MC, V. U-Bahn: Uhlandstrasse. **Amenities:** Restaurant; nonsmoking rooms. *In room:* Hair dryer, no A/C.

Hotel Hackescher Markt 🌟   You'd never know this nugget of charm was newly built in 1998, as everything about it evokes a late-19th-century landmark. Inside, there's a quiet, flagstone-and-ivy covered courtyard that clients use for reading. Rooms are soothing, partially oak-paneled, and equipped for wireless access. Bathrooms have heated floors. Some guests appreciate the romantic overtones of rooms on the upper-most floor, whose walls are angled due to the building's mansard roof. Nightlife, the attractions on Museum Island, and the S-Bahn are a short walk away.

Grosse Präsidentenstrasse 8, 10178 Berlin. ☎ **030/28 03-0.** Fax 030/280 03-111. www.hackescher-markt.com. 31 units. 130€–180€ ($169–$234) double; 175€–205€ ($228–$267) suite. AE, DC, MC, V. S-Bahn: Hackescher Markt. **Amenities:** Bar; laundry, nonsmoking rooms. *In room:* Hair dryer, no A/C.

Hotel Luisenhof 🌟   One of the most desirable small hotels in Berlin's eastern dis-trict but with an out-of-the-way location, the Luisenhof occupies a dignified house, built in 1822. Its five floors of high-ceilinged rooms will appeal to those desiring to escape modern Berlin's sterility. Rooms range greatly in size, but each is equipped with good queen or twin beds and offers touches of Renaissance decor. Bathrooms, though small, are nicely appointed.

Köpenicker Strasse 92, 10179 Berlin. ℂ 030/246 28 10. Fax 030/246 28 160. www.luisenhof.de. 27 units. 119€–250€ ($155–$325) double; 230€–350€ ($299–$444) suite. Buffet breakfast 12€ ($16). AE, DC, MC, V. U-Bahn: Märkisches Museum. **Amenities:** Restaurant; bar; laundry; nonsmoking rooms. *In room:* Hair dryer, no A/C.

Savoy Berlin 🏵🏵🏵   This small, classy hotel, within walking distance of the Ku'-damm and Bahnhof Zoo, has been welcoming international guests for more than 70 years. Any writer worth his or her salt has stayed here while in Berlin, including Thomas Mann and Henry Miller. Rooms, most equipped with bidets, are cozy and come in various styles and furnishings, including four-poster beds. Its clubby bar, the venerable Times Bar, offers Cuban cigars from its own humidors, and the elegant restaurant offers terrace dining in summer. You can't go wrong here.

Fasanenstrasse 9-10, 10623 Berlin. ℂ 030/311 03-0. Fax 030/311 03-333. www.hotel-savoy.com. 125 units. 152€–295€ ($198–$384) double. Buffet breakfast 15€ ($19.50). AE, DC, MC, V. S-/U-Bahn: Bahnhof Zoologischer Garten. **Amenities:** Restaurant; bar; nonsmoking rooms; rooms for those w/limited mobility. *In room:* Hair dryer.

Tiergarten Berlin 🏵🏵 *Finds*   This intimate hotel possesses all the makings of a first-rate hotel: a polite and efficient staff, early 1900s charm and elegance, and light and airy rooms sporting tall stucco ceilings. The bathrooms are modern and spotless. Even the breakfast room, with its great buffet, is something to write home about. In short, it's the kind of place that appeals to both business and pleasure travelers despite its out-of-the way location two subway stops north of Bahnhof Zoo.

Alt-Moabit 89, 10559 Berlin. ℂ 030/39 98 96. Fax 030/39 98 97 35. www.hotel-tiergarten.de. 60 units. 125€–155€ ($163–$202) double. Rates include buffet breakfast. AE, DC, MC, V. U-Bahn: Turmstrasse. **Amenities:** Bar; laundry; nonsmoking rooms. *In room:* Hair dryer, no A/C.

TOP ATTRACTIONS & SPECIAL MOMENTS

The great art collections of Old Berlin suffered during and after World War II. Although many paintings were saved by being stored in salt mines, many larger works were destroyed by fire. Part of the surviving art stayed in the East, including a wealth of ancient treasures that remind us of the leading role played by German archaeologists during the 19th and early 20th centuries. The paintings that turned up in the West and were passed from nation to nation in the late 1940s have nearly all been returned to Berlin.

Berlin has three major museum centers: **Charlottenburg,** with its palace and two significant museums; **Museum Island (Museumsinsel),** with the world-famous Pergamon Museum; and the **Tiergarten,** a center for European art, including the Gemälde-galerie. It makes sense to cover Berlin section by section—saving time and money on transportation.

CHARLOTTENBURG PALACE & MUSEUMS

Schloss Charlottenburg (Charlottenburg Palace) 🏵🏵🏵   Berlin's most beautiful baroque building, Charlottenburg Palace was built in 1695 for Sophia Charlotte, the popular wife of the future king of Prussia, Frederick I. Later it was expanded and served as the summer residence of the Prussian kings, the Hohenzollerns. The main wing (**Altes Schloss,** also known as the Nering-Eosander Building) contains the ground-floor **Historical Rooms,** once the quarters of Sophia Charlotte and her husband. Of these, the Porcelain Cabinet is the most striking (and kitschy), filled with more than 2,000 pieces of porcelain. Also of note is the baroque chapel. You have to join a 50-minute guided tour to visit these rooms. Alternatively, you can skip the tour and head to the upper floor, where you can wander on your own through rooms containing tapestries; goblets; swords; portraits of Sophie Charlotte, her husband, Frederick, and their

---

⌐Value Saving Money on Museums

If you're in Berlin 3 days, save money by buying the 3-day 15€ ($20) SchauLUST Museen Berlin ticket, which allows entry to all state-owned museums and dozens of others on 3 consecutive days. It's a great value, but keep in mind that every Thursday, admission is free to all state-owned museums during the last 4 hours before closing. Also, children under 16 always get into state-owned museums free.

---

son (the so-called Soldier King); and other royal possessions, including the Hohenzollern insignia and a stunning silver place setting. If you join the guided tour, a visit to these rooms is included.

To the right of this building is the **Neuer Flügel (New Wing),** also called the Knobelsdorff Flügel), where you can wander with an audio guide through more royal quarters, the state dining hall, and the elaborate Golden Galerie, one of the prettiest rococo ballrooms in Germany. Behind the palace is a beautiful baroque-style park, which contains the **Neuer Pavilion,** a delightful summer house built in 1825 by Karl Friedrich Schinkel, Berlin's most important early-19th-century architect, and the **Belvedere,** a former teahouse containing 18th- and 19th-century KPM (Königliche Porzellan-Manufaktur) Berlin porcelain.

Spandauer Damm. ✆ 030/320 91-440. www.spsg.de. Altes Schloss (including guided tour) 10€ ($13) adults, 7€ ($9.10) students/children. Neuer Flügel 6€ ($7.80) adults, 5€ ($6.50) students/children; Neuer Pavilion or Belvedere 2€ ($2.60) adults, 1.50€ children. Altes Schloss Tues–Sun 9am–5pm; Neuer Flügel Tues–Sun 10am–5pm (11am–5pm Jan–Mar); Neuer Pavilion Tues–Sun 10am–5pm; Belvedere summer Tues–Fri noon–5pm and Sat–Sun 10am–5pm, winter Tues–Sun noon–4pm. U-Bahn: Sophie-Charlotte-Platz or Richard-Wagner-Platz (then a 10-min. walk). Bus: 109, 309, or M45.

Bröhan Museum ★★ (Finds This wonderful museum specializes in decorative objects of the Art Nouveau (*Jugendstil* in German) and Art Deco periods (1889–1939), with exquisite vases, figurines, glass, furniture, carpets, silver, paintings of artists belonging to the Berlin Secession, and other works of art arranged in drawing-room fashion, including an outstanding porcelain collection. You'll see glassware by Emile Gallé, furniture by Eugene Gaillard and Hector Guimard, and works by Belgian Art Nouveau artist Henry van de Velde and Vienna Secession artist Josef Hommann.

Schlossstrasse 1a. ✆ 030/326 906 00. www.broehan-museum.de Admission 5€ ($6.50) adults, 4€ ($5.20) students/children; more for special exhibits. Tues–Sun 10am–6pm. U-Bahn: Sophie-Charlotte-Platz or Richard-Wagner-Platz (then a 10-min. walk). Bus: 109, 309, or M45.

Museum Berggruen ★★★ Beside the Bröhan Museum, this outstanding collection was previously on display in London's National Gallery but was moved here in 1996 after Berlin offered the collection a home of its own, in renovated former barracks built by August Stüler in 1859. It contains an astonishing 100 works by **Picasso,** from his student years in Madrid through his major periods to late in his life. There are also works by contemporaries like **Cézanne, Matisse** (with one room devoted to about 12 of his works), **Braque,** and **Klee.**

Schlossstrasse 1. ✆ 030/326 958-15. www.smb.museum. Admission 6€ ($7.80) adults, 3€ ($3.90) students/children. Tues–Sun 10am–6pm. U-Bahn: Sophie-Charlotte-Platz or Richard-Wagner-Platz (then a 10-min. walk). Bus: 109, 309, or M45.

BERLIN-MITTE

Start with a stroll down **Unter den Linden** beginning at the Reichstag and Brandenburg Gate (S-Bahn: Unter den Linden; bus: 100). During the decades of the Wall, the
Brandenburg Gate, built in the 18th century as the grand entrance to Unter den Linden, stood in no-man's-land, marking the boundary of East and West Berlin and
becoming the symbol of a divided Germany. After the November 1989 revolution and
the fall of the Wall, many Berliners gathered here to rejoice and dance on top of the
Wall. Near the Brandenburg Gate is the 5-acre (2-hectare) **Holocaust Memorial,** consisting of 2,751 concrete blocks of different sizes and an underground information
center dedicated to victims and their families.

Deutsches Historisches Museum (German Historical Museum) ✿✿   Housed

in the oldest building on Unter den Linden, the 1695 Zeughaus (Arsenal), the
national museum of German history tackles the ambitious goal of chronicling Germany's tumultuous past from the Middle Ages to the present day, utilizing both historic artifacts and audiovisual displays. Clothing, items used in daily life, photographs,
furniture, maps, posters, military uniforms, weapons, and more breathe life into the
political events, social upheavals, wars, and cultural blossoming that have shaped German history over the past several centuries. The architectural gem of the museum is
the inner courtyard with the masks of dying warriors by Andreas Schlüter, now topped
by a glass roof. An addition by I. M. Pei houses special exhibitions.

Unter den Linden 2. ✆ 030/20 304-0. www.dhm.de. Admission to the permanent exhibit 4€ ($5.20) adults, free
for children under 18. Daily 10am–6pm. S-Bahn/U-Bahn: Friedrichstrasse, Hackescher Markt. Bus: 100, 200, or 348 to
Staatsoper.

Altes Museum   Resembling a Greek temple and designed in 1822 by Berlin's great-

est architect, Karl Friedrich Schinkel, this is Berlin's oldest museum. On its main floor
is the **Antikensammlung,** a collection of ancient arts and crafts, primarily Greek and
Roman antiquities, including pottery, figurines, statues, busts, glassware, jewelry,
Greek helmets, and wood and stone sarcophagi. Outstanding are the **Attic red-figure
vases** of the 5th century B.C. (the best known is a large Athenian wine amphora, or
jar, found in Vulci, Etruria, dating from 490 B.C., which shows a satyr with a lyre and
the god Hermes) and the **treasury** with its silver and exquisite gold jewelry from about
2000 B.C. to late antiquity.

On the upper floor is the temporary home of the Egyptian Museum, which houses
Berlin's most famous art object (and probably the world's best-known single piece of
Egyptian art): the **bust of Queen Nefertiti.** Created more than 3,300 years ago, the
bust amazingly never left the sculptor's studio but rather served as a model for all other
portraits of the queen and was left on a shelf when the ancient city was deserted. The
bust was discovered in the early 1900s by German archaeologists. In 2009, the bust
will move into its final resting place, the Neues Museum, currently undergoing
restoration on Museum Island.

On Museum Island. ✆ 030/20 90 55 77. www.smb.museum. Admission 8€ ($10) adults, 4€ ($5.20) students/
children. Daily 10am–6pm. S-Bahn: Hackescher Markt (the closest), Alexanderplatz, or Friedrichstrasse. Bus: 100 or
200 to Lustgarten.

Pergamon Museum ✿✿✿   Berlin's most famous museum is named after its most

prized possession, the **Pergamon Altar,** a magnificent masterpiece of Hellenistic art of
the 2nd century B.C. and certainly one of the wonders of the ancient world. This
Greek altar (180–160 B.C.) has a huge room all to itself, with some 27 steps leading

---

Moments Strolling the Historic Nikolai Quarter

The historic **Nikolaiviertel** (S-/U-Bahn: Alexanderplatz or Klosterstrasse), a symbol of East Berlin's desire to bounce back after war damage, was restored in time for the city's 750th anniversary in 1987. Here, on the banks of the Spree River, is where Berlin was born. Many of the 16th-century neighborhood's medieval and baroque buildings were completely and authentically reconstructed after World War II. Subsequently, some of the city's old flavor has been recaptured here. Period taverns, cozy restaurants, souvenir shops, and churches make it ideal for a leisurely stroll down narrow streets illuminated by gas lanterns.

---

up to the colonnade. Most fascinating is the frieze around the base, tediously pieced together over a 20-year period. Depicting the struggle of the Olympian gods against the Titans as told in Hesiod's _Theogony,_ the relief is strikingly alive, with figures projecting as much as a foot from the background.

Essentially a museum of architecture and antiquities, the Pergamon also contains the impressive 2nd-century **Roman Market Gate of Milet,** as well as the dazzling **Babylonian Processional Way** leading to the **Gate of Ishtar,** created during Nebuchadnezzar's reign in 600 B.C. Greek and Roman sculpture and Islamic art are also on display, including the incredible **facade of Mshatta Palace** from Jordan. If you see only one museum on Museum Island, this should be it.

Bodestrasse 1–3 (entrance on Kupfergraben), Museum Island. © **030/20 90 55 77.** www.smb.museum. Admission 8€ ($10) adults, 4€ ($5.20) students/children. Daily 10am–6pm (Thurs to 10pm). S-Bahn/U-Bahn: Friedrichstrasse, Hackescher Markt. Bus: 100, 200, or 348 to Staatsoper.

Reichstag (Parliament)   Completed in 1894 in neo-Renaissance style to serve as the German house of parliament, the Reichstag had its darkest hour on the night of February 17, 1933, when a mysterious fire broke out that was blamed on the German Communist Party and was used as an excuse by the Nazi government to arrest dissidents and abolish basic democratic rights. Heavily damaged in World War II, it was rebuilt with the exception of a glass cupola that had adorned its center.

The Reichstag again became home of German lawmakers after the fall of the Wall and German reunification in 1990. Following a ceremonial wrapping by artist Christo in 1995, it underwent extensive renovation, including a new glass dome by British architect Sir Norman Foster. Today, you can enter the main (west) entrance for an elevator ride up to the impressive glass dome and its spiraling ramp, with panoramic views from an observation platform and a rooftop restaurant (the view is better than the food). A photographic display chronicles the Reichstag's history. Try to arrive early in the morning; until every German has visited, you can expect long lines at the entrance.

Platz der Republik 1. © **030/22 73 21 52.** www.Reichstag.de. Free admission. Daily 8am–midnight (you must enter by 10pm). S-Bahn: Unter den Linden. Bus: 100 or M41 to Reichstag.

KREUZBERG

Jüdisches Museum Berlin (Jewish Museum Berlin) _ЖЖЖ_   Opened in 2001, this addition to the city's roster of impressive museums was designed by Daniel Libeskind, the son of Holocaust refugees. The zinc-clad building's jagged, zigzagging structure (resembling, perhaps, a deconstructed Star of David, and slashed by hundreds of asymmetrical windows) houses collections chronicling 2,000 years of German-Jewish history, from Roman times to the present. Through photographs, artwork, historic artifacts, religious objects, and audiovisual displays, visitors learn about Jewish emigration to Europe 2,000 years ago, the persecution of Jews in medieval times, the integration of Jews in Germany, Jewish life in Berlin, the development of Jewish community and religious life, and Jewish contributions to German culture, politics, economy, and science. Small rooms scattered throughout the museum are designed especially for children, allowing them to enjoy the museum on a different level. Although the Holocaust is addressed, this is far more than a Holocaust museum.

Lindenstrasse 9–14. (C) 030/259 93 300. www.juedisches-museum-berlin.de. Admission 5€ ($6.50) adults, 2.50€ ($3.25) students/children/seniors, 10€ ($13) families. Mon 10am–1pm; Tues–Sun 10am–8pm. U-Bahn: Hallesches Tor or Kochstrasse. Bus: M29, M41, or 265.

Mauermuseum—Haus am Checkpoint Charlie ✮✮✮ *(Moments* This is by far the best museum for gaining an understanding of what life was like before, during, and after the fall of the Wall—if you have never been to Berlin before, don't miss it. Near what was once the most frequently used border crossing into East Berlin, Checkpoint Charlie, this collection documents events that took place around the Berlin Wall, including successful and failed attempts to escape East Berlin. With displays in English, the museum aptly illustrates these years in Berlin's history with photographs, items used in escape attempts (such as cars with hidden compartments), videos, artwork, and newspaper clippings. The fall of the Wall and the demise of Communism in East Germany, Russia, Poland, and Hungary are also documented, and part of the museum is devoted to nonviolent struggles for human rights around the world, including those led by Gandhi, Walesa, and Martin Luther King, Jr.

Friedrichstrasse 43–45. (C) 030/25 37 25-0. www.mauermuseum.de. Admission 9.50€ ($12) adults, 5.50€ ($7.15) students/children. Daily 9am–10pm. U-Bahn: Kochstrasse. Bus: M29.

TIERGARTEN

Gemäldegalerie (Picture Gallery) ✮✮✮ Housed in a modern structure utilizing natural light, Berlin's top art museum offers a comprehensive survey of European painting from the 13th to the 18th century, presented in chronological order and grouped geographically. Exhibits begin with German paintings of the 13th to the 16th century and include works by **Albrecht Dürer, Lucas Cranach,** and **Holbein the Elder** and **the Younger.** Look for **Cranach's** *Fountain of Youth (Der Jungbrunnen),* which shows old women being led to the fountain, swimming through, and emerging youthful and beautiful. Note that apparently only women need the bath—men apparently regain their youth through relations with younger women. Other highlights are **Cranach's** *The Last Judgement,* eight paintings by **Dürer,** and **Holbein the Younger's portrait of merchant Georg Gisze.**

The next sections contain one of the museum's most important collections, Netherlandish paintings of the 15th and 16th centuries, with works by Jan van Eyck, Rogier van der Weyden, and Pieter Bruegel. Look for Bruegel's *100 Proverbs (100 Sprichwörter),* a delight with peasants engaged in proverbial activities—see how many proverbs you can detect, such as "No use crying over spilled milk." The top attractions of the Flemish and Dutch paintings collection are works by Peter Paul Rubens and some 20 paintings by Rembrandt. Finally, the art lover is treated to works by English,

Moments A New Wall

The hideous 100-mile-long (161km) **Berlin Wall,** built in 1961 to prevent East Germans from fleeing into the sanctity of West Berlin, was reinforced by hundreds of guardhouses, 293 watchtowers, patrol dogs, and a vast swath of no-man's-land. Today the wall is history, but there are several places that recall its notoriety.

The **Mauermuseum—Haus am Checkpoint Charlie** (p. 343) is the best place to gain an understanding of what life was like during the Cold War. If you have time, there's also the **Berlin Wall Documentation Center** on Bernauer Strasse (② 030/464 10 30; www.berliner-mauer-dokumentations zentrum.de; U-Bahn: Bernauer Strasse; S-Bahn: Nordbahnhof). Bernauer Strasse was one of Berlin's most notorious streets during the Cold War, divided its entire length into east and west, with buildings on the east empty and boarded up. Here you'll find a chapel (built on the site of a former church blown up by the Communists in 1985), a Berlin Wall memorial, and a Documentation Center with photographs and other items chronicling in English the historical and political background of the Wall and presenting a personal view of what the Wall meant for Berliners on both sides. The center is open Tuesday to Sunday 10am to 6pm (to 5pm Nov–Mar), and admission is free.

A few sections of the Wall have been left standing, most notably on **Niederkirchnerstrasse** (not far from the Museum Haus am Checkpoint Charlie; S-Bahn/U-Bahn: Potsdamer Platz), where a 820-ft. (250m) section remains. But the most colorful remainder of the Wall is in former East Berlin on **Mühlenstrasse** (S-Bahn: Ostbahnhof; U-Bahn: Warschauer Strasse). Called the **East Side Gallery** (www.eastsidegallery.com), this ⅔-mile-long (1km) section on the banks of the Spree was painted on its east side with more than 100 murals by international artists in 1990. The murals are now a bit faded and chipped, though some artists restored their murals in 2000.

French, and Italian masters, including Gainsborough, Watteau, Botticelli, Raphael, Tiepolo, Titian, Murillo, and Velázquez.

Matthäiskirchplatz 4. ② 030/266 29 51. www.smb.museum. Admission 8€ ($10) adults, 4€ ($5.20) students/children. Tues–Sun 10am–6pm (to 10pm Thurs). U-/S-Bahn: Potsdamer Platz. Bus: 123, 148, 200, M29, or M41.

NEAR THE KU'DAMM

Kaiser-Wilhelm Gedächtniskirche (Kaiser Wilhelm Memorial Church)

Completed in 1895 as a memorial to Kaiser Wilhelm I, this church was destroyed by bombs during World War II and left in ruins as a reminder of the horrors of war. Today it contains a small museum with displays and photos related to war and destruction. Beside the ruined church is a new church designed by Prof. Egon Eiermann and finished in 1961; come here for free organ concerts Saturday at 6pm.

Breitscheidplatz. ② 030/218 50 23. www.gedaechtniskirche.com. Free admission. Ruined church Mon–Sat 10am–4pm; new church daily 9am–7pm; organ concerts in new church Sat 6pm. U-Bahn: Zoologischer Garten or Kurfürstendamm.

Käthe-Kollwitz Museum ⭐⭐ *(Finds)* This small but significant museum shows the powerful drawings, sketches, and sculptures of Käthe Kollwitz (1867–1945), a Berliner who managed to capture human emotions both tender and disturbing in her subjects, mostly the working class. War, poverty, death, hunger, love, grief, and happiness are all deftly rendered with just a few strokes. Who can forget Kollwitz's portrayal of horror on the face of a mother whose child has just been run over, or the wonderment expressed by a young mother and her infant gazing into each other's eyes? Because she routinely took up causes of the suppressed, her work was outlawed by the Nazis.

Fasanenstrasse 24 (just off Ku'damm). ✆ 030/882 52 10. www.kaethe-kollwitz.de. Admission 5€ ($6.50) adults, 2.50€ ($3.25) students/children. Wed–Mon 11am–6pm. U-Bahn: Uhlandstrasse.

The Story of Berlin ⭐ This multimedia extravaganza ambitiously attempts to portray 8 centuries of the city's history through photos, films, sounds, and colorful displays. Beginning with the founding of Berlin in 1237, it chronicles the plague, the Thirty Years' War, Frederick the Great's reign, military life, the Industrial Revolution and the working poor, the Golden 1920s, World War II, divided Berlin during the Cold War, and the fall of the Wall. Hidden loudspeakers heighten the effects: In a 19th-century tenement courtyard, for example, you hear a dog barking, a baby crying, and other sounds of a densely packed neighborhood, while the sound of breaking glass accompanies a display on Nazis and their treatment of Jews. Lights flash in a media blitz as you enter the display on the fall of the Wall, making you feel like one of the first East Berliners to wonderingly cross to the West. Conclude your tour on the 14th floor with a panoramic view over today's Berlin. Be sure, too, to join the 30-minute tour of the underground bunker built in 1974 at the height of the Cold War to house 3,500 people. Luckily it was never used, as there was only enough food, water, and self-generated power to last 2 weeks. Although the displays are a bit jarring and the historical information is too jumbled to be truly educational, the museum does leave a lasting impression.

Ku'damm-Karree, Kurfürstendamm 207–208 (at the corner of Uhlandstrasse). ✆ 030/887 20 100. www.story-of-berlin.de. Admission 9.80€ ($13) adults, 8€ ($10) students/seniors, 3.50€ ($4.55) children, 21€ ($27) families. Daily 10am–8pm (you must enter by 6pm). U-Bahn: Uhlandstrasse.

Zoologischer Garten (Berlin Zoo) ⭐ *(Kids)* Founded in 1844 and just a short walk from the Ku'damm and Bahnhof Zoo, the Berlin Zoo is Germany's oldest zoo and one of Europe's most attractive. Until World War II, it boasted thousands of animals of every imaginable species and description—many familiar to Berliners by nicknames. The tragedy of the war struck here as well, and by the end of 1945, only 91 animals remained. Since the war, the city has been rebuilding its large and unique collection; today more than 11,000 animals are housed here. The zoo has Europe's most modern birdhouse, featuring more than 550 species. The most valuable inhabitants are giant pandas. The **Aquarium** is as impressive as the adjacent zoo, with more than 9,000 fish, reptiles, amphibians, insects, and other creatures, including sharks, crocodiles and Komodo dragons. The "hippoquarium" is a new attraction.

Budapester Strasse 32 and Hardenbergplatz 8. ✆ 030/25 40 10. www.zoo-berlin.de. Combination ticket for zoo and aquarium 16.50€ ($21) adults, 13€ ($17) students, 8.50€ ($11) children; zoo only 11€ ($14) adults, 8€ ($10) college students, 5.50€ ($7.15) children. Summer daily 9am–6:30pm (to 5pm in winter). S-/U-Bahn: Zoologischer Garten.

WHERE TO DINE

Brasserie Desbrosses ⭐ FRENCH   The Ritz-Carlton may be much too ritzy for most budgets, but this classic brasserie—built in 1875 in a French village but dismantled and reassembled here—offers casual dining in a traditional setting as well as alfresco dining on a terrace. A good choice if you're visiting museums in the Tiergarten or the shops around Potsdamer Platz, it offers a reasonably priced weekday business lunch for 13€ ($17), home-baked pastries and breads, seafood and meat dishes, a Sunday champagne brunch for 54€ ($70), and more. Keep in mind, however, that even though dining here is casual, the rest of the hotel is so upscale it's not the kind of place you want to visit on a bad hair day.

The Ritz-Carlton, Potsdamer Platz 3. © **030/33 77 77.** www.desbrosses.de. Meals 14€–20€ ($18–$26). AE, DC, MC, V. Daily 7am–11pm. S-Bahn: Savignyplatz.

Calcutta ⭐ INDIAN   Berlin's first Indian restaurant has been in business for almost 40 years. This small, cheerful establishment with colorful murals and the obligatory Indian background music offers curries, tandoori from a wood-fired clay oven imported from India, and vegetarian dishes. Just a short walk north of the Ku'damm, it's a good place for a relaxing, unhurried meal.

Bleibtreustrasse 17. © **030/883 62 93.** Main courses 10€–16€ ($13–$21). DC, MC, V. Daily noon–midnight. S-Bahn: Savignyplatz.

Dressler CONTINENTAL   Resembling an arts-conscious bistro of the sort that might have entertained tuxedo-clad clients in the 1920s, Dressler is set behind a wine-colored facade and outfitted with leather banquettes, black-and-white tile floors, mirrors, and film memorabilia from the great days of early German cinema. Waiters scurry around with vests and aprons, carrying trays of everything from hefty portions of lobster salad to duck. It's located near Brandenburg Gate.

Unter den Linden 39. © **030/204-44-22.** www.restaurant-dressler.de. Meals 15€–23€ ($19.50–$30). AE, DC, MC, V. Daily 8am–midnight. S-Bahn: Unter den Linden or Friedrichstrasse. Bus: 100 or 200.

Le Buffet im KaDeWe _Value_ INTERNATIONAL   On the sixth floor of the immense KaDeWe department store (see "Shopping," below), you'll find continental Europe's biggest food emporium. It's so amazing that it alone may be worth a trip to Berlin—more types of sausages than you can count, cheeses, teas, breads, jams, sweets, coffees, and more. Interspersed throughout the floor are small dining counters specializing in specific cuisines, but an even greater selection is available one floor up at a glass-enclosed self-service restaurant reminiscent of a greenhouse. The restaurant offers daily specials of Berlin favorites, pasta, an extensive salad bar, an antipasti buffet, desserts, and more.

In KaDeWe, Wittenbergplatz. © **030/217 77 39.** Meals 10€–15€ ($13–$19.50). AE, DC, MC, V. Mon–Fri 9:30am–7:30pm; Sat 9am–7:30pm. U-Bahn: Wittenbergplatz.

Lubitsch CONTINENTAL   Deeply entrenched in the consciousness of many local residents, Lubitsch is considered in some quarters to have a degree of conservative chic. Expect platters of grilled lamb with rosemary and green beans and fried potatoes, or red snapper filet with Mediterranean vegetables and potatoes, though the simpler daily set meal for 10€ ($13) is a steal. Count on an indifferent staff, a black-and-white decor with Thonet-style chairs, and a somewhat arrogant environment that, despite its drawbacks, is very, very _Berliner_.

Bleibtreustrasse 47. © **030/882 37 56.** Meals 9€–18€ ($12–$23). AE, DC, MC, V. Mon–Sat 10am–midnight; Sun 6pm–midnight. U-Bahn: Kurfürstendamm.

Luisen-Bräu *Value* GERMAN   Near Charlottenburg Palace, Luisen-Bräu brews its own beer on the premises and sells German dishes to go with it. An English menu is offered weekdays until 5pm with such items as grilled pork knuckle, sausages, roast pork, and chicken, all with side dishes. After 5pm weekdays, and all day on weekends, you have to order food from a counter. You can also come just for the beer. Dining is at long wooden tables (which fosters conversation with neighbors) or, in summer, outside.

Luisenplatz 1 (at the corner of Spandauer Damm). ✆ 030/341 93 88. www.luisenbraeu.com. Meals 5.80–10€ ($7.55–$13). AE, DC, MC, V. Daily 11am–11:30pm. U-Bahn: U-2 to Sophie-Charlotte-Platz or U-7 to Richard-Wagner-Platz (then a 10-min. walk). Bus: 109 or M45.

Lutter & Wegner Seit 1811 *★★* AUSTRIAN/GERMAN   This wine bar/restaurant dates from 1811, when it first opened as a wine cellar in East Berlin. With its dark wainscoting, candles on white tablecloths, and changing art exhibits, it still exudes an old-world charm, although tables are too close together in the tiny restaurant for much intimacy. In addition to a standard English menu, there's a more interesting daily menu in German with offerings of fresh fish, grilled meats, and more, so be sure to ask for a translation.

Schlüterstrasse 55. ✆ 030/881 34 40. www.restaurantlutterundwegner.de. Reservations recommended. Meals 16.50€–20€ ($21–$26). AE, MC, V. Daily 6pm–midnight. S-Bahn: Savignyplatz.

Marjellchen *★* EAST PRUSSIAN   This is the only restaurant in Berlin specializing in the cuisine of Germany's long-lost province of East Prussia, along with those of Pomerania and Silesia. Amid a Bismarckian ambience of vested waiters and oil lamps, you can enjoy savory old-fashioned fare (marinated elk, for example) of a type that Goethe and Schiller favored. Marjellchen isn't the place to go, however, if you want to keep tabs on your cholesterol intake.

Mommsenstrasse 9. ✆ 030/883 26 76. www.marjellchen-berlin.de. Reservations recommended. Meals 10.10€– 20.20€ ($13–$26). AE, DC, MC, V. Daily 5pm–midnight. U-Bahn: Uhlandstrasse. S-Bahn: Savignyplatz.

Mutter Hoppe GERMAN   This cozy, wood-paneled basement restaurant still serves the solid Teutonic cuisine favored by a quasi-legendary matriarch (Mother Hoppe) who used to churn out vast amounts of food to members of her extended family and entourage. Within a quartet of old-fashioned dining rooms, you'll enjoy heaping portions of such rib-sticking fare as *Sauerbraten* (marinated beef in sauce) with roasted potatoes, and braised filet of pork in mushroom-flavored cream sauce. On weekend nights there's live music from the 1920s and '30s.

Rathausstrasse 21, Nikolaiviertel. ✆ 030/241 56 25. www.prostmahlzeit.de/mutterhoppe. Meals 8€–18€ ($10–$23). MC, V. Daily 11:30am–midnight. U-Bahn/S-Bahn: Alexanderplatz.

Oranium *★★* *Finds* INTERNATIONAL   A 7-minute walk north of Museum Island in the midst of Mitte's main nightlife scene, this lively bistro offers a varied, intriguing menu that hits the spot for those seeking escape from the heavier German cuisine. Hearty breakfasts (served until 4pm), salads, wraps, sandwiches, tapas, fish, and more are listed on the extensive menu.

Oranienburgerstrasse 33–34. ✆ 030/308 82 967. www.oranium.de. Main courses 5.60€–15€ ($7–$19.50). AE, MC, V. Sun–Thurs 9am–midnight; Fri–Sat 9am–2am. S-Bahn: Oranienburgerstrasse. U-Bahn: Oranienburger Tor.

Zur Letzten Instanz GERMAN   Open since 1621, this tiny restaurant claims to be Berlin's oldest *Gaststätte* (neighborhood pub) and has supposedly been frequented by everybody from Napoleon to Beethoven. Its rooms are rustic, with plank floors, wainscoting, and a few antiques. The English menu offers traditional, hearty Berlin specialties, all served with side dishes like dumplings, potatoes, or red cabbage. Be sure to save room for Berlin's famous dessert, *rote Grütze* (cooked fruits with vanilla sauce). Tables are placed outside in summer.

Waisenstrasse 14–16. ✆ **030/242 55 28.** www.zurletzteninstanz.de Meals 9€–14€ ($12–$18). AE, DC, MC, V. Mon–Sat noon–11pm. U-Bahn: Klosterstrasse.

Zwölf Apostel *Value* PIZZA/PASTA   If you're hungry for pizza or pasta after visiting the Pergamon on Museum Island, there's no more popular (or packed) place than this very successful local chain. Catering to everyone from business types to students and occupying colorfully painted vaulted rooms underneath the S-Bahn tracks (you can hear the trains rumble as they pass overhead), it offers very good pastas and pizzas, with reduced prices available until 4pm. There's also a branch near the Ku'Damm at Bleibtreustrasse 49 (✆ **030/312 14 33;** S-Bahn: Savignyplatz).

Georgenstrasse 2 (underneath the S-Bahn tracks near the Pergamon). ✆ **030/201 02 22.** www.12-apostel.de Reservations recommended. Pizzas and pastas 8€–12€ ($10–$16). No credit cards. Sun–Thurs noon–midnight; Fri–Sat noon–1am. S-/U-Bahn: Friedrichstrasse.

SHOPPING

The **Ku'damm** (or Kurfürstendamm) is the Fifth Avenue of Berlin. It's filled with quality stores but also has outlets hustling cheap souvenirs and T-shirts. Although Berliners themselves shop on the Ku'damm, many prefer the specialty stores on the side streets, especially between **Breitscheidplatz** and **Olivaer Platz.** Lovers of porcelain should make a point of visiting the prestigious emporium **KPM (Königliche Porzellan-Manufaktur [Royal Porcelain Factory]),** in the Kempinski Hotel Bristol, Kurfürstendamm 27 (✆ **030/88-67-21-10;** U-Bahn: Kurfürstendamm). Founded in 1763, KPM has become famous the world over for its exquisite hand-painted, hand-decorated items.

Another major shopping street is nearby **Tauentzienstrasse,** with a wide array of stores that are often cheaper than on the Ku'damm, many specializing in German fashions and accessories for women. Anchoring one end of Tauentzienstrasse is the **Europa Center,** once *the* address for mall shopping in West Berlin but now overshadowed by bigger and better malls. At the other end of the street is the 100-year-old **Kaufhaus des Westens,** Tauentzienstrasse 21 (✆ **030/21-210;** U-Bahn: Kurfürstendamm or Wittenbergplatz), a huge luxury department store (the largest in continental Europe), known popularly as **KaDeWe** (pronounced *Kah*-day-vay). It's best known for its food department, where more than 1,000 varieties of German sausages are displayed along with delicacies from all over the world, but there are many equally eye-popping displays on its six floors of merchandise.

If you're looking for serious bargains, head to where the natives shop—**Wilmersdorferstrasse,** with a vast number of discount stores and department stores. Try to avoid Saturday morning, when it's often impossibly overcrowded.

In eastern Berlin, not that long ago, you couldn't find much to buy except a few souvenirs. All that is changed now. The main street, **Friedrichstrasse,** offers some of Berlin's most elegant shopping, including the **Galeries Lafayette** department store and the upscale **Quartier 206** shopping mall. Upmarket boutiques—selling everything from quality women's fashions to Meissen porcelain—are found along **Unter den Linden.** The cheaper stores in eastern Berlin are around the rather bleak-looking

Alexanderplatz. Many souvenir, specialty, and clothing shops are found in the **Nikolai Quarter.** The largest shopping mall in eastern Berlin, with outlets offering a little bit of everything, is at the **Berliner Markthalle,** at the corner of Rosa-Luxemburg-Strasse and Karl-Liebknecht-Strasse. **Potsdamer Platz,** once Berlin's busiest intersection and a no-man's-land during the Cold War, is home to the **Arkaden,** an American-style shopping mall with more than 120 stores and restaurants.

Most stores in Berlin are open Monday to Saturday from 9 or 10am to 6pm, though department stores remain open until 8pm.

Berlin's best-known and biggest outdoor market is the **Grosser/Berliner Trödelmarkt und Kunstmarkt (Art and Junk Market),** on Strasse des 17 Juni (© 030/26 55 00 96), a minute's walk east of the Tiergarten S-Bahn station. A staggering selection of books, CDs, silverware, coins, stamps, china, glass, original artwork, jewelry, clothing, and junk is sold at this market divided into two parts, one with antiques and junk, the other, across the bridge, with arts and crafts. The market is open Saturday and Sunday 10am to 4pm.

NIGHTLIFE

Berlin never sleeps. There are no mandatory closing hours for nightclubs, dance clubs, and bars, so you can stay out all night if you want. Nightlife in Berlin means everything from far-out bars and dance clubs to world-renowned opera and theater. To find out what's going on in the performing arts, pick up a copy of *Berlin in Your Pocket.*

If you don't mind taking a chance on what's available, the best bargain for last-minute tickets is **Hekticket,** with outlets at Hardenbergstrasse 29d, across from Bahnhof Zoo on Hardenbergplatz on the corner of Deutsche Bank (© 030/230 99 30; www.heckticket.de; S-/U-Bahn: Bahnhof Zoologischer Garten), and Karl-Liebknecht-strasse 12, opposite McDonald's near Alexanderplatz (© 030/24 31 24 31; S-/U-Bahn: Alexanderplatz). Unsold tickets for that evening's performances are available for more than 200 venues, including the Staatsoper, Komische Oper, classical concerts, pop concerts, and cabaret—most at up to 50% off.

PERFORMING ARTS   Performances of the world-renowned Berliner Philharmonisches Orchester (Berlin Philharmonic Orchestra), founded in 1882, take place at the **Philharmonie** in the Kulturforum, Herbert-von-Karajan-Strasse 1 (© 030/25488-999; www.berlin-philharmonic.com; U-/S-Bahn: Potsdamer Platz). Tickets for most performances cost 18€ to 61€ ($23–$79), but those for the Berlin Philharmonic usually sell out months in advance (if you're staying in a first-class hotel, the concierge may be able to get seats for you). The **Konzerthaus Berlin,** on beautiful Gendarmenmarkt in Berlin-Mitte (© 030/203-09-21-01; U-Bahn: Französische Strasse), serves as the venue of the Berlin Symphonic Orchestra, founded in 1952 in the former East Germany, and hosts other musical events.

The **Deutsche Oper Berlin,** Bismarckstrasse 35, Charlottenburg (© 030/341 02 49 for information, or 0700-67 37 23 75 46 for tickets; www.deutscheoperberlin.de; U-Bahn: Deutsche Oper), is the largest of Berlin's three opera houses. Works by Mozart, Verdi, and Wagner are perennial favorites, but it also cultivates forgotten operas and works of the 20th century, staging opera virtually every evening except when there's ballet. Tickets for most performances run 17€ to 65€ ($22–$84.50). The **Staatsoper Unter den Linden,** Unter den Linden 7, Berlin-Mitte (© 030/20 35 44 38 for information, or 030/20 35 45 55 for tickets; www.staatsoper-berlin.de; U-Bahn: Friedrichstrasse or Französische Strasse; bus: 100 or 200), has long been one of Berlin's famous opera houses, featuring opera, ballet, and concerts under the musical direction of conductor Daniel Barenboim. Tickets go for 8€ to 80€ ($10–$104) for most performances. The **Komische Oper (Comic Opera),** Behrenstrasse 55–57, Berlin-Mitte (© **030/20 260-666** for information, or 030/47 99 74 00 for tickets; www.komische-oper-berlin.de; S-Bahn: Unter den Linden; U-Bahn: Französische Strasse; bus: 100), an innovative musical theater company, serves as an alternative to the grander mainstream productions of the two other opera houses, presenting a varied program of opera, operetta, symphony concerts, ballet, and even modern dance. Tickets here cost 8€ to 31€ ($10–$40) for most performances.

CLUBS Berlin's oldest jazz club is **Quasimodo,** Kantstrasse 12a, Charlottenburg (© **030/312 80 86;** www.quasimodo.de; S-/U-Bahn: Zoologischer Garten). Although many different styles of music are offered here, including rock, Latin, blues, funk, and soul, jazz is the focus. Cover ranges from 9€ to 32€ ($12–$42). The club is open Tuesday to Saturday 9pm to 3am, with shows beginning at 10pm. A small and smoky jazz house, **A Trane,** Bleibtreustrasse 1, at the corner of Bleibtreustrasse and Pestalozzistrasse (© **030/313 25 50;** www.a-trane.de; S-Bahn: Savignyplatz), features musicians from around the world performing everything from contemporary and mainstream jazz to bebop and swing. It's open daily from 9pm to 2am, but Friday and Saturday are open-ended, with free late-night jam sessions beginning Saturdays after midnight. Otherwise, cover generally ranges from 8€ to 15€ ($9.20–$17.25).

Long before there was online dating, there was **Cafe Keese Ball Paradox,** Bismarckstrasse 108 (© **030/312 91 11;** www.cafekeese-berlin.de; U-Bahn: Ernst-Reuter-Platz), which was founded in 1966 as a dance hall where women get to ask the men to dance. Little has changed since then, except now there are telephones at each table and there's an hourly Men's Choice for dance partners (when the green light goes on). The cavernous place, with live music, is often jammed with the mostly middle-aged, especially on Saturday nights, and formal attire is requested. It's open Tuesday to Saturday from 7:30pm to 3am and Sunday and Monday (senior night) 3 to 10pm. There's no cover, but there is a one-drink minimum.

BARS & CAFES Those in search of a beer near the Ku'damm might try **Zillemarkt,** Bleibtreustrasse 48a (© **030/881 70 40;** S-Bahn: Savignyplatz), which dates from the early 1900s and is a popular neighborhood joint for drinks, weekend brunch, and backyard outdoor seating in nice weather. **Zwiebelfisch,** Savignyplatz 7–8 (© **030/312 73 63;** S-Bahn: Savignyplatz), is a neighborhood bar that's been around for more than 30 years and still enjoys great popularity, especially in the wee hours of the night. Although definitely tourist-oriented and a bit too corny for most sensibilities, **Joe's Wirtshaus zum Löwen,** Hardenbergstrasse 29 (© **030/262 10 20;** S-/U-Bahn: Zoologischer Garten), does a brisk business due to its convenient location (between Bahnhof Zoo and the Kaiser-Wilhelm Gedächtniskirche); huge, multilevel beer hall; and even larger beer garden and occasional music. But on a fine summer's day, nothing beats a beer under the trees at **Loretta's Garden** on Lietzenburger Strasse 89 (© **030/882 33 54;** U-Bahn: Uhlandstrasse), a huge beer garden open April to September.

Many hip locals cite **Bar am Lützowplatz,** Lützowplatz 7 (© **030/262 68 07;** U-Bahn: Nollendorferplatz), as their favorite bar, partly because it manages to be beautiful, chic, breezy, and artsy, and partly because it provides a concentrated kind of conviviality within a prosperous but staid neighborhood. It presents an almost reverential portrait of Mao Tse-tung at the end of its astonishingly long bar, the humor of which cannot be lost on the devoted capitalists and bons vivants who come here to see, be seen, and choose from one of the city's most impressive offerings of cocktails and champagne.

In the eastern part of Berlin, the **Fernsehturm** on Alexanderplatz is a top pick for both the best bird's-eye view of the city and a romantic early evening drink. After paying the 7€ ($9) admission fee to the tower, head straight for the revolving **Telecafe** (© 030/242 33 33; S-Bahn: Alexanderplatz), which at 650 feet (195m) high offers a terrific view during its 30-minute spin.

In the heart of the Nikolai Quarter, **Georg Bräu,** Spreeufer 4 (© 030/242 42 44; S-/U-Bahn: Alexanderplatz), is a popular microbrewery that offers German fare, along with outdoor seating and live music weekends from 10am to 1pm. **Zum Nussbaum,** Am Nussbaum 3 (© 030/242 30 95), is a small, cozy, and comfortable establishment, modeled after a bar built in 1507 but destroyed in World War II.

Kurvenstar, Kleine Präsidentenstrasse 3 (© 030/247 2311-5; S-Bahn: Hackescher Markt), featuring retro furnishings and a curved bar, is popular for its happy hour (Tues–Sat 7–10pm) and nightly happenings, including live music on Thursdays and DJs spinning hip-hop and reggae on Saturdays.

AN EXCURSION TO POTSDAM

If you take only one excursion outside Berlin, it should be to the beautiful baroque town of **Potsdam,** 15 miles (24km) southwest of the city. It served as a garrison and residence of Prussia's kings and royal families from the 17th to the 20th century. Its most famous resident was Frederick the Great, who succeeded in uniting Germany under his rule and built himself the delightful rococo palace **Schloss Sanssouci** ("without care"), which he used as a place for quiet meditation away from the rigors of war and government. His palace still stands, surrounded by a 750-acre (300-hectare) estate, Park Sanssouci, with several other magnificent structures, including the Neues Palais.

GETTING THERE   Potsdam Hauptbahnhof is 20 minutes from Bahnhof Zoo via the **RE1** commuter line, with departures every half hour. Otherwise, you can also reach Potsdam by **S-Bahn** in about 30 minutes.

VISITOR INFORMATION   Potsdam's Tourist Information Centre, Brandenburger Strasse 3 (© 0331/27 55 80; www.Potsdam-tourism.com), at the Brandenburger Gate, is the place to go for information and maps. The office is open April to October, Monday to Friday from 9:30am to 6pm, Saturday and Sunday from 9:30am to 4pm; November to March, Monday to Friday from 10am to 6pm, and Saturday and Sunday from 9:30am to 2pm.

GETTING AROUND   From Potsdam Hauptbahnhof, you can board **bus no. 695 directly for Schloss Sanssouci or Neues Palais. Otherwise, for the most dramatic approach to the palace, take any **tram** departing from in front of the station going in the direction of *"Zentrum"* and get off at Platz der Einheit. From there, you can walk 30 minutes through the heart of the historic town via the pedestrian Brandenburger Strasse, passing delightful shops, cafes, and restaurants along the way. A day transportation pass for Greater Berlin, including Potsdam, is 6€ ($7.80).

TOP ATTRACTIONS & SPECIAL MOMENTS

Potsdam's star attraction is **Schloss Sanssouci** ✿✿✿, Zur Historischen Mühle (© 0331/96 94 202; www.spsg.de). Built in the 1740s by Georg von Knobbelsdorff, it served as Frederick the Great's summer residence for almost 40 years. (He died here and is buried on the grounds.) With only a dozen rooms, the one-story rococo palace is exceedingly modest compared to most royal residences, yet its rooms are a delight, filled with paintings, marble, and gold leaf, with playful motifs of grapes, wine, and images of Bacchus. The elliptically shaped **Marble Hall** is the largest in the palace, but the **music salon** is the supreme example of the rococo style. A small bust of Voltaire commemorates the writer's sojourns here. Don't miss the most dramatic view of the palace—from its park side, it sits atop six grassy terraces, cut into the side of a hill like steps in a pyramid, created for Frederick's vineyards (if you walk through town to the palace, this is the view you'll be treated to first). You can visit only on a 40-minute guided tour in German (an English pamphlet is available), departing every 20 minutes and costing 8€ ($10.40) adults and 5€ ($6.50) students/children. Schloss Sanssouci is open Tuesday to Sunday: April to October 9am to 5pm and November to March 9am to 4pm. *Tip:* It is best (especially in summer) to show up before noon to buy your tickets for the palace tour.

At the other end of Sanssouci Park, about a 25-minute walk away, is the estate's largest building, the extravagant **Neues Palais** (© 0331/96 94 202; www.spsg.de), built 20 years after Schloss Sanssouci as a show of Prussian strength following the devastation of the Seven Years' War. Also serving as a summer residence for the royal Hohenzollerns, it's much more ostentatious than Schloss Sanssouci and in comparison seems grave, solemn, and humorless. Of note is the Grotto Room, its walls and ceiling smothered with shells, mica, minerals, fossils, and semiprecious stones. The Neues Palais is open Saturday to Thursday: April to October 9am to 5pm and November to March 9am to 4pm. Admission here is 5€ ($6.50) for adults and 4€ ($5.20) students/children. It is usually less crowded than Sanssouci.

WHERE TO DINE
The most romantic dining choice in town is **Juliette** *&*, Jägerstrasse 39 (© 0331/270 17 91; tram: 94 or 96), in the heart of the historic city just off Brandenburger Strasse. The cozy and intimate restaurant is set inside a restored old house, with blazing fireplace, low ceilings, exposed beams, and tiny windows. The excellent waiters—many of them hail from France—expertly serve a traditional French menu, which features some wonderful chicken dishes. Fixed-price meals cost 49€ to 79€ ($64–$103). It's open daily noon to 3:30pm and 6pm to midnight.

The most convenient place for a meal if you're visiting Schloss Sanssouci is the Mövenpick chain's **Zur Historischen Mühle,** across from the palace at An der Orangerie (© 0331/28 14 93; bus: 695 to Sanssouci). It offers a variety of continental and traditional German and Swiss meals priced from 10€ to 18€ ($13–$23). In summer there's a shaded outdoor terrace, children's playground, and a beer garden with simpler, less expensive fare ranging from sausage to chicken. It's open daily 8am to 11pm.

3 Munich *&&*

Named after the Munichen monks who settled more than 1,200 years ago on the banks of the Isar River, **Munich** is the capital of the state (or land) of Bavaria and a sprawling city of 1.3 million. Home of industrial giants like BMW and Siemens, it's one of Germany's important cultural capitals, with four symphony orchestras, two opera houses, dozens of world-class museums, more than 50 theaters, and one of Germany's largest universities. The diverse student population and the foreign residents who make up more than 22% of the citizenry ensure an active avant-garde cultural scene and a liberal attitude in an otherwise conservative region.

Munich is striking, largely the product of the exuberant imagination and aspirations of past Bavarian kings and rulers. Royal residences, majestic museums, steepled churches, and ornate monuments celebrate architectural styles from baroque and Gothic to neoclassical and postmodern. Add wide boulevards, spacious parks, thriving nightlife, at least six breweries, and the world's largest beer fest, and you have what amounts to one of Germany's most interesting, exciting, and festive cities.

Munich is a prime rail destination, and though we rate Berlin first in importance, Munich is definitely more picturesque and, in many ways, is more strategically located. Not only are its train connections to the rest of Germany superb, but its link to several high-speed international rail lines makes it an easy stop for anyone on a multicountry tour of Europe. And with an international airport offering direct flight connections with North America, it also makes a good starting or stopping point on a rail trip through Europe.

STATION INFORMATION
GETTING FROM THE AIRPORT TO THE TRAIN STATION
About 25 miles (40km) northeast of central Munich, the **Flughafen München Franz Josef Strauss Airport** (☎ 089/97 52 13 13; www.munich-airport.de), inaugurated in 1992, is among the most modern, best-equipped, and most efficient airports in the world. The airport, Europe's seventh-busiest in terms of passenger volume, handles more than 1,100 departures and landings daily and serves at least 65 cities worldwide. Passengers can fly nonstop from several North American gateways, including New York, Atlanta, and Chicago.

The easiest way to get into town is via the **S-Bahn,** with lines S-8 or S-1 traveling to Marienplatz (the city center) and the Hauptbahnhof (main train station). Trains leave every 10 minutes, and the trip to the Hauptbahnhof takes about 40 minutes. If you have a valid railpass you can ride for free. Otherwise, a ticket is 8.80€ ($11). Alternatively, you can buy a 9.60€ ($12) **1-day transportation pass (Tageskarte)** for greater Munich, advisable if you plan on using public transportation at least once more the remainder of the day. A taxi to the city center costs about 60€ ($78).

INSIDE THE STATION
Munich's main rail station, the **Hauptbahnhof** (☎ 089/1308 58 90), on Bahnhofplatz near the city center, is one of Europe's largest. It contains a hotel, restaurants, shopping, and banking facilities. All major German cities are connected to this station. Some 18 daily trains connect Munich directly to Frankfurt's main train station or its airport (trip time: 3¾ hr.). In addition, there are a half dozen direct trains from Heidelberg to Munich (trip time: 3 hr.) and trains from Berlin depart once or twice an hour (trip time: 6 hr.). For information about long-distance trains, call ☎ **11861.** You can also drop by **EurAide,** a special service for English-speaking travelers providing free train and sightseeing info and selling various rail tickets. It's located off the main hall (behind the Reise Zentrum). Summer hours are Monday to Saturday 7:45am to 12:45pm and 2 to 6pm and Sunday 8am to noon; winter hours are Monday to Friday 9am to noon and 1 to 4pm. It's closed in January.

You'll find a branch of Munich's **Tourismus Information** just outside the Hauptbahnhof's main exit at Bahnhofplatz 2. It distributes city maps for .30€ (40¢) and

Munich

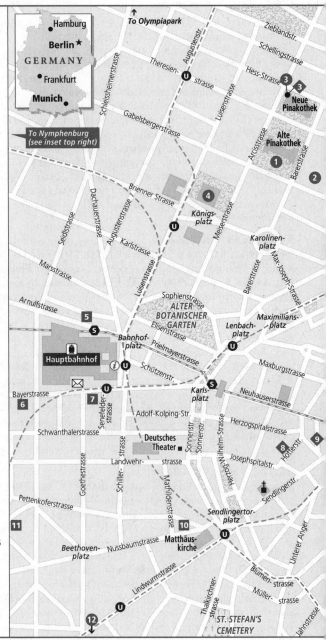

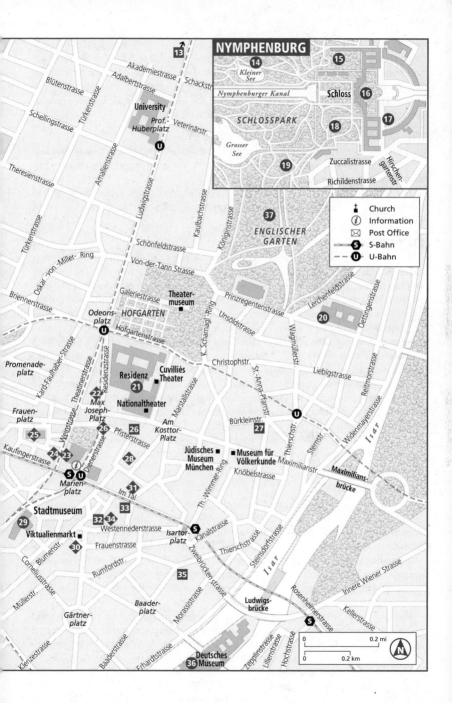

NYMPHENBURG

14 Kleiner See

15

Nymphenburger Kanal

Schloss **16**

17

SCHLOSSPARK

18

Grosser See

Zuccalistrasse

Richildenstrasse

19

Hirschgartenstr.

13

Akademiestrasse

Adalbertstrasse

Schackstr.

Blütenstrasse

Türkenstrasse

Schellingstrasse

University

Prof.-
Huberplatz

Veterinärstr.

U

Theresienstrasse

Amalienstrasse

Ludwigstrasse

Kaulbachstrasse

Königinstrasse

37

ENGLISCHER
GARTEN

Schönfeldstrasse

Von-der-Tann Strasse

Türkenstrasse

Oskar- von-Miller- Ring

Galeriestrasse

Theater-
museum

Prinzregentenstrasse

Lerchenfeldstrasse

Oettingenstrasse

Brienner strasse

Odeons-
platz

HOFGARTEN

U

Hofgartenstrasse

K. Scharnagl -Ring

Unsöldstrasse

20

Wagmüllerstr.

Promenade-
platz

Karl-Faulhaber-Strasse

Theatinerstrasse

Residenzstrasse

Christophstr.

St.-Anna-Pfarrstr.

Liebigstrasse

Reitmorstrasse

Residenz

Cuvilliés
Theater

21

22

Max
Joseph-
Platz

Nationaltheater

Marstallstrasse

U

Bürkleinstr.

27

Thierschstr.

Sternstr.

Widenmayerstrasse

Isar

Frauen-
platz

Wienstrasse

26

Pfisterstrasse

Am
Kosttor-
Platz

Jüdisches
Museum
München

Museum für
Völkerkunde

Maximilianstr.

Maximilians-
brücke

25

Kaufingerstrasse

24

23

Dienerstrasse

28

Knöbelstrasse

S

Marien-
platz

i

Th. Wimmer-Ring

31

Im Tal

33

Stadtmuseum

29

32 **34**

Westenriederstrasse

Kanalstrasse

Isartor-
platz

S

Thierschstrasse

Isar

Steinsdorfstrasse

Innere Wiener Strasse

Viktualienmarkt

30

Frauenstrasse

Cornelius strasse

Blumenstr.

Rumfordstr.

Zweibrückenstrasse

Morassistrasse

35

Ludwigs-
brücke

Rosenheimerstrasse

Kellerstrasse

Müllerstr.

Baader-
platz

Gärtner-
platz

Klenzestrasse

Baaderstrasse

Erhardtstrasse

Deutsches
Museum

36

Zeppelinstrasse

Lilienstrasse

Hochlstrasse

S

	Church
i	Information
✉	Post Office
S	S-Bahn
U	U-Bahn

0   0.2 mi

0   0.2 km

N

brochures. For a 10% deposit that goes toward the cost of the room, the staff will also find you a hotel room. It's open April to October Monday to Saturday 9am to 8pm and Sunday and holidays 10am to 6pm; November to March Monday to Saturday 9:30am to 6:30pm and Sunday and holidays 10am to 6pm.

The **Hauptbahnhof** serves as a nucleus for the many tram, bus, U-Bahn (underground subway), and S-Bahn (metropolitan railway) lines.

INFORMATION ELSEWHERE IN THE CITY

In addition to the tourist office at the Hauptbahnhof, there's another convenient office in the **Neues Rathaus (New Town Hall)** on Marienplatz, open Monday to Friday 10am to 8pm and Saturday 10am to 4pm.

For more information, call ✆ **089/233 96 500** Monday to Friday 8am to 7pm and Saturday 9am to 5pm. You can also get information on the Internet at **www.muenchen.de**.

CITY LAYOUT

The heart of Munich, the **Altstadt (Old Town),** is east of the Hauptbahnhof. Its very center is **Marienplatz,** a cobblestone plaza a 15-minute walk from the train station and connected to the rest of the city by an extensive subway network. Over the centuries, it has served as a market square, a stage for knightly tournaments, and the site of public executions. Today it's no less important, bordered on one side by the impressive Neues Rathaus (New Town Hall), famous for its chimes and mechanized figures appearing daily at 11am and noon (also 5pm in summer). Much of the Old Town is a **pedestrian zone** where you'll find the smartest boutiques, most traditional restaurants, and oldest churches, plus the Viktualienmarkt outdoor market. Most of Munich's museums are within an easy walk or short subway ride from the center.

As for other areas worth exploring, the **Englischer Garten** with its wide green expanses and beer gardens stretches northeast from the city center. Oktoberfest is held at **Theresienwiese,** just south of the Hauptbahnhof, while **Schwabing,** north of the city center. is home to Munich's university and nightlife. **Schloss Nymphenburg,** once the royal family's summer residence, is northwest of town, accessible by streetcar from the train station.

GETTING AROUND

Munich's wonderful underground network, created in conjunction with the 1972 Summer Olympics, is the ultimate in German efficiency. It's divided into the **U-Bahn** (underground subway) and **S-Bahn** (metropolitan railway), with the most convenient connection between the two at Marienplatz. Buses and trams go everywhere the subway doesn't. Munich's public transport system operates daily about 5am to 1am, with some S-Bahn lines, including one to the airport, operating frequently throughout the night. In addition, a handful of bus and tram lines run nightly about 1:30 to 5am, designated by an *N* in front of their number.

Because the S-Bahn is part of the German Federal Railroads, you can use a valid railpass on these lines. Otherwise, you'll have to buy a ticket, which is good for all forms of transportation in Munich and includes transfers. Validate the ticket yourself by inserting it into one of the little blue machines at the entrance to the underground track or on board the bus or tram.

A **single journey** to most destinations costs 2.20€ ($2.85). Shorter journeys—trips of at most two stops on the subway or four on the tram or bus—require a ticket called

Munich U-Bahn & S-Bahn

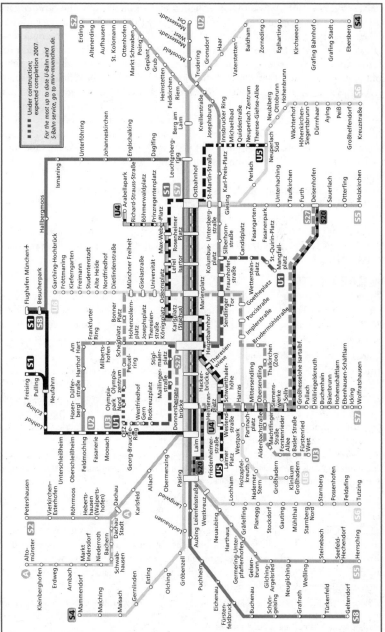

a *Kurzstrecke* at only 1.10€ ($1.45). Slightly more economical is the *Streifenkarte,* a stripeticket allowing multiple journeys and saving the hassle of buying individual tickets each time you travel. It costs 10.50€ ($14) and consists of 10 stripes worth 1.05€ ($1.35) each. For short journeys (a Kurzstrecke), you use one stripe. Most trips in the city, however, require two stripes (a total of 2.10€/$2.75 for the ride). Simply fold up two segments of the *Streifenkarte* and insert them into the validating machine.

A simpler solution still is to buy a *Tageskarte* (day ticket), allowing unlimited travel on all modes of transport for 1 day. A 4.80€ ($6.25) *Tageskarte* is valid for most of Munich's inner city and includes the entire U-Bahn network. If you want to travel to the outskirts, buy the 9.60€ ($12) card for the metropolitan area (about a 50-mile/80km) radius, including the airport and Dachau. The Parnter-Tageskarte, valid for up to five adults (two children count as one adult), costs 8.50€ ($11) and 17€ ($22) respectively.

For more information on Munich's public transportation system (MVV), call ⓒ **089/41 42 43 44;** www.mvv-muenchen.de) or drop by the MVV Kundencenter kiosk inside the Hauptbahnhof or Marientplatz subway station.

Cabs begin at 2.60€ ($3.40), plus 1.20€ ($1.55) per kilometer for the first 5km (3 miles) and 1.45€ ($1.90) per kilometer after that. If you need to call a taxi, phone ⓒ **089/216 10** or 089/194 10.

WHERE TO STAY

The area surrounding the Bahnhof doesn't have many recommendable hotels, but hotels in the Altstadt center of town tend to be very expensive. We list the best hotels closest to the train station, as well as some of our favorite value selections for the rest of the city.

Advokat Hotel   This hotel occupies a six-story apartment house originally constructed in the 1960s. Although its curbside appeal is nil, its stripped-down, streamlined interior borrows in discreet ways from Bauhaus and minimalist models. The result is an aggressively simple, clean-lined, and artfully spartan hotel, with such welcoming extras as free sherry on offer in the '50s-style lounge and a rooftop terrace great for summer evenings. Rooms, half with balconies, offer such perks as fresh flowers, apples, candy, and free drinks in the minibar.

Baaderstrasse 1, 80469 München. ⓒ **089/21 63 10.** Fax 089/21 63 190. www.hotel-advokat.de. 50 units. 160€–200€ ($208–$260) double. Weekend discounts available. Rates include buffet breakfast. AE, DC, MC, V. S-Bahn: Isartor. **Amenities:** Nonsmoking rooms. *In room:* Hair dryer, no A/C.

Am Markt *Value*   Next to Munich's colorful outdoor market, the Viktualienmarkt, this hotel has a nostalgic flair and is a good choice for budget travelers. Though rooms are a bit plain and small, they're modern and neat, with whitewashed walls and bold splashes of color. The old-fashioned breakfast room is tastefully decorated and the entry displays photos of celebrities who have stayed here—and most who haven't. At any rate, the hotel looks more expensive than it is, and you can't beat its location, just a few minutes' walk from Marienplatz.

Heiliggeistrasse 6, 80331 München. ⓒ **089/22 50 14.** Fax 089/22 40 17. www.hotel-am-markt.eu. 31 units, 21 with bathroom. 79€ ($103) double without bathroom; 109€ ($145) double with bathroom. Rates include continental breakfast. MC, V. S-Bahn: Marienplatz. **Amenities:** Lounge.

An der Oper   This five-floor hotel, just steps from the Bavarian National Theater in the Altstadt but tucked away on an overlooked side street, is superbly located for sightseeing and shopping. In spite of its basic decor, there are touches of elegance. Rooms, bathed in white and a bit kitschy with overstated chandeliers, range from small to medium. Bathrooms tend to be small, but are well organized and come mainly with just a shower. What you're paying for here is location.

Falkenturmstrasse 10 (just off Maximilianstrasse, near Marienplatz), 80331 München. ℭ **089/290 02 70**. Fax 089/29 00 27 29. www.hotelanderoper.com. 68 units. 180€–270€ ($234–$351) double. Rates include buffet breakfast. AE, MC, V. Tram: 19. **Amenities:** Restaurant, nonsmoking rooms. *In room:* Hair dryer, no A/C.

Eden Hotel Wolff ⓕ

If you must stay in the train station area, this family-owned hotel across from the station's north side is your best bet. Built in 1890, its interior is richly traditional, with chandeliers and dark-wood paneling, and the staff is attentive and efficient. Most rooms are spacious, and all are tastefully furnished in a decor that runs the gamut from extremely modern to rustic. After sightseeing, guests can use an exercise room, sauna, solarium, steam room, and rooftop terrace.

Arnulfstrasse 4, 80335 München. ℭ **089/55 11 50**. Fax 089/55 115-555. www.ehw.de. 210 units. 178€–292€ ($231–$380) double. Rates include buffet breakfast. AE, DC, MC, V. S-/U-Bahn: Hauptbahnhof. **Amenities:** Restaurant; bar; laundry, nonsmoking rooms. *In room:* Hair dryer.

Europäischer Hof

If you're tired of lugging around baggage and you don't give a darn about charm, you can't get much closer to the train station than this modern hotel with a functional lobby and a courteous staff. Across from the Hauptbahnhof's south side, it offers various room types with varying levels of comfort, from "tourist class" bathroomless rooms with sinks to luxurious "business class" doubles with mini-bars, trouser presses, and hair dryers.

Bayerstrasse 31, 80335 München. ℭ **089/55 15 10**. Fax 089/551 51 14 44. www.heh.de. 145 units, 135 with bathroom. 62€–142€ ($81–$185) double without bathroom, 92€–312€ ($120–$406) double with bathroom. Rates include buffet breakfast. *Frommer's readers:* Discounts available except during major trade fairs and Oktoberfest (the highest rates given above). AE, DC, MC, V. S-/U-Bahn: Hauptbahnhof. **Amenities:** Restaurant; laundry; nonsmoking rooms. *In room:* Minibar (some rooms), hair dryer (some rooms), no A/C.

Gästehaus Englischer Garten ⓕⓕ *Finds*

This is an oasis of charm and tranquillity, separated from the Englischer Garten only by a bubbling brook yet just a short walk away from Schwabing's nightlife. A dozen rooms (half without private bathroom) are located in a 130-year-old converted mill, where breakfast is served outside in fair weather and where small to medium rooms offer "Bavarian grandmotherly" furnishings, including genuine antiques, old-fashioned but comfortable beds, and Oriental rugs. The rest of the units are located in an apartment complex down the street, complete with kitchenettes. There are rental bikes (10€/$13 per day) to explore the expansive English Gardens.

Liebergesellstrasse 8, 80802 München. ℭ **089/383 94 10**. Fax 089/383 94-133. www.hotelenglischergarten.de. 27 units, 21 with bathroom. 71€–97€ ($92–$126) double without bathroom; 98€–149€ ($127–$194) double with bathroom; 103€–172€ ($134–$224) apt. double. Buffet breakfast 9.50€ ($12) extra. AE, MC, V. U-Bahn: Münchener Freiheit. *In room:* No A/C.

Hotel Exquisit

One of the most appealing hotels in this quiet residential neighborhood, the Exquisit lies behind a wine-colored facade only a 10-minute walk from the Hauptbahnhof and Marienplatz. It has a paneled lobby whose focal point is a lounge that gets busy around 6 or 7pm, as well as a sauna and solarium. Rooms are spacious and comfortably furnished, with about half overlooking an ivy-draped garden. The shower-only bathrooms have adequate shelf space, and some have double basins.

Pettenkoferstrasse 3, 80336 München. ℂ **089/551 99 00.** Fax 089/551 99 499. www.hotel-exquisit.com. 50 units. 170€–265€ ($221–$345) double; 225€–305€ ($293–$397) suite. Rates include buffet breakfast. AE, DC, MC, V. U-Bahn: Sendlinger Tor. **Amenities:** Restaurant; bar; nonsmoking rooms; rooms for those w/limited mobility. In room: Hair dryer, no A/C.

Hotel Opera ⭐⭐⭐ (Finds)

This charming little gem is so palatially decorated from the inside out that could be mistaken for the home of a baroness. Marbled floors lead from the richly decorated lobby to an enclosed courtyard reminiscent of Tuscany, where breakfast is served in summer. Each room is beautifully and individually decorated, often with antiques from the countryside or period furniture. Those overlooking the courtyard contain French doors leading to small balconies. Although this hotel is not as centrally located as most of the other choices here, it's still just a 15-minute walk from Marienplatz

St. Anna Strasse 10, 80538 München. ℂ **089/21 04 94-0.** Fax 089/21 04 09-77. www.hotel-opera.de. 25 units. 190€–275€ ($247–$358) double; 285€–365€ ($371–$475) suite. AE, MC, V. nearby. U-Bahn: Lehel. **Amenities:** Restaurant; bar; laundry; nonsmoking rooms. In room: Hair dryer, no A/C.

Hotel Schlicker

In spite of its location between a McDonald's and a Burger King, this hotel exudes a certain kind of charm. Its pedigree dates from 1544, and the same family has managed it for five generations. Due to extensive renovation, however, only the breakfast room suggests that this was once an ancient inn. The midsize bedrooms are comfortable and traditional, but the hotel's main selling point is its location, in the heart of Munich just steps away from the Marienplatz.

Tal 74, 80331 München. ℂ **089/24 288 70.** Fax 089/29 60 59. www.hotel-schlicker.de. 69 units. 115€–200€ ($150–$260) double. AE, DC, MC, V. S-/U-Bahn: Marienplatz. In room: Hair dryer, no A/C

Jedermann ⭐ (Value)

Those in awe of the high prices of Munich hotels find comfort at this pleasant and deftly run hotel, just a 10-minute walk from the Hauptbahnhof and owned by the English-speaking Jenke family since 1962. The old-fashioned Bavarian rooms are generally small but cozy and comfortable; nice touches include flowers, antiques, traditional Bavarian furniture, and chocolates left on the pillows. The cheapest rooms don't have private bathrooms. A computer in the lobby offers free Internet access.

Bayerstrasse 95, 80335 München. ℂ **089/54 32 40.** Fax 089/54 32 41 11. www.hotel-jedermann.de. 55 units, 48 with bathroom. 49€–89€ ($64–$116) double without bathroom; 67€–157€ ($87–$204) double with bathroom. Rates include buffet breakfast. MC, V. 10-min. walk from Hauptbahnhof (turn right on Bayerstrasse from south exit). **Amenities:** Bar. In room: Hair dryer.

Uhland ⭐⭐

The facade of this 100-year-old building, in a quiet residential neighborhood near the Oktoberfest field and a 10-minute walk from the Hauptbahnhof, is welcoming—ornate neo-Renaissance with flower boxes of geraniums at all the windows. A former apartment complex, it was converted into a hotel more than 50 years ago and has kept up with the times, adding such things as a computer for guest use in the communal living room and free wireless Internet connections. Each room is unique, with some decorated in Bavarian style and others in high-tech modern (two even have waterbeds).

Uhlandstrasse 1, 80336 München. ℂ **089/543 35-0.** Fax 089/54 33 52 50. www.hotel-uhland.de. 30 units. 85€–185€ ($111–$241) double. Rates include buffet breakfast. DC, MC, V. U-Bahn: Theresienwiese. Bus: 58 from Hauptbahnhof to Georg-Hirth-Platz. **Amenities:** Laundry; nonsmoking rooms. In room: Hair dryer, no A/C.

TOP ATTRACTIONS & SPECIAL MOMENTS

Munich is stocked with so many treasures that any visitor who plans to "do" the city in a day or two will not only miss out on many major sights but will also fail to grasp the city's spirit and absorb its special flavor. Below you'll find a few vital highlights to help you make the best of your time in the city.

MUSEUMS

Alte Pinakothek ★★★   If you visit only one art museum in Munich, this should be it. Begun as the collection of the royal Wittelsbach family in the early 1500s, it ranks as one of Europe's most important galleries and contains virtually all European schools of painting from the Middle Ages to the early 19th century, with one of the world's largest collections of Rubens, plus galleries filled with German, Dutch, Flemish, Italian, Spanish, and French masterpieces. You'll also find galleries of religious allegorical paintings, portraits of peasants and patricians, Romantic landscapes, still lifes, and scenes of war and hunting.

Although it's difficult to pick the collection's stars, Dürer is well represented with *Four Apostles, The Baumgartner Altar, Lamentation for the Dead Christ,* and, probably most famous, his *Self-Portrait (Selbstbildnis im Pelzrock).* Watch for Titian's *Crowning with Thorns (Die Dornenkrönung),* Rembrandt's *Birth of Christ* with his remarkable use of light and shadows, and Bruegel's *Land of Cockaigne.* Among the many Rubens are the rather frightening *Last Judgment (Das Grosse Jüngste Gericht)* and *The Damned's Descent into Hell (Der Höllensturz der Verdammten),* sure to make a convert of the most avowed sinner. In Albrecht Altdorfer's *Battle of Alexander,* which took him 12 years to complete, notice the painstaking detail of the thousands of lances and all the men on horseback. Another favorite is Adriaen Brouwer of the Netherlands, one of the best painters of the peasant genre. The Alte Pinakothek has 17 of his paintings in Room 11, the largest collection in the world. Brouwer's skill at capturing the life of his subjects as they drink at an inn, play cards, or engage in a brawl is delightful.

Barer Strasse 27 (entrance on Theresienstrasse). (℗) **089/238 05-216.** www.pinakothek.de. Admission 5.50€ ($7.15) adults, 4€ ($5.20) seniors, students, and children. Tues 10am–8pm; Wed–Sun 10am–6pm. U-Bahn: Theresienstrasse. Tram: 27 to Pinakotheken.

Bayerisches Nationalmuseum ★   The Bavarian National Museum emphasizes the historical and cultural development of Bavaria, as well as the rest of Europe, from the Middle Ages to the early 19th century. It complements the Alte Pinakothek, showing what was happening in other genres of art and crafts at the same time that painters were producing their masterpieces. Glass, miniatures, musical instruments, wood and ivory carvings, jewelry, clothing, textiles and tapestries, porcelain, medieval armor and weaponry, furniture, stained-glass windows, sculpture, and religious artifacts and altars are some of the 20,000 items. Outstanding are the **wood sculptures** from the Gothic through rococo periods, especially carvings by **Tilman Riemenschneider**

Value **Saving Money on Museums**

On Sundays, several of Munich's major museums, including all the Pinakothek museums and the Bayerishes Nationalmuseum, charge an admission of only 1€ ($1.30) to their permanent exhibitions, while the Münchener Stadtmuseum is absolutely free.

(notice the facial expressions of the 12 Apostles in Room 16), as well as works by **Erasmus Grasser, Michael Pacher, Johann Baptist Staub,** and **Ignaz Günther.**

One delightful thing about this museum is that the architecture complements the objects. The Late Gothic Church Art Room (Room 15), for example, is modeled after a church in Augsburg, providing a perfect background for the religious art it displays. The basement, partly devoted to folk art, includes furniture and complete rooms showing how people lived long ago. Notice the wooden floors and low ceiling (to save heat). The other half of the museum houses an incredible collection of **nativity scenes (Krippe)** ✸✸ from the Alpine region and Italy. Some of the displays are made of paper, but most are amazingly elaborate and lifelike; it's worth visiting the museum for them alone.

Prinzregentenstrasse 3. ✆ **089/211 24 01.** www.bayerisches-nationalmuseum.de. Admission 5€ ($6.50) adults, 3€ ($3.90) seniors/students; free for children under 18; more for special exhibits. Tues–Sun 10am–5pm (to 8pm Thurs). U-Bahn: Lehel. Tram: 17 to Nationalmuseum.

Deutsches Museum ✸✸✸ Munich's most visited museum and the world's largest and oldest technological museum of its kind, the Deutsches Museum contains a huge collection of artifacts and historic originals, divided into 50-some exhibits relating to physics, navigation, mining, vehicle engineering, musical instruments, glass technology, writing and printing, photography, textiles, and weights and measures. There's also a planetarium. If you followed the guideline running through the museum, you'd walk more than 10 miles (16km). You can see a replica of the **Gutenberg press,** and **musical instruments** from electronic drums to a glass harmonica. You can descend into the bowels of a **coal** and a **salt mine**—it takes the better part of an hour just to walk through. Would you like to ponder the meaning behind the prehistoric drawings of the **Altamira Cave?** What makes the museum fascinating for adults and children alike is that there are buttons to push, gears to crank, and levers to pull (though in today's high-tech world, children used to virtual reality arcades might find the displays a little too tame). There's also a children's section, the **Kinderreich,** geared toward youngsters 8 and younger. In any case, you could easily spend a half day here. Because the museum has outgrown its present facilities, there are branches: The **Deutsches Museum Verkehrszentrum,** Theresienhöhe 14a (✆ **089/500 80 61;** U-Bahn: Schwanthalerhöhe), houses a fleet of automobiles, trains, streetcars, and locomotives, including the first automobile (Benz, 1886); and **Flugwerft Schleissheim,** Effnerstrasse 18 (✆ **089/31 57 14-0;** S-Bahn: Oberschleissheim), which features airplanes, helicopters, engines, simulators, and other displays related to aviation and space travel. A ticket to all three museums costs 15€ ($20).

Museumsinsel 1 (Ludwigsbrücke). ✆ **089/2179-1.** www.deutsches-museum.de Admission 8.50€ ($11) adults, 3€ ($3.90) students/children, 15€ ($19.50) families. Daily 9am–5pm. S-Bahn: Isartor. Tram: 18 to Deutsches Museum.

Münchner Stadtmuseum ✸ Centrally located in the Altstadt (Old Town) and often overlooked, the eclectic Munich City Museum is a great repository of the city's history—but that's not all. The **Puppet Theater Collection** is outstanding, with puppets and theater stages from around the world, as well as fairground art (including the Oktoberfest), while the **Musical Instrument Collection** displays European instruments from the 16th to the 20th centuries and primitive instruments from around the world, including African drums, South American flutes, Indian sitars, and Javanese gamelans. There's also a section devoted to the **history of photography** with original photographs and cameras from 1839 to 1919. The exhibits on Munich cover the history of the city from the late 15th century to the present day with maps, models, paintings, photographs, and furniture, while a section on National Socialism in Munich from 1918 to 1945 covers the Nazi era with photographs, propaganda posters, and documents (unfortunately only in German). But the most valuable pieces are **Erasmus Grasser's** *10 Morris Dancers,* carved in 1480 for display in Munich's old town hall. The morris (or morrice) dance, popular in the 15th century, was a rustic ambulatory dance performed by companies of actors at festivals.

St. Jakobsplatz 1. (℃ **089/233-223 70**. www.stadtmuseum-online.de. Admission 4€ ($5.20) adults, 2€ ($2.30) seniors/students/children, 6€ ($7.80) families; free for children under 6; more for special exhibits. Tues–Sun 10am–6pm. S-/U-Bahn: Marienplatz.

Neue Pinakothek ✿✿   Across from the Alte Pinakothek is the Neue Pinakothek, with its comprehensive view of European painting in the late 18th and 19th centuries. It begins with art from around 1800 (**Goya, Turner,** and **Gainsborough**) and works through early romantic landscape painters **Caspar David Friedrich** and **Leo von Klenze,** then continues with works of the Biedermeier era (**Waldmüller's** romanticized renditions of peasant life are wonderful), German and French impressionism, symbolism, and Art Nouveau. **Corinth, Courbet, Delacroix, Liebermann, Menzel, Cézanne, Gauguin, Rodin, van Gogh, Degas, Manet, Monet,** and **Renoir** all have canvases here. The building itself is a delight, designed by Alexander von Branca and opened in 1981 to replace the old museum destroyed in World War II. Using the natural lighting of skylights and windows, it's the perfect setting for the paintings it displays, and perimeter ramps make the works accessible by wheelchair or stroller.

Barer Strasse 29 (entrance on Theresienstrasse). (℃ **089/238 05-195**. www.pinakothek.de. Admission 5.50€ ($7.15) adults, 4€ ($5.20) seniors/students/children Wed 10am–8pm; Thurs–Mon 10am–6pm. U-Bahn: Theresienstrasse. Tram: 27 to Pinakotheken.

Pinakothek der Moderne ✿✿   This spacious, modern museum brings together four major collections under one roof—art, graphics, architecture, and design—making it Germany's largest museum of art from the 20th and 21st centuries. Foremost is the art collection, which features changing exhibitions that might include German expressionists such as Ernst Ludwig Kirchner and Max Beckmann (the museum possesses Europe's largest collection of his works), surrealists like René Magritte and Dalí, and some of the most important names in modern art, including Picasso, Warhol, Beuys, Rauschenberg, Jasper Johns, and Bruce Nauman. The Architecture Museum displays temporary exhibits on the history of architecture and current developments, while the State Graphic Art Collection stages temporary displays from the beginning of classical modernism to the present. The New Collection is always interesting for its visually pleasing displays of industrial design and applied arts, which can run the gamut from automobiles and computers to teapots and chairs.

Barer Strasse 40. (℃ **089/238 05-360**. www.pinakothek.de. Admission 9.50€ ($12) adults, 6€ ($7.80) seniors/students/children Tues–Sun 10am–6pm (to 8pm Thurs). U-Bahn: Odeonsplatz or Theresienstrasse. Tram: 27 to Pinakotheken.

Städtische Galerie im Lenbachhaus ✿✿   The City Gallery is the showcase for Munich's artists from the Gothic period to the present. Its setting couldn't be more perfect: the former Italianate villa of artist Franz von Lenbach, built at the end of the 19th century. Some rooms have been kept as they were then. Although landscape paintings from the 18th and 19th centuries (particularly interesting are the cityscapes of Munich) and examples of German Jugendstil (Art Nouveau) are part of the collection, the great treasure is the **Blaue Reiter (Blue Rider)** ✮✮✮ group of artists. **Wassily Kandinsky,** one of the great innovators of abstract art, was a key member of this Munich-based group, and Lenbach House has an outstanding collection of works of his early period, from shortly after the turn of the 20th century to the outbreak of World War I. Other Blue Rider artists represented are **Paul Klee, Franz Marc, August Macke,** and **Gabriele Münter.**

In Lenbach House, Luisenstrasse 33 (off Königsplatz). ☎ 089/233 32 000. www.lenbachhaus.de. Admission 5€–10€ ($6.50–$13) adults, 2.50€–5€ ($3.25–$6.50) seniors/students/children; more for special exhibits. Tues–Sun 10am–6pm. U-Bahn: Königsplatz. Tram: 27 to Karolinenplatz.

PALACES

Nymphenburg Palace ✮✮✮   The former summer residence of the Wittelsbach family, who ruled over Bavaria, Nymphenburg is Germany's largest baroque palace. Construction began in 1664 but took more than a century to complete. The first room you'll see is the glorious two-story **Steinerner Saal (Stone Hall),** richly decorated in late-rococo style with stucco work and frescoes, used for parties and concerts, with subsequent rooms containing portraits of the royal family, period furniture, tapestries, and paintings. Probably the most interesting room is Ludwig I's **Gallery of Beauties:** The 36 portraits, commissioned by Ludwig, represent the most beautiful women in Munich in his time. Among them are Queen Marie of Bavaria (mother of Ludwig II), Helene Sedlmayr (daughter of a shoemaker, who later married a footman and had 10 children), and Lola Montez (a dancer whose scandalous relations with Ludwig prompted an 1848 revolt by a disgruntled people who forced his abdication).

To the south of the palace buildings is the **Marstallmuseum,** with a splendid collection of state coaches, carriages, and sleds used for weddings, coronations, and special events. Housed in what used to be the royal stables, the museum culminates in the fantastic fairy-tale carriages of Ludwig II, which are no less extravagant than his castles. On the floor above the Marstallmuseum is the **Museum of Nymphenburg Porcelain,** with a fine collection of delicate figurines, tea services, plates, and bowls from the mid–18th century through the 1920s.

Nymphenburg's park, first laid out as a geometrical baroque garden but transformed into an English landscape garden in the early 19th century, contains statues, artificial hills, lakes, canals, botanical gardens, and a number of pavilions. **Amalienburg,** a small pink hunting lodge unlike anything you've ever seen, is one of the world's great masterpieces of rococo art. Though the first couple of rooms are simple enough, the rest take off in a flight of fantasy, with an amazing amount of decorative silver covering almost every inch of the walls with vines, grapes, and cherubs. Its **Hall of Mirrors** is as splendid a room as you're likely to find anywhere, far surpassing anything in the main palace. In the park are three other pavilions (closed in winter): the **Magdalenenklause,** a meditation retreat, complete with artificial cracks in the walls to make it look like a ruin; the **Pagodenburg,** an elegant two-story tea pavilion; and **Badenburg,** a bathhouse with Europe's first heated indoor pool.

Schloss Nymphenburg 1. ☎ 089/179 08-0. www.schloesser.bayern.de Combination ticket to everything 10€ ($13) adults, 8€ ($10) seniors/students/children in summer, 8€ ($10) and 6€ ($7.80) respectively in winter. Nymphenburg Palace only 5€ ($6.50) adults, 4€ ($5.20) seniors/students/children. Apr to mid-Oct daily 9am–6pm; mid-Oct to Mar daily 10am–4pm. Badenburg, Pagodenburg, and Magdalenenklause closed mid-Oct to Mar. Tram: 17 to Schloss Nymphenburg.

Moments The World's Greatest Beer Fest

Munich's most famous event is the **Oktoberfest (www.muenchen.de)**, held from mid-September to the first Sunday in October. The celebration began in 1810 to honor Ludwig I's marriage, when the main event was a horse race in a field called the Thereisenwiese. Everyone had so much fun the celebration was held again the following year, and then again and again. Today the Oktoberfest is among the largest fairs in the world. Every year the festivities get under way with a parade on the first Oktoberfest Sunday, with almost 7,000 participants marching through the streets in folk costumes. Most activities, however, are at the Theresienwiese, where huge beer tents sponsored by local breweries dispense both beer and merriment, complete with Bavarian bands and singing. Each tent holds up to 6,000, which gives you some idea of how rowdy things can get. During the 16-day period, an estimated six million visitors guzzle more than a million gallons of beer and eat 700,000 broiled chickens! In addition to the beer tents, there are carnival attractions and amusement rides. Entry to the fairgrounds is free, but rides cost extra.

Residenz, Residenzmuseum & Schatzkammer ★★   While Nymphenburg Palace was the Wittelsbach summer home, the Residenz was the Bavarian rulers' official town residence for 4 centuries until 1918. The **Residenzmuseum,** a small part of the residence, is open to the public. A mere fraction of the total palace, it's so large that only half the museum's 80-some rooms are open to the public in the morning; the other half are open in the afternoon. No matter when you come, you'll see state rooms, apartments, bedchambers, and arcades in everything from Renaissance and baroque to rococo and neoclassical. The stunning **Antiquarium** is the largest secular Renaissance room north of the Alps; in the **Silver Chamber** is the complete table silver of the House of Wittelsbach—some 3,500 pieces. The **Ancestors Hall** contains the portraits of 121 members of the family—eerie because of the way their eyes seem to follow you as you walk down the hall. Be sure to see the **Emperor's Hall,** the **Ornate Chapel,** the **Green Gallery,** and the **Ornate Rooms** by François de Cuvilliés the Elder, one of the best examples of South German rococo.

In the Residenz is also the **Schatzkammer (Treasury)** ★★, housing an amazing collection of jewelry, gold, silver, insignia, and religious items belonging to the Bavarian royalty and collected over 1,000 years, including the royal crown, swords, scepters, goblets, bowls, toiletry objects, serving platters, treasures from other countries, and more. The highlight is the 1586 jewel-studded _Statue of St. George_ on his horse.

Max-Joseph-Platz 3. ⓒ **089/290 67-1.** www.schloesser.bayern.de. Combination ticket for Residenzmuseum and Schatzkammer, 9€ ($12) adults, 8€ ($10) seniors/students; free for children under 18. Ticket for either Residenzmuseum or Schatzkammer, 6€ ($7.80) adults, 5€ ($6.50) seniors/students. Daily 9am–6pm in summer; daily 10am–4pm in winter. You must enter 30 min. before closing time. S-Bahn: Marienplatz. U-Bahn: Odeonsplatz. Tram: 19 to Nationaltheater.

A PARK, A ZOO & A SPA

The **Englischer Garten** ★ is one of Europe's largest city parks (larger than New York's Central Park). Despite its name, it owes its existence to an American rather than an Englishman. Benjamin Thompson, who fled America during the Revolution because of his British sympathies, was instrumental in the park's creation and landscaping. Stretching 3 miles (5km) along the Isar in the heart of the city, it offers beer gardens, sunbathing (including nude sunbathing, a surprise to quite a few unsuspecting visitors—some claim these areas are Munich's most popular tourist attraction), and recreation. For a break, stop for a beer at the Chinese pagoda beer garden.

For even more relaxation, head to **Therme Erding,** located near Munich's airport in the suburb or Erding at Thermenallee 1 (© **08122/22 70 200;** www.therme-erding. de; S-Bahn: Erding, then a 15-min. walk or bus no. 550 or 560), which claims to be the largest thermal spa in Europe. It's divided into two areas: the Thermenparadies with a large indoor hot-spring pool, numerous mineral and sulfur baths, free fitness programs like water aerobics, an outdoor pool, and play areas for kids, including 12 water slides (concentrated in an area called Galaxy Rutschenparadies); and the Vitaltherme for visitors 16 years and older, with various baths, saunas, and relaxation rooms. Therme Erding is open Monday to Friday 10am to 11pm and weekends and holidays 9am to 11pm. There are many options for admission, depending on length of stay, time of day, and whether you opt for the Thermenparadies or Vitaltherme. Four hours in the Thermenparadies and Galaxy costs 15€ ($19.50; weekends and holidays cost 3€/$3.90 extra); but weekdays before 1pm it's 9.50€ ($12) for 2 hours.

Tierpark Hellabrunn (Munich Zoo) stands in Tierpark Hellabrunn, about 4 miles (6km) south of the city center, at Tierparkstrasse 30 (© **089/62 50 80;** www. zoo-munich.de; U-Bahn: Thalkirchen). It's home to 5,000 animals and includes the Elephant House (built in 1913); Europe's largest walk-through aviary; an aquarium; the Tropical House for gorillas and chimps; and all the usual inhabitants including penguins, rhinos, polar bears, and lions, in environments that mimic native habitats. It also has a petting zoo and playgrounds. You can visit the zoo daily 8am to 6pm (Oct–Mar 9am–5pm); admission is 9€ ($12) for adults, 6.50€ ($8.45) for seniors, 6€ ($7.80) for students, and 4.50€ ($5.85) for children ages 4 to 14, and free for children 3 and under.

WHERE TO DINE

Alois Dallmayr ✦ CONTINENTAL   Alois Dallmayr, which traces its history from 1700, is the most famous delicatessen in Germany. Its tempting array of delicacies from around the globe has been sampled by many a royal court. The upstairs dining room, seating only 42 and with views of the Frauenkirche's towers, offers Mediterranean fare, served on Nymphenburg porcelain and best enjoyed with wine from the very ample cellar.

Dienerstrasse 14–15. © **089/21 35-100.** www.dallmayr.de. Reservations required. Meals 21€–35€ ($27–$46). AE, DC, MC, V. Tues–Sat noon–2pm and 7–10pm. S-/U-Bahn: Marienplatz. Tram: 19.

Bratwurstherzl am Viktualienmarkt _Value_ GERMAN   Good, hearty food is what you get at this down-to-earth local favorite just a stone's throw from the market. It's famous for its Nürnberger-style bratwurst, fresh from the restaurant's family-owned butcher shop and grilled over a beech-wood flame. Munich's own _Weisswurst_ (a delicacy of veal, spices, lemon, and parsley) is available until it runs out, a bargain at only 1.90€ ($2.45) apiece. Daily special platters (in German only; ask for a translation) are a steal at 6€ ($7.80).

Dreifaltigkeitsplatz 1. © **089/29 51 13.** www.bratwurstherzl.de. Meals 5.80€–11€ ($7.55–$14). AE, DC, MC, V. Daily 10am-9:30pm. S-/U-Bahn: Marienplatz.

Caffé Greco ✦ GREEK/MEDITERRANEAN/GERMAN   Located on the lower level of the Neue Pinakothek with its own outdoor entrance, this casual yet classy restaurant is your best bet for a satisfying meal when visiting the many nearby museums. Gleaming dark woods, photographs hung on white walls, black bentwood chairs, and white tablecloths set the mood for a meal from a limited but satisfying menu, including a classic Greek salad, various spaghetti dishes, fish of the day, and Bavarian specialties.

Barer Strasse 29 (entrance on Theresienstrasse). ✆ **089/2867 57 50.** Meals 8€–13€ ($10–$17). AE, DC, MC, V. Daily 10am–6pm (to 8pm Wed). U-Bahn: Theresienstrassez. Tram: 27.

Donisl (*Value* GERMAN   Open since 1715, Donisl is popular with visitors because of its convenient location near the Neues Rathaus, comfortable atmosphere, typical Bavarian decor, live music every evening, local specialties, English menu, and meals that are all bargain priced at 7.35€ ($9.55). Try the *Weisswurst, Leberkäse* (a kind of German meatloaf that looks like a huge slab of bologna), *Schweinsbraten* (pot-roasted pork), or Wiener schnitzel, each served with a side dish and best washed down with the freshly tapped beer.

Weinstrasse 1 (off Marienplatz). ✆ **089/22 01 84.** www.bayerischer-donisl.de. Meals 7.35€ ($9.55). AE, DC, MC, V. Daily 9am–11pm. S-/U-Bahn: Marienplatz.

Hundskugel ✦✦ GERMAN   Opened in 1440, this is probably Munich's oldest restaurant. Its facade, brightly lit and decorated with flower boxes, hints at what's waiting inside: a tiny dining room with a low-beamed ceiling, little changed over the centuries. It serves Bavarian and German traditional food, including *Spanferkel* (roast suckling pig), *Tafelspitz* (boiled beef), and the *Hundskugel Spezial* (broiled pork tenderloin with potatoes, mushrooms, and vegetables, baked with cheese). Dining here is an experience you won't soon forget.

Hotterstrasse 18. ✆ **089/26 42 72.** Reservations required. Meals 9.50€–20€ ($12–$26). AE, MC, V. Daily 11am–11pm. S-/U-Bahn: Marienplatz.

Nürnberger Bratwurst Glöckl am Dom ✦✦ (*Finds* GERMAN   This is Bavaria at its finest: a rough wooden floor, wooden tables, hooks for hanging coats, beer steins and tin plates lining a wall shelf, Bavarian specialties grilled over an open wood fire, and beer served from wooden barrels. In summer, there's limited outdoor seating in the shadow of the majestic Frauenkirche church. An evening here, dining on specialties like grilled pork knuckle *(Schweinshaxe)* or Nürnberger-style sausages, could possibly be your most memorable in Munich.

Frauenplatz 9. ✆ **089/29 52 64.** www.bratwurst-gloeckl.de. Meals 9€–20€ ($12–$26). MC, V. Daily 11am–10pm. S-/U-Bahn: Marienplatz.

Pfistermühle GERMAN   The country comes right into the heart of Munich at this authentic and old-fashioned restaurant, a series of charmingly decorated dining rooms in a converted 1573 mill. Add outdoor seating in summer, and this ranks as one of the prettiest spots in the Altstadt, just a block from the Hofbräuhaus. Many of the perfectly prepared roasts and fresh fish from the lakes and rivers of Bavaria would be familiar to your Bavarian grandmother, and portions are generous.

Pfistermühle 4. ✆ **089/23 703-865.** Reservations recommended. Meals 14€–22€ ($18–$29). AE, DC, MC, V. Mon–Sat noon–11pm. S-/U-Bahn: Marienplatz.

Prinz Myshkin ✿✿ VEGETARIAN This trendy restaurant serves vegetarian dishes in a refined setting of high vaulted ceilings, artwork, candles, and background music that's likely to be soft jazz. You'll find a variety of changing salads, soups, pizza, and innovative dishes inspired by the cuisines of Asia, Italy, Greece, Mexico, and beyond, ranging from miso soup and vegetarian sushi to spinach gnocchi and tofu stroganoff. It's a great alternative to heavier Bavarian food.

Hackenstrasse 2 (off Sendlinger Strasse, a few minutes' walk from Marienplatz). ✆ 089/26 55 96. www.prinz myshkin.com. Main courses 10€–16€ ($13–$21). AE, MC, V. Daily 11:30am–11:30pm. S-/U-Bahn: Marienplatz.

Ratskeller München ✿✿ GERMAN/CONTINENTAL Throughout Germany, you'll find *Ratskellers,* traditional cellar restaurants in Rathaus (city hall) basements, but this cavernous restaurant with its low, vaulted, painted ceilings is one of the best. Besides Bavarian and Franconian specialties such as roast suckling pig, Wiener schnitzel, and sausages, it has a few vegetarian dishes, sandwiches, and salads, as well as changing specials featuring national dishes from other countries. This is also a good choice for an afternoon coffee and dessert, or a glass of Franconian wine in the adjoining wine cellar.

In Town Hall's cellar, on Marienplatz. ✆ 089/21 99 89-0. www.ratskeller.com. Reservations recommended. Meals 11.50€–24€ ($15–$31). AE, MC, V. Daily 10am–11pm. S-/U-Bahn: Marienplatz.

Spatenhaus an der Oper GERMAN/INTERNATIONAL One of Munich's best-known beer restaurants, across from the Residenz and Nationaltheater, Spatenhaus offers typical, rustic Bavarian atmosphere, regional specialties, and generous portions at reasonable prices. If you want to know what this fabled Bavarian gluttony is all about, order the "Bavarian plate" (Schmankerlplatte), which is loaded down with various meats, including pork and sausages. Top it off with the restaurant's own beer, Spaten-Franziskaner-Bier.

Residenzstrasse 12. ✆ 089/290 706-0. Reservations recommended. Main courses 13€–24€ ($17–$31). AE, MC, V. Daily 9:30am-11:30pm. S-/U-Bahn: Marienplatz or Odeonsplatz.

Weisses Bräuhaus GERMAN This boisterous place is famous for its wheat beer (*Bräuhaus* means "brewery"), which Bavarians will drink even for breakfast. With an informal, smoke-blackened front room outfitted with long wooden tables (you'll have to share your table, but that's part of the fun) and a more formal back dining room with white tablecloths, it serves typical Bavarian fare from a lengthy menu. If you're hungry, go for the Bavarian Farmer's Feast (Bayrischer Bauernschmaus)—roast and smoked pork, pork sausage, dumplings, and sauerkraut. It's a less touristy choice than the Hofbräuhaus.

Tal 7. ✆ 089/290 13 80. www.weisses-brauhaus.de. Meals 8.90€–17€ ($12–$22). MC, V. Daily 8:30am–11pm. S-/U-Bahn: Marienplatz.

Wirtshaus zum Straubinger GERMAN Consistently crowded, this typical Bavarian restaurant near the Viktualienmarkt in the Altstadt has been a popular local choice for decades. The traditionally dressed staff in dirndl and lederhosen delivers steaming platters of pork knuckles, grilled duck, Nürnberger-style sausages, and other dishes that cater to nostalgia—you may see the term *Oma's Küche* ("Grandmother's kitchen") on the menu. For the health conscious, there are also salads and lighter fare for lunch. There's a weekday lunch for 6.20€ ($8.05); in summer, there's an inviting beer garden.

Moments Beer Gardens

The city's beer gardens (biergarten) are as fickle as the weather—if the weather's bad, the beer gardens don't open. By the same token, if the weather suddenly turns gloriously warm in the middle of February, the beer gardens start turning on the taps. Generally speaking, beer gardens are open on sunny days from spring through autumn, usually 10am to 11pm. Ranging from tiny neighborhood gardens accommodating a few hundred to those seating several thousand, they number about 30 in and around Munich, making it the world's beer garden capital. There are self-serve counters for food, or you can bring your own food with you.

These are some of Munich's most famous beer gardens: **Augustiner Keller,** Arnulfstrasse 52 (© **089/59 43 93**), about a 10-minute walk northwest of the Hauptbahnhof; **Viktualienmarkt,** in the city center near Marienplatz (© **089/29 75 45**); **Chinesischer Turm,** with a lovely location in the Englischer Garten (© **089/38 38 73 0**; U-Bahn: Giselastrasse); **Hirschgarten,** Hirschgartenstrasse 1 (© **089/17 25 91**; S-Bahn: Laim), one of Europe's largest, near Nymphenburg Palace. In the Old Town, the famous **Hofbräuhaus,** Platzl 9 (© **089/22 16 76**), also has a beer garden.

Blumenstrasse 5. © **089/23 23 83-0.** Reservations recommended. Main courses 7.50€–17.50€ ($9.75–$23). AE, MC, V. Mon–Sat 10am–midnight; Sun 11am–9:30pm (closed Sun June–Aug). S-/U-Bahn: Marienplatz.

SHOPPING

As Germany's fashion center, Munich boasts upscale boutiques, department stores, and designer names, primarily in the pedestrian-zoned Altstadt (all the following shops are near the S-/U-Bahn Marienplatz station). For traditional Bavarian clothing, stylish **Dirndl-Ecke,** Am Platzl 1/Sparkassenstrasse 10 (© **089/22 01 63**), has been a leading choice for high-grade dirndls, feathered alpine hats, and all clothing associated with the Alpine regions for more than 50 years. The very upscale **Loden-Frey,** Maffeistrasse 7–9 (© **089/21039-0**), offers the world's largest selection of *Loden* clothing and traditional Bavarian costumes, along with Armani and other modern designer fashions.

If you're looking for German and Bavarian souvenirs, a good place to hunt is **Orlandostrasse,** about a 5-minute walk from Marienplatz near the Hofbräuhaus. This small pedestrian lane is lined with shops selling T-shirts, beer steins, dolls in Bavarian costume, pipes, postcards, Christmas tree ornaments, and nutcrackers. Other specialty shops, all in the Altstadtalt, include **Max Krug,** Neuhauser Strasse 2 (© **089/22 45 01**), which has been selling beer mugs, nutcrackers, and cuckoo clocks since 1926; **Münchner Romantix's,** near the Hofbräuhaus at Pfisterstrasse 6 (© **290 40 91**), with Christmas decorations year-round and traditional crafts; and **Leute,** Viktualienmarkt 2 (© **089/26 82 48**), with a wide selection of bowls, trays, boxes, toys, and other finely crafted items made from wood. Germany's oldest miniature pewter foundry, the **Münchner Puppenstuben und Zinnfiguren-Kabinett,** Maxburgstrasse 4 (© **089/29 37 97**), dates from 1796 and is a great source for miniature houses, furniture, and people, all cunningly crafted from pewter or carved wood. Some of the figures are made from 150-year-old molds that are collector's items in their own right.

Since the early 1800s, Munich's most famous market has been **Viktualienmarkt** in the Altstadt, where you can buy bread, cheese, honey, cakes, fruit, wine, vegetables, flowers, and much more.

Store hours in Munich are generally Monday to Saturday from 9 or 10am to 6pm, though department stores stay open until 8pm. In addition, some specialty stores close at 2pm on Saturday.

NIGHTLIFE

To find out what's happening in Munich, go to one of the two tourist offices and get a copy of the monthly *Monatsprogramm* for 1.65€ ($2.15), a complete cultural guide that tells you not only what's being presented—including concerts, opera, special exhibits, and museum hours—but also how to purchase tickets. In addition, *Munich Found,* an English-language publication selling for 3€ ($3.90), list operas, plays, classical concerts, rock and jazz concerts, movies, and more.

THE PERFORMING ARTS   Munich celebrated 350 years of opera in 2004, and the neoclassical-style **Nationaltheater** on Max-Joseph-Platz (© **089/21 85-1920;** S-/U-Bahn: Marienplatz), is Germany's largest opera house. The Nationaltheater's **Bavarian State Opera** (www.bayerische.staatsoper.de) performs mostly Mozart, Wagner, Verdi, and Strauss, though it also stages works from the baroque period (all operas are performed in their original language, though some have German subtitles). The Nationaltheater also stages ballets. Its box office, at Marstallplatz 5, is open Monday to Saturday 10am to 7pm. Tickets for most productions range from about 10€ to 132€ ($13–$172).

The **Gasteig,** Rosenheimer Strasse 5 (© **089/480 98-0;** S-Bahn: Rosenheimer Platz; tram: 18 to Gasteig), serves as the stage for major concerts. Its largest concert hall, the Philharmonie, seats 2,400 and features performances of the **Munich Philharmonic Orchestra** (www.mphil.de) and guest orchestras and ensembles. The Kleiner Konzertsaal (Small Concert Hall) features a wide range of musical talent, from flamenco guitar or piano recitals to concerts of Renaissance and baroque music. Tickets for the Munich Philharmonic Orchestra are 11.10€ to 54.20€ ($14–$70).

BEER HALLS   A *Bierhalle* (beer hall) is a traditional Munich institution, offering food, entertainment, and, of course, beer. Without a doubt, the **Hofbräuhaus,** Platzl 9 (© **089/29 01 36-0;** www.hofbraeuhaus.de; S-/U-Bahn: Marienplatz), which celebrated its 415th birthday in 2004, is the world's most famous beer hall. Everyone who has ever been to Munich has probably spent at least one evening here. There are several floors in this huge place, but the main hall is the massive ground-floor Schwemme, with room for 1,300 people. It features your typical Bavarian brass band, waitresses in dirndls, and tables full of friendly Germans who often break into song and link arms as they sway. A beer garden with room for 500 people under spreading chestnut trees is open in fine weather. If you've never been to the Oktoberfest, this place will give you an idea of what it's like. It's open daily 9am to 11:30pm.

The **Augustiner Bierhalle,** Neuhauser Strasse 27, on the main pedestrian lane in the Old Town (© **089/23 18 32 57;** S-/U-Bahn: Karlsplatz/Stachus or Marienplatz), is much smaller than the Hofbräuhaus, with correspondingly lower prices. It still, however, has typical Bavarian decor, with dark paneled walls, wooden tables, simple hooks for hats and coats, and an English menu listing Bavarian specialties. It's open Monday to Saturday 9am to 11:30pm and Sunday 10am to 11:30pm.

CLUBS & BARS   Munich's premier spot for serious jazz is **Jazzclub Unterfahrt,** Einsteinstrasse 42 (© **089/448 27 94;** www.unterfahrt.de; U-Bahn: Max-Weber-Platz), with a varied program from traditional jazz to crossover hip-hop, blues, Brazilian jazz, and other international acts. Reaching it requires wandering down a labyrinth of underground cement-sided corridors that might remind you of a bomb shelter during the Cold War. Once inside, the space opens to reveal flickering candles, a convivial bar, high ceilings, and clusters of smallish tables facing the stage. It opens daily at 7:30pm, with live music generally from 9pm. Admission ranges from 12€ to 16€ ($16–$21) for most performances.

Kultfabrik, located next to Ostbahnhof Station at Grafingerstrasse 6 (© **089/49 00 90 70;** www.kultfabrik.de), is one of Europe's largest youth entertainment districts, with 20-some concert venues, themed bars, and dance clubs featuring everything from heavy metal and hip-hop to Latino. People tend to move randomly from venue to venue (admission to most clubs costs 5€–6€/$6.50–$7.80). Most venues are open only Fridays and Saturdays, though a few are open other days as well.

In the Altstadt, one of the most convivial spots for an evening out is **Jodlerwirt,** Altenhofstrasse 4 (© **089/22 12 49;** www.jodlerwirt-muenchen.net; S-/U-Bahn: Marienplatz), featuring a musician who plays an accordion, sings traditional Bavarian tunes, tells jokes, and yodels. It's packed to the rafters, elbow-to-elbow here, making it impossible to ignore the other merrymakers at your table and creating a partylike atmosphere every night. It's open Monday to Saturday 6pm to 3am (closed Mon May–Aug). Nearby, the sophisticated **Vinorant Alter Hof,** Alterhof 3 (© **089/24 24 37 33;** www.alter-hof-muenchen.de; S-/U-Bahn: Marienplatz), is a stark contrast with its vaulted ceilings, candles, and jazz playing softly in the background. In a town known mostly for its beer, this wine cellar is a welcome addition for its 24 wines by the glass, mostly Franconian whites. It's open daily 3pm to 1am.

AN EXCURSION TO MAD KING LUDWIG'S NEUSCHWANSTEIN

Of the dozens of castles dotting the Bavarian countryside, none is as famous as **Neuschwanstein** ✹✹✹), created by the extravagant Bavarian King Ludwig II. No doubt you've seen pictures of this fairy-tale castle, perched on a cliff above the town of Hohenschwangau, but even if you haven't, it'll seem familiar, for this is the castle that served as the model for Walt Disney's Sleeping Beauty Castle at Disneyland.

Construction on Ludwig II's most famous castle began in 1869, but only a third of the original plans had been completed at the time of his mysterious death in 1886 (his body, as well as the body of his doctor, was found floating in a lake, but no one has ever proved whether he was murdered or committed suicide). Neuschwanstein, one of several overly ornate castles Ludwig left to the world, is a lesson in extravagance and fantasy, with almost every inch covered in gilt, stucco, woodcarvings, and marble mosaics. Swans are used as a motif throughout, and Ludwig's admiration of Richard Wagner is expressed in operatic themes virtually everywhere, including murals illustrating *Tristan and Isolde* in his bedroom, the most opulent room in the palace—it took 14 artisans more than 4 years to produce the elaborate woodcarvings.

You can see the castle by joining a 35-minute guided tour, available in English, but be aware that the tour requires climbing 165 stairs and descending 181 stairs. This is in addition to the 35 minutes it takes to walk up the steep hill to even reach the castle.

Although overshadowed by Neuschwanstein and not quite as fanciful, there's another worthwhile castle here offering 35-minute tours: **Hohenschwangau Castle** ✹, built in the 1830s by Ludwig II's father, Maximilian II. Young Ludwig spent much of his childhood here, where he was greatly influenced by the castle's many murals depicting the saga of the Swan Knight Lohengrin, immortalized in an opera by Wagner.

To reach Neuschwanstein, take the **train** from Munich's Hauptbahnhof to Füssen, a 2-hour trip costing 18.80€ ($24) one-way. Better yet, if you don't have a railpass, buy a **Bayern Ticket,** allowing travel on local trains throughout Bavaria after 9am. It costs 19€ ($25) for one person or 27€ ($35) for up to five people traveling together. Inquire at **EurAide** at the Hauptbahnhof for more information.

In Füssen, you must take a **bus** from in front of the train station 15 minutes onward to the town of Hohenschwangau. Tickets for Neuschwanstein and Hohenschwangau castles must be purchased at the **Hohenschwangau Ticket-Center,** Alpseestrasse 12 (© **08362/93 08 30;** www.hohenschangau.de); which you'll see upon disembarking from the bus. Tours of either Neuschwanstein or Hohenschwangau are 9€ ($12) for adults and 8€ ($10) for seniors and students; children under 18 are free. Combination tickets to both cost 17€ ($22) and 15€ ($19.50) respectively. Tours are for a specific time (avoid weekends in summer, when the wait for a tour can be as long as 3 hr., or book online to avoid the wait). Both castles are open daily: April to September 9am to 6pm (last tour) and October to March 10am to 4pm.

AN EXCURSION TO DACHAU

About 12 miles (19km) from Munich is **Dachau,** site of Germany's first concentration camp under the Hitler regime and now a memorial to those who died under the Nazis. Some 200,000 prisoners from 34 countries—primarily political and religious dissidents, Jews, Gypsies, and other undesirables—passed through Dachau's gates between 1933 and 1945, of whom 32,000 lost their lives from disease, starvation, torture, execution, slave labor, and medical experiments.

At the **KZ-Gedenkstätte Dachau (Concentration Camp Memorial)** ✷✷, Alte Römerstrasse 75 (© **08131/66 99 70;** www.kz-gedenkstaette-dachau.de), a few of the camp's original buildings have been preserved or reconstructed, including a couple of barracks with rows of bunkers, guard towers, morgue, and crematorium, in a landscape that's bleak and desolate. But what really makes a visit here a sobering experience is the museum, with photograph after photograph illustrating the horrors of the Holocaust and detailed explanation as to how such atrocities came to pass. Photographs show bodies piled high on top of one another and prisoners so malnourished they can't walk. Be sure to see the museum's 20-minute English documentary, shown at 11:30am and 3:30pm. In addition, 2½-hour guided tours in English and audio guides are available for 3€ ($3.90), but the museum provides so much information and everything is so well documented, I don't think they're necessary unless you want more detailed information.

Visiting the Dachau concentration camp, which takes about 3 hours, isn't pleasant, but perhaps it's necessary: A plaque near the museum exit reminds us that those who forget the past are destined to repeat it. Note that the memorial isn't recommended for children under 12.

Admission to the Dachau memorial is free, and it's open Tuesday to Sunday 9am to 5pm. To get there, take **S-Bahn S-2** going in the direction of Petershausen to Dachau (about a 20-min. ride). In Dachau, transfer to **bus no. 726** to the KZ-Gedenkstätte stop or **bus no. 724** to the K-Z Gedenkstätte-Parkplatz, both a 10-minute ride.

4 More Highlights of Germany

HEIDELBERG ☆☆☆

Heidelberg, 55 miles (88km) south of Frankfurt, has an idyllic location on the Neckar River and rates as one of Germany's most romantic cities. One of the few German cities not leveled by air raids in World War II, it boasts a historic, picturesque Altstadt (Old Town), with winding, narrow cobblestone streets lined with medieval and early Renaissance buildings. Above the town looms Heidelberg Castle, while across the Neckar is the Philosophers Pathway with its panoramic views of the city. Above all, however, Heidelberg is a university town and has been since 1386 (the oldest such municipality in Germany). Students make up much of the city's population, imparting a vibrancy that's especially apparent in the Altstadt's colorful student quarter with its narrow streets and lively inns. Finally, Heidelberg's close proximity to Frankfurt's international airport, together with its small-town atmosphere, makes it an ideal first or final stop on a rail tour of Europe.

ESSENTIALS

GETTING THERE   Heidelberg's nearest international airport is Frankfurt (see "Essentials," at the beginning of this chapter). Trains from Frankfurt Hauptbahnhof reach **Heidelberg Hauptbahnhof** (© 06221/52 53 41) in about 1 hour, with departures approximately every half hour. Heidelberg Hauptbahnhof is an important railroad station, lying on the Mannheim line, with frequent service to both regional towns and major cities. Travel time to and from Munich is about 3¼ hours, with seven direct trains departing daily. For information about train schedules, call © **11861.** The station is 1⅔ miles (2.7km) southwest of the Altstadt; take the bus to get to the town center (see "Getting Around," below).

VISITOR INFORMATION   Heidelberg's **Tourist Information** is located just outside the Hauptbahnhof, in a pavilion at Willy-Brandt-Platz 1 (© **06221/1 94 33;** www.cvb-heidelberg.de). It's open April through October, Monday to Saturday 9am to 7pm and Sunday and holidays 10am to 6pm; November through March, Monday to Saturday 9am to 6pm, closed Sunday and holidays. It distributes city maps for 1€ ($1.30), sells the Heidelberg Card (see "Getting Around," below), and makes hotel reservations for a 3€ ($3.90) fee and 10% deposit.

GETTING AROUND   Heidelberg is crisscrossed by a network of trams and buses, many of which intersect at Bismarckplatz in the town center. Although you can walk to the Altstadt (Old Town) in about 30 minutes, bus nos. 41 and 42 travel at frequent intervals between the railway station and Universitätsplatz in the Altstadt. To gain a better appreciation for the town's atmosphere, however, consider disembarking earlier at Bismarckplatz and walking along the pedestrian Hauptstrasse (Main St.). Bus nos. 11 and 33 go directly from the Hauptbahnhof to the castle (bus stop: Rathaus/Bergbahn). Bus or tram fares cost 2.10€ ($2.75) for a single ride, or purchase a **Ticket 24,** good for 24 hours on public transportation and costing 5€ ($6.50) for one person and 8.50€ ($11) for up to five persons traveling within a group. Otherwise, consider purchasing the **Heidelberg Card,** which provides unlimited travel on public transportation, free admission to various attractions (including the castle), and a reduction in prices to other sights. Available at Tourist Information, it costs 10€ ($13) for 1 day, 14€ ($18) for 2 days; a family card for 2 days costs 28€ ($34).

TOP ATTRACTIONS & SPECIAL MOMENTS

Heidelberg's most famous landmark is the hard-to-miss **Heidelberg Castle** ★★★ (© **06221/65 44 29;** www.heidelberg-schloss.de), a huge red-stone structure that spreads along the top of a ridge directly above the Altstadt. A 17th-century fire destroyed much of the castle, and even though parts of it remain a dignified ruin, it's still one of the finest Gothic-Renaissance castles in Germany.

You can reach the castle, set amid woodlands and terraced gardens, by a 2-minute cable-car ride from a platform near Kornmarkt in the Altstadt, with a round-trip costing 5€ ($6.50) for adults and 4€ ($5.20) for children. More rewarding, however, is the journey by foot (it's a very steep climb, though) for the views it affords of the town along the way. From Klingentor, the walk takes about 20 minutes.

First erected as a fortress in the early 16th century and enlarged into a sprawling castle in the 16th and 17th centuries, the castle and its gardens suffered several devastating blows, first during the 30 Years' War, then by French troops, and finally by lightning in 1764. In the years that followed, castle rocks were regularly carted down to construct new homes in Heidelberg, until preservation efforts brought an end to the practice in 1800. Today, part of the castle has been restored and can be seen during a do-it-yourself audio tour. Since there's otherwise little to see other than the few sights mentioned below, be sure to opt for the tour, which allows you to see various rooms, halls, the ballroom, and the chapel while imparting information about castle life.

Afterwards, stop by the late-16th-century **Wine Vat Building,** worth a visit for a look at the **Great Cask.** This huge barrel-like monstrosity, built in 1751 and thought to be the world's largest wine vat, is capable of holding more than 55,000 gallons of wine. Be sure, too, to tour the **Deutsches Apotheken-Museum (Germany Pharmacy Museum;** © **06221/258 80;** www.deutsches-apotheken-museum.de). It describes the history of medicine and treatments, contains four reconstructed pharmacies, and displays various plants, minerals, spices, and other materials (including animal and human body parts) that have served as treatments for various ailments through the ages.

Admission to castle grounds, including the Wine Vat Building and Deutsches Apotheken-Museum, costs 3€ ($3.90) for adults and 1.50€ ($1.95) for children. Cost of the audio tour is 4€ ($5.20) extra. The castle grounds are open daily 8am to 6pm, with castle tours available 9:30am to 6pm March through November and 10am to 5pm December through February. The Pharmacy Museum is open daily: 10:15am to 6pm April through October, and 10am to 5:30pm November through March.

In the town itself, a tour of the main attractions begins at the **Marktplatz** in front of the Rathaus. On market days, the square is filled with stalls of fresh flowers, fish, and vegetables. At the opposite end of the square is the late Gothic **Heiliggeistkirche,** built around 1400, the largest Gothic church in the Palatinate.

If you have time, consider swinging by the **Kurpfälzisches Museum (Museum of the Electoral Palatinate),** Hauptstrasse 97 (© **06221/58 34 020;** bus: 11, 12, 35, 41, or 42). It contains items pertaining to Heidelberg's long history, including Roman pots, tools, and other finds from the time of Heidelberg's important status as a Roman military outpost; medieval objects; and paintings and sculptures from the late 15th to 20th century. The most significant work of art is Tilman Riemenschneider's late-Gothic Altar from Windsheim (1509), depicting Christ and the 12 Apostles, with amazing details in their facial expressions. Another section of the museum, housed in the baroque Morass Palace, features period rooms as they might have appeared in the

Moments Boating in the Neckar

Heidelberg is a good point from which to explore the romantic Neckar Valley. From April to mid-October, you can take a boat tour along the river as far as Neckarsteinach. There are usually four to seven round-trips daily, and you need not return on the same boat. Boats are operated by the **Rhein-Neckar Fahrgastschiffahrt GmbH** (© 06221/20181; www.rnf-schifffahrt.de). Trips between Heidelberg and Neckarsteinach cost 10.50€ ($14) for adults and 6€ ($7.80) for children round-trip. You can order drinks or snacks on the boat. Some of the people operating the boats are descended from the Neckar fishers who helped Mark Twain when he rafted down from Hirschhorn, and the same families have been working the Neckar since the early 1600s. The boat dock, just a short walk from the Altstadt, can also be reached by taking bus nos. 12, 35, 41, or 42 to Kongresshaus/Stadthalle.

18th and 19th centuries, complete with furniture and decorative arts. Unfortunately, explanations in the museum are only in German. The museum is open Tuesday to Sunday 10am to 6pm. Admission is 3€ ($3.90) adults, 1.80€ ($2.35) students, and 1.20 ($1.55) children.

Also of interest is the **Studentenkarzer (Student Prison)** in the Old University off Universitätsplatz, Augustinergasse 2 (© **06221/54 35 54**), where students were held in detention from 1712 to 1914. In those days, students could be punished only by the university, not town officials, so those caught disturbing the peace through drunkenness or misbehavior, chasing citizens' pigs through the alleys, or fighting against members of other student fraternities were incarcerated here. Most students, who were allowed to attend classes and receive outside visitors, considered it an honor to be imprisoned at least once during their studies. The walls and ceilings are covered with graffiti, drawings, portraits, engraved names, dates, and funny verses. It's open April to September, Tuesday to Sunday from 10am to 6pm; October, Tuesday to Sunday 10am to 4pm; November to March, Tuesday to Saturday 10am to 4pm. Admission is 2.50€ ($3.25) for adults, 2€ ($2.60) for seniors and students, and .50€ (65¢) for children.

All the important sights of Heidelberg lie on or near the south bank of the Neckar. However, you should cross to the north side of the river (via the ornately decorated 18th-c. Karl Theodore Bridge) for the best overall view, especially from the **Philosophenweg (Philosophers' Way),** a footpath halfway up Heilegenberg hill.

SHOPPING

The main shopping street is the traffic-free **Hauptstrasse,** which is filled with stores selling glass, crystal, handcrafts, and other items. For a wide assortment of handcrafts from all over Germany, head to **Michael Kienscherff,** Hauptstrasse 177 (© **06221/24255**), filled with music boxes, Christmas decorations, nativity scenes, nutcrackers, wooden toys, and teddy bears.

Heidelberg is also known for its **markets,** including the one held on Wednesday and Saturday mornings at Marktplatz and another held Tuesday and Friday mornings at Friedrich-Ebert-Platz.

WHERE TO STAY & DINE

A glorious old inn right out of the German Renaissance, the **Zum Ritter St. Georg** ✿, Hauptstrasse 178 (✆ **06221/135-0;** www.ritter-heidelberg.de; bus: 10, 11, or 12), is a well-preserved rarity just a stone's throw from the colorful Marktplatz. Built in 1592 by a French merchant, the gabled house is considered a major sightseeing attraction due to its ornately decorated facade. Inside, modernization has robbed some of its 39 rooms of character, particularly the cramped standard rooms. Better are the deluxe rooms facing the main street and the beautiful Heiliggeistkirche. Rates are 144€ to 220€ ($187–$286) for a double.

On the other side of the Neckar, **Hotel Hirschgasse** ✿✿✿, Hirschgasse 3 (✆ **06221/454-0;** www.hirschgasse.de; bus: 34), is tops in Heidelberg for its tranquil and romantic setting, nestled on the hillside of a lane adjoining Philosophers' Way. Heidelberg's oldest inn, the historic country-style home dates from 1472 and counts Mark Twain and Bismarck among its distinguished guests. Its 20 rooms (all non-smoking) are all suites, each different in Laura Ashley designs and some boasting four-poster beds, whirlpool baths, or a balcony. Its two restaurants are considered among the best in town. Rates are 195€ to 335€ ($253–$436) for two people.

Travelers on a budget might consider **Weisser Bock,** Grosse Mantelgasse 24 (✆ **06221/90 00-0;** www.weisserbock.de; bus: 10, 11, or 12), located on one of the town's most picturesque lanes in the heart of the Altstadt. A simple hotel (the reception desk is in the hotel restaurant's kitchen!), it nonetheless has flair, with 23 tall-ceilinged, wood-floored rooms (all nonsmoking) tastefully furnished with all the basic creature comforts. Double rates here are 115€ ($150), and suites cost 135€ ($176).

When visiting Heidelberg Castle, there's no better place for dinner than in the castle itself, at **Schlossweinstube** ✿✿✿ (✆ **06221/97 97 97**). An elegant venue with gleaming floor parquetry and old-fashioned tile ovens, it specializes in fresh duck, stuffed with apples and herbs. Also recommended is the grilled steak, gratinéed with herbs and a red wine sauce. Main courses run 25€ to 35€ ($32.50–$45.50), and reservations are required. It's open Thursday to Tuesday 6pm to midnight; from noon to 5pm, the neighboring Bistro offers reasonably priced traditional German fare (open only Fri–Sun in winter).

The **Ritterstube** ✿, Hauptstrasse 178 (✆ **06221/1350-0;** bus: 10, 11, or 12), is located in one of Heidelberg's most famous Renaissance buildings—Zum Ritter St. Georg—with vaulted ceilings, wainscoting, and starched linen tablecloths topped with flower vases. It's popular among locals for its good German cooking and such seasonal dishes as venison. Main courses cost 12€ to 35€ ($16–$45.50). It's open daily noon to 2:30pm and 6 to 10pm.

The family-owned **Zur Herrenmühle,** Hauptstrasse 239 (✆ **06221/60 29 09;** bus: 11 or 33) occupies a 17th-century house, with thick walls, heavy exposed beams, and antique paneling. The sophisticated maitre d' adds both glamour and an appropriate theatricality along with great service. The classical German cuisine is based on fresh ingredients, offering good quality at reasonable prices. Try the rack of lamb with herbs, salmon, or *Tafelspitz* (boiled beef with vegetables), all with side dishes and ranging from 12.50€ to 22.50€ ($16–$29) for most meals. It's open Monday to Saturday from 6pm to midnight.

No other place in Heidelberg captures bygone days quite like the **Mensurstube** ✿, in the Hotel Hirschgasse, Hirschgasse 3 (✆ **06221/454-165;** bus: 34). In this rustic and cozy spot, you sit at tables more than 2 centuries old—you can still see where

Bismarck and others carved their names. Swords hang from the ceiling—in the past, when dueling was the regular sport of the student fraternities, duels were fought in what is now the dining room. Traditional recipes are served, from a limited menu. Main courses run 15€ to 21€ ($20–$27). Open hours are Monday to Saturday 6 to 10pm.

NIGHTLIFE

Nights here are alive with the youthful enthusiasm of Heidelberg's students. Nowhere is that more apparent than at Heidelberg's many student taverns. Most famous is **Zum Roten Ochsen (Red Ox Inn),** Hauptstrasse 217 (© **06221/2 09 77;** bus: 11 or 33), opened in 1703. It's been in the Spengel family for six generations, and they've welcomed everybody from Bismarck to Mark Twain to Marilyn Monroe. It seems that every student who has attended the university has left his or her mark (or initials) on the walls. There's live piano music nightly, and as the evening progresses, the songs become louder and louder. Hearty German meals are also available. It's open Monday through Saturday from 5pm to midnight; from April to October, it's open from 11:30am to 2pm as well.

Next door is Heidelberg's oldest student pub, **Zum Sepp'l,** open since 1634, Hauptstrasse 213 (© **06221/23085;** bus: 11 or 33). It's also packed with photographs and carved initials of former students, along with memorabilia that ranges from old Berlin street signs to Alabama license plates. There's live piano music most nights from 7 to 10pm, and a menu offers traditional German pub grub like sausages. It's open daily noon to 11pm.

DRESDEN ✮✮✮

Dresden, once known as the "Florence on the Elbe," was celebrated throughout Europe for its impressive baroque architecture and stunning art treasures. Then came the night of February 13, 1945, when Allied bombers rained down phosphorus and high-explosive bombs on the city. By morning, the Dresden of legend was only a memory, and more than 50,000 people had lost their lives. After the war, when Germany was divided by the victors, Dresden landed in the Soviet sector and languished under Communist rule. Today, the capital of Saxony is experiencing a renaissance, after a painstaking reconstruction of its beautiful historic core just in time for the city's 800th birthday bash in 2006. While Dresden is hardly undiscovered, especially among Germans, it lies off the beaten path of most traveling North Americans, despite its convenient location approximately halfway between Prague and Berlin.

ESSENTIALS

GETTING THERE The Dresden Airport (© **0351/881 33 60;** www.dresden-airport.de) lies 6 miles (10km) north of the city center. A suburban rail line that's linked to Dresden's S-Bahn network stretches from the airport to the city's main train station, the Hauptbahnhof, with a stop also at the Bahnhof Neustadt train station. The trip takes about 13 minutes to Neustadt and 21 minutes to the Hauptbahnhof and costs 1.80€ ($2.35) one-way. A taxi from the airport to the center of Dresden costs about 15€ ($20).

Dresden has two main rail stations, the **Hauptbahnhof** main station, which is on the Berlin-Prague line, and **Bahnhof Neustadt.** Some trains stop at both stations, but otherwise tram 11 connects the two. Trains depart Frankfurt Hauptbahnhof approximately every hour directly for Dresden (trip time: 4 hr., 45 min.). From Berlin and Prague, direct trains depart approximately every 2 hours (trip time: 2 hr. from Berlin, 3 hr. from Prague). For information on train schedules, call © **11861.**

VISITOR INFORMATION Dresden's **Tourist Information Center** is located a 5-minute walk from the Hauptbahnhof, at Pragerstrasse 2A. It's open Monday to Saturday 10am to 6pm. Here you can book accommodations for a 3€ ($3.90) per-person fee, purchase a city map for .30€ (40¢), get information booklets in English, and obtain tickets for theater, opera, and concerts. There's a branch tourist office in the Altstadt at the Schinkelwache, Theaterplatz, open Monday to Friday 10am to 6pm and Saturday and Sunday 10am to 4pm. For more information, call ✆ **0351/49 19 21 00,** or search the website at **www.dresden.de**.

GETTING AROUND Dresden's Altstadt and attractions can be reached on foot from either the Hauptbahnhof or Bahnhof Neustadt in about 20 minutes. Otherwise, both trams and buses are available. A single ride, good for 1 hour, costs 1.80€ ($2.35). Or, you can purchase a 24-hour pass for 4.50€ ($5.85). For trams, tickets must be purchased in advance at vending machines. If you're in town longer than a day, another option is the **Dresden City-Card** for 21€ ($27), available at the Tourist Information Center and good for 48 hours of unlimited travel, plus free access to all of the city's best museums.

TOP ATTRACTIONS & SPECIAL MOMENTS

Tip: If you don't plan on using public transportation, your best bet (instead of the Dresden City-Card) is to buy a **Museum Day Ticket,** valid for 1 day and including admission to all museums listed below except the Historic Green Vault and special exhibits. It costs 12€ ($16) for adults, 7€ ($10) for students and children, and 25€ ($33) for families. It's available at the Tourist Information Center.

Dresden's major attractions are concentrated in two famous buildings in the Altstadt. Foremost is the newly restored **Residenzschloss (Royal Palace),** a stately building with an imposing neo-Renaissance facade. First erected some 700 years ago and rebuilt and enlarged over the centuries, it contains the magnificent **Grünes Gewölbe (Green Vault)** ✿✿✿, Sophienstrasse 1 (✆ **0351/491 42 000;** www.skd-dresden.de; tram: 4, 8, or 9 to Theaterplatz). Although there are royal treasuries throughout Europe, this may well be the most stunning and is the most important thing to see in Dresden. Most of the collection stems from the private possessions of Augustus the Strong (1670–1733), Saxon elector and Polish king. The collection is divided into two parts, each with its own admission. The Neues Grünes Gewölbe, which costs 6€ ($7.80) for adults and 3.50€ ($4.55) for students and children, contains an amazing collection of gem-encrusted bowls and dishes, an incredibly ornate coffee set, a fantastic ivory-carved sailing ship, stone-inlaid pictures, ivory goblets, etched glass, ornamental clocks, game sets, and much, much more. The Historic Green Vault, consisting of historic rooms restored to their Baroque splendor, houses more treasures, including items made of silver, gold, and bronze, and jewelry dripping with precious stones, all displayed out in the open rather than behind glass cases. For this reason, admission here is restricted to 100 persons per hour, with tickets issued for a specific time (you can reserve in advance by phone or online). The cost here, including audio guide, is 10€ ($13), 11.50 € ($15) if purchased in advance. The New Green Vault is open Wednesday to Monday 10am to 6pm, while the Historic Green Vault is open Wednesday to Monday 10am to 7pm.

Also in the Royal Palace is the **Kupferstich-Kabinett (Collection of Prints and Drawings;** ✆ **0351/491 42 11;** www.skd-dresden.de), with changing exhibitions drawn from its collection of more than 500,000 drawings, watercolors, lithographs,

Dresden

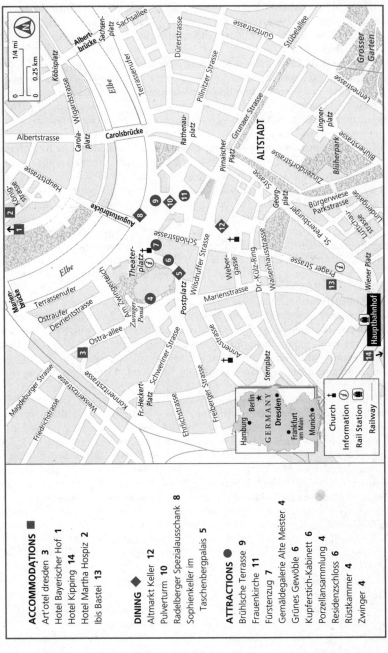

ACCOMMODATIONS ■
Art'otel dresden **3**
Hotel Bayerischer Hof **1**
Hotel Kipping **14**
Hotel Martha Hospiz **2**
Ibis Bastei **13**

DINING ◆
Altmarkt Keller **12**
Pulverturm **10**
Radeberger Spezialausschank **8**
Sophienkeller im
    Taschenbergpalais **5**

ATTRACTIONS ●
Brühlsche Terrasse **9**
Frauenkirche **11**
Fürstenzug **7**
Gemäldegalerie Alte Meister **4**
Grünes Gewöble **6**
Kupferstich-Kabinett **6**
Porzellansammlung **4**
Residenzschloss **6**
Rüstkammer **4**
Zwinger **4**

etchings, illustrated books, and photographs dating from the 15th century to the present and created by more than 11,000 artists. Admission is usually 3€ ($3.90) for adults and 2€ ($2.60) for students and children. It's open Wednesday to Monday 10am to 6pm.

Just a stone's throw away is Dresden's other imposing building, the **Zwinger.** Augustus the Strong built this baroque masterpiece in 1719, and it's where he staged tournaments and reputedly kept dozens of concubines. His physique was called Herculean, his temperament Rabelaisian, but the king was also a lover of the arts. Today, this artfully symmetrical complex of buildings holds a collection of museums and, in its center courtyard, a formal garden of fountains and promenades.

The most important museum in the Zwinger is the **Gemäldegalerie Alte Meister (Old Masters Picture Gallery)** 𝕽𝕽𝕽, located in the Semperbau part of the complex, with an entrance at Theaterplatz 1 (© **0351/491 42 000;** www.skd-dresden.de; tram: 4, 8, or 9 to Theaterplatz). This gallery, one of the best on the Continent, concentrates on great masterpieces of the 16th to 18th centuries. Italian Renaissance and baroque art is strongly represented, with works by Raphael (look for Raphael's showpiece, *Sistine Madonna*), Giorgione *(Sleeping Venus),* Titian, Correggio, and others. Of equal significance are Dutch and Flemish paintings of the 17th century, with works by Rembrandt, Vermeer, and Rubens (the Rubens collection includes his spectacular *Neptune,* full of rearing horses, and an exquisite *St. Jerome*), and old German masterpieces by such artists as Albrecht Dürer.

It's open Tuesday to Sunday 10am to 6pm and charges an admission of 6€ ($7.80) for adults and 3.50€ ($4.55) for children. Included in the admission price is the **Rüstkammer (Armory;** same telephone and website as above), with a vast collection of decorative weapons and costumes, including suits of armor, shields, swords, sabers, rifles, jousting sticks, and more. (*Note:* The Armory will eventually move to more spacious quarters in the Royal Palace; contact the Tourist Information Center for updated information).

Finally, one more museum worth seeing in Zwinger is the sumptuous **Porzellansammlung (Porcelain Collection)** 𝕽𝕽 (© **0351/491 42 000;** www.skd-dresden.de), which also owes its existence to Augustus the Strong (Augustus called his love of the fragile, costly decorative arts a "porcelain sickness"). It boasts an outstanding collection of Chinese, Japanese, and early Meissen porcelain, including Chinese burial objects from the 3rd century B.C. Chinese pieces from the Song and Ming dynasties, and a very valuable collection of Japanese Imari ware. Its Meissen collection, beginning from the time of its invention in 1708, is unparalleled. Even if you've never had much interest in porcelain before, you might find yourself infected with "porcelain sickness" after a visit here. It's open Tuesday to Sunday 10am to 6pm. Admission is 5€ ($6.50) for adults and 3€ ($3.90) for students and children.

Any stroll of Dresden should also take in the **Frauenkirche (Church of Our Lady;** © **0351/498 11 10;** www.frauenkirche-dresden.de; tram: 1, 2, or 4 to Altmarkt), dedicated to Jesus' mother. Although a church has stood on this spot since the 11th century, the church in its present form was first erected in the early 1700s as one of Germany's most important Protestant churches, destroyed during World War II, left as a ruined shell by the East German government as a reminder of the war, and then painstakingly restored in celebration of Dresden's 800th birthday. Visiting hours are generally Monday to Friday 10am to noon and 1 to 6pm, with weekend visitation dependant on church services, weddings, and other functions. You can also climb its

Moments A Cruise on the Elbe

You can take a cruise on the historic Elbe River from central moorings below the Brühlsche Terrasse, aboard the oldest and largest paddle-steamer fleet in the world. Throughout the year, there are 2¾-hour round-trip cruises that pass several imposing castles along the way, including Pillnitz Castle, a former baroque summer residence of Saxon kings. These depart most days of the week at 11am and cost 14.50€ ($19) for adults and 7.25€ ($9.45) for children. There are also shorter 1½-hour trips that go only as far as the Blaues Wunder (Blue Wonder), one of Dresden's most celebrated bridges, completed in 1893 and never destroyed during the wartime bombings.

From the end of March through October, there are longer cruises along the Elbe from Dresden to Rathen, a German village at the border of the Czech Republic, and beyond, with several departures daily. These trips take you through some of the finest river scenery in eastern Germany, including an area known as **"Swiss Saxony,"** one of Germany's most popular natural wonders. It's a land of table-shaped outcrops, isolated pillars, deep gorges, and sheer sandstone cliffs. Because each leg of this waterborne journey to Rathen requires 4½ hours, you'll have to block out an entire day for this experience if you opt for round-trip transport by boat. Alternatively, you can opt for one-way transit by boat, with a return back to Dresden from Rathen by train, a 40-minute ride, with trains departing every 30 minutes or so. The trip to Rathen costs 14.50€ ($19) one-way or 20€ ($26) round-trip. Tickets are available at the kiosk on the bank of the Elbe below the Altstadt, or contact the **Sächsische Dampfschiffahrt** (© **0351/866 09-0;** www.saechsische-dampfschiffahrt.de).

tower for a view over Dresden, open daily 10am to 6pm (to 4pm in winter) and costing 8€ ($10) for adults and 5€ ($6.50) for children.

Nearby, on a narrow lane linking the Frauenkirche with Schlossplatz, is the **Fürstenzug (Procession of Princes),** one of the world's longest friezes, composed of 25,000 Meissen porcelain tiles depicting the rulers of the local dynasty over 800 years. On the banks of the Elbe is the **Brühlsche Terrasse,** a promenade celebrated as the "Balcony of Europe" for its views over the valley. On the other side of the Elbe is the picturesque **Neustadt,** popular for shopping and dining.

SHOPPING

After gaining an appreciation of Meissen porcelain at the Porcelain Collection, you might be drawn to the **Meissener Porzellan am Fürstenzug,** An der Frauenkirche 5 (© **0351/864 29 64**), to start your own collection. The largest shopping center in the Altstadt is the **Altmarkt Galerie Dresden,** located on the Altmarkt at Webergasse 1 (© **0351/482 04-0**), which boasts more than 100 shops. The Altmarkt is best known, however, for **Striezelmarkt,** Germany's oldest Christmas market and a great place to find handmade regional crafts and food. If you miss the market, console yourself at **Weihnachtsland am Zwinger,** Kleine Brüdergasse 5 (© **0351/862 12 30**), which stocks Christmas gifts, decorations, and ornaments year-round.

On the other side of the Elbe, in Neustadt, the most fashionable shopping mecca is the elegant **Königstrasse,** lined with unbroken rows of baroque patrician houses that give an inkling of how Dresden used to look prior to 1945. Tony boutiques and restaurants now occupy the houses. The nearby **Die Halle,** Metzer Strasse 1 (© **0351/ 810 54 45**), is a century-old former market hall filled with vendors selling wine, sausages, vegetables, clothing, and souvenirs.

WHERE TO STAY & DINE

Ibis Bastei, Prager Strasse 5 (© **0351/48 56 54 45;** www.ibishotel.com), is a colorless but convenient choice, just a 3-minute walk away from the Hauptbahnhof (main train station). It's the first in a row of three blocky Communist-era Ibis hotels; each has 306 rooms and caters largely to groups. Double rooms are small, but functional and bright, with modern furnishings and tiny bathrooms. They go for 78€ to 84€ ($101–$109).

On the other side of the Hauptbahnhof (and also just a 3-min. walk away), is **Hotel Kipping** ★, Winckelmannstrasse 6 (© **0352/478 50-0;** www.hotel-kipping.de). This 20-room find was built in neo-Renaissance style in 1884 by a local businessman and was one of the few neighborhood buildings left standing after 1945. It offers attractive, high-ceilinged rooms and a restaurant serving local Saxon cuisine. Doubles here cost 95€ to 120€ ($124–$156), including buffet breakfast.

Just a 2-minute walk from the Bahnhof Neustadt, the city's other train station, is the **Hotel Bayerischer Hof,** Antonstrasse 33–35 (© **0351/82 93 70;** www.bayerischer-hof-dresden.de). Set in a stately 1864 building, it offers 50 spacious rooms, simple but with modern furnishings. Its public spaces, including a restaurant and a bar, are elegant with a bit of flair, leading one to assume the hotel would be more expensive than the 120€ to 138€ ($156–$179) cost of a double room, including buffet breakfast.

A 5-minute walk from Bahnhof Neustadt, near the classy Königstrasse, **Hotel Martha Hospiz** ★★, Nieritzstrasse 11 (© **0351/81 76-0;** www.marthahospiz.dresden. vch.de), is a great choice for those seeking cozy quarters in a quiet residential neighborhood. Its history stretches back more than 100 years, when two nuns set up a hostel for young women arriving from the countryside in search of work who might otherwise be led astray. After World War II, it became a hotel for women travelers; in 1991 it began accepting men. Each of the 50 rooms is spotless and offers such cheerful touches as plants; seven rooms are wheelchair-accessible. Eating in the sunny breakfast room is like dining in a greenhouse, and a basement restaurant specializes in potato dishes. Double rooms here cost 109€ to 121€ ($142–$157), including buffet breakfast.

In between the two train stations, near the Altstadt, **art'otel dresden,** Ostra-Allee 33 (© **0351/49 22-0;** www.artotel.de; tram: 11 to Haus der Presse), is the most self-consciously "arty" hotel in Dresden. The 174 stylish rooms, which eschew the usual box shape in favor of sensuous curves, are full of design surprises, from chairs that can be pulled up to form bar stools to voyeuristic bathroom windows that become opaque when the light is turned on. Naturally, artwork fills the white walls and the in-house art gallery, all by cutting-edge native artist A. R. Penck. Doubles are 155€ ($202).

Theme restaurants are big in Dresden, but few carry it off as well as **Sophienkeller im Taschenbergpalais** ★, Taschenberg 3 (© **0351/497 26-0;** www.sophienkeller-dresden.de; tram: 4, 8, 9, or 11), near the Zwinger and Residenzschloss. Located in the vaulted cellars of a historic palace, it takes its decorating cue from Augustus the

Strong, with a medieval setting and hearty feasts that might have been served in the Royal Saxon Court. There are four distinct dining areas, including one outfitted like a medieval torture chamber. Waitresses in traditional dirndl haul steaming platters of suckling pig fresh off the spit, venison goulash, or roast duck, with most meals costing 10€ to 13€ ($13–$17). It's open daily 11am to midnight.

Sister restaurant to the Sophienkeller, **Pulverturm,** an der Frauenkirche 12 (© 0351/ 26 26 0-0; www.pulverturm-dresden.de; tram: 1, 2, or 4), is also based on a medieval theme and is located in the vaulted cellar of a former tower used to store gunpowder. It offers many of the same dishes as above (at the same prices) and is open the same hours.

Less touristy but very popular is the **Altmarkt Keller,** Altmarkt 4 (© 0351/481 81 30; www.altmarktkeller-dresden.de; tram: 1, 2, or 4), located on the east side of the old market square. This huge, historic cellar with a vaulted ceiling and cozy side rooms is a boisterous venue for Saxon and Bohemian (Czech) cuisine, with platters going for 7€ to 16.50€ ($9.10–$21.45). Can't decide? How about sauerkraut soup, followed by pork goulash with Bohemian dumplings and braised cabbage? It's open daily 11am to midnight. In summer, tables are set up in the historic square.

The two-level **Radelberger Spezialausschank,** Terrassenufer 1 (© 0351/48 48 660; tram: 4, 8, or 9), is a small venue, with gleaming wood-paneled walls and a brewing tank of its own Pilsner beer. In summer, its rooftop beer garden beside the Brühlsche Terrasse is one of the most enviable spots in all of Dresden, with fine views over the Elbe and hearty Saxon dishes such as *Sauerbraten* (marinated beef in sauce), suckling pig, and sausages. Main courses range from 7.90€ to 15€ ($10–$19.50). It's open 10am to 1am in summer and 11:30am to 11pm in winter.

NIGHTLIFE

Between the Elbe River and the Zwinger, on the west side of grand Theaterplatz, stands the imposing **Semper Opera House,** Theaterplatz 2 (© 0351/49 11 705; www.semperoper.de; tram: 4, 8, or 9). Gottfried Semper, the same architect who mapped out the famous picture gallery in the Zwinger, designed the Renaissance-style building, known for its fine acoustics. Opera seats range from 8€ to 74.50€ ($10– $97). The opera company takes a vacation mid-July to mid-August.

For a drink in the Altstadt, **Busmann's,** near the Zwinger at Kleine Brüdergasse 5 (© 0351/862 12 00; tram: 4, 8, 9, or 11), is a lively bar and restaurant with multi-level seating, a large outdoor terrace, an international menu (from roast beef in a red wine sauce to Brazilian-style halibut), more than 300 cocktails, and live music most nights. It's open daily 11am to 2pm.

HIGHLIGHTS OF THE ROMANTIC ROAD

The aptly named Romantic Road, or *Romantische Strasse,* is one of Germany's most popular tourist routes. Stretching 180 miles (290km) between Würzburg in the north and Füssen in the foothills of the Bavarian Alps, it links a series of medieval villages and 2,000-year-old towns. The entire length of the Romantic Road is best done by car or bus and could take days to see in its entirety. That said, several of the top cities along the route can easily be reached by rail, and we highlight the best of those cities in this section (for a description of Neuschwanstein castle near Füssen, see the section on Munich, earlier). Both Frankfurt and Munich are convenient gateways for exploring the road by rail

Moments   Traveling the Romantic Road by Bus

If you have only a limited amount of vacation time allotted for your rail trip to Germany, have a railpass, and would like to see the Romantic Road in a more convenient fashion than that afforded by public transportation (some of the smallest towns do not have train stations and can be reached only by bus), the best option for traveling the route is aboard the comfortable and modern **Romantic Road Europabus,** which links all towns and cities along the route daily in both directions from April through October. Travelers who arrive by air can join the Europabus easily at Frankfurt, Munich, or Augsburg, but the most scenic part of the trip is from Würzburg to Füssen, passing through many of the route's charming villages and towns. In fact, it's probably one of the most scenic bus rides on the planet.

The trip between Würzburg and Füssen takes about 9 hours and costs 58.50€ ($76) one-way, but if you have a railpass you'll get a 60% discount off the fare. If you travel the entire distance of the Europabus, which departs daily at around 8am from both Frankfurt and Munich train stations, the trip will take roughly 13 hours from start to finish and costs 98.80€ ($128) one-way, 39.50€ ($51) if you have a railpass. However, I suggest you break your stop with an overnight stay, in, say, Rothenburg or Augsburg. Seats should be reserved at least 2 working days in advance through **Deutsche Touring GmbH** (© 069/7903-50). For timetables, fare information, and further route details, see the company's website at **www.deutsche-touring.de/id/index.html.**

Note: The Romantic Road Association will provide information on sights and attractions and mail information packs in English. Contact the **Romantische Strasse Arbeitsgemeinschaft,** Waaggässlein 1, 91550 Dinkelsbühl (© **0700 9027 1000;** www.romantischestrasse.de).

WÜRZBURG 🐦🐦

For Germans, the south begins at Würzburg, one of the loveliest baroque cities in the country and the best starting point for the Romantic Road. About 174 miles (280km) northwest of Munich, it not only has excellent rail connections to most of Germany's major cities and to major cities along the Romantic Road route, but also is an interesting town in and of itself. A lively university town, Würzburg, known for its baroque architecture and its Franconian wine, has a 1,300-year history and occupies an idyllic setting surrounded by vineyards. Although 86% of the city's center was destroyed on March 16, 1945, by bombs of the Royal Air Force, the old town has been lovingly restored.

The **Würzburg Hauptbahnhof** is connected to several major rail lines, with departures every hour or so from Frankfurt (trip time: 1¼ hr.) and from Munich (trip time: 2 hr.). For rail information and schedules, call © **11861.** The main train station is just outside and to the north of the old town center, about a 15-minute walk away.

For tourist information, contact the **Verkehrsbüro tourist office,** Am Marktplatz 9 (© **0931/37 23 98;** www.wuerzburg.de). It's open April to December Monday to Friday 10am to 6pm, Saturday 10am to 2pm (May–Oct, it's also open Sun and holidays 10am–2pm); January to March Monday to Friday 10am to 4pm, Saturday 10am to 1pm. The tourist office is in the central square, at the heart of the old town.

Top Attractions & Special Moments

In spring and summer, the liveliest place in town is the **Marktplatz (central marketplace),** where street performers entertain and vendors hawk their wares, ranging from fresh fruit to souvenir trinkets.

Würzburg's cathedral, **Dom St. Kilian,** Domstrasse (© **0931/321 18 30;** www. dom-wuerzburg.de), begun in 1040 and dedicated to a 7th-century Irish missionary to Franconia, is the fourth-largest Romanesque church in Germany and served as the final resting place of Würzburg's bishops. It was destroyed in 1945 and completely rebuilt. An imposing row of prince-bishops' epitaphs adorn the pillars of the main nave, including Gottfried von Spitzenberg (ca. 1190), who was one of the first prince-bishops to rule over the town, and Rudolf von Scherenberg, who died in 1495 and whose epitaph is by the most famous wood sculptor of his time, Tilman Riemenschneider (more on him below). The Dom is open Easter to October, Monday to Saturday from 10am to 5pm, and Sunday from 1 to 6pm; November to Easter, Monday to Saturday from 10am to noon and 2 to 5pm, and Sunday from 1 to 6pm. Admission is free.

If you have time, the **Museum am Dom,** around the corner from the Dom on Kiliansplatz (© **0931/386 65 600;** www.museum-am-dom.de), displays an intriguing combination of "old" and contemporary art from the 10th to 21st centuries, including works by Joseph Beuys, Käthe Kollwitz, Otto Dix, and Tilman Riemenschneider. It's open Tuesday to Sunday 10am to 6pm (to 5pm Nov–Mar). Admission is 3.50€ ($4.55) for adults and 2.50€ ($3.25) for students and children.

The most important thing to see in Würzburg is the **Residenz** ★★, Residenzplatz 2, Tor B (© **0931/355 17-0;** www.residenz-wuerzburg.de; tram: 1, 3, 4, or 5), one of Germany's most important baroque palaces and a UNESCO World Heritage Site. Seat of Würzburg's prince-bishops, it was begun in 1720 to satisfy Prince-Bishop Johann Philipp Franz von Schönborn's passion for elegance and splendor. At its center is the masterful **Treppenhaus (staircase),** above which a high, unsupported vaulted ceiling is decorated with one of the world's largest contiguous ceiling frescos, painted by Tiepolo. It represents the four known continents of the world, with North America depicted by a crocodile and Indian. Beyond the staircase are the palace rooms containing furniture, tapestries, paintings, and other treasures, as well as the Court Gardens. Time your visit to coincide with one of the English tours (given at 11am and 3pm), which allows you to see seven extra rooms (including the famous Mirror Cabinet) and is included in the price of admission (otherwise, you can join a German tour every 15–30 min.). Be sure to see the **court chapel,** a rectangular room divided into five oval sections, three with domed ceilings; window arches are placed at oblique angles to coordinate the windows with the oval sections. Colored marble columns define the sections, their gilded capitals enriching the ceiling frescoes by Johann Rudolf Byss. At the side altars, Tiepolo painted two important works: *The Fall of the Angels* on the left and *The Assumption of the Virgin* on the right. During the summer, a **Mozart festival** is held in the upper halls of the Residenz. The castle is open April to October, daily from 9am to 6pm; November to March, daily from 10am to 4:30pm. Admission is 5€ ($6.50) for adults, 4€ ($5.20) for students and seniors, and free for children under 15.

Finally, another sight worth seeing if there's time is the city's landmark, **Festung Marienberg (Fortress Marienberg)** ⚔ (② **0931/355 17-0;** www.schloesser. bayern.de; bus: 9 Apr–Oct only), located across from the Altstadt over the Alte Mainbrücke stone bridge (which is adorned with statues of saints). This imposing fortress, almost completely destroyed in 1945 and completely restored in 1990, served as the residence of the local prince-bishops from 1253 to 1719. Within its walls is the 8th-century **Marienkirche,** one of the oldest churches in Germany. In the former baroque armory is the **Mainfränkisches Museum** (② **0931/20 59 40;** www. mainfraenkisches-museum.de), with the world's largest collection of sculptures by the great flamboyant Gothic master, Tilman Riemenschneider (1460–1531), called "the master of Würzburg." The sculptor came to live here in 1483 and was the town's mayor in 1520 and 1521. Never a totally decorative artist, Riemenschneider concentrated on the reality of people's appearance, highlighting their hands, faces, and clothing. After siding with the farmers in a 1525 uprising, Riemenschneider was imprisoned for 2 months and after his release never received another large commission. The museum also displays paintings by Tiepolo and Lucas Cranach and sandstone figures from the rococo gardens of the prince-bishops' summer palace. A tribute to one of the few industries of the city, winemaking, is paid in the press house, which contains historic casks and carved cask bases and a large collection of glasses and goblets. It's open Tuesday through Sunday 10am to 5pm (to 4pm in winter).

Fürstenbaumuseum (② **0931/355 17-0**), situated in the restored princes' wing of the fortress, illustrates the history of Würzburg and the prince-bishops. The urban-history section offers a stroll through 1,300 eventful years of Würzburg's history, including an exhibit relating to the discovery of X-rays by Wilhelm Conrad Röntgen in 1895. A model of the town shows its appearance in 1525, and another shows the destruction after the bombing of 1945. It's open Mid-March through October, Tuesday through Sunday 9am to 6pm.

Admission is free for the fortress. Tickets for either the Fürstenbaumuseum or the Mainfränkisches Museum are 4€ ($5.20) each.

Where to Stay & Dine

A 5-minute walk from the train station in the direction of the old town, **Hotel Würzburger Hof,** Barbarossaplatz 2 (② **0931/53814;** www.hotel-wuerzburgerhof.de), is an ornately (some might say over-the-top) decorated hotel. Each of its 34 rooms is different, with frescoes on the walls and rich furnishings, and even those that face the bustling main street are quiet with double-paned windows. Rates run 115€ to 150€ ($150–$195) for a double, including a buffet breakfast.

The 500-year-old **Ratskeller Würzburg,** Langgasse 1 (② **0931/13021;** www. ratskeller-wuerzburg.de; tram: 1, 2, 3, or 5), in the town hall, is not only an interesting place to visit, but also serves tasty Franconian fare at reasonable prices. Country cookery is an art here, as you'll discover if you order the boiled breast of beef with horseradish sauce, noodles, and cranberry jam. The English menu is limited, but the English-speaking host will help you with German menu selections. Game is featured in season. They also specialize in local beer and Franconian white wines. Main courses are 8.70€ to 19€ ($11–$25). It's open daily 10am to midnight.

ROTHENBURG OB DER TAUBER ✩✩✩

If you have time for only one town on the Romantic Road, make it Rothenburg, the best-preserved medieval city in Germany. Inside its undamaged 13th-century city walls, the old town center seems untouched by the passage of time from its heyday as a free imperial city in the 14th century. The only drawback is that Rothenburg, about 32 miles (52km) southeast of Würzburg, suffers from serious overcrowding, especially in summer.

There are no direct trains from Würzburg, but you can reach Rothenburg in about 1 hour, with a change of trains in Steinach. The trip from Frankfurt, including train changes, is about 3 hours. From the train station it's about a 10-minute walk to the old town center. For tourist information, contact **Rothenburg Tourismus Service,** Marktplatz (✆ **09861/404 800;** www.rothenburg.de). November to April, it's open Monday to Friday 9am to noon and 1 to 5pm and Saturday 10am to 1pm; May to October, it's open Monday to Friday 9am to noon and 1 to 6pm and Saturday and Sunday 10am to 3pm.

Top Attractions & Special Moments

For an excellent view, take a walk on the **town ramparts** ✩. This pleasant walk, from the massive 16th-century Spitaltor (at the end of the Spitalgasse) to the Klingentor, takes about a half hour, with panoramic views over the city along the way.

Rothenburg's **Rathaus (Town Hall)** ✩, Marktplatz (✆ **09861/404 177**), consists of an older Gothic section from 1240 and a newer Renaissance structure facing the square, built in 1572 to replace a portion destroyed in a fire. It's decorated with intricate friezes and a large stone portico opening onto the square. From the 165-foot (50m) tower of the Gothic hall, the highest spot in town, you get a great **view** ✩ of the town below. The tower, reached through the town hall's main entrance on Marktplatz, is open April to October daily 9:30am to 12:30pm and 1 to 5pm; November and January to March Saturday and Sunday noon to 3pm; and December daily noon to 3pm. It will cost you 1€ ($1.30) to climb to the top; children pay .50€ (65¢).

The most important church in town, the Gothic **St. Jakobskirche (Church of St. Jacob),** Klostergasse 15 (✆ **09861/7006-20**), dates from 1336. In the west gallery is the **Altar of the Holy Blood** ✩✩, a masterpiece by the famous Würzburg sculptor Tilman Riemenschneider (ca. 1460–1531). The work was executed between 1499 and 1505 to provide a worthy setting for its Reliquary of the Holy Blood. This relic, venerated in the Middle Ages, is contained in a rock-crystal capsule set in the reliquary cross (ca. 1270) in the center of the shrine. The church is open April to October, daily 9am to 5:15pm; December, daily from 10am to 5pm; November and January to March, daily from 10am to noon and 2 to 4pm. Admission is 2€ ($2.60) for adults and .50€ (65¢) for children.

The historical collection of Rothenburg is housed at the **Reichsstadtmuseum (Imperial City Museum),** Klosterhof 5 (✆ **09861/93 90 43;** www.reichsstadt museum.rothenburg.de), in a 13th-century Dominican nunnery. The cloisters are well preserved, and you can visit the convent hall, kitchen, and apothecary. The museum collection includes period furniture and art from Rothenburg's more prosperous periods, a section on medieval Jewish life, weaponry (including flintlock rifles and sabers that once belonged to Marie Antoinette and Napoleon's brother), and archaeological finds from prehistoric times up to the Middle Ages. Among the artistic exhibits is the 1494 *Rothenburg Passion* series, 12 pictures by Martinus Schwartz that depict scenes from the suffering of Christ. An interesting object is a historic tankard that holds more than 6 pints. The museum is open April to October, daily from 10am to 5pm; November to March, daily from 1 to 4pm. Admission is 3€ ($3.90) for adults, 2€ ($2.60) for seniors and students, and 1.50€ ($1.95) for children.

An unusual museum is the **Kriminalmuseum (Medieval Crime Museum),** Burggasse 3 (© **9861/5359;** kriminalmuseum.rothenburg.de), which documents 1,000 years of legal history in Germany. On display are historic documents related to German law and instruments of torture during the Middle Ages, providing a different kind of insight into medieval life. There was, for example, a torture chair just for bakers who shortchanged their customers by baking bread smaller than the prescribed size. It's open daily: April to October 9:30am to 6pm; December and March 10am to 4pm; and November, January, and February 2 to 4pm. Admission is 3.80€ ($4.95) for adults, 2.60€ ($3.40) for students, and 2.20€ ($2.85) for children.

On a much lighter note is the **Deutsches Weihnachtsmuseum (German Christmas Museum),** Herrngasse 1 (© **9861/40 93 65;** www.weihnachtsmuseum.de), which relates the history of German Christmas traditions and is filled with decorations through the ages, including a huge collection of nutcrackers. It's open April to December daily 10am to 5:30pm and January to March Saturday and Sunday 10am to 5pm. Admission is 4€ ($5.20) for adults and 2€ ($2.60) for children.

Where to Stay & Dine

The 45-room **Flair-Hotel Reichs-Küchenmeister** ✧, Kircheplatz 8 (© **09861/97 00;** www.reichskuechenmeister.com), is one of the town's oldest structures and was salvaged from a World War II firestorm through a massive, thoroughly sensitive restoration. It's both stylish and well equipped, with dining options ranging from a main restaurant and a wine tavern to a seasonal garden restaurant. Rooms in the main building are furnished in a variety of styles, from rustic with regional wooden furniture to contemporary. Seventeen identical-looking rooms are available in the less desirable annex across the street. Bathrooms are a bit small, but maintenance is tidy and each comes with a tiled shower. Rates include a buffet breakfast and cost 75€ to 135€ ($97.50–$175) double.

The **Baumeisterhaus** ✧, Obere Schmiedgasse 3 (© **09861/947 00**), is housed in an ancient patrician residence, built in 1596. It contains Rothenburg's most beautiful courtyard (you can dine in it if you reserve in advance). The patio has colorful murals, serenely draped by vines. Frankly, although the Franconian menu is good, the romantic setting is the main attraction. One of the chef's best dishes is *Sauerbraten* (braised beef marinated in vinegar and served with *Spätzle,* small flour dumplings). The food for the most part is the rib-sticking fare beloved by Bavarians. Main courses cost 6.50€ to 20€ ($8.45–$26). It's open daily 10am to 9pm (closed Jan–Feb).

AUGSBURG

Augsburg's 2,000 years of history (it's Germany's second-oldest city and was founded by the Roman emperor Augustus in 15 B.C.) have made it one of southern Germany's major sightseeing attractions. The city is especially noteworthy for its picture-perfect Renaissance and baroque architecture. About 42 miles (68km) northwest of Munich, it's the Romantic Road's largest town and serves also as a gateway to the Alps and the south. It's well connected to area rail lines and has especially good connections to Munich, so if you can't travel the entire Romantic Road, you can do it as an easy day trip out of Munich.

There are more than 60 trains a day from Munich (trip time: 33–46 min.); direct trains depart every hour or so from Frankfurt (trip time: 3–3½ hr.) and every hour from Würzburg (trip time: 2 hr.). The main station is ⅔ mile (1km) west of the center of town, about a 15-minute walk away or a short ride by tram. It's quite easy to get around on foot. For visitor information, contact the **Regio Augsburg Tourismus Tourist-Information,** Maximilianstrasse 57 (② **0821/50 20-70;** www.augsburg-tourismus.de), open April to October Monday to Friday 9am to 6pm, Saturday 10am to 5pm and Sunday 10am to 2pm; November to March Monday to Friday 9am to 5pm and Saturday 10am to 2pm.

Top Attractions & Special Moments

Extending southward from the Rathaus is the wide **Maximilianstrasse** ⧲, lined with shops and old burghers' houses and studded with fountains by the Renaissance Dutch sculptor Adrien de Vries.

One of the most famous buildings here is the **Schaezlerpalais,** Maximilianstrasse 46 (② **0821/324 41 02;** tram: 2), a 60-room rococo mansion facing the Hercules Fountain and constructed between 1765 and 1770. It contains an amazing art collection, mostly by regional German artists of the Renaissance and baroque periods, including Hans Holbein the Elder and Hans Burgkmair. Albrecht Dürer's famous portrait of Jakob Fugger is here. Rubens, Veronese, Tiepolo, Cranach, and others are also represented. The palace contains a rococo ballroom, with gilded and mirrored wall panels and a ceiling fresco, *The Four Continents,* as well as a period garden. It's open Tuesday 10am to 8pm and Wednesday to Sunday 10am to 5pm. Admission is 7€ ($9.10) for adults and 5.50€ ($7.15) for seniors, students, and children.

Anchoring the northern end of the historic old town is the Romanesque and Gothic cathedral of Augsburg, **Dom St. Maria,** Hoher Weg (② **0821/316 63 53;** tram: 2), with records dating from 823. It's famous for four stained-glass windows, the oldest in Germany, dating from the 12th century. They're located at the top of the nave and depict Old Testament prophets in a severe but colorful style. The south bronze door, dating from the 14th century, features 25 bas-relief panels with scenes from the Old Testament. Outside the church are remains of a Roman wall. The Dom is open Monday to Saturday from 7am to 6pm; Sunday from 9:30am to 6pm. Admission is free.

About a 10-minute walk east of the city center, the **Fuggerei,** Vorderer Lech (② **0821/ 31 98 81-0;** www.fuggerei.de; tram: 1), was founded in 1521 to house Augsburg's needy citizens. It was established by Jakob Fugger, one of the most powerful bankers, merchants, and businessmen of his time (he financed the popes in Rome and the Habsburgers' climb to power). Surviving today as the world's oldest social settlement, the Fuggerei is a miniature, self-contained town, enclosed by its own wall and with entry gates and eight narrow lanes. Approximately 150 people—mostly the elderly—occupy the Fuggerei's 140 apartments. Since its founding, residents have had to pay a nominal rent of only one Rhenish guilder (.90€/$1.15) per year. The only obligation is that tenants say three prayers daily for the souls of their founders. Be sure to make a stop at Mittlere Gasse 13, which now serves as the Fuggerei's museum. Not only can you watch a film highlighting Jakob Fugger's life and times, but you can also tour an original apartment consisting of a living room, kitchen, and bedroom, showing what it was like to live here in the days of yore. The museum is open April to October 8am to 8pm and November to March 9am to 6pm. Admission to the Fuggerei, including the museum, is 2€ ($2.60) for adults and 1€ ($1.30) for children.

Where to Stay & Dine

The Steigenberger Drei Mohren ✻✻, Maximilianstrasse 40 (© **0821/5036-0;** www.augsburg.steigenberger.de; tram: 2), is Augsburg's most famous hotel, with a history stretching back several centuries and counting Mozart, Goethe, Napoleon, and various royalty among its guests. Its 105 rooms are comfortable and spacious, but the real draws here are the hotel's prime location, its elegant lobby, and its two restaurants, one decked out like a French bistro and the other serving Mediterranean cuisine. Rooms cost 151€ to 240€ ($196–$312) double, with weekend discounts available.

Also with an enviable location but with cheaper rates is **Hotel Am Rathaus,** Am Hinteren Perlachberg 1 (© **0821/346 49-0;** www.hotel-am-rathaus-augsburg.de; tram: 2). Located behind the imposing town hall yet amazingly quiet, this 32-room property offers small rooms with contemporary furnishings. Rates for a double here are 110€ to 125€ ($143–$163), including breakfast buffet. Weekend discounts are available.

Die Ecke ✻✻ (look for the building's traditional name, Ecke Stube, on its facade), Elias-Holl-Platz 2 (© **0821/51 06 00;** www.restaurantdieecke.de; tram: 2), is the town's finest dining choice, making it a good bet for a special occasion. Located behind the town hall, this restaurant's guests have included Hans Holbein the Elder, Mozart, and, in more contemporary times, Rudolf Diesel (of engine fame), and Bertolt Brecht. There are two floors of dining, as well as courtyard seating out back. The chef is renowned for his presentations, and the venison dishes in season, a specialty, are the best in town. Reservations are a must. Main courses run 20€ to 26€ ($26–$34), but weekday business lunches cost 16€ ($21) and fixed-price dinners start at 44€ ($57). It's open daily 11am to 2pm and 5:30 to 10pm.

The **Ratskeller,** located in the basement of town hall at Rathausplatz 2 (© **0821/319 88 238;** www.ratskeller-augsburg.de; tram: 2), combines its historic setting of high, vaulted ceilings with contemporary beige decor, giving it a hip, edgy atmosphere. It offers typical Bavarian fare, including Weisswurst, Schnitzel, trout, boiled beef, and Leberkäse (a kind of meatloaf), with most meals costing 7.50€ to 18.90€ ($9.75–$25). It's open daily 11am to 11pm.

Nearby, the lively **König von Flandern,** Karolinenstrasse 12 (© **0821/15 80 50;** www.koenigvonflandern.de; tram: 2), is a basement brewery, serving wurst, roast pork, and other hearty fare in addition to its own brews. You can dine here for 8€ to 12€ ($10–$16), and it's open daily 11am to midnight.

10

Great Britain & Ireland

Great Britain is made up of England, Scotland, and Wales, three ancient kingdoms that are today part of the United Kingdom (Northern Ireland is the final member of the U.K.). It might be small—just 88,150 square miles (228,300 sq. km)—but thanks to its history and landscape it consistently ranks among the top destinations for travelers across the globe. Yes, the weather can be a little damp, but the summer brings with it sunshine and long evenings. And the food is really rather good now, with gastropubs and delis sprouting up everywhere from villages to cities. Speaking of which, London is still Europe's center of cool, and the once-grim industrial cities up north—such as Leeds and Newcastle—have been reborn as buzzing cultural hubs. Even farther up, Edinburgh remains Scotland's capital, both politically and artistically, while Ireland is an altogether separate nation—with a different currency, laws, and even its own Gaelic language—but is still a destination easily added to a rail tour of the British Isles.

HIGHLIGHTS OF GREAT BRITAIN

You could spend weeks exploring this fascinating country and still have plenty more to see. Mighty castles, stately homes, magnificent gardens, soaring cathedrals, romantic landscapes, and historic cities are flung across the far corners of Great Britain like so many jewels. But if time is an issue, you couldn't do any better than to limit yourself to London, Edinburgh, and Dublin, the great capital cities of England, Scotland, and the Republic of Ireland. **London** is a dizzying delight, full of pomp and pedigree, a place where high culture and cutting-edge trends feed off one another. London is sedate and raucous, a time-tested background for legendary sites harking back to the earliest days of the kingdom. **Edinburgh,** crowned by its famous castle, is almost as royal as London, and far more dramatically situated, but it's much smaller and easier to digest in a short period. With its unique combination of medieval and neoclassical districts, Edinburgh invites exploration. Scotland's greatest national museums and art collections are concentrated here. The town is suffused with creative energy that blossoms during the famed Edinburgh International Festival. With 40% of the Republic of Ireland's population living within 61 miles (97km) of **Dublin,** this capital is by far the largest and most workaday of all Irish cities. It's also booming thanks to the economic expansion of Ireland over the last couple of decades and consequently packed with great shopping, wonderful restaurants and pubs, and such historic treasures as the Book of Kells, the National Museum, Dublin Castle, and the bucolic pleasures of St. Stephen's Green and Phoenix Park.

(Moments) Festivals & Special Events in Great Britain

On the Saturday closest to her official birthday in mid-June (her real birthday is Apr 21, and is celebrated with gun salutes in Hyde Park), Elizabeth II inspects her regiments from an open carriage and receives the salute during the **Trooping the Colour.** The event dates back to the 1600s when a regiment's colors or flag were trooped in front of the infantry soldiers so they would recognize them on the battlefield. Now it is an opportunity for certain regiments to pay tribute to the queen. With huge military bands, its quintessential English pageantry draws big crowds—many of them waiting to see a wretched young soldier faint in the heat under his ridiculous bearskin hat. Tickets cost £20 ($38) and are allocated in the early part of the year by public ballot. If you can't get tickets to the event (otherwise known as The Queen's Birthday Parade) you could always try the Major General's Review (tickets: free) or the Colonel's Review (tickets: £10/$19). These events happen on the Saturday before the Queen's Birthday Parade and are very similar, albeit lacking the queen. Call © **020/7414-2479** for more details on all three events or look online at **www.army.mod.uk**.

The thrilling **Wimbledon Lawn Tennis Championships,** just outside London, is the event where the posh and the people rub shoulders, and you can get right up close to the world's top tennis players. You can queue for a ticket on the day of the event, but it's very competitive, with people lining up from the previous evening. August 1 to December 31, you can apply to enter the public lottery for next year's tickets by simply sending a self-addressed stamped envelope to **All England Lawn Tennis Club,** P.O. Box 98, Church Rd., Wimbledon, London SW19 5AE. The club will then send you an application form. For more information, call © **020/8971-2473** or visit **www. wimbledon.com** on the Web. The tournament takes place from late June to early July.

The **Henry Wood Promenade Concerts,** the famous summer musical season at London's Royal Albert Hall, dates from 1895. It runs the gamut from ancient to modern classics, and jazz, too. Tickets go from £6 ($11.40) (© **020/ 7589-8212;** www.royalalberthall.com or www.bbc.co.uk/proms). The season runs from mid-July to mid-September.

The **Edinburgh International Festival** is the highlight of the Edinburgh year and turns the city into a nonstop celebration. The festival attracts artists and companies of the highest international standard in all fields of the arts, including music, opera, dance, and theater. Around the same time as the festival runs the exciting spectacle of the **Military Tattoo** on the floodlit esplanade in front of Edinburgh Castle, high on its rock above the city. The city is jammed during this period, and it's essential to book a hotel in advance. For more details on the festival, see "The Edinburgh Festival: Art & Tattoos" on p. 433.

Great Britain & Ireland

1 Essentials

GETTING THERE
The main international airports serving the U.K. are Heathrow and Gatwick, both near London.

Heathrow Heathrow (© **0870/000-0123;** www.baa.co.uk), the main international airport, is 15 miles (24km) west of Central London. It's served by **Air Canada** (© **888/247-2262;** www.aircanada.ca), **American Airlines** (© **800/433-7300;** www. aa.com), **British Airways** (© **800/AIRWAYS;** www.britishairways.com), **Continental Airlines** (© **800/231-0856;** www.continental.com), **Icelandair** (© **800/223-5500** in the U.S.; www.icelandair.com), **United Airlines** (© **800/538-2929;** www. united.com), and **Virgin Atlantic Airways** (© **800/821-5438;** www.virgin-atlantic. com).

The majority of flights from North America arrive at Terminals 3 and 4, with flights from some U.S. destinations touching down at Terminal 1 (when Terminal 5 opens in March 2008, flights will be redistributed). There is a **Tourist Information Centre** in the Tube station concourse that connects with **Terminals 1, 2, and 3,** open daily from 8am to 6pm (to 7pm Mon–Sat June–Sept). You can find **British Hotel Reservation Centre** desks (© **020/7340-1616;** www.bhrc.co.uk) in the arrivals area of every terminal, open daily.

Gatwick Gatwick (© **0870/000-2468;** www.baa.co.uk) is a smaller airport about 25 miles (40km) south of London. It's served by American Airlines; British Airways; Delta; Continental; Northwest; and Virgin Atlantic.

BRITAIN BY TRAIN
Getting to London from the Continent by train used to involve at least one ferry transfer. Not anymore. With the 1994 opening of the Chunnel, running underneath the English Channel between England and France, one can now travel between London and Paris with relative ease. The **Eurostar** (**www.eurostar.com**) train offers direct service from Paris's Gare du Nord and Brussels' Gare du Midi to St. Pancras in London in about 2 hours, making London (or Paris) a day-trip destination. More than a dozen Eurostar trains travel both to and from the Continent daily. **Rail Europe** (© **877/272-RAIL** [7245] in North America; www.raileurope.com) sells Eurostar tickets, allowing you to combine a trip to London with a rail tour of the Continent. Eurail passholders do get a discount when purchasing a Eurostar ticket.

Should you wish to go the slow train route from the Continent to London, you'll need to get off your train in France near the English Channel and take a ferry or hovercraft across the water (up until the 1980s certain trains would board a ferry, but this seamless travel route has now been replaced by the Eurotunnel). You'll disembark at one of the U.K channel ports—those closest to London are Dover, Ramsgate, and Folkestone to the east, and Southhampton, Portsmouth, and Newhaven to the south—and from there you'll board a British train for the journey onward to London. This can actually end up costing more than some of the supersaver round-trip Eurostar fares, and is a lot more of a hassle, but some people may just want to see the fabled white cliffs of Dover from the English Channel.

PASSES
The **Eurail Global Pass** is not accepted on British trains. If you're going to be traveling by train around England, Wales, and Scotland—perhaps taking a few train excursions

out of London—then consider buying a **BritRail Pass.** If you're going to Great Britain in winter, this may be a very economical option as the pass is often discounted for January and February travel. For information on the various BritRail pass options available, including the **BritRail Pass,** the **BritRail Flexipass,** and the **Britrail Plus Ireland Pass,** see chapter 2.

Note that BritRail passes are not for sale in the U.K., so you must obtain them before you leave home. You can purchase BritRail passes on the phone or online through **Rail Europe** (② 877/272-RAIL [7245] in North America; www.raileurope. com); and in person at the **British Travel Shop** next to the VisitBritain office in Manhattan, 551 Fifth Ave., 7th floor, New York, NY (② 212/490-6688).

Note: If you plan to travel for only a day or two to Edinburgh out of London, it may be more economical to purchase Rail Europe's Edinburgh Overnight or Day Trip to Edinburgh excursion packages instead of a pass. For more information on these, call Rail Europe or check their website.

TICKET TYPES

You won't encounter any incomprehensible train terms in England (although it might help to remember the U.K. uses the terms **return** rather than round-trip and **single** rather than one-way), but there are several ticket types you might be unfamiliar with. Broadly speaking, ticket types divide into three groups: **Advance** (booked ahead with restrictions), **Cheap Day/Saver** (bought same day and has restrictions), and **Open** (bought same day, but doesn't have restrictions). Within these groups are various subcategories. It's ridiculous to try and memorize them all. Instead, let the ticket seller know your travel plans in detail (especially which parts are flexible and which parts are not) and question him closely to determine your best option. If you can plan your travel in advance and stick to set times, it can often be cheaper to buy two advance, single tickets than to buy a return ticket. If you input your journey details into **www.nationalrail.co.uk**, the website will tell you which tickets are still available for your desired route. For a list of all available ticket types go to **www.nationalrail.co. uk/times_fares/purchasing_tickets/ticket_types.htm**.

PRACTICAL TRAIN INFORMATION

The entire British railway system was privatized under Margaret Thatcher, so there are now a number of different companies operating trains to specific parts of the country. Virgin, First, and GNER are three of the major names you might encounter.

The sleek high-speed **InterCity** trains running between London and heavily traveled main-line routes (such as Edinburgh) are the most dependable and the most comfortable. For shorter trips (to Brighton or Cambridge, for example) **commuter trains** are used. In some cases you might need to transfer to a **local train** to reach your destination. The local trains connect small towns between larger towns and are very basic. Local stations are small and sometimes (particularly on Sun) there's no one to help with information or ticket sales. You will always find train schedules posted in local stations, and if there is no window service you can buy your ticket on the train. There is no smoking on British trains; even the tobacco-friendly French have forbidden smoking on the Eurostar.

An announcement is (usually) made before a train arrives at each station; some trains will have a digital sign in each car announcing the stop. Station stops are short, so be ready to disembark when the train comes to a halt. In newer trains there will be a well-marked push button that will open the door automatically. In older trains, you'll need to open the door yourself. It may open from the inside, or you may have to open the window and reach outside to turn the door handle.

Trains have a two-tiered ticket system: first class and standard (second) class. First-class tickets cost about one-third more than standard class. The first-class cars have roomier seats and fewer people, but you can travel quite comfortably in standard class. There is no first-class service on local trains. There are toilets on board all but local trains.

First-class service on InterCity trains (such as those between London and Edinburgh) includes free coffee, tea, beverages, and snacks served at your seat; some trains offer a free newspaper and a higher standard of personal service. Standard-class passengers can buy sandwiches and drinks in a cafe car. On most lines an employee comes through with a food and beverage cart. There is no food service on local trains.

TICKETS & RESERVATIONS   You can purchase your ticket with cash or a credit card at a ticket window in any British train station, and you can get your BritRail passes validated there as well. You can also buy a ticket on a train (cash only) if there is not a staffed ticket office or a Permit to Travel machine (these enable you to pay some money towards your fare, avoid a penalty fare, and then upgrade to a full ticket on board the train) at your departure station. If you have a validated BritRail Pass (see "Passes," above), just board your train. Seat reservations are not required on most trains, but they are a good idea on some InterCity trains, especially if you're traveling on a weekend or on journeys longer than 3 hours. They are pretty much a must on the night and weekend trains between Edinburgh and London in the summer. Reservations can be purchased (usually for about £2/$3.80, though they are often free if you have a BritRail Pass) at the same time you buy your ticket, or you can make them inside the train station up to a couple of hours before departure. Should you wish to reserve a seat on a British train before arriving in the U.K., you can do so through Rail Europe (see "Passes," above) for around $11.

FAST FACTS: **Great Britain**

Area Codes Every telephone number in England and Scotland is prefaced by an area code that must be used if you are dialing long distance (London's area code, for example, is **20**; Edinburgh's is **131**). If you're calling long distance but within the United Kingdom, preface the area code with a zero (in other words, London would be **020**), followed by the number. See "Telephone," below.

Business Hours Banks are usually open Monday through Friday 9:30am to 3:30pm. Business offices are open Monday through Friday 9am to 5pm. English pubs used to only be allowed to stay open Monday through Saturday 11am to 11pm and Sunday noon to 10:30pm but since 2005 drinking establishments can apply for a license to serve alcohol longer. And many do. Especially in the cities, where many bars go on until midnight or 1 am and clubs often stay open until 4 or 6am. Scottish licensing laws have always been more flexible with many pubs and bars staying open until midnight but most closing at 11pm. Stores generally open at 10am and close at 6pm Monday through Saturday, staying open until 7 or 8pm on Wednesday or Thursday. Outside of the large cities, shops may be open for only a half day on Saturday and shut one afternoon a week, often Wednesdays. Nowadays, more stores open on Sunday in London and Edinburgh.

Climate Unpredictable is the best that can be said about the weather in England and Scotland. Great Britain is an island and its climate is influenced by the often-stormy North Atlantic. Precipitation is frequent; so are gray skies. Year-round, it tends to be wetter, windier, and colder in Edinburgh than in London. Without question, the best times to visit the U.K. are late spring or early autumn and summer.

Currency Britain's decimal monetary system is based on the pound (£), which is made up of 100 pence (written as "p"). Scotland has its own notes, which can legally be used in England though some smaller storekeepers may be suspicious of them. The exchange rate used in this chapter is £1=$1.90, though fluctuations are constant. Currency exchange services can be found in railway stations, some banks, at most post offices, and in many tourist information centers.

Documents Required All U.S. citizens and Canadians must have a passport with at least 2 months validity remaining. No visa is required. The immigration officer may also want proof of your intention to return to your point of origin (usually a round-trip ticket) and visible means of support while in Britain.

Electricity British current is 240 volts, AC cycle, roughly twice the voltage of North American current. You will need an electrical transformer and a plug adapter to use electric equipment from the U.S. in Great Britain (available at electrical supply or travel shops), or you'll destroy the inner workings of your appliances. Most laptops and some cellphone and digital camera chargers come with transformers built in, but always check carefully before plugging anything in.

Embassies & High Commissions All embassies, consulates, and high commissions are located in London, the capital of the U.K. The **U.S. Embassy** is at 24 Grosvenor Sq., W1 (© 020/7499-9000; www.usembassy.org.uk; Tube: Bond St.) Open Monday to Friday 8:30am to 5:30pm, although not all sections will be open throughout these hours. The **Canadian High Commission** is at MacDonald House, 38 Grosvenor Sq., W1 (© 020/7258-6600; www.canada.org.uk; Tube: Bond St.), open Monday to Friday 8am to 11am.

Health & Safety There are no major health risks associated with traveling in Britain. Pharmacies are called chemists in the United Kingdom; **Boots** is a chain with outlets all over the country. Any prescriptions you bring with you should use generic, not brand names. England and Scotland are generally safe countries, although London is a teeming metropolis subject to petty crimes such as pickpocketing and con games, and more serious offenses such as mugging and rape. Be cautious at night; don't carry all your valuables on you when you go out, and be alert when taking money from ATMs. For police, fire, or an ambulance, dial © 999.

Holidays **Bank Holidays** (there's two in May and one in Aug) celebrate various events, and fall on a Monday, making for a nice long weekend. All banks and many shops, museums, historic houses, and other places of interest are closed and public transport is radically reduced. The same holds true for other holidays:

New Year's Day, Good Friday, Easter Monday, Christmas, and Boxing Day (Dec 26). Crowds swell during school holidays: mid-July to early September, 3 weeks at Christmas and at Easter, and a week in mid-October and in mid-February.

Legal Aid Your consulate, embassy, or high commission (see above) will give you advice if you run into trouble. They can advise you of your rights and even provide a list of attorneys (for which you'll have to pay if services are used), but they can't interfere on your behalf in the legal processes of Great Britain. For questions about American citizens arrested abroad, including ways of getting money to them, call the **Citizens Emergency Center of the Office of Special Consulate Services,** in Washington, D.C. (② **202/647-5225**). Other nationals can go to their nearest consulate or embassy.

Mail Post offices and sub–post offices throughout England and Scotland are open Monday through Friday 9am to 5pm and Saturday 9am to noon. Many sub–post offices and some main post offices close for an hour at lunchtime. Post offices are identified by a big red sign, and may be tucked inside office supply or souvenir shops. An airmail letter or postcard to North America costs 54p ($1) for 10 grams and should arrive within 5 days. Mail within the U.K. can be sent first (to arrive the next day) or second class (to arrive in 2–3 days).

Police & Emergencies The best source of help and advice in emergencies is the police. For non-life-threatening situations, dial ② **118118** and ask for the local police telephone number; dial ② **999** for emergencies only (no coin required). If the local police can't assist, they'll have the address of a person who can. Losses, thefts, and other crimes should be reported immediately; just don't expect to retrieve your stolen goods.

Telephone The Directory Inquiries system has been privatized and its new numbers begin with 118. The easiest to remember is ② **118 118,** where the average call costs 69p ($1.30). One of the cheapest is ② **118 180,** which charges 25p (50¢) basic, plus 30p (60¢) per minute. If you allow the service to connect you, you'll pay more for your phone call than if you get the number from them and call it yourself.

The country code for the United Kingdom is **44.** To call England or Scotland from the United States, dial **011-44,** then the area or city code, and then the six-, seven-, or eight-digit phone number. (Drop the first zero.) If you're in England or Scotland and dialing a number within the same area code, put the zero back on (that is, ② 020/7123-1234).

Nearly all BT Pay Phones in the U.K. now accept credit cards and coins, except for some in rural areas, which only accept credit cards. The minimum charge is 40p (75¢).

To make an international call from the U.K., dial the international access code **(00),** then the country code, then the area code, and finally the local number (dropping any parenthesized zeros). Or call through one of the following long-distance access codes: **AT&T USA Direct** (② 0800/890-011) and **Canada Direct** (② 0800-/890-016). The country code for the **U.S.** and **Canada** is 1.

Tipping In restaurants, **service charges** of 12.5% to 15% are often added to the bill. Sometimes this is clearly marked; at other times it isn't. When in doubt, ask. If service isn't included, it's customary to add 10% to 15% to the bill. Tipping in pubs isn't usually done (unless you're eating), but in **cocktail bars** the server usually gets about £1 or £2 ($1.90 or $3.80) per round of drinks. Try not to tip by credit card or check in England and Wales as—thanks to a 2002 court ruling—this money can then be used by the owner to make up serving staff's pay. Instead, tip with cash to ensure your money rewards the right people. It's standard to tip **taxi drivers** 10% to 15% of the fare. **Barbers and hairdressers** will be happy to get 10% to 15% but won't expect anything. **Tour guides** appreciate £2 ($3.80), though it's not mandatory. **Theater ushers** are not tipped.

2 London

London is one of the world's great cities, with attractions for visitors of every age. It has a 2,000-year-old history and yet is as culturally cutting edge as tomorrow. There's no end of things to do and ways to enjoy the pulsating capital of the United Kingdom. Famous monuments such as the Tower of London and Westminster Abbey draw flocks of visitors every day, as they have for centuries. Pomp and ceremony still define Royal London, with its palaces and protocols. London's museums, nothing short of fabulous, are unrivaled in the scope and quality of their collections. And when it comes to nightlife, London has got it all: theater, dance, music of every kind, pubs, and late-night clubs—take your pick. Most important of all for the rail traveler, London's the major transit point to and from the Continent, and Great Britain's largest rail hub.

STATION INFORMATION
GETTING FROM THE AIRPORT INTO TOWN
The odds are that you will arrive in London at either Heathrow or Gatwick, London's two main international airports (though it's possible that you'll land at Stansted, which now has some trans-Atlantic flights). The other airports—Luton and London City—do not service scheduled international flights, only charters and European destinations.

From Heathrow   There are several ways to get into London from Heathrow. The cheapest way into town is the **Underground** or **Tube,** London's subway system. There are two airport Tube stations on the Piccadilly Line: one for Terminals 1, 2, and 3, and one for Terminal 4. The journey into Central London takes 40 to 50 minutes. A one-way fare to Central London is £4 ($7.60).

The quickest and most comfortable way into town is via **Heathrow Express** (© 0845/ 600-1515; www.heathrowexpress.co.uk), the luxury nonstop rail service to Paddington Station, which takes 15 minutes from Terminals 1, 2, and 3, and 20 to 25 minutes from Terminal 4. Trains leave Heathrow from 5am to midnight and arrive there from 5:30am to midnight. The standard-class one-way tickets cost £14.50 ($27.55); BritRail Passes may be used on the Heathrow Express. Simply go to the ticket office to have your pass validated before boarding the train.

Finally, the **Airbus** (© 0870/574-7777; www.nationalexpress.com), operated by National Express, leaves twice an hour from just outside each Heathrow terminal and goes to 23 stops in central London; there are three buses traveling different routes through London. Ask your hotel or B&B if there's one close by because this may be

London

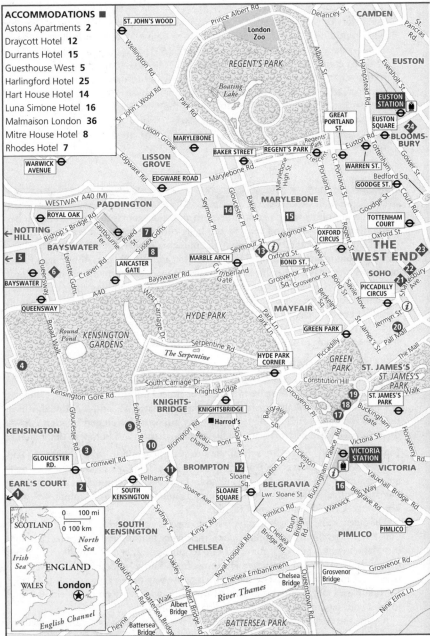

ACCOMMODATIONS ■
Astons Apartments **2**
Draycott Hotel **12**
Durrants Hotel **15**
Guesthouse West **5**
Harlingford Hotel **25**
Hart House Hotel **14**
Luna Simone Hotel **16**
Malmaison London **36**
Mitre House Hotel **8**
Rhodes Hotel **7**

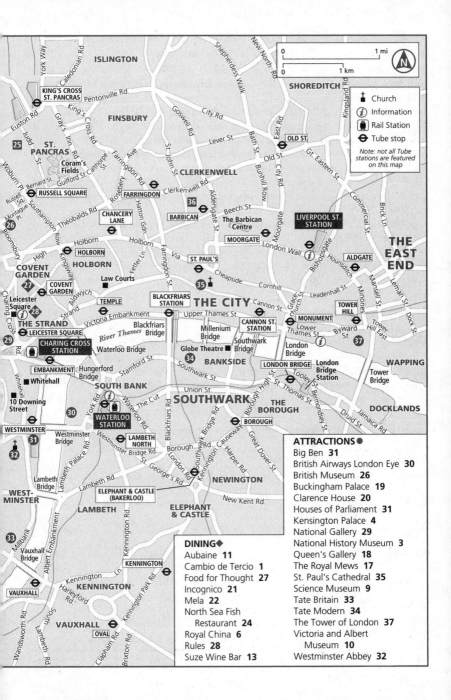

LEGEND

- ✝ Church
- ⓘ Information
- 🚉 Rail Station
- ⊖ Tube stop

Note: not all Tube stations are featured on this map

ATTRACTIONS ●

Big Ben **31**
British Airways London Eye **30**
British Museum **26**
Buckingham Palace **19**
Clarence House **20**
Houses of Parliament **31**
Kensington Palace **4**
National Gallery **29**
National History Museum **3**
Queen's Gallery **18**
The Royal Mews **17**
St. Paul's Cathedral **35**
Science Museum **9**
Tate Britain **33**
Tate Modern **34**
The Tower of London **37**
Victoria and Albert Museum **10**
Westminster Abbey **32**

DINING◆

Aubaine **11**
Cambio de Tercio **1**
Food for Thought **27**
Incognico **21**
Mela **22**
North Sea Fish Restaurant **24**
Royal China **6**
Rules **28**
Suze Wine Bar **13**

the most convenient option. One-way tickets cost £4 ($7.60). **Black taxis** are always available at Heathrow. The approximate fare to London is £50 ($95).

From Gatwick There are four ways of making the 25-mile (40km) trek into London from Gatwick. The best is the **Gatwick Express** (**www.gatwickexpress.co.uk**), which takes around 30 minutes to reach Victoria station, and costs an unwarranted and extortionate £14.90 ($22.80) one-way. You can buy tickets online; give the conductor your e-ticket confirmation number once you're aboard the train. The station is below the airport, and trains depart every 15 minutes from 5am to 12:35am weekdays; till 11:45pm on weekends. A slightly cheaper option is **South Central Trains,** which charges £8.90 ($16.90) one-way for a train that takes 35 to 45 minutes, depending how often it stops between Victoria station and the airport. BritRail passes can be used on both trains. For information on both, call **National Rail Enquiries** (© 0845/748-4950).

Hotelink (© 01293/532244; www.hotelink.co.uk) runs a minibus service and charges £24 ($38.20) to take you directly to your hotel from Gatwick (after your ride on the Gatwick Express, included in the price), or just £19 from Heathrow. **Checker Cars** (© 01293/567700; www.checkercars.com) provides 24-hour taxi service between Gatwick and Central London; expect to pay about £85 ($162) for the 90-minute journey.

INSIDE THE STATIONS

The British Rail train network connects London to all the major cities and most towns within the U.K. (and some European destinations; see "Britain by Train," earlier in this chapter). There are nine major British Rail train stations in London, each serving different parts of the U.K. For more information on the destinations each station serves, see "London's Major Train Stations," below. The station you travel to or from will be determined by where you're coming from or where you want to go.

London's Major Train Stations*

Station	Destinations Served
Charing Cross	Trains travel southeast to Canterbury, Hastings, Dover, and English Channel ports that connect with ferry service to the Continent.
Euston	Trains head northwest to the Lake District and up to Scotland (overnight service to Scotland).
King's Cross	Trains travel to destinations in the east and north of England, including York, and up to Edinburgh.
Liverpool Street	Trains head east to English Channel ports with continuing service to the Netherlands, northern Germany, and Scandinavia.
Paddington	Trains travel to Heathrow airport and southwest to Bath, the West Country, and South Wales.
St. Pancras	Handles Eurostar trains to Paris and Brussels as well as trains to the midlands.
Victoria	Trains head for Gatwick airport and the southeast, including Canterbury and Brighton.
Waterloo	Trains go primarily to the south of England.

In addition to the mainline stations, there are also numerous regional stations, including Blackfriars, Charing Cross, London Bridge, Marylebone, Stratford, and Clapham Junction.

(*Value*) Discount Transportation Passes

Anyone planning to use public transport should check out the range of money-saving passes that can be used on both the Tube and buses. You can buy all of them at Tube stations and any sundry shop or newsagents with a light blue **Ticket Stop** or **Oyster Ticket Stop** sticker in their window. The former will sell only paper tickets, such as One-Day Travelcards (see below). The latter will sell the full range of tickets and passes including Oyster Cards (see below). Here's a sample of the most useful passes for visitors to London:

One-Day Travelcards can be used for unlimited trips before 9:30am (peak-card) or after 9:30am (off-peak) Monday to Friday, and all day on Saturday, Sunday, and holidays, and on N-prefixed night buses. Adults traveling within zones 1 and 2 pay £5.10 ($9.70) off-peak and £6.60 ($12.55) peak. In contrast, the **One-Day LT Card** is available for all zones at peak travel times and costs £13.20 ($25.10).

One-Week Travelcards are good for any number of trips at any hour of the day, and on night buses. A One-Week Travelcard for Zones 1 and 2 costs £23.20 ($44.10).

Oyster Cards are prepaid, reusable "smart" cards that deduct the cost of a trip each time you touch your card to the yellow card-reader found on all public transportation (including the Docklands Light Railway and National Rail). Single journeys on the bus and tube are always cheaper than buying a single ticket (oyster bus fares are £1/$1.90 compared to £2/$3.80 if you buy a cash single, and oyster tube fares are £1.50/$2.85 in zone 1 compared to £4/$7.60 if you buy a cash single), and if you make several trips per day, the amount deducted from your card is capped at the price of a One-Day Travelcard. The Oyster Card can be purchased at any Tube station or online. You simply pay a £3 ($5.70) returnable deposit for the card and add funds to it as you need them. For more information, call ✆ **0870/849-9999** or check out **www.oystercard.com**.

All train stations are also part of the London Underground public transport network, making it fairly easy to travel from one station to another. You can obtain 24-hour train information by calling **National Rail Enquiries** at ✆ **0845/748-4950.**

Facilities and amenities at each station differ but most include ATMs, currency exchange desks, shops, cafes, and pubs. Most stations have large information boards with arrival and departure information for all the destinations they service. Tickets can be purchased at each station (ticket desks and machines) before boarding the train. Waterloo station has a Tourist Information Centre (✆ **020/7620-1550**) in the arrivals hall open from 8am to 10pm daily. For further tourist information visit the Britain and London Visitor Centre (see below).

If all you need is a hotel room, the simplest way to get one is to call the reliable **British Hotel Reservation Centre** (✆ **020/7592-3055;** www.bhrc.co.uk); they book hotel rooms in all price categories, and offer some very attractive discounts.

INFORMATION ELSEWHERE IN THE CITY

The **Britain and London Visitor Centre**, 1 Lower Regent St., SW1 (© **0870/156-6366**), is open Monday 9:30am to 6:30pm, Tuesday to Friday 9am to 6:30pm, Saturday and Sunday 10am to 4pm (June–Sept Sat 9am–5pm). It brings together the English, Welsh, Scottish, and Irish tourist boards. There's also a travel agency and currency exchange service on the premises.

GETTING AROUND

London's a great walking city, but distances are simply too large to make getting everywhere on your own two feet a viable option. Without question, public transportation is the way to go. Tube and bus maps are available at all Underground stations, or you can download them at **www.londontransport.co.uk**. You can also call the 24-hour **travel hot line** (© **020/7222-1234**) for information on how to get from one point to another. There are **LT Information Centres** at several major Tube stations: Euston, Liverpool Street, Piccadilly Circus, and Victoria. They're all open from Monday to Saturday from 7:15am to 9pm (except Euston which closes at 6pm on Sat) and on Sunday from 8:15am to 8pm (except Euston, which closes at 6pm).

BY UNDERGROUND

The London Underground or Tube is easy to use and is generally the quickest way to get around this enormous city. Station signs in the subway tunnels and on the different platforms clearly direct you to eastbound and westbound, or northbound and southbound trains, with the final destinations displayed on the trains. Route maps are posted everywhere and signs above the tracks will let you know how long you'll need to wait before your train arrives.

Except for Christmas Day, Tube trains run every few minutes from about 5:30am Monday to Saturday and 7am or so on Sunday. Nearly all lines stop running somewhere between 11:45pm and 12:30am during the week with tubes running from central London until around 1am on Fridays and Saturdays.

There are two ways to buy tickets for the Tube: at the station ticket window or at a machine (many of which now accept credit cards). Queuing at the window can be phenomenally time-consuming, particularly at West End stations during the summer and at rush hour. You will have to go to the window, though, if you want to buy a pass

---

London Terrorist Attacks

On the morning of Thursday, July 7, 2005, four terrorist bombers hit three London Underground lines and one bus in quick succession, killing scores and wounding hundreds of commuters. If there was any one impression that summed up the attack, it was the measured response of those Londoners caught up in the attack. The grandchildren of the Blitz, who lived with IRA bombings in the '70s and '80s, know how to stiffen their upper lip in catastrophes. People returned somberly to their daily commute the very next day, just "getting on with it," and refusing to kneel to the enemy. The terrorists failed to learn their English history: As the Romans, the Nazis, and the IRA could have told them, London doesn't give up or give in. Indeed, when a bunch of homegrown extremists tried to mirror the Tube attacks just 2 weeks later, they were stopped before any damage could be done.

Moments A Stroll through the City

You may not be able to get around the city by shoe leather alone, but London's still a great walking town when taken in small doses. Stroll in London's great parks: Kensington Gardens, Hyde Park, Green Park, St. James's Park, and Regent's Park offer beautiful paths, fountains, trees, flowers, and meadows. Or pick a neighborhood and stroll down its historic streets, admiring the architecture, the hidden mews, and the garden squares. One of the most pleasant London walks is along the Thames on the South Bank: Starting at the south side of Westminster Bridge you can follow a riverside path all the way down to Tower Bridge, or cut over the Thames to St. Paul's Cathedral on the Millennium footbridge.

valid for longer than 2 days (see "Discount Transportation Passes," above). Ticket machines take coins, banknotes, and sometimes credit cards. Hold onto your ticket throughout your ride because you'll need it to exit. If the turnstile doesn't work on your exit, go to the assistance counter where you may be asked to pay the difference if you have unwittingly bought the wrong ticket.

The London Underground operates on a system of six fare zones. These radiate out in concentric rings from the central zone 1, which is where visitors spend most of their time. Zone 1 covers an area from the Tower of London in the east to Notting Hill in the west, and from Waterloo in the south to Baker Street, Euston, and King's Cross in the north. Single (one-way) tickets starting in zone 1 cost £4 ($7.60) for adults (cash fare) and £2 ($3.80) for children. Journeys starting and ending outside zone 1 cost £3 ($5.70) for adults (cash fare) and £1.50 ($2.85) for children. Oyster fares range from £1.50 ($2.85) within zone 1 to £3.50 ($6.65) to travel between zones 1 and 6. It costs 50p (95¢) for children under 15 with an Oyster Card to travel on the tube at any time between any zones. Children under 10 travel free if traveling with an adult in possession of a valid ticket or Oyster Card. Make sure you buy a ticket or have an Oyster Card before boarding the Tube as fare evaders can be fined £20 ($38).

BY BUS

Traveling by bus is a great way to see London, but it can be dreadfully slow, particularly in rush-hour traffic; the Tube is far more efficient. Normal buses run until around midnight when night buses, with an N in front of the number, take over for the next 6 hours. On most routes, there's one night bus every half hour or hour, and those to, from, and through the West End mostly go via Trafalgar Square, so when in doubt, head there.

Bus routes can be bewildering, however, even if you have a bus map. You'll find routes posted at most bus stops. If you are unsure about where to get off, ask the driver or conductor to let you know when the bus has reached your destination.

To stop a bus when you're on it, press the bell before you get to your stop. Without any signal, the driver won't stop unless passengers are waiting to get on at the next stop. If you're the one waiting, make sure to note whether it is a compulsory (white background on the sign) or a request stop (red background). Just to be safe, wave at the bus to stop no matter what the sign indicates.

You can buy single-trip bus tickets on the bus itself—but only if there is no bus ticket machine at the stop. On older buses, known as the Routemasters (which were all but completely phased out in 2005, apart from two heritage routes: no. 9, running between The Royal Albert Hall and Aldwych; and no. 15, running between Trafalgar Square and Tower Hill), you hop on the back and a conductor comes around, but most new buses are now driver-only so you pay by showing your pass or ticket, using an Oyster Card, or with cash (exact change only). Bus ticket machines can be found at most of the stops in the busy, central parts of London, and you must buy a ticket with exact change before boarding. If inspectors find you without a ticket, the on-the-spot fine is £10 ($19).

Adult single bus fares are £2 ($3.80) within central London. An Oyster Card brings this fare down to £1 ($1.90). Children under 14 go free. Night buses now cost the same as those running during the day. If you don't want to buy an Oyster Card you can buy a book of six Bus Saver tickets for £6 ($11.40).

WHERE TO STAY

Astons Apartments ★★ Behind the redbrick facades of three Victorian town houses, just a couple of minutes from the Gloucester Road Tube station, you'll find this modern and impeccably maintained apartment hotel. Astons is a great choice for those who want to be in charge of their own cooking. These fully equipped studios are in great shape and daily maid service is included. The executive doubles are larger and have some extra amenities, including larger bathrooms. All the studios have kitchenettes and there's a supermarket nearby where you can stock up on supplies.

31 Rosary Gardens, London SW7 4NH. ✆ 800/525-2810 or 020/7590-6000. Fax 020/7590-6060. www.astons-apartments.com. 54 units. £95 ($180) standard double; £132 ($251) executive double. Discount available for Frommer's readers; inquire when booking. Children under 12 stay free in parent's room. AE, DISC, MC, V. Tube: Gloucester Rd. **Amenities:** Nonsmoking rooms. *In room:* Hair dryer, no A/C.

Draycott Hotel ★★ Wonderfully English, this converted town house, with high ceilings and fireplaces galore, features a theatrical theme—each of its well-appointed rooms are named for a towering figure of the English stage. There is a garden square at the back that is divine in spring and summer, and which complements the beauty of the Edwardian-style decor. All the modern conveniences are in place, including increasingly necessary air-conditioning in summer. It's a lovely place for afternoon tea, and is in a great location if you plan to shop Sloane Square or visit the museums of South Kensington. It is a bit pricey, which reflects not only its services but also its aristocratic neighborhood.

26 Cadogan Gardens, London SW3 2RP. ✆ 020/7730-6466. Fax 020/7730-0236. www.draycotthotel.com. 35 units. £205 ($389) double. AE, DC, MC, V. Tube: Sloane Sq. **Amenities:** Lounge. *In room:* Hair dryer.

Durrants Hotel ★ Opened in 1789 off Manchester Square, this 92-room hotel makes for an atmospheric London retreat. It has attractive wood-paneled public areas, a wonderful Georgian room that serves as a restaurant, and even an 18th-century letter-writing room. The guest rooms are generously proportioned (for the most part) and nicely furnished, with decent-size bathrooms. It's an ideal location for the shopping of Oxford Street and for taking quick nips across the street to the Wallace Collection, a jewel of a small museum.

George St., London W1H 6BJ. ✆ 020/7935-8131. Fax 020/7487-3510. www.durrantshotel.co.uk. 92 units. £195 ($371) double. AE, MC, V. Tube: Bond St. **Amenities:** Restaurant; bar; lounge; laundry. *In room:* Hair dryer, A/C (in some rooms).

Guesthouse West ✔ This super-chic B&B is a 25-minutes walk (or a quick taxi ride) from Paddington station. Attracting a young, creative set, the hotel has guest rooms that are minimalist in both design and facilities. Although they cost a little extra, try and get a ground-floor room opening out onto the courtyard. If you can't, there's always the dining terrace out front—great for people-watching. The surrounding area is rich/bohemian, filled with interesting boutiques and organic cafes.

163–165 Westbourne Grove, Notting Hill, London W11 2RS. ✆ 020/7792-9800. Fax 020/7792-9797. www.guesthouse west.com. 20 units. £182–£217 ($346–$412) double. Rates include breakfast. AE, MC, V. Tube: Notting Hill. **Amenities:** Bar; restaurant; laundry; nonsmoking rooms; rooms for those w/limited mobility. *In room:* Hair dryer.

Harlingford Hotel ✔✔ Andrew Davies is the third generation of his family to run this Bloomsbury B&B, a dignified, dove-gray, Georgian-era building not far from Russell Square. He recently oversaw a designer-assisted overhaul of the hotel's rooms. The bathrooms are small but adequate. With their gracious arched windows and high ceilings, the lounge and breakfast room are a real asset. Guests can get a key to unlock and enjoy the communal gardens opposite the hotel. The only downside: no elevator.

61–63 Cartwright Gardens, London WC1H 9EL. ✆ 020/7387-1551. Fax 020/7387-4616. www.harlingfordhotel.com. 43 units. £99 ($180) double. Rates include breakfast. AE, DC, MC, V. Tube: Euston, Russell Sq. **Amenities:** Lounge. *In room:* Hair dryer, no A/C.

Hart House Hotel ✔✔ One of the most welcoming and professionally run B&Bs in London, Hart House occupies a Georgian town house built in 1782, and still retains the dignified entrance hall and polished paneling of its infancy. The rooms (all nonsmoking) are attractive and comfortable, with small but immaculate bathrooms. They all received a renovation—new carpets and furnishings—and plasma TVs in 2007. Double-glazed windows muffle the traffic roar on Gloucester Place, a busy road parallel to Baker Street. There's no elevator.

51 Gloucester Place, London W1U 8JF. ✆ 020/7935-2288. Fax 020/7935-8516. www.harthouse.co.uk. 15 units, all with bathroom (some with shower only). £105 ($199) double. Rates include breakfast. Discounts for 6 nights or more. AE, MC, V. Tube: Marble Arch, Baker St. **Amenities:** Laundry; nonsmoking rooms. *In room:* Hair dryer, no A/C.

Luna Simone Hotel ✔✔ Among the dozens of hotels near Victoria Station, this family-run hotel—renovated from top to bottom in 2002—stands out by a mile. The rooms vary widely in size, but with their fresh decor and tiled bathrooms, they beat all the dowdy, badly designed hotels and B&Bs for miles around. The look throughout is light, simple, and modern, a refreshing change from the many overdecorated faux-Victorian hotels in London.

47–49 Belgrave Rd., London SW1V 2BB. ✆ 020/7834-5897. Fax 020/7828-2474. www.lunasimonehotel.com. 36 units. £70–£90 ($133–$171) double. Rates include breakfast. AE, MC, V. Tube: Victoria, Pimlico. **Amenities:** Lounge; breakfast room; nonsmoking rooms. *In room:* Hair dryer, no A/C.

Malmaison London ✔✔✔ Malmaison is our favorite hotel chain in the U.K., and Malmaison London is good proof why. Situated in a Victorian mansion block—once used as a nursing home—it's now a very slinky boutique hotel boasting huge comfortable beds, friendly English-speaking staff, and a decent brasserie restaurant. It's also near the famous Smithfield meat market—where Scottish freedom fighter William Wallace was executed—if you fancy getting up at dawn to watch the trading take place.

18–21 Charterhouse Square, London EC1M 6AH. ✆ 020/7012-3700. Fax 020/7123-3666. www.malmaison.com. 97 units. £280–£340 ($532–$646) double. AE, MC, V. Tube: Barbican or Farringdon. **Amenities:** Bar; restaurant; laundry; nonsmoking rooms. *In room:* Hair dryer.

Mitre House Hotel ★★   This fine family-run hotel near Paddington Station stretches across four Georgian town houses. It's great for couples with kids because of the varying assortment of accommodations. All the rooms are above average size for London; those at the back are quieter. Free Wi-Fi access was added throughout in May 2007. There's also a big, pleasant lounge, a bar, and an elevator.

178–184 Sussex Gardens, London W2 1TU. ✆ 020/7723-8040. Fax 020/7402-0990. www.mitrehousehotel.com. 67 units. £90 ($171) double. Rates include breakfast. AE, DC, MC, V. Tube: Paddington. **Amenities:** Bar; laundry. *In room:* Hair dryer on request, no A/C.

Rhodes Hotel ★★   The owner of the Rhodes, located on a busy street near Paddington Station, spruced up the entire hotel a few years ago and it's still in tip-top shape. The velvet-curtained lounge and the downstairs dining room boast hand-painted Greek-inspired murals, and painted angels gaze down from the ceiling. There's air-conditioning in the main part of the hotel (though not in the annex, which is why the rooms are cheaper there). The bedroom decor is quite simple and comfortable, all rooms have refrigerators, some have terraces, and the newer rooms have Jacuzzis and DVD players.

195 Sussex Gardens, London W2 2RJ. ✆ 020/7262-0537. Fax 020/7723-4054. www.rhodeshotel.com. 18 units. £75–£90 ($142–$175) double. Rates include continental breakfast. MC, V. Tube: Paddington or Lancaster Gate. **Amenities:** Breakfast room; lounge. *In room:* Hair dryer, A/C (in some rooms).

TOP ATTRACTIONS & SPECIAL MOMENTS

British Airways London Eye ★★   Located on the south bank of the Thames, across from the Houses of Parliament, this 443-foot-high (133m) structure was the world's tallest observation wheel when it opened in 2000 (now wheels in China and Singapore tower over it) and offers panoramic views extending for some 25 miles (40km) when the weather's clear. Passengers are carried in 32 "pods," each making a complete revolution every half hour (a pod holds about 25 passengers and is large enough for everyone to move around in). Along the way you'll see some of London's most famous landmarks from a bird's-eye view. The wheel uses a timed-entry system; book your "boarding ticket" in advance to avoid standing in line.

Jubilee Gardens, SE1. ✆ 0870/500-0600. www.londoneye.com. Admission £14.50 ($27.55) adults, £11 ($20.90) seniors (except weekends and July–Aug), £7.25 ($13.80) children 5–15, children under 5 free. Book online for 10% discount. Daily 10am–8pm (until 9pm June–Sept). Tube: Waterloo, Westminster. River services: Festival Pier.

British Museum ★★★   The British Museum showcases countless treasures of ancient and modern civilizations. The museum is so vast (with 2½ miles/4km of galleries) that you might want to take one of the 90-minute Highlight Tours offered daily at 10:30am, 1pm, and 3pm for £8 ($15.20) or save cash and grab a free eyeOpener tour lead by a museum volunteer around one of the sections, such as The World of Money or Ancient Iraq (contact the museum for a timetable).

The **Great Court,** designed by Lord Norman Foster and completed in 2000, is the largest covered public square in Europe. The inner courtyard is now canopied by a glass roof and houses a bookshop and restaurants. The famous Round Reading Room in the center of the court has been restored to its original Victorian splendor; on either side of the door is a tablet with the names of all the literary luminaries who used this very reading room, and you are welcome to sit and absorb the atmosphere.

Massive winged and human-headed stone bulls and lions that once guarded the gateways to the palaces of Assyrian kings line the **Assyrian Transept** on the ground floor. The star attraction in the angular hall of Egyptian sculpture is the **Rosetta**

Stone, whose discovery led to the deciphering of hieroglyphs. Also on the ground floor is the Duveen Gallery, housing the **Parthenon sculptures** that once decorated the temple on the Acropolis in Athens. They are commonly known as the Elgin Marbles, and for decades the Greek government has tried, without success, to reclaim them. The Department of Medieval and Later Antiquities has its galleries on the first floor (second floor for North Americans). One exhibit, the **Sutton Hoo Anglo-Saxon burial ship** discovered in Suffolk, is a treasure trove of gold jewelry, armor, weapons, bronze bowls and cauldrons, silverware, and a drinking horn.

The featured attractions of the upper floor are the Egyptian Galleries, especially the **mummies.** The galleries of the City of Rome and its empire include exhibits of pre-Roman Italy.

Great Russell St., WC1. ℂ 020/7323-8000. www.thebritishmuseum.ac.uk. Free admission. Galleries: Sat–Wed 10am–5:30pm; Thurs–Fri 10am–8:30pm. Great Court: Sun–Wed 9am–6pm; Thurs–Sat 9am–11pm. Closed Jan 1, Good Friday, Dec 24–26. Tube: Holborn, Tottenham Court Rd., or Goodge St.

Buckingham Palace ℱ   This massive building is the queen's official London residence and one of the most famous buildings in the capital. You can tell Her Majesty is at home when the Royal Standard flies at the masthead. The palace was originally built as a country house for the duke of Buckingham. In 1761, George III bought it and from then on the building was expanded, remodeled, and faced with Portland limestone. The queen occupies only a fraction of its 775 rooms; the rest are used as offices and reception rooms.

The palace is open to the public for 8 weeks in August and September, when the royal family is away on vacation in Scotland. Nothing you see on the self-guided tour, which includes 19 of the state apartments, justifies the exorbitant admission price, although you do get to see some of the famous gardens and Queen Victoria's enormous ballroom. Timed-entry tickets are available in advance or on the day at the ticket kiosk near the palace. You can avoid the long queues (sometimes up to an hour) by purchasing tickets in advance (up to 14 tickets) by credit card (ℂ **020/7766-7300;** www.the-royal-collection.com/royaltickets). **The Royal Mews** ℱ, also on Buckingham Palace Road, is one of the finest working stables in the world today. Gilded and polished state carriages, such as the gold state coach used at every coronation since 1831, are housed here, along with the horses that draw them.

In 2002, as part of her Golden Jubilee celebrations, Queen Elizabeth reopened the **Queen's Gallery** ℱ, whose entrance is right next door to the Royal Mews. In the redesigned galleries you can see paintings and precious objects from the enormous Royal art collection. Items on display change throughout the year.

In 2003, **Clarence House,** the former home of the late queen mother and current London flat of the Prince of Wales and his new wife, Camilla Parker-Bowles, was opened to visitors during the same weeks as Buckingham Palace. It's a stunning home, even if it hasn't been upgraded to any grand degree. Entrance is by guided tour only (using timed-entry tickets).

The Mall, SW1. ℂ **020/7766-7300** for recorded info, credit-card bookings, and for visitors with disabilities; www. royalcollection.org.uk. State Rooms £15 ($28.50) adults, £13.50 ($25.65) seniors/students, £8.50 ($16.15) under 17, under 5 free, £38.50 ($73.15) family ticket for 2 adults and 3 children under 17. Aug–Sept (phone for exact dates) daily 9:45am–6pm (last admittance 3:45pm). Royal Mews £7 ($13.30) adults, £6 ($11.40) seniors/students, £4.50 ($8.55) under 17, under 5s free, £18.50 ($35.15) family ticket. Late Mar to late July and Oct 11am–4pm (last admission 3:15pm); Aug–Sept 10am–5pm (last admission 4:15pm). Queen's Gallery £8 ($15.20) adults, £7 ($13.30) student/senior, £4 ($7.60) under 17, under 5 free, £20 ($38) family. Daily 10am–5:30pm (last admittance 4:30pm),

Moments Changing of the Guard

Buckingham Palace's most famous spectacle, the **Changing of the Guard,** is one of the finest examples of military pageantry you'll ever see. The ceremony begins at 11:30am and lasts for half an hour. The guard, mounted on horses or marching behind a band, comes from either the Wellington or Chelsea barracks and takes over from the old guard in the forecourt of the palace. The guard changes daily from April through July, every other day for the rest of the year. The ceremony may be abruptly canceled during "uncertain" weather conditions. Always consult tourist information offices or local publications for schedules before arriving. Try to get a seat high up on the Victoria fountain in front of the palace for a good view.

closed mid-Feb to end of Mar and other occasional days (phone ahead to check). Clarence House £7.50 ($14.25) adults, students, and seniors, £4($7.60) under 17, under 5 free. Daily Aug–Sept 10am–5:30pm (last admission 4:30pm). Changing of the Guard free (call *(C)* **020/7799-2331** for recorded information). Tube: St. James's Park, Green Park, or Victoria.

Houses of Parliament *(★)*   The Houses of Parliament, along with the clock tower known as Big Ben, are quintessential symbols of London. They're the strongholds of Britain's democracy, the assemblies that effectively trimmed the sails of royal power. Both the House of Commons and the House of Lords were located in the former royal Palace of Westminster, the king's residence until Henry VIII moved to Whitehall. A disastrous fire wiped out all the remnants of that building in 1834. The current Gothic Revival buildings date from 1840 and were designed by Charles Barry. Assisting Barry was A. W. N. Pugin, who designed the paneled ceilings, tiled floors, stained glass, clocks, fireplaces, umbrella stands, and even the inkwells. There are more than 1,000 rooms and 2 miles (3.2km) of corridors. The clock tower at the eastern end houses the world's most famous timepiece. **"Big Ben"** refers not to the clock tower itself, but to the largest bell in the chime, which weighs close to 14 tons.

You may observe parliamentary debates from the **Stranger's Galleries** in both houses. Sessions usually begin in mid-October and run to the end of July, with recesses at Christmas and Easter. The debates in the House of Commons are usually lively and contentious, but your chances of getting into the House of Lords, when it's in session, are generally better. From 1997 to 1999, most of the 700 peers in the House of Lords lost their hereditary posts and were replaced by "people's peers"—considered by many Londoners to be as useless as the old peers. If you want to attend a session, line up at Stephen's Gate, heading to your left for the entrance into the Commons or to the right for the Lords. The London daily newspapers announce sessions of Parliament.

Both houses are open to the general public for 75-minute **guided tours** only during a limited period each year (around the end of July to the beginning of Oct from 9:15am–4:30pm). Tickets can be booked by calling *(C)* **0870/906-3773** and cost £12 ($22.80) for adults, £8.50 ($16.15) for students/seniors, £5 ($9.50) for children, free for under 5 (although tours are not recommended for young kids because there is a large amount of walking and strollers can't be taken everywhere). You must be there 10 minutes before your timed-entry tour begins.

Westminster Palace, Old Palace Yard, SW1. House of Commons ✆ 020/7219-4272. House of Lords ✆ 020/7219-3107. www.parliament.uk. Free admission, subject to recess and sitting times. House of Commons: Mon 2:30–10:30pm; Tues 2:30–10:30pm, Wed 11:30am–7:30pm; Thurs 10:30am–6:30pm; some Fri 9:30am–3pm. House of Lords: Mon–Tues from 2:30pm; Wed from 3pm; Thurs and occasionally Fri from 11am. Line up at St. Stephen's entrance, near the statue of Oliver Cromwell. Tube: Westminster.

Kensington Palace &

Located at the western edge of Kensington Gardens, Kensington Palace was acquired by William and Mary in 1689 and remodeled by Sir Christopher Wren. George II, who died in 1760, was the last king to use it as a royal residence. Princess Diana lived here when in London; the area in front of the palace drew tens of thousands of mourners after her death, a sea of flowers and tributes testifying to a nation's grief.

You can tour the main **State Apartments** of the palace, but many rooms are private and still lived in by lesser Royals, whose "grace and favour" flats are soon to be a thing of the past as the monarchy tries to modernize its operations and trim its expenses. One of the more interesting chambers to visit is Queen Victoria's bedroom, where, on the morning of June 20, 1837, the 18-year-old was roused from her sleep with the news that she was now queen. As you wander through the apartments, you'll see many fine paintings from the Royal Collection. A special attraction is the **Royal Ceremonial Dress Collection,** set in several restored rooms from the 19th century, where you'll find a series of settings with the appropriate court dress of the day and some of Diana's famous frocks. The former apartment of the late Princess Margaret—a fashion icon in her time—is also open to the public.

The Broad Walk, Kensington Gardens, W8. ✆ 0870/751-5170. www.hrp.org.uk. Admission £12 ($22.80) adults, £10 ($19) seniors/students, £6 ($11.40) children 5–16, under 5 free, £33 ($62.70) family. Mar–Oct daily 10am–6pm; Nov–Feb daily 10am–5pm. Tube: Queensway or Bayswater on the north side of the gardens; High St. Kensington on the south side.

National Gallery &&&

One of the finest art museums in the world, Britain's national art collection comprises more than 2,300 paintings dating from 1260 to 1900, supplemented by masterpieces on loan from private collectors. The gallery is arranged in four time bands. The **Sainsbury Wing** shows work from 1260 to 1510 by such artists as Giotto, Botticelli, Leonardo da Vinci, and Raphael. The **West Wing** takes on the next 90 years, with El Greco, Holbein, Bruegel, Michelangelo, Titian, and Veronese. The **North Wing** holds the 17th-century masters, including Rubens, Poussin, Velázquez, Rembrandt, and Vermeer. Works by Stubbs, Gainsborough, Constable, Turner, Canaletto, van Gogh, Corot, Monet, Manet, Renoir, and Cézanne can all be found in the **East Wing.** Very famous works in the museum's collection include Leonardo's *Virgin of the Rocks,* Titian's *Bacchus and Ariadne,* van Eyck's *Arnolfini Marriage,* and El Greco's *Agony in the Garden.* From May to September, the National Gallery lets natural daylight illuminate many of the paintings, particularly in the Sainsbury Wing, to magical effect—the colors are truer, and it cuts down on glare and shadow from the frames. You'll need to choose a sunny day for your visit, though, because artificial help steps in if it gets too gloomy.

There's a free (donation invited) audio guide to every painting on the main floor, and free, guided tours start at 11:30am and 2:30pm every day. Most of the gallery talks are also free.

Trafalgar Sq., WC2. ✆ 020/7747-2885. www.nationalgallery.org.uk. Free admission. Daily 10am–6pm; Wed 10am–9pm. Free guided tours daily 11:30am and 2:30pm. Closed Jan 1, Dec 24–26. Tube: Charing Cross, Embankment, or Leicester Sq.

Natural History Museum ★★ This is a favorite of kids, but adults will find much to please them too, not least of which is the gorgeous and intricate Victorian architecture. Besides dinosaurs and other extinct or exotic creatures, there are earthquake and volcano simulations at the **Earth Galleries** that hint at the terror of the real thing. Kids also love the slithery and slimy critters in the **Creepie-Crawlies** exhibit.

Sir Hans Sloane was such a prolific collector that his treasures overflowed the British Museum, and this magnificent monument was built in 1881 "for housing the works of the Creator." Yet it, too, can display only a fraction of its animal, vegetable, and mineral specimens. Phase Two of the museum's Darwin Centre Project will continue to revolutionize the museum, opening both the storerooms and the science labs, with their 300 white-coated experts, to public view, and offering free tours.

Cromwell Rd., S. Kensington, SW7. ℗ **020/7942-5000**. www.nhm.ac.uk. Admission free. Mon–Sat 10am–5:50pm; Sun 11am–5:50pm. Closed Dec 23–26. Fees for special exhibitions. Tube: South Kensington.

St. Paul's Cathedral ★★ During World War II, newsreel footage showed the famous classical dome of St. Paul's Cathedral standing amid the rubble caused by German bombings. That it survived at all is a miracle: It was badly hit twice during the early years of the Blitz. Then again, St. Paul's is accustomed to calamity, having been burned down three times and destroyed once by invading Norsemen. After the Great Fire of 1666, the old St. Paul's was razed, making way for a new Renaissance structure designed by Sir Christopher Wren and slowly built between 1675 and 1710 (the cathedral is considered the architect's greatest masterpiece).

Inside, the cathedral is laid out like a Greek cross. With the exception of Grinling Gibbons's magnificent choir stalls, the cathedral houses few art treasures. There are, however, many monuments, including one to the duke of Wellington and a memorial chapel to American service personnel who lost their lives in World War II while stationed in the United Kingdom. Encircling the dome is the Whispering Gallery. You can climb to the very top of the dome for a spectacular 360-degree view of London. Wellington and Lord Nelson both lie in the crypt, as does London's most famous architect, Sir Christopher Wren.

St. Paul's will turn 300 years old in 2008 (the last stone was laid on the Lantern in October 1708) and is being spruced up for its birthday with a £40 million ($76 million) restoration project to include internal and external cleaning and the opening of the Triforium Gallery to the public.

Guided "Supertours" last 1½ to 2 hours and include parts of the cathedral not open to the general public. They take place Monday through Saturday at 11am, 11:30am, 1:30pm, and 2pm, for £3 ($5.70) for adults; £2.50 ($4.75) for students/seniors; and £1 ($1.90) for kids 16 and under. Audio tours lasting 45 minutes are available from 9am to 3:30pm and cost £3.50 ($6.65) for adults and £3 ($5.70) for students/seniors.

St. Paul's Churchyard, EC4. ℗ **020/7236-4128**. www.stpauls.co.uk. Cathedral £9.50 ($18.05) adults, £8.50 ($16.15) seniors/students, £3.50 ($6.65) children 16 and under, £22.50 ($42.75) family ticket. Sightseeing Mon–Sat 8:30am–4pm. No sightseeing Sun (services only). Tube: St. Paul's.

Science Museum ★★★ This is one of the best science museums in the world, with some fabulous fun opportunities for kids. With regularly changing exhibits that will surprise you (who would have thought an exhibit about human hair could be so absolutely fascinating?) the curators are constantly thinking up ways to educate and entertain hordes of visitors and kids of all ages. There's a 450-seat IMAX cinema on the first floor, and another huge gallery, **Making the Modern World,** which charts 250 years of technological discoveries and their effects on our culture.

There is an interesting emphasis here on technology as opposed to pure science, with displays of such pioneering machines as Arkwright's spinning machine; Foucault's Pendulum; the Vickers "Vimy" aircraft, which made the first Atlantic crossing in 1919; and the computer that Tim Berners-Lee used to design the World Wide Web. The basement is dedicated to children, with water to play with, construction materials, and various sound and light activities.

Exhibition Rd., SW7. (✆ 0870/870-4868. www.sciencemuseum.org.uk. Admission free. IMAX film £8 ($15.20) adults, £6 ($11.40) children 16 and under, seniors, and students. Daily 10am–6pm. Tube: South Kensington.

Tate Britain 🎨🎨🎨   Founded in 1897, the former Tate Gallery reopened in November 2001 as the Tate Britain, with more exhibition space and a suite of airy new galleries. Having handed International Modernism over to the Tate Modern museum across the Thames, Tate Britain now concentrates on British work dating from 1500. The older works include some of the best of Gainsborough, Reynolds, Stubbs, Blake, and Constable. William Hogarth is well represented, particularly by his satirical *O the Roast Beef of Old England* (known as *The Gate of Calais*). You'll find the illustrations of William Blake, the incomparable mystical poet, including such works as *The Book of Job, The Divine Comedy,* and *Paradise Lost.* The collection of works by J. M. W. Turner is the Tate's largest collection of works by a single artist—Turner himself willed most of his paintings and watercolors to the nation.

Also on display are the works of many major 19th- and 20th-century painters, including Paul Nash, Matisse, Dalí, Modigliani, Munch, Bonnard, and Picasso. Truly remarkable are the several enormous abstract canvases by Mark Rothko, the group of paintings and sculptures by Giacometti, and the paintings by one of England's best-known modern artists, Francis Bacon.

Millbank, SW1. (✆ 020/7887-8888. www.tate.org.uk. Free admission. Fees for special exhibits. Daily 10am–5:50pm (last admission 5pm), first Fri of the month late opening until 10pm (last admission 9pm). Closed Dec 24–26. Tube: Vauxhall.

Tate Modern 🎨🎨🎨   The Tate Modern, London's wildly popular cathedral of modern art, occupies the defunct Bankside Power Station on the South Bank of the Thames opposite St. Paul's Cathedral. You enter through the huge old turbine hall, the scene of some spectacular temporary art installations, and in three floors of galleries the work is arranged thematically rather than chronologically: **Landscape/Matter/Environment, Still Life/Object/Real Life, History/Memory/Society,** and **Nude/Action/Body.** In some rooms, paintings are next to sculptures, which are next to video installations. Others are devoted to a single artist—such as the marvelous Joseph Beuys sculptures.

There's no such thing as a flash visit to Tate Modern. Set aside half a day if you can. Free guided tours start daily at 11am, noon, 2pm, and 3pm, each focusing on one of the four themes and lasting 45 minutes. Be sure to go up to the glass-roofed level seven to see the spectacular views across the Thames.

25 Sumner St., SE1. (✆ 020/7887-8000. www.tate.org.uk. Free admission. Fees for special exhibits. Sun–Thurs 10am–6pm (last admission 5:15pm); Fri–Sat 10am–10pm (last admission 9:15pm). Tube: Southwark, Mansion House, or St. Paul's (cross over the Millennium Bridge).

The Tower of London 🎨🎨🎨 *Moments*   This is the most perfectly preserved medieval fortress in Britain and you'll need at least 2 or 3 hours for your visit. Over the centuries, the Tower has served as a palace and royal refuge; a prison, military base, and supplies depot; home to the Royal Mint and the Royal Observatory; and finally a national monument. The oldest part is the massive **White Tower,** built in 1078 by the Norman king, William the Conqueror, to protect London and discourage rebellion among his new Saxon subjects. Every king after him added to the main structure, so that when Edward I completed the outer walls in the late 13th century, they enclosed an 18-acre (7.2-hectare) square.

The **Crown Jewels** are hugely popular, with people queuing to gape at the glorious gems, which include the Imperial State Crown, encrusted with 3,200 precious stones and one gob-smacking 317-carat diamond. **The Chapel Royal of St. Peter ad Vincula** contains the graves of all the unfortunates executed at the Tower. The Scaffold Site, where the axe man dispatched seven of the highest-ranking victims, including two of Henry VIII's six wives, Anne Boleyn and Catherine Howard, is just outside. Everyone else met their end on **Tower Green** after arriving by boat at **Traitors' Gate.** The **Bloody Tower** was where Richard of Gloucester locked up his young nephews when he usurped his crusading brother Edward IV. The princes' bodies were later mysteriously found near the White Tower. Today, an exhibit re-creates how Sir Walter Raleigh might have lived during his unjust 13-year imprisonment after the Gunpowder Plot against James I.

One-hour guided tours of the entire compound are given by the Yeoman Warders (retired soldiers also known as "Beefeaters") every half hour, starting at 9:30am, from the Middle Tower near the main entrance. Costumed guides also re-create historic happenings, or simply chat you up without breaking character. Booking tickets prior to your visit is a great time-saver.

Tower Hill, EC3. (C) **0870/756-6060** or 0870/756-7070 (box office). www.hrp.org.uk. Admission £16 ($30.40) adults, £13 ($24.70) seniors/students, £9.50 ($17.10) children, free for children under 5, £45 ($85.50) family. Mar–Oct Tues–Sat 9am–6pm, Sun–Mon 10am–6pm; Nov–Feb Tues–Sat 9am–5pm, Sun–Mon 10am–5pm. Last tickets sold 1 hr. before closing. Closed Dec 24–26, Jan 1. Tube: Tower Hill.

Victoria and Albert Museum ★★★ (Moments The Victoria and Albert (V&A) is *the* greatest museum in the world devoted to the decorative arts. Its medieval holdings include such treasures as the early English Gloucester Candlestick; the Byzantine Veroli Casket, with its ivory panels based on Greek plays; and the Syon Cope, a highly valued embroidery made in England in the early 14th century. An area devoted to Islamic art houses the Ardabil Carpet from 16th-century Persia. The V&A houses the largest collection of **Renaissance sculpture** outside Italy and the greatest collection of **Indian art** outside India. One room displays Raphael's giant cartoons for tapestries for the Sistine Chapel. There are suites of furniture, metalwork, and ceramics, and a superb collection of portrait miniatures, including the one Hans Holbein the Younger made of Anne of Cleves for the wife-hunting Henry VIII. The **Dress Collection** includes a collection of corsetry through the ages that's sure to make you wince, and is regularly updated with exhibits from various eras or designers. The exceptional **British Galleries** ★★★ are dedicated to British design from 1500 to 1900, with exhibits ranging from Chippendale to Mackintosh, as well as the "Great Bed of Ware," mentioned in Shakespeare's *Twelfth Night.*

Tip: The V&A is currently undergoing a huge face-lift called FuturePlan. So even if you've been here before it's worth coming back to see the changes. Already finished (in 2005) is a central courtyard garden, a hub from which to explore the museum with lighting by Patrick Woodroffe, the same man who does the Rolling Stones' stage shows.

Cromwell Rd., SW7. ⓒ 020/7942-2000. www.vam.ac.uk. Free admission. Fees for special exhibits. Sat–Thurs 10am–5:45pm; Fri 10am–10pm. Closed Dec 24–26. Tube: South Kensington.

Westminster Abbey 𝒜𝒜𝒜   This ancient building is neither a cathedral nor a parish church, but a "royal peculiar," under the jurisdiction of the Dean and Chapter of Westminster, and subject only to the Sovereign. Mostly dating from the 13th to 16th centuries, Westminster Abbey has played a prominent part in British history, most recently with the funeral of Princess Diana and, in 2002, of the queen mother. All but two coronations since 1066 have taken place here. The oak **Coronation Chair,** made in 1308 for Edward I, can be seen in the **Chapel of Edward the Confessor.** Five kings and four queens are buried in the beautiful, fan-vaulted **Chapel of Henry VII.** In 1400, Geoffrey Chaucer became the first literary celebrity to be buried in **Poets' Corner,** followed by Ben Jonson, Dryden, Samuel Johnson, Sheridan, Browning, and Tennyson. Statesmen and men of science—Disraeli, Newton, Charles Darwin—are also interred in the abbey or honored by monuments.

Guided tours of the abbey cost £5 ($9.50) and start at 10, 10:30, 11am, 2, and 2:30pm during the week and at 10, 10:30, and 11am on Saturdays April through October; at 10:30, 11am, 2, and 2:30pm on winter weekdays and at 10:30 and 11am on winter Saturdays. Audio guides are £4 ($7.60). Arrive early to avoid the crowds.

Dean's Yard, SW1. ⓒ 020/7654-4900 or 020/7222-5152. www.westminster-abbey.org. Admission £10 ($19) adults, £7 ($13.30) seniors/students and children aged 11–16, £24 ($45.60) family ticket, free for children under 11. (Admission covers the Chapter House and Abbey Museum.) The Cloisters, College Garden, and St. Margaret's Church are free. Abbey Mon–Fri 9:30am–4:45pm; Sat 9:30am–2:45pm; last admission 1 hr. before closing; Sun closed for worship. Chapter House 10:30am–4pm. Abbey Museum daily 10:30am–4pm. Cloisters daily 8am–6pm. College Garden Apr–Sept 10am–6pm; Oct–Mar 10am–4pm. Tube: St James's Park, Westminster, Victoria.

WHERE TO DINE

Aubaine 𝒜𝒜 FRENCH BISTRO   This bistro has proved a big hit with locals, thanks to the efficient service, the wondrously delicious bread (try the *pain cereal*), and the authentic perfection of the patisseries. The changing menu features such hearty Gallic mainstays as coq au vin and *coquilles St. Jacques* (scallops with mushrooms and cheese), as well as more modern dishes, such as roasted baby vegetable salad. The potatoes *dauphinois* are arguably the best in London. The relaxed atmosphere lets you enjoy a good French meal without any formality and fuss. It has tables on the street in good weather and serves a nice continental *petit déjeuner.*

260-262 Brompton Rd., SW3. ⓒ 020/7052-0100. www.aubaine.co.uk. Reservations recommended. Main courses £10–£19.50 ($19–$37.05). AE, MC, V. Mon–Sat 8am–10:30pm; Sun 9am–10pm. Tube: South Kensington.

Cambio de Tercio 𝒜𝒜 SPANISH   Several changes of chef have done nothing to dent the standards or popularity of the stylish Cambio de Tercio. The dramatic Spanish-style interior is home to a charming staff that will guide you through a menu of Iberian delights. Ham is the house specialty. You should starve yourself before dining here.

163 Old Brompton Rd., SW5. ⓒ 020/7244-8970. Reservations required for dinner. Main courses £14–£15.50 ($26.60–$29.45). AE, MC, V. Daily noon–2:30pm; Mon–Sat 7–11:30pm; Sun 7–11pm. Tube: Gloucester Rd., South Kensington.

Food for Thought 𝒜 VEGETARIAN CAFE   This place is a veggie institution and the long lines testify to its popularity. Make it inside and you'll be rewarded with a plate full of wholesome salads or a scrumptious quiche or curry. It might sound ordinary, but it's all done really well and the staff is genuinely friendly. The downstairs seating is simple and wooden but you'll have to come pre- or postlunch to get your own table. You can bring your own bottle of wine; there's no corkage fee.

31 Neal St. Covent Garden, WC2. ⓒ 020/7836-0239. Main courses £3–£7 ($5.70–$13.30). No credit cards. Mon–Sat noon–8:30pm; Sun 12:30–5pm. Tube: Covent Garden.

Incognico ⭐⭐ MODERN FRENCH Owned by Michelin-star-winning Nico Ladenis, this brasserie serves superlative French cooking for relatively reasonable prices. The fish is delicious, and there are great vegetarian choices, such as Parmesan risotto with mushrooms. Unlike many of London's restaurants, where the food is only part of the entertainment, eating here feels like a very special gastronomic experience.

117 Shaftesbury Ave., WC2 ⓒ 020/7836-8866. www.incognico.com. Reservations essential. Main courses £12.50–£18.50 ($23.75–$35.15). Fixed-price lunch/pretheater meal, with glass of champagne £25 ($47.50). AE, DC, MC, V. Mon–Sat noon–3pm, 5:30–11pm. Tube: Leicester Sq. or Tottenham Court Rd.

Mela ⭐⭐ INDIAN This festive restaurant—its name means fair—is a huge hit with Indian expats and visiting Bollywood stars. It claims to take its inspiration from Wali Gali, where Delhi's workers go to refuel at midday from a food stall on the street. Lunch here is a fantastic deal: curry or dal of the day, with bread, pickle, and chutney for between £3 ($5.70) and £6 ($11.40). This is a great way for curry novices to have a cheap taste—and to see it being made in an open kitchen. But do come back in the evening for a proper go at the innovative Indian country cuisine.

152–156 Shaftesbury Ave., WC2. ⓒ 020/7836-8635. www.melarestaurant.co.uk. Main courses £6–£15 ($11.40–$28.50); fixed-price meal for 2 people £29.95–£36.95 ($57–$70.20). AE, MC, V. Mon–Sat noon–11:30pm; Sun noon–10:30pm. Tube: Leicester Sq.

North Sea Fish Restaurant FISH & CHIPS Locals love North Sea's version of what is, arguably, the national dish (though some claim it's curry now). Here the look is slightly-scuffed-around-the-edges pub complete with stuffed fish on the walls. The best deal is the enormous seafood platter, which comes with bite-size, battered pieces of lots of different sorts of fish and seafood. You can go for straight cod, of course, or skate, haddock, or plaice, all brought in fresh from Billingsgate every morning. And after all that we'll salute any diner who's got room for one of the traditional desserts.

7–8 Leigh St., WC1. ⓒ 020/7387-5892. Reservations recommended for dinner. Main courses £8.50–£16.95 ($16–$32). AE, DC, MC, V. Mon–Sat noon–2:30pm; 5:30–10:30pm. Tube: Russell Sq. or King's Cross.

Royal China ⭐⭐ CHINESE The plaudits keep rolling in for Royal China's dim sum, which is reckoned by many to be the best in London. A dim sum extravaganza is unlikely to set you back more than £15 ($19). The most popular dish, and deservedly so, is the roast pork puff. Service can be moody. Come during the week when it is quieter and the staff seem happier. If it's full, try the group's newer venture, The Royal China Club, at 40–42 Baker St.

24–26 Baker St., W1 ⓒ 020/7487-4688. www.royalchinagroup.co.uk. Reservations recommended. Dim sum £2.30–£4.50 ($4.40–$8.55). Main courses £7.50–£50 ($14.25–$95); fixed-price dinner £30–£38 ($57–$15.20). AE, DC, MC, V. Mon–Thurs noon–11pm; Fri–Sat noon–11:30pm; Sun 11am–10pm; dim sum to 5pm daily. Tube: Marble Arch.

Rules ⭐⭐ TRADITIONAL BRITISH Lillie Langtry and Edward VII used to tryst at this ultra-British restaurant, but despite the hammy quaintness, Rules is a very modern restaurant operation. It markets the house specialty, "feathered and furred game," as healthy, free-range, additive-free, and low in fat. The food is delicious: traditional yet innovative, until you get to the puddings (desserts), which encompass a

Moments **The Delectable Delights of Soho**

The French had to show them how to do it, but Londoners have taken to sweet flaky pastries, tarts, and cakes with a vengeance. There are patisseries all over the city, but it's most fun to go to Soho and people-watch while you eat. The most venerable patisserie is **Maison Bertaux,** 28 Greek St., W1 (© 020/7437-6007), and we defy you to pass by its delectable window without wanting to dunk a brioche in a cup of coffee.

Patisserie Valerie, 44 Old Compton St., W1 (© 020/7437-3466), is *the* place to gawk at greedy film and theater types who've fallen for its chocolate truffle cake. The crowds are smaller at **Amato,** 14 Old Compton St., W1 (© 020/7734-5733), but its alcoholic chocolate-and-coffee mousse cake is to die for.

selection of nursery and dinner-dance classics. The wine list is pricey, but Rules does have native ales and cider, so try one of these instead.

35 Maiden Lane, WC2. © 020/7836-5314. www.rules.co.uk. Reservations essential. Main courses £15.95–£19.95 ($30–$38). AE, MC, V. Mon–Sat noon–11:30pm; Sun noon–10:30pm. Tube: Charing Cross or Covent Garden.

Suze Wine Bar ✿ PACIFIC RIM   There's a comfortable bistrolike ambience at this charming Mayfair wine bar; the walls are maroon and hung with modern art. The food is Australasian with some international crossovers, and it's always simply and well prepared. Try the succulent New Zealand green-tipped mussels, a house specialty, or the New Zealand scallops. There are several sharing platters to choose from: Italian antipasto, seafood, and cheese. And, of course, you can get a fine glass of wine.

41 N. Audley St.,W1. © 020/7491-3237. www.suzeinmayfair.com. Main courses £14–£17.50 ($26.60–$33.25); platters to share £5–£12.95 ($9.50–$24.60). AE, MC, V. Mon–Sat 11am–11pm. Tube: Green Park.

SHOPPING

London is one of the world's great shopping cities, with a vast and enticing array of department stores, boutiques, small shops, and markets. Major shopping areas are found in the West End, Knightsbridge, and Chelsea. Most stores are open Monday through Saturday from 9:30 or 10am to 5:30 or 6pm, and stay open until 8 or 9pm at least one night a week. Major sales are held in January and June. Bargains you will probably not find, given the current murderous dollar-to-pound exchange rate, but there are some things here you won't necessarily find for less money (or even at all) anywhere else, such as antiques, some stationary, and British and European designer goods.

WEST END SHOPPING   Most of the department stores, designer shops, and chain stores have their flagships in the West End. **Oxford Street** is home of many large stores with prices that are more affordable than in other areas in the West End. Two of the department stores you might want to check out are **Marks & Spencer,** 458 Oxford St. (© 020/7935-7954; www.marksandspencer.com; Tube: Marble Arch), where you find well-made, if dull, basics of all kinds and styles, and the much more upscale **Selfridges,** 400 Oxford St. (© 0800/123 400; Tube: Marble Arch), one of the largest department stores in Europe. For affordable, hip clothing—supermodel Kate Moss designed a line here in 2007—brave the teen herds at **Top Shop,** 216 Oxford St. (© 020/7636-7700; www.topshop.com; Tube: Tottenham Court Rd.).

Bond Street (Tube: Bond St.) is the address for all the hot international designers. Here and on adjacent streets you'll find a large selection of very expensive fashion boutiques and jewelry stores. For books head to **Charing Cross Road,** where, among other booksellers, you'll find **Foyles,** 113–119 Charing Cross Rd., WC2 (© 020/ 7437-5660; Tube: Tottenham Court Rd.), once the largest bookshop in the world and still carrying an impressive array of hardcovers and paperbacks, as well as travel maps, records, and sheet music.

The **Covent Garden Market** (© 0870/780-5002; www.coventgardenmarket. co.uk; Tube: Covent Garden, Leicester Sq., or Holborn), in the restored Covent Garden fruit and vegetable market, has a number of interesting shops as well as a Monday antiques market. Tuesday through Saturday there are stalls selling "collectible nostalgia," crafts, clothes, and all manner of whatnot. The streets around the market are chockablock with shops selling everything from clothes and books to aromatherapy and food.

Penhaligon's, 41 Wellington St., WC2 (© 020/7836-2150; www.penhaligons.co. uk; Tube: Covent Garden), has its own line of ladylike and light perfumes as well as a large selection of after-shaves, soaps, candles, and bath oils.

Curving **Regent Street,** just off Piccadilly Circus, is a major shopping street for all sorts of goods. **Liberty,** 214–220 Regent St., W1 (© 020/7734-1234; www.liberty. co.uk; Tube: Oxford Circus), is a six-floor emporium famous for its fine quality fabrics. That old Brit institution, **Burberry,** is so much more than well-made raincoats these days; check out the currently cutting-edge designer digs at 157–167 Regent St., W1 (© 020/7968-0000; www.burberry.co.uk; Tube: Piccadilly). If you're looking for toys or children's gifts, check out **Hamleys,** 188–196 Regent St., W1 (© 0800/280-2444; www.hamleys.com; Tube: Piccadilly Circus), which stocks more than 35,000 toys and games on seven floors. *Be warned:* It gets quite scary pre-Christmas.

KNIGHTSBRIDGE SHOPPING London has plenty of department stores to choose from, but **Harrods,** 87–135 Brompton Rd., SW1 (© 020/7730-1234; www. harrods.com; Tube: Knightsbridge), is the most famous. As firmly entrenched in London life as Buckingham Palace, this enormous store has some 300 departments, delectable Food Halls, and several cafes and eateries. **Beauchamp Place,** running south from Brompton Road, is known for its upscale designer shops.

CHELSEA SHOPPING Chelsea's **King's Road** (Tube: Sloane Sq.) became world famous during the Swinging Sixties and is still popular with younger shoppers, but it's becoming more and more a lineup of predictable chain stores, although the new **Duke of York Square,** just west of Sloane Square, has some interesting smaller shops in a pedestrian-only shopping plaza. Chelsea is also known for its design-trade showrooms and stores of household wares. King's Road begins on the west side of Sloane Square tube station.

PORTOBELLO ROAD MARKET Portobello Road in Notting Hill (Tube: Notting Hill Gate) is London's most famous street market. The market, held on Saturdays from 6am to 5pm, is a magnet for collectors of everything from overpriced junk to valuable antiques. If you're a serious collector, you'd do well to get there at the crack of dawn. Find out more at **www.portobelloroad.co.uk**. Weekdays you can check out the antiques and art shops in the area: Don't miss **Westbourne Grove,** a street off Portobello, now home to dozens of great shops, cafes, and restaurants.

NIGHTLIFE

London is one of the world's great cultural capitals and renowned for its nightlife. Theater, music, and dance performances of all kinds take place every night. You can also spend an evening in a pub or dancing at one of London's many clubs. To find out what's happening, buy a copy of *Time Out* (**www.timeout.com**), an invaluable listings magazine published weekly and sold at all newsagents.

In general, you should be able to buy tickets for almost any show or performance once you arrive by going directly to the theater's box office or by calling the theater directly. Many London theaters accept telephone credit card bookings at regular prices plus a minimal fee. By buying directly from the box office, you don't have to pay the commission fee (up to 30%) charged by ticket agencies. The **half-price ticket booth** in Leicester Square known as **tkts** (no phone; Tube: Leicester Sq.) sells seats for shows available that day (beware of imitators—use this location only). The booth is open Monday through Saturday 10am to 7pm and noon to 3pm on Sundays. There are two lines: one for matinee shows and one for evening shows. You can check on the day's offers by visiting **www.officiallondontheatre.co.uk/tkts/today**.

THEATER   Plays and musicals are staged all over the city in approximately 100 theaters, but the commercial hits are centered in the **West End.** The West End theater district is concentrated in the area around Piccadilly Circus, Leicester Square, and Covent Garden. The **Barbican Centre** (Silk St., EC2; ✆ **020/7638-8891;** www. barbican.org.uk; Tube: Barbican) is a multiarts center in the city that always has something great on offer; a concert, ballet, opera, or a Shakespearean play. Elsewhere, on the south bank of the Thames, is the **National Theatre** (✆ **020/7452-3000;** www.nt-online.org), offering a mix of contemporary and classic plays spread over three theaters. Insightful backstage tours run five times a day from Monday to Saturday and cost £5 ($9.50).

BALLET, OPERA & CLASSICAL MUSIC   London is home base to two major opera and dance companies. The **Royal Opera** and **Royal Ballet** perform at the **Royal Opera House** (Covent Garden, WC2E; ✆ **020/7304-4000;** www.royalopera.org; Tube: Covent Garden). The **English National Opera** and occasionally the **English National Ballet** perform at the **London Coliseum** (St. Martin's Lane, WC2; ✆ **0870/145-0200;** www.eno.org; Tube: Leicester Sq.).

The home base for the **London Symphony Orchestra** (**www.lso.co.uk**) is **Barbican Hall** at the Barbican Centre, Silk Street, EC2 (✆ **020/7638-8891;** Tube: Barbican). You may also catch a performance there by the **Royal Philharmonic Orchestra** (**www.rpo.co.uk**), which plays concerts at the Barbican and at the **Royal Albert Hall,** Kensington Gore SW7 (✆ **020/7589-8212;** www.royalalberthall.com; Tube: High St. Kensington), an enormous circular domed concert hall that has been a landmark in South Kensington since 1871. The **Southbank Centre** (South Bank, SE1; ✆ **0871/663-2500;** www.southbankcentre.co.uk; Tube: Waterloo) is made up of The Royal Festival Hall (re-opened in June 2007), The Hayward, The Queen Elizabeth Hall, and The Saison Poetry Library. Together they put on a diverse program encompassing world music, classical concerts, homegrown literature, and contemporary dance.

PUBS   Pubs used to adhere to strict 11am-to-11pm drinking hours set by Parliament but that all changed at the end of 2005 when new licensing laws came into force. Now many pubs still close before midnight but they can apply for a longer license and many do. *Americans take note:* In a pub, you don't tip the bartender, but you can

Thank You for Not Smoking

Ireland did it first. Then Scotland. Then Wales. And in July 2007 England finally joined the gang and banned smoking in public buildings and workspaces. This means nonsmokers can now enjoy London's pubs and restaurants without having to breathe in secondhand cigarette smoke, while smokers can start "smirting" (flirting while smoking) out in the specially designed courtyards and terraces sprouting up all over the capital.

offer to buy him or her a drink. Ten minutes before closing a bell rings, signaling it's time to order your last round. There are hundreds of pubs in London; the following is a very selective list.

Cittie of Yorke, 22 High Holborn, WC1 (© 020/7242-7670; Tube: Holborn or Chancery Lane), is a wonderfully atmospheric pub with a number of rooms, one of which looks like a great medieval hall—an appropriate appearance because a pub has existed at this location since 1430. **Seven Stars,** 53 Carey St., WC2 (© 020/7242-8521; Tube: Holborn), is tiny and modest with a collection of old Toby mugs and law-related art. The pub is located at the back of the law courts, and lots of legal eagles drink here. **Black Friar,** 174 Queen Victoria St., EC4 (© 020/7236-5474; Tube: Blackfriars), is an Edwardian wonder made of marble and bronze Art Nouveau designs. The interior features bas-reliefs of mad monks, a low-vaulted mosaic ceiling, and seating carved out of gold marble recesses. **Churchill Arms,** 119 Kensington Church St., W8 (© 020/7727-4242; Tube: Notting Hill Gate or High St. Kensington), is loaded with Churchill memorabilia. The pub hosts an entire week of celebration leading up to Sir Winston's birthday on November 30. Visitors will find the overall ambience to be down-to-earth and homey (although the Thai food served there comes as a bit of a surprise).

DANCE CLUBS   Cover charges vary according to day of the week and/or what band is playing. For more options, check out the music and clubs listings in *Time Out* (**www.timeout.com**). The big dance clubs don't really start hopping until after 10pm and typically stay open until 3 or 4am on weekends.

A classic (but still incredibly hip) option is **Fabric,** 77a Charterhouse St., EC1 (© 020/7336-8898; www.fabriclondon.com; Tube: Farringdon), located in a refurbished Victorian meat storage unit opposite London's historic Smithfield market. Big name DJs and super-cool unknowns frequently keep the party going until dawn (or even later). For gay action, **Heaven,** Under-the-Arches, Villiers St., WC2 (© 020/7930-4480; Tube: Embankment), is an old-time favorite with great DJs, live bands, and acres of dance floors. Not too far away, **Guanabara,** Parker St., WC2 (© 0207/242-8600; www.guanabara.co.uk; Tube: Holborn) is a thrilling and friendly Brazilian dance club that also serves up authentic Brazilian food at very affordable prices. Down the road, **Bar Rumba,** 36 Shaftesbury Ave., W1 (© 020/7287-6933; www.bar rumba.co.uk; Tube: Piccadilly Circus), is all over the map musically, featuring a different type every night including jazz fusion, phat funk, hip-hop, soul, R&B, and swing. Vibe-wise, it's small but easygoing. Meanwhile **Ronnie Scott's,** 47 Frith St. W1 (© 020/7439-0747; www.ronniescotts.co.uk: Tube: Tottenham Court Rd.), is a must-go for jazz aficionados, who will be entertained every night of the week by the coolest musicians in the universe.

BARS   If you want to slip into an elegant mode and mood, head for one of these classy hotel bars for your favorite cocktail.

The **American Bar** in the Savoy Hotel, The Strand, WC2 (© **020/7836-4343;** Tube: Charing Cross Rd. or Embankment), is one of London's most sophisticated gathering places and reportedly serves the best martini in town. After 8pm it charges £5 ($9.50) for nonresidents (except on Sun), but you will get to hear a jazz pianist (except on Sun). Reservations are recommended (but are only accepted noon–5pm). **The Library** in the Lanesborough Hotel, 1 Lanesborough Place, SW1 (© **020/7259-5599;** Tube: Hyde Park Corner), one of London's poshest drinking retreats, is famous for its unparalleled collection of ancient cognacs and rare cigars. There's no cover charge, and no reservations are taken.

3 Edinburgh

Edinburgh (pronounced *Edin*-burra) is one of the most beautiful and fascinating cities in Europe. Located near the Firth of Forth (try saying that four times fast), an inlet from the North Sea, and surrounded by rolling hills, lakes, and forests, Scotland's capital enjoys an unparalleled setting with panoramic views from every hilltop. The looming presence of Edinburgh Castle lends a romantic, historic air to this fair city, but Edinburgh is also very much an international city of today, where you'll find chic cafes and modern architecture within the city's quaint core. Edinburgh is divided into two distinct areas: **Old Town,** where the medieval fortress city began, and **New Town,** an elegant example of 18th-century urban planning. It's a wonderfully strollable city full of fine museums, galleries, historic attractions, and real character.

GETTING THERE

By Plane   Edinburgh Airport (© **0870/040-0007;** www.edinburghairport.com), 7 miles (11km) west of the city center, receives flights from within the British Isles, the rest of Europe, and some flights from locations in America and Canada. An **Airlink** bus (© **0131/555-6363;** www.flybybus.com) makes the 25-minute trip from the airport to the city center every 10 minutes (every 30 min. at night), letting you off near Waverley Station; the fare is £3 ($5.70) one-way or £5 ($9.50) round-trip. A taxi into the city costs about £17 ($32.30), depending on traffic, and also takes about 25 minutes.

By Rail   Fast trains operated by **GNER** (© **0845/722-5225;** www.gner.co.uk) link London with Edinburgh's **Waverley Station,** at the east end of Princes Street, right in the middle of the city. The station is the central rail hub for all of Scotland and has a train information center, a couple of restaurants, and a luggage storage facility. All fast trains to Waverley provide restaurant, buffet, and trolley service; complimentary beverages and snacks are available in first class. BritRail Passes (but not Eurail passes) may be used for the trip between London and Edinburgh.

Nearly all trains depart from London **King's Cross** Station, except for the **overnight train,** which departs from London **Euston** and an earlier afternoon service also leaving from Euston. The regular journey takes 4½ hours and costs from £28 ($53.20) return, if you buy an **advance** ticket (see "Ticket Types" on p. 395) up to £323 ($604) for a same-day first-class return ticket with no restrictions on when you can travel. GNER (© **0845/722-5225;** www.gner.co.uk) runs the service from King's Cross. Overnight trains are run by **First Scot Rail** (© **0845/601-5929;** www.first group.com), take 7¼ hours, and have sleeper berths you can reserve from £99 ($188)

Edinburgh

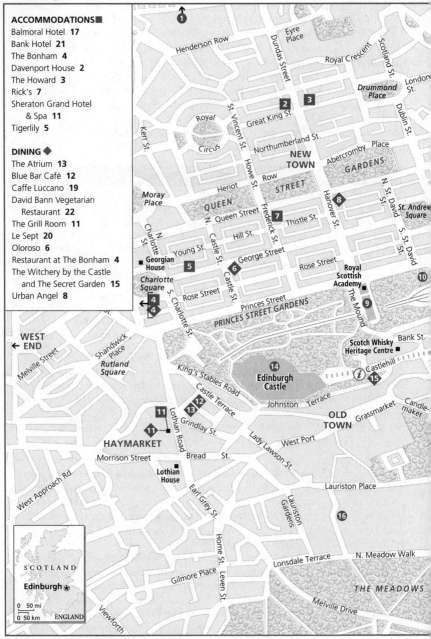

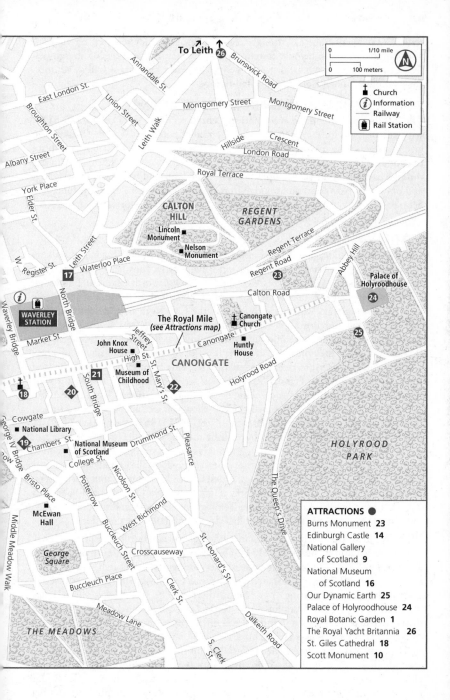

return. Seat reservations are strongly recommended but not required on all London–Edinburgh trains. If you're traveling around the same time as the Edinburgh Festival or on a summer weekend, we advise getting a seat reservation well in advance. Reservations are obtainable through Rail Europe.

VISITOR INFORMATION & ROOM RESERVATIONS

The **Edinburgh & Scotland Information Centre,** 3 Princes St. (© **0845/225-5121;** www.edinburgh.org), above the Waverley Shopping Centre near Waverley Station, can give you sightseeing information, exchange currency, and also book hotels in all price categories. The center sells bus tours and theater tickets as well. It's open Monday through Saturday from 9am to 6pm (to 7pm May, June, and Sept; to 8pm July–Aug; and only 5pm Nov–Mar) and Sunday from 10am to 6pm (to 7pm May, June, and Sept; to 8pm July–Aug; and 5pm Nov–Mar). There's also an information and accommodations desk at Edinburgh Airport.

GETTING AROUND

ON FOOT   Edinburgh is divided into a New Town and an Old Town, and walking is the best way to see both. Most of the city's major attractions lie along or near the **Royal Mile,** the main thoroughfare of the **Old Town,** which begins at Edinburgh Castle and runs all the way to the Palace of Holyroodhouse. Because of its narrow lanes and passageways, you can only explore the Old Town in any depth on foot. Lying below the Old Town and separated from it by a deep leafy ravine is the **New Town,** an extraordinary adventure in urban planning built between 1766 and 1840. It takes in most of the northern half of the heart of the city and is made up of a network of squares, streets, terraces, and circuses, reaching from Haymarket in the west to Abbeyhill in the east. **Princes Street,** famed for its shopping, is the New Town's main artery. Expect to do some climbing because parts of Edinburgh are quite hilly.

If you want a qualified professional guide to show you around, contact (in advance) the **Scottish Tourist Guides Association** (© **01786/451953;** www.stga.co.uk). Different guides charge different prices but usually roughly around £75 ($143) for a half day to £120 ($228) for a full day. For a trip out into the surrounding countryside to learn more about Scotland's ancient history, head out with Jackie Queally on one of her **Celtic Trails** (© **0131/448-2869;** www.celtictrails.co.uk). She leads tours focusing on Celtic spirituality and sacred Scottish sites, a visit to Rosslyn Chapel (made famous by *The Da Vinci Code* thanks to its Knights Templar connections), and the dramatic surrounding glen costs £33 ($62.70) for a half day or £50 ($95) for a full day.

BY BUS   If you're traveling any distance, the bus will be your least expensive mode of transport. **Lothian Buses** (© **0131/555-6363;** www.lothianbuses.co.uk) operates a comprehensive system of double-decker buses throughout Edinburgh. There is a flat fare of £1 ($1.90), whatever distance you ride, but you must make sure you have the exact change if you're paying your fare on the bus. The **Day Ticket** allows 1-day unlimited travel on city buses for £2.50 ($4.75) and can be purchased from the bus driver. A **Ridacard** allows unlimited travel on all buses (except tour buses) for £13 ($24.70) for 1 week, plus a £1 ($1.90) discount on night buses, bringing them down to £1.50 (£2.85) per journey. For an introduction to the principal attractions in and around Edinburgh, consider the **Edinburgh Tour** (www.edinburghtour.com), which allows you to hop on and off at any of 15 stops. Buses start from the Waverley Bridge near the Scott Monument daily at 9:15am, departing every 15 minutes in summer and about every 30 minutes in winter. If you remain on the bus without getting off, the trip will take about 2 hours. The cost is £9 ($17.10) for adults, £8 ($15.20) for seniors/students, £3 ($5.70) for kids 5 to 15, and £20 ($38) for a family ticket. You can get information, tour tickets, and Ridacards at the **Waverley Bridge Travel Shop,** beside Waverley Station.

BY TAXI   You can hail a taxi or pick one up at a taxi stand. Meters begin at £1.50 ($2.85) and increase 25p (50¢) every 52 seconds. On weekends and between 6pm and 6am the meter starts at £2.50 ($4.75). Taxi ranks are at Hanover Street, North Street, Andrew Street, Waverley Station, Haymarket Station, and Lauriston Place. Fares are displayed on the meter and charges posted, including extra charges for night drivers or destinations outside the city limits. To call for a taxi, try **City Cabs (**© **0131/228-1211;** www.citycabs.co.uk).

WHERE TO STAY

Edinburgh offers a full range of accommodations throughout the year. Hotels fill up during the 3-week period of the Edinburgh International Festival in August, so if you're coming then, be sure to reserve far in advance.

Ardmore House ✦✦✦   The owner of this gay-owned, straight-friendly B&B used to work in advertising, which is perhaps why the place is so super-stylish. Sitting in a Victorian row of overly floral B&Bs, it distinguishes itself with a liberal use of neutral tones and the odd dash of bold color. Guests tend to be cool 20- to 30-something types, all smug about having discovered a real gem. The surrounding area is residential and less grand than the city center.

74 Pilrig St., Edinburgh EH2 2EQ. ©/fax **0131/554-4944.** www.ardmorehouse.com. 5 units. £85 ($162) double. Rates include breakfast. MC, V. Bus: 11. **Amenities:** Breakfast room; all rooms are nonsmoking. *In room:* Hair dryer, no A/C.

Bank Hotel ✦ *Value*   This unusual hotel is located right in the heart of Old Town and offers better value than all of its competitors along the Royal Mile. Built in 1923 as a branch of the Royal Bank of Scotland, it now offers a handful of individually decorated theme rooms (each named for a famous Scotsman) above Logie Baird's Bar, a lively ground-floor bar and restaurant. There are delightful touches throughout, and the bathrooms are as nice and comfortable as the rooms. Be warned, there is no elevator to the higher floors.

Royal Mile at 1–3 S. Bridge St., Edinburgh EH1 1LL. © **0131/622-6800.** Fax 0131/622-6822. www.festival-inns. co.uk. 9 units. £85–£140 ($162–$266) double. Rates include breakfast. AE, DC, MC, V. Bus: 4, 15, 31, or 100. **Amenities:** Bar; laundry. *In room:* Hair dryer, no A/C.

The Bonham ✦✦✦   Style is pumped up to a very high level at this New Town hotel, which was Scotland's Boutique Hotel of the Year in 2005. The high-ceilinged, large-windowed guest rooms are spread across three Victorian town houses and feature the best of contemporary furnishings against a bold palette of colors. The beds are huge, and the bathrooms excellent. The hotel is very technofriendly and every room has its own communication and entertainment center. The Restaurant at the Bonham is reviewed on p. 432.

35 Drumsheugh Gardens, Edinburgh EH3 7RN. © **0131/226-6050.** Fax 0131/226-6080. www.thebonham.com. 48 units. £105–£245 ($200–$465) double. AE, MC, V. Bus: 41 or 42. **Amenities:** Restaurant; bar; lounge; laundry; nonsmoking rooms. *In room:* Hair dryer, no A/C.

Davenport House   A fine B&B located on a cobblestone street in the New Town, Davenport House was built in the 1820s and has retained many elegant period touches.

All the bedrooms are nonsmoking and individually decorated with inspiration taken from the 19th century (prepare for chandeliers and swathes of velvet). The best rooms are located on the first and second floors but all have been updated with such modern conveniences as Wi-Fi access and big-screen TVs.

58 Great King St., Edinburgh EH3 6QY ✆ 0131/558-8495. Fax 0131/558-8496. www.davenport-house.com. 6 units. £75–£110 ($143–$209) double. Rates include full breakfast. MC, V. Bus: 23 or 27 from Princes St. **Amenities:** Lounge; nonsmoking rooms, breakfast room. *In room:* Hair dryer, no A/C.

The Howard ⭐⭐   Classic elegance, impeccable service, and gorgeous furnishings combine to make this one of Edinburgh's finest small deluxe hotels. Occupying three Georgian terrace houses in New Town, the Howard is refined but relaxed about it. The public areas were spruced up in 2007, while the spacious guest rooms are impeccable and the bathrooms fabulous (some have freestanding Georgian-style bathtubs). Your "dedicated butler" is on call 24/7.

34 Great King St., Edinburgh EH3 6QH. ✆ 800/323-5463 in the U.S., or 0131/557-3500. Fax 0131/557-6515. www.thehoward.com. 18 units. £180–£295 ($342–$522) double. Rates include breakfast. AE, DC, MC, V. Bus: 13, 23, 27, or C5. **Amenities:** Restaurant; laundry. *In room:* Hair dryer, no A/C.

Rick's ⭐⭐   Rick's was one of Edinburgh's original boutique hotels. Age had taken its toll but a recent refurbishment has freshened things up, ensuring Rick's remains a real classic, with a handful of no-nonsense minimalist rooms done out in neutral woody tones above a bar/eatery. The staff is hip and friendly. Guests are largely businesspeople, but with soul.

55a Frederick St. ✆ 0131/622-7800. Fax 0131-622-7801. www.rickedinburgh.com. 10 units. £129 ($247) double. AE, MC, V. Bus: 3, 10, 11, 16, 17, 22, 25, 26, or 33. **Amenities:** Restaurant; bar; laundry; nonsmoking rooms. *In room:* Hair dryer.

Sheraton Grand Hotel & Spa ⭐   A short walk from Princes Street and directly across from the Lyceum Theatre, this upscale hotel offers spacious, traditionally furnished guest rooms that are extremely comfortable and have nice bathrooms; the castle-view rooms on the top floors are the best. What really makes this hotel stand out, however, is its spa—one of Europe's greatest—which contains a state-of-the-art gym, gorgeous indoor and outdoor pools, steam room and sauna, and a complete array of spa treatments.

1 Festival Sq., Edinburgh EH3 9SR. ✆ 800/325-3535 in the U.S. and Canada, or 0131/229-9131. Fax 0131/221-9631. www.starwoodhotels.com. 260 units. £139–£270 ($264–$513) double. Children under 17 stay free in parent's room. AE, MC, V. Bus: 4, 15, or 44. **Amenities:** 3 restaurants; bar; laundry; nonsmoking rooms. *In room:* Hair dryer.

Tigerlily ⭐⭐⭐   This incredibly hip hotel might give you interior design fever and have you itching to get back home and redecorate. Things like the ball-bearing curtains in the restaurant and the mirrored disco ball in the stairwell might sound crazy in a grand old Georgian house but they really do work. It's not all about design, however; beds are hugely comfortable, bathrooms large (although ask if you want a room with a tub), and the downstairs restaurant/bar is delicious and buzzy.

125 George St., Edinburgh. ✆ 0131/225-5005. Fax 0131/225-7046. www.tigerlilyedinburgh.co.uk. 33 units. £175 ($333) double. AE, MC, V. Bus: 11, 22, 25,10,16,17, 33, 26. **Amenities:** Restaurant; 2 bars; laundry; nonsmoking rooms; rooms for those with limited mobility. *In room:* Hair dryer.

THE TOP ATTRACTIONS & SPECIAL MOMENTS

Old Town's **Royal Mile** ⭐⭐⭐ stretches from Edinburgh Castle all the way to the Palace of Holyroodhouse and bears four names along its length: Castlehill, Lawnmarket,

Moments Great Scott!

Looking more like a neo-Gothic church spire than a monument to a famous writer, the **Scott Monument** in the East Princes St. Gardens (© **0131/529-4068**) is secretly a super place to get some of the best views in the city. In the center of this 200-foot (60m) spire completed in the mid–19th century is a large seated statue of novelist Sir Walter Scott and his dog, Maida. Some of Scott's characters are carved as small figures in the monument. Climb the 287 steps to the top to see the views. Admission to the Scott Monument is £3 ($5.70). It's an easy walk from Waverley station, or take any city center bus along Princes Street.

High Street, and Canongate. Walking along it, you'll see some of the most interesting old structures in the city, with turrets, gables, and towering chimneys.

Edinburgh Castle *&&*   No place in Scotland is filled with as much history, legend, and lore as Edinburgh Castle. Its early history is vague, but it's known that in the 11th century, Malcolm III (Canmore) and his Saxon queen, later venerated as St. Margaret, founded a castle on this spot; the oldest structure in Edinburgh is **St. Margaret's Chapel,** a small stone structure on the castle grounds dating from the 12th century. The somber and sparsely furnished **State Apartments** include Queen Mary's Bedroom, where Mary Queen of Scots gave birth to James VI of Scotland (later James I of England). Scottish Parliaments used to convene in the **Great Hall.** For most visitors, the highlight is the **Crown Chamber,** housing the Honours of Scotland (Scottish Crown Jewels), used at the coronation of James VI, along with the scepter and sword of state of Scotland. The storerooms known as the **French Prisons** were used to incarcerate captured French soldiers during the Napoleonic wars. Many of them made wall carvings you can see today. **Mons Meg,** a 15th-century cannon weighing more than 5 tons, is the most famous of the batteries of cannons that protected the castle. The famous **Stone of Scone** (or, **Stone of Destiny**) is a symbol of Scottish sovereignty stolen as war booty by King Edward I, the "hammer of the Scots," and victoriously displayed in Westminster Abbey for 700 years, until it was ceremoniously returned to Edinburgh Castle in 1996.

Castlehill. © **0131/225-9846.** www.historicscotland.gov.uk. Admission £11 ($20.90) adults, £9 ($17.10) seniors/students, £5.50 ($10.45) children under 16. Apr 1–Sept 30 daily 9:30am–6pm; Oct 1–Mar 31 daily 9:30am–5pm. Bus: Traveline.

National Gallery of Scotland *&&*   This gallery may be small, but it has several important works of art. Italian paintings include Verrocchio's *Ruskin Madonna* and works by Raphael and Titian. Also worth a look are works by El Greco, Velázquez, Degas, van Gogh, Renoir, Gauguin, Cézanne, Monet, Rubens, and Rembrandt. So there's the art history lesson out of the way. Yes, they are all world-class paintings but that's almost the problem; when you're looking at them you could be anywhere in the world. Personally, we think the exciting stuff lies downstairs in The Scottish Collection. Here you get a real sense of the mountains and weather bashing up against this handsome city and the wild terrain that has shaped and inspired the Scottish people. Not to be missed is Peter Graham's *Wandering Shadows*—such an utterly convincing depiction of a wind-blown day, it almost has you believing you're out on a drama-packed hillside watching clouds chase across a sky. McTaggart's raging seas, and quirky paintings such as *The Nativity* by William Bell Scott—a pre-Raphaelite depiction of Jesus being born in a Scottish barn—illustrate how Scottish painters took international themes and made them their own. The beautiful (and oh-so-Scottish) *St Bride* by John Duncan was part of the Celtic revival movement, which began at the end of the 19th century. Elsewhere, ask nicely at the Weston Link Information desk to be shown 38 Turner watercolors and thousands of other drawings and sketches (scribblers include Blake, Goya and Leonardo)—all holed away in the private study rooms.

The Mound. ℂ 0131/624-6200. www.nationalgalleries.org. Free admission. Daily 10am–5pm (until 6pm during the Edinburgh Festival); Thurs till 7pm. Study room opening hours are 10am–12:30pm and 2–4:30pm Mon–Fri (book ahead to guarantee an appointment). Bus: 23, 27, 41, 42, or 45. A free gallery bus connects the Gallery of the Modern Art, The National Gallery, and The Portrait Gallery every 45 min 10:45am–5pm.

National Museum of Scotland ⚔⚔   Scotland's premier museum, built of pale Scottish sandstone, opened in 1998 and houses the nation's greatest treasures. You can follow a chronological trail through the centuries in galleries called "Beginnings," "Early People," "Industry and Empire," and so on up to the "Twentieth Century Gallery." Highlights include wonderful examples of ancient jewelry displayed in modern sculptures by Sir Eduardo Paolozzi; the Trappan treasure horde of silver objects found buried in East Lothian; 11 pieces of the 12th-century Lewis chessmen (82 are in the British Museum); and, gruesomely, the "Maiden"—an early guillotine.

Chambers St. ℂ 0131/247-4422. www.nms.ac.uk. Free admission. Daily 10am–5pm. Bus no. 23, 27, 28, 41, or 42.

Our Dynamic Earth   A former brewery was converted into this multimedia amphitheater capped by a translucent tentlike roof. Its galleries explain the natural diversity of the earth, elaborating on the seismological and biological processes that led from the Big Bang to the world we know today. The presentation features audio and video clips; buttons you can push to simulate earthquakes, meteor showers, and views of outer space; time capsules winding their way back through the eons; and a series of specialized aquariums, some with replicas of primordial life forms, some with living sharks, dolphins, and coral. Also on the premises are a restaurant, a cafe, and a gift shop.

Holyrood Rd. ℂ 0131/550-7800. www.dynamicearth.co.uk. Admission £8.95 ($17) adults, £6.95 ($13.20) seniors/students; £5.75 ($10.90) children 5–15; £1.95 ($3.70) children 2–4. Apr–Oct daily 10am–5pm (last entry 3:50pm); July–Aug daily 10am–6pm (last entry 5.50pm); Nov–Mar Wed–Sun 10am–5pm (last entry 4:50pm). Bus: 30 or 35.

Palace of Holyroodhouse ⚔⚔   Early in the 16th century, this palace was built by James IV adjacent to a 12th-century Augustinian abbey; now it's the Queen's official residence in Edinburgh and used for state entertaining. The nave of the abbey church still remains, but only the north tower of James's palace is left. Most of what you see today was built by Charles II after Scotland and England were united in the 17th century.

One of the more dramatic incidents at Holyroodhouse occurred in 1566 when David Rizzio, the Italian secretary of Mary Queen of Scots, was stabbed 56 times in front of her by her jealous husband, Lord Darnley, and his accomplices. A plaque marks the spot. And one of the more curious exhibits is a piece of needlework done by Mary depicting a cat-and-mouse scene—her cousin, Elizabeth I, happens to be the cat. Some of the rich tapestries, paneling, massive fireplaces, and antiques from the 1700s are still in place. The Throne Room and other drawing rooms are still used for state occasions. In the rear of the palace is the richly furnished King's Bedchamber. The Picture Gallery contains many dubious portraits of Scottish monarchs painted by

Dutch artist Jacob De Witt, who in 1684 signed a contract to turn them out at the rate of one a week for 2 years.

Behind Holyroodhouse begins **Holyrood Park,** Edinburgh's largest. With rocky crags, a loch, sweeping meadows, and the ruins of a chapel, it's a wee bit of the Scottish countryside in the city, and a great place for a picnic. From the park you can climb up a treeless, heather-covered crag called **Arthur's Seat** ✶✶✶ for breathtaking panoramas of the city and the Firth of Forth.

Canongate, at the eastern end of the Royal Mile. ✆ 0131/556-7371. www.royal.gov.uk. Admission £9.50 ($18.05) adults, £8.50 ($16.15) seniors/students, £5.50 children 5–17, under 5 free, £24.50 ($46.55) family. Apr–Oct daily 9:30am–6pm (last admission 5pm); Nov–Mar daily 9:30am–4:30pm (last admission 3:30pm). The palace is closed for periods during the summer months and during royal visits. It's best to phone ahead and check. Bus: 30 or 35.

Royal Botanic Garden ✶✶✶   One of the grandest gardens in Great Britain, the Royal Botanic Garden sprawls across 70 acres (28 hectares) on the north side of the Water of Leith. It dates from the late 17th century, when it was originally used to grow and study medicinal plants. The collection grew dramatically between 1904 and 1932 with plants collected in southwestern China and brought to Edinburgh by George Forrest. Today, the new Chinese Garden contains the largest collection of Chinese plants outside of China. The gardens are particularly famous for their rhododendrons, at their most spectacular in April and May. Plant enthusiasts should consider taking one of the guided tours that leave from the West Gate on Arboretum Place at 11am and 2pm, April through September. You can enjoy fabulous views of Edinburgh's Old Town skyline from the Terrace Café.

Entrances at 20A Inverleith Row and Arboretum Place. ✆ 0131/552-7171. www.rbge.org.uk. Free admission. Guided tours £3 ($5.70). Glasshouse admission £3.50 ($6.65) adults, £3 ($5.70) students/seniors, £1 ($1.90) children. Nov–Feb daily 10am–4pm; Mar and Oct daily 10am–6pm; Apr–Sep daily 10am–7pm. Guided tours Apr–Sept daily 11am, 2pm. Bus: 8, 17, 23, or 27.

The Royal Yacht *Britannia* ✶✶✶   Used by Queen Elizabeth II and the royal family since 1952, this luxurious 412-foot (124m) yacht was decommissioned in 1997, berthed in Leith (2 miles/3km from Edinburgh's center), and opened to the public. You reach the famous vessel by going through a rather dreary shopping mall to a visitor center where you collect a portable audio guide keyed to the major staterooms and working areas on all five decks. You can visit the drawing room and the little-changed Royal Apartments, and explore the engine room, the galleys, and the captain's cabin. An air of the 1950s still permeates the vessel.

Ocean Terminal, Leith. ✆ 0131/555-5566. www.royalyachtbritannia.co.uk. £9.50 ($18.05) adults, £7.50 ($14.25) seniors/students, £5.50 ($10.45) kids 5–17, under 5 free, £26.50 ($50.35) family. Apr–Oct daily 9:30am–4:30pm (last admission); Nov–Mar 10am–3:30pm (last admission). Bus: 11, 22, 34, 35, 36, or 49.

St. Giles Cathedral   A short walk downhill from Edinburgh Castle, this dark and somewhat grim-looking stone church is one of the principal landmarks along the Royal Mile. Dating mostly from the late 15th century, but with sections that date from the 12th century, it is usually referred to as a cathedral but is officially a "high kirk" of Scottish Presbyterianism. It was from here that the famous Scottish minister John Knox preached and directed the Scottish Reformation in the 16th century. The walls are covered with funerary monuments, including one to Edinburgh-born Robert Louis Stevenson. Thistle Chapel houses beautiful stalls and notable heraldic stained-glass windows from 1911. There's a shop and restaurant on-site. The latter turns out good—if a bit old-fashioned—rolls and quiches at a much more affordable price than many of the cafes on the Royal Mile.

High St. ⑦ **0131/225-9442.** www.stgilescathedral.org.uk. Free admission (donations gladly accepted). Easter–Sept Mon–Fri 9am–7pm, Sat 9am–5pm, Sun 1–5pm; Oct–Easter Mon–Sat 9am–5pm, Sun 1–5pm. Guides are available at all times to conduct free tours. Bus: 23, 27, 28, 35, 41, or 42.

WHERE TO DINE

Edinburgh boasts the finest restaurants in Scotland and a wide variety of available cuisines, including Scottish, French, Asian, Italian, and modern European. The Scottish-French culinary connection dates from the time of Mary Queen of Scots, though it's been much refined over the centuries. More and more restaurants are catering to vegetarians, too. Some of the dishes Edinburgh is known for include fresh salmon and seafood, game from Scottish fields, and Aberdeen Angus steaks.

Atrium ✦✦ MODERN SCOTTISH/INTERNATIONAL This trend-setting restaurant next to the Traverse Theatre has been one of Edinburgh's top dining spots since 1993. Chef Neil Forbes, drawing inspiration from Scotland and all over the world, has won numerous awards for the fresh, inventive dishes on his daily-changing menu. Typical dishes include Scottish wild mushroom and rabbit terrine for starters and breast of Gressingham duck for mains.

10 Cambridge St., next to Traverse Theatre. ⑦ **0131/228-8882.** www.atriumrestaurant.co.uk. Reservations recommended. Main courses £17–£21 ($32.30–$38.95); tasting menu £47–£50 ($89.30–$95), or fixed-price dinner menu from £25 ($47.50). AE, DC, MC, V. Mon–Fri noon–2pm and 6–10pm; Sat 6–10pm. Bus: 11 or 15.

Blue Bar Café INTERNATIONAL In a cool circular room on the second floor of the Traverse Theatre, this hip bistro is a less expensive alternative to the Atrium (see above). The fresh and informal menu changes monthly. You can find anything from Thai beef salad with glass noodles to a flavorsome mix of field mushrooms on toast. On theater nights, this is a crowded, fun place to dine. All mains are also served in smaller portions as light options.

10 Cambridge St., on the 2nd floor of the Traverse Theatre. ⑦ **0131/228-1222.** www.bluebarcafe.com. Reservations recommended. Light menu £2.50–£7.50 ($4.75–$14.25); main courses £10.50–£12.50 ($19.95–$23.75). AE, DC, MC, V. Mon–Sat noon–2:30pm; Mon–Thurs 5:30–10:30pm; Fri–Sat 5:30–11pm. Bus: 1, 10, 11, or 15.

Caffé Lucano (Finds) PASTA/CAFE Just around the corner from the Museum of Scotland, this cafe is a bargain spot for lunch or a cuppa. It's not fancy but it does serve Italian specialties—risotto, spaghetti, ravioli, and tortellini—made with fresh ingredients. The soup of the day and bread is only £3 ($5.70), and after 3pm all ready-made rolls are half price, leaving enough spare change for a French-style strawberry tart. It's also good for people-watching and stocks daily papers.

37–39 George IV Bridge. ⑦ **0131/225-6690.** www.caffelucano.co.uk. Main courses £5.50–£14.95 ($10.45–$28.40). MC, V. Mon–Fri 7am–10pm; Sat 8am–10pm. Bus: 23, 27, or 41.

David Bann Vegetarian Restaurant & Bar ✦ (Finds) VEGETARIAN All the current trends in vegetarian cooking are wonderfully summarized in this hip vegetarian restaurant around the corner from the Scottish Parliament building. The chef creates vegetarian dishes inspired and influenced by the foods of India, China, Italy, and the Mediterranean. The menu changes often, but possible choices include Malaysian vegetable curry or baked polenta with Gorgonzola. This is a good spot to come for a meatless Sunday brunch (£5.50/$10.45). The fresh organic juices are delicious.

Moments   Oh, Give It a Try!

Haggis, the much-maligned national dish of Scotland, is certainly an acquired taste. But you've come all this way—why not be brave and give it a try? **Macsween of Edinburgh Haggis (www.macsween.co.uk)** is a long-established family business specializing in haggis. Macsween haggis includes lamb, beef, oatmeal, onions, and a special blend of seasonings and spices cooked together. There's also an all-vegetarian version. Both are sold in vacuum-packed plastic bags. Haggis is sold precooked and requires only reheating in a microwave or oven. You can find this company's product at food stores and supermarkets throughout Edinburgh. Two central distributors are **Peckham's Delicatessen,** 155–159 Bruntsfield Place (© **0131/229-7054**), open Monday to Saturday 8am to midnight, Sunday 9am to 11pm (there's a restaurant in the cellar), and **Jenners Department Store,** 48 Princes St. (© **0870/607-2841**), open daily from 9am to 6pm (until 8pm Thurs).

56–58 St. Mary's St. © **0131/556-5888.** www.davidbann.co.uk. Reservations recommended weekend dinner. Main meals £8.50–£11.90 ($16.15–$22.60). AE, DC, MC, V. Daily 11am–1am. Bus: 30 or 35.

The Grill Room 𝒜𝒜 FUSION/SCOTTISH   For a very fine and memorable meal, The Grill Room in the Sheraton Grand Hotel is a standout. You can expect impeccably high standards and attentive service, though the restaurant is also pleasantly relaxed. English chef Malcolm Webster sticks to in-season local produce to create contemporary dishes that are flavorful and fascinating, without sacrificing the grill-room heartiness of the mahogany-paneled dining room. Don't order too much up front, desserts are also splendid.

In the Sheraton Grand Hotel, 1 Festival Sq. © **0131/229-9131.** Reservations required. Fixed-price lunch £13.50–£17.95 ($25.65–$34.10); dinner main courses £17–£44 ($32.30–$83.60). AE, MC, V. Tues–Fri noon–2pm; Tues–Sat 7–10pm. Bus: 1, 10, 11, or 15.

Le Sept 𝒜 *Finds* FRENCH/SCOTTISH   Although this popular bistro moved from the address that gave it its name (its new quarters are cozy and welcoming), it remains Le Sept, as it has for 20-odd years. It's one of the best places to go for a small but satisfying array of traditional French and Scottish dishes (plus a vegetarian choice). You can try roast haunch of venison or one of the daily fish dishes, such as grilled salmon. The steaks are good, and so are the dessert crêpes.

5 Hunter Sq. © **0131/225-5428.** Reservations recommended at dinner. Main courses £11.50–£19.75 ($21.85–$37.50). AE, DC, MC, V. Mon–Thurs noon–2pm and 6–10:30pm; Fri–Sat noon–11pm; Sun 12:30–10pm. Bus: 3, 7, 14, or 21.

Oloroso INTERNATIONAL   The big reason to eat here is the view. Sitting above the shops, on the fourth floor of this modern building, you can see over the city's chimney pots to the River Forth below. The food, while not quite as spectacular as the view, is a contemporary mix of simple char-grilled steaks and fresh fish, such as the whole John Dory in a sweet soy sauce. The outdoor terrace makes this a great choice in summer.

33 Castle St. (on the corner of George St.). © **0131/226-7614.** www.oloroso.co.uk. Reservations recommended. Main courses £14.50–£29.50 ($27.55–$56.05). AE, MC, V. Daily 12–2:15pm and 7–10pm. Bus: 24, 29, or 42.

Restaurant at the Bonham ⚔ SCOTTISH/CONTINENTAL   The dining room at the chic Bonham Hotel combines 19th-century oak paneling and deep ceiling coves with modern paintings and oversize mirrors. On the oft-changing menu you might encounter butternut squash soup with pumpkin oil, pan-fried Scottish beef, or roasted wild sea bass. Novel desserts include rhubarb cheesecake and praline crème brûlée with a lemon macaroon. They try to keep the ingredients organic, local, and free of genetically modified produce.

In the Bonham Hotel, 35 Drumsheugh Gardens. ✆ 0131/623-9319. www.thebonham.com. Reservations recommended. Main courses £13–£20.50 ($33–$41.80); fixed-price lunches £15 ($28.50) for 2 courses. AE, DC, MC, V. Mon–Sat noon–2:30pm and 6:30–10pm; Sun 12:30–3pm and 6:30–10pm. Bus: 13, 19, 29, or 35.

The Witchery by the Castle and The Secret Garden ⚔⚔ (Finds) SCOTTISH/ FRENCH   This is where the celebs eat when they're in town. Stop by and you'll see why. Two theatrically enchanting dining rooms combine to form one enormously impressive restaurant, originally built as a merchant's house in 1595 and later named after the unfortunate women burned nearby on Castlehill between 1470 and 1722. Either room is a fabulous place for a romantic dinner with unfussy Scottish food such as red mullet poached in star anise and duo of border lamb or, most delectable and expensive of all, a platter of Scottish seafood and crustaceans. Some 1,000 wines and 40 malt whiskies are available.

The Witchery by the Castle/The Secret Garden, Castlehill, Royal Mile. ✆ 0131/225-5613. www.thewitchery.com. Reservations recommended. Main courses £14.95–£50 ($28.40–$95). AE, MC, V. Daily noon–4pm and 5:30–11:30pm. Bus: 23, 27, or 28.

Urban Angel ⚔⚔ CAFE/DELI   Since it opened in 2004 this fresh and light deli has proved a huge hit with locals. The owners really believe in the whole local-and-organic movement and make a big show of supporting their suppliers. The food is just as easy to swallow as their philosophies, including such dishes as organic smoked salmon with a *tattie* (potato) scone, or a salad of baby beetroot and sprouts, plus plenty of other veggie options and a scrumptious all-day brunch.

121 Hanover St. ✆ 0131/225-6215. www.urban-angel.co.uk. All-day brunch from £1 ($1.90) per item, mains £6.95– £11.50 ($13.20–21.85). AE, MC, V. Mon–Thurs 10am–10pm; Fri–Sat 10am–11pm; Sun 10am–5pm. Bus: 23 and 27.

SHOPPING

New Town's **Princes Street** is the main shopping artery. **George Street** and Old Town's **Royal Mile** are also major shopping areas. The best buys are in tartans and woolens, along with bone china and Scottish crystal. Shopping hours are generally Monday through Saturday from 9am to 5 or 5:30pm and Sunday from 11am to 5pm. On Thursdays, many shops remain open to 7 or 8pm.

James Pringle Woolen Mill, 70–74 Bangor Rd., Leith (✆ 0131/553-5161), produces a large variety of top-quality wool items, including cashmere sweaters, tartan and tweed ties, blankets, and tam-o'-shanters. In addition, it boasts one of Scotland's best Clan Tartan Centres, with more than 5,000 tartans accessible. **Shetland Connection,** 491 Lawnmarket (✆ 0131/225-3525), promotes Shetland Island knitwear, and is packed with sweaters, hats, and gloves in colorful Fair Isle designs; the shop also sells hand-knitted mohair, Aran, and Icelandic sweaters. A wide range of Celtic jewelry and gifts makes this shop a top-priority visit.

Geoffrey (Tailor) Highland Crafts, 57–61 High St. (✆ 800/566-1467 in the U.S. and Canada, or 0131/557-0256; www.geoffreykilts.co.uk), is the most famous kilt

Moments   The Edinburgh Festival: Art & Tattoos

The brightest highlight of Edinburgh's year comes in August during the **Edinburgh International Festival,** whose main information and ticket office is **the Hub,** Castle Hill, Edinburgh EH1 2NE (© **0131/473-2000;** www.eif.co. uk), open Monday through Friday 9:30am to 5:30pm. Since 1947, the festival has attracted artists and companies of the highest international standard in all fields of the arts, including music, opera, dance and theater. Usually happening around the same time as the festival is another exciting event, the **Military Tattoo** taking place on the floodlit esplanade in front of Edinburgh Castle, high on its rock above the city. The Tattoo features the precision marching of the British Army's Scottish regiments and performers from some 30 countries, including bands, dancers, drill teams, gymnasts, and motorcyclists, even horses, camels, elephants, and police dogs. The music ranges from ethnic and pop to military and jazz. Schedules are released each year about 6 months before the festival. Tickets are available from the **Edinburgh Military Tattoo Office,** 32 Market St., Edinburgh EH1 1QB (© **0870/755-5118;** www.edintattoo.co.uk).

Less predictable in quality but greater in quantity is the **Edinburgh Festival Fringe** (© **0131/226-0026;** www.edfringe.com), an opportunity for anybody—professional or nonprofessional, an individual, a group of friends, or a whole company—to put on a show wherever they can find an empty stage or street corner. Ticket prices vary from £5 to £50 ($9.50–$95).

maker in the Scottish capital. Geoffrey is also one of the few kilt makers to actually weave the object; watch the process at the **Edinburgh Old Town Weaving Company,** 555 Castlehill (© **0131/226-1555;** bus: 35), Monday through Friday 9am to 5pm. Some of the most stylish tartans are found at **Anta,** 91-93 West Bow, Victoria Street (© **0131/225-4616;** www.anta.co.uk), where you'll find a series of them newly invented in unique styles. The woolen blankets with hand-purled fringe are woven on old-style looms. **Tartan Gift Shops,** 54 High St. (© **0131/558-3187**), has a chart indicating the Scottish origin of family names, and offers a bewildering array of hunt and dress tartans, sold by the yard. There's also a line of lambs wool and cashmere sweaters.

NIGHTLIFE

For 3 weeks in August, the **Edinburgh International Festival** brings world-class cultural offerings to the city, but there are plenty of choices year-round, whether you prefer theater, opera, ballet, symphony concerts, or other diversions. The waterfront district, featuring many jazz clubs and restaurants, is especially lively in summer, and students flock to the pubs and clubs around Grassmarket. Dance clubs are found off High and Princes streets, and in the city's numerous pubs you can often hear live traditional Scottish folk music for the price of a pint. Pick up the free biweekly paper *The List* (available at the tourist office or see **www.list.co.uk**) or see **www.ents24.com** for a schedule of entertainment events.

THE PERFORMING ARTS

THEATER   Edinburgh has a lively theater scene. In 1994, the **Festival Theatre,** 13–29 Nicolson St. (© **0131/529-6000;** www.eft.co.uk; bus: 3, 31, or 33), opened on the eastern edge of Edinburgh. It boasts the largest stage in Britain and is used for theatre, dance, opera, and presentations of all kinds. Tickets are £7 to £50 ($13.30–$95). The **King's Theatre,** 2 Leven St. (© **0131/529-6000;** www.eft.co.uk; bus: 10 or 11), is a 1,600-seat Victorian venue offering a wide repertoire of classical entertainment, including ballet, opera, and productions from London's West End. The resident company of the **Royal Lyceum Theatre,** Grindlay Street (© **0131/248-4848;** www.lyceum.org.uk; bus: 11 or 15), presents everything from Shakespeare to new Scottish playwrights. The **Traverse Theatre,** 10 Cambridge St. (© **0131/228-1404;** www.traverse.co.uk; bus: 11 or 15), is one of the few theaters in Britain funded solely to present new plays by British writers and first translations into English of international works.

BALLET, OPERA & CLASSICAL MUSIC   The **Scottish Ballet** (www.scottish ballet.co.uk) and the **Scottish Opera** (www.scottishopera.org.uk) perform at the **Edinburgh Playhouse,** 18–22 Greenside Place (© **0870/606-3424;** www.edinburgh-playhouse.co.uk; bus: 7 or 10), the city's largest theater. The **Scottish Chamber Orchestra** (www.sco.org.uk) makes its home at the **Queen's Hall,** Clerk Street (© **0131/668-2019;** www.thequeenshall.net; bus: 3, 33, or 31), also a major venue for the Edinburgh International Festival.

4 Irish Rail Essentials

HIGHLIGHTS OF IRELAND

Traveling in Ireland by train is a breeze. It takes you to many of Ireland's top towns and cities (Cork, Belfast, Galway) as well as some of the lesser known gems (Athlone, Portrush) and getting train information is easy for English speakers (although watch out for the accent and slang). On the down side, the ferry journey to (or from) the U.K. or France can take the best part of the day (once you've added in the journey to the ferry port), and the Irish Sea is known for setting stomachs a-jumbling. But brave these minor irritations and you'll be rewarded with stunning rural scenery and a lively cultural welcome.

Ireland is a separate nation from the United Kingdom, and you'll find they do things differently here. All the public notices are written in English and Gaelic; the euro is the currency; the Irish have no problem electing a female president (while still following the dictates of the Catholic pope); and Ireland was the first country in Europe to ban smoking in public places. Add to that the astonishing number of great writers, playwrights, and musicians produced here, and you've got yourself an interesting foreign climate. But don't come expecting a nation of farming folk sipping Guinness in the afternoons. Yes, there are places where this happens, but Ireland has undergone massive economic expansion in the past few years and is now a young, wealthy nation, with hip Dublin at the center of the action.

GETTING THERE
BY PLANE

About half of all visitors from North America arrive in Ireland on direct transatlantic flights to Dublin Airport. The other half fly first into Britain or Europe, then "back-track" into Ireland by air or sea. **Dublin Airport** lies about 6½ miles (10km) to the

> **Moments Festivals & Special Events**
>
> The most up-to-date listings of events in Ireland can be found at **www. ireland.ie** and **www.entertainment.ie**.
>
> **St. Patrick's Dublin Festival** is a massive 4-day fest (Mar 15–18) that's open, free, and accessible to everyone. Street theater, carnival acts, sports, music, fireworks, and other festivities culminate in Ireland's grandest parade, with marching bands, drill teams, floats, and delegations from around the world. For information, call ✆ **01/676-3205** or surf the Web to **www.st patricksday.ie**. *Warning:* The popular hotels in Dublin often fill up a year in advance of the festival. Book a long way ahead to get a good room.

north of the city (**01/814-1111;** www.dublinairport.com). It's a small and very busy airport offering all the usual comforts and services of an international hub.

FROM NORTH AMERICA   The Irish national carrier, **Aer Lingus** (✆ **800/ 474-7424;** www.aerlingus.com), is the traditional leader in providing transatlantic flights to Ireland. Other carriers flying directly to Ireland from the U.S. are **American Airlines** (✆ **800/433-7300;** www.aa.com), **Delta Airlines** (✆ **800/241-4141;** www. delta.com), and **Continental Airlines** (✆ **800/231-0856;** www.continental.com).

FROM BRITAIN   The following carriers offer direct flights from London to Ireland: **Aer Lingus** (✆ **800/474-7424** in the U.S., or 0870/876-5000 in Britain; www. aerlingus.com); **British Airways** (✆ **800/AIRWAYS** in the U.S., or 0870/ 850-9850 in Britain; www.ba.com); **Lufthansa** (✆ **800/645-3880** in the U.S., or 0870/837-7747; www.lufthansa.com); and **British Midland** (✆ **800/788-0555** in the U.S., or 0870/607-0555 in Britain; www.flybmi.com).

Two low-cost airlines making the London-Dublin hop are **CityJet** (✆ **084/5084-5111** in Britain; www.cityjet.com) and **Ryanair,** for which Dublin is the hub city (✆ **0541/569569** in Britain; www.ryanair.com).

FROM THE CONTINENT   Major direct flights into Dublin from the Continent include service from Amsterdam on **KLM** (✆ **800/447-4747** in the U.S.; www.klm. com); Madrid and Barcelona on **Iberia** (✆ **800/772-4642** in the U.S.; www.iberia. com); Brussels on **Sabena** (✆ **800/952-2000** in the U.S.; www.sabena.com); Copenhagen on **Aer Lingus** and **SAS** (✆ **800/221-2350** in the U.S.; www.scandinavian. net); Frankfurt on **Aer Lingus** and **Lufthansa** (✆ **800/645-3880** in the U.S.; www.lufthansa.com); Paris on **Aer Lingus** and **Air France** (✆ **800/237-2747** in the U.S.; www.airfrance.com); and Rome on **Aer Lingus.**

BY FERRY

The Irish Sea has a reputation for making seafarers woozy, so it's always a good idea to consider an over-the-counter pill or patch to guard against seasickness if you choose to take this route.

FROM BRITAIN   There are two ports for the Dublin-bound sea craft: **Dun Laoghaire,** pronounced "dun lehry," is used exclusively by the Stena Line (see info below), and **Dublin Port** (✆ **01/872-2777;** www.dublinport.ie), which is about 2 miles (3.2km) outside of Dublin. The following ferries have a wildly varying number of ticket prices, discounts, packages, and special offers, so always check the websites for the most up-to-date information.

Irish Ferries (© 0870/517-1717 in the U.K., or 818/300-400 in Ireland; www. irishferries.ie) sails between Dublin and Holyhead in North Wales. Travel time is 2 hours on a fast boat, and close to 4 hours on a more sedate ship, with foot-passenger round-trip tickets starting at €58 ($75). Their other route connects Rosslare in southern Ireland to Pembroke in southern Wales, takes 3 hours and 45 minutes and costs the same as the Dublin-Holyhead route. The Eurail Global Pass gives holders a 30% discount on standard passenger fares on both routes. Book online to save €6 ($7.80) on handling charges.

Stena Line (© 0870/570-7070 in the U.K., or 01/204-7777 in Ireland; www.stena line.com) travels between Holyhead in Wales and Dun Laorghaire, which is just south of Dublin. The trip takes about 99 minutes, and costs from €60 ($78) round-trip for a foot passenger. Another route connects Rosslare (in southern Ireland) to Fishguard (in southern Wales). It takes 2 to 3½ hours and prices start at €60 ($78) round-trip. The Eurail Global Pass entitles holders to a 30% discount on standard passenger fares on both routes.

FROM THE CONTINENT **Irish Ferries** (www.irishferries.ie) sails from Roscoff and Cherbourg, France, to Rosslare, which is about 60 miles (97km) south of Dublin. Transit time between the two ports is 18 hours. For reservations, call **Scots-American Travel** (© 561/563-2856 in the U.S.; info@scotsamerican.com) or **Irish Ferries** (© 0870/517-1717 in the U.K., or 818/300-400 in Ireland). Round-trip tickets start at €112 ($145). Eurail Global Pass holders get a 30% discount on this ferry trip.

Brittany Ferries (© 021/427-7801 in Cork; www.brittany-ferries.com) connects Roscoff, France, to Cork (crossing time is about 14 hr.). A ship only sails once each week. The round-trip price for a foot passenger is €78 ($101). For more prices and information on these ferries, see the "Major European Ferry Lines" chart on p. 64.

IRELAND RAILPASSES

The **Eurail Ireland Pass** is valid for 5 days of second-class travel in a period of 1 month and costs $217. It can be purchased in advance from **Rail Europe** (© 877/272/RAIL [7245] in North America; www.raileurope.com) or your travel agent.

The Ireland-only passes listed below are available from booking offices of **Iarnrod Eireann** (© 1850/366222; www.irishrail.com) and the Dublin Tourism office on Suffolk Street (p. 444). *Note:* Discounted passes are available for children.

Irish Explorer Rail Only For use only in the Republic of Ireland, this pass is good for 5 days of rail-only travel within 15 consecutive days for €138 ($179). It's valid for unlimited travel on InterCity, DART, and Suburban Rail.

Emerald Card Rail and Bus Valid for second-class rail and bus service throughout Ireland and Northern Ireland, this pass costs €406 ($528) for 15 days of travel within a 30-day period, or €236 ($307) for 8 days of travel within a 15-day period.

Irish Explorer Rail and Bus For use only in the Republic of Ireland, this pass is good for 8 days of second-class rail and bus travel within 15 consecutive days for €210 ($273).

READY-MADE RAIL GETAWAYS

Iarnrod Eireann (© 01/856-0045; www.railtours.ie), the Irish rail network, also offers a variety of ready-made day tours and getaways departing by train from Dublin.

Ireland

ATLANTIC OCEAN

Irish Sea

St. George's Channel

WALES

They can be purchased at booking offices of Iarnrod Eireann and at the Dublin Tourism office on Suffolk Street (see "Information Elsewhere in the City," later).

RailTours   These 1-day or half-day tours are a convenient way to see a hefty portion of the country. The fare includes reserved seats on InterCity rail services with full dining facilities. For some itineraries, special coaches with qualified driver/guides take you where rail lines don't. There are various itineraries available, including: Connemara and Galway Bay for €89 ($116); The Ring of Kerry for €99 ($129); The Cliffs of Moher, Burren, and Galway Bay for €99 ($129); and The Aran Islands for €119 ($155), including flights.

RailBreaks   These ready-made 2- or 3-day vacations include train travel and accommodation and let you take in a specific region. There are various options to choose from, with rates starting as low as €219 ($285) per person for a 2-day break covering

Cork, The Ring of Kerry, Blarney Castle, and Killarney including rail travel, B&B accommodation, and breakfast daily. A 5-day Royal Atlantic Tour taking in Cork, Cobh, Blarney Castle, Cliffs of Moher, Galway Bay, Connemara, and The Aran Islands including rail travel, flights, and hotel accommodation costs €569 ($740) per person.

FOREIGN TRAIN TERMS

Booking tickets in Ireland is self-explanatory for English speakers, aside from the occasional variance in vocabulary. *One piece of useful information:* The Irish, like the British, use the term "return" instead of round-trip, and "single" instead of one-way.

PRACTICAL TRAIN INFORMATION

Iarnrod Eireann (© **1890/778899;** www.irishrail.com), aka Irish Railways, runs all of the train routes in the Republic of Ireland. The company's website is loaded with valuable information and has timetables, route maps, station information, and tips for rail travelers with disabilities.

RESERVATIONS   Holders of Eurail, BritRail + Ireland, Emerald Card, and Irish Explorer passes do not need to make reservations on trains. Ireland is a small country, and there are no overnight trains or sleeper coaches. Be aware, however, that trains on the more popular routes can be very crowded, with standing room only, especially on Bank Holiday weekends. It's a good idea to arrive at least 45 minutes before departure time to ensure that you get a seat.

Note: Don't worry if a station's booking office is closed or unstaffed as your train readies for departure, should you decide to make a spur-of-the-moment trip and haven't got a pass; you can always buy your ticket on board the train.

SERVICES & AMENITIES   All InterCity train stations are staffed during rush hours and during the day Monday through Saturday; Dublin city stations are staffed around the clock daily and stations in larger cities, such as Cork and Limerick, are staffed virtually around the clock. Tickets can be purchased during booking hours using cash or major credit cards. Stations in cities and larger towns have public restrooms, shops, telephones, lockers, luggage carts, and taxi stands. Stations in smaller suburbs and small towns have public restrooms, telephones, and taxi stands. You can view the list of amenities offered in each station on **www.irishrail.com**.

Most InterCity trains offer some kind of food service, be it a restaurant car or a snack cart. If you're traveling first class, you may even be able to get tableside meal service (albeit for a high price) on some routes.

Trains & Travel Times in Ireland

From	To	Type of Train	# of Trains	Frequency	Travel Time
Dublin Heuston	Cork	IC	16	Mon–Sat	2 hr., 50 min.
Dublin Heuston	Cork	IC	10	Sun	2 hr., 50 min.
Dublin Heuston	Killarney	IC	7	Mon–Sat	3 hr., 30 min.
Dublin Heuston	Killarney	IC	5	Sun	3 hr., 30 min.
Dublin Heuston	Galway	IC	7	Mon–Sat	2 hr., 42 min.
Dublin Heuston	Galway	IC	6	Sun	2 hr., 42 min.
Dublin Connolly	Rosslare Europort	IC	3	Daily	3 hr.
Dublin Connolly	Wexford	IC	2	Daily	2 hr., 30 min.

FAST FACTS: Ireland

Area Codes The country code for Ireland is **353**. The area code for Dublin is **01**.

Business Hours **Banks** are open 10am to 4pm Monday to Friday, with some banks staying open until 5pm on Thursday.

Post offices (known as **An Post**) in city centers are open from 9am to 5:30pm Monday to Friday and 9am to 1pm Saturday. Post offices often close for lunch between 1 and 2:15pm, even in Dublin.

Museums and sights are generally open 10am to 5pm Tuesday to Saturday, and 2 to 5pm Sunday.

Shops are generally open 9am to 6pm, Monday to Friday with late opening on Thursdays until 7 or 8pm. In Dublin's city center most department stores and many shops are open noon to 6pm Sundays.

Currency The Republic of Ireland has adopted the single European currency, the **euro**, symbolized in this chapter by the € sign. In converting prices to U.S. dollars, we used the rate €1 = $1.30. The euro is divided into 100 cents.

Electricity The Irish electric system operates on 220 volts with a plug bearing three rectangular prongs. To use standard North American 110-volt appliances without destroying them or causing a fire, you'll need both a transformer and a plug adapter. Most laptops have built-in transformers and require only a plug adaptor, available at travel and electronic shops.

Embassies/Consulates The **American Embassy** is at 42 Elgin Rd., Ballsbridge, Dublin 4 (© **01/668-8777**; www.dublin.usembassy.gov); the **Canadian Embassy** is at 65 St. Stephen's Green, Dublin 2 (© **01/417-4100**; www.canada.ie).

Health & Safety The Republic of Ireland has enjoyed a traditionally low crime rate, particularly when it comes to violent crime. Those days do regrettably seem to be passing, especially in the cities. By U.S. standards, Ireland is still very safe, but not safe enough to warrant carelessness. Travelers should take normal precautions to protect their belongings from theft and themselves from harm.

In recent years, the larger cities have been prey to pickpockets, purse-snatchers, car thieves, and drug traffickers. Some neighborhoods that are mild mannered by day change character at night, especially if they are home to pubs and nightclubs. Ask at your hotel about which areas are dodgy and when. After midnight, you're best off using a taxi for transport.

Ireland poses no major health risks to the rail traveler.

Mail In Ireland, mailboxes are painted green with the word POST on top. From the Republic, an airmail letter or postcard to the United States, Canada, Australia, or New Zealand, not exceeding 50 grams, costs €.80 ($1) and takes 5 to 7 days to arrive.

Telephone In the Republic, the telephone system is known as Eircom. Phone numbers in Ireland are currently in flux, as digits are added to accommodate expanded service. Every effort has been made to ensure that the numbers and information in this guide are accurate at the time of writing. If you have difficulty reaching a party, the Irish toll-free number for directory assistance is © **11811**; www.11811.ie.

Local calls from a phone booth in the Republic require a **Callcard,** a prepaid computerized card that you insert into the phone instead of coins. They can be purchased in a range of denominations at phone company offices, post offices, and many retail outlets (such as newsstands). There's a local and international phone center at the General Post Office on O'Connell Street.

To place a call from your home country to Ireland, dial the international access code (**011** in the U.S.), plus the country code (**353** for the Republic), and finally the number, remembering to omit the initial 0, which is for use only within Ireland (for example, to call Dublin Castle from the United States, you'd dial 011-353-1/677-7129).

To place a direct international call from Ireland, dial the international access code (**00**) plus the country code (U.S. and Canada 1), the area or city code, and the number. The toll-free international access code for **AT&T** is ✆ 1-800-550-000; for **Sprint** it's ✆ 1-800-552-001; and for **MCI** it's ✆ 1-800-55-1001.

Tipping Most hotels and guesthouses add a service charge to the bill, usually 12.5% to 15%, although some smaller places add only 10% or nothing at all. Always check to see what amount, if any, has been added to your bill. If it is 12.5% to 15%, and you feel this is sufficient, then there is no need for further gratuities. If a smaller amount has been added, however, or if staff members have provided exceptional service, it is appropriate to give an additional tip. For porters or bellhops, tip €1 ($1.30) per piece of luggage. For taxi drivers, hairdressers, and other providers of service, tip as you would at home, an average of 10% to 15%.

For restaurants, the policy is usually printed on the menu—either a gratuity of 10% to 15% is automatically added to your bill or it's left up to you ("service not included" may be written on the bill). Always ask if you are in doubt. As a rule, bartenders do not expect a tip, except when table service is provided.

5 Dublin

Dublin isn't an immediate beauty. Compared to cities such as Edinburgh and Paris, it seems rather squat and lacking in oh-wow architecture. But the inhabitants—the city is home to more than a third of the entire population of Ireland—are the real reason to visit this city. They have a knack for making even everyday living seem poetic, and excel in storytelling and music-making. And Dublin offers far more than just old-style hospitality; it's also packed with young people (not all of them Irish—the booming economy has seen immigrants flood in from throughout the world), and is now one of the trendiest cities in all of Europe. It's also the rail hub of the Republic and home to a major international airport, making it the logical first stop for rail travelers touring the country. Another bonus: Compared to other European capitals, Dublin is a relatively small metropolis and easily traversed. The city center—identified in Irish on bus destination signs as AN LAR—is bisected by the River Liffey flowing west to east into Dublin Bay. Canals ring the city center: The Royal Canal forms a skirt through the north half, and the Grand Canal the southern half. The buzzing, prosperous hub of Dublin lies mostly south of the Liffey. The area containing most of the best hotels, restaurants, shops, and sights is a small, well-defined compound easily walked in a half hour.

Which Dublin Station?

Connolly Station InterCity routes to Sligo, Belfast; Rosslare; Longford; DART service to Malahide, County Dublin (north) and Greystones, County Wicklow (south).

Heuston Station InterCity routes to Cork, Tralee, Limerick, Waterford, Ballina/Westport, Galway, Kildare, Clonmel; No DART service.

On the downside, Dublin's an expensive place to visit, but it's still cheaper than some other cities in Europe.

STATION INFORMATION
GETTING FROM THE AIRPORT TO THE TRAIN STATION

Dublin International Airport (© **01/814-1111;** www.dublinairport.com) is 6.2 miles (10km) north of the city center. A tourist information office located in the Arrivals Concourse provides information on public bus and rail services throughout the country.

If you need to connect immediately with the Irish rail service, the **Airlink Express Coach** (© **01/873-4222** [telephone info line open Mon–Sat 8:30am–6pm]; www.dublinbus.ie) provides express bus service (nos. 747 and 748) from the airport to the two main rail stations, **Connolly** and **Heuston.** Service runs daily from 5:15am until 11:30pm (Sun 7:15am–11:30pm), with departures every 10 to 20 minutes, but is restricted in the early morning and late evening, so check on the phone or Web to find out what time your route runs. One-way fare is €6 ($7.80) for adults and €3 ($3.90) for children under 12. Buy a ticket before boarding the bus from the pay machine just on your left as you exit the airport. The buses leave from the lay-by opposite the pay machine. The journey takes 30 to 35 minutes.

An excellent airport-to-city bus service called **AirCoach** operates 24 hours a day, making runs at 15-minute intervals. AirCoach runs direct from the airport to Dublin's city center and south side, serving all the key hotel and business districts. The one-way fare is €7 ($9.10) and €1 ($1.30) for children under 12; buy your ticket from the driver. Although AirCoach is slightly more expensive than the **Express Coach** (above), it is faster because it makes fewer intermediary stops and it brings you right into the hotel districts. To confirm AirCoach departures and arrivals, call © **01/844-7118** or find it on the Web at **www.aircoach.ie**.

Dublin Bus (© **01/873-4222;** www.dublinbus.ie) services 16A, 41, and 746 also run between the airport and the city center between 6am and 11:30pm. The one-way trip takes about 30 minutes, and the fare is just €1.90 ($2.50). Consult the Travel Information Desk located in the Arrivals Concourse to figure out which bus will bring you closest to your hotel.

If you have a lot of luggage, a **taxi** is the best way to get directly to your hotel or guesthouse. Depending on your destination in Dublin, fares average between €16 and €25 ($20.80–$32.50). Each additional passenger is charged €1 ($1.30). For more information on fares see "Getting Around" section (below). Depending on traffic (which can be horrendous), a cab should take between 20 to 45 minutes to get into

Dublin

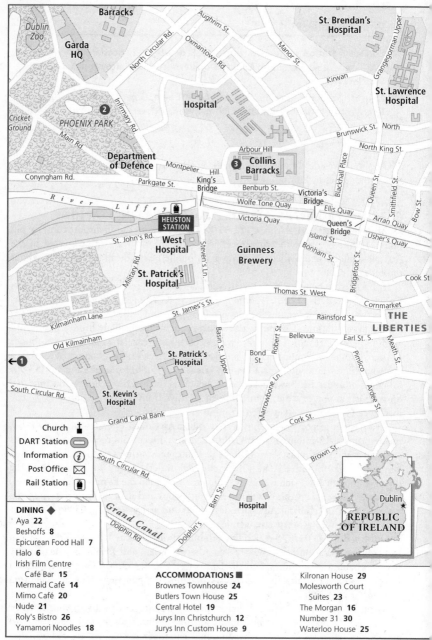

Dublin Zoo

Barracks

Garda HQ

Cricket Ground

PHOENIX PARK ❷

Aughrim St.

North Circular Rd.

Oxmantown Rd.

Manor St.

St. Brendan's Hospital

Grangegorman Upper

Kirwan

St. Lawrence Hospital

Brunswick St. North

Hospital

Infirmary Rd.

Main Rd.

Arbour Hill

North King St.

Department of Defence

Montpelier Hill

King's Bridge

Collins Barracks ❸

Blackhall Place

Queen St.

Smithfield St.

Bow St.

Conyngham Rd.

Parkgate St.

Benburb St.

Wolfe Tone Quay

Victoria's Bridge

Ellis Quay

Arran Quay

River Liffey

HEUSTON STATION

Victoria Quay

Island St.

Queen's Bridge

Usher's Quay

St. John's Rd.

West Hospital

Steven's Ln.

Guinness Brewery

Bonham St.

Bridgefoot St.

Cook St.

Military Rd.

St. Patrick's Hospital

Thomas St. West

Cornmarket

THE LIBERTIES

Kilmainham Lane

St. James's St.

Rainsford St.

Basin St. Upper

Robert St.

Bellevue

Earl St. S.

Meath St.

Old Kilmainham

←❶

St. Patrick's Hospital

Bond St.

Pimlico

Ardee St.

South Circular Rd.

St. Kevin's Hospital

Marrowbone Ln.

Cork St.

Grand Canal Bank

Brown St.

Church ✝
DART Station ⊖
Information ⓘ
Post Office ✉
Rail Station 🚉

South Circular Rd.

Grand Canal

Dolphin's

Barn St.

Hospital

Dublin ★

REPUBLIC OF IRELAND

Dolphin Rd.

DINING ◆
Aya **22**
Beshoffs **8**
Epicurean Food Hall **7**
Halo **6**
Irish Film Centre
   Café Bar **15**
Mermaid Café **14**
Mimo Café **20**
Nude **21**
Roly's Bistro **26**
Yamamori Noodles **18**

ACCOMMODATIONS ■
Brownes Townhouse **24**
Butlers Town House **25**
Central Hotel **19**
Jurys Inn Christchurch **12**
Jurys Inn Custom House **9**

Kilronan House **29**
Molesworth Court
   Suites **23**
The Morgan **16**
Number 31 **30**
Waterloo House **25**

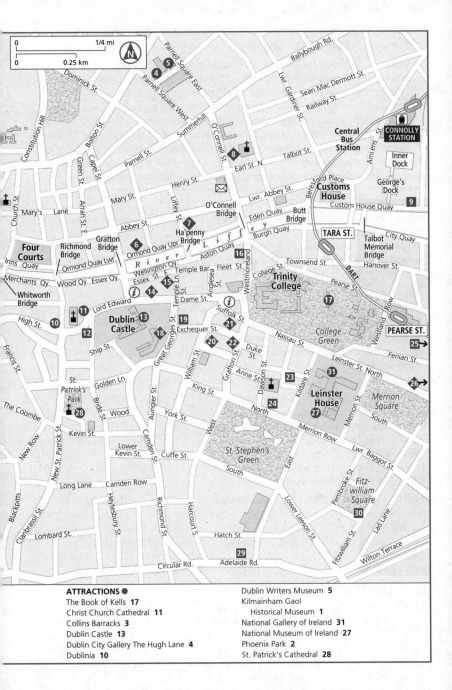

ATTRACTIONS ●

The Book of Kells **17**
Christ Church Cathedral **11**
Collins Barracks **3**
Dublin Castle **13**
Dublin City Gallery The Hugh Lane **4**
Dublinia **10**

Dublin Writers Museum **5**
Kilmainham Gaol
  Historical Museum **1**
National Gallery of Ireland **31**
National Museum of Ireland **27**
Phoenix Park **2**
St. Patrick's Cathedral **28**

⌐Warning Late-Night Crime

Dublin is a booze-fueled city. This is particularly noticeable on weekends around the Temple Bar/Grafton Street/O'Connell Street areas. The Guarda do their best to keep the public order incidents under control, but rowdy herds of men can turn nasty and have been known to attack passersby without any provocation. Although there are no official police warnings about walking back to your hotel alone at certain times of night, we get a taxi if we're arriving at the train station after 10pm (if nothing else it avoids the possibility of inadvertently stepping in vomit), and make sure we don't walk back home alone around pub/club closing time (anywhere between 11pm and dawn).

---

the city center. Taxis are lined up on a first-come, first-served taxi stand outside the arrivals terminal.

Passenger and car ferries from Britain arrive at the **Dublin Port** (© **01/855-0888;** www.dublinport.ie), on the eastern end of the North Docks, and at the **Dun Laoghaire Ferryport** (www.dlharbour.ie). There is bus and taxi service from both ports.

INSIDE THE STATIONS

Dublin has two major train stations—**Heuston Station,** Kingsbridge, off St. John's Road, and **Connolly Station,** Amiens Street—and an additional two minor ones. To determine which station works best for your rail itinerary, see "Which Dublin Station?" below. Both stations are staffed 24 hours daily and will book tickets Monday through Saturday 7am to 10:20pm and Sunday 8am to 10:20pm at Connolly Station and 6:30am to 10:30pm and Sunday 7:45am to 10:30pm at Heuston Station.

CONNOLLY STATION   The major train station for points north of Dublin, Connolly is on the eastern side of Dublin, just a block away from the city's Central Bus Station. Station facilities include luggage lockers, fast-food restaurants and cafes, a taxi stand, ATMs, public bathrooms, newsagents, and ticket vending machines. A visitor information desk is located at track level in the station. There are maps and brochures, but no room reservation service. For more information about this station, call © **01/703-2358** or see **www.irishrail.ie.**

HEUSTON STATION   On the western side of the Dublin, Heuston appropriately handles a lot of the trains heading west out of the city. A visitor information desk is located at track level in the station. Station facilities include fast-food restaurants and cafes, a taxi stand, ATMs, public bathrooms, newsagents, and ticket vending machines. There are maps and brochures, but no room reservation service. For more information about this station, call © **01/703-3299** or see **www.irishrail.com.**

INFORMATION ELSEWHERE IN THE CITY

Dublin Tourism (© **01/605-7700;** www.visitdublin.com) operates six walk-in visitor centers in greater Dublin. The principal center is in the wonderfully restored Church of St. Andrew on Suffolk Street, Dublin 2, open in June and September Monday to Saturday 9am to 7pm, Sunday 10:30am to 3pm; July and August Monday to Saturday from 9am to 8pm, Sunday 10:30am to 3pm, and the rest of the year Monday to Saturday 9am to 5:30pm, Sunday 10:30am to 3pm and Bank Holidays 10:30am to 3pm throughout the year. The Suffolk Street office is about ½ mile (.8km) from Connolly

Station and includes a currency exchange counter, a car-rental counter, an accommodations reservations service, bus and rail information desks, a gift shop, and a cafe.

The other centers are in the **Arrivals Hall** of Dublin Airport; **O'Connell Street,** 14 Upper O'Connell St., Dublin 1; **Baggot Street Bridge,** Baggot Street, Dublin 2; and the ferry terminal at **Dun Laoghaire Harbor** (all telephone inquiries should be directed to the number listed above). All centers are open year-round (except Christmas) for at least the following hours: Monday to Friday 10am to 5pm (excluding a 30- to 60-min. lunch break noon–2pm at some centers).

GETTING AROUND

Getting around Dublin is a breeze. Public transportation is good and getting better, taxis are plentiful and reasonably priced, and walking is a pleasure. In fact, with its current traffic and parking problems, it's a city where the foot is mightier than the wheel.

ON FOOT Small and compact, Dublin is ideal for walking, as long as you remember to look right and then left (in the direction opposite your instincts) for oncoming traffic before crossing the street, and to obey traffic signals. Each traffic light has timed "walk–don't walk" signals for pedestrians. Pedestrians have the right of way at specially marked, zebra-striped crossings; as a warning, there are usually two flashing lights at these intersections.

BY BUS Dublin Bus operates a fleet of green double-decker buses, single-deck buses, and minibuses (called "imps") throughout the city and its suburbs. Most buses originate on or near O'Connell Street, Abbey Street, and Eden Quay on the north side, and at Aston Quay, College Street, and Fleet Street on the south side. Bus stops are located every 2 or 3 blocks. Destinations and bus numbers are posted above the front windows; buses destined for the city center are marked with the Irish Gaelic words AN LAR.

Bus service runs daily throughout the city, starting at 6am (10am on Sun), with the last bus at 11:30pm. Monday to Saturday, Nitelink service runs from the city center to the suburbs from midnight to 3am, with more frequent services on Friday and Saturday nights. Buses operate every 10 to 15 minutes for most runs; schedules are posted on revolving notice boards at each bus stop.

Inner-city fares are calculated based on distances traveled. The minimum fare is €1 ($1.30); the maximum fare (for outer suburbs) is €4.10 ($5.30). The Nitelink fare is €4 ($5.20), or €6 ($7.80) if you are traveling to the outer 'burbs. There is a new **Auto-fare** system in place to eliminate the driver having to deal with cash. You buy a ticket (or use one of your passes) from any of the hundreds of shops or kiosks that sell them and insert it into the fare **validator** on the bus. On some buses, you can still buy your tickets from the driver as you enter the bus, but exact change is required, so have it available: Notes will not be accepted. You can also get 1-day, 3-day, 5-day, and 7-day passes. The 1-day bus-only pass costs €6 ($7.80); the 3-day pass costs €11 ($14.30); the 5-day pass goes for €17.30 ($22.50); and the 7-day pass costs €21 ($27.30). For more information, contact **Dublin Bus,** 59 Upper O'Connell St., Dublin 1 (© **01/ 872-0000;** www.dublinbus.ie).

BY DART While Dublin has no subway in the strict sense, there is an electric rapid-transit train, known as the **DART (Dublin Area Rapid Transit).** It travels mostly at ground level or on elevated tracks, linking the city-center stations at **Connolly Station, Tara Street,** and **Pearse Street** with suburbs and seaside communities as far as Malahide to the north and Greystones to the south. Trains run roughly every 5 to 10 minutes Monday to Saturday from 7am to midnight and Sunday from 9:30am to 11pm. The minimum fare is €1.40 ($1.80). One-day tickets are also available for €7.20 ($9.40) and 3-day tickets for €15.30 ($19.90). For further information, contact **DART,** Pearse Station, Dublin 2 (② **1850/366222** in Ireland, or 01/836-6222; www.irishrail.com).

BY TRAM   The newest addition to Dublin's public transportation network is the sleek light-rail tram known as **Luas,** which means "speed" in Gaelic. Traveling at a maximum speed of 45 mph (70kmph) and departing every 5 minutes in peak hours, Luas has helped ease Dublin's congestion problems; an estimated 120,000 people use it each day. There are two lines: The green line goes from Sandyford in the south east to St. Stephen's Green; the red line starts at the southwest suburb of Tallaght and terminates at Connolly Station. Fares are calculated by length of trip, starting at €1.40 ($1.80) for a single central Dublin trip; round-trip is €2.70 ($3.50). Your best bet is a 1-day travel card that is good for all zones and costs €4.50 adults ($5.85), and €2 ($2.60) for kids. The cards are slightly more expensive if bought direct from LUAS at the tram stops, so you'll save if you buy from one of the agents (usually convenience stores such as Spar and Centra located near the tram stops). Whichever way you go be sure to have a valid ticket when you board or you could be fined €45 ($58.50). For further information, contact **Luas** at ② **01/800-300-604** (in Ireland only) or visit **www.luas.ie.**

BY TAXI   Taxis don't usually respond to being hailed on the street; instead, they line up at stands. Stands are located outside all of the leading hotels, at bus and train stations, and on prime thoroughfares such as Upper O'Connell Street, College Green, and the north side of St. Stephen's Green near the Shelbourne Hotel. You can also phone for a taxi. Here are some companies: **Access Metro Cabs** (② 01/668-3333), **A to B Cabs** (② 01/677-2222), **Castle Cabs** (② 01/831-9000), **Checkers Cabs** (② 01/834-3434), **Speed Cabs** (② 01/475-0800), and **VIP Taxis** (② 01/478-3333; www.viptaxis.ie). If you need a wake-up call, VIP offers that service, along with especially courteous dependability.

Taxi rates are fixed by law and posted in each vehicle. The minimum fare is €3.80 ($4.90) for 1km or about 3 minutes, with the price rising by €.95 ($1.24) for each further kilometer traveled or €.35 (45¢) per minute, if the taxi drops below a speed of 13 mph (21kmph) (rates are slightly higher 8pm–8am, Sun, and bank holidays, and if you travel farther than 9⅓ miles/15km the taxi will switch onto a higher tariff to compensate the driver for having to return with an empty cab). An average ride in the center of Dublin runs from €6 to €11 ($7.80–$14.30).There's an additional charge for each extra passenger of €1 ($1.30). And it costs an extra €2 ($2.60) to book a taxi in advance. *Be warned:* Some hotel staff members will tack on as much as €4 ($4.60) for calling you a cab, although this practice violates city taxi regulations. Complaints can be registered at the **Garda Siochana** at ② **01/659-3800.**

WHERE TO STAY
Brownes Townhouse ⚔   This gorgeous, traditional Georgian hotel overlooks St. Stephen's Green. The rooms were all refurbished in 2005 using warm, muted paints to give a classic yet contemporary feel. It's lovely to wake up in the morning and look out over the park, but there is no double-glazing, so if you're the sort who gets woken by traffic noise opt for one of the back rooms. The sweet attic-like room, 210, is our particular favorite.

22 St Stephen's Green, Dublin 2. © **01/638-3939.** Fax 01/638-3900. www.brownesdublin.com. 11 units. €250–€280 ($325–$364) double. MC, V. DART: Pearse. Bus: 10, 11A, 11B, 13, or 20B. **Amenities:** Restaurant; lounge. *In room:* Hair dryer.

Butlers Town House ★★ *Value*   This beautifully restored and expanded Victorian town house B&B feels like a grand family home. The atmosphere is semiformal yet invitingly elegant, classy without the starched collar. Rooms are richly furnished with four-poster or half-tester beds, using top-quality fabrics and an eye for blending rich colors. The sheets are of two-fold Egyptian cotton, the water pressure is heavenly, and staff is gracious. There's free tea and coffee all day.

44 Lansdowne Rd., Ballsbridge, Dublin 4. © **800/44-UTELL** in the U.S., or 01/667-4022. Fax 01/667-3960. www.butlers-hotel.com. 20 units. €145–€175 ($188–$227) double. Rates include full breakfast. AE, DC, MC, V. Closed Dec 23–Jan 8. DART: Lansdowne Rd. Bus: 7, 7A, 8, or 45. **Amenities:** Breakfast room; laundry. *In room:* Hair dryer.

Central Hotel ★   In the heart of Dublin, between Grafton Street and Dublin Castle, this century-old five-story hotel is now part of the Best Western chain. The public areas retain a Victorian atmosphere, enhanced by an impressive collection of contemporary Irish art. Guest rooms are high-ceilinged, with cheerful and colorful fabrics, and sturdy, Irish-made furnishings. The tucked-away Library Bar is a cozy haven for a drink and a moment's calm.

Exchequer St. (at the corner of Great Georges St.), Dublin 2. © **800/780-1234** in the U.S., or 01/679-7302. Fax 01/679-7303. www.centralhotel.ie. 70 units. €130–€165 ($169–$314) double. Rates include full Irish breakfast and service charge. AE, DC, MC, V. Bus: 22A. **Amenities:** Restaurant; bar; laundry; lounge; nonsmoking rooms. *In room:* Hair dryer, no A/C.

Jurys Inn Christchurch ★ *Value*   Despite its uninspiring architecture, this hotel enjoys a good location in Old City, facing Christ Church cathedral, and is a fine budget option. The rooms are larger than you'd expect and bright, though the decor is as ho-hum as every other chain hotel you've ever visited. Request a fifth-floor room facing west for a memorable view of Christ Church. Wi-Fi is available in the public areas and there's Internet access in all guest rooms.

Christ Church Place, Dublin 8. © **800/44-UTELL** in the U.S., or 01/454-0000. Fax 01/454-0012. www.jurys-dublin-hotels.com. 182 units. €97–€150 ($126–$195) double. Breakfast €13 ($16.90). AE, MC, V. Bus: 21A, 50, 50A, 78, 78A, or 78B. **Amenities:** Restaurant; pub; laundry; nonsmoking rooms. *In room:* Hair dryer, no A/C.

Jurys Inn Custom House ★★ *Value*   Ensconced in the new financial services district and facing the quays, this Jurys Inn follows the chain's successful formula of affordable comfort without frills. Double rooms offer both a double and a twin bed. Twenty-two especially spacious rooms, if available, cost nothing extra. Rooms facing the quays also enjoy vistas of the Dublin hills, but those facing the financial district are quieter. Wi-Fi is available in the public areas and there's Internet access in all guest rooms.

Custom House Quay, Dublin 1. © **800/44-UTELL** in the U.S., or 01/607-5000. Fax 01/829-0400. www.jurys-dublin-hotels.com. 239 units. €97–€150 ($126–$195) double. Rates include service charge. Full Irish breakfast €13 ($16.90). AE, DC, MC, V. Discounted parking available at adjacent lot. DART: Tara St. Bus: 27A, 27B, or 53A. **Amenities:** Restaurant; bar; laundry; nonsmoking rooms. *In room:* Hair dryer, no A/C.

Kilronan House ★★   This extremely comfortable and award-winning B&B is set on a peaceful, leafy road just a 5-minute walk from St. Stephen's Green. Much of the Georgian character remains, such as the ceiling cornicing, hardwood parquet floors,

and the fine staircase. The rooms are brightly inviting in white and yellow, and those facing the front have big bay windows. There's no elevator, so get a room on a lower floor. Breakfast here is especially good, featuring homemade breads.

70 Adelaide Rd., Dublin 2. ℭ **01/475-5266.** Fax 01/478-2841. www.dublinn.com. 12 units, 9 with private bathroom (shower only), 3 with just toilet and basin. €152–€170 ($175–$3323) double en suite, €110 ($143) double with shower and hand basin but no toilet. Rates include full breakfast. AE, MC, V. Bus: 14, 15, 19, 20, or 46A. *In room:* Hair dryer, no A/C.

Molesworth Court Suites ⩗ Hate hotels? Tucked away behind Mansion House, Molesworth Court is a 5-minute walk to Stephens Green. These tastefully decorated, comfortable apartments offer everything you need to set up your own base in Dublin, whether for a night or a month. They all have kitchens, small balconies, and the bi-level penthouses have spacious verandas. The staff is helpful, and there's a maid service every few days. The internal phone system provides you with your own voice mail.

Schoolhouse Lane (off Molesworth St.), Dublin 2. ℭ **01/676-4799.** Fax 01/676-4982. www.molesworthcourt.ie. 12 units. €180 ($234) 1-bedroom apt., €225 ($293) 2-bedroom apt., €415 ($540) 3-bedroom apt. Nonrefundable booking deposit of €100 ($130) due 4 weeks before arrival. AE, MC, V. DART: Pearse. Bus: 10, 11A, 11B, 13, or 20B. **Amenities:** Laundry. *In room:* No A/C.

The Morgan ⩗⩗ In just a few short years, this stylized little boutique hotel in Temple Bar has developed a cult following among folks in fashion and music. Rooms are so airy and minimalist, they almost seem futuristic. A touch of decadence is added by the unique mirrored wardrobes and lavish gold headboards. The place nearly doubled in size in 2005, with more groovy eating and drinking areas added downstairs. Ask for a quiet room if you want some sleep; The Morgan is the midst of the nightclub district.

10 Fleet St., Dublin 2. ℭ **01/643-7000.** Fax 01/643-7060. www.themorgan.com. 106 units. €150–€215 ($195–$280) double. AE, DC, MC, V. Bus: 78A or 78B. **Amenities:** Cafe; bar; laundry; nonsmoking rooms. *In room:* A/C (deluxe rooms only).

Number 31 ⩗⩗ This award-winning town house B&B, in the heart of Georgian Dublin, is actually two beautifully renovated architectural show houses featuring a fabulous sunken fireside seating area with mosaic tiles in the main lounge. In the main house, rooms vary from grand, high-ceilinged affairs to cozier nests. The smaller coach house has lower ceilings, but some rooms have their own patios. All the rooms are a triumph of quiet, good taste. Breakfast is magnificent.

31 Leeson Close, Lower Leeson St., Dublin 2. ℭ **01/676-5011.** Fax 01/676-2929. www.number31.ie. 20 units (all with bathroom). €150–€280 ($195–$364) double. Rates include breakfast. AE, MC, V. Free parking. Bus: 11, 11A, 11B, 13, 13A, or 13B. **Amenities:** Bar; lounge. *In room:* Hair dryer.

Waterloo House ⩗ Waterloo House (actually not one, but two Georgian town houses) is one of the most popular B&Bs in Dublin. The place is charming in an old-world kind of way, with classical music wafting through the lobby, and the elegant, high-ceilinged drawing room looking like a parlor out of an Agatha Christie novel. Guest rooms are comfortable and large (some have two double beds), and breakfast is a high point.

8–10 Waterloo Rd., Ballsbridge, Dublin 4. ℭ **01/660-1888.** Fax 01/667-1955. www.waterloohouse.ie. 17 units. €80–€200 ($104–$260) double. Rates include full breakfast. AE, MC, V. Closed Christmas week. DART: Lansdowne Rd. Bus: 5, 7, or 8. **Amenities:** Breakfast room; all rooms are nonsmoking. *In room:* Hair dryer, no A/C.

TOP ATTRACTIONS & SPECIAL MOMENTS
The Book of Kells ⩗⩗⩗ The jewel in Ireland's tourism crown is the Book of Kells, a magnificent 9th-century manuscript of the four Gospels, painstakingly scripted and

illuminated by talented monks. It's the most majestic work of art to survive from the early centuries of Celtic Christianity, and has often been described as "the most beautiful book in the world." Its fascination derives from the dignified but elusive character of its main motifs, and the astonishing variety and complexity of the linear ornamentation that adorns every one of its 680 pages. This famous treasure and other early Christian manuscripts are on permanent public view at Trinity College, in the Colonnades, an exhibition area on the ground floor of the Old Library. The oldest university in Ireland, Trinity was founded in 1592 by Queen Elizabeth I. It occupies a beautiful 40-acre (16-hectare) site just south of the River Liffey, with cobbled squares, gardens, a picturesque quadrangle, and buildings dating from the 17th to the 20th century. This is one of Dublin's busiest visitor attractions, meaning it can be heaving in summer months. The quietest times are from October to April; if you have to go during the summer, get here as soon as it opens to avoid the crowds.

The Old Library, College Green, Dublin 2. (𝄞 **01/896-2320.** www.tcd.ie/info/trinity/bookofkells. Free admission to college grounds. €8 ($10.40) adults, €7 ($9.10) seniors/students, €16 ($20.80) families, free for children under 12. Mon–Sat 9:30am–5pm; Sun noon–4:30pm (opens at 9:30am May–Sept). Bus: All city buses stop here.

Christ Church Cathedral 𝄞𝄞   Standing on high ground in the oldest part of the city, this cathedral is one of Dublin's finest historic buildings. It dates from 1038, when Sitric, Danish king of Dublin, built the first wooden Christ Church here. The present structure dates mainly from 1871 to 1878, when a huge restoration took place. Highlights of the interior include magnificent stonework and graceful pointed arches, with delicately chiseled supporting columns. This is the mother church for the diocese of Dublin and Glendalough of the Church of Ireland. The Treasury in the crypt is open to the public, and you can hear bells pealing in the belfry.

Christ Church Place, Dublin 8. (𝄞 **01/677-8099.** www.cccdub.ie. Admission €5 ($6.50) adults, €2.50 ($3.25) students and seniors, children under 15 free. June–Aug daily 9am–6pm; Sept–May 9:45am–5pm. Closed Dec 26. Bus: 21A, 50, 50A, 78, 78A, or 78B.

Collins Barracks   Officially part of the National Museum, Collins Barracks is the oldest military barracks in Europe. Even if it were empty, it would be well worth a visit for the structure itself, a splendidly restored early-18th-century masterwork by Colonel Thomas Burgh, Ireland's chief engineer and surveyor general under Queen Anne. The collection housed here focuses on the decorative arts. Most notable is the extraordinary display of Irish silver and furniture. Until the acquisition of this vast space, only a fraction of the National Museum's collection could be displayed, but that's changing, and more and more treasures find their way here, including temporary touring exhibits.

Benburb St., Dublin 7. (𝄞 **01/677-7444.** Free admission. Guided tours at 3pm daily €2 ($2.60) adults, free for children under 16. Tues–Sat 10am–5pm; Sun 2–5pm. Bus: 90, 25, 25A, 66, or 67.

Dublin Castle 𝄞𝄞   Built between 1208 and 1220, this complex displays some of the oldest surviving architecture in the city. It was the center of British power in Ireland for more than 7 centuries, until the new Irish government took it over in 1922. Highlights include the 13th-century Record Tower; the State Apartments, once the residence of English viceroys; and the Chapel Royal, a 19th-century Gothic building with particularly fine plaster decoration and carved oak gallery fronts and fittings. The atmospheric and ancient Undercroft is an excavated site on the grounds where an early Viking fortress stood; and the Treasury, built between 1712 and 1715, is believed to

be the oldest surviving office building in Ireland. There are two restaurants and an interesting gift shop on the premises.

Palace St. (off Dame St.), Dublin 2. © **01/677-7129**. www.dublincastle.ie. Admission €4.50 ($5.85) adults, €3.50 ($4.55) students/seniors, €2 ($3.60) children 6–12, children under 6 free. Mon–Fri 10am–4:45pm; Sat–Sun and holidays 2–4:45pm. Free guided tours every 10–15 min. Bus: 50, 50A, 54, 56A, 77, 77A, or 77B.

Dublin City Gallery The Hugh Lane 🎨 Housed in a finely restored 18th-century building known as Charlemont House, this gallery is situated next to the Dublin Writers Museum. It is named after Hugh Lane, an Irish art connoisseur who was killed during the sinking of the *Lusitania* in 1915 and who willed his collection (including works by Courbet, Manet, Monet, and Corot) to be shared between the government of Ireland and the National Gallery of London. The gallery also has Impressionist paintings, sculptures by Rodin, impressive stained glass, and works by modern Irish artists. In 2001, the museum opened the studio of Irish painter Francis Bacon; it was moved piece by piece from Bacon's original studio and reconstructed at the museum, dust and all. Visitors once had to pay extra to enter Bacon's studio but now it's free. In 2006, the gallery underwent a massive expansion program, doubling its exhibition space, gaining €9 million ($11.7 million) worth of new art, and creating a permanent show on Irish-born abstract painter Sean Scully. The bookshop has the best fine arts book selection in the city and there is also a good cafe.

Parnell Sq. N., Dublin 1. © **01/222-5550**. Fax 01/872-2182. www.hughlane.ie. Free admission. Tues–Thurs 10am–6pm; Fri–Sat 10am–5pm; Sun 11am–5pm. DART: Connolly or Tara stations. Bus: 3, 10, 11, 13, 16, or 19.

Dublinia 🎨 What was Dublin like in medieval times? This historically accurate presentation of the Old City from 1170 to 1540 is re-created through a series of theme exhibits, spectacles, and experiences. Highlights include an illuminated Medieval Maze, complete with visual effects, background sounds, and aromas that lead you on a journey through time from the arrival of the Anglo-Normans in 1170 to the closure of the monasteries in the 1530s. Another segment depicts everyday life in medieval Dublin in a diorama, as well as a prototype of a 13th-century quay along the banks of the Liffey. The medieval Fayre displays the wares of medieval merchants from all over Europe. You can try on a flattering new robe, or, if you're feeling vulnerable, stop in at the armorer and be fitted for chain mail.

St. Michael's Hill, Christ Church, Dublin 8. © **01/679-4611**. www.dublinia.ie. Admission €6 ($7.80) adults, €5 ($6.50) seniors and students, €3.75 ($4.80) children (free for under 5), €16 ($20.80) family. AE, MC, V. Apr–Sept daily 10am–5pm; Oct–Mar Mon–Fri 11am–4pm, Sat–Sun and bank holidays 10am–4pm. Bus: 50, 78A, or 123.

Dublin Writers Museum 🎨🎨 Housed in a stunning 18th-century Georgian mansion with splendid plasterwork and stained glass, the museum is itself an impressive reminder of the grandeur of the Irish literary tradition. A fine collection of personal manuscripts and mementos that belonged to Yeats, Joyce, Beckett, Behan, Shaw, Wilde, Swift, and Sheridan are among the items that celebrate the written word. There is also a children's literature room.

18–19 Parnell Sq. N., Dublin 1. © **01/872-2077**. www.writersmuseum.com. Admission €7 ($9.10) adults, €5.95 ($7.75) seniors and students, €4.40 ($5.72) children, €20 ($26) families. AE, DC, MC, V. Mon–Sat 10am–5pm (6pm June–Aug); Sun and holidays 11am–5pm. DART: Connolly Station. Bus: 11, 13, 16, 16A, 22, or 22A.

Kilmainham Gaol Historical Museum 🎨 This is a key sight for anyone interested in Ireland's struggle for independence from British rule. Within these walls political prisoners were incarcerated, tortured, and killed from 1796 until 1924, when

President Éamon de Valera left as its final prisoner. To walk along these corridors, through the exercise yard, or into the main compound is a moving experience that lingers hauntingly in the memory.

Kilmainham, Dublin 8. © 01/453-5984. www.heritageireland.ie. Guided tour €5.30 ($6.90) adults, €3.70 ($4.80) seniors, €2.10 ($2.75) children and students, €11.50 ($14.95) family. AE, MC, V. Apr–Sept daily 9:30am–4:45pm; Oct–Mar Mon–Fri 9:30am–4pm, Sun 10am–4:45pm. Bus: 51B, 78A, or 79 at O'Connell Bridge.

National Gallery of Ireland 𝒜𝒜𝒜

This museum houses Ireland's national art collection, as well as a superb European collection of art spanning the 14th to the 20th century. Every major European school of painting is represented, including fine selections by Italian Renaissance artists (especially Caravaggio's *The Taking of Christ*), French Impressionists, and Dutch 17th-century masters. In 2007 the gallery gained its first van Gogh, *Rooftops of Paris*. The highlight of the Irish collection is the room dedicated to the witty and shimmering works of Jack B. Yeats, brother of the poet W. B. Yeats. The museum has a fine gallery shop and an excellent self-service restaurant.

Merrion Sq. W., Dublin 2. © 01/661-5133. Fax 01/661-5372. www.nationalgallery.ie. Free admission. Mon–Sat 9:30am–5:30pm; Thurs 9:30am–8:30pm; Sun noon–5pm. Free guided tours Sat 3pm, Sun 2, 3, and 4pm. Free public lectures Sun 3pm, Tues 10:30am. Closed Good Friday and Dec. 24–26. DART: Pearse. Bus: 5, 6, 7, 7A, 8, 10, 44, 47, 47B, 48A, or 62.

National Museum of Ireland 𝒜𝒜𝒜

Established in 1890, this museum is a reflection of Ireland's heritage from 2000 B.C. to the present, with sections devoted to archaeology, decorative arts, and natural history. It is the home of many of the country's greatest historical finds, including the Treasury exhibit, which features the Ardagh Chalice, Tara Brooch, and Cross of Cong. Other highlights include the artifacts from the Wood Quay excavations of the Old Dublin Settlements, and an exhibition of Irish Bronze Age gold ornaments dating from 2200 to 700 B.C. *Note:* The National Museum encompasses Collins Barracks (see above).

Kildare St. and Merrion St., Dublin 2. © 01/677-7444. www.museum.ie. Free admission. Tours (hours vary) €2 ($2.60) adults, free for children. MC, V. Tues–Sat 10am–5pm; Sun 2–5pm. DART: Pearse. Bus: 7, 7A, 8, 10, 11, or 13.

Phoenix Park 𝒜𝒜

Just 2 miles (3.2km) west of the city center, Phoenix Park, the largest urban park in Europe, is the playground of Dublin. A network of roads and quiet pedestrian walkways traverses its 1,760 acres (704 hectares), which are informally landscaped with ornamental gardens and nature trails. Avenues of trees, including oak, beech, pine, chestnut, and lime, separate broad expanses of grassland. The homes of the Irish president and the U.S. ambassador are on the grounds, as is the Dublin Zoo. Livestock graze peacefully on pasturelands, deer roam the forested areas, and horses romp on polo fields. The **Phoenix Park Visitor Centre,** adjacent to Ashtown Castle, offers exhibitions and an audiovisual presentation on the park's history. The cafe/restaurant is open 10am to 5pm weekdays, 10am to 6pm weekends.

Phoenix Park, Dublin 8. © 01/677-0095. www.heritageireland.ie. Visitor Centre: Admission €2.90 ($3.80) adults, €2.10 ($2.75) seniors, €1.30 ($1.70) children and students, €7.40 ($9.60) families. Apr–Sept 10am–6pm (call for off-season hours). Bus: 37, 38, or 39.

St. Patrick's Cathedral 𝒜

It is said that St. Patrick baptized converts on this site, and consequently a church has stood here since A.D. 450, making it the oldest Christian site in Dublin. The present cathedral dates from 1190, but because of a fire and 14th-century rebuilding, not much of the original foundation remains. It is mainly early English in style, with a square medieval tower that houses the largest ringing peal bells in Ireland, and an 18th-century spire. The plaques, monuments, and sarcophagi throughout its 300-foot (90m) interior make it as fascinating a church as any in Europe. St. Patrick's is closely associated with Jonathan Swift, who was dean from 1713 to 1745 and whose tomb lies in the south aisle. Patrick's is the national cathedral of the Church of Ireland. Look for special, changing exhibits of an architectural, fine art, or religious nature.

21–50 Patrick's Close, Patrick St., Dublin 8. ✆ 01/475-4817. Fax 01/454-6374. www.stpatrickscathedral.ie. Admission €5 ($6.50) adults, €4 ($5.20) students and seniors, €15 ($19.50) family. MC, V. Mon–Fri 9am–6pm year-round; Mar–Oct Sat 9am–6pm, Nov–Feb Sat 9am–5pm; Sun Mar–Oct 9–11am, 12:45–3pm, 4:15–6pm, Sun Nov–Feb 10–11am, 12:45–3pm. Closed except for services Dec 24–26 and Jan 1. Bus: 65, 65B, 50, 50A, 54, 54A, 56A, or 77.

WHERE TO DINE

AYA ✿✿✿ JAPANESE   This fashionable eatery across the street from the Brown Thomas department store is very much a good-time destination for chic Dubliners with a yen for sushi. Classics on offer include tempura, *gyoza* (dumplings), *tatsuta* (deep-fried marinated meat or fish), and, of course, plenty of sushi, as well as yakitori, steaks, and noodle salads. Be prepared for the 12.5% service charge added to all tables and the €2 ($2.60) charge to sit at the conveyor belt.

49–52 Clarendon St., Dublin 2. ✆ 01/677-1544. www.aya.ie. Reservations recommended for dinner. Set lunch of starter, main course, and hot drink €19 ($24.70); main courses €17–€45 ($22.10–$58.50). AE, DC, MC, V. Mon–Sat 12:30–11pm; Sun 2–10pm. DART: Tara St. Bus: 16A, 19A, 22A, 55, or 83.

Beshoffs ✿ FISH & CHIPS   The Beshoff name has been synonymous with fresh fish in Dublin ever since Ivan Beshoff hopped over to Ireland from Russia in 1913 and started the fish business that developed into this fast-food cafe. Crisp french fries are served with a choice of fresh fish, from the original recipe of cod to classier variations using salmon, shark, prawns, and other local sea fare. The potatoes are grown on a farm in Tipperary and freshly cut each day. You can get a filling fish dinner and beverage for only €9.50 ($12.35).

6 Upper O'Connell St., Dublin 1. ✆ 01/872-4400. All items €3.25–€9.50 ($4.25–$10.40). MC, V. Mon–Sun 9:30am–9:30pm. DART: Tara St. Bus: Any city-center bus.

Epicurean Food Hall FOOD COURT   A small food hall with a market feel selling food from all over the globe. Favorites include a gourmet Italian deli **La Corte**; a kitsch mini sushi bar, **Sushi gogo;** and **Itsabagel,** with its delicious bagels, imported from H&H Bagels in New York City. Other options include crêpes and waffles from **Milis** and kabobs from the Turkish **Istanbul.** Seating is limited and gets crammed during midweek lunchtimes. Instead head here later in the afternoon.

Lower Liffey and Middle Abbey sts., Dublin 1. No phone. All items €2–€15 ($2.60–$19.50). Credit cards accepted depends on the vendor. Mon–Wed 8am–8pm; Thurs 8am–9pm; Fri–Sat 8am–7pm; Sun 10am–7pm. Bus: 70 or 80.

Halo ✿✿ IRISH/INTERNATIONAL   This is one of Dublin's hippest restaurants, sitting inside the Morrison Hotel on the banks of the Liffey. The superefficient and knowledgeable staff makes dining here a real pleasure, and the food is almost as good as the service, featuring mains such as oven-roasted guinea fowl supreme and pan-fried pike on a purple potato puree. But it was the soft, sweet, warm bread that really stole our hearts.

Morrison Hotel, Ormond Quay, Dublin 1. ✆ 01/887-2400. www.morrisonhotel.ie. Lunch and dinner €23–€27 ($30–$35.10). AE, DC, MC, V. Mon–Sun 6–10:30pm. Dart: Connolly. Bus: 70 or 80.

Irish Film Centre Cafe Bar ✿ IRISH/INTERNATIONAL   One of the most popular drinking spots in Temple Bar, the hip Cafe Bar (in the lobby of the city's coolest place to grab a movie) features an excellent, affordable menu that changes daily. The food is a real mix of nationalities and influences ranging from Irish to Asian with plenty of stops in between. Actual dishes can include anything from spicy meatballs on noodles to beef and Guinness hotpot. Head out the back to find the fab Gallery of Photography.

6 Eustace St., Temple Bar, Dublin 2. ✆ 01/677-8788. www.ifc.ie. Lunch and dinner €7–€10 ($9.10–$13). MC, V. Mon–Sun 10am–9pm. Bus: 21A, 78A, or 78B.

Mermaid Café ★★★ MODERN   The cooking here is downright terrific—think classic cooking with a fresh, eclectic twist. The smoked fish and mussel chowder, New England crab cakes and slow-roasted pork belly with parsnip mash are all flawlessly prepared. On top of all that, the wine list is one of the best in Ireland and the desserts—especially the pecan pie—are divine. Our favorite time to visit is Sunday brunch for sourdough pancakes, gravlax-topped bagels, and eggs benedict.

70 Dame St., Dublin 2. ✆ 01/670-8236. www.mermaid.ie. Reservations required. Dinner main courses €10–€29 ($13–$37.70). Sun brunch €11–€16 ($14.30–$20.80). MC, V. Mon–Sat 12:30–2:30pm and 6–11pm; Sun brunch 12:30–3:30pm and dinner 6–9pm. Bus: 50, 50A, 54, 56A, 77, 77A, or 77B.

Mimo Cafe ★★ (Value) MODERN CONTINENTAL   This chic cafe takes up the center of a whole floor in the Powerscourt Townhouse shopping mall. Don't be put off by the mall location, it's stylish and a surprisingly budget-minded place to stop for terrific salads, pasta dishes, and sandwiches. Try the warm goat's cheese crostini with caramelized figs, wild honey, and beetroot dressing. Or stop by earlier in the day for a late breakfast.

Powerscourt Townhouse, Dublin 2. ✆ 01/674-6712. Main courses €12–€13.50 ($15.60–$17.55). MC, V. Mon–Wed and Fri 10am–5:30pm; Thurs 10am–7:30pm; Sun noon–5:30pm. Bus: Any city-center bus.

Nude (Value) MODERN CAFE   Healthy food for when you're in a hurry and don't want to spend a fortune. Part of a small chain, this Nude is kitted out canteen style with long communal benches of light wood and dark metal. Your fellow diners are likely to be students and local office workers. The food—exhibiting both Asian and Mediterranean influences—consists of soups, salads, wraps, and paninis, served with an array of freshly squeezed juices.

21 Suffolk St., Dublin 2. ✆ 01/672-5577. www.nude.ie. Main courses €4.50–€6.15 ($5.85–$8). AE, MC, V. Mon–Wed 7:30am–9pm; Thurs 7:30am–10pm; Fri 7:30am–9pm; Sat 8am–9pm; Sun 10am–8pm. Bus: 50, 54, or 56.

Roly's Bistro ★★ IRISH/INTERNATIONAL   This two-story shop-front restaurant is a Dublin institution, with wonderful dishes that include roast filet of monk fish with green beans and chorizo, seared lamb's liver with crispy bacon and onion gravy, and a traditional lamb and vegetable pie. The main dining room, with a bright and airy decor and lots of windows, can be noisy when the house is full, but there's also a quiet enclave of booths laid out Orient Express–style for those who prefer a quiet tête-à-tête.

7 Ballsbridge Terrace, Dublin 4. ✆ 01/668-2611. www.rolysbistro.ie. Reservations required. Main courses €20–€29 ($26–$37.70). Set-price lunch €23 ($29.90). AE, DC, MC, V. Daily noon–3pm and 6–10pm. DART: Lansdowne Rd. Station. Bus: 5, 6, 7, 8, 18, or 45.

Yamamori Noodles ★★ JAPANESE   If you're skeptical about Japanese cuisine, Yamamori will make you an instant believer. In a pop, casual, and exuberant atmosphere, you may just be startled by how good the food is here. The splendid menu is a who's who of Japanese cuisine, and the prices range from budget to splurge. On a raw, drizzly Dublin day, the chili chicken ramen is a pot of bliss, while the Yamamori Yaki Soba offers—in a mound of wok-fried noodles—a well-rewarded treasure hunt for prawns, squid, chicken, and roast pork.

71–2 S. Great George's St., Dublin 2. (℗ 01/475-5001. www.yamamorinoodles.ie. Reservations only for parties of 4 or more persons. All dishes €2.50–€22 ($3.25–$28.60). AE, MC, V. Sun–Wed 12:15–11pm; Thurs–Sat 12:15–11:30pm. Bus: 50, 50A, 54, 56, or 77.

SHOPPING

Ireland is known the world over for its handmade products and fine craftsmanship, and Dublin sells the country's best wares. **Kilkenny Design Centre** (5-6 Nassau St.; (℗ 01/677-7066; www.kilkennyshop.com) is a one-stop shop for original Irish designs and quality products, including pottery, glass, candles, woolens, pipes, knitwear, jewelry, books, and prints.

There are many good shopping malls in Dublin, but our favorite is the **Powerscourt Townhouse Centre,** 59 S. William St. (℗ 01/671-7000; www.powerscourt centre.com), housed in a restored Georgian town house. This four-story complex consists of a central skylit courtyard and more than 60 boutiques, craft shops, art galleries, cafes, and restaurants. The wares include all kinds of crafts, antiques, paintings, prints, ceramics, leather goods, jewelry, clothing, hand-dipped chocolates, and farmhouse cheeses.

The Temple Bar area (**www.temple-bar.ie**) has three excellent weekend markets. **Temple Bar Book Market** is held every Saturday and Sunday from 10am to 5:30pm in Temple Bar Square and has enough of everything to make for some great browsing—old and new titles, classics and contemporary novels, science fiction and mysteries, serious biographies, and pulp fiction. **Temple Bar Food Market** is held every Saturday on Meeting House Square from 10am to 5:30pm and is a great picnic shopping spot. Everything here is organic, from fruits and veggies to a delicious selection of homemade cheeses, chutneys, breads, and jams. And then there's the **Cow's Lane Fashion and Design Market,** a fashionista's delight, held every Saturday on Cow's Lane, Old City Temple Bar from 10am to 5:30pm and packed with jewelry and clothes from up-and-coming Irish designers.

NIGHTLIFE

One general fact to keep in mind concerning Dublin's nightlife is that there are very few fixed points. Apart from a handful of established institutions, venues come and go, change character, open their doors to ballet one night and cabaret the next. *In Dublin* (**www.indublin.ie**) and *The Event Guide* (**www.eventguide.ie**) offer the most thorough and up-to-date listings. They can be found on almost any magazine stand.

The award-winning website of the *Irish Times* (**www.ireland.com**) offers a "what's on" daily guide to cinema, theater, music, and whatever else you're up for. The **Dublin Events Guide,** at **www.dublinevents.com**, also provides a comprehensive listing of the week's entertainment possibilities. *Time Out* now covers Dublin as well; check their website at **www.timeout.com/Dublin.**

PUBS The mainstay of Dublin social life is unquestionably the pub. In January 2004, Ireland banned smoking in most public places, a move smokers darkly predicted would kill pub life. It didn't. Below we list a few the city's most distinctive pubs.

For conversation and atmosphere, head to the **Brazen Head,** 20 Bridge St. (℗ 01/ 679-5186; www.brazenhead.com). This brass-filled, lantern-lit pub claims to be the city's oldest, and it might very well be, considering that it was originally opened as a coaching inn back in 1668 and occupies the site of an even earlier tavern dating from 1198. Nestled on the south bank of the River Liffey, it is at the end of a cobblestone courtyard with castellated ramparts and was once the meeting place of Irish freedom fighters such as Robert Emmet and Wolfe Tone. **The Long Hall,** 51 S. Great George's St. (© **01/475-1590**), is one of the city's most photographed pubs, with a beautiful Victorian decor of filigree-edged mirrors, polished dark woods, and traditional snugs (private rooms). The hand-carved bar is a wonder in itself. The choice of trendsetters is **The Market Bar,** Fade Street (off South Great George's St.), Dublin 2 (© **01/613-9094;** www.marketbar.ie). Opened in 2003, this huge old sausage factory is a big hit with the locals. There's no blaring music mix, which means the Irish gift of gab can be indulged without shouting, and the civilized covered courtyard has proven irresistible to outcast smokers.

If you like live Irish traditional music **O'Donoghue's,** 15 Merrion Row (© **01/660-7194;** www.odonoghues.ie), tucked between St. Stephen's Green and Merrion Street, is widely celebrated as the granddaddy of traditional music pubs. A spontaneous session is likely to erupt at almost any time of the day or night. **Oliver St. John Gogarty,** 58–59 Fleet St. (© **01/671-1822;** www.gogartys.ie), in the heart of Temple Bar, has an inviting and quirky old-world atmosphere, and offers hostel quarters on the upper floors, where you would need to be stone deaf, very drunk, or otherwise noise-resistant to fall asleep. There are traditional music sessions every day from 3pm until 2:30am, and it serves oysters and mussels to go with the Guinness.

THEATER   Dublin has a venerable and vital theatrical tradition, which has lately seen a renaissance erupting (along with gentrification and cost-of-living expenses). The new playwrights must wrestle with the titanic Irish ghosts of G. B. Shaw, Beckett, W. B. Yeats, J. M. Synge, Sean O'Casey, and Oscar Wilde, but they manage to hold their own. The online booking site Ticketmaster (**www.ticketmaster.ie**) is an excellent place to get a quick look at what's playing where and for buying tickets.

The **Abbey Theatre,** 26 Lower Abbey St. (© **01/878-7222;** www.abbeytheatre.ie), has been the national theater of Ireland since 1904. The original theater, destroyed by fire in 1951, was replaced in 1966 by the current uninspired 600-seat house. The box office is open Monday to Saturday 10:30am to 7pm; shows run Monday to Saturday at 8pm, and also at 2:30pm on Saturday. Tickets cost €14 to €30 ($18.20–$39). There are senior, student, and children's discounts available Monday to Thursday evening and for the Saturday matinee.

Just north of O'Connell Street off Parnell Square, the restored 370-seat **Gate Theatre,** 1 Cavendish Row (© **01/874-4045;** www.gate-theatre.ie), was founded in 1928 to provide a venue for a broad range of plays. That policy prevails today, with a program that includes a blend of modern works and the classics. The box office is open Monday to Saturday 10am to 7:30pm; shows run Monday to Thursday at 8pm. Tickets cost €26 to €28 ($33.80–$36.40) or €20 ($26) for previews and matinees.

11

Greece

Greece may be best known for its islands, but there are ample attractions on its rail-served mainland (albeit with a few asphalt diversions) to make a superb vacation. Greek train journeys also offer surprisingly diverse landscapes, whether traveling along the coast or through mountains and valleys and across quaint stone bridges.

Road networks were heavily promoted over the country's iron track (laid down from the late 1800s until about 1910) for a very long time, but rail travel is once again gaining popularity. In Athens, a 2004 tram network links the city center to the south coast, and the underground metro grid continues to be extended to outer suburbs, easing transport and road congestion.

With the 2004 Olympics as the impetus, much of the rail network and stations around Greece also received upgrades; main routes have been upgraded so that they are fast, convenient, and comfortable, and line improvements and extensions are planned or in progress.

The Hellenic Railway Organization (OSE) has a bilingual website for schedule information (but not always up-to-date on routes currently in service), augmented by a help line with English-speaking operators to assist travelers. But not all is perfect in Greece for rail travelers and visitors should take that into account. You can only speak to operators when you're inside the country. Furthermore, there is no system to reserve seats or sleepers directly with OSE online or if you are outside the country (even through Rail Europe), although you can try and reserve through a hotel or OSE-affiliated travel agency. Tickets must be paid within 48 hours of departure; otherwise your reservation will be canceled. It's not exactly tourist-friendly for a European Union country that relies on tourism for some 15% of its GDP. (For example, I could book a sleeper long-distance to Victoria Falls in Zimbabwe 8 years ago.)

Note: Some railroad projects are still in progress and new routes are announced seasonally; avoid disappointment by confirming routes before setting off.

HIGHLIGHTS OF GREECE

If you're flying into Greece, your first stop will likely be **Athens,** the capital and a major airport hub. It is home to about half of the country's 11 million people, the nation's total more than doubling in summer with tourists. Rail travelers may be limited to the mainland, but taking a bus, boat, or plane to other destinations is of course an option (and sometimes a necessity) once inside the country. **Eurail Global Pass** holders also receive discounts on domestic ferries, tours and hotels when the terra firma iron grid is not enough.

Domestic rail travel may offer spectacular sightseeing, but do note that there are places here you just cannot reach by train. Excursions or side trips are therefore noted that may require bus or taxi transport, at least for part of the journey.

Greece

Athens is the center of the country's north-south railway axis. The city's underground **metro** lines, some with antiquities on display at the stations, have made it easy to explore the city's ancient glory on modern public transport. A quick ride will take you near the **Acropolis** hill and the renowned monuments upon it, including its crown jewel, the 2,500-year-old **Parthenon.** In the shadow of the ancient hill, the touristy **Plaka** and **Monastiraki** districts provide ample opportunities to shop, eat, and relax amid scattered antiquities. A pedestrian walkway loops around the Acropolis past **Thissio,** with arguably one of the best views in the world, and links many of the sites, including classical Athens's cemetery, **Kerameikos,** and the trendy/sophisticated **Gazi** district across the street (Pireos). In the summer, enjoy a concert or theatrical performance at the **Herodion Atticus Theater** built around A.D. 160 and located below the Acropolis, or head to the **Technopolis** in Gazi, the converted old gasworks opposite Kerameikos, for more contemporary happenings and exhibits.

For a mini-escape, take the **tram** to Athens's south coast. With more than two dozen stops along the seafront, including at organized (pay) **beaches,** the tram is the best mode of transport to cruise for a swim or coffee by the sea.

When you've had enough of the city buzz and chaos, it's time to head to the train station.

Moments   Festivals & Special Events

Carnival (Karnavali, Apokri-es) is celebrated nationwide with costume parades, drinking, dancing, and a general loosening of inhibitions, depending on the locale. The city of Patras's parade is the biggest, while other towns and villages dust off their own unique customs, including the use of animal masks and skins in Macedonian celebrations, a phallic festival in Tyrnavos, Thessaly, on the first day of Lent, and fire-walking on hot coals in Thrace—a throwback to Dionysian worship, but nowadays done in the name of saints Constantine and Helen on May 21. People bop each other with plastic bats in Athens's Plaka. Celebrations last the 3 weeks preceding Lent (Orthodox).

Independence Day and the **Feast of the Annunciation** are celebrated on the same day, March 25, the former with military parades, especially in Athens. For other festivals around the country, look up **www.greecetravel.com/holidays**.

From May to October, the **Athens Epidaurus Festival** features superb domestic and international productions of ancient drama, opera, orchestra performances, ballet, modern dance, and popular entertainers in the ancient **Herodion Atticus Theater** (© **210-324-2121** or 210/323-2771) at the foot of the Acropolis, events at other venues around town, and in the ancient **Epidaurus theater** (© **27530/22-026**, 27530/22-666, or 27530/23-009). Contact the **Athens Epidaurus Festival's central box office**, Panepistimiou 39 (sign-posted El. Venizelou) in the arcade; © **210/327-2000; www.greekfestival.gr**).

Traveling southwest, enjoy a bird's-eye-view of the impressive **Corinth Canal** as you head toward **Corinth** to visit the ancient sites; the ancient theater at **Epidaurus** can be experienced with a theatrical performance by night or as an archaeological site by day, perhaps together with **Mycenae** as an excursion from Athens.

If natural scenery is more your thing, at **Diakofto,** between the port city of Patras and Athens, you can have a swim and take one of the most scenic train rides in Greece on the rack-and-pinion railroad up the mountain to **Kalavryta,** a wintertime ski destination.

The port town of **Patras** will likely be the starting point of your trip if you come to Greece via ferry from Italy. You can head straight to Athens and beyond, or go west or south to the **beaches** along the Peloponnesian coast, taking a detour at Pyrgos to **Ancient Olympia,** birthplace of the Olympic Games. The archaeological site—where the Olympic flame is lit and the ancient Olympics were held—and the superb archaeological museum with its unique Olympics-related contents, are some of Greece's prime attractions.

If you take the main line north from Athens you'll reach Greece's second largest city, **Thessaloniki,** which is also accessible by plane and ferry, and serves as a rail base for east-west trips in northern Greece as well as points north and east out of the country.

Southwest of Thessaloniki, **Mount Olympus,** where Zeus and the other mythological gods dwelled, can prove a challenge to hikers and a rewarding escape for nature lovers, with **beaches** located less than 4 miles away from the mountain town of **Litohoro** "base camp" and other interesting sites nearby, such as **Ancient Dion, Pella,** and **Vergina.** Or travel east from Thessaloniki through the breathtaking **Nestos river valley,** which looks even better when hiked.

1 Essentials

GETTING THERE

BY PLANE   **Athens International Airport Eleftherios Venizelos** (© **210/353-0000;** www.aia.gr), 17 miles (27km) east of Athens at Spata. It is a destination airport for all major European airlines. **Delta Air Lines** (www.delta.com), and Greece's **Olympic Airlines** (www.olympicairlines.com) operate direct flights from New York's JFK, and **Continental** (www.continental.com) flies from Newark. Delta flies nonstop from Atlanta, while **US Airways** (www.usairways.com) flies direct from Philadelphia during the summer. All other European airlines departing the United States make a stop before arriving in Athens, usually at their national hub. Canada's **Air Transat** (www.airtransat.ca) and Olympic operate nonstop flights from Toronto and Montreal.

   Makedonia Airport (© **2310/473-212**), 10 miles (16km) from the northern port city of Thessaloniki, has scheduled and chartered flights to Thessaloniki from numerous European cities.

BY TRAIN   Greece is connected to the Balkans, Eastern Europe, and Turkey by rail; however, the trip can be a long and difficult adventure, where safety precautions (clip your bag to the rack and so on) may also be imperative. It *might* be shorter than the traditional route of taking the ferry from Italy, but it is still off the beaten path, and you may face long, boring border delays. Sleepers or couchettes are recommended for long journeys and overnights, and these are available for all international journeys, though if you're searching the **OSE** website (**www.ose.gr**), they won't show up. You're better off consulting the English-language page of the German website **Die Bahn** (**http://reiseauskunft.bahn.de**), which also shows which trains have sleepers—imperative for journeys that take 3 days or so. You can reserve up to a month in advance, but you must buy your ticket at a domestic station or OSE-affiliated travel agency, or get someone in the country to do it for you, no less than 48 hours in advance of your journey.

   Two trains a day leave Thessaloniki for Skopje, Macedonia, with one continuing on to Zagreb, Croatia, and Ljubljana, Slovenia; the other going on to Belgrade and Serbia. There are also trains to Prague, Czech Republic, and Bratislava, Slovakia. Russia also has a train that goes back and forth from Moscow to Thessaloniki in summer via Kiev and Ukraine. Check if the route is in service before your journey.

   A train that leaves Thessaloniki daily at midnight goes to Sofia, Bulgaria, which continues on to Bucharest, Romania, and Budapest, Hungary. Bring food and water with you, as these may not be offered until you reach Budapest. Two trains a day leave from Thessaloniki to Istanbul, Turkey, the day one with seats, the night one with beds. *Warning:* Some Balkan cities on the OSE website are spelled in their native language (Belgrade is Beograd, Sofia is Sofija, and so forth), if you do a schedule search. Athens is Athina.

   Note: Railpasses are not accepted in Turkey or Russia. For more information on rail travel in Eastern Europe and Turkey, see the appendix.

BY BOAT   Most rail travelers will reach Greece not by train but via ferry from Italy. Boats from Ancona, Bari, Brindisi, and Venice arrive daily to the ports of Patras and Igoumenitsa. Trip times vary depending on the ferry you take and your departure and arrival points. Eurail passholders should consult **www.raileurope.com** or their pass booklets for which operators honor their passes that year; note that you'll have to pay port tax, fuel fees, and a seasonal surcharge (16€–26€/$21–$34) even if you do have a pass.

Trains from Patras will take you east and south around the Peloponnese as far as Kalamata, or, with a change at Kiato, to Athens (3½hr.; 5.30€/$6.70) to continue your rail journey north from there. There is no direct rail service out of Igoumenitsa on the mainland west coast, but you can take an intercity public bus (KTEL) to the train station at Kalambaka (Meteora) for 17.70€ ($23); at press time, only one bus a week, on Sunday at 12:30pm, makes the 4-hour trip from the Igoumenitsa bus station (© **26650/22-309**) to Kalambaka. Avoid this route in winter as bad weather may close roads.

GREECE BY RAIL

If your rail journey is limited to the Greek mainland, buying point-to-point tickets or an in-country pass instead of an international pass might be cheaper, as train travel in Greece is inexpensive. For information on the **Eurail Global Pass, Eurail Global Pass Flexi, Eurail Select Pass,** and **Eurail Saver,** see chapter 2.

Eurail Greece Pass   This pass provides 3 to 10 days of nonconsecutive, first-class travel in Greece. Prices start at $132 for adults.

Eurail Greece-Italy Pass   Get 4 days of nonconsecutive, first- or second-class travel in Greece and Italy within 2 months. Prices start at $274 for adults.

Balkan Flexipass   Rail Europe no longer sells a Greek Flexipass Rail 'n Fly pass, but it has added some bonus options to the Balkan Flexipass to make up for the former's cancellation. A 5-day pass in first class costs $240 for adults, $120 for kids; extra days are available. In addition to discounts on ferry trips between Greece and Italy, day cruises, and other tours, passholders also get discounted airfares between Athens and many of the Greek islands. One-way flights run about 62.40€ ($81.10) for adults, 31.20€ ($40.55) for kids ages 4 to 12; note that you should always check with other airfare discounters to compare flight prices before going this route. Flight arrangements must be made with **Ionian Travel,** Pireos 4, 1st floor, Omonia Square, Athens (© **210/523-4774**), and cannot be exchanged at the airport. Ionian can also purchase point-to-point train tickets for you, if you want to reserve while out of the country. Other OSE-affiliated travel agents may also oblige. For more on this pass, see p. 53.

All of the above passes should be purchased before departing for your trip; you can buy them from **Rail Europe** (© **877/272-RAIL** [7245] in North America; www.rail europe.com).

Domestic **discount railpasses** can also be purchased through OSE once you are in Greece. If you buy six journeys on InterCity trains, you get one bonus trip. There are also family discount cards; cards for people over 60; and for multiple journeys used within 10, 20, or 30 days anywhere in Greece, but only in second class on regional trains. The **Multiple Journey Card** (*Karta Polaplon Taxidion* or *Karta Sindromis*) for one person for 10 days costs 48.10€ ($62.50); a card for two people costs 79.80€ ($104). A 20-day card for one person costs 72.20€ ($93.90), and 30-day card costs 96.30€ ($125.20). There are no discount cards for those under 26, but you get a discount if you show ID.

FOREIGN TRAIN TERMS

A lot of people can speak or understand English in Greece, especially in the main cities, which is a major bonus for travelers. All signs on the rail network are in both Greek and English, but, with the exception of the Athens metro system and airports, announcements—usually inaudible anyway—are only in Greek. Most people are happy to assist if asked (and even if not asked), as trying to communicate by phone to local stations might be a challenge. Contact the railway's customer service (© 1110) or a tourist information office, and get them to find out information for you. Schedules are posted at stations, while railway staff will certainly understand "ticket," "information," "how much," and the usual (polite) sign language for "how many." *Note:* What you might want to ask, however, is if there is a toilet on the train (*E*-hi toe *tre*-no tooa-*le*-ta?). As with the long-distance buses, often there are not, especially on the newer trains, such as the suburban to Corinth.

PRACTICAL TRAIN INFORMATION

There are different types of trains in Greece, notably the fast and modern **InterCity (IC)** and **InterCity Express (ICE)** trains connecting the country's urban centers, and

---

OSE Railway-Affiliated Travel Agencies

Apart from the train stations and OSE ticket offices, you can buy rail tickets from OSE-affiliated travel agents; note that not all agencies sell all types of tickets. Here's a selection of agencies and the ticket types they sell.

Athens

- **Ionian,** Pireos 4, Omonia (© 210/523-4774). Select ticket types.
- **Meliton,** Apollonos 23B, Syntagma (© 210/324-7235-7). All ticket types.
- **Gonidis,** Panepistimiou (El. Venizelou) 57, Omonia (© 210/331-0661). InterCity only.
- **Dimidis,** Kifissias 68, Ambelokipi (© 210/692-7240). All ticket types.
- **Meteor,** Akadimias 43, University (© 210/362-9521). Domestic and international tickets.
- **Zorpidis,** Panepistimiou (El. Venizelou) 25-29, University (© 210/321-5026). InterCity and domestic only.

Piraeus

- **Karapannidis,** Akti Miaouli 11 (© 210/422-1810-1). All ticket types.

Thessaloniki

- **Loukidis,** Aristotelous 22 (© 2310/277-802; www.loukidis.gr); Tsimiski 89 (© 2310/253-232). All ticket types.
- **Zorpidis,** Egnatia 76 (© 2310/244-400); Aristotelous 27 (© 2310/282-600). Athens-Thessaloniki InterCity tickets only.

Greek Train Station Phone Numbers

Information and customer service	✆ 1110
Athens Larissa/Larissis Station	✆ 210/529-8829
New Corinth	✆ 27410/22-522
Diakofto	✆ 26910/43-206
Isthmus	✆ 27410/49-070
Kalavryta	✆ 26920/22-245
Olympia	✆ 26240/22-677
Patras	✆ 2610/639-102
Pyrgos	✆ 26210/22-525
Thessaloniki	✆ 2310/599-049
Toxotes (Nestos)	✆ 25410/93-290
Xanthi	✆ 25410/22-581

Regional (R) trains that serve local and regional routes. There is also a .75m-gauge **rack-and-pinion railway** in the Peloponnese, and two .60m-gauge **steam train** routes in the Pelion peninsula, as well as the **suburban Proastiakos** express train that plies routes from the airport to Piraeus, Athens and Corinth, with plans to reach Thebes (Thiva) and Chalkis (Halkida), Evia, as well as the ports of Rafina and Lavrio in Attica.

The **Hellenic Railway Organization** (**OSE; www.ose.gr**) publishes a Greek and English pamphlet with timetables, available at train stations and OSE offices. Note that some routes in the pamphlet may not be in operation due to renovation work in progress.

Route information, prices, and so on can be obtained in English by dialing ✆ **1110** from any phone in Greece. Operators at 1110 can also take reservations for domestic trains up to a month in advance. You need to have your passport or ID handy, and you must buy the ticket up to 48 hours before departure.

In Athens, tickets can be purchased at all stations, or the two Hellenic Railways Organization ticket offices: Karolou 1, open Monday to Friday 8am to 3pm; and Sina 6 (international travel ✆ **210/362-7947;** domestic travel ✆ **1110,** or **210/362-1039** if calling from abroad), open Monday to Saturday 8am to 3:30pm. You can also buy tickets from OSE-affiliated travel agencies (see "OSE Railway-Affiliated Travel Agencies," above).

Tickets can also be purchased and received (in Athens only) through OSE's **Courier service** by calling ✆ **1110.** Press #5 to be connected to the service. It operates from 8am to 2:30pm Monday through Saturday. Delivery is same-day or next working day; the tickets, plus a small fee, can be paid cash-on-delivery or by credit card. The service is for InterCity and InterCity Express trains, as well as the popular Diakofto–Kalavryta rack-rail line.

Rail tickets must be purchased before boarding. Once a train has left a station, inspectors hole-punch to validate tickets. If you don't have one, the inspector will sell you a ticket and charge you a fine, ranging from 50% of the ticket's cost for long-distance trips, to 20 times as much for regional travel. If you're sure of your schedule, opt for a round-trip ticket and save 20% over the cost of two one-ways.

Even though a train might have a sign saying where it's headed, ask anyway to double-check. Announcements (in Greek) sometimes overrule the destination sign, meaning a train might detour, or terminate before or after the posted destination. Trains also run pretty much on schedule, so if there are two trains at the station leaving a few minutes apart, it is easy to get on the wrong one.

Your ticket will indicate whether you have a first- or second-class seat, the car number your seat is in (in other words, 1, 2, 3, and so on, usually indicated on each train car by a small square plate placed next to the door) and your actual seat number. In major cities, the announcement before the train arrives includes the order of the cars. Pay attention or ask for assistance because cars don't always come in numerical order. All OSE trains have reserved seats, except for two trains on the Athens–Thessaloniki route that have standing-room tickets if seats are sold out.

RESERVATIONS   The Greek railway company, OSE, is one of the few railways that doesn't offer the option of making out-of-country train reservations, except for the few international lines that travel to the country, although you can buy most tickets up to a month in advance from either Rail Europe or the Hellenic Railways offices in Athens. Reserved tickets must be purchased no less than 48 hours in advance. An OSE-affiliated travel agent might be able to help you purchase a ticket before your arrival.

SERVICES & AMENITIES   Before the rail system was upgraded, first-class travel in Greece was worth the extra cost, but second-class seating is now equally comfortable, at least on routes with new cars. You can call ✆ **1110** for information on which lines have new "wagons," as train cars are called here in English. Overhead rails for duffle bags and small suitcases are available; larger baggage should be checked.

There are three sleeper services on the Athens–Thessaloniki route, prices ranging from 54€ ($70.20) in a single compartment to 24€ ($31.20) in a six-bed. The Thessaloniki–Ormenio line that crosses into Bulgaria (Plovdiv-bound) has two trains with couchettes, and the night train to Turkey has sleepers. A single sleeper compartment is an additional 31.40€ ($40.80), a double is 19.80€ ($25.75) per person, and a three-bed is an extra 17.30€ ($22.50). Four-bed and six-bed couchettes cost 12.70€ ($16.50) and 8.60€ ($11.20) per person respectively.

InterCity trains have a food stand run by one of the country's top snack shops or attendants selling sandwiches, chips, and refreshments. Some InterCity trains offer restaurant coaches with fairly good and inexpensive food.

Trains & Travel Times in Greece

From	To	Type of Train	# of Trains	Frequency	Travel Time
Athens	Corinth	Suburban	18	daily	1 hr., 20 min.
Athens	Kiato	Suburban	18	daily	1 hr., 30 min.
Athens	Thessaloniki	ICE/IC	6	daily	4 hr., 15 min.–5 hr.
Kiato	Diakofto	IC/R	8	daily	50 min.–1 hr.
Kiato	Patras	IC	4	daily	1 hr., 40 min.
Patras	Olympia	IC	4	daily	Approx. 2 hr.
Thessaloniki	Katerini	IC	13	daily	40 min.
Thessaloniki	Xanthi	IC	8	daily	3 hr., 35 min.

IC = InterCity; ICE = InterCity Express, R = Regional. Routes with IC service listed may offer additional regional service.

FAST FACTS: **Greece**

Area Codes The international country code for Greece is **30**. To call Greece from abroad, dial the international access code from your base country plus 30, followed by the Greek city code, then the number. Domestically, ten digits are needed. All area codes begin with "2" and most end with "0":

Athens/Piraeus 210, 211; **Diakofto** 26910; **Corinth/Isthmus** 27410; **Kalambaka** 24320; **Kalavryta** 26920; **Katerini/Litohoro** 23520; **Olympia** 26240; **Patras** 2610; **Pyrgos** 26210; **Thessaloniki** 2310; **Toxotes** 25410; **Volos** 24210; **Xanthi** 25410.

Business Hours Work hours in Greece differ by season, day of the week, and type of business. Banks are generally open Monday to Thursday 8am to 2:30pm and Friday 8am to 2pm. Shops are generally open Monday, Wednesday, and Saturday from 8:30am to 2pm; Tuesday, Thursday, and Friday from 8:30am to 2pm and again from 5:30 to 8:30pm. Chain stores, supermarkets, and department stores remain open through the midday siesta Mondays through Saturdays. In tourist areas, stores are generally open longer, as well as on Sundays, when other shops are closed.

Climate The weather in Greece is generally mild in the winter and hot in the summer. Rain is more frequent in western and northern Greece in the winter months, but storms and torrential rains all over the country can occur surprisingly quickly, and sometimes signal a change of season/mean temperature. In the mountainous part of the country, which covers most of the mainland, snowfall can disrupt road and rail travel, though this is infrequent. Spring and fall are the best times to visit Greece for sightseeing: Sites and museums are not crowded, and the temperatures are pleasant for strolling. Prices for travel and accommodations are also lower, compared to the peak summer season from mid-June to mid-September. If you're looking to beat the heat at the beach, head to Greece from mid-June to September.

Documents Required A valid passport is required for entry to Greece. No visa is needed for most foreigners, including North Americans who stay less than 3 months; authorization must be obtained for longer stays. Contact the **Immigration division** (© 210/340-5969). A passport or other form of identification may be required when registering in a hotel.

Electricity Electric current in Greece is 220 volts AC, alternating at 50 cycles. Appliances from North America that are not dual voltage will require a transformer and a round two-prong adapter plug.

Embassies/Consulates The embassies for the U.S. and Canada are in Athens: **United States,** Vas. Sofias 91 (© 210/721-2951); **Canada,** Ioannou Gennadiou 4 (© 210/727-3400).

Health & Safety Make sure to bring (or buy here) a hat and sunscreen to protect yourself from the much-worshipped Greek sun. Aside from that, there are no specific health concerns you need to worry about in Greece. Should you get sick, embassies can provide information on English-speaking physicians. Except for emergencies, hospital admittance is possible through a doctor. Major hospitals rotate emergency duty daily; call © **1434** to hear recorded information in Greek on whose turn it is, © **112** for the multilingual European Union emergency hot line, or consult the English edition of the *Kathimerini* daily newspaper, distributed with the *International Herald Tribune,* sold wherever you see the foreign press (kiosks, outlets, and so on), and online at **www.ekathimerini. com**. Pharmacies, identified by green or sometimes red crosses, are usually open 8am to 2pm on weekdays but reopen on Tuesdays, Thursdays, and Fridays from 5 to 8:30pm. Most neighborhoods also have a pharmacy on emergency duty that's open after hours and on weekends. A list (in Greek) is posted in pharmacy windows, and in the *Kathimerini* English edition and its website.

While Greece is considered to be a safe country, reports of pickpocketing and purse snatching, mostly in Athens, have increased. Walk against the traffic to avoid motorcycle-riding bag-grabbers. Don't accept offers of possibly drugged food or water from strangers at tourist sites, and avoid touts that take lone males to hostess bars, or fast friends who promise hotel-room parties. You will pay exorbitant bills if you succumb.

Holidays Greece celebrates the following national holidays: **New Year's Day,** January 1; **Epiphany** (Baptism of Christ), January 6; **Clean Monday** *(Kathari Deftera)* or Ash Monday, first day of Lent; **Independence Day,** March 25; **Good Friday** to **Easter** (Orthodox calendar), including Easter Monday; **May Day** (Labor Day), May 1; **Whit Monday** *(Agiou Pnevmatos),* day after Pentecost, the 7th Sunday after Easter; **Assumption of the Virgin,** August 15; *Ochi* **Day,** October 28; **Christmas and the following day,** December 25 and 26.

Legal Aid Foreigners should contact their embassies or consulates for legal assistance while in Greece.

Mail Post offices (ELTA) are distinctively blue and yellow. Stamps are available at many kiosks around Greece as well as at shops that sell postcards. An overseas postcard stamp costs .65€ (85¢). In Athens the main **post offices** are at Aeolou 100, just southeast of Omonia Square; at Syntagma Square at Mitropoleos Street; and farther down at Mitropoleos 60, where you can also send parcels. They're open Monday to Friday 7:30am to 8pm, and Saturday 7:30am to 2pm, except the parcel post office, which is only open Monday to Friday. The Syntagma post office is also open Sunday 9am to 1:30pm. All other post offices close at 2pm Monday through Friday and do not open on weekends.

Police & Emergencies For emergencies throughout Greece dial ✆ **100** for **police** assistance and ✆ **171** for the **Tourist Police.** Dial ✆ **199** to report a **fire** and ✆ **166** for an **ambulance.** The EU-wide ✆ **112** is a multilingual service line for all kinds of emergencies.

Telephone The country code for Greece is **30.** All mobile phone numbers start with **69.** All fixed-line numbers comprise 10 digits with an area code that begins with **2** and usually ends with **0** before the number (see "Area Codes," above).

Most public phones only accept phone cards, which are available at kiosks, a few of which still have metered phones. **Telecards** come in denominations from 3€ ($3.90) to 18€ ($23.40). Local calls cost .03€ (4¢) per minute. International rates vary, with calls to the U.S., Canada, and Australia (Zone I) costing .29€ (38¢) per minute.

It's better to use prepaid **calling cards** for your international calls. These are available at kiosks, post offices, OTEshop (phone company) outlets, and money exchange bureaus, the latter of which can also tell you what card gives the best rate for the country you want to call. Denominations are usually 5€ ($6.50), 10€ ($13), and 20€ ($26). For **international phone assistance**, dial ⓒ **139.**

Tipping Restaurants include a service charge in the bill, but many add a 10% tip. Hotel chambermaids should get at least 1€ ($1.30) per day and bellhops 1€ to 2€ ($1.30–$2.60), depending on the service. Most Greeks don't give a percentage tip to taxi drivers but instead round up the fare to the nearest euro.

2 Athens

Claiming the world's first democracy title, Athens (*Attica/Attiki* prefecture) was little more than a village when modern Greece was founded in the 1820s following 400 years of Ottoman rule. The city has since sprawled, ballooning to some four million inhabitants—surpassing Rome—after accommodating a mass influx from Asia Minor in the 1920s; people from the countryside as a result of the 1944–49 civil war, which in turn caused the current concrete carpet of apartment blocks; and most recently, migrant workers from Eastern Europe, the Middle East, and Africa.

The "Big Village's" latest physical transformation is the result of the 2004 Summer Olympics. Neoclassical buildings were restored, museums revamped, more green and pedestrian zones were carved out, along with modern highways, ring roads, and public transport. Light industry was moved out and smoke-belching cars and buses scrapped, all helping to dissipate the notorious pollution *(nefos)* cloud hanging over the Athens basin. While it may never be rid of the chaos, traffic jams, and parking problems, historic Athens has once more become a desired city destination, as the dearth of prime-locale hotel rooms, creeping ever further into the shoulder seasons, attests. As one stunned British visitor (who'd read numerous bad reviews of the city for years) said in 2006, "Why, I had no idea it was so beautiful!"

STATION INFORMATION
GETTING FROM THE AIRPORT TO THE TRAIN STATION
Two rail options are available to get you from **Athens International Airport Eleftherios Venizelos** (ⓒ **210/353-0000;** www.aia.gr) and on your journey: the **suburban railway** (Proastiakos; ⓒ **210/527-2000;** www.proastiakos.gr) takes you direct to Corinth's New Corinth station (1½ hr.); to the main Larissis/Larissa Station in Athens (40 min.); or to the port of Piraeus (1 hr.). Or you can take the **metro** (ⓒ **210/519-4012;** www.ametro.gr) straight into the center of Athens (45 min.). Take care, as both trains share a platform; tickets for either (but bought at separate windows) are 6€ ($7.80), and the metro journey is not covered by a railpass. The metro does have a 10€ ($13) ticket for two people, and a 15€ ($19.50) ticket for three. Neither the suburban rail nor the metro operate on a 24-hour basis: Lines run from about 6am to 11pm. You can check schedules with the suburban rail or metro before your trip.

If you opt to take a **taxi** into town or to the main train station, the ride will cost you around 30€ ($39), or 40€ ($52) if it's between midnight and 5am; trip time is 30 minutes to an hour, depending on traffic. That unscrupulous cab drivers try to overcharge tourists is no secret, and many succeed. Get an estimate before getting in. If a driver seems annoyed or is evasive, move on to the next one in the queue. When you do get in, the meter should be turned on and set to tariff 1 (a "1" appears); it should be set on 2 only between midnight and 5am, or if you take a taxi outside the city limits, but this does *not* include the airport. There is no extra charge *to* the train or bus stations, only *from* them (.90€/$1.15). Also note that the following rate add-ons are standard when traveling to and from the airport: a 3.20€ ($4.15) airport surcharge, highway tolls between the airport and the city (currently 2.70€/$3.50), and a .35€ (45¢) charge for each piece of luggage weighing over 22 lb. (10 kilos).

Public bus service from the airport to the city center (no. X95) is available on a 24-hour basis every 10 to 30 minutes, depending on the time of day for 3.20€ ($4.15). Trip time is about an hour. Tickets can be purchased from the driver or at the booth at the bus stop just outside airport arrivals. To go direct to the train station from the airport by bus, take the X95 to its final stop at Syntagma Square, and from there walk across the street and take the metro to Larissa Station, the fourth stop on the red line toward Aghios Antonios, or else cross Amalias Avenue in front of Parliament to catch trolley bus no. 1 to Larissa Station. Get bus tickets from kiosks or booths at the bus stop. Bus tickets cost .50€ (65¢); metro tickets cost .80€ ($1) and can be purchased at the station. Make sure to validate your ticket before reaching the platform. A validated metro ticket from the airport is good for 90 minutes for trips throughout the public transportation network (bus, trolley, all lines of the metro, tram, and suburban railway) within city limits. Validate the reverse side of the ticket on the next mode of transport before the ticket expires.

INSIDE THE STATION

Larissa Station *(Stathmos Larissis),* which shares its name with the metro station in front of it, is the hub for northern Greece rail lines as well as the Peloponnese in the south. A luggage storage office, restaurant, and platform cantina are pretty much all the facilities this relatively small station has to offer, as well as a train information desk. There is no currency exchange, visitor information, or hotel reservation desk.

Warning: Buying tickets just before departure is risky, as you may find the train you want is already full. Same-day journey tickets are sold from windows in the main entrance; for advance/reserved tickets, you must go next door in the same building by going back outside, towards the restaurant and kiosk. Or call © **1110** to make reservations, remembering to pick up your tickets 48 hours before you travel.

INFORMATION ELSEWHERE IN THE CITY

For train-related info, see "Practical Train Information," above. Otherwise, for a country so dependent on tourism, visitor information is woefully lacking, often to the point of contempt, whether you're searching for assistance online, in the main cities, or even at tourist destinations.

A desk of the **Greek National Tourism Organization** (**GNTO,** also known by its Greek initials, EOT) at the arrivals terminal of **Athens International Airport** (© **210/ 353-0445**), is open from 9am to 7pm on weekdays; 10am to 4pm on weekends in high season. The private hotel and tour booking agencies alongside it are arguably more helpful, and are open longer.

There is a GNTO outlet at Amalias 26 (© **210/331-0392;** www.gnto.gr), just a few minutes' walk from Syntagma Square. It's open Monday through Friday from 9am to 7pm and weekends 10am to 4pm. Its staff can provide maps, transportation schedules, and glossy booklets on Athens as well as more general information on other parts of Greece, although that information may not always be up-to-date. For more detailed

Athens

To Larissis Station

METAXOURGIO

Maizonos
Anexartisias
Square
VATHI

Chiou
Akominatou
Marni
Karolou
Veranzerou
Satovriandou
Ayiou
Konstantinou
Zinonos

Tritis Septembriou
Patission
Solomou
Kapodistriou

Aiolou
Akadimias

Omonia
Square

OMONIA

Lenorman
Kolokynthous
Leonidou
Kolonou
Deligiorgi
Myllerou
Keramikou
Ayisilaou
P. Tsaldari

Menandrou
Aristofanous
Sofokleous

(Pireos)
City Hall
Kotzia
Square

Athinas
Stadiou
El. Venizelou
(Panipistimiou)

Central
Market

Evripidou

Dipilou
Asomaton
Sarri
Sarri
Miaouli

PSIRRI

Athinas
Aiolou
Miltiadou
Praxitelous
Kolokotroni

THISSIO

Ermou
Adrianou

MONASTIRAKI

Monastiraki
Square
Mitropoleos
Ermou
Perikleos

Ancient Agora

GRAND PROMENADE (Apostolou Pavlou)
Akamantos
Aktaiou
Ersychthonos
Dimofontos
Kymaion
Observatory

Roman
Agora
Aiolou
Adrianou

Metropolitan
Cathedral
Apollonos

Vyssakiou
AREOPAGUS

Minisikleous
Lysiou
Nikodimou
Voulis
Adrianou
Tripodon
Ragkava
Thespidos
PLAKA

HILL OF
THE PNYX

Pnyx

THE
ACROPOLIS
Parthenon

NYMPHON
HILL

Theatre of
Dionysus
GRAND PROMENADE
(Dionissiou Areopayitou)

Dora Stratou
Theater

FILOPAPPOU
HILL
Filopappou
Monument

Propylaion
Rovertou Galli St.
Parthenonos
Hatzichristou
Makrigianni

MAKRIGIANNI

AKROPOLI

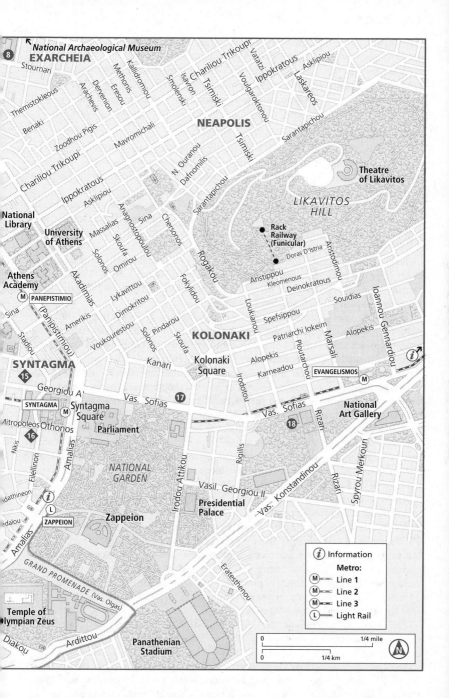

useful and practical info, they may tell you to find out for yourself once you get to the destination rather than being bothered to find out for you.

Other sources for visitors are the **city's hotels**—most have stands with various brochures and maps. Another option is to call the **Tourist Police** (© 171), who are on-call 24 hours a day. They speak English among other languages, and will help with problems or emergencies.

GETTING AROUND

BY PUBLIC TRANSPORTATION   Public transport in the city is cheap if not always speedy. The city's blue-white-and-yellow **buses** run regular routes in Athens and its suburbs daily from around 5am to 10pm or later, depending on the line. The yellow-and-purple **trolleys** serve the city center daily 4:30am to midnight.

Tickets for both buses and trolleys cost .50€ (65¢) and must be bought in advance from kiosks *(periptera)* or at bus ticket booths at some bus stops. The tickets are sold individually and in packets of 10; they are good for a single ride on any bus or trolley. When you board, stamp your ticket in the validation machine, and hold onto it. Casually dressed inspectors periodically board and check, and levy a fine 60 times the ticket price if a passenger doesn't produce one that's validated. Call © 185 for information on all public transport, or visit the **Athens Urban Transport Organization** site (www.oasa.gr), which also has a route map.

The much older **green line** (or **line 1**) of the urban rail (www.isap.gr) links the northern suburbs—including the Olympic stadium at Irini and the National Archaeological Museum at Victoria or Omonia stations—with the port of Piraeus. There are two additional metro lines (www.ametro.gr) that have been expanded, and will continue to do so, resulting in changes in destination names. The **blue line (line 3)** connects Monastiraki and Syntagma stations in the heart of Athens's shopping and tourist districts with the airport. The north-south **red line (line 2)** crosses the Acropolis and the central squares of Syntagma and Omonia. The metro website has a map of all three lines.

Tickets for the metro can also be used on the green line, which is divided into zones and has slightly cheaper tickets. Tickets can be purchased at all stations. Trains on the red and blue lines run frequently from 5:30am to midnight; green line trains start a half hour earlier. Validate your ticket in the machines as you enter and hang on to it or risk a fine of 48€ ($62) to 80€ ($104). You can use the .80€ ($1) ticket to travel on the blue, red, and green lines interchangeably, but only if you're heading in one direction within 90 minutes of validation. Simple metro and bus tickets aren't interchangeable.

A 1€ ($1.30) ticket is available for all modes of public transport within the city for 90 minutes, and a 3€ ($3.90) ticket is good for 24 hours. These can be purchased at bus-ticket booths, kiosks, tram, metro, and suburban rail stations. Longer-term ticket options are described on the metro and OASA websites, including a **hop-on sightseeing bus** ticket for 5€ ($6.50), purchased on the bus (no. 400), which is good for 24 hours on all public transport within the city. This bus does a circuit of all the main sites (the full circuit takes 80–90 min.).

The **tram** (www.tramsa.gr) provides service from central Syntagma Square to the coast, where it branches west to Neo Faliro and the nearby Peace and Friendship stadium, or southeast past the beaches at Alimos and Hellenikon to Glyfada.

Tram tickets can be purchased at station vending machines or at staffed ticket booths at some stations. Validate your ticket and hold on to it. Tickets cost .60€ (80¢) and are valid for 60 minutes for a single journey in one direction. If you plan on taking the tram for five or less stops, get a .40€ (50¢) ticket, which can also be used as a supplement (onward, transfer) ticket from another mode of public transport, provided that that transport's ticket has been retained and it is within 90 minutes of its validation. The tram runs from 5am to midnight.

BY TAXI The more than 15,000 taxis in Athens are notorious for their poor service, even though the majority of cabbies are honest, if not overly friendly. It's also not unusual for cabs to double up on passengers. If you want to be the only customer, you can request your driver not to pick up anyone else along the route, but it is a tacit (and ecofriendly) agreement between customers and drivers in exchange for cheap fares (each party still pays full fare though). If you're in a hurry, call out your destination to one that's occupied but not full; if your stop is on the way, the driver will take you.

There are about 15 radio taxi companies in Athens that you can call to reserve a cab ahead of time. Two established ones are **Attika** (© 210/341-0553), and **Ikaros** (© 210/515-2800). Charges between companies may vary slightly, but if you're trying to make travel connections during rush hour, the service will be well worth the 2€ ($2.60) or thereabouts surcharge for an on-the-spot call or the 3€ to 5€ ($3.90–$6.50) extra for an appointment (usually not more than a few hours later, however). Your hotel can make the call for you and make sure that the driver knows where you want to go. Most restaurants will call a taxi for you without charge. *Warning:* Don't assume there will always be a taxi on call, as there are some periods (such as rush hour) when even radio taxis are unavailable.

At press time, the meter starts at 1€ ($1.30), the minimum fare is 2.70€ ($3.50), and the meter rate (tariff 1) is .35€ (45¢) per kilometer (tariff 2 is .65 (85¢)), with a surcharge of .90€ ($1.15) for service *from* (not to) a port or railway or bus station. A luggage surcharge of .35€ (45¢) is charged for each piece weighing more than 22 lb. (10 kilos). Note that passengers pay all tolls where applicable, and there is also a time charge in addition to the tariff rate per kilometer, which is 9.10€ ($12) per hour. In other words, you really have to trust the driver. You can also arrange a nonmetered amount to sightsee by taxi. For tipping, round up to the nearest euro or two. Drivers get a mandatory extra tip (posted on the dashboard) during holidays.

Warning: Charges should be displayed on a card on your taxi's dashboard. Drivers should not be charging for anything that is not on the list, such as turning on the air conditioner. All hotels are also accessible by car, no matter what the driver might say. Do not pay or get out until you are at your hotel. If you dispute the cost, don't pay the driver; enlist the assistance of your hotel clerk, call the tourist police (© **171**), or ask the driver to take you to the nearest police station, which should have the desired effect.

ON FOOT Even before the pedestrian cobblestone walkway that loops around the Acropolis was completed in 2004, most of Athens's must-see sites were best seen on foot. *But beware:* A red traffic light or stop sign is no guarantee that cars will stop for you. And Athens is one of those places where you must look both ways before crossing a one-way street or pedestrian road. The (supposedly) car-free pedestrian zones in sections of **Plaka,** the **historic center,** and **Kolonaki** do, however, make strolling, window-shopping, and sightseeing infinitely more pleasant.

WHERE TO STAY

Acropolis House Hotel *(Value* This small hotel, housed in a renovated 150-year-old villa, is located on a relatively quiet pedestrian-only side street in Plaka. The newer wing (only half as old) isn't particularly special, but its bargain price counts for a lot. You'll be within walking distance of everything you'll want to see and you won't be

> **Tips** **Location, Location, Location**
>
> Look for a room in the tourist-friendly areas of **Syntagma** (10551, 10555, 10563), **Plaka** (10557, 10558), **Thissio** (11851), **Makriyanni** (11527), or **Koukaki** (10558, 11742), or in **Monastiraki** and **Psirri,** if the hotel is near Ermou Street rather than closer to Sofocleous or Pireos (P. Tsaldari) streets. The latter two areas border the seedy Omonia Square and Central Market (agora) districts, which are best avoided, especially at night. They may not be dangerous, but they do host a steady population of prostitutes, migrants, and drug addicts, even though they rarely approach "outsiders."
>
> Be wary of Olympics-refurbished hotels that play up (or don't) their location, and note that some hotel websites also have incorrect map markers, or show availability when there isn't. Make advance reservations where possible on a trusted website or else directly with the hotel, and double-check the location by post code (noted above), or by downloading a map of Athens from the Greek National Tourism Organization at **www.gnto.gr.**

spending too much time in your room anyway. Rooms without air-conditioning are cheaper.

Kodrou 6–8, 10558 Plaka. ✆ 210/322-2344. Fax 210/324-4143. www.acropolishouse.gr. 25 units. 67€–87€ ($87–$113) double. Rates include continental breakfast. MC, V accepted for deposit/reservation, but total must be paid in cash. Walk 2 blocks down Mitropoleos St. from Syntagma Square and turn left on Voulis, which becomes pedestrianized Kodrou. Metro: Syntagma (red and blue lines), 5-min. walk to station. *In room:* No A/C (some rooms).

Acropolis View Hotel   This nicely maintained hotel is on a residential side street off Rovertou Galli, not far from the Herodion Atticus theater and thus, the Acropolis. The quiet neighborhood at the base of Filopappou Hill is a 10- to 15-minute walk from the heart of Plaka. Rooms (most freshly painted each year) are small but clean and pleasant, with good bathrooms; 16 have balconies. Some, like no. 405, overlook Filopappou Hill, and others, like no. 407, face the Acropolis.

Webster (aka Wemster, Gouempster) 10 and Rovertou Galli St., 11742 Koukaki. ✆ 210/921-7303-5. Fax 210/923-0705. www.acropolisview.gr. 32 units. 95€ ($124) double. Rates include generous buffet breakfast. Substantial reductions Nov–Apr 1. MC, V. Metro: Acropolis (red line), less than 10-min. walk to station. On pedestrian Dionysiou Areopagitou head west. Just opposite the Herodion Atticus theater go left onto Propylaion; take a right onto Rovertou Galli St. The first little street you'll intersect is Webster. **Amenities:** Breakfast room; rooftop bar. *In room:* Hair dryer on request.

Electra Palace ✧   The Electra Palace, not to be confused with the **Electra** hotel on Ermou Street at nearby Syntagma Square, is just a few blocks southwest of the square. Rooms get proportionally smaller and balconies bigger the higher the floor in this luxury-class Plaka hotel, which also has an indoor pool, gym, and steam room. In deluxe rooms you get an Acropolis view and can escape traffic noise. If you don't get a high floor, you can always see the view from the terrace roof. Take advantage of special offers by booking online.

Nikodimou 18, 10557 Plaka. ✆ 210/324-1401 or 210/337-0000. Fax 210/324-1875. www.electrahotels.gr. 150 units. 282€–342€ ($234–$325) double. Rates include breakfast. AE, DC, MC, V. Metro: Syntagma (red and blue lines), 5-min. walk to station. Walk 2 blocks down Mitropoleos St. from Syntagma Sq. and turn left on Voulis until you reach Nikodimou, then right. **Amenities:** Laundry; restaurant; bar, nonsmoking rooms. *In room:* Hair dryer.

Jason Inn Hotel *Value*   Well located on the edge of trendy Psirri and Thissio districts and within walking distance of the Agora, the Acropolis, Kerameikos, Gazi, and so on, the Jason Inn is perfectly situated for Acropolis-gazing from its roof garden. It's also near lots of good restaurants and cafes. Rooms are clean and comfortable. You'll get great value for your money.

Agion Asomaton 12, 10553 Psirri. ☎ 210/325-1106, or 210/520-2491 for reservations. Fax 210/523-4786. www.douros-hotels.com. 57 units. 65€–95€ ($85–$124) double. Rates include American buffet breakfast. MC, V. Metro: Thissio (green line), 5-min. walk (330 ft./100m) to station. Exit the station and turn left, pass the small below-street-level church (Agion Asomaton) bearing left. The hotel is on the right. **Amenities:** Restaurant; bar; nonsmoking rooms. *In room:* Hair dryer.

Parthenon Hotel ★ *Value*   This first-class hotel has cut-rate prices (depending on availability), a great location near Plaka and the Acropolis, a helpful staff, and good amenities. The hotel's website even has a rare, up-to-date events calendar. Management can help get you a room in the affiliated **Alexandros** or **Stratos Vassilikos** hotels if the Parthenon is full, but both are outside the center near the Megaron Mousikis metro station (two stops from Syntagma) in the American Embassy district.

Makri 6, 11527 Makriyianni. ☎ 210/923-4594. Fax 210/923-5797. www.airotel.gr. 79 units. 114€–128€ ($148–$166) double. AE, DC, MC, V. Metro: Acropolis (red line), 2-min. walk to station. Just off pedestrian Dionyssiou Areopagitou, Makri is the first street left from Ath. Diakou, where one of the 2 metro exits is located. **Amenities:** Restaurant; bar; laundry; nonsmoking floors. *In room:* Hair dryer.

Thission Hotel   Near all the main sites, the family-run Thission is at the base of Pnyx Hill in Thissio, with outstanding views of the Acropolis and Lycabettus Hill. The hotel itself is plain but the rooms are adequate. Try for one with a view. Otherwise take in the area from the rooftop garden or one of the numerous sidewalk cafes just outside the door. The hotel is central to Monastiraki, Psirri, and Plaka. Bonus: If there's no room here, the owner can inquire at the Erechthion hotel next door—they're related.

Apostolou Pavlou 25/Agias Marinas 2, 11851 Thissio. ☎ 210/346-7634 or 210/346-7655. Fax 210/346-2756. www.hotel-thission.gr, 18 units. 50€–85€ ($65–$111) double. MC, V. Metro: Thissio (green line), 5-min. walk to station. At Thissio station, walk over the train bridge and up pedestrian Apostolou Pavlou (south, toward the Acropolis) past the Ancient Agora, park, and cafe-table-filled square on your left. The hotel is a little farther up on your right. **Amenities:** Rooftop dining/breakfast; bar; cafe.

TOP ATTRACTIONS & SPECIAL MOMENTS

It's hard not to stare or at least glance at antiquities in Athens, whether they appear as open-air attractions such as the Acropolis or Agora, recessed in the roadside, or behind glass cases at one of the city's three dozen museums or metro stations. The finds are endless, certainly more than could be seen in a single visit. Below are the highlights.

Note: It is wise to call the sites listed below to confirm opening hours. The Culture Ministry announces the summer-schedule hours for each year in spring, about a month before the change, and holidays may also affect the schedule.

The Acropolis ★★★   The **Parthenon,** dedicated to Athena Parthenos (the Virgin), patron goddess of Athens, was the most important religious monument in the ancient city. Climbing up, you first pass through the **Beule Gate,** built by the Romans but known by the name of the French archaeologist who discovered it in 1852. Next comes the **Propylaia,** the monumental 5th-century B.C. entranceway. The little **Temple of Athena Nike (Athena of Victory),** a beautifully proportioned Ionic temple built in 424 B.C., is perched above the Propylaia; it was restored in the 1930s and is being rebuilt once more. Off to the left of the Parthenon is the **Erechtheion,** which the Athenians honored as the tomb of Erechtheus, a legendary king of Athens. Be sure to see the original **Caryatids** (the monumental female figures that served as columns on the Erechtheion's porch) in the Acropolis Museum.

The Parthenon's entire roof and much of the interior were blown up in 1687 when a party of Venetians attempted to take the Acropolis from the Turks, causing appalling damage to the building and its sculptures. Most of what remained was crudely hacked off, and carted off to Britain by Lord Elgin in the early 19th century. Those sculptures—known as the **Elgin Marbles**—are on display in the British Museum, and are a constant point of friction between Greeks and Britons. A **new Acropolis Museum,** just off Dionysiou Areopagitou at **Makriyianni 2–4** and expected to be open by the time you read this, includes an area set aside in anticipation of the Parthenon Marbles'—as they are also known—return. Four of the original Caryatids from the Erechtheion (one disappeared during the Ottoman occupation, and one is in the British Museum) will be on view, together with the entire collection from the old museum on the hilltop, including sculptures from the Parthenon burned by the Persians, statues of **korai** (maidens) dedicated to Athena, figures of **kouri** (young men), and many other finds from the Acropolis comprising some 4,000 works—10 times the amount on display at the hilltop museum.

Dionysiou Areopagitou St. C 210/321-0219. Admission 12€ ($15.60) adults; many categories, including archaeology students, are admitted free (ask, or check www.culture.gr, also for free-admission days). Admission—a coupon booklet—is valid for 4 days, and includes admission coupons to the Acropolis, Acropolis Museum (at time of writing), Ancient Agora, Theater of Dionysos and south slope, Kerameikos cemetery, Roman Forum, north slope, and the Temple of Olympian Zeus. You can buy individual site tickets if you don't want to see the Acropolis; prices vary from 2€ ($2.60) to 4€ ($5.20). Daily 8am–7pm; reduced winter hours. The ticket booth, along with a small post office and a snack bar, are just opposite the Acropolis entrance on the west side of the hill. From Syntagma Sq., take Amalias Ave. onto pedestrian-only Dionysiou Areopagitou St., and follow the marble path veering right up to the Acropolis. Metro: Acropolis (red line).

Ancient Agora ✿   The Agora was Athens's commercial and civic center and where democracy was first practiced, its buildings used for a wide range of political, educational, philosophical, theatrical, and athletic purposes. This is a nice place to wander around and enjoy the views up toward the Acropolis. Be sure to see the herb garden and flowers planted around the 5th century B.C. **Temple of Hephaistos** (better known as the **Thission**); peek into the restored 11th-century Byzantine **Church of the Agii Apostoli (Holy Apostles);** and admire the 2nd-century B.C. **Stoa of Attalos,** a monument built by King Attalos of Pergamon and reconstructed by the Rockefeller-funded American School of Classical Studies in the 1950s.

The **museum** inside the Stoa has finds from 5,000 years of Athenian history, including sculpture and pottery, as well as a voting machine and a child's potty seat. The museum closes 15 minutes before the site.

Just beyond the fenced-in south side of the Agora is a path from Plaka leading to the pedestrian promenade in **Thissio,** and just before the exit is **Areopagus hill** on the left (north side of the Acropolis), where Saint Paul preached. It is also opposite the Acropolis entrance. On the other side of the promenade in Thissio is **Pnyx** hill, site of the first legislative assemblies, where Pericles and other statesmen held their political jousts. Pnyx, and indeed the other hills of **Filopappou,** are also wonderful places to wander freely among antiquities and nature, right in the city's heart.

Below the Acropolis (north side) on the edge of Monastiraki. C 210/321-0185. This site is part of the 12€ ($15.60) Acropolis ticket package. Site and museum: 4€ ($5.20) adults. May–Oct Tues–Sun 8am–7pm; Mon 11am–7pm; reduced winter hours. Entrance/exits on Adrianou St. and Ay. Philipou in Monastiraki; west end of Polignotou St., Plaka; and Thissio Sq., Thissio. Metro: Monastiraki (blue, green line) or Thissio (green line).

Moments   An Evening in Thissio

For some reason this historic station (Athens's first terminus, ca. 1868) is rarely marked in guidebook maps, but the area south of **Thissio** station, one short stop past Monastiraki, is also the most "happening" part of town, as is nearby **Psirri (www.psirri.gr)**, which turns into a lively bar and restaurant quarter at night. Exiting onto the cobblestone walkway (Apostolou Pavlou), head left across Ermou Street and east into Psirri; for the Thissio district, go south (right) towards the cafes and past the ancient Thission (Hephaestos) temple, which is dramatically flood-lit at night, along with the Acropolis. Soon you will see one of the most remarkable views in the world: The Parthenon, and its other pole attraction, Lycabettus Hill, also lit up.

Stop and have a coffee or drink at the square at the west entrance of the Ancient Agora opposite of where three streets meet: pedestrian Iraklidon, aka the old tram street and now chocablock with outdoor cafes; and Nileos, which does a hairpin turn into Akamandos Street. Walk back to Monastiraki and Plaka along pedestrian Adrianou, beside the tracks between Thissio and Monastiraki metro stations, or, during the day, along the pebble pathway. The entrance is opposite the **outdoor Thission cinema (© 210/342-0864** or 210/347-0980). Check what's playing: Seeing a movie outdoors on a balmy summer night is another Athens tradition that shouldn't be missed.

Benaki Museum   You'll find all of Greek history under one roof here. This stunning private collection includes treasures from the Neolithic era to the 20th century. The folk art collection (including magnificent costumes and icons) is superb, as are two rooms decorated in the style of 18th-century northern Greek mansions, ancient bronzes, gold cups, Fayum portraits, and rare, early Christian textiles. A new wing has doubled the exhibition space of the early-20th-century neoclassical house that belonged to the wealthy Benaki family. It's a very pleasant place to spend time. *Note:* The Benaki's massive collection of Islamic art is contained in a museum near Thissio metro station.

Koumbari 1 (at Leoforos Vasilissis Sofias, Kolonaki, 5 blocks east of Syntagma Sq.). © 210/367-1000. www.benaki. gr. Admission 6€ ($7.80) adults, 3€ ($3.90) seniors, students free. Thurs free (except guided tours and temporary exhibitions). Mon, Wed, Fri–Sat 9am–5pm; Thurs 9am–midnight; Sun 9am–3pm; closed Tues. Metro: Syntagma or Evangelismos (blue line). The **Museum of Islamic Art** is located at Ag. Asomaton 22 and Dipilou 12, Psirri. © 210/325-1311. www.benaki.gr. Admission 5€ ($6.50) adults, 3€ ($3.90) seniors, students free. Thurs free (except guided tours). Tues and Thurs–Sun 9am–3pm; Wed 9am–9pm; closed Mon. Metro: Thissio (green line).

Byzantine and Christian Museum   This museum, which underwent a revamp in 2004 and is housed in a 19th-century, Florentine-style villa, is devoted to the art and history of the Byzantine and post-Byzantine eras (roughly 3rd–20th c. A.D.). Selections from Greece's most important collection of icons and religious art—along with sculptures, altars, mosaics, religious vestments, Bibles, and a small-scale reconstruction of an early Christian basilica—are exhibited on several floors, including new exhibition areas, centered around a courtyard.

Vasilissis Sofias 22, Rigillis. © 210/721-1027. Admission 4€ ($5.20). Tues–Sun 8am–7:30pm; reduced winter hours. Metro: Evangelismos (blue line); bus stop: Rigillis.

Kerameikos Cemetery   A cemetery may not be a sightseeing priority, but this ancient site has a number of well-preserved funerary monuments as well as ruins of the colossal **Dipylon Gate,** the main entrance to the ancient city of Athens. There's also a section of the **Sacred Way** (Iera Odos), which still exists in name and route just outside the cemetery, reaching Ancient Eleusis (modern Elefsina), 14 miles (22km) west, where Demeter was worshipped. You can also see substantial remains of the 5th-century B.C. fortifications known as the "Long Walls" that ran from Athens to the port of Piraeus. Pericles eulogized Athens in his famous **funeral oration** for Athenian soldiers killed in the Peloponnesian War here. Bring a book if you're so inclined—it's also a pleasant spot to sit and read.

Ermou 148, Kerameikos. ⓒ **210/346-3552.** This site is part of the 12€ ($15.60) Acropolis ticket package. Museum and site 2€ ($2.60). Mon–Sun 8am–7:30pm. Walk west along Ermou St. past Thissio station toward Gazi (look for the smokestacks); cemetery is on the right. Metro: Thissio.

National Archaeological Museum *★★★*   Home to some of the world's most precious treasures, this Athens must-see has been upgraded, making a visit here a pleasure. Highlights are the bronze *Horse and Jockey* and *Poseidon of Artemision* statues, the golden death mask known as the "Mask of Agamemnon," and Virgin Mary look-alike *Lady of Kalymnos,* from around 2nd-century B.C. Prehistoric clay and marble figurines that look decidedly modern, bronze objects, and gold jewelry are also on show behind nonglare glass cases. Plan to spend hours here while soaking up a visual extravaganza of Greek history.

Patission 44, Museo. ⓒ **210/821-7717.** Fax 210/821-3573. Admission 7€ ($9.10) adults; discounts available for other categories such as students and seniors. Mon 1–7:30pm; Tues–Sun and holidays 8:30am–7:30pm. The museum is ⅓ mile (½km/10 min. on foot) north of Omonia Sq. on 28 Oktovriou St. (known as Patission, which is what it becomes farther north). Metro: Omonia or Victoria; many buses/trolleys can be taken from Omonia Sq. on Panepistimiou St. (marked as El. Venizelou).

Moments   **An Athenian Stroll**

Athens's 19th-century **First Cemetery,** near the all-marble **Panathenian Stadium** or Kallimarmaro, itself the site of the first modern Olympics in 1896, is located inside a huge hilltop garden. Notables are entombed there, many with elaborate sculptures marking their graves. The most famous work is that of Tinos islander Yannoulis Halepas's *Sleeping Lady* on the tomb of Sophia Afentaki, the 18-year-old daughter of a wealthy Athenian. Halepas is said to have gone mad after creating this flawless masterpiece in 1877. From Syntagma southbound (in front of McDonald's or the post office), take bus A3, A4, 103, 108, 111, 155, 206, 208, 237, 856, 057, or 227. Bus stop: A' ("Proto") Nekrotafio.

Or make a walking tour of it, going through the **National Gardens/ Zappeion** from Syntagma, past the stadium, and on to the cemetery. On your way back (or do the reverse), stop at or go by the **Temple of Olympian Zeus** (ⓒ 210/922-6330). Taking some 600 years to build between 515 B.C. and A.D. 132, Greece's one-time largest temple measures just under 51,500 sq. ft. (4,785 sq. m). Fifteen of the original 104 columns are still standing, each 56 feet (17m) high. Then walk past **Hadrian's Arch** (on Amalias Ave.), through which the Roman emperor marched in A.D. 132 to dedicate the giant temple.

WHERE TO DINE

Health Ecology (Ygeias-Ecologias) *(Value)* VEGETARIAN   Meatless starters and salads or dips are widely available in Greece, but this health-food shop, which also sells organically grown produce, has a thriving cafeteria-style restaurant on its premises as well. Well known to locals and organic-food enthusiasts, it serves Greek-style vegetarian food and freshly squeezed juices in the busy, commercial Omonia Square district. Prices are reasonable if not downright cheap. Just don't come here for the atmosphere or for a late dinner.

Panepistimiou (El. Venizelou) 57, near Omonia. ℂ **210/321-0966.** Main courses 4€–6€ ($5.20–$7.80). Daily 8am–9:30pm; Sat 8am–8pm; Sun 9am–4pm. Metro: Omonia.

Kentrikon GREEK/INTERNATIONAL   An Athens institution for daytime dining, Kentrikon is an oasis in the hectic shopping district. With hall-like high ceilings and good air-conditioning, it has an extensive menu, excellent food, and top-notch service (waiters in bow-ties; cloth napkins). It's not pretentious, but on the downside, there is no view. It closes at night, so it's best for lunch.

Kolokotroni 3, near Syntagma Sq., just west of Stadiou St. (turn at the shoe store opposite the park/Old Parliament bldg.), in the arcade. ℂ **210/323-2482.** Main courses 9€–22€ ($12–$28). AE, DC, MC, V. Mon–Sat noon–6pm. Metro: Syntagma.

Kouklis (Scholarhio) Ouzeri ★ *(Value)* GREEK   Kouklis is the best, and perhaps only, "tray taverna" for *mezedes* (appetizers) of all kinds in Plaka. No entrees here; instead you choose from a selection of appetizers brought to your table. Ten dishes, a liter of wine (or a substitute), mineral water, and dessert goes for only 12€ ($15.60) per person for a group of four or more.

Tripodon 14, (between Flessa and Thespidos), Plaka. ℂ **210/324-7605.** www.sholarhio.gr. Meze 2.50€–5€ ($3.25–$6.50). V, MC. Daily 11am–2am. Metro: Syntagma or Monastiraki.

Mamacas ★ MODERN GREEK   Mamacas is a notch above the usual taverna, with traditional dishes prepared with fresh ingredients and given a contemporary twist. It sprawls across much of the block beside the Gazi exit of Kerameikos metro station, in a trendy neighborhood where a former gas factory has been turned into a cultural center. Tables are set out in good weather, and an enclosed rooftop dining area with an Acropolis view is open year-round.

Persefonis 41 at Triptolemou, Gazi. ℂ **210/346-4984.** www.mamacas.gr. Reservations recommended. Main courses 20€–25€ ($26–$32.50). Daily 2pm–2am. AE, MC, V. Alongside the old gasworks factory (Gazi) on Pireos St. at Persefonis. Metro: Kerameikos.

Platanos Taverna GREEK   Platanos is a classic Greek taverna located on a tree-shaded, residential street near the Tower of the Winds. Sheltered tables are set outside, and an old-fashioned Greek ambience pervades inside. The taverna serves fresh, good-quality food in substantial portions.

Dioyenous 4, Plaka (end of Aeolou St., adjacent to Adrianou). ℂ **210/322-0666.** Main courses 8€–9€ ($10.40–$11.70); full meal 15€ ($19.50). No credit cards. Mon–Sat noon–4:30pm and 7:30pm–midnight. Closed Sun and for 2 weeks in Aug. Metro: Monastiraki or Syntagma.

Zeidoron ★ GREEK/STARTERS   One of many restaurants in the lively Psirri district across from Monastiraki, Zeidoron serves lots of delicious *mezedes*, such as vegetable croquettes, eggplant dishes, and heartier meat dishes. Traditionally accompanied by ouzo, an aniseed-flavored liqueur diluted with water or ice, you can have a varied meal—and keep the price tab reasonable—by avoiding the more expensive options, such as shrimp. A wide variety of wines, beers, and ouzos is available.

Taki 10 and Agion Anargiron, Psirri. ℂ 210/321-5368. Reservations recommended. Main courses around 10 ($13); appetizers around 6€ ($7.80). AE, V, MC. Mon–Thurs 6pm–2am; Fri–Sun noon–2am. Closed for a week in Aug. Metro: Monastiraki.

SHOPPING

Between **Plaka** and **Monastiraki** you'll find everything Greece is known for—from the stunning to the kitsch—that you might want to buy: from modern Greek art to replicas of ancient masterpieces to ouzo bottles that look like temples. Be careful of prices and attempt to bargain, especially if you're buying a lot from the same shop or a big-ticket item. Also check out the flea market between Monastiraki and Thissio metro stations, reaching right down to Gazi on pedestrianized Ermou St., which draws huge crowds on Sundays when other shops are closed. To see old hands at work, wander through Psirri (tanneries, metalwork, shoemakers) and the area from Monastiraki metro station to Evripidou St. east of Athinas St. (textiles, bits, and bobs). All kinds of old-fashioned specialist shops and their real-deal staff can be found here. Bargaining is less acceptable outside Plaka and Monastiraki.

Stavros Melissinos, Athens's **poet sandalmaker,** Aghias Theklas 2 (ℂ **210/321-9247;** www.melissinos-art.com), is an international favorite who has handed the reigns over to his artist son, Pantelis. Some two dozen strappy leather designs are available to choose from. They cost 22€ to 35 € ($27.30–$35.10), depending on your shoe size. You'll find him near Ermou Street (north side) at Monastiraki metro station in Psirri.

Try **Nikolaos Paschalidis's** shop in Monastiraki, Hephaistou 11 (ℂ **210/321-0064**), for all things copper, including long-handled coffee pots and wine jugs. **Pelekanos,** Adrianou 115, Plaka (there are two Adrianou streets; ℂ **210/331-0968**), also has traditional objects made of metal, but carries other folk art as well.

Handmade jewelry and ceramics line the walls of **Archipelagos,** Adrianou 142, Plaka (ℂ **210/323-1321**), while **Vergina,** Kidathineon 24, Plaka (ℂ **210/324-5304**), carries artwork and stunning contemporary jewelry by modern Greek artists. The **Center of Hellenic Tradition,** with two entrances, Mitropoleos 59 or Pandrossou 36, Monastiraki (ℂ **210/321-3023**), is a wonderful place for quality traditional Greek art, including icons, pottery, woodcarvings, embroideries, and prints. And you can take a coffee/snack break from shopping at the **Orea Hellas cafe** (ℂ **210/321-3842**) here, complete with an Acropolis view.

NIGHTLIFE

Athens's nightlife, and its accompanying traffic jams, runs through the early hours, year-round. The only thing that changes is the locale: the city center and northern

---

Tips **Shoe-Lover Heaven**

Whether you're male or female (but especially if you're female), it will be hard to leave Athens without buying a beautiful pair of leather shoes. The "shoe mall" is pedestrian Ermou Street, from Syntagma Square down to the little Byzantine church in the middle of the road, Kapnikareas. You can rest your feet here and admire your purchase accompanied by a frappe (iced coffee) at one of the outdoor cafes on the tree-shaded cross-street. Sales start in August.

suburbs in the winter; the seaside restaurants and outdoor bars in the summer. Many bars and clubs move their operations seasonally. Some clubs feature DJs, others live performers. The choices—no matter what the season—are endless.

Check the weekly *Athens News* or the daily *Kathimerini* insert in the *International Herald Tribune* for current cultural and entertainment events, including films, lectures, theater, music, and dance. Unfortunately, up-to-date **club and bar** listings magazines are in Greek only, so you'll have to enlist the assistance of your hotelier or some other Greek-speaker if you want to pursue a summer night beach-club option with a guest foreign DJ. Keep your eyes open for billboard posters advertising upcoming gigs, such as on Ermou St., between the Monastiraki and Thissio metro stations, and scan the free tabloids set out in boxes alongside metro station exits.

THE PERFORMING ARTS The acoustically superior **Megaron Mousikis (Athens Concert Hall),** Vas. Sofias and Kokkali streets, next to the American Embassy (© **210/729-0391** or 210/728-2333; www.megaron.gr), hosts a wide range of classical music programs from September to June (closed July–Aug). The box office is open Monday through Friday from 10am to 6pm, Saturday from 10am to 2pm; open longer on performance nights, including Sunday 6pm to 8:30pm. Tickets are also sold Monday through Friday from 10am to 6pm in the Megaron's convenient downtown kiosk at Ermou 1 (© **210/324-3297**). Ticket prices run from 14€ to 100€ ($18.20–$130), depending on the performance.

The **Greek National Opera** performs at the **Olympia Theater,** Akadimias 59 (© **210/361-2461**). The summer months are usually off season at the theater, but the ensemble often performs at other events, including the Athens Festival.

The **Hellenic American Union,** Massalias 22, Metro: Panepistimiou (© **210/368-0000** or 210/368-0900), periodically hosts performances of English-language theater and American-style music. Check their site **www.hau.gr** for a list of future events.

The **Athens Center,** Archimidous 48 (© **210/701-2268;** www.athenscentre.gr), stages an annual summer theater festival featuring performances of ancient Greek plays in English translation. The website lists upcoming performances.

The **Dora Stratou Theater** has been staging traditional Greek folk dances on Filopappou Hill since 1953. Performances take place May through September, Tuesday through Saturday at 9:30pm, Sunday at 8:15pm. There are no performances on Monday. You can buy **tickets** at the office, Scholiou 8, Plaka (© **210/324-4395;** www.grdance.org), from 9am to 4pm; or before performances at the theater (© **210/ 921-4650;** 7:30pm–9pm). Tickets are 15€ ($19.50).

TRADITIONAL MUSIC Walk the streets of Plaka on any night and you'll find plenty of tavernas offering pseudo-traditional live music. But beware! Many are serious clip joints, where if you sit down and ask for a glass of water, you'll be charged 100€ ($130) for a bottle of Scotch.

Taverna Mostrou, Mnissikleos 22, Plaka (© **210/322-5558**), is large, old, and best known for traditional *laika* (bouzouki) Greek music and dancing. The taverna operates daily from mid-April to late October; 6pm to 2am or later; live music begins at 8:15pm. In winter it's open from Friday to Sunday with known Greek performers. Dinner is a la carte, around 30€ ($39); a bottle of wine and *mezé* (to share) costs 75€ ($97.50); a seat at the bar (a drink) starts at 10€ ($13). In summer you can order drinks at the roof garden, which is also a restaurant. Credit cards accepted.

Palia Taverna Kritikou, Mnissikleos 24, Plaka (© **210/322-2809**), is a lively open-air taverna with music and dancing.

Tips **Sustainable Tourism**

Like many countries, Greece has a serious garbage problem, exacerbated by a lack of waste-disposal facilities. Embryonic efforts are being made to encourage recycling, and visitors, who more than double the country's population of 11 million each year, can help by disposing of their recyclables, such as the ubiquitous plastic (water) bottles, tin cans, and paper, inside the blue containers/bins found on Athens streets alongside the regular metal ones. Recyclable refuse can all go in the same container, but rinsing them out is appreciated.

Several appealing tavernas that usually offer low-key music include fashionable **Daphne's** (but not live), Lysikratous 4 (© **210/322-7971**); **Diogenis** (live in winter), Lysikratous Square © **210/324-7933**); **Stamatopoulos,** Lissiou 26 (© **210/322-8722;** www.stamatopoulostavern.gr); and **Xinos,** Angelou Geronta 4 (© **210/322-1065**).

Or head to the trendy **Psirri** district and follow your ears. The live bouzouki music emanates from tavernas.

3 Highlights of the Peloponnese

Once known as the Morea, the mulberry-leaf-shaped Peloponnese—a silk producer for the ancient and medieval world—is said to incorporate the best of Greece. Mountain ranges and valleys, unspoiled beaches, and some of the most famous cultural sites: ancient Mycenae, Corinth, Olympia, and the acoustically perfect Epidaurus theater are all found here. Nature lovers (and winter skiers) will want to detour up the mountain on the cog railway to Kalavryta, and those in transit can visit a genuine Turkish bath while waiting for a ferry in Patras.

Seeing the sights however, requires careful planning for rail travelers, as service is not particularly fast or frequent, and lines may not be operational due to construction, sometimes for years. It will therefore likely be necessary to take other means of transport to get to some of these wonderful places, at least for part of the journey.

CORINTH & EPIDAURUS

Corinth is regularly served by suburban transport, but only one OSE train goes to the central Corinth town and Isthmus (canal) stations—in the middle of the night. The ancient site at Corinth, as well as the sanctuary, museum, and ancient theater at **Epidaurus,** also cannot be reached by rail. However, discounted tours to both destinations (together with ancient **Mycenae**) are offered to rail passholders by Ionian Travel in Athens (see the "Greece by Rail" section, earlier in this chapter). The theater can also be seen and experienced as part of the Athens Epidaurus Festival (see below). The two other options for getting to Epidaurus are via long-distance bus, as well as a boat on ancient-theater-performance evenings. There is also bus service from the charming port town of Nafplio, but modern Greece's first capital is not served by the rail network, and won't be for the foreseeable future.

ISTHMUS AND ANCIENT CORINTH *(KORINTHOS)*

Just 55 miles (88km) west of Athens, Corinth (Corinth/Korinthos prefecture) is the major gateway to the Peloponnese for those traveling by train out of the capital. For the rail traveler, this city makes an excellent day-trip from Athens or a good stopover point on the way to Diakofto, Patras, or Olympia. It is not, however, a good base city, so don't think about spending the night here.

GETTING THERE   OSE only operates one overnight train that stops at **Isthmos** (Isthmus: the canal) and (old) **Corinth station** in town—also the only time these stations are open. For more information on that train, call the **OSE** help line at ✆ **1110.** Corinth is otherwise served by the suburban **Proastiakos** (✆ **210/527-2000**) that stops at **New Corinth station** (✆ **27410/22-522**). It costs 6€ ($7.80) from Athens. There are 18 daily trains.

To get to the archaeological site and museum, you need to get off the train (1½ hrs. from Athens, 2 hrs. from Patras) at New Corinth station and take a local **bus** into town—a 5- to 10-minute journey—that leaves hourly; from there you can take a frequent **KTEL bus** (✆ **27410/75-425;** info for both local and KTEL buses) for the 4-mile (6km) ride to Ancient Corinth, as well as to Isthmus (the canal). You can also take a **taxi** (✆ **27410/73-000**) from the station to the ancient site (about 5€/$6.50 or 6€/$7.80), or to the canal for a euro or two more.

VISITOR INFORMATION   There's an EOT (GNTO) **tourist information** office at Kolokotroni 6, 3rd floor (✆ **27410/72-662**), 1 block west of Ethnikis Antistasios at Pilarinou Street, close to the seafront and the courthouse in Corinth town. EOT is open 8:30am to 3pm Monday to Friday. You can also contact the **tourist police** at Ermou 51 (✆ **27410/23-282**), near the large park in the city center, if you need assistance.

TOP ATTRACTIONS & SPECIAL MOMENTS

The 4-mile-long (6km) **Corinth Canal,** a dream since antiquity and finally completed in 1893 by Panama and Suez Canal engineers from France and Hungary, revolutionized shipping in the Mediterranean by shaving 185 nautical miles from around the Peloponnese. It is also where the first ancient "railway" was used—the *diolkos* or portage rut railway—built in the 7th century B.C. and in use for some 1,300 years, using animal- or slave-pulling flatbeds to convey ships across the strip of land. You can see sections of the excavated track on the south side, west entrance. Check out the dramatic view of the dug-out cliffs reaching 259 feet (79m), as the train crosses the bridge.

Want to take a **boat trip through the canal?** Contact **Periandros** (✆ **27410/30-880;** www.corinthcanal.com), whose excursion vessel *Canal Vista* makes the 1-hour, 15-minute journey 4 days a week in summer, twice on Thursdays at press time. It costs 17€ ($22).

At **Ancient Corinth,** the most noteworthy feature is the handsome, 6th-century B.C. **Temple of Apollo,** which stands on a low hill overlooking the extensive remains of the **Roman Agora** (marketplace). Only seven of the temple's 38 monolithic Doric columns are standing, the others having long since been toppled by earthquakes. The *Vima* **(public platform),** located in the Agora, is the spot where St. Paul had to plead his case when the Corinthians, irritated by his constant criticisms, hauled him up in front of the Roman governor Gallo in A.D. 52.

The **Archaeological Museum** (✆ **27410/31-207**) on the site of Ancient Corinth has a fine collection of the famous Corinthian pottery that is often decorated with charming red and black figures of birds and animals. There are also a number of statues of Roman worthies and several mosaics, including one in which Pan is shown piping away to a clutch of cows. Admission to the museum and archaeological site is 6€ ($7.80). Both are open in summer Monday through Sunday from 8am to 7:30pm; winter Monday through Sunday from 8am to 3pm or 5pm (changes annually).

Last but not least among important Corinth sites is the imposing fortress of **Acro-corinth** (© **27410/31-266**) on a natural acropolis towering 1,885 feet (566m) above the plain of Corinth. On a clear day, the views from the summit are superb, but the hike up is still formidable. The Acrocorinth features ancient and medieval fortifications built by Greeks, Byzantines, Franks, Venetians, and Turks. Today, there are three courses of outer walls, massive gates with towers, and a jumble of ruined houses, churches, and barracks. Some 2½ miles (4km) from the ancient site, it is open daily 8am to 3pm. Admission is free.

WHERE TO DINE

Restaurants near the ancient sites and the canal tend to have high prices and mediocre food. That said, try **Niko's Ancient Corinth restaurant,** located on the main square (© **27410/31-361**) near the ruins. It offers a wide range of standard Greek fare, from moussaka to chops, and costs around 12€ ($15.60). It's open daily until midnight. There are also a couple of roadside restaurants on the Peloponnese side at the canal—a popular canal-viewing point on the old road—that also sell souvenirs and grocery/gift items.

EPIDAURUS (EPIDAVROS)

The theater of Epidaurus (Argolid/Argolida prefecture) is one of the most impressive sights in Greece. Probably built in the 4th century B.C., this acoustically renowned theater seats some 14,000 spectators. Unlike so many ancient buildings, the theater was not pillaged for building blocks. As a result, it is astonishingly well preserved; restorations have been both minimal and tactful.

GETTING THERE   From Athens, two **buses** (KTEL [Argolid] Terminal A, Kifissou 100, © **210/512-2513,** 210/512-2516, or 210/513-4588), to Epidaurus leave at 8:45am and 4pm; and one leaves at 5:15pm on Sunday. Tickets cost 10.40€ ($13.50) one-way, and the journey takes 2 hours. On performance days a **return bus** trip from Athens leaves at 4pm and costs 20€ ($26). Take local bus no. 051 from Menandrou Street at Zinonos Street just west of Omonia Square, or if you don't mind a bit of a walk, take the blue line of the metro to Eleonas station on Iera Odos (Sacred Way) and walk north to Leof. Athinon (known as "Kavalas"), then west/left to Leof. Kifissou, and turn right.

There is also a **boat** (Hydraiki Naval Co., Ermou 18/Diomias 4–6, 3rd floor, office no. 15, Syntagma; © **210/323-0100;** Mon–Fri 9am–4pm) that sails from Piraeus (M/V *Georgis,* gate E1) at 5:15pm to Ancient Epidaurus on performance days, arriving at 7:30pm. It costs 60€ ($78), which includes a shuttle bus from the port to the theater and back, as well as an orchestra-accompanied candlelit dinner on the return voyage. Buses to the port leave from Klafthmonos Square on Stadiou Street at 4:20pm and at Filellinon Street in front of the parking lot at Xenofontos Street, at 4:35pm. Contact the **Athens Epidaurus Festival** box office (© **210/327-2000;** www.greek festival.gr) for more details, and also check out "Festivals and Special Events," on p. 458.

VISITOR INFORMATION   There are information booths at the entrance to the site, which also have books for sale (by day).

TOP ATTRACTIONS & SPECIAL MOMENTS

Climb up to the top of the **ancient theater** ★★★ and you'll tower over 55 rows of seats: The lower, original section has 34 rows; the upper section of 21 rows was added in a 2nd-century B.C. expansion. The theater's acoustics are famous: You'll almost certainly see someone demonstrating how a whisper can be heard all the way from the round orchestra pit to the top row of seats. Epidaurus is considered a living monument and hosts the summer-long Epidaurus Festival, consisting mostly of performances of classical Greek plays on Friday and Saturday nights. Performances are staged in Greek and translations aren't offered, though most visitors don't mind the language barrier and come to see them anyway. They can usually follow along because the plays are almost always well-known ancient Greek tragedies or comedies.

The **Epidaurus Festival Museum,** near the entrance to the site, with its displays of props, costumes, programs, and memorabilia from past performances is a great supplement to a tour of the theater. It is open the same time as the other attractions but only for the duration of the festival, roughly May to September.

A stop at the site's other museum before roaming through the rest of the area will help to put some flesh on the bones of the sanctuary's scant remains.

The **Sanctuary of Asklepios,** who was worshipped in other parts of Greece as well, served as a religious center for his cult and as a spa, where the sick would come to be cured and the healthy to relax. Accommodations for visitors, **bathhouses,** a **gymnasium, stadium, temples,** and **shrines** are among the ruins. It is unclear why the round **tholos** has labyrinthine foundations, but scholars suspect Asklepios's healing serpents lived there. Two long **stoas** nearby provided a sleeping spot for patients hoping to see Asklepios in a dream. Those who were cured dedicated the votive offerings and inscriptions on display at the museum.

The **excavation museum** features architectural fragments from the sanctuary, votive offerings of terra-cotta body parts, and surgical implements.

Combined admission to the **site, theater,** and **museums** (☎ **27530/22-009**) is 6€ ($7.80). The hours for all the attractions in summer are 8am to 7:30pm daily; in winter, from 8am to 5pm daily.

For **theater tickets** call ☎ **210/327-2000** in Athens, or 27530/22-026 at Epidaurus. It's also possible to buy tickets at the theater itself, starting at 5pm on the day of a performance.

WHERE TO DINE

There is a trailer canteen (sandwiches, refreshments) where the buses park at the ancient site entrance. The site is isolated, so there are no other dining options. Bring picnic fare along with you if you want more options.

DIAKOFTO/KALAVRYTA ☎

The scenic seaside rail route from Athens to the coastal village of Diakofto (also spelled Diakopto) in the northern Peloponnese is nothing compared to the view from the line's mountain-hugging branch from Diakofto to Kalavryta (Achaia prefecture). Arguably one of the best rail excursions in Europe, the famous rack-and-pinion railroad *odontotos,* literally "toothed" track in Greek, travels up the mountain to Kalavryta, offering stunning views of the steep rocks and rich vegetation engulfing the gorge through which the Vouraikos River winds below. One of the narrowest railways at 0.75-meter gauge, the cog railway was completed in 1896 for the practical purpose of transporting ore down from Kalavryta. Today the rail is considered an engineering feat and provides a scenic journey through the region's thick vegetation, caves, and waterfalls as the train weaves along either side of the Vouraikos, navigating through roughly cut tunnels, picturesque bridges, and hanging cliffs. You may even pass a few hikers along the way. A steam engine originally plied the 14-mile (23km) track until it was replaced around 1960 by a diesel one. The track has now been upgraded and new trains are on standby; however, the line was not yet operational at time of writing. Hopefully it will be by the time you read this. Check beforehand—it's a very popular trip.

GETTING THERE   A one-way, first-class ticket costs 12.10€ ($15.75); second class is 10.70€ ($13.90). Change at Corinth from the suburban Proastiakos from Athens. The trip lasts 2 hours and 45 minutes to 3 hours, depending on the type of train. Normally, three trains commute between Diakofto and Kalavryta daily but do check, as the line was inoperative at time of writing. The cost of the 70-minute trip is 4.50€ ($5.85) for first class and 3.70€ ($4.80) for second class. Rail passes are good on all of the above trains.

   Warning: Because there are few trains to Kalavryta on this popular route, if you get off the train at Diakofto without having made reservations on the cog railway before setting off on your trip, especially on holiday weekends, you risk not getting on the Kalavryta train. For further information, contact the stations at **Diakofto** (© 26910/ 43-206), **Kalavryta** (© 26920/22-245), or OSE customer service (© 1110). If the train isn't running, a **taxi** (© 6972/663-864) from Diakofto to Kalavryta costs around 30€ ($39) and takes about 45 minutes. Reserve 2 to 3 hours ahead, such as when you start your journey from Athens, Patras, and so on. A KTEL **bus** originating from Aegio (© 26910-22423) also makes the journey twice a day for 4€ ($5.20), leaving Aegio at 7am and 2:10pm, arriving in Diakofto 10 to 15 minutes later. The bus stop for Kalavryta is beside the train station.

VISITOR INFORMATION   There are no tourist information centers in either Diakofto or Kalavryta, but the local KEP (citizen's information) center in Kalavryta (© 26920/22-666) is helpful, as is Diakofto's municipality (© 26910/41-270).

TOP ATTRACTIONS & SPECIAL MOMENTS

Just past the halfway mark on the train route from Diakofto to Kalavryta, around 8 miles (13km) into the trip, you'll be able to spot the pretty village of **Zahlorou** on the banks of the Vouraikos River. If you get off at the nearby **Mega Spilaio** station (the only one on the route) about 45 minutes into the trip, you will soon see the **Monastery of the Great Cave,** or *Moni Megalou Spilaiou* (© 26920/22-401) after a short walk. Built into the steep walls of **Mount Helmos,** tradition holds that the monastery was founded in the 4th century by two brothers on the site where an icon of the Virgin Mary, said to have been painted by St. Luke, was found. The monastery has been destroyed and rebuilt many times throughout its history, most recently following a 1934 fire. The museum, which may not be open due to ongoing renovations at press time, contains holy relics, Byzantine-era gospels, and intricately carved icon stands from all epochs of Christianity. The monastery is open daily from 6am to 1pm and 2 to 8pm.

   Note: Inform the engineer of your desire to disembark at Mega Spilaio station, and the station attendant when you're ready to leave. The train will stop if there is a passenger on the platform, but be sure to hail the train.

   Kalavryta is about 20 minutes from of Mega Spilaio station, located 2,461 feet (738m) up the mountain. A historic town with a traditional character, stone houses, and well-kept old buildings, it is a popular ski destination in winter. Kalavryta is also near the domestically famed **Aghia Lavra monastery,** credited with being the first to raise the banner of independence against Ottoman rule in 1821. A **monument** in

Kalavryta commemorates a 1943 Nazi massacre of some 1,300 men and boys over the age of 12 both within and around the town; the main church's clock still reads the time the massacre took place, 2:34pm.

About 11 miles (17km) outside of town, but well worth the trip, is the **Cave of the Lakes,** or *Spilaio ton Limnon* (© **26920/31-001**). A natural wonder with stalactites and stalagmites, the cave features more than a dozen lakes on three levels. Excavations have limited public access to part of the cave. A walking tour that lasts just over 30 minutes costs 8€ ($10.40) for adults, 4€ ($5.20) for children aged 6 to 16. The cave has two faces, depending on the season: rivers and waterfalls gush in winter and spring; the lakes are still in the summer and in prerain fall. Ongoing excavations since its rediscovery in 1964 have yielded finds dating from prehistoric times. There is no public transportation from the station to the caves; call a **taxi** (© **26920/22-127**). It's open Monday to Friday 9am to 5:30pm (last group at 4:30pm); July and August 9am to 5:30pm; Saturday, Sunday, and holidays 9am to 6:30pm.

WHERE TO STAY & DINE

Note: Unlike many other places in Greece, in Kalavryta and Diakofto peak season is winter and prices are lower in summer.

You'll probably want to stay in Diakofto for the beach, and/or to be on the main train line to Patras or Athens. Close to the station and some 1,590 feet (500m) from the sea, the two-floor **Chris Paul Hotel** (© **26910/41-715;** www.chrispaul-hotel.gr) is a good place for an overnight stop and a swim. The air-conditioned rooms are simply furnished; doubles cost 55€ to 65€ ($71.50–$84.50).

If nature and isolation are what you're after, take the train to Zahlorou (see above), on the Diakofto–Kalavryta line, where you'll find the **Romantzo Hotel** (© **26920/22-758**), right next to the picturesque Mega Spilaio train station. Located in a forested gorge and surrounded by natural beauty, the old wooden hotel is, as its name suggests, romantic. There are several hiking trails nearby; a trail that goes to the nearby Monastery of the Great Cave is just a few steps away. The hotel has few rooms and they go fast, so reserve well in advance. Its restaurant offers great home-cooked meals, although if you wish to dine elsewhere, many tavernas are located in the village. Rooms run 25€ to 35€ ($32.50–$45.50) for a double.

In Kalavryta, one of the top housing options is the **Xenonas Fanara** (© **26920/23-665**), a year-round guesthouse built in 1995. With nine apartments suitable for two to four people, it has all the expected amenities, including kitchens, heating, and televisions, as well as balconies with views. The hotel is 990 feet (300m) from the station. Rooms cost 60€ to 100€ ($78–$130) for a double with breakfast. As for dining, **Stani** (© **26920/23-000**) is a popular taverna on the main square. Main courses run about 7€ ($9.10).

OLYMPIA ★★

The birthplace of the ancient Olympic Games, Olympia (Ilia prefecture) hosted the top athletic event for more than 1,000 years beginning in 776 B.C. For the modern Games held in 2004, the town received an extensive face-lift that included new stretches of pedestrian walkways and refurbished museums. Unfortunately, the site sustained damage—mainly to the surrounding trees—during the terrible fires of 2007 that ravaged the country, but authorities have made efforts to restore the area in time for the Olympic flame-lighting ceremony ahead of the Beijing Summer Games.

Various venues, temples, and other structures were constructed throughout Olympia's history, the ruins of which can be seen at the archaeological site today, including the Games' original stadium, the gi-normous temple of Zeus, and the temple of Hera, where the Olympic flame is lit for the modern Olympics. The contents of the on-site museum are unique and superlative, including a battering ram in the shape of a ram's head.

GETTING THERE   One of five trains a day from Athens to Pyrgos costs 20.10€ ($26.15) in first class and 16.30€ ($21.20) in second; you'll need to take the Athens–Kiato Proastiakos suburban train first, then transfer to the Intercity train at Kiato for the final leg to Pyrgos. More trains leave from nearby Patras to Pyrgos, where five regional trains shuttle the half-hour distance to Olympia daily. Call ⓒ 1110 for details. Tickets from Pyrgos to Olympia cost .70€ (90¢). Railpasses are valid on all the train options. *Note:* If you miss the train to Olympia at Pyrgos, **KTEL buses** (ⓒ 26210/20-600) also make the short journey to Olympia to avoid wasting time in this unremarkable farming town. The ancient site is less than a 15-minute walk from Olympia village and the train station. Olympia is a walkable town with no public transportation, so you can stroll to all the attractions or take a **taxi** (ⓒ 26240/22-555).

VISITOR INFORMATION   The municipality can help with tourism information via phone (ⓒ 26240/22-549) or in person at the Dimarchio (Town Hall) on the main street. Hours are Monday to Friday, 7:30am to 3pm. The tourist police are also available at ⓒ 26240/22-550; they are most helpful.

TOP ATTRACTIONS & SPECIAL MOMENTS

Between the museum and archaeological site, you'll need the better part of a day to tour Ancient Olympia. If hitting a **beach** is also in your plans, the long and sandy, Blue-Flagged beach at **Zacharo** is about 12 to 15 miles (20–25km) away on the coast (six trains a day run southbound from Pyrgos; 45 min.). The train station is about 1,300 feet (400m) from the shoreline, but you could also stay at one of the few guesthouses.

Olympia's **Archaeological Museum** (ⓒ 26240/22-742), overlooking the ancient site, houses two of antiquity's major statues: Praxiteles's *Hermes* and Paeonios's *Winged Victory,* or *Nike*—the Athens 2004 Olympic medals depicted his winged goddess. Other highlights include sculpted ornaments from the massive Temple of Zeus, prehistoric terra cotta, bronzes, and a collection of marble sculptures dating from Archaic to Roman times.

Most interesting are the objects used in the ancient games. Hundreds of pieces of ancient athletic paraphernalia related to the Olympics are on display, including stone discuses, weights used for balance by long jumpers, and objects commemorating Hercules (Heracles in Greek), the Olympics' mythological founder.

Across the road, the **ancient site** (ⓒ 26240/22-517) is divided into two distinct parts: the religious sanctuary and the athletic facilities. The **religious sanctuary** is dominated by the Temple of Hera and the massive Temple of Zeus. With its three standing columns, the **Temple of Hera** is the older of the two, built around 600 B.C. The *Hermes of Praxiteles* statue was found here, buried under the mud that covered Olympia for so long due to the repeated flooding of the Alfios and Kladeos rivers. The **Temple of Zeus,** which once had 34 massive Doric columns, was built around 456 B.C. Inside the temple stood one of the Seven Wonders of the Ancient World: an enormous gold-and-ivory statue of Zeus on an ivory-and-ebony throne. Not only do we know that Phidias made the 43-foot-tall (13m) statue, we know where he made it: The **Workshop of Phidias** was on the site of the well-preserved brick building clearly visible west of the temple, just outside the sanctuary. A cup with the inscription "I belong to Phidias" was found inside that building.

On the sporting side, in addition to the famed stadium, there are also the remains of the **gymnasium** and **palestra,** where athletics and wrestling were practiced. The remains of a shrine to Philip of Macedon, father of Alexander the Great, and Roman baths and fountains can also be seen.

Admission to both the archaeological museum and the ancient site is 9€ ($11.70); or 6€ ($7.80) separately. The ancient site and museum are open 8am to 7:30pm daily, except the museum opens at noon on Mondays. Reduced winter hours are usually 8:30am until 3pm or 5pm.

Back in the town, the **Museum of the Olympic Games** (✆ **26240/22-544**), commemorates the modern games, displaying commemorative stamps and photos of winning athletes, such as former King Constantine of Greece and the great American athlete Jesse Owens. Admission is 2€ ($2.60); it's open Tuesday to Sunday, 8am to 3:30pm.

WHERE TO STAY & DINE

For a village, the nearly two dozen hotels around Olympia may seem excessive, and they probably would be if not for the massive flood of tourists the city sees in July and August. Note that some hotels in town close in the winter, though both the hotels mentioned below are open year-round.

Perhaps the best hotel in town, **Hotel Europa** ★★, Drouva 1 (✆ **26240/22-650;** www.hoteleuropa.gr), part of the Best Western chain, is a 3-minute cab ride from the station, and sits high on a hill overlooking both the modern village and the ancient site. Most of the large rooms look out onto a large pool and garden, and several have views of the ancient site. All have balconies, refrigerators, and air-conditioning. The 115€ ($150) rate for a double includes breakfast.

Hotel Neda, Karamanli 1 (✆ **26240/22-563;** www.hotelneda.gr), is on the quieter end of the noisy hotel scale and features a pleasant rooftop cafe. The air-conditioned rooms are large; some of the doubles have double beds, but most have twins, so specify your preference when reserving. All units have balconies. Double rooms run 55€ to 80€ ($71.50–$104) with breakfast. The hotel is about 985 feet (300m)—an easy walk—from the train station; and the same distance from the ancient site.

The excellent and reasonably priced **Taverna Praxiteles** ★, Spiliopoulou 7 (✆ **26240/23-570**), is on the ground floor of the refurbished **Pension Leonideon** (same phone number), which reopened in 2007 and has doubles for 30€ ($39); 40€ ($52) with breakfast. The centrally located restaurant is packed almost every evening, first by visitors eating unfashionably early, then with locals, who start showing up around 10pm. Although the entrees are good, it's easy to make a meal of the delicious and varied appetizers. A sampling plate costs 6€ ($7.80) to 12€ ($15.60), and might include octopus, eggplant salad, *taramosalata* (fish-roe dip), *saganaki* (fried cheese), and a handful of olives. In good weather, tables are set outside.

PATRAS

Greece's third-largest city, the port of Patras (Achaia prefecture) is a busy transit point, providing ferry connections to Italy and the islands of the Ionian Sea. Like the port of Piraeus near Athens, the only reason to come to Patras is basically to catch a ferry. But once a year the city offers visitors a different incentive to visit—its famous (in Greece) annual **Carnival,** organized by the city's cultural development body (© **2610/222-157**). The event is celebrated during the 3 weeks before Lent (Orthodox), with lively parades, costumes, and floats. Reserve a room well in advance if you'll be staying here during that time.

Patras received a major upgrade to its landscape just days before the Olympics began in 2004: the nearby **Rio-Antirio suspension bridge,** with the world's longest main span (7,388 ft./2,252m). The bridge links the western Peloponnese with mainland Greece and hence, Europe, which was only possible via shuttle ferries or by looping around the Gulf of Corinth until the bridge opened.

GETTING THERE   Eight trains leave from Athens to Patras, including four Inter-City trains, which take around 3½ hours; the slower ones take just under 4 hours. A first-class, one-way ticket on an IC train from Kiato (taking the suburban Proastiakos from Athens to Kiato) costs 15.10€ ($19.60) and a second-class ticket is 12.40€ ($16.15). Railpasses are good for travel on these trains.

The Patras **train station,** Othonos Amalias 14 (© **2610/639-102**), is on the waterfront near the boat departure piers. Patras is one of the arrival and departure points for ferry service between Greece and Italy. *Note:* If you are taking the train to Patras for the sole purpose of catching a ferry, leave plenty of time to get to the city and your boat in case of a train delay.

VISITOR INFORMATION   A municipality run information center is located at Othonos Amalias 6, about 1,620 feet (495m) from the train station, across from the pier (© **2610/461-740**). Its friendly staff will answer any questions you have year-round, from 8am to 10pm daily.

TOP ATTRACTIONS & SPECIAL MOMENTS

Everything in Patras revolves around the port, which understandably dominates the city because it is a major entry and exit point for passengers and goods to and from Western Europe. Other than its pretty setting, bounded by mountains behind and the sea in front, there are only some offbeat attractions to keep your interest. But if you do decide to check out the town or have time to kill before a train, bus, or boat takes you on to your next destination, here are some good options.

The **Fortress of Patras** (© **2610/623-390**) is located ½ mile (1km) from the port. Once surrounded by a moat, the multitowered structure dates from the 6th century, using material from the ancient acropolis that was previously on the site. The fort was used, albeit by various invaders and defenders, for its original function up until World War II. Since 1973, under the auspices of the Byzantine Antiquities Ephorate, it now holds cultural events at a theater within its walls. The fortress is open daily from 8:30am to 3pm, except Mondays; admission is free.

West of the fortress is one of the country's remaining Ottoman-era hamams or **Turkish baths.** Dating from 1400, **Loutra-hamam Patron,** Boukaouri 29 at Pan-tokratoros Street (© **2610/274-267**), is one of only two in the country—and likely in all of Europe—that, incredibly, is still in use as a public bathhouse. (The other is on the island of Rhodes.) On foot from the train station, head down Ayiou Nikolaou St., which becomes Papadiamantopoulou Street until you reach Boukaouri and turn right. Women can use the baths Monday 9am to 9pm; Wednesday 9am to 2:30pm and 5pm to 9pm; Friday 9am–9pm; and Tuesday, Thursday, and Saturday 2:30pm to 5pm. Men are welcome Tuesday, Thursday, and Saturday 9am to 2:30pm and 5 to 9:30pm; and Wednesday 2:30 to 5pm. The entrance fee is 6€ ($7.80), plus a tip for

Patras

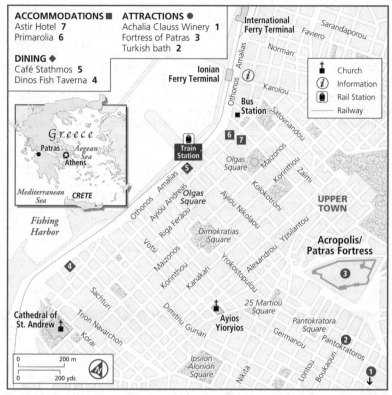

ACCOMMODATIONS ■
Astir Hotel **7**
Primarolia **6**

DINING ◆
Café Stathmos **5**
Dinos Fish Taverna **4**

ATTRACTIONS ●
Achalia Clauss Winery **1**
Fortress of Patras **3**
Turkish bath **2**

✝ Church
ⓘ Information
🚉 Rail Station
Railway

the cleaner. Bring your own toiletries and towel, and remember that this is a public bathhouse and not a luxury spa.

The city's **Archaeological Museum,** Mezonos 42 (① **2610/220-829** or 2610/276-207), features artifacts uncovered from the area, with discoveries spanning the period from 3000 B.C. and 800 B.C., as well as the city's first Roman finds. A new location, on the National Road entrance to Patras (from Athens), was expected to open in 2006 but construction was still ongoing at press time. The museum is open Tuesday through Sunday from 8:30am to 3pm; closed Mondays. Admission is free.

Hovering above the city is the **Achaia Clauss Winery** (① **2610/368-276**), founded in the mid-1800s by Bavarian vintner Gustav Clauss. Free daily tours of the place where some of Europe's oldest wines sit in massive barrels, many carved with works of art, are available year-round on the hour from 11am until 3pm. Try the winery's famed Mavrodafni (akin to sweet sherry), and enjoy the view of the city below. The winery is accessible by **taxi** (① **2610/425-201**) from the train station (less than 7€/$9.10), or by bus no. 7 from the city bus station for 1€ ($1.30). A bus leaves every half hour from 6am to 10pm to the winery 5 miles (8km) away; call the **bus station** (① **2610/453-930** or 2610/273-936) or ask at tourist information to confirm times. To return from the winery, wait for the bus or call a taxi, which will charge extra (on top of the meter) for the pickup.

WHERE TO STAY & DINE

Conveniently located on the waterfront across from the railway station, **Primarolia** ★★, Othonos Amalias 33 (© **2610/624-900**), is within easy walking distance of almost everything you'd want to see in Patras. One of Greece's first boutique hotels, it show-cases artwork and furniture by well-known artists and designers throughout the prem-ises, and each of its 14 rooms sport a different decor. Rooms overlook the harbor or the city. Prices begin at 129€ ($168) for a city-view double including breakfast, and 157€ ($204) for the sea view. During Carnival the prices are 280€ to 360€ ($364–$468).

Its decor may be 1970s, but the 120-room **Astir Hotel,** Agiou Andrea 16 (© **2610/277-502**), has a central location and is within easy walking distance of the train sta-tion, a pool (check that it's open), and views of the harbor and a rooftop terrace that make it worth an overnight stay, especially if you've got an early ferry or train to catch. A double costs 108€ ($140), including breakfast.

You won't have to look further than the train station for a great meal. **Café Stath-mos** (© **2610/622-550**) puts all other station cafeterias and snack bars to shame. Its grilled sandwiches and salads can compete with any bistro, and you'll pay less than 10€ ($13) for a complete meal, including appetizers.

If seafood is what you're after, try **Dinos Fish Taverna,** Othonos Amalias 102 (© **2610/336-500**), a local favorite, where you can choose your own fish. Prices depend on the size of the fish and the day's market rate, but figure a main course will cost about 10€ ($13). It stays open late.

4 Thessaloniki & the Northeast

With no single jaw-dropper like the Acropolis or Eiffel Tower to make its mark, Thes-saloniki compensates with numerous lesser monuments scattered throughout its bor-ders. Traces of the port town's Greek, Roman, Byzantine, Turkish, and Jewish heritage are visible on every other corner of this bustling modern city of one million. Thessa-loniki's multicultural past is legendary: from hosting one of the largest pre-war Jewish populations in Eastern Europe, to being the birthplace of Kemal Ataturk, founder of modern Turkey.

Unlike Greece's "Big Village" capital to the south—a magnet for rural job-seekers since the 1950s—Thessaloniki (aka Salonica) has been cosmopolitan for centuries, and Thessalonicans' sophistication shows. Today it offers rich nightlife, good and rel-atively inexpensive traditional and multi-ethnic food, cultural treasures that include numerous Byzantine churches, and a 2½-mile-long (4km) seaside boardwalk (if you don't mind being subjected to the unusually high humidity). Most important for the rail traveler, the city is a springboard for rail excursions to the whole of northern Greece as well as the country's gateway to Turkey and the Balkans.

STATION INFORMATION
GETTING FROM THE AIRPORT TO THE TRAIN STATION

There are no direct flights from the U.S. to Thessaloniki, so you'll have to make a con-nection from at least one European city to get here. Located 10 miles (16km) from the city center, **Makedonia Airport** (© **2310/473-212**) is linked to the city center and the train station by a public bus line. Taking a taxi, however, will get you to the train sta-tion on the other side of town far quicker, and costs 10€ to 15€ ($13–$19.50), depending on traffic.

INSIDE THE TRAIN STATION

Most visitors arrive by train. Nearly a dozen trains a day run on the popular Athens–Thessaloniki route on newly laid tracks, resulting in fast and efficient service. The InterCity trains are air-conditioned, clean, roomy, and almost soundproof. Only two of the older, slower trains are used on the route from Athens to Alexandroupoli in the northeast. Depending on the type of train, the trip can take from 4 hours and 15 minutes to 8 hours. The overnight train has sleeper and couchette compartments for one to six passengers. Reservations for sleepers should be made many days in advance. The cost of a second-class seat can run from 15.10€ to 48.50€ ($19.60–$63) and a business-class seat from 23.30€ to 63.50€ ($30.30–$82.55), depending on whether the train is a regional, InterCity, or InterCity Express. You can use a rail-pass on these trains.

For information on sleeper compartment pricing on Thessaloniki trains, see "Services & Amenities," at the beginning of this chapter. The Thessaloniki **train station** (© 2310/599-049), Greece's largest, is at the edge of the city on Monastiriou Street, which is the extension of Egnatia west of Dimokratias Square, the location of numerous shady bars. Some unexciting restaurants, cafes, shops, and newsstands are on the premises, as well as a luggage storage office. Head southeast towards the port in trendy **Ladadika** instead for a meal or to rest at an outdoor cafe/bar; southwest to reach popular nightspots. A taxi ride to central **Aristotelous Square** from the station takes less than 10 minutes and costs around 4€ ($5.20). *Warning:* Beware of pickpockets while inside and around the station.

INFORMATION ELSEWHERE IN THE CITY

The main office of the **Greek National Tourism Organization (EOT/GNTO)** in Thessaloniki is at Tsimiski 136 and Dagli (© 2310/221-100). It's open Monday to Friday 8am to 2:45pm and Saturday to Sunday 8:30am to 2pm. From mid-June to the end of August, the hours are daily 9am to 9pm.

There is also a desk in the **Makedonia Airport** domestic arrivals hall (© 2310/471-170), open 8am to 8pm weekdays and 8am to 2:30pm on Saturday.

GETTING AROUND

In the city center, most of the attractions, restaurants, and shops are easily reachable on foot in no more than 20 minutes. Otherwise, you'll need to use public transportation or take a taxi.

BY BUS   Thessaloniki has only one public transportation option: the bus. The network is good, but boarding with backpacks or luggage during rush hour will be a challenge. Tickets can be purchased from kiosks for .50€ (65¢) or on board the bus from machines for .60€ (80¢). Exact fare is required. Validate your ticket upon boarding and hold on to it in case a conductor boards the bus to check if you've paid your fare.

BY TAXI   Cabs are slightly easier to hail here than in Athens. Tell them your destination, take along a map, or have someone write your destination in Greek to show the driver where you want to go. Rates are cheap; round up the fare for a modest tip. Make sure, however, that the driver turns on his meter and that, within the city limits, the tariff rate is set on number 1. Tariff 2 is for outside the city limits. There's an extra 2€ ($2.60) charge for trips from the airport (the meter starts at 1.30€/$1.70 in town), and a small extra charge per bag put in the trunk. After midnight, all fares on the meter are charged at the higher tariff 2 rate.

Thessaloniki

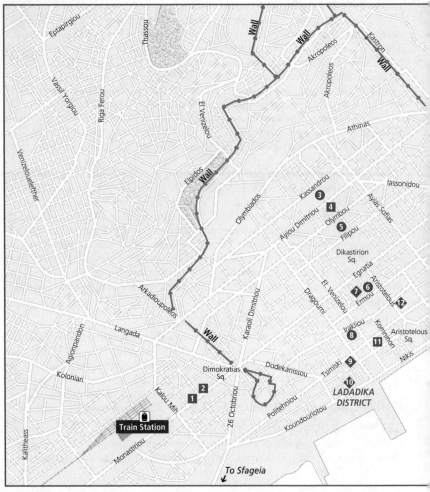

WHERE TO STAY

There are a number of hotels along Monastiriou Avenue leading from the train station into town (eastbound), the street changing names to Egnatia at Dimokratias Square. *Note:* In Thessaloniki, a big convention town, high season is in September during the international trade fair.

Capsis Hotel ✦   Just 650 feet (200m) from the train station, the Capsis is also a convention center and attracts many business travelers. Buts its location on busy Monastiriou makes it just as good for leisure visitors, who can stroll to the city center and sightsee along the way. The rooms are rather average, but the hotel has some accessible rooms for those with mobility issues and a welcome rooftop pool and gym. Another bonus: late check out (5:30pm), and even later—until 8pm—for an extra 10€ ($13).

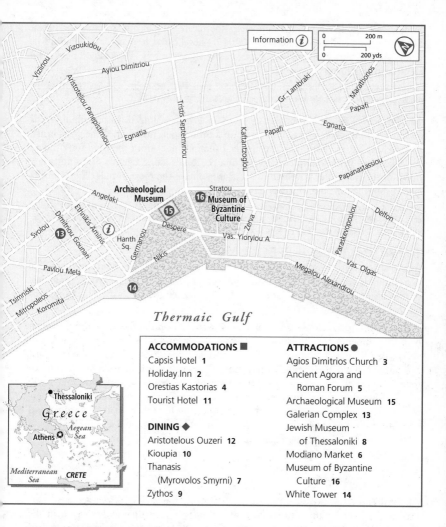

Monastiriou 18, 54629 Thessaloniki. ☏ **2310/596-800.** Fax 2310/510-555. www.capsishotel.gr. 412 units. 125€–180€ ($163–$234) double. Rates include breakfast. AE, DC, MC, V. **Amenities:** Restaurant; 2 bars. *In room:* Hair dryer.

Holiday Inn   Like the Capsis, this well-known hotel chain is an obvious choice for the rail traveler, being some 985 feet (300m) from the station. Its modern rooms, including rare nonsmoking ones, have a luxurious feel to them and soundproof windows. Business- and family-friendly, it has all the necessary hookups, as well as cots, cribs, and babysitting. One room is wheelchair accessible. An on-site gym is free.

Monastiriou 8, 54629 Thessaloniki. ☏ **2310/563-100.** Fax 2310/563-101. www.holiday-inn.com/thessaloniki. 177 units. 149€–276€ ($194–$359) double. Rates include breakfast. AE, DC, MC, V. **Amenities:** Restaurant; bar; laundry; nonsmoking rooms; 1 room for those w/limited mobility. *In room:* Hair dryer.

Orestias Kastorias ⟨Value⟩   This budget hotel has a super location on a quiet street leading from the Ancient Agora (Forum) to Agios Dimitrios church, right in the middle of Thessaloniki's sightseeing area. Rooms are spartan but spacious and clean. Something of a well-kept secret, the 1920s-era hotel caters to many families and Mt. Athos visitors. Front rooms have views of the ancient ruins. *Warning:* There is no elevator in this three-story walk-up.

Agnostou Stratiotou 14, 54631 Thessaloniki. ✆ 2310/276517. www.okhotel.gr. 37 rooms. 49€–64€ ($63.70–$83.20) double; group discounts available. Rates include cookies, tea, and coffee all day. MC, V.

Tourist Hotel ✿   This three-story hotel in a high-ceilinged, historic building is another good budget choice. It's located in a prime spot, just west of the city's heart, Aristotelous Square. Although it is nearly 1.6km (1 mile) from the train station, you can take a bus (there's frequent service) or a cheap taxi along Egnatia Street and walk down to the hotel. Book well ahead, as this is one of the most popular hotels in the city for both leisure and business travelers.

Mitropoleos 21 and Komninon, 54624 Thessaloniki. ✆ 2310/270-501. Fax 2310/226-865. www.touristhotel.gr. 37 units. 80€–100€ ($104–$130). Rates include breakfast. Ask about discounts for extended stays and groups. AE, MC, V. **Amenities:** Laundry. *In room:* Hair dryer on request.

TOP ATTRACTIONS & SPECIAL MOMENTS

As is true for most trips, no matter how much time you have, you won't be able to see everything. If you're planning a short stint during your rail journeys, you'll get a taste of the cultural and historic offerings on a do-it-yourself tour with the sites from various epochs listed below.

Agios Dimitrios Church   A small church was built on the site of a former Roman bath to commemorate Dimitrios, the city's patron saint, in the 4th century. Some 100 years later, the church was expanded to its current five-aisled basilica form, but a 1917 fire burned down the original, prompting the construction of the church you see today. Almost all the mosaics are restorations of what was lost in the fire, but a few survive from the 5th to 7th century A.D. The **crypt** ✿, which you enter down a narrow, twisting staircase, is pleasantly mysterious, with several small anterooms and remains of the **Roman baths.** Particularly venerated are the spots where Dimitrios is believed to have been martyred and the area of the holy water font.

Corner of Agiou Dimitriou and Agiou Nikolaou sts. (1 block north of the Roman Forum, at the base of the Upper City). ✆ 2310/270-591 (crypt). Free admission. Crypt open Mon 12:30–7pm; Tues–Fri 8:30am–8pm; Sat 8am–3pm; Sun 11am–3pm. Reduced winter hours.

Ancient Agora and Roman Forum ✿   Initially the ancient Greek agora or marketplace, it later became the location of a Roman forum. It was discovered in the 1960s by accident when work crews were digging the foundations for the city's courts. You can see the arched remains of the **cryptoporticus,** a retaining wall that supported part of the upper forum. The best-preserved ruin here is the large **Odeum,** or Odeon, a theater where Romans watched athletic, musical, and gladiator contests. Today it is used for summertime concerts.

Behind (north of) Dikasterion Sq., between Filippou and Olimbou sts. ✆ 2310/221-266. Free admission. Tues–Sun 8:30am–3pm; closed Mon.

Archaeological Museum ✿✿✿   The treasures found at the Royal Tombs at Vergina, including the gold *larnax* (box) with the 16-pointed star that held the bones believed to belong to Alexander the Great's father, Philip of Macedon, have been moved to Vergina, where the tombs are located. They have been replaced, however, by finds from the Egnatia highway—the ancient Rome-to-Constantinople road of the

Heading outside the City

If seeing important sites in the vicinity of Thessaloniki is also on your agenda, head to a travel agent such as **Zorpidis** (Egnatia 76, 1st floor; ✆ **2310/244-400**; www.zorpidis.gr), which does a half-day tour to **Vergina-Pella** (tombs of Philip of Macedon and Ancient Pella), a full-day tour to **Meteora** (natural wonder "hoodoo" mountains with monasteries perched on top), a cruise around the all-male monastic **Mt. Athos** peninsula, and a 3-day trip to the **Sporadic islands** (Skiathos and Skopelos) at good prices.

Or you could negotiate a tailored tour with a taxi driver for mainland destinations, which shouldn't cost much more than an organized excursion, or take the train to personal points of interest, west or east, where possible. For instance, from Thessaloniki you can visit the three major locations connected to Alexander the Great:

Ancient Dion (43 miles/70km), an enchanting and enormous site is located at the foot of Mt. Olympus and named after Zeus (Dias in Greek), where the Macedonian Games were also held. Take a train to Katerini (1½ hr.) and then a local bus from the nearby KTEL station or a taxi to the site, some 9 miles (15km) away. Or travel from Litohoro, the base for a **Mt. Olympus** trek and nearby **beaches;** Dion is 4 miles (6km) from there by taxi. For more information on Mt. Olympus, see "An Excursion to Mount Olympus," on p. 498.

Ancient Pella (18 miles/30km), the ancient capital of Macedonia and birthplace of Alexander and his father, Philip II, has an interesting little museum with elaborate mosaics, and an archaeological site. Take a train detour and/or stay in pretty Edessa, and then take a KTEL bus from there.

Vergina (43 miles/70km) is where the enormous, exquisite tomb of Philip II and other renowned historical objects (excavated in 1977) are located. Detour by train to Veria and take a local "blue" bus from the out-of-the-way station to Veria town, where you can catch a KTEL bus to Vergina.

Note: Accommodation in Dion and Vergina is sparse. There is nothing to see or do in modern Pella, and nowhere to stay.

---

same name—the Thessaloniki–Skopje highway, and a new railway line. Exhibits also showcase Thessaloniki's history, from prehistoric to Roman times. Impressively detailed sarcophagi; archaic, classical, and Hellenistic statues from the surrounding region; and unbelievable amounts of gold jewelry dating from the 6th through 2nd century B.C. unearthed from excavations at cemeteries are all on display.

Manoli Andronikou 6, HANTH Sq. ✆ **2310/830-538**. Admission 6€ ($7.80), combined ticket with Byzantine Culture museum is 8€ ($10.40). Tues–Sun 8am–7:30pm; Mon 1–7:30pm. Reduced winter hours.

Galerian Complex   The Roman Tetrarch Galerius went on a construction spree in the 4th century A.D., but it wasn't until about 2 decades ago that many of the structures were rediscovered. **The Arch of Galerius** was built in A.D. 305 by Galerius, to commemorate a victory over the Persians a few years earlier. Only a part of the original structure remains, with bas-reliefs depicting Galerius's battles. The arch, located right next to busy Egnatia Street, was recently restored after traffic pollution began eroding some of the detail.

Nearby stands the **Rotunda;** aka *Agios Georgios* or St. George church, a typical round-shaped Roman construction. Some think it was built as Galerius's mausoleum, others as a temple. It eventually became a church under Byzantine rule, when its mosaic ornamentation was commissioned. The Turks turned it into a mosque in the 15th century. The structure was restored over the course of a decade to repair damage from a 1978 earthquake and was opened to the public in 1999.

Take the boho-chic pedestrian walkway (Gounari St.) to Navarinou Square, flanked by eateries, small boutiques, and book and record shops, and you'll see what remains of Galerius' **palace.** The best-preserved part of the complex is the **Octagon,** a mysterious building that some archaeologists think may have been Galerius' throne room.

The arch is located on Egnatia and Gounari sts.; the Rotunda (© 2310/968-860) is north of it, off Sintrivaniou Sq. Free admission. May–Oct Tues–Fri 8:30am–7pm; Sat–Sun 8am–3pm; closed Mon. Reduced winter hours.

Jewish Museum of Thessaloniki   This small museum portrays Jewish life in Thessaloniki with photographs and artifacts. Jews established the city's first printing press in the early 1500s, and founded the city's first newspaper, *El Lunar,* in 1865. The Sephardic community, which came to Thessaloniki following the 15th-century Spanish Inquisition, thrived under the Ottoman Empire, and by 1900, 80,000 of Thessaloniki's 173,000 inhabitants were Jews. Just before World War II, there were 60,000 Jews here; 2,000 survived the death camps. Today there are almost none.

Agiou Mina 13. © 2310/250-406. www.jmth.gr. Admission 3€ ($3.90). Tues, Fri, Sun 11am–2pm; Wed–Thurs 11am–2pm and 5–8pm. Closed Mon and Sat. Groups of more than 10 people are asked to call ahead.

Modiano Market   You could easily spend a morning in this glass-roofed market, which covers an entire square block, happily wandering from stall to stall and eyeing the fish, meat, fruit, vegetables, flowers, spices, and baked goods on sale. A number of cafes and tavernas are located in and around it so browse, buy, and binge at leisure.

The block bounded by Aristotelous, Ermou, Vassileos Irakleiou, and Komninon sts. Mon–Sat 7am–3pm.

Moments   **Scenic Route through the Nestos**

The **Nestos river delta,** featuring freshwater lakes, rare plant species, and birds, is a European Union special protection area. The migratory rest area is home to endangered birds such as the Dalmatian pelican and white-tailed eagle, 27 orchid varieties, and many other kinds of flora and fauna. The watershed can be seen en route on trains heading from **Thessaloniki** (© 2310/599-049) to Xanthi, farther east. The train runs past the river valley, winding its way through the scenic area on a breathtaking ride, ducking in and out of tunnels and trees. Sit on the right side of the train for a better view as you head east toward Xanthi; on the opposite side for the return journey.

Visitors can **hike into the valley** starting at the village of Toxotes, 9 miles (15km) from Xanthi. Three trains make the 10-minute run from **Xanthi** (© 25410/22-581) to **Toxotes** (© 25410/93-290) at 11am, 5pm, and 2am. Return times from Toxotes are noon, 6:05pm, and 3:50am. Tickets are 1€ ($1.30).

Museum of Byzantine Culture ✸✸✸ Spanning Roman times until the end of the 19th century, this museum, awarded the Council of Europe's 2005 museum prize, has one of the best collections of its type. Paraphernalia from the early Christian Church are on display, as well as priceless icons, intricate jewelry, and religious embroidery. The museum shop offers a range of books on Byzantine culture as well as museum reproductions and postcards. It's just next door to the Archaeological Museum.

Leof. Stratou 2. ✆ **2310/868-570.** www.mbp.gr. Admission 4€ ($5.20); combined ticket with Archaeological Museum is 8€ ($10.40). Check the website for discounts. Tues–Sun 8am–7:30pm; Mon 1–7:30pm; Agiou Pnevmatos (Whit Monday) 8am–1pm.

White Tower This 98-foot (29m) tower is the city's most famous landmark. The cylinder-shaped stone structure was built by the Ottoman Turks in the 16th century as part of the city's walls, but was later used as a place of execution. In the 1980s it was restored and turned into a museum during celebrations for the 2,300th anniversary of the city's founding. Its steep, winding staircase goes up six floors and offers terrific views of the city and harbor. Each floor has a round room with alcoves, some of which were used as prison cells. At the very end of the staircase, a rooftop cafe rewards you for your climb.

Nikis St. and Pavlou Mela St. (on the seaside promenade just south of the Archaeological Museum). ✆ **2310/267-832.** Contact the Museum of Byzantine Culture for hours of operation and admission fees (it was closed at press time, but should be open by the time you read this).

WHERE TO DINE

Note: Most Thessaloniki restaurants do not accept credit cards.

Aristotelous Ouzeri ✸✸ GREEK/STARTERS Its central location, charming atmosphere, creative Greek food, and cosmopolitan service make Aristotelous a well-loved favorite of patrons ranging from artists to academics to business people. It is considered one of the best ouzo (and appetizer) places in town, with seating spilling out into a quiet, enclosed cul-de-sac. Expect to wait for a table if you arrive at 9pm or later.

Aristotelous 8, through the gate on the east side of Aristotelous, between Tsimiski and Irakliou sts.; be careful, as the street numbers repeat at Aristotelous Sq. farther south. ✆ **2310/233-195.** Reservations accepted. Appetizers 12€–30€ ($15.60–$39). MC, V. Mon–Sat noon–midnight; Sun noon–6pm.

Kioupia ✸ GREEK Easily reached on foot from the train station, this is one of the trendy warehouse district's more upscale restaurants. The varieties of food reflect regional cuisines of both Greece and Asia Minor, from where a large proportion of Thessalonicans originated. The house *retsina* is excellent, and there's an extensive wine list.

Note: The same management runs the nearby **Amorgos,** Pagaiou 4 and Doxis, Ladadika (✆ **2310/557-161**), which specializes in fresh fish.

Morihovou Sq. 3–5, Ladadika. ✆ **2310/553-239.** Fax 2310/553-579. www.kioupia.gr. Reservations recommended after 9pm; possible to make online. Appetizers 15€–20€ ($19.50–$26). AE, DC, MC, V. Mon–Sat 1pm–1am; Sun noon–6pm.

Thanasis (Myrovolos Smyrni) ✸✸ GREEK For nearly 50 years, Thessalonicans have beaten a path to this small, family-owned taverna, which serves Greek home-style cooking—including stuffed squid and mussels, both fried and steamed—with zest. During the day, local workers, especially from the attached Modiano Market, fill the restaurant. At night, be ready to grab a tambourine and dance on the table. The music—Greek, of course—gets very loud, especially in winter when seating is solely indoors.

Komninon 32 (between Ermou and Vas. Irakleiou, just outside the Modiano Market). (©) **2310/274-170.** Fax 2310/347-062. Reservations necessary after 10pm. Main courses 6€–8€ ($7.80–$10). No credit cards. Mon–Sun 8am–2am.

Zythos ⊕ GREEK/CONTINENTAL   This was one of the first restaurants to open in Thessaloniki's restored warehouse district, and it's still very popular with ladies who lunch, young lovers, and harried businessmen. The decor is lots of wood and brick, just as you'd expect in a former warehouse. There are usually two daily specials, including one vegetarian choice, on the menu.

Katouni 5, Ladadika. (©) **2310/540-284.** Main courses 8€–15€ ($10.40–$19.50). MC, V. Daily 11am–1am.

SHOPPING

Thessaloniki has great shopping, with a wide variety of shops located in a relatively small area. Stroll along **Tsimiski, Mitropoleos,** and **Proxenou Koromila** streets between **Pavlou Mela** (the diagonal street connecting the church of Ayia Sofia with the White Tower) and the north-south vertical of **Venizelou.** In this area are the city's few department stores, many boutiques selling the latest in expensive haute couture, shops selling jeans and casual clothing, *lots* of shoe stores, jewelry and antiques stores, and a number of confectioneries.

Don't expect to find touristy souvenirs. Instead you'll come across a number of shops displaying the work of local artisans, such as coppersmiths and jewelers, often at bargain prices. Many of these shops are around **Athonos Square,** a warren of alleys bounded by Egnatia, Aristotelous, Ermou, and Karolou Dil streets. More copper and antiques shops are near the church of the Panayia Chalkeon (Virgin of the Copper Makers) at **Dikasterion Square,** particularly behind (north of) it and up Tossitsa and Olimbou streets.

At **Skitso,** Grigori Palama 11 ((©) **2310/269-822**), handmade wooden objects are the highlight, including puppets, ships, crosses, and children's toys. It's a block west of the intersection of Pavlou Mela and Tsimiski. **Ergasterio Kouklis,** Mitropolitou Gennadiou 2 ((©) **2310/236-890**), has wonderful dolls—for collectors, as well as for children. At **Ergani,** Vas. Irakleiou 32 ((©) **2310/222-592**), near the Modiano Market, you'll find a selection of handcrafted items, including decorative objects for your home and jewelry for you.

NIGHTLIFE

Within the grounds of a restored flour mill, the **Mylos** (*mee*-los) complex ⊕, Andreadou Georgiou 56, Sfageia ((©) **2310/551-838;** www.mylos.gr), off 26 Oktovriou St., southwest of the train station, contains a club for blues, folk, jazz, and pop groups; a nightclub featuring Greek singers and comedians; a bar; an outdoor concert stage; exhibition areas and art galleries; a cafe; and an appetizer-serving ouzeri. Almost as soon as it opened in 1991, Mylos became one of the top musical venues in the country and is a permanent fixture on Thessaloniki's nightlife scene year-round. The ouzeri, cafe, and galleries are open from about 11am until late. The clubs are open from 10pm to about 3am.

For more highbrow entertainment, see what's playing at the **Thessaloniki Concert Hall** (Megaron Mousikis), 25th Martiou and Paralia streets ((©) **2310/895-800;** www.tch.gr).

AN EXCURSION TO MOUNT OLYMPUS

The home of Greece's ancient gods, Mount Olympus is actually a range of peaks that includes Mytikas, the country's highest at 9,570 feet (2,917m), rising above the plains of Thessaly and Macedonia. The whole area is a national park that features wildlife and more than 1,500 plant species, many particular to the area.

GETTING THERE   All trails begin from the mountain town of **Litohoro,** which has a small, rarely manned station about 3 miles (4.8km) away, making it rather inconvenient, although you can call a **taxi** (© **23520/82-333** or 6932/671-481; 6€/$7.80; trip time: 10 min.) if your train stops and you get out here. It's better to get off at **Katerini** a little farther north on the Larissa–Thessaloniki line, and take a KTEL (long-distance) **bus** (© **23510/46720** in Litohoro, or 23520/81-271), which leaves every hour. Tickets cost 2€ ($2.60) and the trip takes 20 minutes.

VISITOR INFORMATION   The **Alpine and Ski Club (EOS;** © **210/364-5904** in Athens, 2310/278-288 in Thessaloniki, or 23520/81-944 after 8pm in Litohoro; www.eosthessalonikis.gr; Mon, Wed–Fri 10am–3pm and 8–11pm; Tues 10am–3pm), can provide information about Mt. Olympus, from weather conditions to shelter reservations. **Trekking Hellas** at Filellinon 7, Syntagma, Athens (© **210/331-0323;** www.trekking.gr), organizes excursions, and **Anavasi (www.mountains.gr)** has the best maps of the area, available in bookstores in Greece and abroad.

TOP ATTRACTIONS & SPECIAL MOMENTS

The hike straight to the top will take about 6 hours. It's an ambitious effort to do all at once, and the last bit is a hard and scary scramble. Better to spend the night at a mountain refuge, such as **Spilios Agapitos** (© **23520/81-800;** www.mount olympus.gr; 6,758 ft./2,060m), for about 10€ ($13). It's open from mid-May to the end of October. Bring sheets, a flashlight, towel and toiletries; slippers are recommended. The restaurant is open from 6am to 9pm. **Stavros** (© **23520/84-100;** 3,096 ft./944m) is about 6 miles (10km) from Litohoro and functions more as a restaurant. It's best to call first and make a reservation if you plan on staying at a shelter.

Unique for a mountain excursion, Mount Olympus is also near some pretty nice **beaches,** just 2½ to 4 miles away on the coast. Take a taxi or bus to popular Plaka beach (umbrellas, lounge chairs, amenities). The Plaka-beach-terminating bus leaves hourly in summer from Litohoro KTEL station (2.50€/$3.25 round-trip). Or go to Gritsa beach on the Litohoro-Katerini bus route, which also leaves hourly in summer. Tickets cost 2.20€ ($2.90) round-trip. Get out at "Camping Mitikas" and go straight through the campsite to reach it. Your hotel can also recommend a number of good local beaches.

WHERE TO STAY & DINE

If you stay in Litohoro, **Villa Pantheon** ✿✿, Terma (end) Agiou Dimitriou, 60200 Litohoro (© **23520/83-931**), is arguably the best place, with outstanding views. Rates are 50€ ($65) year-round; add 6€ ($7.80) for breakfast.

The **Olympus Mediterranean** ✿, Dionyssou 5, 60200 Litohoro (© **23520/81-831;** www.olympusmed.gr), is an upscale spa hotel that has an indoor pool and offers

---

Moments   Don't Forget the Sweet ✿✿✿

While in town, the sweet-toothed must get a pastry from one or more of Thessaloniki's renowned bakery chains (there are many store locations spread out all over the city), such as **Agapitos** (www.agapitos.gr), **Averof** (www.averof.gr); **Terkenlis** (www.terkenlis.gr), or **Hatzi** (www.chatzis.gr). A cream-filled cone called a *trigono panoramatos* is a specialty, as is *kazandibi*—a flan deliciously burned on one side—plus many more unusual treats influenced from the surrounding Macedonian region and Turkey.

rooms that come with a Jacuzzi or fireplace at very good prices. Rates are 75€ to 120€ ($97.50–$156) with breakfast.

The hotel is located in town, right beside **To Pazari** taverna (© **23520/82-540** or 23520/84-185), which is up past the main square and around the corner to your left. Take the opportunity to eat fresh fish at excellent prices at this well-signposted taverna, which also serves local meat dishes. It's open daily from noon to 4pm and 7pm until late in the evening. Main courses run about 15€ ($19.50) per person.

12

Hungary

Hungary has a long, rich history that includes membership in the Roman, Turkish and Austro-Hungarian empires, and a gloomy spell trapped behind the Iron Curtain. Today, Hungary has once again regained its position as a vibrant Eastern European country and is one of the Continent's hottest travel destinations. Though the Lake Balaton region has lost much of its allure in recent years, Hungary's infrastructure as a whole has developed measurably. The country's geographic placement makes it a perfect stopover for the train traveler crisscrossing the Continent. For visitors looking for more bang for their buck, the country is still a little cheaper than most of its Western counterparts, though it is not the true budget destination it once was. Still, in a land of expensive gasoline and hefty highway tolls, trains are the principal means of long-distance travel for most of the population; the best way to see this remarkable little country is by rail.

HIGHLIGHTS OF HUNGARY

All rails in Hungary lead into and out of **Budapest,** lively capital and undisputed transportation hub, a proud city sitting astride the Danube River in the middle of the country. Savor Budapest, one of Europe's most appealing cities. But you should also go beyond the capital and explore the smaller cities and the countryside. Hop a train up the Danube to the "Danube Bend" towns of Szentendre, Esztergom, or Visegrád. In the artists' village of **Szentendre,** wander the winding streets and visit some interesting museums or galleries; in **Visegrád** don't miss the ruins of King Matthias's Renaissance Palace; ascend the steep stairs to the cupola at **Esztergom's** cathedral from where you can see deep into the Slovak countryside across the Danube. Ride to Lake Tisza, where you will find beautiful fauna and flora. Explore the little villages around the lake, tucked away in the rolling countryside, grapes of the popular Balaton wines ripening.

1 Essentials

GETTING THERE

BY PLANE The Hungarian airline **Malév** (© 1/235-3888; www.malev.hu) is the local flagship carrier from North America to Budapest. Other airlines offering service to the area include Delta, Lufthansa, and British Airways.

All flights that originate in North America arrive at **Ferihegy II Airport** (© 1/296-7000), located in the XVIII district in southeastern Pest.

An increasing number of low-cost European airlines (14 at press time) has made Hungary more accessible by air from the rest of the Continent. Fly cheaply to, say, London, and you might find a bargain fare to hop over to Budapest. Book early for

Moments Festivals & Special Events

Both the 2-week **Budapest Spring Festival** and **Autumn Festival** feature opera, ballet, classical music, and drama performances in all the major halls and theaters of Budapest. It's advisable to purchase tickets for the performances months in advance, when they are listed. Simultaneous to each festival's performing arts events, temporary exhibitions are also open in many of Budapest's museums. You can buy tickets at the **Budapest Festival Center,** V. 1053 Egyetem tér 5 (© 1/486-3311; www.festivalcity.hu), at the individual venues, or online. The action happens in mid- to late March and mid- to late October.

Every year on the second weekend in July, the ancient town of **Visegrád,** on the Danube, hosts the **International Palace Tournament,** an authentic medieval festival replete with dueling knights on horseback, early music, and dance.

On **King St. Stephen's Day,** August 20, the country's first king and patron saint is celebrated nationwide with cultural events and a display of fireworks over the Danube. Hungarians also celebrate their constitution on this day, as well as ceremoniously welcome the first new bread from the recent crop of July wheat.

The **Budapest Summer Music Festival** starts in July and runs through mid-August. Celebrating the opening of the fall season, special classical music and dance performances are held for 3 weeks starting in late September and going through October, in all the city's major halls during **Music Weeks in Budapest.** For information on the summer and autumn programs, contact the **Hungarian Arts Festivals Federation** (© 36/1-202-1095; www.arts festivals.hu). The latter festival's traditional start is September 25, the day of Béla Bartók's death.

the best-priced tickets. Be prepared for delays, however, and be sure to check which airport your carrier flies out of—it may be on the outskirts of town. Budget airlines that offer flights to Hungary out of many European countries now fly into **Ferihegy I,** also in district XVIII (© 1/296-9696). These include **Wizzair** © 1/470-9499; www.wizzair.com); **SkyEurope** (© 1/777-7000; www.skyeurope.com); **EasyJet** © 0871/244-2366; www.easyjet.com); and **Air Berlin** (© 80/017110; www.airberlin. com) as well as others. For the most current information on budget airlines within Europe, visit **www.skyscanner.com**.

HUNGARY BY RAIL
PASSES

For information on the **Eurail Global Pass, Eurail Global Pass Flexi,** and **European East Pass** and other multicountry options, see chapter 2.

The **Eurail Hungary Pass** offers first-class travel within Hungary for either 5 nonconsecutive days in a 15-day period or 10 nonconsecutive days in a 1-month period. The 5-day pass costs $97; the 10-day pass is $138. The pass is best obtained in North

America before departing for your trip. You can buy it from **Rail Europe** (© 877/ **272-RAIL** [7245] in North America; www.raileurope.com) or your travel agent. Pass discounts for travelers under 26 and those traveling in groups of five or more are available.

FOREIGN TRAIN TERMS

Hungarian ticket agents speak little English, so you will need to know some basic terminology in Hungarian. For a list of the most words for train travelers, see "Useful Hungarian Train Terms," below.

⌒ *Warning* Service Outages

MÁV, the government-owned train service, announced in the summer of 2007 that it would be cutting back service. The intent is to cut 14 branch lines, with another 60 lines also up for cutbacks. Although we don't believe it will change any of the information listed here, it is best to check train schedules and routes online at **www.elvira.hu**.

PRACTICAL TRAIN INFORMATION

Timetables for arrivals are displayed in stations on big white posters, while departures are on yellow posters in glass cases.

Train service in Hungary is generally reliable and usually runs according to schedule, though it's somewhat slower than in Western Europe. Its rail network is extensive, totaling more than 4,800 miles (7,740km), but you should keep in mind that the network is oriented on Budapest, so that city will almost always be both your arrival and your departure point from Hungary. Numerous international trains stop in Budapest, and several daily trains arrive in the city from Vienna, Prague, Warsaw, Zagreb, Bratislava, and Berlin.

Aside from international express trains, the best choices within Hungary are the **InterCity (IC)** express trains, which stop less often en route between major cities. These modern trains are clean and the only trains in Hungary with air-conditioning.

After the InterCity trains come the *gyors* fast trains, which are almost as fast as the IC trains, but are older and grittier. Avoid the slow *személy* and *sebes* trains, as they stop at all local stations, making a ride seem interminable.

Unfortunately, the Hungarian railway authority **MÁV Hungarian Railways** is poorly run and out of date. Ticketing still relies on antiquated systems and tickets purchased at the stations are in Hungarian only; the destination is not even indicated—simply the amount of kilometers you're authorized to travel. The ticketing service people are surly; don't be surprised if you are faced with an unfriendly, unilingual, grumpy Hungarian. At press time, you'd be better off going to a travel agency to buy

---

Useful Hungarian Train Terms

Indul	departure
Érkezik	arrival
Honnan	from where
Hová	to where
Vágány	platform
Munkanap	weekdays
Hétvége	weekend
Szombat	Saturday
Ünnepnap	legal holiday
Gyors	fast train or express
Jegy	ticket
Oda	one-way
Oda-vissza	round-trip
Helyjegy	reservation
Első Osztály	first class
Másodosztály	second class
Nem Dohányzó	nonsmoking
Ma	today
Holnap	tomorrow

Trains & Travel Times in Hungary

From	To	Train type	# of Trains	Frequency	Travel Time
Budapest	Esztergom	Reg.	26	Daily	1 hr., 35 min.– 2 hr., 33 min.
Budapest	Nagymaros-Visegrád		29	Daily	1 hr.

Reservations compulsory on InterCity trains between Budapest and Veszprém and Budapest and Keszthely. Numerous regional trains also travel these routes, but the travel time is longer.

your tickets, though in July 2007 MÁV announced that it's in the process of privatizing and hopes to allow travelers to purchase and print tickets online. You can access a timetable on the Web at **www.elvira.hu**, which can be searched in English.

RESERVATIONS You must reserve a seat on some international express trains and on all InterCity trains. You should ask if a reservation is needed when buying a ticket, but if you want to be guaranteed a seat, spend the extra money. Note that Hungarian trains are often crowded during the summer high season and weekends, so lines for reservations can get very long. You might want to reserve a seat several days in advance (the inefficient pricing and reservations system is currently so complicated that you'll need to head to the ticket office to sort out your options).

SERVICES & AMENITIES Generally speaking, most trains in Hungary do not have as many amenities as their Western European counterparts, and other than the new InterCity trains, they can be downright dirty (and covered in graffiti). You will find a snack bar and eatery on IC and international express trains, but not on other trains in Hungary. Occasionally, on trains other than IC trains, you will encounter a snack cart. Note also that trains do not have potable water, so you'll need to bring your own. Eating on trains is customary, so don't hesitate to bring food along. Load up on drinks and eats before you depart on your trip; every station has snack bars. Bear in mind that on many local trains, the bathrooms are kept locked if they are out of order, so you may have to walk through a few cars to find one available.

Some international trains that pass through Hungary have sleeping cars, but none of the local trains or regional trains have sleeper options of any sort.

FAST FACTS: Hungary

Area Codes See "Telephone," below.

Business Hours **Banks** are usually open from Monday to Thursday 8am to 5pm and Friday 8am to 1pm. Most **stores** are open Monday to Friday 10am to 6pm and Saturday 9 or 10am to 1 or 2pm (except many shopping malls, which keep later hours). As a rule, only stores in central tourist areas are open Sunday. Many shops and restaurants close for 2 weeks in August.

Climate Hungary's climate is fairly mild—the annual mean temperature is 50°F (10°C). That said, summers can get sweltering hot and humid, especially in July and August (when flash storms are possible), and winters can be damp and chilly, especially December and January. Fall and spring are generally pleasant and mild, though it can get wet in May and June.

Currency The basic unit of currency in Hungary is the **forint (Ft).** The rate of exchange used to calculate the dollar values given in this chapter is $1 = 185 Ft. Hungary won't adopt the euro before 2012, but many Hungarian hotels and restaurants already quote their rates in either euros or U.S. dollars as a hedge against inflation. Their rates are never to your advantage.

Documents Required A valid passport is the only document required for citizens of the U.S., Canada, Australia, and New Zealand.

Electricity Most hotels use 220 volts AC (50 cycles) and a European two-prong plug. Electrical equipment operating on 110 volts AC requires the use of an adapter and/or voltage converter.

Embassies & Consulates The embassy of the **United States** is at V. Szabadság tér 12 ((©) **1/475-4400;** Metro: Kossuth tér); the embassy of **Canada** is at II. Ganz u. 12–14. ((©) **1/392-3360;** Metro: Moszkva tér).

Health & Safety For medical treatment, try the **First Med Center,** across from the Mammut shopping center at I. Hattyu u. 14 ((©) **1/224-9090;** www.firstmed centers.com; Metro: Moszkva tér).

By U.S. standards, Hungary is a relatively safe country—muggings and violent attacks are rare. Nevertheless, foreigners are always prime targets. Beware of pickpockets, especially on crowded trams, Metros, and buses. Avoid being victimized by wearing a money belt under your clothes instead of wearing a fanny pack or carrying a wallet or purse. No valuables should ever be kept in the outer pockets of a backpack.

Holidays National holidays include: January 1; March 15 (National Day); Easter Sunday and Monday; May 1 (May Day); Pentecost (Whitsun); August 20 (St. Stephen's Day); October 23 (1956 Remembrance Day); November 1 (All Saints' Day); December 25 (Christmas); December 26 (Boxing Day).

Legal Aid Contact your embassy for legal assistance.

Mail If you need to receive or send mail, it's best to arrange it with your hotel.

Police & Emergencies Call (©) **1/438-8080** to reach a 24-hour hot line service in English, or call (©) **104** for an ambulance, (©) **105** for the fire department, or (©) **107** or 112 for the police.

Telephone The **country code** for Hungary is **36.** The **city code** for Budapest is **1;** use this code when you're calling from outside Hungary. If you're within Hungary but not in Budapest, first dial **06;** when you hear a tone, dial the city code and phone number. If you're calling within Budapest, simply leave off the code and dial only the regular seven-digit phone number. Dial (©) **198** for domestic directory assistance and (©) **199** for international queries.

Numbers beginning with **06-20, 06-30,** or **06-70** followed by a seven-digit number, are **mobile phone numbers.** The number **06-80** is toll free. Public **pay phones** charge varying amounts for local calls depending on the time of day you place your call; it's cheapest in the evenings and on weekends. Most public phones are now operated by the T Com phone company and operate with coins or, more commonly, phone cards that you can buy from post offices, newsstands, and convenience stores. Note that many pay phones are not maintained well and often do not work, so we caution against using them unless it is necessary.

You can reach the **AT&T** operator at ✆ **06/800-01111,** the **MCI Worldphone** operator at ✆ **06/800-01411,** and the **Sprint** operator at ✆ **06/800-01877.**

Tipping The general tipping rate is usually 10%. Among those who welcome tips are waiters, taxi drivers, hotel employees, barbers, cloakroom attendants, toilet attendants, masseuses, and tour guides.

2 Budapest

Budapest came of age in the 19th century, when the two towns of Buda and Pest were little more than provincial outposts on the Danube. Indeed, Budapest, notwithstanding its long and tattered history of Roman, Mongol, and Turkish conquest, is very much a late-19th-century city, with its characteristic coffeehouse and music hall culture. But, along with its extraordinary ambience, the city also has most of the modern conveniences one expects of a European capital.

As the central rail hub of Hungary, and the home of the region's major airport, this remarkably unpretentious city is a must-stop location on any rail tour of the country. On a rail journey that spans Europe's eastern and western halves, Budapest is an ideal stopover—a city that combines the best of both worlds. *Note:* Relatively stable and affordable Internet service is new to Hungary. Many businesses and attractions have jumped on the bandwidth wagon, and then let their websites sit forgotten. For the most reliable information, always call or e-mail. The exception to this rule is hotels, which maintain accurate websites.

STATION INFORMATION
GETTING FROM THE AIRPORT TO THE TRAIN STATIONS
The **Airport Minibus** (✆ 1/296-8555; www.bud.hu), a service of the Budapest Airport Authority, leaves **Ferihegy 2** (✆ **1/296-7155** for general info, 1/296-5052 for arrivals, or 1/296-5883 for departures), located in the XVIII district in southeastern Pest, every 10 or 15 minutes throughout the day. It will take you directly to any city address and costs 2,300 Ft ($12.45/£6.55) one-way, or 3,900 Ft ($21.10/£1.10) round-trip.

The airport has a new official airport taxi service called **Zóna Taxi** (✆ **1/365-5555**), which has a kiosk by the curb as you exit the airport. They charge using a zone system and the fixed rates range from 3,000 Ft ($16.20/£8.55) for zone 1 to 4,300 Ft ($23.25/£12.25) for zone 4. If you want to use a different service, phone from the terminal (see "By Taxi," on p. 517) and a cab will be there in a matter of minutes. There is a separate pickup area for other taxis, so look for the posted sign. For two people traveling together, a taxi from a recommended fleet to the city will be comparable in price to the combined minibus fares, at about 4,500 Ft ($24.30/£12.80). The ride should take 20 to 30 minutes.

Budapest

There is a rail link from **Ferihegy I** to **Nyugati** train station. Travel time is 30 minutes and the cost is 300 Ft ($1.60/85p), and trains depart regularly. **Bus 200** can be used to get from **Ferihegy II** to **I** to connect with the train, though further track construction is planned to allow a direct train link with both airports in the future. This bus requires a regular transport ticket of 230 Ft ($1.25/60p).

Another cheap way into the city is by public transportation; the bus-to-Metro-to-town trip takes about an hour's time in total. Take **bus 200** to the last stop, Kobánya-Kispest. From there, the Blue Metro line runs to the Inner City of Pest and Nyugati pályaudvar, one of the city's major train stations. The bus trip takes a transit ticket, which costs 260 Ft ($1.40/75p) when bought from the driver. News kiosks in the airport lobby also sell tickets for 230 Ft ($1.25/60p). Note that **bus 93** also runs a similar route, but has more stops and less room for passengers and luggage. You will need a new ticket for the Metro ride and one for each successive mode of transport thereafter. A public transportation pass is the most convenient option (see "Getting Around," below).

INSIDE THE STATIONS

Budapest has three major train stations: Keleti pályaudvar (Eastern Station), Nyugati (Western Station), and Déli (Southern Station), though there is no actual correlation between their names and their geographic locations. Each has a Metro station beneath it and an array of accommodation booking offices (see "Information Elsewhere in the City," below), currency-exchange booths, and other services.

Most international express trains pull into and depart from bustling **Keleti Station** (© 1/313-6835; Metro: Keleti pu.), a lovely, classic, steel-girdered structure, built in the eclectic style between 1881 and 1884, that's unfortunately located in Pest's run-down Baross tér. In addition to the Metro (the Red line), numerous bus, tram, and trolleybus lines serve Baross tér. Digital information boards will keep you apprised of arrivals and departures at the platforms at the main entrance and in the international ticketing area. Note that international tickets sales are to the left side of the station on the main floor; domestic tickets for north and northeastern destinations are sold on the lower level. Some international trains call at **Nyugati Station** (© 1/461-5400 for domestic routes, or 1/461-5500 for international routes; Metro: Nyugati pu.), another classic designed by the Eiffel company and built in the 1870s. Numerous tram and bus lines serve busy Nyugati tér, and the Blue Metro line stops underneath the station. This is the only train station with an official **Tourinform** visitor information office (© 1/302-8580; www.tourinform.hu), which dispenses advice, free brochures, maps, and will make hotel reservations. It's located in the station's main hall and open from 9am to 7pm.

Two major hotel reservation services have offices here. **Cooptourist,** Nyugati Station (© 1/458-6200), is open 9am to 4:30pm Monday through Friday. **Budapest Tourist,** Nyugati Station (© 1/318-6552), is open 9am to 5pm Monday through Friday, 9am to noon Saturday. Neither office accepts credit cards.

A few international trains arrive at **Déli Station** (© 1/375-6293; Metro: Déli pu.), an ugly modern building in central Buda. The Red Metro line terminates just beneath the station. Besides the usual tourist amenities, the station has a number of kiosks where you can stock up on snacks before your train journey.

The train station phone numbers listed above are good from 8pm to 6am. During the day, MÁV operates a call center called **MÁVDIREKT** (© 1/371-9449) that will give you information about timetables, prices, reductions, and offers in English. You can also book supplement tickets, including seat reservations.

INFORMATION ELSEWHERE IN THE CITY

The city's best source of visitor information is **Tourinform,** the official Budapest Tourism offices. They have a booth at each of the airports, plus three offices in the city: V. Liszt Ferenc tér 11, in Pest (© 1/322-4098; www.tourinform.hu; Metro: Opera, Yellow line; tram: Oktogon, no. 4–6), open daily from 10am to 6pm; V. Sütő Street 2 (Deák sq.; Metro: Deák tér), with hours from 8am to 8pm daily, with these exceptions: Dec 24 8am to 1pm, Dec 25, Dec 26, and Jan 1 10am to 6pm, and at the Castle (Var bus), where hours are daily 9am to 8pm May 5 to October 31 and daily 9am to 6pm November 2 to April 30, but closed May 1 to 4 and November 1.

The most established hotel reservation agencies are the former state-owned travel agents **Ibusz, Cooptourist,** and **Budapest Tourist.** These tend to have the greatest number of rooms and apartments listed and all have offices in the airport. The main **Ibusz reservations office** is at Ferenciek tere 10 (© 1/485-2767; fax 1/337-1205; www.ibusz.hu. Metro: Ferenciek tere), open year-round from Monday to Friday 9am to 6pm, Saturday 9am to 1pm. All major credit cards are accepted. The other agencies have offices at Nyugati Station (see above).

It's a good idea before you even arrive in Budapest to consult one of the many websites that offer tourist information in English. The site **www.gotohungary.com** has a wealth of tourist information, as does **www.hungarytourism.hu**. Local news, entertainment listings, and the like can be found at **www.funzine.com**, **www.budapestsun. com**, **www.search4.hu**, and **www.budapestinfo.hu/en**.

GETTING AROUND

Budapest has an extensive and inexpensive public transportation system; it's the best way to get around town. The Metros and trams start at 4:30am, but all three Metros stop running at 11pm and most of the trams cease around 11:30pm. Night buses substitute for the major tram lines. All night buses start with a 9; hence the 906 bus is the night replacement for the number 6 tram. There are 34 night bus routes, but they are limited compared to daytime transport. Note that the Red Metro line undergoes periodic reconstruction, and the stations on the line can close down for stretches of up to 8 weeks (often during very inconvenient times, such as the holiday season). Closure notices are posted in Metro cars and at stations, and during these times M2 buses act in place of the closed stations. Also adding to the public transportation chaos is the construction of a new fourth Metro line; buses also replace trams on routes that have been disrupted because of the ongoing work (signs are posted in English where substitutions have been made).

All forms of public transportation require the self-validation of prepurchased **tickets** *(vonaljegy),* costing 230 Ft ($1.25/60p) apiece (children under 6 travel free). Purchase single tickets at Metro ticket windows and newspaper kiosks, and at major transportation hubs. We do not recommend using the machines at tram stops or on buses, for they rarely work. You can buy a 10-pack *(tizes csomag)* for 2,050 Ft ($11.25/ £5.95), and for 3,900 Ft ($21.10/£11.10) a 20-pack *(huszas csomag).* During the process of validating tickets, you must keep the pack intact. The covers are the control ID for that pack. Do not tear individual tickets off as you use them.

If you will be here for a day or more, the best and least expensive choice is a pass. A **1-day pass** is 1,350Ft ($7.30/£3.85) and is valid until midnight of the day of purchase.

Buy passes at Metro ticket windows; the clerk validates the pass at the time of purchase. A **3-day pass** *(turistajegy)* costs 3,100 Ft ($16.75/£8.80) and a **7-day pass** *(hetibérlet)* costs 3,600 Ft ($19.45/£10.25).

Uniformed inspectors, generally wearing a blue or red armband will frequently be checking for valid tickets, particularly at the top or bottom of the escalators to Metro platforms. Fare dodgers face on-the-spot fines of 5,000 Ft ($27/£14.20). Inspectors have a reputation for being abusive to tourists, but employees are being trained to be more tourist-friendly. All public transport operates on rough schedules, posted at bus and tram shelters and in Metro stations.

BY METRO   The Metro is clean and efficient, with trains running every 3 to 5 minutes from about 4:30am until about 11:30pm. The three lines are known by color—Yellow, Red, and Blue. Officially, they have numbers as well, but all signs are color-coded. All three lines converge at **Deák tér.** This is the only station where all lines are available.

The **Yellow (1) line,** the oldest Metro on the European continent, lies just a few steps underground, and runs from Vörösmarty tér in the heart of central Pest, under the length of Andrássy út, and past the Városliget (City Park). Tickets for the Yellow line are validated in red or orange machines as you enter the station. The **Red (2)** and **Blue (3) lines** are modern subways, set deep underground and most stations are accessible by escalator. The Red line runs from eastern Pest, through the city center, across the Danube to Déli Station. The Blue line runs from southeastern Pest, through the city center, to northern Pest. Tickets must be validated at the automated time-stamp boxes before you descend the escalator. When changing lines at Deák tér, you must validate a new ticket at the orange machines in the hallway between lines. A fourth Metro line is under construction, but won't be completed until 2009 at the earliest.

BY BUS   Many parts of the city, most notably the Buda Hills, are best accessed by bus *(busz)*. Most lines are in service from about 4:30am to about 11:30pm, with less frequent weekend or holiday service on some. You must validate your bus ticket on board at the red box found by each door. Tickets for Budapest buses cannot be purchased from the driver. You can board the bus by any door.

Black-numbered local buses constitute the majority of bus lines. Red-numbered buses are express. If an *E* follows the red number on a bus, the bus runs nonstop between terminals. All night buses start with a "9" followed by two more digits. A few buses are labeled by something other than a number; one you'll probably use is the **Várbusz** (Palace Bus), a minibus that runs between Várfok utca, off Buda's Moszkva tér, and the Castle District; other buses labeled *V* (for *villamos*/tram) occasionally run in place of a tram that is down.

BY TRAM   You'll find Budapest's bright-yellow trams *(villamos* in Hungarian) very useful, particularly the **4** and **6,** which travel along the city's Outer Ring (Nagykörút) section. You must validate your ticket on board in the red box. As with buses, tickets are valid for one ride, not for the line itself. Trams stop at every station, and all doors open, regardless of whether anyone is waiting to get on. *The red buttons near the tram doors are for emergency stops, not stop requests.* Some of the tram lines commonly used by tourists (47, 49, 2, and 2A) may have buses running in their place at various times due to the ongoing construction of the fourth Metro line.

BY HÉV   The HÉV is a suburban railway network that connects Budapest to various points along the city's outskirts. There are four HÉV lines; only one, the **Szentendre**

line, is of serious interest to tourists. The terminus for the Szentendre HÉV line is Buda's Batthyány tér, also a station on the Red Metro line. On the Pest side, you can catch the HÉV from the Margit Híd, Budai Híd Fő. To reach Óbuda's Fő tér (Main Sq.), get off at the Árpád híd (Árpád Bridge) stop. The HÉV runs regularly between 4am and 11:30pm. If you have a valid day pass, you do not need to buy a ticket for trips within the city limits; otherwise, a single ticket is needed. For Szentendre, you will need to buy a supplemental ticket for the portion beyond the Budapest boundary only. Show the cashier your transportation pass, if you have one, when asking for the tickets. The supplemental tickets are 270 Ft ($1.45/75p) each way and will be checked and punched by a conductor after you pass the city limits. You may be asked to show your pass again to prove you only needed the supplemental ticket. A full-price ticket is 500 Ft ($2.70/£1.40) each way.

BY TAXI   Budapest taxis have become better regulated, but there are still rogue taxis roaming, especially at the train stations. Never take a taxi from a driver who approaches you in the station. Many drivers are experts at fleecing foreigners. Fares can vary tremendously, but there are two legal pricing schemes, for the reliable services. If you hail a taxi or take one from the curb, the rate is higher than if you were to call the dispatcher. You may be standing in front of it when you call, but the rate will be cheaper. They will often ask for your name and you need to tell the driver. It is illegal for a driver to pick up the wrong customer if you have called in. The law dictates that you be provided with a paper receipt; ask for it if the driver does not offer one, making the driver accountable. Several fleet companies have good reputations, honest drivers, and competitive rates. There is no standard rate across the various companies, but each should have its own rates displayed on the meter. So take the front seat (which is the standard practice in Hungary) and check the rates before you start your journey. We particularly recommend **Fő Taxi** (© 1/222-2222). Other reliable fleets are **Volántaxi** (© 1/466-6666), **City Taxi** (© 1/211-1111), **Tele5** (© 1/355-5555), and **6×6** (© 1/266-6666).

WHERE TO STAY

Budapest has seen a proliferation of new accommodations for various budgets. The better choices among these used to be outside the city center, but as tourism has risen so have the prices of the outer accommodations; we have chosen those places that are near or easily accessible to train stations, by public transportation. In high season, it can be difficult to secure a room, so make reservations and get written confirmation well ahead if possible.

Note that most hotels and pensions in Budapest divide the year into three seasons. **High season** is roughly from March or April to September or October and New Years. **Low season** is roughly from November to February, except the days before New Years. **Special season** includes the Hungarian Formula One race and Sziget Festival in August. Most hotels offer discounts and special package deals on their website if you book early, so be sure to check it.

Andrássy Hotel ✶✶✶ *(Finds)*   This luxury boutique hotel (one of only two in Hungary that merit Small Luxury Hotels of the World membership), is just a few minute's walk from Heroes' Square and the City Park, and 1 minute from the Metro. The rooms have been redecorated and have an eclectic Asian scheme. Double rooms are generous, but the suites are grandly spacious, some with artificial fireplaces in the living room.

The holistic atmosphere lends itself to a Zen feel, making this the perfect place to relax after a long train journey.

VI. Andrássy út 111. ℂ **1/462-2100.** Fax 1/322-9445. www.andrassyhotel.com. 70 units. High season 229€–289€ ($297–$376/£157–£198) double, 329€–409€ ($428–$532/£255–£280) suite; low season 109€–149€ ($142–$194/£75–£102) double, 209€–239€ ($272–$311/£143–£164) suite. AE, DC, MC, V. Metro: Bajza utca (Yellow line). **Amenities:** Restaurant; lounge; laundry. *In room:* Hair dryer.

Art'Otel Budapest ✧✧✧
This is the first branch of a German lifestyle hotel chain to be situated outside of that country and it's a successful one, especially for art lovers. Each of the chain's properties highlights the work of one particular artist, enabling guests to stay in a virtual gallery of modern art. At this hotel, the artist is Donald Sultan, an American modernist. More than 600 pieces of his work grace the hotel's walls, from the lobby to the hallways to the well-equipped guest rooms. Sultan also designed everything from the carpets to the dinnerware.

I. Bem Rakpart 16–19, Budapest. ℂ **800/814-7000** in the U.S. and Canada, 0800/169-6128 in Britain, or 1/487-9487-5500. Fax 1/487-9488. www.artotels.hu. 164 units. High season 155€–180€ ($202–$235/£107–£124) double, 185€–210€ ($241–$273/£127–£144) suite; low season 125€–150€ ($163–$196/£86–£103) double, 155€–185€ ($202–$241/£107–£127) suite. Rates include VAT; weekend and Internet discounts available. Children 12 and under stay free in parent's room. Breakfast 12€ ($15.60/£8.20) extra. AE, DC, MC, V. Metro: Batthyány tér (Red line). **Amenities:** Restaurant; bar. *In room:* Hair dryer.

Atrium Hotel ✧✧
Opened in March 2007, this ultramodern hotel is a breath of fresh air and great for travelers of all ages. The greenish-gray walls mix with blues in the carpet to make the rooms feel airy and roomy, yet they exude a warmth that will welcome even finicky guests. Soundproof windows guard against noise. Attention to detail was taken when converting this former post office to its current incarnation, and it's completely smoke free. It's a block from the Red Metro, close to Keleti station.

VIII. Csokonai u.14. ℂ **1/299-0777.** Fax 1/215-6090. www.hotelatrium.hu. 57 units. High season 39,000 Ft ($211/£111) double; low season 31,200 Ft ($169/£89) double; special season 46,800 Ft ($253/£133) double. Rates include full breakfast. AE, MC, V. Metro: Keleti (Red line). **Amenities:** Bar; dry cleaning. *In room:* Hair dryer.

Baross Hotel ✧
For rail travel convenience, you couldn't ask for a better location than this hotel, right across the street from Keleti train station. The hotel is located on different floors of an otherwise residential building. In addition to the regular rooms, there are eight apartments, whose different configurations can accommodate two to three adults with a double bed and a couch; each has a fully equipped kitchen. As a bonus, the Metro is just outside the door, along with four bus lines. Negatively, Baross tér is one of the less attractive neighborhoods. This hotel is still a little gem in the rough with good-size, comfortable rooms. And the area is trying hard to clean its face.

VII. Baross tér 15. ℂ **1/461-3010.** Fax 1/343-2770. www.barosshotel.hu. 48 units. High season 98€ ($127/£67) double, 160€–200€ ($208–$260/£111–£137) apt.; low season double 78€ ($101/£53); 125€–165€ ($163–$215/£86–£113) apt. Rates for regular rooms are double the price during special season. Rates include full breakfast. AE, MC, V. Metro: Keleti (Red line). **Amenities:** Nonsmoking rooms. *In room:* Hair dryer upon request.

City Hotel Mátyás ✧
Flowing with simple, old-world charm, this hotel caters to guests 40 and older. The comfortable rooms are plain, with minimal decor and clean white walls, and there's adequate space for two people. Some rooms have a fantastic view of the Buda castle district. Note that the hotel's apartments do not have kitchens. A renovation is scheduled for 2008 to the front of the building's exterior, but we hope not much is changed—it has great character. Breakfast is served in the adjoining famous Mátyás Pince Restaurant.

V. Marcius 15 tér. ⓒ **1/338-4711.** Fax 1/317-9086. www.cityhotels.hu. 85 units. High season 35,500 Ft ($192/£101) double, 48,500 ($262/£138) apt.; low season: 25,000 Ft ($135/£71) double, 35,000 Ft ($189/£100) apt.; special season 46,500 Ft ($251/£132) double, 71,500 Ft ($387/£203)˙apt. Rates include full breakfast. AE, MC, V. Metro: Ferenciek tere (Blue line). **Amenities:** Restaurant; bar; laundry; nonsmoking rooms. *In room:* Hair dryer upon request.

City Ring Hotel ๛๛
Perfectly located for the train traveler, this hotel is only 1 block from Nyugati train station, making it an ultraconvenient base with easy access to transportation, shopping, and restaurants. The rooms will comfortably fit two people, but are not overly spacious. They are modestly decorated, with an emphasis on functionality, but are tasteful. You stay here for the location and cleanliness, not the decor. One nitpick: The showers in the bathrooms are on the small side. The staff is incredibly helpful and friendly.

XIII. Szent István krt. 22. ⓒ **1/340-5450.** Fax 1/340-4884. www.cityhotels.hu. 39 units. High season 27,000 Ft–30,750 Ft ($146–$166/£77–£88) double; low season: 19,000 Ft–21,500 Ft ($103–$116/£54–£61) double; special season 31,500 Ft–37,750 Ft ($170–$219/£90–£115) double. Rates include full breakfast. AE, MC, V. Metro: Nyugati (Blue line) or trams 4 or 6. **Amenities:** Laundry, nonsmoking rooms. *In room:* Hair dryer upon request.

Délibáb Hotel ๛
Built at the turn of the 20th century, this small hotel was once the neo-Renaissance home of the famous Hungarian Eszterházy family, and is ideal for the traveler spending a short amount of time in the city. It's situated a block from Heroes Square, with ready access to many sights and the Metro. The rooms border on dowdy, but are fastidiously clean. For a beautiful night view, book rooms 210 through 212, or try rooms 310 through 312 for a spectacular panorama of Heroes Square. *Note:* There's no elevator, and the second floor in Hungary is the equivalent of the third floor in North America.

VI. Délibáb u. 35. ⓒ **1/342-9301.** Fax 1/342-8153. www.hoteldelibab.hu. 34 units. High season 83€ ($108/£57) double; low season 68€ ($88/£47) double; special season 115€ ($150/£79) double. Extra bed 15 € ($19.50/£10.30) per person per night. Rates include full breakfast. AE, MC, V. Metro: Hősök tér (Yellow line). **Amenities:** Laundry, nonsmoking rooms. *In room:* No A/C, TV, hair dryer upon request.

!bis Budapest Centrum ๛
The location of this hotel is top-notch; it's at the foot of Ráday u., one of the major dining streets in the city and a cultural hot spot. Museums and shopping are also within easy walking distance. Rooms are basic, adequately sized, and impeccably clean. There is a peaceful garden terrace on the first floor where you can sit and relax. Light sleepers should request a room overlooking the terrace rather than Ráday.

IX. Ráday u. 6. ⓒ **1/456-4100.** Fax 456-4116. www.ibishotel.com. 126 units. High season 19,550 Ft ($108/£56.75) double; low season 16,250 Ft ($88/£46) double; special season 37,500 Ft ($203/£107) double. Breakfast 2,000 Ft ($10.80/£5.70). AE, MC, DC, V. Metro: Kálvin tér (Blue line). **Amenities:** Bar; laundry; nonsmoking rooms.

Leo Panzio ๛ *Finds*
This small pension sports a fantastic location in the downtown area of Budapest, just minutes from Váci utca's shopping opportunities, and a stone's throw from the Metro. Rooms are comfortable but not spacious, decorated in dark woods and with framed antique postcards on the walls. If charm and location are more important than living space, this is the place to stay.

V. Kossuth Lajos u. 2/A. ⓒ **1/266-9041.** Fax 1/266-9042. www.leopanzio.hu. 14 units. High season 89€ ($116/£60.90) double; low season 76€ ($98.80/£52) double; special season 119€ ($155/£81.40) double. Rates include breakfast. DC, MC, V. Metro: Ferenciek tere (Blue line). **Amenities:** Laundry. *In room:* Hair dryer.

NH Hotel ๛๛๛
We don't usually associate modern elegance with a homey atmosphere, but this hotel near Nyugati station has it. Built from the ground up in 2003 directly behind the Vigszinház Theater, this hotel has taken a modern, minimalist

approach but still has a warm, welcoming feeling. By the end of 2007, they plan to have solar panels installed on the roof to generate their own electricity, making this one of the most ecofriendly hotels in the city.

XIII. Vigszinház u. 3. ✆ **1/814-000.** Fax 814-0100. www.nh-hotels.com. 160 units. High and special season 191€ ($248/£131) double; low season 131€ ($170/£89.65) double. Breakfast 16€ ($20.80/£10.95). AE, DC, MC, V. Metro: Nyugati (Blue line) or tram 4 or 6. **Amenities:** Restaurant; bar; laundry. *In room:* Hair dryer.

TOP ATTRACTIONS & SPECIAL MOMENTS

Note: Almost all museums and attractions allow photography and video recording without a flash, but most museums require that you purchase a photo ticket for still photography or video, with videotaping costing much more. Keep your ticket visible and the guards will not continually ask you to produce it. Photo ticket prices are listed in each entry below.

Budapesti Történeti Múzeum (Budapest History Museum) 🎖 This museum,
also known as the Castle Museum, is the best place to get a sense of once-great medieval Buda. Many of the museum's descriptions are written in English, but not throughout, so it's probably worth splurging for an audio tour. The history of the palace's repeated cycles of destruction and reconstruction is so arcane that it's difficult to understand what you're really seeing, but it is worth it for those who have the time.

I. In Buda Palace, Wing E, on Castle Hill. ✆ **1/225-7809** or 1/225-7810. www.btm.hu. Admission 1,100 Ft ($5.95/£3.10); audio guides 850 Ft ($4.60/£2.40), photo ticket 600 Ft ($3.25/£1.70) video ticket 1,600 Ft ($8.65/£4.55). Daily 10am–6pm Mar 16–Sept 15; Wed–Mon 10am–6pm Sept 16–Oct 31, Wed–Mon 10am–4pm Nov 1–Feb 28. Metro: Moszkva tér (Red line), then bus "Várbusz" or Deák tér, then bus no. 16. Funicular: From Clark Ádám tér to Castle Hill.

Nemzeti Múzeum (Hungarian National Museum) 🎖🎖 This enormous neo-
classical structure, built from 1837 to 1847, played a major role in the beginning of the Hungarian Revolution of 1848 and 1849; on its wide steps on March 15, 1848, poet Sándor Petőfi and other young radicals are said to have exhorted the people of Pest to revolt against the Habsburgs. The two main museum exhibits on view are "The History of the Peoples of Hungary from the Paleolithic Age to the Magyar Conquest" and "The History of the Hungarian People from the Magyar Conquest to 1989."

VIII. Múzeum krt. 14. ✆ **1/338-2122.** www.hnm.hu. Free admission, but photo ticket is 3,000 Ft ($16.20/£8.55), video 5,000 Ft ($27/£14.20). ✆ 1/327-7773 for guided tours; book a week in advance. Tues–Sun 10am–6pm. Metro: Kálvin tér (Blue line) or Astoria (Red line).

Széchenyi Baths 🎖🎖🎖 Part of an immense health spa located in the City Park, the
Széchenyi Baths are second to none in terms of facilities and popular appeal. On a nice day, crowds of bathers, including many families and tourists, visit the palatial unisex outdoor swimming pool. Look for older gentlemen, concentrating intently on their floating chess boards, as they play half immersed in the steaming pool. Turkish-style thermal baths are segregated and located off to the sides of the pool. In warm weather, there is segregated nude sunbathing on the roof. Massages are available at a rate of 3,500 Ft ($18.90/£9.95) for 30 minutes.

XIV. Állatkerti út 11–14, in City Park. ✆ **1/363-3210.** www.spasbudapest.com. Admission to the thermal baths 2,400 Ft ($13/£6.80), dressing cabins 400 Ft ($2.15/£1.15) extra. Daily 6am–10pm, some pools close earlier on Sat–Sun. Metro: Széchenyi fürdő (Yellow line).

Szépművészeti Múzeum (Museum of Fine Arts) 🎖🎖 Opened in 1906, this
neoclassical behemoth is situated on the left side of huge Heroes' Square. A significant part of the collection was acquired in 1871 from the Esterházys, an enormously wealthy

noble family that spent centuries amassing great art. The museum's holdings consist of more than 15,000 works, including the largest number of Spanish paintings in Europe outside of Madrid. Trained docents offer daily (and free) 1-hour tours in English of one gallery at 11am and 2pm; the featured gallery is changed on a rotating basis.

XIV. Hősök tere. ✆ 1/469-7100. www.szepmuveszeti.hu. Free admission for permanent collection; other exhibits are variable depending. Tues–Sun 10am–5:30pm. Metro: Hősök tere (Yellow line).

HISTORIC BUILDINGS

Magyar Állami Operaház (Hungarian State Opera House) ✮✮✮   Designed by Miklós Ybl in the neo-Renaissance style, Budapest's Opera House was completed in 1884 and boasts an ornate interior featuring frescoes by two of the best-known Hungarian artists of the day, Bertalan Székely and Károly Lotz. Considered one of the most beautiful in Europe, with a rich and evocative history, it is home to both the State Opera and the State Ballet. Tickets can be purchased here for as little as 800 Ft ($4.30/£2.25) for some performances.

VI. Andrássy út 22. ✆ 1/331-2550. www.operavisit.hu. Admission (by guided tour only, minimum 10 people) 2,500 Ft ($13.50/£7.10), students with international ID 1,300 Ft ($7/£3.70). Photo and video tickets 500 Ft ($2.70/£1.40). Tours daily at 3 and 4pm. Metro: Opera.

Parliament ✮✮✮   Budapest's great Parliament building, the second largest in Europe after London's, is an eclectic design mixing the predominant Gothic revival style with a neo-Renaissance dome. It was completed in 1902. Standing proudly on the Danube bank, visible from almost any riverside point, it has been one of Budapest's symbols from the outset, though until 1989 a democratically elected government convened here only once (just after World War II, before the Communist takeover). The Parliament is home to the "legendary" jeweled crown of King St. Stephen. Historical records have shown that the crown is constructed of two parts and from two different eras—neither from King St. Stephen's time—but Hungarians want to believe it was Stephen's.

V. Kossuth tér. ✆ 1/441-4415. Tourist.office@parliament.hu. Admission (by guided tour only): 50-min. tour in English, 2,300 Ft ($12.45/£6.55) adults, 1,150 Ft ($6.20/£3.25) students. Tickets available at gate X. Prebook by e-mail or phone ✆ 1/441-4904 or 1/441-4415. Photography allowed at no charge. Tours year-round Wed–Sun at 10am, noon, 1pm, and 2pm. Closed when Parliament is in session, usually Mon and Thurs. Metro: Kossuth tér; Tram 2 and 2A Szalay utca.

CHURCHES & SYNAGOGUES

Dohány Synagogue ✮✮✮   Built in 1859, this is the second largest working synagogue in the world (the oldest is in New York). The architect was non-Jewish Lajos Förster, who designed it using Romantic, Moorish, and Byzantine elements. The synagogue's interior pulls its inspiration from a mix of Orthodox and Reformed Judaism. It has a rich, but tragic history. There's a Jewish museum next door that traces the origins of Hungarian Judaism and features exhibits of ceremonial Judaica throughout the centuries. The museum periodically puts on excellent temporary exhibitions. The Holocaust Memorial and Heroes' Temple in the courtyard are well worth visiting.

VII. Dohány u. 2–8. ✆ 1/342-8949. www.bpjewmus.hu. Admission 1,400 Ft ($7.55/£4), photo tickets 500 Ft ($2.70/£1.40) for synagogue, museum free. Mon–Thurs 10am–4:30pm; Fri 10am–2:30pm; Sun 10am–5:30pm, except Jewish holidays. Metro: Astoria or Deák tér; Bus: 74.

Mátyás Templom (Matthias Church) ✮✮✮   Originally founded by King Béla IV in the 13th century, this symbol of Buda's Castle District is officially named the Church of Our Lady. It is popularly referred to as Matthias Church after the 15th-century

King Matthias Corvinus, who added a royal oratory and who was twice married here. Like other old churches in Budapest it has an interesting history of destruction and reconstruction, always being refashioned in the architectural style of the time. Renovation has been an on-going process as financial considerations allow. Do not miss the museum upstairs, often overlooked by travelers who do not realize it is there; it has an interesting history of the royal crown and a wonderful view of the church.

I. Szentháromság tér 2. (C) 1/355-5657. www.matyas-templom.hu. Daytime 650 Ft ($3.50/£1.85) adults, 400 Ft ($2.15/£1.15) students. Photos permitted at no charge. Mon–Fri 9am–5pm; Sat depends on wedding schedules; Sun 1–5pm. Metro: Moszkva tér, then bus "Várbusz" or Deák tér, then bus no. 16. Funicular: From Clark Ádám tér to Castle Hill.

Szent István Bazilika (St. Stephen's Church) 🕏

The country's largest church, this basilica took more than 50 years to build (the 1868 collapse of the dome caused significant delay) and was finally completed in 1906. Szent István Square, a once-sleepy square in front of the church, was elegantly renovated in the autumn of 2002, converted along with several neighboring streets into a pedestrian-only zone. If you wander to the left of the church into the back chapel and spring for 100 Ft (55¢/30p), you can view St. Stephen's mummified hand, or you can wait until August 20, his feast day, and see it for free when it is paraded around the city.

V. Szent István tér 33. (C) 1/318-9159. www.basilica.hu. Church free admission; treasury: 400 Ft ($2.15/£1.15); Panorama tower 500 Ft ($2.70/£1.40). Photos allowed at no charge. Thorough guided tours ($10.80/£5.70) can be requested at the church. Church daily 9am–7pm, except during services; treasury daily 9am–5pm; Szent Jobb Chapel Mon–Sat 9am–5pm, Sun 1–5pm; Panorama tower daily 10am–5pm. Metro: Arany János utca or Bajcsy-Zsilinszky út.

PARKS & PANORAMAS

Gellért Hegy (Gellért Hill) 🕏🕏, towering 750 feet (235m) above the Danube, offers a city panorama (bus: 27 from Móricz Zsigmond körtér). It's named after the Italian Bishop Gellért, who assisted Hungary's first Christian king, Stephen I, in converting the Magyars. He was killed by pagans where his enormous statue now stands. On top of Gellért Hill is the **Liberation Monument,** built in 1947 to commemorate the Red Army's liberation of Budapest from Nazi occupation. Also atop the hill is the **Citadella,** built by the Austrians shortly after they crushed the Hungarian uprising of 1848–49. Views of the city from both vistas are excellent, but the Citadella is spectacular. Don't bother paying extra to get into the upper part, the view is not that much higher, so it is a waste of money.

City Park (Városliget) 🕏🕏 is an equally popular place to spend a summer day (Metro1: Hósök tere/Heroes' Sq. or Széchenyi Fürdó). Heroes' Square, at the end of Andrássy út, is the most logical starting point for a walk in City Park. The lake behind

---

Tips Quick Picnic

For great picnic fare (perfect for your next train excursion or park visit), head over to the **Plus Grocery** store at the Wesselényi u. tram stop (4 or 6 tram). Inside the door to your right, they sell delicious oven-roasted whole chickens for 790 Ft ($4.25/£2.25). If you only want half, ask for fél (pronounced *fail*). To the left of the chicken stand, the deli sells an assortment of salads and will give you plastic utensils. On the other side of the lobby is a bakery where you can pick up dessert, and the grocery section sells drinks.

the square is used for boating in summer and ice-skating in winter. **Gundel,** Budapest's most famous restaurant, is also here, as are the immense Habsburg style **Széchenyi Baths.** One highlight is the **Vajdahunyad Castle** (Vajdahunyad vára), which is in part a replica of a Transylvania castle on **Széchenyi Island.** It is now home to the **Agricultural Museum,** with free entrance to the permanent exhibit. Photo tickets are 500 Ft ($2.70/£1.40).

WHERE TO DINE

Étterem is the most common Hungarian word for restaurant and is used for everything from cafeteria-style eateries to first-class restaurants. A *vendéglő,* or guesthouse, is a smaller, more intimate restaurant, often with a Hungarian folk motif; *café* has blurred meanings with some serving full meals, while others only snacks. An *önkiszolgáló* is a self-service cafeteria, typically open only for lunch. Stand-up *bufes* are often found in transport hubs. A *cukrászda* or *kávéház* is a Central European coffeehouse, where coffee and sweets are served. A *borozó* is a wine bar, a *söröző* a beer bar; sandwiches are usually available at both. Unless stated otherwise, all restaurants listed have menus in English, and all are required to have nonsmoking areas.

Frici Papa Kifőzés *(Value* HUNGARIAN   The staff can be downright surly, but customers keep coming anyway; we think the attitude actually makes for entertainment with your meal if you're prepared for it. This is a plain, homey place with no frills and its prices reflect that. The daily offerings are posted with signs hanging on a peg board near the front windows, and everything is a la carte, even the ketchup. For the best selections, go for lunch or an early dinner; after 7pm, you are taking your chances.

VI. Király u. 55. No phone. Main dishes 559 Ft–600 Ft ($3–$3.25/£1.60–£1.70). No credit cards. Mon–Sat 11am–9pm. Tram 4 or 6 Király u.

Govinda Vegetariánus Étterem *✿* INDIAN/VEGETARIAN   This self-serve restaurant serves delicious vegetarian food in a tranquil, smoke-free environment. Seating is plentiful, but this place can be packed at lunchtime on weekdays, so you may have to wait in line. The staff speaks English and will explain each dish. Another plus: Proceeds from the restaurant help to support efforts to feed the homeless of the city in the form of monthly food giveaways.

V. Vigyázó Ferenc u. 4. *℃* **1/269-1625.** Main dishes 620 Ft ($3.25/£1.70); small sampler meal 1,450 Ft ($7.80/£4.10); large sampler meal 1,7500 Ft ($9.45/£5); student menu 720 Ft ($3.95/£2.05). No credit cards. Mon–Sat noon–9pm. Metro: Kossuth Lajos tér (Red line).

Hemingway *✿✿✿ (Moments* HUNGARIAN   You will feel like you've escaped the city when visiting this restaurant, situated next to a small lake surrounded by plenty of trees. The open and airy interior makes us feel like we've joined Hemingway inside one of his favorite getaways. The piano and bass duo adds to the relaxing Casablanca atmosphere. The food and service are superb. In good weather, eat outside on the terrace overlooking the water for a romantic meal.

XI. Kosztolányi D. tér 2, Feneketlen tó. *℃* **1/381-0522.** www.hemingway-etterem.hu. Reservations recommended. Main courses 2,390 Ft–5,990 Ft ($12.90–$32.40/£6.80–£17). AE, DC, MC, V. Daily noon–midnight. Bus: Take bus no. 7 toward Buda from Ferenciek tér to Feneketlen tó, a small "lake."

M *✿✿✿* HUNGARIAN   This quiet and unassuming restaurant might easily be overlooked, but shouldn't be. There are only three tables inside the entrance, but there's more seating upstairs. The menu, an eclectic mix of Hungarian and international influences, is left to the whims of the chef, who changes the menu (available on the website) every Tuesday but always gets rave reviews. The decor is notable: Every inch of the walls and ceiling is covered in brown wrapping paper with black line drawings of furnishings found in a home. Reserve an outside table or one on the main level in warm weather.

VII. Kertész 48. ☎ 1/342-8991. www.rajzoltetterem.hu. Reservations recommended. Main courses 1,550 Ft–2,450 Ft ($8.35–$13.15/£4.40–£6.90). No credit cards. Daily noon–midnight. Tram: 4 or 6 Király u.

Mátyás Pince ✿✿✿ *Moments* HUNGARIAN   Art, history, and music buffs will love this restaurant, established in 1904 and named for King Mathyás; the myths and legends of his reign grace the walls in magnificent style. The frescoes and stained glass decorating the dining areas were registered as national monuments in 1973. Music is provided by the Lakatos gypsy music dynasty every night but Mondays from 7pm until closing, creating an all-around romantic experience. The combination of excellent Hungarian cuisine (the menu's extensive), entertainment, and service makes for a wonderful evening out.

V. Március 15 tér 7-8. ☎1/266–8008. www.cityhotels.hu. Reservations recommended. Main courses 2,700 Ft–7,900 Ft ($14.60–$42.70/£7.70–£22.50). AE, MC, V. Daily 11am–midnight. Metro: Ferenciek tere (Blue line).

Mosselen Belgium Beer Café ✿✿✿ *Finds* FLEMISH   Mosselen means mussels in Flemish, but this L-shaped restaurant is best known as a beer lovers' paradise; if you love beer, this is the only bar with such a wide selection. There are 10 different beers on tap, plus a further selection of over 50 other brews to choose from, each served in a distinctive glass. The wainscoted walls of deep, rich wood help instill a Belgium country atmosphere. The menu has an interesting selection of fish dishes, ranging from tuna steak to prawns, but meat and vegetarian options are available. Thanks to its combination of excellent food and beer choices, this is a favorite spot.

XIII Pannónia u. 14. ☎ 1/452-0535. Reservations recommended. Main courses 2,790 Ft–4,590 Ft ($15.10–$24.80/£7.95–£13.05); beer 790–5,300 Ft ($4.25–$28.65/£2.20–£15.10). AE, DC, MC, V. Daily noon–midnight. Tram 4 or 6 to Jászai Mari tér.

Paprika Vendéglő ✿✿ HUNGARIAN   If you want to sample the cuisine of the Hungarian countryside without leaving the city, this is the place. The old-fashioned earthen oven, oversized cooking utensils, and log cabin interior will envelop you in rustic comfort. Let yourself go hog wild and try the roasted wild boar with brandy, or the saddle of deer. No matter what you order, the portions will be generous.

VII. Dozsa Gyorgy 72. 4½ blocks from Heroes Sq. ☎ 06/70/574-6508 (cellphone). Reservations recommended. Main courses 1,650–3,200 Ft. ($8.90–$17.30/£4.70–£91.0). No credit cards. Daily 11am–11pm. Metro: Hősők tere (Yellow line).

Pilvax Restaurant ✿✿ HUNGARIAN   This restaurant has opened and closed many times since its 1848 inception because of political regime changes, but it's been operating continuously since 1989. The large dining room is decorated in a renovated Biedermeier style, with old Hungarian prints on the walls and crystal chandeliers hung from the ceilings. It's like eating in your Hungarian granny's dining room, except Granny didn't have strolling musicians playing during a meal like they do here.

V. Pilvax köz 1-3. ☎ 1/266-7660. www.cityhotels.hu. Reservations recommended. Main courses 2,100 Ft –5,000 Ft ($11.35–$27/£6–£14.20). MC, V. Daily noon–midnight. Metro: Deák (All lines).

Tabáni Terasz ✿✿ HUNGARIAN   The dishes here are all prepared with a nice variety of vegetables, which is unusual for traditional Hungarian cuisine, which uses vegetables sparingly. The portions are substantial. The interior is made up of small

Coffeehouse Culture

Budapest, like Vienna, was famous for its coffeehouse culture. Coffeehouses have housed the literary movements and political circles of many a revolution, with their members identified in large part by which coffeehouse they met in. You can still go to several classic coffeehouse-style venues today that more or less resemble their historic counterparts. All offer delicious pastries, coffee, and more in an atmosphere of splendor.

The **Gerbeaud** ★★ is a classic, but it's overrated, overpriced, and frequented mostly by tourists. It's located in the Inner City at V. Vörösmarty tér 7 (© **1/429-9000**). The **Central Kávéház** ★★★ is one of the noblest and most beautifully renovated establishments, and to this day is a haunt for many a writer or thinker. It's at V. Károlyi Mihály u. 9. (© **1/266-2110;** www.centralkavehaz.hu; Metro: Ferenciek tere). **Művész Kávéház** ★★, another historic coffeehouse frequented by the artistic community for decades, is across the street from the Opera House at VI. Andrássy út 29. (© **1/352-1337;** Metro: Opera).

Of major historical importance is the reopened (2006) **Café New York** ★★ in the New York Palace Hotel, located at VII. Erzsébet Krt 9-11. © **1/886-6167.** The building was built by the New York Life Insurance Company in 1894; the cafe was the meeting place of many of Hungary's famous writers, poets, and artists.

rooms with tables and chairs—a layout that makes you feel like you're entering someone's home—and is decorated with wall hangings, paintings, and other regional touches. It is a bit difficult to get to from the Pest side of the city, but worth the effort. In summer, dine on the lovely terrace.

I. Apród utca 10. © **1/201-1086.** www.tabaniterasz.hu. Main courses 1,990 Ft–4,300 Ft ($10.75–$23.25/£5.70–£12.25). AE, MC, V. Daily noon–midnight. Bus: 86 to Döbrentei tér.

Trófea Grill Étterem ★★★ *Finds* HUNGARIAN This is the best all-you-can-eat restaurant in the city, and you get to select from a daily-changing menu of over 100 different dishes and drinks. The hot entrees are Hungarian favorites and usually include some version of beef, chicken, or venison in a hearty sauce. You can also take marinated chicken or pork to the grill to be prepared for you. Everything is included in one price if you don't order wine off of the wine list. *Note:* There are four restaurants of this name in the city, but they are owned by different companies; this location is the only one we recommend.

XIV. Erzsébet Királyné útja 5. © **1/251-6377.** www.trofeagrill.com. Reservations recommended. Lunch 2,499 Ft ($13.50/£7.10); dinner 3,699 Ft ($20/£10.50); Fri dinner, all day Sat–Sun, and holidays 4,199 Ft ($22.70/£11.95). Mon–Fri noon–5:30pm; Mon–Thurs 5:30pm–midnight. Sun playroom for children 11:30am–5pm. Children up to 59 in. (150 cm) get 50% reduction. Metro: Mexikói (Yellow line).

SHOPPING

Shoppers fill the pedestrian-only **Váci utca,** from the stately Vörösmarty tér, the center of Pest, across the roaring Kossuth Lajos utca, all the way to Vámház krt. Prices in this area reflect the touristy feel, so if you are looking for bargains, look here, but shop elsewhere.

The **Castle District** in Buda, with many folk-art boutiques and galleries, is another popular, but overpriced area for souvenir hunters. Locals (and careful travelers) might window-shop in these two neighborhoods, but do their buying elsewhere. One popular street is Pest's **Outer Ring** (Nagykörút); another bustling street is Pest's **Kossuth Lajos utca,** off the Erzsébet Bridge, and its continuation **Rákóczi út,** extending all the way out to Keleti Station.

Hungary's famous folkloric objects are the most popular souvenirs among foreign visitors. The mushrooming number of folk-art shops (Népművészeti Háziipar) have a great selection of handmade goods. Popular items include pillowcases, embroidered tablecloths, runners, wine cozies, pottery, porcelain, dolls, intricately painted or carved eggs, dresses, skirts, and sheepskin vests. The main store, **Folkart Centrum,** is at V. Váci u. 58 (© 1/318-5840), and is open daily from 10am to 7pm. One shop that has a wide selection and helpful staff is **Folkart Craftman's House** on the side street, Régiposta u. 12, right off of Váci u. (© 1/318-5143); it's open daily from 10am to 7pm. **Holló Folkart Gallery,** at V. Vitkovics Mihály u. 12 (© 1/317-8103), is an unusual gallery selling handcrafted reproductions of folk-art pieces from various regions of the country. It is open Monday to Friday from 10am to 6pm; Saturday 10am to 2pm. **Csók István Galéria,** located at V. Váci u. 25 (© 1/318-2592) is the perfect place for something a little more upscale, unique, but still affordable, so don't miss browsing. It's open daily from 10am to 8pm.

Another popular Hungarian item is **porcelain,** particularly from the country's two best-known producers, Herend and Zsolnay. Although both brands are available in the West, here you'll find a better selection and perhaps lower prices. At the **Herend Shops,** V. József nádor tér 11 (© 1/317-2622) or VI. Andrássy út 16 (© 1/374-0006), you'll find the widest Herend selection in the capital. Delightfully gaudy Zsolnay porcelain from the southern city of Pécs is Hungary's second most celebrated brand, found in almost all shopping centers and in numerous porcelain shops; one to visit is **Zsolnay Márkabolt in the Duna Plaza,** Váci út 178 (© 1/239-3784).

Budapest also has five **vintage market halls** *(vásárcsarnok)* of historic importance, wonders of steel and glass, built in the 1890s in the ambitious grandiose style of the time. Specifically built to bring food merchants indoors to improve sanitary conditions, they are still in use. They provide a measure of local color you won't find in the grocery store. The **Központi Vásárcsarnok** (Central Market Hall), on IX. Vámház körút (on the Pest side of the Szabadság Bridge), is the largest and most spectacular market hall. Visit the second floor for a large selection of common souvenirs at better prices than elsewhere in the city.

NIGHTLIFE

The weekly English-language newspapers *The Budapest Sun* (**www.budapestsun. com**) and *The Budapest Times* (**www.budapesttimes.hu**) are good all-round resources that can be found at TourInform or newsstands. The free *Funzine* magazine can be found just about everywhere in the city.

The **Cultur-Comfort Ticket Office** (Cultur-Comfort Központi Jegyiroda; www.cultur-comfort.hu), VI. Paulay Ede u. 31. (© 1/322-0000; Metro: Opera), sells tickets to just about everything, from theater and operetta to sports events and rock concerts. It's open from Monday to Friday 9am to 6pm. For **opera and ballet,** go to the **Hungarian State Opera Ticket Office** (Magyar Állami Opera Jegyiroda), VI.

> ### (Moments Music for a Summer Evening
>
> During the hot, hazy, lazy days of summer, you'll find special venues for classical music. **St. Stephen's Church** (Bazilika) **Plaza** hosts outdoor symphony concerts. The **Hungarian State Opera House** hosts opera and symphony performances, usually in August.
>
> Margaret Island is also the scene of many musical events, but they change from year to year. Check *Funzine* or *The Budapest Sun* for a current schedule.
>
> The Castle District's beautiful **Matthias Church** (Mátyás Templom), at I. Szentháromság tér 2, holds regular Tuesday- and Friday-night series of organ concerts from June to September. Concerts start at 7:30pm. Tickets can be purchased before the performance at the church's entry.

Andrássy út 22 (© **1/353-0170;** Metro: Opera). For **rock, pop, and jazz concert** tickets, try Ticket Express, VI. Jókai u. 40 (© **1/353-0692;** www.tex.hu; Metro: Opera) as well as **Concert & Media,** XI. Üllői út 11–13 (© **1/455-9000;** www.jegyelado.hu; Metro: Kalvin tér).

THE PERFORMING ARTS   Many of the city's indoor venues do not offer regular programming during the summer because they are not air-conditioned; the newer **Palace of Arts** is the exception. When these venues do have special summer events, keep the cooling situation in mind.

Completed in 1884, the **Magyar Állami Operaház** (Hungarian State Opera House), VI. Andrássy út 22 (© **1/331-2550;** Metro: Opera), is Budapest's most famous performance hall. Hungarians adore opera, and a large percentage of seats are sold on a subscription basis; buy your tickets a few days or weeks ahead, if possible. If a performance is sold out, go to the box office an hour before the opening curtain to obtain "no-show" tickets. The box office is open from Monday to Friday 11am to 6pm. Ticket prices range from 300 Ft to 10,300 Ft ($1.60–$55.65/85p–£29.30).

The relatively new **Palace of Arts,** Budapest, Komor Marcell u. 1 (© **1/555-3000;** www.muveszetekpalotaja.hu; tram 2: Közvágóhíd station) is a place where the classical music tradition and the avant-garde (in the form of contemporary dance and art) coexist. Adjacent to Hungary's National Theater, the building is home to the elegant **National Concert Hall** and the **Festival Theater.** The **Ludwig Museum,** home to a mix of period and contemporary pop art from geographic regions ranging from the U.S. to Central Europe, is also housed here. You can buy tickets to concerts or to the museum on the first floor in the Palace of Arts.

The Great Hall (Nagyterem) of the **Zeneakadémia** (Ferenc Liszt Academy of Music), VI. Liszt Ferenc tér 8 (© **1/341-4788,** ext. 179; Metro: Oktogon), is the city's premier music hall. The box-office is open whenever the school is open. Tickets range from 1,000 Ft to 12,000 Ft ($5.40–$64.85/£2.85–£34.15), though there are often student recitals where visitors can be part of the audience for free.

LIVE-MUSIC CLUBS   **Fat Mo's Music Club,** always a hot place, is at V. Nyári Pál u. 11 (© **1/267-3199;** Metro: Kálvin tér [Blue line]). There's no cover charge. The live jazz concerts start at 9pm and dancing starts at 11pm. The best night is definitely Sunday, with *Hot Jazz Band* performing in the style of the '20s and '30s. Make sure you book a table if you wish to enjoy their superb food as well. **TRAFO,** XI. Liliom u. 41 (© **1/215-1600;** tram: 4 or 6 to Üllöi út), is an old electric power station that was transformed into a cultural center. It also hosts a hip disco. *The* nights are Wednesday and Sunday with the party starting at 10pm, but on Fridays dance to the '60s and '70s greatest hits; Trafo is closed during summers. **Old Man's Pub,** VIII. Akácfa u. 13 (© **1/322-7645;** Metro: Blaha Luzja tér), is the place to take in the best jazz and blues in Hungary. This very hip spot is open daily from 3pm to 3am. The **Columbus Pub,** opposite the Intercontinental Hotel (© **1/266–9013**), is a docked boat restaurant/nightclub on the Pest side of the Danube; the best of local jazz musicians play nightly.

EXCURSIONS TO THE DANUBE BEND

The delightful towns along the Danube Bend—Szentendre, Esztergom, and Viseg-rád—are easy day trips from Budapest. The great natural beauty of the area, where forested hills loom over the river, makes it a welcome departure for the city weary.

SZENTENDRE

Szentendre (pronounced *Sen*-ten-dreh), 13 miles (21km) north of Budapest has been populated since the Stone Age by Illyrians, the Celtic Eraviscus tribe, Romans, Lom-bards, Avars, and, naturally, Hungarians. Serbians settled here in the 17th century, embellishing the town with their unique characteristics. **Szentendre,** counts half a dozen Serbian churches among its rich collection of historical buildings. Since the turn of the 20th century, Szentendre has been home to an artist's colony. Museums here do not have stable hours, even when posted on their door. Think of a museum as icing on the cake, if it is open. The town is an extremely popular tourist destina-tion, which is sometimes a turn-off for visitors, but it really is a treasure. To appreci-ate the rich flavor of the town, look beyond the touristy shops and wander the streets looking at the architecture, the galleries, and the churches. Don't miss walking along the river for a lovely and relaxing view. Almost all of the streets are cobblestone, so choose comfortable footwear.

GETTING THERE   The HÉV suburban railroad connects Budapest's Batthyány tér with Szentendre. On the Pest side, you can catch the HÉV from the Margit Híd, Budai Híd Fö.Trains leave daily, year-round, every 20 minutes or so from 4am to 11:30pm (trip time: 45 min.). The one-way fare is 500 Ft ($2.70/£1.40); subtract 230 Ft ($1.25/60p) if you have a valid Budapest public transportation pass. The trip takes 45 minutes.

VISITOR INFORMATION   The information office **Tourinform** is at Dumtsa Jenő u. 22. (© **26/317-965;** www.szentendre.hu). It is open April through October Monday to Wednesday from 9:30am to 6pm and Thursday to Sunday 9:30am to 7:30pm; in the off season it's open Monday to Friday from 9:30am to 5pm. To get here, just follow the flow of pedestrian traffic into town on Kossuth Lajos utca. Like all things in this town, the staff marches to the beat of its own drummer, not always keeping to the posted schedule.

Top Attractions & Special Moments

If you want to visit a unique shop, make it **Handpets** ✸✸✸ Dumsta Jeno u. 15 (© **26/ 373-746;** www.handpets.hu). Made for three or five fingers and designed by Kati Szili, Handpets are the most creative hand puppets we have ever seen. The hand-made puppets are of high quality and are sure to delight children of all ages. This is the only shop where the entire collection is available, though there are poor imitations sold elsewhere.

The most widely known museum in this village is the **Marzipan Museum** ✵✵ Dumsta Jeno u. 12 (© **26/311-931**). Here's your chance to see a 5¼ ft (1.6m) -long reproduction of the Hungarian Parliament made entirely in marzipan. Kids will love the Disney characters. It's open May to September daily from 10am to 7pm and October to April daily from 10am to 6pm. Admission is 400 Ft ($2.15/£1.15). The **Margit Kovács Museum** ✵✵✵, Vastagh György u. 1 (© **26/310-244**), is a must-see, displaying the exceptional and highly original work of Hungary's best-known ceramic artist. Her sculptures of elderly women and friezes of village life are particularly moving. The museum is open March to September Tuesday to Sunday from 9am to 5pm. Admission is 700 Ft ($3.80/£2).

The **Serbian Orthodox Blagovestenska Church** at Fo tér 4 is a fine example of an orthodox church built in the 1700s. It is open Tuesday through Sunday from 10am to 5pm. Admission is 250 Ft ($1.35/70p); an extensive collection of Serbian Icons are housed in a nearby hilltop museum. **Szántó Jewish Memorial House and Temple** ✵✵✵, Albotmány u. 4, is the first temple built in Hungary after World War II and is probably the smallest synagogue in the world. It was dedicated on May 17, 1998 by the Chief Rabbi of Hungary. Men are given a yarmulke to wear when entering. It's open Tuesday to Sunday from 11am to 5pm. Donations are accepted.

Where to Dine

For a full sit-down meal, try **Chez Nicolas Restaurant** ✵✵, Kígyó utca 10. (© **26/311-288;** www.cheznicolas.hu). It offers intimate, romantic dining with an outdoor terrace looking out on the river. You can choose from Hungarian or French dishes. Main courses vary from 1,790 Ft to 3,800 Ft ($9.65–$20.55/£5.10–£10.80). Open Tuesday through Sunday from noon to midnight.

Aranysárkány Vendéglő (Golden Dragon Inn) ✵, Alkotmány u. 1/a (© **26/301-479;** www.aranysarkany.hu), just east of Fő tér on Hunyadi utca, is always crowded. Choose from such enticing offerings as spicy leg of lamb, roast leg of goose, and venison ragout. A tasty vegetarian plate is also offered. Various traditional Hungarian beers are on tap. Main courses are 2,400 Ft to 3,600 Ft ($13–$19.45/£6.80–£10.25) with special tourist menus for 3,300 Ft ($17.85/£9.40). It's open daily from noon to 10pm.

Vidám Szerzetesek Vendéglo (Restaurant of Merry Friars) ✵, Bodgadányi u. 3–5 (© **26/310-544**), offers first-rate ambience, and fine quality fare. The traditional Hungarian menu consists of a bewildering number of imaginative dishes. Main courses run from 1,700 Ft to 3,900 Ft ($9.20–$21.10/£4.85–£11.10). Open Tuesday through Sunday from noon to 10pm.

ESZTERGOM

Formerly a Roman settlement, **Esztergom** (pronounced *Ess*-tair-gome), 29 miles (46km) northwest of Budapest, was the seat of the Hungarian kingdom for 300 years. Hungary's first king, István I (Stephen I), received the crown from the pope in A.D. 1000. He converted Hungary to Catholicism, and Esztergom became the country's center of the early church. Although its glory days are long gone, this quiet town remains the seat of the archbishop-primate—the "Hungarian Rome."

GETTING THERE Twenty-five trains make the run daily between Budapest's Nyugati Station and Esztergom (trip time: 1½ hr.); IC trains are not available on this route. Train tickets cost 900 Ft ($4.85/£2.55).

VISITOR INFORMATION   Gran Tours, Széchenyi tér 25 (© **33/502-001**), is the best source of information. Summer hours are from Monday to Friday 8am to 4pm and Saturday 9am to noon; winter hours are from Monday to Friday 8am to 4pm. The station is on the outskirts of town, while the tourist info center is in the city center. Take bus no. 1 or 6 to Széchenyi tér. Local buses depart from outside the train station.

Top Attractions & Special Moments

The massive, neoclassical **Esztergom Cathedral** ✿✿ (© **33/402-354**), in Szent István tér on Castle Hill, is the largest church in Hungary. It is Esztergom's most popular attraction and one of Hungary's most impressive buildings. Built in the last century, it was to replace the cathedral ruined during the Turkish occupation. It claims the world's largest altarpiece painted on one continuous piece of canvas. The cathedral **Treasury (*Kincstár*)** ✿ contains a stunning array of ecclesiastical jewels and gold works. The cupola provides unparalleled views of Esztergom and the surrounding Hungarian and Slovak countryside. The cathedral is open daily, summer from 8am to 7pm, winter from 8am to 4pm. The treasury, crypt, and cupola are open daily, summer from 9am to 4:00pm, winter from Tuesday to Sunday noon to 4pm. Admission to the cathedral is free, but to see the crypt costs 100 Ft (.55¢/30p). The treasury is 550 Ft ($2.95/£1.40), and to see the cupola, which is only open during summer, costs 200 Ft ($1.10/£55p). To get here, take bus no. 6 from the train station and get off at the cathedral or in good weather, it is a nice walk.

Where to Dine

Hungarian specialties abound at **Anonim Vendéglő,** Berényi u. 4 (© **33/411-880**), which is an intimate restaurant housed in an ancient monument near the cathedral. Well-prepared meat dishes are coupled with outstanding vegetarian dishes and attentive service. It's open Tuesday through Sunday noon to midnight, but doesn't accept credit cards. Main courses run from 1,200 Ft to 3,000 Ft ($6.50–$16.20/£3.40–£8.55).

VISEGRÁD

Halfway between Szentendre and Esztergom, **Visegrád** (pronounced *Vee*-sheh-grod) is the smallest town in the country, making it historically fascinating. The Romans built a fort here, which was still extant when Slovak settlers gave the town its present name (meaning "High Castle") in the 9th or 10th century. After the Mongol invasion (1241–42), construction began on both the present ruined hilltop citadel and the former riverside palace. Visegrád boasted one of the finest royal palaces ever built in Hungary. Only one king, Charles Robert (1307–42), actually used it as his primary residence, but monarchs from Béla IV, in the 13th century, through Matthias Corvinus, in the late 15th century, spent time in Visegrád and contributed to its development, the latter expanding the palace into a great Renaissance center known throughout Europe.

GETTING THERE   There's no direct train service to Visegrád. Instead, take 1 of 28 daily trains departing from Nyugati Station for Nagymaros (trip time: 40 min.–1 hr.). From Nagymaros, take a ferry across the river to Visegrád. The ferry dock (RÉV; © 26/398-344) is a 5-minute walk from the train station. A ferry leaves every hour throughout the day. The train ticket to Nagymaros costs 900 Ft ($4.85/£2.55); the ferryboat ticket to Visegrád costs 200 Ft ($1.10/55p) for adults and 100 Ft (55¢/30p) for students.

VISITOR INFORMATION   Visegrád Tours, RÉV u. 15 (© **26/398-160**), is located across the road from the RÉV ferry boat landing. It is open daily 8am to

5:30pm; from November to March they are open, but they use the hotel next door as their winter office.

Top Attractions & Special Moments

Once covering much of the area where the boat landing and Fő utca (Main St.) are now found, the ruins of the Royal Palace and the Salamon tower are all that remain today for visitors to explore. The entrance to the open-air ruins of the **King Matthias Museum** 𝕬𝕬 is at Fő u. 27 (𝕮 **26/398-026**). Admission is free and the museum is open Tuesday to Sunday from 9am to 5pm. The buried ruins of the palace, having achieved a near-mythical status, were not discovered until this century. The Salamon Tower is open Tuesday to Sunday from 9am to 5pm, May through September.

The **Cloud Castle (Fellegvár)** 𝕬𝕬𝕬 (𝕮 **26/398-101**), a mountaintop citadel above Visegrád affords one of the finest views you'll find over the Danube. Admission to the Citadel is 800 Ft ($4.30/£2.25). It is open daily from 9:30am to 5:30pm. The "City Bus," a van taxi that awaits passengers outside Visegrád Tours, takes people up the steep hill for the steep fare of 2,000 Ft ($10.80/£5.70) apiece. If you stay less than 30 minutes, you can ride down again for 1,000 Ft ($5.40/£2.85); otherwise, you'll again pay 2,000 Ft ($10.80/£5.70). Note that it is not a casual walk to the Citadel; consider it a day hike and pack accordingly.

Where to Dine

In keeping with its name, **Renaissance Restaurant,** at Fő u. 11, across the street from the MAHART boat landing (𝕮 **26/398-081**), specializes in authentic medieval cuisine. Food is served in clay crockery without silverware (only a wooden spoon) and guests are offered paper crowns to wear. A meal is 4,500 Ft ($24.30/£12.80) per person. If you're big on the medieval theme, come for dinner (July–Aug only), when a six-course "Royal Feast" is celebrated following a 45-minute duel between knights. It's only is available to groups of not less than 30 people, but if you call, they will include you in a group if one is scheduled. It's open daily, from noon to 10pm. Tickets for this special evening are handled by the restaurant directly or Visegrád Tours (see above).

13

Italy

This boot-shaped peninsula is called *La Bell'Italia* (Beautiful Italy), and so it is, stretching from the Alpine peaks in its north to the offshore island of Sicily. The works left by Leonardo da Vinci, Raphael, Michelangelo, and all the gang are waiting to dazzle you, along with the ruins of Rome, the decaying but still magnificent *palazzi* of Venice, and the Renaissance treasures of Florence. You'll find enough Duomos, Madonnas, masterpieces, and scenery to dazzle the eye. And that's not all: Italy is a citadel of style and fashion and serves, at least in the view of Italians, the world's greatest cuisine. Each of the country's 20 regions has its own distinctive kitchen.

In our very limited space, we can only preview some of the highlights of this vast, diversified land, with its more than 5,000 miles (8,046km) of coastline, from the Ligurian Sea in the northwest to the Adriatic Sea washing eastward. The most hurried visitor with a railpass usually confines his or her itinerary to Rome, Florence, and Venice, and that's not a bad idea, as this trio of cities ranks among the top 10 in the world for attractions. Just seeing those cities will easily eat up a week's vacation. And if you have extra time, you can venture into other major cities, such as Milan or Naples, or explore some of Italy's charming towns, such as Pisa and Turin, or the scenic Lake Como. The good news is that visiting these cities by rail is a breeze thanks to thoroughly improved rail network. And though the cities themselves may not be cheap, rail travel in Italy is relatively inexpensive, making it a good destination for travelers trying to conserve their euros.

HIGHLIGHTS OF ITALY

On international flights, chances are you'll fly into **Rome** to begin your rail journey through Italy, though some people will find themselves flying into Milan (from which you can easily connect to Rome by train or plane). Rome deserves as much of your time as your schedule allows. It is one of the planet's great historical cities and is filled with museums, monuments, and a *joie de vivre* unlike any other city in Italy.

Allow at least 3 or 4 days to skim the highlights. You can divide your time among the ancient, papal, and modern attractions the city has to offer. Visit the Colosseum, the Roman Forum, and Palatine Hill; then take in St. Peter's Basilica and the Sistine Chapel before tossing in a few coins at the Trevi Fountain. And these are just a tiny few of the sights the city has to offer.

After Rome, if you have time for the south, you can take the train to Naples for a day of exploring. If you can spare an extra day, stay overnight and spend the following day wandering around the ruins of **Pompeii** or **Herculaneum.**

Once back in Rome, grab a train north to **Florence,** where a minimum of 3 days is needed to explore the glories of the city of the Renaissance. Here are all the churches, museums, historic squares, panoramic views, and galleries you would ever want to see, beginning with the masterpieces of the Uffizi Gallery, one of the world's

largest and greatest repositories of art. Other highlights include the multicolored Duomo or cathedral, Giotto's bell tower, the Palazzo Pitti, Michelangelo's *David* in the Galleria dell'Accademia, the massive Palazzo Vecchio (another Medici residence) opening onto Piazza della Signoria (where you'll want to have a coffee in a cafe), and the Medici Chapels. Walk the Ponte Vecchio, shop at San Lorenzo Market, and look into some of the world's greatest churches to occupy your final day or hours.

From Florence, head northeast by train to **Venice,** the queen of the Veneto and one of the world's most dazzling cities, built on 118 islets linked by 400 bridges with 150 canals cut through the maze. Venice is filled with attractions, including *palazzi* and churches but it is the glorious city itself that is its major allure. It shouldn't exist but does, like a preposterous dream.

Moments Festivals & Special Events

At the riotous **Carnevale,** theatrical presentations and masked balls take place throughout Venice and on the islands in the lagoon. The balls are by invitation only (except the Doge's Ball), but the street events and fireworks are open to everyone. The festivities take place the week before Ash Wednesday, the beginning of Lent. Contact the **Venice Tourist Office,** San Marco, Ex Giardini Reali, Palazzo Selva, 30124 Venezia (© **041/5298711**).

Processions and age-old ceremonies—some from pagan days, some from the Middle Ages—are staged during the **Holy Week observances** held nationwide. The most notable procession is led by the pope, passing the Colosseum and the Roman Forum up to Palatine Hill; a torch-lit parade caps the observance. The events kick off 4 days before Easter Sunday, sometimes at the end of March but often in April.

Palio fever grips the Tuscan hill town of Siena from early July to mid-August for a wild and exciting horse race that originated in the Middle Ages. Pageantry, costumes, and the celebrations of the victorious *contrada* (sort of a neighborhood social club) mark the spectacle. It's a "no rules" event: Even a horse without a rider can win the race. For details on Il Palio, contact the **Azienda di Promozione Turistica,** Piazza del Campo 56, 53100 Siena (© **0577/280551**).

After Venice, your rail journey takes you northwest to the sprawling metropolis of **Milan.** You'll need a full day for Milan, capital of Lombardy and a city of glitz and glamour. It doesn't have the attractions of the "royal trio," but is rich in sights, nonetheless, highlighted by its Gothic Duomo, its famous opera house of La Scala; Leonardo's masterpiece, *The Last Supper,* in Santa Maria delle Grazie; and the Brera Palace and Art Gallery, one of northern Italy's greatest showcases of art.

After Milan, all of Italy's lake district, especially Como, is at your doorstep. You can also take the train northwest to the Piedmontese city of **Turin,** famous as the resting place of the controversial Holy Shroud, or else go to the port city of **Genoa,** birthplace of Columbus, to survey its many monuments and to tour its port facilities.

1 Essentials

GETTING THERE

High season on most airlines' routes to Italy is usually June to the beginning of September. This is the most expensive and most crowded time to travel. **Shoulder season** is April to May, early September to October, and December 15 to 24. **Low season** is November 1 to December 14, and December 25 to March 31.

Alitalia (© **800/223-5730;** www.alitalia.com) is the Italian national airline, with nonstop flights to Rome from a number of North American cities. Most flights arrive in either Milan or Rome.

Major North American carriers offering direct flights to Italy include **American Airlines** (© 800/433-7300; www.aa.com), **Delta** (© 800/241-4141; www.delta.com), **United** (© 800/538-2929; www.united.com), **US Airways** (© 800/428-4322;

www.usairways.com), **Continental** (© **800/231-0856;** www.continental.com), and **Air Canada** (© 800/247-2262; www.aircanada.ca). **British Airways** (© 800/AIR-WAYS; www.britishairways.com), **Virgin Atlantic Airways** (© 800/821-5438; www.virgin-atlantic.com), **Air France** (© 800/237-2747; www.airfrance.com), **Northwest/KLM** (© 800/225-2525; www.klm.com), and **Lufthansa** (© 800/645-3880; www.lufthansa-usa.com) offer some attractive deals for anyone interested in combining a trip to Italy with a stopover in, say, Britain, Paris, Amsterdam, or Germany.

Depending on your departure city, flying time to Italy ranges from 8 to 12 hours.

ITALY BY RAIL
PASSES
For information on the **Eurail Global Pass, Eurail Global Pass Flexi,** and other multicountry options, see chapter 2. Information on the **Eurail Italy Pass** and **Eurail Italy Rail 'n Drive** options is also available in chapter 2. All of these passes should be purchased in North America and are available through **Rail Europe** (© **877/272-RAIL** [7245] in North America; www.raileurope.com).

Italy also has a number of other railpasses that can be purchased at most of the country's major train stations. Seniors 60 and over can avail themselves of the **Cartaviaggio Relax** if they present proof of age. Costing 30€ ($39), this card can be purchased only in Italy, and grants a 15% discount off the price of any first- or second-class ticket. A similar pass, **Cartaviaggio Smart,** costs 40€ ($52), and grants persons up to 26 years of age a 10% discount in either first- or second-class seats. Finally, the **Cartaviaggio Executive** costs 80€ ($104) for a 10% discount on the price of first-class tickets on all trains. All of these passes are valid for a year from the date of purchase.

FOREIGN TRAIN TERMS
A station is a *stazione,* and trains are *Espresso,* meaning an express, or *Diretto,* meaning direct. Additional charges are referred to as *supplemento.* These *Diretto* and *Espresso* trains can also be called *Regionali* or *Interregionali.* The train to avoid, especially on long-distance journeys, is a *locali,* which stops at all stations.

Tickets are called *biglietti,* with a single ticket labeled an *andata* or a round-trip *andata e ritorno.* First class is *prima;* second class is *seconda classe.* Ticket offices are called *la biglietteria.* For journeys up to 155 miles (250km), you can often make ticket purchases at newsstands or even a station tobacconist. Such a ticket is called *un biglietto a fascia chilometrica.*

PRACTICAL TRAIN INFORMATION
The train is the way to go in Italy. Train travel is inexpensive, the service is frequent, and the trains among the most modern in Europe. Most of Italian trains have been integrated into the state system, and are operated by **Trenitalia.** Information on the rail network is available online at **www.trenitalia.it** in Italian and English. Most trains, except in deep rural areas of the south, are modern and air-conditioned.

Trains provide an excellent means of transport, even if you don't buy a railpass or one of the special Italian railway tickets (see above). As a rule of thumb, second-class travel usually costs about two-thirds the price of an equivalent first-class trip. Unless you're riding Eurostar Italia, you're better off opting for first class when traveling by rail in Italy. The newly reconditioned IC Plus and Eurostar City trains (reservations a must) run the fastest schedules with conventional equipment. The **InterCity (IC)** trains are modern, air-conditioned trains that make limited stops when compared to the far slower direct or regional trains (which should be avoided). Newly reconditioned IC

Trains & Travel Times in Italy

From	To	Type of Train	# of Trains	Frequency	Travel Time
Rome	Bari	Eurostar Italia	4	Daily	4 hr., 43 min.
Rome	Ancona	Eurostar Italia	4	Daily	3 hr., 20 min.
Rome	Florence	Eurostar Italia	26	Daily	1 hr., 35 min.
Rome	Milan	Eurostar Italia	15	Daily	4 hr., 30 min.
Rome	Naples	Eurostar Italia	15	Daily	1 hr., 35 min.
Rome	Palermo	InterCity	1	Daily	10 hr., 35 min.
Rome	Salerno	Eurostar Italia	11	Daily	2 hr., 31 min.
Rome	Salerno	InterCity	5	Daily	2 hr., 42 min.
Rome	Venice	Eurostar Italia	5	Daily	4 hr., 32 min.
Milan	Venice	InterCity	9	Daily	3 hr., 5 min.

Plus and Eurostar City trains (reservations a must) run the fastest schedules with conventional equipment. The best of the Italian trains are unquestionably the high-speed **Eurostar Italia (ES)** trains (don't confuse these with the Eurostar trains that run from Britain to France—they aren't the same!). Using the same tilting technology as the German ICE T and Pendolino trains, these trains are modern, exceptionally comfortable, and though passholders pay a supplement to ride them, they are definitely the way to go in Italy.

Children 4 to 11 receive a discount of 50% off the adult fare, and children 3 and under travel free with their parents. Seniors and travelers under age 26 can also purchase discount cards.

New Electric trains (known collectively as **Artesia** trains) have made travel between France and Italy faster and more comfortable than ever. **France's TGVs** travel at speeds of up to 185 mph (297kmph) and have cut travel time between Paris and Turin from 7 to 5½ hours and between Paris and Milan from 7½ to 6¾ hours. **Eurostar Trains** travel at speeds of up to 145 mph (233kmph) and currently run between Milan and Lyon (5 hr.), with a stop in Turin. Riviera trains connect the French Riviera to Milan just as quickly.

Tilting **Cisalpino** (*Chee*-sahl-peeno) trains are some of the world's most advanced and speed from northern Italy (primarily Venice, Florence, and Milan) to major cities in Switzerland. Though aimed mostly at business travelers, they're a great way to get from Italy to Switzerland. To ride these trains, passholders must buy a Passholder Ticket that includes a seat reservation (mandatory).

A luxurious overnight train (the *Salvador Dalí*), connects Milan and Turin with Barcelona in Spain. **Artesia de Nuit** trains connect Paris to various cities in Italy. And **EuroNight (EN)** trains service both international and domestic routes. Riviera night trains connect Nice to Venice, Florence, and Rome. **InterCity Night (ICN)** trains essentially offer the same services as EuroNight trains, but travel only within Italy's borders.

RESERVATIONS   When you purchase either a single or a round-trip ticket, the validity is for a period of 2 months from the date you bought the ticket. The date you want to travel is stamped on the ticket at the time of purchase, providing you make a seat reservation. Undated tickets purchased at newsstands or from tobacconists need to be validated on the day you plan to take the journey.

Even though reservations are optional on most rail journeys, it's still wise to book a ticket and a seat on runs between such major cities as Florence and Venice, Rome and Naples, or Rome and either Florence or Milan. Italian trains are very crowded on public holidays, and reservations are almost mandatory during these peak periods. A regular seat reservation runs between $11 and $17, depending on the train and class you've selected. Big rail depots, such as the Stazione Termini in Rome, often have separate windows for making reservations—labeled *prenotazioni*. Reservations are mandatory on all ES, Artesia, Cisalpino, IC Plus, Riviera, ES City, and night trains.

If you're traveling at night, it's wise to reserve a *couchette* (foldaway bed) or sleeper (private sleeping cabin), especially for long distances, such as the train that goes from Paris to Rome or vice versa. A wide variety of sleeping accommodations are available depending on the night trains that you choose. If you ask for *Superiore* or *Finestrino* when booking, you'll get a top bunk giving you more legroom and greater privacy. When reserving, try not to get a seat next to the corridor, as passengers here are the most likely to get robbed.

The supplement you'll pay for access to a couchette aboard an Italian night train varies considerably depending on how many others you'll be sharing a compartment with. For a couchette within a compartment shared by six, you'll pay a supplement of $35 per person. For a couchette within a compartment shared by four (and these are available only on an increasingly limited number of trains), you'll pay a supplement of $45 per person. And for a sleeper shared with only one other person, you'll pay a supplement of between $56 and $68 per person, depending on the train and the itinerary (single sleepers are available on Ellipsos night trains—the supplement varies). You can and should prereserve sleeper options (and pay the supplement), through Rail Europe as soon as you have your trip dates figured out, especially if you're traveling during high season. If you're already within Italy, you can reserve these in advance by heading for the ticket window of any railway station.

Note: Seat reservations are not always marked on seats and some people may try and claim your reserved seat as their own. Firmly but politely insist they vacate (and if you haven't reserved and sit in an apparently unreserved seat, be advised that you may actually be sitting in someone else's seat).

SERVICES & AMENITIES   Most InterCity trains have facilities for persons with limited mobility. There are dining facilities on all major trains, though prices are lethal. If you're on a strict budget, do as the Italians do and pack your own picnic for consumption while riding the rails and taking in the scenery. It's a great way to travel. ES trains offer better seating and are one of the only domestic trains in Italy where second-class travel won't be a less-grand experience than first class. First-class passengers on ES trains get a free drink and snack served at their seats.

Overnight accommodations on Italian trains range from "Gran Class" single-sleeper cabins with private bathrooms and showers on the Ellipsos hotel train from Milan to Barcelona, to six-berth economy couchettes on the Artesia de Nuit trains from Paris to Rome, to reclining sleeperette seats on ICN trains from Rome to Venice. Note that although sleeper cabins are segregated by sex (except for families taking a whole cabin), couchettes are not segregated by sex. First-class sleeper cabins usually include a continental breakfast in their rates. All sleeping accommodations require the payment of a supplement in addition to your railpass—and must be reserved well in advance. We recommend reserving through Rail Europe (© **877/272-RAIL** [7245]; www.raileurope.com) before you leave home. Note that to reserve some classes of sleeper cabins, you'll need to have a first-class railpass.

Warning: Theft on some Italian trains is a problem. If you opt for a couchette or sleeper on an Italian train, make sure your belongings are well secured.

FAST FACTS: Italy

Area Code The country code for Italy is **39**. Today, city codes (or area codes for cities) have been folded into each phone number. Therefore, you must dial the whole number, whether you're calling from outside or inside Italy, or even within a city such as Rome itself.

Climate It's warm all over Italy in summer; it can be very hot in the south, especially inland. The high temperatures (measured in Italy in degrees Celsius) begin in Rome in May, often lasting until sometime in October. Winters in the north of Italy are cold, with rain and snow, but in the south the weather is warm all year, averaging 50°F (10°C) in winter. For the most part, it's drier in Italy than in North America, so high temperatures don't seem as bad because the humidity is lower. In Rome, Naples, and the south, temperatures can stay in the 90s for days, but nights are most often comfortably cooler.

Documents Required U.S. and Canadian citizens with a **valid passport** don't need a visa to enter Italy if they don't expect to stay more than 90 days and don't expect to work there. If after entering Italy you want to stay more than 90 days, you can apply for a permit for an extra 90 days, which as a rule is granted immediately. Go to the nearest *questura* (police headquarters) or to your home country's consulate. If your passport is lost or stolen, head to your consulate as soon as possible for a replacement.

Electricity The electricity in Italy varies considerably. It's usually alternating current (AC), varying from 42 to 50 cycles. The voltage can be anywhere from 115 to 220. It's recommended that any visitor carrying electrical appliances obtain a transformer. Check the exact local current at the hotel where you're staying. Plugs have prongs that are round, not flat; therefore, an adapter plug is also needed.

Embassies/Consulates In case of an emergency, embassies have a 24-hour referral service.

The **U.S. Embassy** is in Rome at Via Vittorio Veneto 119A (📞 **06/46741**; fax 06/46742356). **U.S. consulates** are in Florence, at Lungarno Amerigo Vespucci 38 (📞 **055/266951**; fax 055/284088), and in Milan, at Via Principe Amedeo 2-10 (📞 **02/290351**; fax 02/29001165). There's also a consulate in Naples on Piazza della Repubblica 1 (📞 **081/5838111**). For consulate hours, see individual city listings.

The **Canadian Embassy** in Rome is at Via Zara 30 (📞 **06/854441**). The Canadian Consulate in Milan is at V.V. Pisani 19 (📞 **02/67581**).

Health & Safety Italy has a low rate of violent crime, little of which is directed at tourists. Petty crimes such as pickpocketing, theft from parked cars, and purse-snatching, however, are serious problems, especially in large cities. Most reported thefts occur at crowded tourist sites, on public buses or trains, or at the major railway stations: Rome's Termini, Milan's Centrale, Florence's Santa Maria Novella, and Naples's Centrale. Clients of Internet cafes in major cities have been targeted. Elderly tourists who have tried to resist petty thieves on motor scooters have suffered broken arms and collarbones.

On trains, a commonly reported trick involves one or more persons who pretend to befriend a traveler and offer drugged food or drink. Also, thieves have been known to impersonate police officers to gain the confidence of tourists. The thief shows the prospective victim a circular plastic sign with the words "police" or "international police." If this happens, the tourist should insist on seeing the officer's identification card *(documento),* as impersonators tend not to carry forged documents. Tourists should immediately report thefts or other crimes to the local police.

Medical facilities are available, but may be limited outside urban areas. Public hospitals sometimes do not maintain the same standards as hospitals in the United States, so travelers are encouraged to obtain insurance that would cover a stay in a private Italian hospital or clinic. It is almost impossible to obtain an itemized hospital bill from public hospitals, as required by many U.S. insurance companies, because the Italian National Health Service charges one inclusive rate (care services, bed, and board).

Holidays Offices and shops in Italy are closed on the following **national holidays:** January 1 (New Year's Day), Easter Monday, April 25 (Liberation Day), May 1 (Labor Day), June 2 (Anniversary of the Republic), August 15 (Assumption of the Virgin), November 1 (All Saints' Day), December 8 (Feast of the Immaculate Conception), December 25 (Christmas Day), and December 26 (Santo Stefano).

Closings are also observed in the following cities on **feast days** honoring their patron saints: Venice, April 25 (St. Mark); Florence, Genoa, and Turin, June 24 (St. John the Baptist); Rome, June 29 (Sts. Peter and Paul); Palermo, July 15 (St. Rosalia); Naples, September 19 (St. Gennaro); Bologna, October 4 (St. Petronio); Cagliari, October 30 (St. Saturnino); Trieste, November 3 (St. Giusto); Bari, December 6 (St. Nicola); and Milan, December 7 (St. Ambrose).

Legal Aid The consulate of your country is the place to turn for legal aid, although offices can't interfere in the Italian legal process. They can, however, inform you of your rights and provide a list of attorneys. You'll have to pay for the attorney out of your pocket—there's no free legal assistance. If you're arrested for a drug offense, about all the consulate will do is notify a lawyer about your case and perhaps inform your family.

Mail Mail delivery in Italy is notoriously bad. Your family and friends back home might receive your postcards in 1 week, or it might take 2 weeks (sometimes longer). Postcards, aerogrammes, and letters weighing up to 20 grams sent to the United States and Canada cost .85€ ($1.10). Stamps *(francobolli)* can be bought at *tabacchi* (tobacco stores). You can buy special stamps at the **Vatican City Post Office,** adjacent to the information office in St. Peter's Square; it's open Monday to Friday 8:30am to 7pm and Saturday 8:30am to 6pm. Letters mailed at Vatican City reach North America far more quickly than mail sent from elsewhere for the same cost.

Police & Emergencies Dial ⓒ **113** for ambulance, police, or fire. In case of a breakdown on an Italian road, dial ⓒ **803116** at the nearest telephone box; the nearest Automobile Club of Italy (ACI) will be notified to come to your aid.

Telephone To call Italy from the United States, dial the **international prefix, 011;** then Italy's **country code, 39;** and then the actual **phone number** (which has a city code built in).

A **local phone call** in Italy costs around .10€ (10¢). **Public phones** accept coins, precharged phone cards (*scheda* or *carta telefonica*), or both. You can buy a *carta telefonica* at any *tabacchi* (tobacconists; most display a sign with a white *T* on a brown background) in increments of 1€ ($1.30), 2.50€ ($3.25), 3€ ($3.90), 5€ ($6.50), 7.50€ ($9.75), and 10€ ($13). To make a call, pick up the receiver and insert .10€ (15¢) or your card (break off the corner first). Most phones have a digital display that'll tell you how much money you've inserted (or how much is left on the card). Dial the number, and don't forget to take the card with you after you hang up.

To call the **national telephone information** (in Italian) in Italy, dial ✆ **1240.** It costs .40€ (50¢) and .10€ (15¢) every additional 2 seconds.

Tipping In **hotels,** a service charge of 15% to 19% is already added to a bill. In addition, it's customary to tip the chambermaid 1€ ($1.30) per day, the door-man (for calling a cab) .50€ (65¢), and the bellhop or porter 1.50€ to 2.50€ ($1.95–$3.25) for carrying your bags to your room. A concierge expects about 15% of his or her bill, as well as tips for extra services performed, which could include help with long-distance calls.

In **restaurants and cafes,** 15% is usually added to your bill to cover most charges. If you're not sure whether this has been done, ask, *"È incluso il servizio?"* (ay een-*cloo*-soh eel sair-*vee*-tsoh?). An additional tip isn't expected, but it's nice to leave the equivalent of an extra couple of dollars if you've been pleased with the service. Checkroom attendants expect .75€ ($1), and washroom atten-dants should get .50€ (65¢). Restaurants are required by law to give customers official receipts. Taxi drivers expect at least 15% of the fare.

2 Rome

The city of Rome is simultaneously strident, romantic, and sensual. And although the romantic poets would probably be horrified at today's traffic, pollution, overcrowding, crime, political discontent, and barely controlled chaos of modern Rome, the city endures and thrives in a way that is called "eternal."

It would take a lifetime to know a city filled with 27 centuries of artistic achieve-ment. A cradle of Western civilization, timeless Rome is home to more treasures of ancient history, art, and architecture per square foot than any other city in the world. Caesar was assassinated here, Charlemagne crowned, and the list of the major events goes on and on.

In between all that absorption of culture and history, take time to relax and meet the Romans. Savor their succulent pastas while enjoying a fine glass of wine on one of the city's splendid squares where one of the reigning Caesars might have gone before you, or perhaps Michelangelo or Raphael.

For the rail traveler, Rome, though too far south to be considered truly central, is easily reached by rail and its ultra modern **Stazione Termini** is well connected to most other Italian cities, as well as several major European destinations. It's unquestionably the best starting point for a rail trip of Italy and it makes an excellent starting or ter-mination point for a rail tour of Europe.

STATION INFORMATION

GETTING FROM THE AIRPORT TO THE TRAIN STATION

The gateway for most visitors beginning a rail journey of Italy is **Leonardo da Vinci Airport** (© **06/65951**), also called Fiumicino.

After you leave Passport Control, you'll see two **information desks** (one for Rome, one for Italy). At the Rome desk, you can pick up a general map and some pamphlets Monday to Saturday 8:15am to 7pm; the staff can also help you find a hotel room if you haven't reserved ahead. A *cambio* (money exchange) operates daily 7:30am to 11pm, offering surprisingly good rates.

There's a **train station** in the airport. To get into the city, follow the signs marked TRENI for the 30-minute shuttle to Rome's main station, **Stazione Termini** (arriving on Track 22). The shuttle runs 6:37am to 11:37pm for 9.50€ ($12.35) one-way. On the way, you'll pass a machine dispensing tickets, or you can buy them in person near the tracks if you don't have small bills on you. When you arrive at Termini, get out of the train quickly and grab a baggage cart. (It's a long schlep from the track to the exit or to the other train connections, and baggage carts can be scarce.)

A **taxi** from Da Vinci airport to the city costs 45€ ($58.50) and up for the 1-hour trip, depending on traffic. The expense might be worth it if you have a lot of luggage or just don't want to be bothered with the train trip. Call © **06/6645,** 06/3570, or 06/4994 for information.

INSIDE THE STATION

Trains and buses (including trains from the airport) arrive in the center of old Rome at the silver **Stazione Termini,** Piazza dei Cinquecento (© **892021**); this is the train, bus, and subway transportation hub for all Rome and is surrounded by many hotels (especially cheaper ones). If you're taking the **Metropolitana (subway),** follow the illuminated red-and-white M signs. To catch a bus, go straight through the outer hall and enter the sprawling bus lot of **Piazza dei Cinquecento.** You'll also find **taxis** there.

The Roma Termini is a virtual city within a city. On the lower level of the two-level station is a vast array of services such as a drugstore, ATMs, clothing shops, fast food, lounges, hairdressers, a bookstore, and barbershops. On-site is a **tourist office** (no phone), open daily 8:15am to 7:15pm. You can get minor information here but for hotel reservations go to the kiosk across from track no. 20, open daily 7am to 10pm. A deposit is taken from you (the amount based on your selection of hotel), and you're supposed to arrive at your selected hotel within the hour. There's always a line, but you can pick up one of the nearby phones and make a reservation for free by dialing © **06/97745496.**

A **24-hour luggage storage** office is located on the underground floor of the Termini wing. **Train information** is available from three computer touch screens at tracks 1, 9, and 22 in the center of the station. Train reservations are made at ticket windows no. 30 to no. 45. Windows no. 30 to no. 38—*Prenotazioni Posti–WL–Cuccette–Pendolino*—make reservations, and also arrange sleeper and couchette reservations. Windows no. 7 to no. 29—*biglietti Ordinari e Ridotti*—actually sell tickets. **Informazioni ferroviarie** (in the outer hall) dispenses information on rail travel to other parts of Italy.

INFORMATION ELSEWHERE IN THE CITY

The chief tourist office is the **Azienda Provinciale di Turismo (APT)** at **Via Parigi 5** (© **06/82059127**). The headquarters is open Monday to Saturday 9am to 7pm.

Rome

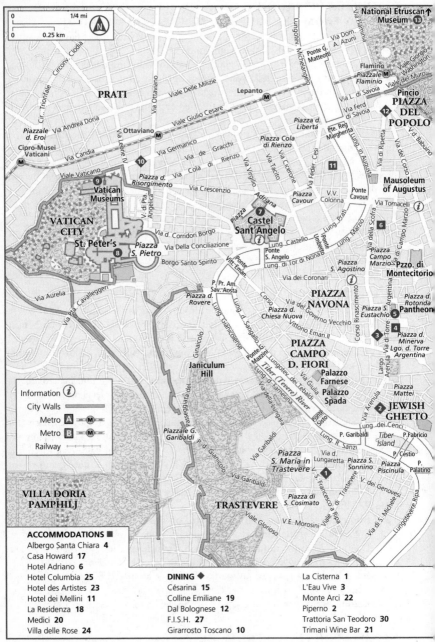

ACCOMMODATIONS ■
Albergo Santa Chiara **4**
Casa Howard **17**
Hotel Adriano **6**
Hotel Columbia **25**
Hotel des Artistes **23**
Hotel dei Mellini **11**
La Residenza **18**
Medici **20**
Villa delle Rose **24**

DINING ◆
Césarina **15**
Colline Emiliane **19**
Dal Bolognese **12**
F.I.S.H. **27**
Girarrosto Toscano **10**

La Cisterna **1**
L'Eau Vive **3**
Monte Arci **22**
Piperno **2**
Trattoria San Teodoro **30**
Trimani Wine Bar **21**

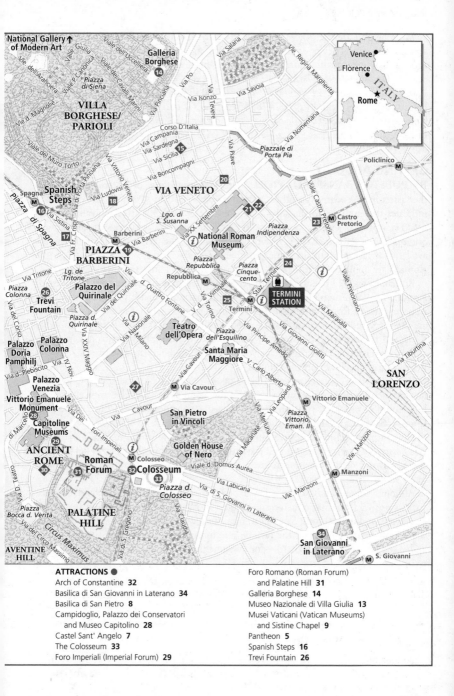

ATTRACTIONS ●

More helpful are the offices maintained by the **Comune di Roma** at various sites around the city. They're staffed daily 9:30am to 7:30pm and dispense maps and brochures. Here are the addresses and phone numbers: in Piazza dei Cinquecento, outside Termini (© **06/47825194**); on Lungo Tevere Vaticano (© **06/68809707**); in Piazza San Giovanni, in Laterano (© **06/77203535**); on Via Nazionale, near the Palazzo delle Esposizioni (© **06/47824525**); on Via del Tempio della Pace, near the Colosseum (© **06/69924307**); on Piazza Sonnino in Trastevere (© **06/58333457**); on Piazza Cinque Lune, near Piazza Navona (© **06/68809240**); and on Via dell'Olmata (© **06/4740955**).

GETTING AROUND

BY PUBLIC TRANSPORTATION   The **Metropolitana,** or **Metro,** for short, is the fastest means of transportation, operating daily 5:30am to 11:30pm. A big red M indicates the entrance to the subway. Tickets are 1€ ($1.30) and are available from *tabacchi* (tobacco shops), many newsstands, and vending machines at all stations. Some stations have managers, but they won't make change. Booklets of tickets are available at tabacchi and in some terminals. *Tip:* Avoid riding the trains when the Romans are going to or from work or you'll be mashed flatter than fettuccine.

Roman buses are operated by **ATAC (Azienda Tramvie e Autobus del Comune di Roma),** Via Volturno 65 (© **06/46951** for information). For 1€ ($1.30) you can ride to most parts of Rome, although it can be slow going in all that traffic and the buses are often very crowded. Your ticket is valid for 75 minutes, and you can get on many buses and trams during that time by using the same ticket. Buy bus tickets in tabacchi or bus terminals. You must have your ticket before boarding because there are no ticket-issuing machines on the vehicles.

Buses and trams stop at areas marked FERMATA. At most of these, a yellow sign will display the numbers of the buses that stop there and a list of all the stops along each bus's route in order, so you can easily search out your destination. Bus service runs from 5:30am to midnight and the night service is from 12:10 to 5:30am; an N after the line number defines buses running at night. It's best, however, to take a taxi in the wee hours—if you can find one. At the **bus information booth** at Piazza dei Cinquecento, in front of the Stazione Termini, you can purchase a directory complete with maps summarizing the routes.

Although routes change often, a few old reliable routes have remained valid for years, such as **no. 75** from Stazione Termini to the Colosseum, **H** from Stazione Termini to Trastevere, and **no. 40** from Stazione Termini to the Vatican. But if you're going somewhere and are dependent on the bus, be sure to carefully check where the bus stop is and exactly which bus goes there—don't assume that it'll be the same bus the next day.

BY TAXI   Don't count on hailing a taxi on the street or even getting one at a stand. If you're going out, have your hotel call one. At a restaurant, ask the waiter or cashier to dial for you. If you want to phone for yourself, try one of these numbers: © **06/6645,**

⌒Value Traveler's Tip

At Stazione Termini, you can buy a special **tourist pass,** which allows you to ride on the ATAC network and the Metro. It costs 4€ ($5.20) for a day or 16€ ($20.80) for a week.

06/3570, or **06/4994.** The meter begins at 3€ ($3.90) for the first 2 miles (3km) and then rises .75€ ($1) per kilometer. Every suitcase costs 1.05€ ($1.35), and on Sunday a 3.35€ ($4.35) supplement is assessed. There's another 4.90€ ($6.35) supplement 10pm to 7am.

WHERE TO STAY

Albergo Santa Chiara   This is one of the best located hotels in the inner core of historic Rome, right in back of the Pantheon and opening onto the Piazza della Minerva. The Corteggiani family has been welcoming visitors to this hotel since 1838. Marble columns evoke the elegance of yesterday. The comfortable and well-maintained bedrooms are furnished with classic simplicity and range in size from the very small to the very large, the latter spacious enough to be classified as Roman apartments. If you face Piazza della Minerva, you'll have a grand view but can also anticipate noise late at night.

Via Santa Chiara 21, 00186 Roma. ✆ 06/6872979. Fax 06/6873144. www.albergosantachiara.com. 98 units. 223€–280€ ($290–$364) double; 415€–550€ ($540–$715) junior suite. Rates include buffet breakfast. AE, DC, MC, V. Metro: Piazza di Spagna. **Amenities:** Bar; laundry service; 1 room for those w/limited mobility. *In room:* Hair dryer.

Casa Howard ✻✻ *(Finds)*   It's rare to make a discovery in the tourist-trodden Spanish Steps area, which is why Casa Howard comes as a pleasant surprise. The little B&B occupies about two-thirds of the second floor of a historic structure in an ideal location for shoppers. The welcoming family owners maintain beautifully furnished guest rooms, each with its own private bathroom (although some bathrooms lie outside the bedrooms in the hallway). The Pink Room is the most spacious, with its own en suite bathroom. Cristy at reception can "arrange anything" in Rome for you and will also invite you to use the house's private Turkish *hammam* (steam bath).

Via Capo le Case 18, 00187 Roma. ✆ 06/69924555. Fax 06/6794644. www.casahoward.com. 5 units. 160€–230€ ($208–$299) double. MC, V. Metro: Piazza di Spagna. **Amenities:** Bar; laundry service; massage; all rooms non-smoking. *In room:* Hair dryer.

Hotel Adriano ✻   Stay here if you want elegance and top-notch living in a converted palace from the 15th century that's close to the Spanish Steps, the Piazza Navona, and the Pantheon. Even some members of the Italian Parliament, which is nearby, check in here. Bedrooms are simply furnished but tasteful, with excellent beds usually resting on hardwood floors. You can enjoy breakfast on the hotel's roof terrace.

Via di Pallacorda 2, 00186 Roma. ✆ 06/68802451. Fax 06/68803926. www.hoteladriano.com. 82 units. 160€–250€ ($208–$325) double; 260€–400€ ($338–$520) suite. Rates include breakfast. AE, DC, MC, V. Bus: 95 or 175. **Amenities:** Bar; laundry service; 1 room for those w/limited mobility.

Hotel Columbia ✻✻ *(Finds)*   This is one of the most modern hotels in the neighborhood, with a hardworking multilingual staff. Originally built around 1900, the hotel keeps up-to-date with the times. The interior contains Murano chandeliers and conservatively modern furniture. The compact and cozy guest rooms have shower-only bathrooms and compare well against the accommodations in the best hotels nearby. The appealing roof garden has a view over the surrounding rooftops.

Via del Viminale 15, 00184 Roma. ✆ 06/4883509. Fax 06/4740209. www.hotelcolumbia.com. 45 units. 150€–235€ ($195–$306) double; 203€–317€ ($264–$412) triple. Rates include buffet breakfast. AE, DC, MC, V. Metro: Repubblica. **Amenities:** Bar; laundry service; nonsmoking rooms. *In room:* Hair dryer.

Hotel dei Mellini ✻   Pilgrims planning to explore the Vatican area can splurge on this hotel, situated on the right bank of the Tiber between the Spanish Steps and St.

Peter's Basilica. It's the most popular address in Rome for visiting actors and enter-tainers. The handsome public rooms are tastefully elegant. Guest rooms are spacious and have a classic Art Deco styling in their choice of furnishings and fixtures, includ-ing beautiful private bathrooms. Its roof terrace opens onto panoramic nighttime views of the floodlit city.

Via Muzio Clementi 81, 00193 Roma. ⓒ **06/324771.** Fax 06/32477801. www.hotelmellini.com. 80 units. 159€–300€ ($206.70–$390) double; from 345€ ($448.50) suite. Rates include breakfast. AE, DC, MC, V. Metro: Lepanto. **Amenities:** Restaurant; bar; cafe; laundry service; rooms for those w/limited mobility; nonsmoking rooms. *In room:* Hair dryer.

Hotel des Artistes *Value*   A few steps from Termini Station, this hotel is frequently renovated and is looking good. Asian carpets and velvet draperies along with spotless maintenance have made this one of the best values in the area. Mahogany furnishings and marble-clad bathrooms make this a worthy choice. For the really frugal rail trav-eler, one part of the hotel is actually a hostel with dormitory-style rooms, bathrooms in the corridors, and a TV and ceiling fan in each room. Charges for these units start at 65€ ($84.50) double and are the best deal in the Termini area. The rooftop garden at night is a magnet for guests.

Via Villafranca 20, 00185 Roma. ⓒ **06/4454365.** Fax 06/4462368. www.hoteldesartistes.com. 45 units. 122€–199€ ($159–$259) double. Rates include buffet breakfast. AE, DC, MC, V. Metro: Castro Pretorio. Bus: 310. **Amenities:** Bar; all rooms nonsmoking. *In room:* Hair dryer.

La Residenza *ⓕⓕ*   In a glamorous location (admittedly far from the Termini area) 10 minutes from the Spanish Steps, this little hotel successfully combines intimacy and elegance. A bit old-fashioned and homelike, the converted villa has an ivy-covered courtyard and a series of grand public rooms with Empire divans, oil portraits, and rattan chairs. Terraces are scattered throughout. The guest rooms are generally spa-cious, containing bentwood chairs and built-in furniture, including beds. The dozen or so junior suites boast balconies. The bathrooms have robes and even come equipped with ice machines.

Via Emilia 22–24, 00187 Roma. ⓒ **06/4880789.** Fax 06/485721. www.hotel-la-residenza.com. 29 units. 200€–220€ ($260–$286) double; 240€–250€ ($312–$325) suite. Rates include buffet breakfast. AE, MC, V. Metro: Piazza Barberini. **Amenities:** Bar; laundry service. *In room:* Hair dryer.

Medici   Near Termini and the shops along Via XX Settembre, this hotel dates from 1906, when it was built to house passengers arriving by rail in Rome. Many of its bet-ter rooms overlook an inner patio garden. Accommodations (last renovated in 2003) are generously sized and decorated in a classic Roman style. The cheapest units (stan-dard) are a good buy because they're only slightly smaller than the superior units (though the latter offer air-conditioning, more antiques, and better furnishings).

Via Flavia 96, 00187 Roma. ⓒ **06/4827319.** Fax 06/4740767. www.hotelmedici.com. 69 units (showers only). 80€–200€ ($104–$260) double; 110€–250€ ($143–$325) triple. Rates include buffet breakfast. AE, DC, MC, V. Metro: Piazza della Repubblica. **Amenities:** Bar; laundry service; 1 room for those w/limited mobility; nonsmoking rooms. *In room:* A/C (in some rooms), hair dryer.

Villa delle Rose   Long a favorite with rail passengers, this hotel is only 2 blocks from Termini Station and is an acceptable, if not exciting, choice. In the late 19th cen-tury it was a private villa but has been much altered and modified over the years to receive guests. Much of its old architectural allure is still in evidence, including the Corinthian-capped marble columns in the lobby and the luxuriant garden in back.

Redecorating and upgrading of the bedrooms and the tiled bathrooms has made them more comfortable than ever, though the overall look is still one of faded grandeur.

Via Vicenza 5, 00185 Roma. ✆ **06/4451788.** Fax 06/4451639. www.villadellerose.it. 38 units. 124€–170€ ($161–$221) double. Rates include buffet breakfast. AE, DC, MC, V. Metro: Termini or Castro Pretorio. **Amenities:** Breakfast garden; bar; all nonsmoking rooms. *In room:* A/C (in some rooms), hair dryer.

TOP ATTRACTIONS & SPECIAL MOMENTS

Basilica di San Giovanni in Laterano ✿   This church—not St. Peter's—is the cathedral of the diocese of Rome. Catholics all over the world refer to it as their "mother church." Originally built in A.D. 314 by Constantine, the cathedral has suffered many vicissitudes and was forced to rebuild many times. The present building is characterized by its 18th-century facade by Alessandro Galilei (statues of Christ and the Apostles ring the top). Borromini gets the credit—some say blame—for the interior, built for Innocent X.

The most unusual sight is across the street at the "Palace of the Holy Steps," called the **Santuario della Scala Santa** ✿, Piazza San Giovanni in Laterano (✆ **06/7726641**). It's alleged that these were the actual steps that Christ climbed when he was brought before Pontius Pilate. These steps are supposed to be climbed only on your knees, which you're likely to see the faithful doing throughout the day. Visiting hours are daily from 6:15am to noon and 3:30 to 6:30pm. Admission is free. *Note:* **Santuario della Scala Santa** is open daily from 6:15am to noon and 3:30 to 6:30pm.

Piazza San Giovanni in Laterano 4. ✆ 06/69886433. Basilica free; cloisters 2€ ($2.60). Summer daily 9am–6:45pm (off season to 6pm). Metro: San Giovanni. Bus: 4, 16, 30, 85, 87, or 174.

Basilica di San Pietro (St. Peter's Basilica) ✿✿✿   As you stand in Bernini's **Piazza San Pietro (St. Peter's Sq.)**, you'll be in the arms of an ellipse; like a loving parent, the Doric-pillared colonnade reaches out to embrace the faithful. Holding 300,000 is no problem for this square. Inside, the size of this famous church is awe-inspiring—though its dimensions (about two football fields long) are not apparent at first. St. Peter's is said to have been built over the tomb of the crucified saint. The original church was erected on the order of Constantine, but it threatened to collapse and the present structure is 17th-century Renaissance and baroque; it showcases the talents of some of Italy's greatest artists—Michelangelo and Raphael, among others.

In such a grand church, don't expect subtlety. But the basilica is rich in art. Under Michelangelo's dome is the celebrated **baldacchino** ✿✿ by Bernini. In the nave on the right (the 1st chapel) is the best-known piece of sculpture, the ***Pietà*** ✿✿✿ that Michelangelo sculpted while still in his early twenties. Just before the altar, and on the right, you'll see **a bronze statue of St. Peter** ✿. It has been the custom for centuries for the faithful to kiss the saint's right foot, which today has literally been kissed smooth. You can visit the **treasury** ✿, filled with jewel-studded chalices, reliquaries, and copes. One robe worn by Pius XII strikes a simple note in these halls of elegance. The sacristy now contains a **Museo Storico (Historical Museum)** ✿ displaying Vatican treasures, including the large 1400s bronze tomb of Pope Sixtus V by Antonio Pollaiuolo and several antique chalices. In addition you can visit the **Vatican grottoes** ✿✿ with their tombs, both ancient and modern (Pope John XXII gets the most adulation).

The grandest sight is yet to come: the climb to **Michelangelo's dome** ✿✿✿, which towers about 375 feet high (113m). Although you can walk up the steps, we recommend the elevator as far as it'll carry you (you'll still face 320 steps). You can walk along the roof, from which you'll be rewarded with a panoramic view of Rome and the Vatican.

To tour the area around **St. Peter's tomb,** you must apply several days in advance to the excavations office (© **06/69885318**), open Monday to Saturday from 9am to 3:30pm. Pass under the arch to the left of the facade of St. Peter's to find it.

Piazza San Pietro. © **06/69881662** (for information on celebrations). Basilica (including grottoes) free. Guided tour of excavations around St. Peter's tomb 10€ ($13); children younger than 15 are not admitted. Stairs to the dome 4€ ($5.20); elevator to the dome 5€ ($6.50); Sacristy (with Historical Museum) free. Basilica (including the sacristy and treasury) Oct–Mar daily 9am–6pm; Apr–Sept daily 9am–7pm. Grottoes daily 8am–5pm. Dome Oct–Mar daily 8am–5pm; Apr–Sept 8am–6pm. Bus: 46. Metro: Ottaviano/San Pietro.

Campidoglio ✵✵✵, Palazzo dei Conservatori ✵✵✵, and Museo Capitolino ✵✵

The summit of the Capitoline Hill, the most sacred of ancient Rome, is where the Temples of Jupiter and Juno once stood. This was the spiritual heart of Rome, where triumphant generals made sacrifices to the gods who had given them their victories, and where the earthly homes of the king and queen of heaven stood.

One side of the piazza is open; the others are bounded by the **Senatorium (Town Council),** the statuary-filled **Palace of the Conservatori (Curators),** and the **Capitoline Museum.** These museums house some of the greatest pieces of classical sculpture in the world.

On the left is the **Capitoline Museum,** based on an architectural plan by Michelangelo, with an enormous collection of marble carvings from the ancient world. Many of them are just statues—notable for their age, but that's about it. In the first room is *The Dying Gaul* ✵✵, a work of majestic skill; in a special gallery all her own is *The Capitoline Venus,* who demurely covers herself—this statue (a Roman copy of the Greek original) has been a symbol of feminine beauty and charm through the centuries. The famous statue of *Marcus Aurelius* ✵✵ is kept in the museum to protect it from pollution. This is the only bronze equestrian statue to have survived from ancient Rome, mainly because it was thought for centuries that the statue was that of Constantine the Great, and papal Rome respected the memory of the first Christian emperor.

The Palace of the Conservatori, across the way, is rich in classical sculpture and paintings. In the courtyard are fragments of a colossal statue of Constantine. One of the most notable bronzes is the *Spinario* ✵✵✵ (little boy picking a thorn from his foot), a Greek classic from the 1st century B.C. In addition, you'll find *Lupa Capitolina* ✵✵✵ (Capitoline She-Wolf), a rare Etruscan bronze possibly from the 5th century B.C. (Romulus and Remus, the legendary twins that the she-wolf suckled, were added at a later date.) The entrance to the courtyard is lined with the remains (head, hands, a foot, and a kneecap) of an ancient colossal statue of Constantine the Great.

Piazza del Campidoglio 1. © **06/67102071.** Admission (to both museums) 6.50€ ($8.45). Tues–Sun 9am–8pm. Bus: 44, 81, 95, 160, 170, 715, or 780.

Castel Sant'Angelo ✵

This overpowering castle on the Tiber was built in the 2nd century as a tomb for Emperor Hadrian; it continued as an imperial mausoleum until the time of Caracalla. If it looks like a fortress, it should—that was its function in the Middle Ages. It was built over the Roman walls and linked to the Vatican by an underground passage that was much used by the fleeing pontiff, Pope Clement VII, who escaped from unwanted visitors such as Charles V during his 1527 sack of the city. In the 14th century, it became a papal residence, enjoying various connections with Boniface IX, Nicholas V, and Julius II, patron of Michelangelo and Raphael.

But its legend rests largely on its link with Pope Alexander VI, whose mistress bore him two children (those darlings of debauchery, Cesare and Lucrezia Borgia). Even those on a rushed visit might want to budget time for a stopover here because it's a most intriguing sight, an imposing fortress that has seen more blood, treachery, and turmoil than any other left in Rome. It is Rome's chief citadel and dungeon. An audio guide is available to help you understand what you're seeing.

The highlight here is a trip through the Renaissance apartments with their coffered ceilings and lush decoration. Their walls have witnessed some of the most diabolical plots and intrigues of the High Renaissance. Later, you can go through the dank cells that once echoed with the screams of Cesare's victims of torture. The most famous figure imprisoned here was Benvenuto Cellini, the eminent sculptor/goldsmith, remembered chiefly for his *Autobiography.* Now an art museum, the castle halls display the history of the Roman mausoleum, along with a wide-ranging selection of ancient arms and armor. You can climb to the top terrace for another one of those dazzling views of the Eternal City.

Lungotevere Castello 50. ℭ **06-399-676-00.** Admission 8€ ($10.40). Tues–Sun 9am–7pm. Bus: 23, 40, 46, 49, 62, 80, 87, 280, 492, or 910. Metro: Ottaviano, then a long stroll.

Colosseo (Colosseum) ★★★
In spite of the fact that it's a mere shell, the Colosseum remains the greatest architectural inheritance from ancient Rome. The completed stadium, called the Amphitheatrum Flavirum, was dedicated by Titus in A.D. 80 with a weeks-long bloody combat between gladiators and wild beasts. At its peak, the Colosseum could seat 80,000 spectators; exotic animals—humans also—were shipped in from the far corners of the empire to satisfy their jaded tastes. The games were quite an event, and everybody went. A day at the Colosseum was rather formal—the toga was de rigueur dress for men, even though many resented it much the way modern suburbanites hate to put on a tie on Saturday. The seating arrangement was a strictly social arrangement. The higher you were in society, the lower your seat was—even if you had the money, it was out of the question to "buy" a better seat if your birth didn't warrant it.

Next to the Colosseum is the intricately carved **Arch of Constantine** ★★, erected in honor of Constantine's defeat of the pagan Maxentius (A.D. 306). Many of the reliefs have nothing whatsoever to do with Constantine or his works, but tell of the victories of earlier Antonine rulers—they were apparently lifted from other, long-forgotten memorials.

Piazzale del Colosseo, Via dei Fori Imperiali. ℭ **06/39967700.** Admission 10€ ($13) all levels (includes Palatine Hill). Nov–Feb 15 daily 8:30am–4:30pm; Feb 16–Mar 15 daily 8:30am–5pm; Mar 16–Mar 27 daily 8:30am–5:30pm; Mar 28–Aug daily 8:30am–7:15pm; Sept daily 8:30am–7pm; Oct daily 8:30am–6pm. Guided tours in English with an archaeologist 7 times per day (9:30am, 10:15am, 11:15am, 11:45am, 12:30pm, 1:45pm, and 3pm) 3.50€ ($4.55).

Fontana di Trevi (Trevi Fountain) ★★★
As you elbow your way through the summertime crowds around the Trevi Fountain, it's hard to believe that this little piazza was nearly always deserted before the film *Three Coins in the Fountain* brought

---

⟨Moments⟩ The Greatest View in Rome

Before leaving the Campidoglio, walk around the right corner (as you face it) of the Senatorial Palace for a look at the Forum. This is a great vantage point for viewing the ruins below, and on a summer's evening you'll find small groups of visitors mixed with Roman couples leaning on the railing surveying the softly lit columns and crumbling temples.

---

the tour buses. Today, it's a must on everybody's itinerary. The fountain is an 18th-century extravaganza of baroque stonework ruled over by a large statue of Neptune. While some of the statuary is the work of other artists, the man who gets the credit for the entire project is Nicola Salvi. The tradition of throwing coins into the fountain is an evolution of earlier customs. At one time, visitors drank water from the fountain; later they combined that with an offering to the spirits of the place. In our inflationary world, all we get to do is make the offering.

Piazza di Trevi. Metro: Barberini.

Fori Imperiali (Imperial Forums) ✿✿✿   The Imperial Forums were constructed by a succession of emperors to make commerce more comfortable for the merchants of Rome, and to provide new libraries, and more room for assembly, since the original Roman Forum had become too small.

With your back to the Colosseum, begin walking up the Via dei Fori Imperiali (built by the Fascists in the '30s) keeping to the right side of the street. Those ruins across the street are what's left of the colonnade that once surrounded the **Temple of Venus and Roma.** Next to it, you'll recognize the back wall of the Basilica of Constantine. Shortly, you'll come to a large outdoor restaurant, where Via Cavour joins the boulevard you're on. Just beyond the small park across Via Cavour are the remains of the **Forum of Nerva,** built by the emperor whose 2-year reign (A.D. 96–98) followed that of the paranoid Domitian. Nerva's Forum is best observed from the railing that skirts it on the Via dei Fori Imperiali. The only really intelligible remnant is a wall of the Temple of Minerva with two fine Corinthian columns.

The next forum up was that of **Augustus** ✿✿, and was built before the birth of Christ to commemorate the emperor's victory over the assassins Cassius and Brutus in the Battle of Fillippi (42 B.C.).

You can enter the **Forum of Trajan** ✿✿ on Via Quattro Novembre near the steps of Via Magnanapoli. Once through the tunnel, you'll emerge into the newest and most beautiful of the Imperial Forums, built between A.D. 107 and 113. There are many statue fragments and pedestals bearing still-legible inscriptions, but more interesting is the great Basilica Ulpia, whose gray marble columns rise roofless into the sky. This forum was once regarded as one of the architectural wonders of the world.

Beyond the Basilica Ulpia is **Trajan's Column** ✿✿✿, in magnificent condition, with intricate bas-relief sculpture depicting Trajan's victorious campaign (though, from your vantage point, you'll be able to see only the earliest stages). The next stop is the **Forum of Julius Caesar** ✿✿, the first of the Imperial Forums. It lies on the opposite side of Via dei Fori Imperiali. This was the site of the Roman stock exchange, as well as the Temple of Venus; restored columns stand cinematically in the middle of the excavations.

Via de Fori Imperiali. Free admission. Metro: Colosseo. On view 24 hr.

Foro Romano (Roman Forum) ✿✿✿   The Roman Forum was built in the marshy land between the Palatine and the Capitoline hills (where legend has it that Romulus and Remus were suckled by the she-wolf). It flourished as the center of Roman life in the days of the Republic, before it gradually lost prestige to the Imperial Forum. By day the columns of now-vanished temples and the stones from which long-forgotten orators spoke are mere shells. But at night, when the Forum is silent in the moonlight, it isn't difficult to imagine that Vestal Virgins still guard the sacred temple fire.

Moments   I Left My Heart on the Piazza Navona

One of the most beautifully baroque sites in all of Rome, **Piazza Navona** ✿✿✿ is like an ocher-colored gem, unspoiled by new buildings, or even by traffic. The shape results from the Stadium of Domitian, whose ruins lie under-neath the present constructions. Great chariot races were once held here (some rather unusual, such as the one in which the head of the winning horse was lopped off as it crossed the finish line and was then carried by runners to be offered as a sacrifice by the Vestal Virgins atop the Capito-line). In medieval times, the popes used to flood the piazza to stage mock naval encounters. Today the piazza is packed with vendors and street per-formers, and lined with pricey cafes where you can enjoy a cappuccino or gelato and indulge in unparalleled people-watching.

Besides the twin-towered facade of 17th-century Santa Agnes, the piazza boasts several baroque masterpieces. The best known, in the center, is Bernini's **Fountain of the Four Rivers (Fontana dei Quattro Fiumi)** ✿✿✿, whose four stone personifications symbolize the world's greatest rivers: the Ganges, Danube, della Plata, and Nile. It's fun to try to figure out which is which. (*Hint:* The figure with the shroud on its head is the Nile, so repre-sented because the river's source was unknown at the time.) At the south end is the **Fountain of the Moor (Fontana del Moro),** also by Bernini. The **Fountain of Neptune (Fontana di Nettuno),** which balances that of the Moor, is a 19th-century addition; it was restored after a demented 1997 attack by two men who broke off the tail of one of its sea creatures.

If you want the stones to have some meaning, you'll have to purchase a detailed plan, as the temples can be hard to locate. Arm yourself with a good map sold at the entrance and allow at least 3 hours for wandering about. The best of the lot is the handsomely adorned **Temple of the Dioscuri** ✿✿✿, erected in the 5th century B.C. in honor of a battle triumph and dedicated to the Gemini twins Castor and Pollux. The **House of the Vestal Virgins** ✿✿ is a popular attraction; some of the statuary, mostly headless, remains. Head toward the Colosseum and you'll encounter the **Arch of Titus** ✿✿, which depicts Rome's sacking of Jerusalem's temple—look closely and you'll see a menorah among the booty.

From the arch it's a long walk up to the **Palatine Hill** ✿✿✿, one of the seven hills of Rome; your ticket from the Forum will admit you to this attraction (it's open the same hours). The Palatine, tradition tells us, was the spot on which the first settlers built their huts, under the direction of Romulus. In later years, the hill became a patri-cian residential district that attracted citizens such as Cicero. It's worth the climb for the panoramic, sweeping view of both the Roman and Imperial forums, as well as the Capitoline Hill and the Colosseum. Of the ruins that remain, none is finer than the so-called **House of Livia** ✿✿, whose frescoes are in miraculous condition.

When the glory that was Rome has completely overwhelmed you, you can enjoy a respite in the cooling **Farnese Gardens** ✿, laid out in the 16th century, which incor-porate some of Michelangelo's designs.

Largo Romolo e Remo. ⓒ **06/39967700.** Forum free admission; Palatine Hill 10€ ($13). Apr–Sept daily 8:30am–7pm; Oct daily 8:30am-6:30pm; Nov to mid-Feb daily 8:30am–4:30pm; mid-Feb to Mar 8:30am–5pm; guided tour in English 4:15pm 3.50€ ($4.55). Last admission 1 hr. before closing. Closed holidays. Metro: Colosseo. Bus: 27, 81, 85, 87, or 186.

Galleria Borghese 🌟🌟🌟   Most visitors come here to see Canova's famous **statue of Pauline Bonaparte Borghese** 🌟🌟🌟, the sister of Napoleon. But there are numerous other works of art worth seeing here. This treasure trove of art, housed in an opulent 17th-century palace, includes such masterpieces as Bernini's *David, The Rape of Persephone,* and his *Apollo and Daphne.* Also on the ground floor of the palace are interesting 17th-century busts of Roman emperors, and a few pieces of Roman statuary from antiquity. Upstairs is a treasure house of painting including works of Raphael (*Young Woman with a Unicorn* and a famous ***Deposition from the Cross*** 🌟🌟🌟), Pinturicchio, Botticelli, Correggio, Titian, Veronese, Bellini, and even some non-Italians, such as Bruegel and Albrecht Dürer. Two of the greatest paintings in all of Rome are showcased here—***Madonna del Palafrenieri*** 🌟🌟🌟 by the "divine" Caravaggio, showing the Virgin, Jesus, and St. Anne; and Domenichino's ***Diana the Huntress*** 🌟🌟🌟, with its rich, lush detail.

Important information: No more than 360 visitors at a time are allowed on the ground floor, and no more than 90 are allowed on the upper floor. Reservations are essential, so call ⓒ **06/32810** (Mon–Fri 9am–6:30pm; Sat 9am–1pm). However, the number always seems to be busy. If you'll be in Rome for a few days, try stopping by in person on your first day to reserve tickets for a later day. Better yet, before you leave home, contact **Select Italy** (ⓒ **847/853-1661;** www.selectitaly.com).

Piazza Scipione Borghese 5 (off Via Pinciano). ⓒ **06/32810** for information. www.galleriaborghese.it. Admission 8.50€ ($11.05) plus 2€ ($2.60) for reservation fee. Tues–Sun 9am–7pm. Bus: 5, 19, 52, 53, 116, or 910.

Musei Vaticani (Vatican Museums) 🌟🌟🌟   This is a repository of one of the world's greatest art collections, especially rich in treasures from antiquity and the Renaissance. Too many visitors try to squeeze the Vatican Museums into a day's itinerary that includes a half dozen other sights. This is utter foolishness. There are many museums in the Vatican in addition to Michelangelo's Sistine Chapel, and several papal apartments you'll want to see. It would require much more time than a day to examine all that's here, so if all you have is a day, pick a few spots to concentrate on.

The **Pinacoteca** 🌟🌟🌟, or picture gallery's art collection is arranged chronologically, starting with gilded polyptiques in the style of Byzantium, and progressing through the Renaissance up to the 21st century. There are some 15 rooms containing the works of such masters as Giotto, Beato Angelico, Raphael, da Vinci, Titian, Veronese, Caravaggio (the splendid *Deposition*), Murillo, and Ribera. The gallery rooms are arranged in a circle, so you'll exit through the same door you entered.

The handsomely decorated rooms of the **Pius Clementine Museum** 🌟🌟🌟 contain a vast collection of Greek and Roman sculpture. Of particular note are the porphyry sarcophagi of the mother and daughter of Constantine the Great (4th c.), Hercules (a gilded bronze of the 1st c.; note also the magnificent room it's in), the ***Apollo Belvedere*** 🌟🌟🌟 (a Roman copy of a 4th-c. B.C. Greek original), mosaics from the floor of the Villa Hadrian outside Tivoli, and the ***Belvedere Torso*** 🌟🌟🌟 (a fragment of a Greek statue from the 1st c. B.C. that was carefully studied by Michelangelo). There are literally hundreds of other statues lounging in the halls.

Moments A Lazy Afternoon at the Villa Borghese

The **Borghese Gardens** (encompassing the Galeria Borghese), now a perfectly exquisite 17th-century estate, were developed by Cardinal Scipio Borghese, a high churchman belonging to another of Rome's mighty families. The most striking feature of the Borghese Gardens is its trees—stark and eerie looking, their trunks rising some 50 feet (15m) into the air without a single branch, only to burst forth in an evergreen canopy high above. Few activities are quite as pleasant as a slow stroll through the Villa Borghese on a sunny afternoon, pausing to admire carefully planned 17th-century vistas, ornamental fountains, and the magnificent trees.

The **Raphael Rooms** ✷✷ are one of the highlights of the museums. While still a young man, Raphael was given one of the greatest assignments of his short life: to decorate a series of rooms in the apartments of Pope Julius II. The decoration was carried out by Raphael and his workshop from 1508 to 1524. In these works, Raphael achieves the Renaissance aim of blending classic beauty with realism. In the important Stanza della Segnatura, the first room decorated by the artist, you'll find the majestic *School of Athens* ✷✷✷, one of his best-known works, depicting such philosophers from the ages as Aristotle, Plato, and Socrates.

Michelangelo devoted 4½ years to painting the beautiful ceiling frescoes of the majestic **Sistine Chapel** ✷✷✷ for Pope Sistus IX. The epic work was so physically taxing that it permanently damaged his eyesight. Glorifying the human body as only a sculptor could, Michelangelo painted nine panels taken from the pages of Genesis, and surrounded them with prophets and sibyls. Today, throngs of visitors walk around bumping into one another, faces pointed ceiling-ward, admiring the frescoes at the expense of a crick in the neck. Michelangelo not only did the ceiling but also the monumental fresco of *The Last Judgment* ✷✷✷ on the altar wall. The chapel, in danger of collapse, underwent a controversial restoration in the 1990s that some purists say altered Michelangelo's original figures.

Vatican City, Viale Vaticano (a long walk around the Vatican walls from St. Peter's Sq.). ✆ **06/69883332.** Admission is 13€ ($16.90) adults, 8€ ($10.40) children. Mid-Mar to late Oct Mon–Fri 10am–3:45pm; Sat 10am–2:45pm. Off season Mon–Sat and last Sun of the month 10am–12:30pm. Closed all national and religious holidays (except Easter week) and Aug 15–16. Metro: Ottaviano/San Pietro, then a long walk.

Pantheon ✷✷✷   Of all the great buildings of ancient Rome, only the Pantheon ("All the Gods") remains intact today. It was built in 27 B.C. by Marcus Agrippa, and later reconstructed by the emperor Hadrian in the first part of the 2nd century A.D. This remarkable building is among the architectural wonders of the world because of its dome and its concept of space. The Pantheon was once ringed with niches containing white marble statues of Roman gods. Animals were sacrificed and burned in the center, and the smoke escaped through the only means of light, an opening at the top 27 feet (8.1m) in diameter. Michelangelo came here to study the dome before designing the cupola of St. Peter's, whose dome is only 2 feet (.6m) smaller than the Pantheon's.

Piazza della Rotonda. ✆ **06/68300230.** Free admission. Mon–Sat 8:30am–7:30pm; Sun 9am–6pm. Bus: 40, 87, 170, or 492 to Largo di Torre.

Scalinata di Spagna (Spanish Steps) ★★★   The Spanish Steps and the adjoining Piazza di Spagna both take their name from the Spanish embassy, which was housed in a palace here during the 19th century. The Spanish, however, had nothing to do with the construction of the steps. They were built by the French, and lead to the French church in Rome, Trinita' dei Monti. The twin-towered church behind the obelisk at the top of the Steps is early 16th century. The steps themselves are early 18th century.

Piazza di Spagna. Metro: Spagna.

Museo Nazionale di Villa Giulia (Etruscan) ★★★   Like the Palazzo Borghese, the 16th-century Villa Giulia was built as a country house, and today houses a priceless collection of art and artifacts left by the mysterious Etruscans, who predated the Romans in Italy (arriving around 800 B.C.).

If you have time only for the masterpieces, head for Sala 7, which has a remarkable *Apollo* from Veio from the end of the 6th century B.C. (clothed, for a change). Two other widely acclaimed pieces of statuary in this gallery are *Dea con Bambino (Goddess with a Baby)* and a greatly mutilated, but still powerful, *Hercules* with a stag. In the adjoining Sala 8, you'll see the lions' sarcophagus from the mid–6th century B.C., which was excavated at Cerveteri, north of Rome. Finally, in Sala 9, is one of the world's most important Etruscan art treasures, the bride and bridegroom coffin from the 6th century B.C., also from Cerveteri. Near the end of your tour, another masterpiece of Etruscan art awaits you in room 33: the *Cista Ficoroni,* a bronze urn with paw feet, mounted by three figures, dating from the 4th century B.C.

Piazzale di Villa Giulia 9. ✆ 06/3226571. Admission 4€ ($5.20). Tues–Sat 8:30am–6:30pm. Metro: Flaminio.

WHERE TO DINE

Césarina EMILIANA-ROMAGNOLA/ROMAN   This restaurant perpetuates the culinary traditions of the late Césarina Masi in a newer manifestation of her famous original hole-in-the-wall, which catered to Rome's fashionable set in the 1960s. Today this favorite of Roman families serves excellent versions of *bollito misto* (an array of well-seasoned boiled meats), rolled from table to table on a cart; and *misto Césarina*—three kinds of pasta, each handmade and served with a different sauce. If anything, her food tastes better than ever.

Via Piemonte 109. ✆ 06/4880828. Reservations recommended. Main courses 7€–20€ ($9.10–$26). AE, DC, MC, V. Mon–Sat 12:30–3pm and 7:30–11pm. Metro: Barberini. Bus: 52, 53, or 910.

Colline Emiliane ★★ *Finds* EMILIANA-ROMAGNOLA   This small local favorite right off Piazza Barberini serves *classica cucina Bolognese* in a bustling, trattoria setting. It's a family-run place where everybody helps out. The owner is the cook and his wife makes the pasta, which, incidentally, is about the best you'll find in Rome. The enticing menu is loaded with old favorites and delicacies—none finer than an inspired *tortellini alla panna* (cream sauce) with truffles.

Via Avignonesi 22 (off Piazza Barberini). ✆ 06/4817538. Reservations highly recommended. Main courses 14€–19€ ($18.20–$24.70). MC, V. Sat–Thurs 12:45–2:45pm and 7:45–10:45pm. Closed Aug. Metro: Barberini.

Dal Bolognese ★ BOLOGNESE   If *La Dolce Vita* were being filmed now, this restaurant would be used as a backdrop, its patrons photographed in their latest Fendi drag. It's one of those rare dining spots that's not only chic, but noted for its Bolognese cuisine as well. To begin your meal, we suggest *misto di pasta*—four pastas, each flavored with a different sauce, arranged on the same plate. The chefs also turn out the town's best veal cutlets Bolognese topped with cheese—simply superb.

Piazza del Popolo 1–2. ⓒ **06/3611426.** Reservations required. Main courses 10€–20€ ($13–$26). AE, DC, MC, V. Tues–Sun 1–3pm and 8:15pm–midnight (last dinner order at 11:15pm). Closed 20 days in Aug. Metro: Flaminio.

F.I.S.H. ✿ *(Finds* SEAFOOD   One of Rome's hottest restaurants, F.I.S.H. stands for "Fine International Seafood House," and it definitely lives up to its billing. An array of beautifully executed pasta dishes is served nightly but we prefer to stick to the market-fresh fish and shellfish dishes, which are among the finest served in Rome. The chic dining spot has a sleek but elegant decor, and it's tiny—reserve well in advance and count yourself lucky if you get a table.

Via dei Serpenti 16. ⓒ **06/47824962.** Reservations imperative. Main courses 12€–20€ ($15.60–$26). AE, DC, MC, V. Tues–Sun 7:30pm–midnight. Closed Aug 7–Sept 2 and Dec 25. Metro: Cavour.

Girarrosto Toscano ✿ *(Value* TUSCAN   If you're calling on the pope, you can stop off for lunch at this popular place near the Vatican, which serves some of the most memorable Tuscan dishes in Rome. The atmosphere is old, including a vaulted cellar ceiling in the dining room, but the food is market-fresh, especially the mammoth selection of antipasti. Oysters and fresh fish from the Adriatic are also served daily. Meat and fish dishes are priced according to weight, and costs can run considerably higher than the prices quoted below.

Via Germanico 58. ⓒ **06/39725717.** Reservations required. Main courses 10€–16€ ($13–$20.80). AE, DC, MC, V. Tues–Sun 12:30–3pm and 8–11pm. Metro: Ottaviano.

La Cisterna ROMAN   Consider having at least one meal in the ancient district of Trastevere across the Tiber, as it's the most typical and atmospheric of all Roman districts. For more than 75 years, the Simmi family has been turning out real Roman cookery—and serving it fresh from the ovens. In summer, guests like to sit at the restaurant's sidewalk tables as they devour fresh fish and other delectable dishes, including homemade pastas and well-flavored meats.

Via della Cisterna 13. ⓒ **06/5812543.** Reservations recommended. Main courses 10€–20€ ($13–$26). AE, MC, V. Mon–Sat 7pm–1:30am. Bus: H, 75, 170, 280, or 710.

L'Eau Vive ✿ *(Finds* INTERNATIONAL   In a 17th-century *palazzo* (the frescoed ceilings are gorgeous), this discovery—a favorite dining spot of the late Pope John Paul II—is run by a lay sisterhood of Christian missionaries from five different continents who dress in traditional costumes. The sisters sing hymns at 10pm nightly and act as the waitresses; tips are used for religious purposes. The beautifully balanced menu of well-prepared dishes is as international in flavor as the servers. Main dishes range from guinea hen with onions and grapes in a wine sauce to couscous.

Via Monterone 85. ⓒ **06/68801095.** Reservations recommended. Main courses 8€–20€ ($10.40–$26); fixed-price menus 15€–30€ ($19.50–$39), AE, MC, V. Mon–Sat 12:30–2:30pm and 7:30–10:30pm. Closed Aug 1–20. Bus: 46, 62, 64, 70, or 115.

Monte Arci ROMAN/SARDINIAN   This restaurant is set behind a sienna-colored facade on a cobblestone street near Piazza Indipendenza. It features Roman and Sardinian specialties (you'll spend even less for pizza) such as *nialoreddus* (a regional form of gnocchetti); pasta with clams, lobster, or the musky-earthy notes of porcini mushrooms; and delicious lamb sausage flavored with herbs and pecorino cheese. The best pasta dish we sampled was *paglia e fieno al Monte Arci* (homemade pasta with pancetta, spinach, cream, and Parmesan). It's all home cooking—hearty but not that creative.

Via Castelfirdardo 33. © **06-4941220.** Reservations recommended. Main courses 6€–13€ ($7.80–$16.90); fixed-price menu 25€ ($32.50). AE, DC, MC, V. Mon–Fri 12:30–3pm; Mon–Sat 7–11:30pm. Closed Aug. Metro: Stazione Termini or Repubblica.

Piperno ⏥ ROMAN/JEWISH   In the heart of the old Jewish ghetto, this trattoria has been open and running since 1856, and every year it makes new fans of visitors to this historic part of old Rome. Its celebrated Jerusalem artichokes (which isn't really an artichoke) are deep-fried but they appear on your plate flaky and dry—not greasy. The time-tested recipes are prepared with market-fresh ingredients—count yourself lucky if the stuffed squash blossoms appear on the menu. You'll be served by a uniformed crew of hardworking waiters, whose advice and suggestions are worth considering.

Via Monte de' Cenci 9. © **06/68806629.** Reservations recommended. Main courses 17.50€–20€ ($22.75–$26). DC, MC, V. Tues–Sat 1–2:30pm and 8–10:30pm; Sun–Mon 1–2:30pm. Bus: 23.

Trattoria San Teodoro ⏥ ROMAN   At last there's a good place to eat in the former gastronomic wasteland near the Roman Forum and Palatine Hill. The helpful staff at this top-rated trattoria welcomes visitors and locals to a shady terrace or a dimly lit dining room. The market-fresh menu includes succulent homemade pastas, some excellent seafood (try the carpaccio made with tuna, turbot, or sea bass), and any number of well-flavored and tender meat dishes.

Via dei Fienili 49–51. © **06/6780933.** Reservations recommended. Main courses 15€–40€ ($19.50–$52). AE, MC, V. Daily 12:30–3:30pm and 7:30pm–midnight. Metro: Circo Massimo.

Trimani Wine Bar ⏥ CONTINENTAL   Opened as a tasting center for French and Italian wines, spumantis, and liqueurs, this is an elegant wine bar with a lovely decor (stylish but informal) near Stazione Termini. More than 30 wines are available by the glass. To accompany them, you can choose from a bistro-style menu, with dishes such as salad niçoise, vegetarian pastas, herb-laden bean soups *(fagiole),* and quiche. Also available is a wider menu, including meat and fish courses. The specialty is the large choice of little "bruschette" with cheese and radicchio—the chef orders every kind of prosciutto and cheese from all over Italy. The dishes are matched with the appropriate wines.

Via Cernaia 37B. © **06/4469630.** Reservations recommended. Main courses 9€–18€ ($11.70–$23.40); glass of wine (depending on vintage) 2€–14€ ($2.60–$18.20). AE, DC, MC, V. Mon–Sat 11:30am–3pm and 6pm–12:30am (in Dec open also on Sun). Closed 2 weeks in Aug. Metro: Repubblica or Castro Pretorio.

SHOPPING

We won't pretend that Rome is Italy's finest shopping center (Florence and Venice are), nor that its shops are unusually inexpensive—many of them aren't. But even on the most elegant of Rome's thoroughfares, there are values mixed in with the costly boutiques. On a short visit the best method is to stroll the major shopping streets (see below), ferreting out the best values.

The posh shopping streets **Via Borgognona** and **Via Condotti** begin near Piazza di Spagna. For the most part, the merchandise on both is chic and very, very expensive. Wise shoppers are advised to take a look at the goods displayed on the Spanish Steps before a tour of Via Condotti. Here, craftspeople good and bad lay out their wares on old velvet cloths—usually paintings, beads, silver and turquoise jewelry, some of it quite good—and bargain for the best offer. **Via Frattina** runs parallel to Via

Ancona & Bari: Gateways to Greece

The port cities of Ancona (190 miles/304km northeast of Rome) and Bari (284 miles/454km southeast of Rome) are the two major embarkation points for passholders crossing the Adriatic to Greece. Ferries from both these cities run to Patras in Greece (usually via Igoumenitsa).

For trains running between Rome and Bari and Rome and Ancona, refer to "Trains & Travel Times in Italy," earlier. If you don't want to use a day on your pass, one-way rail fares from Rome to Bari cost $65 to $95 when bought in advance through Rail Europe; fares to Ancona run $40 to $53. Ferries generally depart in the afternoon and arrive on the afternoon of the following day in Greece; when planning your schedule, be sure to leave plenty of time to catch the ferry.

Ferry routes are operated by **Superfast Ferries/Blue Star Lines** (www.superfast.com) and **Minoan Lines** (www.minoan.gr). Transit aboard one of these ferries costs 18€ ($23.50) one-way in an airline-style seat. If you want a private cabin, it'll cost you approximately 98€ ($127) for a double, or 54€ ($70) in a quad. Ask about family discounts if you're traveling with children. *Warning:* Snack bars aboard these ferries charge outrageous prices, so cost-conscious travelers should purchase their own food in Ancona or Bari and bring it aboard.

Note: The Eurail Global Pass and the Eurail Greece–Italy Pass are accepted on these ferries for deck passage only (cabins cost extra), though a supplement of 15€ to 30€ ($19.50–$39) is assessed during the summer high season. Port taxes and fuel surcharges may also be assessed. If you have a Flexi version of a pass, you will lose one day on the pass (either at arrival or departure) to cover the ferry trip. For more on ferries covered by the Eurail Global Pass, see chapter 2; for more on the ferries to Greece, see chapter 11.

Bookings can be made at **info.athens@superfast.com** for the Superfast/Blue Star lines. Bookings for Minoan Lines must be made through one of their local agents; for a current list of their agents in Italy, Greece, and the United States, check the "For Passengers" section of the company's website.

Condotti, its more famous sibling, and is the hippest and busiest shopping street in town. You'll frequently find it closed to traffic, converted into a pedestrian mall thronged with shoppers moving from boutique to boutique.

Beginning at the top of the Spanish Steps, **Via Sistina** runs to Piazza Barberini. It houses the city's densest concentration of boutiques and expensive dress shops. It's good for browsing, and women visitors will occasionally find exciting items on sale. Most shoppers reach **Via Francesco Crispi** by following Via Sistina 1 long block from the top of the Spanish Steps. Near the intersection of these streets are several shops full of unusual and not overly expensive gifts. Evocative of *La Dolce Vita,* **Via Veneto** is filled these days with expensive hotels and cafes, and an array of relatively expensive stores selling shoes, gloves, and leather goods.

Traffic-clogged **Via Nazionale**—just crossing the street is no small feat—begins at Piazza della Repubblica and runs down almost to Piazza Venezia. Here you'll find an abundance of leather stores—more reasonable in price than those in many other parts of Rome—and a welcome handful of stylish boutiques.

Via dei Coronari, should be seen whether or not you buy. Buried in a colorful section of the Campus Martius (Renaissance Rome), Via dei Coronari is an antiquer's dream, literally lined with magnificent vases, urns, chandeliers, breakfronts, chaises, refectory tables, candelabra, you name it. You'll find the entrance to the street just north of the Piazza Navona.

NIGHTLIFE

Evenings in Rome always begin at one of the cafes, the most famous of which line the **Via Veneto.** Two other popular gathering places for cafe-sitting are **Piazza della Rotonda** and **Piazza del Popolo.** For the cost of an espresso, the people-watching is free.

There are few evening diversions quite as pleasurable as a stroll past the solemn pillars of old temples or the cascading torrents of Renaissance fountains glowing under a blue-black sky. Of the **fountains,** the Naiads (Piazza della Repubblica), the Tortoises (Piazza Mattei) and, of course, the Trevi are particularly beautiful at night. The **Capitoline Hill** is magnificently lit after dark, with its Renaissance facades glowing like jewel boxes. Behind the Senatorial Palace is a fine view of the **Roman Forum.** If you're staying across the Tiber, **Piazza San Pietro,** in front of St. Peter's Basilica, is impressive at night without tour buses and crowds. And a combination of illuminated architecture, Renaissance fountains, and frequent sidewalk shows and art expositions is at **Piazza Navona.** If you're ambitious and have a good sense of direction, try exploring the streets to the west of Piazza Navona, which look like a stage set when lit at night.

The minimagazine ***Wanted in Rome*** has listings of jazz, rock, and such and give an interesting look at expatriate Rome. The daily ***Il Messaggero*** lists current cultural news. And ***Un Ospite a Roma,*** available free from the concierge desks of top hotels, is full of details on what's happening. Even if you don't speak Italian, you can generally follow the listings of special events and evening entertainment in ***La Repubblica,*** one of the leading Italian newspapers.

THE PERFORMING ARTS   If you're in the capital for the opera season, usually late December to June, you might want to attend the historic **Teatro dell'Opera (Rome Opera House),** Piazza Beniamino Gigli 1, off Via Nazionale (© **06/481601;** Metro: Repubblica). In summer the venue switches to the Baths of Caracalla. Call ahead or ask your concierge before you go. Tickets are 20€ to 130€ ($26–$169). The **Rome Opera Ballet** also performs at the Teatro dell'Opera. Look for announcements of classical concerts that take place in churches and other venues.

CAFES & BARS   Along the Via Veneto, **Harry's Bar,** at #150 (© **06/484643**), is the choicest watering hole. It has no connection with other famous Harry's bars, such as the one in Venice, and in many respects, the Roman Harry's is the most elegant of them all. **Cafè de Paris,** Via Vittorio Veneto 90 (© **06/4815631**), is a local landmark and a good place to get the night started. Tables spill out onto the sidewalk in summer, and the passing crowd walks through the maze.

The fashion-conscious descend on the Piazza de Popolo, where there is always an aura of excitement, especially after midnight. The best place for a drink here is **Café Rosati,** Piazza del Popolo 5A (© **06/3225859**), in business since 1923. The preferred tables are out front where growling Maseratis cruise by while young Italian men in silk shirts hang from the car windows. Its rival, **Canova Café,** Piazza del Popolo 16 (📞 **06/ 3612231**), is another great place for people-watching. We also gravitate to the Piazza della Rotonda, across from the Pantheon, which is dramatically lit at night. The top cafe here is **Di Rienzo,** Piazza della Rotonda 8–9 (📞 **06/6869097**). The best coffee in Rome is brewed at **Caffè Sant'Eustachio,** Piazza Sant'Eustachio 82 (📞 **06/68802048**), where the water supply is funneled into the city by an aqueduct built in 19 B.C.

Alternately, you could try **Antico Caffè Greco,** 86 Via Condotti (📞 **06/6791700**), which has been serving drinks since 1760. Over the years it has attracted such habitués as Goethe, Stendhal, and D'Annunzio. Half a block from the foot of the Spanish Steps, it still retains a 19th-century atmosphere. The waiters wear morning coats— most effective looking—and seat you at small marble tables. Beyond the carved wooden bar are a series of small elegant rooms hung with oil paintings in gilded frames.

CLUBS   Arciliuto, Piazza Monte Vecchio 5 (📞 **06/6879419;** bus: 42, 62, or 64), is a romantic candlelit spot within walking distance of the Piazza Navona that was reputedly once the studio of Raphael. From 10pm to 2am, Monday through Saturday, guests enjoy a musical salon ambience, listening to a guitarist, a pianist, and a violinist. The evening's presentation also includes live Neapolitan songs and new Italian madrigals, even current hits from Broadway or London's West End. The cover is 19€ ($24.70), including the first drink; it's closed July 15 to September 5.

In a high-tech, futuristic setting, **Alien,** Via Velletri 13–19 (📞 **06/8412212**), provides a bizarre space-age dance floor, bathed in strobe lights and rocking to the sounds of house/techno music. The crowd is young. It's open Tuesday to Sunday 11pm to 5am, with a cover of 16€ to 18€ ($20.80–$23.40) that includes the first drink.

Piper, Via Tagliamento 9 (📞 **06-8555398;** bus: 63), opened in 1965 in a former cinema and became the first modern disco of its kind in Italy. Many dances such as "the shake" were first introduced to Italy at this club. No longer what it was in those La Dolce Vita years, the Piper is still going strong. Today it lures with fashion shows, screenings, some of the hottest parties in town, and various gigs, drawing a casual and mixed-age crowd. The pickup scene here is hot and heavy. The kind of music you'll hear depends on the night. Open Monday to Saturday 11pm to 4am, charging a cover of 20€ to 25€ ($26–$32.50), including one drink.

Big Mama, Vicolo San Francesco a Ripa 18 (📞 **06/5812551**), is a hangout for jazz and blues musicians where you're likely to meet the up-and-coming stars of tomorrow and sometimes even the big names. For big acts, the cover is 10€ to 30€ ($13–$39), plus 13€ ($16.90) for a seasonal membership fee.

AN EXCURSION TO TIVOLI 😊😊

An ancient town 20 miles (32km) east of Rome, Tivoli, known as Tibur to the ancient Romans, was the playground of emperors, who maintained lavish villas here near the famous woods and waterfalls. Today its reputation continues unabated: It's the most popular half-day jaunt from Rome.

GETTING THERE   From Rome, take Metro Line B to Ponte Mammolo. After exiting the station, board a Cotral bus for the rest of the way to Tivoli (it will drop you off in front of the tourist information office). A bus marked TIVOLI also leaves every 15 to 20 minutes during the day from Via Gaeta (west of Via Volturno), near the Stazione Termini. Both buses are part of the regular public transportation system. A one-way fare from Rome to Tivoli costs 2€ ($2.60).

VISITOR INFORMATION   For information about the town and its attractions, go to **Azienda Autonoma di Turismo,** Vicolo Barchetto (© **0774/334522**), open Monday to Friday 9am to 1pm and 3 to 5pm, and Saturday 9am to 7pm.

TOP ATTRACTIONS & SPECIAL MOMENTS

Four miles (6.5km) from the foothills on which Tivoli is built lies a gently sloping plain, the site of **Villa Adriana** or **Hadrian's Villa** ✶✶✶, Via di Villa Adriana (© **06/39967900**). Of all the Roman emperors dedicated to *la dolce vita,* the globe-trotting Hadrian spent the last 3 years of his life in the grandest style. Today the ruins of his estate cover 180 acres of rolling terrain. The estate was built as a heaven on earth in which to spend a long and luxurious retirement. Hadrian himself designed a self-contained world for a vast royal entourage, the guards required to protect them, and the hundreds of servants needed to bathe them, feed them, and satisfy their libidos. On the estate were theaters, baths, temples, fountains, gardens, and canals bordered with statuary. Much of the ruin is readily recognizable, and it's easy to wander around the hot and cold baths and experience a real sense of the villa as it once was (though if you wish to see what it looked like during its heyday, see the plastic reconstruction at the entrance). Admission is 6.50€ ($8.45). It's open daily 9am to sunset (about 6:30pm in summer, 4pm Nov–Mar). To get here, take bus no. 2 or 4 from the center of Tivoli.

At Tivoli itself, the clutter and clamor of 21st-century Italy is forgotten in a perfect gem from the Renaissance: **Villa d'Este** ✶✶, Piazza Trento, Viale delle Centro Fontane (© **199-766-166** in Italy), so named after the 16th-century cardinal who transformed it from a government palace (it had been built in the 13th c. as a Benedictine convent) into a princely residence, which remained in the cardinal's family until 1918. The 16th-century frescoes and decorations of the place itself are attractive, but unexceptional. The garden on the sloping hill beneath is another story—a perfect fairy tale of the Renaissance, using water as a medium of sculpture, much the way the ancients used marble. Pathways are lined with 100 fountains of every imaginable size and shape. Admission is 6.50€ ($8.45). It's open Tuesday to Sunday at 9am; closing times vary according to the season (1 hr. before sunset). November to January it closes at 4pm; closing times may be as late as 6:45pm in summer.

3 Naples

Nestled by a blue bay in the shadow of Mount Vesuvius, Naples, just 136 miles (219km) southeast of Rome, has been known to seafarers since the 6th century B.C. It remains one of the Mediterranean's foremost port cities to this day, its streets teeming with life—shirtless dockworkers, prostitutes, scampering children, throngs of pedestrians, huge open markets, and apartment houses whose facades are all but obscured with laundry. It has its towering castles and elegant palaces, too, as befits a town whose past enthusiasts have included the Emperor Nero and the poet Virgil.

Naples is also an ideal jumping-off point for some of the most popular vacation and sightseeing attractions in southern Italy. From here you can explore the ruins of Pompeii and Herculaneum, or sail to the fabled Isle of Capri. But the city itself has its own impressive sights, including some excellent museums. We rank it behind Florence and Venice, but if you're in the area and can spare a day or two, Naples has excellent rail connections to Rome and makes for a good 1- or 2-day rail excursion out of the capital city.

GETTING THERE   The rail lines between Rome and Naples are among the most frequently used in Italy. You can take either a regular train or a Eurostar Italia train to go from Rome to Naples. Some 16 express trains run daily from Rome's Stazione Termini to the **Stazione Centrale** in Naples, the trip taking only 1 hour and 45 minutes and costing 33€ ($42.90) one-way. Tickets may be booked through Rail Europe or by calling ✆ **892021.** Regular train service is slower but cheaper, taking about 2½ hours and costing 10.50€ ($13.65) one-way.

Trains from Rome usually pull into Stazione Centrale in the heart of Naples. Here you will find many services, including a 24-hour pharmacy, plus a train information and reservations office right off the main hall that's open daily from 7am to 9pm. There is also a money exchange kiosk here (charging very expensive rates) and various food services. The office for storing luggage is open daily from 6am to 11pm, and charges 4.40€ ($5.70) per bag for 12 hours.

Some 656 feet (200m) outside the station is the **Ente Provinciale per il Turismo,** the local tourist office at Piazza Garibaldi (✆ **081/268779**), open Monday to Saturday 9am to 1pm and 3 to 8pm, Sunday 9am to 1pm. It does not make hotel reservations.

VISITOR INFORMATION   The main tourist office, **Ente Provinciale per il Turismo,** is at Piazza dei Martiri 58 (✆ **081/4107211**), open Monday to Friday 9am to 2pm. The staff does not make hotel reservations, which you'll need to make by yourself or through a travel agency.

GETTING AROUND   The **Metropolitana** line will deliver you from Stazione Centrale in the east all the way to the suburb of Pozzuoli. Get off at Piazza Piedigrotta if you want to take the funicular to Vómero. The Metro uses the same tickets as buses and trams. It's dangerous to ride **buses** at rush hours—never have we seen such pushing and shoving. Many people prefer to leave the buses to the battle-hardened Neapolitans and take the subway or **tram** 1 or 4, running from Stazione Centrale to Stazione Mergellina. For a ticket valid for 75 minutes with unlimited transfers during that time, the cost is 1€ ($1.30). A ticket for a full day of unlimited travel costs 3€ ($3.90).

If you survive the **taxi** driver's reckless driving, you'll have to do battle over the bill. Many cab drivers claim that the meter is broken and assess the cost of the ride, always to your disadvantage. Some legitimate surcharges are imposed, such as night drives and extra luggage. Many drivers, however, deliberately take the scenic route to run up costs. You can call a radio taxi at ✆ **081/5564444,** 081/5560202, or 081/5707070.

Funiculars take passengers up and down the steep hills of Naples. **Funicolare Centrale** (✆ **081/6106400**), for example, connects the lower part of the city to Vómero. Departures, daily 6:30am to midnight, are from Piazzetta Duca d'Aosta, just off Via Roma. The same tickets valid for buses and the Metro are good for the funicular.

TOP ATTRACTIONS & SPECIAL MOMENTS

Charles III of Spain took over a 16th-century building and turned it into **Museo Archeologico Nazionale (National Archaeological Museum)** ★★★, Piazza Museo Nazionale 18–19 (✆ **081/292823**), when he became king of Naples in the mid–18th century. Installed in the mansion was his exquisite Farnese collection. Since that time, the museum has added art and artifacts from the excavations at Pompeii and

Moments Sicily: Land of Myth & Legend

Sicily is the largest of Mediterranean islands, 110 miles (178km) north to south and 175 miles (282km) wide, and a land of dramatic intensity. For centuries, its beauty and charm have attracted the greedy eye of foreign invaders: the Greeks, Romans, Vandals, Arabs, Normans, Swabians, and the Houses of Bourbon and Aragon. Luigi Barzini wrote: "Sicily is the schoolroom model of Italy for beginners, with every Italian quality and defect magnified, exasperated and brightly colored." Of course, it is the people themselves—bound by tradition and local customs—that provide the greatest interest. Most rail travelers on their first journey to Italy won't have time to visit Sicily, but it's well worth exploring on subsequent excursions.

The best centers for touring are Palermo, Syracuse, and Taormina. If you're considering anchoring into Sicily for a holiday, then Taormina is the best site, with the finest choice of hotels in all price ranges. If you stick to the main road that skirts the coast, encircling the island, you'll get to see most of the major sights, veering inland for such attractions as the active volcano of Mount Etna.

Trains from all over Italy arrive at the port at Villa San Giovanni, near Reggio di Calabria on the Italian mainland, and roll onto enormous barges for the 1-hour crossing to Sicily. Passengers remain in their seats during the short voyage across the Strait of Messina, eventually rolling back onto the rail tracks at Messina, Sicily. From Rome, the trip to Palermo takes 11 to 12 hours, depending on the speed of the train; the rail route from Naples takes 9 to 11 hours. Aboard any of the trains pulling into Palermo, you can book a couchette. For fares and information, call ☏ **892021**.

Palermo, the capital of Sicily and also its largest port lies 447 miles (721km) south of Naples and 579 miles (934km) south of Rome, and is reached by rail, part of it involving a sea crossing as mentioned above. Its major attractions include the **Cathedral of Palermo** ✿✿, on the Corso Vittorio Emanuele (☏ **091/334373**), built in the 12th century on the foundation of an earlier basilica that had been converted by the Arabs into a mosque. The **Palace of the Normanni (Palace of the Normans)** ✿✿, at the Piazza Parlamento (☏ **091/7051111**), contains one of the greatest art treasures in Sicily, the **Cappella**

Herculaneum as well as the Borgia collection of Etruscan and Egyptian antiquities, making its contents the most valuable archaeological collection in Europe.

Among the outstanding works in the Farnese collection are the gigantic marble *Hercules,* dating from the 1st century B.C., and the *Farnese Bull,* a sculptured group from the Greek Apollonius of Tralles. The original dates from the 2nd century B.C., and this work, a copy, once stood in the Baths of Caracalla in Rome. Also from the collection is a bas-relief of Orpheus and Eurydice, whose original dates from the 5th century B.C.

Several galleries on the mezzanine level are given over to mosaics recovered from Pompeii and Herculaneum, the most magnificent of which depicts Alexander battling

Palatina (Palatine Chapel) ⟨⟨⟨. Erected at the request of Roger II in the 1130s, it is the finest example of the Arabic-Norman style of design and building. In a former convent, **Museo Archeologico Regionale** ⟨⟨⟨, Via Bara all'Olivella 24 (② 091/6116805), houses one of the greatest archaeological collections in southern Italy. Many works displayed here were excavated from Selinunte, once one of the major towns in *Magna Graecia* (Greater Greece).

Taormina, 155 miles (250km) east of Palermo, is the greatest holiday resort south of Capri. Dating from the 4th century B.C., Taormina hugs close to the edge of a cliff overlooking the Ionian Sea. The sea—and the railroad track—is down below, connected to the town by bus routes. Looming in the background is Mount Etna, the active volcano. Noted for its mild climate, the town enjoys a year-round season. The **Taormina Tourist Office** is in the Palazzo Corvaja, Piazza Santa Caterina (② 0942/23243), open Monday to Saturday 8am to 2pm and 4 to 7pm.

Syracuse is 35 miles (56km) southeast of Catania, the leading city along the coast of eastern Sicily and a transportation hub for rail lines in the area. From other major cities in Sicily, Syracuse is best reached by **train.** It's 1½ hours from Catania, 2 hours from Taormina, and 5 hours from Palermo. Usually you must transfer trains in Catania. For information, call ② **892021.** Trains arrive in Syracuse at the station on Via Francesco Crispi, centrally located midway between the archaeological park and Ortygia.

The main **tourist office** is at Via San Sebastiano 43A (② **0931/481211**), with a branch office at Via Maestranza 33 (② **0931/65201**). Both are open Monday to Saturday 9am to 1:30pm and 3 to 6:15pm.

Syracuse's **Archaeological Park** ⟨⟨⟨ lies west of the modern town reached along Viale Rizzo. It is peppered with the most important attractions, beginning with **Teatro Greco** ⟨⟨⟨ or the Greek Theater on Temenite Hill. Although in ruins, this is one of the great Greek theaters remaining from the classical era. The **Roman Amphitheater** ⟨ nearby was erected at the time of Augustus. It ranks among the top live amphitheaters left by the Romans in Italy.

with the Persian forces. Admission is 9€ ($11.70), and hours are Monday and Wednesday to Sunday 9am to 8pm. Metro: Piazza Cavour.

Museo e Gallerie Nazionale di Capodimonte (National Museum & Gallery of the Capodimonte) ⟨⟨, in the Palazzo Capodimonte, Parco di Capodimonte lying off Amedeo di Savoia and entered at Via Miano 2 (② 081/7499111), stands near the outskirts of the city. The Capodimonte Galleries are housed in an 18th-century palace, surrounded by its own attractive gardens. The State Apartments contain a rich collection of ivories, porcelains, glass, and china, as well as the **Farnese Armory.** The real attraction of the palace, however, is the National Gallery, which occupies the top floor. One of the finest galleries in Italy, it is especially rich in paintings of the 14th century and the early Italian Renaissance.

One of the best of the 14th-century group is a coronation scene painted by Simone Martini, a leader of the Sienese School. The Renaissance is well represented by the greatest artists of that period: Raphael with *The Holy Family and Saint John,* Filippino Lippi with *Annunciation and Saints,* Michelangelo, Botticelli, Titian, and Mantegna. Hours are Thursday to Tuesday 8:30am to 7:30pm. Admission is 10€ ($13).

Museo Nazionale di San Martino (National Museum of San Martino) ✿✿, Largo San Martino 8 (© **081/5781769**), in the Vomero district, is worth the trip if you do nothing more than stand on the balcony overlooking the Bay of Naples and gaze in awe at the panorama that includes Vesuvius and Capri. Reconstructed in the 17th century in a Neapolitan baroque style on the site of a 14th-century monastery, the museum is on the grounds of the Castel Sant'Elmo, and houses a broad collection of costumes, armor, carriages, documents, and 19th-century Campania paintings. Of special interest is the elaborately decorated Nativity scene by Curiniello. Admission is 6€ ($7.80); it's open Thursday to Tuesday 8:30am to 7:30pm. Funicular: Stazione Centrale from Via Toledo or Montesanto.

Castelnuovo (New Castle) ✿✿, Piazza del Municipio (© **081/4201241**), is marked by three massive turrets towering above the square. Although it was begun in 1279 by Charles of Anjou, most of what you see today dates from its mid-15th-century restoration (after Alfonso the Magnanimous drove the House of Anjou from its premises). The castle's most celebrated feature is the Arch of Triumph by Francesco Laurana, commemorating Alfonso's victory. Among the rooms you can visit are the massive Hall of the Barons, now used by the Naples City Commission, and the 14th-century Palatine Chapel, at the core of the castle. Admission is 5€ ($6.50). Hours are Monday to Saturday 9am to 7pm; tram: 1 or 4; bus: R2.

WHERE TO STAY & DINE

Hotel Britannique ✿, Corso Vittorio Emanuele 133, 80121 Napoli (© **081/7614145;** www.hotelbritannique.it), is known for its central location close to the satellite rail station of Mergellina, and for its attractive bedrooms overlooking the Bay of Naples. Personally managed by the owners, it remains charmingly old-fashioned, although it has been modernized. An oasis is the hotel's flower-filled garden. Many guest rooms, ranging from small to large, have some antiques, although most of the furnishings are functional. The bathroom plumbing is aging but still humming along. Doubles cost 190€ ($247), with a junior suite going for 220€ ($286); rates including breakfast; Metro: Piazza Amedeo; bus: C16 or C28.

In the Santa Lucia area near the waterfront, the 10-story **Hotel Royal** ✿, Via Partenope 38-44, 80121 Napoli (© **081/7644800;** www.hotelroyal.it), has long been a favorite of Naples visitors. Because this is a noisy part of Naples, bedrooms have been soundproofed. Each of the guest rooms has a balcony, though not all of them open onto the Bay of Naples. The hotel is especially noted for its "restaurant with a view," and for its well-stocked wine cellar. Facilities include a pool and a health club. Doubles cost from 190€ to 410€ ($247–$533), with a suite going from 800€ ($1,040); rates include breakfast; tram: 4.

Alloggio dei Vassalli ✿, Via Donnalbina 56, 80134 Napoli (© **081/5515118;** www.bandbnapoli.it), is small but one of the best and most upscale of Naples' B&Bs. It's set on the second floor of the historic 18th-century Palazzo Donnalbina. In the heart of Naples, the B&B is imbued with some of the building's original architectural details, including ceilings of antique wooden rafters and decorative stucco work. Bedrooms are spacious and bright, each tastefully and comfortably furnished. Doubles cost 99€ to 119€ ($129–$155), with triples going for 124€ to 130€ ($161.20–$169); bus: 152.

Near the seafront, **Don Salvatore** *&*, Strada Mergellina 4A (☏ **081/681817**), naturally specializes in seafood and does so exceedingly well. The fish, which comes from the Bay of Naples, is then either grilled or shaped into an array of dishes, including linguine with shrimp or squid. The wine cellar here is the best in Naples. Main courses cost 10€ to 15€ ($13–$19.50); Metro: Mergellina. Another favorite for seafood, **Giuseppone a Mare** *&*, Via Ferdinando Russo 13 (☏ **081/5756002**), is known for serving some of the best and freshest seafood in Campania. Diners make their fishy choices—ranging from fresh crabs to eels—from a trolley wheeled by each table. Often the day's catch is deep-fried as many locals like it that way. Main courses cost 12€ to 16€ ($15.60–$20.80); bus: 140. The grilled seafood is even better at the more highly rated **La Cantinella** *&&*, Via Cuma 42 (☏ **081/7648684**), on a bustling street opening onto the bay in the romantic Santa Lucia area. The *antipasti* table is one of the most alluring in town, and you can include all sorts of other dishes—not just fish. Main courses cost 13€ to 24€ ($16.90–$31.20); bus: 104, 140, or 150.

1-DAY EXCURSIONS FROM NAPLES

The most exciting sightseeing attractions in southern Italy lie within a 15-mile (24km) radius of Naples, making that city an ideal home base for many excursions into the surrounding countryside. We list the three most compelling places to visit below in order of their importance.

POMPEII *&&&*

Buried in its heyday in A.D. 79 by the eruption of Mount Vesuvius, the city of Pompeii, 15 miles (24km) south of Naples, offers visitors a glimpse of life as it was lived 2,000 years ago. The volcanic ash and lava that destroyed the city also helped to preserve the ruins until their rediscovery in 1748.

GETTING THERE   The **Circumvesuviana Railway** (☏ **081/7722111**) departs Naples every half hour from Piazza Garibaldi. However, be sure you get on the train headed toward *Sorrento* and get off at Pompeii/Scavi (*scavi* means "ruins"). Beware pickpockets on the circumvesuviana platforms! If you get on the Pompeii train, you'll end up in the town of Pompeii and will have to transfer there to the other train to get to the ruins. A round-trip ticket costs 4.60€ ($6); trip time is 35 minutes each way. Circumvesuviana trains leave Sorrento every half hour for Pompeii, costing 1.80€ ($2.35) one-way. There's an entrance about 150 feet (45m) from the rail station at the Villa dei Misteri. At the rail station in the town of Pompeii, **bus** connections take you to the entrance to the excavations.

VISITOR INFORMATION   The **tourist office** is at Via Sacra 1 (☏ **081/8507255**). It's open Monday to Friday 8am to 3:40pm (until 7pm Apr–Sept), and Saturday 8am to 2pm.

Top Attractions & Special Moments

Most people visit the **Ufficio Scavi di Pompeii,** Piazza Esedra (☏ **081/8610744**), the best-preserved 2,000-year-old ruins in Europe, on a day trip from Naples (allow at least 4 hr. for even a superficial look at the archaeological site). The ruins are open November to March daily from 8:30am to 5pm (last admission at 3:30pm), April to October daily 8:30am to 7:30pm (last admission at 6pm). Admission is 11€ ($14.30).

Of particular interest are the elegant patrician villas, some of which are in an amazing state of preservation. The finest of these is the **House of the Vettii (Casa dei Vettii)** ⋇⋇⋇, built around an attractive Etruscan courtyard and adorned with handsome statuary. The dining room, frescoed with cupids, is decorated in the traditional Pompeiian black and red. Among the statues still remaining in the villa is a sculpture of Janus, the two-faced household god. The **House of the Mysteries (Villa dei Misteri)** ⋇⋇, near the Herculaneum Gate, just outside the city walls, is an unusual villa—in appearance and purpose. As a cult center for the mysterious sect of Dionysus, it is decorated with murals and frescoes depicting some of the sacred—and very secret—initiation rites of this popular, but strange religion.

The **Stabian Thermae (baths)** ⋇⋇⋇, near the center of town, are a surprisingly intact example of public baths in an early Roman town. If you miss seeing the small household accessories in the Pompeiian homes, you'll find them on display in the **Antiquarium,** where pottery, utensils, sculptures, and kitchen equipment are exhibited. Flanked by the Temples of Jupiter and Apollo and the huge Basilica is the physical and political core of Pompeii, the **Forum** ⋇. Damaged in the earthquake that crippled the city 16 years before Mount Vesuvius finished the job, this important edifice was never completely restored. As you wander through the ruins, you can try your hand at translating the graffiti and campaign slogans immortalized on the walls and columns.

VESUVIUS ⋇⋇⋇

It may not look as sinister as it did in A.D. 79 when it buried Pompeii, Herculaneum, and Stabiae in a flood of lava and volcanic ash, but Vesuvius is still an active volcano. It has erupted more than once since the dawn of the Christian era, including a tragic spouting of lava in 1631 that killed thousands, and a less fatal explosion in 1906 when it simply blew the ring off its crater. The last spectacular eruption was on March 31, 1944.

It might sound like a dubious invitation, but it's possible to visit the rim of the crater's mouth. As you look down into its smoldering core, you might recall that Spartacus, a century before the eruption that buried Pompeii, hid in the hollow of the crater, which was then covered with vines.

To reach Vesuvius from Naples, take the Circumvesuviana Railway from Piazza Garibaldi to Ercolano (Herculaneum). Seven Vesuviana Trasporti (© **081/5592582**) buses per day go from Herculaneum to the crater of Vesuvius, costing 3.10€ ($4.05) round-trip. Once at the top, you must be accompanied by a guide, which will cost 7€ ($9.10). Assorted tour guides are found in the bus parking lot; they are available daily from early in the morning to about 4:30pm in winter, 6pm in the summer.

HERCULANEUM ⋇⋇

If you've a yen to explore more ruins, you can head for this seaside resort buried in the same eruption that doomed Pompeii. The site of Herculaneum is much smaller—only about one-fourth the size of Pompeii—and a portion of it remains unexcavated because it is covered by the sprawling slums of Resina. According to legend, Hercules himself founded the city, which was covered in A.D. 79 by much thicker volcanic mud than the lava layer that buried Pompeii. This mud acted as an excellent preservative until 1709 when Prince Elbeuf began "mining" the town for all the treasures he could carry away. In spite of the harm caused by this destructive looting, subsequent excavations have revealed a remarkably well-preserved town, whose buildings are frequently of a higher quality than those found in Pompeii.

Casa dei Cervi (House of the Stags) ✶, the finest house in Herculaneum, was named for the sculpture found inside it. Important private homes to seek out are the **House of the Bicentenary (Casa del Bicentenario)** ✶, the **House of the Wooden Cabinet (Casa a Graticcio)** ✶✶, and the **House of the Wooden Partition (Casa del Tramezzo di Legno)** ✶. Inside the **House of Poseidon and Amphitrite** is an excellent mosaic depicting the god and goddess of the sea.

In addition to the private homes and villas, Herculaneum contains some fascinating public buildings, including the large **Municipal Baths** *(terme)* ✶✶✶, and the more lavish **Suburban Baths (Terme Suburbane)** ✶, built near the elegant villas at the outskirts of the city.

From April to October, the ruins are open daily 8:30am to 7:30pm (last admission at 6pm); from November to March open daily 8:30am to 5pm (last admission at 3:30pm). Admission is 11€ ($14.30). To reach the archaeological zone, take the regular train service from Naples on the Circumvesuviana Railway, a 20-minute ride that leaves about every half hour from Corso Garibaldi 387, just south of the main train station (you can also catch Circumvesuviana trains underneath Stazione Centrale itself; follow the signs). This train will also get you to Vesuvius (same stop), Pompeii, and Sorrento.

4 Florence & Tuscany

On the banks of the Arno, Florence had been a Roman stronghold since the 1st century B.C., but it was not until after A.D. 1200 that it began to come into its own as a commercial and cultural center. During the 13th century, the merchants and tradesmen organized the guilds, which were to control the economy and government of Florence for nearly 150 years. These guilds supervised the construction of several important buildings of the city, and, with their newfound wealth, commissioned works of art that were to adorn the churches and palaces.

This revival of interest in art and architecture brought about the Italian Renaissance, an amazing outburst of activity between the 14th and 16th centuries that completely changed the face of the Tuscan town. During its heyday under the benevolent eye (and purse) of the Medicis, the city was lavishly decorated with churches, palaces, galleries, and monuments, making it the world's greatest repository of art treasures. The list of geniuses who lived or worked here reads like a who's who in the world of art and literature: Dante (he "invented" the Italian language here), Boccaccio, Fra Angelico, Brunelleschi, Donatello, da Vinci, Raphael, Cellini, Michelangelo, Ghiberti, Giotto, and Pisano.

Smack in the middle of the country, Florence sits on one of the country's major high-speed rail lines and offers good connections to Rome, Milan, and Venice, as well as several foreign cities (Artesia de Nuit trains, for example, connect the city to Paris). It's the best spot to explore the Tuscany region by rail. Aside from its good train links, the city is a fabulous destination for rail travelers because of its compact nature—nearly everything, from the city's attractions to its hotels, is within walking distance of the city's train station.

STATION INFORMATION
GETTING FROM THE AIRPORT TO THE TRAIN STATION
If you fly into the Tuscany region (usually through a connection from another Italian city), you can take an express train into the city from **Galileo Galilei Airport** at Pisa

Florence

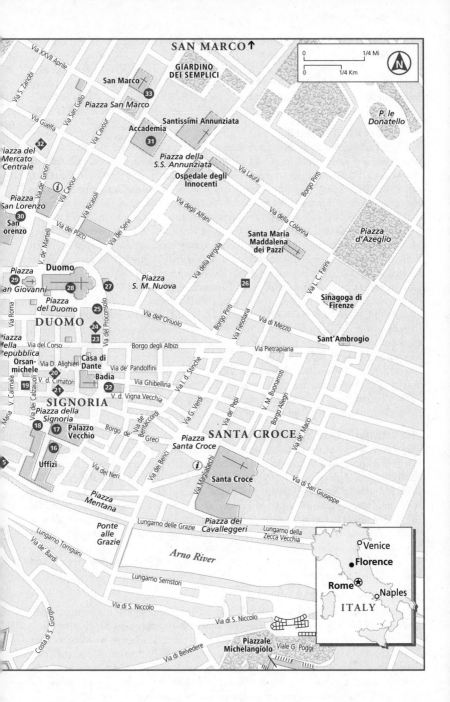

(© **050/849111**), 58 miles (93km) west of Florence. It costs 5.20€ ($6.75) one-way into Florence.

There's also a small domestic airport, **Amerigo Vespucci,** on Via del Termine, near A-11 (© **055/30615**), 3½ miles (5.5km) northwest of Florence, a 15-minute drive. From the airport, you can reach Florence by the ATAF shuttle bus ("Vola in bus"), which stops at the main Santa Maria Novella rail terminal. The fare is 4.50€ ($5.85).

INSIDE THE STATION

If you're coming north by train from Rome, count on a trip time of 1 to 2¾ hours, depending on your connections. In Florence, **Santa Maria Novella rail station,** Piazza della Stazione, adjoins Piazza Santa Maria Novella. For railway information, call © **892021.** Some trains into Florence stop at the **Stazione Campo di Marte,** on the eastern side of Florence. A bus service (no. 12) runs between the two rail terminals and costs 1.20€ ($1.55). Hours of service are from 6:20am to midnight daily.

Santa Maria Novella station has all the usual amenities. A train reservations office on-site is open daily from 7am to 9pm, and a money exchange center (open Mon–Sat 8:20am–7:20pm) is right inside the main station hall. A luggage storage facility is located at track #16, and charges 4.40€ ($5.70) per bag for 12 hours; it's open daily 6am to midnight. A 24-hour pharmacy, **Farmacia Comunale** (© **055/216761**), lies just outside the station opening onto Piazza della Stazione.

A small **Ufficio Informazioni Turistiche** (© **055/212245**) at the station is located directly across the square from the main exit. It dispenses free maps and a listing of the hours for city attractions but doesn't make hotel reservations. It's open daily 9am to 7pm and Sunday 8:30am to 2pm.

For hotel reservations, visit **Imprese Alberghiere** (no phone) in the train station. You can't reserve rooms over the phone but must show up in person daily 8:30am to 7pm. The staff here charges a commission ranging from 3€ to 8€ ($3.90–$10.40), depending on your choice of hotel. In the busy season, expect long lines.

INFORMATION ELSEWHERE IN THE CITY

The main tourist office is the **Azienda Promozione Turistica** at Via Manzoni 16 (© **055/23320**; www.firenzeturismo.it) near the Uffizi galleries; it's open Monday to Friday 9am to 1pm. There is another branch at Via Cavour 1R (© **055/290832**), open Monday to Saturday 8:30am to 6:30pm and Sunday 8:30am to 1:30pm. There is yet another branch just south of Piazza Santa Croce, at Borgo Santa Croce 29R (© **055/2340444**), open April to October Monday to Saturday 9am to 7pm and Sunday 8:30am to 2pm; November to March Monday to Saturday 9am to 5pm and Sunday 8:30am to 2pm. None of these information offices make hotel reservations.

Two useful websites with information about Florence include **www.mega.it** and **http://english.firenze.net**.

GETTING AROUND

Florence is a city designed for walking, with all the major sights in a compact area. The only problem is that the sidewalks are almost unbearably crowded in summer.

If you plan to use **public buses,** you must buy your ticket before boarding, but for 1.20€ ($1.55) you can ride on any public bus for a total of 70 minutes. A 24-hour ticket costs 5€ ($6.50). You can buy bus tickets at *tabacchi* (tobacconists) and newsstands. Once on board, you must validate your ticket in the box near the rear door, or you stand to be fined 40€ ($52)—no excuses accepted. The local **bus station** (which serves as the terminal for ATAF city buses) is at Piazza della Stazione, behind the train station.

Bus routes are posted at bus stops, but the numbers of routes can change overnight because of sudden repair work going on at one of the ancient streets—perhaps a water main broke overnight and caused flooding. We recently found that a bus route map printed only 1 week beforehand was already outdated. Therefore, if you're dependent on bus transport, you'll need to inquire that day for the exact number of the vehicle you want to board.

You can find **taxis** at stands at nearly all the major squares. Rates are a bit expensive: The charge is .90€ ($1.15) per kilometer (⅔ mile), with a 3.20€ ($4.15) minimum. If you need a **radio taxi,** call ✆ **055/4390** or 055/4798.

WHERE TO STAY

Grand Hotel Cavour   Opposite the Bargello Museum, this hotel was converted from a private mansion and has retained much of the original pristine beauty, such as frescoed and coved ceilings. The hotel is known for its atmospherically decorated wine bar and restaurant, and for its roof terrace, "Michelangelo," which offers a panoramic sweep over the Duomo, Palazzo Vecchio, and more. The rooms, unlike the building, are contemporary in styling and comfort, although a bit small. Regrettably, this hotel lies in a particularly noisy part of town, and even the soundproofed windows can't quite block out the sounds.

Via del Proconsolo 3, 50122 Firenze. ✆ **055/266271.** Fax 055/218955. www.albergocavour.it. 105 units. 245€–400€ ($319–$520) double. Rates include buffet breakfast. AE, DC, MC, V. Bus: 14, 23, or 71. **Amenities:** Restaurant; laundry service; nonsmoking rooms; rooms for those w/limited mobility. *In room:* Hair dryer.

Hermitage Hotel ✿ *Finds*   No hotel in Florence is better located than this offbeat charmer, situated right on the Arno at the foot of the Ponte Vecchio. The hotel's rooms are pleasantly furnished with antiques from the 17th to the 19th centuries. Bathrooms are superb and contain lots of gadgets; some have Jacuzzi tubs. Those rooms overlooking the Arno offer the most scenic view, and they've been fitted with double-glazed windows. The intimate lounge has a bar to one side and a fireplace for that nippy evening, but the main allure is the roof terrace planted with flowers, which offers wonderful views.

Vicolo Marzio 1, Piazza del Pesce I, 50122 Firenze. ✆ **055/287216.** Fax 055/212208. www.hermitagehotel.com. 28 units. 120€–245€ ($156–$319) double. Rates include breakfast. MC, V. Bus: B. **Amenities:** Bar; laundry service; rooms for those w/limited mobility, nonsmoking rooms. *In room:* Hair dryer.

Hotel Bellettini ✿ *Value*   Midway between the Duomo (cathedral) and the rail station, this 32-room hotel was carved out of a 14th-century palace with a history of innkeeping going back 3 centuries. Run by two Tuscan-born sisters, it's one of the more traditional choices in the center of Florence, and filled with atmospheric trappings such as carved wood, wrought-iron beds, stained-glass windows, antiques, and terra-cotta tiles. The small to midsize bedrooms are furnished minimally but comfortably. Only two accommodations per floor share the corridor bathrooms, so you'll rarely have to wait in line.

Via di Conti 7, 50123 Firenze. ✆ **055/213561.** Fax 055/283551. www.hotelbellettini.com. 32 units, 28 with bathroom (shower only). 105€ ($137) double without bathroom; 140€ ($182) double with bathroom. Rates include buffet breakfast. AE, DC, MC, V. Bus: 1, 9, 14, 17, 23, 36, or 37. **Amenities:** Laundry service; nonsmoking rooms.

Hotel Monna Lisa ✿   This privately owned Renaissance palazzo has been well preserved and tastefully furnished, and it's exceptionally located—just 4 blocks east of the Duomo. Most of the great old rooms (some are spacious, others cramped) overlook either an inner patio or a modest rear garden. Each room is handsomely furnished with antiques and artwork; many have their original painted wooden ceilings. Some of the tiled bathrooms have Jacuzzi tubs.

Borgo Pinti 27, 50121 Firenze. (© **055/2479751.** Fax 055/2479755. www.monnalisa.it. 45 units. 193€–370€ ($251–$481) double; 262€–460€ ($341–$598) triple; 438€–740€ ($569–$962) suite. Rates include buffet breakfast. AE, DC, MC, V. Bus: A, 6, 31, or 32. **Amenities:** Bar; laundry service; rooms for those w/limited mobility; nonsmoking rooms. *In room:* Hair dryer.

Hotel Porta Rossa ⚔

An inn on this spot has allegedly been putting up wayfarers to Florence since 1386, making Porta Rossa the second-oldest hotel in Florence. The hotel occupies the top three floors of a six-story structure. In spite of its antiquity, the hotel has kept abreast of the times, installing modern conveniences, good beds, and ample bathrooms—some with showers only, others with a tub. Most of the bedrooms are spacious. An attractive feature is a terrace with panoramic views of Florence.

Via Porta Rossa 19, 50123 Firenze. (© **055/287551.** Fax 055/282179. www.hotelportarossa.it. 79 units. 148€–212€ ($192–$276) double; 185€–248€ ($241–$322) triple. Rates include breakfast. AE, DC, MC, V. Bus: A. **Amenities:** Bar; laundry service; nonsmoking rooms; rooms for those w/limited mobility. *In room:* Hair dryer.

Hotel Tornabuoni Beacci ⚔

Near the Arno and Piazza S. Trinità, on the principal shopping street, this near-century-old pensione occupies the top three floors of a 16th-century *palazzo*. The hotel still bears an air of old-fashioned gentility and a lot of atmosphere. The rooms are moderately well furnished with period pieces in an old Florentine style, though still a trifle worn. Rooms at the top are smaller but have better views. The roof terrace for breakfast or drinks is a delight, opening onto scenic vistas of the skyline of Florence.

Via Tornabuoni 3, 50123 Firenze. (© **055/212645.** Fax 055/283594. www.tornabuonihotels.com. 28 units. 130€– 280€ ($169–$364) double; from 250€ ($325) suite. Rates include buffet breakfast. AE, DC, MC, V. Bus: B, 6, 11, or 36. **Amenities:** Restaurant; bar; laundry service. *In room:* Hair dryer.

Hotel Torre Guelfa ⚔⚔

Only 164 feet (50m) from the Ponte Vecchio, this hotel is crowned with a 13th-century tower offering panoramic views of the city. The structure dates from 1280 although there have been many alterations over the years. The midsize accommodations are inviting and have pastel-washed walls, paisley carpeting, and good bathrooms; some have canopied cast-iron beds.

Borgo SS. Apostoli 8 (between Via dei Tornabuoni and Via Per Santa Maria), 50123 Firenze. (© **055/2396338.** Fax 055/2398577. www.hoteltorreguelfa.com. 39 units. 150€–210€ ($195–$273) double; 180€–255€ ($234–$332) suite. Rates include breakfast. AE, MC, V. Bus: D, 11, 36, 37, or 68. **Amenities:** Bar; laundry service; nonsmoking rooms. *In room:* Hair dryer.

Hotel Vasari ⚔ *Value*

Before it was completely revamped into an excellent hotel in 1993, this inn enjoyed a long history, having served as a monastery in the 16th century and as the town house mansion of the 19th-century French poet Alfonse de Lamartine. Much of the old charm remains, including ceiling frescoes and an original stone fireplace in the breakfast room. Bedrooms are small to midsize and are comfortably but minimally furnished. The tiled bathrooms are small but immaculate. The central location, just 1,000 feet (304m) from the Duomo is a plus.

Via B. Cennini 9–11, 50123 Firenze. (© **055/212753.** Fax 055/294246. www.hotelvasari.com. 27 units. 110€–155€ ($143–$202) double; 150€–201€ ($195–$261) triple. Rates include breakfast. AE, DC, MC, V. Bus: 4, 7, 10, 13, 14, 23, or 71. **Amenities:** Bar; laundry service; rooms for those w/limited mobility. *In room:* Hair dryer.

TOP ATTRACTIONS & SPECIAL MOMENTS

To truly see the city at less than a breakneck pace, you need at least 3 days in Florence. If you have less time than that, make sure to see the **Uffizi** and the **Galleria dell'Accademia.** Don't forget to have a meal in one of the city's excellent Tuscan restaurants, and try to make time to view the city (especially the Ponte Vecchio) at sunset—it's a truly memorable experience.

One other noteworthy spot worth your attention is the **Piazza della Signoria** ⟨⟨. As the "front yard" of Florence's city hall, Palazzo Vecchio, Piazza della Signoria was the center of the city's political life from around A.D. 1300. Today the square is a favorite attraction, not only because of its historical significance, but for its wealth of artistic sights as well. On the piazza itself is the **Fountain of Neptune** ⟨, a massively detailed work by Ammannati. Created in the 16th century, it portrays the sea god surrounded by his following of water creatures and woodland nymphs. Also on the plaza is a copy of Michelangelo's *David,* substituted for the original after it was removed to the safety of the Academy Gallery in 1873. Opening onto the square is the **Loggia dei Lanzi** ⟨⟨, a spacious open hallway dating from the 14th century. It is lined with several important sculptures, all of them outshined by Cellini's brilliant masterpiece of *Perseus* ⟨⟨⟨ holding the head of Medusa.

Baptistery (Battistero San Giovanni) ⟨⟨⟨
Facing the Duomo, the octagonal Baptistery is a splendid example of Romanesque architecture as only the Florentines could interpret it. Dating from the 5th century, it was virtually rebuilt in the 11th and 12th centuries with particularly Florentine innovations. The facade is covered with green and white marble, and set into three sides are magnificent bronze doors decorated with gilded bas-reliefs. The greatest treasures here are the reproductions of the **East and North Doors** ⟨⟨⟨, artistically created by Ghiberti under a commission awarded him by the cloth guild of Florence. The enterprise, one of the curtain raisers on the Renaissance, cost the guild 22,000 florins (a 15th-c. Florentine could live in luxury on only 200 florins a year), and took Ghiberti a total of 52 years. After the second door was unveiled in 1452, Michelangelo adjudged it so beautiful that he dubbed it "The Gateway to Paradise."

Piazza San Giovanni. ⟨ 055/2302885. Admission 3€ ($3.90). Mon–Sat noon–7pm; Sun 8:30am–2pm. Bus: 1, 6, or 17.

Bargello Museum (Museo Nazionale del Bargello) ⟨⟨
Begun in 1254, this medieval palace was once a powerful military fortress. Today, as a museum, it exhibits the arms and armor used during the more violent periods of its history, along with a fine collection of decorative art. But the real attraction at the Bargello is the splendid array of medieval and Renaissance sculpture. There's another *David* by Michelangelo here, though not nearly as virile as the famous one in the Accademia. Nor does it stand up to the most famous *David* ⟨⟨ here—Donatello's free-standing bronze creation, nude (except for boots and bonnet) atop the severed head of Goliath. Also by Donatello is his heroic and extremely lifelike interpretation of *St. George* ⟨. Michelangelo is represented in several works, including his *Bacchus,* a bust of *Brutus,* and a bas-relief of *Madonna and Child with John the Baptist.*

Via del Proconsolo 4. ⟨ 055/294883. Admission 4€ ($5.20). Mon–Sat 8:15am–1:50pm; Sun 8:15am–1:50pm. Closed Jan 1, May 1, Christmas, and the 2nd and 3rd Mon and the 1st, 3rd, and 5th Sun of the month. Bus: A, 14, or 23.

Basilica di San Lorenzo ⟨⟨
This church was begun in 1442 by Brunelleschi, and the interior completed by Manetti in 1460. Shaped like a Latin cross, the church was the favorite of the Medicis (the adjoining New Sacristy contains the tombs of the

clan), so a great deal of money and artistic effort went into decorating it. The **Old Sacristy,** at the left of the nave, was partially decorated by Donatello, including some terra-cotta reliefs. The adjoining **Laurenziana Library** ☆☆ was designed by Michelangelo to contain the huge Medici collection of manuscripts. It boasts an unusual staircase and an intricately carved and paneled reading room.

Piazza San Lorenzo. (℃) **055/216634.** Free admission; 2.60€ ($3.40) for special exhibitions. Mon–Sat 10am–5:30pm. Bus: 1, 6, 7, 11, 17, 33, 67, or 68.

Basilica di Santa Maria Novella ☆☆   Right near the rail station, on the Piazza Santa Maria Novella, this landmark is a large Dominican edifice built between 1278 and 1350. Its geometric facade, made of inlaid marble, was added in the 15th century by Alberti. The church is especially interesting for its frescoes by Masaccio, Ghirlandaio, Orcagna, and Filippo Lippi. The adjoining cloisters are also worth a visit, especially the Spanish Chapel with frescoes by Andrea di Bonaiuto and his assistants.

Piazza Santa Maria Novella. (℃) **055/215918.** Church free; Spanish Chapel and cloisters 2.70€ ($3.50). Church Mon–Fri 7am–noon and 3–6pm. Spanish Chapel and cloisters Mon–Sat 9am–5pm, Sun 9am–2pm. Bus: A, 6, 9, 11, 36, 37, or 68.

Duomo Museum (Museo dell'Opera del Duomo) ☆☆   Across the street from but facing the apse of Santa Maria del Fiore, is this museum beloved by connoisseurs of Renaissance sculptural works. It shelters the sculpture removed from the campanile and the Duomo. A major reason for visiting the museum is to see the world–famous marble **choirs** ☆☆—*cantorie*—of Donatello and Luca della Robbia (both works face each other, and are housed in the first room you enter after climbing the stairs). One of Donatello's most celebrated works, *Magdalene* ☆☆, is in the room with the *cantorie*. A major attraction is an **unfinished** *Pietà* ☆☆, **by Michelangelo,** in the middle of the stairs. It was carved between 1548 and 1555, when the artist was in his 70s. The premier attraction, however, is the **restored panels of Ghiberti's Gates of Paradise** ☆☆☆, which were removed from the baptistery. In gilded bronze, each is a masterpiece of Renaissance sculpture, the finest low-relief perspective in all Italian art.

Piazza del Duomo 9. (℃) **055/2302885.** Admission 6€ ($7.80). Year-round Mon–Sat 9am–7:30pm; Sun 9am–1:40pm. Bus: B, 14, 23, or 71.

⟨Tips⟩ How to Avoid Those Endless Lines

Select Italy offers the possibility to reserve your tickets for the Uffizi, Boboli Gardens, Galleria dell'Accademia, and many other attractions in Florence. The cost varies from 16€ to 30€ ($20.80–$39), depending on the museum, and several combination passes are available. Contact **Select Italy** at (℃) **847/853-1661,** or buy online at **www.selectitaly.com.**

If you're already in Florence and don't want to waste half a day waiting to enter the Galleria degli Uffizi, Galleria dell'Accademia, Boboli Gardens, Pitti Palace, and many others, call **Firenze Musei** ((℃) **055/294883;** www.firenze musei.it). The service operates Monday to Friday from 8:30am to 6:30pm, and Saturday to 12:30pm. Requests must be made a minimum of 5 days in advance; you pick up the tickets at the museum booth on the day your visit has been approved. There's a service charge of 3€ ($3.90), plus, of course, the regular price of the museum admission.

Moments A Stroll across Italy's Most Famous Bridge

Miraculously spared by the Nazis in their bitter retreat from the Allied advance in 1944, the **Ponte Vecchio (Old Bridge)** ⚜⚜ is the last remaining medieval *ponte* that once spanned the Arno (the Germans blew up the rest). The existence of the Ponte Vecchio was again threatened in the flood of 1966—in fact, the waters of the Arno swept over it, washing away a fortune in jewelry from the famous goldsmiths' shops that flank the bridge.

Today the Ponte Vecchio is back in business, closed to traffic except the *pedoni* or foot passenger type. The little shops continue to sell everything from the most expensive of Florentine gold to something simple—say, a Lucrezia Borgia poison ring.

Galleria degli Uffizi ⚜⚜⚜ Few art museums in the world can compare with the Uffizi, home to Italy's finest collection of art. The 16th-century building stretches from the Palazzo Vecchio to the Arno. In spite of its size and multitudinous works of art (about 2,500 paintings alone, plus miniatures, statues, and more than 100,000 drawings and prints), the museum is easily navigated because the galleries are grouped by periods and schools. But don't expect to see everything in 1 day. Laid out progressively, the galleries begin with Room 1 (classical sculptures) and extend through Room 42 (Italian and French paintings of the 18th c.). The largest concentration of paintings is on Italian works of the 15th and 16th centuries (more than 400 of these alone). Room 10 is the most popular in the entire gallery. Here you'll find the works of Botticelli, including his ***Birth of Venus*** ⚜⚜⚜ and ***Primavera,*** two of the most famous paintings in the world.

Room 18, the octagonal Tribune, is the most splendid in the museum, even when it contains no exhibits. The floor is inlaid with marble in geometric designs, and the domed ceiling studded with pearl shells. The room's most prominent spot is occupied by the ***Medici Venus*** ⚜⚜, a magnificent Greek sculpture, along with later copies of 4th-century Greek sculptures of *The Wrestler* and *Apollo.*

Piazzale degli Uffizi 6. © 055/23885. www.uffizi.firenze.it. Admission 6.50€ ($8.45). Tues–Sun 8:15am–7pm (last entrance 45 min. before closing). Advance booking necessary. Bus: A, B, 23, or 71.

Galleria dell'Accademia ⚜⚜ This museum is visited mainly for one exhibit: Michelangelo's awesome statue of ***David*** ⚜⚜⚜. For years the 17-foot (5.1m) statue weathered the elements on the Piazza della Signoria, but was finally moved to the Accademia in 1873 and placed beneath the rotunda of a room built exclusively for its display. When he began work, Michelangelo was just 29. In the connecting picture gallery is a collection of Tuscan masters, such as Botticelli, and Umbrian works by Perugino (teacher of Raphael).

Via Ricasoli 60. © 055/2388609. Admission 6.50€ ($8.45). Tues–Sun 8:15am–6:50pm. Bus: B, D, or 12.

Giotto's Bell Tower (Campanile di Giotto) ⚜⚜ Although better known for his great skill in fresco painting, Giotto left to posterity the most beautiful campanile (bell tower) in Europe, rhythmic in line and form. The 274-foot (82m) tower, a "Tuscanized" Gothic, with bands of colored marble, can be scaled for a truly memorable **panoramic view** ⚜⚜⚜ of the sienna-colored city and the blue-green Tuscan hills in the distance.

Piazza del Duomo. ⓒ **055/2302885**. Cathedral free; excavations 3€ ($3.90); cupola 6€ ($7.80). Daily 8:30am–6:30pm. Bus: 1, 6, or 17.

Il Duomo (Cattedrale di Santa Maria del Fiore) 🌟🌟🌟   The cathedral of Florence, called simply the *Duomo,* is the crowning glory of Florence. But don't rush inside too quickly, as the view of the exterior, with its geometrically patterned bands of white, pink, and green marble, is, along with **Brunelleschi's dome** 🌟🌟🌟, the best feature. One of the world's largest churches, the Duomo represents the flowering of the "Florentine Gothic" style. Begun in 1296, it was finally consecrated in 1436, yet finishing touches on the facade were applied as late as the 19th century. Inside, the overall effect is bleak, except when you stand under the cupola, frescoed in part by Vasari. Some of the stained-glass windows in the dome were based on designs by Donatello (Brunelleschi's friend) and Ghiberti (Brunelleschi's rival). The overall effect of the cathedral's famous dome atop its octagonal drum is one of the most striking sights of the city—and its most famous landmark. If you resist scaling Giotto's bell tower, you may want to climb Brunelleschi's ribbed dome. The view is well worth the trek.

Piazza del Duomo. ⓒ **055/2302885**. Cathedral free; excavations 3€ ($3.90); cupola 6€ ($7.80). Thurs 10am–3:30pm; Sat 10am–4:45pm; Sun 1:30–4:45pm. 1st Sat of the month 10am–3:30pm. Bus: 1, 6, or 17.

Medici Chapels (Cappelle Medicee) 🌟🌟   Michelangelo left his mark on Florence in many places, but nowhere can you feel so completely surrounded by his works as in the Medici Chapels, adjoining the Basilica di San Lorenzo (see above). Working from 1521 to 1534, Michelangelo created the Medici tomb in a style that foreshadowed the baroque. Lorenzo the Magnificent was buried in the **New Sacristy** 🌟🌟🌟 near Michelangelo's uncompleted *Madonna and Child* group. Ironically, the finest groups of sculpture were reserved for two of the lesser Medicis, who are represented as armored, idealized princes. The other two figures on Lorenzo's tomb are most often called *Dawn* (represented as woman) and *Dusk* (as man). The best-known figures are *Night* 🌟🌟🌟 (chiseled as a woman in troubled sleep) and *Day* 🌟🌟🌟 (a man of strength awakening to a foreboding world) at the feet of Giuliano, the duke of Nemours.

Piazza Madonna degli Aldobrandini 6. ⓒ **055/2388602**. Admission 6€ ($7.80). Apr 1–Nov 10 daily 8:15am–5pm; Nov 11–Mar 31 daily 8:15am–1:50pm. Closed 2nd and 4th Sun, and 1st, 3rd, and 5th Mon of each month. Bus: 1, 6, 7, 11, 17, 33, 67, or 68.

Palazzo Pitti and the Giardini di Boboli (Boboli Gardens) 🌟🌟   Just 5 minutes from the Ponte Vecchio, The Pitti, built in the mid–15th century (Brunelleschi was the original architect), was once the residence of the powerful Medici family. Today it contains several museums, the most important of which is the **Galleria Palatina** 🌟🌟, a

---

⟮*Moments*   **A Garden Stroll**

Behind the Pitti Palace are the extensive **Boboli Gardens** 🌟, Piazza de'Pitti 1 (ⓒ **055/2388786**), designed and executed by Triboli, a landscape artist (on canvas and in real life), in the 16th century. Studded with fountains and statues, it provides an ideal setting for a relaxing break between museum visits. The gardens are also the setting for Fort Belvedere, an imposing structure that dominates the hillside and offers a spectacular view of Florence. For opening times, see above.

Moments **One of the World's Greatest Views**

The best overall view of the city is from the **Piazzale Michelangelo** (bus no. 13 from the Central Station), an elevated plaza on the south side of the river. If you can ignore the milling crowds and souvenir peddlers who flood the square, you can enjoy a **spectacular view** ✰✰✰ of old Florence, circled by the hazy hills of Tuscany. It's like looking at a Renaissance painting. We prefer the view at dusk when the purple-fringed Tuscan hills form a frame for Giotto's bell tower, Brunelleschi's dome, and the towering hunk of stones that stick up from the Palazzo Vecchio. If you look up into the hills, you can also see the ancient town of Fiesole, with its Roman ruins and cathedral. Another copy of Michelangelo's famous statue, *David,* dominates Piazzale Michelangelo, giving the wide square its name. Crown your view with some of the delectable ice cream served on the square at **Gelateria Michelangelo** (✆ 055/2342705), open daily 7am to 2am.

repository of old masters. Devoted mainly to Renaissance works, the Palatine is especially rich in Raphaels, including his world-famous *Madonna of the Chair.* Other works by Titian, Botticelli, Fra Bartolomeo, Filippo Lippi, Tintoretto, Rubens, Van Dyck, and Velázquez round out the collection.

The **Royal Apartments (Appartamenti Reali)** ✰ boast lavish reminders of the time when the Pitti was the home of the kings of Savoy. Reopened in 1993 after a restoration, these apartments in all their baroque sumptuousness, including a flamboyant decor and works of art by del Sarto and Caravaggio, can be viewed only on a guided tour, usually Tuesday and Saturday (also on an occasional Thurs) 9 to 11am and 3 to 5pm. Tours leave every hour. Reservations are needed, so call ✆ 051/2388614.

Other museums are the **Museo degli Argenti (Museum of Silver)** ✰ (✆ 055/2388761), 16 rooms devoted to displays of the "loot" acquired by the Medici dukes; and the **Galleria d'Arte Moderna** (✆ 055/2388601).

Piazza Pitti, across the Arno. ✆ 055/2388614. Palatina and Modern Art Gallery 8.50€ ($11.05); 4€ ($5.20) for both Argenti and Boboli Gardens. Combination ticket to all museums and Boboli Gardens 11.50€ ($14.95). Galleria Palatine and Appartamenti Reali Tues–Sun 8:15am–6:45pm; Museo degli Argenti Nov–Feb Tues–Sun 8:15am–4:30pm; Mar Tues–Sun 8:15am–5:30pm; Apr–May and Sept–Oct Tues–Sun 8:15am–6:30pm; June–Aug Tues–Sun 8:15am–7:30pm. Galleria d'Arte Moderna Tues–Sun 8:15am–7pm. Boboli Gardens June–Sept daily 8:30am–7:45pm; Apr–May and Oct daily 8:30am–6:45pm; Nov–Mar daily 9am–5:45pm. Ticket office closes 1 hr. before the gardens. Bus: B, 11, 36, 37, or 68.

St. Mark's Museum (Museo di San Marco) ✰✰   This state museum is a handsome Renaissance palace whose cell walls are decorated with magnificent 15th-century **frescoes** ✰✰✰ by the mystical Fra Angelico. In the days of Cosimo dei Medici, San Marco was built as a Dominican convent. It originally contained bleak, bare cells, which Angelico and his students then brightened considerably. One of his better-known paintings here is *The Last Judgment* ✰✰, contrasting the beautiful angels and saints on the left with the demons and tortured sinners of hell on the right. Among his other works are a masterful *Annunciation* ✰✰✰, and a magnificently colorful *Virgin and Child.*

Piazza San Marco 1. ✆ 055/294883. Admission 4€ ($5.20). Mon–Fri 8:15am–1:50pm; Sat–Sun 8:15am–6:50pm. Ticket office closes 30 min. before the museum. Closed 2nd and 4th Mon of the month; 1st, 3rd, and 5th Sun of the month; Jan 1, May 1, and Christmas. Bus: 1, 6, 7, 10, 11, 17, or 20.

WHERE TO DINE

Buca dell'Orafo 🍴 *finds* FLORENTINE   This little dive is one of many cellar (*buca*)-type joints beloved by Florentines. The trattoria is usually stuffed with regulars and travelers so if you want a seat, go early. Over the years the chef has made little concession to the foreign palate, turning out genuine Florentine specialties, such as tripe and mixed boiled meats with a green sauce.

Via Volta dei Girolami 28R. 🕐 **055/213619.** Main courses 10€–13€ ($13–$16.90). No credit cards. Tues–Sat 12:30–2:30pm and 7:30–10:30pm. Closed Aug and 2 weeks in Dec. Bus: B.

Cafaggi TUSCAN/SEAFOOD   Set in a converted palazzo, this 100-seat trattoria has been a Florentine tradition since 1922, its tables spread across two old-fashioned dining rooms. This charming and atmospheric eatery is securely ensconced on the Florentine dining circuit, its kitchen adhering to time-tested Tuscan recipes, including some of the town's best seafood. Some of the recipes appear a bit startling at first but can quickly become addictive as exemplified by the spaghetti with sardines, pine nuts, and raisins.

Via Guelfa 35R. 🕐 **055/294989.** Reservations recommended. Main courses 9€–17€ ($11.70–$22.10). AE, MC, V. Mon–Sat 12:30–3:30pm and 7–11pm. Bus: 1, 6, 7, 11, 17, 33, 67, or 68.

Cantinetta Antinori 🍴 *finds* FLORENTINE/TUSCAN   The menu at one of Florence's most highly rated wine bars changes with the seasons, and is it ever good. You can visit this 15th-century palazzo for complete meals or else snacks. Regardless of what you order, your food is most often accompanied by one of the best-stocked cellars in town from a company that has been hawking wines for 6 centuries. The food is standard but satisfying, and many of the ingredients come directly from the Antinori farms.

Piazza Antinori 3. 🕐 **055/292234.** Reservations recommended. Main courses 13€–22€ ($16.90–$28.60). AE, DC, MC, V. Mon–Sat 12:30–2:30pm and 7–10:30pm. Closed Aug and Dec 24–25. Bus: 6, 11, 14, 36, 37, or 68.

Da Ganino 🍴 FLORENTINE/TUSCAN   Both the *New York Times* and the Paris *Herald Tribune* have lavished justified praise on this intimate little trattoria, which is run by the Ganino family across from an American Express office midway between the Uffizi and the Duomo. Succulent pastas, well-flavored and perfectly cooked meats, classic T-bone *Fiorentina* steaks, and some of the best of regional ingredients, such as white truffles, keep foodies and locals coming back for more.

Piazza dei Cimatori 4R. 🕐 **055/214125.** Reservations recommended. Main courses 6€–20€ ($7.80–$26). AE, DC. Mon–Sat 12:30–3pm and 7:30–10:30pm. Bus: 14, 23, or 71.

Il Latini 🍴 TUSCAN/FLORENTINE   Latini is loud and claustrophobic, and the service borders on hysterical. Still, this is an enduringly popular place with locals and visitors, who pack the place for the enormous portions served at communal tables. A waiter will arrive to recite a list of items corresponding to antipasti, pasta, main course, and dessert. If you insist on seeing a printed menu, someone will probably find one, but it's more fun just to go with the flow. We can't pretend the food is subtle—it isn't— but it's filling, relatively cheap, and made with fresh ingredients.

Via del Palchetti 6R (off Via Vigna Nuova). 🕐 **055/210916.** Reservations recommended. Main courses 10€–17€ ($13–$22.10). AE, DC, MC, V. Tues–Sun 12:30–2:30pm and 7:30–10:30pm. Closed Dec 24–Jan 7. Bus: C, 6, 11, 36, or 37.

Le Mossacce *Value* TUSCAN/FLORENTINE   Near the Duomo or cathedral, this small *osteria* is known for serving tasty, affordable home cooking in generous portions to hungry Florentines. Many of the delights of the Florentine menu appear here, including such classics as *ribollita* (a thick vegetable soup) or those justly celebrated slices of *bistecca* (beefsteak) *alla fiorentina*. A tradition since 1942, Le Mossacce hires waiters who prefer to tantalize you with the offerings of the day instead of presenting you with a menu—we had a great meal following their advice.

Via del Proconsolo 55R. ✆ 055/294361. Reservations unnecessary. Main courses 6€–10€ ($7.80–$13). AE, DC, MC, V. Mon–Fri noon–2:30pm and 7–9:30pm. Closed Aug. Bus: 14.

Osteria di Giovanni ✿ INTERNATIONAL/FLORENTINE   Near the train station, this is a winning choice installed in a palace dating from the 1400s. Under vaulted ceilings with a decor of musical instruments and original paintings, you are served well-prepared Florentine and international dishes based on market-fresh ingredients. Most diners come here to order big slabs of the tender and well-flavored beefsteak, which will usually feed at least two people.

Via del Moro 22R. ✆ 055/284897. Reservations recommended. Main courses 8€–25€ ($10.40–$32.50). AE, DC, MC, V. Mon 7pm–12:30am; Wed–Sat noon–3pm and 7pm–midnight. Closed 3 weeks in Aug. Bus: C, 6, 9, 11, 36, 37, or 68.

Paoli ✿✿ TUSCAN/ITALIAN   Paoli, between the Duomo and Piazza della Signoria, is one of Florence's finest restaurants. It turns out a host of specialties, but could be recommended almost solely for its atmospheric medieval-tavern atmosphere. All pastas are homemade, and the fettuccine alla Paoli is served piping hot and full of flavor. The chef also does a superb *rognoncino trifolato* (thinly sliced kidney cooked with oil, garlic, and parsley) and sole meunière. It's worth saving room for one of the yummy desserts.

Via dei Tavolini 12R. ✆ 055/216215. Reservations required. Main courses 11€–20€ ($14.30–$26). AE, DC, MC, V. Wed–Mon noon–2:30pm and 7–10:30pm. Closed 3 weeks in Aug. Bus: A.

Sabatini ✿✿ FLORENTINE   Locals and visitors alike extol this restaurant's classic Tuscan cuisine, served in an antique house only 600 feet (180m) from the Duomo. Understated and traditional, it offers all the old-time favorites Florentines have grown to love, including *bistecca alla fiorentina*—arguably the finest in the city—and classics such as boiled Valdarno chicken in a savory green sauce. The wine cellar is particularly notable here for both its Tuscan and Umbrian vintages—one habitué called it "seductive."

Via Panzani 9A. ✆ 055/282802. Reservations recommended. Main courses 12.50€–30€ ($16.25–$39). AE, DC, MC, V. Tues–Sun 12:30–2:30pm and 7:30–10:30pm. Bus: 1, 6, 14, 17, or 22.

Trattoria Garga ✿✿ TUSCAN/FLORENTINE   Some of the most creative cuisine in Florence is served at this restaurant, set midway between the Ponte Vecchio and Santa Maria Novella. This local favorite's postage-size kitchen turns out dishes based on old Tuscan recipes that have been given a new twist. The walls are from the days of the Renaissance, and they are decorated with contemporary paintings. Save room for dessert: The chef prepares a cheesecake so good that even New Yorkers give it a thumbs-up.

Via del Moro 48R. ✆ 055/2398898. Reservations required. Main courses 15€–27€ ($19.50–$35.10). AE, DC, MC, V. Tues–Sun 7:30–11pm. Bus: 6, 9, 11, 36, 37, or 68.

SHOPPING

Florence is a city of high fashion, and it's also known for its leather goods, straw products, and magnificently crafted gold jewelry, much of the latter sold at the pint-sized shops along the Ponte Vecchio. Note, however, that it's not a city for bargains—prices are almost always appropriately up there.

Located away from the Ponte Vecchio, **Mario Buccellati,** Via dei Tornabuoni 69-71R (© **055/2396579**), a branch of the Milan store that opened in 1919, specializes in exquisite handcrafted jewelry and silver.

Intrepid shoppers head for the **Mercato della Paglia** or **Mercato Nuovo (Straw Market** or **New Market**), 2 blocks south of Piazza della Repubblica. (It's called Il Porcellino by the Italians because of the bronze statue of a reclining wild boar, a copy of the one in the Uffizi.) Tourists pet its snout (which is well worn) for good luck. The market stands in the monumental heart of Florence, an easy stroll from the Palazzo Vecchio. It sells not only straw items but also leather goods (not the best quality), along with typical Florentine merchandise: frames, trays, hand-embroidery, table linens, and hand-sprayed and -painted boxes in traditional designs.

Even better bargains await those who make their way through the pushcarts to the stalls of the open-air **Mercato Centrale (Mercato San Lorenzo),** in and around Borgo San Lorenzo, near the rail station. If you don't mind bargaining, which is imperative, you'll find an array of merchandise such as raffia bags, Florentine leather purses, sweaters, gloves, salt-and-pepper shakers, straw handbags, and art reproductions.

For one-stop shopping the best outlet is **La Rinascente,** Piazza della Repubblica 2 (© **055/219113**), right in the heart of Florence. This is where frugal but taste-conscious Florentines go to shop. Their clothing for men and women features some of the big names but also talented and lesser-known Italian designers. You'll also find good buys in china, perfumes, and jewelry, along with a "made in Tuscany" department that sells everything from terra-cotta vases to the finest virgin olive oils.

NIGHTLIFE

For theatrical and concert listings, check at the tourist office.

THE PERFORMING ARTS From May to July, the city welcomes classical musicians for its **Maggio Musicale** festival of cantatas, madrigals, concertos, operas, and ballets, many of which are presented in Renaissance buildings. The main venue for the festival is the **Teatro Comunale di Firenze/Maggio Musicale Fiorentino,** Corso Italia 16 (© **055/27791**), which also presents opera and ballet from September to December and a concert season from January to April. Schedule and ticket information for the festival is available from **Maggio Musicale Fiorentino/Teatro Comunale,** Corso Italia 12, 50123 Firenze (© **055/2779350**). Tickets to theatrical productions and the festival cost 20€ to 100€ ($26–$130). For further information, visit the theater's website, at **www.maggiofiorentino.com**.

CAFES & CLUBS **Café Rivoire,** Piazza della Signoria 4R (© **055/214412**), offers a classy and amusing old-world ambience with a direct view of the statues on one of our favorite squares in the world. You can sit at one of the metal tables on the flagstones outside or at one of the wooden tables in a choice of inner rooms filled with marble detailing and unusual oil renderings of the piazza outside.

The oldest and most beautiful cafe in Florence, **Gilli's,** via Roma 1, adjacent to Piazza Repubblica 39R, Via Roma 1 (© **055/213896**), is a few minutes' walk from the Duomo. It was founded in 1789, when Piazza della Repubblica had a different name. You can sit at a brightly lit table near the bar or retreat to an intricately paneled pair of rooms to the side and enjoy the flattering light from the Venetian-glass chandeliers.

At **Space Electronic,** Via Palazzuolo 37 (© **055/293082**), the decor consists of wall-to-wall mirrors and an imitation space capsule that goes back and forth across the dance floor. If karaoke doesn't thrill you, head to the ground-floor pub, which stocks an ample supply of imported beers. On the upper level is a large dance floor with a wide choice of music and a high-energy row of laser beams. This place attracts a lot of foreign students who want to hook up with Florentine men and women on the prowl. The disco opens Tuesday to Sunday at 10pm and usually goes until 3am. The 15€ ($19.50) cover includes the first drink.

Rio Grande, Viale degli Olmi 1 (© **055/331371**), is Florence's best, biggest, and most international disco. A 15-minute cab ride from Piazza del Duomo, near Parco della Cascine, it has an indoor/outdoor setting that includes century-old trees, a terrace, and three dance floors. The music includes everything from punk to rock to funk to garage. Gays mix with the mostly straight crowd with ease, and the typical age range is 18 to 32. For the disco only, a cover of 11€ to 16€ ($14.30–$20.80) is imposed.

AN EXCURSION TO PISA ✿✿

No longer the powerful port it was in the western Mediterranean in the 12th century, Pisa is still visited for its magnificent buildings, especially the Leaning Tower of Pisa, a building that is one of the most recognizable on earth. The silting up of its harbor marked Pisa's decline in 1284, and it suffered even greater devastation in the Allied bombings of 1944. Nonetheless, there is much here to celebrate at a point lying 47 miles (76km) west of Florence and easily visited on a day trip from that city.

GETTING THERE   Chances are you might land in Pisa to begin your descent on Florence. Both domestic and international flights land at Pisa's **Galileo Galilei Airport** (© **050/849111**). From the airport, trains depart every 15 to 30 minutes, depending on the time of day, for the 5-minute ride into Pisa, costing 1€ ($1.30) each way. As an alternative, bus no. 3 leaves the airport every 20 minutes heading for Pisa, costing .90€ ($1.15) one-way.

Trains make the 1-hour journey between Pisa and Florence every 1½ hours; the ride costs 5.20€ ($6.75) one-way. Trains running along the coast link Pisa with Rome, a trip of 3 hours. Depending on the time of day and the speed of the train, one-way fares are 16€ to 28€ ($20.80–$36.40). In Pisa, trains arrive at the **Stazione Pisa Centrale** (© **892021**), about a 10- to 15-minute walk from the Leaning Tower. Otherwise, you can take bus no. 1 from the station into the heart of the city.

TOURIST INFORMATION   The **tourist office** at Piazza Duomo 1 (© **050-560464**) is open daily 9:30am to 6:30pm. A second branch is at Piazza Vittorio Emanuele II, next to the train station (© **050/42291**); it's open Monday to Friday 9am to pm, and Saturday 9am to 1:30pm.

TOP ATTRACTIONS & SPECIAL MOMENTS

Seemingly every visitor heads first for the **Leaning Tower of Pisa (Campanile)** ✿✿✿, Piazza del Duomo 17 (© **050/3872210**). Construction began on the eight-story campanile in 1174 by Bonanno, and there has been a persistent legend that the architect deliberately intended that the bell tower lean (that claim is undocumented). If it stood up straight, the tower would measure about 180 feet (54m). The tower was closed for many years as Pisans worked to stabilize it. Tons of soil were removed from under the foundation, and lead counterweights were placed at the monument's base.

Admission is 15€ ($19.50), and hours April 1 to June 13 and September 4 to September 30 are daily 8:30am to 8:30pm; June 14 to September 4 8:30 am to 11pm; October daily 9am to 7pm; November to February daily 9:30am to 5pm; March 1 to March 13 9am to 6pm; March 14 to March 20 daily 9am to 7pm; March 21 to March 31 daily 8:30am to 8:30pm. Only 40 people are admitted at one time. Reservations are a necessity; you can call for one or reserve online at **www.duomo.pisa.it**.

Also at the Piazza del Duomo, the **Baptistery (Battistero)** ✿✿✿ (𝄐 **050/3872210**), is circular in shape, dating from 1152 when it was constructed along Romanesque lines, the work taking 100 years. It was finished in a more ornate Gothic style by Nicola and Giovanni Pisano. Its greatest treasure is the **hexagonal pulpit** ✿✿, designed by Nicola Pisano. Supported by pillars, it rests on the backs of a trio of marble lions, containing bas-reliefs of the *Crucifixion,* the *Adoration of the Magi,* the *Presentation of the Christ Child at the Temple,* and *The Last Judgment.*

The **Duomo** ✿✿ (𝄐 **050/3872210**) itself, dominating the so-called Campo dei Miracoli (Field of Miracles), was begun by Buscheto in 1064, and is today one of the finest Pisan-Romanesque buildings in Tuscany, with a **west front** ✿✿✿ that is light and graceful with three tiers of marble columns. The south transept door has impressive Romanesque **bronze panels** ✿✿ from the late 12th century, the work of Bonanno Pisano. Yet another **impressive pulpit** ✿✿✿ found here was the creation of Giovanni Pisano who worked on it from 1302 to 1311. Admission is 2€ ($2.60). It's open April to September daily 10am to 8pm; March and October daily 10am to 7pm, and November to February daily 10am to 1pm and 3 to 5pm.

Camposanto ✿✿, Piazza del Duomo (𝄐 **050/3872210**), is a cemetery that was begun in 1277 by Giovanni di Simone, one of the architects of the Leaning Tower. Called the Holy Field, the vast marble arcades of this long building, or so legend has it, contain soil brought back from the Holy Land. Allied bombings in 1944 destroyed most of its once-lavish frescoes, although scenes depicting *The Triumph of Death* remain (1350–80). Admission costs 5€ ($6.50). Hours are April to September daily 8am to 8pm; March and October daily 9am to 7pm, and November to February daily 10am to 5pm.

WHERE TO DINE

Because of its well-prepared food and its proximity to Piazza del Duomo, **Emilio,** Via Cammeo 44 (𝄐 **050-562141**), is always packed. Inside, a large, high window, similar to what you'd find in a church, filters light down upon the brick-walled interior. The menu (it serves lunch only) features a fresh assortment of antipasti, spaghetti with clams, risotto with mushrooms, perfectly prepared grilled fish, and Florentine beefsteaks. In season, try one of the game dishes with polenta. The chef's dessert specialty is *crema limoncello,* a mousse prepared with limoncello liqueur. Main courses cost 5.50€ to 15€ ($7.15–$19.50), with fixed-price menus going for 9.50€ to 14€ ($12.35–$18.20). Open Saturday to Thursday noon to 3:30pm.

Another good choice for Pisan cuisine is **Antica Trattoria Da Bruno,** Via Luigi Bianchi 12 (𝄐 **050/560818**), which has been in business for some 50 years at its location close to the Leaning Tower. The recipes may be old-fashioned but the food is completely fresh and well prepared. Local favorites include *zuppa pisana,* a minestrone made with black cabbage, or wild boar with olives and polenta. Main courses cost 8€ to 15€ ($10.40–$19.50). It's open Monday noon to 2:30pm, Wednesday to Sunday noon to 3pm and 7 to 10:30pm.

AN EXCURSION TO SIENA

Although such a point of view may be heretical, one can almost be grateful that Siena lost its medieval battles with Florence. Had it continued to expand and change after reaching the zenith of its power in the 14th century, chances are it would be remarkably different today, influenced by the rising tides of the Renaissance and the baroque (represented today only in a small degree). But Siena retained its uniqueness (certain Sienese painters were still showing the influence of Byzantium in the late 15th c.) and is a showplace of the Italian Gothic.

GETTING THERE   The rail link between Florence and Siena is a bit inconvenient because you often have to change trains and wait at other stations, such as the one at the town of Empoli. Trains arrive every hour from Florence, however, costing 5.70€ ($7.40) one-way. Trains pull in at Siena's station at Piazza Fratelli Rosselli (© **892021**), a difficult 30-minute climb uphill to the monumental center unless you take bus no. 2, 4, 6, or 10, depositing you at Piazza Gramsci in the heart of Siena.

TOURIST INFORMATION   The **Siena Tourist Office** at Piazza del Campo 56 (© **0577/280551**), is open daily 9am to 7pm, and dispenses information and good, free maps.

TOP ATTRACTIONS & SPECIAL MOMENTS

The Town Hall of Siena, **Palazzo Comunale,** stands in the virtual heart of Siena at the shell-shaped **Piazza del Campo** ✿✿✿, described by Montaigne as "the finest of any city in the world." Pause to enjoy **Fonte Gaia,** which locals sometimes call the Fountain of Joy because it was inaugurated to great jubilation throughout the city, with embellishments by Jacopo della Quercia (the present sculptured works are reproductions—the badly beaten-up original ones are found in the town hall). The square is truly stunning, designed like a sloping scalloped shell; you'll want to linger in one of the cafes along its edge. You'll hardly be able to miss the lithe **Torre (tower) del Mangia** ✿✿✿, dating from the 14th century, which soars to a height of 335 feet (101m) over the skyline of the city.

The brick-built **Palazzo Pubblico** (1288–1309) on the square is filled with important art works by some of the leaders of the Sienese school of painting and sculpture. Upstairs in a museum is the *Sala della Pace,* frescoed from 1337–39 by Ambrogio Lorenzetti, and showing allegorically the idealized effects of good government and bad government. In this depiction, the most notable figure of the Virtues surrounding the King is *La Pace* (Peace). To the right of the King and the Virtues is a representation of Siena in peaceful times. The tower and museum at Piazza del Campo (© **0577/226230**) are open mid-March to October daily 10am to 7pm; November to mid-March daily 10am to 5pm, charging an admission of 7€ ($9.10).

Southwest of Piazza del Campo stands **Il Duomo** ✿✿✿, Piazza del Duomo (© **0577/283048**), built from 1136 to 1382; it's one of the great cathedrals of Italy, with a Pisan-influenced Romanesque-Gothic architecture. The impressive facade is from the 13th century, as is the Romanesque campanile or bell tower. The interior is a series of black and white zebralike striped designs. Black and white marble pillars support the vault. The chief treasure is the **octagonal pulpit** ✿✿✿ of the 13th century, the work of Nicola Pisano. The pillars of the pulpit are held up by a quartet of marble lions, evocative of the Pisano pulpit at Pisa.

On Piazza San Giovanni, the **Battistero (Baptistery)** ✿ (© **0577/283048**) lies behind the Duomo. Its Gothic facade left unfinished by Domenico di Agostino, it is nonetheless an impressive site. Inside its chief attraction is the **baptismal font** ❀❀ from 1417, the work of Jacopo della Quercia, containing some bas-reliefs by such Tuscan masters as Donatello and Lorenzo Ghiberti. It is a Renaissance work of superb design and craftsmanship. Admission is 6€ ($7.80). It's open March to May, September, and October daily 9:30am to 7pm; June to August daily 9:30am to 8pm.

Pinacoteca Nazionale ❀❀, in the Palazzo Buonsignori, Via San Pietro 29 (© 0577/281161), displays an amazing and extensive collection from the Sienese school ranging from the 13th to the 16th century, everything housed in a 15th-century *palazzo*. Displayed here are many of the Italian masters of the pre-Renaissance era. The principal treasures are found on the second floor, where you'll contemplate the artistry of Duccio in the early salons. The gallery is rich in the art of the two Lorenzetti brothers, Ambrogio and Pietro, who painted in the 14th century. Ambrogio is represented by an *Annunciation* and a *Crucifix*. But one of his most celebrated works, carried out with consummate skill, is an almond-eyed Madonna and her bambino surrounded by saints and angels. Pietro's most important entry here is an altarpiece—*Madonna of the Carmine*—made for a church in Siena in the 1320s. There is also Simone Martini's *Madonna and Bambino,* damaged, but one of the most famous paintings in the entire collection. Admission is 4€ ($5.20). It's open Monday from 8:30am to 1:30pm; Tuesday to Saturday from 8:15am to 7:15pm; and Sunday from 8:15am to 1:15pm.

WHERE TO DINE

On Siena's most historic square stands **Al Mangia,** Piazza del Campo 43 (© 0577/281121), which serves seasonally adjusted menus of refined Tuscan and international cuisine, and offers outside tables opening onto the landmark town hall. In a building whose origins date from the 12th century, you are served artfully prepared food. The service and the cooking are first rate, with main courses costing 18.50€ to 26€ ($24.05–$33.80). It's open daily from noon to 3:30pm and 7 to 10pm.

Equally good is **Al Marsili,** Via del Castoro 3 (© 0577/47154), serving a Sienese and Italian cuisine in its atmospheric setting between the cathedral and Via di Città. Some of the best antipasti in town is offered here, and you get such unusual but tasty dishes as smoked venison or wild boar. Their risottos—such as one made with four different cheeses—are superb, as are the tender and well-flavored meat and poultry dishes. Main courses cost 8€ to 18€ ($10.40–$23.40). It's open Tuesday to Sunday 12:30 to 2:30pm and 7:30 to 10:30pm.

5 Venice & the Northeast

Venice is a fairy-tale city of islands and gondolas, where the canals are lined with wedding cake palaces. The "Serene Republic" of Venice had a turbulent and fascinating history. As Attila the Hun swept through 5th-century Italy toward trembling Rome, he spread proverbial death and destruction in his path. Attila was on his way to claim the emperor's stepsister, Honoria, as his "bride," and though his ultimate sack of Rome was averted, the swath of desolation he left in his wake was real enough. One particularly unfortunate town was razed to the ground, and its terrified inhabitants fled into the marshes on the shores of the Adriatic. The political climate of the times was so insecure that the population deemed it wisest to remain in the swamps and build their houses on stilts in the water, and so Venice got her start.

The Venice we know today is from a much later era though, an era rich with the accumulated spoils of Crusaders and merchantmen. The wizardlike rulers of Renaissance

Venice shrewdly—sometimes unscrupulously—parlayed Venice into mistress of the Adriatic, and the many monuments and palaces erected in those days attest to the profit inherent in such a position.

The city is an excellent rail destination, though you'll naturally have to take to the water once you get to the city proper. Venice is easily reached by train from all parts of Italy (it's the northeast rail hub for Italy) and several other European countries. And rail travelers actually have the easiest time getting into the city, as the main railway station on Piazzale Roma is right in the thick of things.

STATION INFORMATION

GETTING FROM THE AIRPORT TO THE TRAIN STATION

You can fly nonstop from North America to Venice on Delta. You'll land at the **Aeroporto Marco Polo** (© 041/2606111) at Mestre, north of the city on the mainland. The **Consorzio Motoscafi** (© 041/5222303) operates a *motoscafo* (shuttle boat) service that can deliver you from the airport directly to the center of Venice at Piazza San Marco in about 30 minutes. The boats wait just outside the main entrance, and the fare begins at 80€ ($104) for up to six passengers (if there are only two of you, find some fellow travelers to share the ride and split the fare with you). If you've got some extra euros to spend, you can arrange for a **private water taxi** by calling © 041/5415084. The cost of the ride to the heart of Venice is 80€ ($104).

Buses from the airport are less expensive, though they can only take you as far as Piazzale Roma; from here you will need to take a vaporetto to reach your hotel. The **Azienda Trasporti Veneto Orientale** (© 0421/383671) shuttle bus links the airport with Piazzale Roma (where the main train station is located) for 3€ ($3.90). The trip takes about half an hour, and departures are about every 30 minutes daily 8:20am to 8:40pm. Even cheaper is a local bus company, **ACTV** (© 041/2424), whose bus no. 5 makes the run for 1€ ($1.30). The ACTV buses depart every half hour and take about 20 minutes to reach Piazzale Roma.

INSIDE THE STATION

Trains pull into the **Stazione di Santa Lucia,** at Piazzale Roma, from Rome (trip time: 5¼ hr.), Milan (3½ hr.), Florence (4 hr.), and Bologna (2 hr.). For information and timetables, contact **FS** (© 892021; www.trenitalia.it) or Rail Europe. The best and least expensive way to get from the station to the rest of town is to take a vaporetto, which departs near the main entrance to the station.

The station has all the expected amenities, including a currency exchange desk, luggage storage, restaurants, and ATMs. The vaporetto departs near the station's main entrance.

A **tourist office** (© 041/5298711), located just off the station's main hall, dispenses information and maps but does not make hotel reservations. It's open 8am to 6:30pm daily.

Anyone between the ages of 14 and 29 is eligible for a **Rolling Venice pass,** entitling you to discounts for museums, restaurants, stores, language courses, hotels, and bars. Valid for 1 year, it costs 4€ ($5.20) and can be picked up at a special Rolling Venice office set up in the train station during summer.

INFORMATION ELSEWHERE IN THE CITY

From spring to autumn hotel reservations in overcrowded Venice should be made as far in advance as possible, either through a travel agent or independently. The tourist office (see above) does not make reservations. **Azienda di Promozione Turistica,** San

Venice

Marco 71F (© **041/5298711**), is open daily 9am to 3:30pm. Posters around town with exhibit and concert schedules are more helpful. Ask for a schedule of the month's special events and an updated list of museum and church hours because these can change erratically and often.

GETTING AROUND

BY VAPORETTO   Much to the chagrin of the once-ubiquitous gondoliers, Venice's **motorboats** *(vaporetti)* provide inexpensive and frequent, if not always fast, transportation in this canal city. The vaporetti are called "water buses," and they are indeed the "buses" of Venice because traveling by water is usually faster than traveling by land. The service is operated by **ACTV (Azienda del Consorzio Trasporti Veneziano)**, Cannaregio 3935 (© **041/2424**). An *accelerato* is a vessel that makes every stop; a *diretto* makes only express stops. The average fare is 3.50€ ($4.55). ACTV also sells a ticket valid for 1 hour on all vaporetti, costing 6€ ($7.80). Tickets can be bought on board. Note that, in summer, the vaporetti are often fiercely crowded. Pick up a map of the system at the tourist office. They run daily up and down the Grand Canal, with frequent service 7am to midnight and then hourly midnight to 7am. To save money you can buy a 24-hour ticket for 15€ ($19.50) or a 3-day ticket for 30€ ($39).

BY MOTOR LAUNCH (WATER TAXI)   Motor launches *(taxi acquei)* cost more than public vaporetti, but you won't be hassled as much when you arrive with your luggage if you hire one of the many private ones. You might or might not have the cabin of one of these sleek vessels to yourself because the captains fill their boats with as many passengers as the law allows before taking off. Your porter's uncanny radar will guide you to one of the inconspicuous piers where a water taxi waits. The price of a transit by water taxi from the train station to Piazza San Marco begins at 60€ ($78) for up to four passengers. The captains adroitly deliver you, with luggage, to the canal-side entrance of your hotel or on one of the smaller waterways within a short walking distance of your destination. You can also call for a water taxi; try the **Consorzio Motoscafi** at © **041/5222303.**

WHERE TO STAY

Hotel Abbazia   The benefit of staying here is that there's no need to transfer to any vaporetto—you can walk here from the rail station, about 10 minutes away. This hotel was built in 1879 as a monastery for barefooted Carmelite monks, who established a verdant garden in what's now the courtyard; it's planted with subtropical plants that thrive, sheltered as they are from the cold Adriatic winds. You'll find a highly accommodating staff and comfortable but very plain guest rooms with well-kept bathrooms. Twenty rooms overlook the courtyard, ensuring quiet in an otherwise noisy neighborhood.

Calle Priuli ai Cavaletti, Cannaregio 68, 30121 Venezia. © **041/717333.** Fax 041/717949. www.abbaziahotel.com. 50 units. 90€–250€ ($117–$325) double; 200€–300€ ($260–$390) junior suite. Rates include buffet breakfast. AE, DC, MC, V. Vaporetto: Ferrovia. **Amenities:** Nonsmoking rooms. *In room:* Hair dryer.

Hotel ai do Mori *Value*   Since Venice is one of the globe's most expensive cities, many visitors put up with some inconveniences to stay at this affordable choice in the central tourist zone near Piazza San Marco. The town house dates from the mid–15th century, and you'll have to balance your need for space with your desire for a view (and your willingness to climb stairs because there's no elevator): The lower-level rooms are larger but don't have views; the third- and fourth-floor rooms are cramped but have sweeping views over the basilica's domes. Furnishings are in a simple modern style. In lieu of any food service here, numerous cafes and trattorie lie outside your door.

Calle Larga San Marco, San Marco 658, 30124 Venezia. ℂ 041/5204817. Fax 041/5205328. www.hotelaidomori. com. 11 units, 9 with bathroom. 60€–90€ ($78–$117) double without bathroom; 80€–140€ ($104–$182) double with bathroom. MC, V. Vaporetto: San Marco. **Amenities:** All nonsmoking rooms. *In room:* Hair dryer.

Hotel Bernardi-Semenzato

This remains a budget favorite north of the Ponte Rialto. It doesn't please everyone, and it's hardly state of the art in spite of renovations; but it's an affordable option in a ridiculously expensive city. The facade looks a little battered, but there is comfort to be found inside. Guests are housed in the main building, with lots of hand-hewn ceiling beams exposed, or else in an annex 3 blocks away. If you're given a room in the annex, you're not being sentenced to some Venetian Siberia; it evokes a Venetian nobleman's apartment. Bedrooms are tastefully furnished, with retiled bathrooms. Murano chandeliers and parquet floors add Venetian grace notes.

Calle de l'Oca, Cannaregio 4366, 30121 Venezia. ℂ **041/5227257.** Fax 041/5222424. www.hotelbernardi.com. 26 units. 95€–105€ ($124–$137) double. AE, MC, V. Rates include breakfast. Vaporetto: Ca' D'Oro. **Amenities:** Nonsmoking rooms.

Hotel do Pozzi ⓐ

This antique building, just a short walk from Piazza San Marco and its basilica, feels more like a country tavern than a hotel. It's more than 2 centuries old but has been modernized and brought up-to-date. The hotel is really old Venice, with lots of atmosphere, and in summer breakfast is served out on a characteristic little square surrounded by flowers. Antiques are mixed with functional modern furniture in the small to midsize bedrooms, some of which have showers in the bathrooms, others with tub and shower.

Corte do Pozzi, San Marco 2373, 30124 Venezia. ℂ **041/5207855.** Fax 041/5229413. www.hoteldopozzi.it. 35 units. 130€–280€ ($169–$364) double. Rates include breakfast. AE, DC, MC, V. Vaporetto: Santa Maria del Giglio. **Amenities:** Bar; laundry service; nonsmoking rooms. *In room:* Hair dryer.

Hotel Marconi

Just 50 feet (15m) from the Rialto Bridge, this old relic is still going strong though its heyday was in the 1930s. When Venice is in high season and overcrowded, it's very expensive—otherwise, it's one of the bargains in town. The building itself was constructed at the beginning of the 16th century, and the drawing room still evokes that era. The four most desirable rooms (and the most expensive) open onto dramatic views of the Grand Canal. Bedrooms range from small to midsize, each with a tiled shower-only bathroom. Sidewalk tables are placed outside in fair weather to take in a lovely view of the Grand Canal.

Riva del Vin, San Polo 729, 30125 Venezia. ℂ **041/5222068.** Fax 041/5229700. www.hotelmarconi.it. 26 units. 119€–450€ ($155–$585) double; 149€–320€ ($194–$416) triple. Rates include breakfast. AE, DC, MC, V. Vaporetto: Rialto. **Amenities:** Laundry; all nonsmoking rooms. *In room:* Hair dryer.

Hotel Montecarlo

Just a 2-minute walk from Piazza San Marco, this Best Western hotel is installed in a much-upgraded 17th-century town house. The owners have given it Venetian flair, lining its upper halls with the work of some of the city's most outstanding old masters and decorating the small guest rooms with Venetian-styled antique reproductions and glass chandeliers from the neighboring island of Murano. Some are quite dark, the curse of many Venetian hotels. All have well-kept bathrooms.

Calle dei Specchieri, San Marco 463, 30124 Venezia. ℂ **800/780-7234** in the U.S. and Canada, or 041/5207144. Fax 041/5207789. www.venicehotelmontecarlo.com. 48 units. 185€–350€ ($241–$455) double. Children 12 and under stay free in parent's room. Rates include buffet breakfast. AE, DC, MC, V. Vaporetto: San Marco. **Amenities:** Restaurant; bar; laundry; nonsmoking rooms. *In room:* Hair dryer.

Hotel San Cassiano Ca'Favretto ⓐ

San Cassiano Ca'Favretto was once the studio of 19th-century painter Giacomo Favretto. The views from the hotel's gondola pier and from the dining room's porch encompass the lacy facade of the Ca' d'Oro. The hotel was constructed in the 14th century as a palace, and many of its architectural details, including 20-foot (6m) ceilings, have been retained. There's no elevator, but the Murano chandeliers, the rooms filled with antique reproductions, the 18th-century stucco work in the breakfast room, and a wood-beamed bar with a canal view do much to compensate.

Calle della Rosa, Santa Croce 2232, 30135 Venezia. ⓒ **041/5241768.** Fax 041/721033. www.sancassiano.it. 35 units. 130€–450€ ($169–$585) double. Rates include breakfast. AE, DC, MC, V. Vaporetto: San Stae. **Amenities:** Bar; laundry; rooms for those w/limited mobility; nonsmoking rooms. *In room:* Hair dryer.

Hotel Savoia & Jolanda ⓕ   Better-heeled rail passengers seeking a taste of the Venetian luxury for which the city is renowned, will find solace in this hotel, just a few minutes walk from Piazza San Marco right off a Venetian lagoon. It's truly a special place for lodgings and very romantic. Try for one of the midsize and well-furnished guest rooms opening onto a view of the lagoon. Well-chosen fabrics, paintings, and Venetian glass from the island of Murano add to the luster of the hotel, as do the old wooden beams and the flower-decked terraces. The suites have panoramic balconies and terraces.

Riva degli Schiavoni, Castello 4187, 30122 Venezia. ⓒ **041/5206644.** Fax 041/5207494. www.hotelsavoiajolanda. com. 51 units. 208€–422€ ($270–$549) double; from 350€ ($455) suite. Rates include buffet breakfast. AE, DC, MC, V. Vaporetto: San Zaccaria. **Amenities:** Restaurant; laundry. *In room:* Hair dryer.

La Residenza ⓕⓕ   One of our all-time favorite nests in Venice occupies a 14th-century palazzo overlooking an evocative square of old Venice a few steps from Piazza San Marco. The legend and lore of old Venice is kept alive in this palace, which has also been kept abreast of the times. Bedrooms are spacious and well furnished with stylistic Venetian reproductions, contemporary pieces, and small shower-only bathrooms. There's no elevator, so be prepared. Because the address is known by some of the world's most discerning hotel shoppers, book well in advance if arriving in season.

Campo Bandiera e Moro, Castello 3608, 30122 Venezia. ⓒ **041/5285315.** Fax 041/5238859. www.venicelaresidenza. com. 15 units. 80€–180€ ($104–$234) double. Rates include breakfast. MC, V. Vaporetto: Arsenale. **Amenities:** Nonsmoking rooms.

TOP ATTRACTIONS & SPECIAL MOMENTS

You really need 2 to 3 days to properly take in the city, but if you have only 1 day, be sure to watch the sun rise over **Piazzetta San Marco** ⓕ. Adjacent to the Palace of the Doges is this landmark little square, noted for its fabulous statue of the winged lion of St. Mark. It stands atop a granite column (which was also ripped off from Constantinople), and is flanked by a similar column, on whose capital stands St. Theodore, former patron of Venice until he was supplanted by St. Mark.

In what has been called the "antechamber" of Venice, you have the best view of the southern facade of St. Mark's Basilica. Imbedded in the facade is a *Virgin and Bambino* in mosaics, honoring a poor baker—that is, Pietro Fasiol, who was unjustly accused and executed on a false charge of murder. At the left of the entrance to the Palace of the Doges stands a world-famous collection of four porphyry figures called *The Moors*. Naturally puce colored, they are huddled together in fear.

Ca' d'Oro ⓕⓕⓕ   The grandest setting for any art gallery is Ca' d'Oro, formerly a private palace, donated to the Italian state after the First World War by the owner, Baron Franchetti. The collection ranges from Van Dyck to Carpaccio, and the lush appointments of the palace itself compete with the works of art on the walls.

The "House of Gold" was so named because it was once gilded (imagine what that would cost today). Today the pink-and-white stone exterior has a lacy Gothic look, making it almost appear like a candy box. Opposite the entrance door you can go into a salon to see Titian's voluptuous *Venus*. The masterpiece on this floor is Andrea Mantegna's *St. Sebastian*. Another equally renowned work of art is Anthony Van Dyck's *Portrait of a Gentleman*. At some point you emerge onto a loggia where you can enjoy a panoramic view of the Grand Canal.

Cannaregio 3931–3932. © **041/5238790**. Admission 5€ ($6.50). Mon 8am–2pm; Tues–Sun 8:15am–7:15pm. Closed Jan 1, May 1, and Dec 25. Vaporetto: Ca' d'Oro.

Campanile di San Marco ✹✹
The bell tower of St. Mark's Basilica is a reconstruction of the original, which dramatically collapsed into the Piazza in the summer of 1902. No one was hurt because the night before the fall the tower had emitted a telltale groan that sent everyone within earshot racing to safety. It collapsed the next day when the populace was kept at a safe distance. The Venetians rebuilt their belfry, and it's now safe to ascend. A modern elevator takes you up for a splendid view of the city.

Piazza San Marco. © **041/5224064**. Admission 6€ ($7.80). Nov–Mar daily 9:30am–4:15pm; Apr–June, Sept–Oct daily 9am–7pm; July–Aug 9am–9pm. Closed Jan 7–31. Vaporetto: San Marco.

Ca' Rezzonico ✹✹
At this 17th- and 18th-century palace along the Grand Canal, Robert Browning lived as a widower in rooms once occupied by Clement XII. Nowadays, it's a museum of baroque furnishings and paintings. A **Throne Room** contains an allegorical ceiling by Tiepolo. Here are all the rich props that characterized Venice in the 18th century, including ebony blacks carrying torches, elaborate chandeliers, gilded furniture, and the inevitable chinoiserie. The best paintings are by Pietro Longhi, including his well-known work, *The Lady and the Hairdresser*. Majolica and Venetian costumes are exhibited on the top floor.

Fondamenta Rezzonico, Dorsoduro 3136. © **041/2410100**. Admission 6.50€ ($8.45) adults. Nov–Mar Wed–Mon 10am–5pm; Apr–Oct Wed–Mon 10am–6pm. Vaporetto: Ca' Rezzonico.

Collezione Peggy Guggenheim ✹✹✹
This is one of the most comprehensive and brilliant modern-art collections in the Western world, and it reveals the foresight and critical judgment of its founder. The collection is housed in an unfinished palazzo, the former home of Peggy Guggenheim. In the tradition of her family, Guggenheim was a lifelong patron of contemporary painters and sculptors. As her private collection increased, she decided to find a larger showcase and selected Venice. Displayed here are works not only by Pollock and Ernst but also by Picasso (see his cubist *The Poet* of 1911), Duchamp, Chagall, Mondrian, Brancusi, Delvaux, and Dalí, plus a garden of modern sculpture that includes works by Giacometti.

In the Palazzo Venier dei Leoni, Calle Venier dei Leoni, Dorsoduro 701. © **041/2405411**. Admission 10€ ($13); 5€ ($6.50) for children and students. Free for children under 10. Wed–Mon 10am–6pm. Vaporetto: Accademia.

Ducale Palace & Bridge of Sighs (Palazzo Ducale & Ponte dei Sospiri) ✹✹✹
This Venetian landmark is around the corner from the Basilica of St. Mark. It is a 16th-century reconstruction of the original 14th-century palace, which had been gutted by a great fire. Here sat the Council of Ten, that rather arbitrary administrative body of Renaissance Venice that meted out justice at the height of the republic. Justice was unfortunately characterized largely by torture and execution, and not always for the best of reasons. The room in which the old men sat is a great gloomy chamber, decorated with somber oil paintings, and reached via an antechamber with a lion's

mouth, into which letters of accusation were dropped. The famous resident of the place was the Doge himself, whose private apartments are aglow with frescoed walls and ceilings with magnificent paintings.

Dungeons are connected to the palace by the Bridge of Sighs or **Ponte dei Sospiri** 𝕬𝕬. The bridge was named because of the sad laments of the prisoners led across to torture and even death. Casanova was imprisoned here in 1775, but he managed to escape.

Piazzetta San Marco. ℂ 041/2715911. Admission 12€ ($15.60) adults. Apr–Oct daily 9am–7pm; Nov–Mar daily 9am–5pm. Vaporetto: San Marco.

Galleria dell'Accademia 𝕬𝕬𝕬 The pomp and circumstance, the glory that was Venice, lives on in this remarkable collection of paintings spanning the 14th century to the 18th century. The hallmark of the Venetian school is color and more color. From Giorgione to Veronese, from Titian to Tintoretto, with a Carpaccio cycle thrown in, the Accademia has samples—often their best—of its most famous sons.

You'll first see works by such 14th-century artists as Paolo and Lorenzo Veneziano, who bridged the gap from Byzantine art to Gothic (see the latter's *Annunciation*). Next, you'll view Giovanni Bellini's *Madonna and Saint* (poor Sebastian, not another arrow), and Carpaccio's fascinating yet gruesome work of mass crucifixion. Two of the most important works with secular themes are Mantegna's armored *St. George,* with the dragon slain at his feet, and Hans Memling's 15th-century portrait of a young man. Giorgione's *Tempest* is the most famous painting at the Accademia. Lastly, seek out the cycle of narrative paintings that Vittore Carpaccio did of St. Ursula.

Campo della Carità, Dorsoduro. ℂ 041/5222247. Admission 6.50€ ($8.45). Mon 8:15am–2pm; Tues–Sun 8:15am–7:15pm. Vaporetto: Accademia.

Museo Civico Correr 𝕬𝕬 This museum traces the development of Venetian painting from the 14th century to the 16th century. On the second floor are the red and maroon robes once worn by the doges, plus some fabulous street lanterns. There's also an illustrated copy of *Marco Polo in Tartaria.* You can see Cosmé Tura's *La Pietà,* a miniature of renown from the genius in the Ferrara School. This is one of his more gruesome works, depicting a bony, gnarled Christ sprawled on the lap of the Madonna. Farther on, search out a Schiavone *Madonna and Child* (no. 545), our candidate for ugliest bambino ever depicted on canvas (no wonder the mother looks askance). One of the most important rooms at the Correr is filled with three masterpieces: Antonello da Messina's *Pietà,* Hugo van der Goes's *Crucifixion,* and Dieric Bouts's *Madonna and Child.* The star attraction of the Correr is the Bellini salon, which includes works by

---

(Moments **A Ride along the Grand Canal**

The main street of town is the **Grand Canal** 𝕬𝕬𝕬, thronged with gondolas and *vaporetti* (those motorized boat-buses), spanned by graceful bridges and lined with palaces. Many of those palaces house fabulous museums, with collections encompassing art from the Renaissance to the present.

The best way to see the Grand Canal is to board vaporetto no. 1 (push and shove until you secure a seat at the front of the vessel). Settle yourself in, make sure that you have your long-distance viewing glasses, and prepare yourself for a view that can thrill even the most experienced world traveler.

Moments A Ride in a Gondola

In *Death in Venice,* Thomas Mann wrote: "Is there anyone but must repress a secret thrill, on arriving in Venice for the first time—or returning thither after long absence—and stepping into a Venetian gondola? That singular conveyance, come down unchanged from ballad times, black as nothing else on earth except a coffin—what pictures it calls up of lawless, silent adventures in the plashing night; or even more, what visions of death itself, the bier and solemn rites and last soundless voyage!"

Mann reflected the point of view of German romanticism, but he didn't tell the whole story. The voyage on a gondola isn't likely to be so soundless—at least not when the time comes to pay the bill. When riding in a gondola, two major agreements have to be reached—one, the price of the ride; two, the length of the trip.

The official rate is 62€ ($80.60) per hour, but we've never known anyone to honor it. The actual fare depends on how well you stand up to the gondolier, *beginning* at 100€ ($130) for up to 50 minutes. Most gondoliers will ask at least double the official rate and reduce your trip to 30 to 40 minutes or even less. Prices go up after 8pm. Two major stations where you can hire gondolas are **Piazza San Marco** (© 041/5200685) and **Ponte di Rialto** (© 041/5224904).

founding padre Jacopo and his son, Gentile. But the real master of the household was the other son, Giovanni, the major painter of the 15th-century Venetian school (see his *Crucifixion* and compare it with his father's treatment of the same subject).

In the Procuratie Nuove, Piazza San Marco. © 041/2405211. Admission (including admission to the Ducale Palace, above) 12€ ($15.60). Apr–Oct daily 9am–7pm; Nov–Mar daily 9am–5pm. Vaporetto: San Marco.

Scuola di San Giorgio degli Schiavoni ⟨★★⟩

At St. Antonino Bridge (Fondamenta dei Furlani), off the Riva degli Schiavoni, is the second important school to visit in Venice. Between 1507 and 1509, Vittore Carpaccio painted a pictorial cycle here of exceptional merit and interest. Of enduring fame are his works of *St. George and the Dragon* ⟨★★⟩, our favorite art in Venice—certainly the most delightful. In one frame, St. George charges the dragon on a field littered with half-eaten bodies and skulls. Gruesome? Not at all. Any moment you expect the director to call "Cut!"

Calle dei Furiani, Castello. © 041/5228828. Admission 3€ ($3.90). Nov–Mar Tues–Sat 10am–12:30pm and 3–6pm, Sun 10am–12:30pm; Apr–Oct Tues–Sat 9:30am–12:30pm and 3:30–6:30pm, Sun 9:30am–12:30pm. Last entrance 20 min. before closing. Vaporetto: San Zaccaria.

Scuola di San Rocco ⟨★★★⟩

This dark, early-16th-century "school" was richly decorated by the great Tintoretto. *Scuole* were Venetian institutions throughout the various quarters in which the patricians met. The best-known one is San Rocco, in which Tintoretto won a commission to do 56 canvases, a task that took 18 years. Paintings cover the Upper and Lower Halls, including the well-known *Flight into Egypt.* The school owns Tintoretto's masterpiece, his huge *Crucifixion.* Other scenes also illustrate episodes from the life of Christ.

Campo San Rocco, San Polo. ✆ **041/5234864**. Admission 7€ ($9.10) adults, free for children up to 18 years old. Mar 28–Nov 2 daily 9am–5:30pm; Nov 3–Mar 27 daily 10am–5pm. Closed Easter and Dec 25–Jan 1. Ticket office closes 30 min. before last entrance. Vaporetto: San Tomà.

St. Mark's Basilica (Basilica di San Marco) ✿✿✿ Dominating Piazza San Marco is the **Basilica of St. Mark,** named for the patron saint of the city, whose body was carried here from Alexandria in A.D. 828. It is called the "Church of Gold" and is one of the most fabulously embellished structures in Europe. A great central dome and satellite cupolas form the silhouette, and inside is a profusion of mosaics depicting biblical scenes.

The **Presbytery** is said to contain the sarcophagus of St. Mark under a green marble "blanket." Here you'll find the ***Pala d'Oro*** ✿✿✿, a fabulous altar screen made of beaten gold and liberally encrusted with diamonds, rubies, emeralds, and pearls. You're also admitted to the **Treasury** ✿, filled with some of the loot the Crusaders brought back from Constantinople.

After leaving the basilica, head up the stairs in the atrium to the **Marciano Museum** and the **Loggia dei Cavalli.** The star of the museum is the world-famous ***Triumphal Quadriga*** ✿✿, four horses looted from Constantinople by Venetian crusaders during the sack of that city in 1204. These horses once surmounted the basilica but were removed because of pollution damage and were subsequently restored. The museum, with its mosaics and tapestries, is especially interesting, but also be sure to walk out onto the loggia for a view of Piazza San Marco.

Piazza San Marco. ✆ **041/5225205**. Basilica free; treasury 2€ ($2.60); presbytery 1.50€ ($1.95); Marciano Museum 3€ ($3.90). Basilica and presbytery May–Sept Mon–Sat 9:30am–4:30pm, Sun 2–5:30pm; Oct–Apr Mon–Sat 10am–4:30pm, Sun 2–4pm. Treasury Mon–Sat 9:30am–5pm; Sun 2–5pm. Marciano Museum Apr–Oct Mon–Sat 10am–5pm, Sun 2–4pm; Nov–Mar Mon–Sat 10am–4pm, Sun 2–4pm. Vaporetto: San Marco.

WHERE TO DINE

Al Covo ✿✿ VENETIAN/SEAFOOD   Al Covo has a special charm because of its atmospheric setting, sophisticated service, and the fine cooking of Cesare Benelli and his Texas-born wife, Diane. Look for a reinvention of a medieval version of fish soup, potato gnocchi flavored with local whitefish, seafood ravioli, linguine blended with zucchini and fresh peas, and delicious fritto misto with scampi, squid, a bewildering array of fish, and deep-fried vegetables such as zucchini flowers. Al Covo prides itself on not having any freezers, guaranteeing that all food is prepared fresh every day.

Campiello della Pescaria, Castello 3968. ✆ **041/5223812**. Reservations recommended for dinner. All main courses 15€–38€ ($19.50–$49.40); tasting menu 68€ ($88.40). MC, V. Fri–Tues 12:45–2:15pm and 7:45–10pm. Vaporetto: Arsenale.

Al Mascaron VENETIAN   Crowd into one of the three loud, boisterous dining rooms, where you'll probably be directed to sit next to a stranger at a long trestle table. The waiters will come by and slam down copious portions of fresh-cooked local specialties: deep-fried calamari, spaghetti with lobster, monkfish in a salt crust, pastas, savory risottos, and Venetian-style calves' liver (which locals prefer rather pink), plus the best seafood of the day made into salads. There's also a convivial bar, where locals drop in to spread the gossip of the day, play cards, and order vino and snacks.

Calle Lunga Santa Maria Formosa, Castello 5225. ✆ **041/5225995**. Reservations recommended. Main courses 13€–22€ ($16.90–$28.60). No credit cards. Mon–Sat noon–3pm and 7:30–11pm. Vaporetto: Rialto or San Marco.

Le Bistrot de Venise ✿ *finds* VENETIAN/FRENCH   Young artists and others flock to this local favorite, enjoying the change-of-pace fare—some recipes here have been handed down for generations and date from the 14th century. Many of the dishes have been all but forgotten, such as a soup made with rice flour, pomegranates, chicken, and slivered almonds. Of course, you can also order traditional and more familiar fare (especially fresh fish), and can virtually count on it being good.

Calle dei Fabbri, San Marco 4685. ✆ 041/5236651. Main courses 24€–28€ ($31.20–$36.40); fixed-price menus 40€–60€ ($52–$78). MC, V. Daily noon–3pm and 7pm–1am. Vaporetto: Rialto.

Osteria alle Testiere ✿ (Finds) VENETIAN/ITALIAN

A restaurant for the young at heart, this 24-seat trattoria seats you at tables covered with butcher paper and feeds you well at affordable prices. Beefed up by a wine list of some 100 selections, you can enjoy well-prepared dishes in a tavernlike setting. When you ask for a recipe here—the food is that good—you're often told it's a secret. The young couple we shared a table with claimed that they'd sampled everything on the menu and were coming back to start all over again.

Castello 5801 (on Calle del Mondo Novo). ✆ 041/5227220. Reservations required. Main courses 14€–21€ ($18.20–$27.30). MC, V. Tues–Sat noon–2pm and 7–10pm. Closed Aug and Dec 20–Jan 15. Vaporetto: San Marco or Rialto.

Ristorante Corte Sconta VENETIAN/SEAFOOD

This restaurant lies on a narrow alley, whose name is shared by at least three other streets in Venice (this particular one is near Campo Bandiere Moro and San Giovanni in Bragora). The modest restaurant's plain wooden tables are often filled with artists, writers, and filmmakers who come here for one of the biggest and most varied selection of freshly caught seafood in Venice. The fish is flawlessly fresh, including, for example, *gamberi*—tiny baby shrimp placed live on the grill.

Calle del Pestrin, Castello 3886. ✆ 041/5227024. Reservations required. Main courses 15€–30€ ($19.50–$39); fixed-price menus 65€ ($84.50). MC, V. Tues–Sat 12:30–2:30pm and 7:30–9:30pm. Closed Jan 7–Feb 7 and July 15–Aug 15. Vaporetto: Arsenale.

Ristorante da Raffaele ✿ ITALIAN/VENETIAN

One of our favorite canal-side restaurants, named for the famous artist, is a 5-minute stroll from Piazza San Marco. It's often overrun with tourists, though the veteran kitchen staff handles the onslaught well. Against an atmospheric backdrop of Old Venice (high-beamed ceilings, wrought iron chandeliers, and hundreds of copper pots), you can feast on such treats as deep-fried fish from the Adriatic, wonderful grilled meats, and the city's best bean soup.

Calle Larga XXII Marzo (Fondamenta delle Ostreghe), San Marco 2347. ✆ 041/5232317. Reservations recommended Sat–Sun. Main courses 13€–24€ ($16.90–$31.20). AE, DC, MC, V. Fri–Wed noon–3pm and 7–10:30pm. Closed Dec 10–Feb. Vaporetto: San Marco or Santa Maria del Giglio.

Ristorante Noemi VENETIAN

Since 1927, discerning Venetian foodies have been making their way to this simple trattoria for its friendly service, affordable midrange prices, and market-fresh ingredients. Some of its dishes are inspired by *nuova cucina,* but many rely on old-fashioned recipes known to everybody's mamma mia. The cooks are known for their infallible skill in the kitchen and marvelous fish dishes such as "black" spaghetti with cuttlefish in its own sauce or a filet of sole Casanova (a white wine sauce, fresh mushrooms, and Adriatic shrimp).

Calle dei Fabbri, San Marco 912. ✆ 041/5225238. Reservations recommended. Main courses 17€–25€ ($22.10–$32.50). AE, DC, MC, V. Tues–Sun 11:30am–midnight. Vaporetto: San Marco.

Trattroria da Fiore ✿ (Value) VENETIAN

This affordable place is an eagerly sought out address because of its take on really typical local cookery, including some of the best regional fare served in the Accademia area. The house specialty is *pennette all Fiore*, which is served with seven fresh vegetables in season, a hearty, filling pasta dish. If you have more room, you can taste some very fresh and well-prepared fish dishes from the Adriatic, including a savory kettle of fish soup.

Calle delle Botteghe, San Marco 3461. (©) 041/5235310. Reservations suggested. Pastas 10€–20€ ($13–$26); main courses 15€–35€ ($19.50–$45.50). MC, V. Wed–Mon noon–3pm and 7–10pm. Vaporetto: Accademia.

SHOPPING

There's virtually a shop—or shops—in every block, selling Venetian crafts, such as glass and lace, and oh, so much more. Most of the shopping is concentrated around **Piazza San Marco** or **Ponte Rialto.**

The best place to buy Carnevale masks is **Mondonovo,** Rio Terrà Canal, Dorsoduro 3063 (© **041/5287344**), where talented artisans labor to produce copies of both traditional and more modern masks, each of which is one-of-a-kind and richly nuanced with references to Venetian lore and traditions. Prices start at 25€ ($32.50) for a fairly basic model. The studio/shop **Bambole di Trilly,** Fondamenta dell'Osmarin, Castello 4974 (© **041/5212579**), offers dolls with meticulously painted porcelain faces (they call it a "biscuit") and hand-tailored costumes, including dressy pinafores. Prices begin at 15€ ($19.50) and reasonably priced dolls are made with the same painstaking care as the most expensive ones. Select outlets in Venice sell some of the greatest fabrics in the world. **Norelene,** Calle della Chiesa, Dorsoduro 727 (© **041/5237605**), features lustrous hand-printed silks, velvets, and cottons, plus wall hangings and clothing.

One of the oldest (founded in 1866) and largest purveyors of traditional Venetian glass is **Pauly & Co.,** Ponte Consorzi, San Marco 4392 (© **041/5209899**), with more than two dozen showrooms. Part of the premises is devoted to something akin to a museum, where past successes (now antiques) are displayed. Antique items are only rarely offered for sale; but they can be copied and shipped anywhere, and chandeliers can be electrified to match your standards. They begin at about 1,000€ ($1,300).

The art glass sold by **Venini,** Piazzetta Leoncini, San Marco 314 (© **041/5224045**), has caught the attention of collectors from all over the world. Its best-known glass has a distinctive swirl pattern in several colors, called a *venature.* This shop is known for the refined quality of its glass, some of which appears almost transparent. Much of it is very fragile, but the shop learned long ago how to ship it anywhere safely. To visit the furnace, call © **041/2737204.**

NIGHTLIFE

The tourist office distributes a free pamphlet (part in English, part in Italian), called *Un Ospite di Venezia.* A section of this useful publication lists events, including any music and opera or theatrical presentations, along with art exhibitions and local special events.

In January 1996, a dramatic fire left the fabled **Teatro de La Fenice** at Campo San Fantin, the city's main venue for performing arts, a blackened shell and a smoldering ruin. Opera lovers around the world, including the late Luciano Pavarotti, mourned its loss. The Italian government pledged $12.5 million for its reconstruction. **Teatro Le Fenice** *€€€* (© **041/786511;** www.teatrolafence.it), reopened on November 12, 2004, presenting *La Traviata* by Giuseppe Verdi. The total cost of the renovation came to $90 million. New seating gives the renovated concert hall a total of 1,076 seats, and the stage curtain was donated by Italian fashion designer Laura Biagiotti. Tickets and subscriptions can be purchased directly from the theater's box office open daily 10am to 6pm.

In olden days, wealthy Venetians were rowed down the Grand Canal while being serenaded by gondoliers. To date, no one has improved on that age-old but now very expensive custom. Strolling through St. Mark's Square, having a cup of espresso at one of the two famous cafes (see below) and listening to a band concert may be even better.

CAFES & BARS   Venice's most famous spot is **Caffè Florian,** Piazza San Marco, San Marco 56–59 (© **041/5205641**), built in 1720 and elaborately decorated with plush red banquettes, elaborate murals under glass, and Art Nouveau lighting. The Florian has hosted everyone from Casanova to Lord Byron and Goethe. Light lunch is served noon to 3pm, and an English tea is offered 3 to 6pm, when you can select from a choice of pastries, ice creams, and cakes. It's open Thursday to Tuesday 9:30am to midnight; it's closed the first week in December and the second week in January.

Its rival, **Quadri,** Piazza San Marco, San Marco 120–124 (© **041/5222105**), stands on the opposite side of the square from Florian's and is as elegantly decorated in antique style. It should be: It was founded in 1638. Wagner used to drop in for a drink when he was working on *Tristan und Isolde.* The bar was a favorite with the Austrians during their long-ago occupation. From April to October, it's open daily 9am to 1am; off-season hours are Tuesday to Sunday from 9am to midnight.

The single most famous of all the watering holes of Ernest Hemingway is **Harry's Bar,** Calle Vallaresso, San Marco 1323 (© **041/5285777**). Harry's is known for inventing its own drinks and exporting them around the world, and it's said that *carpaccio,* the delicate raw-beef dish, was invented here. Fans say that Harry's makes the best Bellini in the world, although many old-time visitors still prefer a vodka martini. Harry's Bar is now found around the world, but this is the original (the others are unauthorized knockoffs). Celebrities frequent the place during the various film and art festivals. Harry's is open daily 10:30am to 11pm.

The hippest cafe in Venice today is funky little **Cip's** ✿, on Isola della Giudecca within the Cipriani Hotel (© **041-5207744**). Pronounced *chips* (as in potato), this cafe with its summer terrace frames one of the grandest views of Piazza San Marco. If you arrive between May and August, ask for a Bellini, made from prosecco and white-peach purée. You can also order the best bitter chocolate gelato in Venice here. Cip's also serves terrific international and Venetian dishes. To reach the place, take the vaporetto to Zittelle.

CLUBS   Near the Accademia, **Il Piccolo Mondo,** Calle Contarini Corfu, Dorso-duro 1056A (© **041/5200371**), is open during the day but comes alive with dance music at night. The crowd is often young. It's open daily 10pm to 4am, but the action actually doesn't begin until after midnight. Cover, including the first drink, is 7€ ($9.10) Thursday and Friday, and 10€ ($13) Saturday. **Martini Scala Club,** Campo San Fantin, San Marco 1980 (© **041/5224121**), is an elegant restaurant with a piano bar (and a kitchen that stays open late). The piano bar gets going after 10pm and stays open until 3am (it's closed Tues–Wed at lunch).

AN EXCURSION TO PADUA

The most popular day trip out of Venice and a spot easily reached by rail, is the ancient university city of Padua, 25 miles (40km) west of Venice. Padua remains a major art center of the Venetia region. A university that grew to fame throughout Europe was founded here as early as 1222 (in time, Galileo and the Poet Tasso were to attend).

Padua itself is sometimes known as *La Città del Santo* (the city of the saint), the reference being to St. Anthony of Padua, who is buried at a basilica the city dedicated to him. *Il Santo* was an itinerant Franciscan monk (who is not to be confused with St. Anthony of Egypt, the monastic hermit who could resist all temptations of the Devil).

GETTING THERE Padua-bound trains depart for and arrive from Venice once every 30 minutes (trip time: about 30 min.), costing 8€ ($10.40) for a one-way ticket. For information and schedules, call *©* **892021.** Padua's main rail terminus is at the **Piazza Stazione,** north of the historic core and outside the 16th-century walls. Frequent buses run to the center from the station.

TOURIST INFORMATION The **Padua Tourist Office** is at Galleria Pedrocchi (*©* **049/8767927;** www.turismopadova.it), and open Monday to Saturday from 9:15am to 1:30pm and 3 to 7pm. Bus nos. 3, 8, and 12 run between the trains station and tourist office. The one-way fare is 1€ ($1.30). You can also go by taxi for around 10€ ($13).

TOP ATTRACTIONS & SPECIAL MOMENTS

Many visitors arrive just to visit **Cappella degli Scrovegni,** Piazza Eremitani 8, off Corso Garibaldi (*©* **049/2010020**), to see the celebrated *Giotto frescoes* 🏵🏵🏵. Sometime around 1305 and 1306, Giotto did a cycle of more than 35 (remarkably well-preserved) frescoes inside, which (along with those at Assisi) form the basis of his claim to fame. Like an illustrated storybook, the frescoes unfold Biblical scenes. The third bottom panel (lower level on the right) depicts Judas kissing a most skeptical Christ, perhaps the most reproduced and widely known panel in the cycle. On the entrance wall is Giotto's *Last Judgment,* with Hell winning out in sheer fascination. The chapel is open daily from 9am to 7pm, and charges an admission fee of 12€ ($15.60) for adults and 5€ ($6.50) for ages 6 to 17. The fee includes entrance to the nearby **Museo Civico di Padova** 🏵, Piazza Eremitani 8 (*©* **049/8204550**), open Tuesday to Sunday from 9am to 7pm. Of the museums sheltered in this building, the picture gallery is the most important—filled with minor works by major Venetian artists, dating from the 14th century.

The art world lost heavily on March 11, 1944, when Allied bombs rained down on **Chiesa degli Eremitani** 🏵, Piazza Eremitani 9 (*©* **049/8756410**). Before that time, it housed one of the greatest art treasures in Italy, the Ovetari Chapel frescoed by Andrea Mantegna. The cycle of frescoes was the first significant work by Mantegna (1431–1506). The church was rebuilt, but you can't resurrect 15th-century frescoes, of course. Inside, in the chapel to the right of the main altar, are fragments left after the bombing, a preview of what we missed in Mantegna's work. The most interesting fresco saved is a panel depicting the dragging of St. Christopher's body through the streets. Note also the *Assumption of the Virgin.* Mantegna is recommended even to those who don't like "religious painting." In the chancel chapel are some **splendid frescoes** 🏵🏵 attributed to Guarineto, a Venetian student of the great Giotto. The chapel is admission free and open Monday to Saturday from 8am to 12:30pm and 4 to 7pm; Sunday from 10am to 1pm and 4:30 to 7pm.

At Piazza del Santo, **Basilica di Sant'Antonio** 🏵🏵 (*©* **049/8242811**), dates from the 13th century when it was dedicated to St. Anthony of Padua interred inside. The basilica is a hodgepodge of styles, with mainly Romanesque and Gothic features. It has as many cupolas as Salome had veils. *Campanili* and minarets combine to give it a curious Eastern appearance. Inside, the **interior** 🏵🏵 is richly frescoed and decorated—and usually swarming with pilgrims devoutly ritualistic to the point of paganism, touching "holy" marble supposed to have divine power. The greatest art treasures are the **Donatello bronzes** 🕮🕮 at the main altar, with a realistic *Crucifix* (fluid, lyrical line) towering over the rest. Seek out, too, the Donatello relief depicting the removal of Christ from the cross, a unified composition expressing in simple lines the tragedy of Christ and the sadness of the mourners—an unromantic approach.

WHERE TO DINE

At some point, head for **Caffè Pedrocchi** 🕮, via VIII Febbraio 15 (© **049/8781231**), off Piazza Cavour in a neoclassical landmark hailed as the most elegant coffee house in Europe when it opened its doors in 1831. It's open Tuesday through Sunday from 8am to midnight.

For a special lunch, visit **Antico Brolo** 🕮🕮, Corso Milano 22 (© **049/664555**), across from the town's Civil Theater. Installed in a Renaissance-style dining room, with tables on its garden terrace, this restaurant serves the best food in town, a combination of the Veneto and Italian in general. Seasonal ingredients are used to shape the changing menu of classic dishes, many given a modern twist. Main courses cost 18.50€ to 33€ ($24.05–$42.90), and hours are Tuesday to Sunday from 12:30 to 2:30pm and 7:30 to 11pm.

AN EXCURSION TO VERONA

The fictional home of Shakespeare's "pair of star-cross'd lovers," Romeo and Juliet, Verona is 71 miles (114km) west of Venice. In the city's medieval "age of flowering" under the despotic, often cruel, Scaligeri princes, Verona reached the pinnacle of its influence and prestige, developing into a town that even today is among the great art cities of Italy. The best-known member of the ruling Della Scala family, Can Grande I, was a patron of Dante. His sway over Verona has often been compared to that of Lorenzo the Magnificent over Florence.

GETTING THERE A total of 34 trains a day make the 2-hour run between Venice and Verona, charging 13.50€ ($17.55) for a one-way ticket. From Milan and points west, some 40 trains a day make the 2-hour journey to Verona. Tickets cost 14.50€ ($18.85) one-way. Four daily trains come up from Rome, the 5-hour journey costing 40€ ($52) one-way.

Trains arrive at Verona's **Stazione Porta Nuova,** Piazza XXV Aprile, south of the centrally located arena and Piazza Brà; call © **892021** for schedules and information. A branch of the **Verona Tourist Office** (© **045/8000861**) is located at the rail station. It's open in summer Monday to Saturday from 9am to 6pm and Sunday 9am to 3pm.

TOURIST INFORMATION The **Verona Tourist Office** is at Via Degli Alpini 9, at Piazza Brà (© **045/8068680**). It's open Monday to Saturday from 9am to 7pm. Off-season hours are Monday to Saturday 8am to 2pm. The tourist office and its railway branch don't make hotel reservations.

TOP ATTRACTIONS & SPECIAL MOMENTS

The most famous and most beautiful square in Verona is **Piazza dei Signori** 🕮🕮, dominated by the Palazzo del Governo, where Can Grande extended the shelter of his "hearth and home" to that fleeing Ghibelline, Dante Alighieri. The marble statue in the center of the square is of the "divine poet." Facing Dante's back is the later 15th-century **Loggia del Consiglio,** surmounted by five statues. The most attractive building on the square, the loggia is frescoed. Five different arches lead into the Piazza dei Signori, the innermost chamber of the heart of Verona.

The **Arche Scaligere** are outdoor tombs surrounded by wrought-iron gates that form a kind of open-air pantheon of the Scaligeri princes. One tomb, that of Cangrande della Scala, rests directly over the door of the 12th-century **Santa Maria Antica.**

Basilica San Zeno Maggiore *ᏭᏭ*, Piazza San Zeno (© **045/8006120**), is a near-perfect Romanesque church and *campanile,* graced with a stunning entrance—two pillars supported by puce-colored marble lions and surmounted with a rose window. On either side of the portal are bas-reliefs depicting scenes from the Old and New Testaments, as well as a mythological story portraying Theodoric as a huntsman lured to hell (the king of the Goths defeated Odoacer in Verona). The panels—nearly 50 in all—on the bronze doors are truly a remarkable achievement of primitive art, sculpted perhaps in the 12th century. Admission is 2€ ($2.60), and hours are Monday to Saturday from 8:30am to 6pm, and Sunday 1 to 6pm. It's closed Monday from noon to 3pm.

Arena di Verona *ᏭᏭ*, Piazza Brà (© **045/8003204**), evoking the Colosseum in Rome, is an elliptically shaped amphitheatre dating from the 1st century A.D. Four arches of the "outer circle" and a complete "inner ring" still stand, which is rather remarkable because an earthquake hit this area in the 12th century. For nearly half a century, it's been the setting of a summer opera house, usually from mid-July to mid-August. More than 20,000 people are treated to, say, Verdi, Mascagni, or a performance of *Aïda,* the latter considered by some to be "the greatest operatic spectacle in the world." Admission is 4€ ($5.20). It's open Tuesday to Sunday from 8:30am to 7:30pm (on performance days 9am–3pm), Monday 2 to 7:30pm.

The 14th-century **Castelvecchio (Old Castle)** *ᏭᏭ*, Corso Castelvecchio 2 (© **045/8062611**), is situated alongside the Adige River (and reached by heading out the Via Roma). It stands near the Ponte Scaligera, the famous bridge bombed by the Nazis in World War II and subsequently reconstructed. The former seat of the Della Scala family, the restored castle has now been turned into an **Art Museum,** with important paintings from the Veronese school. Admission is 4€ ($5.20), and hours are Monday 1:30 to 7:30pm, Tuesday to Sunday 8:30am to 7:30pm.

WHERE TO DINE

While not the gourmet citadel of Italy, Verona is blessed with a series of good restaurants, notably **Ristorante 12 Apostoli** *ᏭᏭ*, Vicolo Corticella San Marco 3 (© **045/596999**), which, at 250 years old, is the city's oldest. The present owners, the Gioco brothers, keep it humming with Giorgio being the culinary whiz in the kitchen and Franco welcoming you to the table. This is Italian cookery with a flair prepared with market-fresh ingredients; main courses cost 13€ to 22€ ($16.90–$28.60). Open Tuesday to Sunday 12:30 to 2:30pm and Tuesday to Saturday 7 to 10pm. Closed the first week in January and June 15 to July 5.

Another choice, almost as good, is **Ristorante Re Teodorico** *Ᏼ*, Piazzale Castel San Pietro 1 (© **045/8349990**), serving a finely honed regional and international cuisine at a site on the edge of town, opening onto vistas of Verona and the Adige. At a table under an arbor, you can partake of some of the finest and most imaginative dishes in Verona, featuring the freshest of fish and meat dishes, with main courses costing 16€ to 25€ ($20.80–$32.50). It's open Thursday to Tuesday (closed Sun night) from noon to 3pm and 7 to 10pm. It's closed January.

Rewriting its Italian and international menu every 6 months, **Brunello Lounge,** in the Due Torri Hotel Baglioni, Piazza Sant'Anastasia 4 (© **045/595044**), serves impeccably fresh ingredients fashioned into a series of palate-pleasing dishes that transcend the ordinary. Spicings and flavorings are subtle, and sometimes seemingly ill-matched ingredients are cooked into harmonious platters of delight. Main courses cost 16€ to 18.50€ ($20.80–$24.05), and hours are Monday to Saturday from 12:30 to 2:30pm and 7 to 10:30pm.

6 Milan & the Northwest

Busy Milan is a commercial powerhouse and, partly because of its banks and major industrial companies, Italy's most influential city. It's the center of publishing, silk production, TV and advertising, and fashion design; it's also close to Italy's densest collection of automobile-assembly plants, rubber and textile factories, and chemical plants. The industry and prosperity of the capital of the Lombardy region, has imbued it with a 21st-century commercial atmosphere unlike Italy's other large cities, where the past is so tangible.

The city's commercialism, combined with World War II bombings, have spared very few of the city's oldest buildings, but those that do remain are definitely worth visiting. And Milan also boasts La Scala, one of Europe's most prestigious opera houses.

For the rail traveler, Milan is an ideal stopover during a grand tour of Europe, as several of Europe's most strategic rail lines converge here and most international trains heading into Italy stop in the city. It's also home to one of the major airports welcoming arriving traffic from North America, so many people start off their Italian rail journeys in this metropolis. From Milan, you can make connections (many of them high speed) to all of the major cities in Italy. Though we rank this the fourth-best city in the Italian scheme of things, Milan is definitely the busiest and best of Italy's rail hubs.

STATION INFORMATION
GETTING FROM THE AIRPORT TO THE TRAIN STATION
Milan has two airports: **Aeroporto di Linate,** 4¼ miles (7km) east of the inner city and the **Aeroporto Malpensa,** 31 miles (50km) northwest. Malpensa is used for most transatlantic flights, whereas Linate is used for flights within Italy and Europe. For general airport and flight information, call ✆ **02/74852200.**

Malpensa Express trains connect Malpensa airport with the minor rail station, Stazione Cadorna, in the center of Milan. The trip takes 40 minutes, and trains run every half hour daily from 5:50am to 9:50pm. A one-way fare costs 11€ ($14.30) for adults and 5.50€ ($7.15) for children 4 to 12. The trip is not covered by a railpass. For more information call ✆ **02/85114382.**

Buses run between Linate and Milan's Centrale station every 30 minutes daily from 6am to 11:45pm. A bus (no. 73) also runs between Piazza San Babila and Linate airport every 10 minutes daily from 6:05am to 12:55am. Buses run from Malpensa to Stazione Centrale daily every 30 to 45 minutes. Buses from Linate to Milan's Centrale Station cost 3€ ($3.90) one-way. Bus no. 73 from Linate to Piazza San Babila costs only 1€ ($1.30) one-way. For information about buses from Linate to Centrale Station and Piazza San Babila, call ✆ **02/58587237** or 800/808181. For information about buses from Malpensa to Stazione Centrale, call ✆ **02/33910794** or 0331/519000. Note that both the bus and train options are much cheaper than taking a taxi, which could run you a whopping 70€ ($91).

Milan

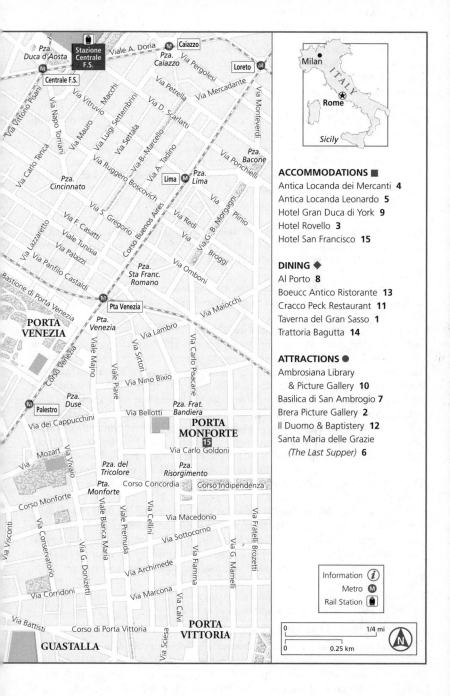

ACCOMMODATIONS ■

Antica Locanda dei Mercanti **4**

Antica Locanda Leonardo **5**

Hotel Gran Duca di York **9**

Hotel Rovello **3**

Hotel San Francisco **15**

DINING ◆

Al Porto **8**

Boeucc Antico Ristorante **13**

Cracco Peck Restaurant **11**

Taverna del Gran Sasso **1**

Trattoria Bagutta **14**

ATTRACTIONS ●

Ambrosiana Library
   & Picture Gallery **10**

Basilica di San Ambrogio **7**

Brera Picture Gallery **2**

Il Duomo & Baptistery **12**

Santa Maria delle Grazie
   (The Last Supper) **6**

Information	ⓘ
Metro	Ⓜ
Rail Station	🚉

INSIDE THE STATION

Milan has the finest rail connections in Italy. The main rail station for arrivals is Mussolini's mammoth **Stazione Centrale**, Piazza Duca d'Aosta (© **892021**), where you'll find the National Railways information office open daily from 7am to 9pm.

One train per hour arrives from both Genoa and Turin (trip time: 1½–2 hr.), costing 15€ ($19.50) one-way. Fifty-four trains arrive daily from Venice (trip time: 3 hr.), costing 24€ ($31.20) one-way; and one train per hour arrives from Florence (trip time: 2½ hr.), costing 17€ to 28€ ($22.10–$36.40) one-way. Trains from Rome (trip time: 5½ hr.) arrive every hour; the fare is 51€ ($66.30) one-way. Three Artesia trains arrive daily from Paris and Lyon. Contact Rail Europe for more information.

The station is directly northeast of the heart of town; trams, buses, and the Metro link the station to Piazza del Duomo in the very center.

At the train station, you can arrange for luggage storage daily from 6am to midnight; the cost is 4.40€ ($5.70) per 12 hours. Baggage-check facilities are labeled *Deposito Bagagli* and can be reached by taking the exit at the end of tracks #6 and #7. In the same location is a branch of the lost property office, **Ufficio Oggetti Smarriti Comune** (© **02/63712212**), open daily from 8am to 6pm. There are also a supermarket and ATMs.

For currency exchange, head along the archway leading to tracks—called *binario* in Italian—#10 to #15 until you get to the office. Money is converted daily from 7am to 10:30pm.

For train information, look for a black "i" sign. The office is located at the extreme right end of the station as you enter from the tracks. The British flag indicates that an English-speaking clerk is there to help you daily from 7am to 9pm. Note, however, that this is not the office at which to make reservations for EuroCity, InterCity, Rapido Express, or Eurostar Italia trains. To reach that office, go through the main station hall and down the stairs to the foyer on the lower street level. Look for a door marked *Biglietteria Est*, meaning ticket office east, and go through that entrance, then take a number from the machine and wait your turn. This reservation office—counters no. 49 and 53—is called *Prenotazioni*, and the hours are Monday to Friday from 8am to 10pm and Saturday and Sunday from 8am to 1pm. For Railpass validation, you must go to another office at the station's street level. It's marked *Biglietteria Ovest*; reservations are processed at windows no. 20 or 22. These windows are marked "International Tickets" (yes, in English).

A branch of the **Milan Tourist Office** at Stazione Central (© **02/77404318**), is open Monday through Saturday from 9am to 6pm, and Sunday from 9am to 1pm and 2 to 5pm. The staff here will give you a list of hotels but will not make reservations. Because Milan is a city of commerce that's often filled with business clients or hosting conventions, a hotel reservation should be made before you ever get to the city.

Note: The area surrounding the train station is not the safest after dark; caution should be used when leaving or arriving here at night.

INFORMATION ELSEWHERE IN THE CITY

The main tourist office, **Azienda di Promozione Turistica del Milanese,** is at Piazza del Duomo (the very heart of Milan) at Via Marconi 1 (© **02/72524301**). It's open Monday to Saturday 8:45am to 1pm and 2 to 6pm, and Sunday 8:45am to 1pm and 2 to 5pm in summer (closes 1 hr. earlier in winter). The staff will provide a listing of hotels but won't make reservations.

GETTING AROUND

The **Metro subway** system is extensive and efficient, covering most of Milan; in addition, there are buses and trams, making it fairly easy to navigate. Regular tickets cost 1€ ($1.30) and are sold at Metro stations and newsstands. Some subway tickets are good for continuing trips on city buses at no extra charge, but they must be used within 75 minutes of purchase. You must stamp your ticket when you board a bus or tram, or risk incurring a fine. The tourist office and all subway ticket offices sell a **travel pass** for 3€ ($3.90) for 1 day, or 5.50€ ($7.15) for 2 days, good for unlimited use on the city's tram, bus, and subway network.

To phone a **taxi,** dial *C* **02/4040,** 02/8585, or 02/4000; fares start at 3.10€ ($4.05), with a nighttime surcharge of 3.10€ ($4.05).

WHERE TO STAY

Antica Locanda dei Mercanti In the historic district, this sophisticated and reasonably priced hotel is a favorite with many movers and shakers in Milan's fashion industry. Former model Paolo Ora gutted the second floor of a building from the 1800s and turned it into this little charmer in 1996. Each midsize room comes with a marble-clad shower-only bathroom, and the design lines are sleek and contemporary with fine use of fabrics. Some rooms have canopied beds and all feature fresh flowers, books, and magazines.

Via San Tommaso 6, 20121 Milano. *C* **02/8054080.** Fax 02/8054090. www.locanda.it. 14 units (showers only). 168€–302€ ($218–$393) double. AE, MC, V. Tram: 1, 14, or 24. Metro: Cairoli, Cordusio, or Duomo. **Amenities:** Laundry; nonsmoking rooms. *In room:* A/C (in some rooms), hair dryer.

Antica Locanda Leonardo *✦ Finds* If you're seeking both atmosphere and comfort, this undiscovered gem is a worthy choice. A restored 19th-century building houses the hotel, whose chief grace note is an inner courtyard and garden that features wildly blooming wisteria in summer. Many of the bedrooms open onto small balconies, and the mostly midsize rooms are individually decorated in styles ranging from Liberty to very modern. Half of the bathrooms come with shower, the rest with tub.

Corso Magenta 78, 20123 Milano. *C* **02/48014197.** Fax 02/48019012. www.leoloc.com. 20 units. 150€–215€ ($195–$280) double; 255€ ($332) triple. Rates include continental breakfast. AE, DC, MC, V. **Amenities:** Bar; laundry; 1 room for those w/limited mobility. *In room:* Hair dryer.

Hotel Gran Duca di York *✦✦* This Liberty-style *palazzo* dates from the 1890s, when it was constructed by the Catholic Church to shelter the clergy from the nearby Duomo. Among them was the cardinal of Milan, who later became Pope Pius XI. Today anyone can rent one of the pleasantly furnished and well-kept rooms. They range from small to medium in size, and each has a tiled bathroom.

Via Moneta 1A (Piazza Cordusio), 20123 Milano. *C* **02/874863.** Fax 02/8690344. www.ducadiyork.com. 33 units. 178€–218€ ($231–$283) double. Rates include buffet breakfast. AE, MC, V. Closed Aug. Metro: Cordusio or Duomo. **Amenities:** Bar; laundry. *In room:* Hair dryer.

Hotel Rovello This affordable hotel's location is ideal, close to the Santa Maria delle Grazie, between Castello Sforzesco and Piazza Duomo. Renovations added soundproofing to the windows and improved the hotel's guest rooms, which are furnished in a minimalist yet comfortable style. Hardwood floors, orthopedic mattresses, and small dressing areas in some units add to this hotel's charm, along with the immaculately kept shower-only bathrooms. The place is not luxurious but is highly commendable.

Via Rovello 18, 20121 Milano. C 02/86464654. Fax 02/72023656. www.hotel-rovello.it. 120€–210€ ($156–$273) double. Children under 6 stay free in parent's room. Rates include continental breakfast. AE, DC, MC, V. Bus: 1, 2, 3, 4, 12, 14, 18, 19, 20, 24, or 27. Metro: Cordusio. **Amenities:** Bar; laundry. *In room:* Hair dryer.

Hotel San Francisco ★ *(Value)*   Near the Central Station, this pleasant and moderately priced hotel is an oasis of tranquility in this high-priced city. Its well-maintained bedrooms are not only comfortable, but warm and inviting. All of the accommodations contain tiled bathrooms with tub or shower. There's also a charming little garden. The English-speaking management will help ease your adjustment into Milan.

Viale Lombardia 55, 20130 Milano. C 02-2361009. Fax 02-26280377. www.hotel-sanfrancisco.it. 31 units. 75€–130€ ($97.50–$169) double; 95€–178€ ($124–$231) triple. Rates include breakfast. AE, DC, MC, V. Metro: Loreto. **Amenities:** Bar; laundry; nonsmoking rooms. *In room:* Hair dryer.

TOP ATTRACTIONS & SPECIAL MOMENTS

Ambrosiana Library & Picture Gallery (Biblioteca–Pinacoteca Ambrosiana) ★★
Near the Duomo, this museum houses one of the leading art galleries in the north of Italy, primarily featuring paintings from the 15th through the 17th centuries. Among its most famous works are *Portrait of a Musician,* by Leonardo da Vinci, and *The Fruit Basket* by Caravaggio. One of the museum's highlights is room 10, with 10 magnificent **cartoons by Raphael** ★★★, which he prepared for the frescoes of the School of Athens in the Vatican. Another room contains a collection of reproductions from the drawings of Leonardo da Vinci's *Codex Atlanticus.* The **Ambrosiana Library** contains many medieval manuscripts that are shown for scholarly examination only.

Piazza Pio XI 2. C 02/806921. Admission 7.50€ ($9.75) adults; seniors and children under 18 are 4.50€ ($5.85). Tues–Sun 10am–5:30pm. Metro: Duomo or Cordusio.

Brera Picture Gallery (Pinacoteca di Brera) ★★★
A 17th-century palace houses one of the finest collections of paintings in Italy. Most of the paintings are religious works, especially by Lombard and other northern Italian painters, but you'll also find representative paintings by El Greco, Rubens, Rembrandt, and Van Dyck. One of the gallery's prize possessions is the *Urbino Altarpiece,* by Piero della Francesca, depicting the Virgin and Child surrounded by a number of saints with the duke of Urbino kneeling in the foreground. Also on display are Mantegna's **The Dead Christ** ★★★, Giovanni Bellini's **Pietà** ★★, and Bernardino's **Virgin of the Rose Bush.** Another masterpiece is Raphael's **Bethrothal of the Virgin** ★★. The Venetian School is well represented in the works of Titian, Tintoretto, and Veronese.

Via Brera 28. C 02/722631. Admission 5€ ($6.50). Tues–Sun 8:30am–7:15pm. Metro: Lanza, or Montenapoleone.

Il Duomo & Baptistery ★★★
Dominating the Piazza del Duomo, Milan's cathedral is the largest Gothic structure in Italy. Begun in 1386, it took nearly 500 years to complete. Work was carried on during this period by architects and master masons from France and Germany, as well as all parts of Italy, giving the Duomo a flamboyant Gothic **exterior** ★★★ more reminiscent of the cathedrals north of the Alps than of its sister churches in Italy. With a floor plan in the shape of a Latin cross and five naves, the cathedral is supported by 40 exterior buttresses and 50 interior columns. Its height, including the spire topped by a gilded statue of the Virgin (added in 1859), is 367 feet (110m). More than 3,000 statues decorate the inside and outside.

To experience the Duomo at its most majestic, you must take the elevator to the **roof** or **visita ai terrazzo** ★★★, where you can walk through a forest of pinnacles, turrets, and marble statuary.

Piazza del Duomo. ℂ **02/86463456.** Cathedral free; roof via stairs 4€ ($5.20), roof via elevator 6€ ($7.80); crypt 1€ ($1.30); baptistery 1.50€ ($1.95). Cathedral daily 7am–7pm. Roof daily 9am–4:30pm. Crypt daily 9:30am–noon and 2:30–6pm. Baptistery daily 9:45am–12:45pm and 2–5:45pm.

Santa Maria delle Grazie & *The Last Supper* ★★

At the same time that Bramante was adding the purely Renaissance dome to the transitional Gothic church on the Piazza Santa Maria delle Grazie, his friend Leonardo da Vinci was working on his great fresco, *The Last Supper* ★★★, in the adjoining refectory of the Dominican convent. Bramante's vast domed crossing with its apsed transepts and choir struck an entirely original note in Milanese architecture. Visitors today often ignore the main church, however, and go directly to the simple refectory next door to gaze in awe at what is the best known and most frequently copied religious painting in the world. Although Leonardo's *Last Supper* miraculously survived such threats as a bombing attack in World War II, it is barely holding its own against the ravages of time. The painting depicts Christ at the moment when he announces that 1 of the 12 will betray him.

Piazza Santa Maria delle Grazie (off Corso Magenta). ℂ **02/4987588.** Free admission to church; 6.50€ ($8.45), plus 1.50€ ($1.95) for reservation to see *The Last Supper.* Church Mon–Sat 9am–noon and 3–6pm; Sun 3:30–6:30pm. *The Last Supper* viewings Tues–Sat 8:30am–6:45pm; Sun 9am–7:15pm. Reservations required for *The Last Supper;* call Mon–Sat 8am–7pm and leave your name. Metro: Cadorna or Conciliazione.

WHERE TO DINE

Al Porto ★★ SEAFOOD Opened in 1907, this lovely restaurant is one of the most popular places to go for seafood, and features a lovely glassed-in garden dining room. Even though Milan is an inland city, the chefs here manage to secure some of the best and freshest fish shipped daily to the local markets. Try their traditional *fritto misto,* a platter of lightly sautéed shellfish and various kinds of fish.

Piazzale Generale Cantore. ℂ **02/8321481.** Reservations required several days in advance. Main courses 12€–25€ ($15.60–$32.50). AE, DC, MC, V. Tues–Sat 12:30–3pm; Mon–Sat 7:30–10:30pm. Closed Dec 24–Jan 3 and Aug. Metro: Porta Genova or Sant'Agostino.

Boeucc Antico Ristorante INTERNATIONAL/MILANESE

This longtime favorite, opened in 1696, features a trio of rooms in an antique *palazzo* that's within walking distance of the Duomo and the major shopping arteries. In summer, guests gravitate to a terrace for open-air dining. You might enjoy spaghetti in clam sauce, a salad of shrimp with arugula and artichokes, or grilled liver, veal, or beef with aromatic herbs.

Piazza Belgioioso 2. ℂ **02/76020224.** Reservations required. Main courses 15€–22.50€ ($19.50–$29.25). AE, DC, MC, V. Mon–Fri 12:40–2:30pm; Sun–Fri 7:40–10:30pm. Closed Aug, Easter, and Christmas. Metro: Duomo, Montenapoleone, or San Babila.

Cracco Peck Restaurant ★★★ MILANESE/ITALIAN

The elegant Peck's is owned by the famous delicatessen, viewed as the Milanese equivalent of Fauchon's in Paris. A Czech immigrant, Francesco Peck, opened the restaurant back in the 19th century and went on to build a food empire. Some of the freshest and tastiest dishes in Milan are served by an efficient staff, including a classic version of risotto Milanese. The wine cellar features 1,800 kinds of wine from around the world.

Via Victor Hugo 4. ℂ **02/876774.** Reservations required. Main courses 30€–45€ ($39–$58.50). Fixed-price menus 90€–130€ ($117–$169). AE, DC, MC, V. Mon–Fri 12:15–2pm and 7:15–10:30pm; Sat 7:15–10:30pm. Closed 3 weeks in Jan and Aug 10–31. Metro: Duomo.

Taverna del Gran Sasso ⊛ ABRUZZI   This tavern sends out a siren call to all gourmands—no chefs serve more bountiful portions in all of Milan. Against a rustic tavern background that includes a tall open hearth, you are treated to a number of specialties from the southern province of Abruzzi. Special dishes include filet of beef with mushrooms and Gorgonzola with arugula; a risotto studded with fresh asparagus and Brie cheese; or else agnolotti (a homemade pasta) with wild boar sauce.

Piazza Principessa Clotilde 10. ✆ **02/6597578.** Reservations not required. Main courses 8.50€–18€ ($11.05–$23.40). Fixed-price menus 33€–39€ ($42.90–$50.70). AE, DC, MC, V. Mon–Fri 12:30–2:30pm and 7:30pm–midnight; Sat and Sun 7:30pm–midnight. Closed Jan 1 and Aug 14–16. Metro: Repubblica.

Trattoria Bagutta ⊛ INTERNATIONAL   Dating from 1927, this bustling trattoria, has long been our favorite in Milan, and we always have at least one or two meals here on every visit. The cuisine is not just from Lombardy, but also borrows heavily from the kitchens of Tuscany and Bologna as well. This is generous, home-style cooking, and the interior is cozy and comfortable, amusingly decorated with caricatures of famous Italians (the rear dining room is the most enticing).

Via Bagutta 14. ✆ **02/76002767.** Reservations required. Main courses 10.50€–22€ ($13.65–$28.60). AE, DC, MC, V. Mon–Sat 12:30–2:30pm and 7:30–10:30pm. Closed Dec 24–Jan 6. Metro: San Babila.

SHOPPING

London has Harrods, Paris has all the big-name boutiques you can think of, and Rome and Florence instill an acquisitional fever in the eyes of anyone who even window-gazes. Milan, however, is blessed with one of the most unusual concentrations of shopping possibilities in Europe. Most of the boutiques are infused with the style, humor, and sophistication that has made Milan the dynamo of the Italian fashion industry, a place where the sidewalks sizzle with the hard-driving entrepreneurial spirit that has been part of the northern Italian textile industry for centuries.

A walk on the fashion subculture's focal point, **via Montenapoleone**—heart of the Golden Triangle and one of Italy's great shopping streets—a mile-long (1.6km) strip that has become a showcase for famous (and high-priced) makers of clothes and shoes, with excursions into the side streets, will quickly confirm that Milan is home to what one shopper we met deemed, "the most unbelievable variety of shoes, clothes, and accessories in the world."

Early morning risers will be welcomed only by silent streets and closed gates. Most shops are closed all day Sunday and Monday (although some open on Mon afternoon). Some stores open at 9am unless they're very chic, and then they're not likely to open until 10:30am. They remain open, for the most part, until 1pm, reopening again between 3:30 and 7:30pm.

Bargain hunters leave the Golden Triangle and head for a mile-long (1.6km) stretch of **Corso Buenos Aires,** where you can find style at more affordable prices. Start off at **Piazza Oberdan,** the square closest to the heart of Milan. Clothing abounds on Corso Buenos Aires, especially casual wear and knockoffs of designer goods. But you'll also find a vast array of merchandise, from scuba-diving equipment to soft luggage. Saturdays are unbelievably crowded here. You'll find more bargains in the **Brera,** the name given to a sprawling shopping district around the Brera Museum. This area is far more attractive than Corso Buenos Aires and has often been compared to New York's Greenwich Village because of its cafes, shops, antiques stores, and art students. Skip the main street, **Via Brera,** and concentrate on the side streets, especially **Via Solferino, Via Madonnina,** and **Via Fiori Chiari.**

NIGHTLIFE

THE PERFORMING ARTS The most complete list of cultural events appears in the large Milan newspaper, the left-wing *La Repubblica.* Try for a Thursday edition, which usually has the most complete listings.

The world's most famous opera house is **La Scala** ✮✮✮, Piazza della Scala (Metro: Duomo). Reopening before Christmas in 2004, after 3 years of renovation, producers presented Mozart's envious antagonist, Antonio Salieri's long forgotten opera, *"Europe Riconosciuta,"* which was an opera commissioned for the house's original opening in 1778. The opera had gone unproduced since that time—many critics felt with good reason. La Scala is fully restored, with a technologically advanced stage and a splendid auditorium. First-night critics raved about the new acoustics. There are now three movable stages and 200 added seats. Tickets are hard to come by for La Scala and should be arranged as far in advance as possible. Costing 10€ to 170€ ($13–$221), tickets can be purchased at **Biglietteria Centrale** (© 02/72003744), in the Galleria Vittorio Emanuele (Piazza della Scala corner), open daily noon to 6pm. Metro: Duomo. For more information, check out **http://lascala.milano.it**.

LIVE-MUSIC CLUBS At **Le Scimmie,** Via Ascanio Sforza 49 (© **02/89402874;** bus: 59), bands play everything from funk to blues to creative jazz. Doors open Monday to Saturday around 8pm, and music is presented 10pm to around 3am.

Rolling Stone, Corso XXII Marzo 32 (© **02/733172;** tram: 54 or 73), features head-banging rock bands. It's open every night, usually 10:30pm to 4am, but things don't get going until at least midnight. It's closed in July and August. Cover ranges from 10€ to 18€ ($13–$23.40).

CAFES The decor of the **Berlin Cafe,** Via Gian Giacomo Mora 9 (© **02/8392605;** tram: 15, 19, or 24), seems straight out of turn-of-the-20th-century Berlin, with etched glass and marble-topped tables. It's a great spot for coffee or a drink, although we've had gruff service here. A variety of simple snack food is available, primarily during the day, although the cafe is open until midnight.

Boasting a chic crowd of garment-district workers and shoppers, **Café Cova,** Via Montenapoleone 8 (© **02/76000578;** Metro: Montenapoleone), has been around since 1817, serving pralines, chocolates, brioches, and sandwiches. The more elegant sandwiches contain smoked salmon and truffles. Sip your espresso from fragile gold-rimmed cups at one of the small tables in an elegant inner room or while standing at the prominent bar. It's closed in August and on Sunday year-round. Closing time is in the early evening.

AN EXCURSION TO LAKE COMO

Flower-bedecked promenades, lemon trees, romantic villas, parks and gardens, and crystal clear blue waters welcome you to Lake Como, 30 miles (48km) north of Milan and stretching 2½ miles (4km) at its widest point. "Everything noble, everything evoking love"—that's how Stendhal characterized fork-tongued Lake Como. Others have called it "the looking glass of Venus."

GETTING THERE At the southern tip of the lake, the town of **Como,** known for its silk industry, makes a good base for exploring. Trains arrive daily at Como from Milan (trip time: 40 min.) every hour; fares cost 8€ ($10.40) one-way. **Stazione San Giovanni,** Piazzale San Gottardo (© **892021**), is at the end of Viale Gallio, a 15-minute walk from the center of Como.

VISITOR INFORMATION In the exact center of town at Piazza Cavour (#17) is where you'll find the **tourist office** (☏ **031/269712;** www.lakecomo.org). It's open Monday to Saturday from 9am to 1pm and 2:30 to 6pm. From June to September it is open on Sunday 9am to 1pm. The staff doesn't make hotel reservations.

TOP ATTRACTIONS & SPECIAL MOMENTS

Touring **Lake Como** ✸✸✸ by boat is the main reason to visit the town of Como. It's easy to take a cruise around the lake; boats departing from the town's piers make calls at every significant settlement along its shores. Stroll down to the **Lungo Lario,** adjacent to Piazza Cavour, and head to the ticket windows of the **Società Navigazione Lago di Como** (☏ 031/304060). Half a dozen ferries and almost as many high-speed hydrofoils embark on circumnavigations of the lake. One-way transit from Como to Colico at the northern end of the lake takes 4 hours by ferry and 90 minutes by hydrofoil, and includes stops at each of the towns or major villages en route. Transit each way costs 9.50€ to 13.10€ ($12.35–$17.05), depending on which boat you take. One-way transit between Como and Bellagio takes 2 hours by ferry and 45 minutes by hydrofoil, and costs 7.80€ to 11€ ($10.15–$14.30) per person. There's no ferry service from Como between October and Easter, but there is hydrofoil service between October and Easter.

To get an overview of the lake area, take the funicular at Lungolario Trieste (near the main beach at Villa Genio) to the top of **Brunate,** a hill overlooking Como and providing a panoramic view. Departures are every 15 minutes daily, and the trip costs 4.10€ ($5.35) round-trip.

Before rushing off on a boat for a tour of the lake, you might want to visit the **Cattedrale di Como** ✸, Piazza del Duomo (☏ 031/265244). Construction on the cathedral began in the 14th century in the Lombard Gothic style and continued on through the Renaissance until the 1700s. Frankly, the exterior is more interesting than the interior. Dating from 1487, the exterior is lavishly decorated with statues, including those of Pliny the Elder (A.D. 23–79) and the Younger (A.D. 62–113), who one writer once called "the beautiful people of ancient Rome." Inside, look for the 16th-century tapestries depicting scenes from the Bible. The cathedral is open Monday to Saturday 7am to noon and 3 to 7pm.

WHERE TO DINE

Close to the cathedral, **Ristorante Imbarcadero,** in the Metropole & Suisse hotel, Piazza Cavour 19, 22100 Como (☏ **031/269444;** www.hotelmetropolesuisse.com), serves an enticing Lombard and Italian cuisine on tables placed near the edge of the lake. All the food, including the pastas, is homemade and much of the fresh fish served here comes from the lake itself. Main courses cost 12€ to 18€ ($15.60–$23.40), with a fixed-price menu at 25€ ($32.50). It's open daily from noon to 3pm and 7 to 10:30pm.

AN EXCURSION TO TURIN ✸✸

Also known as Torino, Turin is one of Italy's richest cities and the automobile capital of the country. It was also the host city for the 2006 Olympic Winter Games. The capital of Piedmont, Turin became the first capital of a united Italy, and much of its history is linked to the House of Savoy. Its chief treasure is the Shroud of Turin, whose mysterious origins have been the subject of much controversy. Was it really the shroud that Joseph of Arimathea wrapped about the body of Christ when his body was removed from the cross?

In addition to being an economic powerhouse, Turin is also a city of grace and elegance, known for its baroque architecture, its bevy of first-rate museums, its Fiat cars, its Juventus soccer team, and its scenic location at the foothills of the Alps.

GETTING THERE   Turin is a major **rail** terminus, with arrivals at **Stazione di Porta Nuova,** Corso Vittorio Emanuele (© **892021;** www.trenitalia.com), or **Stazione Centrale,** Corso Vittorio Emanuele II (© **892021**), in the heart of the city. It takes 1¼ hours to reach Turin by train from Milan, but it takes anywhere from 9 to 11 hours to reach Turin from Rome, depending on the connection. The one-way fare from Milan is 15€ ($19.50); from Rome it's 42€ ($54.60). Direct trains also arrive here from Paris; for more information, contact Rail Europe.

TOURIST INFORMATION   Go to the office of **APT,** Piazza Solferino 1 (© **011/ 535181**), which is open daily 9am to 7pm. There's another office at the Porta Nuova train station (same phone), open daily 9:30am to 7pm. These offices will make "last-minute" hotel reservations for free if you call 48 hours in advance—no sooner than that.

TOP ATTRACTIONS & SPECIAL MOMENTS

To begin your exploration, head first for the **Piazza San Carlo** 𝕮𝕮, the loveliest and most unified square in the city, covering about 3½ acres (1.4 hectares). Heavily bombed in the last war, it dates from the 17th century, and was built to the design of Carlo di Castellamonte. In the heart of the piazza is an equestrian statue of Emanuele Filiberto (1528–80), duke of Savoy and the only child of Charles III, who is known chiefly today for replacing Latin with Italian as the official language of the kingdom. The two churches are those of Santa Cristina and San Carlo. On the square, some of the most prestigious names in Italy have sat sipping coffee and plotting the unification of Italy. The most popular coffee house is the **Caffè Torino,** 204 Piazza San Carlo (© **011/545118**), where under the arcade you'll often see elegant Turinese who turn up for pastries, Campari, and much talk.

The city's most interesting museums are located in the Guarini-designed, 17th-century **Science Academy Building,** 6 Via Accademia delle Scienze (© **011/4406903** or 011/5617776), whose ground floor houses an **Egyptian Museum** 𝕮𝕮𝕮 with a collection so vast that it's surpassed only by the ones at Cairo and the British Museum in London. Of the statuary, that of **Ramses II** is the best known, though there is one of Amenhotel II as well. In the rather crowded wings upstairs, the world of the pharaohs lives on (one of the prize exhibits is the "Royal Papyrus," with its valuable chronicling of the Egyptian monarchs from the 1st through the 17th dynasties). The funereal art is exceptionally rare and valuable, especially the chapel built for Meie and his young wife, and an entirely reassembled tomb (that of Chaie and Merie, 18th dynasty), discovered in an amazingly well-preserved condition at the turn of the 20th century.

In the same building, you can visit the **Sabauda (Savoy) Gallery** 𝕮𝕮, one of the richest in Italy, whose collection was acquired over a period of centuries by the House of Savoy. It keeps the same hours as the Egyptian Museum. The Academy has the largest exhibit of the Piedmontese masters, but is well endowed in Flemish art as well. Of the latter, the most celebrated painting is Sir Anthony Van Dyck's *Three Children of Charles I* (England). Other important works include Botticelli's *Venus,* Memling's *Passion of Christ,* Rembrandt's *Sleeping Old Man,* Titian's *Leda,* Mantegna's *Holy Conversation,* Jan van Eyck's *The Stigmata of Francis of Assisi,* Veronese's *Dinner in the*

House of the Pharisee, and intriguing paintings by the Bruegels. Admission to the Egyptian Museum is 6.50€ ($8.45); to the Galleria Sabauda it's 4€ ($5.20). Hours for both attractions are Tuesday to Sunday 8:30am to 7pm. To get here, take tram 18 from the train station.

Cattedrale di San Giovanni ⋆, Piazza San Giovanni (© **011/4360790**), is a Renaissance cathedral dedicated to John the Baptist. A tragic fire swept across the cathedral in the spring of 1997, but its major treasure, the **Holy Shroud** ⋆⋆⋆ was not damaged. Acquired by Emanuele Filiberto (whose equestrian statue you saw in the Piazza San Carlo), the shroud is purported to be the one that Joseph of Arimathea wrapped around the body of Christ when he was removed from the cross. Detailed charts in front of the holy relic claim to show evidence of a hemorrhage produced by the crown of thorns. The shroud is rarely on view but you can see dramatically lit photographs of the amazing relic. The shroud is contained in the **Museo della Santissima Sindone,** Via San Domenico 28 (© **011/4365832**), which is open daily from 9am to noon and 3 to 7pm, and charges an admission of 5.50€ ($7.15). Entrance to the cathedral is free daily from 7am to noon and 3 to 7pm. To get here from the train station, take bus no. 63.

WHERE TO DINE

Turin is home to some of the best restaurants in northwest Italy, notably **Villa Sassi** ⋆, in the Hotel Villa Sassi, Via Traforo del Pino 47 (© **011/8980556**), a 17th-century villa 3¾ miles (6km) east of the town center but reached easily by tram 15 or bus no. 61. It's worth the extra effort to get here, as its noteworthy Piedmontese and international cuisine is served in elegant, antiques-filled salons. Some of the produce for the meals comes from the villa's own farm. Main courses run 13€ to 24€ ($16.90–$31.20). It's open Monday to Saturday from noon to 2:30pm and 8 to 10:30pm. It's closed in August.

A fast-rising restaurant is **Vintage 1997** ⋆, Piazza Solferino 16 (© **011/535948;** tram: 4 or 10; bus: 5 or 67), which specializes in regional, mainly meat-based Piedmontese fare along with a nightly offering of fresh seafood from the coast. We enjoyed some of our best meals in the region here, including some unusual but successful mixtures such as lamb with tuna sauce. Main courses cost 11€ to 28€ ($14.30–$36.40), and hours are Monday to Friday noon to 3pm and Monday to Saturday 8pm to midnight.

14

The Netherlands

Exploring the Netherlands by train is a snap. In a country barely half the size of Maine and with 16 million inhabitants, few are the towns and places of interest that can't be reached directly by train (or require only a minimal amount of additional traveling by bus or bicycle). Dutch trains are frequent, and invariably both punctual and clean, so traveling from one end of the realm to another, and to points in between, is no great trial.

This means you can stay focused on getting the most out of your time in Amsterdam, The Hague, Haarlem, and other historic Dutch towns and cities, because you won't need to spend too much time on a train. Each of these cities is no more than a short ride away from the other. Even places in relatively remote Zeeland, Friesland, and Limburg provinces are within easy reach, enabling you to get close to a slower-paced way of life in this country that has been wrested acre by acre from the sea.

HIGHLIGHTS OF THE NETHERLANDS

The principal highlight of the Netherlands—the city of **Amsterdam**—also happens to be one of the highlights of the entire world. That's why it's as much a fixture on any well-conceived European rail tour as London, Paris, and Rome. Just 20 minutes by train from Schiphol Airport, Amsterdam is Holland's capital and major city. This high-energy metropolis has a multiethnic population of 740,000 (and 600,000 bicycles), and runs the cultural gamut from the heights of the Van Gogh Museum to legal prostitution and officially tolerated dope dens.

Some visitors to Holland make the mistake of thinking there's no more to the country than Amsterdam. Not so. Just 15 minutes away by train is **Haarlem,** a graceful and historic small city that's well worth a side trip. Your next stop could well be **The Hague,** sophisticated, more than a little stuffy, and the seat of the Dutch government and royal family. Nearby **Delft,** an ancient seat of Dutch royalty (and the hometown of Dutch master Vermeer), is smaller and easier to get to grips with.

Should you feel the need to stretch your legs, metaphorically speaking, head down south to handsome and occasionally raucous **Maastricht,** at the country's borders with Germany and Belgium. A different kind of Dutch spirit and some of the best eating and drinking in the land will be your rewards.

1 Essentials

GETTING THERE

Carriers with flights into Amsterdam from North America include **Air Canada** (© 888/247-2262; www.aircanada.ca), **Continental Airlines** (© 800/231-0856; www.continental.com), **Delta Airlines** (© 800/241-4141; www.delta.com), **KLM** (© 800/225-2525; www.klm.com), **Northwest Airlines** (© 800/225-2525; www.nwa.com), and **United Airlines** (© 800/538-2929; www.united.com).

Moments Festivals & Special Events

Koninginnedag (Queen's Day), April 30, a nationwide holiday for the House of Orange, is vigorously celebrated in Amsterdam. The center city gets so jam-packed with people it's virtually impossible to move. A street market held all over town features masses of stalls, run by everybody from kids selling old toys to professional market folk. Dutch flags and orange ribbons, orange-dyed hair, and orange-painted faces are everywhere. Street music and theater combine with too much drinking, but Koninginnedag remains good-natured, if boisterous. For more information, contact **VVV Amsterdam** (© 0900/400-4040; www.amsterdamtourist.nl).

Among the world's leading gatherings of top international jazz and blues musicians, the **North Sea Jazz Festival** unfolds over 3 concert-packed days in early July at Rotterdam's giant Ahoy venue. Last-minute tickets are scarce, so book as far ahead as you can. Contact **North Sea Jazz Festival** (www.northseajazz.nl) for more information.

Lastly, the **Grachten Festival,** a 5-day festival of chamber music, plays at various intimate and atmospheric venues along Amsterdam's canals in mid-August. Part of the festival is the exuberant Prinsengracht Concert. Contact **Stichting Grachtenfestival** (© 020/421-4542; www.grachtenfestival.nl) for details.

Amsterdam Airport Schiphol (© 0900/0141 for general and flight information; www.schiphol.nl), 8 miles (13km) southwest of the center city, is the principal airport in the Netherlands and handles virtually all of the country's international flights. Schiphol has quick, direct rail links to Amsterdam Centraal Station, and to many more Dutch cities.

THE NETHERLANDS BY RAIL

High-speed **Thalys** trains from France and Belgium, and high-speed **ICE** trains from Germany serve Amsterdam and other Dutch cities. The Thalys travel time from Brussels is 2 hours and 40 minutes; the ICE travel time from Frankfurt is 4 hours. In addition, Amsterdam is linked to many cities around Europe by slower **EuroCity (EC), EuroNight (EN),** and other international trains.

All major Dutch tourist destinations are within 2½ hours of Amsterdam on **Nederlandse Spoorwegen (Netherlands Railways/NS;** © 0900/9292; www.ns.nl), Holland's national rail system. NS trains are a good way to travel with the Dutch, who use them even for short journeys to the next town up the line. In addition to Amsterdam, other destinations easily reached by train from Schiphol include The Hague (30 min.), Rotterdam (40 min.), and Utrecht (1 hr.)—these are the shortest travel times by Inter-City train. The trains run so often you can usually just go to the station and wait for the next one—your wait will be short. At even the smallest stations, there is half hour or hourly service in both directions, and major destinations have between four and eight trains an hour. Service begins as early as 5am (slightly later on Sun and holidays) and runs until around 1am. A special **Night Train** runs between Utrecht and Rotterdam, via Amsterdam, Schiphol, Leiden, and The Hague.

The Netherlands

There are two kinds of national train service in Holland: **InterCity** express trains connecting the main towns and cities; and the ***stoptrein*** (stop train), a slow train that stops at every station on the line—for some services, a *stoptrein* is called, counter-intuitively, a **Sprinter,** which travels faster between stations, yet still stops at all of them.

Note: Should you wish to bike some of your travel route—and Holland is Europe's bicycling country par excellence—Netherlands Railways has some handy arrangements whereby you can rent a bicycle at one station and drop it off at another.

PASSES

For details on purchasing multicountry options, such as the **Eurail Global Pass,** see chapter 2. The **Benelux Pass** allows 5 days of unlimited travel in 1 month in Belgium, the Netherlands, and Luxembourg for $207 in second class and $314 in first class. Two to five adults traveling together should purchase instead the **Benelux Saverpass,** to benefit from a discount of around 18%. For passengers ages 12 to 25, the **Benelux Youth Pass** (available in second class only) costs $158. Children ages 4 to 11 pay about half the adult fare, and children under 4 travel free. These passes must be purchased in North America and can be obtained from **Rail Europe** (© **877/272-RAIL** [7245] in North America; www.raileurope.com) or through your travel agent.

With the multiday **Eurail Holland Pass,** valid only in the Netherlands, you get two options: 3 days or 5 days of unlimited travel within 1 month. The passes are available for both first- and second-class travel; prices start at $92 for 3 days in second class. While there is no children's discount on Eurail Holland pass prices, locally, a 1-day *Railrunner* unlimited travel pass can be purchased for children ages 4 to 11 (up to a maximum three children per adult over 19) for 2€ ($2.60) per child (children under 4 travel free). Passengers ages 4 to 25 traveling in second class can purchase a **Holland Rail Youth Pass** (prices start at $69 for 3 days of travel).

The words "single" and "return" when used in reference to trains in Holland, mean one-way and round-trip respectively. In addition to Netherlands Railways's regular single *(enkele reis),* day return *(dagretour),* and weekend return *(weekendretour)* tickets (note that a round-trip ticket costs less than two one-way tickets), look for the discounted *dagkaart* (day card), *5-dagkaart* (5-day card), and *NS Zomertoer* (Summer Tour)—all three have extra-cost options that also provide free public transportation. These various tickets and passes are valid only in the Netherlands, and can be purchased only at train stations in Holland. You can purchase some tickets from in-station automats, and doing so will save you .50€ (65¢) per ticket over the price at the ticket counter.

Note: Tickets cannot be purchased onboard Dutch trains. The fine for riding a train without a valid ticket is 35€ ($46), plus the fare.

FOREIGN TRAIN TERMS

A train is a *trein* in Dutch. Class is *klas;* second class is *tweede klas,* and first class is *eerste klas.* A station is, easily enough, a *station.* In big cities such as Amsterdam, Rotterdam, and Den Haag (The Hague), which have more than one station, the main station is generally called Centraal Station (Central Station). The Dutch word for platform is *spoor* (it rhymes with "boar"). The bigger stations have separate counters for selling domestic tickets *(Binnenland)* and international tickets *(Buitenland,* or just plain International).

Departure and arrival are *vertrek* and *aankomst* in Dutch (announcements are also made in English in the most important stations). Information is *Informatie.*

PRACTICAL TRAIN INFORMATION

Dutch trains are often crowded, and since reservations are not available (except for international trains) it makes sense not to travel during peak hours, when you may need to stand. On the other hand, distances between stations are short and a bunch of people are sure to get out at whatever the next one is.

All trains, even the smallest, have a first-class section or cars. Smoking is forbidden both on trains and on station platforms.

Due to the country's small size, no Dutch trains have restaurant cars (some international trains do), but on long-distance InterCity trains an attendant pushes around

Train Frequency & Travel Times in the Netherlands

Amsterdam	Haarlem	The Hague	Delft	Rotterdam	Maastricht
Travel Time	15 min.	50 min.	55 min.	58 min.	2 hr., 30 min.
Frequency*	6	6	5	6	2

Frequency is average number of trains per hour during daytime.

a small cart, from which coffee, tea, mineral water, sandwiches, potato chips, and other snack items are dispensed. These are more expensive than the same things bought from a supermarket, so if you are on a tight budget, buy them before boarding the train. Similarly, a lack of long distances means there are no sleeper cars on trains within the Netherlands.

Some trains, employed most often during rush hours in urban areas, are double-deckers; these often get very crowded, but an upstairs window seat affords a great view of whatever there is to be seen.

FAST FACTS: The Netherlands

Area Codes When making local calls in Amsterdam you won't need to use the area codes shown in this chapter. You do need to use an area code between towns and cities. The area code for Amsterdam is **020**. Other area codes are Haarlem **023**, The Hague and Scheveningen **070**, Delft **015**, and Maastricht **043**.

Business Hours Banks are open Monday to Friday from 9am to 4pm (some stay open until 5pm). Some banks also open on late-hour shopping nights and Saturdays. Stores generally are open Monday from 10 or 11am to 6pm, and Tuesday to Saturday from 8:30 or 9am to 6pm. Some stores close for lunch, and nearly all have 1 full closing day or 1 morning or afternoon when they're closed. Many stores, especially in the larger towns, have late hours on Thursday and/or Friday evening, and in the cities some main-street stores are open on Sundays.

Climate Holland has a maritime climate, with few temperature extremes in either summer or winter. Summer temperatures average 67°F (19°C); the winter average is 35°F (2°C). Winters, moderated by the North Sea and the fading glow of the Gulf Stream, most often are rainy (it's driest Feb–May).

July and August are the best months for soaking up rays at sidewalk cafes, dining at an outdoor restaurant in the evening, and going topless on the beach. September usually has a few weeks of fine weather. There are even sunny spells in winter, when brilliant, crisp weather alternates with clouded skies.

Documents Required For stays of up to 3 months, citizens of the U.S. and Canada need only a valid passport. A visa is required for stays of longer than 3 months.

Electricity The Netherlands runs on 230 (220–240) volts electricity (North America uses 110 volts). To use appliances from home without burning them out, you'll need a small voltage transformer (available at your local hardware store) that plugs into the round-holed European electrical outlet and converts the Dutch voltage for any small appliance up to 1,500 watts.

Embassies & Consulates **U.S. Embassy:** Lange Voorhout 102, Den Haag (© **070/310-9209**; http://netherlands.usembassy.gov); **U.S. Consulate** in Amsterdam: Museumplein 19 (© **020/575-5309**; tram: 3, 5, 12, or 16). **Canadian Embassy:** Sophialaan 7, Den Haag (© **070/311-1600**; www.canada.nl).

Health & Safety In the event of a medical emergency, call the national emergency number: © **112**. For 24-hour nonurgent doctor referral and urgent dentist referral in Amsterdam, call the **Central Doctors Service** (© **020/592-3434**).

During regular office hours you will probably be better off checking with your hotel reception desk—most hotels either have an arrangement with, or can point you to, a nearby practice.

Holidays January 1 (New Year's Day); Good Friday; Easter Sunday and Monday; April 30 (Queen's Day/*Koninginnedag*); Ascension Day; Pentecost Sunday and Monday; December 25 (Christmas Day) and December 26. The dates for Easter, Ascension, and Pentecost change each year.

Mail Postage for a postcard or ordinary letter to the U.S. and Canada is .89€ ($1.15).

Police & Emergencies Holland's emergency number to call for the police (*politie*), fire department, and ambulance is ☎ **112**. For routine matters, call the general police number (☎ **0900/8844**), or visit a district police office; in Amsterdam; a centrally located one is at Lijnbaansgracht 219 (tram: 1, 2, 5, 6, 7, or 10), just off of Leidseplein.

Telephone The international access code for the Netherlands is **011** and the country code is **31**. To call the Netherlands from the United States, dial 011, then 31, then the area code of the city you'd like to reach (20 in Amsterdam, for example), followed by the telephone number. So the whole number you'd dial would be 011-31-20-000-0000.

To make international calls from the Netherlands, first dial 00 and then the country code for the U.S. or Canada: 1. Next you dial the area code and number.

For directory assistance: Dial ☎ **0900/8418** for international information. Dial ☎ **0900/8008** for multiple numbers inside Holland and ☎ **118** for a maximum of one number per call. **For operator assistance:** To make an international collect call, dial ☎ **0800/0410**.

Toll-free numbers: Numbers beginning with 0800 within Holland are toll-free, but calling a 1-800 number in the States from Holland is not toll-free. In fact, it is the same as an overseas call. Watch out for special Dutch numbers that begin with 0900. Calls to these numbers are charged at a higher rate than ordinary local calls, and can cost up to .90€ ($1.15) a minute.

You can use pay phones with either a KPN or a Telfort *telekaart* (phone card)—but note that neither company's card works with the other company's phones—which are 5€ ($6.50), 10€ ($13), 20€ ($39), and 50€ ($65) from post offices, train ticket counters, VVV tourist information offices, and some tobacconists and newsstands. Some pay phones take credit cards. A few pay phones take coins.

To charge a call to your calling card, call **AT&T** (☎ **0800/022-9111**), **MCI** (☎ **0800/022-9122**), **Sprint** (☎ **0800/022-9119**), or **Canada Direct** (☎ **0800/022-9116**).

Tipping All taxes and service charges are supposed to be included in the prices of hotels, restaurants, cafes, nightclubs, salons, and sightseeing companies. Even taxi fare includes taxes and a standard 15% service charge. To be absolutely sure in a restaurant that tax and service are included, look for the words *inclusief BTW en service* (BTW is the abbreviation for the Dutch words that mean value-added tax), or ask the waiter. The Dutch are so accustomed to having these charges included that many restaurants have stopped spelling it out.

To tip like the Dutch (no, seriously!), in a cafe or snack bar leave some small change; in a standard restaurant, leave 2€ to 3€ ($2.60–$3.90), and up to a generous 5€ ($6.50) if you think the service was particularly good; for expensive tabs, you may want to leave more—or maybe less! It's enough to round up taxi fares.

2 Amsterdam ★★★

Old Amsterdam's graceful cityscape recalls its 17th-century golden age as the heart of a global trading network and colonial empire, when wealthy merchants constructed gabled residences along neatly laid-out canals. A delicious irony is that today these placid old structures also host brothels, smoke shops, and some extravagant nightlife. The city's inhabitants, proud of their live-and-let-live attitude, which is based on pragmatism as much as on a long history of tolerance, have decided to control what they cannot effectively outlaw. They permit licensed prostitution in the Red Light District, and the sale of hashish and marijuana in designated "coffee shops."

Don't think most Amsterdammers are late-model hippies, though, drifting around town in a drug-induced haze. They are too busy whizzing around on bicycles, jogging through Vondelpark, feasting on arrays of ethnic dishes, or simply watching the parade of street life from a sidewalk cafe. A new generation of entrepreneurs has revitalized old neighborhoods such as the Jordaan, turning some of the distinctive houses into offbeat stores and bustling cafes, hotels, and restaurants. And along the waterfront, old harbor installations have been put to bold new uses, or swept away entirely in favor of large-scale modern cultural, business, and residential developments.

Between dips into Amsterdam's artistic and historical treasures, be sure to take time out to absorb the freewheeling spirit of Europe's most vibrant city.

STATION INFORMATION

GETTING FROM THE AIRPORT TO THE TRAIN STATION
Netherlands Railways **trains** from Amsterdam Airport Schiphol (see "Getting There," earlier in this chapter) for Amsterdam Centraal Station depart from Schiphol Station, downstairs from Schiphol Plaza, attached to the airport. Frequency ranges from eight trains an hour at peak times to one an hour at night. The fare is 3.60€ ($4.70) one-way in second class and 6.10€ ($7.95) in first class (or free if you hold a valid train pass), and the ride takes 15 minutes.

You'll find **taxi** stands in front of Schiphol Plaza. All taxis from the airport are metered. Expect to pay around 40€ ($52) to the center city.

INSIDE THE STATION
Amsterdam Centraal Station is the mammoth hub for all rail travel and public transportation in the city. An office of **VVV Amsterdam** tourist information (© **0900/400-4040,** or 31-20/551-2525 from outside the Netherlands; www.amsterdamtourist.nl) is inside the station on platform 2B, open Monday to Saturday from 8am to 8pm, and Sunday and holidays from 9am to 5pm; it can make last-minute hotel reservations. Another office is right in front of the station on Stationsplein, open daily from 9am to 5pm. In addition, you'll find currency exchange at GWK Travelex; a Netherlands

Amsterdam

ACCOMMODATIONS ■
Agora **13**
Amstel Botel **31**
Amsterdam Wiechmann **9**
Bilderberg Hotel Jan Luyken **18**
Canal House **3**
De Filosoof **15**
Hotel Amsterdam-De Roode Leeuw **21**
Prinsenhof **29**
Seven Bridges **27**
Victoria **22**

DINING ◆
Bolhoed **2**
Café Luxembourg **12**
De Belhamel **1**
De Jaren **26**
De Prins **5**
Kantjil & de Tijger **10**
Rose's Cantina **14**
Spanjer & Van Twist **4**
Tempo Doeloe **28**
Wilhelmina-Dok **32**

ATTRACTIONS ●
Amsterdams Historisch Museum **11**
Amsterdamse Bos **20**
Anne Frankhuis **6**
Hash Marihuana & Hemp Museum **24**
Koninklijk Paleis **8**
Museum Het Rembrandthuis **25**
Oude Kerk **23**
Rijksmuseum De Meesterwerken **19**
Stedelijk Museum CS **30**
Van Gogh Museum **17**
Vondelpark **16**
Westerkerk **7**

NETHERLANDS
Amsterdam

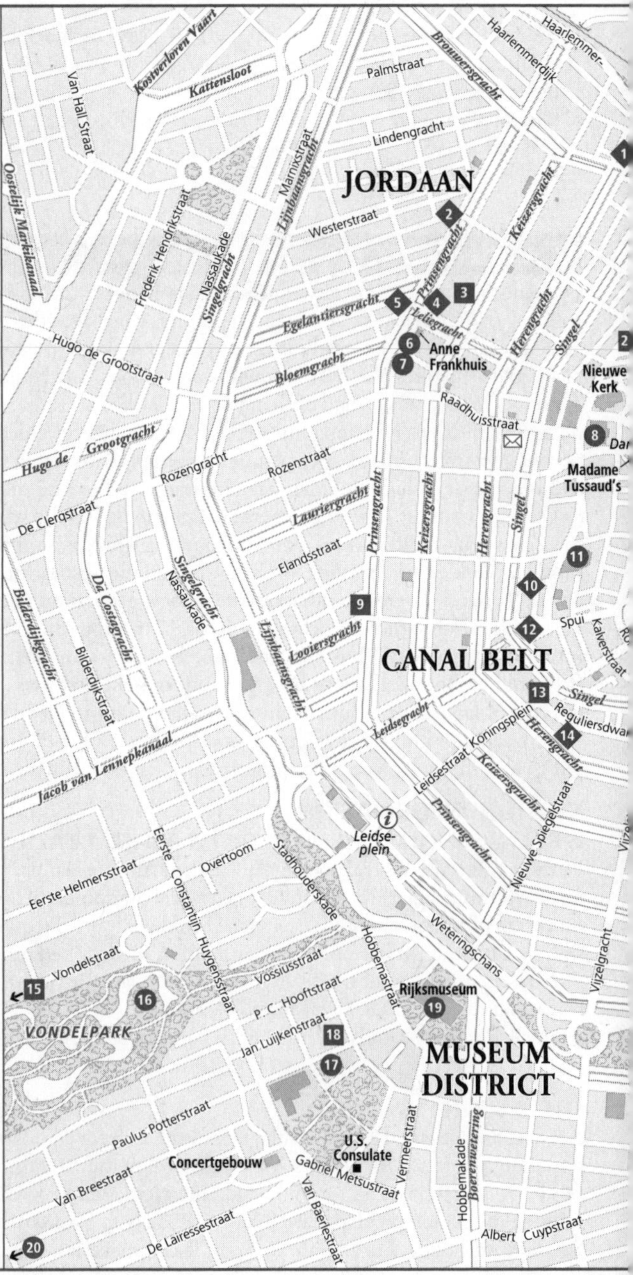

JORDAAN
CANAL BELT
MUSEUM DISTRICT
VONDELPARK
Anne Frankhuis
Nieuwe Kerk
Madame Tussaud's
Leidseplein
Rijksmuseum
U.S. Consulate
Concertgebouw
Haarlemmerdijk
Brouwersgracht
Palmstraat
Lindengracht
Westerstraat
Prinsengracht
Keizersgracht
Herengracht
Singel
Egelantiersgracht
Leliegracht
Bloemgracht
Raadhuisstraat
Rozengracht
Rozenstraat
Lauriergracht
Elandsstraat
Looiersgracht
Spui
Kalverstraat
Leidsegracht
Leidsestraat
Koningsplein
Reguliersdwa
Nieuwe Spiegelstraat
Weteringschans
Vijzelgracht
Marnixstraat
Lijnbaansgracht
Nassaukade
Singelgracht
Frederik Hendrikstraat
Van Hall Straat
Kostverloren Vaart
Kattensloot
Oostelijk Marktkanaal
Hugo de Grootstraat
Hugo de Grootgracht
De Clercqstraat
Da Costagracht
Bilderdijkgracht
Bilderdijkstraat
Jacob van Lennepkanaal
Eerste Constantijn Huygensstraat
Overtoom
Eerste Helmersstraat
Stadhouderskade
Vondelstraat
Vossiusstraat
P. C. Hooftstraat
Jan Luijkenstraat
Hobbemastraat
Paulus Potterstraat
Van Breestraat
De Lairessestraat
Van Baerlestraat
Gabriel Metsustraat
Vermeerstraat
Hobbemakade
Boerenwetering
Albert Cuypstraat

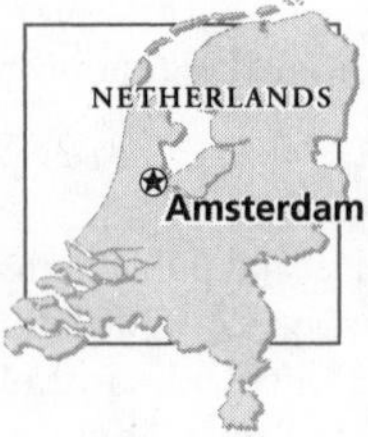

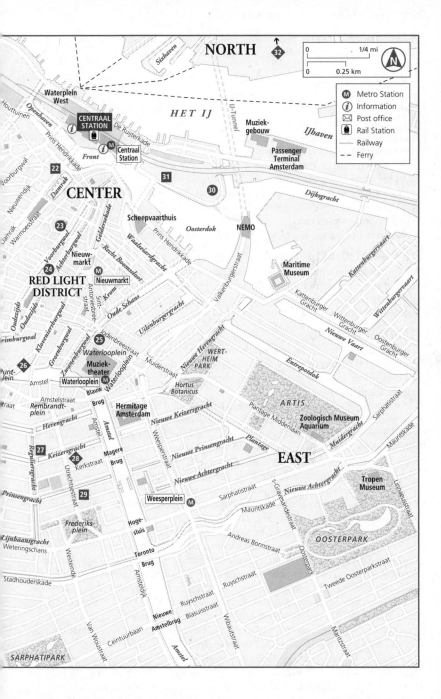

NORTH

Railways office for tickets, reservations, and information, with separate desks for international and national trains; ticket automats; restaurants and snack bars; and a host of small stores.

The station, a Dutch neo-Renaissance architectural monument dating from 1889, is currently—and for some years to come—a confusing construction site. A new Metro station, set to be the hub of the Noord–Zuid line (due to enter service in 2011) is being dug at the front; a new main entrance for the train station and generally improved passenger facilities are being tackled at the same time; and the waterfront zone at the rear is being completely revamped.

When you emerge at the front of the station, you will find a taxi stand; a bunch of stops for trams (streetcars) and buses; the entrance to the existing Metro station; and docks for tour boats, the Water Taxi, the Canal Bus, and the Museum Boat. At the rear of the station are docks for the ferryboats that shuttle passengers around the city's fast-developing waterfront.

Beware: The station is a pickpocket convention that's in full swing at all times.

INFORMATION ELSEWHERE IN THE CITY

VVV Amsterdam also has an office (actually a line of three booths set into a wall) right in the center of town at Leidseplein 1 (tram: 1, 2, 5, 6, 7, or 10), on the corner of Leidsestraat, open Sunday to Thursday from 9:15am to 5pm, and Friday to Saturday from 9:15am to 7pm.

GETTING AROUND

The center city is small enough that the best way to get around Amsterdam is on your own two feet. Be sure to wear good walking shoes, as those charming cobblestones will get under your soles and on your nerves after a while. When crossing the street, watch out for trams and bikes.

Of the city's 16 **tram** (streetcar) lines, 10 begin and end at Centraal Station, and one passes through. An extensive **bus** network complements the trams. The current four **Metro** lines—50, 51, 53, and 54—are mainly useful for getting to and from the suburbs. Most tram/bus shelters and all Metro stations have maps that show the entire transit network. A detailed map is available from VVV tourist information offices and from the GVB Tickets & Info office outside Centraal Station on Stationsplein.

Note: By the start of 2009, all public transportation in the Netherlands is due to be using the new national electronic **OV-chipkaart** in place of tickets. Amsterdam has begun to introduce this smart card, first on Metro trains, and during 2008 on trams and buses too. Three main types of OV-chipkaart are being introduced: a reloadable "personal" card that can be used only by its pictured owner; a reloadable "anonymous" card that can be used by anyone; and a nonreloadable "throwaway" card that can be used by anyone. Electronic readers automatically deduct the correct fare when you ride. The personal and anonymous reusable cards, both valid for 5 years, cost 7.50€ ($9.75) and can be loaded and reloaded with up to 30€ ($39); the throwaway card costs 2.50€ ($3.25). Reduced-rate cards are available for seniors and children.

A transition period will ensure that the following information on the existing tickets and fares will remain valid until the new card is fully up and running.

There are 11 public transportation fare zones in greater Amsterdam, though tourists rarely travel beyond the center-city zone 5700 (Centrum). Tickets are valid for travel on buses, trams, and the Metro. A **day ticket** *(dagkaart),* valid for the entire day of purchase and the following night, can be purchased from any bus or tram driver, conductor, or ticket dispenser for 6.50€ ($8.45). Tickets for **2, 3,** and **4 days,** for 10.50€ ($14), 13.50€ ($18), and 16.50€ ($21) respectively, can be purchased from the **GVB Tickets & Info** office on Stationsplein, in front of Centraal Station.

A **single journey ticket** *(enkeltje)* is 1.60€ ($2.10) for one zone and 2.40€ ($3.10) for two zones. For multiple journeys, buy a **strip card** *(strippenkaart)*. An eight-strip card costs 6.40€ ($8.30) from the driver or conductor. Discount strip cards are available from Metro station ticket counters, the GVB Tickets & Info office, post offices, and many news vendors; you pay 6.80€ ($8.85) for a card with 15 strips, and 20.10€ ($26) for one with 45 strips. On some trams and on Metro trains you are responsible for stamping the required number of strips for your journey, on other trams a conductor does this, and on buses the driver does it. To use the validating machines, just fold at the line and punch in; you don't need to punch in each individual strip—just count down the number of strips you need and punch in the last one.

Officially, you can't hail a **taxi** from the street, but taxis will often stop anyway if you do. Otherwise, find one of the strategically located taxi stands sprinkled around town, marked by distinctive yellow phone boxes. Or, call **Taxi Centrale Amsterdam** (© 020/677-7777). Taxis are metered. Fares—which include a service charge—begin at 3.40€ ($4.40) when the meter starts and run up at 1.95€ ($2.50) a kilometer (or 3.10€/$4.05 a mile), and after 16 miles (25km) at 1.45€ ($1.90) a kilometer (or 2.35€/$3.05 a mile).

Two waterbus services bring you to many of the city's top museums and other attractions. A day ticket for the **Canal Bus** (© 020/623-9886) allows you to hop on and off as many times as you like on three lines until noon the next day, for 18€ ($23) for adults, 12€ ($16) for children ages 4 to 12, and free for children under 4. It's also available through Rail Europe. The **City(S)hopper/Museumboot** (© 020/530-5412)—*"boot"* is pronounced just like *boat*—operates a scheduled service every 30 to 45 minutes from Centraal Station to Prinsengracht, Leidseplein, Museumplein, Herengracht, the Muziektheater, and the Eastern Dock. A day ticket is 17€ ($22) for adults, 13€ ($17) for children ages 4 to 12, and free for children under 4. Special tickets are available that include discounted admission to some museums and attractions.

You can also follow the Dutch example and travel around by bicycle. Bike-rental rates are around 9€ ($12) a day or 30€ ($39) a week; a deposit of 50€ ($65) is generally required. You can rent bikes from Centraal Station when you arrive, and from many rental stores, all of which have similar rates. **MacBike** (© 020/620-0985) rents a range of bikes, including tandems and six-speed touring bikes; it has branches at Centraal Station; Mr. Visserplein 2, close to the Muziektheater; and Marnixstraat 220, close to Rozengracht. **Damstraat Rent-a-Bike** is at Damstraat 20–22 (© 020/625-5029), close to the Dam.

WHERE TO STAY

Agora   Old-fashioned friendliness is the keynote at this efficiently run and well-maintained lodging, a block from the Flower Market, in a fully restored canal house from 1735. Furniture from the 1930s and 1940s mixes with fine mahogany antiques and an abundance of overstuffed furniture. Those rooms that don't have a canal view look out on a pretty garden at the back. There's no elevator, and one room has no bathroom.

Singel 462, 1017 AW Amsterdam. © 020/627-2200. Fax 020/627-2202. www.hotelagora.nl. 16 units. 126€–140€ ($164–$182) double with bathroom; 92€ ($120) double without bathroom. Rates include buffet breakfast. AE, DC, MC, V. Tram: 1, 2, or 5 to Koningsplein. **Amenities:** Lounge. *In room:* Hair dryer, no A/C.

Amstel Botel *(Kids)* Where better to experience a city on the water than by lodging in a boat-hotel, moored so close to Centraal Station you could just about swim there? Its cabins are spread out over four decks connected by elevator. The bright, modern rooms are no-nonsense but comfortable, and the showers small. Be sure to ask for a room with a view on the water, and not on the uninspiring quay side.

Oosterdokskade 2–4, 1011 AE Amsterdam. ✆ **020/626-4247**. Fax 020/639-1952. www.amstelbotel.com. 175 units. 89€–94€ ($116–$122) double. AE, DC, MC, V. Tram: 1, 2, 4, 5, 9, 13, 16, 17, 24, 25, or 26 to Centraal Station. Amenities: Bar. *In room:* No A/C.

Amsterdam Wiechmann *(★)* It takes only a moment to feel at home in the antique-adorned Wiechmann, a classic, comfortable, casual place beside Looiersgracht. Besides, the location is one of the best you'll find in this or any price range. Most of the rooms are standard, with good-size twin or double beds, and some have big bay windows. Furnishings are elegant. The higher-priced doubles, with a view on the canal, have antique furnishings.

Prinsengracht 328–332, 1016 HX Amsterdam. ✆ **020/626-3321**. Fax 020/626-8962. www.hotelwiechmann.nl. 38 units. 130€–150€ ($169–$195) double; 245€ ($319) suite. Rates include continental breakfast. MC, V. Tram: 1, 2, or 5 to Prinsengracht. **Amenities:** Lounge; nonsmoking rooms (all rooms). *In room:* No A/C.

Bilderberg Hotel Jan Luyken *(★)* Close to the Rijksmuseum, this is a small hotel with some of the amenities and facilities of a large one—though without the large rooms. Everything here is done to maintain a balance between a sophisticated lineup of facilities and an intimate and personalized approach appropriate to a 19th-century residential neighborhood. That feel extends to the air-conditioned guest rooms, which look more like those in a well-designed home than in a standard hotel room.

Jan Luijkenstraat 58, 1071 CS Amsterdam. ✆ **020/573-0730**. Fax 020/676-3841. www.janluyken.nl. 62 units. 139€–179€ ($181–$233) double. AE, DC, MC, V. Tram: 2 or 5 to Hobbemastraat. **Amenities:** Wine bar; laundry; nonsmoking rooms. *In room:* Hair dryer.

Canal House *(★★)* A contemporary approach to reestablishing the elegant canalhouse atmosphere has been taken by the proprietor of this small hotel in three adjoining houses from 1630 close to Westermarkt. These were rebuilt to provide private bathrooms and filled with antiques, quilts, and Oriental rugs. A steep staircase still has its beautifully carved old balustrade. Overlooking the back garden, the magnificent breakfast room seems to have been untouched since the 17th century. On the parlor floor is a cozy Victorian-style salon.

Keizersgracht 148, 1015 CX Amsterdam. ✆ **020/622-5182**. Fax 020/624-1317. www.canalhouse.nl. 26 units. 140€–190€ ($182–$247) double. Rates include continental breakfast. DC, MC, V. Tram: 13, 14, or 17 to Westermarkt. **Amenities:** Lounge. *In room:* Hair dryer, no A/C.

De Filosoof *(★)* *(Finds)* On a quiet street facing Vondelpark, this might be the very place if you fancy yourself as something of a philosopher. Each room is dedicated to a mental maestro—Aristotle, Plato, Goethe, Wittgenstein, Nietzsche, Marx, and Einstein are among those who get a look-in—or are based on motifs like Eros, the Renaissance, and astrology. Regular all-round improvements keep the service and amenities up-to-date.

Anna van den Vondelstraat 6, 1054 GZ Amsterdam. ✆ **020/683-3013**. Fax 020/685-3750. www.hotelfilosoof.nl. 38 units. 105€–155€ ($137–$202) double. Rates include buffet breakfast. AE, MC, V. Tram: 1 to Jan Pieter Heijestraat. **Amenities:** Bar. *In room:* Hair dryer, no A/C.

Hotel Amsterdam-De Roode Leeuw 🌟🌟   Close to Centraal Station and right next to the Dam, this family hotel, housed in a 1911 building, is still owned by descendants of the original proprietors. Its rooms are supermodern, though, with thick carpets, air-conditioning, and ample wardrobe space. Rooms at the front get more light, but are also subjected to more street noise; some have balconies. The award-winning De Roode Leeuw restaurant serves classic Dutch cuisine.

Damrak 93–94, 1012 LP Amsterdam. ✆ 020/555-0666. Fax 020/620-4716. www.hotelamsterdam.nl. 79 units. 225€–310€ ($293–$403) double. AE, DC, MC, V. Tram: 4, 9, 14, 16, 24, or 25 to the Dam. **Amenities:** Restaurant; cafe; laundry; nonsmoking rooms. *In room:* Hair dryer.

Prinsenhof *Value*   A modernized canal house close to the Amstel River, this hotel has rooms (two with bathroom) with beamed ceilings and basic yet tolerably comfortable beds. Front rooms look out onto Prinsengracht, where houseboats are moored. The proprietors, Rik and André van Houten, take pride in their hotel and make you feel welcome (check out the hotel's website for a good dose of their humor). There's no elevator, but a pulley hauls your luggage up and down the stairs.

Prinsengracht 810, 1017 JL Amsterdam. ✆ 020/623-1772. Fax 020/638-3368. www.hotelprinsenhof.com. 10 units. 89€ double ($116) with bathroom; 69€ double ($90) without bathroom. Rates include continental breakfast. AE, MC, V. Tram: 4 to Prinsengracht. *In room:* No TV, no A/C.

Seven Bridges 🌟🌟 *Finds*   One of Amsterdam's canal-house gems, not far from Rembrandtplein, gets its name from its view of seven arched bridges. There are antique furnishings, handmade Italian drapes, hand-painted tiles and wood-tiled floors, and Impressionist art posters on the walls. The biggest room, on the first landing, can accommodate up to four and has a huge bathroom with marble floor and double sinks. Attic rooms have sloped ceilings and exposed wood beams, and there are big, bright basement rooms done almost entirely in white.

Reguliersgracht 31, 1017 LK Amsterdam. ✆ 020/623-1329. Fax 020/624-7652. www.sevenbridgeshotel.nl. 11 units. 110€–260€ ($143–$338) double. Rates include full breakfast. AE, MC, V. Tram: 16, 24, or 25 to Keizersgracht. *In room:* Hair dryer, no A/C.

Victoria 🌟   Since 1890, the elegant Victoria has been a turreted landmark at the head of Damrak, overlooking Centraal Station and the canal-boat piers. It can be noisy and tacky out on the busy street below, but you won't notice that once you get inside the hushed, plush interiors. You can survive quite nicely without taking taxis if you stay here, about as close as you can get to Centraal Station. Guest rooms in an adjacent new block lack some of the atmosphere of the old.

Damrak 1–5, 1012 LG Amsterdam. ✆ 888/201-1803 in the U.S. and Canada, or 020/623-4255. Fax 020/625-2997. www.parkplaza.com. 306 units. 290€–325€ ($377–$423) double; from 490€ ($637) suite; add 5% city tax. AE, DC, MC, V. Tram: 1, 2, 4, 5, 9, 13, 16, 17, 24, 25, or 26 to Centraal Station. **Amenities:** Restaurant; cafe; bar; laundry; nonsmoking rooms. *In room:* Hair dryer.

TOP ATTRACTIONS & SPECIAL MOMENTS

For sightseers in Amsterdam, the question is not simply what to see and do, but rather how much of this intriguing city's marvelous sights you can fit into the time you have. There are miles and miles of canals to cruise, hundreds of narrow streets to wander, countless historic buildings to visit, more than 40 museums holding collections of everything from artistic wonders to obscure curiosities, not to mention diamond cutters and craftspeople to watch as they practice generations-old skills . . . the list is as long as every visitor's individual interests.

Amsterdams Historisch Museum (Amsterdam Historical Museum) 🌟🌟
Housed in the rambling 17th-century Burger Weeshuis, the former City Orphanage next to the Begijnhof, this fascinating museum gives you a better understanding of everything you'll see when you go out to explore the city on your own. Gallery by gallery, century by century, you learn how a small fishing village founded around 1200 became a major sea power and trading center. The main focus is on the golden age, a period when Amsterdam was the world's wealthiest city, and some of the most interesting exhibits are of the trades that made it rich in the 17th century. You can also view some famous paintings by the Old Dutch masters in the context of their time and place in history.

When you leave the museum, cut through the **Schuttersgalerij (Civic Guards Gallery),** a covered passageway that leads to the Begijnhof, and is bedecked with 15 enormous 17th-century paintings of the Amsterdam Civic Guards. The open hours are the same as for the museum, and admission is free.

Kalverstraat 92, Nieuwezijds Voorburgwal 357, and Sint-Luciënsteeg 27. ✆ 020/523-1822. www.ahm.nl. Admission 7€ ($9.10) adults, 5.25€ ($6.85) seniors, 3.50€ ($4.55) children 6–18, children under 6 free. Mon–Fri 10am–5pm; Sat–Sun 11am–5pm. Tram: 1, 2, 4, 5, 9, 14, 16, 24, or 25 to Spui.

Anne Frankhuis 🌟🌟🌟   In summer you may have to wait an hour or more to get in, but no one should miss experiencing this house, where eight people from three separate Jewish families lived together in near total silence for more than 2 years during World War II. The hiding place Otto Frank found for his family and friends, next to Westermarkt, kept them safe until it was raided by Nazi forces and its occupants were deported to concentration camps. Anne, whose ambition was to be a writer, kept her famous diary here as a way to deal both with the boredom and her youthful jumble of thoughts, which had as much to do with personal growth as with the war and the Nazi terror raging outside her hiding place. Visiting the rooms where she hid is a moving and eerily real experience.

The rooms of the building, which was an office and warehouse at that time, are still as bare as they were when Anne's father returned, the only survivor of the eight *onderduikers* (divers, or hiders). Nothing has been changed, except that protective Plexiglas panels have been placed over the wall where Anne pinned up photos of her favorite actress, Deanna Durbin, and of the little English princesses Elizabeth and Margaret. As you tour the building, it's easy to imagine Anne's experience growing up in this place, awakening as a young woman, and writing down her secret thoughts in a diary.

Prinsengracht 263 (at Westermarkt). ✆ 020/556-7105. www.annefrank.org. Admission 7.50€ ($9.75) adults, 3.50€ ($4.55) children 10–17, children under 10 free. Mid-Mar to mid-Sept daily 9am–9pm; mid-Sept to mid-Mar daily 9am–7pm. Tram: 13, 14, or 17 to Westermarkt.

Hash Marihuana & Hemp Museum   It wouldn't really be Amsterdam without its fascination with intoxicating weeds, would it? This museum in the Red Light District will teach you everything you ever wanted to know, and much you maybe didn't, about hash, marijuana, and related products. It does not promote drug use but aims to make you better informed before deciding whether to light up and, of course, whether to inhale. One way it does this is by having a cannabis garden in the joint—sorry—on the premises. Hemp plants fill the air with a heady, resinous fragrance, and hemp fiber could be the material of the future if the exhibit on its multifarious uses is anything to go by. Among several artworks in the museum's collection is David Teniers the Younger's painting, *Hemp-Smoking Peasants in a Smoke House* (1660).

Oudezijds Achterburgwal 130. Ⓒ 020/623-5961. www.hashmuseum.com. Admission 5.70€ ($7.15) adults, children under 13 (accompanied by an adult) free. Daily 10am–10pm. Tram: 4, 9, 14, 16, 24, or 25 to the Dam.

Koninklijk Paleis (Royal Palace) ✿

One of the Dam's heavier features is the solid, neoclassical facade of the Royal Palace (1648–55), designed by Jacob van Campen—the Thomas Jefferson of the Dutch Republic—as the city's Stadhuis (Town Hall). Its interior is replete with white Italian marble, sculptures, and painted ceilings. Poet Constantijn Huygens called the then-new Town Hall the "Eighth Wonder of the World." It was built on a foundation of a precisely tabulated 13,659 timber piles—a figure all Dutch schoolchildren are taught. *Note:* The palace is closed for renovations until some time in 2008; until then you can only view the exterior.

Dam. Ⓒ 020/620-4060. www.koninklijkhuis.nl. Tram: 1, 2, 4, 5, 9, 13, 14, 16, 17, 24, or 25 to the Dam.

Museum Het Rembrandthuis ✿

Bought by Rembrandt in 1639 when he was Amsterdam's most fashionable portrait painter, the house, behind Waterlooplein, is a shrine to one of the greatest artists the world has ever known. In this house, Rembrandt's son, Titus, was born and his wife, Saskia, died. The artist was bankrupt when he left in 1658. Not until 1906 was the building rescued from a succession of subsequent owners and restored as a museum. In 1998, a modern wing for temporary exhibits was added. Restoration has returned the old house to the way it looked when Rembrandt lived and worked here, complete with his combined living room and bedroom, the studio he and his pupils used, the artist's cabinet of art and curiosities, a ground-floor kitchen, and the maid's bedroom. The rooms are furnished with 17th-century objects and furniture that, as far as possible, match the descriptions in Rembrandt's 1656 bankruptcy petition. His printing press is back in place, and you can view 250 of his etchings and drawings hanging on the walls. These include self-portraits and landscapes, and several relate to the traditionally Jewish character of the neighborhood. In addition, there are works by contemporaries like Jan Lievens.

Jodenbreestraat 4–6. Ⓒ 020/520-0400. www.rembrandthuis.nl. Admission 8€ ($10) adults, 5.50€ ($7.15) students, 1.50€ ($1.95) children 6–15, children under 6 free. Daily 10am–5pm. Tram: 9 or 14 to Waterlooplein.

Oude Kerk (Old Church) ✿

This late-Gothic church at Oudezijds Voorburgwal—its official name is the Sint-Nikolaaskerk (St. Nicholas's Church), but nobody ever calls it that—was begun in 1250 and essentially completed with the construction of the bell tower in 1566. On its southern porch, to the right of the sexton's house, is a coat of arms belonging to Maximilian of Austria, who, with his son Philip, contributed to the porch's construction. Rembrandt's wife is buried in vault 28K, which bears the simple inscription "Saskia Juni 1642." The church contains a magnificent Christian Müller organ from 1728 that is regularly used for recitals. On hourly guided tours, you can climb the church tower for an outstanding view of Old Amsterdam. Nowadays, the pretty gabled almshouses around the church feature red-fringed windows through which can be seen the scantily dressed ladies of the Red Light District.

Oudekerksplein. Ⓒ 020/625-8284. www.oudekerk.nl. Church: Admission 5€ ($6.50) adults, 4€ ($5.20) seniors, students; children under 12 free. Mon–Sat 11am–5pm; Sun 1–5pm; Tower: Admission 5€ ($6.50). Sat–Sun 1–5pm; guided tours every 30 min.; Ⓒ 020/689-2565. Metro: Nieuwmarkt.

Rijksmuseum De Meesterwerken ✿✿✿

Most of Holland's premier museum is closed for renovation until 2010. During this period, under the heading "The Masterpieces," key paintings and other stellar works from the magnificent 17th-century Dutch Golden Age collections can be viewed in the Philips Wing. The three-star rating given here is justified even for the truncated highlights alone, but you need to remember that most of the collections, which total seven million individual objects (only a fraction of which would be displayed at any given time), will be "invisible" to visitors for some time to come.

Petrus Josephus Hubertus Cuypers (1827–1921), the "grandfather of modern Dutch architecture," designed the brick and gabled museum in a monumental Dutch neo-Renaissance style. Cuypers, a Catholic, slipped in more than a dab of neo-Gothic, too, causing the country's thoroughly Protestant King William III to scorn what he called "that cathedral"; the museum opened in 1885 to a less-than enthusiastic public reception. Since then, many additions have been made to both the collections and the building.

The Rijksmuseum contains the world's largest collection of paintings by the Dutch masters, including the most famous of all, a single work that all but defines the Golden Age. The painting is Rembrandt's *The Shooting Company of Captain Frans Banning Cocq and Lieutenant Willem van Ruytenburch,* better known as *The Night Watch* (1642). The scene so dramatically depicted is surely alien to most of the people who flock to see it: gaily uniformed militiamen checking their weapons and accouterments before moving out on patrol. Works by Jacob van Ruisdael, Maerten van Heemskerck, Frans Hals, Paulus Potter, Jan Steen, Jan Vermeer, Pieter de Hooch, Gerard Terborch, Gerard Dou, and others also grace the walls. The range is impressive—individual portraits, guild paintings, landscapes, seascapes, domestic scenes, medieval religious subjects, allegories, and the incredible (and nearly photographic) Dutch still lifes.

Jan Luijkenstraat 1. ⓒ 020/674-7047. www.rijksmuseum.nl. Admission 10€ ($13) adults, children under 19 free. Daily 9am–6pm (Fri 10pm). Tram: 2 or 5 to Hobbemastraat.

Stedelijk Museum CS 🐦 *Note:* The Stedelijk Museum's regular premises on Paulus Potterstraat at Museumplein are closed until some time in 2009 for renovation and expansion. Until then, the city's modern art museum occupies temporary quarters in the old TPG Post building east of Centraal Station (hence the "CS" in the name). This is the place to see works by such Dutch painters as Karel Appel, Willem de Kooning, and Piet Mondrian, alongside works by the French artists Chagall, Cézanne, Picasso, Renoir, Monet, and Manet, and by the Americans Calder, Oldenburg, Rosenquist, and Warhol. The Stedelijk centers its collection around the De Stijl, Cobra, post-Cobra, Nouveau Réalisme, pop art, color-field painting, zero, minimalist, and conceptual schools of modern art, and it houses the largest collection outside Russia of Kasimir Malevich's abstract paintings.

Oosterdokskade 5. ⓒ 020/573-2911. www.stedelijk.nl. Admission 9€ ($12) adults; 4.50€ ($5.85) seniors, students, children 7–16; children under 7 free. Daily 10am–6pm. Tram: 1, 2, 4, 5, 9, 13, 16, 17, 24, 25, or 26 to Centraal Station.

Van Gogh Museum 🐦🐦🐦 More than 200 paintings by Vincent van Gogh (1853–90), along with nearly every sketch, print, etching, and piece of correspondence the artist ever produced, are housed here. Van Gogh painted for only 10 years, sold only one painting in his lifetime, and was on the threshold of success when he committed suicide at age 37. You can trace this great artist's artistic development and psychological decline by viewing the paintings displayed in chronological order according to the seven distinct periods that defined his short career.

One particularly splendid wall, on the second floor, has a progression of 18 paintings produced during the 2-year period when Vincent lived in the south of France,

Moments   **Special Amsterdam Experiences**

- **For outdoors types:** Rent a bicycle and join the flow of bikers for one of Amsterdam's classic experiences—but go carefully.
- **For shoppers:** Pick up a bunch of tulips from the Flower Market on Singel, even if they're just to brighten up your hotel room.
- **For night owls:** Stroll through the Red Light District, to examine the quaint gabled architecture along its narrow canals—oh, yes, and you might also notice certain ladies watching the world go by through their red-fringed windows.
- **For bar flies:** Spend a leisurely evening in a *bruine kroeg* (brown cafe), the traditional Amsterdam watering hole.

generally considered to be his artistic high point. It's a symphony of colors and color contrasts that includes *Gauguin's Chair; The Yellow House; Self-Portrait with Pipe and Straw Hat; Vincent's Bedroom at Arles; Wheatfield with Reaper; Bugler of the Zouave Regiment;* and one of the most famous paintings of modern times, *Still Life Vase with Fourteen Sunflowers,* best known simply as *Sunflowers.*

Paulus Potterstraat 7 (at Museumplein). ☎ 020/570-5200. www.vangoghmuseum.nl. Admission 10€ ($13) adults, 2.50€ ($3.25) children 13–17, children under 13 free. Daily 10am–6pm (Fri 10pm). Tram: 2, 3, 5, or 12 to Van Baerlestraat.

Westerkerk (West Church)   The Dutch Renaissance–style Westerkerk (1631) is where Rembrandt and his son, Titus, were buried, and where in 1966 Queen (then Princess) Beatrix and Prince Claus said their marriage vows. Architect Pieter de Keyser took over the design work from his father, Hendrick, who died in 1621. The light, spacious interior has a fine organ. The 277-foot-high (83m) tower, the Westertoren, is Amsterdam's tallest, and affords spectacular city views; at its top is the blue, red, and gold imperial crown of the Holy Roman Empire, a symbol bestowed by the Habsburg emperor Maximilian. You can climb the tower on a guided tour.

Westermarkt. ☎ 020/624-7766. www.westerkerk.nl. Church: free admission. Apr–Sept Mon–Fri 11am–3pm. Tower: admission 6€ ($7.80). Apr–Sept Mon–Sat 10am–5:30pm; guided tours every 30 min. Tram: 13, 14, or 17 to Westermarkt.

PARKS

When the sun shines in Amsterdam, people head for the city's parks. The most popular and centrally located is the 122-acre (49-hectare) **Vondelpark** ✿✿ (tram: 1, 2, 3, 5, 7, 10, or 12). Vondelpark lies generally southwest of Leidseplein, with the main entrance adjacent to Leidseplein, on Stadhouderskade. A pattern of ponds and streams surrounded by meadows, trees, and colorful flowers, it hosts skateboarding; Frisbee-flipping; in-line skating; model-boat sailing; pickup soccer, softball, and basketball; open-air concerts and theater; smooching in the undergrowth; parties; picnics; and crafts stalls. Beware the tasty-looking "gâteau" sold here, or you might find yourself floating above the trees: Drug-laced "space cake" is an acquired taste.

To enjoy scenery and fresh air, head out to the giant **Amsterdamse Bos** (bus: 170 or 172 from outside Centraal Station), in the Amstelveen southern suburb. Nature on the city's doorstep, the park was laid out during the Depression years as a public works project. At the main entrance on Amstelveenseweg, stop by the **Bezoekerscentrum**

(Visitor Center), Bosbaanweg 5 (© **020/545-6100;** www.amsterdamsebos.nl), where you can trace the park's history, learn about its wildlife, and pick up a plan of the park. The center is open daily from noon to 5pm, and admission is free. Across the way is a bicycle rental shop (© **020/644-5473**), where bikes are available for from 8€ ($10) a day. Then, follow the path to a long stretch of water called the **Bosbaan,** a 1¼-mile (2km) competition-rowing course. Beyond the course's western end are a pond, the **Grote Vijver,** where you can rent boats, and the **Openluchttheater (Open-Air Theater),** which often has performances on summer evenings.

CANAL-BOAT TOURS

The canals are the best starting point to Amsterdam. Tours last approximately an hour and leave at regular intervals from *rondvaart* (excursion) piers in key locations around town. Most launches are docked along Prins Hendrikkade and Damrak near Centraal Station, on Rokin near Muntplein, and at Leidseplein. Tours leave every 15 to 30 minutes during the summer season (9am–9:30pm), every 45 minutes in winter (10am–4pm). Prices vary, but a basic 1-hour tour costs around 9€ ($12) for adults, 6€ ($7.80) for children 4 to 12, and free for children under 4. Tickets are also available from Rail Europe.

WHERE TO DINE

Bolhoed ⋆ VEGETARIAN   Forget the corn-sheaf 'n' brown-rice image affected by so many vegetarian restaurants. Instead, garnish your healthful habits with tangy flavors and a dash of zest. Latin style, aboriginal art, world music, evening candlelight, and a fine view of the canal from each of the two plant-bedecked, cheerful rooms in this former hat store near Noordermarkt—*bolhoed* is Dutch for bowler hat—distinguish a restaurant for which *vegetarian* is a tad too wholesome-sounding. For outdoors dining in summer, there are a few canal-side tables.

Prinsengracht 60–62. © 020/626-1803. Main courses 13€–17€ ($17–$22); *dagschotel* 13€ ($17); 3-course menu 19€ ($25). No credit cards. Sun–Fri noon–11pm; Sat 11am–11pm. Tram: 13, 14, or 17 to Westermarkt.

Café Luxembourg ⋆ INTERNATIONAL   "One of the world's great cafes," wrote the *New York Times* about this relaxed grand cafe, at Spui, which draws all kinds of people to its large portions of food at reasonable prices. Soups, sandwiches, and such dishes as meatloaf are available. Special attractions are choices like Chinese dim sum and *satay ajam* (Indonesian grilled chicken in a peanut sauce). Sunday in particular, but also on other days, it's a good place to do breakfast over the morning papers and a cup of strong coffee. You're encouraged to linger, and in summer there's sidewalk dining.

Spui 24. © 020/620-6264. www.cafeluxembourg.nl. Salads and specials 7.50€–12€ ($9.40–$15); lunch 4.50€–9.75€ ($5.65–$12); main courses 8.50€–15€ ($11–$19). AE, DC, MC, V. Sun–Thurs 9am–1am; Fri–Sat 9am–2am. Tram: 1, 2, or 5 to Spui.

De Belhamel ⋆ *Finds* CONTINENTAL   Soft classical music complements a graceful Art Nouveau setting at this split-level restaurant overlooking the photogenic junction of the Herengracht and Brouwersgracht canals. The tables fill up quickly on most evenings, so make reservations or go early. Try for a window table and take in the superb canal views. Although generally excellent, De Belhamel does have two minor flaws: The waitstaff is occasionally a bit too laid-back and it can get noisy when it's busy.

Brouwersgracht 60. © 020/622-1095. www.belhamel.nl. Main courses 19€–21€ ($25–$27); fixed-price menu 34€ ($44). AE, MC, V. Daily noon–4pm and 6–10:30pm. Tram: 1, 2, 5, 13, or 17 to Martelaarsgracht.

De Jaren CONTINENTAL   Large and brightly lit De Jaren, across the water from Muntplein, is fashionable without being pretentious. It occupies a solid-looking building on two stories, with unusually high ceilings and a multicolored mosaic floor. Students from the nearby university lunch here, and it's popular with the media crowd. The unique selling point is not so much the fashionable set that hangs out here, but two marvelous open-air patios beside the Amstel River.

Nieuwe Doelenstraat 20–22. ⓒ 020/625-5771. www.cafe-de-jaren.nl. Main courses 13€–17€ ($17–$22); lunch menu 12€ ($16). V. Sun–Thurs 10am–1am; Fri–Sat 10am–2am. Tram: 4, 9, 14, 16, 24, or 25 to Muntplein.

De Prins ⭑⭑ *Value* DUTCH/FRENCH   This companionable restaurant in a 17th-century canal house across the canal from the Anne Frank House, has a smoke-stained, brown-cafe style and food that could easily grace a much more expensive place. This is a quiet neighborhood place—nothing fancy or trendy, and the relatively few tables fill up fast. There's a bar on a slightly lower level than the restaurant. From March to September De Prins spreads a terrace out onto the canal side.

Prinsengracht 124. ⓒ 020/624-9382. www.deprins.nl. Main courses 10€–15€ ($13–$20); *dagschotel* 10€ ($13); specials 11€–16€ ($14–$21). AE, DC, MC, V. Daily 10am–1am. Tram: 13, 14, or 17 to Westermarkt.

Kantjil & de Tijger ⭑ INDONESIAN   Unlike the many Indonesian restaurants in Holland that wear their ethnic origins on their sleeves, with waitstaff decked out in traditional costume, the "Antelope and the Tiger" is chic, modern, and cool. More-over, this eatery near Spui attracts customers who like their Indonesian food not only chic, modern, and cool—but good as well. The 20-item *rijsttafel* (rice table) for two is deservedly a bestseller.

Spuistraat 291–293. ⓒ 020/620-0994. www.kantjil.nl. Reservations recommended on weekends. Main courses 12€–16€ ($16–$21); rijsttafels 43€–55€ ($56–$72) for 2. AE, DC, MC, V. Mon–Fri 4:30–11pm; Sat–Sun noon–11pm. Tram: 1, 2, or 5 to Spui.

Rose's Cantina TEX-MEX   Just off Leidsestraat, Rose's attracts with typical American favorites such as hamburgers and meatballs, though the decor and most of the cuisine are Mexican inspired. The tables are oak, the service is decent but slow—think the basic rate of continental drift—and the atmosphere is Latin American and buzzing with good cheer. Beware of long waiting times for a table, during which, as likely as not, you'll sit at the bar downing one after another of Rose's deadly margaritas.

Reguliersdwarsstraat 38–40. ⓒ 020/625-9797. www.rosescantina.com. Main courses 15€–22€ ($20–$29). AE, DC, MC, V. Mon–Sat 5–11:30pm; Sun 3–11:30pm. Tram: 1, 2, or 5 to Koningsplein.

Spanjer & Van Twist ⭑ *Finds* CONTINENTAL   This place just off Keizersgracht would almost be worth the visit for its name alone, so it's doubly gratifying to find the food good, too. The interior is typical *eetcafé*-style, with the day's specials chalked on a blackboard, a long table with newspapers at the front, and the kitchen visible in back. In fine weather, you can eat on an outdoor terrace next to the tranquil Lelie-gracht canal.

Leliegracht 60. ⓒ 020/639-0109. Reservations not accepted. Main courses 11€–15€ ($14–$20). MC, V. Sun–Thurs 10am–1am; Fri–Sat 10am–2am (only light snacks after 10pm). Tram: 13, 14, or 17 to Westermarkt.

Tempo Doeloe ⭑⭑ INDONESIAN   For authentic Indonesian cuisine, from Java, Sumatra, and Bali—which doesn't leave out much—this place between Prinsengracht and Keizersgracht is hard to beat. You dine in a *batik* ambience that's Indonesian, but restrained. Try out one of the many little meat, fish, and vegetable dishes of the three

---

Moments **Spice of Life**

Even if you're on a tight budget, aim to eat at least one **Indonesian rijsttafel.** This traditional "rice table" banquet of as many as 25 succulent and spicy foods, served in tiny bowls, usually costs around 15€ to 30€ ($20–$39). Pick and choose from among the bowls and add your choice to the pile of rice on your plate. It's a delicious and a true taste of multicultural Amsterdam. For an abbreviated version served on one plate, try *nasi rames.* At lunch, the standard Indonesian fare is *nasi goreng* (fried rice with meat and vegetables) or *bami goreng* (fried noodles prepared in a similar way). A great place to eat rijsttafel is Tempo Doeloe (see below).

---

different rijsttafel options, from the 15-plate vegetarian rijsttafel *sayoeran,* and the 15-plate rijsttafel *stimoelan,* to the sumptuous 25-plate rijsttafel *istemewa.*

Utrechtsestraat 75. (𝒞 020/625-6718. www.tempodoeloerestaurant.nl. Reservations required. Main courses 14€–25€ ($18–$33); rijsttafel 27€–35€ ($35–$46); fixed-price menu 27€–43€ ($35–$56). AE, DC, MC, V. Daily 6–11:30pm. Tram: 4 to Keizersgracht.

Wilhelmina-Dok ⋆ CONTINENTAL   Across the IJ waterway from Centraal Station, this fine waterfront eatery more than justifies a short, free ferryboat ride across the IJ followed by a 5-minute walk. Plain wood, candlelit tables, wood floors, and oak cabinets give the interior an old-fashioned maritime look, and large windows serve up views across the narrow, boat-speckled channel. Tables on the terrace are sheltered from the wind in a glass-walled enclosure.

Nordwal 1. (𝒞 020/632-3701. www.wilhelmina-dok.nl. Main courses 17€–19€ ($22–$25). AE, DC, MC, V. Daily 11am–midnight. Ferry: IJveer from Waterplein West behind Centraal Station to the dock at IJplein, then walk or bike east along the dike-top path.

SHOPPING

Bargain-hunters won't have much luck (except maybe at the flea markets), but shopping in Amsterdam definitely has its rewards. Best buys include diamonds and traditional Dutch products such as Delftware, pewter, crystal, and old-fashioned clocks. No matter what you're looking for, you're sure to be impressed with the range of possibilities.

By far the most ubiquitous items you'll see will be those in the familiar blue-and-white "Delft" colors that have almost become synonymous with Holland. Souvenir stores, specialty stores, and department stores feature Delftware earthenware products in the widest variety of forms imaginable. Be aware that unless it meets certain specifications, that souvenir you bring home with you won't be an authentic piece of the hand-painted earthenware pottery that has made the Delft name famous. A wide selection of Delftware can be found at **Galeria d'Arte Rinascimento,** Prinsengracht 170 (𝒞 020/622-7509), across the canal from the Anne Frank House, and at the four branches of **Delftshop,** Prinsengracht 440 (𝒞 020/627-8299); Spiegelgracht 13 (𝒞 020/421-8360); Rokin 44 (𝒞 020/620-1000); and Muntplein 12 (𝒞 020/623-2271).

De Bijenkorf ⋆, Dam 1 (𝒞 0900/0919), Amsterdam's premier department store, has a vast array of goods in all price ranges.

Amsterdam diamond cutters have an international reputation for high standards. When you buy from them, you'll be given a certificate listing the weight, color, cut, and identifying marks of the gem you purchase. The following stores offer diamond cutting and polishing tours, as well as sales of the finished product: **Amsterdam Diamond Center,** Rokin 1–5 (© **020/624-5787**); **Coster Diamonds,** Paulus Potterstraat 2–8 (© **020/305-5555**); **Gassan Diamonds,** Nieuwe Uilenburgerstraat 173–175 (© **020/622-5333**); **Stoeltie Diamonds,** Wagenstraat 13–17 (© **020/623-7601**); and **Van Moppes Diamonds,** Albert Cuypstraat 2–6 (© **020/676-1242**).

MARKETS

You find just about anything your imagination can dream up, at the **Albert Cuyp Markt,** Albert Cuypstraat, It's open Monday to Saturday from 9am to 6pm. From March to December, Thorbeckeplein hosts a **Sunday Art Market** where local artists show off their wares. **Waterlooplein Flea Market** ✿ is the city's classic market, offering everything from cooking pots to mariner's telescopes to decent prints of Dutch cities; it's open Monday to Saturday from 10am to 5pm. And gardeners will find it well-nigh impossible to leave Amsterdam without at least one purchase from the floating **Flower Market,** on Singel at Muntplein, open daily year-round. Just be certain the bulbs you buy bear the obligatory certificate clearing them for entry into the United States and Canada.

NIGHTLIFE

Like an Indonesian rijsttafel, nightlife in Amsterdam is a bit of this and a bit of that. There's a strong jazz scene, good music clubs, and some enjoyable English-language shows at the little cabarets and theaters along the canals. The club and bar scene can be entertaining if not outrageous; the dance clubs may indeed seem quiet and small to anyone used to the flash of New York, L.A., or London. However, the brown cafes—the typical Amsterdam pubs—have never been better.

Amsterdam's top orchestra is the famed **Royal Concertgebouw Orchestra,** whose home is the **Concertgebouw** ✿✿, Concertgebouwplein 2–6 (© **020/671-8345**; daily 10am–5pm, 24-hr. information line © 020/675-4411). World-class orchestras and soloists are only too happy to appear at the Concertgebouw's Grote Zaal (Great Hall) because of its perfect acoustics. Chamber and solo recitals are given in the Kleine Zaal (Little Hall). Tickets cost from 15€ to 100€ ($20–$130). The main concert season is September to mid-June, and during July and August there is the Robeco Summer Concerts, also world class but with a listener-friendly price tag—all seats are just 25€ ($33).

The **Netherlands Opera** has established an international reputation for mounting daring productions. The company performs at the **Muziektheater** ✿, Waterlooplein 22 (24-hr. information line © **020/551-8100,** or 020/625-5455 box office). This theater is also used by the **National Ballet,** which performs large-scale classical ballet repertoire as well as contemporary work, and by the **Netherlands Dance Theater,** which is based in The Hague and is famous for its groundbreaking contemporary repertoire. Most performances begin at 8:15pm, with opera tickets selling for 25€ to 100€ ($33–$130), and ballet tickets for 15€ to 150€ ($20–$195).

Opened in 2005 in a spectacular piece of modern architecture on the IJ waterfront just east of Centraal Station, the **Muziekgebouw aan 't IJ,** Piet Heinkade 1 (© **020/788-2000**), is the city's new home for avant-garde and experimental music. Look for concerts of modern, old, jazz, electronic, and non-Western music, along with small-scale musical theater, opera, and dance. Tickets are 10€ to 50€ ($13–$65). In a kind of annex is the equally new home of the jazz and improvised music club the **Bimhuis,** Piet Heinkade 3 (© 020/788-2188). Tickets here are 10€ to 20€ ($13–$26).

For several years, **Boom Chicago,** Leidsepleintheater, Leidseplein 12 (© 020/423-0101), has been bringing delightful English-language improvisational comedy to Amsterdam. Dutch audiences don't have much of a problem with the English sketches; they often seem to get the point ahead of the native English speakers in attendance. Tickets are 13€ to 22€ ($17–$29). Spectators are seated around candlelit tables for eight people and can have dinner and a drink while they enjoy the show. The restaurant is open at 7pm, and meals are 16€ to 20€ ($21–$26).

In Amsterdam, jazz and blues groups hold forth in bars, and the joints start jumping at around 11pm. You'll find listings in *What's On.* **Bourbon Street,** Leidsekruisstraat 6–8 (© 020/623-3440), hosts a mix of local and traveling jazz and blues talent. **Maloe Melo,** Lijnbaansgracht 163 (© 020/420-4592), Amsterdam's "home of the blues," features live blues most nights, interspersed with jazz and country evenings, and jams on Tuesday and Thursday nights. It's generally packed every night.

Amsterdam's dance-club scene embraces every type of ambience and clientele, from the sophisticated rooms in large hotels to underground alternative spots. The scene isn't wildly volatile, but places do come and go. Leading clubs include **Akhnaton,** Nieuwezijds Kolk 25 (© 020/624-3396), for African music and salsa; **Melkweg,** Lijnbaansgracht 234A (© 020/624-1777), for a variety of live music plus dance events; and **Paradiso,** Weteringschans 6–8 (© 020/626-4521), which has live music followed by dance parties. At **Odeon,** Singel 460 (© 020/624-9711), set in a 17th-century canal house, you can dance to jazz, funk, house, techno, R&B, and classic disco—all at the same time, since there are three different floors.

BROWN CAFES

You'll find *bruine kroegen* (brown cafes) everywhere: on street corners, at the canal intersections, and down narrow little lanes. They look as if they've been there forever, and they have, practically. These neighborhood bars are the favorite local haunts. Brown cafes will typically sport lace half-curtains at the front window and ancient Oriental rugs on tabletops (to sop up any spills from your beer). Wooden floors, overhead beams, and plastered walls blend into a murky brown background, darkened by the centuries of smoke from Dutch pipes and cigars. Frequently there's a wall rack with newspapers and magazines, but they get little attention in the evening, when conversation flows as readily as *pils* (beer). *Jenever,* the potent Dutch gin, is on hand in several different flavors, some served ice cold—but never on the rocks.

Your hotel neighborhood is sure to have at least one brown cafe close at hand. Far be it for me to set any sort of rigid itinerary for a brown-cafe *kroegentocht* ("pub crawl"), but you just might want to look into the following: **Hoppe,** Spui 18–20 (© 020/623-7849), a student and journalist hangout since 1670, which has sawdust on the floor and is always packed; **'t Smalle,** Egelantiersgracht 12 (© 020/623-9617), in the Jordaan district on the canal side, a bar in a former distillery and tasting house that dates from 1786; **Café Chris,** Bloemstraat 42 (© 020/624-5942), a tap house since 1624; **De Karpershoek,** Martelaarsgracht 2 (© 020/624-7886), which dates from 1629 and was once a favorite hangout of sailors; and **Papeneiland,** Prinsengracht 2 (© 020/624-1989), a 300-year-old establishment filled with character and with a secret tunnel used by 17th-century Catholics.

Smoking Coffee Shops

Visitors often get confused about "smoking" coffee shops and how they differ from "no-smoking" ones. Well, to begin with, "smoking" and "no-smoking" don't refer to cigarettes—they refer to hashish and marijuana. The use of narcotic drugs is officially illegal in the Netherlands, but Amsterdam and some other local authorities permit the sale in licensed premises of up to 5 grams (.2 oz.) of hashish or marijuana for personal consumption.

Smoking coffee shops not only sell cannabis, most commonly in the form of hashish, but also provide a place where patrons can sit and smoke it all day long if they so choose. Generally, these smoking coffee shops are the only places in Amsterdam called "coffee shops"—regular cafes are called cafes or *eetcafes*—so chances are, whether or not you want to smoke, you'll be able to find what you're looking for without too much difficulty.

AN EXCURSION TO HAARLEM ✦

Traditionally the little sister city of Amsterdam, this handsome small city, has a similar 17th-century ambience but gets by fine without the hassles that go with the capital's famously tolerant and often eccentric lifestyle.

ESSENTIALS

GETTING THERE   **Trains** depart at least every half hour from Amsterdam Centraal Station for Haarlem; the trip takes around 15 minutes. The historic center is a 5- to 10-minute walk from the graceful 1908 Art Nouveau train station (which is decorated with painted tiles and has a fine station restaurant).

VISITOR INFORMATION   **VVV Haarlem,** Stationsplein 1 (© **0900/616-1600;** www.vvvzk.nl), is just outside the train station.

TOP ATTRACTIONS & SPECIAL MOMENTS

First-time visitors generally head straight for the **Grote Markt** ✦✦✦, the handsome central market square. Most points of interest in Haarlem are within easy walking distance of the Grote Markt. The monumental buildings around the square date from the 15th to the 19th century and are a visual minicourse in the development of Dutch architecture. Here stands Haarlem's 14th-century **Stadhuis (Town Hall),** a former hunting lodge of the counts of Holland rebuilt in the 17th century.

Adjacent to the Grote Markt, the splendid **Sint-Bavokerk (Church of St. Bavo),** also known as the **Grote Kerk (Great Church)** ✦, Oude Groenmarkt 23 (© **023/532-4399;** www.bavo.nl), soars into the sky. Finished by 1520 after a relatively short building period, it has a rare unity of structure and proportion. Mozart, Handel, Mendelssohn, Schubert, and Liszt all made special visits to Haarlem to play the church's magnificent **Christian Müller Organ** (1738). It has 5,068 pipes and is nearly 98 feet (29m) tall, and when it's going flat out, it's loud enough to blow your socks off. You can hear it played at one of the free concerts on Tuesday evening and Thursday afternoon from April to October. St. Bavo's is open Monday to Saturday from 10am to 4pm. Admission is 2€ ($2.60) for adults, 1.25€ ($1.65) for children ages 12 to 16, and free for children under 12.

The city's finest attraction is the **Frans Hals Museum** ✶✶, Groot Heiligland 62 (✆ **023/511-5775;** www.franshalsmuseum.nl). In the galleries, halls, and furnished chambers of a 1608 home for retired gentlemen, the famous paintings by Frans Hals (ca. 1580–1686) and other masters of the Haarlem school hang in settings that look like the 17th-century houses they were intended to adorn. The museum is open Tuesday to Saturday from 11am to 5pm, and Sunday and holidays from noon to 5pm. Admission is 7€ ($9.10) for adults, and free for visitors under 19.

An ideal way to view the town is by canal boat. Tours by **Woltheus Cruises** (✆ **023/535-7723;** www.woltheuscruises.nl) depart from a jetty on the Spaarne River next to the Gravenstenenbrug, a handsome lift bridge. May to September, cruises are daily every hour from 11am to 6pm (the first and last cruises depart only if the number of passengers is sufficient); October to April, Tuesday to Saturday at the same times. Tickets are 6.50€ ($8.45) for adults, 3.50€ ($4.55) for children ages 3 to 11, and free for children under 3.

WHERE TO DINE

A popular cafe-restaurant, **Jacobus Pieck,** Warmoesstraat 18 (✆ **023/532-6144;** www.jacobuspieck.nl), has a lovely shaded terrace in the garden for fine-weather days, and inside it's bustling and stylish. Outside or in, you'll find excellent food and friendly, efficient service. At lunchtime they serve generous sandwiches and burgers, and their salads are particularly good. Main dinner courses range from pastas and Middle Eastern dishes to wholesome Dutch standards. Main courses are 15€ to 17€ ($20–$22).

3 The Hague ✶✶

Amsterdam is the national capital, but The Hague ('s-Gravenhage, or more commonly Den Haag, in Dutch) is the seat of government and the official residence of the Dutch monarchs. This tradition began in 1248, when Count Willem II of Holland was crowned king of the Romans in the German city of Aachen, but he chose to live at the Binnenhof Palace in what is now The Hague. Sophisticated, full of parks and elegant homes, the city has an 18th-century French look that suits its role as the diplomatic center of the Dutch nation.

GETTING THERE   The Hague is an easy day trip from Amsterdam, with frequent **train** service—including the Thalys international high-speed train—from Amsterdam Centraal Station. Note that The Hague has two main train stations, Centraal and Hollands Spoor; most of the sights are closer to Centraal Station, but some trains stop only at Hollands Spoor. Neither station has a tourist information office, but just outside both are tram and bus stops, and taxi stands.

TOURIST INFORMATION   **VVV Den Haag,** Hofweg 1 (mailing address: Postbus 85456, 2500 CD Den Haag; ✆ **0900/340-3505;** www.denhaag.com; tram: 1 or 16), is across the street from the Binnenhof (Parliament). The office is open Monday to Friday from 10am to 6pm, Saturday from 10am to 5pm, and Sunday from noon to 5pm.

TOP ATTRACTIONS & SPECIAL MOMENTS

The Hague's most notable attraction is the impressive **Binnenhof (Inner Court)** ✶ complex of Parliament buildings, in the center city. Join a tour, to visit the medieval **Ridderzaal (Hall of the Knights).** The queen delivers a speech from the throne here each year on the third Tuesday in September, arriving and departing in her golden

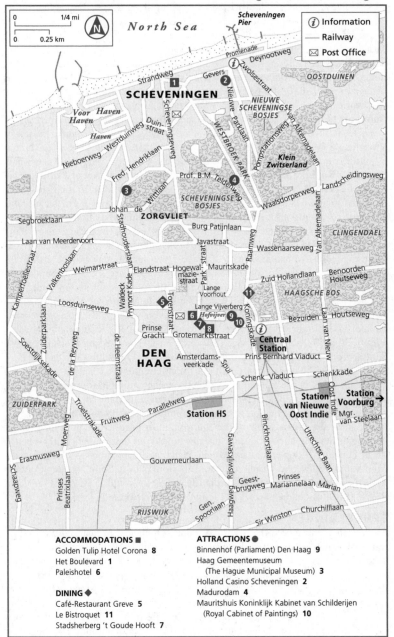

The Hague & Scheveningen

0   1/4 mi
0   0.25 km

North Sea

Scheveningen Pier

ⓘ Information
— Railway
✉ Post Office

Promenade
Deynootweg
Zwolsestraat
Strandweg
Gevers
OOSTDUINEN

1 SCHEVENINGEN
2
Nieuwe Parklaan
NIEUWE SCHEVENINGSE BOSJES
Van Alkemadelaan
Pompstationsweg

Voor Haven
Haven
Duin-straat
Scheveningsweg
Westduinweg
Haven
WESTBROEK PARK
Klein Zwitserland

Nieboerweg
Fred. Hendriklaan
Wittlaan
Prof. B.M. Teldersweg
4
Waalsdorperweg
Landscheidingsweg

3
Johan de Wittlaan
SCHEVENINGSE BOSJES
Raamweg
Van Alkemadelaan
CLINGENDAEL

Segbroeklaan
ZORGVLIET
Burg Patijnlaan

Laan van Meerdervoort
Javastraat
Wassenaarseweg

Weimarstraat
Elandstraat
Hogewal-mazie-straat
Mauritskade
Zuid Hollandlaan
Benoorden Houtseweg

Kamperfoeliestraat
Valkenboslaan
Waldeck Prymont Kade
Park-straat
Lange Voorhout
11
HAAGSCHE BOS

Loosduinseweg
Torenstraat
5
Lange Vijverberg
Hofvijver
9
Koningskade
Bezuiden Houtseweg

Stadhouderslaan
Prinse Gracht
6 **7** **8** **10**
Grotemarktstraat
ⓘ

de la Reyweg
de Heemstraat
DEN HAAG
Amsterdams-veerkade
Spui
Centraal Station
Prins Bernhard Viaduct

Soestdijksekade
Zuiderparklaan
Schenk Viaduct
Schenkkade

ZUIDERPARK
Troelstrakade
Parallelweg
Station HS
Station van Nieuwe Oost Indie
Station Voorburg →
Mgr. van Steelaan

Moerweg
Fruitweg
Binckhorstlaan
Utrechtse Baan

Erasmusweg
Gouverneurlaan

Schaapweg
Prinses Beatrixlaan
RIJSWIJK
Gen. Spoorlaan
Haagweg
Rijswijkseweg
Geest-brugweg
Prinses Mariannelaan
Marian
Sir Winston Churchilllaan

ACCOMMODATIONS ■
Golden Tulip Hotel Corona **8**
Het Boulevard **1**
Paleishotel **6**

DINING ◆
Café-Restaurant Greve **5**
Le Bistroquet **11**
Stadsherberg 't Goude Hooft **7**

ATTRACTIONS ●
Binnenhof (Parliament) Den Haag **9**
Haag Gemeentemuseum
  (The Hague Municipal Museum) **3**
Holland Casino Scheveningen **2**
Madurodam **4**
Mauritshuis Koninklijk Kabinet van Schilderijen
  (Royal Cabinet of Paintings) **10**

coach—like Cinderella—drawn by high-stepping royal horses. Depending on government business, you can tour one or the other of the two chambers of the **Staten-Generaal (States General),** the Dutch Parliament, which is open for guided tours Monday to Saturday from 10am to 4pm. Tours are 7€ ($9.10) or 5€ ($6.50) for adults, and 6€ ($7.80) or 4€ ($5.20) for seniors, students, and children ages 13 and under, depending on the tour being offered at the time. It's requested you book ahead by telephone (© **070/364-6144;** www.binnenhofbezoek.nl) for the guided tour, and that you call ahead to confirm that tours are going on the day you intend to visit. Admission to the Parliament exhibit in the reception room of the Hall of Knights is free.

Adjacent to the Binnenhof is the Italian Renaissance–style **Mauritshuis,** Korte Vijverberg 8 (© **070/302-3435;** www.mauritshuis.nl), built in 1644 as the home of a young court dandy and cousin of the Orange-Nassaus. Today this small palace houses the **Koninklijk Kabinet van Schilderijen (Royal Cabinet of Paintings)** ✚✚, and is the permanent home of an impressive art collection given to the Dutch nation by King Willem I in 1816. Highlights include 13 Rembrandts, 3 Frans Hals, and 3 Vermeers (including the famous *View of Delft*), plus hundreds of other famous works by such painters as Bruegel, Rubens, Steen, and Holbein (including his portrait of Jane Seymour, 3rd wife of King Henry VIII of England). The gallery is open April to August, Monday to Saturday from 10am to 5pm, and Sunday from 11am to 5pm; September to March, Tuesday to Saturday from 10am to 5pm, and Sunday from 11am to 5pm. Admission is 9.50€ ($12) for adults and free for visitors under 19.

The **Gemeentemuseum Den Haag (The Hague Municipal Museum)** ✚, Stadhouderslaan 41 (© **070/338-1111;** www.gemeentemuseum.nl), possesses a world-famous collection of works by Piet Mondrian (1872–1944), including his last work, *Victory Boogie Woogie* (1943), inspired by New York. The museum is open Tuesday to Sunday from 11am to 5pm. Admission is 8.50€ ($11) for adults, 6.50€ ($8.45) for seniors, 5€ ($6.50) for students, and free for children under 19.

Not far away, in the Scheveningen Woods, is enchanting **Madurodam** ✚, George Maduroplein 1 (© **070/416-2400;** www.madurodam.nl; tram: 9), a miniature village in 1-to-25 scale that represents the Dutch nation in actual proportions of farmland to urban areas. It presents many of the country's most historic buildings in miniature, with lights that actually work, bells that ring, and trains that run efficiently—as trains do in Holland. It's open January to mid-March and September to December, daily from 9am to 6pm; mid-March to June, daily from 9am to 8pm; and July to August, daily from 9am to 11pm. Admission is 13€ ($17) for adults, 12€ ($16) for seniors, 9.25€ ($12) for children ages 4 to 11, and free for children under 4.

SCHEVENINGEN ✚

So close to The Hague is the beach resort and fishing port of **Scheveningen**—just 3 miles (5km)—it seems part of the same city. This is probably Holland's most chic seacoast resort and contains an array of international-name boutiques and upscale restaurants. Yet you can still catch a sight of costumed fishermen's wives near the harbor—they dress up in their traditional Dutch garb for special events, like *Vlaggetjesdag* (Flag Day) in early June when the first of the new season's herring are landed.

To get there from The Hague, take tram 1 or 9 from Den Haag Centraal Station to Gevers Deynootplein in Scheveningen (tram 10, 11, and 17 from The Hague stop close to Scheveningen's fishing harbor). Tourist information is available from **VVV Scheveningen,** Gevers Deynootweg 1134 (© **0900/340-3505;** www.denhaag.com), at the Palace Promenade mall.

Moments   **A Right Royal Bus Route**

If you have an interest in royalty and palaces, take a ride on city bus no. 4. Its route passes four Dutch palaces built during the 16th and 17th centuries, among them Huis ten Bosch, the home of Queen Beatrix, in the Haagse Bos (Hague Woods); no visits are permitted.

Among Scheveningen's attractions are biking, strolling on the dunes, fishing in the North Sea, and splashing in the waves at the beach or in a heated wave pool. The beach and bathing zone is called Scheveningen Bad—but it looks pretty good to the Dutch.

Tuxedoed croupiers provide blackjack and roulette at **Holland Casino Scheveningen,** Kurhausweg 1 (© **070/306-7777**), across from the beautifully restored 19th-century Kurhaus Hotel. The dress code is "correct" (collar and tie for men), and the minimum age is 18. You need your passport to get in. The casino is open daily from 10am to 3am. Admission is 3.50€ ($4.55).

WHERE TO STAY

Corona *€*   Centrally located opposite the Parliament, this charming, small hotel, once a lively coffeehouse, features contemporary decor, with touches of handsome marble and mahogany in the lobby. The guest rooms are done in soft pastel colors with graceful window drapes. The elegant main restaurant, full of French Provincial furnishings, is a favorite retreat for the good and the great in government circles. On balmy days, part of the restaurant becomes a sidewalk terrace.

Buitenhof 39–42, 2513 AH Den Haag. © **070/363-7930.** Fax 070/361-5785. www.corona.nl. 36 units. 110€–175€ ($143–$163) double. Rates include buffet breakfast on weekends. AE, DC, MC, V. Tram: 10, 16, or 17 to Buitenhof. **Amenities:** 2 restaurants; bar; laundry. *In room:* Hair dryer, no A/C.

Het Boulevard   Perched atop the sea dunes at Scheveningen within walking distance of the Palace Promenade, this hotel has a commanding sea view from its sun lounge/restaurant and from some of the guest rooms, which all are plainly furnished in a clean-cut, modern style. The hotel has special family rooms for those with young children.

Seinpostduin 1, 2586 EA Scheveningen. © **070/354-0067.** Fax 070/355-2574. www.boulevard-hotel.nl. 30 units. 85€–105€ ($111–$176) double. Rates include buffet breakfast. AE, DC, MC, V. Tram: 1 or 9 to Keizerstraat; or 11 to Scheveningen Haven. *In room:* No A/C.

Paleis Hotel *€*   Behind the royal family's Noordeinde Palace, this intimate hotel has spacious and elegant guest rooms furnished with soft chairs and settees, in a quiet city-center setting. Bathrooms are a bit small but fitted out beautifully. Some rooms are air-conditioned. The location is excellent both for shopping (the pedestrian shopping promenade is nearby) and for sightseeing.

Molenstraat 26, 2513 BL Den Haag. © **070/362-4621.** Fax 070/361-4533. www.paleishotel.nl. 20 units. 195€–245€ ($254–$319) double. AE, DC, MC, V. Tram: 17 to Gravenstraat. **Amenities:** Bar. *In room:* Hair dryer, A/C (in some rooms).

WHERE TO DINE

Café-Restaurant Greve MEDITERRANEAN   A building that once housed a car showroom is now a popular restaurant. The cafe's large windows look out on lively Torenstraat; the restaurant is more intimate, with low ceiling, candlelight, and wooden tables. There's a small a la carte menu and a three-course fixed price option. You can choose to have a dish either as a starter or as a main course—an ideal solution for small appetites or those who want to sample the menu.

Torenstraat 138. (**C**) **070/360-3919.** www.greve.nl. Main courses 12€–22€ ($16–$29); fixed-price menus 20€–30€ ($26–$39). AE, DC, MC, V. Cafe daily 10am–1am; restaurant Mon–Sat 6–11pm, Sun 6–10pm. Tram: 17 to Noordwal.

Le Bistroquet ⭐ CONTINENTAL   This small, popular restaurant in the center city is one of The Hague's finest, its quietly elegant dining room featuring lovely table settings. The menu, though short, is to the point, and covers lamb, fish, and poultry dishes. A fine Dutch menu choice is the three variations of Texel lamb with roasted garlic and a basil sauce.

Lange Voorhout 98. (**C**) **070/360-1170.** www.bistroquet.nl. Main courses 25€–35€ ($33–$46). AE, DC, MC, V. Mon–Fri noon–2pm and 6–10pm; Sat 6–10pm. Tram: 10, 16, or 17 to Kneuterdijk.

Stadsherberg 't Goude Hooft ⭐⭐ DUTCH/CONTINENTAL   There's a definite old Dutch flavor to this wonderful, large restaurant overlooking the city's old market square, yet its 1600s exterior cloaks a 1939 interior installed after a disastrous fire. The wooden beams, brass chandeliers, and rustic chairs and tables blend harmoniously with the stained-glass windows, medieval banners, and wall murals. There's a large sidewalk cafe on the "Green Market" square. An extensive menu covers everything from snacks to light lunches to full dinners.

Dagelijkse Groenmarkt 13. (**C**) **070/346-9713.** www.tgoudehooft.nl. Main courses 14€–20€ ($18–$26); fixed-price menus 16€–24€ ($21–$31). AE, DC, MC, V. Mon noon–6pm; Tues–Wed and Fri–Sat 10am–7pm; Thurs 10am–9:30pm, Sun 11am–6pm. Tram: 17 to Gravenstraat.

AN EXCURSION TO DELFT ⭐⭐

Yes, this is the home of the famous blue-and-white porcelain, and you can visit the factory where it is produced. This small, handsome city is also the cradle of the Dutch Republic and the burial place of the royal family, and was the birthplace and inspiration of artist Jan Vermeer, the 17th-century master of light and subtle emotion.

GETTING THERE   There's frequent **train** service from Amsterdam; the ride takes just under 1 hour. The train station in Delft is only a short walk from the center city, or you can take one of the buses, trams, or taxis that stop right outside the station. **Tram** service is also available from Den Haag Centraal to Delft and costs 4 strips on a *strippenkaart,* or about 1.80€ ($2.35).

VISITOR INFORMATION   Tourist Information Delft, Hippolytusbuurt 4, 2611 HN Delft (© **015/215-4051;** www.delft.nl), is located in the center of town. The office is open April to September, Sunday and Monday from 10am to 6pm, Tuesday to Friday from 9am to 6pm, and Saturday from 10am to 5pm; October to March, Sunday from 11am to 4pm, and Tuesday to Saturday from 10am to 4pm.

TOP ATTRACTIONS & SPECIAL MOMENTS

The house where Vermeer was born, lived, and painted is long gone from Delft, as are his paintings. The artist's burial place, the **Oude Kerk (Old Church),** Roland Holstlaan 753 (© **015/212-3015**), is noted for its 27 stained-glass windows by Joep Nicolas. You should also visit the **Nieuwe Kerk (New Church)** ⭐, Markt (© **015/212-3025**), where Prince William of Orange and other members of the House of Orange-Nassau are buried. Both churches are open April to October, Monday to Saturday from 9am to 6pm; November to March, Monday to Friday from 11am to 4pm and

Saturday from 11am to 5pm. Admission is 3€ ($3.90) for adults, 2.50€ ($3.25) for seniors, 1.50€ ($1.95) for children ages 5 to 14, and free for children under 5 (tickets are valid in both churches).

The **Stedelijk Museum Het Prinsenhof** *ⓕ*, St. Agathaplein 1 (*ⓒ* **015/260-2358;** www.prinsenhof-delft.nl), on nearby Oude Delft, is where William I of Orange (William the Silent) lived and had his headquarters in the years when he helped found the Dutch Republic. He was assassinated here in 1584, and you can see the bullet holes in the stairwell. Today the Prinsenhof is a museum of paintings, tapestries, silverware, and pottery. It's open Tuesday to Saturday from 10am to 5pm, and Sunday and holidays from 1 to 5pm. Admission is 5€ ($6.50) for adults, 4€ ($5.20) for seniors and children ages 12 to 16, and free for children under 12.

In the same neighborhood you can view a fine collection of old Delft tiles displayed in the wood-paneled setting of a 19th-century mansion museum called **Lambert van Meerten,** Oude Delft 199 (*ⓒ* **015/260-2358;** www.lambertvanmeerten-delft.nl). The museum is open Tuesday to Saturday from 10am to 5pm, and Sunday and holidays from 1 to 5pm. Admission is 3.50€ ($4.55) for adults; 3€ ($3.90) for seniors, students, and children ages 12 to 16; and free for children under 12.

To view a demonstration of the traditional art of making and hand-painting Delftware, visit the factory and showroom of **Koninklijke Porceleyne Fles,** Rotterdamseweg 196 (*ⓒ* **015/251-2030;** www.royaldelft.com), founded in 1653. It's open April to October, daily from 9am to 5pm; November to March, Monday to Saturday from 9am to 5pm. Admission is 4€ ($5.20) for adults, and free for children under 12.

WHERE TO DINE

The skillfully prepared dishes at **Le Vieux Jean,** Heilige Geestkerkhof 3 (*ⓒ* **015/213-0433;** www.levieuxjean.nl), draw from the provincial French tradition, using the freshest of top-quality ingredients. The setting is an old churchyard just across from the Oude Kerk, and you receive a warm and friendly welcome. Main courses cost 24€ to 34€ ($31–$44); fixed-price menus 33€ to 55€ ($43–$72).

Some of the best Dutch cooking in the country is dished up at the atmospheric **Spijshuis de Dis** *ⓕ*, Beestenmarkt 36 (*ⓒ* **015/213-1782;** www.spijshuisdedis.com), east of the market. Look out for traditional plates presented in modern variations. A good example is the *Bakke pot*—a stew made from three kinds of meat (beef, chicken, and rabbit) in a beer sauce, served in the pan. An entree will set you back 14€ to 22€ ($18–$29); fixed-price menu 30€ ($39).

4 Maastricht *ⓕ*

A riverside city of cafes and churches, Maastricht (pop. 120,000) is a seductive mixture of historic buildings and monuments, a lighthearted carnival, and some of the finest restaurants to be found in any Dutch city of its size. Somehow—in between eating, drinking, church-going, stepping out for Carnival, and hanging onto their heritage—the people of Maastricht are building a modern, prosperous, and vibrant city. Discovering how they do it all can be quite an education.

GETTING THERE   Trains depart hourly from Amsterdam, Rotterdam, and The Hague for the approximately 2½-hour journey to Maastricht (trains from Amsterdam are direct; those from Rotterdam and The Hague require a transfer in Eindhoven). Maastricht station is a 15- to 20-minute walk from the Vrijthof square in the center city. Outside the station are bus stops and a taxi stand.

VISITOR INFORMATION **VVV Maastricht,** Kleine Staat 1 (© **043/325-2121;** www.vvvmaastricht.nl), is off Grote Straat, a 15-minute walk from the train station, across the Maas River. It's open May to October Monday to Saturday from 9am to 6pm, and Sunday from 11am to 3pm; November to April Monday to Friday from 9am to 6pm, and Saturday from 9am to 5pm.

TOP ATTRACTIONS & SPECIAL MOMENTS

Walking from the train station to the center of town, you head down Stationstraat, cross the Maas on the **Sint-Servaasbrug (St. Servatius Bridge),** which dates from 1280 to 1289 and is one of the oldest bridges in the Netherlands. The **Vrijthof** 𝕮𝕮, the city's most glorious square, is a vast open space bordered on three sides by restaurants and cafes with sidewalk terraces, and on the fourth by the Romanesque Sint-Servaas Basilica and the Gothic Sint-Jan's Church with its soaring red belfry. This is Maastricht's forum, especially in good weather, when the cafe terraces are filled with people soaking up the atmosphere and watching the world go by.

The oldest parts of the majestic cruciform **Sint-Servaasbasiliek (Basilica of St. Servatius),** Keizer Karelplein (© **043/325-2121;** www.sintservaas.nl), date from the year 1000, though the church was considerably enlarged in the 14th and 15th centuries. St. Servatius, Maastricht's first bishop, is buried in the crypt. Over the centuries people have honored the saint with gifts, so the treasury has a collection of incredible richness and beauty that includes two superb 12th-century reliquaries fashioned by Maastricht goldsmiths. The basilica is open Monday to Saturday from 10am to 5pm, and Sunday from 12:30 to 5pm. Admission is 3.50€ ($4.55) for adults, 2.10€ ($2.75) for seniors and students, 1€ ($1.30) for children ages 6 to 12, and free for children under 6.

Next door, the sober, whitewashed interior of the city's main Dutch Reformed (Protestant) church, **Sint-Janskerk (St. John's Church),** dating from the 14th century and given to the Protestants in 1633, makes a study in contrasts with the lavish Catholic decoration at St. Servatius's. But there are murals, sculpted corbels of the 12 Apostles, and grave monuments of local dignitaries and wealthy individuals. Most visitors come here, though, to climb the 218 narrow, winding steps to the 230-foot-high (69m) belfry's windy viewing platform, 141 feet (42m) above the streets, and the fine city views it affords. The church is open Easter to mid-October, Monday to Saturday from 11am to 4pm. Admission to the church is free; and to the tower is 1.50€ ($1.95) for adults, and .50€ (65¢) for children under 13.

The west wing and crypts of the Romanesque cruciform **Onze-Lieve-Vrouwbasiliek (Basilica of Our Lady)** 𝕮, Onze-Lieve-Vrouweplein (© **043/325-1851;** www.sterre-der-zee.nl), date from the 11th century, and there's evidence of an even earlier church and a pagan place of worship on the site. But the side chapel sheltering a statue of Our Lady Star of the Sea is the focus for most pilgrims. The richly robed statue, fronted by a blaze of candles, is credited with many miracles, even during long years when it was hidden away because of religious persecution. The church treasury contains a rich collection of tapestries, reliquaries, church silver, and other religious objects. The basilica is open daily from 11am to 5pm, except during services; the treasury is open Easter to mid-October, Monday to Saturday from 11am to 5pm, and Sunday from 1 to 5pm. Admission to the basilica is free; and to the treasury is 3€ ($2.10) for adults, 2€ ($2.60) for seniors, and 1€ ($1.30) for children under 13.

Designed by Italian architect Aldo Rossi and opened in 1995, the riverside **Bonnefanten Museum** ✿, av. Céramique 250 (© **043/329-0190;** www.bonnefanten.nl), is instantly recognizable from its striking, bullet-shaped dome. Works of art within include pieces from the Maasland School, such as sculpture, silverwork, and woodcarvings produced along the Maas Valley in Limburg and Belgium. This art dates from as far back as the 13th century and had its apogee during the 15th and 16th centuries. Internationalism is illustrated in the museum's collection of Italian and Flemish masters. These include works by Filippo Lippi and Bellini, and Pieter Bruegel the Younger's *Wedding in Front of a Farm* and *Census at Bethlehem.* The museum is open Tuesday to Sunday from 11am to 5pm. Admission is 7.50€ ($9.75) for adults, 3.75€ ($4.90) for children ages 13 to 18, and free for children under 13.

For centuries, marlstone has been extracted from **Sint-Pietersberg (Mount St. Peter)** ✿✿ (© **043/325-2121;** www.pietersberg.nl), on the city's southwestern edge, leaving the hill's interior honeycombed with 20,000 passages. From Roman times to the days of medieval sieges to the 4 years of Nazi occupation during World War II, there passages have served as a place of refuge. The temperature underground is about 50°F (10°C), and it's damp, so bring a cardigan or a coat to protect against the chill. The caves are open July to September, daily at 2:45pm. Guided tours are 4€ ($5.20) for adults and 2.75€ ($3.60) for children under 13.

WHERE TO STAY & DINE

There's been an inn on the site of the **Hotel Du Casque** ✿, Helmstraat 14 (© **043/321-4343;** www.hotelducasque.nl), since the 15th century. The present family-run hotel carries on the proud tradition, with contemporary facilities, comfortable rooms, and good old-fashioned friendliness. It faces the lively Vrijthof square; those rooms overlooking the Vrijthof have the finest view in town. Doubles cost 124€ to 144€ ($161–$188).

At **De Poshoorn,** Stationsstraat 47 (© **043/321-7334;** www.poshoorn.nl), a small corner hotel near the train station, you register with the friendly owner in the ground-floor cafe. You needn't be afraid of being disturbed in your sleep—from the rooms you can hardly hear any of what's going on downstairs. The guest rooms aren't too large, but they're modern and have comfortable beds. Doubles cost 70€ ($91).

One of the city's top restaurants, **Toine Hermsen** ✿✿, Sint Bernardusstraat 2–4 (© **043/325-8400;** www.toinehermsen.com), on the corner of Onze-Lieve-Vrouweplein, is the proud possessor of a Michelin star. The chef creates French cuisine classics and exploits regional seasonal ingredients such as Limburg's asparagus and chicory. You can expect good portions of impeccable food and superb but relaxed service. Reservations are required. Main courses cost 25€ to 45€ ($33–$59); fixed-price menus are 30€ to 65€ ($39–$85).

Local favorite **'t Plenkske** ✿, Plankstraat 6 (© **043/321-8456;** www.hetplenkske.nl), is a fine restaurant in the Stokstraat Quarter, with a light, airy decor and an outdoor patio overlooking the site of the city's ancient Roman baths. Regional specialties from both Maastricht and Liège are prominent on the menu, along with a number of French classics thrown in for good measure. Main courses cost 15€ to 24€ ($20–$31); the fixed-price menu is 25€ ($33).

15

Norway

For the rail traveler, the mountainous and elongated country of Norway is the crown jewel of Scandinavia. From its snowcapped mountains to its scenic fjords warmed by the Gulf Stream, much of the country's varied land- and seascapes can be seen from your train window. The rail ride between the eastern capital city of Oslo and its western outpost of historic Bergen (gateway to the fjord district) is one of the most scenic in Europe, vying with some of the dramatic mountain rail journeys in alpine Switzerland. See "Highlights of Norway," below, for more details on this 7-hour trip.

Norwegian rail engineers have defied nature and laid tracks through dizzying, difficult terrain that was once accessible only to mountain goats and spry adventurers. You are carried quickly and efficiently across the often breathtaking terrain of this beautiful land. Routes are not comprehensive, especially as you go into the far north toward Lapland and the Midnight Sun, but rail lines are gloriously scenic, and the major towns and their myriad attractions are easily reached by train.

Norway has dramatic scenery in abundance, but do bear in mind that it comes at a price; what Norway doesn't have is cheap living. In fact, in 2007, the U.K.'s Economic Intelligence Unit, placed it as *the* most expensive city in the world. High prices, however, shouldn't deter the value-minded rail traveler. In this chapter, we provide some budget-saving tips along with recommendations of moderately priced hotels and restaurants.

Note: A map detailing Norway's rail routes as well as the rail lines of the major Scandinavian countries can be found on p. 197.

HIGHLIGHTS OF NORWAY

With a very small window of opportunity for warm and sunny days, a key factor in timing your rail visit to Norway is, of course, the weather. The summer season is very short, beginning in June (May is still quite cold) and ending by late August, when it's often possible to see snow flurries whirling about your head. Expect long days of sunlight, even at night. North of the Arctic Circle, the Midnight Sun is clearly visible. Once September arrives, days quickly grow cold; open-air museums close down; attractions, including tourist offices, go on reduced hours; and—most important for the rail traveler—trains begin running on less frequent schedules. Winter sports continue under dark, foreboding skies including dog-sledding, ice-fishing, and cross-country and alpine skiing, but these attract only the most hearty (and warmly dressed) travelers.

Average rail passengers will not have much time for exploring the northern reaches of this ancient land of the Vikings and can happily confine themselves to the two greatest cities in Norway: Oslo, the capital, and the "second city" of Bergen. Oslo, one of the world's most beautifully sited capitals, deserves at least 2 or 3 days of your time; as does Bergen, whose charm and history are as compelling as its excellent accessibility to

Moments Festivals & Special Events

Norway's cities and towns stage numerous festivals and special events throughout the year (check with the local tourist office to see what's going on during your visit), but the following three are definitely worth a look if you're in town for them:

The **Holmenkollen Ski Festival** held on the outskirts of Oslo in early March is one of Europe's largest ski festivals, with World Cup Nordic skiing and biathlons, international ski-jumping competitions, and Norway's largest cross-country race for amateurs. For more information, contact **Skiforeningen,** Kongeveien 5, Holmenkollen, 0787 Oslo (© **22-92-32-00;** www. skiforeningen.no).

From mid-May to early June, the world-class **Bergen International Festival (Bergen Festspill)** features musical artists from Norway and around the world. It's is one of the largest annual musical events in Scandinavia. For information, contact the Bergen International Festival, P.O. Box 183, Sentrum, N-5804 Bergen, (© **55-21-06-30;** www.fib.no).

The major event on the Oslo calendar, the **Nobel Peace Prize Ceremony** is held annually at Oslo City Hall on December 10. Attendance is by invitation only. For information, contact the **Nobel Institute,** Henrik Ibsens gate 51, N-0255 Oslo (© **22-12-93-00;** www.nobelpeaceprize.org).

the western fjord district. Both cities are located in the south, where this spoon-shaped country rounds out into a bowl, with Oslo on the east and Bergen on the west.

Most flights to the country land in Oslo, making it the obvious starting point for a rail trip in Norway. A number of world-class attractions await you: **Akershus Castle,** one of the oldest historical monuments in Oslo; the 17th-century **Oslo Cathedral; Vigelandsparken** (a field of sculpture by Norway's greatest, Gustav Vigeland); the *Kon-Tiki* **Museum** housing the world-famous balsa log raft from 1947; the openair **Norwegian Folk Museum;** the **Viking Ship Museum** (with a trio of Viking burial vessels); and, outside of town, the **Henie Onstad Kunstsenter,** a treasure trove of art acquired by former movie star and skating champion Sonja Henie.

One of the great adventures of Norway is to make the 7-hour, 305-mile (490km) rail journey from Oslo to Bergen, one of the most startlingly beautiful in all of Europe. The train after leaving Oslo climbs to the little town of **Gol** at 679 feet (204m) before beginning a much steeper ascent. It reaches the winter resort of **Geilo** at 2,605 feet (782m) and continues to climb until it approaches the village of **Ustaoset** at 3,248 feet (974m). After that the train crosses a foreboding landscape of icy mountain lakes and rock-strewn ridges wearing "snow bonnets." Tickets for this journey are available from **Rail Europe** (© **877/272-RAIL;** www.raileurope.com).

At the tiny mountain village of **Finse,** in the vicinity of the **Hardangerjøkulen Glacier,** you are virtually in polar conditions. At 4,009 feet (1,203m), Finse is the highest station in Norway.

Leaving Finse, the Oslo–Bergen line goes through a 6¼-mile (10km) tunnel emerging near **Hallingskeid** before going on to its next stop at **Myrdal.** The descent then is to the lake town of **Voss,** only 184 feet (55m) above sea level and both a winter and a summer sports resort. The scenery grows tamer as the train begins its descent into Bergen, the last lap of this journey taking about an hour.

The final destination of **Bergen** is one of the great historic centers of Scandinavia, and had been the capital of Norway until it was unseated by Oslo. As the gateway to the fjords, its port was once the source of great power, ruled over by the Hanseatic League, a medieval mercantile guild. Situated on a peninsula, this UNESCO World Heritage Site is surrounded by towering mountains (which can be ascended by funicular) and filled with old cobblestone streets flanked by weather-beaten clapboard houses in various hues; one of these old (17th-c.) neighborhoods is called Chaos City because of its crazy mazes and unplanned buildings (go ahead, get lost in its atmosphere). Be sure to see the city's aquarium (one of the largest and best in Scandinavia), and to tour old Bryggen, a district of Hanseatic timbered houses along the waterfront. You also may want to tour the marketplace, which offers the best fresh seafood you can imagine.

1 Essentials

GETTING THERE

All transatlantic flights from North America land at Oslo's **Gardermoen Airport** (© 81-55-02-50; www.osl.no), 30 miles (48km) north of Oslo. **Continental** (© 800/231-0856;** www.continental.com) flies direct from Newark, New Jersey, to Oslo, taking 7 hours and 35 minutes.

Other airlines flying to Norway through a gateway city in Europe, include **British Airways** (© 800/AIRWAYS in the U.S.; www.britishairways.com), **SAS** (© 800/221-2350 in the U.S.; www.scandinavian.net), **Icelandair** (© 800/223-5500 in the U.S.; www.icelandair.com), and **KLM** (© 800/225-2525 in the U.S.; www.nwa.com).

NORWAY BY RAIL
PASSES

For information on the **Eurail Global Pass, Eurail Global Pass Flexi, Eurail Select Pass, Eurail Scandinavia Pass,** and other multicountry options, see chapter 2.

In addition to the multicountry passes, there is the **Eurail Norway Rail Pass.** The pass offers 3 to 8 days of unlimited second-class train travel in a 1-month period, starting at $243 for adults. Don't worry about it being a second-class pass, as the comfort level of second class on Norwegian trains is equal to first class in many other European countries. Similar passes for travelers under 26 and for seniors (over 60) start at $182. The pass must be purchased before leaving North America. You can buy the pass through **Rail Europe** (© 877/272-RAIL [7245] in North America; www.raileurope.com) or your travel agent.

FOREIGN TRAIN TERMS

Don't bother learning a lot of train terms in difficult-to-pronounce Norwegian. Norwegians start learning English while in grade school, and you can usually learn what you need to know by asking train personnel for help in English. That said, here are a few common terms you may find helpful to know: *Avgaende tog* means departure and *Ankommende tog* means arrival. *Billetter* are tickets.

PRACTICAL TRAIN INFORMATION

The **Norwegian State Railways (NSB)** operates the major rail lines of Norway. Call © 81-50-08-88 (press 4 for English) for timetable info and bookings. For info on the Web, log on to **www.nsb.no**.

⌒Moments The Essence of Norway

The must-do rail experience in this country is the trip from Oslo to Bergen, but those with more time—a total of 24 hours—will find another wonderful option that cuts through the heart of Norway on a northward trek: **A train trip from Oslo to Bodø** that captures what local tourist promoters accurately bill as "the essence" of Norway.

As the train heads north from Oslo, the scenery is bucolic with rolling hills, farmlands, and small villages. The farther north you go, the more dramatic the scenery becomes, especially as you continue north from the resort of Lillehammer, famed for hosting the 1992 Winter Olympics. When you reach Dombås—instead of going to Trondheim—you can detour to the northwest and the town of Åndalsnes. This leg is one of the grandest of all rail journeys in Scandinavia: Your train will plunge through tunnels carved through foreboding mountains, and whiz over bridges and past waterfalls and the highest vertical canyon in Norway.

After arriving in Åndalsnes, you can return to Dombås for a final journey to the north. If possible, plan an overnight stopover in the medieval city of Trondheim, one of the most historic and beautiful in Scandinavia and the ancient capital of Norway.

From Trondheim you can travel to the northern terminus of the rail line at Bodø, a city that lies north of the Arctic Circle. Many rail passengers in summer take this journey to Bodø just to bask in the Midnight Sun.

At Bodø, you can return on the same train to Oslo, or, as an alternative, you can take a bus northeast from Bodø to the city of Narvik. After a stopover in Narvik, you can once again board a train, the Ofoten Line, for a journey eastward into Sweden, where most passengers head southeast to the capital city of Stockholm.

Norway's 2,500-mile (4,044km) network of electric and diesel-electric trains runs as far as Bodø, 62 miles (100km) north of the Arctic Circle. (Beyond that, visitors must take a coastal steamer, plane, or bus to Tromsø and the North Cape.) The fastest express trains, called NSB Regiontog, crisscross the mountainous terrain between Oslo, Stavanger, Bergen, and Trondheim, using a tilting technology to help with the corners. Holders of first-class railpasses don't get to travel first class automatically (this would require payment of a supplement), but they do get access to an upgraded second-class compartment, which is just fine on these trains.

The most popular and most scenic run in the country covers the 305 miles (490km) between Oslo and Bergen. Visitors with limited time often choose this route for its fabled mountains, gorges, white-water rivers, and fjords. The trains often stop for passengers to enjoy breathtaking views. The one-way second-class fare from Oslo to Bergen is 728NOK ($109/£58.25). Seat reservations cost 50NOK ($7.50/£4) and are recommended in the summer season. Another popular run, from Oslo to Trondheim, costs 810NOK ($122/£64.80) one-way in second class.

Trains & Travel Times in Norway

From	To	Type of Train	# of Trains	Frequency	Travel Time
Oslo	Bergen	Regiontog	2	Daily	6 hr., 24 min.–6 hr., 41 min.
Oslo	Bergen	Regiontog	1	Daily	7 hr., 46 min.
Oslo	Bergen	Regiontog	2	Daily	7 hr., 9 min.–7 hr., 23 min.

One of the country's obviously scenic trips, from Bergen to Bodø, is not possible by train because of the rough terrain. Trains to Bodø leave from Oslo (see "The Essence of Norway," above).

If you're traveling direct between cities separated by a long distance and don't have a railpass, a **Minipris Ticket** (available in Norway only) might be a good option. With this ticket, you can travel in second class for 199NOK to 299NOK ($29.85–$44.85/ £15.90–£23.90) one-way, but only on routes that take you more than 93 miles (150km) from your point of origin. No stopovers are allowed except for a change of trains. Tickets are valid only on select trains, for boarding that begins during designated off-peak hours. You can buy Minipris Tickets at any railway station in Norway, by calling **Customer Service** at ✆ 81-56-82-22 (paying a supplement of 50NOK/ $7.50/£4), or online at **www.nsb.no**. The Minipris ticket has some restrictions, and seats sell out quickly.

Travelers over age 67 are entitled to a 50% discount, called an **Honnorrabatt,** on Norwegian train trips of more than 31 miles (49km). Regardless of age, the spouse of someone over 67 can also receive the 50% discount.

RESERVATIONS   Reservations are recommended on most InterCity and NSB Regiontog trains, and on all overnight and international services. A reservation costs 50NOK ($7.50/£4) above the price of your regular ticket or railpass if made in Norway. Sleepers on overnight trains should also be reserved (see below). It's not always necessary to make a reservation on secondary trains, but it's always advised in the summer season, as trains are likely to be filled to capacity.

Timetables are distributed free at all rail stations under the name of *NSB Togruter.* On the more scenic routes, you can often get data in English describing the highlights of the trip.

SERVICES & AMENITIES   Second-class travel on Norwegian trains is highly recommended. In fact, second class in Norway is as good as or better than first-class travel anywhere else in Europe, with reclining seats and various comforts. First-class coaches cost 50% more than second class and are considered "not worth the investment" by the majority of rail riders in Norway.

The sleepers on night trains (called **InterNordNight**) are a good investment because you'll be saving on a regular hotel accommodation. They have recently been refurbished and can now only be booked by the compartment. Each compartment contains two beds and costs 750NOK ($112.50/£60) for a one-way journey, regardless of whether it is occupied by one or two people. Breakfast is 60NOK ($9/£4.80) extra. Passengers can choose to travel in an ordinary seat instead, where they'll be given a pillow, blanket, eye mask, and earplugs. Sleepers can be booked through Rail Europe in North America. Children 4 to 15 years of age and senior citizens pay 50% of the regular adult fare. Group and midweek tickets are also available.

There are special compartments for persons with disabilities on most medium- and long-distance trains. People in wheelchairs and others with physical disabilities, as well as their companions, may use the compartments. Some long-distance trains offer special playrooms ("Kiddie-Wagons") for children, complete with toys and educational items.

The express trains running between Oslo and Bergen (or vice versa) have excellent dining cars, some of the best in northern Europe, but meals are terribly expensive. The secondary express trains have buffets, serving both hot meals and snacks. On the smaller regional trains, expect food wheeled through the cabin on a cart.

FAST FACTS: Norway

Area Code The international country code for Norway is **47**. If you're calling from outside the country, the city code is **2** for Oslo and **5** for Bergen. Inside Norway, no area or city codes are needed. Phone numbers have eight digits.

Business Hours Most **banks** are open Monday to Friday from 8:15am to 3:30pm (Thurs to 5pm), and are closed Saturday and Sunday. Most **businesses** are open Monday to Friday from 9am to 4pm. **Stores** are generally open Monday to Friday from 10am to 5pm (many stay open Thurs until 6 or 7pm) and Saturday 10am to 3pm. Shopping malls will often open later; until 8pm on weekdays and 3pm on Saturday. Most shops close on Sunday.

Climate In summer, the average temperature in Norway ranges from 57°F to 65°F (14°C–18°C). In January, it hovers around 27°F (3°C), ideal for winter sports. The Gulf Stream warms the west coast, where winters tend to be temperate. Rainfall, however, is heavy.

Above the Arctic Circle, the sun shines night and day from mid-May until late July. For about 2 months every winter, the North Cape is plunged into darkness.

Currency The basic unit of currency is the Norwegian krone (crown), or NOK, made up of 100 øre. At this writing, $1=6.5 NOK; £1=12.37 NOK.

Documents Required Citizens of the United States and Canada need a valid **passport** to enter Norway. You need to apply for a visa only if you want to stay more than 3 months.

Electricity Norway uses 220 volts, 30 to 50 cycles, A.C., and standard continental two-pin plugs. Transformers and adapters are needed to use Canadian and American equipment. Always inquire at your hotel before plugging in any electrical equipment.

Embassies & Consulates In case you lose your passport or have some other emergency, contact your embassy in Oslo. The Embassy of the **United States** is at Drammensveien 18, N-0244 Oslo (© **22-44-85-50;** www.usa.no); and **Canada's** is at Wergelandsveien 7, N-0244 Oslo (© **22-99-53-00;** www.canada.no).

Health & Safety Norway offers some of the best medical facilities in Europe, with well-trained, English-speaking doctors. Norway's national health plan does not cover American or Canadian visitors; medical expenses must be paid in cash and costs are generally more reasonable than elsewhere in Western Europe.

You're probably safer in Norway than in your home country; however, you should take the usual precautions you would when traveling anywhere. Guard your possessions (particularly around Oslo's Gardermoen airport and Central Railway Station) and don't become blasé about security. One of the least safe places at night is east Oslo, which has a growing drug problem, but even there it's reasonably safe to walk around at night, though you may encounter some hassle from drug addicts, alcoholics, or beggars.

Holidays Norway celebrates the following public holidays: New year's Day (Jan 1), Maundy Thursday, Good Friday, Easter, Labor Day (May 1), Ascension Day (mid-May), Independence Day (May 17), Whitmonday (late May), Christmas (Dec 25), and Boxing Day (Dec 26).

Legal Aid If arrested or charged with a crime in Norway, you can obtain a list of private lawyers from the U.S. Embassy to represent you.

Mail Airmail letters or postcards to the United States and Canada cost 11NOK ($1.65/88p) for up to 20 grams ($^7\!/_{10}$ oz.). Airmail letters take 7 to 10 days to reach North America. The principal post office in Norway is **Oslo Central Post Office,** Dronningensgate 15, N-0101 Oslo. Mailboxes are vibrant red, embossed with the trumpet symbol of the postal service. They're found on walls, at chest level, throughout cities and towns. Stamps can be bought at the post office, at magazine kiosks, or at some stores. The post office can weigh, evaluate, and inform you of the options for delivery time and regulations for sending parcels. Shipments to places outside Norway require a declaration on a printed form stating the contents and value of the package.

Police & Emergencies Call ⓒ 112 for the **police,** ⓒ 110 to report a **fire,** or ⓒ 113 to request an **ambulance** throughout Norway.

Telephone & Telegrams Direct-dial long-distance calls can be made to the United States and Canada from most phones in Norway by dialing ⓒ 00 (double zero), then the country code (1 for the U.S. and Canada), followed by the area code and phone number. Norwegian coins of 1NOK (15¢/10p), 5NOK (75¢/40p), and 10NOK ($1.55/80p) are used in the increasingly rare pay phones.

Tipping Hotels add a 10% to 15% service charge to your bill, which is sufficient unless someone has performed a special service. Most bellhops get at least 10NOK ($1.55/£80p) per suitcase. Nearly all restaurants add a service charge of up to 15% to your bill. Barbers and hairdressers usually aren't tipped, but toilet attendants and hatcheck people expect at least 5NOK (75¢/40p). Don't tip theater ushers. Taxi drivers don't expect tips unless they handle heavy luggage.

2 Oslo

The oldest Scandinavian capital, founded by the Viking king Harald (also known as Harold Fairhair) in 1048, Oslo is renowned for its spectacular natural beauty, with urban subways connecting you to mountain lakes, evergreen forests, and hiking trails—all within the city limits. Oil rich, it is no longer a provincial capital but has risen to become a metropolis and one of the most cosmopolitan cities of Europe, with a vibrant nightlife and an attitude of tolerance.

At the top of the 60-mile (97km) Oslofjord, Norway encompasses 175 square miles (453 sq. km), although its urban growth covers only about a 10th of that. The rest is a vast outdoor playground.

More and more of Oslo's old wooden structures have given way to tall modern buildings and glass-roofed atriums. It's a great city for wandering as it has incorporated art to decorate both its public and private buildings, with sculpture integral to its public squares and parks, especially the Vigeland Sculpture Park.

STATION INFORMATION

GETTING FROM THE AIRPORT TO THE TRAIN STATION

Most international flights land at **Oslo Airport** in Gardermoen ((C) **81-55-02-50;** www. osl.no), about 30 miles (48km) north of Oslo.

High-speed trains ((C) **81-50-07-77;** www.flytoget.no) run between the airport's train station (right at the air terminal) and Oslo's Central Station. The trip takes a maximum 22 minutes and costs 160NOK ($24/£12.80) per person each way. Trains depart the airport between 5:35am and 12:36am, every 10 minutes. *Note:* A railpass does not cover this train.

There's also frequent bus service, departing at intervals of between 15 and 30 minutes throughout the day, for downtown Oslo (trip time is about 35 to 40 min.). It's maintained by **SAS** (whose buses deliver passengers to the Central Station and to most of the SAS hotels within Oslo) and costs 130NOK ($22.10/£11.70) one-way per person.

If you want to take a taxi (and we don't recommend it unless you're traveling in a large group), be prepared for a lethally high charge of around 600NOK to 700NOK ($90–$105/£48–£56) for up to four passengers plus their luggage. If you need a "maxi-taxi," a minivan suitable for between 5 and 15 passengers, plus luggage, you'll be charged about 900NOK ($135/£72).

INSIDE THE STATION

Trains from the Continent, Sweden, and Denmark arrive at **Oslo Sentralstasjon,** Jernbanetorget 1 ((C) **81-56-82-22** for train information). At the beginning of Karl Johans Gate (the main street of Oslo), the terminal is in the center of the city. From the Central Station, trains leave for Stockholm, Copenhagen, Bergen, Stavanger, Trondheim, and Bodø (the last stop on Norway's northern rail line). You can also catch trams here to all major sections of Oslo (see "Getting Around," below).

In 2006 a new **Tourist Information Office** ((C) **81-53-05-55;** www.visitoslo.com) opened at Trafikanten Service Centre, next to the train station, and the old one inside the station closed down. The new center is open Monday to Friday 7am to 8pm; Saturday and Sunday 8am to 6pm (until 8pm May–Sept); and 10am to 4pm on public holidays. Staff can exchange money, and make hotel reservations at a cost of 45NOK ($6.75/£3.60).

Oslo Central Station is open from 4:30am to 1:20am. Arrival and departure times for trains are displayed on digital bulletin boards inside the station. For train reservations—or to validate a railpass—go to the area marked *Billetter.* Here you can make sleeping car reservations too, and buy both domestic and international tickets. Opening hours for the ticket office are 6am to 11:15pm Monday to Friday, 6:30am to 11:15pm Saturday, and 7am to 11:15pm Sundays and holidays.

Baggage storage lockers are located on a balcony (follow the signs inside the station). They cost 20NOK to 50NOK ($3–$7.50/£1.60–£4), depending on the size of

Oslo

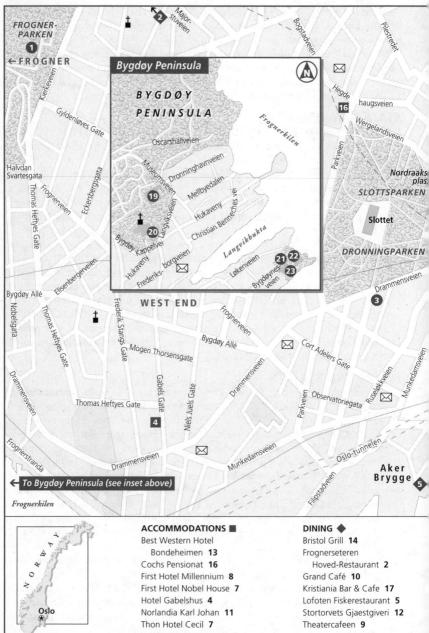

Bygdøy Peninsula

BYGDØY PENINSULA

Frognerkilen

Oscarshallveien

Museumsveien

Dronninghavnveien

Mellbyedalen

Hukaveny

Christian Bennechesvei

Bygdøy Kappelvei

Langviksveien

Hukaveny

Frederiks-borgveien

Langvikbukta

Løkenveien

Bygdøynes-veien

FROGNER-PARKEN

←FROGNER

Kirkeveien

Gyldenløves Gate

Halvdan Svartesgata

Frognerveien

Thomas Heftyes Gate

Eckersbergsgata

Bygdøy Allé

Nobelsgata

Thomas Heftyes Gate

Drammensveien

Frognerstranda

Elisenbergveien

Frederik Stangs Gate

Mogen Thorsensgate

Gabels Gate

Thomas Heftyes Gate

Niels Juels Gate

WEST END

Frognerveien

Bygdøy Allé

Drammensveien

Munkedamsveien

Cort Adelers Gate

Parkveien

Observatoriegata

Ruseløkkveien

Munkedamsveien

Oslo-tunnelen

Filipstadveien

Aker Brygge

← To Bygdøy Peninsula (see inset above)

Frognerkilen

Major-stuveien

Bogstadveien

Pilestredet

Hegde

haugsveien

Wergelandsveien

Parkveien

Nordraaks plas.

SLOTTSPARKEN

Slottet

DRONNINGPARKEN

Drammensveien

Kierkeveien

NORWAY

Oslo

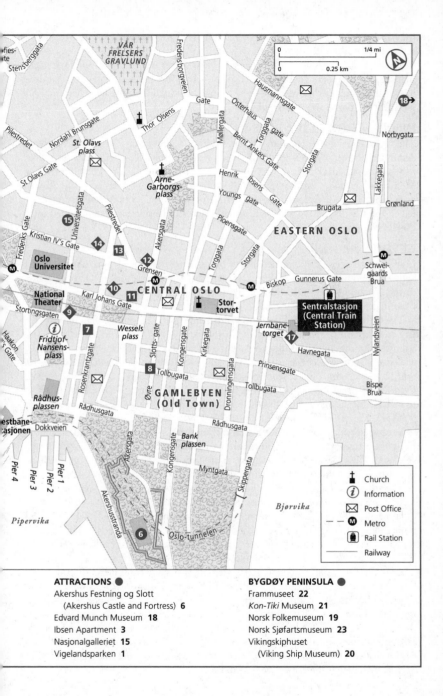

ATTRACTIONS ●

Akershus Festning og Slott
(Akershus Castle and Fortress) **6**
Edvard Munch Museum **18**
Ibsen Apartment **3**
Nasjonalgalleriet **15**
Vigelandsparken **1**

BYGDØY PENINSULA ●

Frammuseet **22**
Kon-Tiki Museum **21**
Norsk Folkemuseum **19**
Norsk Sjøfartsmuseum **23**
Vikingskiphuset
(Viking Ship Museum) **20**

the bag, for 24 hours, with a 7-day maximum. One other amenity of note inside the station is free Internet access.

There are two currency exchange offices (**www.forex.no**) in the station; one in the Airport Express Train Terminal (open 7am–7pm Mon–Fri and 9am–4pm Sat) and one in the main hall (open 8am–8pm Mon–Fri and 9am–5pm Sat). There is also a post office, a bank, and several ATMs.

INFORMATION ELSEWHERE IN THE CITY

The **Oslo Tourist Information Office,** Fridtjof Nansens plass 5, entered on Roald Amundsen Street (© **81-53-05-55;** www.visitoslo.com), is open April and May, Monday to Saturday 9am to 5pm; June to August, daily 9am to 7pm; September, Monday to Saturday 9am to 5pm; and October to March, Monday to Friday 9am to 4pm. The staff will give you free maps, brochures, and make hotel reservations for a fee of 45NOK ($6.75/£3.60). Sightseeing tickets can be purchased and guided tours can also be arranged.

GETTING AROUND

Oslo has an efficient citywide network of buses, trams (streetcars), and subways. Buses and electric trains take passengers to the suburbs. From mid-April to October, ferries to the attraction-filled peninsula of Bygdøy depart from the harbor in front of the Oslo Rådhuset (City Hall).

The **Oslo Pass** (also called the Oslo Card) can help you become acquainted with the city at a fraction of the usual price. It allows free travel on public transportation, free admission to museums and other top sights, discounts on sightseeing buses and boats, and special treats in some restaurants. You can purchase the card at hotels, many shops, tourist information offices, from travel agents, and in the branches of Sparebanken Oslo Akershus. Adults pay 210NOK ($31.50/£16.80) for a 1-day card, 300NOK ($45/£24) for 2 days, and 390NOK ($58.50/£31.20) for 3 days. Children's cards cost 90NOK ($13.50/£7.20), 110NOK ($16.50/£8.80), and 140NOK ($21/£11.20).

Jernbanetorget is Oslo's major **bus and tram** terminal stop, and is located right in front of the train station. Most buses and trams passing through the heart of town stop at Wessels Plass, next to the Parliament, or at Stortorget, the main marketplace. Many also stop at the National Theater or University Square on Karl Johans Gate.

The **subway (T-banen)** has five lines, all running through the city center. All subways stop at the National Theater on Karl Johans Gate.

For schedule and fare information, call **Trafikanten** (© **81-50-01-76;** www. trafikanten.no). Single-trip tickets cost 30NOK ($4.50/£2.40); children 4 to 15 travel for half fare; children 3 and under are free. An eight-coupon Flexi card costs 160NOK (US$24/£13) and is half price for children.

From April 1 to September 30, ferries depart for Bygdøy from Pier 3 in front of the Oslo Rådhuset. For schedules, call **Båtservice Sightseeing** (© **23-35-68-90;** www. boatservicesightseeing.com). The ferry or bus to Bygdøy is a good choice because parking there is limited. Other ferries leave for various parts of the Oslofjord. Tickets on the ferry cost 30NOK ($4.50/£2.40), half price for children. The Båtservice also runs excellent sightseeing cruises beginning the end of April, with prices from 115NOK to 515NOK ($17.25–$77.25/£9.20–£41.20). Inquire at the **Tourist Information Office** or directly through the Båtservice (see above).

WHERE TO STAY

Best Western Hotel Bondeheimen   This restored 1913 building is today an affordable hotel within walking distance of many of Oslo's attractions and transportation hubs. In spite of modernization, it maintains a pleasing old-fashioned Norwegian charm mixed with modern conveniences and comfort. The rooms are a bit small, but space is well used and they are furnished in pinewood pieces. Most bathrooms have showers only (some with tubs). Ask about discount rates and upgrades. The staff aims to please.

Rosenkrantzgate 8 (entrance on Kristian IV's Gate), N-0159 Oslo. © **800/633-6548** in the U.S., or 23-21-41-00. Fax 22-21-41-01. www.bondeheimen.com. 127 units. Mon–Thurs 1,390NOK ($209/£111) double; Fri–Sun 1,090NOK ($164/£87.20) double. Rates include breakfast. Tram: 7 or 11. **Amenities:** Restaurant; bar; laundry; nonsmoking rooms; rooms for those w/limited mobility. *In room:* Hair dryer.

Cochs Pensjonat *Value*   Launched in 1927 by the Coch sisters, this is the most famous and enduring boarding house in Oslo. The building's ornate facade curves around a bend in a boulevard banking on the northern edge of the Royal Palace. It's been greatly expanded over the years, and is now a clean, well-conceived, inexpensive hotel representing excellent value. Expect very few, if any, amenities (even the kitchenettes have only a hot plate and sink) and services at this hotel—rooms don't have telephones.

Parkveien 25, N-0350 Oslo. © **23-33-24-00.** Fax 23-33-24-10. www.cochspensjonat.no. 88 units, 78 with bathroom. Rooms with bathroom, TV, and kitchenette 640NOK ($96/£51.20) double; rooms without kitchenette and private bathroom 540NOK ($81/£43.20) double. MC, V. Tram: 11 or 12. *In room:* TV (some rooms), kitchenette (some rooms), no phone.

First Hotel Millennium *Finds*   Created in 1998 out of a 1930s Art Deco office building, this hotel is both minimalist and stylish, and is hailed for its atmosphere and character. At ¼ mile (.4km) from Central Station, it's close to most of central Oslo's major attractions. Bedrooms are generally spacious, with good-size bathrooms, and combine Art Deco touches with Nordic modern decor. The 10 rooms on the top floor have balconies.

Tollbugata 25, N-0157 Oslo. © **21-02-28-00.** Fax 21-02-28-30. www.firsthotels.no. 112 units 1,145NOK–1,545NOK ($172–$232/£91.60–£124) double. AE, DC, MC, V. Tram: 30 or 42. **Amenities:** Restaurant; bar; laundry; nonsmoking rooms; room for those w/limited mobility. *In room:* Hair dryer.

Hotel Gabelshus *Finds*   Built in 1912, this old-time favorite attracts discerning travelers who know of its relatively secluded location. It's a schlep from the train station, but a worthwhile one. Part of the Choice Hotel Group since 2004, it's been totally remodeled and enlarged while maintaining an old-fashioned charm. The aura of an English manor house is evoked by public lounges filled with art and antiques along with burnished copper and working fireplaces. Both antique reproductions and Nordic design dominate the midsize to spacious bedrooms, some of which have terraces.

Gabels Gate 16, N-0272 Oslo 2. © **23-27-65-00.** Fax 23-27-65-60. www.choicehotels.no. 114 units. Fri–Sun 1,195NOK–1,435NOK ($179–$215/£96–£115) double; Mon–Thurs 1,435NOK–1,995NOK ($215–$299/£115–£160) double; 2,500NOK–3,500NOK ($375–$525/£200–£280) suite. Rates include breakfast and a light supper. AE, DC, MC, V. Tram: 10. **Amenities:** Breakfast room; laundry; nonsmoking rooms. *In room:* Hair dryer.

Norlandia Karl Johan *Finds*   Renovations made in the last few years have made this hotel—a 10-minute walk from Central Station—better, brighter, and more welcoming than ever. Decorators use Norwegian folk art to give it an atmospheric feel, along with some Oriental carpets, antiques, or reproductions. The medium-size bedrooms have double-glazed windows and comfortable furnishings, along with marble bathrooms. We prefer the rooms opening onto the front with French windows giving a panoramic view of the central city.

Karl Johans Gate 33, N-0162 Oslo. ✆ **23-16-17-00**. Fax 22-42-05-19. www.norlandia.no/karljohan. 111 units. Mon–Fri 1,595NOK ($239/£128) double; Sat–Sun 1,000NOK ($150/£80) double; from 2,000NOK ($300/£160) suite. Rates include breakfast. AE, DC, MC, V. T-banen: Stortinget. **Amenities:** Bar; laundry; nonsmoking rooms; rooms for those w/limited mobility. *In room:* Hair dryer.

Thon Hotel Cecil ⭐ The Thon chain represents great value combining comfort with affordability. This contemporary hotel enjoys a central location, with many restaurants, sights, and shops lying within easy walking distance. The well-maintained rooms are bright yet cozy and contain neatly kept bathrooms with showers. Expect relatively simple styling and none of the trappings of more expensive nearby competitors—there's no health club, sauna, or full-fledged room service. For peace and quiet, make sure you don't get one of the street-facing rooms.

Stortingsgata 8 (entrance on Rosenkrantzgate), N-0130 Oslo. ✆ **23-31-48-00**. Fax 23-31-48-50. www.thonhotels. no. 111 units. 995NOK–1,575NOK ($149–$236/£79.60–£126) double. AE, DC, MC, V. T-banen: Stortinget. **Amenities:** Laundry; nonsmoking rooms; rooms for those w/limited mobility. *In room:* Hair dryer.

TOP ATTRACTIONS & SPECIAL MOMENTS

There are those who say a visit to Oslo would be worthwhile if you came just to see the harbor and take a boat ride along the Oslofjord. Because this is the most scenically located capital of Europe, panoramic views are important, especially the one from **Tryvannstårnet,** a 390-foot (117m) observation tower atop 1,900-foot (570m) Tryvann Hill.

On even the most cursory visit, you should see the **Viking ships** on Bygdøy peninsula; explore such famous vessels as the polar ship, *Fram,* or the balsa raft, *Kon-Tiki;* and take in the Norwegian Maritime Museum and the Folk Museum. If you're an art lover, visit the **Munch Museum** and go to the outskirts of town to see the famous **Henie Onstad Art Center.**

Akershus Festning og Slott (Akershus Castle and Fortress)   Built by King Haakon V about 1300, Akershus Castle and Fortress is one of the most important relics of Norway in the Middle Ages, though what you'll see when you visit is mostly a Renaissance palace. A fire in 1527 devastated the northern wing, and the castle was rebuilt and transformed under the Danish-Norwegian king Christian IV in the 1600s. The castle is infamous for having served as a prison during the Nazi regime. Commemorating those dreadful years is the on-site Norwegian Resistance Museum, showing underground printing presses and radio transmitters among other illegal artifacts that trace the German attack on Norway in 1940 until that country's liberation in 1945. In summer season 40-minute English-language guided tours are offered Monday to Saturday at 11am, 1pm, and 3pm, and on Sunday at 1 and 3pm.

Akershus Festning. ✆ **23-09-35-53**. Admission 50NOK ($7.50/£4) adults, 10NOK ($1.50/80p) children. May–Aug Mon–Sat 10am–4pm, Sun 12:30–4pm; Sept–Apr Thurs only noon–2pm. Closed for special events. Tram: 10 or 12. Bus: 60.

Henie Onstad Kunstsenter ⭐⭐   On a site beside the Oslofjord, 7 miles (11km) west of Oslo, ex-movie star and skating champion Sonja Henie and her husband, Niels Onstad, a shipping tycoon, opened this museum in 1968 to display their prodigious art collection. The center's especially good 20th-century collection includes some 1,800 works by Munch, Picasso, Matisse, Léger, Bonnard, and Miró. Henie's Trophy Room is impressive, with 600 trophies and medals, including three Olympic

Moments   Scandinavia's Greatest Painter

Oslo is the city of the great artist, Edvard Munch (1863–1944), and many aficionados make a special pilgrimage here to see his finest works. Although he would grow up to become hailed as "the handsomest man in Norway," he suffered through many childhood illnesses and tragic deaths (such as the early death of his mother). Much of that grief later found expression in his works such as the world-famous *The Scream.*

Heavily influenced by French Realism, Munch studied in Paris in 1885. In time he would reject that movement, succumbing to Impressionism and later Symbolism. His first exhibition in Berlin in 1892 touched off a nationwide scandal. Critics screamed "anarchistic provocation," and the show was forced to close. But Munch was not deterred. He was on a roll in the 1890s, creating some of his most memorable works, including the cycle, *The Frieze of Life,* dedicated to love, death, anxiety, and darkness.

Returning to Norway in 1908, he fell in love with the Oslofjord and painted many memorable seascapes. After a love affair went sour, he suffered a nervous breakdown. Although he helped decorate the auditorium of Oslo University, by 1916 he'd turned inward and led the life of a hermit in a home outside Oslo. He continued to paint, however, often landscapes hailed by critics as "sensuous," and always in bold colors.

The best showcase of Munch's paintings is found at **Edvard Munch Museum** ★★, Tøyengata 53, 0578 Oslo (② **23-49-35-00;** www.munch.museum.no). The museum traces Munch's works from early Realism to latter-day Expressionism. The rotating collection features 1,100 paintings, some 4,500 drawings, and around 18,000 prints, numerous graphic plates, and 6 sculptures.

Admission to the museum is free from October to March and otherwise 65NOK ($9.75/£5.20) adults; 35NOK ($5.25/£2.80) students, seniors, and children 7 and over; children under 7 are free. It is open June to August daily 10am to 6pm; September to May Tuesday to Friday 10am to 4pm, Saturday and Sunday 11am to 5pm (T-banen: Tøyen).

gold medals and 10 world skating championships. In addition to its permanent exhibition, the foundation presents cultural activities—music, theater, film, dance, and poetry readings. There are free tours on Sunday at 2pm.

Høkvikodden, Sonja Henies Vei 31. ② **67-80-48-80.** www.hok.no. Admission 80NOK ($12/£6.40) adults, 60NOK ($9/£4.80) seniors, 50NOK ($7.50/£4) students, 30NOK ($4.50/£2.40) children 7–16, free for children 6 and under. Free for everyone on Wed after 3pm. Tues–Thurs 11am–7pm; Fri–Sun 11am–5pm. Bus: 151.

Nasjonalgalleriet ★★★   Situated behind Oslo University, this is Norway's greatest art gallery and one of the finest in northern Europe. It specializes in Norwegian artists, though there is a noteworthy collection of old European masters, including works by van Gogh, Gauguin, Cézanne, and Degas. Norwegian artists whose work is on display include Johan Christian Dahl, Harriet Backer, and Christian Krohg, the latter earning his fame by painting everyone from mariners to prostitutes. The two

Moments   Ringing the Doorbell at Ibsen's Apartment

Although he sometimes had a troubled relationship with his native country of Norway, **Henrik Ibsen** (1828–1906) today is duly honored as the country's foremost dramatist. Since 1993, it's been possible to visit his **apartment,** just a short walk from the National Theater in Stortingsgate where so many of his greatest plays—including the 1879 *A Doll's House* or the 1881 *Ghosts*—are still performed with a certain devotion.

A blue plaque on the building at the corner of Arbinsgate and Drammensveien marks the apartment where Ibsen lived from 1895 until his death. He often sat in the window, with a light casting a glow over his white hair. People lined up in the street below to look up at him, and he seemed to take delight in the adulation—so long overdue, as far as he was concerned. Italy's greatest actress, Eleanora Duse, came here to bid him a final adieu, but he was too ill to receive her. She stood outside in the snow, blowing him kisses.

The only time Ibsen broke with Norway was when his country did not come to the aid of Denmark in its war with Prussia. Outraged, Ibsen went into a self-imposed exile in 1864 and stayed away in protest for 27 years, returning to settle in Christiania (the old name for Oslo) when memories of his resentment had faded. All is forgiven now, and his memorable *Peer Gynt* is hailed around the world as a forerunner of contemporary drama.

It's an amazing moment to wander through the apartment, which still has its original furniture. It's as if Ibsen still resides in this "living museum." The entrance is at Henrik Ibsens gate 26, (© **22-12-35-50**; www.ibsen.net/ibsen-museum), and admission is 70NOK ($10.50/£5.60) for adults, 45NOK ($6.75/£3.60) students/seniors, and 25NOK ($3.75/£2) for children. The apartment is open mid-May to mid-September Tuesday to Sunday 11am to 6pm, and from mid-September to mid-May from Tuesday to Sunday 11am to 4pm (to 6pm Thurs). Guided tours are given year-round in English. T-banen: Nationaltheatret.

most notable homegrown artists featured in the collection are Gustav Vigeland, Norway's greatest sculptor, and Edvard Munch, Scandinavia's greatest painter. Munch's iconic *The Scream,* one of the world's most reproduced paintings, can be seen here, as can his *Madonna* and *Melancholy.* Alongside the permanent exhibitions, you'll also often find some more contemporary art in the temporary exhibition space on the first floor and in the Art Hall behind the main building.

Universitetsgata 13. © **22-20-04-04.** www.nationalmuseum.no. Free admission. Tues–Wed and Fri 10am–6pm; Thurs 10am–7pm; Sat–Sun 11am–5pm. Closed Mon. Tram: 11, 17 or 18.

Vigelandsparken and Museum ☆☆☆   The work of Norway's greatest sculptor, Gustav Vigeland (1869–1943), is spread across the 75-acre (30-hectare) Frogner Park, whose main entrance is on Kirkeveien. Vigeland died a year before the park was completed but left behind a total of 227 monumental sculptures, of which the most celebrated work is the 52-foot (16m) monolith composed of 121 colossal figures, all carved into one piece of stone. The most photographed sculpture, however, is *The Angry Boy.*

Also at the park is the **Vigeland-museet,** to the south in Nobelsgate. Vigeland's former studio, where he lived and worked from 1924 until his death, features his drawings, plaster casts, and woodcuts among other memorabilia.

Frogner Park, Nobelsgate 32. ℂ 23-49-37-00. Free admission to park. Museum: 45NOK ($6.75/£3.60) adults, 25NOK ($3.75/£2) children under 17, seniors and students. Park daily 24 hr. Museum June–Aug Tues–Sun 10am–5pm; Sept–May Tues–Sun noon–4pm. Tram: 12.

MUSEUMS ON THE BYGDØY PENINSULA

Located south of the city, the peninsula is reached by commuter ferry (summer only) leaving from Pier 3, facing the Rådhuset (Town Hall). Departures during the day are every 40 minutes before 11am and every 20 minutes after 11am, and a one-way fare costs 30NOK ($4.50/£2.40), half price for children. Bus no. 30 from the National Theater also runs to Bygdøy; the museums are only a short walk from the bus stops on Bygdøy.

Frammuseet 𝕬   There's only one exhibit here, but it's world famous: the polar ship *Fram.* The sturdy exploration ship was the vessel Fridtjof Nansen used to sail across the Arctic Ocean (1893–96) at the age of 27. The vessel was later used in the Antarctic by Norwegian explorer Roald Amundsen, when he became the first man to reach the South Pole in 1911.

Bygdøynesveien. ℂ 23-28-29-50. www.fram.museum.no. Admission 50NOK ($7.50/£4) adults, 20NOK ($3/£1.60) students and children 7–16, children under 7 free. Nov–Feb Mon–Fri 10am–3pm, Sat–Sun 10am–4pm; Mar–Apr and Oct daily 10am–4pm; May and Sept daily 10am–5pm; June–Aug daily 9am–6pm. Bus: 30 or 3. Ferryboat: no. 3.

Kon-Tiki Museum 𝕬𝕬   *Kon-Tiki* is the world-famous balsa-log raft that the young Norwegian scientist Thor Heyerdahl and his five comrades sailed in for 4,300 miles (7,000km) in 1947—all the way from Callao, Peru, to Raroia, Polynesia. The museum also houses the papyrus *Ra II,* which Heyerdahl and his comrades used in 1970 to cross the Atlantic from Safi in Morocco to Barbados in the southern Caribbean.

Bygdøynesveien 36. ℂ 23-08-67-67. www.kon-tiki.no. Admission 50NOK ($7.50/£4) adults, 25NOK ($3.75/£2) children, 110NOK ($16.50/£8.80) family ticket. Mar and Oct daily 10:30am–4pm; Apr–May and Sept daily 10am–5pm; June–Aug 9:30am–5:30pm; Nov–Feb daily 10:30am–3:30pm.

Norsk Folkemuseum 𝕬𝕬𝕬   In a beautiful 35-acre (14-hectare) park, this 110-year-old museum traces Norwegian cultural history with both indoor and outdoor exhibitions and activities. Preservation-minded Norwegians scoured the countryside, finding more than 150 old buildings, mostly from the 1600s and 1700s, and moved them to Oslo where they are arranged in an evocative and informative display that's as good as a time-travel machine. Of special note is the museum's **Gamlebyen** (old town), the reproduction of an early-20th-century small village, and a medieval wooden stave church built in 1200. In 2004, the museum merged with the Bygo Royal Farm, enabling visitors to walk through scenic acres of fields and grazing land.

Museumsveien 10. ℂ 22-12-37-00. www.norskfolke.museum.no. Admission mid-Sept to mid-May 70NOK ($10.50/ £5.60) adults, 45NOK ($6.75/£3.60) seniors/students, 25NOK ($3.75/£2) children 6–16, children under 6 free, 150NOK ($22.50/£12) family ticket; mid-May to mid-Sept 90NOK ($13.50/£7.20) adults, 65NOK ($9.75/£5.20) students/seniors, children under 6 free, 200NOK ($30/£16) family ticket. Mid-Sept to mid-May Mon–Fri 11am–3pm, Sat–Sun 11am–4pm; mid-May to mid-Sept daily 10am–6pm.

Norsk Sjøfartsmuseum 𝕬𝕬   This museum, which contains a complete ship's deck with helm and chart house, and a three-deck-high section of the passenger steamer *Sandnaes,* chronicles the maritime history and culture of Norway. The Boat Hall features a fine collection of original small craft. Especially intriguing are the sailing ships

---

Moments **Down by the Old Waterfront**

On the waterfront near Rådhusplassen, the town hall, Oslo's Fishermen's Wharf—called **Aker Brygge**—is a favorite rendezvous point for visitors and Oslovians alike. One of our favorite pastimes is to head down here and approach one of the shrimp boats where you can purchase a bag of freshly caught and cooked shellfish from a fisherman. Buy a beer at one of the harbor-fronting cafes and find a scenic spot where you can shell your feast and eat while taking in a view of the harbor.

After your snack, wander among the little shops, the ethnic food joints, the fast-food stands, or see what's playing in the on-site theater or the multicinema complex. Jazz concerts are often staged outdoors in summer.

---

used in 18th- and 19th-century polar expeditions, including the vessel *Gjøa,* which Roald Amundsen used to sail through the Northwest Passage from 1903 to 1906.

Bygdøynesveien 37. ✆ **24-11-41-50.** www.norsk.sjofartsmuseum.no. Admission to museum and boat hall 40NOK ($6/£3.20) adults; 25NOK ($3.75/£2) students/seniors; free for kids under 16. Mid-May to Aug daily 10am–6pm; Sept to mid-May 14 Mon–Wed, Fri–Sun 10:30am–4pm, Thurs 10:30am–6pm.

Vikingskiphuset (Viking Ship Museum) ✵✵✵ This museum is devoted to one of the rarest finds in the world: three Viking burial vessels that were excavated on the shores of the Oslofjord and preserved in clay. The most spectacular find is the 9th-century *Oseberg* ✵, discovered near Norway's oldest town. This 64-foot (19m) dragon ship features a wealth of ornaments and is the burial chamber of a Viking queen and her slave. The *Gokstad* find is an outstanding example of Viking vessels because it's so well preserved. The smaller *Tune* ship was never restored.

Huk Aveny 35, Bygdøy. ✆ **22-13-52-80.** Admission 50NOK ($7.50/£4) adults, 35NOK ($5.25/£2.80) seniors, 25NOK ($3.75/£2) students/children 7–16, children under 7 free. May–Sept daily 9am–6pm; Oct–Apr daily 11am–4pm.

WHERE TO DINE

Bristol Grill ✵✵ CONTINENTAL   Located in the prestigious Hotel Bristol and open since 1924, this grill has attracted its fair share of celebrities. It's one of the last bastions of courtly formal service in Oslo, with excellent food served in a dining room resembling an elegant hunting lodge from the 1920s. The best Nordic version of bouillabaisse is served here, along with time-tested favorites such as medallions of venison.

In the Hotel Bristol, Kristian IV's Gate 7. ✆ **22-82-60-20.** www.bristol.no. Reservations recommended. Main courses 210NOK–285NOK ($31.50–$42.75/£16.80–£22.80). AE, DC, MC, V. Mon–Sat 5–11pm; Sun 3–10pm. Tram: 10, 11, 17, or 18.

Frognerseteren Hoved-Restaurant NORWEGIAN   This longtime favorite is on the mountain plateau of Holmenkollen, with a view of the famous ski jump, as well as a sweeping panorama of the city and the Oslofjord. In a landmark Viking-Revival lodge constructed in 1896, guests can choose between an affordable cafe and a more formal restaurant, or else opt for beer and snacks on the breezy terrace outside. Specialties, served 1,600 feet (480m) above sea level and 1,000 feet (300m) downhill from the Holmenkollen railway stop, include such country favorites as filet of elk and smoked Norwegian salmon.

Holmenkollveien 200. ☎ **22-92-40-40**. www.frognerseteren.no. Reservations recommended. Cafe platters 60NOK–110NOK ($9–$16.50/£4.80–£8.80); restaurant main courses 240NOK–295NOK ($36–$44.25/£19.20–£23.60). Set-price menus 500NOK–750NOK ($75–$113/£40–£60). DC, MC, V. Restaurant Mon–Sat noon–10pm; Sun noon–9pm. Cafe Mon–Sat noon–10pm; Sun noon–9pm. T-banen: Frognerseteren.

Grand Café ✿✿ NORWEGIAN   This is the most famous cafe in Oslo, once patronized by Edvard Munch and Henrik Ibsen, the latter a devotee of whale steak. Installed on the ground floor of Oslo's grandest hotel, the restaurant serves tasty traditional Norwegian country cuisine with a modern twist (where else could you get reindeer with polenta?) in a quietly swanky setting. The fish dishes are numerous and delicious, and the desserts divine. If the prices are too steep, stop in for breakfast, between 6:30 and 10am, Monday through Saturday.

In the Grand Hotel, Karl Johans Gate 31. ☎ **23-21-20-00**. www.grand.no. Reservations recommended. Main courses: dinner 215NOK–265NOK ($32.25–$39.75/£17.20–£21.20); lunch 115NOK–225NOK ($17.25–$33.75/£9.20–£18). AE, DC, MC, V. Mon–Sat 11am–11:30pm; Sun noon–11pm. T-banen: Stortinget.

Kristiania Bar & Cafe CONTINENTAL   If you want historical grandeur but don't want to pay the steep prices of the Grand Café, this is the place for you. It serves simple, unpretentious food, such as burgers, sandwiches, pastas, and salads in a building that evokes a more gracious era, when train stations were temples to progressiveness. It still feels like a station, albeit one of exceptional beauty. The magnificent Victorian-era bar serves reasonably priced drinks, and attracts a big after-work crowd. You won't get any surprises in the food department (except for a couple of Tex-Mex starters) but neither will you go into shock over the bill.

Østbanen, Jernbanetorget 1. ☎ **22-17-50-30**. www.kristianiabar.no. Reservations recommended. Main courses 75NOK–145NOK ($12.75–$24.65/£6.75–£13.05). AE, DC, MC, V. Mon–Thurs and Sat 11am–1am; Fri 11am–3am; Sun 11am–midnight.

Lofoten Fiskerestaurant ✿ SEAFOOD   Located in the Aker Brygge complex, this restaurant is one of the best choices for dining along the Oslo waterfront, combining a top-notch seafood dinner with one of the most panoramic views of the city's seascape. Nautical accessories decorate the interior, and when the weather's fair guests may dine on the outdoor terrace. Scrupulously seasonal and rigorously precise, the cuisine is based on the favorite fish of the Norwegian palate: lobster, oysters, salmon, halibut, and trout.

Stranden 75, Aker Brygge. ☎ **22-83-08-08**. www.fiskerestaurant.no. Reservations recommended. Lunch main courses 140NOK–265NOK ($21–$39.75/£11.20–£21.20); dinner main courses 179NOK–285NOK ($26.85–$42.75/£14.30–£22.80). AE, DC, MC, V. Mon–Sat 11am–1am; Sun noon–midnight. Bus: 27.

Stortorvets Gjaestgiveri ✿ NORWEGIAN   The oldest restaurant in Oslo, this is one of the city's most atmospheric dining spots. Many of its dining rooms haven't changed much since the early 18th century, when this was an inn for wayfarers, offering both food and lodging. The venue remains a top choice for traditional Norwegian cuisine served in either the cafe up front, a more formal restaurant in the rear, or a secluded courtyard garden during the summer months. To illustrate just how authentic the food is, *Lutefisk*—aged, air-dried cod—a dish abandoned by most chefs as too time-consuming, is still prepared here, as is an equally rare *cassoulet* (bean pot stew). Look for live jazz on weekends.

Grensen 1. ☎ **23-35-63-60**. www.stortorvets-gjestgiveri.no. Small platters and snacks in cafe 65NOK–125NOK ($9.75–$18.75/£5.20–£10). Main courses 160NOK–280NOK ($24–$42/£12.80–£22.40). AE, DC, MC, V. Mon–Sat 11am–10:30pm.

Theatercafeen ⚭⚭ INTERNATIONAL   This Vienna-style eatery captures the opulence of its *fin-de-siècle* heyday, having been meticulously re-created from photographs and the memories of its many devotees. Decorated with portraits of Norwegian artists, actors, painters, and composers, the gorgeous dining room is an experience in itself. But food is the real star here: Options on the huge menu range from humble smørbrød to a five-course dinner that might include Swedish caviar, beef tartar, reindeer steak, or fjord trout. Follow up your meal with a selection from the extensive cheese board.

In the Hotel Continental, Stortingsgaten 24/26. ✆ 22-82-40-50. www.hotel-continental.com. Reservations recommended. Small dishes and sandwiches (served until 5pm or after 9:30pm) 98NOK–170NOK ($14.70–$25.50/£7.85–£13.60); main courses 200NOK–318NOK ($30–$47.70/£16–£25.44). AE, DC, MC, V. Mon–Sat 11am–11pm; Sun 3–10pm. Closed July. T-banen: Nationaltheatret.

SHOPPING

Many of the leading stores are found along **Karl Johans Gate,** the main street of Oslo, and its many side streets. In the core of the city, there are many other shops ringing **Stortovet,** the main square of town. These shops tend to specialize in local goods, such as enameled silver jewelry and handicrafts. If you're interested in Norwegian crafts, check out **Baerum Verk,** Verksgata 15, Baerum Verk (✆ 67-13-00-18; www.baerums verk.no), where you'll find some 65 different shops hawking handicrafts on-site, especially jewelry and woolens. Some of the best crafts are on display at **Den Norske Husfliden,** Møllergata 4 (✆ 22-42-10-75; www.dennorskehusfliden.no), near the marketplace and the cathedral. This is the retail outlet of the Norwegian Association of Home Arts and Crafts, an organization founded in 1891 and devoted to quality work. Here you'll find the finest in Norwegian designs, including furnishings, woodworking, gifts, textiles, glassware, ceramics, embroidery, and wrought iron. Another fine showcase of crafts is **Norway Designs,** Stortingsgaten 28 (✆ 23-11-45-10; www. norwaydesigns.no), with its mostly upmarket merchandise with good buys in pewter, jewelry, crystal, and knitwear.

Folk costumes often interest those with Norwegian ancestors, and the best purveyor is **Heimen Husflid,** Rosenkrantzgate 8 (✆ 22-41-40-50; www.heimen.net), which offers folkloric clothing from all the different regions of the nation, both north and south. The hand-knit sweaters in traditional Norwegian patterns are an especially good buy.

Hadeland Glassverk, Jevnaker (✆ 61-31-64-00; www.hadeland-glassverk.no), is the most famous name in Norwegian glass and has been since 1762. Craftspeople on-site will show you how glass is blown and shaped, and you can also visit an on-site glass museum. All the items here are of the highest quality.

A lot of souvenirs hawked are pure junk, but not at **William Schmidt,** Fr. Nansens Plads 9 (✆ 22-42-02-88; www.williamschmidt.no), the leading vendor of quality Norwegian souvenirs since 1853. Its pewter items range from Viking ships to beer goblets, and many sealskin items, such as moccasins and handbags, are also sold. Prepare for winter with one of the first-class hand-knit cardigans, pullovers, or gloves. All the sweaters are made from 100% Norwegian wool.

NIGHTLIFE

With more than 100 cafes, restaurants, and clubs, Oslo rocks around the clock. From the tourist office or your hotel reception desk, pick up a copy of *What's On in Oslo* to see what's happening at the time of your visit or take a look at the entertainments listings on **www.visitoslo.com**. Note that from June 20 to the middle of August, Oslo goes into a cultural slumber—Oslovians are too busy enjoying their natural surroundings while the summer sun shines to go to the theater.

Their city's **Nationaltheatret,** Johanne Dybwads Plass 1 (© **81-50-08-11;** www. nationaltheatret.no), is world famous but it's only for theater buffs who want to see Ibsen or Bjørnson performed in the original Norwegian language. There are no performances in July and August; otherwise, tickets range from 150NOK to 380NOK ($22.50–$57/£12–£30.40) for adults or 85NOK to 170NOK ($12.75–$34.50/ £6.80–£13.60) for students and seniors.

Even if you don't speak Norwegian, you might want to attend a performance of **Den Norske Opera,** the Norwegian National Opera Company at Storgaten 23 (© **81-54-44-88;** www.operaen.no), the leading venue for ballet and opera, although there are no performances from mid-June to mid-August. Tickets cost 160NOK to 400NOK ($24–$60/£12.80–£32) except for galas.

Although not the equal of Stockholm or Copenhagen, Oslo has its fair share of dance clubs, including the hottest ticket, **Smuget,** Rosenkrantzgate 22 (© **22-42-52-62;** www.smuget.no), behind the Grand Hotel in the center of town. It offers the liveliest dance floor in town and a stage where bands perform. Live music plays from 11pm to 3am, and there's recorded music from 10pm till very late. Cover ranges from 60NOK to 100NOK ($9–$15/£4.80–£8).

A conventional pub most evenings, **Herr Nilsen,** C.J. Hambros Plass 5 (© **22-33-54-05;** www.herrnilsen.no), also hosts some of the world's best jazz musicians—playing everything from prospective to Dixieland. The cover ranges from free to 220NOK ($33/£17.60). It's open Monday to Saturday noon to 3am, Sunday 3pm to 3am. One of the largest venues for jazz and rock is the **Rockefeller Music Hall,** Torggata 16 (© **22-20-32-32;** www.rockefeller.no), where tickets for live concerts range from 100NOK ($15/£8) to as much as 700NOK ($105/£56). Performances are Sunday to Thursday 8pm, Friday and Saturday 9pm. The bar can stay open until 3am but usually shuts down after the show.

Our favorite Oslovian night cafe is **Lorry,** Parkveien 12 (© **22-69-69-04**), a suds-drenched cafe/restaurant established 120 years ago and still going strong at its location across the street from a park flanking the Royal Palace. An outdoor terrace is a magnet in summer, or else you can retreat inside to enjoy 130 different kinds of beer and a young convivial crowd of both locals and visitors. Open Monday to Saturday 11am to 3am, Sunday noon to 1am.

3 Bergen

Many rail passengers bypass Oslo altogether for Norway's second city of Bergen because it's the gateway to the glorious western fjord district. In spite of the fact that it swarms with thousands of visitors and cruise-ship passengers during its short summer, the city at its core manages to retain the feeling of a large country town.

In history, it was the former capital of Norway, having been founded in 1170, and Bergen enjoyed its heyday as the most important trading center for the powerful Hanseatic League of the Middle Ages. Like Oslo, Bergen is scenically located in a sheltered position between a string of islands to the west and the famous silhouette of seven mountains to the east.

Still a maritime city, it is known even today for its fishing industries and shipbuilding. Bergen's unique harborfront, with its old Hanseatic buildings, is today one of UNESCO's World Heritage Sites. Increasingly cosmopolitan in spite of its village-like center, Bergen is more and more becoming a city of culture—in fact, it launched the new millennium as the "European City of Culture" in 2000.

STATION INFORMATION
GETTING FROM THE AIRPORT TO THE TRAIN STATION
Should you opt to fly into Bergen, say, from London or Copenhagen, you'll land at the **Bergen Airport** (© 55-99-80-00) in Flesland, 12 miles (19km) south of the city. Planes operated by **SAS** (© 91-50-54-00; www.scandinavian.net) service Bergen.

Frequent buses connect the airport to the center of town, departing every 15 minutes; a one-way ticket costs 75NOK ($11.25/£6) and takes around 45 minutes to the city center. A taxi from the airport to the city center, including the rail station, costs from 280NOK ($42/£22.40). Chances are, however, that you will not be flying into Bergen and quickly boarding a train for some other destination in Norway, as most visitors head to Bergen and the fjord country as a destination unto itself and not necessarily a stopover en route to somewhere else.

INSIDE THE STATION
The stone-constructed **Bergen Train Station** (© 81-50-08-88) is a 7- to 10-minute walk south of the harbor, along the street from the entrance to the Bergen Storsenter Shopping Mall, which also houses the city's bus station. Trains from Oslo pull in here. On-site is a luggage storage facility, open daily 5:30am to 12:30am, that charges 20NOK to 50NOK ($3–$7.5/£1.60–£4) per 24 hours, depending on size of items. Because the station is so close to the city center, services such as ATMs, restaurants, currency exchange, pharmacies, and so forth are in the immediate vicinity of the station.

There is no tourist office within the station itself, but the city's visitor information center is just a 10-minute walk away (see below).

INFORMATION ELSEWHERE IN THE CITY
The **Bergen Tourist Office,** Vågsallmenningen 1 (© 55-55-20-00; www.visitbergen. com), in the center of town, provides information, maps, and brochures about Bergen and the fjord district. It also makes hotel reservations for 30NOK ($4.50/£2.40). You can exchange foreign currency and cash traveler's checks here when the banks are closed. You can also purchase city sightseeing tickets here or book tours of the fjords. Open June to August daily, from 8:30am to 10pm; May and September daily from 9am to 8pm; October to April Monday to Saturday, from 9am to 4pm.

GETTING AROUND
The **Bergen Card** entitles you to free bus transportation and (usually) free museum admission throughout Bergen, plus discounts on car rentals, parking, and some cultural and leisure activities. It's a good value. Ask for it at the tourist office (see above). A 24-hour card costs 170NOK ($25.50/£13.60) for adults, 70NOK ($10.50/£5.60) for children aged 3 to 15. A 48-hour card is 250NOK ($37.50/£20) or 100NOK ($15/£8). Children under 3 generally travel or enter free.

The **Central Bus Station** (Bystasjonen), Strømgaten 8 (© 55-55-90-70), is the terminal for all buses serving the Bergen and Hardanger areas, as well as the airport bus. The station has luggage storage, shops, and a restaurant. City buses are marked with their destination and route number. For **bus information** in the Bergen area, call © 177. A network of yellow-sided city buses serves the city center only. For information, call © 55-59-32-00.

Bergen

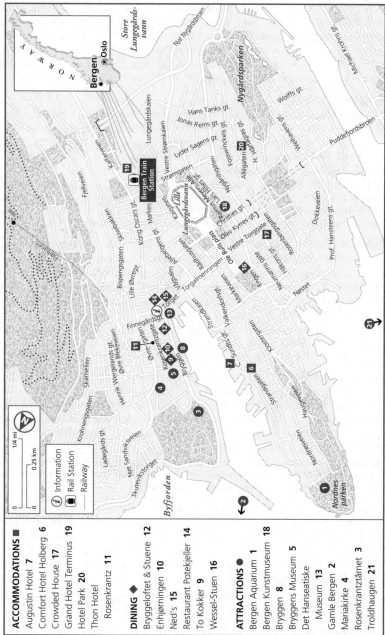

ACCOMMODATIONS ■
Augustin Hotel **7**
Comfort Hotel Holberg **6**
Crowded House **17**
Grand Hotel Terminus **19**
Hotel Park **20**
Thon Hotel
  Rosenkrantz **11**

DINING ◆
Bryggeloftet & Stuene **12**
Enhjørningen **10**
Ned's **15**
Restaurant Potekjeller **14**
To Kokker **9**
Wessel-Stuen **16**

ATTRACTIONS ●
Bergen Aquarium **1**
Bergen Kunstmuseum **18**
Bryggen **8**
Bryggens Museum **5**
Det Hanseatiske
  Museum **13**
Gamle Bergen **2**
Mariakirke **4**
Rosenkrantztårnet **3**
Troldhaugen **21**

You can call a **taxi** by dialing **07000.** Sightseeing by taxi, a bit of a luxury, costs 400NOK ($60/£32) for the first hour and 300NOK ($45/£24) for each additional hour.

You can take a ferry across the harbor Monday to Friday from 7am to 4:15pm; they don't run on Saturday or Sunday. One-way fares are 12NOK ($1.80/95p) for adults, 6NOK (90¢/50p) for children. Ferries arrive and depart from either side of the harbor at Dreggekaien and Munkebryggen. For information, call ℭ **55-55-20-00.**

WHERE TO STAY

Augustin Hotel ℛ *Finds*   Right on the harborfront, this well-run hotel enjoys some of the best scenic views in the city. Owned by the same family for three generations, it was built in 1909 in the Art Nouveau style but added a new wing in 1999. For tradition and old-fashioned comfort, book one of the rooms in the old section; for the latest in amenities, opt for the new wing.

Carl Sundts Gate 24, N-5004 Bergen. ℭ **55-30-40-00.** Fax 55-30-40-10. www.augustin.no. 109 units. Mon–Thurs 1,400NOK–1,510NOK ($210–$227/£112–£121) double, from 2,000NOK ($300/£160) suite; Fri–Sun 800NOK–900NOK ($120–US$135/£64–£72) double, from 1,400NOK ($210/£112) suite. AE, DC, MC, V. Bus: 2 or 4. **Amenities:** Restaurant; bar; laundry; nonsmoking rooms; rooms for those w/limited mobility. *In room:* Hair dryer.

Comfort Hotel Holberg ℛ   This hotel, a 15-minute walk from Bergen's fish market, is named for Holberg, the famous 18th-century Norwegian writer and dramatist, and the lobby is a virtual shrine to the author. The midsize bedrooms are decorated in a modernized Norwegian farmhouse style, with wooden floors, half-paneling stained in forest green, and large windows. Half the tiled bathrooms have tubs and showers; the rest have showers only.

Strandgaten 190, Nordnes, N-5817 Bergen. ℭ **55-30-42-00.** Fax 55-23-18-20. www.choicehotels.no. 140 units. Mon–Thurs 790NOK–1,560NOK ($107–$211) double; Fri–Sat 890NOK ($120) double. Rates include breakfast. AE, DC, MC, V. **Amenities:** Restaurant; bar; laundry; nonsmoking rooms; rooms for those w/limited mobility. *In room:* Hair dryer.

Crowded House   The only reason to stay here is for the price. This is the simplest and most spartan hotel we'll recommend within Bergen, but scores of college students prefer its stripped-down lodgings. Originally built as a conventional-looking five-story hotel in 1923, it was reconfigured in the 1980s as a "backpackers' hotel." Rooms are aggressively plain but well heated in winter, with washbasins, phones, white walls, carpeting, and relatively comfortable beds.

Håkonsgate 27, 5015 Bergen. ℭ **55-90-72-00.** Fax 55-90-72-01. www.crowded-house.com. 33 units (only 1 with bathroom). 590NOK ($88.50/£47.20) double without private bathroom; 690NOK ($104/£55.20) double with private bathroom. AE, DC, MC, V. Bus: 5, 9, 20, or 22. **Amenities:** Cafe/bar; laundry.

Grand Hotel Terminus   Opposite the rail station, this enduring favorite and Bergen landmark opened in 1928 as the city's first luxury hotel. It has attracted many interesting guests over the years, including the great explorer of the Arctic wastelands, Roald Amundsen and playwright Henrik Ibsen. In 2006 it was taken over by the Augustin Hotel (see above) and in 2007 was undergoing a major overhaul, but we're sure the classically elegant atmosphere of the old days will remain.

Zander Kaaesgate 6, N-5001 Bergen. ℭ **55-21-25-00.** Fax 55-21-25-01. www.ght.no. 131 units. 1,650NOK ($248/£132) double. Rates include breakfast. AE, DC, MC, V. Bus: 2 or 4. **Amenities:** Restaurant; bar; laundry; nonsmoking rooms; rooms for those w/limited mobility. *In room:* Hair dryer.

Hotel Park ℛ   A 10-minute walk from the rail station, this family-run hotel is set in a converted 1890s town house. The spacious to midsize rooms are traditionally furnished, and feature some attractive antique pieces. Bathrooms are tiny, but the

Norwegian breakfasts are huge. The Park often has rooms when other central hotels are fully booked. *Note:* In summer, the Park uses a nearby building (furnished in the same style) to accommodate its overflow.

Harald Hårfagresgaten 35 and Allegaten 20, N-5007 Bergen. © **55-54-44-00**. Fax 55-54-44-44. www.parkhotel.no. 33 units. 1,000NOK ($155/£80) double. Rates include breakfast. **Amenities:** Breakfast room; lounge; nonsmoking rooms. *In room:* Hair dryer.

Thon Hotel Rosenkrantz ⭐   Near Bryggen, the historic Hanseatic port, this restored 1921 hotel enjoys a bull's-eye central location. For such a small place, it offers a surprising array of entertainment possibilities, ranging from a lobby bar to a nightclub with live music. The midsize bedrooms have recently been refurbished and are pleasantly and comfortably furnished, each with a good-size bathroom. Laptop owners will find Wi-Fi access in the public areas but not in all the rooms; ask ahead if it matters to you.

Rosenkrantzgate 7, N-5003 Bergen. © **55-31-50-00**. rosenkrantzrainbow-hotels.no. 129 units. 1,495NOK ($224.25/ £120) double. Rates include breakfast. AE, DC, MC, V. Bus: 1, 5, or 9. **Amenities:** Restaurant; bar; laundry; nonsmoking rooms; rooms for those w/limited mobility. *In room:* Hair dryer.

TOP ATTRACTIONS & SPECIAL MOMENTS
On your first day, explore the top attractions of Bergen, including the old Hanseatic Bryggen and its museums, and discover the shops and artisans' workshops along the

Moments Strolling Medieval Bergen

Bryggen ⭐⭐⭐, a row of Hanseatic timbered houses rebuilt along the waterfront after the disastrous fire of 1702 is all that remains of medieval Bergen. Fires have damaged this area repeatedly over the centuries (last in 1955) because of the wooden structures, but much has been restored, enough so that the site has been added to UNESCO's World Heritage list. It's now a center for arts and crafts, where painters, weavers, and craftspeople have their workshops. You'll need at least 2 hours to walk and explore the old wharf.

To see what Bergen was like in the Middle Ages, enter **Det Hanseatiske Museum** ⭐, Finnegårdsgaten 1A, Bryggen (© **55-54- 46-90**), the best preserved of the wooden buildings of old Bryggen. Today the building is furnished with authentic artifacts from the early 18th century. Living conditions, as you can clearly see, were spartan. No heating or lighting was allowed because of the danger of fire. Hours mid-May to mid-September are daily 9am to 5pm; mid-September to mid-May Tuesday to Saturday 11am to 2pm, Sunday 11am to 4pm. Admission is 45NOK ($6.75/£3.60) for adults mid-May to mid-September and 25NOK ($3.75/£2) mid-September to mid-May; free for children year-round. Bus: 1, 5, or 9.

Also at Bryggen, you can visit the **Bryggens Museum** (© **55-58-80-10**), displaying artifacts uncovered in excavations from 1955 to 1972. This museum illustrates the daily life of Bergensers in medieval times. Foundations more than 8 centuries old have been incorporated into today's exhibits. Admission is 40NOK ($6.15/£3.20) for adults, free for children. Open May to August daily 10am to 5pm; September to April Monday to Friday 11am to 3pm, Saturday noon to 3pm, Sunday noon to 4pm. Bus: 1, 5, or 9.

Moments **Norway's Most Dramatic Train Ride**

The train ride from Bergen to the little resort of Flåm has been called "Norway in a Nutshell." This **12-hour tour** ✦✦✦ is the most scenically captivating in the entire country, the breadth and diversity of its landscapes encapsulating the majesty of the country's fjords and mountains.

Several different transit options operate throughout the day. The one most aggressively recommended by Bergen's tourist office operates year-round. It starts at 8:30am at **Bergen's** railway station. After a 2-hour train ride, you'll disembark in the mountaintop hamlet of **Myrdal**, where you can take in the natural wonders for about 20 minutes. In Myrdal you'll board a cog railway for one of the world's most dramatically inclined train rides. The trip down to the village of **Flåm**, a drop of 870m (2,900 ft.), takes an hour and passes roaring streams and seemingly endless waterfalls.

After a 1-hour stopover in Flåm, where you can have lunch or take a brief hike, you'll board a fjord steamer for a ride along the Sognefjord. You'll reach the fjord-side town of Gudvangen after a 2-hour ride. After 30 minutes in Gudvangen, you'll board a bus for the 75-minute ride to Voss. Here you'll spend 30 minutes before boarding a train for the 75-minute ride back to Bergen. Arrival is scheduled for 8:18pm.

Expect only a rushed overview of each town, as there is more scenery than you can digest in a 12-hour day. The round-trip fare, excluding meals, costs 790NOK ($119/£63.20) for adults, 345NOK ($51.75/£27.60) for children 4 to 15, and free for accompanied children under 4. There are discounts for holders of Eurail passes or Scandinavia passes, and a wide availability of options that, for extra fees, allow you to prolong the experience for up to an additional 2 days, thanks to supplemental overnights at panoramic hotels en route. We strongly recommend that you try the more prolonged experience instead of a "quickie." For more information, contact Bergen's **tourist office** (p. 660), call ✆ 81-56-82-22, or go to **www.norwaynutshell.com**.

harborfront. End your day by taking the funicular to Fløien for a panoramic view of Bergen and its waterfront and have a fish dinner in an old tavern. On day two, head out to Troldhaugen, the summer villa of the fabled composer, Edvard Grieg, and return to Bergen in time to walk through Gamle Bergen, a re-created old town from the 18th and 19th centuries.

For orientation purposes and to gain a convenient overview of the attractions of Bergen, on Saturdays and Sundays you can take a 1½-hour walking tour of the city at 3pm from late June to late August. Tickets cost 95NOK ($14.24/£7.60) and the route passes through Bryggen and the fish market. Tickets can be bought from the tourist office at Vågsalmenningen 1 (✆ **55-55-20-00**), which is also where the tours start.

Akavriet (Bergen Aquarium) ✦✦   One of the biggest and most impressive aquariums in Scandinavia is only a 15-minute walk from the historic center. If it swims off the coast of Bergen, it's swimming here. The aquarium's mammoth outdoor tank holds seals and penguins, and some 70 indoor tanks are home to a host of colorful sea life. It's mesmerizing to watch the schools of herring and anglerfish glide by in complete synchronization. Most popular are the penguin feedings scheduled at 12pm and 3pm (and also 6pm May–Sept).

Nordnesbakken 4. ⓒ 55-55-71-71. www.akvariet.no. Admission 150NOK ($22.50/£12) adults, 100NOK ($15/£8) children 3–13, 400NOK ($45/£24) family ticket. May–Aug daily 9am–7pm; Sept–Apr daily 10am–6pm. Bus: 11 from the fish market.

Bergen Kunstmuseum (Bergen Art Museum)   This museum is composed of three galleries situated in three separate buildings overlooking the lake, Lille Lunge- gardsvann. The Lysverket collection houses the bulk of the museum's treasures, displaying some of its 9,000 pieces, which run the gamut from 13th-century Russian icons to works by Yoko Ono. However, we think the Rasmus Meyers collection, housing a parade of **Edvard Munch masterpieces** 𝑅𝑅, is the main attraction. The Stenersen collection—usually housed in the building of the same name, but currently in the Lysverket while the Stenersen is given over to temporary exhibitions—is a close second, with a collection of 20th-century art that includes a fine assemblage of **works by Paul Klee** 𝑅𝑅.

Rasmus Meyers allé 3, 7, and 9. ⓒ 55-56-80-00. www.bergenartmuseum.no. Admission 50NOK ($7.50/£4) adults, free for children 16 and under. Mid-May to mid-Sept daily 11am–5pm; mid-Sept to mid-May Tues–Sun 11am–5pm. Bus: 1, 5, or 9.

Gamle Bergen 𝑅   North of the city center, this open-air museum is one of the finest along the western coast of Norway, re-creating life as lived in the 18th and 19th centuries in a parklike setting. More than 40 wooden buildings were moved here from western Norway and reassembled. This Old Town comes with old-fashioned streets and narrow cobblestone alleyways, all converging on an open square. The houses are furnished with pieces authentic to the era. You can visit such sites as a photographer's studio from the turn of the 20th century, a merchant's living room in the style of the 1870s, a baker's house and shop, and even the abode of a poor seamstress from around 1860.

Elsesro and Sandviken. ⓒ 55-39-43-00. Admission 50NOK ($7.50/£4) adults, 25NOK ($3.75/£2) students/seniors, children free. Houses mid-May to mid-Sept only, guided tours daily on the hour 10am–5pm. Park and on-site restaurant daily noon–6pm. Bus: 1 or 9 from the city center every 10 min.

Mariakirke (St. Mary's Church) 𝑅𝑅   The oldest building in Bergen (its exact date is unknown, but it was built sometime in the 12th c.), this Romanesque church is one of the most beautiful in Norway. It's been in continuous use since the day it opened,

---

Moments **Something Fishy**

There is no livelier place in Bergen than the open-air **Fisketorget (Fish Market)** held every Monday to Saturday 7am to 3pm at the **Torget** 𝑅𝑅 along the harborfront. You can wander at will through the crowds drawn to the colorful stands where a wide variety of fresh fish is hawked, especially kippers, smoked salmon, and shellfish. We prefer to feast here at lunch on freshly made smoked salmon sandwiches. In addition to fish, there are hawkers peddling flowers, vegetables, fruit, and even handicrafts and souvenirs. You can also pick up the makings of a picnic lunch here. And bring your camera—the sight of the vendors in their bright orange rubber overalls makes a great photo op.

having been spared destruction from the numerous fires that swept over this largely wooden city. The oldest artifact is an impressive 15th-century triptych behind the altar, and there's a baroque pulpit, donated by Hanseatic merchants, with carved figures depicting everything from Chastity to Naked Truth.

Dreggen. ⓒ 55-31-59-60. Admission 20NOK ($3/£1.60) for adults, free for children 6 and under. Mid-May to mid-Sept Mon–Fri 9:30–11am and 1–4pm; mid-Sept to mid-May Tues–Fri 11am–12:30pm. Bus: 9, 20, 21, or 22.

Rosenkrantztårnet ★ Scottish masons, who incorporated a mammoth keep from 1270, designed this tower in the 1560s as both a defensive tower and a residence. The tower was named for Erik Rosenkrantz, the governor of Bergen Castle. In 1560, the tower and residence were reconstructed and enlarged. A small octagonal tower, crowned by a cupola, surmounts the Renaissance facade of this five-floor building. Although heavily damaged in an explosion in the harbor during the Nazi era, the tower was reconstructed. From the battlements, a panoramic view of Bergen can be enjoyed.

Bergenhus Bradbenken. ⓒ 55-31-43-80. Admission 30NOK ($4.50/£2.40) adults, 15NOK ($2.25/£1.20) children 5–15, free 4 and under. May 15–Aug 31 daily 10am–4pm; Sept 1–May 14 Sun noon–3pm. Bus: 1, 5, or 9.

Troldhaugen ★★ This Victorian house, high on a hill overlooking Lake Nordås just outside of Bergen, was the summer villa of composer Edvard Grieg. The house contains Grieg's own furniture, paintings, and other mementos. His Steinway grand piano is frequently used at concerts given in the house during the annual Bergen festival, as well as at Troldhaugen's own summer concerts. Grieg and his wife, Nina, are buried in a cliff grotto on the estate—follow the marked pathway across the wooded grounds.

Troldhaugveien 65, Hop. ⓒ 55-92-29-92. www.troldhaugen.com. Admission 60NOK ($9/£4.80) adults, free for children. May–Sept daily 9am–6pm; Oct–Nov and Apr Mon–Fri 10am–2pm, Sat–Sun noon–4pm; mid-Jan to Mar Mon–Fri 10am–2pm; closed Dec. Bus: 23 or 24 to Hop from the Bergen bus station, Platform 20; when you reach Hop exit, turn right, walk about 600 feet (180m), turn left at Hopsvegen, and follow signs (15-min. walk). Hop is 3 miles (4.8km) from Bergen.

WHERE TO DINE

Bryggeloftet & Stuene *Value* NORWEGIAN One of the town's better bargains, this harborfront restaurant is an atmospheric choice, with a street-level bar and eating area evoking 19th-century Bergen, and a more formal restaurant upstairs resting under high ceilings and paneled in wood. Meals here are quintessentially Norwegian—try the grilled filet of reindeer with a creamy wild game sauce.

Bryggen 11. ⓒ 55-30-20-70. www.bryggeloftet.no. Reservations recommended. Main courses 199NOK–350NOK ($29.85–$52.50/£15.90–£28); lunch *smørbrød* 99NOK–125NOK ($14.85–$18.75/£7.90–£10)AE, DC, MC, V. Mon–Sat 11am–11:30pm; Sat 11am–midnight; Sun 1–11:30pm. Bus: 1, 5, or 9.

Enhjørningen (The Unicorn) ★★ SEAFOOD/CONTINENTAL This is one of the best restaurants in town and one of the most atmospheric. You'll dine in one of several old-fashioned rooms set end-to-end railroad-car style in an old Hanseatic clapboard structure on the Bryggen harborfront. The lunchtime buffet is one of the best dining bargains of town, loaded with meat and fish dishes. The seafood and continental menu in the evening is more refined, offering such delights as a cognac-marinated Norwegian salmon.

Bryggen. ⓒ 55-32-79-19. www.enhjorningen.no. Reservations required. Main courses 275NOK–310NOK ($41.25–$46.50/£22–£24.80); set-price menus 490NOK–550NOK ($73.50–$82.50/£39.20–£44). AE, DC, MC, V. June–Sept daily noon–11pm; rest of year 4–11pm. Bus: 4, 5, 80, or 90.

Ned's &&& SEAFOOD/GAME   One of the smallest upscale restaurants in Bergen, housed in an old 19th-century fish market. Intimate and choice, it has an additional 35 outdoor seats for clement weather, and offers stylish, well-prepared food and a panoramic view of the harbor. Dishes might include smoked cod and leek chowder, or medallions of lamb served with wilted spinach and caviar. The staff is one of the friendliest we've encountered in all of Norway.

Zacchariasbrygge 50. ⓒ **98-21-99-51.** Reservations recommended. Main courses 235NOK–340NOK ($35.25–$51/£18.80–£27.20); fixed-price menus 440NOK–580NOK ($66–$87/£35.20–£46.40). AE, DC, MC, V. May–Aug Mon–Sat 11:30am–11pm, Sun 11:30am–10pm; Sept–Apr Mon–Sat 5–11pm. Bus: 1, 5, or 9.

Restaurant Potekjelleren & *Finds* NORWEGIAN/ITALIAN   For deluxe dining, Bergen style, this citadel of fine food and formal service is worth every krone. Set inside an antique wood building just steps from the Fish Market, this is one of the city's oldest restaurants, its foundations dating from the mid–15th century. Guests, dining either in the ancient cellar or the more formal dining room upstairs, can partake of an unusual yet excellent cuisine that combines some of the best dishes from both the Norwegian and Italian kitchens. Light, inventive cookery is the rule of the day.

Kong Oscargate 1A. ⓒ **55-32-00-70.** Reservations required. Set menus 395NOK–585NOK ($59.25–$87.75/£31.60–£46.80). AE, DC, MC, V. Mon–Sat 4–10pm; bar Mon–Sat till 1am. Bus: 1, 5, or 9.

To Kokker (Two Cooks) & FRENCH/NORWEGIAN   Visiting celebrities and savvy local foodies frequent this bastion of good eating, set in a 1703 building adjacent to the old piers and wharves along the harborfront. Start, perhaps, with the velvety smooth lobster soup before going on to, say, reindeer with lingonberry sauce. The chefs here know their craft well and the solid staff offers delightful service in a lovely antique setting.

Enhjørninggarden. ⓒ **55-30-69-55.** www.tokokker.no. Reservations required. Main courses 265NOK–315NOK ($39.75–$47.25/£21.20–£25.20). AE, DC, MC, V. Mon–Sat 5–10pm. Bus: 1, 5, or 9.

Wessel-Stuen NORWEGIAN   Named for the 18th-century humorist, Johan Herman Wessel, this local favorite evokes a wine cellar from the 1700s and is decorated in an old tavern style, with beamed ceilings and an adjoining pub. We are impressed with the recent menu changes, noting that the chefs are becoming more inventive and more attuned to modern taste. You'll still find the classic sirloin steak with Béarnaise sauce, but also a pesto-gratinéed filet of lamb with ratatouille.

Engen 14. ⓒ **55-55-49-49.** www.wesselstuen.no. Reservations recommended. Dinner main courses 199NOK–259NOK ($29.85–$38.85/£15.90–£20.70); lunch items 119NOK–139NOK ($17.85–$20.85/£9.50–£11.10). AE, DC, MC, V. Mon–Sat 11am–12:30am; Sun 2–11:30pm. Bus: 2, 3, or 4.

SHOPPING

One of the best displays of handicrafts from the western fjord district is the **Torget** or marketplace (p. 665) along the waterfront, the site of a lively fishing market Monday to Saturday. Good buys here include rugs, handmade tablecloths, and woodcarvings.

For one-stop shopping head to **Galleriet,** Torgalmenningen 8 (ⓒ **55-30-05-00;** www.galleriet.com), the largest shopping complex in western Norway, with some 70 different shops.

For good buys in local clothing, head for **Berle Bryggen,** Bryggen (ⓒ **55-10-95-00**), along the harbor at the historic core of the old waterfront. The well-stocked emporium offers great buys in sweaters for men and women as well as souvenirs such as troll dolls, pewter, and other gift items.

Close to the fish market and harbor, the four-story **Kloverhuset,** Strandgaten 13–15 (© **55-31-37-90;** www.kloverhuset.com), offers the biggest inventory of fashion, including gloves, wool sweaters, and Sami jackets from the north of Norway. Opposite the Flower Market, **Viking Designs,** Strandkaien 2A (© **55-31-05-20**), has a prize-winning selection of upmarket knitwear.

The best outlet for handicrafts is in and around **Bryggen Brukskunst,** the Old Town near the wharf. Here local craftspeople have taken over the old buildings and ply their trades in the colorful atmosphere. Some of the items being crafted are based on designs that might go back 3 centuries, even as much as 1,500 years, the latter exemplified by a Romanesque cruciform pilgrim's badge.

The leading purveyor of glassware and ceramics is **Prydkunst-Hjertholm,** Olav Kyrres Gate 7 (© **55-31-70-27**). Much of the merchandise comes directly from artisans' studios, including textiles, pewter, and wood items, along with gifts and souvenirs.

NIGHTLIFE

From mid-June to mid-August, **Bergen Folklore** performs at Schøtstuene (The Hanseatic Assembly Rooms), Øvregaten 50, at 9pm daily. Tickets cost 100NOK ($15/£8) for adults (free for children) and can be bought from the tourist office (p. 660). The performance lasts 1 hour and consists of traditional folk dances and music from rural Norway. Bergen's major cultural venue is **Grieghallen,** Lars Hillesgate 3A (© **55-21-61-50;** www.grieghallen.no), the 1978 performance hall that is the most prestigious venue in western Norway for music, drama, and other cultural events. Tickets cost 100NOK to 465NOK ($15–$69.75/£8–£37.20).

For a refined late-night drink the best option is **Engelen,** in the Radisson SAS Royal Hotel, Bryggen (© **55-54-30-00;** bus: 1, 5, or 9), open Wednesday to Saturday 9am to 3am. During the week it's largely those in their 40s, 50s, and 60s; on the weekend the crowd is younger and more raucous. Covers range from 60NOK to 80NOK ($9–$12/£4.80–£6.40). **Rick's Café,** Veiten 3 (© **55-55-31-31;** www.7nights. no; bus: 1, 5, or 9), is also popular locally, with its rooms devoted to cabaret, comedy, or just drinking. Open daily 10pm to 3am; no one under 24 permitted.

The biggest sports pub in Bergen is **Fotballpuben (Football Pub),** Vestre Torggate 9 (© **55-33-66-61;** www.fotballpuben.no; bus: 1 or 9), a sudsy joint where soccer and rugby ignite passions. Its inner rooms are crowded with a heavy-drinking, sports-loving crowd who watch games on the TV screens up above. Known for its inexpensive beer, the club is open Monday to Thursday 9am to 1am, Friday and Saturday 9am to 3am, and Sunday noon to 1am. The town's most frequented pub is **Kontoret Pub,** Kong Olav Vs Plass 4 (© **55-36-31-30;** www.dickensbergen.no; bus: 2, 3, or 4), next to the Dickens Restaurant and Pub. You can order the same food at the Kontoret as in the Dickens, though most people come here to drink. It's open Monday to Thursday 11am to 12:30am, Friday and Saturday 11am to 2:30am, and Sunday 1pm to 12:30am.

Portugal

Occupying the Iberian Peninsula with the much larger country of Spain, Portugal is a world unto itself, lying in one of the most remote and least explored corners of Western Europe. In no way are you visiting a "suburb of Spain," as Portugal's harshest critics charge. In history, language, culture, and cuisine, Portugal, in spite of its diminutive size, is very much a nation with a distinctive and remarkable heritage and identity.

For such a small country, the regional diversity is immensely varied and of compelling interest, from the beach resorts of the Algarve to the historic capital of Lisbon and onward into the north, embracing not only the city of Porto but the rural Minho, where old traditions still prevail, and even the most remote province, Trás-os-Montes, where country life goes on much as it has for decades.

Of all the Western European countries reviewed in this book, Portugal has the least developed rail system, but what there is will easily, quickly, conveniently—and cheaply— get the train traveler to the country's scenic highlights. Portugal's rail system, **Caminhos de Ferro Portugueses (CP),** runs InterCidade trains that link a total of 60 Portuguese cities to Lisbon. To rush you to the north, the high-speed Alfa train connects Lisbon, Porto, and the far northern city of Braga and offers both first- and second-class seating. If there is a real downside to the country for the international rail traveler, it's that Portugal has few major international train links. You can travel by rail between Lisbon and Madrid via the Lusitânia Comboio Hotel train, and from Lisbon to the French/Spanish border (where you can connect to a TGV to Paris) on the Sud-Expresso sleeper train. The only other links are from Lisbon to Badajoz, Spain, and Porto and the northwestern Galician city of Vigo, Spain. Because the number of rail connections is limited, it's best to make Portugal either your first or last stop on a train tour of Europe.

HIGHLIGHTS OF PORTUGAL

The areas of Portugal most easily reached by rail, and most likely to leave lasting and evocative memories, are the capital city of **Lisbon** (of course), situated on the western coast of the country; the sun belt southern coast of the **Algarve;** the enchanting medieval walled town of **Óbidos;** the university city of **Coimbra,** seat of one of the oldest universities in the world and the center of the Portuguese Renaissance; and **Porto,** at the mouth of the River Douro, whose vineyards in the hinterlands beyond support the country's thriving port wine trade.

In Portugal, your choice of rail itineraries is more limited: From Lisbon you can go south to the Algarve or north to Óbidos, Coimbra, Porto, and beyond, unless you plan to visit the remote provinces in the eastern plains. No matter which route you choose to take, you won't feel deprived.

Moments   Festivals & Special Events

The **Festas dos Santos Populares** is celebrated throughout Lisbon. Celebrations begin on June 13 and 14 in the Alfama, with feasts honoring Saint Anthony. Parades commemorating the city's patron saint feature *marchas* (parading groups of singers and musicians) along Avenida da Liberdade, singing, dancing, drinking wine, and eating grilled sardines. On June 23 and 24, for the Feast of St. John the Baptist, bonfires brighten the night and participants jump over them. The night of the final celebration is the Feast of St. Peter on June 29. The **Lisbon Tourist Office** (© **808/781-212**) supplies details about where some of the events are staged, although much of the action is spontaneous. Mid-June to June 30.

On the first weekend in July, the **Colete Encarnado ("Red Waistcoat")** takes place at Vila Franca de Xira, north of Lisbon on the River Tagus. Like the more famous feria in Pamplona, Spain, this festival involves bulls running through narrow streets, followed by sensational bullfights in what aficionados consider the best bullring in Portugal. Fandango dancing and rodeo-style competition among the Ribatejo *campinos* (cowboys) mark the event. For more information, call © **26/328-56-05**.

The **Estoril Festival,** at the seaside resort outside of Lisbon, is a festival of classical music usually run from mid-July to the first week in August (dates vary), which occupies two concert halls that were built for the 500th anniversary of Columbus's first voyage to the New World. For information, call the **Associação International de Música da Costa do Estoril** (© **21/468-5199;** www.estorilfestival.net).

The northern route is the most scenic, taking you up the Atlantic coast to Óbidos, on to Coimbra, and even farther north to Porto.

The journey south from Lisbon to the Algarve doesn't go through the lush green countryside of Portugal the way the trip north does. It takes you across the country's drier but dramatic plains in a land that its former Moorish rulers called *Al-Gharb.* Much of the terrain you'll see outside your train window evokes the northern tier of the African coastline. You'll pass a countryside fabled for its rice paddies, wheat fields, Arabian horses, and black bulls, and can often gaze upon *campinos,* the region's sturdy horsemen dressed in regional garb.

The capital city of Lisbon, even though not central to Portugal the way Madrid is to Spain, is nonetheless the hub of its vast rail networks. Regardless of where you're going in Portugal by rail, you can reach the destination from Lisbon. When the rail lines run out, buses take over to carry you the rest of the way, but that holds true only for the remotest towns and villages.

To make the most of your trip, it's best to spend 3 days in Lisbon. Most of the first day will be used up merely getting to Lisbon. If you arrive in time, you can walk around the **Alfama** (the oldest and most historic district) and end your tour seeing the fantastic panorama afforded by a sunset visit to Castel de São Jorge (St. George's Castle). Start off your next day with a tour of Belém, a suburb of Lisbon, and view the famous Mosteiro dos Jerónimos (Jerónimos Monastery). Toss in some artistic highlights in the

afternoon, including the must-see **Museu da Fundacão Calouste Gulbenkian,** one of Europe's artistic treasure troves. Your third day can be spent exploring the satellite town of **Sintra,** Lord Byron's "glorious Eden," and visiting its two national palaces.

For many rail travelers that will be all the time allotted for Portugal. Those with another 3 days usually explore the history-rich **Algarve** coast, which stretches for some 100 miles (160km) from Henry the Navigator's Cape St. Vincent to the border town of Vila Real de Santo Antonio adjacent to Spain. This is the region we focus on most in this chapter. To reach the Algarve, take a train from Lisbon to either **Lagos** or **Faro** (from which you can take buses to all the major resorts). Both of these cities make logical bases because of their convenient rail links to Lisbon, and you can spend some time exploring remote coastal villages to the east and west of either city. A distinct Arabic flavor still prevails in the region, with its fret-cut chimneys, mosque-like cupolas, and cubist houses.

If you seek culture more than time at a beach, you can spend 3 days taking in the major sightseeing targets north of Lisbon—Óbidos, Coimbra, and Porto. If you only have 1 day, we'd cast our vote for Coimbra. The rail connections from Coimbra and Porto are easy but less so for Óbidos, although the latter is worth the effort to reach it if you have the time. See "Northward Ho!" on p. 696 for more information on Portugal's northern highlights.

1 Essentials

GETTING THERE

Lisbon, the country's capitol, is the major gateway city for flights into Portugal. International flights land at **Aeroporto de Lisboa** (② 21/841-3500) on the northern edge of Lisbon, 4 miles (6.4km) from the heart of the city. (Instead of flying, however, many rail passengers prefer to get to Lisbon by taking the train west from Madrid after their visit to Spain.)

Flying time from New to York to Lisbon is about 6½ hours.

When it was established in 1946, **TAP** (② 800/221-7890; www.tap-airportugal. pt), the national airline of Portugal, flew only between Lisbon and Angola and Mozambique (then Portuguese colonies). Today, TAP flies to four continents and has one of the youngest fleets in the airline industry—its aircraft have an average age of only 4 years. Its U.S. gateway is Newark, New Jersey. In Portugal, it flies to three destinations, the most popular of which are Lisbon, Porto, and Faro, the capital of the Algarve along Portugal's southern coast.

Continental Airlines (② 800/525-0280; www.continental.com) flies direct to Lisbon out of Newark International Airport.

Air Canada (② 800/247-2262; www.aircanada.ca) no longer offers direct flights to Lisbon, but it does offer daily flights from Toronto and Montréal to Paris, where you can transfer to another carrier to reach Lisbon.

A lot of passengers fly into London and then head to Portugal from there. For flights from the U.K., contact **British Airways** (② 800/247-9297 in the U.S., or 80/820-0125 in Portugal) or **TAP**, Gillingham House, 3844 Gillingham St., London SW1V 1JW (② 0845/601-0932).

TAP also has frequent flights on popular routes from major cities in Western Europe. Its flights to Lisbon from London are an especially good deal; sometimes they're priced so attractively that one might combine a trip to England with an inexpensive rail vacation in Portugal.

PORTUGAL BY RAIL

PASSES

Both the **Eurail Global Pass** and **Eurail Global Pass Flexi** are good for use on Portuguese trains; the **Eurail Spain–Portugal Pass** is good on both Spanish and Portuguese trains. See chapter 2 for more details on these passes.

Portugal also has its own railpass: the **Portuguese Railpass** allows any 4 days of unlimited first-class train travel in a 1-month period, costing $165 per person. Children ages 4 to 11 pay a discounted fare. Kids under 4 ride free.

Note: All of the passes we mention above should be purchased in North America prior to your departure. Passes can be ordered through **Rail Europe** (② 877/272-RAIL [7245] in North America; www.raileurope.com) or your travel agent.

FOREIGN TRAIN TERMS

Posted schedules—called *horarios* in Portuguese—aren't always accurate, so you should go to the station ticket booths, called *bilheteiras,* instead.

Suburbano trains, as you might have guessed, run to the environs of any city, such as Lisbon. On timetables, the rail line's long-distance international links are marked *IN.*

If you prefer to purchase your rail tickets abroad, the words *Bilhetes turisticos* indicate a tourist ticket, which invariably offers a discount. Families should ask about a *cartão de família,* which offers good discounts to families traveling together.

The complete rail timetable in Portugal, available at train stations, is called *Guia Horario a Oficial.* In larger stations, you'll see ticket windows divided between *Camboios de amanhã e doas segiomtes,* meaning ticket offices for purchasing advance tickets, and *Só para comboios de hoje,* meaning offices in which you buy tickets on the day of travel. Travelers 65 and over should inquire about a *cartão dourado* or senior citizens card. At rail stations, know that *partida* indicates a departure gate and that *chegada* means arrival.

PRACTICAL TRAIN INFORMATION

Portuguese trains are run by **Caminhos de Ferro Portugueses (CP; ✆ 800/208-208;** www.cp.pt), the national railway. Originally built by the British, the country's network of rail lines consists mostly of wide-gauge lines for more comfort, and much of the 2,236-mile (3,600km) network is electrified. In some of the more remote parts of Portugal, however, the rail lines are narrow gauge, resulting in slow travel times.

Whenever possible, board an **Alfa** train. These high-speed carriers run between the most important cities in the north and make only major stops. The best of these trains are the **Alfa Pendular** express trains racing between Lisbon and Porto; these trains are as good as any competitor in Europe, with air-conditioning, fine food service, and airline-type seating. The Alpha Pendular trains also offer special sections equipped for the mobility impaired. Far less luxurious and much slower are the **InterCidade (IC)** trains linking most major towns and cities of Portugal. The air-conditioned IC trains offer dining and drinking facilities, but passengers for years have complained about the poor quality of the cuisine. The fastest trains that carry no supplements are the **Inter-Regionals (IR).** On less popular routes, you'll likely find yourself aboard one of the slow-moving **Regionals** or **Suburbanos** trains, which stop at every hamlet—travel aboard these lines is spartan at best.

Trains & Travel Times in Portugal

From	To	Type of Train	# of Trains	Frequency	Travel Time
Madrid	Lisbon	Tren	1	Daily	9 hr., 15 min.
Lisbon	Lagos	IC	1	Daily	4 hr., 30 min.
Lisbon	Faro	IC	5	Daily	4 hr.
Lisbon	Óbidos	Regional	1	Daily	2 hr., 10 min.
Lisbon	Óbidos	Urbano (Regional)	5	Daily	2 hr., 30 min.
Lisbon*	Coimbra	ALFA/Urbano	10	Daily	1 hr., 51 min.–2 hr., 30 min.
Lisbon*	Coimbra	IC/Urbano	3	Daily	2 hr., 3 min.–2 hr., 15 min.
Lisbon*	Porto	ALFA	2	Daily	2 hr., 47 min.
Lisbon*	Porto	ALFA/Urbano	9	Daily	2 hr., 56 min.–3 hr., 5 min.
Lisbon	Porto	IC/Urbano	8	Daily	3 hr., 21 min.
Coimbra	Porto	ALFA	7	Daily	58 min.
Coimbra*	Porto	IC/Urbano	7	Daily	1 hr., 14 min.–1 hr., 30 min.

Train transfer required. Trains schedules and travel times in Portugal are constantly in flux. This chart's info was correct at press time, but you should always confirm travel times for your dates of travel before finalizing any plans.

There are two main sleeper trains that service Portugal. The **Lusitânia Hotel train** runs from Lisbon to Madrid, and costs 76€ ($98.80) per person, one-way in first class. Your reservation is included in your ticket, and passes are accepted on these trains. The second sleeper train, the **Sud-Expresso,** runs between Lisbon and the Spanish/French border, and costs 117€ ($152) per person, one-way in first class. The Sud-Expresso connects with the Paris TGV train at the border station at Hendaye/Irún.

Second-class travel is jokingly referred to in Portugal as "an experience, but I'll go by car next time." Because second-class service tends to be spartan on most trains, most passengers opt to spend 40% more per ticket and travel first class, where they get better service and more leg room. We highly recommend that you do the same.

RESERVATIONS These are mandatory on most Portuguese trains and should be made as far in advance as possible. Likewise, railpass validation should be made at designated windows at rail stations. Tickets for IC or Alfa trains can often be booked up to 20 days ahead; in some cases, only 10-day bookings are allowed. You can make reservations through travel agents or else go to the station where you'll often have to wait in long lines. You can also make reservations for most Portuguese trains before you leave home through Rail Europe (see "Passes," above). If you don't have a ticket before boarding, the conductor may fine you. Riding without a ticket *(sem bilhete)* can lead to exorbitant fines in some cases. Reservations are essential on international and express trains, but on many trains they are optional; nevertheless, because all Portuguese trains are likely to be crowded, reservations are advised. They are free if made on the day before departure, though you'll pay $15 if you make them in the U.S. Also note that even if you hold a railpass, you'll need to pay a supplement (15€/$19.50) when traveling the express routes.

SERVICES & AMENITIES Couchettes—actually foldout bunk beds—are available in Portugal, and advance reservations are absolutely essential for one of these compartments. Couchettes are rented on the Sud Expresso from Paris to Lisbon and on the Lusitania Express from Madrid to Lisbon. On most trains, couchettes cost around $36 per person. On major runs, you'll also encounter *wagons-lit* or sleepers—compartments with one to three beds. Most night trains offer full restaurant service, and stewards provide drinks and snacks around the clock. If you need food and drink, always inquire before boarding a train because there's no guarantee they will be available on Portuguese trains. If services aren't available, carry the food and drink you'll need for the journey. Most trains in Portugal are air-conditioned and have adequate restroom facilities.

FAST FACTS: Portugal

Area Codes The most used area code in Portugal is **21** in Lisbon. Other area codes include **28** for both Lagos and Faro (the capital of the Algarve).

Business Hours Hours vary throughout the country, but there is a set pattern. Banks are generally open Monday to Friday from 8:30am to 3pm. Currency exchange offices at airports and rail terminals are open longer hours, and the office at Portela Airport outside Lisbon is open 24 hours a day. Most museums open at 10am, close at 5pm, and often close for lunch between 12:30 and 2pm. Larger museums with bigger staffs often remain open at midday. Shops are open, in general, Monday to Friday from 9am to 1pm and from 3 to 7pm, and Saturday from 9am to 1pm. Most restaurants serve lunch from noon until 3pm and dinner from 7:30 to 11pm; many close on Sunday. Many nightclubs open at 10pm, but the action doesn't really begin until after midnight and often lasts until the wee hours of the morning.

Climate Summer may be the most popular time to visit Portugal, but for the traveler who can chart his or her own course, spring and autumn are the best seasons. To use a North American analogy, the climate of Portugal most closely parallels that of California. There are only slight fluctuations in temperature between summer and winter; the overall mean ranges from 77°F (25°C) in summer to about 58°F (14°C) in winter. The rainy season begins in November and usually lasts through January. Because of the Gulf Stream, Portugal's northernmost area, Minho, enjoys mild (albeit very rainy) winters, even though it's at approximately the same latitude as New York City.

Snow brings many skiing enthusiasts to the Serra de Estrêla in north central Portugal. For the most part, however, winter means only some rain and lower temperatures in other regions. The Algarve enjoys temperate winters and is somewhat of a winter Riviera, attracting sun worshippers from North America and Europe. Summers everywhere tend to be long, hot, clear, and dry.

Lisbon and its satellite resort of Estoril enjoy 46°F to 65°F (8°C–18°C) temperatures in winter and temperatures between 60°F and 82°F (16°C–28°C) in summer.

Documents Required If you have a valid passport from the U.S. or Canada and plan to stay no more than 90 days, you do not need a visa to enter Portugal. If you'd like to stay more than 90 days, you can apply for an additional stay at the nearest Portuguese embassy. As a rule, the extension is granted immediately.

Electricity Voltage is 200 volts AC (50 cycles), so you'll need a transformer and an adapter plug—available at most hardware stores in North America—to use electrical appliances from the U.S. and Canada in Portugal. The concierge desks at most large hotels can often lend you a transformer and plug adapters, or tell you where you can buy them nearby. To be on the safe side, ask at your hotel before plugging in anything.

Embassies & Consulates If you lose your passport or have some other pressing problem, you'll need to get in touch with your embassy. The Embassy of the **United States,** on Avenida das Forças Armadas (Sete Rios), 1600 Lisboa (② 21/ 727-3300), is open Monday to Friday from 8am to noon and from 1:30 to 4pm. The Embassy of **Canada** is at Avenida da Liberdade 198–200, 1269 Lisboa (② 21/ 316-4600). It's open Monday to Friday from 8:30am to 12:30pm and from 1:30 to 4pm (embassy closes at 1pm on Fri July–Aug).

Health & Safety Portugal does not offer free medical treatment to visitors except for citizens of certain countries, such as Great Britain, which have reciprocal health agreements. Nationals from such countries as Canada and the United States have to pay for medical services rendered.

You should encounter few health problems traveling in Portugal. The tap water is generally safe to drink, the milk is pasteurized, and health services are good. Occasionally, the change in diet may cause some minor diarrhea, so you may want to take some antidiarrhea medicine along.

Limit your exposure to the sun, especially during the first few days of your trip and, thereafter, from 11am to 2pm. Use a sunscreen with a high protection factor and apply it liberally. Remember that children need more protection than adults do and should wear a hat.

Though Portugal has a relatively low rate of violent crime, petty crime against tourists is on the rise in continental Portugal. Travelers may become targets of pickpockets and purse-snatchers, particularly at popular tourist sites, restaurants, and on public transportation such as trains. Travelers should also avoid using ATMs in isolated or poorly lit areas. In general, visitors to Portugal should carry limited cash and credit cards, and leave extra cash, credit cards, and personal documents at home or in a hotel safe.

Pickpocketing and purse-snatching in the Lisbon area occur in buses, restaurants, the airport, trains, train stations, and trams, *especially tram 28 to the Castle of São Jorge.* Gangs of youths have robbed passengers on the Lisbon–Cascais train. At restaurants, thieves snatch items hung over the backs of chairs or placed on the floor, so keep a careful eye on your belongings. There have been reports of theft of unattended luggage at the Lisbon Airport. Special care should also be taken at the Santa Apolónia and Rossio train stations, the Alfama and Bairro Alto districts, the Castle of São Jorge, and Belém.

Holidays Watch for these public holidays, and adjust your banking needs accordingly: January 1 (New Year's Day and Universal Brotherhood Day); Carnaval, early March (dates vary); Good Friday, March or April (dates vary); April 25 (Liberty Day, anniversary of the revolution); May 1 (Labor Day); Corpus Christi, June (dates vary); June 10 (Portugal Day); August 15 (Feast of the Assumption); October 5 (Proclamation of the Republic); November 1 (All Saints' Day); December 1 (Restoration of Independence); December 8 (Feast of the Immaculate Conception); and December 25 (Christmas Day). June 13 (Feast Day of St. Anthony) is a public holiday in Lisbon, and June 24 (Feast Day of St. John the Baptist) is a public holiday in Porto.

Legal Aid Contact your local consulate for a list of English-speaking lawyers if you run into trouble with the law. After that, you're at the mercy of the local courts.

Mail While in Portugal, you may have your mail directed to your hotel (or hotels), to the American Express representative, or to General Delivery *(Poste Restante)* in Lisbon. You must present your passport to pick up mail. The general post office in Lisbon is on Praça do Comércio, 1100 Lisbon (© **21/346-3231**); it's open Monday to Friday from 8am to 10pm, Saturday, Sunday, and holidays 9am to 6pm.

Police & Emergencies For emergencies in Portugal, call the **Red Cross** (© **21/942-1111**) if you need an ambulance and © **21/771-4000** to find a hospital.

Telephone Portugal Telecom phones accept coins or a prepaid phone card (see below). Calling from a booth with the right change or card allows you to avoid high hotel surcharges. For long-distance (trunk) calls within the country, dial the city code followed by the local number. *Note:* If you see a city code that begins with a zero, drop this initial zero and substitute a "2."

At "CrediFone" locations and at post offices, special phones take prepaid cards sold at post offices.

Telephone calls can also be made at all post offices, which also send telegrams. International calls are made by dialing **00** (double zero), followed by the country code, the area code (not prefaced by 0), then the local phone number. The country code for the United States and Canada is **1**. The country code for Portugal is **351**.

Tipping Most service personnel in Portugal expect a good tip rather than a small one, as in the past. Hotels add a service charge (known as *serviço*), which is divided among the entire staff, but individual tipping is also the rule. Tip .75€ ($1) to the bellhop for running an errand; .50€ (65¢) to the doorman who hails you a cab; .75€ ($1) to 1€ ($1.30) to the porter for each piece of luggage carried; 2.50€ ($3.25) to the wine steward if you've dined often at your hotel; and 1.50€ ($1.95) to the chambermaid. In first-class or deluxe hotels, the concierge will present you with a separate bill for extras, such as charges for bullfight tickets. A gratuity is expected in addition to the charge. The amount will depend on the number of requests you've made.

Figure on tipping about 20% of your taxi fare for short runs. For longer treks—for example, from the airport to Cascais—15% is adequate. Restaurants and nightclubs include a service charge and government taxes of 17.5%. As in hotels, this money is distributed among the entire staff—not to mention the waiter's mistress and the owner's grandfather—so extra tipping is customary. Add about 5% to the bill in a moderately priced restaurant, up to 10% in a deluxe or first-class establishment. For hat check in fado houses, restaurants, and nightclubs, tip at least .50€ (65¢). Washroom attendants also get .50€ (65¢).

2 Lisbon

This capital city's greatest glory came in the 15th and 16th centuries during Portugal's age of discovery when mariners such as Vasco da Gama sailed from here to explore the uncharted seas of the world. Those discoveries, such as the first sea route from Western Europe around Africa to the Indies, launched the spice trade and brought great wealth to the city, ushering in the golden age of Lisbon when it became known as the "Queen of the Tagus River."

Trouble was on the way in the centuries ahead, including a devastating earthquake in 1755, but Lisbon has bounced back from its many disasters and is waiting to greet you today. In spite of extensive rebuilding and modernization, the old charm of Lisbon still remains, especially in its most traditional quarter, the Alfama.

Lisbon is still benefiting from the 1998 face-lift it gave itself when it hosted the World Expo. Many construction projects were completed for that spectacle, and most of these have been recycled to benefit today's visitor.

Allow at least 3 days to skim the highlights of Portugal's capital, sitting on the north bank of the Tagus estuary, some 10 miles (16km) from the Atlantic. With a population of some 700,000, it is a busy, bustling metropolis and port, noted for its cuisine (especially seafood), monuments, great art, fado music cafes, fashionable bars and clubs, and great shops. It is also the best center for touring Portugal by rail, including spectacular Sintra, located in the immediate environs of Lisbon.

STATION INFORMATION
GETTING FROM THE AIRPORT TO THE TRAIN STATIONS
There is no direct rail service from Portugal's airport. After a long flight many passengers arriving at the Aeroporto de Lisboa prefer to take a taxi to meet a connecting train. The average taxi fare to one of the city's main train stations ranges from 12€ to 20€ ($15.60–$26), depending on how heavy traffic is; an additional charge of 1.50€ ($1.95) is leveled for each piece of luggage. Less expensive is the AERO-BUS that takes passengers between the airport and the Cais do Sodré train station, departing every 20 minutes from 7am to 10:30pm. The cost is 3€ ($3.90) one-way.

INSIDE THE STATIONS
Lisbon has a confusing number of rail stations—some with a full range of services such as Estação Rossio or Estação Santa Apolónia, others with more meager offerings.

Estação Rossio lies between Praça Restauradores and Praça Dom Pedro IV (Metro: Rossio or Restauradores). Trains from here mostly service day-trippers and commuters from the bedroom communities around Lisbon, including the former royal palaces at Quéluz and Sintra. Rossio is the smallest, oldest, and most lavishly decorated of the stations in Lisbon, and is also the site of the grand dowager hotel, Avenida Palace. It's set in the heart of the city, so you don't need to worry about public transport links to it.

Rossio remains a vintage, somewhat outmoded piece of architecture, evoking the Manueline style of the great Portuguese kings, and is a sightseeing attraction in its own right. On the ground floor is a small information office dispensing routine advice daily from 10am to 1pm and 2:30 to 6pm. For domestic travel, a window is open daily from 7am to 3:30pm, with an international window open daily from 9am to noon and 1 to 5:30pm. Both of these are staffed by English-speaking attendants. There is a tourist office located nearby (see below) in addition to money exchange kiosks, restaurants, and bars. Most visitors to Lisbon pass through here to catch a train to Sintra. Trains depart on tracks 4 and 5 every 15 to 30 minutes from 6:30am to 1am daily, the trip taking 45 minutes and costing 2€ ($2.60) for a one-way ticket. Luggage storage is available here daily from 8:30am to 11:30pm; a locker costs 3€ ($3.90) for 48 hours.

Estação Santa Apolonia, Avenida Infante Dom Henrique, lies east of the Alfama on the banks of the Tagus River, and 2 miles (2½km) east of the center of Lisbon. Depending on traffic, it takes a taxi from 5 to 10 minutes to reach the center of town from this station, with an average fare costing 6€ ($7.80). It's also possible to go by bus no. 9, 28, 46, 59, or 90, a one-way fare going for 1.15€ ($1.50). Major national and international trains pull in here, including those from Paris and Madrid. Major cities of Lisbon are also served, including Coimbra (the university city) and Porto (home of port wine). Facilities include ATMs, restaurants, bars, and money exchange kiosks. Luggage storage is also available daily from 8:30am to 11:30pm and costs 3€ ($3.90) for 48 hours. You can get both rail and tourist information at offices to the right as you exit from the trains and walk past ticket window no. 1. These offices are open daily from 9am to 10pm. Hotel reservations can be made here, and there is no commission charged.

Lisbon

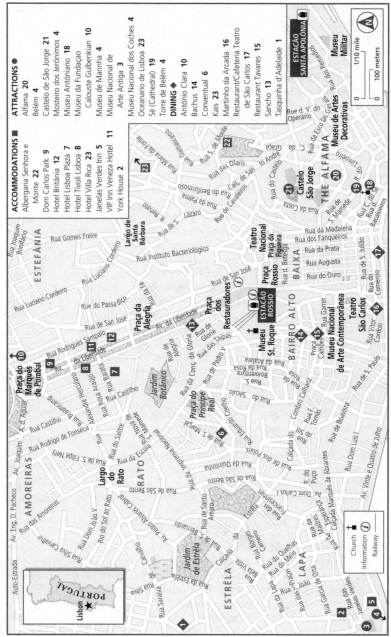

ACCOMMODATIONS ■
Albergaria Senhora e Monte **22**
Dom Carlos Park **9**
Hotel Britânia **12**
Hotel Lisboa Plaza **7**
Hotel Tivoli Lisboa **8**
Hotel Villa Rica **23**
Janelas Verdes Inn **5**
VIP Inn Veneza Hotel **11**
York House **2**

ATTRACTIONS ●
Alfama **20**
Belém **4**
Castelo de São Jorge **21**
Mosteiro dos Jerónimos **4**
Museu Antóniano **18**
Museu da Fundação Calouste Gulbenkian **10**
Museu de Marinha **4**
Museu Nacional de Arte Antiga **3**
Museu Nacional dos Coches **4**
Oceanário de Lisboa **23**
Sé (Cathedral) **19**
Torre de Belém **4**

DINING ◆
Antonio Clara **10**
Bachus **14**
Conventual **6**
Kais **23**
Martinho da Arcada **16**
Restaurant/Cafeteria Teatro de São Carlos **17**
Restaurant Tavares **15**
Sancho **13**
Tasquinha d'Adelaide **1**

Church
Information
Railway

Estação Oriente (Metro: Oriente) is Lisbon's newest and most modern railway station. Designed by a Spanish architect in 1998 as part of the city's Expo 98 improvements, it links together railway spurs and railway lines that were previously never connected. Set in the Olivais neighborhood, near Lisbon's southern edge within the showplace park, Parque das Naçaos, it's an industrial-looking structure made of white-painted steel that looks both stylish and post-modern. Prior to its construction, passengers arriving in Rossio had to take a bus, tram, or taxi, with their luggage, if they wanted to continue their rail journey from the north to the south of the country. Today some long-distance and suburban trains stop here. For example, all trains heading for Santa Apolónia make a brief stop here. Trains leave from here to such northern destinations as Porto, the Beiras (Central Portugal), the Minho (in the north), and the Douro of port wine fame. This is also a departure point for Sintra. This railway station's opening coincided with the construction of 10 additional subway stations, and Oriente Station is interconnected with the entire subway system.

Estação Cais do Sodré (Metro: Cais do Sodré) lies just beyond the end of Rua Alecrim, to the west of Praça Comércio. The station, a 5-minute walk from the Baixa district, is so small in scale that it's easy to mistake it for a tram station. To reach the center, such as the landmark Praça dos Restauradores, take the Metro or bus no. 1, 44, or 45. If you're connecting with trains at the Estação Santa Apolónia, take bus no. 28. Most passengers exploring Lisbon stop off here to reach the many attractions of Belém, including Mosteiro dos Jerónimos. Trains depart for Belém every 15 minutes during the day, costing 1.15€ ($1.50) for the one-way, 10-minute trip. It's also possible to get trains here for the country's two most famous resorts along the Costa do Sol, Estoril and Cascais, both immediately north of Lisbon.

Estação Entrecampos (Metro: Entrecampos) is an intermediate railway station, a sort of "way station" that's set strategically on a spur line emanating outward from the city's newest, blockbuster railway station, Estação Oriente (see above). Passengers departing from Lisbon for points south of the Tagus, including Faro and Lagos, can board their trains here. They are routed on the lower level of the older of the two bridges traversing the Tagus, Ponte XXV Abrile (locals also refer to this bridge as the "Ponte Sobre Tejo"; its upper level is reserved for cars). Trains from this station go to Barreiro on the south bank of the Tagus, where passengers headed for the Algarve—specifically Faro—must transfer. At Barreiro, passengers cross a platform to board trains headed to points in Portugal's "Deep South." Barreiro is also linked by a ferry to Lisbon. Ferries depart from Terminal Fluvial (also known as Sul e Sueste), adjacent to Praça do Comércio. The ferry ride is included in rail tickets to the Algarve, and departures are every half hour (trip time: 30 min.).

For rail information at any of these terminals, call © **80/820-8208.**

INFORMATION ELSEWHERE IN THE CITY

Hotel reservations, for which no commission is levied, can be made at all local tourist offices. The main office is at Palacio da Foz, Praça dos Restauradores (© **808/781-212;** www.visitportugal.com), at the Baixa end of Avenida da Liberdade. The office dispenses information about Lisbon as well as Portugal in general, and is open daily from 9am to 8pm (Metro: Restauradores). Here you can also purchase the **Lisbon Card,** which provides free city transportation and entrance fees to many museums and attractions, plus discounts to certain events. For adults, a 1-day pass costs 14.85€ ($19.30); 2 days, 25.50€ ($33.15); 3 days, 31€ ($40.30). Children 5 to 11 pay 7.50€ ($9.75), 12.75€ ($16.60), and 15.50€ ($20.15), respectively. There is another tourist office across from the general post office in Lisbon on Rua do Arsenal 15 (© **21/031-2700;** www.visitlisboa.com). Hours are daily 9am to 7pm.

GETTING AROUND

Lisbon is a vast urban sprawl, with many of its most visited attractions, including Belém and Sintra, lying in the environs. You'll need to rely on public transportation, which more or less runs pretty well. In the heart of town, the best way to cover Lisbon, especially the ancient districts of the Alfama and Baixa, is on foot. Wear sturdy walking shoes along these often cobbled and narrow streets, which haven't changed much from the days when donkeys walked them.

The public transportation system is operated by **CARRIS** (© **21/361-3000;** www.carris.pt), which supervises the network of funiculars, trains, subways (the Metro), and buses. Consider buying a *bilhete de assinature turistico,* which covers all forms of transportation. A 1-day pass sells for 3.50€ ($4.55); a 5-day pass goes for 13.50€ ($17.55). Fares must be loaded onto a 7 Colinas Card, which costs .50€ (65¢) and can be purchased at CARRIS booths in terminals and transportation hubs, which are open daily from 8am to 8pm, and at most Metro stations.

The Metro subway system's stations are designated by large M signs. A single ticket costs .75€ ($1); a packet of 10 tickets goes for 6.65€ ($8.65). Service is daily from 6:30am to 1am. For more information, call © **21/350-01-15,** or visit **www.metro lisba.pt**.

Lisbon still operates an old-fashioned tram system, with trolley cars called *eléctricos* making the steep run from the heart of town up to the Bairro Alto section. Buses or tram tickets cost from 1.15€ to 1.50€ ($1.50–$1.95) each, and you can purchase tickets from the driver. The fare depends on how far you're traveling, as Lisbon is divided into five different zones. Buses and *eléctricos* run daily from 6am to 1am.

The city is linked to its Riviera by a smooth-running, electric train system that will take you from Lisbon to such resorts as Estoril and Cascais. There's only one class of seat, with a one-way fare ranging from 1.50€ to 3.35€ ($1.95–$4.35). There is also a trio of funiculars, including the Glória, which goes from Praça dos Restauradores to Rua São Pedro de Alcântara; the Bica, from Calçada do Combro to Rua do Boavista; and the Lavra, from the eastern side of Avenida da Liberdade to Campo Martires de Pátria. A one-way ticket on any of these funiculars costs 1.15€ ($1.50).

Finally, taxis are often the preferred means of transport, as fares are reasonable, beginning with a basic charge of 2.15€ ($2.80) with increments thereafter. Between 10pm to 6am daily, fares go up by 20%. For a **Radio Taxi,** call © **21/811-9000,** or visit **www.retalis.pt**.

WHERE TO STAY

Albergaria Senhora de Monte ✦ *Finds*   Near St. George's Castle, in the oldest part of Lisbon, this inn is welcoming and unpretentious. It's a hidden gem perched on a hilltop near a belvedere, opening onto panoramic views in all directions. The junior suites all have terraces, though all the bedrooms are comfortable and inviting. The restored accommodations are imbued with decorator's touches such as gilt-edged door panels and bronze fixtures.

Calçada do Monte 39, 1170-250 Lisboa. © **21/886-6002.** Fax 21/887-7783. www.maisturismo.pt/sramonte. 28 units. 120€–145€ ($156–$189) double; 140€–175€ ($182–$228) suite. Rates include continental breakfast. AE, DC, MC, V. Metro: Socorro. **Amenities:** Breakfast room; bar; laundry. *In room:* Hair dryer.

Dom Carlos Park *(Value)* Just off the landmark Praça do Marquês de Pombal, this hotel is known for its central location and affordable prices. The midsize bedrooms are more functional than stylish, all of them paneled in Portuguese redwood. Facing a little park, the hotel is well run with a friendly, accommodating staff who will direct you to all the points of interest and tell you the best way to get to where you're going.

Av. Duque de Loulé 121, 1050-089 Lisboa. ✆ **21/351-2590.** Fax 21/352-0728. www.domcarlospark.com. 76 units. 126€ ($164) double; 152€ ($198) triple; 214€ ($278) suite. Rates include buffet breakfast. AE, DC, MC, V. Metro: Marquês de Pombal. **Amenities:** Restaurant; bar; laundry. *In room:* Hair dryer.

Hotel Britânia ✿ *(Value)* Only 1,640 feet (500m) from the Rossio, a block from Avenida da Liberdade (the main boulevard), this long-time favorite was carved out of a 1942 Art Deco office building. In the mid-1990s all the spacious bedrooms were massively upgraded and renovated, although many of its vintage architectural features were retained. The property features high ceilings, tasteful carpeting, comfortable furnishings, and carved headboards on twin- or king-size beds. The hotel's service is like that provided by a small, well-run inn.

Rua Rodrigues Sampaio 17, 1150-278 Lisboa. ✆ **21/315-5016.** Fax 21/315-5021. www.heritage.pt. 32 units. 165€– 250€ ($215–$325) double. AE, DC, MC, V. Metro: Avenida. **Amenities:** Bar; laundry; nonsmoking rooms. *In room:* Hair dryer.

Hotel Lisboa Plaza ✿✿ In the heart of the city, this seven-floor, family-owned hotel sits on a quiet side street a ½ mile (1km) north of Rossio. Built in 1953, the hotel was extensively restored by top designers in the '90s, and much of its charm, evoking Edwardian elegance, was retained and touched up. The traditionally styled accommodations range from standard rooms, to much larger superior units, to roomy and tastefully furnished suites (try for one at the rear overlooking botanical gardens). All rooms feature double-glazed windows and marble bathrooms.

Travessa do Salitre 7, Avenida da Liberdade, 1269-066 Lisboa. ✆ **21/321-8218.** Fax 21/347-1630. www.heritage.pt. 106 units. 165€–240€ ($215–$312) double; 260€–450€ ($338–$585) suite. Children under 12 stay free in parent's room. AE, DC, MC, V. Metro: Avenida. **Amenities:** Restaurant; bar; laundry, nonsmoking rooms. *In room:* Hair dryer.

Hotel Tivoli Lisboa ✿✿ Located in a prime spot about ⅔ mile (1.1km) north of Rossio, this hotel, opened in 1933, is a conservative, cosmopolitan, and enduring favorite of both vacationers and business travelers thanks to such enticing features as the only hotel pool in central Lisbon. A large, dramatically decorated two-floor lobby sets a welcoming tone, and a top-floor restaurant opens onto a terrace for panoramic dining. Tasteful carpeting, stylish chintz, and comfortable furnishings decorate the spacious, bright, and inviting bedrooms, which offer many amenities, including marble bathrooms.

Ave. da Liberdade 185, 1269-050 Lisboa. ✆ **21/319-8900.** Fax 21/319-8950. www.tivolihotels.com. 329 units. 420€ ($546) double; from 570€ ($741) suite. Rates include continental breakfast. AE, DC, MC, V. Metro: Avenida. **Amenities:** 2 restaurants; 2 bars; laundry; nonsmoking rooms; rooms for those w/limited mobility. *In room:* Hair dryer.

Hotel Villa Rica ✿✿ Located in Entrecampos, the city's new financial district, this supremely modern property caters to the business set. The midsize bedrooms are decorated in a sleek, contemporary style and are exceedingly comfortable. The trio of restaurants caters to a wide range of tastes and pocketbooks. Facilities are strictly deluxe, ranging from a health club with Turkish bath and indoor swimming pool to a piano bar.

Ave. 5 de Outubro, 301–319, 1600-035 Lisboa. ℂ **21/0043-000.** Fax 21/004-43-33. www.hotelvillarica.com. 171 units. 126€–143€ ($164–$186) double. AE, DC, MC, V. Metro: Entrecampos. Bus: 32 or 83. **Amenities:** 3 restaurants; 2 bars; laundry service; nonsmoking rooms. *In room:* Hair dryer.

Janelas Verdes Inn ✿✿ *Finds*   Set 1¼ miles (2km) from Rossio, between the harbor and Bairro Alto, this is one of Lisbon's most atmospheric and charming hotels. It's installed in an 18th-century town house that was once home to Eça de Queiroz, the Portuguese novelist. Rooms are spacious and elegantly furnished with a combination of antiques and reproductions. The best rooms are in the rear and on the upper levels, as they open onto sweeping views of the Tagus River.

Rua das Janelas Verdes 47, 1200-690 Lisboa. ℂ **21/396-8143.** Fax 21/396-8144. 29 units. www.heritage.pt. 235€– 295€ ($306–$384) double. AE, DC, MC, V. Bus: 27, 40, 49, or 60. **Amenities:** Bar; laundry; nonsmoking rooms; rooms for those w/limited mobility. *In room:* Hair dryer.

VIP Inn Veneza Hotel ✿ *Finds*   Housed in one of the few remaining old palaces that once lined Avenida da Liberdade (it's a splendid structure that dates from 1886), this hotel opened in 1990 and is a real discovery. A grand staircase leads to a trio of upper floors where you'll find handsomely furnished and up-to-date guest bedrooms. The service and friendly welcome are top rate.

Ave. da Liberdade 189, 1250-141 Lisboa. ℂ **21/352-2618.** Fax 21/352-6678. www.viphotels.com. 37 units. 89€– 98€ ($116–$127) double. Rates include continental breakfast. AE, DC, MC, V. Metro: Avenida. **Amenities:** Bar; laundry. *In room:* Hair dryer.

York House ✿✿   An even more atmospheric choice than the Janelas Verdes Inn (see above), the York House was carved out of a 17th-century convent and is filled with more charm and character than any other hotel in Lisbon. Long a celebrity favorite, it lies on a cobbled street between Bairro Alto and the waterfront 1¼ miles (2km) west of the Rossio. Mazelike public rooms, filled with antiques, lead to bedrooms that vary in size, although each is beautifully furnished, often with a four-poster bed and antiques.

Rua das Janelas Verdes 32, 1200-691 Lisboa. ℂ **21/396-2435.** Fax 21/397-2793. www.yorkhouselisboa.com. 32 units. 150€–260€ ($195–$338) double. AE, DC, MC, V. Bus: 27, 40, 49, 54, or 60. **Amenities:** Restaurant; bar; laundry. *In room:* Hair dryer.

TOP ATTRACTIONS & SPECIAL MOMENTS

If you only have a day in Lisbon, take a stroll through the Alfama, the city's most interesting district. Visit the 12th-century **Sé (cathedral),** and take in a view of the city and the River Tagus from the **Santa Luzia Belvedere.** Climb up to the **Castelo de São Jorge (St. George's Castle).** Take a taxi or bus to Belém to see the **Mosteiro dos Jerónimos (Jerónimos Monastery)** and the **Torre de Belém.** While at Belém, explore one of the major sights of Lisbon, the **Museu Nacional dos Coches (National Coach Museum).**

IN THE ALFAMA

Castelo de São Jorge ✿✿   This hilltop fortress, a former citadel of Portuguese kings, towers over Lisbon. It became a royal abode when Afonso Henriques chased out the Moors in 1147, and remained so until 1511, when Manuel I constructed a more lavish palace closer to the harbor. The 1755 earthquake struck it badly, but in 1938 the dictator Salazar ordered the old walls rebuilt and gardens added.

Today's visitors can climb the towers and walk along the **battlements** ✿, the reconstructed ramparts, later taking in the **view from the Observation Platform** ✿✿, a large shaded square opening onto Lisbon and the river beyond. You can stroll the

Moments Strolling the Alfama

It's old and decaying, but the **Alfama** 🎇🎇 is one of the most history-rich and evocative old quarters of any European capital. Give it at least a morning or an afternoon. Now mired in large part in poverty, the Alfama used to be the toniest neighborhood in Lisbon, inhabited in part by the aristocracy, its closely knit alleyways built around a fortified castle on the hilltop.

The rich fled after Lisbon's 1755 earthquake, leaving the district to the families of fishermen and paupers. The Alfama was allowed to decay gracefully, and it is because of this poverty that its casbah-like layout remains intact today.

Balconies are strung with laundry; music emanates from tavernas filled with immigrants from such former colonies as Mozambique or Cape Verde; crumbling churches have terraces with panoramic views; hidden restaurants spill out onto open-air courtyards; and black-shawled widows grill sardines on open braziers, tossing a fish head to a passing cat.

One of the best views is from **Largo das Portas do Sol** 🎇, one of the gates to the old city. A lively fish market takes place every morning at Rua de São Pedro.

Another great panoramic sweep is possible from **Miradouro de Santa Luzia** 🎇🎇, whose bougainvillea-clad terrace spans the tiled roofs of the Alfama toward the Tagus River.

grounds, taking in the landscaping of olive, pine, and cork trees, all graced by elegant peacocks strutting their feathers or white-bodied swans gliding by.

Rua da Costa do Castelo. 📞 21/880-0620. 5€ ($6.50) adults, free for children under 10. Mar–Oct daily 9am–9pm; Oct–Mar daily 9am–6pm. Bus: 37. Tram: 12 or 28.

Museu Antóniano This Alfama church, so it is said, stands on the spot where St. Anthony of Padua, an itinerant Franciscan monk who became the patron saint of Portugal, was born in 1195. Only the crypt remains from the original church. The present structure dates from 1757 and was based on the design of the architect Mateus Vicente. The church is a medley of styles, including baroque overtones and neoclassical Ionic columns standing on each side of the principal portal. Married couples visit the church on their wedding day, leaving flowers for St. Anthony. The saint was born and reared in Lisbon but spent the last months of his life in Padua. Next to the church, the museum displays ancient manuscripts, ex-votos, and images, all related to St. Anthony.

Largo de Santo António de Sé 24. 📞 21/886-9145. Free admission. Daily 10am–1pm and 2–5pm. Metro: Rossio. Bus: 37. Tram: 12 or 28.

Sé (Cathedral) 🎇 It's not one of the grand cathedrals of Europe, but this blend of Romanesque and Gothic architecture, characterized by twin towers flanking its entrance, merits 30 or so minutes of your time if you're exploring the Alfama. The cathedral was begun in 1147 when Afonso Henriques ordered it built for the first bishop of Lisbon after he'd kicked out the Moors. Over the years the cathedral has had a rough time of it, as it was devastated by a series of earth tremors in the 14th century.

It also shook at its foundations during the earthquake of 1755. The austere interior is a bit gloomy, but there are treasures here, including the font where St. Anthony of Padua is said to have been christened in 1195. Other notable features include the Gothic chapel of Bartholomeu Joanes plus a crib by Machado de Castro. If time remains, visit the cloister, built on the orders of King Dinis in the 14th century. It's of ogival construction with garlands and a Romanesque **wrought-iron grille** ✿. The sacristy contains valuable images, relics, and other treasures from the 15th and 16th centuries.

Largo de Sé. ✆ **21/886-6752**. Cathedral entrance free; cloister 2.50€ ($3.25). Daily 9am–7pm; holidays 9am–5pm. Tram: 28. Bus: 37.

IN BELÉM

At the mouth of the Tagus River, Portuguese caravels set sail on their voyages of discovery, changing the maps of the world and even the world itself. These voyages led to trade with India and the East, the capture of Goa, the colonization of Brazil, and the granting of Macao as a trading post with China, among other adventures. Portugal was indeed launched upon its golden age.

You can journey to the suburb of Belém in the southwestern district to see where Portuguese mariners such as Ferdinand Magellan, Vasco de Gama, and Barolomeu Dias set out on their voyages across the Sea of Darkness.

Belém is easily reached by public transportation. Take tram 15 for the 20-minute ride from Praça do Comércio in the center of Lisbon, or else bus nos. 29 and 43, which also leave from Praça do Comércio. The slow trains from Cais do Sodré marked "Cascais" also stop at Belém.

You can spend an entire day at Belém enjoying its monuments, parks, and gardens, as well as strolling its setting along the Tagus. If your time is very limited, try to see at least Mosteiro dos Jerónimos, Museu Nacional dos Coches, and Museu de Marinha—all reviewed below, along with some more minor attractions.

Mosteiro dos Jerónimos ✿✿   This is the jewel of the age of Manueline art. Manuel I, called "The Fortunate," launched this monastery to commemorate the success of Vasco da Gama's voyage to India. Bearing the king's name, Manueline architecture blends the most flamboyant Gothic aspects with Moorish influences. "Pepper money," meaning profits from the spice trade with India, helped finance this magnificent monument.

A former small chapel built by Henry the Navigator is today **Ingreja de Santa Maria** ✿✿, with one of the most beautiful interiors of any of Lisbon's churches, particularly evocative for its **network vaulting** ✿ over the aisles and naves. The pinnacle of Manueline expression is achieved in the **cloisters** ✿✿✿, reached through the west door. Completed in 1544, these cloisters are filled with delicate tracery and lushly carved images adorning their arches and balustrades. The church boasts three naves noted for their delicate columns; several of the ceilings are graced with ribbed barrel vaulting. Many of Portugal's greatest national heroes are entombed here, including Vasco da Gama and the land's national poet, Luís Vas de Camões, author of the epic *Os Lusíadas* (The Lusiads), in which he glorified the triumphs of his compatriots.

Praça do Império. ✆ **21/362-0034**. www.mosteirojeronimos.pt. Church entrance free; cloisters 4.50€ ($5.85) adults, 2.25€ ($2.95)15–25 years old, free 14 and under. May–Sept Tues–Sun 10am–6pm; Oct–Apr Tues–Sun 10am–5pm. Tram: 15. Bus: 27, 28, 29, 43, 49, or 51.

Museu de Marinha ✿✿   One of Europe's greatest maritime museums depicts Portugal's seafaring past and is installed in the west wing of Mosteiro dos Jerónimos. It was in the chapel here that mariners took Mass before embarking on their fabled voyages, including Vasco da Gama's sail around the Cape of Good Hope to open the sea route to India. Navigational instruments, replicas of maps from the 1500s, and astrolabes evoke the mariners' past and what was known at the time of their discoveries. Royal galleys re-create an age of opulence, with depictions of everything from the heads of dragons to sea monsters. The most elaborate of these galleys was the one ordered built by Queen Maria I in honor of her son's marriage in 1785 to a Spanish princess—the crew consisted of 80 oarsmen. On display are many models of sailing ships ranging from the 15th to the 19th centuries, including pleasure boats and river crafts. Of special interest is a model of the queen's stateroom on the royal yacht of Carlos I, the Bragança king assassinated at Praça do Comércio in 1908. It was on this craft that the queen mother, Amélia, and her son, Manuel II, escaped to Gibraltar.

Praça do Império. ☏ 21/362-0019. www.museu.marinha.pt. Admission 3€ ($3.90) adults, 1.50€ ($1.95) students, free for children under 5. Apr–Sept Tues–Sun 10am–6pm; winter Tues–Sun 10am–5pm. Train: Belém. Tram: 15. Bus: 27, 28, 29, 43, 49, or 51.

Museu Nacional dos Coches 𝕶𝕶   This is the world's greatest coach museum and is one of the most visited attractions in Portugal. Founded by Amélia, wife of Carlos I, it's installed in a riding academy built in the 1700s. Gilded coaches, four-wheelers, litters—they are all found here. The most ancient is the splendidly painted **four-wheeler** 𝕶 that Philip of Spain brought to Portugal in the late 16th century. The coaches range from the very simple to the most ostentatious, the latter being the three outrageously adorned coaches built in 1716 for the Marquês de Abrantes, Portugal's ambassador to Pope Clement XI. Their interiors are lined with gold and red velvet, and the coaches are carved and decorated with royal coats-of-arms along with allegories.

Praça de Afonso de Albuquerque. ☏ 21/361-0850. www.museudoscoches-ipmuseus.pt. Admission 3€ ($3.90) adults, 1.50€ ($1.95) students 14–25, free for children under 14. Tues–Sun 10am–6pm. Train: Belém. Tram: 15. Bus: 14, 27, 28, 29, 43, 49, or 51.

⌒**Moments**   **To Market, to Market . . .**

The big market of **Ribeira Nova** 𝕶𝕶 is as close as you can get to the heart of Lisbon. Behind the Cais do Sodré train station, an enormous roof shelters a collection of stalls offering the produce used in Lisbon's finest restaurants. Foodstuffs arrive each morning in wicker baskets bulging with oversize carrots, cabbages big enough to be shrubbery, and stalks of bananas. Some of the freshly plucked produce arrives by donkey, some by truck, some balanced, in Mediterranean fashion, on the heads of Lisboan women. The country's rich soil produces the juiciest peaches and the most aromatic tomatoes.

At the market, women festively clad in voluminous skirts and calico aprons preside over mounds of vegetables, fruit, and fish. On cue, the vendors begin howling about the value of their wares, stopping only to pose for an occasional snapshot. Fishing boats dock at dawn with their catch. The fishermen deposit the cod, squid, bass, hake, and swordfish on long marble counters. The *varinas* (fishwives) balance wicker baskets of the fresh catch on their heads as they climb the cobblestone streets of the Alfama or the Bairro Alto to sell fish from door to door.

Torre de Belém ⚑⚑ This quadrangular tower is one of Portugal's greatest monuments to its Age of Discovery. Built by Manuel I, the tower was a fortress in the early 16th century and the starting point for the famous Portuguese mariners. The **decoration** ⚑⚑ of the tower's exterior is magnificent, adorned with rope carved of stone and balconies. Moorish-styled watchtowers guard it and the battlements appear in the shape of shields. A monument to Portugal's great naval past, the tower is often used to symbolize Portugal itself. Along the balustrade of the loggias, stone crosses represent the Portuguese crusaders. From the ramparts you're rewarded with a **panorama** ⚑⚑ of the Tagus and its vessels. In the center of the square on which the tower sits is the **Fonte Luminosa** ⚑ or Luminous Fountain, whose water jets strike up some 70 original patterns every evening, creating a show that lasts for about an hour.

Praça do Império, Avenida de Brasília. ⓒ **21/362-0034.** www.mosteirojeronimos.pt. Admission 3€ ($3.90) adults, 1.50€ ($1.95) 15–25 years old, free for children under 14. Sun free until 2pm. May–Sept Tues–Sun 10am–6:30pm; Oct–Apr Tues–Sun 10am–5pm. Tram: 15. Bus: 27, 28, 29, 43, 49, or 51.

OTHER GREAT MUSEUMS
Museu da Fundaçao Calouste Gulbenkian ⚑⚑⚑
Hailed by art critics as one of the world's finest private art collections, this magnificent treasure trove was formed from a nucleus of art acquired by Calouste Gulbenkian, an oil magnate with an eye for art, who died in 1955 and willed his collection to the state. The modern museum was constructed on a former private estate that once belonged to the Count of Vilalva and opened in 1969. Allow at least 3 hours for a romp through this varied collection, which covers Egyptian, Greek, and Roman antiquities among other treasures, even a rare (for Europe) assemblage of Islamic art, including Syrian glass and ceramics and textiles from Turkey and old Persia. The **medieval illuminated manuscripts and ivories** ⚑ form a stunning display, as do the French Impressionist paintings, 18th-century decorative works, antiques, silverware, and jewelry.

In a move requiring great skill in negotiation, Gulbenkian managed to buy art from the Hermitage in St. Petersburg. Among his most notable acquisitions are two Rembrandts: *Portrait of an Old Man* and *Alexander the Great.* Two other well-known paintings are *Portrait of Hélène Fourment* by Peter Paul Rubens and *Portrait of Madame Claude Monet* by Pierre-August Renoir. In addition, we suggest that you seek out Mary Cassatt's *The Stocking.* The French sculptor Jean-Antoine Houdon is represented by a statue of Diana. Silver made by François-Thomas Germain, once used by Catherine the Great, is here, as well as a piece by Thomas Germain, the artist's father.

As a cultural center, the Gulbenkian Foundation sponsors plays, films, ballets, and concerts, as well as a rotating exhibition of works by leading modern Portuguese and foreign artists.

Av. de Berna 45. ⓒ **21/782-3000.** www.museu.gulbenkian.pt. Admission 3€ ($3.90), free for seniors (65 and over), students, and teachers. Free to all Sun. Tues–Sun 10am–5:45pm. Metro: Sebastião or Praça de Espanha. Bus: 16, 26, 31, 46, 56.

Museu Nacional de Arte Antiga ⚑⚑⚑
Set inside the 17th-century palace of the Counts of Alvor, this great museum, one of the finest in Iberia, was founded in part from rare collections taken from monasteries that were suppressed in 1833. The greatest paintings to be found in Portugal are displayed here in a carefully laid out collection, with the major European paintings from the 14th to the 19th centuries on the ground floor. On the top floor is one of the country's finest displays of Portuguese art and sculpture. The gallery has some celebrated works, including a **polyptych** ⚑⚑⚑ from St. Vincent's monastery, a work attributed to Nuno Gonçalves between 1460

Finds **If It Swims, It's Here**

A legacy left by Expo '98, the second biggest aquarium in the world (the largest is in Osaka, Japan), **Oceanario de Lisboa** ☆☆ ((℗ **21/891-7002;** www. oceanario.pt), helps you realize what a seafaring nation Portugal was and still is. The centerpiece of this amazing glass-and-stone building is a 1.3-million-gallon holding tank. That's about the equivalent of four Olympic swimming pools strung together. From shoals of sardines to menacing sharks, the displays consist of four distinct ecosystems that replicate the Atlantic, Pacific, Indian, and Antarctic oceans. Each is supplemented with above-ground portions on which birds, amphibians, and reptiles flourish. Look for otters in the Pacific waters, penguins in the Antarctic section, trees and flowers that might remind you of Polynesia in the Indian Ocean section, and puffins, terns, and seagulls in the Atlantic division.

Don't underestimate the national pride associated with this huge facility. Most Portuguese view it as a latter-day reminder of their former mastery of the seas. Admission is 10.50€ ($13.65) adults, 5.25€ ($6.85) students and children under 13. Open daily 10am to 8pm (closes at 7pm in winter). Metro: Estaçao do Oriente.

and 1470. A triptych, *The Temptation of St. Anthony* ☆☆☆, is the gallery's other celebrated treasure. Other notable works include the portrait of St. Jerome in his old age by Albrecht Dürer, a great work of Renaissance humanism from 1521. Hans Holbein the Elder weighs in with his masterly *The Virgin and Child and Saint* from 1519. A series of 16th-century **Namban screens** ☆ form one of the museum's other treasures, as does a ceramics collection and many decorative items made for the royal family, including a strikingly unusual faience violin.

Rua das Janelas Verdes. (℗ **21/391-2800.** www.mnarteantiga-ipmuseus.pt. Admission 3€ ($3.90) adults, 1.50€ ($1.95) students, free for children under 14. Tues 2–6pm; Wed–Sun 10am–6pm. Tram: 15 or 18. Train: Santos. Bus: 27, 49, 51, or 60.

WHERE TO DINE

António Clara ☆☆ PORTUGUESE/INTERNATIONAL   One of the most celebrated restaurants in Lisbon is located just off the Praça do Marquês de Pompal. This upmarket establishment occupies a late-19th-century villa that was the home of the Miguel Ventura Terra (1866–1918), a famous architect of his day. In one of the most beautiful dining rooms of the city, you can enjoy top-notch cooking that is a modern and inspired rendition of classic recipes. Meals include such specialties as paella for two, monkfish rice, cod, and beef Wellington. The dishes might be familiar, but only the highest-quality ingredients are used. The seafood is especially good here.

Ave. da República 38. (℗ **21/799-4280.** Reservations recommended. Main courses 12€–30€ ($15.60–$39). AE, DC, MC, V. Mon–Sat 12:30–3pm and 7:30–10:30pm. Metro: Saldainha.

Bachus ☆☆ INTERNATIONAL/PORTUGUESE   In Bairro Alto, a short distance south of Rossio station, this amusing and sophisticated restaurant has an ambience evocative of a turn-of-the-20th-century British club. Classic favorites are dished up by classy waiters who service their tables well. The menu is adjusted to take advantage of seasonal produce, and old and new influences are combined to produce appetizing fare that might range from shrimp Bachus to mountain goat.

Largo da Trindade 8–9. ⑦ **21/342-2828**. Reservations recommended. Main courses 15€–24€ ($19.50–$31.20). AE, DC, MC, V. Tues–Fri noon–2pm and 7pm–midnight; Sat–Sun 6pm–2am. Metro: Chiado.

Conventual ⭐⭐ *Finds* PORTUGUESE

One of Lisbon's finest restaurants (the prime minister of Portugal is a fan) is west of Rossio Station, off Praça de Principe Real. This exemplary dining room is comfortably spaced with white-clothed tables evoking a 1930s style and is overseen by a graceful, welcoming staff. The menu is beautifully balanced between rich game favorites such as stewed partridge in port and fish dishes such as grilled monkfish in an herb-flavor cream sauce.

Praça das Flores 45. ⑦ **21/390-9246**. Reservations required. Main courses 17€–25€ ($22.10–$32.50). AE, DC, MC, V. Mon–Fri 12:30–3:30pm; Mon–Sat 7:30–11:30pm. Closed Aug. Metro: Avenida.

Kais ⭐ INTERNATIONAL

Located at the docks, this bar and restaurant opens onto an esplanade by the river. It's installed in a late-19th-century warehouse that has been amazingly converted into one of the most beautiful restaurants in Lisbon. Against a backdrop of Frank Lloyd Wright–inspired furniture, you can select from a dazzling array of fresh foodstuffs deftly handled by the skilled chefs in the kitchen. Shrimp in champagne sauce is just one of the many tempting dishes that await you.

Rua da Cintura-Santos. ⑦ **21/393-2930**. Reservations recommended. Main courses 25€–30€ ($32.50–$39); prix-fixe menus 50€–60€ ($65–$78). Mon–Thurs 8pm–midnight; Fri–Sat 8pm–1am. Closed first 2 weeks in Aug. Metro: Cais do Sodré.

Martinho da Arcada PORTUGUESE

It's one of the city's most famous restaurants, thanks to its age (it was established in 1782) and its association with Portugal's beloved poet, Fernando Pessoa, whose photos hang on the wall. There are three distinct sections to this place. There's a cafe section for drinks and sandwiches; an outdoor terrace, where the menu is less complete than what you'll find inside; and an inside dining room with antecedents that go back more than 225 years. The menu here is long and varied, but if you ask for what the kitchen is the most proud of, a staff member will talk abut the house-style cod (a thick "tenderloin" of cod served with twice-cooked onions and fried potatoes) and house-style filet steak with coffee sauce and fresh vegetables.

Praça di Comercio 3. ⑦ **21/887-9259**. Reservations recommended for dinner. Main courses 13.50€–18€ ($17.55–$23.40). AE, DC, MC, V. Mon–Sat 8am–11pm. Metro: Terreiro do Paço.

Restaurant/Cafeteria Teatro Nacional de São Carlos CONTINENTAL

Just after the turn of the millennium, one of the formal "showcase" salons within Lisbon's Opera House, originally built in 1765, was transformed into a restaurant, the kind of airy, appealingly formal venue where sparkling wine might be served with fresh fish and a rundown on the plot of an upcoming or past opera performance. It's made even more appealing by the tables set up under parasols within the traffic-free square outside. The best menu items include cod with pesto sauce and red cabbage risotto, magret of duck with green peppers, tournedos with three kinds of mushrooms and cream sauce, and grilled beef with three different kinds of Portuguese cheese.

Largo São Carlos. ⑦ **21/346/8082**. Salads, pastas, and risottos 10€–14€ ($13–$18.20); main courses 12.50€–18€ ($16.25–$23.40). Mon–Sat 9am–midnight. AE, DC, MC, V. Metro: Baixo/Chiado.

Restaurant Tavares ✦✦✦ INTERNATIONAL   Established as a cafe in the 18th century, Lisbon's oldest restaurant once reigned supreme and is still going strong today, despite its many challengers. Against an elegant backdrop with splendid furnishings, the restaurant serves the finest interpretation of regional cuisine mixed harmoniously with classic French-inspired dishes including classic scallops of veal *viennoise*. The refined cooking is firmly rooted to the seasons, and the top-notch welcome and service continue to lure the diplomats and literati who patronize this swank rendezvous.

Rua das Misericórdia 35. ✆ **21/342-1112.** Reservations required on weekends. Main courses 20€–40€ ($26–$52). AE, DC, MC, V. Mon–Fri 12:30–2:30pm; Mon–Sat 8–10:30pm. Closed Aug. Bus: 15. Metro: Chiado.

Sancho PORTUGUESE/INTERNATIONAL   This cozy and rustic dining room in the heart of Lisbon, close to Rossio Station, is one of the city's most atmospheric. The restaurant serves longtime favorites such as pan-broiled Portuguese steak in a dining room equipped with blessed air-conditioning in summer and a roaring fireplace in winter. The shellfish is some of the best and freshest in town, and for something really local, opt for *churrasco de cabrito ao piri-piri* (goat with a fiery pepper sauce).

Travessa da Glória 14. ✆ **21/346-9780.** Reservations recommended. Main courses 12€–19€ ($15.60–$24.70). AE, DC, MC, V. Mon–Fri noon–3pm and 7–10:30pm; Sat 7–10:30pm. Metro: Avenida or Restauradores.

Tasquinha d'Adelaide ✦ *Finds* PORTUGUESE   This unusual restaurant is known for serving the culinary specialties of Trás-os-Montes, the most rugged and remote province of Portugal. The restaurant itself is on the western edge of the Bairro Alto, and a table here is a coveted commodity among Lisboan foodies who appreciate its homelike atmosphere and unpretentious but good-tasting cuisine. This food is not for the faint of heart, and attracts those who deliberately seek out its hearty regional fare, which includes such daunting courses as tripe with collard greens and rice. There are options for less adventurous palates as well.

Rua do Patrocinio 70–74. ✆ **21/396-2239.** Reservations recommended. Main courses 14€–27€ ($18.20–$35.10). AE, DC, MC, V. Mon–Sat 12:30–4pm and 8pm–2am. Metro: Rato.

SHOPPING

Portugal is known for its handicrafts, including exquisite embroideries, decorative glazed tiles, china, fishermen's sweaters, fado recordings, lightweight baskets—and the best buys of all, regional pottery in all types, shapes, and forms. The single best buy in the country is gold, as jewelers are required by law to put in a minimum of 19.2 karats into each piece of jewelry. Many of the ornamental designs of fine gold or silver pieces date from ancient times.

Run by the same family for more than a century, the leading center for silver, gold, and filigree is **W. A. Sarmento,** Rua Aurea 251 (✆ **21/347-0783** or 21/342-6774), at the foot of the Santa Justa elevator. The most distinguished silver- and goldsmiths in Portugal, their specialty is lacy filigree jewelry. Also worthy is **Joalharia do Carmo,** Rua do Carmo 87B (✆ **21/342-4200**), which sells handmade silver pieces and even platinum jewelry in stunning designs.

Just for fun, even if you don't buy anything, head for the open-air street market, **Feira da Ladra** ✦✦, the sprawling flea market where Portuguese vendors peddle their wares on Tuesday and Saturday. It's best to go in the morning. One of the best selections of Portuguese baskets and one of the widest displays of regional handcrafts are sold here. The market activity begins about a 5-minute stroll from the Lisbon waterfront as you head into the Alfama sector, beginning your search at Campo de Santa Clara and following your instinctive shopping nose up and down the hilly streets.

Founded in 1824, **Vista Alegre,** Largo do Chiado 18, in the Chiado district (© 21/ 346-1401), is the most famous porcelain producer in the country. If you don't see what you want in the main showcase, know that there is a large inventory warehouse at the rear of this two-floor outlet. **Ana Salazar,** Rua do Carmo 87, also in the Chiado district (© 21/347-2289), is the most avant-garde designer of women's clothing in Portugal. Known for her "stretch fabrics," Salazar designs clothes that critics have called "body conscious yet wearable."

Fábrica Viuva Lamego, Largo do Intendente 25, in the Graça district (© 21/885-2408), founded in 1879, sells the largest and best selection of tiles and pottery in Lisbon. The tiles are contemporary but based on old Portuguese motifs.

NIGHTLIFE

What's On in Lisbon, available at most newsstands, is your best companion for an up-to-the-minute preview of what's going on in the Portuguese capital.

Cultural Lisbon is best showcased at **Teatro Nacional São Carlos,** Rua Serpa Pinto 9 (© 21/325-3045), attracting opera and ballet lovers from across the country, its season lasting from mid-September to July. Some of the best concerts and recitals are presented at **Museo da Fundacão Calouste Gulbenkian,** Ave. De Berna 45 (© 21/782-3000), which stages occasional ballets or jazz concerts as well.

To get your evening in Lisbon going, you can head for one of two evocative institutions. **A Brasileira,** Rua Garrett 120 (© 21/346-9541), in the Chiado district, is the oldest surviving coffeehouse in Lisbon and a tradition since 1905, when it was the gathering place for the city's literati. Sitting here having a demitasse of strong coffee is like wandering back in a time capsule to Lisbon's yesterday. Other than coffee, the most typical drink of Lisbon is port wine, and **Solar do Vinho do Porto,** Rua de São Pedro de Alcantâra 45 (© 21/347-5707), is devoted just to this enticing drink. In a setting from 3 centuries ago, you can peruse the menu of 200 types of port wine— sweet or dry, red or white.

Lisbon abounds with bars and dance clubs, many offering live music. In a former factory and warehouse beside the river, **Bar of the Café Alcántara,** Rua Maria Luisa Holstein 15 (© 21/363-7176), evokes a railway car in turn-of-the-20th-century Paris. The club is a lot of fun and caters to gay, straight, and everything in between. Another cafe, **Blues Café,** Rua Cintura do Puerto do Lisboa 3–4 (© 21/395-7085), is also by the river with an eagle's nest balcony encircling one floor. The latest hip-hop and garage music is played here every night Tuesday through Saturday.

A two-story warehouse near the Apolónia has been converted into **Lux,** Avenida Infante Don Henrique (© 21/882-0890), on the banks of the Tagus. This counter-culture joint is filled with hip patrons and cutting-edge music, including both a disco and a bar, with the dance club charging a 12€ ($15.60) cover after midnight.

If you like a drink with a view, there is no better spot than the aptly named **Panorama Bar,** in the Lisboa Sheraton Hotel, Rua Latino Coelho 1 (© 21/312-0000), on the top floor of Portugal's tallest building (30 stories high). Against the backdrop of a cosmopolitan decor, you can enjoy views over the city and the Tagus. The bar stays open Sunday to Wednesday 12:30pm to 2am, Thursday to Saturday 12:30pm to 3am. One of the most popular watering holes in the Barrio Alto is **Portas Largas,** Rua da Atalaia 105 (© 21/346-6379), a hip hangout attracting a mixture

Moments The Songs of Sorrow

Unless you have experienced the nostalgic sounds of **fado,** the songs of sorrow, you do not know Portugal—certainly not its soul. Fado is Portugal's most vivid art form; no visit to the country should be planned without at least 1 night spent in a local tavern where this traditional folk music is heard.

A rough translation of *fado* is "fate" from the Latin *fatum,* meaning "prophecy." Fado usually tells of unrequited love, jealousy, a longing for days gone by. As one expert put it, it speaks of "life commanded by the Oracle, which nothing can change." It's usually sung by females but is also performed by male singers, both known as *fadistas.*

Fado found its earliest fame in the 19th century when Maria Severa, the beautiful daughter of a gypsy, took Lisbon by storm, singing her way into the hearts of the people—and especially the heart of the count of Vimioso, an outstanding bullfighter of his day. Legend has it that she is honored by present-day fadistas who wear a black-fringed shawl in her memory.

In this century the most famous exponent of fado has been Amália Rodrigues, who was introduced to American audiences in the 1950s at the New York club La Vie en Rose. She was discovered while walking barefoot and selling flowers on the Lisbon docks, near the Alfama.

Clutching black shawls around themselves, the female *fadistas* pour out their emotions, from the tenderest whisper of hope to a wailing lament of life's tragedies. As they sing, accompanied by a guitar and a viola, standing against a black gas street lamp, without benefit of backdrops or makeup, they seem to lose all contact with the surrounding world—they just stand there, seemingly outdoing the Rhine's Lorelei in drawing you into their world of tenderness and fire. Though much enjoyment can be derived from understanding the poetic imagery, a knowledge of Portuguese is not essential. The power

of straight and gay that's open until 3:30am daily. The most charming bar of Lisbon is **Procópio,** Alto de São Francisco 21 (© **21/385-2851**), which attracts actors, journalists, and politicos.

AN EXCURSION TO SINTRA

To Lord Byron, it was a "glorious Eden." To today's visitor, it is the single most rewarding day trip from any city within Portugal. Once a favorite summer retreat of Portuguese kings, Sintra is set among fresh water springs, wooded ravines, and lush vegetation of exotic trees and shrubs. In the blistering summer months, Sintra is a cool mountain retreat, especially in the evening.

The natural beauty of this land, located 18 miles (29km) northwest of Lisbon, is enhanced by country manor houses, cobbled streets, horse-drawn carriages, and national palaces. In 1995, UNESCO recognized its charm by naming it a World Heritage Site.

GETTING THERE   Trains depart from Estação Rossio (p. 678) from tracks 4 and 5, leaving every 15 to 30 minutes daily from 6am to 2am. The trip time is 45 minutes, and a one-way ticket costs 1.40€ ($1.80). Trains arrive in Sintra at **Estação de Caminhos de Ferro,** Avenida Dr. Miguel Bombarda (© **808/208-208**). The station of the lyrics, the warmth of the voices, and the personalities of the singers communicate a great deal.

Fado is sung all over Lisbon and its environs, but the best clubs for this art form include **Adega Machado,** Rua do Norte 91 (© **21/322-4640**), the city's most beloved fado club where some of the greatest of today's *fadistas* appear. A dinner show starts at 8pm with music beginning at 9:15pm. Open Tuesday to Sunday, the club charges 16€ ($20.80), including two drinks.

Another cherished favorite is **A Severa,** Rua das Gaveas 51 (© **21/346-4006**), featuring top-notch male and female *fadistas* alternating with folk dancers. You can also dine here on fine regional dishes. The meals are a la carte, costing 15€ to 30€ ($19.50–$39). There are two shows daily from 9pm to 2am.

One of the most famous and enduring clubs in Bairro Alto is **Luso,** Travessa de Queimada 10 (© **21/342-2281**), converted from a vaulted network of 17th-century stables. Great fado shows and good regional food is served, with dinners costing 39€ ($50.70). Dinner (includes a show) is served at 8:30pm daily. For a cover of 25€ ($32.50), including two drinks, you can come just for the second show (10:30pm).

Close to the waterfront and the Alfama, **Parreirinha da Alfama,** Beco do Espirito Santo 1 (© **21/886-8209**), is an old-time cafe that offers one of the purest forms of fado (no folkloric shows here). A favorite since the 1950s, it presents classic fado and serves a good regional dinner for 38€ ($49.40). If you don't want to dine, you pay a modest cover of 15€ ($19.50), which is credited toward your drink bill. Open daily from 8pm to 1am, with music beginning at 9:30pm.

is ⅔ mile (1.1km) downhill from the center of town. Buses run frequently back and forth; the fare is 1€ ($1.30). A taxi into town costs 6€ ($7.80) for up to four passengers. For more information, call © 808/208-208.

TOURIST INFORMATION   The **Sintra Tourist Office** is at Praça da República 23 (© **21/923-1157**), in the center of town. From June to September it is open daily 9am to 8pm; October to May daily 9am to 7pm.

TOP ATTRACTIONS & SPECIAL MOMENTS

Even those on the most rushed of schedules try to budget time to see two of Portugal's greatest palaces. **Palacio Nacional de Sintra** ✦✦✦, Largo da Rainha Dona Amélia (© **21/910-6840** or 21/910-6841; www.ippar.pt), was a royal palace until 1910, when the Portuguese monarchy fled town in the face of revolution. In the heart of *Sintra Vila*, the Old Town, the landmark structure is dominated by a pair of conical chimneys rising above it. Much of it was constructed by João I in the late 1300s and built upon the site of a palace constructed by Moorish sultans that had been torn down. A favorite summer retreat of Portuguese royalty, it has seen much rebuilding and enlarging over the years, and the building is now an interesting conglomeration of architectural styles.

Moments **Back to Glorious Eden**

If you'd like to see Sintra the way Lord Byron did when working on his autobiographical *Childe Harold's Pilgrimage,* you can rent a horse-drawn carriage in front of the National Palace of Sintra at Largo da Rainha Dona Amélia. Carrying up to five passengers, these romantic tours last less than an hour but are worth the price. You'll be following trails blazed by Moorish sultans centuries ago along bougainvillea-lined streets, and can look up at little balconies aflame with red geraniums. Once you've gotten the view the carriage ride has shown you, you can wander about making your own discoveries. Prices must be negotiated with the driver as there are no fixed rates, but an average ride through town usually costs about 10€ to 25€ ($13–$32.50).

Inside, the domed ceiling of **Sala does Brasões (Stag Room)** ✦ makes for a splendid salon. Stags hold the coats-of-arms of nearly 75 Portuguese noble families, and the lower walls are lined with Delft-like tiled panels from the 1700s. The other splendid chamber is the **Sala dos Cisnes (Swan Room)** ✦ of the former banquet hall, painted in the 17th century. This room was a favorite of King João I, the father of Prince Henry the Navigator. The ceiling was covered with magpies, a reference to the gossipy ladies of the courts. The Room of the Sirens or Mermaids is one of the most elegant in the palace. It's decorated with intricate Arabesque designs. Admission is 4€ ($5.20) for adults, 2€ ($2.60) for children 14 to 25, free for kids under 13. Open Thursday to Tuesday 10am to 5:30pm. Free admission on Sunday and holidays.

The other great palace in Sintra is **Palacio Nacional de Pena** ✦✦, Estrada de Pena (© **21/910-5340;** www.ippar.pt), standing on a plateau of 1,500 feet (457m) on one of the loftiest peaks in the Serra de Sintra mountain chain. Built in the 19th century, the palace is a blend of various architectural styles and was the royal abode of the young queen, Maria II, and her husband, Ferdinand Saxe-Coburg-Gotha. Ferdinand took charge of the building, appointing Baron Von Eschwege, a German architect, to construct this cool summer place for the royal family. It's set on parklike grounds and is a monument to a faded royal life. Allow 2 hours to tour the whole place, including the oval-shaped bedroom (adorned with bright red walls) of Manuel II, the last king of Portugal. Decorated with German stained-glass windows, the elegant **Ballroom** ✦ is a major highlight, with its Asian porcelain and life-size torchbearers supporting a mammoth candelabra. The **Arab Room** ✦ is a stunner with its magnificent *trompe l'oeil* frescoes.

The notable **Chapel Altarpiece** ✦ is from the 16th century and is made of alabaster and marble, each niche depicting a scene from the life of Christ. If time remains, explore the gardens.

Admission is 4€ ($5.20) for adults, 2€ ($2.60) children 6 to 17 years old, 2€ ($2.60) adults 65 and older, and free for children 5 and under. The palace is open June to September Tuesday to Sunday from 10am to 6:30pm; October to May Tuesday to Sunday 10am to 4:30pm.

WHERE TO DINE

In the hillside village right below Sintra, **Cantinho de São Pedro,** Praça Dom Fernando II 18 (© **21/923-0267**), is known for its savory French and Portuguese-inspired cuisine, and is found right off the main square of this little satellite to Sintra. Daily specials, *pratos do dia,* are some of the finest fare in the area, and the menu always offers something enticing, perhaps salmon and shrimp au gratin or pork with an unusual mixture of clams. Main courses cost 15€ to 30€ ($20–$39), with a fixed-price menu going for 20€ ($26). Open daily noon to 3pm and 7:30 to 10pm.

Uphill from the Praça de República in Sintra, **Tacho Real** ⭑⭑, Rua da Ferraria 4 (© **21/923-5277**), serves well-prepared Portuguese and French meals in a stylish setting reached after climbing some steep steps. Both meat and fish dishes are handled equally well by a well-trained staff. The fish stew is the best in the area, and the fixed-price menu is one of Sintra's dining bargains. Main courses cost 14€ to 30€ ($18.20–$39), with a fixed-price menu costing 18€ ($23.40). Open Thursday to Tuesday noon to 3pm and 7:30 to 10:30pm.

3 The Algarve

This strip of beachfront property is a great amphitheater facing the sea, stretching for 100 miles (160km) from Cape St. Vincent of Prince Henry the Navigator fame to the border town of Vila Real de Santo António overlooking the Spanish frontier. Called *Al-Gharb* by the Moorish conquerors, the Algarve is celebrated for the pink blossoms of its almond trees in bloom from the middle of January until the end of February.

Fishing is still a buoyant source of income for this region, although nearly all the coast has been given over to tourism. Those lonely beaches backed up by tiny, white-washed fishing hamlets are getting harder and harder to find as developers take over. The Algarve consists of two sections. The *barlavento* lying to the west of Portimão is a coastal strip—mainly a rock-strewn coast—that is humid and has cliffs rising 246 feet (75m), with sandy shores and hidden coves often separated by strange grottoes. East of Faro (the capital), the *sotavento* is riddled with salty lagoons, sandy dunes, and broken spits of beaches filled mainly with European sunbathers from June to October.

Lagos and Faro are the best base cities in the Algarve for train travelers because both offer easy rail access to Lisbon.

GETTING THERE

Faro, 192 miles (309km) southeast of Lisbon, is the rail hub of the Algarve with five IC trains arriving daily from Lisbon. The trip takes 4 hours and a one-way ticket costs about 19.50€ ($25.35). If you're connecting with Lagos in the west, six trains make the 2-hour journey out of Faro each day. Fares cost 6.40€ ($8.30) one-way.

Estación Faro, Largo Estaçao (© **808/208-208**), lies near the town center, adjacent to the bus station and close to the intersection of Avenida de República and Praça de Estação. Built as an architectural showcase in the 1890s, but dimmed by age, it is the most important and strategic rail junction in the south of Portugal thanks to its position astride lines that interconnect it to the north-south lines from Lisbon and the east-west lines from Vila Real in the east and Lagos in the west. Faro is Portugal's second most used railway transfer point after Lisbon.

There are no tourist offices within the station, but the **Faro Tourist Office,** Rua da Misericórdia 8–12 (© **28/980-3604;** www.visitalgarve.pt), is just a few minutes' walk away. It's open June to August daily 9:30am to 7pm, September to May daily 9:30am to 5:30pm. The staff does not make hotel reservations but will provide data about what lodging is available (what's cheap, what's luxurious, and so on). Although there is no ATM at the station, there are banks along Avenida de Rua de Santo António and Avenida de República, all a short walk from the station. For luggage storage, you'll

Moments Northward Ho!

Although we focus more on Portugal's southern region in this chapter (its northern region is really more suited to a driving tour than a rail trip), if you have 3 extra days on your itinerary, you can ride the rails north from Lisbon to experience three widely different jewels in the Portuguese crown: the walled medieval city of **Óbidos,** followed by the ancient university city of **Coimbra,** and topped by several glasses of port wine drunk on home turf in the old city of **Porto** (second-largest in Portugal). Unlike the arid but historical plains to the south, these towns and cities lie in lush "Atlantic green" Portugal.

Óbidos

Dominated by the keep and towers of its ancient castle, the walled city of **Óbidos** ⭐⭐ is only 58 miles (93km) north of Lisbon, but it's a comparatively long train ride away. From the Estaçao do Rossio in Lisbon, frequent daily commuter trains run to the rail junction at Cacém, where you can change trains for the final lap into Óbidos. The entire trip takes 2 to 3 hours and costs 7.60€ ($9.90) for a one-way ticket. The tourist office is located on Rua Direita, Aprtado 42 (© **262/955-060;** www.rt-oeste.pt).

Óbidos so captivated Queen Isabella in 1228 that her husband, King Denis, presented it to her as a gift, a token of his devotion. You can spend 3 or 4 hours wandering behind its 14th-century castellated walls, viewing the whitewashed houses and old churches and finding good food and overnight lodging at its converted stone castle, now the **Pousada do Castelo,** Paço Real (© **26/295-5080;** www.pousadas.pt), which offers 12 air-conditioned rooms and suites. Rates range from 190€ to 300€ ($247–$390) double; 257€ to 405€ ($334–$527) suite.

Coimbra

Most rail passengers skip Óbidos and head straight from Lisbon to the romantic city of **Coimbra** ⭐⭐⭐, 123 miles (198km) to the north. Some 16 high-speed trains per day make the 2-hour trek north from Lisbon to Coimbra at a cost of 23€ ($29.90) for a one-way ticket.

The birthplace of six kings and the seat of Portugal's oldest university, Coimbra, on the right bank of the Mondego River, is a city rich in attractions—not only its university, but one of the country's greatest Romanesque cathedrals, **Sé Velha;** and a 12th-century Gothic monastery. The renowned 18th-century **Quinta das Lagrimas** (Estate of Tears), or "Garden of Tears," was the former abode of the ill-fated Inês de Castro, mistress of Pedro the Cruel, who was murdered here on order of Pedro's father, King Alfonso IV. The gardens are a favorite pilgrimage spot for romantics and the house is now the best hotel in the region (see below).

have to go next door to the bus station, which doesn't store bags for more than 24 hours. Depending on size, the cost is from 2€ to 4€ ($2.60–$5.20) per bag. Note that the kiosk here isn't staffed on Saturday and Sunday. Taxis line up outside the rail

Stop in at the **Coimbra Tourist Office,** Largo da Portagem (© **23/948-8120;** www.turismo-centro.pt), a 5-minute walk from the train station, and you'll be given a map of the town, a list of the monuments with opening hours, and the names of the leading hotels and restaurants. Our favorite place to stay in town is the luxurious and romantic 35-room manor **Quinta das Lagrimas,** Rue Antonio Agusto Gonçalves (© **23/980-2380;** www.quinta daslagrimas.pt). The rooms are decorated in traditional Portuguese style but offer every modern comfort. Rates are 142€ to 210€ ($185–$273) double; 315€ to 406€ ($410–$528) suite.

Porto

The final stop on your rail journey north is **Porto** ✸✸, 195 miles (314km) north of Lisbon. A settlement known as Portucale since the 8th century B.C., the town eventually lent its name to the whole country. Once the base of the Portuguese shipping fleet, Porto (literally, "the port") helped Portugal evolve into a great maritime power. Today, however, the city on the Douro River is known mainly for housing the lodges or wine storehouses of the world-famous port wine made across Ponte Dom Luis in the satellite suburb of Vila Nova de Gaia.

The rail traveler can explore some of Porto's notable tourist highlights, including its Romanesque **Sé (Cathedral);** its 15th-century church, **Ingreja de Santa Clara;** its even more impressive 14th-century Gothic **Ingreja de São Francisco;** and its **Fundaçao de Serralves** museum devoted to modern art. Later in the day, you can take a boat trip up the Douro to sail by the vineyards where the grapes used to make the port are grown.

From Estaçao Santa Apolónia in Lisbon, five daily Alfa trains make the trip to Porto. The journey takes about 3 hours and costs 27.50€ ($35.75) for a one-way ticket. If you spend the night in Coimbra (see above), you can take one of several high-speed trains to Porto (trip time: 1 hr., 10 min.); a one-way ticket costs 16.10€ ($20.95). Be sure to take a train to the **Estação de São Bento** station (© **808/208-208**), which is in the center of town, and not Porto's other rail station, which is south of the city.

For a list of hotels, restaurants, and attractions, stop in at the **Porto Tourist Board,** Rua do Clube Fenianos 25 (© **22/339-3472;** www.portoturismo.pt), just a few minutes' walk from the train station. One good hotel within 5 or 10 minutes' walk of the station is the 149-room **Mercure Batalha Hotel,** Porto Praca de Batalha (© **22/204-3300;** www.mercure.com). It offers traditional and tastefully decorated rooms. Rates run 90€ to 120€ ($117–$156) double, but the hotel often discounts it prices.

station, with fares to most points within the environs of Faro ranging from 6.50€ to 21€ ($8.45–$27.30).

Caminho Ferro Português, Largo da Estação (© 808/208-208), is the second major rail hub for the Algarve. It's in Lagos, 43 miles (69km) west of Faro and 164

Finds **The Algarve's Most Beautiful Spot**

Directly south of the port of Lagos stands **Ponta da Piedade** ⋆⋆⋆, an area of such stunning beauty that it's unmatched anywhere along the coast. This gem is filled with towering cliffs and hidden grottoes carved eons ago by turbulent waves, which make them look like flamboyant examples of Manueline architecture.

At the lighthouse here, the **view** ⋆⋆ stretches from Cabo de São Vincente on the west to Cabo Carvoeiro in the east. Ponta de Piedade is 2 miles (3km) south of the Lagos harbor. To get here, take a taxi down from Lagos.

---

miles (264km) south of Lisbon. The station, in the eastern part of Lagos, is reached via a pedestrian suspension bridge, and is about 2,100 feet (630m) from the town's main square at Praça Gil Eanes. Four IC trains run from Lisbon to Lagos, taking 4½ hours and costing 21.50€ ($27.95) one-way. There are also 2 daily ALFA trains going from Lisbon to Lagos in 3 hours and 40 minutes, costing 24.50€ ($31.85) one-way. Faro is the westernmost terminus of rail lines that stretch east to west across the Algarve. Points farther west, including Sagres, require access by bus from either Lagos or Faro.

There are no ATMs within the station, but there are a number of them along Avenida dos Descobrimentos, one of the city's busiest and most visible avenues, just a short walk away. The bus station is directly across the street; neither station offers luggage storage. Taxis are available at the entrance to the station; it will cost about 5€ to 17€ ($6.50–$22.10) to go virtually anywhere within Lagos.

There is no tourist office within the station. The **Lagos Tourist Office** lies along Rua Vasco da Gama, Sitio de São João (© **28/276-3031**), open daily from 9:30am to 1pm and 2 to 5:30pm. The staff will make reservations but only if the client shows up in person or if the client requests this service by phone at least 2½ weeks in advance. Reservations cost 2€ ($2.60) per person.

TOP ATTRACTIONS & SPECIAL MOMENTS

Other than the beaches, the chief man-made attractions in the Algarve lie within the towns of Faro and Lagos. The exception to this is **Sagres** ⋆, or "The End of the World," lying 21 miles (34km) west of Lagos and 71 miles (114km) west of Faro. At the extreme southwestern corner of Europe, it is a rocky escarpment jutting into the Atlantic Ocean. It was from this remote point that Prince Henry the Navigator launched Portugal onto the seas of exploration, establishing a school where mariners such as Vasco da Gama, Magellan, Diaz, and Cabral apprenticed. We find the sunsets here among the most dramatic in Europe. Ancient mariners thought that when the sun sank from here beyond the cape, it plunged over the edge of the world.

Henry's windswept fortress, **Fortaleza de Sagres,** Ponte de Sagres (© **28/262-0140**), has been reconstructed and turned into a small museum documenting the area's naval history. It's open May to September daily from 9:30am to 8pm; October to April daily from 9:30am to 5:30pm. Admission is 3€ ($3.90) for adults, 1.50€ ($1.95) for ages 15 to 25, and free for children 14 and under. Far more dramatic than this man-made attraction are the surrounding pathways that open onto vertigo-inducing panoramas of the turbulent sea and towering cliffs.

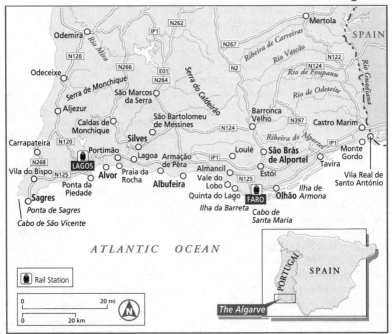

Lying 3 miles (4.8km) to the west is the lonely **Cabo de São Vicente,** with the second most powerful lighthouse in Europe. This lighthouse beams illumination 60 miles (97km) across the ocean. Tours of the actual lighthouse are not generally available.

Lagos ✦, your rail hub for the western Algarve, is also the principle resort of the western Algarve, opening onto Baia de Lagos, one of the widest bays of the Portuguese coast. You can spend a morning or an afternoon exploring its attractions, including **Antigo Mercado de Escravos,** Praça do Infante Dom Henríques, an arcaded slave market, the only one of its kind in Europe. Captives were once sold here to the highest bidder. It can be viewed at any time and admission is free.

Sitting just off the waterfront stands the 18-century church, **Igreja de Santo António** ✦, Rua General Alberto Carlos Silveira (© **28/276-2301**). This church is a real Algarvian gem, its lower part covered with the blue-and-white tiles or *azulejos* of Portugal. The rest is in carved, painted, or gilded wood. A series of eight paneled paintings depict so-called miracles performed by Saint Anthony. At the altar are impressive **gilt carvings** ✦ created with gold imported from Brazil. Admission is 3€ ($3.90) adults, 1€ ($1.30) students and seniors 65 and older; children 12 and under are free. Hours are Tuesday to Sunday 9:30am to 12:30pm and 2 to 5pm.

Next door to the church of Saint Anthony stands the **Museu Municipal Dr. José Formosinho,** Rua General Carlos Silveira (© **28/276-2301**), the regional museum of the western Algarve. Of particular interest here are the replicas of the fret-cut chimneys of the Algarve, with exhibitions of various regional handcrafts and artifacts ranging from ecclesiastical sculpture to a numismatic collection. Pickled freak animals are among its more exotic attractions, and there's even a funky pair of 19th-century sunglasses.

Admission is 2.20€ ($2.85) for adults, 1.10€ ($1.45) for students (not college age), and free for children under 12. Hours are Tuesday to Sunday 9:30am to 12:30pm and 2 to 5pm.

The capital city of **Faro** is a bit lean on man-made attractions. If you're caught between trains, you can occupy 2 to 3 hours of time by visiting such sights as **Igreja de Nossa Senhora do Monte do Carmo do Faro,** Largo do Carmo, erected in the 19th century. The church could be easily skipped were it not for its bizarre **Capela d'Ossos** or "Chapel of Bones." The chapel is lined with an estimated 1,245 human skulls and bones. These bones were dug up from graves around the church in 1816. Entrance to the chapel costs 1€ ($1.30). It's open 10am to 12:30pm and 3 to 5:30pm.

The **Sé (Cathedral),** Largo da Sé (© **28/987-0870**), the major cathedral for the Algarve, should be more impressive than it is. Nonetheless, it merits 30 minutes or so of your time. This Renaissance cathedral took the tower of its Gothic predecessor, and its wide nave is flanked by *azulejos* from the 18th-century. Its chief attraction is its Capela do Rosário, which is loaded with *azulejos* from the 17th-century. Admission is 3€ ($3.90), and the building is open daily 10am to 5:30pm.

Museo Municipal de Faro, Largo Dom Afonso III 14 (© **28/989-7400**), is housed in the 16th-century edifice of the former Convento de Nossa Senhora da Assuncão. Artifacts recovered from the Algarve are on display in the cloister galleries with some intriguing sights—including a tomb—excavated at nearby Milreu, where the Romans built a temple dedicated to Ossonoba in the 1st century A.D. Other displays include Mudéjar tiles from the Muslim era, ancient weapons and coins, and a 16th-century bishop's throne. Admission is 3€ ($3.90) adults, 1.50€ ($1.95) for children ages 13 to 18, and free for 12 and under. Open in winter Tuesday to Friday 9:30am to 5:30pm, Monday and Saturday 2 to 5:30pm; summer Tuesday to Friday 10am to 8pm, Monday and Saturday 2:30 to 8pm.

WHERE TO STAY & DINE

A good choice for Lagos-bound travelers is the 324-room **Tivoli Lagos** ⚐, Rua António Crisógano dos Santos, Lagos 8600-678 (© **28/279-0079**), the town's leading hostelry, housed in a 20th-century castle of Moorish and Portuguese design that's set within its own ramparts and moats. Removed from the beach, the hotel lies at the eastern side of town and has its own pool, all on 3 acres (1.2 hectares) of prime hilltop real estate. Both standard and deluxe rooms are rented and each is well maintained and attractively furnished. Doubles average 103€ ($134), with suites going for 190€ ($247).

Down the scale a bit, but still very inviting, is the 36-room **Albergaria Marina Rio,** Avenida dos Descobrimentos, Lagos 8600-645 (© **28/276-9859**), in the very heart of Lagos opposite the marina. Its most dramatic feature is a panoramic top-floor swimming pool with a broad sun terrace. A courtesy bus takes guests to the beaches. Bedrooms are neatly kept and range in size from small to medium, with doubles averaging 95€ ($124); rates include a buffet breakfast.

For the finest lodgings in the Lagos area, head over to **Romantik Hotel Vivenda Miranda** ⚐⚐⚐, Porto de Mos, Lagos 8600-282 (© **28/276-3222**), a Moorish-inspired hotel standing on a cliff that opens onto the rugged coastline, 1¾ miles (2.8km) south of Lagos, close to a good sandy beach at Praia do Porto de Mos. The hotel offers well-furnished and somewhat stylish bedrooms ranging from midsize to spacious, and its outdoor pool opens onto lush gardens and sun terraces. Doubles rent for 114€ to 184€ ($148–$239), with a suite costing 128€ to 290€ ($166–$377).

Even though it's a bit uninspired, **Eva** ⚑, Avenida da República, Faro 8000-078 (② **28/900-1000**), is the best of the lodgings in the capital city of Faro. This modern, eight-floor, 148-room hotel stands at the harborfront, not at the beach, but offers a rooftop swimming pool. Bedrooms are furnished in a restrained style, the finer accommodations containing balconies opening onto the water. Doubles average 120€ ($156), with suites costing 190€ ($247); all rates include breakfast. The best overnight value in town is found at **Residential Algarve** ⚑, Rua Infante Dom Henrique 62, Faro 8000-363 (② **28/989-5700**), which opened in 1999, having been created out of an 1880s private home that was once owned by a local mariner. Before it became a hotel, it had to be practically demolished but was reconstructed in the original style. The hotel, only a short walk from the center of town, offers midsize to spacious bedrooms, each well furnished. Rates average 70€ ($91) double and 85€ ($111) triple.

In the very heart of Lagos, the undiscovered **A Lagosteira,** Rua do 1 de Maio 20 (② **28/276-2486**), is one of the best restaurants in town, serving seafood and regional Portuguese cuisine with an Algarvian slant. We always gravitate to this place for our first meal in town, devouring the fish soup and the savory clams—lobster is also a specialty. Main courses cost from 9€ to 23€ ($11.70–$29.90). Another local favorite is **Don Sebastião** ⚑, Rua do 25 de Abril 20–22 (② **28/276-2795**), which serves savory Portuguese and Algarvian cuisine that's an equal match for the food dished out at A Lagosteira. It too is in the heart of town, lying to the west of the main waterfront, bordering Avenida dos Descobrimentos on the opposite bank from the rail station. The menu is varied and tasty, with a good selection of local wines. In summer, there's outdoor dining. Main courses cost from 7€ to 25€ ($9.10–$32.50).

The greatest restaurants in the Algarve are not found in Faro, but you are likely to find yourself here because it's a rail hub. Don't despair, as you can order hearty, typical Algarvian cuisine at **Adega Nortenha,** Praça Ferreira de Almeida 25 (② **28/982-2709**), in the heart of the city and convenient to bus and rail connections. The restaurant's regional dishes, such as bits of seafood cooked with chunks of pork in a casserole, also make it one of the most affordable bargains in town, with main courses costing 5.50€ to 12.50€ ($7.15–$16.25). A tradition since 1925, **Dois Irmãos,** Largo do Terreiro do Bispo 13–15 (② **28/982-3337**), is a modest but a good choice for its Algarvian cuisine of freshly grilled fish and shellfish dishes—most likely the catch was harvested that morning. Service is slow, but it's worth the wait. Main courses cost 10€ to 24€ ($13–$31.20).

To avoid a constant diet of regional fare, you can retreat to **Casa Velha** ⚑⚑⚑ (② **28/939-4983**), outside Faro, 12 miles (20km) to the east, in the direction of Almancil. This grand coastal restaurant serves refined French cuisine based on market-fresh ingredients deftly handled by an experienced kitchen staff. Dishes are beautifully balanced, featuring everything from foie gras or lobster to sea bass or a delectable breast of duck seasoned with a dozen spices. Main courses cost 18€ to 30€ ($23.40–$39). A fixed-price menu is 65€ ($84.50).

17

Spain

Riding the rails in Spain is a grand adventure that offers travelers an ideal way to see one of the most diverse landscapes in Europe—from the snowcapped peaks surrounding Granada and the rivers enveloping Toledo to the Moorish-flavored Andalusia to the modern artistry of Catalonia. Traveling through Spain by rail is the cheapest way to see the country—especially if you opt for a railpass—and a relatively inexpensive venture when compared to train travel in other Western European countries. Value-conscious travelers looking for a diverse destination without sacrificing comfort will be hard-pressed to find a better choice on the Continent.

Since the mid-1990s, there has been an almost Herculean improvement in the Spanish state railway system, aka **RENFE** *(Red Nacional de Ferrocarriles Espanoles)*. Spain now offers more options for the rail traveler than ever before. Its high-speed Talgo trains and the speedy and luxurious AVE trains, running between Madrid and Seville/Barcelona, have almost buried the country's reputation for sluggish rail service, though the notoriously slow *regionales y cercanías* (regional and local trains) still remain.

RENFE's network of trains is now so vast that all the major sections of Spain are linked to Madrid with efficient high-speed trains. To reach some of the more remote provinces or areas, you still must rely on slow-moving trains, but if you stick to the main cities, you can be anywhere in Spain within a matter of hours, including Andalusia in the south (Seville and Granada) or Barcelona (the country's second major rail hub) in the east.

HIGHLIGHTS OF SPAIN

Every major region of Spain, from the Basque country in the northeast to the southern cities of Andalusia, such as Granada and Seville, is within hours of **Madrid** by rail. The capital of Spain is at the geographical center of the country and is the hub of all its major rail networks. Madrid makes the best base for a rail tour of Spain because you can branch out to virtually anywhere in the country.

The country's second major rail transportation hub, **Barcelona,** is in the remote northeast of the country and is a long way from some of Spain's frequently visited cities, such as Toledo. Barcelona is a good launch pad for rail travelers only if they are coming from the east, through the south of France, or are flying first into Barcelona to begin their rail journey.

Madrid's attractions are year-round, including three internationally famous art galleries—**the Prado, Centro de Arte Reina Sofia,** and **Museo Thyssen–Bornemisza**—along with a royal palace, grand public squares, and museum after museum stuffed with treasures. Its 17th-century square, **Plaza Mayor,** lies at the focal point of Madrid's historic core. While in Madrid, be sure to budget a 1-day trip by rail to **Toledo,** the capital of old Castile and one of the five most fascinating cities of Spain.

After seeing Madrid, most rail passengers head south to Andalusia, specifically Seville. Those with an extra 2 or 3 days to spare, however, can continue to take train rides from Madrid to several art cities that lie on its doorstep. In just 2 hours you can travel 54 miles (87km) northwest of Madrid to **Segovia.** If you leave early enough from Madrid, you can visit Segovia's Cabildo Catédral de Segovia, the last Gothic cathedral built in Spain (1515), and its fabled Alcázar dating from the 12th century. Although it would be a long day, you can return to Madrid by nightfall. Another long day trip from Madrid is to the walled city of **Avila,** 68 miles (109km) northwest of Madrid. Some two dozen trains leave daily from Madrid for Avila, taking 1½ to 2 hours each way. The main attraction in this city forever linked to St. Teresa, born here in 1515, are the medieval walls, averaging 33 feet (9.9m) tall.

An even longer day trip out of Madrid (2½ hr.) is an excursion to the ancient university city of **Salamanca,** 127 miles (204km) northwest of Madrid. Labeled a World Heritage City by UNESCO, Salamanca's major attractions, including its Plaza Mayor (the most beautiful in Spain) and both its old and new cathedrals, can be visited in 3 hours.

Although the city of **Bilbao,** capital of the Basque country, is a popular tourist destination now that its Guggenheim Museum has opened, a train ride here from Madrid can take 5½ to 8½ hours, making it very inconvenient for rail travelers with limited

Moments   Festivals & Special Events

One of the biggest draws on Spain's cultural calendar, **ARCO** (Madrid's International Contemporary Art Fair) showcases the best in contemporary art from Europe and America. At the Nuevo Recinto Ferial Juan Carlos I, the exhibition brings together galleries from throughout Europe, the Americas, Australia, and Asia, who showcase the works of regional and internationally known artists. To buy tickets, contact Parque Ferial Juan Carlos I at ℓ **94-722-3000**. The cost is between 32€ and 63€ ($41.60–$81.90). You can get schedules from the tourist office closer to the event. Dates vary, but it's usually held mid-February. For more information, call ℓ **91-722-3000**, or visit **www.ifema.es**.

The **Feria de Sevilla (Seville Fair)** is the most celebrated week of revelry in all of Spain, with all-night flamenco dancing, entertainment booths, bullfights, horseback riding, flower-decked coaches, and dancing in the streets. The action takes place the second week after Easter, and you'll need to reserve a hotel well in advance. For general information and exact festival dates, contact the Office of Tourism in Seville (ℓ **95-422-14-04**).

Madrileños run wild during the 10-day **Fiesta de San Isidro** celebration honoring their city's patron saint. Food fairs, Castilian folkloric events, street parades, parties, music, dances, bullfights, and other festivities mark the occasion, which starts the second week of May. Make hotel reservations early. Expect crowds and traffic (and beware of pickpockets). For information, contact the **Oficina Municipal de Información y Turismo**, Plaza Mayor 3, 28012 Madrid (ℓ **91-588-1636**; www.munimadrid.es).

time on their hands. The same goes for the sea resort of San Sebastian and for the medieval city of Pamplona, made famous by its running of the bulls.

It's far easier for rail travelers to head south, and we concentrate on options in that area of the country. From Madrid, high-speed trains rush you south to the vast sprawling lands of Andalusia, which takes up the southern tip of Spain, opening onto the Mediterranean. This once-great stronghold of Muslim Spain is rich in history and tradition, containing some of the country's most celebrated treasures: the world-famous Mezquita (mosque) in Córdoba, the Alhambra in Granada, and the great Gothic cathedral in Seville. It also has many smaller towns just waiting to be discovered—Ubeda, Jaén, gorge-split Ronda, Jerez de la Frontera, and the gleaming white port city of Cádiz. Give Andalusia at least a week, and you'll still have only skimmed the surface.

This dry mountainous region also embraces the overbuilt and often tacky Costa del Sol (Málaga, Marbella, and Torremolinos), or Sun Coast, a strip of beach resorts that's popular with Europeans, but one that we suggest skipping.

Seville, the capital of Andalusia, is of major interest to the rail traveler, as this city ranks along with Madrid, Barcelona, and Toledo as one of the five most visited—and justifiably so—cities of Spain.

On the banks of Río Guadalquivir, Seville flourished under Muslim rule and again in the 16th century. Many architectural treasures remain from those epochs, including a celebrated cathedral, which contains the tomb of Columbus, and **La Giralda,** the minaret of a mosque constructed from 1184 to 1198. This is Spain's most perfect Islamic building. Seville's **Barrio de Santa Cruz,** or medieval Jewish quarter, is alone worth the train ride from Madrid, with its tangle of quaint and winding streets. Because of the sultry climate, July and August are the worst months to visit here.

A total of 22 AVE trains make the 45-minute trip from Seville to the historic city of **Córdoba** each day. A visit to the city's famous mosque is one no traveler will likely forget.

After a visit to Seville, passengers wanting to see the world-famous **Alhambra,** a palace left over from the days of Moorish occupation, can take one of four trains heading east from Seville. The journey takes you along one of Andalusia's most scenic train rides into the snowcapped Sierra Nevada mountains before reaching the palace's home, the city of **Granada.** After Granada, a traditional rail tour of Spain heads northeast to **Barcelona,** although this is a long journey that will take 12 to 13 hours depending on the train.

Barcelona, the capital of Catalonia, is one of the busiest ports in the Mediterranean. In culture, business, and sports, it rivals Madrid and is on par with many of the distinguished capitals of Europe. Barcelona is known for its **Las Ramblas,** the most famous street in Spain, alive at all hours, and for the architecture of Gaudí, best represented by his unfinished masterpiece, **Sagrada Familia,** a cathedral. In the heart of town, the evocative **Barri Gotic,** or Gothic quarter, is reason enough to visit the city, crowned by the 14th-century **Barcelona Cathedral.** Historical monuments and museums, including one dedicated to Picasso, abound here, but the city is celebrated for the scores of structures in its Eixample District, left over from the artistic explosion of *modernista.*

After Barcelona, rail passengers can either fly out of the city or continue by train up the rugged coastline, **Costa Brava,** and into France.

1 Essentials

GETTING THERE

The major gateway cities for international and domestic flights into Spain are Barcelona and Madrid. Madrid's international airport, **Barajas** (© **91-305-8343**), lies 9 miles (15km) east of the center and has two terminals—one for international flights, the other for domestic traffic. The airport for Barcelona is **El Prat de Llobregat,** Prat de Llobregat (© **93-298-3838**), about 7½ miles (12km) southwest of the city.

Iberia Airlines (© **800/772-4642;** www.iberia.com) offers more routes into and within Spain than any other airline. It features daily nonstop service to Madrid from such North American cities as New York, Chicago, and Miami. **Air Europa** (© **800/238-7672;** www.air-europa.com) is Iberia's chief Spanish-based competitor, serving Madrid from New Jersey's Newark Airport, with continuing service to major cities in Spain.

Note: Barcelona-bound passengers often land in Madrid, which is linked by Iberia flights departing at 15-minute intervals during peak hours on weekdays. Iberia flights also leave Madrid frequently for Seville, which is the gateway air city to Andalusia.

Other North American carriers with direct service to Spain include **American Airlines** (© **800/433-7300;** www.aa.com); **Delta** (© **800/241-4141;** www.delta.com); **Continental Airlines** (© **800/231-0856;** www.continental.com); and **US Airways** (© **800/622-1015;** www.usairways.com).

United Airlines (© **800/241-6522;** www.ual.com) does not fly into Spain directly but offers airfares from the United States to Spain in conjunction with a host of European airlines.

SPAIN BY RAIL
PASSES

Both the **Eurail Global Pass** and **Eurail Global Pass Flexi** are good for use on Spanish trains. See chapter 2 for more details on these and other multicountry passes.

Spain also has its own national railpasses, all issued by **RENFE.** For information on train fares, schedules, and destinations, contact RENFE (© **90-224-0202;** www.renfe.es) or Rail Europe (© **877/272-RAIL** [7245] in North America; www.raileurope.com). Children 4 to 11 pay approximately half the adult fare, and tots under 4 ride free. For train tickets, go to the principal office of RENFE in Madrid at Alcalá 44 (© **90-224-0202;** Metro: Banco de España), open Monday to Friday 9:30am to 8pm.

Warning: If you purchase a round-trip ticket in Spain, you must hang onto both parts of the ticket until you've completed your entire journey or you might be fined severely when the conductor comes around to check tickets on your return leg.

The only trains in Spain not run by RENFE are a few narrow-gauge lines, such as the one from Barcelona to Montserrat and the lines along the north coast of Spain; these do not accept railpasses.

The **Eurail Spain Pass** offers 3 to 10 days of unlimited train travel within a 2-month period, with a choice of both first- and second-class travel. First-class travel costs $253 for 3 days or $529 for 10 days; second class, $197 for 3 days or $427 for 10 days. The **Eurail Spain–Portugal Pass** also allows 3 to 10 days of unlimited first- or second-class travel in both Spain and Portugal. In first class the cost is $289 for 3 days or $565 for 10 days; in second class, $258 for 3 days or $488 for 3 days.

The **Eurail Spain Rail 'n Drive** pass combines 3 days of unlimited train travel and 2 days in your own rental car, costing $318 to $486 per person, depending on the car. Reductions are granted if two adults travel together.

The two most popular countries in Europe with American travelers, Spain and France, are combined in the **Eurail France 'n Spain Pass,** offering 4 to 10 days of unlimited train travel in a 2-month period, with a choice of first- or second-class seats. For 4 days, the cost is $352 per person in first class or $305 in second class. Discounts apply when two or more adults travel together.

All railpasses should be purchased in North America before you depart for Europe. Passes can be ordered in North America through **Rail Europe** (© **877/272-RAIL** [7245]; www.raileurope.com) or your travel agent.

FOREIGN TRAIN TERMS

All stations in Spain post train timetables, *llegadas* indicating arrivals and *salidas* meaning departures. For other information, ask at a ticket window or *taquilla.* Nearly all long-distance trains *(largo recorrido)* offer first- and second-class tickets, the slowest (also the least expensive) of these being the *regionales.*

Regular long-distance interregional trains are known as *diurnos.* When these trains travel at night, they become *estrellas.* Talgos (Tren Articulado Ligero Giocoechea Oriol) are the fastest, most expensive, and also the most comfortable trains in Spain. Talgos stop only at major cities, not outposts. The classic and best version is a **Talgo 200,** featuring both a standard *turista* class and a luxurious *preferente* class. The high-speed train between Madrid and Seville/Barcelona is called AVE. Other high-speed trains include the Alvia, Alaria, Altaria, Avant, and Euromed. Bigger cities such as Madrid have trains making short runs, and these local networks are called *cercanias*.

PRACTICAL TRAIN INFORMATION

Talgo and **AVE** trains are the fastest and most efficient in Spain, but there are a number of other special trains that run in Spain as well. Altaria trains are high-speed lines that will get you from Madrid to Córdoba in a little more than 2 hours, or Madrid to Seville in slightly more than 3 hours.

For speed, stick to the fast AVE trains linking Barcelona with Madrid. The two most important cities of Andalusia, Seville and Granada, are linked by TRD trains (Regional Diesel Trains), incorporating the latest technology in the field of diesel engines. TRD trains require reservations (available only in Spain).

If you're on a strict budget, opt for second-class seats on trains; they are reasonably comfortable and usually well maintained.

RESERVATIONS Reservations are a very good idea in Spain if you're traveling on holidays, on Friday afternoons, or on Sunday nights. Reservations are required for all fast and long-distance trains, and are required for passengers who book couchettes or sleeper accommodations. Only slow regional and local trains do not require reservations. All reservations should be made as far in advance as possible. Unless you're fluent in Spanish and can navigate RENFE's website, the best way to make reservations in advance of your trip is through Rail Europe. The cost of these advance reservations is built into the ticket price. Prices also vary depending on whether you pay by cash or credit card and whether you have a railpass or not. It's a confusing situation, best discussed on an individual basis with a Rail Europe reservations agent.

If you're traveling on the same day you purchase your ticket and need a reservation, go to the window marked *venta immediata*. For future travel, head for the window called *venta anticipada*. Expect long lines at either window. Sometimes you'll have to take a number from a vending machine and watch for that number to appear on a digital display board. Before leaving the window, be certain that the *fecha* (date) and the *hora salida* (departure time) are correct on your reservation. Railpass validation can

Trains & Travel Times in Spain

From	To	Type of Train	# of Trains	Frequency	Travel Time
Madrid	Barcelona	AVE	15	Daily	2 hr., 35 min.
Madrid	Cordoba	AVE	21	Daily	1 hr., 42 min.
Madrid	Cordoba	Talgo 200	6	Daily	1 hr., 57 min.– 2 hr.
Madrid	Cordoba	Altaria	5	Daily	2 hr., 5 min.– 2 hr., 9 min.
Madrid	Seville	AVE	19	Daily	2 hr., 30 min.
Madrid	Seville	Altaria	2	Daily	3 hr., 12 min.
Madrid	Algeciras	Altaria	2	Daily	5 hr., 50 min.
Madrid	Malaga	Talgo 200	6	Daily	4 hr., 2 min.– 4 hr., 20 min.
Madrid	Granada	Altaria	2	Daily	4 hr., 32 min.
Seville	Granada	T.R.D.	4	Daily	3 hr.–4 hr.
Seville	Cordoba	AVE	18	Daily	40 min.
Granada	Barcelona	Trenhotel	1	Daily	11 hr., 40 min.

also be made at any of these designated windows. For both regular ticket holders and passholders, standard seat reservations start at 9.55€ ($12.40) per passenger for both adults and children and are nonrefundable. Reservation prices for more luxurious trains can be higher, beginning at 13.90€ ($18.05) per passenger.

SERVICES & AMENITIES   Couchettes—actually foldout bunk beds—are called *literas* in Spain. We have found that many of these couchettes, which sleep six, are old and dirty. They're inexpensive, but you might not feel comfortable sleeping in them. If you're taking a long-distance night train—called an *estrella*—you can see if a *Tren-hotel* (train hotel) option is available for you. These are clean sleeping compartments with their own shower and toilet. Advance reservations are absolutely essential for one of these compartments.

Based on distance, sleeper fares—in addition to the regular ticket—range from 19.10€ to 175€ ($24.85–$228) per passenger, with couchette reservations costing a flat 24.35€ ($31.65) per person. Reservations can be confirmed up to 2 months prior to the date of travel, but are nonrefundable and nonexchangeable.

Most night trains have full restaurant service, and stewards also provide drinks and snacks at all hours. Inquire in advance about dining facilities or services. If they don't exist, bring your own food and drink to be on the safe side.

Most Spanish trains are air-conditioned with adequate toilet facilities. Tickets for *gran clase* (*preferente* on the Talgo) feature sleeping cars with private showers and toilets. In *turista* class cars, you'll find berths that sleep four. In economy class, expect a "sleeperette" seat.

FAST FACTS: Spain

Area Codes   In Spain, you must always dial the entire phone number, including the area code, no matter where you are located. Area codes are as follows: **91** for Madrid; **93** for Barcelona; **95** for Seville, Córdoba, Marbella, and Málaga.

Business Hours   Banks are open Monday to Friday 9:30am to 2pm and Saturday 9:30am to 1pm. Most offices are open Monday to Friday 9am to 5 or 5:30pm; the longtime practice of early closings in summer seems to be dying out. In restaurants, lunch is usually from 1 to 4pm and dinner from 9 to 11:30pm or midnight. There are no set rules for the opening of bars and taverns, many opening at 8am, others at noon; most stay open until 1:30am or later. Major stores are open Monday to Saturday 9:30am to 8pm; smaller establishments, however, often take a siesta, doing business from 9:30am to 1:30pm and 4:30 to 8pm. Hours can vary from store to store.

Climate   Spring and fall are ideal times to visit nearly all of Spain, with the possible exception of the Atlantic coast, which experiences heavy rains in October and November. May and October are the best months in terms of both weather and crowds. In summer it's hot, hot, and hotter still, with the cities in Castile (Madrid) and Andalusia (Seville and Córdoba) heating up the most. Madrid has dry heat; the average temperature can hover around 84°F (29°C) in July and 75°F (24°C) in September. Seville has the dubious reputation of being about the hottest part of Spain in July and August, often baking under average temperatures of 93°F (34°C). Barcelona, cooler in temperature, is very humid in July and August.

Documents Required Visas are not needed by U.S. and Canadian citizens for visits of less than 3 months.

Electricity Most hotels use 220 volts AC (50 cycles). Some older places have 110 or 125 volts AC. Carry an adapter with you, and always check at your hotel desk before plugging in any electrical appliance.

Embassies & Consulates If you lose your passport, fall seriously ill, get into legal trouble, or have some other serious problem, your embassy or consulate can help. These are the Madrid addresses and hours: The **United States Embassy,** Calle Serrano 75 (© **91-587-2200;** Metro: Núñez de Balboa), is open Monday to Friday 9am to 6pm. The **Canadian Embassy,** Núñez de Balboa 35 (© **91-423-3250;** Metro: Velázquez), is open Monday to Thursday 8:30am to 5:30pm, Friday 8:30am to 2:30pm.

Health & Safety Spain should not pose any major health hazards. The rich cuisine—garlic, olive oil, and wine—may give some travelers mild diarrhea, so take along some anti-diarrhea medicine, moderate your eating habits, and, even though the water is generally safe, drink mineral water only. Fish and shellfish from the horrendously polluted Mediterranean should only be eaten cooked.

If you are traveling around Spain (particularly southern Spain) over the summer, limit your exposure to the sun, especially during the first few days of your trip and, thereafter, from 11am to 2pm. Wearing a hat is a good idea. You should also use a sunscreen with an SPF rating of at least 25, and apply it liberally and often. Remember, if you're traveling with kids, they need more protection than adults do.

Water is safe to drink throughout Spain, though you should not drink the water in mountain streams, regardless of how clear and pure it looks.

While most of Spain has a moderate rate of crime, and most of the North American tourists who visit it each year have trouble-free visits, the principal tourist areas have been experiencing an increase in violent crime. Madrid and Barcelona, in particular, have reported growing incidents of muggings and violent attacks, and older tourists and Asian Americans seem to be particularly at risk. Criminals frequent tourist areas and major attractions such as museums, monuments, restaurants, hotels, beach resorts, trains, train stations, airports, subways, and ATMs. In Barcelona, violent attacks have occurred near the Picasso Museum and in the Gothic Quarter, Parc Güell, Plaza Real, and Mont Juic. In Madrid, reported incidents occurred in key tourist areas, including the area near the Prado Museum and Atocha train station, and areas of old Madrid such as Sol, the El Rastro flea market, and Plaza Mayor. Travelers should exercise caution both day and night, carry limited cash and credit cards, and leave extra cash, credit cards, passports, and personal documents in a safe location.

Holidays These include January 1 (New Year's Day), January 6 (Feast of the Epiphany), March 19 (Feast of St. Joseph), Good Friday, Easter Monday, May 1 (May Day), June 10 (Corpus Christi), June 29 (Feast of St. Peter and St. Paul), July 25 (Feast of St. James), August 15 (Feast of the Assumption), October 12 (Spain's National Day), November 1 (All Saints' Day), December 8 (Immaculate Conception), and December 25 (Christmas).

Legal Aid If you're in trouble with the law, contact your embassy or consulate (see "Embassies & Consulates," above) for a list of English-speaking lawyers in your area.

Mail Airmail letters to the United States and Canada cost .78€ ($1) up to 20 grams; letters within Spain .30€ (40¢). Postcards have the same rates as letters. Allow about 8 days for delivery to North America; in some cases, letters take 2 weeks to reach North America. Rates change frequently, so check at your local hotel before mailing anything. As for surface mail to North America, forget it. Chances are you'll be home long before your letter arrives.

Police & Emergencies The national emergency number is © 112 throughout Spain.

Telephones If you don't speak Spanish, you'll find it easier to telephone from your hotel, but remember that this is often very expensive because hotels impose a surcharge on every operator-assisted call. In some cases it can be as high as 40% or more. On the street, phone booths (known as *cabinas*) have dialing instructions in English; you can make local calls by inserting a .25€ (35¢) coin for 3 minutes.

For directory assistance: Dial © 1003 in Spain.

For operator assistance: If you need operator assistance in making an international call, dial © 025.

Toll-free numbers: Numbers beginning with **900** in Spain are toll-free, but calling an 800-number in the States from Spain is not toll-free. In fact, it costs the same as an overseas call.

Each number is preceded by its provincial code for local, national, and international calls. For example, when calling to Madrid from Madrid or another province within Spain, telephone customers must dial **91-123-45-67**. Similarly, when calling Valladolid from within or outside the province, dial **979-123-45-67**.

When in Spain, the access number for an **AT&T** calling card is © **900/99-0011**. The access number for **Sprint** is © **900/99-0013**.

More information is also available on the Telefónica website at **www.telefonica.es**.

To call Spain: If you're calling Spain from the United States, dial the international access code **(011),** then the country code for Spain **(34),** followed by the city code and the telephone number. So the whole number you'd dial would be **011-34-00-000-0000**.

To make international calls: To make international calls from Spain, first dial **00** and then the country code (U.S. or Canada **1**), followed by the city area code and number.

Tipping The government requires restaurants and hotels to include their service charges—usually 15% of the bill. That does not, however, mean that you should skip out of a place without dispensing an extra euro or two. The following are some guidelines:

Your hotel porter should get 1€ ($1.30) per bag. Maids should be given 1.50€ ($1.95) per day, more if you're generous. Tip doormen 1€ ($1.30) for assisting with baggage and .50€ (65¢) for calling a cab. In top-ranking hotels the concierge will often submit a separate bill, showing charges for newspapers and other services; if he or she has been particularly helpful, tip extra. For cab drivers, add about 10% to the fare as shown on the meter. At airports, such as Barajas in Madrid and major terminals, the porter who handles your luggage will present you with a fixed-charge bill.

In both restaurants and nightclubs, a 15% service charge is added to the bill. To that, add another 3% to 5% tip, depending on the quality of the service. Waiters in deluxe restaurants and nightclubs are accustomed to the extra 5%, which means you'll end up tipping 20%. If that seems excessive, you must remember that the initial service charge reflected in the fixed price is distributed among all the help.

Barbers and hairdressers expect a 10% to 15% tip. Tour guides expect 2€ ($2.60), although a tip is not mandatory. Theater and bullfight ushers get .50€ (65¢).

2 Madrid

At an altitude of 2,165 feet (660m), lofty Madrid is the geographical center of Spain and the hub of both its rail and highway networks. Since 1561, the city has presided over one of the most volatile and fast-changing countries in the world, going from kingdom to dictatorship to democracy.

Madrid is not the most beautiful or charming of European capitals, but it is home to some of the greatest art museums in the world and is also a good base for exploring some of the finest art cities of antiquity, especially Toledo to its immediate south.

Even more than museums, it is the spirit and lifestyle of the Castilians that provoke interest, even passion, in those who view the city as a grand place to visit. Once night falls, *la movida* (roughly, "the movement") flows until dawn in more bars, cafes, *tascas,* and clubs than there would seem to be stars in heaven.

For the train traveler, Madrid is Valhalla, the "center of the universe" for riding the rails. Trains fan out from Madrid to all the major cities, regions, and provinces of Spain. There are good connections to the "cities of the heartland," such as Segovia and Toledo, and express links to such major cities and attractions as Seville or Barcelona.

STATION INFORMATION
GETTING FROM THE AIRPORT TO THE TRAIN STATIONS

In lieu of adequate bus connections, many passengers arriving in Madrid at its Barajas airport rely on a taxi to take them to the two major rail terminals. To the station at Chamartín, the cost of a ride ranges from 20€ to 25€ ($26–$32.50). Trip time is 15 to 20 minutes, depending on traffic. From Barajas to the Atocha station, the cost ranges from 25€ to 30€ ($32.50–$39), with trip time varying from 20 to 40 minutes, based entirely on traffic conditions.

If you are traveling light and want to save money, you can take a subway from Barajas into central Madrid. Take line 8 to Mar de Cristal and switch to line 4; a one-way trip costs 1.10€ ($1.45). Air-conditioned buses also take you from the arrivals terminal to the bus depot under Plaza de Colón, a central point. The fare is 2.50€ ($3.25), and buses leave every 10 to 15 minutes daily from 6am to 10pm. From Plaza de Colón, you can take one of the frequent *cercanias* trains (railpasses are valid) for the short hop to either Atocha or Chamartín station.

Maddrid

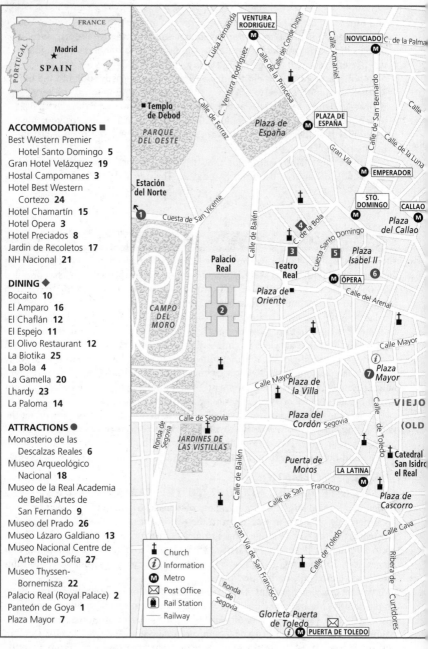

ACCOMMODATIONS ■
Best Western Premier
  Hotel Santo Domingo **5**
Gran Hotel Velázquez **19**
Hostal Campomanes **3**
Hotel Best Western
  Cortezo **24**
Hotel Chamartín **15**
Hotel Opera **3**
Hotel Preciados **8**
Jardin de Recoletos **17**
NH Nacional **21**

DINING ◆
Bocaito **10**
El Amparo **16**
El Chaflán **12**
El Espejo **11**
El Olivo Restaurant **12**
La Biotika **25**
La Bola **4**
La Gamella **20**
Lhardy **23**
La Paloma **14**

ATTRACTIONS ●
Monasterio de las
  Descalzas Reales **6**
Museo Arqueológico
  Nacional **18**
Museo de la Real Academia
  de Bellas Artes de
  San Fernando **9**
Museo del Prado **26**
Museo Lázaro Galdiano **13**
Museo Nacional Centre de
  Arte Reina Sofía **27**
Museo Thyssen-
  Bornemisza **22**
Palacio Real (Royal Palace) **2**
Panteón de Goya **1**
Plaza Mayor **7**

Madrid Metro

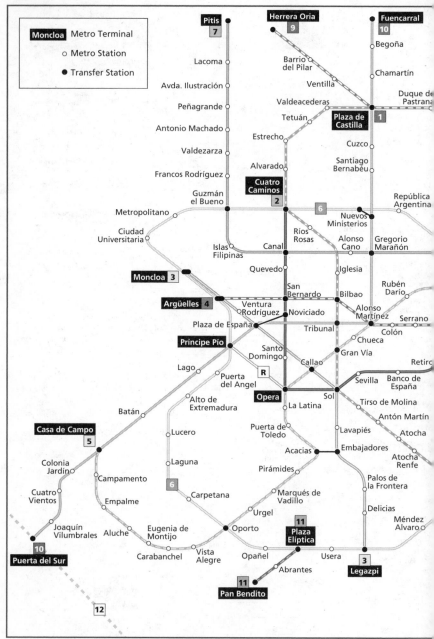

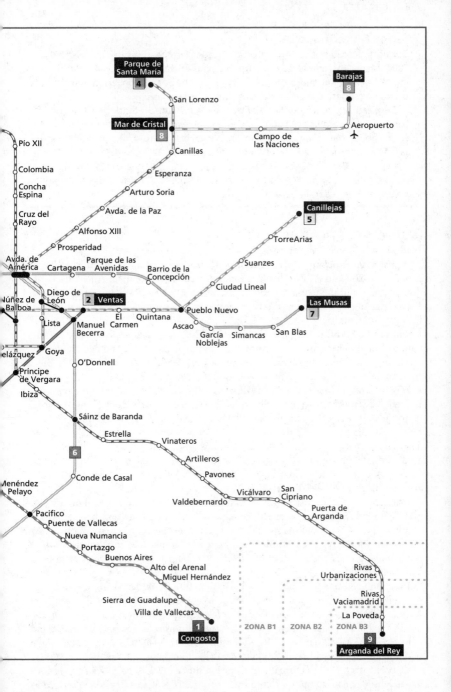

Parque de
Santa María
4

Barajas
8

San Lorenzo

Mar de Cristal
8

Aeropuerto

Campo de
las Naciones

Pío XII

Canillas

Colombia

Esperanza

Concha
Espina

Arturo Soria

Canillejas
5

Cruz del
Rayo

Avda. de la Paz

Alfonso XIII

TorreArias

Prosperidad

Avda. de
América

Parque de las
Avenidas

Barrio de la
Concepción

Suanzes

Cartagena

Diego de
León

Ciudad Lineal

Núñez de
Balboa

2 Ventas

Pueblo Nuevo

Las Musas
7

Lista

El
Carmen

Quintana

Manuel
Becerra

Ascao

San Blas

García
Noblejas

Simancas

Velázquez

Goya

O'Donnell

Príncipe
de Vergara

Ibiza

Sáinz de Baranda

Estrella

Vinateros

6

Artilleros

Conde de Casal

Pavones

Vicálvaro

San
Cipriano

Menéndez
Pelayo

Valdebernardo

Puerta de
Arganda

Pacífico

Puente de Vallecas

Nueva Numancia

Portazgo

Buenos Aires

Rivas
Urbanizaciones

Alto del Arenal

Miguel Hernández

Rivas
Vaciamadrid

Sierra de Guadalupe

La Poveda

Villa de Vallecas

ZONA B1   ZONA B2   ZONA B3

1

9

Congosto

Arganda del Rey

Terror & the Trains

During the deadliest terrorist attack in recent European history, on March 11, 2004, Islamic extremists bombed four commuter trains entering Madrid, causing 191 deaths and more than 1,400 injuries. The Spanish government continues to investigate the attacks and to arrest suspects.

Despite the publicity generated by the Madrid attacks (and the subsequent London Tube bombings in 2005), by and large, chances are there's no need to worry about day-to-day safety on Spain's trains. Up-to-date information on safety and security can be obtained by calling © **888/407-4747** toll-free in the U.S. and Canada. Outside the U.S. and Canada, call © **202/501-4444.** Both numbers operate from 8am to 8pm Eastern Standard Time, Monday to Friday, except on U.S. federal holidays.

INSIDE THE STATIONS

Madrid has two major rail stations, Atocha and Chamartín.

At **Estación Atocha,** Glorieta Carlos V (© **90-224-0202;** Metro: Atocha), high-speed Talgo 200 and AVE trains link Madrid with major points in Andalusia (Córdoba, Seville, and the Costa del Sol, for example), as well as AVE and Alvia trains to Barcelona. Atocha is linked to the city's second major station, Chamartín (see below), by *cercanías* trains.

The local **RENFE ticket office** (© **90-224-0202**) in the station is open daily from 6am to 1am. Go here for train information, seat reservations, and railpass validation. For money exchange, use the on-site offices of **Caja Madrid** (© **91-506-2800**), open Monday to Friday 8:15am to 8pm, Saturday 10:30am to 2pm.

A branch of the **Madrid Tourist Office** (© **91-528-4630**) is also found here, and is open daily from 9am to 9pm. This office doesn't make hotel reservations. For that, go to the on-site travel agency, **Viajes El Corte Inglés** (© **91-528-4408**), open daily from 7am to 10pm. You pay your hotel bill on the spot and are issued a voucher. There is no charge for hotels booked within Madrid; outside of the city, the cost is 15€ ($19.50) per booking. **Luggage lockers** *(consignas automáticas),* operated by RENFE, are also at the station. Luggage can be stored daily from 6:30am to 10:30pm at a cost of 2€ to 4.50€ ($2.60–$5.85).

Atocha is a virtual tourist attraction in itself, a 19th-century palace built of iron and glass, with a restaurant, a botanical garden, and numerous cafes and bars. Signs are clearly marked throughout the station, and there are excellent links to public transport such as the Metro. Atocha is far more central than Charmartín, lying directly south of the famous Parque del Buen Retiro and within walking distance of such attractions as Museo del Prado.

Estación Charmartín, San Agustin de Foxa (© **902-24-0202;** Metro: Charmartín), is the international rail station for Madrid. Major destinations reachable from here include Lisbon and Paris. Chamartín is also the depot for domestic destinations in the northwest and parts of southern Spain. For **train information,** seat reservations, and railpass validation, go to the local RENFE office (© **902-24-0202**), in the center of the station between tracks 11 and 12. Hours are daily from 5:30am to midnight.

Opposite track 19 is the **tourist information office** (© **91-315-9976**), open Monday to Saturday 8am to 8pm. Next to the tourist office is **Viajes Brujula** (© **91-315-7894**), a travel agency that will make reservations in Madrid hotels for 2.50€ ($3.25) per person. It's open daily 7:30am to 9:30pm. You can also visit the **Oficina Municipal de Información y Turismo,** Plaza Mayor 3 (© **91-588-16-36**). It's open Monday to Saturday 10am to 8pm, and Sunday 10am to 3pm. For **money exchange,** go to Caja Madrid (© **91-732-0155**), open Monday to Friday 8:15am to 8pm and Saturday 10:30am to 2pm.

Chamartín lies in the north of Madrid, a 15- to 20-minute ride from the center (longer if traffic is bad).

INFORMATION ELSEWHERE IN THE CITY

The major and most convenient **tourist office** in Madrid is on Duque de Medinaceli 2 (© **91-429-4951;** Metro: Banco de España), open Monday to Saturday from 9am to 7pm; Sunday and holidays 9am to 3pm. The staff does not make reservations but will provide you with a list of hotels and *hostales,* as well as a good street map.

GETTING AROUND

Madrid is a vast urban sprawl. To get around, you'll need to rely on public transportation. The good news is that many of the city's major tourist sights lie in the historic core, which can be covered on foot. In fact, the only way to explore the narrow cobblestone streets of old Madrid is by walking (wear sturdy shoes).

For most attractions, the Metro (or subway) system is the way to go. It's safe, speedy, well maintained, and also inexpensive. Fares and schedules are posted at every one of Madrid's 158 subway stations. Eleven lines, totaling 106 miles (171km), service Greater Madrid, with individual Metro tickets costing 1.75€ ($2.30).

It's cheaper to purchase a *bonotransporte* at any station, giving you 10 rides on either the Metro or the bus system at a cost of 6.40€ ($8.30). Trains run daily from 6am to 1:30am. Violent crime is almost unheard of in the subway, but pickpocketing is common. For **Metro information,** call © **90-244-4403.**

Buses pick up the slack caused by gaps in the Metro system, and these vehicles are usually fast and efficient, traveling in special lanes. The cost of a one-way ticket is the same as the Metro (see above). A bus guide, *Madrid en Autobús,* is distributed free at bus kiosks. Buses run daily from 6am to 11:30pm. Late-night revelers rely on the *Búho,* or "owl," a late-night bus service. For schedules and information about Madrid buses, call **Empresa Municipal de Transportes** at © **91-406-8810.**

Taxis operate around the clock. The base fare is 1.85€ ($2.40); for every kilometer thereafter, the fare increases by .85€ to 1.10€ ($1.15–$1.45). Supplements are charged: 2.50€ ($3.25) to a bus or train station or 5€ ($6.50) to the airport. There is also a 1.10€ ($1.45) supplement on Sundays, holidays, and after 10pm. Taxis are most often hailed in the street; otherwise, call **Radio Taxi** (© **91-447-5180**) or **Teletaxi** (© **91-371-3711**). *Warning:* Make sure the meter is turned on.

WHERE TO STAY

Best Western Premier Hotel Santo Domingo ⭐⭐   A 2-minute walk from the Plaza de España, this five-story hotel opened in 1994 and has been overhauled several times since. The atmospheric public rooms feature lots of antiques and artwork. The guest rooms are the strong point, however, and are impressively decorated with tapestry wall coverings, marble bathrooms, fine bedding, and brocade draperies. The best units are the fifth-floor doubles, especially those with furnished balconies and views over the tile roofs of Old Madrid.

Plaza Santo Domingo 13, 28013 Madrid. ✆ **91-547-9800.** Fax 91-547-5995. www.hotelsantodomingo.com. 120 units. 100€–140€ ($130–$182) double. Breakfast free Sat–Mon mornings; otherwise 11€ ($14.30) extra. AE, DC, MC, V. Metro: Santo Domingo. **Amenities:** Restaurant; bar; laundry; nonsmoking rooms. *In room:* Hair dryer.

Gran Hotel Velázquez ✿   One of the most attractive of Madrid's moderately priced hotels, this appealing choice is found behind a 1930s Art Deco–style facade on an affluent residential street. It lies in the chic Salamanca shopping district, just a 5-minute taxi ride from Atocha station. Bedrooms vary in size (some of the larger ones have separate sitting areas), but all have a sleek 1940s decor and feature marble bathrooms.

Calle de Velázquez 62, 28001 Madrid. ✆ **91-575-2800.** Fax 91-575-2809. www.chh.es. 143 units. 110€–295€ ($143–$384) double; 165€–360€ ($215–$468) junior suite; 320€–440€ ($416–$572) executive suite. AE, DC, MC, V. Metro: Velázquez. **Amenities:** 2 restaurants; laundry. *In room:* Hair dryer.

Hostal Campomanes *(Value)*   A great location near the opera house and Palacio Real (Royal Palace) and affordable prices combine to make this one a winner. It's a clean, decent choice with Philippe Stark minimalist furnishings. The folks at the desk are especially helpful in decoding rail timetables.

Calle Campomanes 4, 28013 Madrid. ✆ **91-548-8548.** Fax 91-559-1288. www.hh-campomanes.com. 30 units. 87€–111€ ($113–$144) double; 111€–149€ ($144–$194) suite. Rates include continental breakfast. AE, DC, MC, V. Metro: Opera. **Amenities:** Laundry; rooms for those w/limited mobility. *In room:* Hair-dryer, safe.

Hotel Best Western Cortezo   Just off Calle de Atocha, which leads to the railroad station of the same name, the Cortezo is a short walk from Plaza Mayor and Puerta del Sol. Although it has been renovated many times since, it still has a lingering aura of the 1950s when it was built. The accommodations are comfortable but simply furnished, with contemporary bathrooms containing tub/shower combos. Beds are springy and the furniture is pleasantly modern; many rooms have sitting areas with a desk and armchair. The public rooms match the guest rooms in freshness.

Doctor Cortezo 3, 28012 Madrid. ✆ **91-369-01-01.** Fax 91-369-37-74. www.hotelcortezo.com. 85 units. 105€–135€ ($137–$176) double; 155€–200€ ($202–$260) suite. AE, DC, MC, V. Metro: Tirso de Molina. **Amenities:** Restaurant; laundry service. *In room:* Hair dryer.

Hotel Chamartín   If you're staying overnight near the Chamartín station, this nine-story business hotel is your best bet. The hotel is part of a massive shopping center linked to the actual station—in fact, its owner is RENFE, the Spanish government rail system. The good-size and well-appointed bedrooms are soundproofed. It's a 15-minute taxi ride from the airport.

Augustin de Foxá, 28036 Madrid. ✆ **91-334-4900.** Fax 91-733-0214. www.husa.es. 378 units. 90€–142€ ($117–$185) double; 175€–220€ ($228–$286) suite. AE, DC, MC, V. Metro: Chamartín. **Amenities:** Restaurant; cafeteria; bar/lounge; laundry; rooms for those w/limited mobility. *In room:* Hair dryer.

Hotel Opera   Set close to the royal palace and the opera house, this hotel isn't regal, but offers standard comfort and a warm welcome from its English-speaking staff. Guest rooms range from medium to surprisingly spacious, each with first-rate furnishings and excellent bathrooms. The Opera remains one of Madrid's relatively undiscovered boutique hotels.

Cuesta de Santo Domingo 2, 28013 Madrid. ✆ **91-541-2800.** Fax 91-541-6923. www.hotelopera.com. 79 units. 99€–149€ ($129–$194) double. AE, DC, MC, V. Metro: Opera. **Amenities:** Restaurant; bar; laundry; nonsmoking rooms. *In room:* Hair dryer, Wi-Fi.

Hotel Preciados ✿ *(Finds)*   Only a 10-minute taxi ride from Atocha Station, this centrally located hotel is one of the city's less discovered. Housed in a converted 1881 building, the hotel retains much of its architectural past but was completely over-hauled to include all the requisite modern comforts. Children are catered to here (even the restaurant offers a kid's menu). The midsize to spacious bedrooms with shiny new bathrooms and double-glazed windows make this one a winner.

Preciados 37. ⓒ **91-454-44-00.** Fax 91-454-44-01. www.preciadoshotel.com. 73 units. 125€–150€ ($163–$195) double; 190€–320€ ($247–$416) suite. MC, V. Metro: Puerta del Sol. **Amenities:** Restaurant; bar; nonsmoking rooms; rooms for those w/limited mobility. *In room:* Hair dryer, Wi-Fi.

Jardín de Recoletos 🌟 (Value)   This Salamanca District hotel, known for its afford-able prices, is close to the Plaza Colón, one of Madrid's major traffic arteries. Rooms are rather spacious and are attractively and comfortably decorated. All have a well-equipped kitchenette, an advantage that makes this hotel popular with families.

Gil de Santivañes 6, Madrid 28001. ⓒ **91-781-1640.** Fax 91-781-1641. www.jardinderecoletos.com. 43 units. 130€–205€ ($169–$267) double; 196€–263€ ($255–$342) suite. Rates include buffet breakfast. AE, DC, MC, V. Metro: Colón or Serrano. **Amenities:** Restaurant; cafe; laundry. *In room:* Hair dryer.

NH Nacional   At the turn of the 20th century, this stately hotel was built to service overnight passengers arriving at the nearby Atocha rail station. The restored hotel con-tinues to serve travelers, but now has a smooth, seamless decor that takes maximum advantage of the building's tall ceilings and large spaces. Although not the grand monument it used to be, it still offers comfortable, modernized bedrooms and a wel-coming ambience.

Paseo del Prado 48, 28014 Madrid. ⓒ **91-429-6629.** Fax 91-369-1564. www.nh-hotels.com. 214 units. 90€–225€ ($117–$293) double; 235€ ($306) junior suite. AE, DC, MC, V. Metro: Atocha. **Amenities:** Restaurant; bar-cafeteria; laundry; rooms for those w/limited mobility. *In room:* Hair dryer.

TOP ATTRACTIONS & SPECIAL MOMENTS

Monasterio de las Descalzas Reales 🌟🌟   This magnificent building was once a royal palace. In 1559, Juana of Austria, sister of Felipe II, converted the building into a convent where aristocratic women could retreat to become "the bride of Christ." When the pope learned that the sisters in the convent were starving, he allowed them to open the monastery to visitors wanting to see its rich treasure trove of art. Each noblewoman who entered the convent brought a dowry, and those precious relics form the nucleus of the collection today. The most valuable painting is Titian's *Cae-sar's Money*, along with art works from Old Masters such as Bruegel the Elder sheltered in The Flemish Hall. Tapestries on display are from Ruben's cartoons with his chubby matrons. A small cloister on the second floor is ringed with chapels containing art-work and precious objects, including bits of wood said to be from the cross on which Christ was crucified.

Plaza de las Descalzas Reales s/n. ⓒ **91-542-0059.** Admission 5€ ($6.50) adults, 2.50€ ($3.25) children. Tues–Thurs and Sat 10:30am–12:45pm and 4–5:45pm; Fri 10:30am–12:45pm; Sun 11am–1:45pm. Bus: 1, 2, 5, 20, 46, 50, 51, 52, 53, 74, 150, M1, M2, M3, or M5. From Plaza del Callao, off Gran Via, walk down Postigo de San Martín to Plaza de las Descalzas Reales; the convent is on the left.

Museo Arqueológico Nacional 🌟🌟   This stately mansion houses one of Iberia's great archaeological museums. Founded by Queen Isabella II in 1867, the museum features exhibits spanning history from unrecorded times to the 19th century. The Iberian artifacts are supplemented by finds at digs from Ancient Greece, Italy at the time of the Etruscans, and Egypt.

The most notable and impressive sculpture is *La Dama de Elche,* a primitive carv-ing from the 4th century B.C. discovered along the southeastern coast of Spain. The

Moments   Death in the Afternoon

Blood sports may not be your thing, but the art of bullfighting is as old as pagan Spain, and reveals much about the character of the Spaniard. Bull-fighting's most avid aficionados claim it is a "microcosm of death, catharsis, and rebirth." It remains one of the most evocative and memorable events in Spain, although the action at the *corrida* may horrify the faint of heart.

Madrid draws the finest matadors in Spain. If a matador hasn't proved his worth in the **Plaza Monumental de Toros de las Ventas,** Alcalá 237 (© **91-356-2200;** www.las-ventas.com; Metro: Ventas), he won't be recognized as a top-flight artist. The major season begins during the Fiestas de San Isidro, patron saint of Madrid, on May 15. This is the occasion for a series of fights with talent scouts in the audience. Matadors who distinguish themselves in the ring are signed up for Majorca, Málaga, and other places.

The best way to get tickets to the bullfights is at the stadium's box office (open Fri–Sun 10am–2pm and 5–8pm). Alternatively, you can contact one of Madrid's most competent ticket agents, **Localidades Galicia,** Plaza del Car-men 1 (© **91-531-2732;** Metro: Puerta del Sol). It's open Tuesday through Saturday from 9:30am to 1:30pm and 4:30 to 7pm, Sunday from 10am to 1pm. Regardless of where you buy them, tickets to bullfights range from 2€ to 120€ ($2.60–$156), depending on the event and the position of your seat within the stadium. Concierges for virtually every upper-bracket hotel in Madrid can acquire tickets, through inner channels of their own, to bull-fights and other sought-after entertainment. Front-row seats at the bull-fights are known as *barreras. Delanteras* (third-row seats) are available in both the *alta* (high) and the *baja* (low) sections. The cheapest seats sold, *filas,* afford the worst view and are in the sun *(sol)* during the entire per-formance. The best seats are in the shade *(sombra).*

Bullfights are held on Sunday and holidays throughout most of the year, and every day during certain festivals, which tend to last around 3 weeks, usually in the late spring. Starting times are adjusted according to the antic-ipated hour of sundown on the day of a performance. Late-night fights by neophyte matadors are sometimes staged under spotlights on Saturday around 11pm.

austere beauty of the statue reveals traces of Greek influence. Another notable sculp-ture is *La Dama de Baza*. The museum is especially rich in artifacts in the epoch between Roman and Mudéjar Spain.

The mosaics from the Roman period are notable, especially *Monks and Seasons* from the Albacete period, with outstanding pieces from the Visigothic era also on display. Outside the museum is an exact reproduction of the Altamira cave paintings discov-ered near Santander in northern Spain in 1868.

Calle Serrano 13. © **91-577-7912.** Admission 3€ ($3.90), free for children and adults over 65; free Sat–Sun (2:30–8:30pm). Tues–Sat 9:30am–8:30pm; Sun 9:30am–2:30pm. Metro: Serrano or Colón. Bus: 1, 9, 19, 51, or 74.

Museo de la Real Academia de Bellas Artes de San Fernando ⚔   A short stroll from the Puerta del Sol (the exact center of Madrid), this leading Iberian fine arts museum is set in a 17th-century baroque palace. When the building was an art academy, its alumni included the likes of Salvador Dalí and Picasso. This is hardly the grandest art museum in Madrid, but there are superb works, including a collection of old master paintings ranging from Rubens to Van Dyck, plus excellent drawings by Titian and Raphael. The best selection is the array of Spanish paintings from the 1500s to the 1800s, including works by Velázquez, El Greco, Ribera, and Murillo. Also here is one of the best monk paintings Zurbarán ever did, *Fray Pedro Machado*. A former director of the academy, Goya has a room devoted entirely to his art. Our favorite is his *Burial of a Sardine*.

Alcalá 13. Ⓒ **91-524-0864**. Admission 3€ ($3.90) adults, 1.50€ ($1.95) students, free Wed and for children 18 and under. Tues–Fri 9am–7pm; Sat–Mon 9am–2:30pm. Metro: Puerta del Sol or Sevilla. Bus: 3, 15, 20, 51, 52, 53, or 150.

Museo del Prado ⚔⚔⚔   This museum, one of the world's greatest repositories of art, began as a royal collection and was later beefed up by the Habsburgs. The range of art is mainly from the 12th to the 19th centuries, and the collection quite naturally features the greatest assembly of Spanish paintings in the world, notably the impressive works by the great Velázquez and Goya. The annex of the Prado, Cason del Buen Retiro, contains late-19th-century and 20th-century sculpture and painting.

Those who can't see everything might want to enter through the Puerta de Goya, opening onto Calle Felipe IV. This leads to the second floor (called first floor in Spain). The artwork is arranged by school, with the oldest works displayed on the lower floors. Especially notable is the Goya Collection featuring both his *Clothed Maja* and *Naked Maja* (both ca. 1800). The artist who depicted "blatant" nudity was charged with obscenity.

You'll find a splendid array of works by the incomparable Diego Velázquez (1599–1660). The museum's most famous painting, in fact, is his *Las Meninas,* a triumph for its use of light effects and perspective. The faces of the queen and king are reflected in the mirror in the painting itself. The artist in the foreground is Velázquez, of course.

The Prado is a trove of the work of El Greco (ca. 1541–1614), the Crete-born artist who lived much of his life in Toledo. You can see a parade of "The Greek's" saints, Madonnas, and Holy Families—even a ghostly *John the Baptist.*

The Flemish painter Peter Paul Rubens (1577–1640), who met Velázquez while in Spain, is represented by the peacock-blue *Garden of Love* and by the *Three Graces.* Also worthy is the work of José Ribera (1591–1652), a Valencia-born artist and contemporary of Velázquez whose best painting is the *Martyrdom of St. Philip.* Seville-born Bartolomé Murillo (1617–82)—often referred to as the "painter of Madonnas"—is represented by three versions of the Immaculate Conception.

The Prado has an outstanding collection of the work of Hieronymus Bosch (1450?–1516), the Flemish genius. *The Garden of Earthly Delights,* the best-known work of "El Bosco," is here. You'll also see his *Seven Deadly Sins* and his triptych *The Hay Wagon. The Triumph of Death* is by another Flemish painter, Pieter Bruegel the Elder (1525?–69), who carried on Bosch's ghoulish vision.

Major Italian works are exhibited on the ground floor. You'll see art by Italian masters—Raphael, Botticelli, Mantegna, Andrea del Sarto, Fra Angelico, and Correggio. The most celebrated Italian painting here is Titian's voluptuous Venus being watched by a musician who can't keep his eyes on his work.

Thanks to a massive $92-million expansion, the once stuffy museum has doubled its floor space and is even making room for children's workshops. Much of the expansion is found below ground level. The main structure from 1785 is linked underground to the Prado's modern annex; the passageway runs beneath a garden and a plaza. The Prado has also branched out to incorporate surrounding buildings, including the Casón del Buen Retiro overlooking Retiro Park. It is filled with the work of 19th-century Spanish painters. The former Army Museum nearby was transferred to Toledo. Modern galleries hosting temporary exhibits have opened around a cloister, creating 20% more floor space to display the works of Bosch, Botticelli, Rubens, and the like.

Paseo del Prado. ⓒ **91-330-28-00**. www.museoprado.es. Admission 6€ ($7.80) adults, 3€ ($3.90) students; free on Sun and for kids under 18. Tues–Sun 9am–8pm; holidays 9am–2pm. Guided tours are Tues 1pm and 5:30pm; Wed–Sat 9am–5:30pm. Closed Jan 1, Good Friday, May 1, and Dec 25. Metro: Atocha or Banco de España. Bus: 9, 10, 14, 19, 27, 34, 37, or 45.

Museo Lázaro Galdiano ★★ *Finds*   Bequeathed to the nation in 1947, this is one of the grandest collections of art in Castile, housed in the former manse of the author José Lázaro Galdiano. The original museum, added to over the years, began from the writer's own impressive collection of fine and applied art. Imagine 37 rooms bulging with art, including many of the most famous and reproduced masters of Europe.

We like to take the elevator to the top floor and work our way down, taking in, at our leisure, everything from Goya portraits to a cross-shaped pocket watch worn by Charles V. The *Saviour* is a portrait attributed to Leonardo da Vinci. Surprisingly, the collection is rich in English landscapes, notably by Turner, Gainsborough, and Constable, and also contains paintings from Spain's greatest masters, including El Greco, Murillo, Velázquez, and Zubarán. Of macabre interest is Salon 30 devoted to Goya, including some notorious paintings from his "black period."

Calle Serrano 122. ⓒ **91-561-60-84**. www.flg.es. Admission 4€ ($5.20) adults, 3€ ($3.90) students, free 12 and under. Wed–Mon 10am–4:30pm. Closed holidays and Aug. Metro: Ruben Dario or Núñez de Balboa. Bus: 9, 16, 19, 27, 45, 51, 61, 89, or 114.

Museo Nacional Centro de Arte Reina Sofia ★★   A former 18th-century general hospital, once called "the ugliest building in Spain," is today a repository of modern art in Spain. The museum has completed a $95-million expansion, creating far more exhibition space and installing everything from an art bookstore to a cafeteria offering reasonably priced meals and snacks. When work is done, there will be more space for art in the permanent collections, plus galleries for temporary exhibitions. It's worth the trip alone just to see Picasso's *Guernica* ★★★, the single most famous work of the 20th century. Taking his inspiration from the German attack on the Basque town of Guernica in 1937, this masterpiece represents Picasso's glaring indictment of the destruction of war.

Picasso is also represented by other works, including one of our all-time favorites, *Woman in Blue,* painted in 1901. When it failed to win in a national competition, Picasso disowned the painting. The permanent collection is housed on the second and fourth floors, featuring works by such famous Spanish artists as Dalí and Miró. Sometimes the temporary exhibits are even more stunning than the permanent collection.

Santa Isabel 52. ⓒ **91-467-5062** or 91-468-30-02. www.museoreinasofia.es. Admission 6€ ($7.80) adults, 3€ ($3.90) students, free after 2:30pm Sat, all day Sun, and for ages 17 and under. Wed–Sat and Mon 10am–9pm; Sun 10am–2:30pm. Free guided tours Mon and Wed at 5pm; Sat at 11am. Metro: Atocha. Bus: 6, 10, 14, 18, 19, 26, 27, 32, 34, 36, or 37.

Museo Thyssen-Bornemisza ✿✿✿   Installed in Madrid's 18th-century Villahermosa Palace in 1992, this collection grew from one of the greatest private art collections in the world—the assemblage of the late Baron Heinrich Thyssen-Bornemisza and his son, Hans Heinrich. Beginning in the 1920s, the collection was intended to illustrate the history of Western art, and in that it succeeds brilliantly with some 800 representative works of art, including masterpieces by the likes of Picasso, Goya, van Gogh, and Titian.

As a privately owned collection, the Thyssen museum's treasure trove was rivaled only by that of Queen Elizabeth II. Spain acquired the collection for $350 million, outbidding Walt Disney World and others. Rooms are arranged so that the logical sequence of European paintings can be traced from the 13th to the 20th centuries, a parade of greatness from El Greco to Velázquez and Rembrandt to Caravaggio. The walls are rich with the work of notable French Impressionists, including major American works by such artists as Jackson Pollock and Edward Hopper.

The galleries are arranged around a covered central courtyard, the top floor starting with early Italian and going on to the 1600s. By the time you reach the ground floor, you'll be surrounded by works from the 20th century.

Like the Prado, the museum is also expanding—in this case into two adjoining buildings—providing more room for its permanent collection as well as space for prestigious road shows of art.

Palacio de Villahermosa, Paseo del Prado 8. ⓒ **91-369-0151.** www.museothyssen.org. Admission 6€ ($7.80) adults, 4€ ($5.20) students and seniors, free for children 13 and under. Tues–Sun 10am–7pm. Metro: Banco de España. Bus: 1, 2, 5, 9, 10, 14, 15, 20, 27, 34, 37, 45, 51, 52, 53, 74, 146, or 150.

Palacio Real (Royal Palace) ✿✿   During the reign of the dictator, Franco, this palace was just a monument, but now has taken on more meaning after the restoration of the monarchy. The lavishly decorated complex is vast, constructed high on a bluff opening onto Río Manzanares. For centuries the site was a royal fortress, but following a fire in 1734, the present palace was built on orders of Felipe V.

Today's royal family resides elsewhere, but this palace was occupied until 1931, when Alfonso XIII abdicated. King Juan Carlos comes here only for state occasions.

Most impressive is the **Throne Room** ✿, with its gold and scarlet thrones, exact reproductions of those once used by Charles V. The **Porcelain Room** ✿ is a stunner, both its walls and ceiling entirely covered by porcelain from the royal factory. It's a romp of cherubs and wreaths.

Decorated in 1879, the **Dining Gallery** ✿, with its ceiling paintings and handsome tapestries, evokes the heyday of the Bourbon dynasty. Today, there are some 2,000 rooms in the palace, not all of them open to the public. You can visit such highlights as the Reception Room, the State Apartments, the Armory, and the Royal Pharmacy. A special discovery, often overlooked, is the **Gasparini Room** ✿, named after the Neapolitan designer and decorated with rococo and chinoiserie. In the antechamber is a portrait of Charles IV by Goya. After touring the palace, you can stroll through its garden, Campo del Moro.

Plaza de Oriente, Calle de Bailén 2. ⓒ **91-542-6947.** www.patrimonionacional.es. Admission 10€ ($13) adults, 3.50€ ($4.55) students and children 16 and under. Oct–Mar Mon–Sat 9:30am–5pm; Sun 9am–2pm; Apr–Sept Mon–Sat 9am–4pm, Sun 9am–3pm. Metro: Opera or Plaza de España. Bus: 3, 25, 39, or 148.

Panteón de Goya   Outside the city center, Goya's Tomb still attracts his fans, as it contains one of his masterpieces, an elaborate **fresco** ✿✿✿ depicting the miracles of St. Anthony on the dome and cupola of the little hermitage of San Antonio de la

Florida. Critics have hailed the work as "Goya's Sistine Chapel." Built in the reign of Carlos IV in the neoclassical style, the hermitage is dedicated to St. Anthony. In 1798, Goya spent 4 months painting the cupola with this mammoth fresco. In the background the artist peopled his work with ordinary street characters from the 1700s. In the chapel rests the tomb of the artist, his remains shipped here from Bordeau, where he died as an expatriate in 1828. In 1799, Goya became court painter to Carlos IV but pictured the royal family with grotesque accuracy.

Glorieta de San Antonio de la Florida 5. © **91-542-0722.** Free admission. Tues–Fri 9:30am–8pm; Sat–Sun 10am–2pm. Metro: Príncipe Pío. Bus: 41, 46, 75, or C.

Plaza Mayor ★★★   This is the most famous and most historic square in Spain. The plaza is enveloped by 17th-century, three-story buildings with arcades at their base. These arcades are filled with cafes and craft shops. Some of the building facades are graced with allegorical paintings, as well as balconies, pinnacles, and dormer windows. The square was the center of life in old Madrid, staging everything from bullfights and executions to pageants and trials by the Inquisition. In 1621, the square was the venue for the beautification of St. Isidore, Madrid's patron saint. In the center of the plaza stands a statue of Felipe III, who is responsible for the construction of the square. A coin and stamp market is held every Sunday morning, along with stalls hawking used books, old badges, and other collectibles.

In the southwest corner of the square you can take a flight of steps leading down to the Calle de Cuchilleros, site of a bevy of *mesones* (traditional restaurants). The most famous of these is **Restaurante Botín,** Calle de Cuchilleros 17 (© **91-366-4217**), which Hemingway made famous in the pages of *The Sun Also Rises.* Dating from 1725, the kitchen specializes in roast suckling pig.

Plaza Mayor. Daily 24 hr. Metro: La Latina or Opera.

WHERE TO DINE

Bocaito *(Value* SPANISH/TAPAS   We are so in love with the perfectly prepared and tasty tapas served here that it's hard to get around to ordering a main course. In a typical Madrid tavern with bullfighting posters, the chefs prepare tapas "to die for," including the likes of such delicacies as salt cod pâté with caviar. Don Luis Benavente, the chef and owner, has a devoted following who likes his imaginative take on typical Andalusian and Castilian dishes.

Calle Libertad 4–6. © **91-532-1219.** Reservations recommended. Tapas 5.40€–8€ ($7–$10.40); main courses 8€–18€ ($10.40–$23.40). DC, MC, V. Mon–Fri 1–4pm; Mon–Sat 8:30pm–midnight. Closed Aug. Metro: Banco de España, Chueca.

El Amparo ★★ BASQUE   A former carriage house was converted into this elegant enclave of refined Basque cuisine, which some food critics hail as the finest provincial food in Spain. The cuisine has a real modern accent, made with top-notch ingredients that are fashioned into imaginative and flavorful platters. Under rough-hewn wooden beams, you can partake of such specialties as ravioli with crayfish or roulades of lobster flavored with soy sauce.

Callejón de Puigcerdà 8. © **91-431-6456.** Reservations required. Main courses 24€–36€ ($31.20–$46.80). AE, DC, MC, V. Mon–Fri 1:30–3:30pm; Mon–Sat 9–11:30pm. Closed Easter week. Metro: Serrano. Bus: 19, 21, or 53.

El Chaflán ★ SPANISH   This restaurant is the showcase for the culinary talents of one of Madrid's hottest chefs, Jean Pablo Felipe Tablado, who draws enthusiastic diners and rave reviews. He puts his own spin on every dish that comes out of his kitchen,

Moments Tasca Hopping

Madrid's equivalent of London's pub-crawl is *tasca* hopping. *Tascas* are local taverns serving tapas along with beer and wine (the hard stuff, too). Many *tascas* specialize in one dish, perhaps mushrooms or else shrimp, although most of them serve a wide array of tasty appetizers. Since the dining hour is late in Madrid, often around 10pm, Madrileños patronize these *tascas* and satisfy their predinner appetites with one "small plate" after another. It's amazing they are still hungry when it's time for dinner.

Our favorite *tascas* include **Casa Mingo,** Paseo de la Florida 34 (② **91-547-7918**), where you can pair the best cider in town with a piece of *cabrales* or goat cheese from the northwestern province of Asturias. Roast chicken, served at communal tables, is the other specialty of the kitchen. A tankard of cider goes for 3.90€ ($5.05), a serving of *cabrales* for 5.20€ ($6.75), and a whole roast chicken for 9€ ($11.70). Service is daily 11am to midnight. No credit cards. Metro: Principe Pio, then a 5-minute walk.

One of the most patronized *tascas* in Old Madrid is **Taberna Toscana,** Manuel Fernández y Gonzales 10 (② **91-429-6031**), where you sit on country stools and order some of the best tapas in town. These include *chorizo* (the spicy Spanish sausage), *lacón y cecina* (boiled ham), and tasty *habas* or broad beans. The kidneys in sherry sauce and the snails in hot sauce are also delectable. A glass of wine starts at 1€ ($1.30), and tapas range from 3.60€ to 16€ ($4.70–$21). MasterCard and Visa are accepted, and hours are Tuesday to Saturday noon to 4pm and 8pm to midnight. Metro: Puerta del Sol or Sevilla.

Cervecería Santa Barbara, Plaza de Santa Barbara 8 (② **91-319-0449**), set in one of old Madrid's most colorful squares, is the outlet for a beer factory. The two most popular brews are *cerveza negra* (black beer) and *cerveza dorada* (golden beer). This *cerveza* is consumed with homemade potato chips and such seafood delights as barnacles, fresh lobster or shrimp, or crabmeat. Tapas cost 2€ to 10€ ($2.60–$13), with a beer going for 1.75€ ($2.30). MasterCard and Visa are accepted. Open daily 8am to midnight. Metro: Alonzo Martínez. Bus: 3, 7, or 21.

Another well-patronized tapas outlet, **Cervecería Alemania,** Plaza de Santa Ana 6 (② **91-429-7033**), opens onto an even more colorful square. Evocative of the turn of the 20th century, it offers little tables that are jam-packed nightly with locals sampling the fried sardines or a Spanish omelet. A beer costs 2€ to 3€ ($2.60–$3.90), with tapas going from 4€ to 10€ ($5.20–$13). No credit cards are accepted. Open Sunday and Thursday 11am to 12:30am, Friday and Saturday 11am to 2am. Metro: Tirso de Molina or Puerta del Sol.

emphasizing flavor and texture. The best fish, local meats, and produce attract native foodies and discerning visitors alike—try the perfectly prepared roast suckling pig.

Av. Pio XII 34. ② **91-350-6193.** Reservations required. Main courses 27€–45€ ($35.10–$58.50). Fixed-price menu 80€ ($104). AE, DC, MC, V. Mon–Fri 1:30–4pm; Mon–Sat 9–11:30pm. Metro: Pio XII.

El Espejo ✦ *Value* INTERNATIONAL   Located near Plaza de las Cortés, this restaurant features one of the best menu values in town, the list of international specialties changing daily. The chefs enhance the pristine flavors of food with skill and restraint, and dish after dish, such as guinea fowl flavored with Armagnac, has won our enthusiasm. The setting is a beautiful Art Nouveau dining room, with outdoor tables available during most months of the year.

Paseo de Recoletos 31. ⓒ **91-308-2347**. Reservations required. Fixed-price menu 27.50€ ($35.75). AE, DC, MC, V. Daily 1–4pm and 9pm–midnight. Metro: Colón. Bus: 5, 27, 45, or 105.

El Olivo Restaurant ✦✦ MEDITERRANEAN   This chic restaurant is for devotees of olive oil and Spanish sherry. It took a Frenchman, Jean-Pierre Vandelle, to exploit two of Spain's culinary resources in this showcase of fine cuisine. A cart stocked with 40 regional olive oils is wheeled from table to table so diners can select a variety to soak up with chunks of bread. The cooking shows imagination and solid technique. The sherry bar features 100 different brands, one of the largest selections in Spain.

General Gellgos 1. ⓒ **91-359-1535**. Reservations recommended. Main courses 24€–30€ ($31.20–$39). Fixed-price menus 48€ ($62.40). AE, DC, MC, V. Tues–Sat 1–4pm and 9pm–midnight. Closed Aug 15–31 and 4 days around Easter. Metro: Plaza de Castilla or Cuzco.

La Biotika ✦ *Value* VEGETARIAN   Vegetarian cuisine doesn't get a lot of attention in most Madrid restaurants, but this discovery is a rare exception. Opening east of the landmark Plaza Santa Ana, La Boitika is intimate and charming. It serves the capital's best macrobiotic vegetarian cuisine, and does so exceedingly well. We always begin with one of the homemade soups, which are made fresh daily, then have one of the large, fresh salads. One specialty is a "meatball without meat" (made with vegetables but shaped like a meatball).

Amor de Dios 3. ⓒ **91-429-07-80**. Main courses 7.50€–13€ ($9.75–$16.90); *menú del dia* 9€–14.50€ ($11.70–$18.85). No credit cards. Daily 1–5pm and 8–11:30pm. Metro: Antón Martin.

La Bola *Finds* MADRILEÑA   When Ava Gardner was filming *The Barefoot Contessa* in 1954 (with Bogie), she would show up here with an entourage of matadors. Ava's long gone, but this remains one of the most evocative of the 19th-century red-doored restaurants of Madrid. Against a backdrop of Venetian crystal, ever-loyal fans show up to dine on *cocido madrilène*, the traditional Castilian Sunday boiled dinner. The tried-and-true recipes of Old Castile are still served here.

Calle de la Bola 5. ⓒ **91-547-6930**. Reservations required. Main courses 18€–27€ ($23.40–$35.10). AE, DC, MC, V. Daily 1:30–5pm; Mon–Sat 8:30–11pm. Metro: Opera or Santo Domingo. Bus: 25 or 39.

La Gamella ✦✦ *Finds* CASTILIAN/INTERNATIONAL   An unusual mix and successful offering of Californian and Castilian cuisine is delectably served at this expat outpost under the guidance of Ohio-born Dick Stephens. In the 19th-century building where Ortega y Gasset, the Spanish philosopher, was born, Stephens has cooked for such notable personas as the king and queen of Spain. The chefs here know just how to coax the most flavor out of the premium ingredients used, and you can invariably count on a delightful evening.

Alfonso XII 4. ⓒ **91-532-4509**. www.lagamella.com. Reservations required. Main courses 17€–21€ ($22.10–$27.30). AE, DC, MC, V. Mon–Fri 1:30–4pm; Mon–Sat 9pm–midnight. Metro: Retiro or Banco de España. Bus: 19, 27, 34, 45, 51, or 52.

La Paloma ✦ BASQUE/FRENCH   Two of Europe's greatest cuisines—French and Basque—are wed harmoniously at this exclusive retreat in the elegant Salamanca district. The chef and owner, Segundo Alonso, is known for his perfectly prepared and "robust" dishes, specializing in various meats, such as pigs' trotters, which he fashions into divine concoctions. The welcome and the service are flawless.

Jorge Juan 39. © **91-576-8692.** Reservations required. Main courses 50€–55€ ($65–$71.50); *menú de degustación* 56€ ($72.80). AE, DC, MC, V. Mon–Sat 1:30–4pm and 9pm–midnight. Metro: Vergara or Velázquez.

Lhardy ✿✿ SPANISH/INTERNATIONAL   A Madrid legend since its opening in 1839, this was once the preferred dining choice of the capital's cognoscenti, especially its literary and political leaders. In an antique setting of marble and hardwood, a ground-floor deli still dispenses cups of steaming consommé from silver samovars into little porcelain cups. On the second floor, in an ornate Belle Epoque–styled restaurant, specialties that might have been known to Queen Isabella II are still prepared—and done so exceedingly well.

Carrera de San Jerónimo 8. © **91-521-3385.** Reservations recommended for the upstairs dining room. Main courses 30€–40€ ($39–$52). AE, DC, MC, V. Mon–Sat 1–3:30pm and 8:30–11pm. Closed Aug. Metro: Puerta del Sol.

SHOPPING

Some call it Madrid's **El Rastro** ✿ or flea market. Other more discerning critics refer to it as the thieves market. It's said that virtually everything stolen in Madrid turns up here at some point. Set in a triangle of streets a few minutes' walk south of Plaza Mayor, this flea market dates from the Middle Ages and is centered around Plaza de Cascorro. The main action takes place along Calle Ribera de Curtidores, or "tanner's riverbank," once the headquarters of the tanning industry and the slaughterhouse district. The other major street of vendors hawking their wares is along Calle de Embajadores. The time to go is after 8am on a Sunday morning. What's for sale? Everything from an "original" El Greco for 10€ ($13) to antiques, bric-a-brac, and a vast array of fascinating junk. Plaza de Cascorro and Ribera de Curtidores (Metro: La Latina; bus: 3 or 17).

The leading department store of Madrid—in fact, the flagship of the largest department store chain—is **El Corte Inglés,** Preciados 3 (© **91-379-8000**). A lot of the merchandise here is of interest mainly to locals, but you'll also find a large selection of Spanish handcrafts, including damascene steelwork from Toledo, embroidered shawls, and flamenco dolls. You can also preview a wide selection of Spanish fashion for both women and men. Open Monday to Saturday 10am to 10pm; Metro: Puerta del Sol.

An excellent center for crafts is **El Arco de los Cuchilleros Artesania de Hoy,** Plaza Mayor 9, Basement Level (© **91-365-2680**), set within one of the 17th-century vaulted cellars off the historic Plaza Mayor. An unusual and varied collection of one-of-a-kind merchandise from all over Spain has been assembled here, including everything from textiles to pottery and leather items. Daily 11am to 8pm. Metro: Puerta del Sol or Opera. Devotees of antiques, Iberian style, gravitate to **Centro de Anticuarios Lagasca,** Lagasca 36 (© **91-577-3752**), where they discover about a dozen different outlets under one arcade. The attics of Spain were raided for this assemblage of furnishings, porcelain, and bric-a-brac. Open Monday to Friday 11am to 2pm and 5 to 8:30pm, Saturday 11am to 2pm; Metro: Serrano or Velázquez.

The quality leather products at **Loewe,** Serrano 26 (© **91-577-6056**), have made this exclusive outlet a Madrid legend since 1846. Its designers have won many gold medals for their tasteful, chic leather designs. The store carries a deluxe assortment of luggage and handbags along with both leather and suede jackets for men and women. Open Monday to Saturday 9:30am to 8:30pm; Metro: Banco de España or Gran Vía.

NIGHTLIFE

Following a $160-million renovation in the late 1990s, **Teatro Real,** Plaza Isabel II (© **91-516-0660**), is the showcase for cultural Madrid. It first opened in 1850 under the reign of Queen Isabel II, and its acoustics are the best in Iberia. The building is the home for Compañía del Teatro Real, which specializes in opera but is also a major venue for classical music, with tickets beginning as low as 15€ ($19.50) and climbing to as much as 145€ ($189); Metro: Opera.

Palacio Gaviria, Calle Arenal 9 (© **91-526-6069**), was built in 1847 by Marqués de Gaviria, one of the paramours of Queen Isabella II. It remains today as the greatest *Isabelino* (a jumble of neoclassical and baroque styles) palaces in Madrid. Today it is both a venue for classical music and a late-night cocktail bar. Guests wander from one elegant salon to another. Wednesday is cabaret night. The cover ranges from 10€ to

---

Moments The Exotic Sound of Flamenco

No art form, other than bullfighting, is more evocative of Spain than flamenco dancing. Although it may have been created by "lowlife roots,"
including taverns catering to hoodlums, brothels, gypsies, and what one
critic called "whoopee hedonism," flamenco has long grown respectable
and is heard in the most elegant of clubs today.

The finest flamenco singers and dancers appear in Madrid, accompanied
by the guitar music, castanets, and the ritualized clapping of the audience.
The earliest performers might have been dancer-prostitutes, but today
some of the finest talent in all the land, both female and male, pursue the
art of flamenco. If you have only 1 night in Madrid, try to take in a flamenco
show, notably at the sizzling **Corral de la Morería,** Morería 17 (© **91-365-
8446**), charging a 32€ ($41.60) cover, including one drink. The show with
dinner costs 75€ to 85€ ($97.50–$111). Although it's touristy, some of the
best flamenco performers in Spain appear here nightly in colorful costumes.
Open daily 8:30pm to 2:30am; Metro: La Latina or Opera.

If you prefer a less touristy atmosphere, check out the scene at **Casa
Patas,** Cañizares 10 (© **91-369-0496**), which is also a bar and restaurant. Perhaps the best flamenco shows in Madrid are presented here daily. The cover
ranges from 25€ to 30€ ($32.50–$39). Two shows are presented Friday and
Saturday at 9pm and midnight, with one show Monday to Thursday at
10:30pm; Metro: Tirso de Molina or Anton Martín.

Should you become crazed for flamenco during your stay in Madrid, you
might also head for **Café de Chinitas,** Torija 7 (© **91-547-1502**), a club of
long-enduring popularity. One of Madrid's best flamenco clubs, the cafe lies
in an old structure set at midpoint between the Gran Vía (the main drag)
and the Opera. Some of the best gypsy flamenco dancers from Andalusia
appear here. A dinner and show costs 75€ ($97.50); the cover for the show
without dinner, but with one drink included, is 34€ ($44.20). Shows are pre-
sented Monday to Saturday from 10:30pm to 2am; Metro: Santo Domingo
or Opera; bus: 1 or 2.

15€ ($13–$19.50), including a first drink. Open Monday to Wednesday and Sunday 11pm to 4am, Thursday to Saturday 11pm to 6am; Metro: Puerta del Sol or Opera.

The mammoth **Kapital,** Atocha 125 (© **91-420-2906**), is one of the top dance clubs of Madrid, drawing an under-35 dancing crowd. From hip-hop to house, *terrazas* to cinemas, there is action going on at all times on seven floors of this "mad, mad world" *discoteca.* The action doesn't really get going until 2am. Open Thursday to Sunday midnight to 6am, with afternoon sessions Saturday and Sunday from 5:30 to 11pm. Admission ranges from 2€ to 10€ ($2.60–$13), including the first drink; Metro: Atocha.

Another hot, hot dance club set near the Puerta del Sol is **Joy Eslava,** Arenal 11 (© **91-366-5439**), which goes on in spite of passing fads and fancies. Attracting a wide range of clients, mostly in their 30s and 40s, it pulsates to a lively disco beat nightly from 11:30pm to 6:30am. Admission is 15€ ($19.50), including your first drink; Metro: Puerta del Sol or Opera.

Jazz aficionados flock to **Café Central,** Plaza del Angel 10, off Plaza de Santa Ana (© **91-369-4143**), which has a turn-of-the-20th-century Art Deco decor. Some of the country's leading jazz performers entertain you at their nightly sessions. Open Sunday to Thursday 1:30pm to 3:30am, Friday and Saturday 1:30pm to 3am. Live jazz is featured daily from 10pm to midnight, with a cover ranging from 7€ to 15€ ($9.10–$19.50), depending on the show (Metro: Antón Martín or Puerto del Sol). Those seeking jazz also descend on **Clamores,** Albuquerque 14 (© **91-445-7938**), with its dark and smoky interior. Dating from the 1980s, this is one of the biggest and most frequented jazz clubs in Iberia. Spanish jazz bands appear regularly in addition to some excellent artists from the United States. Jazz is presented only Tuesday to Saturday; call for times. Jam sessions are staged on Sunday night. A cover of 8€ to 25€ ($10.40–$32.50) is imposed Tuesday to Saturday (Metro: Bilbao).

Casino action is found at **Casino Gran Madrid,** Km29 Carretera La Coruña, Apartado 62, the A-6 highway running between Madrid and La Coruña (© **91-856-1100**). The largest casino in Spain, it also attracts non-gamblers to its restaurant and entertainment facilities, featuring everything from four bars to a disco. Games of chance include both French and American roulette, blackjack, *punto y banco,* baccarat, and chemin de fer. Entrance costs 3€ ($3.90), and you must present a passport. Open daily 4pm to 5am.

AN EXCURSION TO TOLEDO

Reached by train in only 35 minutes from Madrid (it's about 42 miles/68km to the south of the capital), this is Iberia's greatest imperial city. Toledo stands atop a hill enveloped on three sides by a bend in the River Tagus, a scene immortalized by the city's most famous painter, El Greco, in his *View of Toledo,* currently hanging in New York's Metropolitan Museum of Art.

Toledo's history is ancient. The Visigoths made it their capital in the 6th century A.D., leaving behind churches extant even today. In medieval times, Toledo was a melting pot of Muslim, Jewish, and, of course, Christian cultures. The Toledo cathedral, one of the greatest in Europe, dates from those times. Even on the most rushed of schedules, try to visit this cathedral along with the Iglesia de Santo Tomé (with El Greco's masterpiece), and most definitely Charles V's fortified palace, the Alcázar. With time remaining, you can see El Greco's house in the old Jewish quarter.

GETTING THERE

Nine to 12 trains per day run to Toledo from either the Atocha or Chamartín stations in Madrid. These short-distance, high-speed trains require reservations (available only in Spain). The earliest departure Monday to Friday is at 6:50am, but not until 9:20am on Saturday and Sunday. A one-way fare costs 8.60€ ($11.20). For schedules and more information, call **RENFE** at ⓒ **90-224-0202.**

Arrivals are at **Estación Toledo,** Paseo de la Rosa 2 (ⓒ **90-224-0202**), a beautiful neo-Mudéjar station lying just over the bridge, Puente de Azarquiel, from the center of town. From the station, bus no. 5 or 6 run into the center. Buses depart every 15 minutes from the station during the day, taking you to the main square of town, Plaza de Zocodover, the ancient marketplace. A one-way fare costs 1€ ($1.30); the ride is only 5 minutes. The train station has drinking and dining facilities but no tourist information office. There is a luggage storage kiosk, however, charging 3€ ($3.90) per bag. Open Monday to Friday 5:45am to 9:20pm, Saturday and Sunday 6:30am to 10pm.

TOURIST INFORMATION

The **Toledo Tourist Office** is at Puerta de Bisagra (ⓒ **92-522-0843;** www.jccm.es), and is open Monday to Friday 9am to 6pm, Saturday 9am to 7pm, and Sunday 9am to 3pm.

TOP ATTRACTIONS & SPECIAL MOMENTS

One of the great Gothic structures of the world, the **Catedral de Toledo** ✸✸✸, Cardenal Cisneros 1 (ⓒ **92-522-2241**), dates from 1226 when King Ferdinand III laid the first stone. Today, the cathedral is renowned for its art and architecture, along with its five naves and stunning stained glass. It makes no apologies for its ostentation. The cathedral is the seat of the primate of Spain and the spiritual heart of the Spanish Catholic church. Its chief treasures are its **choir stalls** ✸✸✸, the carvings on its wooden lower stalls depicting the fall of Granada, and a **series of paintings by El Greco** ✸ in the Sacristy. The masterpiece here is El Greco's *Denuding of Christ* above the marble altar. A splendid 16th-century **silver gilt monstrance** ✸✸ by Enrique de Arfe is found beneath a Mudéjar ceiling in the Treasury. At the High Altar, a **polychrome reredos** ✸ is one of the most magnificent in Spain, depicting scenes from the life of Christ. Admission to the cathedral is free, but if you visit its treasury the cost is 4.95€ ($6.45). Open Monday to Saturday 10:30am to 6:30pm and Sunday 2 to 6:30pm.

The second great edifice of Toledo is the **Alcázar,** Cuesta de Carlos V 2, near Plaza de Zocodover (ⓒ **92-522-1673**), close to the eastern edge of the old city, its architectural line dominating the skyline. Charles V ordered this fortified palace built on the site of Roman, Visigoth, and even Muslim fortifications. The Alcázar became world famous in 1936 when it was practically destroyed by Republicans. Holding down the fortress, the Nationalists survived a 70-day siege. Today the Alcázar houses an army museum. Admission is 3€ ($3.90), and hours are Tuesday to Sunday 9:30am to 2pm.

In a 16th-century hospital founded by Cardinal Mendoza, **Museo de Santa Cruz** ✸✸, Calle Miguel de Cervantes 3 (ⓒ **92-522-1036**), is a museum of art and sculpture, one of the finest in Seville. The museum is celebrated for its **collection of 16th and 17th century paintings** ✸, 18 of which are by El Greco himself. *The Assumption of the Virgin* ✸ is El Greco's last known work. Paintings by Ribera, Goya, and other great Spanish artists are also on display, along with medieval and Renaissance tapestries and masterful sculptures. Admission is free, and the museum is open Monday to Saturday 10am to 6:30pm, Sunday 10am to 2pm.

At **Iglesia de Santo Tomé,** Plaza del Conde 4 (© **92-525-6098**), you can gaze upon El Greco's masterpiece, ***The Burial of the Count of Orgaz*** ✿✿✿, painted in 1586. The chapel itself is modest, dating from the 14th century, and stands in the old Jewish quarter. Admission is 2€ ($2.60), and hours are daily 10am to 6:45pm (closes at 5:45pm in winter).

Founded by Queen Isabella and King Ferdinand in 1477, **Monasterio de San Juan de los Reyes** ✿, Calle Reyes Católicos 17 (© **92-522-3802**), is in the Isabelline style, with both flamboyant Gothic, traces of Mudéjar, and even Renaissance influences. The church is noted for its **sculptured decoration** ✿ by Juan Guas, the Flemish architect who designed the church. Its Gothic cloister from 1510 is stunningly beautiful with a multicolored Mudéjar ceiling. Admission is 2€ ($2.60) adults and free for children under 9. Hours are daily 10am to 7pm, November to March daily 10am to 6pm.

It's not known for sure if El Greco actually lived at this address, but even so **Casa y Museo de El Greco,** Calle Samuel Leví 3 (© **92-522-4046**), remains one of the most enduring attractions of Toledo. In the old Jewish quarter, the house is a museum sheltering a collection of the Crete-born artist's works, including his magnificent series, ***Christ and the Apostles*** ✿. The museum also displays a copy of his famous *A View of Toledo,* plus three portraits and many other works of art. Admission is 2.40€ ($3.10), and hours are Tuesday to Saturday 10am to 2pm and 4 to 6pm, Sunday 10am to 2pm.

The oldest and largest of Toledo's eight original synagogues, **Sinagoga de Santa Maria la Blanca,** Calle Reyes Católicos 2 (© **92-522-7257**), dates from the 12th century. By 1405 it was taken over by the Catholic Church, but in modern times it has been restored, as much as it's possible, to its pristine beauty, with carved stone capitals and white horseshoe arches, along with ornamental, horizontal moldings. Its five naves and much of its elaborate Mudéjar decorations remain. Admission is 1.90€ ($2.45). Hours April to September are daily 10am to 6:45pm (otherwise daily 10am–5:45pm).

WHERE TO DINE

Just a minute's walk north of the cathedral, **Asador Adolfo** ✿, Calle Hombre de Palo 7 (© **92-522-7321**), is one of the finest in town and serves typical Toledan cuisine. In a building dating in part from the Middle Ages, chefs turn out savory meals, including some of the province's best game dishes, such as partridge or venison. Reservations are recommended, and main courses range from 18€ to 28€ ($23.40–$36.40). Open Tuesday to Saturday 1 to 4pm and 8pm to midnight, Sunday 1 to 4pm.

As you're in the heart of old Castile, you might want to sample some of that province's fabled fare. It doesn't get any better than **Casón de los López** ✿✿, Sillería 3 (© **90-219-8344**). A short walk from the Plaza de Zocodover in the center of town, this restaurant serves the lightest and most sophisticated cuisine in Toledo. The building itself is a virtual antiques museum, but it's the fresh food from the bounty of the agricultural countryside that keeps this place packed. Reservations are required. Main courses cost 16€ to 25€ ($20.80–$32.50), with set-price menus ranging from 37€ to 52€ ($48.10–$67.60). Open daily 1:30 to 4pm and Monday to Saturday 8:30 to 11:30pm.

SHOPPING

Toledo is known for its *damasquinado,* or damascene, work—that is, the Moorish art of inlaying gold, and even copper or silver threads, against a matte black steel backdrop. Stores all over town hawk these objects, none better than **Casa Bermejo,** Calle

Airosas 5 (© **92-528-5367**), established in 1910 and still going strong. Some 50 artisans here turn out beautiful objects in Mudéjar designs, including platters, pitchers, swords, and other gift items. Open Monday to Friday 9am to 1pm and 3 to 6pm, Saturday 10am to 2pm. A worthy rival is **Felipe Suarez,** Circo Romano 8 (© **92-522-0027**), in business since 1920s. It also produces quality damascene work, some objects of rare beauty. Open daily 10am to 7pm. You'll also find superb craftsmanship in damascene at **Santiago Sanchez Martín,** Calle Río Llano 15 (© **92-522-77-57**), which specializes in the elaborately detailed arabesques whose techniques are as old as the Arab conquest of Iberia. Look for everything from decorative tableware (platters, pitchers, and so on) to mirror frames, jewelry, letter openers, and ornamental swords. It's open Monday to Friday 9am to 1:30pm and 4 to 6:30pm.

3 Seville

The capital of Andalusia, Seville launched itself into greatness after the Christian conquest of the south in the 13th century. The most exciting times to visit are during *Semana Santa* (Holy Week, which leads up to Easter) and for the *Feria de Abril* (April Fair). The religious processions at Holy Week, when sacred images are paraded through the streets, are world famous.

Visitors flock to Seville to see its *Catedral* (third largest in the world) and its Alcázar complex, the Moorish fortress enlarged by the Christians in the 14th century to resemble the Alhambra in Granada. The maze of streets east of the cathedral and the Alcázar is called the Barrio de Santa Cruz, the old Jewish quarter. It's Seville at its most romantic, filled with strolling guitarists, secret plazas, flower-bedecked patios, and tapas bars. This old ghetto is reason enough to visit here.

GETTING THERE   Located to the north of the city, **Estación Santa Justa,** Avenida Kansas City (© **90-224-0202**), is the major transportation hub of Andalusia with trains, including AVE and *Trenhotel* runs, arriving from all over Spain. It offers especially good connections to Córdoba, Madrid, Barcelona, and Málaga, even Valencia and Granada. For a preview of trains serving the area, refer to the "Trains & Travel Times in Spain" chart on p. 707.

The tourist information office at the train station (© **95-478-2003**) is open daily from 8am to 8pm. The staff provides information about hotels available in the area but do not make reservations themselves. The station is easy to navigate, with three ATMs available as well as a money exchange kiosk. There are three bars and a cafe, plus a restaurant. Bus no. 32 runs to the center, costing 1€ ($1.30). You can also take **TeleTaxi** (© **95-462-2222**) or **Radio Taxi** (© **95-458-0000**); the base rate for a taxi is 2.15€ ($2.80). There is a luggage storage facility at the station that charges 3€ ($3.90) per bag per day.

VISITOR INFORMATION   The main office for tourist information is at Avenida de la Constitución 21B (© **95-422-1404**), open Monday to Saturday 9am to 7pm, Sunday and holidays 10am to 2pm. The staff here doesn't make hotel reservations.

TOP ATTRACTIONS & SPECIAL MOMENTS

Catedral de Sevilla ✸✸✸, Plaza del Triunfo, Avenida de la Constitución (© **95-421-4971**), was constructed in the 12th century on the site of the great mosque of the Almohads. The celebrated cathedral is the largest Gothic building in the world and the third largest church in Europe. Construction began in 1401 and lasted for a century. The stated goal of its architects was simply this: "Those who come after us will

Seville

ACCOMMODATIONS ■
Hotel Murillo **6**
La Casa de la Judería **8**

DINING ◆
La Albahaca **7**
El Fogon de Leña **9**
Taberna del Alabardero **2**

ATTRACTIONS ●
Catedral de Sevilla **4**
Hospital de la Santa
   Caridad **3**
Museo Provincial de Bellas
   Artes de Sevilla **1**
Reales Alcázares **5**

take us for madmen." The towering edifice claims to shelter the Tomb of Columbus, his coffin held up by bearers evoking the kings of Navarra, Aragón, Castile, and León. The towering monument to Christian beliefs is filled with objets d'art and architectural monuments, including the *Capilla Mayor* ✿, with its huge iron grilles forged in the 16th century. At the Retablo Mayor, a statue of Santa Maria de la Sede, the patron saint of the cathedral, sits at the main altar before a "waterfall" of gold brought back from the New World. Other treasures include **15th-century stained-glass windows** ✿, elaborate choir stalls from the same century, and paintings by Murillo, Goya, and Zurbarán, among other Spanish artists. After touring the dark cathedral, you can take delight in the **Patio de los Naranjos** ✿, with its fresh citrus scent of orange blossoms and sound of chirping birds.

The major landmark on the Seville skyline is **La Giralda** ✿✿✿, the bell tower that adjoins the cathedral. Visitors climb this tower for one of Andalusia's most panoramic city views. The Arabs built the tower as a minaret in 1198, crowning it with bronze spheres. Instead of tearing the tower down as a pagan monument, the Catholic conquerors removed these spheres and crowned La Giralda with Christian symbols, such as a bronze weathervane (called *giraldillo*) portraying Faith. The tower has seen other additions over the centuries, including the addition of bells in the 1500s. To ascend it, you walk a seemingly endless ramp.

Admission to the tower and cathedral is 7.50€ ($9.75) for adults, 2€ ($2.60) for students and children 16 and under. Hours in July and August are daily 9:30am to 3:30pm; September to June Monday to Saturday 11am to 5pm.

Hospital de Santa Caridad, Calle Temprado 3 (© **95-422-3232**), was once the haunt of Miguel de Manara, whose notorious life was said to have been the inspiration for the story of Don Juan. A charity hospital founded in 1674, it still cares for the elderly and the infirm. It can be visited by the general public, who come here to delight in the glory of the building's baroque Sevillana style. Nuns will show you through two beautiful courtyards filled with plants. On the tour you can see some Dutch tiles from the 18th century and impressive fountains. In the church itself are many Old-Masters-type paintings by some of the leading artists of the 17th century. Especially ghoulish is the *End of the World's Glory* by Valdés Leal, picturing an archbishop being devoured by maggots. Admission is 5€ ($6.50), free for children under 12. Open Monday to Saturday 9am to 1:30pm and 3:30 to 7:30pm, Sunday 9am to 12:30pm.

Museo Provincial de Bellas Artes de Sevilla ✿✿, Plaza del Museo 9 (© **95-478-6482**), lies off a main artery, Calle de Alfonso XII, and is a former convent. Today it shelters a gallery devoted to some of the most important works of art in Seville. One gallery showcases two of El Greco's best-known works, and many other leading Spanish painters are on parade, including Zurbarán. Note especially Zurbarán's *San Hugo en el Refectorio* (1655), painted for the monastery at La Cartuja. The most fascinating of these is by the artist, Valdés-Leal, a 17th-century painter with a macabre style as exemplified by his painting of John the Baptist's head. More contemporary paintings are displayed on the top floor. Admission is 1.50€ ($1.95); free for students and children under 12. Open Tuesday 2:30 to 8:30pm, Wednesday to Saturday 9am to 8:30pm, Sunday 9am to 2:30pm.

Reales Alcázares ✿✿✿, Plaza de Triunfo s/n (© **95-450-2323**), is a complex of magnificent buildings that has been the home of Spanish royalty for almost 7 centuries. The palace was the sometimes residence of Queen Isabella I, who sent navigators from Seville to the New World in search of gold and other treasures. Mudéjar courtyards and elegantly decorated corridors remain from the Alcázar's imperial heyday. Over the years subsequent monarchs have added their own architectural touches, including the lavishly decorated **state apartments** ⚔ ordered built by Charles V. Beautiful 16th-century tiles and elaborate tapestries decorated the halls where Charles once trod. The palace contains many notable features such as the **Patio de las Doncellas** ⚔, or maidens, with its elaborate plasterwork by the top artisans brought in from Granada, and the **Salon de Embajadores** ⚔, dating from 1427. This salon is celebrated for its splendid dome of carved and gilded, interlaced wood. Wind down in the sumptuous **gardens** ⚔ with their Moorish fountains, pavilions, and terraces. Admission is 7€ ($9.10); free for students and children under 16. Open April to September Tuesday to Saturday 9:30am to 7pm, Sunday 9:30am to 5pm; October to March Tuesday to Saturday 9:30am to 5pm, Sunday 9:30am to 1:30pm.

SHOPPING

One of the best selections of Andalusian ceramics is found at **El Postigo,** Calle Arfe (☎ **95-456-0013**), in the vicinity of the cathedral. The display of hand-painted tiles is exceptional. Open Monday to Saturday 10am to 1:30pm.

For general merchandise, head for **El Corte Inglés,** Plaza Duque de la Victoria 13B (☎ **95-459-7000**), in the commercial center of town. In addition to its regular line of items for the home, it also hawks a vast array of handicrafts as well. Open Monday to Saturday 10am to 10pm.

Works by some of the best of the southern Spanish artists are on display at **Rafael Ortiz,** Marmolles 12 (☎ **95-421-4874**), where exhibitions are frequently changed. Open Monday 6pm to 9pm, Tuesday to Friday 11am to 1:30pm and 6 to 9pm, and Saturday 11am to 1:30pm.

The fashions of southern Spain are showcased at **Iconos,** Ave. de la Constitución 21A (☎ **95-422-1408**), a boutique appealing to a wide age group of women, with an array of items from costume jewelry to silk scarves. Open Monday to Saturday 10am to 8:30pm and Sunday 11am to 7pm.

Souvenirs of the city, T-shirts, hammered wrought-iron what-nots, and ceramics are available at **Matador,** Ave. De la Constitución 28–30 (☎ **95-422-62-47**). The shop is open Monday to Friday 10am to 8:30pm, Saturday 10am to noon and 4:30 to 8:30pm.

NIGHTLIFE

The people of Seville begin their evening early by touring all the tapas bars. The most typical of the old-fashioned tapas joints is **Casa Ramón,** Plaza de los Venerables 1 (☎ **95-422-8483**), in Barrio de Santa Cruz. Since 1934, this landmark bar has served delectable tapas along with local wine. Try *pata negra,* a ham from the fabled black-hoofed Iberian breed of pig, celebrated for its sweet flavor caused by a diet of acorns. On the northern edge of Barrio de Santa Cruz stands **El Rinconcillo,** Gerona 40 (☎ **95-422-3183**), a *tasca* dating from 1670, making it the oldest bar in town. The selection of cheeses here is especially tempting. For the best seafood tapas, head over to **La Alicantina,** Plaza del Salvador 2 (☎ **95-422-6122**), lying 5 blocks north of the cathedral. We can personally vouch for the fried calamari, the clams marinara, and the garlic-flavored grilled shrimp.

If you like bars instead of *tascas,* head for **Abades,** Calle Pío 42–43 (☎ **95-571-8279**), set in a mansion in the Santa Cruz barrio that dates from the 1800s. It is an architectural jewel box from the Spanish *Romantico* era, with classical music playing in the background. Later you can enjoy authentic Andalusian flamenco at **Club Los**

Gallos, Plaza de Santa Cruz 11 (© **95-421-6981**), which is one of the most reputable of the joints, attracting top talent for its impassioned performances. The cover charge of 27€ ($35.10) includes the first drink.

Its major competition, with shows almost equally as good, is **El Arenal,** Calle Rodó 7 (© **95-421-6492**). There is a cover charge of 35€ ($45.50), which includes one drink. Show times at both clubs are usually nightly at 8:30 and 10:30pm, but call to confirm that. For a fiesta every night, head for **El Patio Sevillano,** Paseo de Cristobal Colón 11 (© **95-421-4120**), where exotically costumed Andalusian dancers entertain you with flamenco songs and dance, Spanish folk songs and dance, and occasional classical pieces by such composers as Chueca. Two shows nightly begin at 7:30 and 10pm, and the cover of 33€ ($42.90) includes the first drink.

There's something really special about attending operas inspired by Seville, especially Mozart's *Marriage of Figaro* or Verdi's *La Forza del Destino* in Seville itself. Since the 1990s, the city has boasted its **Teatro de la Maestranza,** Paseo de Colón 22 (© **95-422-6573**), which is also the setting for other musical presentations ranging from jazz to classical. Spanish *zarzuelas* (operettas) are also performed here. Tickets depend on the event and can be purchased at the box office, open daily from 10am to 2pm and 6 to 9pm.

WHERE TO STAY & DINE

In the heart of the Santa Cruz district, the 57-room **Hotel Murillo,** Calle Lope de Rueda 7–9 (© **95-421-60-95;** www.hotelmurillo.com), is easy on the purse. Named after the artist who used to live in the district, it lies near the gardens of the Alcázar. The nonsmoking rooms are small, but neatly kept and comfortably furnished. Rates range from 65€ to 130€ ($84.50–$169) double, 71€ to 162€ ($92.30–$211) in a triple.

La Casa de la Judería 𝓕𝓕, Plaza Santa Maria la Blanca, Callejón de dos Hermanos 7 (© **95-441-5150;** www.casasypalacios.com), is installed inside a 17th-century palace, the former abode of the dukes of Beja, and is within easy walking distance of the cathedral and Seville's other major attractions. The 119 bedrooms are individually decorated, most often with antiques or reproductions, and some have four-poster beds. All the units have balconies, and some of the better units also have whirlpool tubs and living rooms. Doubles cost 133€ to 255€ ($173–$332), with suites going for 225€ to 380€ ($293–$494).

La Albahaca 𝓕𝓕, Plaza Santa Cruz 12 (© **95-422-0714**), serving grand Andalusian and Basque cuisine, is housed in one of the best-preserved structures in the Santa Cruz barrio. The house was designed by famed architect Juan Talavera, and the setting is elegant—it's long been a favorite of visiting royalty, including the king and queen of Spain. The French-style menu is skillfully tailored to incorporate the bounty of the Andalusian countryside, and no chef in town does better desserts—wait until you try the fig soufflé or the bitter orange mousse. Main courses cost 15€ to 30€ ($19.50–$39), and hours are Monday to Saturday 1 to 4pm and 8pm to midnight.

An unusual blend of Argentine and Andalusian cuisine is served at the relatively unknown **El Fogon de Leña** 𝓕, Santo Domingo de la Calzeda 13 (© **95-453-1710**), located near the old town. The setting of antique tiles and regional artifacts forms an appropriate backdrop to the skilled cooking of the talented chefs, who turn out savory dishes night after night. Inside the two-story interior you can stop at the entrance and pay your respects to the mounted head of the last bull killed in the ring by José Luís Vasquez, the celebrated bullfighter. The meat dishes, such as the ox steak, are especially succulent. Main courses cost 15€ to 18€ ($19.50–$23.40), and hours are daily 1:30 to 4:30pm and 8:30 to 11:30pm.

Three blocks from the cathedral, **Taberna del Alabardero** 𝕽𝕽, Calle Zaragoza 20 (𝒞 **95-450-2721**), is one of the city's most prestigious restaurants. Set in a 19th-century town house, the restaurant serves refined Andalusian cuisine to politicians, diplomats, and royalty. Against a backdrop of art and antiques, formalized service takes place in two main salons, with additional seating in the rear garden. Devotees of fine food in Seville swear by this place. Main courses cost 20€ to 30€ ($26–$39). Hours are daily 1 to 4:30pm and 8pm to midnight.

AN EXCURSION TO CÓRDOBA

Julius Caesar, Pompey, and Agrippa used to stop off in Córdoba when it was the capital of a Roman province called Baetica, established in 151 B.C. But it was under the Moors in the 8th century that the city reached the apex of its power, second only to glittering Constantinople. A visit to its Mezquita (Great Mosque)—still standing today—was said to have been comparable to a pilgrimage to Mecca.

GETTING THERE   Eighteen daily AVE trains depart from Seville for Córdoba—a trip of only 40 minutes. For more information and schedules, contact RENFE (𝒞 **90-224-0202;** www.renfe.es).

Trains arrive at Estación Córdoba, Glorieta de las Tres Culturas, which has a 24-hour luggage storage area with coin-operated lockers. The cost ranges from 3€ to 5€ ($3.90–$6.50) depending on your type of luggage. Also inside the station is a restaurant and cafeteria. There is not, however, a tourist information office (it's a 10- to 12-min. walk, or you can take bus no. 3).

The train station is a 10-minute walk from the city center. If you don't want to walk, you can head into town by taxi for about 6€ to 7€ ($7.80–$9.10). Taxis usually meet arriving trains, or you can call **Radio Taxi** (𝒞 **95-776-4444**).

Bus no. 3 makes the run from the train station through Plaza Tendillas and along the river up Calle Doctor Fleming. A one-way ticket costs .80€ ($1.05).

TOURIST INFORMATION   The **Córdoba Tourist Office** is at Calle Torrijos 10 (𝒞 **95-747-1235;** www.andalusia.com), open Monday to Friday from 9:30am to 6:30pm, Saturday 10am to 2pm, Sunday and holidays 10am to 2pm. The staff does not make hotel reservations.

TOP ATTRACTIONS & SPECIAL MOMENTS

It's worth the train trip to Andalusia to visit the **Mezquita-Catedral de Córdoba** 𝕽𝕽𝕽, Torrijos and Calle Cardenal Herrero (𝒞 **95-747-0512**). This magnificent edifice was the Arabs' crowning architectural achievement in the West during their 8th-century heyday. The original mosque, built between 785 and 787, changed and evolved over the centuries using many different styles. The field of more than **850 columns** 𝕽𝕽𝕽 was crafted mainly from jasper, granite, and marble, often taken from Roman and Visigothic structures. The richly ornamented prayer niche, the **mihrab** 𝕽𝕽𝕽, is a stunning work. This domed shrine of Byzantine mosaics once housed the Koran.

In the 16th century, a cathedral was placed awkwardly in the middle of this mosque. Highlights of the cathedral include **two pulpits** 𝕽𝕽 of mahogany, jasper, and marble, and the **baroque choir stalls** 𝕽𝕽 of Pedro Duque Cornejo from the mid–18th century. Not quite as impressive is the **Capilla de Villaviciosa** 𝕽, the first Christian chapel constructed in the mosque in 1371 with magnificent multi-lobed arches. For a charming walk, head through the Patio de los Naranjos, a courtyard of orange trees where the faithful once washed before prayer. Admission is 7.50€ ($9.75) adults, 3.25€ ($4.25) children (ages 10–14); kids 9 and under free. Open June to September Monday to Saturday 10am to 7pm, and Sunday 9 to 10am and 2 to 5:30pm; October to April daily 10am to 6pm.

The second great edifice of Córdoba is the **Alcázar de los Reyes Cristianos** ✿, Plaza Santo de los Mártires (© **95-742-0151**), 2 blocks southwest of the Mezquita. This fortress was commissioned in 1328 by Alfonso XI and remains one of the finest examples of military architecture in all of Iberia. It became the palace-fortress of the Catholic monarchs, its severity softened by its beautiful gardens, fountains, and water terraces. Wander at leisure across the Moorish patios, taking in salons with **Roman mosaics** ✿ and an impressive **sarcophagus** ✿ from the 3rd century A.D. Admission to the Alcázar is 4€ ($5.20) adults; free for children under 14. Hours mid-May to September are Tuesday to Sunday 8:30am to 2:30pm and 6 to 8pm; October to mid-May Tuesday to Saturday 10am to 2pm and 4:30 to 6:30pm. The gardens are illuminated July to September daily 10am to 1am.

After seeing the city's two major edifices, you will have viewed the best of Córdoba. If you still have some time remaining before you have to head back to Seville, check out the narrow streets of the old **Judería** ✿✿, the former Jewish quarter. This ancient barrio lies directly north of the Mezquita, and is filled with 18th-century whitewashed houses with delicate window grilles.

Of the private palaces of Córdoba, one is open to the public. **Palacio Museo de Viana** ✿✿, Plaza de Don Gome 2 (© **95-749-6741**), is an impressive example of the civil architecture of Córdoba in the 15th century. With its beautiful garden and a dozen courtyards, it's a stunner outside and in, as it's filled with opulently rich furnishings and objets d'art. Note especially the stunning **Mudéjar** *artesonado* **ceiling** ✿ constructed of cedar. The tapestry collection is rich and evocative—many of the hangings were made in royal workshops based on cartoons by Goya. Admission is 6€ ($7.80). It's open June to September Monday to Saturday 9am to 2pm; October to May Monday to Friday 10am to 1pm and 4 to 6pm, Saturday 10am to 1pm.

Other minor museums include the **Museo Arqueológico Provincial** ✿, Plaza Jerónimo Páez 7 (© **95-735-5517**), 2 blocks northeast of the Mezquita. This is one of Andalusia's most important treasure troves of archaeological digs in the area. In a palace from 1505, it displays artifacts, many from Paleolithic and Neolithic times, along with Roman sculptures, bronzes, mosaics, and ceramics, even some Visigothic finds. Admission is 1.50€ ($1.95). Children 17 and under free. Open Tuesday 2:30 to 8:30pm, Wednesday to Saturday 9am to 8:30pm, and Sunday 9am to 2:30pm.

Another distinguished museum is **Museo de Bellas Artes de Córdoba,** Plaza del Potro 1 (© **95-735-5550**), housed in an old hospital. This is an impressive regional fine arts museum, housing some outstanding examples of Spanish baroque art, sculpture, and other art objects. The museum lies to the immediate east of the Mezquita. Admission is 1.50€ ($1.95); free for children under 11. Open Tuesday 3 to 8pm, Wednesday to Saturday 9am to 8pm, and Sunday 9am to 3pm.

WHERE TO DINE

Just a 10-minute walk from the Mezquita, **Campos de Córdoba** ✿, Calle de los Lineros 32 (© **95-749-7500**), is a wine cellar *(bodega)* and top-notch restaurant that's been around since 1908. The tapas bar in front is filled with wine drinkers, and you can retreat to the rear, following in the footsteps of numerous celebrities, to dine on fresh and well-prepared Spanish and Andalusian cuisine. Main courses cost 15€ to 20€ ($19.50–$26), and reservations are recommended. Open daily 1 to 4pm and Monday to Saturday 8pm to midnight.

Serving even better but more expensive food is **La Almudaina** ★★★, Jardines Plaza de los Santos Mártires 1 (📞 **95-747-4342**), set in a 15th-century palace near the Alcázar. Fronting the river in the former Jewish barrio, this is one of Andalusia's finest restaurants, though it's moderate in price when you consider its quality. Fresh Spanish and French dishes served in generous portions are the hallmarks of the place. Reservations are required, with main courses costing 12€ to 20€ ($15.60–$26) and a fixed-price menu going for 21€ ($27.30). Hours are daily from noon to 4pm and Monday to Saturday 8:30pm to 12pm. June 15 to September 1, the restaurant is closed all day Sunday and for the rest of the year only on Sunday night.

Around the corner from the Mezquita, **Taberna Casa Pepe de la Judería,** Calle Romero 1 (📞 **95-720-0744**), is a typical Andalusian restaurant that serves Córdoban recipes of exceptional merit. Spread across three floors, it also offers rooftop dining from May to October. The fare is hearty and regional, and all dishes use first-rate ingredients. Try the Andalusian gazpacho to start. Reservations are recommended, and main courses cost 12€ to 23€ ($15.60–$29.90). Open daily 1 to 4:30pm, Sunday to Thursday 8:30 to 11:30pm, and Friday and Saturday 8:30pm to midnight.

4 Granada ★★★

In the foothills of the snowcapped Sierra Nevada, Granada, at 2,200 feet (671m), sprawls over two main hills, the Alhambra and the Albaicín, and is crossed by two rivers, the Genil and the Darro. The location is 258 miles (415km) south of Madrid, 164 miles (261km) east of Córdoba, and 155 miles (250km) southeast of Seville. This former stronghold of Moorish Spain is full of folklore. Washington Irving *(Tales of the Alhambra)* used the symbol of this city, the pomegranate *(granada),* to conjure up a spirit of romance.

Most visitors head to this city with one goal in mind—to see the famous Alhambra Palace. Though the palace is the city's must-see attraction, visitors should definitely take the time to soak up the Moorish atmosphere in the old Arab Quarter and take in the other top sites. *Tip:* A good way to tour the city for the rail traveler heading here from Seville (the most popular departure point for Granada) is to schedule one's arrival in the city for late afternoon, overnight in Granada, and then spend the next day touring the wonders of the city before departing on the overnight *Trenhotel* to Barcelona. Be sure to reserve a spot on the overnight train well in advance (see "Practical Train Information," at the beginning of this chapter).

GETTING THERE   Most rail passengers head east to Granada after a visit to Seville (see earlier section). Four TRD trains run from Seville to Granada daily taking between 3 and 3½ hours. Instead of launching your Andalusian rail adventure in Seville, you can also take one of two daily Altaria trains leaving from Madrid's Atocha Rail Station and heading south to Granada; the trip takes around 4½ hours.

The **train station** in Granada is at Avenida de Los Andaluces (📞 **90-224-0202**) in the southwesterly part of the city, away from the city center. A taxi from the train station to the center of Granada costs 3€ to 6€ ($3.90–$7.80), but a one-way bus fare is only 1€ ($1.30). A stop for bus lines 1, 3, 4, 5, 6, 7, 9, 11, and 33 is about 330 feet (99m) from the entrance to the train station.

The station is open daily from 6:30am to 11:10pm. Immediate tickets can be purchased daily from 8:30am to 9:30pm, and advance tickets from 8:30am to 11:30pm. There is a luggage storage office open daily from 6:30am to 11:10pm, which costs 2.75€ ($3.60), but no tourist office. ATMs are available inside the station.

VISITOR INFORMATION   The **tourist office,** Plaza de Mariana Pineda 10 (© **95-824-7128;** www.granadatur.com), is open Monday to Saturday 9am to 7pm, Sunday 10am to 2pm. The staff here will supply you with a list of hotels but will not make hotel reservations. Another tourist office is located at Calle de Santa Ana 4 (© **95-857-5204**). Hours are Monday to Saturday 9am to 7pm and Sunday 10am to 2pm. It's a 20-minute walk from the train station, or you can take bus no. 3, 9, or 11 from the station.

GETTING AROUND

Walking is a viable option once you arrive in the center of town, and is the preferred method for exploring Old Granada and the Arab Quarter. Cuesta de Gomérez is one of the most important streets in Granada. It climbs uphill from the Plaza Nueva, the center of the modern city, to the Alhambra. At the east-west artery of Plaza Nueva, Calle de los Reyes Católicos goes to the heart of the 19th-century city and the towers of the cathedral. The main street of Granada is the Gran Vía de Colón, the principal north-south artery.

Calle de los Reyes Católicos and the Gran Vía de Colón meet at the circular Plaza de Isabel la Católica, graced by a bronze statue of the queen offering Columbus the Santa Fe agreement, which granted the rights to the epochal voyage to the New World. Going west, Calle de los Reyes Católicos passes near the cathedral and other major sights in the downtown section of Granada. The street runs to Puerta Real, the commercial hub of Granada with many stores, hotels, cafes, and restaurants.

Taxis can be summoned by calling © **95-776-44-44.** Otherwise you can rely on **public buses** (© **95-881-37-11**). The most useful bus is Bus Alhambra going from Plaza Nueva in the center to the Alhambra (which is a steep climb of almost ¾ mile/1.2km from the city center). Rides cost 1€ ($1.30), or you can purchase a packet of 10 tickets costing 10€ ($13).

TOP ATTRACTIONS & SPECIAL MOMENTS

Later enriched by Moorish occupants into a lavish palace, the **Alhambra and Generalife** ⟨⟨⟨, Palacio de Carlos V (© **95-822-0912;** www.alhambra.org), was originally constructed for defensive purposes on a rocky hilltop outcropping above the Darro River. The modern city of Granada was built across the river from the Alhambra, about half a mile (.8km) from its western foundations.

When you first see the Alhambra, you may be surprised by its somewhat somber exterior. You have to walk across the threshold to discover the true delights of this Moorish palace. Tickets are sold in the office at the Entrada del Generalife y de la Alhambra. Enter through the incongruous 14th-century **Gateway of Justice** ⟨. Most visitors don't need an expensive guide but will be content to stroll through the richly ornamented open-air rooms, with their lacelike walls and courtyards with fountains.

The most-photographed part of the palace is the **Court of Lions** ⟨⟨⟨, named after its highly stylized fountain. This was the heart of the palace, the most private section where the sultan enjoyed his harem. Opening onto the court are the Hall of the Two Sisters, where the favorite of the moment was kept, and the Gossip Room, a

Granada & the Alhambra

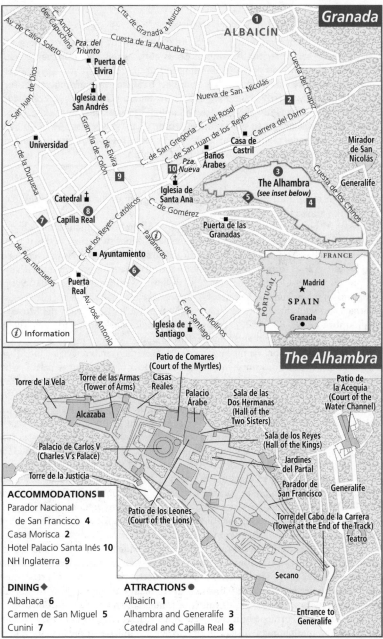

Granada

ALBAICÍN

Crta. de Granada a Murcia
C. Ancha de Capuchins
Av. de Calvo Soleto
Pza. del Triunto
Cuesta de la Alhacaba
■ Puerta de Elvira

Cuesta del Chapiz

† Iglesia de San Andrés
Nueva de San Nicolás
❷

C. San Juan de Dios
Gran Vía de Colón
C. de Elvira
C. de San Gregoria C. del Rosal
C. de San Juan de los Reyes
Carrera del Darro
Mirador de San Nicolás

■ Universidad
C. de la Duquesa
Pza. Nueva ❿ †
Baños Árabes ■
■ Casa de Castril
❸ The Alhambra
(see inset below)
Generalife
Cuesta de los Chinos

❾
Iglesia de Santa Ana †
❺ ❹

■ Catedral †
❽ Capilla Real
❼
C. de Gomérez
C. de los Reyes Católicos
C. Pavaneras

■ Puerta de las Granadas

■ Ayuntamiento
❻
C. de Pue ntezuelas
Puerta Real
Av. José Antonio
Iglesia de Santiago †
C. Molinos
C. de Santiago

ⓘ Information

FRANCE
PORTUGAL
Madrid ★
SPAIN
Granada ●

The Alhambra

Torre de la Vela
Torre de las Armas (Tower of Arms)
Casas Reales
Patio de Comares (Court of the Myrtles)
Palacio Árabe
Sala de las Dos Hermanas (Hall of the Two Sisters)
Patio de la Acequia (Court of the Water Channel)

Alcazaba

Palacio de Carlos V (Charles V's Palace)
Sala de los Reyes (Hall of the Kings)
Jardines del Partal

Torre de la Justicia

Patio de los Leones (Court of the Lions)
Parador de San Francisco
Generalife

Torre del Cabo de la Carrera (Tower at the End of the Track)
Teatro

Secano

Entrance to Generalife

ACCOMMODATIONS ■
Parador Nacional
 de San Francisco 4
Casa Morisca 2
Hotel Palacio Santa Inés 10
NH Inglaterra 9

DINING ◆
Albahaca 6
Carmen de San Miguel 5
Cunini 7

ATTRACTIONS ●
Albaicín 1
Alhambra and Generalife 3
Catedral and Capilla Real 8

> **Tips**   **Reserving for the Alhambra**
>
> Because of the overwhelming crowds, the government limits the number of people who can enter the Alhambra. Go as early as possible, but even if you get here at 10am you may not be admitted until 1:30pm. If you arrive after 4pm, it's unlikely you'll get in at all. Your best bet is to make arrangements for tickets before you arrive by calling the **Banco Bilbao Vizcaya** (© **90-222-4460**) within Spain. Tickets can also be reserved online at **www.alhambratickets.com**. You can charge tickets to your MasterCard or Visa. Tickets cost 10€ ($13) but with an additional service fee of .88€ ($1.15). Once reserved, these tickets can be picked up at the main entrance to the Alhambra.

factory of intrigue. Entertainment was provided nightly in the **Hall of Kings'** dancing room to amuse the sultan's party.

Charles V built a Renaissance palace at the Alhambra—which, although quite beautiful, is terribly out of place in such a medieval Moorish setting. Today it houses the **Museo Bellas Artes en la Alhambra** (© **95-822-4843**), open November to February Tuesday 2:30 to 6pm, Wednesday to Saturday 9am to 6pm, Sunday 9am to 2:30pm; March to October Tuesday 2:30 to 8pm, Wednesday to Saturday 9am to 8pm, and Sunday 9am to 2:30pm. Of minor interest, it displays mostly religious paintings and sculpture from the 1500s to the present. It also shelters the **Museo de la Alhambra** (© **95-822-7527**), devoted to Hispanic-Muslim art and open Tuesday to Saturday 9am to 2:30pm and Sunday 9am to 2pm.

Exit from the Alhambra via the Puerta de la Justicia, then circumnavigate the Alhambra's southern foundations until you reach the gardens of the summer palace, where Paseo de los Cipreses quickly leads you to the main building of the **Generalife** ✻✻, built in the 13th century to overlook the Alhambra. The sultans used to spend their summers in this palace (pronounced Heh-neh-rah-*lee*-feh), safely locked away with their harems. The Generalife's glory is its gardens and courtyards. Don't expect an Alhambra in miniature: The Generalife was always meant to be a retreat, even from the splendors of the Alhambra. Comprehensive tickets, including Alhambra and Generalife, are 10€ ($13); Museo Bellas Artes 1.50€ ($1.95); Museo de la Alhambra 1.50€ ($1.95); illuminated visits 6.75€ ($8.80). March to October daily 8:30am to 8pm, floodlit visits Tuesday to Saturday 10pm to 11:30pm; November to February daily 8:30am to 6pm, floodlit visits Friday and Saturday 8 to 9:30pm (bus: 30 or 32).

Once you've finished touring the Alhambra, head for the **Albaicín** ✻. The city's old Arab quarter is on one of the two main hills of Granada and stands in marked contrast to the city center's 19th-century buildings and wide boulevards. It and the surrounding gypsy caves of Sacromonte are holdovers from an older past. The Albaicín once flourished as the residential section of the Moors, even after the city's reconquest, but it fell into decline when the Christians drove them out. This narrow labyrinth of crooked streets escaped the fate of much of Granada, which was torn down in the name of progress. Fortunately it has been preserved, as have its cisterns, fountains, plazas, whitewashed houses, villas, and the decaying remnants of the old city gate. To begin your tour of the Albaicín, take bus no. 31 or 32.

In the center of town, **Catedral and Capilla Real** ✻✻, Plaza de la Lonja, Gran Vía de Colón 5 (© **95-822-2959**), is a richly ornate Renaissance cathedral begun in 1521 and completed in 1714. Its **spectacular altar** ✿✿ is one of the country's architectural highlights, acclaimed for its beautiful facade and gold-and-white interior. Behind the cathedral (entered separately) is the Flamboyant Gothic **Royal Chapel** ✿✿, where the remains of Queen Isabella and her husband Ferdinand lie. It was their wish to be buried in recaptured Granada, not Castile or Aragón. Accenting the tombs is a wrought-iron grille, itself a masterpiece. In the sacristy you can view Isabella's personal **art collection** ✿✿, including works by Rogier Van der Weyden and various Spanish and Italian masters such as Botticelli. Admission to the cathedral is 3.50€ ($4.55); as is admission to the chapel. The cathedral is open Monday to Saturday 10:30am to 1:30pm and 4 to 8pm (4–7pm in winter), Sunday 4 to 8pm. The chapel is open Monday to Saturday 10:30am to 1pm and 4 to 7pm, Sunday 11am to 1pm and 4 to 7pm.

WHERE TO STAY & DINE

Because the rail station is inconveniently located with respect to the center of the city, all of the following hotels and restaurants are about a 10- to 12-minute taxi or bus ride from the train depot.

Parador Nacional de San Francisco ✿✿✿, Real Alhambra, 18009 Granada (© 95-822-1440; www.parador.es), is the most famous *parador* (special state-owned inn) in Spain—and the hardest to get into—set on the grounds of the Alhambra. The decor is tasteful and the place evokes a lot of history with its rich Andalusian ambience. The 36-room *parador* is housed within a former convent founded by the Catholic monarchs after they conquered the city in 1492. The guest rooms are generally roomy and comfortable. Rooms in the older section are furnished with antiques; units in the more modern wing are less inspired. Rates vary considerably throughout the year, but average about 260€ ($338) double. *Note:* The hotel also advertises itself as Parador de Granada, so don't be confused if you see that name.

A real find, the 14-room **Casa Morisca** ✿✿, Cuesta de la Victoria 9, 18010 Granada (© 95-822-1100; www.hotelcasamorisca.com), is in the historic lower district of Albaicín, at the foot of the Alhambra. The house dates from the end of the 15th century and the original interior has been kept and restored, although the facade was given a 17th-century overlay. Local craftsmen worked only with the original materials of the building, including clay tiles and lime mortar. Bedrooms are individually decorated in an old style but with all modern comforts. Rates are 118€ to 148€ ($153–$192) double; 198€ ($257) suite.

The NH chain runs the 36-room **NH Inglaterra,** Cettie Meriem 4, 18010 Granada (© 95-822-1559; www.nh-hoteles.es), 2 blocks northeast of the cathedral and 5 minutes from the Alhambra. In 1992, they completely refurbished the run-down place. Its five-floor property is set well back from the thundering traffic of the main drag, Gran Vía de Colón. The air-conditioned rooms are moderately spacious and comfortably furnished with good beds and bright decorations. Rates are 125€ ($163) for a double.

Hotel Palacio Santa Inés ✿✿, Cuesta de Santa Inés 9, 18010 Granada (© 95-822-2362; www.palaciosantaines.com), in the colorful Albaicín district, is one of the most enchanting places to stay in Granada and about a 5-minute walk from the Alhambra. The painstakingly restored little palace was in complete ruins until the mid-1990s. Now it's a lovely, graceful inn that's even a bit luxe. The 35 medium-size rooms have air-conditioning and lots of antique furniture; some are duplexes and have small sitting rooms, and several open onto views of Granada. The suites have full kitchens. Rates are 130€ to 160€ ($169–$208) for a double; 250€ ($325) for a suite.

   Albahaca ⭐, Calle Varela 17 (© **95-822-4923**), is a locally beloved bistro housed in a century-old building. Owner Javier Jiménez seats 30 diners at 10 tables in this old-fashioned restaurant, decorated in a rustic style with bare white walls. The traditional dishes he serves are unpretentious and tasty, especially the *salmorejo* (creamy tomato gazpacho). It's a real find! Main courses run 8€ to 17€ ($10.40–$22.10).

   On the sloping incline leading up to the Alhambra, **Carmen de San Miguel,** Plaza de Torres Bermejas 3 (© **95-822-6723**), offers spectacular views of the city center. The restaurant is proud of its glassed-in dining room and patio-style terrace. The food, although good, doesn't quite match the view. Main courses are 16€ to 23€ ($20.80–$29.90); tasting menu 30€ to 50€ ($39–$65).

   The array of seafood served at **Cunini,** Plaza de la Pescadería 14 (© **95-826-7587**), perhaps 100 selections, extends even to the tapas offered at the long stand-up bar. Even though Granada is inland, it's not that far from the Mediterranean, and some of the freshest and best fish in town is served here. Specialties include a *zarauela* (seafood stew), smoked salmon, and grilled shrimp. Main courses cost 15€ to 36€ ($19.50–$46.80). Most dishes are reasonably priced except for the very expensive shellfish platters.

NIGHTLIFE

A good place to begin your night is along the **Campo del Príncipe,** where at least seven old-fashioned tapas bars do a rollicking business during the cool of the evening. Our favorite is **La Esquinita,** Campo del Príncipe (© **67-901-5974**). Small, atmospheric, and sometimes claustrophobic, it serves a crowd that mostly eats standing up, sometimes spilling into the street. A perennial favorite directly in front of the cathedral is **Antigua Bodega Castañeda,** Elvira 3–5 (© **95-822-6362**). Inside, rows of antique wine barrels and exposed masonry attract the city's wine connoisseurs. Another contender for your bar business is **Casa Henrique,** Calle Acera de Darro 8 (© **95-825-5008**), an old-fashioned, masonry-sided hole-in-the-wall lined with antique barrels of wine and sherry. Its specialty tapas consist of thin-sliced Serrano ham and heaping platters of steamed mussels with herbs and white wine.

5 Barcelona

One of the Mediterranean's busiest and most bustling ports, Barcelona is the capital of Catalonia, a province with its own rich language and culture that lies in the northeast of Spain and leans more to continental Europe in spirit than it does to the peninsula of Iberia.

   If your schedule is so rushed that you have to choose either Barcelona or Madrid, that's a tough call. It's like someone saying you can visit either London or Paris. When it comes to sights, food, monuments, and shopping, the rival cities are in a neck-and-neck race. If you want to see the traditional land of bullfights and flamenco, make it Madrid. For wild nightlife, bronzed nude beaches, whimsical and daring *modernista* architecture, and the work of Surrealistic painters such as Dalí or Joan Miró, make it Barcelona. The city, which was revitalized in 1992 when it hosted the Summer Olympics, is fast emerging as one of continental Europe's hottest tourist destinations.

   Barcelona is also the gateway to Catalonia; the eastern coast Spanish ports along the Mediterranean such as Valencia; and the Pyrenees, which are not that distant.

   It is not, however, a good center for touring much of Spain. Madrid is in the exact center and is a much better rail hub. Keep that in mind if you prefer to base yourself in a place that offers easy access to day excursions by rail.

STATION INFORMATION
GETTING FROM THE AIRPORT TO THE TRAIN STATIONS

You can reach Estaçio Barcelona-Sants by a local train that runs at half-hour intervals between the airport and the train station daily from 5:38am to 10:11pm, the 30-minute trip costing 2.25€ ($2.95). For 3.90€ ($5.05), you can also take one of the **Aeróbuses** running daily from the airport to the Estaçio Sants every 12 minutes daily 6pm to midnight. To get to the station by taxi, expect a fare ranging from 20€ to 30€ ($26–$39).

There is no Metro line that runs to the Estaçio de França station and no Aérobus. Taxis meet all arriving flights at the Barcelona airport and a trip to Estaçio de França by taxi costs 20€ to 30€ ($26–$39). You can, of course, reach Plaça de Catalunya by bus or Metro. From this transportation hub, bus no. 17 runs out to the Estaçio França. If you're carrying heavy luggage, however, it will be a difficult jaunt.

INSIDE THE STATIONS

Like Madrid, Barcelona has two major rail stations: Estaçio Barcelona-Sants and Estaçio França.

Estaçio Barcelona-Sants, in Plaça Paisos Catalans (© **90-224-0202;** Metro: Sants-Estaçio), is Barcelona's public transportation hub, with most bus lines, all Metro lines, and both long-distance and regional trains converging here. Direct trains link you to Montpellier, France, with ongoing connections to Paris and Geneva on TGV (high-speed) trains.

You can also catch trains here for Valencia and the Levante, Zaragoza, Madrid, Seville, and faraway Milan in Italy. For general rail information, call © **90-224-0202,** or visit **www.renfe.es**.

The two-level station offers many services and facilities, including banks for exchanging money, ATMs, a pharmacy, travel agents for making hotel reservations, restaurants, a phone center, and shops. The tourist office (© **93-285-3834**) is open in the off season Monday to Saturday 8am to 8pm and Sunday 8am to 2pm. In summer, it is open daily 8am to 8pm. Luggage storage is available: Large lockers rent for 4.60€ ($6), small lockers for 3.10€ ($4.05). The luggage storage facility is open daily from 7am to 11pm.

The station's 12 tracks lie beneath the main floor of the station and are accessible by both elevators and escalators. Video screens posted over the tracks list information.

Estacio de França, Avenida Marqués de l'Argentera (© **90-224-0202**), is southeast of the center of Barcelona, close to Ciutadella Park, the zoo, the port, and Vila Olímpica. It is linked by frequent buses to the Plaça de Catalunya. Take bus no. 17, which costs 1.10€ ($1.45) for a one-way fare. There is neither a tourist office here nor travel agents for making hotel reservations, and no currency exchange is available either. There are, however, ATMs, a restaurant, a bar, and a cafe at this two-level station. RENFE trains serving such cities as Madrid or Tarragona in Catalonia or Zaragoza in Aragón are the ones that frequent França. Express night trains from Paris, Zurich, Milan, and Geneva also pull in here, as does the Barcelona–Montpellier Talgo day train.

INFORMATION ELSEWHERE IN THE CITY

The main tourist office for Barcelona is at **Palau de Rubert,** Passeig de Gràcia 107 (© **93-238-4000**), open Monday to Friday 10am to 7pm and Saturday, Sunday, and holidays 10am to 2pm. The staff does not make hotel reservations but will provide a list of dozens of local travel agents who do. They will also give you a list of Barcelona

Barcelona

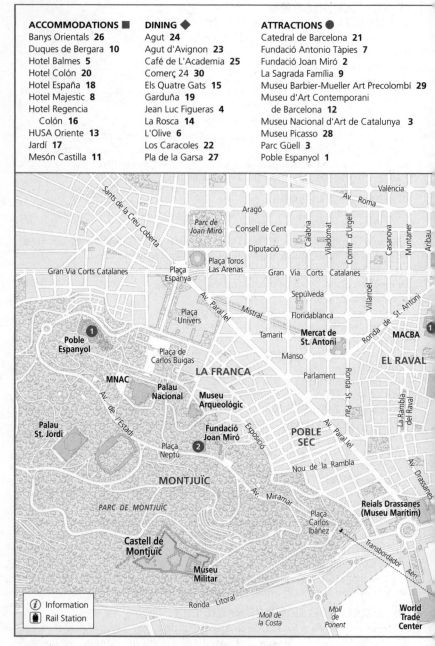

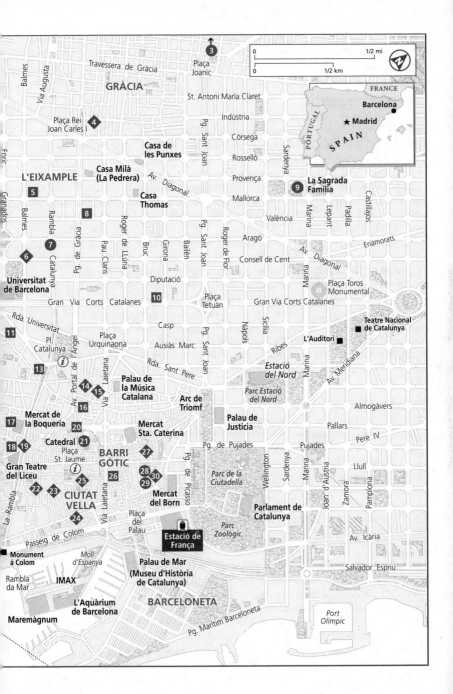

hotels in all price ranges. Another organization, **Oficina de Informaçio de Turisme de Barcelona,** Plaça de Catalunya 17-S (© **80-711-72-22** from inside Spain; www. barcelonaturisme.com), also provides detailed information—but no hotel reservations—daily from 9am to 9pm.

GETTING AROUND

To save money on public transportation, a *carte* good for 10 trips, the *Tarjeta T-10,* sells for 6.90€ ($8.95). This pass is available at Transports Metropolita de Barcelona, Plaça de la Universitat, open Monday to Friday 8am to 5pm, Saturday 8am to 1pm.

Another money-saver is a ride on *Bus Turistic,* which travels by 24 of the city's most visited attractions. You can get on and off the bus as you please, and your single ticket also covers the Montjuïch and Tibidabo cable car and funicular. The *Bus Turistic* can be purchased on the bus or at the tourist office at Plaça de Catalunya, and costs 19€ ($24.70) for 1 day or 23€ ($29.90) for 2 days. Children pay 11€ ($14.30) for 1 day or 15€ ($19.50) for 2 days.

Five **Metro** lines service greater Barcelona Monday to Thursday from 5am to midnight, Friday to Saturday 5am to 2am, and Sunday 6am to 2am. A one-way fare is 1.35€ ($1.75), and all major Metro lines converge at Plaça de Catalunya.

Barcelona also has daily bus service from 6:30am to 10pm, with some night buses running between 11pm and 4am. The one-way fare is 1.25€ ($1.65).

Look for the letters SP (meaning *servicio público*), the designation for taxis, which charge a basic rate of 1.75€ to 1.85€ ($2.30–$2.40), with each additional kilometer costing .78€ to 1€ ($1–$1.30). Supplements are assessed for certain items, including rides to the airport and extra-large pieces of luggage. Most taxis can be hailed on the street, or you can call **Autotaxi Mercedes** (© **93-307-0707**) or **Miramar** (© **93-433-1020**).

WHERE TO STAY

Banys Orientals *(Value)*   This hotel, off the Vía Laietana in the heart of the city, is one of the old city's best buys. Within walking distance of many of Barcelona's major monuments, the hotel is a league above your typical no-frills lodgings. Even though the accommodations are rather minimalist, there are such whimsies as four-poster beds and prints on the walls depicting everything from Egyptian monuments to scenes in a Turkish harem. Bedrooms are beautifully maintained and offer every convenience, from bathtubs to bedside tables.

Carrer Argentaria 37, 08003 Barcelona. © **93-268-84-60.** Fax 93-268-84-61. www.hotelbanysorientals.com. 50 units. 98€ ($127) double; 129€ ($168) suite. AE, DC, MC, V. Metro: Jaume I. **Amenities:** All nonsmoking rooms; 1 room for those w/limited mobility. *In room:* Hair dryer.

Duques de Bergara *(★)*   This town house, built for the duke of Bergara in 1898, has been successfully transformed into an inviting five-story hotel with a modern seven-story tower. All of the bedrooms are generally large and sport elegant fabrics and traditional comforts, including some especially inviting marble bathrooms. The public rooms are dramatically furnished in a decorative *modernista* style. This is that rare Barcelona hotel that has a pool.

Bergata 11, 08002 Barcelona. © **93-301-5151.** Fax 93-317-3442. www.hoteles-catalonia.com. 149 units. 150€–250€ ($195–$325) double; 225€–285€ ($293–$371) triple. AE, DC, MC, V. Metro: Plaça de Catalunya. **Amenities:** Restaurant; bar; laundry; rooms for those w/limited mobility. *In room:* Hair dryer.

Barcelona Metro

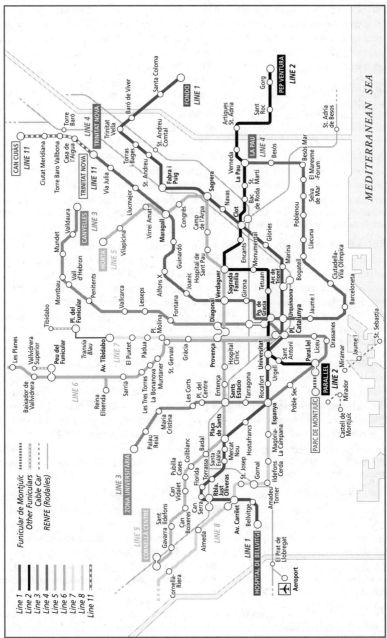

Hotel Balmes   In the Eixample district, north of Plaça de Catalunya, this seven-story hotel dates from the 1980s and is chain operated but highly efficient and welcoming. Bedrooms are the strong attraction here, as they are exceedingly comfortable, tastefully furnished, and contain marble-trimmed bathrooms. The more tranquil units open onto a small garden in the rear. There is also a pool.

Carrer Mallorca 216, 08008 Barcelona. ☎ **93-451-1914.** Fax 93-451-0049. www.derbyhotels.es. 100 units. 90€–195€ ($117–$254) double. AE, DC, MC, V. Metro: Diagonal or Paseo de Gracia. **Amenities:** Restaurant; bar; laundry. *In room:* Hair dryer.

Hotel Colón ✦✦   If you want to stay in the heart of Gothic Barcelona, there is no better location than this hotel opposite the main entrance to the cathedral. You parade through old-fashioned public rooms to modernized and good-size bedrooms that are comfortably and traditionally furnished. The sixth-floor rooms with balconies overlooking the square are the most sought after; rooms on the lower floors can be rather dark.

Avinguda de la Catédral 7, 08002 Barcelona. ☎ **800/845-0636** in the U.S., or 93-301-1404. Fax 93-317-2915. www.hotelcolon.es. 145 units. 255€ ($332) double; from 385€ ($501) suite. AE, DC, MC, V. Bus: 16, 17, 19, or 45. **Amenities:** Restaurant; bar; laundry. *In room:* Hair dryer.

Hotel España   Stay here for the low rates, although you will get comfort and some architectural style. The building itself is a relic of the city's turn-of-the-20th-century splendor, as it was built in 1902 by fabled architect Doménech i Montaner. Guests have included Salvador Dalí and other luminaries. The well-scrubbed bedrooms are mostly medium in size and are comfortably but rather functionally furnished.

Carrer Sant Pau 9–11, 08001 Barcelona. ☎ **93-318-1758.** Fax 93-317-1134. www.hotelespanya.com. 80 units. 105€–135€ ($137–$176) double. AE, DC, MC, V. Metro: Liceu or Drassanes. **Amenities:** Restaurant; rooms for those w/limited mobility. *In room:* Hair dryer.

Hotel Majestic ✦   A landmark since it was built in 1918, this hotel boasts a central location that's only a 10-minute walk from the transportation hub at Plaça de Catalunya. It was modernized and upgraded during the 1990s, though it has retained the dignified stateliness of the original public areas. Bedrooms are better than those at many nearby competitors, with tasteful color schemes, chic upholsteries and carpets, and artwork. Special amenities include a pool, fitness center, and sauna.

Passeig de Gràcia 68, 08007 Barcelona. ☎ **93-488-1717.** Fax 93-488-1880. www.hotelmajestic.es. 303 units. 410€–470€ ($533–$611) double; 540€–690€ ($702–$897) suite. AE, DC, MC, V. Metro: Passeig de Gràcia. **Amenities:** 2 restaurants; bar; laundry. *In room:* Hair dryer.

Hotel Regencia Colón *Value*   In back of the Hotel Colón (see above), this six-story property is a less expensive sibling, though it still enjoys a great location in the Gothic Old Town near the cathedral. It's a bit stodgy and gets a lot of tour groups, but nevertheless remains a favorite and is comfortable. Rooms are insulated against sound and are well maintained and inviting, as is the welcome from the staff here.

Sagristans 13–17, 08002 Barcelona. ☎ **93-318-9858.** Fax 93-317-2822. 50 units. www.hotelregenciacolon.com. 170€ ($221) double; 195€ ($254) triple. AE, DC, MC, V. Metro: Plaça de Catalunya or Urquinaona. **Amenities:** Restaurant; bar; laundry. *In room:* Hair dryer.

HUSA Oriente   If you want to find lodgings on Barcelona's colorful and most famous boulevard, Les Rambles, consider this hotel. It dates from 1842 and in its heyday was one of the grand hotels of the city (celeb guests included Errol Flynn and Maria Callas). Much of its original architectural grandeur remains, though it's been considerably modernized and changed over the decades. Today, it offers modestly furnished but tasteful and comfortable bedrooms.

Les Rambles 45, 08002 Barcelona. ✆ **93-302-2558.** Fax 93-412-3819. www.husa.es. 142 units. 171€ ($222) double. AE, DC, MC, V. Metro: Liceu. **Amenities:** Restaurant; bar.

Jardí *(Value)* This hotel's location, in the heart of the Gothic quarter near many of the city's most visited monuments, is its most attractive feature. The five-story hotel rests on ancient Roman foundations and has been considerably modernized and improved. Rooms, though somewhat austere, are furnished comfortably; the quieter accommodations are on the upper floors.

Plaça Sant Josep Oriol 1, 08002 Barcelona. ✆ **93-301-5900.** Fax 93-342-5733. 42 units. 86€–96€ ($112–$125) double; 108€ ($140) triple. AE, DC, MC, V. Metro: Liceu. **Amenities:** Lounge.

Mesón Castilla *(★)* *(Value)* Operated by the Spanish hotel chain, HUSA, this hotel, a real bargain, was carved out of a former apartment building near the center of Les Rambles, Barcelona's main boulevard. The antiques-stuffed hotel features a wealth of Art Nouveau detailing. Bedrooms are medium in size and quite comfortable, furnished with tasteful pieces such as Catalán-style headboards. The best accommodations open onto private terraces.

Valldoncella 5, 08001 Barcelona. ✆ **93-318-2182.** Fax 93-412-4020. www.husa.es. 56 units. 144€ ($187) double. AE, DC, V. Metro: Plaça de Catalunya or Universitat. **Amenities:** Breakfast room; lounge; laundry. *In room:* Hair dryer.

TOP ATTRACTIONS & SPECIAL MOMENTS

Before wandering the narrow, labyrinthine streets of old Barcelona, consider a panoramic view of it first to get your bearings. That's possible from **Tibidabo Mountain** *(★)*, just north of the port, and reached by a funicular taking you up to 1,600 feet (487m). **Mirador Torre de Collserola** (✆ **93-406-9354**) was built at the time of the 1992 Barcelona Olympics, and from it the most stunning vistas unfold. It costs 5€ ($6.50) to climb the tower. From Plaça de Catalunya, take bus no. 58 to Avinguda del Tibidabo, where you can board a special bus to take you to the funicular. The funicular runs daily and costs 4.40€ ($5.70) one-way. The tower is open July to September Monday to Friday 11am to 2:30pm and 3:30 to 7pm, Saturday and Sunday 11am to 7pm. During other months, hours are more limited, with most closings at 6pm.

Catedral de Barcelona *(★★★)* The most acclaimed example of Catalán architecture and one of the great Gothic cathedrals of Europe, this church was begun in 1298 under the reign of Jaime II, but was not completed until 1889. Called "the loveliest oasis in Barcelona" by historian Cirici, it is distinguished by a Gothic interior with a single, wide nave, with 28 side chapels branching off of it. Among the most distinguished of these is **Capella de Sant Benet,** dedicated to the patron saint of Europe and housing a splendid altarpiece depicting the *Transfiguration* by Bernat Martorell in 1452. The **choir stalls** *(★)* are especially notable, the top tier of this 15th-century art displaying the coats-of-arms of the 12 knights of the Order of Toisón del Oro. The **cloisters** *(★)* are another notable feature; they're in the Gothic style and decorated with a statue of St. George slaying the dragon. The cloister contains a museum of medieval art. Beneath the main altar is the impressive **crypt** *(★)*, with its alabaster sarcophagus (1339) of the martyred St. Eulalia. The twin octagonal bell towers date from 1386, although the bells were installed in 1545. You can take an elevator to the roof for one of the grand panoramic views of Barcelona's Gothic barrio. At noon on Sunday, the most typical folkloric dance of Catalonia, the *sardana,* is performed in front of this edifice.

Plaça de la Seu. ✆ **93-315-1554.** Admission free to the cathedral; museum 1.25€ ($1.65); global ticket to museum, rooftop terraces, and towers 4.50€ ($5.85). Cathedral daily 8am–1pm and 5–7pm. Cloister museum daily 9am–1pm and 5–7pm. Metro: Jaume I.

Fundació Antoni Tàpies ✿   This museum is devoted to the work of a single artist, Antoni Tàpies. Born in 1923, Tàpies has become one of the best-known artists in Catalonia. He was a devotee of Surrealism and used any number of unconventional materials in the creation of his work, including concrete and metal. A landmark building, the museum lies near Passeig de Gràcia in the Eixample district and was designed by Lluis Domenech I Montaner, the leading exponent of Catalán Art Nouveau. A full range of Tàpies works is on display, including drawings, sculptures, and ceramics, as well as paintings. His most controversial and rather gigantic sculpture, *Cloud and Chair,* is on top of the building. It was made from 9,000 feet (2,700m) of metal wiring and tubing.

Aragó 255. ✆ **93-487-0315.** www.fundaciotapies.org. Admission 6€ ($7.80) adults, 4€ ($5.20) students, free for children under 16. Tues–Sun 10am–8pm. Metro: Passeig de Gràcia.

Fundació Joan Miró ✿   One of Spain's greatest artists, Joan Miró (1893–1983), was from Catalonia. A stark white building was designed by Josep Lluís Sert to house a permanent collection of the paintings, sculptures, graphics, and tapestries of this world-class artist, including his amusing *Flame in Space* and *Named Woman,* painted in 1932. The artist donated many of the 10,000 works housed here. Trained in Paris and an admirer of Gaudí's *modernista,* Miró is known for his whimsical abstract forms, brilliant colors, and surrealism. Using multimedia, one wing charts the evolution of Miró's art from the age of 8 until his final works in the 1970s.

Plaça de Neptú, Parc de Montjuïc. ✆ **93-443-9470.** www.bcn.fjmiro.es. Admission 7.50€ ($9.75) adults, 5€ ($6.50) students, free for children under 15. July–Sept Tues–Wed and Fri–Sat 10am–8pm, Thurs 10am–9:30pm, Sun 10am–2:30pm; Oct–June Tues–Wed and Fri–Sat 10am–7pm, Thurs 10am–9:30pm, Sun 10am–2:30pm. Bus: 50 at Plaça d'Espanya or 55.

La Sagrada Família ✿✿   This, the symbol of Barcelona, is Antoni Gaudí's unfinished masterpiece and the most unconventional church in Europe. The architect lived like a recluse at the site for 16 years and is buried in the **crypt** ✿, which was actually constructed by the cathedral's original architect, Francesc de Paula Villar I Lozano. Those who have seen Gaudí's finished plan for Sagrada Família can only lament that the architect died before carrying out his final dream. At the time of his death only one tower on the Nativity Facade had been completed. Financed by public contributions, work continues to this day. The apse remains the first part of the church completed by Gaudí. The controversial **Passion Façade** ✿ was finished in the late 1980s by Josep María Subirach. It is often criticized because of its "sinister" figures. Finished in 1904, the **Nativity Façade** ✿ is the most complete part of the church, its doorways representing faith, hope, and charity. A steep climb, 400 steps lead to the towers and upper galleries, opening onto **panoramic views of Barcelona** ✿✿. There's an elevator for those unable to make the climb.

Majorca 401 (entrance from Carrer de Sardenya or Carrer de la Marina). ✆ **93-207-3031.** www.sagradafamilia.org. Admission 8€ ($10.40). Elevator 2€ ($2.60). Apr–Oct daily 9am–8pm; Nov–Mar daily 9am–6pm. Metro: Sagrada Família.

Moments A Journey Back in Time

Barcelona's **Barri Gòtic** ★★★, or Gothic quarter, is filled with narrow, winding streets that take you back to the Middle Ages. Every street offers something of interest, a historic sight and most definitely dozens of shops, restaurants, and cafes, some of which may have been patronized by Picasso. The chief attraction is the **Cathedral of Barcelona** (p. 751), but there are dozens of other historic buildings as well, along with countless squares to discover on your own. None is more notable than Plaça de Sant Jaume, which has been the city's political center since Roman times. Today this square is dominated by the **Palau de la Generalitat,** headquarters of the autonomous government of Catalonia; and by the **Ajuntament,** the Barcelona city hall. If you need guidance in approaching this warren of fascinating old streets, the tourist office leads popular walking tours of the barrio in summer. Tours in English are conducted daily at 10am; the cost is 9€ ($12.20) for adults, 3€ ($4.05) for ages 4 to 12, kids 3 and under are free. For more information, call ✆ **93-285-3832.**

Museo Barbier-Mueller Art Precolombí ★★   In the medieval Palacio Nadal, this 1997 museum showcases one of the most important collections of pre-Columbian art. On display are some 6,000 exhibitions of tribal art, the first pieces acquired by the museum's namesake, Josef Mueller (1887–1977) in 1908. Of much interest are the artifacts left over from the Mayan culture, dating from 1000 B.C. A vast array is on display, including stone sculpture, ceramic and ornamental objects of great style, and funerary artifacts. Seek out, in particular, the artifacts of the Olmecs, a tribe that settled on the Gulf of Mexico in the 1st millennium B.C. and was known for its impressive stone sculpture and figures carved out of jade.

Carrer de Montcada 12–14. ✆ **93-310-4516.** www.barbier-mueller.ch. Admission 3€ ($3.90) adults, 1.50€ ($1.95) students and seniors, free for children under 12 and to all the first Sun of every month. Tues–Sat 10am–6pm; Sun and holidays 10am–3pm. Metro: Jaume I. Bus: 14, 17, 19, 39, 40, 45, or 51. Tourist bus: Ruta Sur (Azul).

Museu d'Art Contemporani de Barcelona ★   One of the leading showcases of modern art in eastern Spain, this museum houses masterpieces from a wide range of artists including Tàpies and Paul Klee. It is especially rich in the works of Catalán painter Joan Miró, who was known for his surrealistic style, vivid colors, and fantastical forms. The museum itself is an architectural statement of Richard Meier, an American architect. Some critics say, and we agree, that the building is a work of art, particularly in its manipulation of natural light.

Plaça dels Angels 1. ✆ **93-412-0810.** Admission 7.50€ ($9.75) adults, 6€ ($7.80) students, free for children under 14 and seniors over 65. Wed–Sat 11am–7:30pm; Sun 10am–3pm. Metro: Plaça de Catalunya.

Museo Nacional d'Art de Catalunya ★★★   Built for the 1929 World's Fair in Montjuïc Park, this museum, one of Spain's major art showcases, is not only the major repository of Catalán art, but also displays the most significant collection of Romanesque art in the world. Some 100 Romanesque pieces range from icons to sculptures, and also include some splendid frescoes from the 12th century. To round out the collection, churches, monasteries, and other centers were "raided" throughout Catalonia for their treasures. One of the most remarkable exhibitions here features wall paintings from Sant Climent de Taüll and Santa Maria de Taüll. The museum is also rich in Gothic art, especially from Catalonia. Paintings by many great Spanish masters, from Velázquez to Zurbarán, are featured.

Palau Nacional, Parc de Montjuïc. ✆ **93-622-0360**. Admission 8.50€ ($11.05) adults, 3.50€ ($4.55) youths 7–20, free for children 6 and under. Tues–Sat 10am–7pm; Sun 10am–2:30pm. Metro: Espanya, lines 1 or 3.

Museu Picasso ✦✦　Pablo Picasso (1881–1973) was born in Málaga but arrived in Barcelona at the age of 14. He fell in love with the city and in time would donate some 2,500 of his paintings, drawings, and engravings. They are now housed in this museum carved out of several old mansions on this street from the Middle Ages. The greatest attraction here is in the early drawings of the teenage Picasso, including *The First Communion* painted in 1896. A few paintings from his Blue and Rose periods are displayed, but his most celebrated work is the series, *Las Meninas,* based on the Velázquez masterpiece hanging in Madrid's Prado (p. 721). Scenes from Picasso's old notebooks depict street life in Barcelona. It is said that Picasso found inspiration among Barcelona's prostitutes for his *Les Demoiselles d'Avignon,* which some art historians view as the wellspring of modern art.

Montcada 15–19. ✆ **93-256-3000**. Admission 6€ ($7.80) adults (8.50€/$11.05 temporary and permanent exhibits), 3€ ($3.90) students and visitors 16–25 (8.50€/$11.05 temporary and permanent exhibits), free for children under 16. Tues–Sun 10am–8pm. Metro: Jaume I.

Parc Güell ✦✦　Like Sagrada Família, Gaudí's eccentric park was never completed. Even so, UNESCO has designated it as a World Heritage Site. The park was commissioned in the 1890s by Count Eusebi Güell and set on 50 acres (20 hectares) as a "garden city." Even though the park opened in 1922, little of Gaudí's grand design had been realized. On-site today is **Casa-Museu Gaudí,** Carrer del Carmel 28 (✆ **93-219-3811**), designed by the architect Ramon Berenguer. The museum contains drawings and furnishings by Gaudí. Admission to the museum is 4.50€ ($5.85), and it is open April to September daily 10am to 7:45pm, October to March daily 10am to 5:45pm. Gaudí did complete several of the public areas in the park, which evoke a Surrealist Disney World, complete with a mosaic pagoda and a lizard fountain spitting water. A mosaic-encrusted chimney by Gaudí can be seen at the entrance to the park, and the **Room of a Hundred Columns,** with 84 crooked pillars, is the most atmospheric attraction.

Carrer d'Olot. ✆ **93-219-3810**. Free admission. May–Sept daily 10am–9pm; Oct–Apr daily 10am–6pm. Bus: 24, 25, 31, or 74.

Poble Espanyol ✦　This re-created Spanish village was originally constructed for the 1929 World's Fair. A total of 116 houses illustrate architectural styles from all the Spanish provinces, ranging from Galicia in the northwest to Valencia along the southeastern coast (known as the Levante). Some of these life-size reproductions of typical buildings date in style from the 10th century. The living museum is an entertainment complex with more than a dozen restaurants, "musical" bars, and even a dance club, along with numerous shops selling typical Spanish handicrafts. In some of these artisan havens, you can see craftspeople at work, perhaps blowing glass or printing colorful fabrics. Toledo damascene work along with sculpture and even Catalán canvas sandals are made here. There's also a children's theater.

Avgda Marqués de Comillas 13, Parc de Montjuïc. ✆ **93-325-7866**. Admission 7.50€ ($9.75) adults, 4€ ($5.20) children 7–12, free for children 6 and under. Mon 9am–8pm; Tues–Thurs 9am–2am; Fri–Sat 9am–4am; Sun 9am–midnight. Metro: Espanya. Bus: 13 or 50.

WHERE TO DINE

Agut ⚑ *Finds* CATALAN   Only 3 blocks from the waterfront, this longtime favorite is set in the colorful Barri Xinés district. A family-run business for most of the 20th century, the restaurant is decorated with paintings by Catalán artists. It serves good food at very reasonable prices, the cuisine based on time-tested recipes and fresh ingredients. One of our favorite dishes is *soufle de rape amb gambes* (soufflé of monkfish with shrimp).

Gignas 16. ☎ **93-315-1709.** Reservations required. Main courses 20€–35€ ($26–$45.50). Fixed-price lunch 10.50€ ($13.65) Tues–Fri only. AE, MC, V. Tues–Sun 1:30–4pm; Tues–Sat 9pm–midnight. Closed Aug. Metro: Jaume I.

Agut d'Avignon ⚑ CATALAN   Near Plaça Reial in the old town, this is one of our favorite restaurants in Barcelona and also one of the oldest. In business for more than 40 years, it keeps its devotees happy and attracts new converts by turning out savory Catalán cuisine. Long a choice of writers, newspaper people, artists, and politicians, it offers time-tested meals served in generous portions and made with quality ingredients. Start with the fishermen's soup and proceed through the menu (ask a waiter to help you translate)—whatever you order, you'll get a special meal.

Trinitat 3. ☎ **93-317-7552.** Reservations required. Main courses 40€–60€ ($52–$78). AE, DC, MC, V. Daily noon–midnight. Metro: Jaume I or Liceu.

Café de L'Academia ⚑⚑ *Value* MEDITERRANEAN   A short walk from Plaça Sant Jaume, one of the most famous squares in the Gothic quarter, this affordable restaurant is housed in an elegant 15th-century building. The chef serves succulent Catalán and Mediterranean dishes and terms his cuisine "kitchen of the market," an accurate appraisal of his use of the freshest of ingredients gathered early in the morning. Recipes are imaginative and nearly always palate pleasing, as exemplified by the partridge stuffed with onions and duck liver.

Carrer Lledó 1. ☎ **93-315-8253.** Reservations required. Main courses 11€–17€ ($14.30–$22.10). AE, MC, V. Mon–Fri 9am–noon, 1:30–4pm, and 8:45–11:30pm. Closed last 2 weeks Aug. Metro: Jaume I.

Comerç 24 ⚑⚑ *Finds* CATALAN/INTERNATIONAL   Chef Carles Abellan earns culinary laurels with his light, imaginative, and original renderings of old-time Catalonia favorites. Set in a renovated salting house along the Barceloneta waterfront, the restaurant features an attractive minimalist and modern decor. Dishes are cooked to order as the chef believes in "split-second" timing. Try the fresh salmon perfumed with vanilla and served with yogurt.

Carrer Comerç 24, La Ribera. ☎ **93-319-2102.** www.comerc24.com. Reservations required. Main courses 8€–14€ ($10.40–$18.20); tasting menu 54€ ($70.20). MC, V. Tues–Sat 1:30–3:30pm and 8:30–11:30pm. Closed 10 days in Dec, 10 days in Aug. Metro: Arco de Triompho, Estacion de Francia.

Els Quatre Gats *Value* CATALAN   Since 1897, this former gathering place of the literati and artistic elite (Picasso was a regular) has been a favorite for drinking and dining in the Gothic barrio close to the cathedral. Today the restored *fin-de-siècle* cafe is visited for its atmosphere, good food, and reasonable prices. The cookery is unpretentious but prepared from fresh ingredients, and the menu is seasonally adjusted.

Montsió 3. ☎ **93-302-4140.** Reservations required Sat–Sun. Main courses 10€–20€ ($13–$26); fixed-price menu 21€ ($27.30). AE, DC, MC. Daily 9am–12:30am. Metro: Plaça de Catalunya.

Garduña *Value* CATALAN   In the rear of Catalonia's most famous food market, La Boquería, this somewhat ramshackle eatery is known for its crowd-pleasing food, large

Moments **Rambling Les Rambles**

Commonly called **La Rambla** ⭐⭐⭐, this winding street is the most famous promenade in Spain. It actually consists of five different sections—each a rambla—Rambla de Canaletes, Rambla dels Estudis, Rambla de Sant Josep, Rambla dels Caputxins, and Rambla de Santa Mónica. It begins in the north at the transportation hub, Plaça de Catalunya, and runs all the way to the port and the monument to Columbus. Day and night, this is the most active street in Barcelona. It can be walked at any time, and you'll always see something new, as the street is forever changing. Caged birds and flower stalls greet you, as do street musicians and mime *artistes* and tarot card readers. Hotels, town houses, endless shops, and many cafes and restaurants also flank this fabled boulevard. The most famous building you'll pass along the 1-mile (1.6km) boulevard is Gran Teatre del Liceu on Rambla dels Caputxins.

portions, and reasonable prices. Food here is superfresh—you'll likely pass some of the produce stalls that provided the ingredients for your meal when you walk through the market. The restaurant offers you a choice of dining downstairs at a bustling bar or more formally in the room upstairs.

Jerusalem 18. ☎ **93-302-4323**. Reservations recommended. Main courses 13€–30€ ($16.90–$39); fixed-price menu lunch 13€ ($16.90), dinner 16€ ($20.80). AE, DC, MC, V. Mon–Sat 1–4pm and 8pm–midnight. Metro: Liceu.

Jean Luc Figueras ⭐⭐⭐ CATALAN   Jean Luc Figueras is one of our favorite chefs in Catalonia—and of most local food critics, too. The former studio of Balenciaga in the Gràcia district has been elegantly converted into a backdrop for the refined cuisine of this talented chef, who respects tradition but is also innovative. The emphasis is on seafood, and market-fresh ingredients are cleverly fashioned into velvety smooth dishes. Be sure to try the homemade desserts, and definitely sample one of the seven varieties of freshly made bread.

Santa Teresa 10. ☎ **93-415-2877**. Reservations required. Main courses 30€–45€ ($39–$58.50). AE, DC, MC, V. Mon–Sat 1:30–3:30pm and 8:30–11:30pm. Metro: Diagonal.

La Rosca *Value* SPANISH/CATALAN   In the Gothic barrio, close to the transportation hub of Plaça de Catalunya, this is an old-fashioned restaurant where the owner, Don Alberto Vellve, respects Catalán traditions of good food and service. Against a nostalgic backdrop of bullfighter posters and pictures of old Barcelona, a hearty, regional fare is served at most affordable prices. Most of the dishes served here would have been familiar in the kitchen of Grandmother Catalonia—and that's a very good thing.

Julía Portet 6. ☎ **93-302-5173**. Reservations recommended. Main courses 7€–12€ ($9.10–$15.60); fixed-price menu 8.50€–14€ ($11.05–$18.20). No credit cards. Sun–Fri 9am–4pm and 8–9:30pm; summer Sun–Fri 9am–4pm. Closed Aug 20–30. Metro: Plaça de Catalunya.

L'Olive ⭐ CATALAN/MEDITERRANEAN   You assume that this two-floor restaurant is named for the olive that figures so prominently in its Mediterranean cuisine, but it's actually named for the owner, Josep Olive. The dining room is designed in a modern Catalán style, and the overall feeling is one of elegance with a touch of intimacy. You won't be disappointed by anything on the menu, especially the *salsa maigret* of duck with strawberry sauce. Monkfish flavored with roasted garlic is always a palate pleaser, and you can finish with a *crema catalán* (a flan) or one of the delicious Catalán pastries.

Calle Balmes 47 (corner of Concéjo de Ciento). ℂ 93-452-1990. Reservations recommended. Main courses 13€–20€ ($17–$26); *menú completo* 45€ ($58.50). AE, DC, MC, V. Daily 1–4pm; Mon–Sat 8:30pm–midnight. Metro: Passeig de Gràcia.

Los Caracoles CATALAN   "The Snails" (as it translates into English) was founded back in 1835 in the heart of the Gothic Quarter near the Rambles, and the tantalizing aroma of roasting chicken is still wafting through this seedy street after all these years. The founding Bofarull family is still in charge of this time-mellowed favorite, which is seemingly visited by every tourist in town. Even though Los Caracoles hasn't been acclaimed the best restaurant in Barcelona since the time of the American Civil War, it remains a bastion of local culture and a favorite of old-time locals who mingle with diners from Japan to the Yukon territories. The food on the menu at this old favorite—which was featured in the inaugural edition of *Spain on $5 a Day* and recommended for many years—has never been altered. For longtime visitors to Barcelona, the memories might be an important lure.

Escudellers 14. ℂ 93-302-31-85. Reservations recommended. Main courses 8€–30€ ($10.40–$39). AE, DC, MC, V. Daily 1pm–midnight. Metro: Drassanes.

Pla de la Garsa ⓕ *Value* CATALAN/MEDITERRANEAN   Close to the cathedral in the Gothic quarter, Ignacio Sulle, an antiques seller, has assembled an intriguing collection of furnishings and objets d'art to serve as a backdrop for his succulent menu of old-time Mediterranean and Catalán favorites. Backed up by one of the best wine lists in Barcelona, Sulle searches far and wide for choice ingredients, which his chefs concoct into a series of imaginative dishes, starting with marvelous terrines and the fish and meat pâtés.

Assaonadors 13. ℂ 93-315-2413. Reservations recommended Sat–Sun. Main courses 6€–15€ ($7.80–$19.50). AE, MC, V. Daily 8pm–1am. Metro: Jaume I.

⟮*Moments* **A Taste of Catalán Bubbly**

Catalonia is famous for its *cava*, the local name for champagne. Throughout Barcelona champagne bars are called *xampanyerías*. For a fun night on the town, go on a champagne bar crawl sampling the local bubbly. Our favorites include **El Xampanyet,** Carrer Montcada 22 (ℂ **93-319-7003;** Metro: Jaume I), close to the Picasso Museum in the old town on an ancient street. Revelers go here to drink the champagne at marble tables and to feast on tapas. Open Monday to Saturday noon to 4pm and 7 to 11:30pm, Sunday 11am to 4pm. Closed in August. At the corner of Plaça de Tetuan is **Xampú Xampany,** Gran Vía de les Corts Catalanes 702 (ℂ **93-265-0483;** Metro: Girona). Against a backdrop of abstract paintings, you can enjoy glass after glass of the bubbly Monday to Saturday 8pm to 1:30am.

SHOPPING

The best one-stop shopping is at **El Corte Inglés,** at Avinguda Diagonal 617–619 (© **93-366-7100;** Metro: María Cristina), one of the finest department stores along the eastern Spanish seaboard, selling everything from high fashion to regional handcrafts. Enjoy food and drink in a rooftop cafe. Open Monday to Saturday 10am to 10pm. There's a branch at Avinguda Diagonal 471 (© **93-493-4800;** Metro: Hospital Clinic), which keeps the same hours.

As a city of art, Barcelona is known for its galleries. Especially interesting for visitors is **Art Picasso,** Tapinería 10 (© **93-268-3240;** Metro: Jaume I), which has excellent lithographic reproductions of works by Joan Miró, Dalí, and Picasso, all the homegrown artists. Open daily 11am to 8pm. Summer hours are 9:30am to 8pm. The best artwork by Catalonia's living artists and sculptors is sold at **Sala Parés,** Petritxol 5 (© **93-318-7020;** Metro: Liceu or Placa de Catalunya), established in 1840. Artwork is shown in a two-floor amphitheater, and exhibitions of contemporary works change every 3 weeks. Open Monday to Saturday 10:30am to 2pm and 4:30 to 8:30pm. Antique collectors head for **Antiguedades Artur Ramón,** Palla 23 (© **93-302-5970;** Metro: Jaume I), a three-story emporium filled with rare pieces from the attics of Catalonia, and also 19th- and 20th-century artwork and sculpture, including many decorative objects and rare ceramics. Open Tuesday to Saturday 10am to 1:30pm and 5 to 8pm.

Barcelona is not Milan or Paris but is increasingly known for its fashion, best represented by **Adolfo Domínguez,** Passeig de Gràcia 32 (© **93-487-4170;** Metro: Passeig de Gràcia), an outlet celebrated as the Spanish Armani. Their style, as summed up by one local fashion critic—"Austere but not strict, forgivingly cut in urbane earth tones." Open Monday to Saturday 10am to 8:30pm. **Textil I d'Indumentaria,** Carrer Montcada 12 (© **93-319-7603;** Metro: Jaume I), is a showcase of regional design under the auspices of the Museum of Textile and Fashion. Across from the Picasso Museum, it sells well-designed clothing, shoes for men and women, jewelry, and an array of other merchandise. Open Tuesday to Saturday 10am to 8:30pm and Sunday 10am to 3pm.

Catalonia has long been celebrated for its handmade pottery, which is showcased best at **Itaca,** Carrer Ferran 26 (© **93-301-3044;** Metro: Liceu), which has a wide array of ceramics and other works. Open Monday to Saturday 10am to 8:30pm. The best center for designer housewares is **Vincón,** Passeig de Gràcia 96 (© **93-215-6050;** Metro: Diagonal), selling some 10,000 different wares including beautifully designed household items along with sleekly designed modern furnishings. Open Monday to Saturday 10am to 8:30pm.

The hurried rail passenger on a tight schedule may have time to visit only the pick of the city's malls, which house a wide variety of Catalonian merchandise under one roof. The best of these includes **Maremagnum,** Moll d'Espanya (© **93-225-8100;** Metro: Drassanes or Barceloneta), near the Columbus Monument. In addition to its many shops, there are also a dozen theaters, an IMAX theater, and many restaurants, pubs, and dance clubs. Open daily 10am to 10pm. The largest shopping center in Barcelona is **Centre Comercial Barcelona Glòries,** Avinguda Diagonal 208 (© **93-486-0404;** Metro: Glòries), a three-story emporium with some 100 shops, many of them posh. This mall is filled with some treasures, but also lots of lesser merchandise. Open Monday to Saturday 10am to 10pm.

NIGHTLIFE

Begin your *tasca* crawl of the Gothic barrio by sitting on the terrace of **La Vinya del Senyor,** Plaça Santa María 5 (© 93-310-3379), enjoying the magnificent facade of Santa María del Mar. There are some 300 selections of wine here (many sold by the glass), along with select *cavas* (Catalán champagne), *moscatells,* and sherries. Open Tuesday to Saturday noon to 1:30am and Sunday noon to midnight (Metro: Jaume I or Barceloneta).

Before attending the theater, head for **Café de la Opera,** La Rambla 74 (© 93-317-7585; Metro: Liceu); the city's most fabled cafe has been in business since the beginning of the 20th century. Operagoers flock here, as do one of the widest cross-sections of people. It's open daily from 8:30am until the early morning hours. After a drink, head for the **Gran Teatre del Liceu,** La Rambla dels Caputxins 51-54 (© 93-485-9900; Metro: Liceu), a Belle Epoque–style, 2,700-seat opera house, one of the greatest theaters in the world. It was rebuilt following a devastating fire in 1994. Today it's the venue for the major cultural events of Catalonia.

At the top of the Ramblas, you can patronize **Café Zurich,** Plaça de Catalunya 1 (© 93-317-9153; Metro: Plaça de Catalunya), another traditional meeting point and one of the best places in the old city for people-watching. Going strong since the early 1920s, it's known for its *bocadillos,* or little sandwiches.

The evening begins early in Barcelona in the bars, with **Molly's Fair City,** Carrer Ferran 7 (© 93-342-4026; Metro: Liceu), being the favorite hangout of ex-pats. Evoking a Dublin beer hall, it's open Monday to Thursday from 8pm till 2:30am; Friday, Saturday, and Sunday 5pm to 3am. For a typical old-town bar, head for **El Born,** Passeig del Born 26 (© 93-319-5333; Metro: Jaume I or Barceloneta), a converted former fish shop. You can also enjoy an inexpensive dinner; meals start at 18€ ($23.40). Open Monday to Saturday 6pm to 2am (until 3am Fri–Sat). Near Plaça Reial, **Schilling,** Carrer Ferran 23 (© 93-317-6787; Metro: Liceu), is an old cafe and bar that looks like something from Gaudí's era, with its iron columns and marble tables. Both gays and straights mix harmoniously here. Open Monday to Thursday 10am to 2:30am, Friday and Saturday 10am to 3am, and Sunday noon to 2am.

As the evening progresses, the cabarets and jazz clubs start to fill up. One of the oldest and best jazz clubs is **Harlem Jazz Club,** Comtessa de Sobradiel 8 (© 93-310-0755; Metro: Jaume I or Liceu). Small and intimate, the club often attracts top jazz artists from Europe and America. Open Tuesday to Thursday and Sunday 8pm to 4am, until 5am Friday and Saturday. There's a one-drink minimum but no cover. Closed 2 weeks in August. Another premier venue for good blues and jazz is **Jamboree,** Plaça Reial 17 (© 93-314-1789; Metro: Liceu), in the heart of the Gothic old city. Jazz is not always scheduled here; sometimes a Latin dance band will perform. Cover is 6€ to 10€ ($7.80–$13), and it's open daily 10:30pm to 5am, with shows beginning at 11pm.

In the showplace rooms of the Palau Dalmases, **Espai Barroc,** Carrer Montcada 20 (© 93-310-0673; Metro: Jaume I), holds forth in the Barri Gòtic. It's one of the most elegant venues on the after-dark circuit. The best night is Thursday at 11pm when nearly a dozen singers perform songs from assorted operas. For the opera aficionado, this is a grand evening out. Cover is charged only on Thursday, costing 20€ ($26) and including a drink. Open Tuesday to Thursday 8pm to 2am, Friday and Saturday 10pm to 2am, and Sunday 6 to 9pm.

Luz de Gas, Carrer de Muntaner 246 (© **93-414-1699**), is a theater and cabaret with some of the best jazz in Barcelona on weekends. Weekdays at this Art Nouveau club are given over to cabaret. A wide range of music is presented here weekly, including pop, soul, jazz, rhythm and blues, and salsa. The cover of 15€ ($19.50) includes the first drink. Open Monday and Sunday 11pm to 4am, Wednesday 11pm to 5am, Thursday 11pm to 5:30am, and Friday and Saturday 11pm to 5:45am. **Barcelona Pipa Club,** Plaça Reial 3 (© **93-301-1165;** Metro: Liceu), is a final venue for jazz devotees. You ring the buzzer as if being admitted to an old speakeasy, and inside the music ranges from Brazilian rhythms to New Orleans jazz. There's no cover, and hours are daily 10pm to 3am.

Barcelona is not associated with flamenco the way Madrid or Andalusia are, but there are some excellent clubs, including a highly rated flamenco cabaret at **El Tablao de Carmen,** Poble Espanyol de Montjuïc (© **93-325-6895;** Metro: Espanya). You can go early and explore this re-created Spanish village. The first show (Tues–Thurs, and Sun) is presented at 9:30pm; the second show at 11:30pm Tuesday to Thursday and Sunday, or else midnight on Friday and Saturday. A drink and show costs 30€ ($39). The oldest flamenco club in Barcelona is **Los Tarantos,** Plaça Reial 17 (© **93-319-1789**), which presents the best of Andalusian flamenco. Each show lasts around 1¼ hours, beginning at 8:30pm, 9:30pm and 10:30pm Monday to Saturday. The 5€ ($6.50) cover includes your first drink.

Late at night, especially into the early hours, dance clubs prevail, including **La Paloma,** Tigre 27 (© **93-301-6897;** Metro: Universitat), the most famous dance hall in Barcelona. It's for an older crowd and those who remember the mambo or the fox trot. The hall is open Thursday to Sunday with matinees lasting from 6 to 9:30pm, and night dances taking place from 11:30pm to 5am. A much younger crowd is drawn to **Up and Down,** Numancia 179 (© **93-280-2922;** Metro: Maria Cristina). This is a two-level dance club, with the members of the flaming youth hanging out downstairs. A cosmopolitan place, the dance club is open Tuesday to Saturday midnight to 6am, charging a cover ranging from 15€ to 20€ ($19.50–$26), including your first drink.

AN EXCURSION TO MONTSERRAT

At a point 35 miles (56km) northwest of Barcelona, the monastery of Montserrat is the most visited attraction outside Barcelona. One of the major pilgrimage centers in Spain, it sits atop at 4,000-foot-high (1,200m) mountain that's 7 miles (11km) long and 3¼ miles (5.5km) wide. A popular venue for weddings, the site possesses the medieval statue of "The Black Virgin" *(La Moreneta),* the patron saint of Catalonia. Thousands upon thousands of the faithful flock here annually to touch the statue.

GETTING THERE   From Barcelona, Montserrat is reached via the Manresa line of Ferrocarrils de la Generealitat de Catalunya, with 10 trains leaving daily from Plaça d'Espanya in Barcelona (trip time: 1 hr.). The central office at Plaça de Catalunya (© **93-205-1515**) sells tickets for 13€ ($16.90) round-trip. The train connects with the aerial cable car, Aeri de Montserrat, whose fare is included in the round-trip. *Note:* Railpasses are not accepted for this journey, so passholders will have to purchase a ticket.

VISITOR INFORMATION   The visitor information center is at Plaça de la Creu (© **93-877-7777;** www.gencat.net). It's open daily 9am to 6pm.

TOP ATTRACTIONS & SPECIAL MOMENTS

Consecrated in 1592, the Montserrat Monastery is entered at Plaça Santa María. Although the French destroyed the monastery in 1811 during their attack on Catalonia, it was reconstructed and repopulated in 1844. During the Franco regime, when the dictator tried to obliterate Catalán culture, the monastery remained a beacon of enlightenment.

One of its noted attractions is the 50-member **Escolania** ᐖᐖ, one of the oldest and most renowned boys' choirs in Europe, having been founded in the 13th century. Crowds flock here at 1pm daily to hear the choir sing "Salve Regina" and "Virolai" in the basilica. Hours are daily 8 to 10:30am and noon to 6:30pm, charging no admission. For a view of the **Black Madonna,** enter the church through a side door to the right and follow the crowds.

Museu de Montserrat stands at Plaça de Santa María (© **93-877-7777;** www. montserratvisita.com). It contains important works of art, including paintings by old masters such as El Greco and Caravaggio. Even more modern painters such as Picasso are shown here, and you'll also find pieces by French Impressionists, including Monet and Degas. Many ancient artifacts are also shown. Hours are daily Monday to Friday 10am to 6pm and Saturday and Sunday 10am to 7pm. Admission is 5€ ($6.50) for adults, 4.50€ ($5.85) seniors, and 3.50€ ($4.55) for students and children.

A funicular takes you in just 9 minutes to the peak, **Sant Joan,** at 4,119 feet (1,255m); it operates every 20 minutes daily from 10am to 5:45pm April to June, and September; 10am to 7pm July to August; and 10am to 4:45pm October to November, and March; and 11am to 4:45pm December to February. The cost is 6.30€ ($8.20) round-trip. One of the **greatest panoramas in all of Spain** ᐖᐖᐖ can be seen from this point—from the distant Pyrenees to the Balearic Islands.

18

Sweden

Clean and fresh are useful adjectives when describing Sweden's cities, furniture, trains, politics, and its huge expanse of wilderness groaning with dark pine forests and gleaming blue lakes.

Twice the size of Britain, this large country sits on the northern edge of Europe, and although it requires some effort for the rail traveler to get here (though easier now, thanks to the Oresund Bridge linking Denmark and Sweden), it's definitely worth the trip. Stockholm and Gothenburg are increasingly fashionable, offering up plenty of urban delights—bars, galleries, first-class restaurants, clubs, and so on. But urban areas only take up a little more than 1% of the country, and beyond that is a wonderfully varied landscape featuring everything from the mountainous Arctic reaches of northern Lapland to the sandy white beaches of Skåne in the south. And wherever you go you'll meet the friendly and efficient residents of Sweden, and get an inspiring thrill from traveling through one of the most modern, liberal, and eco-friendly countries in the world.

Plus, the good news for rail travelers is that Sweden's trains are among the most efficient and high tech in Europe, with easy rail access to all the top sights, along mostly scenic routes in a country that is relatively underpopulated compared to the rest of Europe. English speakers will have no trouble finding someone to help them out— nearly the whole country speaks English—making this a trouble-free destination in the language department. And, to ease the eco-guilt of traveling, most of Sweden's trains are run on electric power, all of which is harvested from renewable resources.

The bad news: Its trains run on time with utter efficiency, and the natural sights are great, but the prices in Scandinavia are a killer. To travel deluxe or first class in Sweden is a costly undertaking (though cheaper than in other Scandinavian countries). We do, of course, recommend a number of moderate choices in this chapter, but one should keep in mind that Sweden's not the best place for a rail trip on a strict budget.

If you have a choice, come here in summer when the Midnight Sun extends the days in June and July. The climate is generally cool during this brief summer period, except on the southern coast, which, thanks to the effects of the Gulf Stream, can heat up like the Mediterranean. Winter, on the other hand, when the days are gray and too short, can be a horrible experience, and even Stockholm can feel like the deep freeze. On the positive side, the air is clean, crisp, and fresh.

Note: For a detailed look at Sweden's rail routes, as well as the rail lines in all of the major Scandinavian countries, see the map on p. 197.

HIGHLIGHTS OF SWEDEN

The average rail traveler usually allots 3 to 5 days for Sweden. If all you have is 3 days and Sweden's the first stop on your rail itinerary, we recommend you fly to Stockholm. You can also travel into Stockholm by rail from Copenhagen, but you'll lose an extra day

Moments Festivals & Special Events

Some 30 operas and ballets, from the baroque to early romantic era, are presented in Stockholm's unique 1766 **Drottningholm Court Theater,** with original decorative paintings, stage sets, and machinery. Call ✆ **08/660-82-25** for tickets or go to **www.dtm.se**. The season runs from late May to late September. Take the T-bana to Brommaplan, and then bus no. 301, 323, 176, or 177. A steamboat runs here from Stockholm in the summer; call ✆ **08/587-14-000** for information.

Swedes celebrate **Midsummer Eve** all over the country with maypole dancing to fiddle and accordion music, among other events. It's celebrated on the Saturday falling between June 20 and June 26.

Another of the city's top summer festivals is **The Stockholm Jazz Festival** (✆**08/505-33-170**; www.stockholmjazz.com). Taking place annually, in the middle of July, the lineup is usually bulging with emerging Scandinavian talent and big names such as Stevie Wonder and Lauryn Hill. The setting is the romantic downtown island of Skeppsholmen. Day tickets cost 450SEK ($63/£31.50).

---

in transit. If you have 5 days, we suggest you spend your extra time on the country's west coast in Gothenburg. The rail journey from Gothenburg to Stockholm takes slightly more than 3 hours and you'll cut through the heartland of the country, passing some of its most soul-stirring landscapes, including rich forestland, and glistening blue lakes.

Even those doing a cursory tour of Northern Europe are wise to include **Stockholm,** the capital of Sweden, on their rail itineraries. The city is the rail hub of Sweden, with high-speed trains branching out to the south, north, and west.

Though a city of 1.5 million—Ingmar Bergman called it "simply a rather large village"—Stockholm is filled with wide, open spaces and expanses of water. The city spreads across 14 islands in Lake Mälaren, marking the beginning of a mammoth archipelago taking in 24,000 islands, skerries, and islets stretching all the way to the Baltic Sea. Founded more than 7 centuries ago, it didn't become the official capital until the mid-1600s.

As cities go, Stockholm is one of the most beautiful in Europe, and you can easily budget 3 days to take in the highlights, especially if you include a side trip to Uppsala. Walk the streets of its Old Town, **Gamla Stan,** visit one of the city's many fine museums, and tour the must-see royal warship *Vasa,* a 17th-century man-of-war pulled from the sea and arguably Scandinavia's top attraction. The open-air park, **Skansen,** filled with some 150 historical dwellings, is another attraction well worth your time.

And when you need a change of scenery, take a day-trip from Stockholm to the ancient city of **Uppsala,** Sweden's major university town, easily reached by train. It not only has a great university but a celebrated 15th-century cathedral that is still the seat of the archbishop. Nearby is **Gamla Uppsala,** the capital of the Svea kingdom about 15 centuries ago.

If you have the time and you've finished touring the east coast of Sweden, hop on a train and head west to the city of **Gothenburg** (Göteborg in Sweden), the best center for exploring the western coast of Sweden, and the country's major port. Stockholm, of course, is the far greater attraction, but Gothenburg is not without its charm. Like Stockholm, it is a lively, bustling place riddled with canals, parks, and gardens, a wealth of museums, and the largest amusement park in Scandinavia. And from here, you can easily catch a train to whisk you off to your next international destination.

1 Essentials

GETTING THERE

SAS (© **800/221-2350** in the U.S.; www.scandinavian.net) flies direct to Stockholm from Chicago and New York daily. **Continental** (© **800/231-0856;** www.continental. com) also flies direct between New York and Stockholm.

Other airlines fly to gateway European cities and then connect to flights into Stockholm. **British Airways** (© **800/AIRWAYS** in the U.S.; www.britishairways.com) flies to London and offers connecting flights to Sweden. **Icelandair** (© **800/223-5500** in the U.S.; www.icelandair.com) is an excellent choice for travel to Stockholm, thanks to connections through Reykjavik, and usually offers good deals.

To reach Stockholm or Gothenburg by rail, you'll likely pass through Copenhagen, which is the main rail hub connecting Scandinavia to the rest of Europe. There are several daily trains from Copenhagen to Stockholm and Copenhagen to Gothenburg.

If you're traveling out of Norway, there are at least three trains a day between Oslo and Stockholm. Travel time is about 6½ hours. There are also several trains a day from Oslo to Gothenburg. Travel time is about 4 hours.

SWEDEN BY RAIL
PASSES

For information on the **Eurail Global Pass,** the **Eurail Global Pass Flexi,** the **Eurail Scandinavia Pass,** and other multicountry options, see chapter 2. The **Eurail Sweden Pass** offers 3 to 8 days of unlimited first- or second-class travel within a 1-month period. Adult prices start at $243 for 3 days of second-class travel; discounts are available for children. Passes should be purchased in North America through your travel agent or **Rail Europe** (© **877/272-RAIL** [7245]; www.raileurope.com).

FOREIGN TRAIN TERMS

The Swedish word for train is *tåg.* Beyond that one word, don't bother learning a lot of train terms in difficult-to-pronounce Swedish. Swedes start learning English at a young age, and you can usually find out what you need to know by asking train personnel for help.

Trains & Travel Times in Sweden

From	To	Type of Train	# of Trains	Frequency	Travel Time
Stockholm	Uppsala	SJ Reg/IC	33	Mon–Fri	40 min.
Stockholm	Uppsala	SJ Reg/IC	24–26	Sat–Sun	40 min.
Stockholm	Gothenberg	X2000	8	Mon–Fri	3 hr., 7 min.
Stockholm	Gothenberg	X2000	7	Sat–Sun	3 hr., 7 min.
Stockholm	Gothenberg	InterCity	6	Daily	4 hr., 51 min.

Moments Sweden's Most Famous Rail Journey

The most famous rail route in Sweden during summer is the 621-mile (1,000km) run from Mora to Gallivare—called *Inlandsbanan* (© 0771/53-53-53; www.inlandsbanan.se) or "Inland Railway." It crawls along at a speed of 30 mph (48kmph) through unspoiled Swedish landscapes of blue lakes and deep green forests. From your window you can often see bear, reindeer, and elk. The train makes several stops along the way for photo ops. Passengers can sometimes get off and pick wild berries or take a quick dip in a mountain lake (take care to avoid hungry bears!). You can reach Mora from Stockholm by train in about 4 hours. If you figure in a return trip to Stockholm, the whole journey takes about a week. From mid-June through to the end of August, you can buy an Inland Railway Card valid for 14 days for the entire railway for 1,395SEK ($195/£97.65) plus an optional 50SEK ($7/£3.50) for each seat reservation, but all the extras will add up. One-week packages are available that include rail fare, hotels, and breakfast, and start at 4,320SEK ($605/£302) per person double, with a 1,440SEK ($202/£101) single supplement, and go as high as 9,250SEK ($1,295/£648) for tours that include boat trips (single supplement is 3,185SEK/$446/£223). The final return to Stockholm is on an overnight train in a two-bed sleeping compartment.

PRACTICAL TRAIN INFORMATION

Swedish trains follow tight schedules and travel often—usually every hour, or every other hour—between most of the big Swedish towns. Trains leave Malmö, Helsingborg, and Gothenburg for Stockholm every hour throughout the day, Monday through Friday, with slightly restricted services at the weekend.

Swedish trains are among the most modern and efficient in Europe, and the network spans the entire country. The Swedish high-speed train is called the **X2000,** and travels at speeds of 125 mph (200kmph) on all major routes. The fleet has recently been refurbished with new trains offering Wi-Fi access and electrical sockets at every seat. Modern and comfortable overnight trains operate on the longer routes going from north to south (some even have onboard cinemas), or to international destinations such as Oslo and Berlin.

Trains are operated by **Swedish State Railways (Statens Järnvagär).** For train information, call © **0771/75-75-75,** or visit **www.sj.se.**

RESERVATIONS   At train stations in Sweden, ask for a free copy of *SJ Tagtider,* the rail timetable. Unlike many of its fellow European countries, Swedish trains are generally devoid of surcharges and reservations are not mandatory except on the high-speed X2000 train and the night trains. If you purchase a regular rail ticket on the X2000, a seat reservation will be included in the price as it will on the night trains. On other trains a seat reservation costs extra.

For those with a railpass, typical reservations cost around 35SEK ($4.90/£2.45) for a seat on an InterCity train, 65SEK ($9.10/£4.55) on an X2000, and 150SEK ($21/£10.50) for a couchette. Railpass holders don't have to pay a supplement on regional trains and often aren't charged on IC trains either.

Policies may differ slightly on non-SJ trains in Sweden. More than two-dozen regional train services are called *Länstrafik* and are run by the various provinces of Sweden, though these are run in close cooperation with SJ. Your international railpass should be valid on most regional trains.

SERVICES & AMENITIES   In first-class compartments, passengers are served hot meals in their seats (and on the X2000 a light meal comes as part of the seat price). In second-class cars, meals are served in a bistro coach. All InterCity trains sell meals and refreshments such as snacks and drinks, and many have family cars with play facilities for kids. The X2000 trains offer audio channels and computer outlets, as well as a wireless network for those who have a laptop and want to access the Internet.

Overnight accommodation, where available, ranges from clean and comfortable couchettes to exclusive two-bed compartments with a shower and toilet. Generally speaking, sleepers in Scandinavia aren't a particularly expensive venture and cost less than in other European countries.

Note: Second class on Swedish trains is the same as first class in many countries to the south so you may want to save the extra kronor.

FAST FACTS: Sweden

Area Code The international country code for Sweden is **46**. The local city code for Stockholm is **08**; for Uppsala, it's **18**; and for Gothenberg, it's **31**.

Business Hours Generally, **banks** are open Monday through Friday from 10am to 3pm (Thurs until 4:30 or 5pm). In some larger cities banks extend their hours, usually on Thursday or Friday, until 5:30 or 6pm. Most **offices** are open Monday through Friday from 8:30 or 9am to 5pm (sometimes to 3 or 4pm in the summer); on Saturday, offices and factories are closed, or open for only a half day. Most **stores and shops** are open Monday through Friday between 9:30am and 6pm, and on Saturday from 9:30am to somewhere between 1 and 4pm. Once a week, usually on Monday or Friday, some of the larger stores are open from 9:30am to 7pm (July–Aug to 6pm). Some city stores also open on a Sunday between noon and 4pm.

Climate It's hard to generalize Sweden's climate. The country as a whole has many sunny summer days, but it's not super hot. July is the warmest month, with temperatures in Stockholm and Gothenburg averaging around 64°F (17°C). February is the coldest month, when the temperature in Stockholm averages around 26°F (–3°C), and Gothenburg is a few degrees warmer. It's not always true that the farther north you go, the cooler it becomes. During the summer, the northern parts of the country (Halsingland to northern Lapland) may suddenly have the warmest weather and bluest skies. The southern coast, warmed by the Gulf Stream, can be pleasantly hot in the summer, but don't count on it.

Currency The country's currency is the Swedish krona (SEK), which has 100 ore to the krona (plural form is *kronor*). The exchange rate in this book is calculated at 7.20SEK = $1 and 13.70SEK = £1.

Documents Required U.S. and Canadian citizens with a **valid passport** don't need a visa to enter Sweden if they don't expect to stay more than 90 days and don't expect to work there.

Electricity In Sweden, the electricity is 220 volts AC (50 cycles). To operate North American hair dryers and other electrical appliances, you'll need an electrical transformer or converter, and adaptor plugs that fit the two-pin round continental electrical outlets that are standard in Sweden. Transformers and adaptors can be bought at hardware stores or travel shops.

Embassies & Consulates All embassies are in Stockholm. The Embassy of the **United States** is at Dag Hammarskjölds Väg 31, S-115 89 Stockholm (© **08/783-53-00**; www.stockholm.usembassy.gov); the **Canadian Embassy** is at Tegelbacken 4, S-103 23 Stockholm (© **08/453-30-00**; www.canadaemb.se).

Health & Safety Sweden is viewed as a "safe" destination, although problems, of course, can and do occur anywhere. You don't need to get shots, the produce is safe, and the water in cities and towns potable. It is easy to get a prescription filled in towns and cities, and nearly all cities and towns throughout Sweden have hospitals with English-speaking doctors and well-trained medical staffs. Watch out for pickpockets in the cities where travelers are targeted for their passports and cash.

Holidays Sweden celebrates the following public holidays: New Year's Day (Jan 1); Epiphany (Jan 6); Good Friday; Easter Sunday; Easter Monday; Labor Day (May 1); Ascension Day (mid-May); Whitsunday (late May); National Day (June 6); Midsummer Eve and Day (late June); All Saints' Day (late Oct/early Nov); Christmas Eve, Christmas Day, and Boxing Day (Dec 24–26); and New Year's Eve (Dec 31). Inquire at a tourist bureau for the dates of the holidays that vary.

Legal Aid While traveling in Sweden, you are, of course, subject to that country's laws. If arrested or charged, you can obtain a list of private lawyers from the U.S. Embassy to represent you.

Mail Post office services are now incorporated in shops and kiosks so their hours vary. To send a postcard or letter not weighing more than 20 grams ($^7/_{10}$ oz.) to North America costs 10SEK ($1.40/70p) by airmail, which takes about 5 days. Mailboxes carry a yellow post horn on a blue background. You also can buy stamps in most tobacco shops and stationers.

Police & Emergencies In an emergency, dial © **112** anywhere in the country. These calls are free from payphones.

Telephone Instructions in English are posted in public phone boxes, which can be found on street corners. Payphones in Sweden take credit cards or phone cards, which can be purchased at most newspaper stands and tobacco shops.

Tipping Hotels include a 15% service charge in your bill. Restaurants, depending on their class, add 13% to 15% to your tab. Taxi drivers are entitled to 10% of the fare, and cloakroom attendants usually get 7SEK ($1/50p).

2 Stockholm

Stockholm has the biggest airport in the country, so many rail passengers fly into Stockholm and then use the time saved to explore not only Sweden's capital, but other major rail destinations in the country, including Gothenburg. And, as the country's rail hub, Stockholm also has the best rail connections in Sweden; all of the major

Stockholm

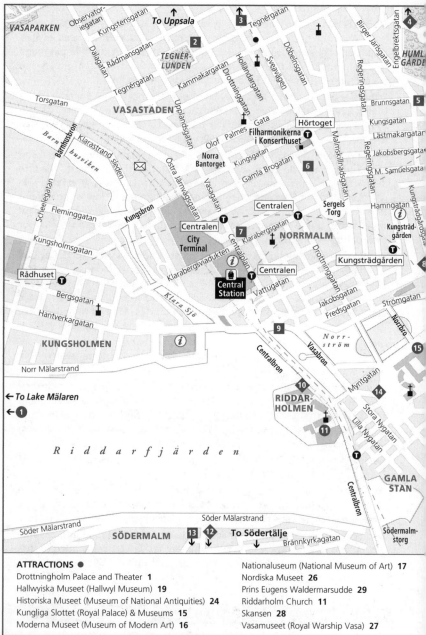

ATTRACTIONS ●

Drottningholm Palace and Theater **1**
Hallwyiska Museet (Hallwyl Museum) **19**
Historiska Museet (Museum of National Antiquities) **24**
Kungliga Slottet (Royal Palace) & Museums **15**
Moderna Museet (Museum of Modern Art) **16**

Nationaluseum (National Museum of Art) **17**
Nordiska Museet **26**
Prins Eugens Waldermarsudde **29**
Riddarholm Church **11**
Skansen **28**
Vasamuseet (Royal Warship Vasa) **27**

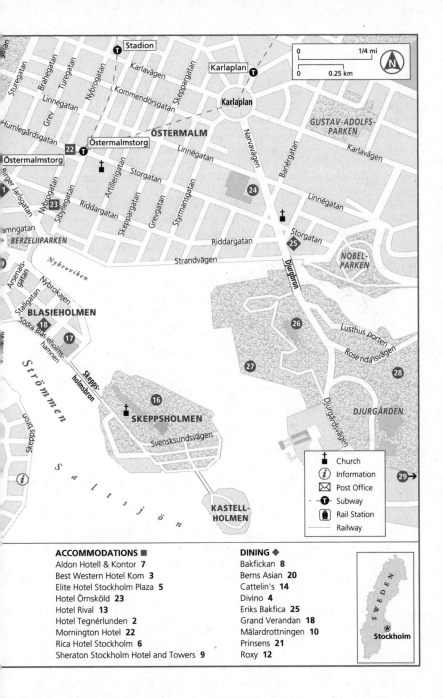

ACCOMMODATIONS ■
Aldon Hotell & Kontor **7**
Best Western Hotel Kom **3**
Elite Hotel Stockholm Plaza **5**
Hotel Örnsköld **23**
Hotel Rival **13**
Hotel Tegnérlunden **2**
Mornington Hotel **22**
Rica Hotel Stockholm **6**
Sheraton Stockholm Hotel and Towers **9**

DINING ◆
Bakfickan **8**
Berns Asian **20**
Cattelin's **14**
Divino **4**
Eriks Bakfica **25**
Grand Verandan **18**
Mälardrottningen **10**
Prinsens **21**
Roxy **12**

tourist destinations are within easy reach, many no more than 3 hours or so away. And thanks to the natural beauty of the country, every major train journey out of the capital is scenic.

Stockholm effortlessly combines more than 7 centuries' worth of beautiful architecture, from the crazy cobblestone streets of its medieval old town to the clean lines of the granite, marble, and glass towers of its modern new town. It's located at a point where the waters of Lake Mälaren join the Baltic Sea, right on the doorstep of an archipelago of 24,000 islands, skerries, and islets. But even more than its well-tended past and forward-looking present, Stockholm is most famously a world showcase of democratic socialism. It is a city that is both clean and well planned, a savvy and sophisticated metropolis whose cultural attractions and entertainment venues rival those of Europe's other great capitals.

Give it at least 3 days and know that you will have scratched only the surface of its allure. Note, however, that rail passengers should avoid a winter visit, when many of Stockholm's major attractions, including all the outdoor ones, close down. The cold weather sets in by October, and you'll need to keep heavily wrapped up well past April.

STATION INFORMATION
GETTING FROM THE AIRPORT TO THE TRAIN STATION
You'll wing your way into Stockholm's **Arlanda Airport** (© 08/797-60-00; www.arlanda.com), approximately 28 miles (45km) north of the city center on the E4 highway. A long covered walkway connects the international and domestic terminals should you be flying in from Gothenburg or some other Swedish city.

For rail travelers, the fastest and cheapest way to go from the airport to the Central Station within Stockholm is on the high-speed **Arlanda Express** train (trip time: 20 min.), which is covered by the Eurail Pass. Trains run every 15 to 30 minutes daily from 5am to 1am. If you don't have a railpass, the cost of a one-way ticket is 200SEK ($28/£14), although there are often deals during the summer. For more information, call **020/22-22-24** or go online to **www.arlandaexpress.com.**

Another option is to take the Flygbussarna Bus (**www.flygbussarna.com**) outside the airport entrance to Central Station. A round-trip ticket costs 175SEK ($24.50/£12.25); one-way fare is 95SEK ($13.30/£6.65). Buses run from 4:50am to 12:30am. The trip takes 40 minutes or so depending on traffic. A taxi from the airport costs 400SEK to 600SEK ($56–$84/£28–£42). Most cab companies have an airport-to-city fixed price of around 445SEK to 475SEK ($62.30–$66.50/£31.15–£33.25); a 10% tip is standard.

At the **Centralstationen** (Central Station; © **0771/75-75-75**) you can connect with Stockholm's efficient subway system, called the T-bana. The Central Station is directly across from the bus station, **Cityterminalen (City Terminal)** at Klarabergsviadukten 72 (© **08/440-85-70**). Both the bus and train stations are serviced by the T-bana Centralen stop.

INSIDE THE STATION
The Central Station is convenient to any number of affordable hotels in the area and is one of the better equipped stations in the north of Europe, featuring a number of shops on its lower level, and kiosks selling everything from food and beverage to tobacco and newspapers—there's even a casino. There are also cafes, pubs, restaurants, and fast-food chains, plus a **Konsum,** evocative of an American supermarket. The food service ranges from a cafeteria to a first-class restaurant.

Train information is prominently displayed on bulletin boards in several key places just inside the main entrance to the Central Station. In the main hall is a large ticket office where train reservations can be made, including reservations for sleeper-car accommodations. Hours are Monday to Sunday 5am to 12:30am.

Also at the station is a currency exchange kiosk, **Forex** (© **08/416-67-34;** www.forex.se), open daily 7am to 9pm. Lockers at the station cost 30SEK to 60SEK ($4.20–$8.40/£2.10–£4.20) per day.

INFORMATION ELSEWHERE IN THE CITY

The **Tourist Center** is at Sverigehuset (Sweden House), Hamngatan 27 (© **08/50-82-85-08;** www.stockholmtown.com). It's open Monday to Friday 9am to 7pm, Saturday 10am to 5pm and Sunday 10am to 4pm. Maps and other free tourist materials are available, and the staff can help you find the perfect hotel for your budget. If done in person, this service costs 75SEK ($10.50/£5.25), but it is free via phone or e-mail.

GETTING AROUND

You can travel throughout Stockholm by bus, local train, subway (T-bana), and tram, going from Singö in the north to Nynäshamn in the south. Routes are divided into zones, and one ticket is valid for all types of public transportation in the number of zones you have paid to travel in within an hour of being stamped. Subway entrances are marked with a blue T on a white background.

The basic fare for public transportation (subway, tram, streetcar, or bus) is 20SEK ($2.80/£1.40) per coupon, and you will need a minimum of two for most of Stockholm; the farther you go, the more coupons you need. To travel in all three zones you will need four units. Purchase a ticket for a tram or streetcar at the tollbooth found at every stop. You can transfer for free (or double back and return to your starting point) within an hour of your departure.

For information on all services, including buses, subways *(Tunnelbana),* and suburban trains *(pendeltåg),* call © **08/600-10-00** or head online to **www.sl.se/English**.

The SL Center, on the lower level of Sergels Torg (east of Central Station), provides transportation information. It also sells a map of the city's system, including suburban trains, and day and discount passes for public transportation. It's open Monday to Friday from 7am to 6:30pm, and Saturday and Sunday 10am to 5pm. In 2008, a new office is set to open in the lower hall of Central Station and will be open from Monday to Saturday 6:30am to 11:15pm and Sunday 7am to 11:15pm.

Your best transportation bet is to get a **travelcard.** A 1-day card costs 90SEK ($12.60/£6.30) and is valid for 24 hours of unlimited travel by T-bana, bus, and commuter trains within Stockholm. Most visitors will probably prefer the 3-day card for 190SEK ($26.60/£13.30), valid for 72 hours in Stockholm and the adjacent county. The 3-day card is also valid for reduced admission to the Skansen Museum, and free entry to the Kaknäs Tower and Gröna Lunds (Fun Fair). A card for a child 8 to 19 costs 55SEK ($7.70/£3.85) for 1 day or 115SEK ($16.10/£8.05) for 3 days. Kids under 7 travel free with an adult. Tickets are available at tourist information offices, in subway stations, and from most news vendors.

Stockholmskortet (Stockholm Card) is a discount card allowing unlimited travel by bus (except airport buses), subway, and local trains throughout the city and the surrounding county. Admission to 75 attractions is included in the package, as is a 1-hour sightseeing boat tour exploring either the royal or historical canals. The card is also good for ferry travel to Djurgården, a recreation area packed with museums and cafes. The card is an excellent buy, especially if you plan to do a lot of traveling by public transport around Stockholm to visit a lot of attractions.

You can buy the card at several places in the city, including the Tourist Center in Sweden House. The cards are stamped with the date and time of the first use. For a 24-hour card adults pay 290SEK ($40.60/£20.30), for 48 hours 420SEK ($58.90/£29.40), and for 72 hours 540SEK ($75.60/£37.80), with children paying 120SEK ($16.80/£8.40), 160SEK ($22.40/£11.20), and 190SEK ($26.60/£13.30), respectively.

Taxis in Stockholm are expensive, with fares varying between different firms. Meters start at around 45SEK ($6.30/£3.15), and even a short ride within the city can cost as much as 200SEK ($28/£14). You can hail cabs displaying the sign LEDIG, or you can order one by phone. **Taxi Stockholm** (© **08/15-00-00;** www.taxistockholm. se) is a large, reputable company.

WHERE TO STAY

By the standards of U.S. and Canadian cities, hotels in Stockholm are very expensive. But dozens of hotels in Stockholm offer reduced rates on weekends all year, and daily from around mid-June to mid-August. And, conveniently, many of the least expensive lodgings in the city are located near the Central Station.

Adlon Hotell & Kontor   This 1880s structure has seen many improvements and changes over the years, but much of the old architecture has been retained. It's a little short on style but big on comfort. The small to midsize bedrooms sport tiny bathrooms but have been modernized with functional Nordic furnishings. The hotel is just a few blocks away from Central Station and is convenient to public transportation. There's also free broadband Internet in every room.

Vasagatan 42, S-111 20 Stockholm. © 08/402-65-00. Fax 08/20-86-10. www.adlon.se. 94 units. 1,300SEK–2,295SEK ($182–$321/£91–£161) double. Rates include breakfast. T-bana: Centralen. **Amenities:** Bar; lounge; laundry; nonsmoking rooms; room for those w/limited mobility. *In room:* Hair dryer.

Best Western Hotel Kom *Value*   In the city center, about a 20-minute walk to Central Station, this hotel was carved out of a modernized hostel built in 1972 and it's still owned by the YMCA and YWCA. In May 2003, the hotel added 29 new rooms located in a nearby building equipped with its own breakfast room. Reflecting their hostel backgrounds, many rooms are quite small, but they are nicely furnished with a host of modern amenities and immaculate shower-only bathrooms.

17 Döbelnsgatan, S-111 40 Stockholm. © 08/412-23-00. Fax 08/412-23-10. www.komhotel.se. 128 units. 1,220–2,045SEK ($171–$286/£85.40–£143) double, budget rooms (with bunks) 600SEK ($84/£42) double. Rates include breakfast. Hostel-type shared rooms cost 500SEK–800SEK ($70–$112), without breakfast. **Amenities:** Breakfast room; bar; laundry; nonsmoking rooms; rooms for those w/limited mobility. *In room:* Hair dryer.

Elite Hotel Stockholm Plaza *&*   This top-rated and well-run hotel is set on a triangular piece of land about a 15-minute walk northeast of Central Station. The building is more than a century old but has kept abreast of the times with frequent modernizations. Since 1984, it's been one of the most respectable midbracket hotels of central Stockholm. The renovated bedrooms are small to midsize, and furnished functionally but comfortably, each with a tiled bathroom. The hotel has a sauna available for private use.

Birger Jarlsgatan 29, S-103 95 Stockholm. © 08/566-22-000. Fax 08/566-22-020. www.elite.se. 143 units. 1,100SEK–2,700SEK ($154–$378/£77–£189) double; from 1,900SEK ($266/£133) suite. Rates include breakfast. AE, DC, MC, V. T-bana: Hötorget or Östermalmstorg. **Amenities:** Restaurant; bar; laundry, nonsmoking rooms. *In room:* Hair dryer.

Hotel Örnsköld *(Value)*   Near the Royal Dramatic Theatre (it attracts an artistic crowd), this hotel is east of Central Station but still convenient to the city center. Built in 1910, it's undergone frequent renovations but nevertheless retains a slightly old-fashioned appeal. The high-ceilinged rooms, on the floor above street level, have modern furnishings, some a little worn, but all immaculately kept. Some of the larger rooms have space for extra beds, and each room comes with a neat little shower-only bathroom.

Nybrogatan 6, S-114 34 Stockholm. © **08/667-02-85.** Fax 08/667-69-91. www.hotelornskold.se. 27 units. 1,295SEK–2,195SEK ($181–$307/£90.65–£154) double. Rates include breakfast. AE, MC, V. T-bana: Östermalmstorg. **Amenities:** Nonsmoking rooms. *In room:* Hair dryer.

Hotel Rival   This charming boutique hotel—once the grand Aston Hotel, which had its heyday in the 1930s—was opened in 2003 by Benny Anderson of ABBA. The decor is first class, elegant, and modern. Rooms sport high-tech conveniences such as plasma-screen TVs and DVD players (there's an ever-changing and up-to-date library of free English-language DVDs downstairs), along with marble bathrooms and Egyptian cotton linens. Other alluring extras include a comfortable movie theater. It's just south of the Old Town.

Mariatorget 3, SE-118 91 Stockholm. © **08/54-57-89-00.** Fax 08/754-57-89-24. www.rival.se. 99 units. Mon–Thurs 2,190SEK–3,090SEK ($307–$433/£153–£216) double; Fri–Sun 1,440SEK–3,090SEK ($202–$433/£101–£216). Weekend rates include breakfast. AE, DC, MC, V. **Amenities:** Restaurant; bar; lounge; laundry; nonsmoking rooms; rooms for those w/limited mobility. *In room:* Hair dryer.

Hotel Tegnérlunden *(★)*   Like a London town house hotel, this hidden gem lies next to a leafy park, which is unusual for Stockholm. It features an airy rooftop breakfast room, and despite a big expansion, retains a personal atmosphere. Rooms are tasteful and functionally furnished but a long way from cutting edge. Those we saw were well maintained and blissfully quiet, especially those opening out onto the rear. The bathrooms, equipped with shower units, are small but beautifully kept.

Tegnérlunden 8, S-113 59 Stockholm. © **08/5454-5550.** Fax 08/5454-5551. www.hoteltegnerlunden.se. 102 units. 1,775SEK ($233/£123) double. Rates include buffet breakfast. AE, DC, MC. Bus: 40, 47, 53, or 65. **Amenities:** Breakfast room; bar; laundry; nonsmoking rooms. *In room:* hair dryer.

Rica Hotel Stockholm   This first-class hotel is just 1,290 feet (387m), and an easy walk, from Central Station. Built in the early 1980s, it offers rooms large on international style and comfort but short on local charm. The midsize bedrooms are tasteful and functionally furnished. The large bountiful breakfast buffet is served in a lovely winter garden.

Slöjdgatan 7, S-111 57 Stockholm. © **08/723-72-00.** Fax 08/723-72-09. www.rica.se. 292 units. 1,220SEK–2,245SEK ($171–$314/£85.40–£157) double, with the cheaper prices on the weekend. Rates include breakfast. AE, DC, MC, V. **Amenities:** Lunch restaurant; bar; lounge; laundry; nonsmoking rooms; rooms for those w/limited mobility. *In room:* Hair dryer.

Sheraton Stockholm Hotel and Towers   Just a 2-minute walk from the Central Station, this eight-story hotel looks out on the Old Town, Lake Mälaren, and City Hall. It went through a total renovation in 2007 and what it lacks in old-fashioned Swedish charm, it makes up for with strikingly modern facilities, including a new fitness center. Bedrooms are spacious and luxuriously furnished; all the important amenities—and then some—are here. Because it has lots of rooms to fill, rates here can vary wildly.

Tegelbacken 6, S-101 23 Stockholm. ℂ **800/325-3535** in the U.S., or 08/412-34-00. Fax 08/12-34-09. www.sheraton. com/stockholm. 464 units. 1,295SEK–1,950SEK ($181–$273/£90.65–£137) double; from 4,400SEK ($616/£308) suite. AE, DC, MC, V. T-bana: Centralen. **Amenities:** Restaurant; bar; laundry; nonsmoking rooms; rooms for those w/limited mobility. *In room:* Hair dryer.

TOP ATTRACTIONS & SPECIAL MOMENTS

Even on the most cursory visit to the city, take the ferry to **Djurgården** to visit the **Vasa Ship Museum,** the city's most celebrated attraction, and the open-air **Skansen Folk Museum.** In the afternoon take a walking tour of **Gamla Stan (Old Town)** and perhaps have dinner here. On the second day get up early and go for a boat cruise of the archipelago and catch such cultural highlights as **Kungliga Slottet (Royal Palace)** or the **National Museum of Art.** If you have a third day, prepare to descend on the **Drottningholm Palace and Theater** or take a day tour to the ancient university city of **Uppsala.**

Drottningholm Palace and Theater ★★★ On an island in Lake Mälaren, Drottningholm (Queen's Island) has been dubbed the Versailles of Sweden. The majesty of this 17th century Renaissance palace was enlivened by additional elements of the French baroque and rococo trends of later years. It is about 7 miles (11km) from Stockholm and is easily reached by boat (the best method), bus, or subway. The palace—loaded with courtly art and furnishings—is surrounded by fountains and parks, and still functions as one of the official residences of the country's royal family.

Nearby is the **Drottningholm Slottsteater (Drottningholm Court Theater),** which grew to fame under Gustavus III, himself an accomplished playwright and actor. The best-preserved 18th-century theater in the world, it still uses its original stage, sets, and machinery. Each summer, between May and September, operas and ballets are staged in full 18th-century regalia, complete with period costumes and wigs. In addition to touring the stage, auditorium, and dressing rooms, visitors can also pop into the gift shop.

One other item of interest: The **Chinese Pavilion** is located on the palace grounds and must not be missed. It was built during the rococo conquest of Europe, when everything Oriental came into fashion, and rivals the Brighton Pavilion for its whimsical splendor.

Ekerö, Drottningholm. Palace: ℂ 08/402-62-80. www.royalcourt.se. 70SEK ($9.80/£4.90) adults, 35SEK ($4.90/ £2.45) students and children under 19, free for children under 7; Chinese Pavilion 60SEK ($8.40/£4.20) adults, 30SEK ($4.20/£2.10) students and children under 19, free for children under 7. Theater: ℂ 08/759-0406. www.dtm.se. 60SEK $(8.45) adults, 40SEK ($5.60) students. Free for children under 16. Palace and Chinese Pavilion Oct–Apr Sat–Sun noon–3:30pm; May–Aug daily 10am–4:30pm; Sept daily noon–3:30pm. Theater, guided tours in English every hour on the hour, May daily 12:30–4:30pm; June–Aug daily 11am–4:30pm; Sept daily 1–3:30pm. T-bana: Brommaplan, then bus no. 301 or 323 to Drottningholm. Ferry from the dock near City Hall.

Hallwylska Museet (Hallwyl Museum) ★ *Finds* To visit the former home of Countess Wilhelmina von Hallwyl is to wander back into a time capsule of the Belle Epoque. The countess was a world-class collector of art and objets d'art, and she spent the better part of 7 decades acquiring an astonishing collection of priceless paintings, silver, armor, weapons, rare tapestries, glass, and more—she collected virtually anything, even buttons and umbrellas. The house was built to Wilhelmina's specifications in the 1890s and despite its Renaissance- and Gothic-inspired design, it had all the mod conveniences of the day: indoor plumbing, electricity, telephone, even an elevator. It was donated to the state in 1920, and that is precisely when the clock stopped running inside this fascinating, eccentric museum.

Hamngatan 4. © 08/519-55-599. www.lsh.se. Guided tours 60SEK ($8.40/£4.20) adults, children under 18 free. Guided tours in English July–Aug Tues–Sun at 1pm; Sept–June Sun at 1pm. T-bana: Östermalmstorg.

Historiska Museet (Museum of National Antiquities) ✰✰

Among other allures, this museum boasts one of the most precious collections of gold in the world. The *Guldrummet* or **Gold Room** ✰✰✰ is an underground vault accessed to the right of the main entrance. In all, there are 3,000 gold and silver objects displayed in this room, dating from about 2,000 B.C. to A.D. 1520. The room also displays Viking silver and gold jewelry, and other precious items, many unearthed from ancient burial sites. Collections include Viking stone inscriptions and coins minted in the 10th century.

Narvavägen 13–17. © 08/519-556-00. www.historiska.se. 50SEK ($7/£3.50) adults; 40SEK ($5.60/£2.80) students/seniors; free for children under 19. May–Sept daily 10am–5pm; Oct–Apr Tues–Sun 11am–5pm (late view Thurs till 8pm). T-bana: Karlaplan or Östermalmstorg. Bus: 44, 47, 56, 69, or 76.

Kungliga Slottet (Royal Palace) & Museums ✰✰

The pride of Gamla Stan (Old Town), this 608-room showcase is one of the few palaces in Europe still in use as the official home for a monarch (though the king and queen prefer Drottningholm) that may be visited by the general public. Built principally in the Italian baroque style, between 1691 and 1754, it can easily take up to 3 hours to tour.

The highlights here are the **Royal Apartments** ✰✰, with their magnificent baroque ceilings and fine tapestries. The State Apartments have the oldest palace interiors, having been decorated in 1690 by French artists; look for at least three magnificent baroque ceiling frescoes and fine tapestries.

Nearly all visitors head for the **Royal Armoury** *(Livrustkammaren)* ✰✰ in the cellars of the palace. Here you can view weapons and armor, check out the gilded coaches ridden in by kings, and look at coronation outfits, some dating from the 16th century. *Skattkammaren,* the **Royal Treasury** ✰✰, contains one of the best-known collections of crown jewels in Europe, including a dozen crowns, scepters, and orbs along with stunningly beautiful pieces of antique jewelry. The most outstanding exhibit here is King Erik XIV's coronation regalia from 1561. Gustav III's collection of sculpture from the Roman Empire can be viewed in the **Antikmuseum (Museum of Antiquities).**

Slottsbacken 1, Gamla Stan (Old Town). © 08/402-61-30. www.kungahuset.se. Combination ticket to all parts of palace except the Royal Armory 130SEK ($18.20/£9.10) adults, 65SEK ($9.10/£4.55) students and children under 19. Entrance to the Royal Armory 50SEK ($7/£3.50); free for students and children under 19. May close without warning for state visits and royal receptions. Generally opening hours are as follows: Apartments and Treasury Feb 1–May 14 Tues–Sun noon–3pm; May 15–Aug 31 daily 10am–5pm; Sept 1–Sept 14 Mon–Sat 10am–4pm, Sun noon–3pm; Sept 15–Jan 7 Tues–Sun noon–3pm. Closed mid-Jan to end of Jan and during government receptions. Museum of Antiquities May 15–31 and Sept 1–14 daily 10am–4pm; June–Aug daily 10am–5pm. Royal Armory Sept–Apr Tues–Sun 11am–4pm; May–Aug daily 11am–4pm. T-bana: Gamla Stan. Bus: 2, 43, 55, 71, or 76.

Moderna Museet (Museum of Modern Art) ✰✰

On the tiny island of Skeppsholmen, this museum focuses on contemporary works by Swedish and international artists, including kinetic sculptures. In addition to changing exhibitions that have been known to kick up controversy, there's a small but excellent collection of cubist art by Picasso, Braque, and Léger; Matisse's *Apollo* decoupage; the famous *Enigma of William Tell* by Salvador Dalí; and works by Brancusi, Max Ernst, Giacometti, Arp, and more. Other works include the 12-foot-high (3.6m) *Geometric Mouse* by Claes Oldenburg; *Fox Trot,* an early Warhol; and *Total Totality All,* a huge sculpture by Louise Nevelson.

Skeppsholmen. © 08/519-55-200. www.modernamuseet.se. 80SEK ($11.20/£5.60) adults; 60 SEK ($8.40/£4.20) students/seniors; free for children under 19. Tues 10am–8pm; Wed–Sun 10am–6pm. T-bana: T-Centralen. Bus: 65.

Moments   A Walk Back into Time

Gamla Stan ✦✦✦, or the Old Town of Stockholm, is spread over four islands and contains two of our top sights: the Royal Palace and Riddarholm Church. But with its narrow lanes and medieval buildings, Gamla Stan is a major attraction in its own right. The old shops are well worth the trip, and they are backed up by a number of attractive, mainly expensive restaurants.

Stortorget, the old marketplace, is the center of Gamla Stan. Dominated by a rococo palace, most of its buildings date from the 16th and 18th centuries (the red building was constructed during the reign of the famous queen Christina). The **Stock Exchange** is housed in an 18th-century building and contains a museum (©08/534-81-818; www.nobelmuseum.se) open to the public.

The **Storkyrkan Church** ✦✦, or **Great Church,** the oldest church in Stockholm, was founded in the 13th century, but has been rebuilt many times since. It became Lutheran Protestant in 1527, 7 years after its darkest event, in which a Danish king invited 80 Swedish noblemen to dinner and had them beheaded in the courtyard, leaving their heads in a pile to warn dissidents. It is the scene of royal coronations, christenings, and weddings. The most celebrated sculpture is the immense *St. George and the Dragon* ✦✦✦, dating from 1489. The royal pews have been in service for 3 centuries, and the ebony and silver altar, dating from 1652, is stunning. You can also see the *Last Judgment,* which is said to be one of the largest paintings on earth. This is still an operating church, so confine your sightseeing to times when no services are being conducted. It's open from 9am to 7pm Monday through Saturday, 9am to 5:30pm on Sunday; admission is free.

Nationalmuseum (National Museum of Art) ✦✦   Had Queen Christina retained her crown and continued building her collection, Stockholm would surely have had a Prado or a Louvre. This museum isn't the Prado—nor is it the Uffizi—but it does contain a vast Swedish collection of masterpieces and is one of the most outstanding art museums in Northern Europe, filled with the works of old masters such as Rembrandt and Rubens.

Located at the tip of a peninsula on Södra Blasieholmshamnen, a short walk from the Royal Opera House, the Renaissance-style building houses world-class masterpieces from the early Renaissance to the beginning of the 20th century.

The first floor is devoted to applied arts (silverware, handcrafts, porcelain, Empire furnishings, and the like), but first-time visitors may want to head directly to the second-floor collection of masterpieces, which includes a notable collection of rare 16th-century Russian icons and Lucas Cranach's most amusing painting, *Venus and Cupid.*

The most important room in the entire gallery has one wall devoted to the works of Rembrandt (*Portrait of an Old Man* and *Portrait of an Old Woman*), along with his impressions of a maid (one of the more famous works in Stockholm). Other rooms offer exceptional paintings by Flemish, English, and Venetian masters. Exhibited also are important modern works—Manet's *Parisienne;* Degas's dancers; Rodin's nude male

(Copper Age); van Gogh's *Light Movements in Green;* and paintings by Renoir, notably *La Grenouillère.*

Södra Blasieholmshamnen. ✆ **08/519-54-300.** www.nationalmuseum.se. 80SEK ($11.20/£5.60) adults; 60 SEK ($8.40/£4.20) students/seniors; free for children under 19. Tues 11am–8pm (also on Thurs Sept 1–May 31); Wed–Sun 11am–5pm. T-bana: Kungsträdgården. Bus: 2, 55, 59, 62, 65, or 76.

Nordiska Museet (Nordic Museum) ⭐⭐
On the island of Djurgården, the outstanding Nordic Museum houses an impressive collection of more than a million implements, costumes, and furnishings depicting life in Sweden from the 1500s to the present day. Highlights of the rich and varied collection include dining tables laid with food and all the implements, one from each century, and period costumes ranging from matching garters and ties for men to the purple flowerpot hats of the strolling ladies of the 1890s. Anglers head for the basement, where there's an extensive exhibit of the tools of the Swedish fishing trade, plus relics once used by nomadic Lapps.

Djurgårdsvägen 6–16, Djurgården. ✆ **08/519-546-00.** www.nordiskamuseet.se. 60 SEK ($8.40/£4.20) adults; free for children under 19; free to all Wed Aug 1–May 30 4–8pm. June–Aug daily 10am–5pm; Sept–May Mon–Fri 10am–4pm (Wed 10am–8pm), Sat–Sun 11am–5pm. T-bana: Karlaplan. Bus: 44 or 47.

Prins Eugens Waldemarsudde ⭐⭐
The once-royal residence of the "painting prince," Prince Eugen (1865–1947), is today an art gallery, surrounded by a sculpture garden and overlooking the water. Donated by the prince to the city in his will, Waldemarsudde is on Djurgården. The prince was one of Sweden's major landscape painters and his most high-profile works are the murals inside City Hall. In the garden are statues by such sculptors as Rodin, and the house itself is a treasure to behold. At one time Prince Eugen possessed the largest art collection in Sweden, and some of it—works by Edvard Munch, for one—is on display.

Prins Eugens Väg 6. ✆ **08/545-837-00.** www.waldemarsudde.se. Admission 80SEK ($11.20/£5.60) adults, 60SEK ($8.40/£4.20) seniors/students, free for children under 19. Tues–Sun 11am–5pm (Thurs until 8pm). Bus: 47.

Riddarholm Church ⭐
The second-oldest church in Stockholm is on the tiny island of Riddarholmen, next to Gamla Stan. It was founded in the 13th century as a Franciscan monastery. Almost all the royal heads of state are entombed here, except for the elusive Christina, who is buried in Rome. Her father, Gustavus Adolphus II, who saw Swedish power reach its peak, is buried in a Dutch Renaissance chapel. There are three principal royal chapels, including one, the Bernadotte, that belongs to the present ruling family.

Riddarholmen. ✆ **08/402-61-30.** www.royalcourt.se. Admission 30SEK ($4.20/£2.10) adults, 10SEK ($1.40/70p) students and children 7–18, children under 7 free. June–Aug daily 10am–5pm; May 15–31 and Sept 1–14 daily 10am–4pm; closed rest of year. T-bana: Gamla Stan.

Skansen ⭐⭐⭐
Stockholmers call this 75-acre (30-hectare) open-air museum, with more than 150 antique buildings from the 17th and 18th centuries, "Old Sweden in a Nutshell," because it represents all of Sweden's provinces, from Lapland in the north to Skåne in the south. Founded in 1891, Skansen is the world's oldest open-air museum and comes complete with a zoo featuring Scandinavian fauna. Exhibits range from a windmill to a manor house to an entire town quarter. Browsers can explore the old workshops where craftspeople such as silversmiths and glassblowers plied their trade. These handicrafts are demonstrated here, along with more humble occupations such as weaving and churning butter. In summer, international stars perform at the auditorium here, and special events such as folk dancing and concerts are staged.

Djurgårdsslätten 49–51. ℂ **08/442-80-00.** www.skansen.se. Admission varies seasonally. 40SEK–100SEK ($5.60–$14/£2.80–£7) adults, 30SEK–40SEK ($4.20–$5.60/£2.10–£2.80) children 6–15, free for children 5 and under. Special events attract higher charges. Historic buildings Jan–Feb and Nov Mon–Fri 10am–3pm, Sat–Sun 10am–4pm; Mar–Apr and Oct daily 10am–4pm; May to late June daily 10am to 8pm; late June to Aug daily 10am to 10pm; Sept daily 10am–5pm; Dec daily 10am–3pm. Bus: 47 from central Stockholm. Ferry from Slussen.

Vasamuseet (Royal Warship Vasa) 𝓕𝓕𝓕   On a bright sunny Sunday, August 10, 1628, the Royal Flagship *Vasa*—ordered built by Gustavus Adolphus II—set sail on her maiden voyage and, much to the horror of onlookers, promptly keeled over and sank into the murky Stockholm harbor.

The *Vasa* was finally salvaged by Anders Franzén, an amateur marine archaeologist, in 1961. To everyone's amazement, she was fantastically well preserved. More than 4,000 coins, carpenter's tools, "Lübeck gray" sailor pants, fish bones, and other seagoing articles for the truncated trip were found aboard. All of the *Vasa* sculptures—97% of the 700 were found—are back on the ship, which looks stunning now that it is once again carrying grotesque faces, lion masks, fish-fashioned bodies, and other carvings, some with the original paint and gilt still gleaming.

The great cabin of the ship has been rebuilt with the original oak panels decorated with elegant woodcarvings and ingenious foldout beds. Visitors can walk right through the cabin. Also, a 16-foot-long (4.8m) interior exposed-view model has been built; 90 dolls representing soldiers and crew show life aboard.

Galärvarvsvägen 14, Djurgården. ℂ **08/519-54-800.** www.vasamuseet.se. Admission 80SEK ($11.20/£5.60) adults, 40SEK ($5.60/£2.80) students, free for children under 19. June–Aug daily 8:30am–6pm; Sept–May daily 10am–5pm. Closed Jan 1, Dec 23–25 and 31. Bus: 44, 47, or 69. Ferry from Slussen year-round, from Nybroplan in summer only.

WHERE TO DINE

Bakfickan 𝓕 *Finds* SWEDISH   In-the-know local foodies gravitate to Bakfickan, which is far more affordable than it's more glamorous neighbor, Operakällaren, even though both restaurants use the same kitchen. Self-titled "the hip pocket," it's a help-yourself affair handing over authentic Swedish specialties such as reindeer, elk, and even delectable saffron-gold Arctic cloudberries. With only 28 eating stools set up around a counter, it fills up quickly in winter but has space outside during the warmer months.

Jakobs Torg 12. ℂ **08/676-58-09.** www.operakalleren.com. Reservations not accepted. Main courses 140SEK–245SEK ($19.60–$34.30/£9.80–£17.15). AE, DC, MC, V. Mon–Fri 11:30am–11:30pm, Sat noon–11:30pm. Closed Jan 1, 6–7, and Dec 24–26, 31. T-bana: Kungsträdgården.

Berns Asian 𝓕 MODERN ASIAN   Located in the swank Bern Hotel, this classic restaurant might have opened in 1860 as a "pleasure palace," but it's changed with the times and now looks to Asia for its inspiration. Three monumental chandeliers light the main hall, while the plush furniture described by August Strindberg in the Red Room (*Röda Rummet*) is still here. Dishes are plucked from across the Continent and range from dim sum to tempura to raw meats and fish.

Näckströmsgatan 8. ℂ **08/566-32-222.** www.berns.se. Reservations recommended. Main courses 150SEK–425SEK ($21–$59.50/£10.50–£29.75). AE, DC, MC. Sun–Thurs 11:30am–11pm; Fri–Sat 11:30am–1am. T-bana: Östermalmstorg.

Cattelin's *Value*   Since 1897, this old favorite has been feeding frugal Stockholmers—and feeding them well—from its location on a historic street about a half-mile (.8km) south of Central Station. Cattelin has survived not only wars but also changing tastes and still sticks to the tried and true, using fresh ingredients laced into grandmother's favorite salmon, veal, chicken, and beef dishes—all served in a convivial but noisy setting.

Storkyrkobrinken 9. © 08/20-18-18. Reservations recommended. Main courses 170SEK–220SEK ($23.80–$30.80/ £11.90–£15.40). AE, DC, MC, V. Mon–Fri 11am–10pm; Sat–Sun noon–10pm. T-bana: Gamla Stan.

Divino ⚑ TUSCAN   This elegant and pricey Italian restaurant is one of Stockholm's finest. The Tuscan menu, which includes dishes such as suckling pig with cauliflower and truffles, grilled tuna with lukewarm early spring salad, and scallops with avocado puree, is light-years away from your local trattoria. The wine cellar is particularly noteworthy. If the prices frighten you, check out the adjacent Divino Deli & Bar (same address) for something less elaborate, and for the best cappuccino in Stockholm.

Karlavägen 28. © 08/611-02-69. www.divino.se. Reservations recommended. Main courses 275SEK–295SEK ($38.50–$41.30/£19.25–£20.65). Fixed-price menus from 455SEK ($63.70/£31.85). AE, DC, MC, V. Mon–Sat 6–11pm. Bus: 1, 42, 44, 55, or 56.

Eriks Bakfica ⚑ (Value) SWEDISH   Swedes looking for *husmanskost* (wholesome home cooking) have been coming here since 1979. We always check out the array of daily herring appetizers, but what really attracts us is the tantalizing "archipelago stew," a ragout of fresh fish (it varies daily) prepared with tomatoes and served with garlic mayonnaise. If you drop in for lunch, ask for Erik's cheeseburger with "secret sauce" (it's not on the menu, so you need to request it).

Fredrikshovsgatan 4. © 08/660-15-99. www.eriks.se. Reservations recommended. Main courses 120SEK–295SEK ($16.80–$41.30/£8.40–£20.65). AE, DC, MC, V. Tues–Fri 11:30am–midnight; Sat 5pm–midnight; Sun 5–11pm. Bus: 47.

Grand Verandan ⚑ SWEDISH   Opposite the Royal Palace, the 1874 Grand Hotel, the finest in Sweden, is the setting for this first-class restaurant with panoramic views of the harbor. The chefs here are celebrated for their fabled smörgåsbord, offering up all the classic meats, fish, and cheeses, including herring and gravalax, plus some hot options. An a la carte menu is also served, with dishes ranging from sirloin of reindeer with artichoke terrine to seared filet of pike-perch with roasted beetroot.

In the Grand Hotel, Blasieholmshamnen 8. © 08/679-35-86. www.grandhotel.se. Reservations required. Main courses 145SEK–335SEK ($20.30–$46.90/£10.15–£23.45). Swedish buffet 395SEK ($55.30/£27.65). AE, DC, MC, V. Daily 11am–11pm. T-bana: Kungsträdgården. Bus: 46, 55, 62, or 76.

Mälardrottningen ⚑ (Finds) INTERNATIONAL   A rare chance to dine aboard the famous motor yacht once owned by Woolworth heiress Barbara Hutton, who entertained her husbands, including Cary Grant, aboard the vessel. Converted into a hotel and restaurant, it is an atmospheric dining choice with an international menu that changes seasonally but always uses very fresh produce. Service is formal and you can feast upon an array of top-notch dishes. Choose the less expensive option of breakfast to get a cheaper look at the boat.

Riddarholmen. © 08/545-187-80. www.malardrottningen.se. Reservations recommended. Main courses 105SEK– 235SEK ($14.70–$32.90/£7.35–£16.45). AE, DC, MC, V. Mon–Sat 6–11pm. T-bana: Gamla Stan.

Prinsens ⚑ SWEDISH   This enduring (it opened in 1897) and atmospheric restaurant has long been popular with artists and what used to be called "the bohemian fringe," and forcefully emphasizes good Swedish home cooking. Delights such as homemade lingonberry preserves go brilliantly with the game dishes of autumn. Seating is on two levels, but spills out onto the sidewalk when the summer sun shines.

Mäster Samuelsgatan 4. ✆ **08/611-13-31.** www.restaurangprinsen.com. Reservations recommended. Main courses 170SEK–300SEK ($23.80–$42/£11.90–£21). AE, DC, MC, V. Mon–Fri 11:30am–11:30pm; Sat 1–11:30pm; Sun 5–10:30pm. T-bana: Östermalmstorg.

Roxy ✻ INTERNATIONAL A restaurant-bar that's as cool as the surrounding Nytoget neighborhood and a hotspot on the gay scene (though it attracts a mixed and harmonious crowd). The menu is an interesting mix of Mediterranean and Scandinavian influences. Weekends at Roxy are lively, so call ahead to make reservations for the dining room. If you can't get a table, the food in the bar is excellent, and you'll get great music and a friendly staff thrown in for free.

Nytorget. ✆ **08/640-96-55.** www.roxysofo.se. Reservations recommended. Main courses 170SEK–240SEK ($23.80–$33.60/£11.90–£16.80). Dagens (daily) menu 72SEK ($10.10/£5.05). AE, MC, V. Tues–Thurs and Sun 5pm–midnight; Fri–Sat 5pm–1am. T-bana: Medborharplatsen.

SHOPPING

The quality of Swedish glass is known around the world, and functional Swedish design in furniture, often made of blond pine or birch, enjoys equal renown. Many visitors shop for handicrafts, especially woolen items. The favorite place for shopping is the network of cobblestone streets in **Gamla Stan,** near the Royal Palace, especially along **Västerlånggatan.** In central Stockholm, one of the main shopping drags is **Hamngatan.**

For pottery, try **Blås & Knåda,** Hornsgatan 26 (✆ **08/642-77-67;** www.blasknada. com), a cooperative of more than 40 Swedish ceramic artists and glassmakers selling high-quality products.

For one-stop shopping, visit one of Stockholm's major department stores, including its largest, **Åhléns City,** Klarabergsgatan 50 (✆ **08/402-80-00;** www.ahlens.com), which has a celebrated food department and first-class gift shop, along with a department selling Orrefors and Kosta Boda crystal. Its major competitor, in business since 1902, is **Nordiska Kompaniet (NK),** Hamngatan 18–20 (✆ **08/762-80-00;** www. nk.se), which also has a major department devoted to the sale of high-quality Swedish glass. In the basement you'll find thousands of various handicrafts. A final shopping stop that might interest you is **PUB Shopping Arcade,** Hötorget 13 (✆ **08/789-19-39;** www.pub.se), filled with boutiques and specialty departments, selling a lot of middle-priced clothing and high-quality housewares. Greta Garbo worked here before she became a famous actress.

One of the great showcases of Swedish handcrafts is **DesignTorget,** in the Kulturhuset, Sergels Torg 3 (✆ **08/508-31-520;** www.designtorget.se), which retails the work of nearly 200 Swedish craftspeople. This center is especially rich in pottery, furniture, textiles, clothing, pewter, and crystal.

Yet another artisan outlet is **Svensk Hemslojd,** Sveavägen 44 (✆ **08/23-21-15**), headquarters for the Society for Swedish Handcrafts, with a wide selection of elegant glassware, pottery, gifts, and wooden or metal handcrafts by some of Sweden's best-known artisans.

For home furnishings, Swedish style, the best outlet is **Nordiska Galleriet,** Nybrogatan 11 (✆ **08/442-83-60;** www.nordiskagalleriet.se), with two floors of beautifully styled yet functional furniture. One of Sweden's most prominent stores for home furnishings, **Svenskt Tenn,** Strandvägen 5 (✆ **08/670-16-00;** www.svenskttenn.se), has been a tradition since 1924. Look for one of Stockholm's best selections of furniture, printed textiles, lamps, glassware, china, and gifts.

Finally, and just for fun, head for **Östermalms Saluhall,** Nybrogatan 31 (**www. ostermalmshallen.se**). Sweden's most colorful indoor market is filled with vendors hawking cheese, meat, fresh vegetables, just-caught fish, and more. Plan to have lunch at one of the food stalls.

NIGHTLIFE

The greatest after-dark event is a performance at **Drottningholm Court Theater,** Drottningholms (© **08/660-82-25;** www.dtm.se), founded by Gustavus III in 1766 (p. 774). On Lake Mälaren, outside Stockholm, but easily reached by public transportation, it stages operas and ballets with performances in regalia, wigs, and period costumes from the 1700s. The theater's original stage, machinery, and nearly three dozen sets are still in use. Seating 450 patrons, the theater charges 165SEK to 610SEK ($23.10–$85.40/£11.55–£42.70) for its hard-to-get tickets. The season runs from May to September, with performances beginning at 4pm and 7:30pm.

Another major cultural venue, **Kungliga Operan (Royal Opera House),** Gustav Adolfs Torg (© **08/791-44-00;** www.operan.se), was also founded by Gustavus III, who was later assassinated here at a masked ball. This is the home of the Royal Swedish Opera and Royal Swedish Ballet. Tickets cost 100SEK to 410SEK ($14–$57.40/£7–£28.70) for most performances.

In summer, head for **Skansen,** Djurgården 49–51 (© **08/442-80-00;** www. skansen.se), which often stages folk dancing performances from June to August at 7pm. During the same period, outdoor dancing—everything from tango to ballroom—with live music takes place from Monday to Saturday, from 8pm to around midnight. In summer there are also concerts, singalongs, and guest performances by leading artists. See Skansen under "Top Attractions & Special Moments" (p. 777) for information on getting there and entrance fees (although evening events often attract higher prices).

MUSIC CLUBS   One of the most frequented nightclubs in Stockholm is **Café Opéra,** Operahuset, Karl XII's torg (© **08/676-58-07;** www.cafeopera.se), which has an elegant dance floor open nightly from 5pm to 3am, charging a cover of 140SEK ($19.60/£9.80) after 10pm. Another major entertainment emporium is **The Daily News Cafe,** in Sweden House, Kungsträdgården (© **08/21-56-55;** www.dailys.se), with a dance club upstairs and a much-frequented pub in the cellar. It's open Wednesday to Monday 9am to between 4 or 5am; cover is 80SEK to 160SEK ($11.20–$22.40/£5.60–£11.20).

The leading jazz club in town is **Stampen,** Stora Nygatan 5 (© **08/20-57-93;** www.stampen.se), attracting lovers of Dixieland played by the hottest jazz bands around. There's a dance floor downstairs. It's open Monday to Saturday 8pm to 1am, with a cover of 100SEK ($14/£7). **Engelen,** Kornamnstorg 59B (© **08/20-10-92;** www.wallmans.com), is a combination pub and nightclub charging a cover of 50SEK to 80SEK ($7–$11.20/£3.50–£5.60) after 8pm. Live performances—soul, funk, rock, whatever—fill the night. The pub is open Tuesday to Thursday 4pm to 1am, Friday and Saturday 4pm to 3am, Sunday 5pm to 3am; the nightclub's open daily from 10pm to 3am.

BARS   Stockholm's most unusual bar is **Icebar,** Nordic Sea Hotel Vasaplan 4–7 (© **08/505-63-124;** www.nordichotels.se), the world's first permanent ice bar, with temperatures kept at 27°F (–5°C) year-round. Even the cocktail glasses here are made of pure, clear ice shipped down from the Torne River in Sweden's Arctic north. Admission is 160SEK ($22.40/£11.20), which includes warm clothes and a welcome drink. Guests enter in 45-minute shifts. Booking is recommended, although between 9:45pm and 1am on a Friday or Saturday night you can simply stop by without calling ahead. Perhaps Stockholm's favorite bar—certainly the most central—is **Sturehof,** Stureplan 2 (© **08/440-57-30;** www.sturehof.com), a tradition since 1897. Housed in a covered arcade, with a live music and performance venue upstairs in the Obar, it is open Monday to Friday 11am to 2am, Saturday noon to 2am, and Sunday 1pm to 2am. Supermodels and a bevy of TV actors flock to **Blue Moon Bar,** Kungsgatan 18 (© **08/244-700;** www.bluemoonbar.se), with its black leather upholstery and chic atmosphere. You get recorded dance music for the cover of 120SEK ($16.80/£8.40). It's open Thursday to Sunday 10pm to 5am (8pm–4am Fri–Sat only during July).

AN EXCURSION TO UPPSALA

On the Fyrisån River, the ancient university city of Uppsala—easily reached by train—is 42 miles (68km) north of Stockholm and is the most popular day trip outside the capital. An important Viking settlement, Uppsala is also visited for its celebrated 15th-century cathedral and its 16th-century castle.

With its 40,000-plus students, Uppsala still reigns as one of the greatest centers of learning in Europe, as well as the ecclesiastical capital of Sweden. It enjoys a lovely setting in an urban environment of grand old churches and footbridges. One of its attractions is the former home of Swedish botanist Carl von Linné, with a predictably amazing garden. Film buffs already know Uppsala as the birthplace of Ingmar Bergman and the setting for his film classic *Fanny and Alexander.*

GETTING THERE   During the day, trains leave approximately every 45 minutes from Stockholm's Central Station to Uppsala, making the trip in 40 minutes. It's possible to go to Uppsala early in the morning, see the major attractions, and be back in Stockholm for dinner. Those with a valid railpass ride for free; otherwise, a second-class one-way ticket costs 64SEK ($8.95/£4.50).

Trains arrive in the heart of the city at the Uppsala Central Station, which is within easy walking distance of all the city's major attractions except for Gamla Uppsala (see below). The latter can be reached by bus no. 2 departing from the train terminal. The bus costs 20SEK ($2.80/£1.40) per ride. Buy your ticket directly aboard the bus, but note that the driver won't change any bill larger than 100SEK ($14/£7).

VISITOR INFORMATION   The **Uppsala Tourist Information Office** is at Fyris torg 8 (© **018/727-48-00;** www.uppland.nu), a 5-minute walk from the train station. It's open Monday to Friday 10am to 6pm, Saturday 10am to 3pm, and from July to mid-August Sunday noon to 4pm as well.

TOP ATTRACTIONS & SPECIAL MOMENTS

The crowning glory of Uppsala is **Domkyrkan** ★★, Domkyrkoplan 5–7 (© **018/ 18-72-01;** www.uppsaladomkyrka.se), a Gothic cathedral—the largest in Scandinavia—whose twin spires dominate the skyline at 400 feet (120m). Once severely damaged in a fire in 1702, it has been restored in the old style. Finished in 1270, for 3 centuries the cathedral was the coronation church for Sweden's monarchy; a dozen Swedish royals were crowned under the Coronation Vault between 1441 and 1719. Much of the original Gothic work can still be seen in the doorways.

The cathedral's greatest treasure is the 1710 **Baroque pulpit** ★★★, which was carved by Burchardt Precht based on designs of Nicodemus Tessin the Younger. King

Gustav Vasa is buried in the medieval Lady Chapel, and the Finsta Chapel is the setting for the display of the gilt and silver **Reliquary of St. Erik** ✸✸✸, made in 1579 and dedicated to the patron saint of Sweden. A **museum** ✸✸ in the north tower shelters a splendid collection of rare textiles, which date from the 12th century, as well as royal burial regalia from the Vasa tombs. Rare artifacts include a gold embroidered brocaded robe from the early 15th century that once belonged to Queen Margrethe.

Admission to the cathedral is free; admission to the museum costs 30SEK ($4.20/£2.10) adults. Children up to 16 enter free. The cathedral is open daily 8am to 6pm. The museum is open May to September Monday to Saturday 10am to 5pm, Sunday 12:30pm to 5pm. From October to April hours are Tuesday to Saturday 10:30am to 1:30pm, Sunday 12:30 to 4pm.

The Swedish botanist Carl von Linné (1707–78)—also known as Carolus Linnaeus—lived and worked at the **Linnaeus Garden & Museum,** Svartbäcksgatan 27 (📞 **018/471-25-76;** www.linnaeus.uu.se), where he developed a classification system for the world's plants and flowers still used today. His house is now a museum adjacent to a botanical garden with some 1,600 different plants. When von Linné died, curators found detailed sketches and descriptions of his garden, which has been authentically restored. Entrance to the museum and gardens costs 50SEK ($7/£3.50), free for children 15 and under. The museum and shop are open daily 11am to 5pm. The gardens are open May to September daily 11am to 8pm.

At the end of Drottinggatan is the **Carolina Rediviva (University Library),** Drottninggatan (📞 **018/471-39-00;** www.ub.uu.se), which houses over 2 million volumes and more than 40,000 manuscripts, many from the medieval era and among the rarest in Europe. This is the largest library in Sweden, and the home of the celebrated **Silver Bible Codex Argenteus** ✸✸, written in silver and gold letters on 187 leaves of purple parchment sometime around A.D. 520. It is the only extant book in the old Gothic script in the world. Among other rare treasures is the **Carta Marina,** a fairly accurate map of Scandinavia from 1539. Another rare treasure is **Codex Uppsaliensis,** the oldest manuscript (around 1300) of Snorre Sturtasson's *Edda*. Admission is 20SEK ($2.80/£1.40) adults; free for children under 12. It's open mid-June to mid-August Monday to Friday 9am to 5pm, Saturday 10am to 5pm, and Sunday 11am to 4pm; mid-August to mid-June Sunday 10am to 5pm.

If you have time, make your way to **Gamla Uppsala** ✸, 3 miles (4.8km) north of the center of Uppsala, which was the capital of the Svea kingdom some 15 centuries ago. An archaeological site includes a trio of **Royal Mounts** ✸✸✸ dating from the 6th century and believed to contain the pyres of three Swedish kings. On the site of an early pagan temple stands a badly damaged 12th-century parish church that was never properly restored. Swedish kings were crowned here before that role fell to Uppsala Cathedral. **Gamla Uppsala Museum,** Disavägen (📞 **018/23-93-00**), opened in 2000, helps to put the burial mounds and ancient stones in context, offering historical insights into this once-powerful pagan kingdom. Admission is 50SEK ($7/£3.50) for adults, 30SEK ($4.20/£2.10) for children 7 to 18 and students, and free for kids aged 6 and under.

WHERE TO DINE

If you're in Uppsala for lunch, head for the **Domtrappkällaren** ✸✸, Sankt Eriksgränd 15 (📞 **018/13-09-55;** www.domtrappkallaren.se), in the center city, an atmospheric choice constructed on the remains of an ecclesiastical compound from the 12th century. The dining room is made up of a series of rooms, some with vaulted ceilings, as well as one narrow room where unruly students were imprisoned in medieval times. The chefs don't depend on the mellow old atmosphere alone but turn out finely tuned Swedish cuisine made with fresh ingredients, including freshly caught salmon or else reindeer from the north, with game as an autumn specialty. Main courses cost 135SEK to 255SEK ($18.90–$35.70/£9.45–£17.85), and hours are Monday to Friday 11am to 11pm, and Saturday 5 to 11pm.

An alternative choice is **Restaurant Odinsborg** ✎, near the burial grounds in Gamla Uppsala (© 018/323-525; www.odinsborg.com), housed in a farmhouse built in the late 1890s. As befits its setting near a Viking royal graveyard, the restaurant uses an early medieval theme in its decor. Order traditional preparations of Swedish favorites, including smoked eel, fried herring, or marinated salmon. Main courses cost 120SEK to 200SEK ($16.80–$28/£8.40–£14), with the summer smorgasbord (served from May to August) going for 165SEK ($23.10/£11.55). It's open daily from 6pm until late with a cafe providing sustenance during the day.

3 Gothenburg

Göteborg (in Swedish) is Sweden's major port and largest city, as well as the gateway to northern Europe. Located at the mouth of the Göta River, it's especially convenient for the rail traveler as it lies equidistant from three Scandinavian capitals. Stockholm can be reached in 3 hours, Oslo in 4 hours. To get here from Copenhagen, you can take one of the many daily 35-minute train rides to the Swedish city of Malmö, and then travel north by train to Gothenburg (trip time: 3½ hr.).

Although filled with heavy industry, there is much in Gothenburg of interest to the visitor, including numerous museums and a huge summer amusement park. Gothenburg is also the best center for excursions to the fishing villages and holiday resorts strung along the western coast of Sweden.

STATION INFORMATION
GETTING FROM THE AIRPORT TO THE TRAIN STATION
Many residents of Sweden's west coast consider Copenhagen's airport more convenient than Stockholm's for getting to Gothenburg. For information on getting to Copenhagen, see "Getting There" in chapter 6.

Planes arrive from other areas of Europe at **Landvetter Airport** (© 031/94-10-00; www.lfv.se), 16 miles (26km) east of Gothenburg. An airport bus *(Flygbuss)* departs every 20 minutes (during peak times) for the half-hour ride to the city's central bus terminal, just behind Gothenburg's main railway station. Buses run daily between 5am and 12:30am. A one-way trip costs 75SEK ($10.50/£5.25). For more information, see **www.flygbussarna.com**.

INSIDE THE STATION
Trains arrive from all over Scandinavia at **Central Station** (© 0771/75-75-75), on one side of Drottningtorget. The station has an office of the national railroad company, SJ, selling rail and bus tickets for connections to nearby areas. Office hours are 7am to 10pm daily. You will also find all the usual conveniences of a major rail hub station, including currency exchange, luggage storage, and newsstands.

INFORMATION ELSEWHERE IN THE CITY
The **Gothenburg Tourist Office** is at Kungsportsplatsen 2 (© 031/61-25-00; www.goteborg.com). Open June and mid-August to late August daily 9:30am to 6pm; July

Gothenburg

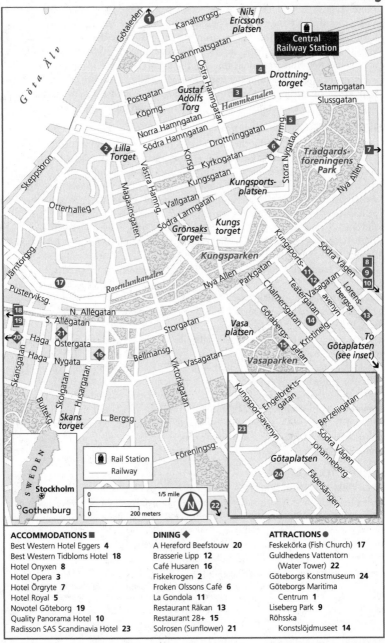

to mid-August daily 9:30am to 8pm; September to April Monday to Friday 9:30am to 5pm, Saturday 10am to 2pm. The staff here can make reservations in a hotel for a fee of 60SEK ($8.40/£4.20) per person, or you can book the Gothenburg Package without a charge. The package includes a stay in a hotel, breakfast, and a Gothenburg Pass (see below). Booking hotels through the tourist office online is also free.

Warning: The area around the station attracts a lot of unsavory characters at night, many intent on baiting visitors into hookups with prostitutes or else mugging them. Take precautions or a cab if you need to get to the station at night.

GETTING AROUND

Visitors usually find that the cheapest way to explore Gothenburg (besides on foot) is to buy a **Göteborgskortet (Gothenburg Pass).** Available at hotels, newspaper kiosks, and the city's tourist office (see above), it entitles you to unlimited travel on local trams, buses, and ferries. The card also covers many sightseeing attractions (including Liseberg Amusement Park), discounts at some shops and restaurants, and other extras (such as two-for-one airport bus travel), which makes the card worthwhile. A ticket valid for 24 hours costs 225SEK ($31.50/£15.75) for adults, 160SEK ($22.40/£11.20) for children; a 48-hour ticket is 310SEK ($43.40/£21.70) for adults and 225SEK ($31.50/£15.75) for children.

A single tram ticket costs 20SEK ($2.80/£1.40); a 24-hour travel pass (the "red day card") is 50SEK ($7/£3.50). If you don't have an advance ticket (recommended as it makes tram travel much cheaper; simply buy them from a Pressbyrån shop or kiosk near the tram stops), you can buy a ticket on board the tram. Make sure you have some change ready.

Taxis are not as plentiful as you might like. However, you can always find one by going to the Central Station. To call a **taxi,** dial Taxi **Göteborg** ✆ **031/65-00-00.** A taxi ride within the city limits costs 155SEK to 275SEK ($21.70–$38.70/£10.85–£19.35). With the Gothenburg Pass, you get a 10% reduction.

Bus and tram numbers and routes are currently in flux in Gothenburg. The bus and tram route numbers below were correct at the time of going to press but may have changed by the time you are reading this. Consequently, we recommend checking transport options with the tourist information office or staff at your chosen destination before you set off.

WHERE TO STAY

Best Western Hotel Eggers ⭐ *Finds*   Built in 1859, this is the second oldest hotel in Gothenburg, and it's still a favorite and going strong. Even better for rail travelers, it's right near Central Station. The hotel retains some of its old architectural allure—wood paneling, elaborate staircases, and stained-glass windows—though everything has been modernized. The individually decorated bedrooms vary in size but are attractive and comfortable, with large bathrooms.

Drottningtorget, S-401 25 Göteborg. ✆ **800/528-1234** in the U.S. and Canada, or 031/333-44-40. www.hotel eggers.se. Fax 031/333-44-49. 67 units. Mid-June to mid-Aug and Fri–Sat year-round 995SEK–1,530SEK ($139–$214/£70–£107) double; rest of year 1,780SEK–2,305SEK ($249–$323/£125–£161) double. Rates include breakfast. AE, DC, MC, V. Tram: 1, 3, 4, 5, 6, 7, 8, or 9. Bus: 40. **Amenities:** Restaurant; bar; laundry; nonsmoking rooms. *In room:* Hair dryer.

Best Western Tidbloms Hotel ⭐ *Finds*   There aren't enough affordable hotels in the city center, so if you're here in summer, you may want to take a tram to this hotel, located in a residential neighborhood 2 miles (3.2km) east of the rail station. The hotel dates from 1897 but has been completely modernized and enjoys the benefits of a tranquil and safe neighborhood. A conical tower, elaborate brickwork, and other 19th-century adornments are still in place. The midsize bedrooms with wooden floors are comfortably furnished, each equipped with a good-size bathroom. Guests like to meet each other in the little British-style library. The on-site restaurant, inspired by Scottish design and set in a cozy and inviting vault, is a local favorite.

Olskrosgatan 23, S-416 66 Göteborg. ⓒ 031/707-50-00. Fax 031/707-50-99. www.tidbloms.com. 42 units. Sun–Thurs 1,450SEK ($203/£102) double; Fri–Sat 940SEK ($132/£65.80) double. Rates include breakfast. AE, DC, MC, V. Tram: 1, 3, or 6. **Amenities:** Restaurant; bar; laundry; nonsmoking rooms; rooms for those w/limited mobility. *In room:* Hair dryer.

Hotel Onyxen *(Value)*   This family-owned and -run hotel is set inside a late-19th-century building that has been reconfigured into a more modern format. It's a good-value choice that's only a short tram ride from Central Station. The decor is more efficient than stylish. The midsize bedrooms rest under white, high ceilings and have shower-only bathrooms that are small but clean.

Sten Sturegatan 23, S-412 52 Göteborg. ⓒ 031/81-08-45. Fax 031/16-56-72. www.hotelonyxen.com. 34 units. Mid-June to mid-Aug and Fri–Sat year-round 990SEK–1190SEK ($139–$167/£69.30–£83.30) double; rest of year 1,190SEK–1,390SEK ($167–$195/£83.30–£97.30) double. Extra bed 200SEK ($28/£14). Rates include breakfast. AE, DC, MC, V. Tram: 4, 5, 6, or 8. **Amenities:** Bar; laundry; nonsmoking rooms. *In room:* Hair dryer.

Hotel Opera   Created from two 19th-century buildings that were joined together, renovated, and modernized, this well-run hotel appeals equally to business and leisure travelers. It's ideal for rail travelers, as it's only a couple of minutes' walk from Central Station. The midsize bedrooms are individually decorated and comfortably furnished; each has a small bathroom.

Norra Hamngatan 38, S-411 06 Göteborg. ⓒ 031/80-50-80. Fax 031/80-58-17. www.hotelopera.se. 75 units. 895SEK–1,450SEK ($125–$203/£62.65–£102) double. Rates include breakfast. AE, DC, MC, V. Tram: 1, 4, 5, 6, 7, 8, or 9. **Amenities:** Restaurant; bar; laundry; nonsmoking rooms. *In room:* Hair dryer.

Hotel Örgryte   This family-owned and -run hotel is a local favorite dating from the 1960s but massively upgraded in the 1990s. It's in the residential district of Örgryte, 1 mile (1.6km) east of the historic district, but is easily reached by a short bus ride. The hotel has streamlined, rather functional midsize bedrooms, although some are large enough to have sitting areas. The bathrooms are a bit small. The place is decent, well maintained, and affordable.

Danska Vägen 68–70, S-416 59 Göteborg. ⓒ 031/707-89-00. www.hotelorgryte.se. Fax 031/707-89-99. www.hotel orgryte.se. 70 units. Sun–Thurs 1,490SEK ($209/£104) double, mid-June to mid-Aug and Fri–Sat 940SEK ($132/£65.80) double. Rates include breakfast. AE, DC, MC, V. Bus: 60 or 62. **Amenities:** Restaurant; bar; laundry; nonsmoking rooms. *In room:* Hair dryer.

Hotel Royal   Just ¼ mile (.4km) from the train station, this is the oldest hotel in Gothenburg, dating back to 1852. The owners, the Oddestad family, have completely renovated it and added all the modern comforts, though the entrance hall is still imbued with a rich aura of the 1800s, with a painted glass ceiling and a staircase with wrought-iron banisters. The guest rooms come in various shapes and sizes, each with a good-size shower-only bathroom.

Drottninggatan 67, S-411 07 Göteborg. ⓒ 031/700-11-70. Fax 031/700-11-79. www.hotel-royal.com. 82 units. 1,395SEK–1,495SEK ($195–$209/£97.65–£105) double. Discounts may apply for weekends and summer. Rates include buffet breakfast. AE, DC, MC, V. Tram: 1, 3, 4, 5, or 6. Bus: 60. **Amenities:** Nonsmoking rooms. *In room:* Hair dryer.

Novotel Göteborg ✦ This stylish, converted brewery is now one of the best hotels in Gothenburg, run by the French outfit Accor. Even though it lies 2½ miles (4km) from the center, it is easily reached by a series of trams and buses. Its style and comfort make it worth the trek outside the suggested inner core of the city. The 148 bedrooms contain many built-in pieces, all tasteful and inviting, and each room has a small bathroom with tub and shower. The sauna is a popular facility here.

Klippan 1, S-414 51 Göteborg. ✆ 800/221-4542 in the U.S., or 031/720-22-00. Fax 031/720-22-90. www.novotel.se. 149 units. Mon–Thurs 1,560SEK–1,690SEK ($218–$237/£109–£118) double; Fri–Sat 940SEK–1,040SEK ($132–$146/£65.80–£72.80) double. Limited number of discounted rooms in summer. Rates include breakfast. AE, DC, MC, V. Tram: 3 or 9. Bus: 91 or 92. **Amenities:** Restaurant; bar; laundry; nonsmoking rooms; rooms for those w/limited mobility. *In room:* Hair dryer.

Quality Panorama Hotel ✦ *Finds* Only a 10-minute walk from the city center, this 13-story hotel is one of the tallest buildings in Gothenburg. The best and most accessorized rooms are on floors 7 to 13. The larger ones were refurbished in 2005. The plant-filled lobby, lit by a skylight, is home to a mezzanine restaurant and a piano bar. Bedrooms are well furnished and bright, each featuring wooden floors and double-glazed windows. Bathrooms, though small, are neatly kept with adequate shelf space.

Eklandagatan 51–53, S-400 22 Göteborg. ✆ 031/767-70-00. Fax 031/767-70-70. www.panorama.se. 338 units (some with shower only). 990SEK–1,995SEK ($139–$279/£69.30–£140) double. Rates include breakfast. AE, DC, MC, V. Closed Dec 21–Jan 7. Tram: 4 or 5. Bus: 40 or 51. **Amenities:** Restaurant; bar; laundry; nonsmoking rooms. *In room:* Hair dryer.

Radisson SAS Scandinavia Hotel ✦✦✦ If you can afford it, this hotel offers some of the best living in Gothenburg and is ideally located opposite the rail station. Surrounding a large atrium, it opened in 1986, but has kept abreast of the times ever since; many of the rooms received a touch-up in 2006/2007. The bedrooms are spacious and luxuriously appointed, with well-maintained bathrooms. The hotel's health club has an indoor pool and the whole building has free Wi-Fi.

Södra Hamngatan 59–65, S-401 24 Göteborg. ✆ 800/333-3333 in the U.S., or 031/758-50-50. Fax 031/758-50-01. www.gothenburg.radissonsas.com. 349 units. 1,390SEK–2,150SEK ($195–$301/£97.30–£151) double; from 2,500SEK ($350/£175) suite. Rates include breakfast. AE, DC, MC, V. Tram: 1, 3, 4, 5, or 7. Bus: 40. **Amenities:** Restaurant; bar; laundry; nonsmoking rooms; rooms for those w/limited mobility. *In room:* Hair dryer.

TOP ATTRACTIONS & SPECIAL MOMENTS

If you're here in summer, be sure to enjoy a cup of coffee at one of the cafes along **Kungsportsavenyn** ✦, the pulsating artery of Gothenburg, which stretches from Götaplatsen north for ⅔ mile (1km) to the canal and Kungsportsplatsen. To walk this tree-lined boulevard (known locally as "The Avenyn") is to experience the "living room" of Gothenburg. Winter visitors can explore some of Gothenburg's numerous museums, including **Göteborgs Konstmuseum,** the **Göteborg Maritime Center,** and the **East India House.**

Göteborgs Konstmuseum ✦✦✦ This is the leading art museum of western Sweden. If your time is limited, take the elevator to the **Fürstenberg Gallery** ✦✦✦, established by arts patron Pontus Fürstenberg (1827–1902) to display works by Scandinavian artists living as expats in Paris in the 1880s. All the big names in Swedish art, including Prince Eugen and Carl Larsson, are on parade here, and the collection is also rich in the National Romantic movement of the 1890s. The other highlight of the museum is the octagonal **Arosenium Room** ✦✦✦, which is a delightful romp showcasing the whimsical paintings of artist Ivar Arosenius (1878–1909).

(Moments) Scenes from Gothenburg Life

Early risers can visit the daily **Fish Auction** ✦ at the harbor, the largest fishing port in Scandinavia. The entertaining sale begins at 7am sharp. You can also visit the **Feskekörka (Fish Church)**, on Rosenlundsgatan (**www.fiskekyrkan.se**), which is in the fish market. It's open Tuesday through Thursday from 9am to 5pm, Friday from 9am to 6pm, and Saturday from 10am to 2pm.

The traditional starting point for seeing Gothenburg is the cultural center, **Götaplatsen**. Its *Poseidon Fountain* is the work of Carl Milles, one of Sweden's most important sculptors. The big trio of buildings here is the Concert Hall, the municipally owned theater, and the Göteborgs Konstmuseum.

For a quick orientation to Gothenburg, visit the 400-foot-tall (120m) **Guldhedens Vattentorn (water tower)**, Syster Estrids Gata (© **031/82-00-09**); take tram 13 or bus 60 from the center of the city, about a 10-minute ride. The elevator ride up the tower is free, and there's a cafeteria/snack bar at the top. The tower is open May to September daily noon to 10pm.

Colorful lyricism explodes in the rooms beyond, as they are devoted to the "Göteborg Colorists," including Karl Isakson (1878–1922) and Carl Kylberg (1878–1952). Old Masters, including Rembrandt and Rubens, are also on exhibit, as are such contemporary achievers as Henry Moore and Francis Bacon. The gallery has an impressive collection of international art, notably French Impressionists, along with Bonnard, Cézanne, van Gogh, and Picasso, as well as sculpture by Carl Milles and Auguste Rodin.

Götaplatsen. © **031/61-29-80**. www.konstmuseum.goteborg.se. Admission 40SEK ($5.60/£2.80) adults, free for children under 20. Tues and Thurs 11am–6pm; Wed 11am–9pm; Fri–Sun 11am–5pm. Tram: 4 or 5. Bus: 40.

Göteborgs Maritima Centrum   This maritime museum is appropriately located on the harbor. This is a true floating museum of nearly a dozen ships, of which the destroyer, *Småland,* is the most formidable. Other highlights of the fleet include the submarine *Nordkaparen,* along with tugboats, a lightship, steamships, and other watercraft. When not sailing to Stockholm, the famous Göta Canal boats are berthed here, including the 1874 *Juno,* the 1912 *Wilhelm Tell,* and the 1931 *Diana.*

Packhuskajen 8. © **031/10-59-50**. www.goteborgsmaritimacentrum.com. Admission 75SEK ($10.50/£5.25) adults, 30SEK ($4.20/£2.10) children 7–15, free for children under 7. Mar–Apr, Sept–Oct daily 10am–4pm; May–Aug daily 10am–6pm; Nov Sat–Sun 10am–4pm. Closed Dec–Feb. Tram: 5 to Lilla Bommen.

Liseberg Park ✦✦   This amusement park is Sweden's number-one tourist attraction, drawing more than three million visitors annually. Launched in 1923, it has been amusing, wining, and dining Gothenburgers ever since, with its "gardens of delight," including splashing fountains, pleasure pavilions, festive lighting, and beds of flowers. Open-air vaudeville shows and musical performances are presented on various stages, and there are dozens of rides, including a brand-new wooden roller coaster—Scandinavia's largest. The park is dominated by the 492-foot-high (148m) **Liseberg Tower** ✦; the ride to the top is accompanied by sound and light and it climaxes with a vast panoramic view of Gothenburg.

Korsvägen. ✆ **031/40-01-00.** www.liseberg.se. Admission 60SEK ($8.40/£4.20), free for children under 7. Ask about special passes. Opening hours are roughly June–Aug Mon–Fri 11am–11pm, Sat 11am–midnight, Sun 11am–10pm; Sept and May Thurs–Sun 11am–10pm; early Oct and late Apr Sat–Sun 11am–8pm. See website for more details. Tram: 4 or 5 from the city.

Röhsska Konstslöjdmuseet 🏛🏛 Two Gothenburgers, the Röhss brothers, launched this leading arts and crafts museum in 1916 with a bequest to the city. Pass through the entrance to this Romantic–style building—flanked by a pair of marine lions from the Ming dynasty—and you'll find temporary exhibitions of modern arts and crafts on the main floor. The highlights of the permanent collection of contemporary arts and crafts are on the second landing, where the exhibits are particularly rich with treasures of the 17th through the 19th centuries. Upstairs are exhibits devoted to silver, glassware, exquisite porcelain, furnishings, and antique textiles. On the top floor is an array of East Asian art.

Vasagatan 37–39. ✆ **031/61-38-50.** www.designmuseum.se. Admission 40SEK ($5.60/£2.80) adults, free for children under 19. Tues noon–8pm; Wed–Fri noon–5pm; Sat–Sun 11am–5pm. Tram: 3, 4, 5, 7, or 10. Bus: 42, 45, or 49.

WHERE TO DINE

A Hereford Beefstouw 🏛 *Value* STEAK Gothenburg's best steakhouse is part of a successful chain serving mostly Australian beef and specializing in a 17-ounce T-bone—finish it at your own risk. Backed up by an excellent salad bar, the menu offers a selection of sauces to go with your beef, including the classic Béarnaise, as well as a garlic butter or parsley sauce. A wide array of other cuts, including filet steaks, tenderloins, and veal sirloins are also featured.

Linnégatan 5. ✆ **031/775-04-41.** www.a-h-b.dk. Reservations recommended. Main courses 145SEK–385SEK ($20.30–$53.90/£10.15–£26.95); salad bar as a main course 150SEK ($21/£10.50). AE, DC, MC, V. Mon–Fri 11:30am–2pm and 5–10pm (Fri until 11pm); Sat 4–11pm; Sun 3–9pm. Closed frequently in July and early Aug. Call ahead to check. Tram: 1, 3, 4, or 9.

Brasserie Lipp SWEDISH/FRENCH On Gothenburg's main promenade, this bustling eatery, established in 1987, is as close as the city gets to having a bistro evocative of the Left Bank in Paris. Although much of the menu is French inspired, such as the escargots in garlic butter and entrecôte of beef with a Dijon mustard sauce, other dishes are strictly homegrown, including fresh fish caught off the coastal waters of Gothenburg. The best *choucroute garnie* (sauerkraut with sausage and pork) in the city is served here.

Kungsportsavenyn 8. ✆ **031/10-58-30.** www.brasserielipp.com. Reservations required. Main courses 200SEK–260SEK ($28–$36.40/£14–£18.20). AE, DC, MC, V. Daily 11:30am–11:30pm. Tram: 1, 4, 5, or 6. Bus: 40.

Café Husaren INTERNATIONAL This former pharmacy/milliner/bank is the best-known and most animated cafe in the Haga district of Gothenburg. The century-old decor includes a reverse-painted glass created in the mid-1890s. Place your order for well-stuffed sandwiches, freshly made salads, and pastries, which include the biggest and most succulent cinnamon roll in town. You carry your food to one of the indoor or, in summer, outdoor tables. The shrimp salad is very good here.

Haga Nygata 28. ✆ **031/13-63-78.** www.cafehusaren.se. Sandwiches 20SEK–45SEK ($2.80–$6.30/£1.40–£3.15); pastries 12SEK–32SEK ($1.70–$4.50/85p–£2.25). Mon–Thurs 9am–8pm; Fri 9am–7pm; Sat–Sun 9am–6pm. Tram: 3, 6, 9, or 11.

Fiskekrogen 🏛🏛 SEAFOOD Across the canal from the Stadtsmuseum, this restaurant is your best choice for seafood in the central city. Against a nautical backdrop, the

Moments A Picnic in the Park

Across the canal from the Central Station is an ideal spot for a picnic: **Trädgårdsföreningen** *ᏨᏨ*, with entrances on Slussgatan. This park boasts a large *rosarium* with some 10,000 rose bushes of 4,000 different species, the centerpiece being the Palm House, a large greenhouse where subtropical plants grow year-round. There's a Butterfly House where these stunning creatures live in a simulation of a natural habitat. Entrance to the park costs 15SEK ($2.10), free for children under 17, and free for all mid-September through mid-April. The park is open daily from 7am to 8pm mid-April to mid-September and 7am to 6pm the rest of the year.

For the makings of an elegant picnic, go to **Suluhallen,** Kungstorget, which was built in 1888. This is the city's colorful indoor market. Shops sell meat, fruit, vegetables, and delicatessen products. You can buy all sorts of game, including moose and reindeer, and even lamb from Iceland. The produce (including exotic fruit) comes from all over the world. There are four restaurants and one coffee bar in the building. Much of the food is already cooked and can be packaged for you to take out. The hall is open Monday to Friday 9am to 6pm, Friday 8am to 6pm, and Saturday 9am to 2pm. Take tram 1, 3, 4, 5, 7, or 10 to Kungsportsplatsen.

restaurant offers a well-stocked fresh seafood bar, with plenty of lobster, clams, crayfish, mussels, and oysters. The chefs take a bold approach to harmonizing flavors and offer fragrant, light sauces as part of their finely tuned repertoire.

Lilla Torget 1. ✆ 031/10-10-05. www.fiskekrogen.se. Reservations recommended. Main courses 275SEK–355SEK ($38.50–$49.70/£19.25–£24.85); set menus (ordered per table) 645SEK–845SEK ($90.30–$118/£45.15–£59.15). AE, DC, MC, V. Mon–Fri 11:30am–2pm and 5:30–11pm; Sat 1–11pm. Tram: 2 or 5.

Froken Olssons Café SWEDISH   This local favorite is conveniently located 2 blocks from Kungsportsavenyn, the major city artery. In summer, tables overflow onto a wide terrace, although there is ample space inside as well. Come here to feast on light cafe cuisine: well-stuffed baguettes and an array of homemade soups and fresh salads, plus desserts such as fruit cheesecakes and meringues. It can get a bit noisy and crowded at lunchtime.

Östra Larmgatan 14. ✆ 031/13-81-93. Coffee 24SEK ($3.35/£1.70); *dagens* (daily) menu 50SEK–69SEK ($7–$9.65/£3.50–£4.85); salad buffet 60SEK ($8.40/£4.20); sandwiches 30SEK–70SEK ($4.20–$9.80/£2.10–£4.90). MC, V. Mon–Fri 9am–10pm. Tram: 1, 4, 5, or 6. Bus: 40.

La Gondola ITALIAN   Some of the best pizzas and classic Italian dishes in Gothenburg are dished up here. It's a little piece of Venice in Scandinavia, with its striped poles, outdoor seating area, and ample menu. All the old favorites turn up, including the house specialty, *saltimbocca* (veal and ham), along with such grilled specialties as tender and juicy steaks. Try the freshly made minestrone and save room for one of the delicious desserts.

Kungsportsavenyn 4. ✆ 031/711-68-28. www.lagondola.se. Reservations recommended. Main courses 105SEK–250SEK ($14.70–$35/£7.35–£17); *dagens* (daily) lunch 80SEK–170SEK ($11.20–$23.80/£5.60–£11.90). AE, DC, MC, V. Daily 11:30am–11pm. Tram: 1, 4, 5, or 6. Bus: 38 or 75.

Restaurang Räkan/Yellow Submarine 🍴 SEAFOOD   This is one of the city's finest seafood joints, as well as a wonderfully goofy treat. Its nautical decor taken to extremes, the restaurant offers not just the usual wooden plank tables and buoy lamps, but also a re-creation of a Swedish "lake." Your seafood platter arrives on a battery-powered boat with you directing the controls. Kids, naturally, adore the place. If all this sounds too gimmicky, know that the fish is fresh, perfectly cooked, and lightly seasoned, especially the prawns, mussels, and Swedish lobster.

Lorensbergsgatan 16. 🕐 031/16-98-39. www.rakan.se. Reservations recommended. Main courses 215SEK–315SEK ($30.10–$44.10/£15.05–£22). AE, DC, MC, V. Mon–Sat 4–11pm; Sun 3–10pm. Tram: 1, 4, 5, or 6. Bus: 40.

Restaurant 28+ 🍴🍴🍴 INTERNATIONAL   Chic and stylish, this restaurant's three dining salons are romantically lit by candles and have soaring ceilings. It's hip, it's fashionable, the service is exceptional, and the food is good if a little pricey. You're assured some of the most imaginative and fabulously fresh cuisine in town, so if you have a demanding palate that needs satisfying, this restaurant is worth the expense.

Götabergsgatan 28. 🕐 031/20-21-61. Reservations recommended. Fixed-price menus 795SEK–895SEK ($111–$125/£55.65–£62.65); main courses 295SEK–445SEK ($41.30–$62.30/£20.65–£31.15). AE, DC, MC, V. Mon–Sat 6–11pm. Bus: 40. Tram: 1, 4, 5, or 6.

Solrosen (Sunflower) *Value* VEGETARIAN   This is the best vegetarian restaurant in Gothenburg. It's been going for decades, but there's still a good wholesome buzz about the place. Diners take advantage of the all-you-can-eat salad bar and the unlimited coffee. Beer and wine are also available. The Sunflower blooms in the Haga district, a low-rise neighborhood of 18th- and early-19th-century buildings. You serve yourself at the counter.

Kaponjärgatan 4. 🕐 031/711-66-97. Main courses 50SEK–130SEK ($7–$18.20/£3.50–£9.10). Daily platters 50SEK–75SEK ($7–$10.50/£3.50–£5.25). AE, DC, MC, V. Mon–Fri 11:30am–1am; Sat 2pm–1am. Tram: 1, 6, or 9.

SHOPPING

For one-stop shopping, visit **Nordstan,** one of the largest shopping malls in Scandinavia, with more than 150 shops, stores, restaurants, coffee shops, banks, a post office, and travel agencies. **Kungsgatan** and **Fredsgatan,** a hugely long pedestrian mall in Sweden, stretches for 2 miles (3.2km). Another major shopping artery is **Kungsportsavenyn,** called the "Avenyn" by Gothenburgers. From early spring to autumn, this is the most bustling avenue in Gothenburg, and it's flanked with shops, restaurants, and cafes. Also check out the recently revitalized working district of **Haga Nygatan,** now home to the rich and trendy, who've been followed by a load of funky/chic shops.

The biggest department store is **Bohusslöjd,** Avenyn 25 (🕐 **031/16-00-72;** www. bohusslojd.se), with one of the city's most carefully chosen selection of Swedish handcrafts, including hand-woven rugs and pine or birch bowls. Since 1866, **C. J. Josephssons Glas & Porslin,** Korsgatan 12 (🕐 **031/17-56-15**), has been a leading name in Swedish glassmaking. Many of its finest pieces are the work of some of the country's best-known designers.

Gothenburg's most popular store is **Nordiska Kompaniet (NK),** Östra Hamngatan 42 (🕐 **031/710-10-00;** www.nk.se), carrying more than 200,000 items for sale. It's especially well stocked in Kosta Boda and Orrefors crystal, along with pewter items, and many, many crafts.

A permanent exhibit center for some 30 potters and glassmakers, **Lerverk,** Västra Hamngatan 24–26 (🕐 **031/13-13-49**), offers beautifully crafted items of the highest quality.

NIGHTLIFE

Liseberg Park (see "Top Attractions & Special Moments," above) is the leading night-time venue in summer, with all sorts of family-style entertainment. The cultural high-light is **Göteborgsoperan** (the Gothenburg Opera House), Packhuskajen (© **031/10-80-00;** www.opera.se), a relatively new opera house opened by the king in 1994 that features opera, operettas, musicals, and ballet. A short walk from Central Station, it opens onto views of the water, and has five bars and a cafe on its premises. Prices depend on the event being staged.

The largest and most comprehensive nightclub in Gothenburg is **Trädgår'n,** Nya Allén (© **031/10-20-80;** www.tradgarn.se), where no one under 25 is admitted. Its two-story interior is filled with a dance club, a cabaret, and a restaurant. The cover charge for the dance club is 100SEK to 140SEK ($14–$19.60/£7–£9.80), with a din-ner and access to the cabaret going for 530SEK ($74.20/£37.10). The dance club is open Friday and Saturday 11pm to 5am, the restaurant Monday to Friday 11:30am to 3:30pm, and Wednesday to Saturday 6 to 10:30pm, with the cabaret kickoff at 8pm.

In a former fire station, **Oakley's Country Club,** Tredje Långgatan 16 (© **031/42-60-80;** www.oakleys.nu), is a supper club offering a changing array of dancers and impersonators who work hard to keep the audience amused. Expect a changing array of musical acts, plenty of musical and show-biz razzmatazz, and imitations of Swedish pop stars you've probably not heard of. An automatic cover charge of 120SEK ($16.80/£8.40) per person is added to the cost of your meal.

For a taste of the local rock scene head to **Sticky Fingers,** Kaserntorget 7, (© **031/701-00-17;** www.stickyfingers.nu), where you'll find four floors of music ranging from hip-hop to hard rock and a band playing live nearly every night. Previous per-formers have included Motorhead and Queens of the Stone Age. Cover sticks at around SEK60 ($8.40/£4.20) but is usually free between 9 and 10pm if you want to simply pop in for a look. It's open Wednesday 8pm to 2am (summer only), Thursday 8pm to 2am, and Friday and Saturday 9pm to 4am.

Finally, one of Gothenburg's newer nightspots is **Tranquilo,** Kungstorget 14 (© **031/13-45-55;** www.tranquilo.se), a fun, colorful Latino spot attracting a super-attractive crowd usually found nibbling on South American dishes or sipping *caipir-inhas,* Brazil's national cocktail. Dining goes on until about 10:30pm, while the bar stays open until between 1 and 3am depending on business.

19

Switzerland

Switzerland occupies a position on the rooftop of the continent of Europe, with the drainage of its mammoth Alpine glaciers becoming the source of such powerful rivers as the Rhine and the Rhône. The appellation "the crossroads of Europe" is fitting, as all rail lines, road passes, and tunnels through the mountains lead here. From the time the Romans crossed the Alps, going through Helvetia (the old name for today's Switzerland) on their way north, the major route connecting northern and southern Europe has been through Switzerland. The old roads and paths have developed into modern highways and railroads.

The tourist industry as we know it started in Switzerland, and the tradition of welcoming visitors is firmly entrenched in Swiss life. The first modern tourists, the British, began to come here "on holiday" in the 19th century, and other Europeans and some North Americans followed suit, so that soon the small federal state became known as "a nation of hotelkeepers." Swiss hospitality, based on years of experience, has gained a worldwide reputation, and the entire country is known for its cleanliness and efficiency.

Switzerland has many great museums and a rich cultural life, but that's not why most people visit. They come mainly for the scenery, which is virtually unrivaled in the world, from Alpine peaks to mountain lakes, from the palm trees of Ticino to the "Ice Palace" of Jungfrau. And, especially important to the rail traveler, Switzerland is renowned for the breadth and number of its scenic train routes (see "Switzerland's Famous Scenic Rail Lines," at the end of this chapter, for the lowdown on eight of our favorites).

HIGHLIGHTS OF SWITZERLAND

Most European capitals completely dominate the attractions list of their countries as in the case of London or Paris. Not so in Switzerland, which has four cities of equal tourist allure—Zurich, Geneva, Bern, and Lausanne—all of which we'll explore by rail in this section. Each city deserves at least 2 days of your time and because Switzerland is so small, you can travel quickly by rail from one city to another in just a matter of a few hours.

Most airplanes from North America arrive in **Zurich**, which is the major rail transportation hub of Switzerland and an ideal place to embark upon your train tour of the Alps. At the foot of the large **Lake Zurich**, the city of Zurich is one of the most beautiful in Europe, spreading out along both banks of the Limmat River. Zurich can be visited for its remarkably preserved **Altstadt** or Old Town alone. You can spend a morning walking the Limmat's right bank and exploring its guild houses from the 16th and 17th centuries.

Switzerland's largest city, the former home of Thomas Mann, James Joyce, and Lenin, is filled with attractions, none more notable than the quays along the river. Its

Switzerland

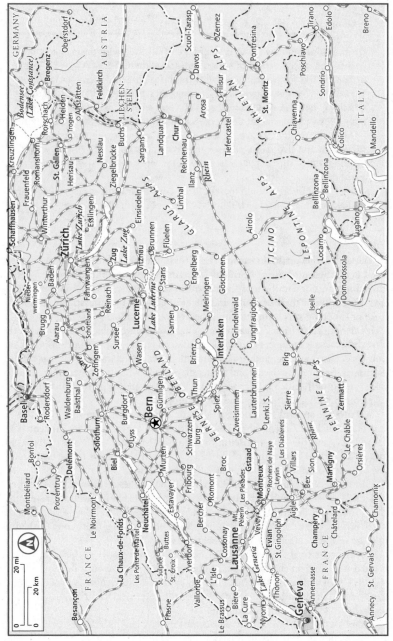

> ⟨*Moments* **Festivals & Special Events**
>
> On the third Monday in April, members of all the guilds dress in costumes and celebrate the arrival of spring at **Sechseläuten** ("Six O'Clock Chimes") in Zurich. The festival climaxes with the burning of Böögg, a straw figure symbolizing winter. There are also children's parades. The **Zurich Tourist Office** (⟨ **044/215-40-00**; www.zuerich.com) shows the parade route on a map. (Böögg is burned at 6pm on Sechseläutenplatz, near Belevueplatz.)
>
> At the **Fêtes de Genève**, in Geneva, highlights include flower parades, fireworks, and live music all over the city. Call ⟨ **022/909-70-00** for more information or surf the Web to **www.fetesdegeneve.ch**. The festival takes place in early August.
>
> Last, the famous "onion market" fair, **Zibelemärit**, takes place in Bern in mid-November. Call ⟨ **031/328-12-12** for more information.

two chief churches are **Fraumünster** and **Grossmünster,** and its greatest museums are the **Landesmuseum (Swiss National Museum)** and **Kunsthaus Zurich,** a fine-arts museum that is one of the most important in Europe. Even on the shortest of visits, save time to walk the beautiful—and superexpensive—**Bahnhofstrasse,** the world's greatest shopping street running from the main train station to the lake.

It's an hour's ride from Zurich to the capital city of **Bern,** which is even lovelier than Zurich because it embraces one of the greatest medieval districts in Europe. In Bern you get scenery, culture, and history, and the most idyllic gateway for exploring the **Bernese Oberland,** a summer and winter playground with its Alpine skiing, clear blue lakes, and **Jungfraujoch** at 11,333 feet (3,399m), where a train from **Interlaken** will take you to the highest railway station in Europe.

Walking the arcaded streets of the **Altstadt** is Bern's major drawing card. The special places include **Bärengraben (Bear Pits),** the **Cathedral of St. Vincent** dating from 1421, and the **Kunstmuseum** or Fine Arts Museum, with one of the world's largest collections of the works of Paul Klee. For a final goodbye to the city, head for the belvedere atop **Mount Gurten** at 2,815 feet (858m).

On your fifth day in Switzerland head by rail to the lakeside town of **Lausanne,** usually a ride of about 1 hour. This is your best center for exploring **Lake Geneva,** one of the world's most beautiful bodies of water. You can spend 1 day discovering Lausanne itself, including Switzerland's most impressive Gothic building (**Lausanne Cathedral),** and the next day touring the lake by boat.

Devote your final 2 days in Switzerland to the serene city of **Geneva,** which is located near the French border and can be reached from Lausanne in about 45 to 50 minutes. Called the most international city in the world, Geneva is the center of the European United Nations, the birthplace of the International Red Cross, and is the capital of French-speaking Switzerland.

Although devoid of world-class attractions, the city and its beautiful lakeside setting is an attraction in and of itself. You come here to buy a watch, walk the lakeside quays, and spend a night in *Vieille Ville* (Old Town) clustered in narrow streets around **Cathédrale St-Pierre.** Geneva is also a good base for exploring the Alps and Lake Geneva.

1 Essentials

GETTING THERE

Switzerland is situated at the center of Europe and thus is a focal point for international air traffic. The busy intercontinental airports of Zurich and Geneva can be reached in 7 to 8 hours from the east coast of North America and in less than 2 hours from London or Paris.

Swiss International Air Lines Ltd. (© **877/359-7947** in the U.S., or 0848/700-700 in Switzerland; www.swiss.com), simply called **Swiss,** is the major carrier for Switzerland. Most flights from North America land in Geneva or Zurich.

Other airlines that offer service to Switzerland out of North America include **American Airlines** (© **800/433-7300;** www.aa.com), **Delta Airlines** (© **800/221-1212;** www.delta-airline.com), and **Air Canada** (© **888/247-2262;** www.aircanada.com).

If none of the major carriers above service your airport, you can also fly into London or Manchester, and from there connect to either Zurich or Geneva on **British Airways** (© **0870/850-4850** in Britain, or 800/AIRWAYS in the U.S.; www.british airways.com), **easyJet** (© **0870/600-000;** www.easyjet.com), or **Aer Lingus** (© **800/ 474-7424;** www.aerlingus.com).

SWITZERLAND BY RAIL
PASSES

For information on the **Eurail Global Pass, Eurail Global Pass Flexi,** and other multicountry options, see chapter 2.

SWISS PASS/SWISS FLEXIPASS   The most practical and convenient ticket for your trip to Switzerland is the **Swiss Pass,** which entitles you to unlimited travel on the entire network of the Swiss Federal Railways, as well as on lake steamers and most postal motor coaches linking Swiss cities and resorts. The pass also provides free entrance to more than 400 museums in Switzerland and provides a 50% discount on most Swiss mountain railways. Note that the **Swiss Flexipass** also offers the 50% mountain railway discount, and you don't have to use a day on your pass to take advantage of this discount. For prices and more information on the Swiss Pass, Swiss Flexipass, and the free **Swiss Family Card** that allows children under 16 to travel free with a paying parent (and only a parent), see chapter 2. All of these passes should be purchased in North America before you leave on your trip and can be obtained through **Rail Europe** (© **877/272-RAIL** [7245] in North America; www.raileurope. com) or your travel agent.

SWISS REGIONAL RAILPASSES   One of the country's most unusual transportation bargains is offered in the form of regional passes that divide Switzerland into about half a dozen districts. Passes, most of which are good for 5 days of unrestricted rail travel, are offered for the Lake Geneva region, the Graubunden (Grisons), the Ticino, central Switzerland, and the Bernese Oberland. If you plan to devote a block of days to exploring one of these specific regions, you might find one of these passes a great savings.

One of the most popular of these passes is the **Bernese Oberland Regional Pass** (Regional Pass für das Berner Oberland), which allows for 3 travel days out of 7 days, and 5 travel days out of 15 days. You can buy the pass at any railway station or tourist office in the Bernese Oberland. You can also purchase it by phone from **Reisezentrum BLS, Bern** (© **031/327-3271**), or on the Web at **www.regiopass-berneroberland.ch.**

The 3-day option sells for 224F ($184/£95.70) in second class and 267F ($219/£114) in first class. The 5-day option costs 270F ($221/£115) in second class and 322F ($264/£137) in first class. The pass provides free transport during the appropriate time frames on all but a handful of the cog railways, buses, cable cars, ferryboats, and SBB trains within the region.

SWISS CARD   This pass, valid for 1 month, entitles the holder to a free transfer from any Swiss airport or border point to any destination within Switzerland and a second free transfer from any destination in Switzerland to any Swiss airport or border point. Each transfer must be completed within 1 day. Additionally, the Swiss Card gives the holder unlimited half-fare trips on the entire Swiss travel system, including trains, postal coaches, lake steamers, and most (but not all) excursions to mountain-tops. The pass costs $187 (£97.25) for first class or $139 (£72.30) for second class and is available from Rail Europe. Children under 16 ride free with a *parent* if you request the free **Swiss Family Card** (see above) when you purchase your Swiss Card.

SWISS TRANSFER TICKET   This offers one round-trip transfer from an airport or border point to any destination in Switzerland. The ticket costs $143 (£74.35) per adult in first class, $94 (£48.90) in second class. Children under 16 ride free with a *parent* if you request the free **Swiss Family Card** (see above) when you purchase your ticket.

FOREIGN TRAIN TERMS

The two most popular languages in Switzerland are German and French. English, however, is widely spoken and understood by Swiss nationals, who learn to speak it in grade school, so there's no need to learn any foreign train terms. Most Swiss timetables in railway stations usually have a section written in English.

PRACTICAL TRAIN INFORMATION

The **Swiss Federal Railway** has one of the most extensive rail systems on the Continent and its trains are noted for their comfort and cleanliness. Most of the electrically operated trains have first-class and second-class compartments. International trains link Swiss cities with other European centers. InterCity trains arriving from Holland, Scandinavia, and Germany usually require a change at Basel's station, where a connection is normally available on the same platform. Most InterCity trains offer the fastest connections and, because trains leave the Basel station hourly, there's never too long a wait.

One of the busiest rail links in Europe stretches from Paris to Geneva and Lausanne. Almost as busy are the rail routes between Paris and Zurich. Most of the trains assigned to these routes are part of Europe's network of high-speed trains. (The French refer to them as *trains à grande vitesse,* or TGV.) From Paris's Gare de Lyon, about four trains a day depart, respectively, for both Geneva and Lausanne. Travel time to Geneva is about 3½ hours; travel time to Lausanne is about 4 hours. Trains from Paris to Zurich depart five times a day from Paris's Gare de l'Est (travel time to Zurich on the TGV is about 4½ hr.).

Ironically, miles traveled by train within Switzerland are proportionately more expensive than equivalent distances within France, so ongoing fares from Zurich or Geneva to other points within Switzerland might come as an unpleasant surprise. Consequently, many travelers who anticipate lots of rail travel are well advised to consider the purchase of any of Rail Europe's passes. Note, however, that a number of

Trains & Travel Times in Switzerland

From	To	Type of Train	# of Trains	Frequency	Travel Time
Zurich	Bern	InterCity	25	Daily	1 hr.
Zurich	Geneva	InterCity	16	Daily	2 hr., 40 min.
Zurich	Lausanne	InterCity	16	Daily	2 hr., 8 min.
Geneva	Lausanne	InterCity	31	Daily	33 min.

Switzerland's best-known trains are privately owned and do not accept Eurail passes, though passholders will get a discount on fares. Swiss railpasses cover all scenic trains.

RESERVATIONS   These are absolutely necessary on Switzerland's special scenic trains (see the last section in this chapter for details). On most Swiss trains, however, reservations aren't usually necessary, although you can make one for about $13 (£6.75) through Rail Europe if you want to ensure yourself a seat, especially during the busy holiday season. Having a railpass doesn't guarantee you a seat. Fares for EuroCity and InterCity trains within Switzerland are included in a railpass, but on most international trains you'll be assessed a supplement (which depends on the train you take and your ultimate destination).

Because rail journeys are short in Switzerland, it will rarely be necessary to book a couchette or sleeper, for which reservation fees begin at $35 (£18.20) and climb higher. Sleepers and couchettes are available on most international routes running through Switzerland, and accommodations on these trains can be reserved at least 60 to 90 days in advance through Rail Europe. These sleeper services aren't available on domestic routes within Switzerland itself.

SERVICES & AMENITIES   All major train stations in Switzerland have food and drink for sale. We'd recommend that you avail yourself of their offerings, taking along bottled water or a picnic lunch to enjoy as you watch Alpine scenery. Most trains have minibars, but they are expensive and not for the frugal rail traveler.

Many trains making longer runs also have self-service buffets, which are far more affordable than eating in one of the dining cars, where prices are lethal. If your train has one, a self-service buffet is the way to go if you didn't bring a picnic lunch.

FAST FACTS: Switzerland

Area Code The country code for Switzerland is **41**. City area codes are as follows: **01 and 044** for Zurich, **031** for Bern, **021** for Lausanne, and **022** for Geneva.

Business Hours **Banks** are usually open Monday to Friday 8:30am to 4:30pm (closed on legal holidays). Foreign currency may be exchanged at major railroad stations and airports daily from 8am to 10pm. Most **business offices** are open Monday to Friday 8am to noon and 2 to 6pm. **Shops** are usually open Monday to Friday 8am to 12:15pm and 1:30 to 6:30pm, and on Saturday 1:30 to 4pm. In large cities, most shops don't close during the lunch hour, although many do so on Monday morning.

Climate The temperature range is about the same as in the northern United States, but without the extremes of hot and cold. Summer temperatures seldom rise above 80°F (27°C) in the cities, and humidity is low. Because of clear air and the lack of wind in the high Alpine regions, sunbathing is sometimes possible even in winter. In southern Switzerland, the temperature remains mild year-round, allowing subtropical vegetation to grow. June is the ideal month for a tour of Switzerland, followed by either September or October, when the mountain passes are still open. In summer, the country is usually overrun with tourist traffic.

Documents Required Every traveler entering Switzerland must have a valid passport, although it's not necessary for North Americans to have a visa if they don't stay longer than 3 continuous months. For information on permanent residence in Switzerland and work permits, contact the nearest Swiss consulate.

Electricity Switzerland's electricity is 220 volts, 50 cycles, AC. Some international hotels are specially wired to allow North Americans to plug in their appliances, but you'll usually need a transformer for your electric razor or hair dryer. You'll also need an adapter plug to channel the electricity from the Swiss system to the flat-pronged American system. Don't plug anything in without being certain your appliances and the electrical outlets are compatible.

Embassies & Consulates Most embassies are located in the national capital, Bern; some nations maintain consulates in other cities such as Geneva. The **Canadian embassy** is at Kirchenfeldstrasse 88, Bern (© **031/357-32-00**). The embassy of the **United States** is located at Jubilaumstrasse 93, Bern (© **043/499-29-60**), with consulates in Zurich at Dufourstrasse 101 (© **044/499-29-60**), and in Geneva at rue Versonnex 7 (© **022/840-51-60**).

Health & Safety Medical care and health facilities in Switzerland are among the best in the world. Note that Swiss authorities require immunization against contagious diseases if you have been in an infected area during the 14-day period immediately preceding your arrival in Switzerland.

Crimes of violence, such as muggings, are rare in Switzerland. It is generally safe to walk the streets of cities day and night. The most common crime reported by visitors is a picked pocket.

Holidays The legal holidays in Switzerland are New Year's (Jan 1–2), Good Friday, Easter Monday, Ascension Day, Whit Monday, Bundesfeier (the Swiss Independence Day; Aug 1), and Christmas (Dec 25–26).

Legal Aid This may be hard to come by in Switzerland. The government advises foreigners to consult their embassy or consulate (see "Embassies & Consulates," above) in case of a dire emergency, such as an arrest. Even if your embassy or consulate declines to offer financial or legal help, it will generally offer advice on how to obtain help locally.

Mail Post offices in large cities are open Monday to Friday from 7:30am to noon and 2 to 6:30pm, and on Saturday 7:30 to 11am. If you have letters forwarded to a post office to be collected after you arrive, you'll need a passport for identification. The words *"Poste Restante"* must be clearly written on the envelope. Letters not collected within 30 days are returned to the sender. Letters are either first class, meaning air mail, or surface mail, rated second class.

Police & Emergencies Dial © **117** for the police (emergencies only) and © **118** to report a fire.

Telephone The telephone system is entirely automatic and connects the entire country. **Helpful numbers** to know are: **111** for directory assistance, **120** for tourist information and snow reports, **140** for help on the road, **162** for weather forecasts, and **163** for up-to-the-minute information on road conditions. Hotels add substantial service charges for calls made from your room; it's considerably less expensive to make calls from a public phone booth.

To use a **coin-operated telephone,** lift the receiver and insert 40 centimes to get a dial tone. Be sure to have enough coins on hand, as you must insert more for each message unit over your initial deposit. If you insert more coins than necessary, the excess amounts will be returned. A pay phone will accept up to 5F ($4.10/£2.15).

To make a local call, dial directly after you hear the dial tone (no area code needed); for other places in Switzerland, dial the area code and then the number. To call a foreign country, dial the code of the country first, then the area code, and then the number.

Tipping A 15% service charge is automatically included in all hotel and restaurant bills, although some people leave an additional tip for exceptional service. For taxis, a tip is usually included in the charges (a notice will be posted in the cab).

2 Zurich ✶✶✶

Zurich is not only the largest city in Switzerland and one of the most beautiful on the Continent, but it is also Switzerland's major rail hub and one of the country's two major airport terminals for air traffic from North America. Most rail passengers fly into Zurich to begin their rail tour of Switzerland.

Zurich is well connected to many of Europe's major cities, with four trains per day arriving from Munich (trip time: 4½ hr.); trains arriving every hour from Milan (trip time 4½ hr.); five TGV trains per day from Paris (trip time: 4½ hr.); five trains from Salzburg (trip time: 6 hr.); and four trains from Vienna (trip time: 9 hr.). Zurich is also a hub for overnight trains to many international cities, including Amsterdam, Rome, Prague, Barcelona, and Vienna. From Zurich, high-speed trains also race you anywhere you're going within Switzerland.

Called the "city by the lake," Zurich lies on both banks of the Limmat River and its tributary, the Sihl. Quays line the riverbanks and the lake, making for some of the grandest scenic promenades in Europe. Though the capital of a canton (district), Zurich has not been the capital of Switzerland since 1848 (that's Bern). It was, however, a great center of liberal thought, having attracted Linen, Carl Jung, James Joyce, and Thomas Mann. The Dadaist school was founded here in 1916.

Even though it's a German-speaking city, nearly all Zurichers speak English. Although there is much here of interest to the visitor, Zurich is essentially a city of commerce and industry, with briefcase-carrying, Armani-attired executives heading for the world's fourth-largest stock exchange or the world's largest gold exchange. Because of all this money changing hands, Zurich also offers some of the most upper-crust shops in Europe along with a bevy of top-quality, posh restaurants. On the downside, the city caters to the wealthy and prices are appropriately up there. No need to worry though— we recommend dining and hotel options for all budgets in this section.

Zurich

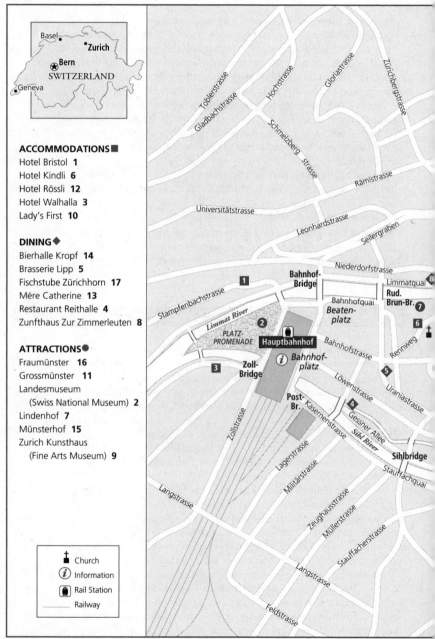

✝ Church
ⓘ Information
🔲 Rail Station
─── Railway

RIGHT BANK

0   1/5 mile
0   200 meters

N

Plattenstrasse

Asylstrasse

Klosbachstrasse

Freiestrasse

Minervastrasse

Zollikerstrasse

Kreuzplatz

Feldeggstrasse

Seefeldstrasse

Dufourstrasse

Hottingerstrasse

Zeltweg

Mühlebachstrasse

Kreuzstrasse

10

Bellerivestrasse

Stadelhofer-
platz

Rämistrasse

9

Falken strasse

Goethestr.

Utoquai

Hirschengraben

Grossmünster-
platz

Oberdorfstr.

Theaterstr.

11

Bellevueplatz

Münsterg.

12

Limmatquai

Quaibr.

Lake Zurich

13

Limmat River

14

Stadthausquai

Bürkli-
platz

Münster-
Bridge

15

Borsenstrasse

16

Bahnhof-
strasse

Gén.-Guisan-Quai

Paradeplatz

Bleicherweg

Tal

ARBORETUM

Claridenstrasse

Beethovenstrasse

Mythenquai

Bastei-
platz

Stocker
strasse

Dreikönigstrasse

Gotthard strasse

Alfred-Escher-Strasse

BELVOIR PARK

17

vulkanstrasse

Tödistrasse

Freigutstrasse

Lavaterstrasse

Seestrasse

Brandschenk

Tessinerplatz

Schulhausstrasse

Gablerstrasse

RIETER PARK

Stauffbridge

estrasse

Tunnelstrasse

Seestrasse

Scheideggstrasse

Bürglistrasse

Enge

Hugelstrasse Kurf

Sihl River

Bederstrasse

Waffenplatzstrasse

LEFT BANK

Nationalstrasse 3

Lessingstrasse

STATION INFORMATION
GETTING FROM THE AIRPORT TO THE TRAIN STATION
Zurich International Airport (© 043/816-22-11; www.zurich-airport.com) is the biggest airport in Switzerland and the most popular gateway to the country; in fact, it's among the 10 busiest airports in Europe. It's located approximately 7 miles (11km) north of the city center.

The best and cheapest way to get to the center of the city is to hop a train at the airport; for 8F ($6.55/£3.40), you'll arrive in less than 10 minutes at the Zurich Hauptbahnhof, the main railway station. The train runs every 15 to 20 minutes between 5am and 12:10am. The ride is covered by your railpass, though it's unwise to waste a day on your pass for such an inexpensive trip.

A trip to the central rail station by taxi will cost you between 50F and 60F ($41–$49/£21.30–£25.50).

INSIDE THE STATION
Zurich Hauptbahnhof (© 0900/300-300) is a major European rail hub and one of the cleanest and safest stations on the Continent. Trains arrive and depart to a number of major European cities, including Munich, Milan, and Paris, from this station.

On the same level as the train tracks is the **Rail Travel Centre,** opposite track 13. You can get your railpass validated here, and the staff provides information for rail travel throughout Switzerland, sells tickets, and makes reservations. It's open daily from 6:30am to 9:30pm. Take a number from the machine as you enter, and wait your turn. A list of departing trains is displayed on digital boards within the station.

On the left side of the main arrival hall is a **Money Exchange** kiosk open daily from 6:30am to 11:30pm. The staff will convert your currency into Swiss francs. The Swiss prefer to use their own francs in transactions, shunning the euro and the dollar. You can store your luggage one level below (take the escalator). The cost is 8F ($6.55/£3.40) per day, and the counter is open daily from 6am to 10:50pm. There are also public showers at the train station, costing 14F ($11/£5.70); they're open 6am to midnight.

The **Zurich Tourist Office,** Bahnhofplatz 15 (© 044/215-40-00; www.zuerich. com), is based inside the main railway station and offers tourist information, maps, and brochures. It's open November to April, Monday to Saturday 8:30am to 7pm and Sunday 9am to 6:30pm; May to October, Monday to Saturday 8am to 8:30pm and on Sunday 8:30am to 6:30pm.

Hotel reservations can be made here, or you can e-mail the staff in advance at **hotel@zuerich.com**. Vacancies in hotels are posted on an electronic hotel reservations board at the front of the station; otherwise the tourist office will find rooms for you after 10:30am.

On the bottom level of the station are a number of shops and fast-food outlets.

The Bahnhof is also the hub for Zurich's public transportation system. You can catch trams or buses here to wherever you are going in the city.

GETTING AROUND
The public transport system of Zurich is operated by VBZ Züri–Linie, or **Zurich Public Transport** (© 0848/988-988 for information) and is the best and cheapest way to get around town. The modern and extensive network of trams and buses (there is no subway) runs daily from 5:30 to 12:30am. You should have to wait no longer

---

> ⌒Value **An Open Sesame & Bargain Pass**
>
> **ZurichCARD** costs 17F ($14/£7.30) for 24 hours or 34F ($28/£14.55) for 72 hours. It's a great deal offering a 50% reduction on public transportation, free visits to 43 museums, reduced prices at the local zoo, and a welcome drink at more than two dozen restaurants. The pass is widely available and is sold at the Zurich Hauptbahnhof, the airport, and certain hotels.

---

than 6 minutes during rush hours. Most trams and buses connect at the Zurich Hauptbahnhof, in the heart of the city.

You can buy tickets from automatic vending machines located at every stop. You must have a ticket before you get on a vehicle; if you're caught without one, you'll pay a fine of 80F ($66/£34.30) on the spot.

For a trip of up to four stops, the fare is 3.80F ($3.10/£1.60), and 4.10F ($3.35/£1.75) for longer journeys. Visitors will get the most for their money by buying a *Tageskarte* (1-day ticket), which costs 7.80F ($6.40/£3.35) and allows you to travel on all city buses and trams for 24 hours.

Taxis are very expensive in Zurich. The budget-conscious will want to use them only as a last resort. Your hotel will usually be glad to call a taxi for you, but if you're making the call yourself, call **Taxi 444** (© **044/444-44-44**). The basic charge before you even get into the vehicle is 6F ($4.90/£2.55), plus 3.50F ($2.85/£1.50) for each kilometer you travel.

Biking is a good way to get around Zurich, especially in the outlying areas. Bikes can be rented at the baggage counter of the railway station for 32F ($26/£13.50) a day, courtesy of **Workfare** (© **043/288-34-45;** www.zuerirollt.ch).

WHERE TO STAY

Hotel Bristol ⌘ ⌒Value   Close to the Bahnhof, this affordable (a rarity in superexpensive Zurich!) hotel is a bit lean on facilities, but the helpful staff will quickly ease you into life in Zurich. The midsize bedrooms are well maintained and frequently renovated. This is also one of the few lower-priced hotels that is accessible to those with limited mobility.

Stampfensbachstrasse 34, CH-8035 Zurich. © **044/258-44-44.** Fax 044/258-44-00. www.hotelbristol.ch. 53 units. 170–240F ($139–$197/£72.30–£102) double; 195–270F ($160–$221/£83.20–£115) triple. Rates include continental breakfast. AE, DC, MC, V. Tram: 11 or 14. **Amenities:** Laundry; rooms for those w/limited mobility. *In room:* Hair dryer.

Hotel Kindli ⌘   This hotel is set inside a restored 16th-century building in the Altstadt's (Old Town) pedestrian zone. The structure might be antique, but the hotel was drastically overhauled and turned into one of the better choices for those seeking good comfort and a bit of atmosphere, enhanced by the use of Laura Ashley fabrics throughout. Bedrooms are midsize, each with a different color scheme and completely modern plumbing.

Pfalzgasse 1, CH-8001 Zurich. © **043/888-76-76.** Fax 043/888-76-77. www.kindli.ch. 20 units. 280–420F ($230–$344/£120–£179) double. Rates include continental breakfast. AE, DC, MC, V. Tram: 7, 11, or 13. **Amenities:** Restaurant. *In room:* Hair dryer.

Hotel Rössli ⌘   This antique building in the Oberdorf section of Zurich, about a mile (1.6km) from the train station, was massively overhauled and turned into a modern hotel that attracts a hip, young crowd. The midsize bedrooms are tastefully and comfortably furnished. A special feature here is a suite with a separate living room, kitchen, three bedrooms, and a roof terrace offering lovely views. The bar is a popular gathering point for Zurich's artists and musicians.

Rössligasse 7, CH-8001 Zurich. ✆ **044/256-70-50.** Fax 044/256-70-51. www.hotelroessli.ch. 18 units. 270–300F ($221–$246/£115–£128) double; 380–430F ($312–$353/£162–£184) suite. Rates include buffet breakfast. AE, DC, MC, V. Tram: 4 or 15. **Amenities:** Bar. *In room:* Hair dryer.

Hotel Walhalla *(Value)*   Only a short walk from the Bahnhof, this hotel is a bargain by Zurich standards. It is spread across two five-floor buildings. One of these structures is relatively modern; the other is a bit more antiquated, although some prefer its higher ceilings and architectural details. The midsize bedrooms are comfortably furnished and well maintained, though beyond a bathroom, expect almost no in-room amenities but a TV.

Limmatstrasse 5, 8005 Zurich. ✆ **044/446-54-00.** Fax 044/446-54-54. www.walhalla-hotel.ch. 48 units. 180–220F ($148–$180/£76.95–£93.60) double. AE, DC, MC, V. Tram: 3 or 14. **Amenities:** Restaurant; nonsmoking rooms; rooms for those w/limited mobility. *In room:* TV, hair dryer.

Lady's First *(Finds)*   Pia Schmid, a well-known local architect, took an 1880s town house and successfully converted it into this charming boutique hotel, equipped with a first-class spa and a rooftop terrace with panoramic views of the cityscape. The midsize to spacious bedrooms are handsomely furnished with high ceilings and parquet floors. The summer rose garden is alluring, as is the blazing fireplace in the winter lounge. One other special feature: The hotel reserves its top two floors just for women.

Mainaustrasse 24, Kreis 8, CH-8008 Zurich. ✆ **01/380-80-10.** Fax 01/380-80-20. www.ladysfirst.ch. 28 units. 250–340F ($205–$279/£107–£145) double. Rates include breakfast. AE, DC, MC, V. Tram: 2 or 4. **Amenities:** Breakfast room; rooms for those w/limited mobility. *In room:* Hair dryer.

TOP ATTRACTIONS & SPECIAL MOMENTS

In the center of Zurich, the world-famous **Bahnhofstrasse** ✶✶✶ is the world's most beautiful shopping street. Planted with linden trees, the street was built on the site of what used to be a "frogs' moat." The exclusive street is relatively free of traffic, except for trams, which Zurichers have labeled "holy cows."

Beginning at the Bahnhofplatz, the street extends for nearly 4,000 feet (1,219m) until it reaches the lake. The drab **Bahnhofplatz,** the hub of Zurich's transportation network, is the railway station square and is home to the Hauptbahnhof (the German word for central railway station), which was built here in 1871.

With your back to this railway terminus, head up Bahnhofstrasse, which is filled with banks and shops selling luxury merchandise, such as Swiss watches. Select a favorite cafe and people-watch when you get tired of shopping. Incidentally, if you do shop, take along plenty of cash or else a gold-plated credit card. The merchandise here is exquisite, but it's also some of the most expensive in the world.

Fraumünster   On the left bank, this church, with its slender blue spire, overlooks the Münsterhof, the former pig market of Zurich. It was founded as an abbey by the Emperor Ludwig (Louis the German, grandson of Charlemagne) in 853, but dates mainly from the 13th and 14th centuries in its present incarnation. In the undercroft are the remains of the crypt of the old abbey church. The chief attractions here are five **stained-glass windows** ✶—each with its own color theme—by Marc Chagall dating from 1970. Obviously, they are best seen in bright morning light. The church is also celebrated for its elaborate organ. The Gothic nave is from the 13th to the 15th centuries, and the basilica has three aisles. In the Romanesque and Gothic cloisters are 1920s paintings depicting old Zurich legends about the founding of the abbey.

Fraumünsterstrasse. (©) **044/211-41-00.** Free admission. May–Sept Mon–Sat 9am–noon, daily 2–6pm; Oct, Mar–Apr Mon–Sat 10am–noon, daily 2–5pm; Nov–Feb Mon–Sat 10am–noon, daily 2–4pm. Tram: 4 to City Hall.

Grossmünster   The Romanesque and Gothic cathedral of Zurich was, according to legend, founded by Charlemagne, whose horse bowed down on the spot marking the graves of three early Christian martyrs. Rising on a terrace above the Limmatquai, the cathedral has twin three-story towers, a city landmark. On the right bank of the Limmat, the present structure dates principally from 1090 to 1180 and from 1225 to the dawn of the 14th century. The cathedral is dedicated to those Christian missionaries and the patron saints of Zurich: Felix, Regula, and Exuperantius.

The cathedral was once the parish church of Zwingli, one of the great leaders of the Reformation. He urged priests to take wives (he'd married himself) and attacked the "worship of images" and the Roman doctrine of Mass. This led to his death at Kappel in a religious war in 1531. The public hangman quartered his body, and soldiers burned the pieces with dung. That spot at Kappel is today marked with an inscription: "They may kill the body but not the soul." If you visit the choir you'll come upon stained-glass windows Giacometti completed in 1933. In the crypt is the original (but weather-beaten) statue of a 15th-century figure of Charlemagne. A copy of that same statue crowns the south tower.

Grossmünsterplatz. (©) **044/252-59-49.** Cathedral free; towers 3F ($2.45/£1.25). Cathedral Mar 15–Oct daily 9am–6pm; Nov–Mar 14 daily 10am–4pm. Towers Mar–Oct daily 9am–6pm (weather permitting); off season Sat–Sun 10am–4pm (weather permitting). Tram: 4.

Moments **A Summer Walk along the Quays of Zurich**

To walk the **Quays of Zurich**   is an attraction rivaled in the city only by the Swiss National Museum. These promenades have been built along the Zurichsee (Lake Zurich) and the Limmat River. The most famous is **Limmat Quai**, in the virtual heart of Zurich, beginning at the Bahnhof Bridge and extending east to the Rathaus (town hall) and beyond. These quays have lovely gardens planted with beautiful trees such as the linden. The Swiss are known for their love of flowers, which is much in evidence as you join Zurichers for a stroll on the promenade, an especially invigorating experience when spring comes to the city.

Uto Quai is the major lakeside promenade, running from Badeanstalt Uto Quai, a swimming pool, to Bellevue Square and Quai Brucke. The graceful swans you see in the lake aren't just a scenic attraction. Zurichers have found that they're an efficient garbage disposal system, keeping the lake from being polluted as it laps up on their shores. If you stroll as far as **Mythen Quai,** you'll be following the lake along its western shore and out into the countryside where vistas open onto the Alps and, on the far horizon, the Oberland massifs.

Moments Discoveries along Medieval Streets

Even if you have to skip a museum or two, head for the **Alstadt (Old Town)** ★★★, known for its romantic squares, narrow cobblestone streets, winding alleyways that aren't as sinister as they look, fountain-decorated corners, medieval houses, art galleries, boutiques, colorfully quaint restaurants, shops, a scattering of hotels, and antiques stores. The Old Town lies on both sides of the Limmat River, and you might begin your exploration at the **Münsterhof** or former swine market. Excavations have turned up houses here that date back to the 1100s. Once it was the tarrying place of Charlemagne, and to walk its old streets is to follow in the footsteps of historic figures ranging from Mozart and Lenin to Einstein and Carl Jung.

Shaded by trees, the belvedere square of **Lindenhof** is one of the most scenic spots in Zurich, especially favored at twilight time by those who believe in "young love." It can be reached by climbing medieval alleyways from the Fraumünster. Once the site of a Celtic and Roman fort, Lindenhof is a good point to watch the crossing of the Limmat River. The lookout point is graced with a fountain, of course. There's also a good view of the medieval Old Quarter, which rises in layers on the right bank. Many excellent restaurants are located in this vicinity.

Directly south of Münsterbrücke is a Gothic church, rather austere, called the **Wesserkirche** or "water church." When it was built in 1479, it was surrounded by water.

Landesmuseum (Swiss National Museum) ★★★ This museum, located in a big, sprawling gray stone Victorian building in back of the Zurich Hauptbahnhof, offers an epic survey of Swiss culture, art, and history. The collection of artifacts starts off in dim unrecorded time and carries you to the present day. It's like a storybook history of all the cantons that you turn page by page as you go from gallery to gallery.

Religious art sounds a dominant theme, and especially noteworthy are the 16th-century stained glass that was removed from Tänikon Convent and the frescoes from the church of Müstair. Some of the museum's Carolingian art dates from the 9th century. Altarpieces—carved, painted, and gilded—bring back the glory of the Swiss medieval artisan. Several rooms from Fraumünster Abbey are also on view.

The museum's prehistoric section is exceptional, dipping back to the 4th millennium. Switzerland's history as a Roman outpost is explored in several exhibits. And the displays of utensils and furnishings of Swiss life over the centuries are staggering: medieval silverware, 14th-century drinking bowls, tiled 18th-century stoves, 17th-century china, Roman clothing, painted furniture, costumes, even dollhouses. Naturally, arms and armor revive Switzerland's military legacy, from 800 to 1800, although some weapons date from the late Iron Age.

Museumstrasse 2. ⓒ **044/218-65-11.** www.musee-suisse.com. Admission 5F ($4.10/£2.15), 3F ($2.45/£1.25) students and seniors, free for children under 16; special exhibitions 8–12F ($6.55–$9.85/£3.40–£5.10). Tues–Sun 10:30am–5pm. Tram: 3, 4, 5, 11, 13, or 14.

Zurich Kunsthaus (Fine Arts Museum) ✔ This museum is devoted to works mainly from the 19th and 20th centuries, although many of its paintings and sculpture dip back to antiquity. Dating from Victorian times, the collection has grown and grown and is today one of the most important in Europe.

As you enter, note Rodin's *Gate of Hell*. Later on you can explore one of our favorite sections, the **Giacometti wing** ✔, showcasing the artistic development of the amazing Swiss-born artist (1901–66), whose works are characterized by surrealistically elongated forms and hallucinatory moods.

All the legendary names of modern art can be found in the galleries, including a collection of the works of Norwegian artist **Edvard Munch** ✔✔, the largest outside of Oslo. Old Masters such as Rubens and Rembrandt are suitably honored, and one salon contains 17 Rouaults.

Heimplatz 1. ☎ **044/253-84-84.** www.kunsthaus.ch. Admission 6F ($4.90/£2.55) adults, 4F ($3.30/£1.70) seniors, free for children 16 and under; special exhibitions 16F ($13/£6.75) adults, 10F ($8.20/£4.25) children. Tues 10am–6pm; Wed–Fri 10am–8pm; Sat–Sun 10am–6pm. Tram: 3 (marked "Klusplatz").

WHERE TO DINE

Bierhalle Kropf ✔ SWISS/BAVARIAN *Der Kropf* is everyone's favorite beer hall, installed in one of the oldest burgher houses in Zurich, only a short walk from Paradeplatz. Locals flock here for the large portions and affordable prices. Against an old-fashioned Swiss backdrop of stag horns and stained glass, robust and well-prepared platters of mountain favorites, such as mammoth pork shanks, stewed meats, chopped veal, and the famous *rösti* (Swiss-style hash browns) are served.

In Gassen 16. ☎ **044/221-18-05.** Reservations recommended. Main courses 22–44F ($18–$36/£9.35–£18.70). AE, MC, V. Mon–Sat 11:30am–11pm. Closed Easter, Dec 25, and Aug 1. Tram: 2, 8, 9, or 11.

Brasserie Lipp SWISS/FRENCH This bustling bistro was inspired by the world-famous Art Nouveau Brasserie Lipp in Paris. The atmosphere of Paris is re-created here, as is the cuisine; you'll find such old-time classics as peppery steaks and sole meunière on the menu. It's a bustling place, with waiters scurrying about, often bringing in heaping platters of sauerkraut with pork products just as they do in the real thing on the Left Bank of Paris.

Uraniastrasse 9. ☎ **044/211-11-55.** Reservations recommended, especially Fri–Sat. Main courses 30–50F ($25–$41/£13–£21.30). AE, DC, MC, V. Mon–Thurs 11am–11pm (to 2:30am Fri–Sat); Sun 11:45am–10pm. Tram: 6, 7, 11, or 13.

Kaufleuten *finds* INTERNATIONAL Only a few steps from the Bahnhofstrasse, this enduring favorite roams the globe for its culinary inspiration, serving everything from a platter-size Wiener schnitzel fried a golden brown to a fiery coconut and chicken curry from Thailand. It is strong in its freshwater fish dishes, especially salmon, sole, and sea bass, which are prepared almost close to perfection and never allowed to dry out. The restaurant is also a nightlife venue.

Pelikanstrasse 18. ☎ **044/225-33-33.** Reservations recommended. Main courses 26–50F ($21–$41/£10.90–£21.30). AE, DC, MC, V. Mon–Fri 11:30am–2pm; daily 7pm–2am (to 3am Fri–Sat). Tram: 6, 7, 11, or 13.

Mère Catherine PROVENÇAL/FRENCH One of the Alstadt's favorite bistros is nestled in a quiet courtyard, its tranquil cafe tables evoking the Left Bank of Paris. The unpretentious French cooking features fresh fish along with an ever-changing roster of daily specials. Try to arrive early for an aperitif at the Bar Philosophe next door before going to your table to partake of delights that will make you salivate with pleasure.

Moments Sailing Lake Zurich

At some point during your stay in Switzerland's largest city, you'll want to take a lake steamer for a tour around Lake Zurich. Walk to Bahnhofstrasse's lower end and buy a ticket at the pier for any of the dozen or so boats that ply the lake waters from late May to late September. The boats are more or less the same so it doesn't matter which one you take. Most of the steamers contain simple restaurant facilities, and all have two or three levels of decks and lots of windows for wide-angle views of the Swiss mountains and shoreline. During peak season, boats depart at approximately 30-minute intervals. The most distant itinerary from Zurich is to **Rapperswil,** a historic town near the lake's southeastern end. A full-length, round-trip tour of the lake from Zurich to Rapperswil takes 2 hours each way, plus whatever time you opt to spend exploring towns en route. Many visitors opt for shorter boat rides encompassing only the northern third of the lake, where the total trip takes about 90 minutes.

A full-length tour of the lake costs 23F ($19/£9.90) in second class and 38F ($31/£16.10) in first class. The shorter boat ride on the northern third of the lake costs only 7.80F ($6.40/£3.35). For information call ✆ 044/487-13-33.

Nägelihof 3. ✆ **044/250-59-40.** Reservations required. Main courses 19F–26F ($16–$21/£8.30–£10.90). MC, V. Mon–Sat 11am–midnight. Tram: 4 or 15.

Restaurant Reithalle *(Value* INTERNATIONAL   In a former stable on a small island in the heart of Zurich, this local favorite is a friend of the frugal rail passenger. In fair weather, its cobblestone courtyard is mobbed with fun-loving drinkers and diners. Expect a robust and hearty cuisine prepared with fresh ingredients, based on recipes from around the world—even from as far away as Iran. The interior becomes a dance club every Saturday from 11pm to 3am, and restaurant patrons enter free (otherwise there's a cover of 12F/$9.85/£5.10).

In the Theaterhaus Gessnerallee, Gessnerallee 8. ✆ **044/212-0766.** Reservations not necessary. Lunch main courses 18–34F ($15–$28/£7.80–£14.55); dinner main courses 22F–34F ($18–$28/£9.35–£14.55). AE, DC, MC, V. Mon–Fri 11am–midnight; Sat–Sun 6pm–midnight. Tram: 3.

Zunfthaus Zur Zimmerleuten ✵ SWISS   The foundations of this 1708 building date from 1336, when it was originally the carpenters' guildhall. An architectural showpiece, it's now one of the Zurich's most enduring restaurants. A flight of baroque stairs leads from the street level to the elegant dining room, which is decorated with rows of leaded-glass windows and an impressive collection of hunting trophies. Menu items include morel toasts; freshwater bouillabaisse; filet of pike-perch poached in Savoy cabbage; and a local specialty, *ratsherrentopf,* composed of three different filets with rösti and butter sauce. The reward for the kitchen's vigilance is a loyal clientele with discerning palates who enjoys the full-bodied dishes.

Limmatquai 40. ✆ **044/250-53-63.** Reservations recommended. Main courses 27F–55F ($22–$45/£11.45–£23.40). AE, DC, MC, V. Mon–Sat 11:30am–2pm and 6–11pm. Closed mid-July to mid-Aug. Tram: 4 or 15.

SHOPPING

Zurich has been called a shopper's Valhalla, if that's not too pagan a term for such a Protestant city. Within the heart of Zurich are 25 acres (10 hectares) of shopping, including the exclusive stores along the **Bahnhofstrasse,** previewed on p. 806. Along this gold-plated street you can walk with oil-rich sheiks and their families in your search for furs, watches, jewelry, leather goods, silks, and embroidery. If your own oil well didn't come in, you can still shop for souvenirs.

Your shopping adventure might begin more modestly at the top of the street, the **Bahnhofplatz.** Underneath this vast transportation hub is a complex of shops known as **"Shop Ville."**

Bally Schuhfabriken AG, Bahnhofstrasse 66 (© **044/224-39-39**), is the largest official outlet of the famous Swiss chain, occupying a prominent place in a big-windowed store on this shopping artery. For lovers of Bally shoes, this is the place to buy them, although the merchandise is not necessarily cheaper than at other Bally outlets. You'll find the most complete line of Bally shoes here in the world, along with accessories and clothing (most, but not all, of which are made in Switzerland).

If your heart is set on buying a timepiece in Zurich, try **Beyer,** Bahnhofstrasse 31 (© **043/344-63-63**), located midway between the train station and the lake. Besides carrying just about every famous brand of watch made in Switzerland, such as Rolex and Patek Philippe, they also have a surprising museum in the basement, containing timepieces from as early as 1400 B.C. Another sure bet in Zurich would be **Bucherer AG,** Bahnhofstrasse 50 (© **044/211-26-35**). A longtime name in the Swiss watch industry, this store carries an impressive collection of jewelry as well.

Jelmoli Department Store, Seidengasse 1 (© **044/220-44-11**), is a Zurich institution, selling everything a large department store should, from cookware to clothing. Founded 150 years ago by the Ticino-born entrepreneur Johann Peter Jelmoli, the store and the success of its many branches is a legend among the Zurich business community.

Musik Hug, Limmatquai 28–30 (© **044/269-41-41**), is the kind of shop that musicians will love, particularly if they need sheet music for anything from flugelhorn concertos to yodeling duets. It might be the largest repository of Alpine musical tradition anywhere, as well as a commercial music shop stocking woodwind recorders of all sizes and pitches along with flugelhorns and French horns.

Schweizer Heimatwerk, Rudolf Brun-Brücke (© **044/217-83-17**), is only one of a chain of similar stores throughout Zurich. Most of them have the same basic collection of, for example, hand-painted boxes in charmingly naive patterns with or without music mechanisms, bookends, china, decorative stoneware plates, a wide range of textiles, and the obligatory cowbells in all sizes. This particular store has a large selection of glass, embroidery, and woodcarvings, among other items. The English-speaking staff is particularly helpful in suggesting "little gifts."

NIGHTLIFE

The Zurich Opera is the most outstanding local company, performing at **Opernhaus,** Falkenstrasse 1 (© **044/268-64-66**), near Bellevueplatz in the center of the city. The opera house is also a repertory theater, hosting ballets, concerts, and recitals, although it shuts down in July and August. Tickets cost 16F to 380F ($13–$312/£6.75–£162), and the box office is open daily 10am to 6:30pm. The **Zurich Tonhalle Orchestra** performs at the Tonhalle Gesellschaft, Claridenstrasse 7 (© **044/206-34-34**), a 1,500-seat theater, which is also the venue for many internationally known soloists.

Tickets range from 15F to 160F ($12–$131/£6.25–£68.10), and the box office is open daily 10am to 6pm.

More boisterous nightlife is found at the 160-seat **Bierhalle Wolf,** Limmatquai 132 (© **044/251-01-30**), the best-known beer hall in the city, known for its "evergreen music" (folk) played by an oompah band. You can also dine here on the kitchen's robust fare. Cover starts at 6F ($4.90/£2.55), and hours are daily 11am to 2am. The largest nightclub in Zurich, and one of the best, is **X-tra,** in the Limmathaus, Limmatstrasse 118 (© **044/448-15-00**). With a long bar and an outdoor terrace, it features some of the best rock groups in Europe. The cover ranges from 30F to 45F ($25–$37/£13–£19.25), depending on the performers.

For the best New Orleans–style jazz, head for **Casa Bar,** Münstergasse 30 (© **044/261-20-02**), where Dixieland is heard Monday to Friday 5pm to 2am, Sunday 8pm to 2am. Some 60 patrons a night, of various ages, crowd into this bar. House and garage music are featured at **Kaufleuten,** Pelikanstrasse 18 (© **044/225-33-22**), which has four different bar areas and an on-site restaurant. British or Irish pubs are all the rage in Zurich, including **James Joyce Pub,** Pelikanstrasse 8 (© **044/221-18-28**), boasting the furnishings and paneling of an 18th-century pub in Dublin, and **Oliver Twist,** Rindermarkt 6 (© **044/252-47-10**), attracting a fun-loving young crowd that overflows into a summer courtyard.

3 Bern ⭑⭑⭑

Bern, set in the heart of Switzerland, has been the country's capital since 1848. A city of diplomats, it is one of the loveliest places to visit in the country, surrounded on three sides by the River Aare, a body of water to which it is linked symbolically as much as Paris is to the Seine.

Built between the 12th and 18th centuries, Bern is one of the few great medieval cities left in Europe that hasn't been destroyed, torn down, or bombed in wars. In 1983, the United Nations declared it a "World Landmark." It's a city of arcades, nearly 4 miles (6.4km) of them running along the streets of the old sector, and they're weatherproof and traffic free. Underneath these arcades are shops, everything from exclusive boutiques to department stores, from antiques dealers to jewelers. It's a city of fountains and oriel windows, and its old sandstone steps have been trodden for centuries.

The city is a stop on many international rail routes. Trains from France, Italy, Germany, and even Spain all pass through Bern, making it a great stopover point on a cross-continental train trip. The TGV high-speed train, for example, connects Paris with Bern in just 4½ hours. Bern is also situated on most major rail lines in Switzerland, particularly those connecting Geneva (90 min.) and Zurich (1 hr.). We place it second on a rail trip through Switzerland because most people fly into Zurich or Geneva first, though Bern has its own airport at Belpmoos.

Bern can also be your gateway to the Alpine region of central Switzerland, the Bernese Oberland. Trains leave every hour for Interlaken, the capital of the Bernese Oberland, where you can make all sorts of rail connections into the mountains, especially if you want to take the train trip to Jungfraujoch, which for many rail passengers is the most dramatic and scenic trip in all of Switzerland.

STATION INFORMATION
GETTING FROM THE AIRPORT TO THE TRAIN STATION
The **Bern-Belp Airport** (© **031/960-21-11;** www.alpar.ch) is 6 miles (9.6km) south of the city in the town of Belpmoos. International flights arrive from London, Paris,

Bern

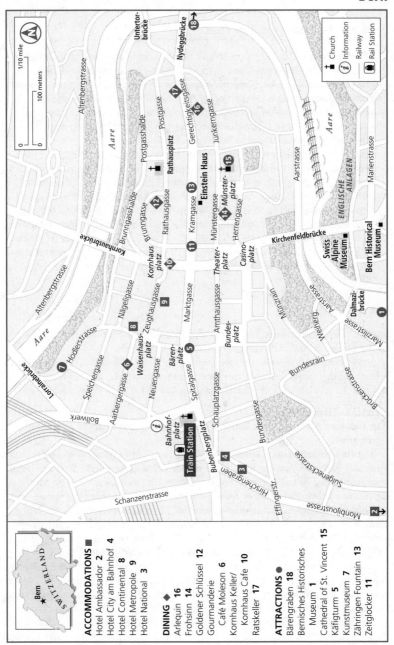

ACCOMMODATIONS ■
Hotel Ambassador **2**
Hotel City am Bahnhof **4**
Hotel Continental **8**
Hotel Metropole **9**
Hotel National **3**

DINING ◆
Arlequin **16**
Frohsinn **14**
Goldener Schlüssel **12**
Gourmanderie
Café Moleson **6**
Kornhaus Keller/
Kornhaus Cafe **10**
Ratskeller **17**

ATTRACTIONS ●
Bärengraben **18**
Bernisches Historisches
Museum **1**
Cathedral of St. Vincent **15**
Käfigturm **5**
Kunstmuseum **7**
Zähringen Fountain **13**
Zeitglocker **11**

Bern: A Center for Rail Trips

Bern is a center for several rail trips that are among the most spectacular in Europe. You'll probably need help from someone at the tourist office to help organize one of these itineraries, but the staff at the Bern Tourist office is now capable of crafting and selling tickets for either one-way or circular itineraries that will take you through some of the most vertiginous landscapes in Europe. One of our favorites involves traveling from Bern through its Oberland region, with rail junctions in towns that include Interlaken, Lauterbrunnen, Wengen, and Kleine Scheidegg, then over the Jungfraujoch via Grindelwald and Interlaken, and back to Bern. Jungfraujoch, at 11,152 feet (3,400m), has the highest railway station in Europe and offers panoramic views over glaciers and the Alps, including the so-called Ice Palace. The cost for this particular itinerary, which is self-conducted, self-guided, and self-scheduled, assuming that participants begin and end their journeys in Bern, is 146F ($120/£62.40) in second class and 227F ($186/£96.70) in first class. For anyone holding a valid Swiss Pass, the price of this itinerary is reduced to 52F ($43/£22.35) for second-class travel, and 80.50F ($66/£34.30) for first-class travel.

and Nice, but transatlantic jets are not able to land here. Fortunately, it's a short hop to Bern from the international airports in Zurich and Geneva.

A taxi from the airport to the city center costs about 38F ($31/£16.10), so it's better to take the shuttle bus that runs between the airport and the Bahnhof (train station) in the city center. The shuttle trip costs 15F ($12/£6.25) one-way.

INSIDE THE STATION

The **Bahnhof** rail station, on Bahnhofplatz, is right in the center of town near all the major hotels.

The **Rail Information Center** inside the station is open Monday to Friday 8am to 7pm and Saturday 9am to 5pm. Here you can also make reservations and validate your railpasses. The location of the office is across the passageway from the tourist center. Many visitors who arrive in Bern choose to visit the Jungfrau, the famous mountain outside Interlaken, whose train station, at 13,638 feet (4,158m) is the highest in Europe. Your railpass will take you from Bern to Interlaken but at the Interlaken station you must purchase a separate ticket on a private railroad for the final trip to Jungfrau. For more rail information and schedules, call © **0900/300-300.**

On the ground level of the station there are money exchange offices including an ATM. The Swiss Railroad operates one of these offices, labeled Change SBB, which is open daily from 6:30am to 9pm. The station also offers a 24-hour baggage storage facility downstairs, charging 4F to 8F ($3.30–$6.55/£1.70–£3.40) for lockers.

The **Bern Tourist Office** is located inside the Bahnhof, on Bahnhofplatz (© **031/328-12-12;** www.bernetourism.ch). It's open June to September daily 9am to 8:30pm; October to May Monday to Saturday 9am to 6:30pm, and on Sunday 10am to 5pm. If you need help finding a hotel room, the tourist office can make a reservation for you for 3F ($2.45/£1.25) in the price range you select. The office also sells hotel packages for 2, 3, or 4 nights in hotels rated anywhere from two to five stars, the latter almost paralyzingly priced.

If your luggage is light, you can walk to your hotel; otherwise, take one of the taxis waiting outside the station.

GETTING AROUND

The public transportation system, **Stadtische Verkehrsbetriebe (SVB),** is a reliable, 48-mile (77km) network of buses and trams. Before you board, purchase a ticket from one of the automatic machines (you'll find one at each stop) because conductors don't sell tickets. If you're caught traveling without one, you'll be fined 80F ($66/£34.30) on the spot in addition to the fare for the ride. A short-range ride (within six stations) costs 1.90F ($1.55/£80p); a normal ticket, valid for 45 minutes one-way, goes for 2.70F ($2.20/£1.15).

To save time and money purchase a **Bern Card** for 20F ($16/£8.30) which entitles you to unlimited travel on the SVB network for 24 hours. Forty-eight- and 72-hour cards are also available. One-day tickets are available at the **ticket offices** at the Railcity Tourist Center, the railway station, and in some hotels and museums. The card also gives you discounts at museums and the zoo.

You can catch a taxi at the public cab ranks, or call a dispatcher; two cab companies you can try are **Nova Taxi** (© **031/331-33-13**), and **Bären Taxi** (© **031/371-11-11**). The first kilometer of any taxi ride in Bern costs from 6.80F to 12F ($5.60–$9.85/£2.90–£5.10), and every kilometer after that costs an additional 3.40F ($2.80/£1.45), depending on how fast the traffic is moving and the time of day. The "average" taxi ride within Bern will probably cost about 18F to 26F ($15–$21/£7.80–£10.90).

WHERE TO STAY

Hotel Ambassador ✿ This nine-floor hotel close to the Bundeshaus, the seat of the Swiss government, is one of the best and most affordable of the moderately priced hotels in Bern. True, its rooms are a bit small and the furnishings are only functional, but they are reasonably comfortable and very well maintained. Rooms like this you expect in Switzerland, but what comes as a surprise is the on-site teppan restaurant with Japanese specialties, including a garden evocative of Tokyo. Unusual for Bern, the hotel also has a private pool with sauna. It's a 5-minute tram ride from the train station (the tram stops right in front of the hotel).

Seftigenstrasse 99, CH-3007 Bern. © 031/370-99-99. Fax 031/371-41-17. www.fhotels.ch. 99 units. 220F–350F ($180–$287/£93.60–£149) double. AE, DC, MC, V. Tram: 9. **Amenities:** 2 restaurants; laundry. *In room:* Hair dryer.

Hotel City am Bahnhof This hotel takes its name from the train station, which is only 2 blocks away. If your luggage is light, you can walk straight here from the depot. The hotel is equally popular with business clients and visitors to Bern. The midsize bedrooms with acceptable—hardly exciting—furnishings are far from luxurious, but the maintenance level is high. Rooms come with a minibar and TV but little else. Breakfast is the only meal served.

Bahnhofplatz 7, CH-3011, Bern. © 031/311-53-77. Fax 031/311-06-36. www.fhotels.ch. 58 units. 180F–240F ($148–$197/£76.95–£102) double. AE, DC, MC, V. **Amenities:** Breakfast lounge; laundry.

Hotel Continental This is one of the better, though still fairly impersonal, government-rated, three-star hotels clustered around the Bern Bahnhof. It charges very fair prices—at least by the standards of high-priced Bern—for its comfortably furnished bedrooms. The rooms, although small, are well maintained and outfitted in both contemporary and traditional pieces; flower boxes outside the bedroom windows are a nice touch. In fair weather, breakfast is taken under a canopied terrace.

Zeughausgasse 27, CH-3011 Bern. ✆ **031/329-21-21.** Fax 031/329-21-99. www.hotel-continental.ch. 43 units. 165F–195F ($135–$160/£70.20–£83.20) double. Rates include buffet breakfast. AE, DC, MC, V. Tram: 3 or 9. **Amenities:** Lounge; nonsmoking rooms; laundry.

Hotel Metropole   This hotel is situated between the Bern Bahnhof and the Altstadt, so it's convenient to most attractions and all transportation. The hotel's small bedrooms are comfortably furnished in both traditional and contemporary style, and have equally small bathrooms. Don't expect too many amenities—minimalism is the word here.

Zeughausgasse 26, CH-3011 Bern. ✆ **031/311-50-21.** Fax 031/312-11-53. www.hotelmetropole.ch. 58 units. 160F–180F ($131–$148/£68.10–£76.95) double. Rates include buffet breakfast. AE, DC, MC, V. Tram: 9. **Amenities:** Nonsmoking rooms.

Hotel National *Value*   Originally built in 1908 as a brewery, and later transformed into a textile factory, this simple but dignified hotel enjoys a consistently high occupancy thanks to its good value and well-scrubbed interior. The reception area lies one floor above street level, and to reach it, you'll either take the stairs or a "historically significant" elevator that might remind you of a rather quaint birdcage. The hotel will look even better in 2008, thanks to the radical restoration of the neighborhood around the Bahnhof, which, at the time of this writing, was a dusty construction site. Accommodations are sober but reliable, utterly devoid of any contemporary fashion statements or accessories, and occupied by a value-conscious clientele. Of particular note are the bedrooms on the uppermost floor, where a recent renovation exposed some of the massive timber trusses that form the exterior's mansard roof.

Hirschengraben 24, CH-3011 Bern. ✆ **031/381-1988.** Fax 031/381-6878. www.nationalbern.ch. 46 units, 32 with private bathroom. Double with shared bathroom 120F ($98/£50.95); double with private bathroom 140F–160F ($115–$131/£59.80–£68.10). AE, MC, V. Tram: 3, 5, or 9. **Amenities:** Restaurant. *In room:* No phone in rooms w/no bathroom.

TOP ATTRACTIONS & SPECIAL MOMENTS

Marktgasse is the principal artery of the Old Town, and it's lined with luxurious shops and boutiques—the number of florists revealing the Bernese love of flowers. In this traffic-free sector you can stroll at your leisure, shopping and admiring the 17th- and 18th-century houses. Eventually you'll come to **Junkerngasse,** the most prestigious street in Bern, lined with patrician houses.

Marktgasse rolls on until it becomes **Kramgasse,** the first street to the right of the city's clock tower. It has many antiques shops and art galleries. You'll also view many turrets and oriel windows, and you'll come upon the 1535 **Zähringen fountain,** showing a bear, the city's mascot, in armor. The **Käfigturm** (prison tower) on Marktgasse marked the boundary line of Bern in the 13th century. Restored in the 18th century, it stands at the top of the Marktgasse.

To the east stands the **Zeitglocken** or Clock Tower, which was built in the 12th century and restored in the 16th century. Until 1250 it was the west gate of Bern. Four minutes before every hour, crowds gather for what has been called "the world's oldest and biggest horological puppet show." Mechanical bears (the little bear cubs are everybody's favorite), jesters, and emperors put on an animated show—it's one of the longest running acts in show business, staged since 1530.

Bärengraben *(?)*   The famous bear pits are a deep, moon-shaped den where the bears, those mascots of Bern, have been kept since 1480. Beloved by the Bernese, the bears are pampered and fed. Everybody seemingly drops by here, throwing these hungry beasts a carrot. The pits are reached by going across Nydegg Bridge, which has a great view of the city. It was built over a gorge of the river and its major stone arch has a span of 180 feet (55m). The bears have long been adopted as the heraldic symbol of Bern.

East end of Nydeggbrücke. Free admission. 3F ($2.45/£1.25) to feed the bears. June–Sept daily 9am–5:30pm; Oct–May daily 9:30am–4:30pm.

Bernisches Historisches Museum (Bern Historical Museum) ✿✿   This neo-Gothic castle, built in the Swiss fortress style of the 16th century, contains historical relics, along with archaeological, ethnographic, and numismatic collections. The main attraction is a series of seven 15th-century tapestries. A tapestry called *The Thousand Flowers,* plus four others telling the story of Julius Caesar, once belonged to the dukes of Burgundy. A number of rural and urban rooms, filled with period furnishings and artifacts, are also open to the public.

Helvetiaplatz 5. ✆ 031/350-77-11. Admission 8F ($6.55/£3.40) adults, 5.50F ($4.50/£2.35) students and seniors, free for children 16 and under. Tues–Sun 10am–5pm. Tram: 3 or 5.

Cathedral of St. Vincent ✿   The church was begun in 1421, although its tower wasn't completed until 1893. Its **belfry** ✿✿, dominating Bern, is 300 feet high (91m), and at the top a panoramic sweep of the Bernese Alps unfolds. You can climb a staircase, some 270 steps, to the platform tower. You'll also have a great vista over the Old Town and its bridges and a view of the **Aare.**

The cathedral or Münster is one of the newer of the Gothic churches of Switzerland. Its most exceptional feature is the **tympanum** ✿✿ over the main portal, with more than 200 figures. Some of them are painted, and the vanquished ones in this Last Judgment setting are singled out for particularly harsh treatment. The mammoth stained-glass windows in the chancel were created in the 15th century. The choir stalls (c. 1523) brought the Renaissance to Bern. Inside the Matter Chapel is a curious stained-glass window, the *Dance of Death,* constructed in the closing year of World War I but based on a much older design.

Münsterplatz. ✆ 031/312-04-62. Cathedral free; viewing platform 3F ($2.45/£1.25) adults, 1F (80¢/£40p) children. Cathedral Easter Sun–Oct Tues–Sat 10am–5pm, Sun 11:30am–5pm; off season Tues–Fri 10am–noon and 2–4pm, Sat 10am–noon and 2–5pm, Sun 11:30am–2pm. Viewing platform closes half an hour before cathedral. Bus: 12.

Kunstmuseum ✿   The museum has both Swiss and foreign works, placing its emphasis on the 19th and 20th centuries. Some of its paintings, however, go back to the 14th century. There is a collection of Italian "primitives," such as Fra Angelico's *Virgin and Child.* Swiss primitives include one from the Master of the Carnation (Paul Löwensprung, d. 1499), who signed his work with either a red or a white carnation.

The romantic painter Hodler is represented by allegorical frescoes, depicting *Day* and, conversely, *Night.* Several Impressionists are represented, including Monet, Manet, Sisley, and Cézanne; you'll also find works by such artists as Delacroix and Bonnard.

Hodlerstrasse 12. ✆ 031/328-09-44. Permanent collection 7F ($5.75/£3) adults, 5F ($4.10/£2.15) seniors; special exhibitions up to 18F ($15/£7.80) extra. Tues 10am–9pm; Wed–Sun 10am–5pm. Bus: 20.

The Paul Klee Collection (Zentrum Paul Klee) ✿✿✿   The painter was born in Switzerland in 1879. The local collection of his works includes 40 oils, 2,000 drawings, and many gouaches and watercolors. Klee had a style characterized by fantasy forms in line and light colors. Until around 2004, most of the artworks within this museum were contained within an overcrowded series of rooms within the also-recommended

> ### Moments   On the Hoof through Bern
>
> Bern is a walking city and your own two feet are the only practical means of exploring Altstadt and its many attractions. You can see what there is to see here in about 2½ hours.
>
> Don't overlook the possibility of walks in Greater Bern, including Bern's own mountain, **Gurten,** a popular day trip destination reached in 25 minutes by tram 9 and a rack railway. Eurail passholders and Swiss Passholders get a 50% discount on the railway. Once here, you'll find many walking paths and can enjoy a panorama over the Alps. There's also a children's playground.
>
> In and around Bern you'll find 155 miles (250km) of **marked rambling paths.** One of the most scenic runs along the banks of the Aare through the English gardens, the Dählhölzli Zoological Gardens, Elfenau Park, and the Bremgarten woods.
>
> For **jogging and running,** the best spots are the Aare River Run (Dalmaziquai), stretching 2¼ miles (4km), or the Aare River Run–Bear Pits, which is 3 miles (5km) long.

Kunstmuseum. That was before they were moved into a museum created expressly for them by Renzo Piano, one of the most celebrated architects of Italy. Today, in a location about 5km (3 miles) east of Bern's Alstadt, more than 4,000 works by the artist are proudly displayed as a kind of homage to Bern's "local son who made good."

Monument in Fruchtland 3. (C) **031/359-0101.** Entrance 16F ($13/£6.75) adults, 14F ($11/£5.70) children 6–16. Free for persons 5 and under. Tues–Sun 10am–5pm; Thurs till 9pm. Tram: 5. Bus: 12.

WHERE TO DINE

Arlequin SWISS/ITALIAN   Artists, writers, and frugal diners frequent this informal restaurant, which sets out tables on a pergola-shaded, open-air terrace in summer. From Wednesday to Friday, the chef sautés a platter-wide Wiener schnitzel—the best in town—a golden brown. At other times of the week you can dig into a lot of old-time Swiss favorites, such as goulash soup, and even some specialties from south of the border in Italy.

Gerechtigkeitsgasse 51. (C) **031/311-39-46.** Reservations recommended. Main courses 15F–30F ($12–$25/£6.25–£13); fixed-price meal 20F ($16/£8.30). AE, MC, V. Tues–Sat 11am–1pm and 5–10pm. Tram: 9.

Frohsinn *(Finds* SWISS/CONTINENTAL   Small and intimate, this bistro sits in the shadow of the Bern Clock Tower. Its intimate atmosphere and good, moderately priced food has attracted a loyal following of journalists and national politicians. Sometimes the chefs dip across the borders into neighboring countries, especially France and Italy, for their recipes, which are prepared with first-rate ingredients purchased at the market that day.

Münstergasse 54. (C) **031/311-37-68.** Reservations required. Main courses 22F–52F ($18–$43/£9.35–£22.35). AE, DC, MC, V. Tues–Sat 8am–2pm and 6–11:30pm. Tram: 54.

Gourmanderie Café Moleson *(Finds* INTERNATIONAL   This looks like your basic cafe but the food at this joint is rather un-cafe-like. Market-fresh ingredients and skilled preparation combine to produce good-tasting dishes that attract everyone from politicians to artists. The friendly English-speaking staff will guide you through the specials of the day. Try such dishes as a sautéed filet of beef in a paprika cream sauce with fresh mushrooms, or else grilled organic chicken breast with a rich salad bowl of bacon, eggs, pineapple, cashew nuts, and a homemade dressing.

Aarbergerasse 24, 3011 Bern. © 031/311-44-63. www.moleson-bern.ch. Reservations not required. Main courses 26F–45F ($21–$37/£10.90–£19.25); fixed-price dinner 59F ($48/£24.95) 3 courses, 69F ($57/£29.65) 4 courses. AE, DC, MC, V. Mon-Fri 11:30am–2:30pm; Mon–Sat 6-11:30pm.

Kornhaus Keller/Kornhaus Café SWISS/MEDITERRANEAN   With a pedigree dating from the 1700s, this is the most famous restaurant and beer cellar in Bern. Installed in a converted grain warehouse, this veteran favorite hardly serves the best food in Bern, although the acceptable, rib-sticking fare is dished out in heaping portions. The 450-plus-seat dining room is filled every night and the restaurant keeps patrons in a convivial mood by presenting folk music from the Alps. Most diners come here for the good times under the soaring vaulted ceilings—you won't find a more jovial atmosphere elsewhere in Bern.

Kornhausplatz 18. © 031/327-72-72. Reservations recommended in cellar-level restaurant, not necessary in cafe. Main courses in cellar 36F–48F ($30–$39/£15.60–£20.30); platters and snack items in cafe 15F–27F ($12–$22/ £6.25–£11.45); glasses of wine and tea in cafe 6F–8F ($4.90–$6.55/£2.55–£3.40) each. AE, DC, MC, V. Cafe daily 8:30am–12:30am; cellar Mon–Sat noon–2pm; daily 6–11pm (last order). Cellar-level bar 6pm–12:30am or 2am, depending on business.

Ratskeller Kids SWISS   This historic establishment offers old masonry, modern paneling, and a battalion of busy waitresses serving ample portions of good, rib-sticking food. This dining room has long been the family favorite of generations of locals. Specialties include rack of lamb *a la diable* for two, an omelet soufflé aux fruits, veal kidneys Robert, and *côte de veau* (veal steak) in butter sauce. Your best bet is the tiny filet of perch (*egli* in German) with white sauce on a bed of spinach. Prized by gourmets, this tiny fish is native to the lakes around Bern.

Gerechtigkeitsgasse 81. © 031/311-17-71. Reservations recommended. Main courses 28F–50F ($23–$41/£11.95– £21.30). AE, DC, MC, V. Daily 11:30am–2pm and 6–11pm. Tram: 9.

SHOPPING

You'll find stores of all types along Bern's 4 miles (6km) of arcades. The main shopping streets are **Spitalgasse, Kramgasse, Postgasse, Marktgasse,** and **Gerechtigkeitsgasse.**

With a few exceptions, stores in the city center are open on Monday from 2 to 6:30pm; on Tuesday, Wednesday, and Friday from 8:15am to 6:30pm; on Thursday from 8:15am to 9pm; and on Saturday from 8:15am to 4pm. They're closed on Sundays.

You might begin your shopping excursion at **Globus,** Spitalgasse 17 (© **031/313-40-40**), a major department store that has been compared to Bloomingdale's, with departments for everything. Many people from the Bernese Oberland come into Bern just to shop at Globus.

The best handicrafts, souvenirs, and gifts are found at **Heimatwerk,** Kramgasse 61 (© **031/311-30-00**), located on a historic street near the Clock Tower. This outlet sells handicrafts from all over Switzerland, including textiles, woodcarvings, music boxes, and jewelry.

NIGHTLIFE

Bern Guide, distributed free by the tourist office, keeps a current list of cultural events.

The **Bern Symphony Orchestra,** one of the finest orchestras in Switzerland, is conducted by the acclaimed Russian-born Dmitrij Kitajenko, whose services are supplemented by frequent guest conductors from around the world. Concerts by the orchestra are usually performed at the concert facilities in the **Bern Casino,** Herrengasse 25 (© 031/328-02-28). Except for a summer vacation usually lasting from July until mid-August, the box office is open Monday through Friday from 12:30 to 3pm. Tickets range from 20F to 65F ($16–$53/£8.30–£27.55).

Major opera and ballet performances are usually staged in what is Bern's most beautiful theater, the century-old **Stadttheater,** Kornhausplatz 20 (© 031/329-51-11). Performances are often in German, and to a lesser degree in French, but the language barrier usually won't get in the way of enjoying a performance.

Klötzlikeller, Gerechtigkeitsgasse 62 (© 031/311-74-56), the oldest wine tavern in Bern, is near the Gerechtigkeitsbrunnen (Fountain of Justice), the first fountain you see on your walk from the Bärengraben (Bear Pits) to the Zytgloggeturm (Clock Tower). Watch for the lantern outside an angled cellar door. The well-known tavern dates from 1635 and is leased by the city to an independent operator. Some 20 different wines are sold by the glass, with prices starting at 9F ($7.40/£3.85). The menu is changed every 6 weeks. In summer hours are Tuesday to Friday 4 to 11:30pm; off-season Monday to Saturday 4 to 11:30pm.

Marians' Jazzroom, Engerstrasse 54 (© 031/309-61-11), has its own separate entrance from the Innere Enge Hotel. Unique in Bern, it serves up not only food and drink, but the finest traditional jazz performed live by top artists from around the world. From Tuesday to Thursday, hours are 7pm to midnight, Friday 7:30pm to 1am, Saturday 7pm to 2am. On Saturday, there is a Concert Apéro from 4:30 to 6:30pm, and on some Sundays there is a Jazz Brunch from 10am to 1:30pm. Cover ranges from 15F to 47F ($12–$39/£6.25–£20.30), depending on the act. Closed June 6 to September 7.

Come Back Bar, Rathausgasse 42 (© 031/311-77-13), is a tavern that's cosmopolitan and tolerant, and likely to attract lots of genuinely cool artists and hipsters in Bern. It occupies the cellar vaults below the medieval buildings of the Rathausgasse. Inside, blinking lights frame a discreet dance floor and a long bar functions as a local hangout for many of the gay and gay-friendly residents of the Old Town. It's especially crowded on weekends, with a calmer, more low-key approach to things during weeknights. Open daily 6pm to 12:30am (until 3:30am Fri–Sat).

4 Lausanne ✶✶✶

Lausanne, the second largest city on Lake Geneva and the fifth largest city in Switzerland, rises in tiers from the lake. A haunt of international celebrities, Lausanne is 134 miles (214km) southwest of Zurich and is easily reached by rail. Either Lausanne or Geneva (see later) can be your base for exploring Lake Geneva, which the Swiss call Lac Léman.

Many rail passengers even use Lausanne as a base for a day trip to Geneva, as trains connect these two lakeside cities every 20 minutes (trip time: 35–50 min.). If you're in France and want to visit Switzerland next door, you can also take one of four trains per day (trip time between Paris and Lausanne is approximately 4 hr.).

This university city has been inhabited since the Stone Age and was the ancient Roman town of *Lousanna*. In 1803, it became the 19th canton to join the Confederation, and is today the capital of the canton of Vaud.

Ouchy, once a sleepy fishing hamlet, is now the port and hotel resort area of Lausanne. The lakefront of Lausanne consists of shady quays and tropical plants spread across a lakefront district of about half a mile (.8km). The **Château d'Ouchy** stands on place de la Navigation; from here, place du Port adjoins immediately on the east. **Quai de Belgique** and **quai d'Ouchy** are lakefront promenades bursting with greenery and offering the best views of the lake.

Haute Ville or the Upper Town is the most ancient part of Lausanne and is best explored on foot (see box below). The Upper and Lower towns are connected by a small metro or subway.

STATION INFORMATION

GETTING FROM THE AIRPORT TO THE TRAIN STATION

Lausanne doesn't have an airport, so most visitors fly to Geneva–Cointrin Airport in Geneva (p. 827) and then travel on to Lausanne. The train from Geneva leaves for Lausanne every 20 minutes and the trip takes about 45 minutes. Call ✆ **0900/300-300** for **train** schedules.

In addition, between late May and late September a lake steamer cruises several times a day in both directions between Geneva and Saint-Gingolph, Lausanne, Vevey, Montreux, and Nyon. Sailing time from Geneva is about 3½ hours. Round-trip transit from Geneva costs 75F ($62/£32.25) in first class, 55F ($45/£23.40) in second class, with 50% discounts for children 16 and under; it's free to passholders. For information, contact the **Compagnie Générale de Navigation (CGN),** 17 av. de Rhodanie (✆ **0848-811-848**).

Lausanne's railway station is a steep, 20-minute uphill climb from the ferryboat terminal and recommended only for the enthusiastic and the very fit. More appealing is a 7-minute metro ride, priced at 2.40F ($1.95/£1) per person, between the stations of **Embarcadère** (immediately adjacent to the ferryboat terminal) and **Gare CFF.**

INSIDE THE STATION

Trains arrive at the **Lausanne Train Station,** place de la Gare (✆ **0900/300-300**), with arrivals from Basel every hour (trip time: 2½ hr.) or from Zurich via Biel at the rate of three trains per hour (trip time: 2½ hr.).

The **Lausanne Tourist Office** (✆ **21/613-73-73;** www.lausanne-tourisme.ch) is located in the main hall of the train station and is open daily 9am to 7pm in high season (closes at 6pm off season). The multilingual staff here will make hotel reservations for a 3% commission. They'll also sell you one of two distinctly different passes. The **Lausanne Pass** (also known as a *carte journalière,* a **Lausanne Daily Ticket,** or a **24-Hour Pass**), priced at 7F ($5.75/£3), is good for 24 consecutive hours of free travel on any bus or metro line within the town center.

There is also a **currency exchange kiosk** at the station (✆ **021/312-38-24**), which charges only a 5F ($4.10/£2.15) commission or else no commission on traveler's checks. If your credit card allows it, the office also makes cash advances during its daily business hours of 8am to 7pm.

GETTING AROUND

To avoid the crawling pace of the city's trams, take the metro, the city's subway system. The trip between the heart of the Haute Ville and Ouchy takes 6 minutes. Departures are every 7½ minutes Monday to Friday from 6:15am to 11:45pm. During off-hours and on weekends and holidays, trains run every 15 minutes. A one-way ride from the town center to Ouchy costs 2.40F ($1.95/£1) ; a 24-hour ticket sells for 7F ($5.75/£3).

The **TL (Lausanne Public Transport Company)** has a well-designed network of trams and buses whose routes complement the city's subway line. The tram or bus fare is 2.40F ($1.95/£1), regardless of the distance, for a single trip completed within 60 minutes on lines 1 to 50 of the TL urban network on the Lausanne-Ouchy metro.

You can purchase or stamp your tickets at the automatic machines installed at most stops, or just ask the driver. (A surcharge is collected if you get your ticket from the driver at a stop that has a machine.) A 1-day ticket for unlimited rides costs 7F ($5.75/£3) for adults, 5.70F ($4.65/£2.40) for children.

Lausanne has dozens of taxi stands, where you'll usually find a long line of people waiting for a cab. Alternatively, you can telephone **Allô Taxis** (© **0800/87-08-72**) or **Taxiphone** (© **0800/80-18-02**) for a cab. The meter starts at 8F ($6.55/£3.40); each kilometer traveled adds 3.50F ($2.85/£1.50) during daylight hours in town, or 4F ($3.30/£1.70) in town on weekends or at night between 8pm and 6am. For trips outside the town limits, each kilometer traveled costs 5F ($4.10/£2.15), regardless of the time of day. The first 22 pounds of luggage is free, with 1F (80¢/40p) charged for every suitcase thereafter. You may also use the **Fast Baggage service,** which offers same-day luggage delivery between five destinations in Switzerland (cost starts at about 25F/$21/£10.90). Passengers can check in their luggage at the train station no later than 9am and collect it at the final destination from 6pm or later the same day (hours vary, so check before you use the service). For more information on the service and on luggage restrictions, contact **Rail Europe** (**www.raileurope.com**).

You can rent bikes at the baggage-forwarding counter of the **railroad station** (© **0900-300-300**). It's open daily from 6:50am to 7:50pm. The cost is 32F ($26/£13.50) per day. You can easily bike around the Lower Town—the part that borders the lake is relatively flat—but it isn't recommended in the Upper Town where the streets are very steep.

WHERE TO STAY

Beau-Rivage Palace ✦✦✦ One of Switzerland's most legendary hotels, this *beaux-arts* luxury property sits directly beside Lac Léman, surrounded by 10 acres (4 hectares) of lush gardens. If you plan on splurging on a hotel room in Switzerland, here's the place to do it. Built in 1861, and enlarged in 1908, the hotel has been frequently renovated, but always with a sense of respect (reverence, even), for its original architecture. It's among the last bastions of formal Europe, attracting *la grande bourgeoisie.* In the tradition of the grand hotels of the early 20th century, rooms come in a wide range of styles. Even the least expensive units have Oriental carpets, a mixture of genuine antiques with convincing reproductions, and private balconies overlooking Lac Léman.

17-19 place du Port, CH-1006 Lausanne-Ouchy. © **800/223-6800** in the U.S., or 021/613-33-33. Fax 021/613-33-34. www.brp.ch. 169 units. 470F–780F ($385–$640/£200–£333) double; from 1,050F ($861/£448) suite. AE, DC, MC, V. Parking 25F ($21/£10.90). Metro: Ouchy. **Amenities:** 3 restaurants; 2 bars; laundry. *In room:* Hair dryer.

Hotel Agora ✦ For rail travelers, this hotel is the most convenient base in town as it's only 900 feet (270m) from the Lausanne train depot. Opened in 1987, the six-story structure brings a futuristic look to old Lausanne—its architecture of sculpted marble has been compared by locals to the facade of a spaceship. The small to midsize bedrooms are set behind soundproof windows and offer comfortable furnishings and modern plumbing.

9 av. du Rond-Point, CH-1006 Lausanne. ✆ 021/555-59-55. Fax 021/555-59-59. www.fhotels.ch. 82 units. 215F–260F ($176–$213/£91.50–£111) double; 420F ($344/£179) junior suite. AE, DC, MC, V. Bus: 1, 3, or 5. **Amenities:** Laundry; nonsmoking rooms. *In room:* Hair dryer.

Hotel Aulac *Value*   This hotel, on the Ouchy lakefront, is housed in a mellow old baroque-styled mansion with a three-story Renaissance-influenced porch. It dates from the turn of the 20th century as evoked by its mansard roof with tiles and its towering Victorian clock tower. The bedrooms are among the least expensive along the waterfront, although hardly the best. They never rise to more than those found in a low-rent motel, but maintenance is high and the furnishings comfortable.

4 place de la Navigation, CH-1000 Lausanne-Ouchy. ✆ 021/613-15-00. Fax 021/613-15-15. www.aulac.ch. 84 units. 210F–270F ($172–$221/£89.45–£115) double; 360F ($295/£153) suite. Rates include continental breakfast. AE, DC, MC, V. Metro: Ouchy. **Amenities:** Restaurant; laundry. *In room:* Hair dryer.

Hotel Continental   Across from the Lausanne train station, the Continental competes with the Agora (see above) for the most convenient hotel for passengers arriving by train. Because it's cheaper, the Agora is often fully booked, so the larger Continental is a viable alternative, as it, too, is a contemporary hotel. The accommodations here range from midsize to large, and are well maintained and comfortably furnished with modern pieces, soundproof windows, and tiled bathrooms.

2 place de la Gare, CH-1001 Lausanne. ✆ 021/321-88-00. Fax 021/321-88-01. www.hotelcontinental.ch. 116 units. 335F–390F ($275–$320/£143–£166) double; 460F ($377/£196) junior suite. AE, DC, MC, V. Rates include buffet breakfast. **Amenities:** 2 restaurants; bar; laundry; babysitting; rooms for those w/limited mobility; nonsmoking rooms. *In room:* Hair dryer.

Hotel Elite *&*   Though located in the center of Lausanne and a short uphill walk from the train station, this white-painted, five-story hotel has a tranquil atmosphere and a small garden with fruit trees. Originally built as a villa in the late 1890s, it was turned into a hotel in 1938 and has been successfully run by the same family ever since. The midsize bedrooms, some with air-conditioning and one with a kitchenette, are clean and neatly furnished. Bathrooms have either a shower, a bath, or both. The best units are those on the fourth floor, as they open onto views of the lake.

1 av. Sainte-Luce, CH-1003 Lausanne. ✆ 021/320-23-61. Fax 021/320-39-63. www.elite-lausanne.ch. 33 units. 175F–230F ($144–$189/£74.90–£98.30) double; 365F–410F ($299–$336/£156–£175) junior suite. Rates include buffet breakfast. AE, DC, MC, V. Bus: 1, 3, or 5. **Amenities:** Breakfast lounge; laundry; all nonsmoking rooms. *In room:* Hair dryer.

Minotel AlaGare   Taking its name from the nearby train station *(gare),* this hotel offers affordable and convenient, if basic, accommodations for rail travelers. It's especially inviting in summer when its window boxes burst into bloom with geraniums. The paneled public rooms lead to a series of small but clean and comfortable bedrooms, each with modern plumbing.

14 rue du Simplon, CH-1006 Lausanne. ✆ 021/617-92-52. Fax 021/617-92-55. www.alagare.com. 45 units. 141F–189F ($116–$155/£60.30–£80.60) double. Rates include buffet breakfast. AE, DC, MC, V. Bus: 1, 3, or 5. Closed Dec 29–Jan 5. **Amenities:** Restaurant; nonsmoking rooms. *In room:* Hair dryer.

TOP ATTRACTIONS & SPECIAL MOMENTS

Château de Beaulieu et Musée de l'Art Brut *&*   If you find the bizarre art in this gallery "disturbing," know that it was painted by disturbed individuals. Located on the northwestern side of town, this château dates from 1756 and was once occupied by Madame de Staël. The museum displays what the artist Jean Dubuffet called

Moments   A Walk through the Middle Ages

Lausanne's Upper Town or **Haute Ville** ✶✶ still evokes the Middle Ages—a night watchman even calls out the hours from 10pm to 2am from atop the cathedral's belfry. Walking through the old town of Lausanne is one of its major attractions and the best way to absorb the medieval atmosphere. It's easy to get lost—and that's part of the fun. If you don't want to be so care-free, you can also take an organized walking tour (see below). This area is north of the railroad station; you can reach it by strolling along rue du Petit-Chêne.

The focal point of the Upper Town, and the shopping and business heart of Lausanne, is **place Saint-François.** The Church of St. François, from the 13th century, is all that remains of an old Franciscan friary. Today the square is regrettably filled with office blocks and the main post office. While vehi-cles are permitted south of the church, the area to the north is a pedestrian-only zone; it has more than 1¼ miles (2km) of streets, including **rue de Bourg,** northeast of the church, the best street for shopping. Rue de Bourg leads to the large, bustling rue Caroline, which winds north to **Pont des Bessières,** one of the three bridges erected at the turn of the century to connect the three hills on which Lausanne was built. From the bridge, you'll see the Haute Ville on your right, with the 13th-century **Cathedral of Lau-sanne,** opening onto place de la Cathédrale. From the square, rue du Cité-de-Vant goes north to the 14th-century **Château Saint-Marie,** on place du Château—once the home of bishops and now housing the offices of the canton administration.

From here, avenue de l'Université leads to **place de la Riponne,** with the **Palais de Rumine** on its east side. From place de la Riponne, rue Pierre-Viret leads to the **Escaliers du Marché,** a covered stairway dating from the Mid-dle Ages. You can also take rue Madeleine from the place de la Riponne, continuing south to place de la Palud. On the side of place de la Palud stands the 17th-century **Hôtel de Ville** (town hall).

South of place de la Palud is rue du Pont, which turns into rue Saint-François (after crossing rue Centrale). Nearby, at **place du Flon,** you can catch the subway to Ouchy. In recent years place du Flon, with its cafes and bars, has become a favorite evening hangout.

Lausanne's civic authorities conduct a **guided walking tour** of their city, lasting 1 to 2 hours, Monday to Saturday May to September. Departure is from place de la Palud, adjacent to the city hall, at 10am and 3pm. The cost is 10F ($8.20/£4.25) for adults, 5F ($4.10/£2.15) for seniors. Students and chil-dren are free. For reservations, call ✆ 021/321-77-66.

art brut in the 1940s. This curious mélange of artwork was collected by the painter from prisoners, the mentally ill, and the criminally insane. It's a bizarre twilight zone of art, often dubbed "psychopathological," especially the art by schizophrenics. Dubuffet despised the pretentiousness of the avant-garde art scene around him, and as a form of protest decided to begin this collection of the works of "nonartists," many of whom he found superior to the more established artists of his day.

11 av. des Bergières. ℂ 021/315-25-70. www.artbrut.ch Admission 10F ($8.20/£4.25) adults, 5F ($4.10/£2.15) seniors, students, and children. Free admission first Sat of each month. Tues–Sun 11am–6pm. Bus: 2 to Beaulieu.

Lausanne Cathédrale 🕮🕮🕮   The focal point of the Upper Town is one of the finest medieval churches in Switzerland—in fact, one of the most beautiful Gothic structures in Europe, standing 500 feet (152m) above Lake Geneva. Construction began in 1175; in 1275, the church was consecrated by Pope Gregory X. The doors and facade of the cathedral are luxuriously ornamented with sculptures and bas-reliefs. The architect Eugène Viollet-le-Duc began a restoration of the cathedral in the 19th century—and it's still ongoing. The interior is relatively austere except for some 13th-century choir stalls; the rose window also dates from the 13th century. The cathedral has two towers; you can climb the 225 steps to the observation deck of one of the towers.

Place de la Cathédrale. ℂ 021/316-71-61. Admission cathedral free; tower 2F ($1.65/£0.85). Apr–Sept Mon–Fri 7am–7pm, Sat–Sun 8am–7pm; Oct–Mar Mon–Fri 7am–7pm, Sat–Sun 8am–5:30pm. Visits not permitted Sun morning during services. Bus: 7 or 16.

WHERE TO DINE

À la Pomme de Pin 🕮🕮 TRADITIONAL FRENCH/SWISS   Our favorite restaurant in Lausanne's old town lies within a 17th-century setting between the back side of the cathedral and the château. There are actually two restaurants here, including a brasserie with leather banquettes and a more expensive and formal restaurant, where prices are at least 25% higher and the cuisine is more elaborate and "gastronomic" than in its cheaper counterpart. Main courses in the brasserie are likely to include filet of fera (a whitefish from the nearby lake) prepared with white wine, parsley, and tomatoes. Main courses in the restaurant include rack of Emmenthaler Valley veal with a mousseline of potatoes and foie gras.

11 rue Cité Derrière. ℂ 021/323-4656. Reservations recommended. In the brasserie, main courses 18.50F–32F ($15–$26/£7.80–£13.50); in the restaurant, main courses 28F–58F ($23–$48/£11.95–£24.95). AE, DC, MC, V. Mon–Fri 11:30am–2:30pm; Mon–Sat 7–10:30pm. Closed Aug.

Buffet de la Gare CFF SWISS/FRENCH   Surprising as it may seem, one of the town's best inexpensive restaurants is inside the Lausanne railway station itself, and frugal city dwellers often come here for a good brasserie dinner. This is not a rail station fast-food joint, but an informal restaurant offering well-prepared dishes cooked to order and made from market-fresh ingredients. There is both a brasserie section for more casual dining (it's more fun), as well as a more formal restaurant area (more sedate), although the prices and the kitchens are the same.

In the train station, 11 place de la Gare. ℂ 021/311-49-00. Reservations recommended in the restaurant only. Main courses 16F–62F ($13–$51/£6.75–£26.50); fixed–price menu 32F ($26/£13.50). MC, V. Restaurant daily 6am–midnight; brasserie daily 11am–midnight. Bus: 1, 3, or 5.

Café Beau-Rivage 🕮 SWISS   Reached through the exquisitely maintained gardens of the plush hotel the Beau-Rivage Palace, this *brasserie de luxe* is sheltered in a lakeside pavilion, its dining room evoking a Parisian cafe with a flower-filled summer terrace. In addition to its elegant dinner service, the cafe serves coffee, tea, pastries, and a light menu from Monday to Friday 11am to 1am and on Saturday and Sunday 9am to 1am. After 7:30pm, it also becomes a piano bar. If you come here for food, expect a light and tasty cuisine prepared with the freshest of ingredients, followed by luscious desserts wheeled around on a cart.

In the Beau-Rivage Palace, 18 place du Général-Guisan, Ouchy. © 021/613-33-39. Reservations recommended. Main courses 32F–70F ($26–$57/£13.50–£29.65); fixed–price dinner 82F ($67/£34.85). AE, DC, MC, V. Daily 11:30am–1am. Metro: Ouchy.

Le Jardin d'Asie ⑮ PAN-ASIAN   This is the best Pan-Asian restaurant in the city, drawing heavily from the culinary influences of both Japan and China, but also including some zesty Malaysian specialties for greater variety. The atmosphere appropriately evokes a garden setting and the widely spaced tables allow for private conversations. Servers stylishly present sushi, sashimi, and many specialties such as chicken in peanut sauce to a satisfied clientele. There are also uniformed teppanyaki chefs standing by, knives at the ready, to prepare your dinner in front of you.

7 av. du Théâtre. © 021/323-74-84. Reservations recommended. Main courses 22F–32F ($18–$26/£9.35–£13.50); fixed-price Chinese menu 45F ($37/£19.25); fixed-price Japanese menu 45F ($37/£19.25). AE, DC, MC, V. Mon–Sat 11:45am–2pm and 7–10pm; Sun only 7–9:30pm. Bus: 7 or 16.

SHOPPING

Shoppers in Lausanne tend to be much more concerned with the commercialized glamour of Paris than with kitschy mountain souvenirs. That being the case, you'll find lots of emphasis on high-profile outfits such as luggage and leather maker **Louis Vuitton,** 30 rue de Bourg (© **021/312-76-60**); or haute jeweler **Cartier,** 6 rue de Bourg (© **021/320-55-44**). But if handmade souvenirs from the region appeal to you, head for **Heidi's Shop,** 22 rue du Petit-Chêne (© **021/311-16-89**).

The biggest jeweler in Lausanne, with a well-established international recommendation, is **Bucherer,** 15 place St-François (© **021/312-36-12**). Competitors, especially for Swiss watches, include **Roman Mayer,** 12 place St-François (© **021/312-23-16**), which has especially good buys in Omega watches, and **Junod,** 8 place St-François (© **021/312-27-45**), carrying Blancpain watches among others.

NIGHTLIFE

A good way to spend an evening in Lausanne is by hanging out in any of the cafes and bars ringing the **Espace Flon,** a cluster of restaurants and shops at place Flon. Lots of hideaways, frequented by strollers of all ages, will be here to tempt you, but one of the most appealing is **Le Grand Café,** allée Ernest-Ansermet 3 (© **021/320-40-30**), inside the Casino of Lausanne. Here, in an American-inspired space that contains some of the glitz and razzle-dazzle of a celebrity haunt, you can meet a cross section of virtually every night owl in town.

Attractive and popular discos include **Mad,** rue de Genève 23 (© **021/340-69-69**), where the fads and preoccupations of nocturnal Paris filter quickly in from the west via an under-30 crowd. **Ouchy White Horse Pub,** 66 av. d'Ouchy (© **021/616-75-75**), draws the crowds at night who in summer enjoy the terrace with views of the water. There's beer on tap, and a range of tapas and burgers are sold. It's the most authentic pub atmosphere in town.

Lausanne is also a city of culture. With Geneva it shares the Orchestre de la Suisse Romande and also occasionally hosts the legendary ballet company of Maurice Béjart. For information on what's happening during the time of your visit, contact the local tourist office (discussed earlier). Most performances of major cultural impact take place at the **Théâtre–Municipal Lausanne,** avenue du Theatre (© **021/310-16-00**). **Beaulieu,** at 10 av. des Bergières (© **021/643-21-11;** www.beaulieu.org), is also a venue for dance concerts, operas, and orchestral music presentations. For more information call the Théâtre–Municipal Lausanne.

5 Geneva ⭐⭐⭐

Switzerland's second largest city, French-speaking Geneva is situated at the lower end of Lake Geneva aka Lac Léman. Located on the Rhône at the extreme western tip of Switzerland, but right in the heart of Europe, Geneva is at the crossroads of the Continent. Often deemed the "most international of cities" because of all the international organizations (such as the Red Cross) that have their headquarters in the city, Geneva is linked to the outside world by a vast network of airlines and railways, and is an ultraconvenient stop on any rail passenger's itinerary.

In addition to enjoying good rail connections to all of Switzerland, Geneva receives four trains (all of them requiring at least one connection) per day from Vienna (trip time: 10–12 hr.), and five trains per day from Milan (trip time: 4¼ hr.). The city is also the terminal point for the Paris–Geneva train, eight of which arrive daily in the city after a journey of about 3½ hours. Geneva also rivals Lausanne (see earlier) as the best base for exploring Lake Geneva.

A lively, cosmopolitan atmosphere prevails in Geneva, a city of parks and promenades. In summer it becomes a virtual garden. It's also one of the healthiest cities in the world—the north wind blows away any pollution. The situation, in a word, is magnificent, not only lying on one of the biggest Alpine lakes, but within view of the pinnacle of Mont Blanc.

Geneva is virtually surrounded by French territory. It's connected to Switzerland only by the lake and a narrow corridor. For that and other reasons—the city was actually unwillingly annexed by France in 1798 before being set free during Napoleon's collapse in 1814—Geneva is definitely a Swiss city, but with a decided French accent.

STATION INFORMATION
GETTING FROM THE AIRPORT TO THE TRAIN STATION
The **Geneva-Cointrin Airport** (☎ 022/717-71-11; www.gva.ch), although busy, is quite compact and easily negotiated. The national airline, **Swiss** (☎ 877/359-7947), serves Geneva more frequently than any other airline. Other international airlines that partner with North American–based airlines and fly into Geneva include **Air France** (☎ 800/237-2747), with seven flights daily from Paris; and **British Airways** (☎ 800/ 217-9297), with seven daily flights from London.

You can easily get to the center of Geneva from the airport by rail. Trains leave from the airport terminal about every 8 to 20 minutes from 5:39am to 11:36pm for the 7-minute trip to **Gare Cornavin,** the main train station. The one-way fare is 10F ($8.20/£4.25) in first class and 7F ($5.75/£3) in second class. Railpasses cover this line, though you may not want to waste a day on a pass for such a short and inexpensive trip.

A taxi into town will cost 45F ($37/£19.25) and up, or you can take bus no. 10 for 12F ($9.85/£5.10).

Note: From late May to late September there are frequent daily arrivals in Geneva by Swiss lake steamers from Montreux, Vevey, and Lausanne (you can use a railpass for the trip). If you're staying in the Left Bank (Old Town), get off at the Jardin Anglais stop in Geneva; Mont Blanc and Pâquis are the two Right Bank stops. For more information, call ☎ 022/312-52-23. To get to the Jardin Anglais stop from the railway station, take bus no. 8, getting off (both stops are appropriate) at either the Quai du Mont-Blanc stop or the Metropole stop. If you prefer to go on foot, the walk from the railway station to the quays will take only 5 to 10 minutes.

Geneva

Basel
Zurich
Bern ✪
SWITZERLAND
Geneva

ⓘ Information
🛄 Rail Station
—— Railway

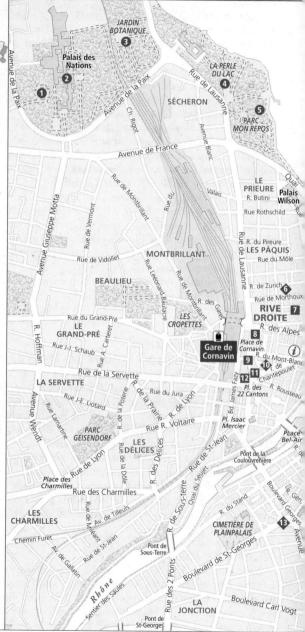

Lac Léman
(Lake Geneva)

FRONTENEX

Quai Cologny

Rampe de Cologny

Route de Vandœuvres

PARC DES
EAUX-VIVES

Plateau de Frontenex

PARC
LA GRANGE

Chemin Frank Thomas

Ch. Av. Rosemont

Avenue W. Favre

MONTCHOISY

Route de Frontenex

Quai Gustave Ador

Rue des Eaux-Vives

Rue de Montchoisy

Rue des Vollandes

26 **27**

Rue Plantamour

Rue du Mont-Blanc

Woodrow Wilson

28
Jet d'Eau

*Rade de
Genève*

25

rue du 31 Décembre

R. de la Mairie

Route de Frontenex

Gare des
Eaux-Vives

Route de Chêne

Ch. de la Petite Boissière

Promenade Martin

Pont du-
Mont-Blanc

JARDIN
ANGLAIS

24
ILE
ROUSSEAU

ont des
ergues

22 **23**

Quai Général Guisan

Av. Pictet De Rochemont

Rue Agasse

Av. de l'Amandolier

Chemin Rieu

Rue du Rhône

21

RIVE
GAUCHE
rd.-pt
de Rive

Rue de la Terassière

RUES BASSES

20   les Rues Basses **19**

R. la Fontaine

R. Lachenal

Route de Malagnou

VIELLE VILLE
(OLD TOWN) **18** **15**

Rue Hodler

Pl. Em.
Guyenot

Grand Rue **17** **16**

R. de l'Hôtel de Ville

Ch. Galland

Corraterie

Hôtel de
Ville

14

Boulevard Helvétique

Bd. Jacques Dalcroze

FLORISSANT

R. de la Croix Rouge

Bd. des Tranchées

Route de Florissant

Place
Neuve

Promenade
des Bastions

Rue de l'Athenée

PARC
A. BERTRAND

Dufour

Université

Cours ses Bastions

Rue de l'Athenée

Avenue Bertrand

avon

R. de Candolle

Philosophes

Place Ed.
Claparède

Avenue Peschier

Avenue Louis Aubert

R. St. Léger

PLAINE DE
LAINPALAIS

Rd-pt. de
Plainpalais

Rue A. Lombard

Avenue de Champel

CHAMPEL

Mail

Henri Dunant

R. de Carouge

Boulevard du Pont d'Arve

R. Prévost-
Martin

Rue Bd. de la Cluse

Avenue de Miremont

LA CLUSE

0   1/5 mile
0   200 meters
N

INSIDE THE STATION

Geneva's **CFF (Chemins de Fer Fédéraux)** train station in the town center is **Gare Cornavin,** place Cornavin (① **0900/300-300** for ticket information), which is a major international and local hub.

The city's tourist office maintains a free direct phone line to most Geneva hotels at the station, with a digital board listing accommodations available. For comprehensive service and general information, however, you'll need to head for the main tourist office (see below).

Also on-site is a luggage storage kiosk open Monday to Friday 7am to 7:30pm, Saturday and Sunday 8am to 12:30pm and 1:30 to 6:45pm, which charges 9F ($7.40/ £3.90) per day. You may also send your luggage on to your next destination using the **Fast Baggage service** (p. 822). The locker area charges from 4F to 7F ($3.30–$5.75/ £1.70–£3) and is open daily 4:30am to 12:45am. There are also several ATMs at the station.

Public transportation is readily available right outside the train station.

INFORMATION ELSEWHERE IN THE CITY

A 5-minute walk from the rail station, Geneva's tourist office, the **Office du Tourisme de Genève,** is located at 18 rue du Mont-Blanc (① **022/909-70-00;** www.geneve tourisme.ch). The staff provides information about the city, and can also arrange hotel reservations for a 5F ($4.10/£2.15) fee, both in Geneva and throughout Switzerland, and refer you to other establishments specializing in tour bookings. They can also give you details about audio-guided visits to the city's Old Town. The tourist office is open from June 15 to September 15, Monday to Friday from 10am to 6pm and Saturday and Sunday from 9am to 6pm; the rest of the year, Monday to Saturday from 10am to 6pm.

GETTING AROUND

Walking is the cheapest and most practical form of transportation within Geneva, and it's also the most advantageous method for the rail traveler to view this beautiful city. That said, there will be times you'll need to get someplace a little more quickly than a leisurely stroll will allow, and the city has a couple of transportation methods to choose from.

BY PUBLIC TRANSPORTATION   Most of Geneva's public tram and bus lines begin at the central place Cornavin in front of the main railroad station. From here, you can take bus F or 8 to the Palais des Nations. Local buses and trams operate daily from 5am to midnight, and you can purchase a ticket from a vending machine before you board; instructions are given in English. **Transport Publics Genevois** (① **0900/ 022-021;** www.unireso.com), next to the tourist office in Gare Cornavin, offers free maps of local bus routings. Trips that stay within zone 10, enveloping most of Geneva, cost 3F ($2.45/£1.25), with unlimited use of all zones costing 10F ($8.20/£4.25) for 1 day. The latter is particularly useful as most of the city's noteworthy attractions are in the suburbs.

BY TAXI   The meter on whatever cab you take in Geneva will automatically begin calculating your fare at 7F ($5.75/£3), and then add between 2.90F and 3.50F ($2.40–$2.85/£1.25–£1.50) for every kilometer you travel, depending on the time of day or night. No tipping is required. To summon a **taxi,** call ① **022/331-41-33** or 022/320-20-20.

WHERE TO STAY

Best Western Strasbourg & Univers ✦   A 2-minute walk from Gare Cornavin, this is one of Geneva's best moderately priced hotels. The building itself dates from 1900 but has been renovated and modernized over the years. Bedrooms range from large (on the lower floors) to a bit cramped. Rooms are comfortably furnished with a lot of wood pieces, and have decent tiled bathrooms. The hotel is run by a local family and doesn't have the feel of a chain hotel despite its affiliation with Best Western.

10 rue J–J–Pradier, CH-1201 Genève. ℂ 800/780-7234 in the U.S. and Canada, or 022/906-58-00. Fax 022/906-58-14. www.bestwestern.com. 51 units. 250F–270F ($205–$221/£107–£115) double; 400F–500F ($328–$410/£171–£213) suite. Rates include a buffet breakfast. AE, DC, MC, V. Bus: 1, 2, 3, 4, 8, 12, 13, or 44. **Amenities:** Breakfast lounge. *In room:* Hair dryer.

Hotel Bernina   Rail passengers often check in here because of the convenience of its location across from Gare Cornavin and its reasonable prices (considered inexpensive in this costly town). Although guests get clean, comfortably furnished bedrooms under high ceilings, they don't enjoy a lot of style as the place is rather sterile, especially the lobby, which evokes a dull airport waiting room. The soundproof windows, however, are welcome in this heavily congested part of Geneva.

22 place de Cornavin, CH-1211 Genève. ℂ 022/908-49-50. Fax 022/908-49-51. www.bernina-geneve.ch. 80 units. 240F–293F ($197–$240/£102–£125) double. Rates include breakfast. AE, DC, MC, V. Bus: 10.

Hotel Edelweiss   This hotel enjoys a scenic location near quai du President-Wilson, one of the most scenic quays of Geneva, and is about a half mile (.8km) from Gare Cornavin. Built in the 1960s, it was upgraded and renovated in the '90s and is a winning choice for its blend of rustic alpine decor, modern exterior, and completely up-to-date amenities. Most of the bedrooms are small and rather functionally furnished, but they are well kept and comfortable. The friendly staff greets guests in traditional costumes.

2 place de la Navigation, CH-1201 Genève. ℂ 022/544-51-51. Fax 022/544-51-99. www.manotel.com. 42 units. 210F–330F ($172–$271/£89.45–£141) double. AE, DC, MC, V. Bus: 1. **Amenities:** Restaurant; bar; laundry.

Hotel International & Terminus   This hotel, originally built in 1900, is a winning choice for rail travelers as it's just across the street from the main entrance to Gare Cornavin. Maintenance in the spacious accommodations is high, windows are double-glazed, and the furnishings are comfortable and modern—though the bathrooms are rather cramped. The hotel's La Veranda restaurant is frequently patronized by rail travelers tired of the train depot's fast-food outlets.

20 rue des Alpes, CH-1201 Genève. ℂ 022/906-97-77. Fax 022/906-97-78. www.international-terminus.ch. 60 units. 160F–280F ($131–$230/£68.10–£120) double. Rates include buffet breakfast. AE, DC, MC, V. Bus: 6, 10, or 33. **Amenities:** Restaurant. *In room:* Hair dryer.

Hotel Lido   Only 2 blocks from Gare Cornavin, this hotel dates from 1963 and has never overcome the architectural dullness of that era. Nonetheless, the hotel is convenient for train travelers and charges reasonable rates for its basic bedrooms. Furnishings are functional—not stylish—but there is comfort and cleanliness here, along with full bathrooms. Expect very few amenities, however, especially in the rooms, although they are soundproof.

8 rue Chantepoulet, CH-1201, Genève. ℂ 022/731-55-30. Fax 022/731-65-01. www.hotel-lido.ch. 31 units. 150F–210F ($123–$172/£63.95–£89.45) double. Rates include continental breakfast. AE, DC, MC, V. Bus: 10. **Amenities:** Breakfast room; laundry.

Hotel Moderne   One of many acceptable choices near Gare Cornavin, this seven-story hotel is within easy walk of the quays. The hotel's public areas are Nordic style and modern. Behind soundproof windows, the midsize bedrooms are sunny and furnished in a standard but comfortable manner. The small bathrooms are spotless and have either a shower or a bathtub. Breakfast is served in a glassed-in extension.

1 rue de Berne, CH-1211 Genève. ✆ 022/732-81-00. Fax 022/738-26-58. www.hotelmoderne.ch. 55 units. 215F ($176/£91.50) double. Rates include buffet breakfast. AE, DC, MC, V. Bus: 10. **Amenities:** 2 restaurants; laundry; non-smoking rooms.

TOP ATTRACTIONS & SPECIAL MOMENTS

If you arrive in Geneva in summer, begin your tour of the city by heading east from the rail station along rue du Mont-Blanc until you arrive at quai du Mont Blanc and begin a long promenade along the **Quays of Geneva** ⭐⭐⭐. The one sight you can't miss—even if you tried—is the **Jet d'Eau** ⭐⭐, the famous fountain that is the trademark of the city and is located on a concrete platform in the middle of the lake. Visible for miles around from April to September, it throws water 460 feet (140m) into the air above the lake. The *bise* (wind) blows the spume into a feathery, fluttery fan, often wetting those below who stand too close. The Genevese call the fountain the *jeddo*. It dates from 1891, but was much improved in 1951. The engineering behind the fountain used to be a secret, until Saudi Arabia managed to acquire it. It pumps 109 gallons of lake water at 125 mph (200kmph).

The quays, with their luxuriantly planted flower gardens, are dotted with ancient buildings. The aquatic population consists of seagulls, ducks, and swans. A fleet of small boats, called *Mouettes genevoises* (✆ 022/732-29-44), shuttles visitors from one quay to another from mid-March to mid-October. For rides that last 30 minutes or less, the cost is 2.20F ($1.80/£0.95) adults, and 2F ($1.65/£85p) children; rides lasting 30 to 60 minutes cost 3F ($2.45/£1.25) adults and 2.20F ($1.80/£95p) children.

Like the water jet, the **Flower Clock** in the **Jardin Anglais (English Garden)** is another Geneva trademark. Its face is made of flowers, and it keeps perfect time (what else would you expect in this world-famed center of watchmaking?). The Jardin Anglais is at the foot of the Mont Blanc Bridge, which spans the river at the point where the Rhône leaves Lake Geneva. It was rebuilt in 1969. To get here from the Jet d'Eau stroll south on quai Gustave-Ador and then bear right.

After leaving the garden, cross the Mont Blanc bridge and turn left onto the quai des Bergues and stroll as far as the bridge, Pont des Bergues. If you cross this bridge you'll come to **Ile Rousseau,** with a statue of Geneva's most famous son done by Pradier in 1834. This island, the former stamping ground of the philosopher, is home to any number of ducks, swans, and other aquatic fowl such as grebes. In the middle of the Rhône, it was once a bulwark of Geneva's river defenses.

You can continue crossing the bridge and can then turn right on the Bezanson Hugues quay until you reach rue de Moulins and the **Tour-de-l'Ile,** farther downstream. Built in 1219, a château that once stood here was used as a prison by the counts of Savoy. A wall plaque commemorates the visit of Caesar in 58 B.C. The tower is all that remains of the 13th-century castle. It was here that freedom fighter Philibert Berthelier was decapitated in 1519. Nowadays, the Geneva Tourist Office is located on the island. You can also explore the old markets, where there are often exhibitions of the works of contemporary Genevese artists.

If you walk east along the quai des Bergues you'll return to the Pont du Mont-Blanc. To your left, when facing the lake, is the **Brunswick Monument,** the tomb of

Charles II of Brunswick, who died in Geneva in 1873. The duke left his fortune to the city provided it built a monument to him. Geneva accepted the cash and modeled the tomb after the Scalieri tombs in Verona, Italy.

VIEILLE VILLE 𓆱𓆱𓆱

"Old Town" in Geneva is one of the most remarkable in Switzerland and has been called Europe's best-kept secret. It's situated on the city's Left Bank, where the cultural life of Geneva flourishes. Its ancient streets are home to art galleries, antiques shops, booksellers, and tiny bistros. Follow the Grand'Rue, about ¾ mile (1.2km) from Gare Cornavin, where Jean-Jacques Rousseau was born at 40 Grand'Rue, and wander back in time.

The old quarter is dominated by the **Cathedral of St. Pierre** 𓆱, Cour St-Pierre (© 022/311-75-75), originally built between the 10th and 13th centuries and partially reconstructed in the 15th century. The church looks out over Geneva from its hilltop perch. It became Protestant in 1536. The interior is austere, just the way Calvin preferred it (his seat is on the north side). The church has seen much recent renovation, and it has a modern organ with 6,000 pipes. If you don't mind the 157 steps, you can climb to the north tower for a splendid vista of the city, its lake, the Alps, and the Jura mountains.

Recent excavations have disclosed that a Christian sanctuary was located here as early as A.D. 400. To enter the St. Pierre archaeological site, called **Site Archéologique de St-Pierre,** go through the entrance in Cour St-Pierre, at the right-hand corner of the cathedral steps. The underground passageway extends under the present cathedral and the High Gothic (early-15th-c.) **Chapelle des Macchabées,** which adjoins the southwestern corner of the church. The chapel was restored during World War II, after having been used as a storage room following the Reformation. Excavations of the chapel have revealed baptisteries, a crypt, the foundations of several cathedrals, the bishop's palace, 4th-century mosaics, sculptures, and geological strata.

The cathedral and the chapel are open June to September Monday to Saturday from 9:30am to 6:30pm and Sunday noon to 6:30pm; October to May Monday to Saturday 10am to 5:30pm and Sunday noon to 5:30pm. There is no admission charge to visit the cathedral, although donations are welcome; tower admission is 4F ($3.30/£1.70) for adults, 2F ($1.65/85p) ages 6 to 12. Sunday service is held in the cathedral at 10am, and an hour of organ music is presented on Saturdays at 6pm from June to September. The archaeological site is open Tuesday to Saturday from 10am to 5pm; the admission charge is 8F ($6.55/£3.40) adults, 4F ($3.30/£1.70) students and seniors. Take bus no. 3, 5, or 17, or tram 12.

Next door to the cathedral is a Gothic church where Calvin preached, known as the **Temple de l'Auditoire,** or Calvin Auditorium. It was restored in 1959 in time for Calvin's 450th anniversary.

After leaving the cathedral, strike out across the Cour St-Pierre, turning left onto the rue St-Pierre, where at no. 4 you'll encounter **Maison Tavel,** 6 rue du Puits-St-Pierre (© 022/418-37-00), the oldest house in Geneva. First built in 1303, according to dim records, it was apparently rebuilt in 1334. It's decorated with amusing carved heads and a fine turret, and has a 12th-century cellar, which predates the original building. It's open Tuesday to Sunday 10am to 5pm; admission is free. Temporary exhibits cost 3F ($2.45/£1.25) for adults and 2F ($1.65/85p) 18 and under.

Hôtel de Ville (city hall), a short walk from the cathedral, dates from the 16th and 17th centuries. It has a cobbled ramp instead of a staircase. The **Salle d'Alabama** is the

---

Moments **A Lakeside City of Parks & Gardens**

If you head north along rue de Lausanne from Gare Cornavin, you'll arrive at some of the lushest parks in Geneva. **Parc Mon-Repos** ✿✿ is off avenue de France and **La Perle du Lac** is off rue de Lausanne. Directly to the right is the **Jardin Botanique (Botanical Garden)**, which was established in 1902. It has an Alpine garden, a little zoo, greenhouses, and exhibitions, and can be visited free from April to September, daily from 8am to 7:30pm; and October to March, daily from 9:30am to 5pm.

If you leave the **Jardin Botanique** on the Left Bank, you can head west, along avenue de la Paix, to the Palais des Nations in the **Parc de l'Ariana**. It's located about a mile (1.6km) north of Gare Cornavin.

---

salon where arbitration between America and England in 1872 (over England's support of the Confederacy during the American Civil War) was peacefully resolved. Its Baudet Tower was constructed in 1455. Incidentally, the Red Cross originated here in 1864.

Across from the city hall is the **Arsenal,** an arcaded structure dating from 1634. In the courtyard of the building is a cannon cast in 1683.

OTHER ATTRACTIONS

Musée d'Art et Histoire (Museum of Art & History) ✿✿   If you can only visit one museum while in Geneva, make it this one, the city's most important. The collections offer a little bit of everything, and include prehistoric relics, Egyptian relics, Greek vases, medieval stained glass, 12th-century armory, and many paintings of the Flemish and Italian schools. The Etruscan pottery is impressive, as is the medieval furniture. See the altarpiece by Konrad Witz from 1444, showing the "miraculous" draught of fishes. Swiss timepieces are duly honored, and many galleries contain works by such world-famous artists as Rodin, Renoir, Hodler, Vallotton, Le Corbusier, and Picasso.

2 rue Charles-Galland (between bd. Jacques-Dalcroze and bd. Helvétique). ✆ 022/418-26-00. Free admission; 5F ($4.10/£2.15) temporary exhibitions adults, 3F ($2.45/£1.25) for children. Tues–Sun 10am–5pm. Bus: 1, 3, 5, 8, or 17.

Musée de l'Ariana ✿✿   This is one of the top three museums devoted to porcelain and pottery in Europe and the headquarters for the international academy of ceramics. Located west of the Palais des Nations, the museum building is in the Italian Renaissance style, and was built in 1877 for P. F. Revilliod, the 19th-century Genevese writer who began the collection. Here you'll see Sèvres at its best, along with the celebrated Delft faïence, Meissen porcelain, and many superb pieces from Japan and China.

10 av. de la Paix. ✆ 022/418-54-50. http://mah.ville-ge.ch. Free admission permanent collection; temporary exhibitions 5F ($4.10/£2.15) adults, 3F ($2.45/£1.25) for children under 18. Wed–Mon 10am–5pm. Bus: 8 or F.

Palais des Nations ✿✿   The former home of the defunct League of Nations, about a mile (1.6km) north of Mont Blanc Bridge, is the present headquarters of the United Nations in Europe. The monumental compound was constructed between 1929 and 1936, and the complex of buildings is the second largest in Europe after Versailles. Tours, conducted in English, last about an hour and depart from the visitors' entrance at 14 av. de la Paix, opposite the Red Cross building. To join the tour you'll need to show your passport. The highlight of the tour is the Assembly Hall, with a balcony made entirely of marble and lofty bays looking out over the Court of Honor.

A Philatelic Museum displays collections of stamps relating to the League of Nations or the United Nations, and a League of Nations Museum documents the history of the precursor to the United Nations.

Parc de l'Ariana, 14 av. de la Paix. ✆ 022/917-48-96. www.unog.ch. Admission 10F ($8.20/£4.25) adults, 8F ($6.55/£3.40) students, 5F ($4.10/£2.15) for children, free for 5 and under. July–Aug daily 10am–5pm; Apr–June, Sept–Oct daily 10am–noon and 2–4pm; rest of the year Mon–Fri 10am–noon and 2–4pm. Bus: 5, 8, 18, F, V, or Z.

WHERE TO DINE

Brasserie Lipp FRENCH/SWISS   Named after the most famous brasserie on the Left Bank of Paris, this restaurant serves a similar type of cuisine, specializing in fresh oysters— the best in the city—and large platters of sauerkraut. When you see the waiters in long white aprons and black jackets, you'll think you've been miraculously transported over the border. That impression is reinforced when the actual food is served, including all our favorite classics such as a Toulousian cassoulet and three kinds of pot-au-feu.

In Confédération-Centre, 8 rue de la Confédération. ✆ 022/311-10-11. Reservations recommended. Main courses 28F–47F ($23–$39/£11.95–£20.30); plats du jour 19F–37F ($16–$30/£8.30–£15.60) lunch only; fixed-price menus 59F–80F ($48–$66/£24.95–£34.30). AE, DC, MC, V. Mon–Sat 7am–2am; Sun 9am–2am. Bus: 2, 7, 12, or 16.

Café du Centre CONTINENTAL/SWISS   Established in 1871, this is still the busiest cafe in Geneva, with an outdoor terrace that's always packed in fair weather. The atmosphere inside evokes a time-blackened brasserie in Old Lyon. The menu (it comes in English) is the largest in town, with nearly 140 different items offered every day. Carnivores will be especially happy with the tender and well-flavored meat platters (the best and most tender cut is called *onglet*).

5 place du Molard. ✆ 022/311-85-86. Reservations recommended. Main courses 19F–60F ($16–$49/£8.30–£25.50); fixed-price *assiette du jour* 19F ($16/£8.30) at lunch Mon–Fri only. AE, DC, MC, V. Mon 6am–midnight; Tues–Fri 6am–1am; Sat 9am–10pm; Sun 9am–midnight. Tram: 12.

Chez Ma Cousine ⓥalue FRENCH/SWISS   What you'll find here is an amiable but stringently unpretentious venue of spartan-looking wooden tables and chairs, and an open kitchen. Despite a very limited menu, the place does a roaring business. A free salad accompanies most main courses, and the only option for potatoes is "Provençal style." Platters include several variations of grilled chicken, the house specialty.

5 rue Lissignol. ✆ 022/731-9898. Reservations unnecessary. Main courses 15F–16F ($12–$13/£6.25–£6.75). Mon–Fri 11:30am–2:30pm and 6:30–11:30pm. Bus: 1.

La Favola ✦TUSCAN/ITALIAN   The habitués of the finest Italian restaurant in the city, just a few steps from the Cathedral of St. Pierre, complain only that it doesn't serve on weekends. This family-run restaurant is warm and inviting, its tables placed in two cramped—and always packed—rooms, through which waiters scurry back and forth while carrying heaping platters of food. The seasonal menu is small and deliberately limited to ensure fresh ingredients. Look for such delightful dishes as carpaccio of beef; lobster salad; and a luscious version of tortellini stuffed with ricotta, meat juices, red wine, and herbs. Don't even think of coming here without making reservations well in advance.

15 rue Jean-Calvin. ✆ 022/311-74-37. Reservations required. Main courses 24F–60F ($20–$49/£10.40–£25.50). AE, MC, V. Mon–Fri noon–2pm and 7:15–10pm. Closed 2 weeks in July–Aug and 1 week at Christmas. Tram: 12.

Le Sumo Yakitori ✦ finds JAPANESE   This is a dining oddity that's well known to many cost-conscious residents of Geneva, and almost always overlooked by foreign tourists, most of whom might find the culinary format of this tiny place baffling. The

Moments **Sailing the Waters of Lac Léman**

More interesting than the monuments of Geneva itself is a sail across Lake Geneva (Lac Léman). You'll enjoy sweeping waterside views of the surrounding hills, and some of the most famous vineyards in Switzerland, many of which seem to roll down to the historic waters. Because of bad weather and low visibility in winter, cruises only run between April and late October, and in some cases, only between May and September.

Mouettes Genevoises Navigation, 8 quai du Mont-Blanc (© 022/732-47-47; www.swissboat.com), specializes in small-scale boats carrying only 100 passengers at a time. An easy excursion that features the landscapes and bird life along the uppermost regions of the river Rhône draining into the lake is the company's **Tour du Rhône (Rhône River Tour).** The trip originates at a point adjacent to Geneva's Pont de l'Ile, and travels downstream for about 9 miles (15km; 2 hr., 45 min.) to the Barrage de Verbois (Verbois Dam) and back.

Between April and October, departures are daily at 2:15pm, and also on Wednesday, Thursday, Saturday, and Sunday at 10am. The tour costs 17F ($14/£7.30) for adults and 12F ($9.85/£5.10) for children 4 to 12; it's free for children under 4. The same company also offers 1¼-hour tours (four times a day) and 2-hour tours (twice a day) out onto the lake. The longer tour includes a prerecorded commentary on the celebrity residences and ecology of the lake en route. These tours cost 24F ($20/£10.40) for the shorter tour and 30F ($25/£13) for the longer tour. No stops are made en route.

fact that it doesn't serve sushi or sashimi, coupled with its claustrophobic dimensions (it seats only 22 diners at a time) and open galley-sized kitchen makes it unusual. You'll be happiest if you ask lots of questions of the English-speaking Japanese staff at this place before you order. Menu items include marinated and roasted quail, grilled shrimp, Bali-style jasmine rice, and all-vegetarian versions of grilled eggplant with garlic sauce.

15 rue Monthoux. © 022/731-19-50. Reservations not accepted. Brochettes 2F–5F ($1.65– $4.10/£85p–£2.15) each, platters 10F–17F ($8.20–$14/£4.25–£7.30). Fixed-price menus 40F ($33/£17.15). AE, MC, V. Bus: 1.

Windows ✦ CONTINENTAL   Flooded with sunlight from large panoramic windows, and permeated with an undeniably upscale but discreet sense of old-fashioned exclusivity, this charming restaurant attracts a clientele of politicians, film industry personnel, writers, and the merely rich. Menu items change with the seasons, but you might find orange-marinated chicken cutlets with a yogurt-flavored avocado sauce and bulgur wheat; or roasted *omble chevalier,* a whitefish from the nearby lake, served with a reduction of carrot juice and a passion-fruit–flavored butter sauce.

In the Hotel Angleterre, 17 quai du Mont-Blanc. © 022/906-55-55. Reservations recommended. Main courses 49F–64F ($40–$52/£20.80–£27.05). AE, DC, MC, V. Daily noon–10pm. Bus: 1.

SHOPPING

Geneva practically invented the wristwatch. In fact, watchmaking in the city dates from the 16th century. Be sure to avoid purchasing a Swiss watch in one of the souvenir stores; legitimate jewelers will display a symbol of the Geneva Association of

Watchmakers and Jewelers. Here, more than in any other Swiss city perhaps, you should be able to find all the best brands, including Vacheron & Constantin, Longines, Omega, and Blancpain, to name just a few. Most salespeople you'll encounter speak English and are very helpful.

A shopping spree might begin at **place du Molard,** once the harbor of Geneva before the water receded. Merchants from all over Europe used to bring their wares to trade fairs here in the days before merchants immigrated to richer markets in Lyon.

If you walk along rue du Rhône and are put off by the prices, go 1 block south to rue du Marché, which in various sections becomes rue de la Croix-d'Or and rue de Rive, and is sometimes referred to by locals as "la rue du Tram" because of the many trolleys that run along its length. Comparison shopping is the way to go in Geneva—many stores jack up prices for visitors.

Store hours vary. Most are open Monday to Friday from 8am to 6:30pm and Saturday from 8am to 5pm. For one-stop shopping, head for one of the big department stores such as **Bon Genie,** 34 rue du Marché (© 022/818-11-11), located on place du Molard. This department store sells mostly high-fashion women's clothing. Its storefront windows display art objects from local museums alongside designer clothes. There's also a limited selection of men's clothing, as well as furniture, cosmetics, and perfumes. **Globus-Grand Passage,** 48 rue du Rhône (© 022/319-50-50), is one of the largest department stores in Geneva, with many boutique-style departments and a self-image that's firmly patterned after the Galeries Lafayette in Paris. Expect glamour, and lots of upbeat cheerfulness.

Come Prima, 17 rue de la Cité (place Bémont; © 022/310-77-79), is our favorite Geneva shop, with a spectacular array of gift and leather items. This boutique is loaded with top-quality leather bags and carry-ons.

Bucherer, 45 rue du Rhône (© 022/319-62-66), located opposite the Mont Blanc Bridge, is a chrome-and-crystal store selling deluxe watches and diamonds. The store offers such name brands as Rolex, Piaget, Ebel, Baume & Mercier, Omega, Tissot, Rado, and Swatch. The carpeted third floor is filled with relatively inexpensive watches. You'll also find a large selection of cuckoo clocks, music boxes, embroideries, and souvenirs, as well as porcelain pillboxes and other gift items.

Gübelin Jewelers, 1 place du Molard (© 022/310-86-55), dates from 1854. This family-run establishment is known mainly for its brand-name watches, although it also sells beautiful precious stones and jewelry. You can also buy reasonably priced gifts, such as pen and pencil sets.

NIGHTLIFE

Geneva has more nightlife than any other city in French-speaking Switzerland. Most activity centers around **place du Bourg-de-Four,** which used to be a stagecoach stop during the 19th century and is located in the Old Town. Here, you'll find a host of outdoor cafes in the summer.

Geneva has always attracted the culturally sophisticated, including Byron, Jean-Baptiste, Corot, Victor Hugo, Balzac, George Sand, and Franz Liszt. Ernst Ansermet founded Geneva's great **Orchestre de la Suisse Romande,** whose frequent concerts entertain music lovers at **Victoria Hall,** 14 rue du Générale-Dufour (© 022/807-00-17; www.osr.ch). For opera there's the 1,500-seat **Grand Théâtre,** place Neuve (© 022/418-30-00; www.geneveopera.ch), which welcomes Béjart, the Bolshoi, and other ballet companies, in addition to having a company of its own. For a preview of events at the time of your visit, pick up a copy of the monthly *List of Events* issued by the tourist office.

Au Chat Noir, 13 rue Vautier (© **022/343-49-98**), is easy to reach by tram 12 from place Bel-Air. The club lies in the suburb of Carouge, and is the best spot for funk, rock, salsa, jazz, and some good old New Orleans blues. Live music is presented nightly at 9pm (10pm Fri–Sat). The cover ranges from 16F to 20F ($13–$16/£6.75–£8.30).

Le Dancing de la Coupole, 116 rue du Rhône (© **022/787-50-12**), is a much-frequented brasserie that is also a dance club, focusing mainly on the music of the '60s, and doing so Tuesday to Saturday 5pm to 2am. There's no cover.

If you're barhopping, drop in at **Mr. Pickwick Pub,** 80 rue de Lausanne (© **022/ 731-67-97**), which also serves British food. Mostly patrons come here to drink and converse, listen to American or British music, or enjoy an Irish coffee. The best piano bar at night is **Le Francis,** 8 bd. Helvetique (© **022/346-32-52**), which is an elegant place for a rendezvous, with live music beginning at 10pm.

6 Switzerland's Famous Scenic Rail Lines 𝄞𝄞𝄞

Switzerland not only offers Europe's most dramatic Alpine scenery, but eight of the greatest train rides in the world. If you take one or all of these train trips, be assured that they will be among the most memorable of your life. All of the trains below can be booked through **Rail Europe** (© **877/272-RAIL** [7245]; www.raileurope.com) or your travel agent.

GLACIER EXPRESS One of the most evocative trains in the country, the **Glacier Express** connects two fabled ski resorts—St. Moritz in the east and Zermatt in the west—while passing through the resorts of Chur, Andermatt, and Brig. On the 7½-hour trip, your train will pass through 91 tunnels and cross 291 bridges, peaking at 6,669 feet (2,001m) at the towering Oberalp Pass. There is no more memorable way to travel across the Alpine heartland of the country, past mountain lakes, vast forests, and cow-filled pastures. *Note:* Glacier Express trains do not run from late October through early December.

The Swiss Pass covers the full ride, while the Eurail Global Pass offers a discount. Prices start at $291 (£151) one-way in first class or $194 (£101) in second class. Seat reservations are required and cost an additional $33 (£15.60). If you begin your trip in Zermatt, you can reach the resort by rail from Geneva in just 4 hours; otherwise, tack on an additional 3½ hours for the trip from Zurich to St. Moritz.

BERNINA EXPRESS Another dramatic ride is the **Bernina Express,** a 2½-hour trip from St. Moritz through a lunar landscape of ice-age glaciers and stone-studded fields and pastureland to the palms and foliage of Tirano in Italy. All cars on this train (run by the Rhäetische Bahn Authority) have panoramic windows so you won't miss the views. The ride may be short, but you won't soon forget the breathtaking scenery passing by your window as you go through wild gorges, across towering bridges, and into foreboding loop tunnels, moving past dozens upon dozens of snowcapped glaciers. At the rail junction in Tirano, a bus will take you on the 3-hour journey to Lugano (mid-May to mid-Oct only), one of the finest lake resorts of Switzerland's Italian-speaking Ticino district. *Note:* Although we recommend you pick up the Bernina Express in St. Moritz, it actually starts off in Chur.

A one-way fare from St. Moritz to Lugano, including the bus fare is 65F ($53/£27.55) in first class or 47F ($39/£20.30) in second class; the trip is covered by the Eurail Global Pass and the Swiss Pass. Seat reservations on both the train and bus are required and cost an additional $24 (£12.50) when made through Rail Europe.

St. Moritz is a 3½-hour train ride from Zurich. For more information on the Bernina Express, head online to **www.rhb.ch**.

CENTOVALLI RAILWAY   The **Centovalli Railway** offers one of the most dramatic train rides in Ticino, the Italian-speaking part of Switzerland in the south of the country bordering Italy. Running through the region's scenic "Hundred Valleys," the railway links Locarno (one of the country's most popular resorts) with the town of Domodossola in northern Italy, on the southern side of the Alps at the foot of the Simplon Pass.

The 2-hour trip features the lush, wonderful countryside of southern Switzerland, filled with mountain landscapes, flowering meadows, and magnificent forests.

No reservations are required. The trip is covered by the Eurail Global Pass and the Swiss Pass; otherwise, prices start at $65 (£33.80) in first class or $39 (£20.30) in second class. Locarno, the starting point of the trip, is about a 3-hour train ride from Zurich. For more information, check online at **www.centovalli.ch**.

GOLDEN PASS LINE   The **Golden Pass Line** is the natural and panoramic route linking Central Switzerland with Lake Geneva, and because it features some of the country's greatest lakes and evocative mountain scenery, the line is often called "Switzerland in a Nutshell." The train ride covers 149 miles (239km), from the shores of Lake Lucerne and over the Brünig Pass to the chic resort of Montreux on Lake Geneva. Three trains run along various legs of the route and to cover the entire route, you'll need to change trains twice (track variances prevent a single train from running the entire length of the route). The **Brünig Panoramic Express** runs from Lucerne to Interlaken, the **Salon Bleu** from Interlaken to Zweisimmen, and the **GoldenPass Panoramic-MOB** from Zweisimmen to Montreux.

Reservations are required for each leg of the trip (they cost 7F/$5.75/£3) per leg), though if you plan on traveling the whole route, you can get them all for 11F ($9/£4.70) at any Swiss train station or online at **www.goldenpass.ch**. If you buy in advance from Rail Europe, it will cost you $18 (£9.35) per leg. The trip is covered by the Eurail Global Pass and the Swiss Pass; otherwise, the cost for all three legs is 138F ($113/£58.75) in first class or 83F ($68/£35.35) in second class. To start your run in Lucerne, take a 50-minute train to the city out of Zurich. For more schedules and information on this railway line, see **www.goldenpass.ch** and **www.mob.ch**.

CHOCOLATE TRAIN   A real novelty is the so-called **"Chocolate Train,"** which offers luxurious first-class travel in vintage Belle Epoque 1915 Pullman cars or modern panoramic cars from June through October only. You depart from Montreux on Lake Geneva for the medieval city of Gruyères, where you are given time to tour the city's castle and famous cheese factory. Then it's back on the train and off to the Cailler-Nestlé chocolate factory in Broc, where you're given a tour and a tasting of some of the factory's delicious chocolate before reboarding your train and returning to Montreux. Along the way your train will pass stunning views of Lake Geneva vineyards and other beautiful landscapes. Complimentary croissants and coffee are served on the train.

A first-class Swiss Pass or Eurail Global Pass covers the train ride and all entrance fees; passholders can obtain the mandatory seat reservations for $31 (£16.10) on the train's website at **www.mob.ch**, or at **www.raileurope.com**. Those without passes can buy a ticket online or at any Swiss train station for 88F ($72/£37.45) in first class, 58F ($48/£24.95) in second class. The round-trip train ride, including stopovers, takes more than 8 hours to complete, and there's only one train per day. Montreux, the starting point of the trip, is a 1-hour train ride from Geneva. For more information on the train, see **www.mob.ch**.

WILLIAM TELL EXPRESS The **William Tell Express** links the German-speaking part of the Switzerland with the Italian-speaking Ticino region from May to October. Your trip begins in Lucerne when you board a historic paddle-steamer for a 3-hour cruise of Lake Lucerne and a first-rate meal. At the little town of Fluelen, you'll abandon ship and board a panoramic train that runs through towering cliffs and steep ravines of the Reuss Valley, including passage through the Gotthard Tunnel—a historic railway tunnel that is Europe's most important north-south gateway. After passing a number of old-fashioned Swiss villages, the train plunges south into the valleys that open onto the lakeside resorts of Lugano and Locarno.

The journey takes a total of 6 hours and 10 minutes. The trip is free for holders of the Swiss Pass or Eurail Global Pass, though reservations are required, and cost $45 (£23.40; which includes your meal on the boat, and a souvenir). A regular one-way passage (most rail travelers don't do the round-trip) for the journey from Lucerne to Lugano costs $77 (£40.05) in first class (the only class available). To get to the starting point in Lucerne, take a 50-minute train out of Zurich.

MOUNT PILATUS COG RAILWAY One of the most stunning mountain rail journeys in Switzerland is the **Mt. Pilatus Cog Railway,** located about 9 miles (15km) south of Lucerne, a city only a 50-minute train ride from Zurich. The regular round-trip fare on the cog railways is 60F ($49/£25.50). The Swiss Pass offers a 50% discount on the regular fare.

Between May and November, weather permitting, the cog railway operates between Alpnachstad, at the edge of the lake, and the very top of Mount Pilatus. From the quays of Lucerne, take a lake steamer for a scenic 90-minute boat ride to Alpnachstad. If you have a railpass, it will cover this steamer.

At Alpnachstad, transfer to the electric cog railway, which runs at a 48% gradient—the steepest cogwheel railway in the world. Departures are every 45 minutes daily from 8:20am to 4:50pm May to September only, the trip taking 45 minutes. At Pilatus-Kulm you can get out and enjoy the view. There are two mountain hotels and a belvedere offering views of Lake Lucerne and many of the mountains around it. For the descent from Mount Pilatus, some visitors prefer to take a pair of cable cars that terminate at Kriens, a suburb of Lucerne. Here you can take bus no. 1 (covered by the Swiss Pass), which will carry you into the heart of Lucerne. If you opt to go down by the cable cars, the round-trip fare on the cog railway and cable cars is 55F ($45/£23.40). Eurail passholders get a 30% reduction on the cable cars.

A similar excursion to Pilatus is possible in the winter, but because the cog railway is buried in snow, you must alter your plans. You'll have to ascend and descend by cable car, which many visitors find exhilarating. From the train station at Lucerne, take bus no. 1 to the outlying suburb of Kriens. At Kriens, transfer to a cable car that glides over meadows and forests to the village of Fräkmüntegg, 4,600 feet (1,402m) above sea level. The trip takes half an hour. At Fräkmüntegg, switch to another cable car, this one much more steeply inclined than the first. A stunning feat of advanced engineering, it swings above gorges and cliffs to the very peak of Mount Pilatus (Pilatus-Kulm). Unlike the cog railways, these cable cars operate year-round. The round-trip ride by cable car from Kriens to Fräkmüntegg costs 36F ($30/£15.60).

JUNGFRAUJOCH   A train trip from Interlaken to **Jungfraujoch,** at an elevation of 11,333 feet (3,399m), is the most dramatic rail journey in Switzerland. For more than a century it's been the highest railway station in Europe. It's also one of the most expensive: A ticket costs $168 (£87.35) in first class or $158 (£82.15) in second class. Holders of Eurail passes are granted a 25% discount; Swiss Card and Swiss Pass holders get a 50% discount. Note that families can fill out a Family Card form, available at the railway station, which allows children 16 and under to ride free. For more information, see **www.raileurope.com**.

Take a train from either **Zurich** (2 hr.) or **Geneva** (3 hr.) to get to Interlaken's East Station (you'll need to transfer in Bern in both directions) and then allow 2 hours and 20 minutes for the journey from Interlaken to the Jungfraujoch. Departures are usually daily at 8am from the east station in Interlaken; expect to return around 4pm. To check times, contact the sales office of **Jungfrau Railways** (© **033/828-71-11;** www.jungfraubahn.ch).

The trip is comfortable, safe, and packed with adventure. First you'll take the **Wengernalp railway (WAB),** a rack railway that opened in 1893. It will take you to Lauterbrunnen, at 2,612 feet (796m), where you'll change to a train heading for the Kleine Scheidegg station, at 6,762 feet (2,061m)—welcome to avalanche country. The view includes the Mönch, the Eiger Wall, and the Jungfrau, which was named for the white-clad Augustinian nuns of medieval Interlaken (Jungfrau means "virgin").

At Kleine Scheidegg, you'll change to the highest rack railway in Europe, the **Jungfraubahn.** You have 6 miles (9.6km) to go; 4 miles (6.4km) of them will be spent in a tunnel carved into the mountain. You'll stop briefly twice, at **Eigerwand** and **Eismeer,** where you can view the sea of ice from windows in the rock (the Eigerwand is at 9,400 ft./2,865m and Eismeer is at 10,368 ft./3,160m). When the train emerges from the tunnel, the daylight is momentarily blinding, so bring a pair of sunglasses to help your eyes adjust. Notorious among mountain climbers, the Eigernordwand (or "north wall") is incredibly steep.

Once at the Jungfraujoch terminus, you may feel a little giddy until you get used to the air. There's much to do in this eerie world up in the sky, but take it slow—your body's metabolism will be affected and you may tire quickly.

Behind the post office is an elevator that will take you to a corridor leading to the famed **Eispalast (Ice Palace).** Here you'll be walking inside "eternal ice" in caverns hewn out of the slowest-moving section of the glacier. Cut 65 feet (20m) below the glacier's surface, these caverns were begun in 1934 by a Swiss guide and subsequently enlarged and embellished with additional sculptures by others. Everything in here is made of ice, including full-size replicas of vintage automobiles and local chaplains.

After returning to the train station, you can take the Sphinx Tunnel to another elevator. This one takes you up 356 feet (108m) to an observation deck called the **Sphinx Terraces,** overlooking the saddle between the Mönch and Jungfrau peaks. You can also see the **Aletsch Glacier,** a 14-mile (23km) river of ice—the longest in Europe. The snow melts into Lake Geneva and eventually flows into the Mediterranean.

Have a meal in one of the five **restaurants** at the top of the peak. As a final adventure, you can take a **sleigh ride,** pulled by stout huskies.

On your way back down the mountain, you'll return to Kleine Scheidegg station, but you can vary your route by going through **Grindelwald,** which offers panoramic views of the treacherous north wall.

Appendix:
Eastern Europe & the Balkans

Though this book covers the primary rail destinations of Europe, there are a number of other European countries, primarily in Eastern Europe, where change is always in the air, and today's rail traveler can see history in the making.

From the Baltic to the Black Sea, the nations of Eastern Europe stretch across one of the most diverse regions on earth. Freed from the Soviet umbrella, the last in a line of 2 millennia of conquerors, these nations have changed their politics and identities—or have been created from scratch—since the epochal year of 1989. You'll be treated to some remarkable attractions, as every country or region is completely different.

The nations of Eastern Europe are a land of great culture, folklore, and attractions, both man-made and natural. Expect stunning landscapes, a fascinating but turbulent history, and some of the friendliest people in Europe, as you travel from the snow-capped Tatra Mountains of Poland to the wide beaches of the Bulgarian Black Sea coast. Not only that, but you'll encounter prices a lot cheaper than in the West. On the downside, trains in these countries can be unpredictable, slow, less safe, and a whole lot less comfortable than rail service in Western Europe.

1 Bulgaria

Occupying the eastern half of the Balkan Peninsula, Bulgaria is a land of great beauty, from its Black Sea coast to its villages still somewhat living in the Middle Ages, from its rugged and mountainous interior to its fertile Danube plains, from its fishing villages to its Roman ruins and lush valleys. At the crossroads of Europe, it's naturally had a violent history. Its recent past has been blighted by its record as the closest ally of the former Soviet Union, but today it turns toward Western Europe, embracing capitalism and democracy and welcoming visitors to come see what Bulgaria is all about. It's a safe and relatively hassle-free country, unlike many former Eastern Bloc "republics."

Not as touristy as its neighbors, Greece and Turkey, Bulgaria today is a bulwark of Balkan culture, a country existing for 13 centuries with impressive mosques, rustic villages, flamboyantly decorated churches, and an enduring folklore, the latter a holdover from the days when the country fancied itself a "guardian" of Balkan Christian tradition.

Its climate is continental, meaning long, hot, and dry summers when everybody who can afford it races toward the cooling Black Sea coast, followed by bitterly cold winters, which are a less than ideal time to travel. The only travelers who brave Bulgaria's winters are skiers attracted to Bulgaria's major ski resorts, which generally offer plenty of snow from mid-December to mid-April and feature improving but not world-class facilities like those found in Austria and Switzerland. Visitors not at the

Eastern European Rail Routes

beach in summer can be found hiking along 22,991 miles (37,000km) of marked trails, many cutting through virgin national parks and pristine nature reserves.

BULGARIA BY RAIL
PASSES
Rail Europe offers the **European East Pass,** which covers Bulgaria; see chapter 2 for more on this pass. See below for details on the **Balkan Flexipass,** which covers not only Bulgaria but other countries as well.

PRACTICAL TRAIN INFORMATION
The country offers a wide network of some 2,658 miles (4,278km) of rail tracks fanning out to all parts of the country. Buses here generally travel faster and more frequently, but riding the rails is more comfortable and offers far more panoramic views.

Train travel is amazingly cheap by Western standards, and all of the major cities, towns, and resorts are accessible by rail. Facilities and standards, however, lag behind the West, except for **InterCity Express** trains running between Sofia, Varna, and Burgas. There are three types of trains: express called *ekspresen,* fast moving known as *bârz,* and, to be avoided in our view, the snail-like *pâtnicheski* or slow-moving vehicles, that stop at every cow pasture. Slow trains are made even slower because of the often mountainous terrain. It's virtually impossible to find a national rail timetable, and even if you do, don't count on its accuracy. Timetables are written sloppily—in Cyrillic, no less—on a paper hastily pasted to the window of the ticket office. *Note:* Reservations are mandatory on all express trains. A reservation is called *zapazeno myasto* in Bulgarian.

In dire need of lots of cash for improvement, **Bulgarian State Railways (BDZh)** is the state network, blanketing most of the country, with the expected delays on long-distance jaunts. InterCity trains are about the only vehicles that are stocked with a buffet car, so you may need to bring along your own food and water on some runs.

Trains that run long distances at night offer a couchette and/or a sleeper, which are most affordable and far cheaper than a hotel (though admittedly far less comfortable than their western counterparts). Reservations for these accommodations must be made at least 2 days in advance, and possibly earlier in heavily booked July and August.

A daily **Bosphor** train runs between Istanbul, Turkey, and Bucharest, Romania, crossing year-round through Bulgaria, and the **Trans-Balkan Express** travels daily between Thessaloniki, Greece, and Bucharest via Sofia, the capital of Bulgaria. Also, several day trains travel to Thessaloniki, and one overnight train goes to Athens. The Balkan Express also travels between Sofia and Belgrade.

The main train station for rail information—and for the purchase of tickets—is **Tsentralna Gara (Central Station)** in Sofia, at Maria Luiza 112 (© 02/931-11-11), which is your point of arrival for most international trains. Tickets are also sold and information dispensed at **Rila International Travel Agency,** General Gurko 5 (© 02/987-07-77; www.bdz-rila.com), in Sofia. The same service is provided in the center of Sofia at the **Natzionalen Dvoretz na Kulturata (National Palace of Culture),** Pl. Bulgaria 1 (© 02/65-71-85 for international trains, or 02/65-84-02 for domestic journeys).

HIGHLIGHTS OF BULGARIA

Culturally and historically rich, the capital of Bulgaria, the city of **Sofia** ⽊⽊ is ripe for discovery. If you'll overlook its dreary Soviet-era architecture, you'll find Roman churches, Ottoman and Byzantine mosques, superb ballet and opera, varied restaurants, and even an exciting nightlife with enough bars and dance clubs to satisfy a New Yorker. Is a new Prague waiting to be discovered by hipsters?

(*Warning* **Staying Safe**

Petty street crime, much of which is directed against foreigners or others who appear to have money, continues to be a problem in Bulgaria. Pickpocketing and purse-snatching are frequent occurrences, especially in crowded markets and on shopping streets. Con artists operate on public transportation and in bus and train stations. Travelers should be suspicious of "instant friends" and should also require persons claiming to be government officials to show identification. There have been numerous incidents in which visitors have accepted offers of coffee or alcoholic beverages from "friendly people" met by chance at the airport, bus stations, hotels, or train stations and have been drugged or assaulted and robbed.

Value **Your Pass to Exotic Countries**

A trail of ancient cities, mosques, and natural wonders can be made most affordable through a **Balkan Flexipass,** granting you unlimited travel through Bulgaria, Greece, Macedonia, Romania, Turkey, and Serbia/Montenegro. You can travel for 5, 10, or 15 days within a 1-month period, with prices starting at $240. Travel is in first class only, and there are special fares for passengers under 26 or more than 60 years of age. The Balkan Flexipass is available through **Rail Europe** (© 877/272-RAIL [7245] in North America; www.raileurope.com) and most travel agents.

Sitting on a 1,788-foot (536m) plateau, at the foot of Mount Vitosha, Sofia is the highest capital in Europe with a population of around 1.2 million. For centuries the center of trans-European routes, Sofia sits midway between the Black Sea and the Adriatic. The hub of Bulgaria's rail network, Sofia deserves at least 2 days of your time.

The major attraction is **Hram-pametnik Alexander Nevski (Alexander Nevski Memorial Cathedral)** 𝕽𝕽, Ploshtad Alexander Nevski (© 02/987-76-97), a neo-Byzantine structure with glittering interlocking domes, constructed at the dawn of the 20th century. Try to visit the crypt, which is filled with a stunning collection of icons.

The other noteworthy house of worship is **Tsentralna Sofiiska Sinagoga (Central Sofia Synagogue)** 𝕽𝕽, 16 Ul. Ekzarh Yosif at Bul. Washington (© 02/831-273), in a beautifully restored 1909 synagogue celebrated for its Moorish turrets and gilt domes. It's dedicated to Russians who fell liberating Bulgaria from the Ottoman Empire.

Among the city's 10 or so other top attractions, the most notable is **Natzionalen Archeologicheski Musei (National Archaeological Museum),** Ploshtad Alexander Batenberg (© 02/882-405), housed in a former Great Mosque and filled with artifacts of the country's cultural history—notably the gold treasure of **Vulchi Trun** 𝕽𝕽, a masterpiece of Thracian workmanship on 13 vessels of gold.

In summer, most visitors make a dash for the country's Black Sea resorts (the sea is actually a brilliant blue with sandy beaches), centered on the ancient city of **Varna** 𝕽, 282 miles (470km) east of Sofia and 7 hours away by train. Cosmopolitan and cultivated, it is the third largest city of Bulgaria, and is known for its parks, gardens, wide tree-lined boulevards, and a beachfront boardwalk.

Another great city of Bulgaria is **Plovdiv** 𝕽, 104 miles (174km) southeast of Bulgaria on the main route from Sofia to the Turkish border. Skip the tacky environs and head at once to the heart of the old city with some of Bulgaria's most romantic National Revival architecture from the 18th and 19th centuries. Spend a day here wandering its cobblestone streets free of cars. Some of its museums are rich in Thracian artifacts from as far back as 4000 B.C. Plovdiv is 2½ hours by train from Sofia.

If time remains, try to visit one of the most stunning cities in the Balkans—**Veliko Târnovo** 𝕽𝕽𝕽, 144 miles (240km) northeast of Sofia. This was the capital of the Second Bulgarian Kingdom from the 12th to the 14th centuries when it was hailed as "a second Constantinople." Known as the City of the Czars, it's a virtual museum city with panoramic vistas at every turn. The ruined fortress of **Tsarevets** was once a royal palace and cathedral, and in summer the most spectacular sound-and-light show in Bulgaria takes place here. Take the train from Sofia toward Varna and change at the town of Gorna-Orjahovitza. Trip time from Sofia is roughly 5½ hours.

FOR MORE INFORMATION

Tourism information is found at the **Bulgarian Tourism Authority,** 1 Sveta Nedelia Sq. Sofia (© **02/933-58-45;** www.bulgariatravel.org), open Monday to Friday 9am to 5:30pm. Another source of information is **Bulgarian Tourist Chamber,** 8 Sveta Sofia (© **02/987-40-59;** www.btch.org), in Sofia. For information about what's happening in the capital, check **Sofia City Guide (www.sofiacityguide.com).**

2 Croatia

Part of the Austro-Hungarian Empire until World War I, Croatia is, after years of slumber, in vogue once again. Part of its allure is that 10% of its land mass consists of national parks. Thousands of visitors from Western Europe and a scattering of U.S. and Canadian explorers head here each year to see the emerging country's pristine coastlines, low green mountains, and flat but rich agricultural plains.

There are 1,111 miles (1,778km) of beautiful coastline and an astonishing thousand islands, of which 66 are inhabited. Medieval walled towns, most of which are remarkably preserved, add to the big town allure of such new "hot spots" as Zagreb, Split, and Dubrovnik. Beach-goers descend en masse from mid-May to late September, when the country's beaches are ideal for swimming. Naturism—nude bathing to most of us—has long been a popular tradition here.

Wherever you go, fresh seafood will be found on the menu. Of course, as a Balkan nation, Croatia naturally offers such old favorites as spit-roasted lamb and goulash.

Though recognition of its independence came in 1992 from the European Union, for most of the '90s Croatia lived in political isolation because of its conflict with the Serbs. But peace has returned to this land, and Croatia is once again viewed as a safe and desirable travel destination, though a visit here is still something of an adventure.

As the country's capital and transportation hub, Zagreb offers the best road, air, and rail links to other countries and is usually the starting point for most tours.

CROATIA BY RAIL

PASSES

For information on the Eurail Select Pass, see chapter 2. The **Eurail Austria–Croatia–Slovenia Pass** offers 4 days of unlimited first-class travel in Austria, Slovenia, and Croatia within a 2-month period. Passes cost $261 (£136) for adults; children ages 4 to 11 get a discounted rate, and kids under 4 travel free. Longer passes are also available.

Another option is the **Eurail Hungary–Croatia–Slovenia Pass,** which offers anywhere from 5 to 10 days of unlimited first-class travel in Hungary, Slovenia, and Croatia within a 2-month period. Prices start at $242 (£126) and children 4 to 11 get a discounted rate.

Both passes should be purchased either through Rail Europe or a travel agent before leaving North America.

PRACTICAL TRAIN INFORMATION

Rail Europe represents the Croatian railway system through its sales and information network. For more information, contact **Rail Europe** (© **877/272-RAIL** [7245] in North America; www.raileurope.com).

Although Croatia's train network is slow (buses are the preferred option for most locals), international connections are fine and much more comfortable than buses. It is the rail services inside the country that you need to watch out for because internal

> **Warning   Staying Safe**
>
> Vigilance is imperative when dealing with countries with a war-torn past. Although most of the country is safe for visitors, some of the more remote regions remain uncleared of land mines. The Danube region, for instance, is especially hazardous. It is ill advised to wander into fields or abandoned towns during your travels in Croatia.

trips get cut off when going through Bosnia and Serbia. The best routes to take are from Zagreb to Rijeka and Pula, or Zagreb to Split and Zadar. Tickets are much cheaper here than in most other parts of Europe, so you won't get much value for your railpasses. There are three types of trains: fast moving ones called *ubrazni*, locals known as *putnicki*, and first-class-only trains called *poslovni*. The first-class trains of Croatia are capacity controlled, with a rudimentary system of seat reservations that limit the number of passengers so that no one will be without a seat, although that luxury doesn't apply to the *ubrazni* and the *putnicki* trains mentioned above.

Distances in Croatia are short, and the time it takes for even the slowest trains between isolated villages won't gobble up too much of your day. It might be difficult to lay your hands on a hard (printed) copy of a Croatian timetable, even within Croatia, but even if it isn't always accurate, there's an electronic version posted on the Web at **www.hznet.hr**.

The word for arrivals is *dolazak* and departures are *odlazak* or *polazak*. A transfer is known as *presjedanje*.

In dire need of lots of improvement, **Croatian Railways Ltd.,** Mihanovićeva 12, 10000 Zagreb (© **385/1-4577-111**), is the state network, covering most of the country and traveling through Bosnia and Serbia. One bright spot, though, is the renovation of the track between Zagreb and Split. This upgrade allows tilting trains to use the tracks, which has cut down travel time from 9 hours to 4 hours and 45 minutes.

The main train station for rail information—and for the purchase of tickets—is **Zagreb Glavni kolodor** in Zagreb, at Trg kralja Tomislava 12, which is also your point of arrival for most international trains. There are eight other major train stations around the country: **Željeznički kolodvor Knin,** Trg Ante Starčevića 2; **Željeznički kolodvor Metković,** Andrije Hebranga bb; **Željeznički kolodvor Ploče,** Trg Tomislava 19; **Željeznički kolodvor Šibenik,** Fra Jerolima Milete 24; **Željeznički kolodvor Split,** Zlodrina polijano 20; **Željeznički kolodvor Zadar,** Ante Starčevića 3; **Željeznički kolodvor Pula,** Kolodvorska 5, and **Željeznički kolodvor Rijeka,** Trg Kralja Tomislava 1. All of these stations have a uniform telephone number (© **60/333 444**).

HIGHLIGHTS OF CROATIA

The capital of Croatia, the history-rich city of **Zagreb** lies on the fringe of the Pannonian Plain on the Sava River. For most of its centuries of existence, it consisted of two separate towns—one on the high ground and secular, the other religious. These two towns, Kaptol and Gradec, were finally joined in 1850. The population today hovers around 780,000, almost 52,000 of whom are enrolled at the University of Zagreb.

A major attraction is **Hrvatski Povijesni Muzej (Croatian History Museum),** 9 Matoševa (© **385/1-43-10-65;** www.jagor.srce.hr). Located in the 18th-century baroque palace, Vojković-Oršić-Rauch, and the old site of the National Museum, this place now houses more than 140,000 artifacts dating from the Middle Ages. The collection includes fine art, firearms, flags and uniforms, everyday objects, religious artifacts, and a plethora of other relics.

The city's other noteworthy museum is **The Archaeological Museum,** 19 Nikola Subic Zrinski Sq. (© **385/48-73-101;** www.amz.hr). Permanent exhibits here include extensive collections from the prehistoric era and ancient Egypt. There is also a **Numismatic collection** that draws many visitors. The museum itself is beautiful and worth the price of admission.

Among the city's 10 or so other top attractions, the most notable is **Hrvatsko Narodno Kazalište u Zagrebu (Croatian National Theater in Zagreb),** Trg Marsala Tita 15 (© **385/148-88-415;** www.hnk.hr), which was opened in 1895 by Emperor Franz Joseph I. Today it is the cultural epicenter of Zagreb and the site of ballet, musicals, comedies, dramas, contemporary dance, and opera performances. Tickets are practically a steal for North Americans, running $7 to $12 (£3.65–£6.25) for a play and $15 to $30 (£7.80–£15.60) for a ballet or opera.

In summer, most visitors make a dash for **Dubrovnik,** 243 miles (391km) southeast of Zagreb in southern Dalmatia. People refer to this beautiful part of the Adriatic coast as "The New Riviera . . . but cheaper." On a visit here in 1929, George Bernard Shaw explained: "If you want to see heaven on earth, come to Dubrovnik." With its white pebble beaches, craggy shoreline, and pristine sea, today's visitors are finally seeing what Shaw meant. There is no connection to the rail network in Dubrovnik, so your best bet is to take a train to Split and the bus or ferry to Dubrovnik (bus trip time: 1 hr., 20 min.).

Another great city of Croatia is **Split,** 156 miles (256km) south of Zagreb, and reached by a scenic train ride (trip time: 4½ hr.) that is a virtual preview of Croatia in its entirety. Set against a backdrop of crystal-clear waters, dense forests, and barren mountains, Split, founded in the 3rd century A.D., is the second most populous city in Croatia. Thanks to its vibrant cafe life and beach scene, it is still more of a cultural center than a resort.

The city's attractions can easily fill two busy days of your vacation. Chief among these is **Diocletian's Palace (Obala Hrvatskog Norodnog Preporoda).** These ruins are all that remain of the palace that Roman Emperor Diocletian built at the end of the 3rd century on the Bay of Aspalathos. He spent the last 2 years of his life here, following his abdication in A.D. 305. Much altered over the centuries, the remains combine the quality of a luxurious villa with those of a military camp.

Other attractions include the **Cathedral of St. Dominius Peristil,** whose main site is a 3rd-century octagonal mausoleum built as a shrine to Diocletian. Its 60m (200-ft.) bell tower, designed in the Romanesque-Gothic style, dates from the 12th century. At the cathedral, you can ask to visit **Jupiter's Temple,** Kraj Sv. Ivana at Grad, an ancient Roman temple that was converted into a baptistery during medieval times. The city's main museum, **Gradski Muzej,** Papaličeva 1 at Grad, houses a stunning collection of medieval weaponry.

One local tradition is the *Splitski Sir,* which is a nightly trip through the city checking to see who is at which of the cafes and what is going on there. The best cafe for people-watching is the outdoor terrace of the **Luxor Café,** Peristil, at Grad. While enjoying your drink, you'll take in a view of monuments in the distance that go back 2,000 years.

FOR MORE INFORMATION

Tourism information is found at the **Hrvatska Turisticka Zajendica** (Croatian National Tourist Board), Iblerov trg 10/IV, 10000 Zagreb (© **385/146-99-333;** www.croatia.hr), open Monday to Friday 9am to 5:30pm. There is a U.S. office at 350 Fifth Ave., Suite 4003, New York, NY 10118 (© **800/829-4416** or 212/279-8672).

3 Macedonia

A troubled but beautiful land, this province of the former Yugoslavia is now charting an uncertain future as one of Europe's newest republics. West of Bulgaria, this poor and struggling country is a land beset by racial and ethnic tensions—and often violence—as it's inhabited by pockets of Slavs, Turks, Serbs, Bulgars, and Albanians. The political situation remains somewhat unstable and the threat of potential ethnic violence is real; both the U.S. and Great Britain advise its citizens to travel here with great caution and at their own risk.

For rail passengers, Macedonia lies on the main line between European countries in the West and Greece, so many passengers stop here briefly before continuing east. Even though it's been fought over by other nations for centuries—it was once part of the Ottoman Turkish Empire—most of the country's monuments, including ancient monasteries, mosques, old churches, historic buildings, and archaeological "gardens," remain relatively intact. Even so, Macedonia is only for the most adventurous of travelers.

MACEDONIA BY RAIL
PASSES
Macedonia has no railpasses of its own—nor would you need one for the limited amount of travel you're likely to do in the country. Rail Europe offers a **Balkan Flexipass** (see p. 845) that covers travel in Macedonia among several other countries.

PRACTICAL TRAIN INFORMATION
International trains tend to run more or less on time in Macedonia, but domestic trains proceed at a snail's pace. Trains are operated by **Makedonski Aheleznici** (Macedonian Railways). The principal line, and the route the average visitor will travel, is the north/south rail link between Belgrade and Thessaloniki in Greece, stopping off in Skopje (pop. 600,000), the capital of Macedonia.

Thessaloniki (p. 490), incidentally, is the second city of modern Greece also called Macedonia, as opposed to the former Yugoslav province—now country—of Macedonia. There is confusion and rivalry here about which land is entitled to use the name of Macedonia.

Express trains journey three times daily from Belgrade to Skopje in Macedonia (travel time: 3–5 hr.); and there are international links to Vienna, Budapest (via Belgrade), and also from Istanbul (via Sofia) to Skopje. Reservations are required on all international lines passing through Macedonia. For night travel, you must also reserve a couchette or

---

⌜Warning⌟ Staying Safe

Macedonia is not the safest place to visit. Even though the overall level of violence has diminished, interethnic violence, including armed exchanges, continues. Acts of intimidation and violence against British and American citizens are a possibility, and land mines and unexploded ordnance pose a continuing threat. Incidents of theft and other petty crimes aboard trains are constantly reported; travelers should take precautions.

sleeper on any international trains traveling through Macedonia as well. International lines serve food and drink, but if you're traveling on domestic services in Macedonia, bring your own supplies for the trip.

The best source of rail assistance is the **Skopje Railway Station** (© 02/234-255) in the capital. Most of the staff at Feroturist Travel Agency, inside the train station, will provide rail data and sell international and domestic tickets. They also book couchettes and sleepers—say, on the train to Belgrade.

HIGHLIGHTS OF MACEDONIA

Skopje, the capital of Macedonia, is on the banks of the Vardar River in the historic core of the Balkans. Disasters have historically beset the city, none worse than the earthquake of 1963, which destroyed much of Skopje. But there is still much in the rebuilt city to admire, with its minarets, mosques, and Turkish-style domes in the old town.

All the major sights unfold as you make your way out of the train depot, walking northwesterly toward the old city, with its 15th-century **Turkish Baths** and other attractions. The ancient **Oriental Bazaar** is worth an hour of your time, as you shop for regional handicrafts or watch them being made at this atmospheric souk.

Near the Turkish Bridge is Skopje's best museum, the **Municipal Art Gallery.** The **Museum of Macedonia,** filled with regional artifacts, is also worth a visit. The **Church of Sveti Spas** is visited mainly for its impressive collection of icons, many from the 1700s, and there is also a local mosque, **Mustafa Pasha,** where you can scale the minaret for the most panoramic view of Skopje. Across the street from this mosque lies **Fort Kale,** now in ruins but dating from the 10th century.

Outside the capital, the most scenic rail route is a 2-hour trip to the town of **Bitola** ⨂, which is relatively undiscovered and well worth a night or two. You'll definitely feel you're in Turkey here, and there are many relics to explore, including the Roman ruins of **Heraclea** along with an early **Christian palace.** Other highlights—all on Marshal Tito Square (named for Yugoslavia's former dictator)—are the **Mosa Pijade Art Gallery,** installed in an old mosque, and the 16th-century **Bezistan Bazaar.** Wander at your leisure through the district of bazaars known as **Stara Charshiya,** making your way to the city market.

The greatest attraction of Macedonia is not on a rail line but can be reached by frequent buses from Bitola. The old town of **Ohrid** ⨂⨂⨂ is a charmer filled with red-roofed houses, sidewalk cafes, and rustic fish restaurants surrounding the world's second deepest lake after Lake Baikal in Russia. Ohrid is acclaimed as one of the true beauty spots in all of Europe, and UNESCO has declared it a World Heritage Site. Trip time from Bitola to Ohrid is 90 minutes (via bus).

Although you'll want to spend most of your precious time on the lake, you can stroll the streets of Ohrid for hours, taking in such notable churches as **Sveti Kilment** and **Sveti Sofija** before heading west to the **Amphitheater** constructed by the Romans. After a visit, walk over to the walls of the old **citadel** for a panoramic view of the district before continuing south to the ruins of an ancient basilica whose mosaics can still be seen.

FOR MORE INFORMATION

Getting information on rail travel in Macedonia before you get here is almost impossible; it's difficult enough even when you're in the country.

During your visit to Ohrid and its lake, you can obtain information on the area from the **Biljana Tourist Office,** Partizanska 3 (© 046/266-494), in front of the bus station, and also at Automoto Sojuz, Galicica at Lazo Trpkoski (© **02/3181-181**), in the eastern part of Ohrid.

Because it's so hard to obtain information before you go, many visitors often contact their **Macedonian embassy.** In North America, the Embassy of the Republic of Macedonia is at 2129 Wyoming Ave. NW, Washington, DC 20008 (© **202/667-0501**).

4 Poland

A member of NATO since 1999, Poland is shaking off its tragic past at the hands of the Nazis and the Soviet Union, and forging greater ties with Western Europe and a close bond with America. Although it has a troubled image abroad because of its disastrous history, it offers an abundance of natural and cultural attractions. These range from the bustling, post-socialist charm of Warsaw, its capital, to the beautifully restored old city of Gdansk, from the Renaissance arcades of 1,000-year-old Krakow to the grim gas chambers of Auschwitz.

POLAND BY RAIL
PASSES
Unlike most other Eastern European countries, rail travel is not incredibly cheap in Poland, though it's still a lot less expensive than in Western Europe. It's estimated that on some long runs, the cost of a regular rail ticket is practically that of a discounted airplane ticket. Therefore, railpasses are the way to go here if you plan to do extensive rail travel in Poland.

Rail Europe offers a **European East Pass** that covers travel in Poland (see chapter 2), and the **Poland Pass,** which allows unlimited travel on the entire network of the Polish rail system. The Poland Pass varies in duration from 5 to 15 days of travel in a 1-month period; a first-class pass (recommended) starts at $148. Passengers under 26 years old can purchase a Poland Youth Pass for about 30% less.

PRACTICAL TRAIN INFORMATION
Berlin and Warsaw, both virtually destroyed in World War II, today enjoy one of the most famous rail connections in Europe, the fastest train running from Berlin in the west to Warsaw in the east in just 6½ hours. Four trains arrive daily from Berlin; the overnight train, with sleeping and couchette cars only, takes 8 hours. The scenery is pleasant without being spectacular, and the rail lines go along the Piast Trail linking such historic towns as Rzepin and Poznan.

Berlin is the western rail gateway to Warsaw, but there are many other options, notably four daily trains linking Warsaw to Prague in 10 to 12 hours, depending on connections. Two daily trains also run between Vienna and Warsaw (via Katowice) that take 7 to 8 hours, depending on the train. Most North American rail passengers take the train from Berlin.

Polish trains are faster and more efficient than they've ever been, though still lagging behind rail service in, say, Germany. Opt whenever possible for InterCity, EuroCity, or *Ekspresowe* trains, which offer restaurant cars, more comfort (some even have air-conditioning), and fewer delays. Avoid the snail-like *Osobowe* or *Pospieszne* categories, though if you get stuck, make sure to stock up on food and drink before getting on the train. Reservations are vital on all express trains. We definitely recommend that you go first class when traveling in Poland. The extra comfort and the security of actually having a reserved seat are worth the money. If you're taking a night train, opt for a sleeping car instead of a couchette.

> **Warning   Staying Safe**
>
> Regrettably, safety is a grave issue when traveling the rails in Poland. International trains to Poland are said to be crawling with thieves, and theft of valuables, including luggage, is commonplace. The most dangerous route is the Berlin to Warsaw night train where most robberies occur. Our advice: Get a sleeping car and lock the door.

Reservations can be made through Rail Europe or at ticket offices within each of the country's major railway stations. You can also buy rail tickets and make reservations at any branch of the Orbis Polish Travel Bureau, which are found in all major cities and towns. This agency is especially recommended for North Americans as it places great importance on hiring people who speak English. It's sometimes—but not always—possible to pay for a ticket with a credit card. With the purchase of a ticket, reservations are free. When you obtain a ticket, look at it carefully. If there's a letter "R" positioned inside a box, it means that reservations are mandatory; a letter "R" that's not encased within a box means that seat reservations are required in only part of the train.

In Warsaw, the main dispenser of information for rail travel in Poland is **Warszawa Centralna** or Central Station at Jerozolimskie 54, Srodmiescie (© **022/9436**). For domestic rail information, call **022/620-03-61;** for international rail information, call © **022/620-45-12.** International trains arrive at the Central Station. Domestic departures are most often at the adjoining station, Warszawa Srodmiescie, Jerozolimskie, Stromiescie (© **022/628-47-41**). Online, go to the excellent Polish rail website (in Polish) at **www.wars.pl**.

HIGHLIGHTS OF POLAND

Your rail adventure begins in **Warsaw** ✿✿, where you can wander for a day around the Old Town that was destroyed by the Nazis but reconstructed in the 1950s. The city is the political center of the country and its geographical heart since 1611. Try to ignore the drabness of the surrounding Soviet-style architectural horror and concentrate on the nuggets, which include **Rynek Starego Miasta (Old Town Square)** ✿✿✿, the hub of Old Town life where arts and crafts are sold in summer and spontaneous musical performances take place. The best way to see Old Town is to take a horse-drawn carriage from here, which passes by such attractions as **Zamek Krolewski** ✿, Pl. Samkowy 4, Stare Miasto, the royal castle dating from the 14th century.

After a look at Warsaw, most visitors head 170 miles (270km) south to **Krakow** ✿✿✿, home to 100,000 students and almost as many pubs. Thirty-four trains make the 3-hour journey each day from Warsaw. Krakow is more intriguing than Warsaw since its Stare Miasto (Old Town), with its towers, facades, and ancient churches, was spared from Hitler's devastation. The streets of its Old Town are likened to a living museum. On a grim note you can journey to **Auschwitz** ✿, 38 miles (60km) west to visit this infamous death camp for Jews, gypsies, homosexuals, and even Jehovah's Witnesses. Ten buses a day leave from Kraków for Auschwitz; buses will drop you off close to the entrance to the museum at the death camp.

If time remains, try to see the city of **Gdansk** ✿, 219 miles (350km) north of Warsaw. Eighteen trains make the 4-hour trip every day. On the Baltic Coast at the mouth of the Wisla, this was once the free city of Danzig. The birthplace of Solidarity, it is the center of the Polish Riviera and the gateway to "castle country," such as the fortress of the Teutonic Knights of Malbork (easily accessible by train from Gdansk). In the area east of Gdansk (towards Belarus) are 1,000 lakes.

FOR MORE INFORMATION
On the Web, search the **Official Poland Tourist Board** site at **www.poland.pl**.

In Warsaw, information is available at **The Center for Tourist Information,** Pl. Zamkowy 1/13, Stare Miasto (© **022/635-18-81**), and at the **Warsaw Tourist Information Office,** Krakowskie Przedmiescie 89 Srodmiescie (© **022/94-31;** www.warsawtour.pl).

In Krakow, consult **Cultural Information Center,** 7 Ul. Józefa (© **012/429-51-50;** www.karnet.krakow2000.pl), and the **Tourist Information Office,** 7 Ul. Józefa (© **012/429-44-99;** www.krakow.pl).

For information in North America, contact the **Polish National Tourist Office,** 5 Marine View Plaza, Hoboken, NJ, 07030 (© **201/420-9910;** www.polandtour.org).

5 Romania

The most beautiful country in Eastern Europe—a nation the size of Oregon—has a lot going for it: medieval villages, cosmopolitan cities (its capital, Bucharest, was once known as "The Paris of the East"), Count Dracula's Transylvania, a history-rich landscape, snowy peaks, and a Black Sea coastline. There are 2,000 old monasteries alone, including the fabled painted monasteries of Bucovina. From its mysterious Carpathian Mountains to its UNESCO World Heritage Site monuments, Romania calls out for your attention and time.

There are problems here, mainly those caused by the country's painful transition from the Communist dictatorship of the brutal Nicolae Ceauşescu to a market economy and liberal democracy. Sure, there's natural and man-made beauty, but tourist facilities lag far behind and there is much that is derelict, not working, and definitely not operating on a time clock. But if you avoid the smoke-belching industrial area horror—a legacy of the long Communist rule—and escape to the countryside, you'll find picture-perfect castles and fortified villages.

The weather is a big determining factor when timing your visit. Because summers are blistery hot and winters are bitterly cold, spring and fall are ideal.

Note: Americans and Canadians can stay in Romania without visas for 90 days.

ROMANIA BY RAIL
PASSES
Rail Europe offers a **Balkan Flexipass** (p. 845) that covers travel in Romania. They also offer a **Romania Pass** that covers 5 or 10 days of first-class travel in Romania over a 2-month period. Prices start at $176 per adult; children 4 to 11 pay a discounted price, and children under 4 travel free. The passes should be purchased in North America.

The **Eurail Global Pass** is now good for Romania. Also available are the **Eurail Select Pass** and the **Austria–Hungary Pass.** For more information on these passes, see chapter 2.

PRACTICAL TRAIN INFORMATION
Train fares in Romania are moderate, and rail travel is the best way to get to the small towns and villages spread across the country's 7,021-mile (11,300km) network, operated by the **Romanian State Railway,** generally known as CFR. Western travelers find

Romania's timetables confusing or "bizarre," as one irate traveler described them to us. Some trains are in poor condition, often derelict, and passengers are frequently left sweltering in the heat or freezing in the cold. Trains are also crowded, so long journeys are not recommended. To compensate, some rail routes are especially scenic, especially those making their way across the Transylvanian landscape.

Opt for the InterCity and or *rapide* services, which stop at only the major towns, and usually have a dining car (bring some food and drink with you anyway, just to be on the safe side). Advance bookings for these fast trains are vital. Avoid the atrocious *tren de personae* trains like the plague! Most long-distance overnight trains have couchettes or sleeping cars, which require reservations. Tickets are sold at rail depots only an hour, sometimes 2 hours, before departure times—expect long lines.

Bucharest offers numerous international train connections and facilities on these trains are usually quite good. One of the most popular routings from the west is the Budapest-Bucharest train journey, which takes 12 hours. Some of the international trains that run through the Hungarian capital and the Romanian capital include the *Pannonia Express* (out of Prague), the *Dacia Express* (out of Vienna; it offers nice views of the Transylvanian countryside), and the *Ister* (a EuroNight train with modern sleeping compartments). There is also train service between Belgrade and Bucharest (trip time: 12–13 hr.); and a slow train between Sofia and Bucharest, which covers a distance of 319 miles (513km) in 12 hours.

You can seek more information on CFR, the Romanian Railways, at **www.cfr.ro**. In Bucharest, you can check with Agentia de Voiaj CFR at Str. Domnita Anastasia 10–14 (© **021/313-2644** or 021/314-5528), 139 Calea Grivitei (© **021/316 8947**), or 22 Str. Nicolae Grigorescu (© **021/340-1860**). A helpful rail timetable in English is offered online at **www.meresultrenurilorcfr.ro**. Train schedules are available in most cities and towns by calling © **221** for information. As there will no doubt be a language problem, ask an English-speaking member of your hotel staff to make the call for you.

HIGHLIGHTS OF ROMANIA

You will likely arrive in the capital city of **Bucharest** ✮✮. Ceauşescu tried to have bulldozers destroy much of the French flavor of the ancient city with his grotesque Communist state–inspired architecture, but restoration is underway to recapture some of the old essence of Bucharest.

Bucharest boasts five train stations, of which **Gara de Nord,** the biggest and the ugliest, is your most likely arrival point from such cities as Belgrade, Munich, Sofia, Vienna, and Budapest (the most likely point of departure).

Allow at least a day to see the monuments and to partake of some of the city's lively new restaurants and burgeoning nightlife. You can't see it all in a day, but you should definitely see the attractions we list below if your time is limited. **Biserica Stavropoleos** ✮, Strada Stavropoleos, is uniquely Romanian, the best example of what is known locally as Brancovenese architecture, a curvy style created in both stone and wood and blending late Renaissance with Byzantine motifs. The remarkable church, with its fresco-adorned walls and impressive dome, was constructed between 1724 and 1730.

For the best introduction to the varied architecture of Romania, head for **Muzeul Satului** ✮, a village museum at Sos Kiseleff 28–30, filled with workshops of craftspeople, old churches, and the most typical of regional housing, each furnished authentically. Another folkloric museum is **Muzeul Taranului Roman** ✮, a Romanian regional museum with nearly 100,000 artifacts on display at Sos Kiseleff 3. The 19th-century

---

Warning   **Staying Safe**

Traveling by train in Romania is relatively safe but crimes do occur, mostly non-violent ones such as robberies, muggings, pickpocketing, and confidence scams. Organized groups of thieves and pickpockets operate in the train stations, on trains, and on the subways. A number of thefts and assaults occur on overnight trains, including thefts from passengers in closed compartments. One popular scam involves an individual posing as a plainclothes policeman approaching a potential victim, flashing a badge, and asking for his/her passport and wallet, which the thief then grabs and flees with.

Palatul Cotroceni ✵, Blvd. Geniului 1, was the home of the royal family from 1893 until 1947, when they were chased out by the Communists. Rebuilt after a 1977 earthquake, it is lavishly furnished and houses many personal items left by the fleeing royals.

Finally, you might want to go by **Palatul Parlamentului** ✵ or the Parliament Palace, Calea 13 Septembrie, a mammoth contemporary structure that can be blamed on Ceauşescu's megalomania. It is the second largest building in the world, a true Stalinist monstrosity that has 7 of its 3,000 rooms open to the public. Yes, that's 24-karat gold on the ceiling.

The true charm of Romania lies not in Bucharest but in its countryside, especially a trip to Transylvania to call on Count Dracula. A UNESCO World Heritage Site, the **Danube Delta (Delta Dunarii)** ✵✵, is Europe's largest wetland reserve, embracing an area of 3,604 square miles (5,800 sq. km) and sheltering some 300 species of birds and 160 species of fish. One of the best centers for exploring the delta is **Tulcea**, lying 163 miles (263km) northeast of Bucharest, reached by daily express train (trip time: 5 hr.). The western province of Romania, **Transylvania** ✵✵✵, the land of the fictional Count Dracula (inspirer Vlad the Impaler, however, was all too real), continues to spark the imagination of the world. It is a land of forest-covered mountains, historic villages, fortified churches, and an unspoiled landscape. The best way to see this province is to take one of 15 daily trains out of Bucharest and make the 3- to 4-hour trip to **Brasov** ✵✵, a medieval city that's an ideal Transylvanian gateway. From Brasov, your itinerary can continue west to **Sighisoara** and **Sibiu** and north to **Cluj** before pressing on to **Deva, Hundedoara, Arad,** and **Timisoara.** The old Roman colony of **Sibiu** ✵✵ is another good base city and a good place to get information about traveling in Transylvania (see below). As the ancient capital of Transylvania, Sibiu, is serviced by seven trains per day from Bucharest; the trip takes 6 hours.

Romania's northeastern province of **Moldavia** is visited mainly for its fabled monasteries. Regrettably, reaching these major attractions by rail is too cumbersome a process to recommend.

FOR MORE INFORMATION

The **Official Romanian Tourist Board** website is **www.romaniatravel.com**. Amazingly, Bucharest has no tourist office, although there is a booth in the Gara de Nord train station. Many hotels keep helpful brochures to distribute to their clients. Private travel agents fill the gap, as does the **European Union Information Centre** in the Central University Library, Piata Revolutiei at Calea Victoriei 88 (✆ **021/315-3470;** www.infoeuropa.ro).

A good source for information about Transylvania is the **Tourist Information Office** in Sibiu, S. Brukenthal 2 (© **0269/208-913;** www.primsb.ro).

For information before you leave home, contact the **Romanian National Tourist Office,** 355 Lexington Ave., 19th Floor, New York, NY 10017 (© **212/545-8484;** www.romaniatourism.com).

6 Serbia & Montenegro

Only in February 2003 did the Federal Republic of Yugoslavia become two new nations—Serbia and Montenegro, one a turbulent Balkan country and the other a pint-sized state bordering the Adriatic Sea, both undergoing economic upheaval and profound political change. Though still suffering the aftershocks of civil war and NATO bombing, the tourist industry is slowly coming back, although there is unrest in the Serbian province of Kosovo, where travel is still not advised.

There is much to see in both provinces, and for the traveler with a sense of adventure it's worth the effort. With its vast mountains and plateaus, it is a scenic land of great grandeur with rivers flowing north into the Danube. Its only coastline is the Montenegrin coast, stretching for 93 miles (150km). The splendid **Tara Canyon** in Montenegro is the largest in Europe, and the **Bay of Kotor** is the only real fjord in the south of Europe. In Serbia, Belgrade, the capital city, is lively and vibrant, though lagging far behind the other capitals to its west.

Because of the varied terrain the climate is very different in certain regions. In the north, with its fertile plains, a continental climate prevails, meaning hot and very humid summers with bitterly cold winters. To the southeast, moving toward Montenegro and its mountains, an Adriatic climate prevails along the coast, with hot, dry summers lasting until October and cold winters with lots of snowfall inland.

North American citizens don't need a visa. *Note:* It is generally safe to travel to Belgrade (the capital of Serbia), and that city is the major rail terminus from other international destinations.

SERBIA & MONTENEGRO BY RAIL
PASSES
Rail Europe offers a **Balkan Flexipass** (p. 845) and the **Eurail Select Pass** (see chapter 2), which cover rail travel through Serbia and Montenegro. There is no single railpass for the country, nor is one really needed, as most travelers pass through here en route to somewhere else—often Bulgaria.

PRACTICAL TRAIN INFORMATION
International trains run through Serbia (not Montenegro) and go on to some of the former Yugoslav republics and surrounding countries. The main rail link coming down from Hungary arrives in Belgrade and goes on to Macedonia or Bulgaria. Even international lines tend to be slow moving and overcrowded. Domestic trains are often a physical disaster, in poor condition, even more overcrowded than international trains, and subject to endless delays. Reservations made at the departure station are absolutely essential on all international trains.

Two trains link Belgrade with Budapest (7 hr.) and two trains a day run to Vienna (11 hr.). There are also two trains a day to the Greek city of Thessaloniki, going on to Athens, the total journey taking 22 hours. The Balkan Express goes from Belgrade to Sofia in Bulgaria in 9 hours; the trip from Belgrade to Istanbul takes 23 hours.

International trains from Belgrade include stops at Novi Sad and Subotica for places in the north and west, and they also stop at Nis for passengers heading east. Montenegro is serviced by a domestic line from Belgrade, which runs to the coastal town of Bar, the republic's only port. A total of four fast (and we use the term loosely) passenger trains make the run daily between Belgrade and Bar via Podorica. From Belgrade to Bar, figure on a minimum trip time of 8 hours.

Although international lines are generally safe (the usual precautions are advised), domestic train travel through the country should be undertaken with care, as assaults and robberies of visitors have been reported.

For information about rail travel in Serbia and Montenegro, go to the main Belgrade rail station on Savski Trg (© **381/11-3614-811;** www.serbianrailways.com).

HIGHLIGHTS OF SERBIA & MONTENEGRO

From its low mountains off the Adriatic Coast to the highlands of Serbia, there is much to see and explore here, including a wide variety of architectural styles ranging from Romanesque to Gothic, from Renaissance to baroque. Throughout the land are great monuments or else their ruins, including fortresses, ancient churches, Byzantine-style basilicas, and Roman amphitheaters. If you're pressed for time, spend a day exploring Belgrade and the rest of your time taking in Montenegro, which has a far greater scenic allure.

With a population of two million, **Belgrade** ✿, on the southern tier of the Carpathian Basin where the River Sava links up with the Danube, is your gateway to the country. The city has been "the capital of the Serbs" since 1403 when the Turks drove the Serbs northward. The train station lies on the south side of Belgrade. From the station, tram 1, 2, or 13 heads for the **Kalemegdan Citadel** ✿, a major attraction on the north side of town. A Roman camp in the 1st century A.D., today this is a complex of Orthodox churches, Turkish baths, Muslin tombs, and a big military museum presenting a warlike view of the country.

The art and culture of Serbia are showcased at the **National Museum,** Trg Republike 1A, which displays everything from ancient artifacts to Picasso. Serbian folkloric costumes are best seen at the **Ethnographical Museum,** Studentski Trg 13. A section of great charm is **Skadarlija** ✿, originally settled by gypsies but later turned into a retreat for Bohemians. Much of its 19th-century artistic flavor remains intact.

In contrast to Serbia, **Montenegro** ✿✿✿ is optimistically called "the jewel of Europe." Train arrivals are in **Bar,** a port city of only minor interest. From here, buses fan out to the area's major scenic wonders. From June to September, all of Montenegro is a popular holiday spot, centering on the beautiful **Lake Skadar** ✿✿✿, the largest lake in the Balkans and a major bird sanctuary. **Kotor** ✿✿ is a major resort town situated at the head of southern Europe's deepest fjord. It's a walled medieval city that is a UNESCO World Heritage Site. The other town of interest is **Budva** ✿, built by the Venetians in the Middle Ages. Today it is Montenegro's leading beach resort. Its old walled town, destroyed by two earthquakes in 1979, has been reconstructed.

FOR MORE INFORMATION

The **National Tourist Organization of Serbia** operates a helpful website **www. serbia-tourism.org**. The official website for the **National Tourism Organization of Montenegro** is **www.visit-montenegro.com**.

The **Tourist Office Organization of Belgrade** is at 1 Dečanska, Belgrade (© **381/ 11-3248-404;** www.tob.co.yu).

7 Slovakia

Slovakia broke away from Czechoslovakia on January 1, 1993, and has been forging ahead to create its own identity ever since. East of the Czech Republic and about one-third its size, Slovakia doesn't have a world-class city such as Prague and doesn't have the three-star attractions its neighbor does. But what it does have is breadth—it covers nearly 19,000 square miles (49,000 sq. km), which makes it larger than Switzerland.

In addition to its historic capital city of Bratislava, Slovakia is home to the High Tatra Mountains, which are spread over an area of 300 square miles (770 sq. km). With its waterfalls, caves, and canyons, this is one of the great national parks of Europe, the mountains peaking at 2,650m (8,694 ft.). Combined with all this majestic glory are quaint villages and castles on the Danube, charming towns of the Little Carpathians, and beautiful 18th-century churches in the east of the country.

SLOVAKIA BY RAIL
PASSES
Rail Europe offers a **European East Pass** (see chapter 2) that covers travel in Slovakia. No other pass is accepted.

PRACTICAL TRAIN INFORMATION
Zeleznice Slovenskej Republiky (Slovak State Railways) is less developed than the railways in the Czech Republic. However, there is less need for trains, and the mountainous terrain throughout much of the republic makes rail travel difficult. That said, you'll find some of Central Europe's most scenic rail lines in Slovakia, including a stunning ride on an electric train into the High Tatras.

Although it's not the transportation hub for Central Europe that Prague is, Bratislava is well connected. The best routing into Slovakia is the 5-hour trip from Prague to Bratislava's **Hlavná Stanica** (© 52-49-82-75); there are seven trains per day. From Vienna's Sudbahnhof, 20 daily trains make the 1-hour run to Brastislava. If you're in Hungary, seven trains per day make the 3-hour trip from Budapest to Bratislava.

Reservations are essential, especially on express trains, which are labeled **R** or **Míst.** Reservations can be booked ahead of time on Slovakian trains through Rail Europe; the cost is around $12 (£6.25). It's also essential to reserve sleepers—called *lahatkovy vozen*—and couchettes on long trips. These should both be booked as far in advance as possible (again, Rail Europe can book these as well). In all cases, you should book the direct lines, which are called *rýchlik,* as these trains stop only at cities or larger towns. Unless you've got endless time, avoid the local trains called *osobný vlak,* though travel on these snail-paced trains is 50% cheaper. On express trains, and if you're willing to pay 50% more for your tickets, you can go first class—if you can afford it, we advise it, as second-class travel is often overcrowded and uncomfortable. Only express trains have dining cars, so bring food and drink along with you on other trains. In general, the network is reliable, with trains running on time.

Statistics cite Slovakia as having "medium crime," mostly picked pockets, purse and cellular phone snatchings, and muggings. Armed robbery and the drugging and robbing of unsuspecting victims at nightspots or bars does happen, but is rare. Most thefts occur at crowded tourist sites or on trains or buses. Numerous thefts are reported from couchettes on international train journeys, so keep a careful eye on your belongings or get a sleeper car with a lockable door.

For more information, consult the website of **Slovakia State Railways** at **www. zsr.sk**, or call © **02/2029-7582.**

HIGHLIGHTS OF SLOVAKIA

On the banks of the Danube, **Bratislava** ⚔ is the rail hub of Slovakia and also its capital. Its Old Town or **Starý Mesto** is looking better than ever now that it's brightening up its dreary Communist-era gray concrete high-rise projects. Beyond these modern monstrosities, on the city's outskirts, are castles and vineyards. The Old Town, with its cobblestone streets, invites hours of exploration relieved by fashionable cafes, bars, and restaurants.

A highlight is **Bratislava Castle** ⚔ or Brastislavsky Hrad, Zámocka U1, Starý Mesto, a four-towered landmark overlooking Old Town from a hill just outside the city. Its 18th-century glory was reconstructed by the Communists on foundations laid in the 9th century. Under the Hungarian kings and later the Habsburgs, the edifice was further expanded as a fortress against the Turkish menace from the east.

Another gem awaiting you is **Primaciálny Palác** ⚔ or Primates' Palace, Primaciále Nam, 1 Starý Mesto, a pale pink baroque palace celebrated for its **Hall of Mirrors** ⚔⚔ where the peace treaty of Pressburg was signed in 1805 by Napoleon and Franz I, the Austrian emperor. You can also enjoy the lush antiques and intricately woven tapestries from the 1600s. The massive Gothic church of **Dom Svätého Martina** ⚔ or St. Martin's Cathedral, Rudnayovo Nám, Starý Mesto, was consecrated in 1452. Once Hungary's coronation cathedral (Slovakia was part of the Austro-Hungarian Empire until 1918), it witnessed the crowning of 17 royals here between the 16th and 19th century.

After Bratislava, the country's main attraction is the **Tatras Mountains** ⚔⚔⚔, but reaching them by train will take at least 5 hours. Once you finally get here, the district is compact, about 20 miles (32km) from end to end, containing 35 mountain lakes with clear but very cold waters. Your gateway to the Tatras is the city of **Poprad,** located 204 miles (329km) east of Bratislava. The town is a bit of a Soviet-era architectural horror, but there's beauty at its doorstep. An electric railroad here takes you to the more fascinating attractions and tourist facilities that lie 19 miles (30km) to the north.

FOR MORE INFORMATION

On the Web, consult **www.slovakia.org**. In the Tatras Mountains, tourist information is available at all resort towns, including **Satur,** Námestie Sv. Egídia 2950, Poprad (☎ **052/442-2710**). In Bratislava itself, **Satur** is Slovakia's national travel agency, with offices at Jesenského 5, Starý Mesto (☎ **02/5441-0133**).

In North America, contact the **Slovak Commercial & Tourist Office,** 10 E. 40th St., Suite 3606, New York, NY 10016 (☎ **212/679-7044;** www.slovakiatourism.sk).

8 Slovenia

Of all the breakaway republics of old Yugoslavia (it declared its independence from Yugoslavia on June 25, 1991, and met only meager resistance from Belgrade), Slovenia is the most prosperous and the safest to visit. It is also one of the most scenic.

Slovenia, at peace with its neighbors, is bordered by Austria, Hungary, Croatia, and Italy. Seemingly ignoring the neighbors to which it was once united, the country has turned its eyes to the West and joined the European Union and NATO in 2004. About 90% of the population is made up of a single ethnic group, the Slovenes, so the country is not as sharply divided by ethnic minorities as some of its neighbors.

From its Adriatic shores to its Alpine peaks, Slovenia is loaded with natural beauty. Many European vacationers here spend all their time with a beach towel on the country's small strip of emerald blue coast. But there is so much more to see inland, ranging from mountains and lakes to old vineyards and undulating farmland. The standard of living here is much like that of Western Europe. The culture reflects the long occupation of Habsburg control (before the Habsburgs, Slovenia was part of the Roman Empire for nearly 5 c.).

Spring and autumn are the best times to explore this small Slavic nation. July and August are the obvious months to visit if you're planning on spending time at its beaches.

SLOVENIA BY RAIL
PASSES
For information on the **Eurail Select Pass,** see chapter 2.

The **Eurail Austria–Croatia–Slovenia Pass** offers 4 days of unlimited first-class travel in Austria, Slovenia, and Croatia within a 2-month period. Passes start at $261 (£136) for adults, children ages 4 to 11 pay a special rate, and kids under 4 travel free. Up to 6 extra days may be purchased for $20 (£10.40) each. Another option is the **Eurail Hungary–Croatia–Slovenia Pass,** which offers anywhere from 5 to 10 days of unlimited first-class travel in Hungary, Slovenia, and Croatia within a 2-month period. The cost starts at $242 for an adult; children ages 4 to 11 pay a special rate, and kids under 4 travel free.

Both passes should be purchased through either Rail Europe or a travel agent before leaving North America.

PRACTICAL TRAIN INFORMATION
Rail travel isn't the most time-efficient mode of transportation in Slovenia (most locals leave the trains to the tourists, preferring to take buses instead), but it will get you from point A to point B without too many stops. Tickets here are very inexpensive, so if you plan only to travel in Slovenia, purchasing a railpass makes no financial sense. Do not fall into the trap of buying tickets on the train unless you absolutely have to. Supplements for such purchases can run you more than the actual ticket.

Slovenian Railways (© 01-29-13-332; www.Slo-zeleznice.si) operates several types of trains. The modern high-speed tilting trains, known as **InterCity Slovenian trains (ICS),** offer greater comfort than the other rail types. Additional services on these trains include wheelchair transport, telephones, a restaurant, and a free parking place at the rail station. Seat reservations are mandatory. **EuroCity (EC)** trains are high-quality international trains with a superfluity of services. **InterCity trains (IC)** connect long distances within Slovenia. There are also lower-quality international

---

⌈Warning Staying Safe

Political demonstrations have been known to occur in city centers in Slovenia, most often in Ljubljana around *Kongresni Trg* (Congress Sq.). These demonstrations are, for the most part peaceful in nature, but in the past there have been anti-American incidents. Once demonstrators threw paint balloons and eggs at the American Embassy. The U.S. Department of State urges Americans to stay away from such rallies. Information on the security and political climate of the country can be obtained by calling the U.S. Department of State at © **888/ 407-4747** from 8am to 8pm Monday to Friday, except federal holidays.

Tips Changing Currency

Slovenia adopted the euro in 2007 and therefore must keep its debt levels, budget deficits, interest rates, and inflation levels within the EU's Maastrict criteria.

---

trains (designated MV on timetables). Local and regional trains are the slowest of the Slovenian rail network and cover the shortest distances.

Note: Figuring out timetables, if there are any at the station, is a challenge. Departures are usually listed on a yellow chalkboard titled *Odhad* or *Odhodi Vlakov.* Arrivals are listed on a white chalkboard titled *Prihod* or *Prihodi Vlako.* Be forewarned that there is a good chance that the times listed will be wrong. Helpful Slovene words include *peron* (platform), *sedez* (seat), and *smer* (direction). If you're having trouble, many people speak English in Slovenia so try asking for help. Getting off a train at the right spot has also proved tricky for travelers in Slovenia, because no announcements are made over a speaker system to announce a coming stop and smaller stations usually have only one sign. Ticket checkers will be happy to help you find the right stop, or you could go by the estimated travel time, though we don't recommend that.

Tickets are for sale at various tourist agencies, the best and most comprehensive of which are centered in Ljubljana (© 01-29-13-332 for information daily 6am–10pm). If you're traveling from the west into Slovenia, the best crossing is at the town of Jesenice on the Austrian border. This is the town in the west that's closest to Ljubljana. Because railpasses are valid in Austria, but not in Slovenia, you'll have to pay a nominal amount, depending on your ticket, for the short transit.

HIGHLIGHTS OF SLOVENIA

According to an ancient legend, the capital, **Ljubljana** ✿, was founded by the Greek prince Jason and his Argonauts. The story goes that while the motley crew was trying to escape King Aites, the man from whom they had stolen the Golden Fleece, they sailed on the Sava into Ljubljana. Culture and a rich history are two components that have made this city a favorite among both locals and visitors.

Set in a basin between the Karst and Alpine regions, this city is one of the least populous in Slovenia, with only 278,000 inhabitants. Despite the small size, however, Ljubljana has everything that most other European capitals have—just on a smaller scale.

A major attraction is the **National Museum,** 1 Muzejska 1000 (© **386/1-241-4400;** www.narmuz-lj.si). This national landmark was established in 1821 and has been the Slovene center for artifacts and other historical items ever since. In front of the building is a monument honoring nobleman and scholar, Janez Vajkard Valvasor. A member of the Royal Society of London, Valvasor's true fame came when he penned *Slava vojvodine Kranjske (The Glory of the Duchy),* which described Slovenia in great detail, essentially putting it on the map.

The other noteworthy museum is the **Virtualni Muzej,** Ljubljanski grad 1000 (© **386/1-426-43-40;** www.festival-lj.si/virtualnimuzej). This innovative museum presents the visitor with a ticket into the past through virtual reconstructions of the Emona Forum (in A.D. 388), Ljubljana (in 1580), the Town Square (in 1780), Congress Square (in 1886), Marija Square (in 1913), Vegova Street/Napoleon Square (in 1941), and Revolution Square (in 1984). Using virtual technology, visitors can also examine Slovenian artifacts more closely than they would be able to anywhere else because of security restraints.

Among the city's other top attractions, are the **Casino Ljubljana,** 9 Miklošičeva 1000 Ljubljana (© **386/1-436-13-69;** www.casino-lj.si), and the **Domina Hotel Casino,** 154 Dunajska cesta (© **386/1-588-2510;** www.dominahotels.it), both of which have plenty of slot machines and live gaming tables. The latter of the two, Domina, was opened in 2005 and built in accordance with international gaming standards.

The capital of the Štajerska region, **Maribor,** 64 miles (104 km) northeast of Ljubljana, is the second most important city center in Slovenia. Tourist areas have popped up at the feet of the vineyard-covered hills that blanket the city. There are 31 miles (50km) of wine roads lined with shops and restaurants selling homemade treats, allowing visitors a close look at the most dominant product of the region. The area is perfect for cyclists and horseback riders.

Bled ✻✻✻, 34 miles (55km) northwest of Ljubljana, is the best mountain resort in the country. Surrounded by the Julian Alps, it opens onto Lake Bled, which has a small island in its center that's part of Bled itself. The most popular excursion in Bled involves going over to the island to visit the **Church of the Assumption.** Boats can be rented to take you over, or you can take a round-trip on a gondola. Some visitors swim over.

European aristocrats made Bled a fashionable destination in the 1800s, although its thermal springs have been known for their healing powers since the 1600s. Many recreational facilities have opened here in the time since Slovenia achieved its independence, with the lake and its island turned into a virtual playground, offering windsurfing, rowing, and sailing. Horse-drawn carriages carry you for a ride along the lakefront promenade, as swans glide by on the water. Bled is surrounded by the mountains of **Triglav National Park.** Within its borders, you'll find waterfalls, roaring rapids, and nature trails cut through the forests. **Bled Castle,** built in 1004, houses a museum with artifacts unearthed in the region.

FOR MORE INFORMATION

Tourist information is found at the **Slovenian Tourist Information Centre,** 10 Krekov trg, SI-1000 Ljubljana (© **386/1-306-45-75** or 386/1-306-45-76; www.slovenia.info), open Monday to Friday 9am to 5:30pm. There is an office of the Consulate General in the United States at 600 Third Ave., 21st Floor, New York, NY 10016 (© **212/370-3006;** www.slovenia.info).

For information on Bled, head online to **www.bled.si.**

Index

WATCHING AN IN-FLIGHT MOVIE ISN'T MUCH OF A CULTURAL EXPERIENCE.

EVEN WITH SUBTITLES.

RAIL EUROPE™

Instead of flying, take the train and discover the real Europe in style and comfort with Rail Europe. For reservations and information visit raileurope.com.

I don't speak sign language.

A hotel can close for all kinds of reasons.
Our Guarantee ensures that if your hotel's undergoing construction, we'll let you know in advance. In fact, we cover your entire travel experience. See www.travelocity.com/guarantee for details.

travelocity
You'll never roam alone.

There's a parking lot where my ocean view should be.

À la place de la vue sur l'océan, me voilà avec une vue sur un parking.

Anstatt Meerblick habe ich Sicht auf einen Parkplatz.

Al posto della vista sull'oceano c'è un parcheggio.

 No tengo vista al mar porque hay un parque de estacionamiento.

Há um parque de estacionamento onde deveria estar a minha vista do oceano

Ett parkeringsområde har byggts på den plats där min utsikt över oceanen borde vara.

Er ligt een parkeerterrein waar mijn zee-uitzicht zou moeten zijn.

 هنالك موقف للسيارات مكان ما وجب ان يكون المنظر الخلاب المطل على المحيط .

 眼前に広がる紺碧の海・・・じゃない。窓の外は駐車場

停车场的位置应该是我的海景所在。

I'm fluent in pig latin.

Hotel mishaps aren't bound by geography.
Neither is our Guarantee. It covers your entire travel experience, including the price. So if you don't get the ocean view you booked, we'll work with our travel partners to make it right, right away. See www.travelocity.com/guarantee for details.

travelocity
You'll never roam alone.